pamphlet

S0-BRC-118

THE DEVELOPMENT OF
AMERICAN POLITICAL THOUGHT

A DOCUMENTARY HISTORY

THE DEVELOPMENT OF
AMERICAN POLITICAL THOUGHT

A DOCUMENTARY HISTORY

BY

J. MARK JACOBSON, Ph.D.

FORMERLY OF THE DEPARTMENT OF POLITICAL SCIENCE
UNIVERSITY OF WISCONSIN

D. APPLETON–CENTURY COMPANY

INCORPORATED

NEW YORK   LONDON

COPYRIGHT, 1932, BY THE CENTURY CO.
ALL RIGHTS RESERVED, INCLUDING THE
RIGHT TO REPRODUCE THIS BOOK, OR
PORTIONS THEREOF, IN ANY FORM.   4106

PRINTED IN U. S. A.

TO

B. M. W.

PREFACE

The study of political thought should call for no apologies. Despite the contributions of history's greatest minds, this study, nevertheless, does not to-day hold the preëminent position that it formerly held and still deserves. The practical world of the machine age cannot, it appears, discover values in the realm of ideas. Political philosophy, we are told, is vague, ethereal, and unrelated to the workaday world. To an important degree, the charge is well grounded. The subject has frequently been taught merely as the development of ideas without much attention to the relation of ideas and the other realities of human life. The metaphysical approach pictures thought as growing out of thought alone; the second parent to the birth of ideas—environmental realities—is neglected. So long as teachers of political philosophy make the clouds their classrooms, that long will this intellectual food be nectar to the Olympian gods and not nourishment to worldly mortals.

But there is no need for an ethereal approach to human thinking. A definite relation between theory and practice actually exists. In the first place, political theory develops out of the needs and practices of its own age; often it arises out of specific issues and controversies. Unconsciously but realistically, social and economic factors motivate political thinking. In general, there are four important influences upon the development of ideas: the geographic, the economic, the social, and the cultural. The geographic factors include the contour of the earth's surface, the distribution of land and water, soil fertility, and climatic conditions. We can no more study man accurately apart from the ground upon which he lives, the earth from which he wrests a living, or the routes over which he trades, than we can understand the polar bear apart from its habitat. The important differences between Jeffersonian and Jacksonian democracy, as we shall see, were due largely to environmental influences. The economic factors arise from man's possession of property, his desire for such possession, or his use of property as a lever of political power. Such economic factors played an important rôle in the conflict between commercial Federalism and agrarian Jeffersonianism. The social factors in thought arise from the division of men into social groups, from man's membership in an exclusive aristocracy, his desire for ad-

mission into the ranks of the elect, or his insistence that all classes
be reduced to his own level. The Puritan institution of the spiritual
aristocracy developed partially out of social forces. The cultural
factors in philosophy grow out of the ideas—social, ethical, religious,
scientific—that man inherits through education, books, and social
institutions. The system of balanced government adopted by the
Federalist framers of the Constitution came largely from the earlier
writings of Locke and Montesquieu.

Not only does theory grow out of reality, but, in the second place,
it outlives the needs that produced it. The mental habits of man
change infinitely more slowly than do his environment and his workaday problems. Cultural heritage plays an important rôle in political
thought.

And in the third place, theory consequently determines future
practice. This tripartite relation of theory and practice can well be
illustrated by the history of the Monroe Doctrine. At the time of its
inception one hundred years ago, this country was weak and fearful
of its continued existence as an independent nation. Spain planned
the recapture of her rebellious American possessions; Russia desired
the Pacific coast of North America; and the United States was the
subject of European intrigues. Moreover, the wide expanse of the
Atlantic, the slowness of transportation, and the insignificance of
our foreign trade isolated us from Europe. Out of these environmental factors and political needs, the Monroe Doctrine evolved.
The European states are no longer attempting aggrandizement on the
American continents; the steamboat, the cable, and the radio have
reduced the Atlantic to a mere pond; and American trade and investments abroad have destroyed our economic isolation. The Monroe
Doctrine has thus outlived the needs and causes that produced it.
Yet it continues to influence our foreign policy in the interdependent
civilization of the twentieth century.

Since a definite relationship exists between theory and reality, the
study of the history of political thought—provided this relationship
is clearly presented—has certain important values. In the first place,
it teaches us that the political ideas which we hold to-day have a
historical background; to understand our present theories, such as the
doctrine of judicial supremacy, we must understand their origin,
background, and development. In the second place, a historical
analysis of political thought demonstrates the relativity of ideas to
environment and circumstance. Frequent change and flux characterize the realm of thought as well as that of business or politics. For

example, the leaders of the American Revolution feared government and aimed to render their new political institutions weak and harmless; to-day we constantly expand the functions of government. In the third place, such a study teaches us that many of the ideas formerly cherished as gospel truth are now held up to ridicule. The Puritan fathers, for instance, believed that only the "godly" should rule. And in the fourth place, the evolutionary study of political thought consequently makes us more analytical and more critical of those political ideas that are to-day considered as absolute and immutable divine revelations.

A few words concerning the method of this book may be pertinent. An attempt has been made to explain the geographic, economic, social, and cultural forces at work in the development of American political thought. The essays aim to indicate the relation of theory to reality. Much political thought has never been put into definite statement, and must be sought for in the ideals that tacitly underly the forms of actual social institutions and methods. A study of political institutions and of governmental policies is often as essential as an analysis of men's writings. Jacksonian democracy, for example, expressed itself in institutions and trends rather than in literature. The documents added to each chapter illustrate the types of political thinking during each major period of American life. Only through the examination of original writings can the student study political thought satisfactorily. The number of selections has been kept small in order that their length may be sufficient to enable the student to see for himself the type of approach and reasoning employed by each writer. This method has necessarily compelled the omission of many valuable documents.

My thanks are due to many friends who have aided me in the preparation of this book. Without the kind permission of various publishers, the inclusion of the documentary material would have been impossible. Space does not permit the mention of all who have read portions of the manuscript and who have aided with their criticisms. Three, whose suggestions, encouragement, and inspiration proved invaluable, deserve special mention—Professor W. J. Shepard, Professor F. A. Ogg, and Professor J. M. Gaus.

J. MARK JACOBSON

Madison, Wisconsin
June, 1931.

CONTENTS

	PAGE
PREFACE	vii

CHAPTER I.—PURITANISM 3

ESSAY:

1. INFLUENCES ON COLONIAL PURITANISM 3
2. PURITAN THEOCRACY 8
3. GERMS OF DEMOCRACY 13
4. THE REVOLT AGAINST ORTHODOX PURITANISM 17

DOCUMENTS:

JOHN CALVIN, INSTITUTES OF THE CHRISTIAN RELIGION . . . 23
JOHN COTTON, LETTER OF LORD SAY AND SELE, 1636 . . . 32
       ANSWERS TO PROPOSALS MADE BY LORD SAY AND
       SELE, 1636 35
THE PLATFORM OF CHURCH DISCIPLINE, 1649 39
THE MAYFLOWER COMPACT, 1620 61
THE FUNDAMENTAL ORDERS OF CONNECTICUT, 1638 . . . 61
THOMAS HOOKER, A SURVEY OF THE SUMME OF CHURCH DISCIPLINE 65
ROGER WILLIAMS, THE BLOUDY TENENT OF PERSECUTION FOR
       CAUSE OF CONSCIENCE 70
       THE BLOUDY TENENT YET MORE BLOUDY . . 80

CHAPTER II.—THE AMERICAN REVOLUTION 88

ESSAY:

1. THE CAUSES OF THE REVOLUTION 88
2. THE POLITICAL PHILOSOPHY OF THE REVOLUTION . . . 94
3. THE TORY ATTACK UPON THE REVOLUTION 106
4. THE POLITICAL PHILOSOPHY UNDERLYING THE REVOLUTIONARY
       GOVERNMENTS 109

DOCUMENTS:

JOHN ADAMS, NOVANGLUS 112
ALEXANDER HAMILTON, THE FARMER REFUTED 125
THOMAS PAINE, COMMON SENSE 135
DANIEL LEONARD, MASSACHUSETTENSIS 143
JONATHAN BOUCHER, A VIEW OF THE CAUSES AND CONSEQUENCES OF
     THE AMERICAN REVOLUTION 153

PAGE

CHAPTER III.—FEDERALISM 164

ESSAY:

1. POST-REVOLUTIONARY CONDITIONS 164
2. THE CONSTITUTIONAL CONVENTION OF 1787—ITS POLITICAL
   ATTITUDES 168
3. THE CONSTITUTION OF 1787 173
4. *THE FEDERALIST PAPERS* 179
5. JOHN ADAMS 186
6. JOHN MARSHALL AND THE SUPREME COURT 189

DOCUMENTS:

JOHN ADAMS, A DEFENCE OF THE CONSTITUTIONS OF GOVERNMENT
  OF THE UNITED STATES 191
MAX FARRAND (EDITOR), RECORDS OF THE CONSTITUTIONAL CON-
  VENTION 200
THE FEDERALIST PAPERS 212
JOHN MARSHALL, MARBURY V. MADISON 228
                STURGES V. CROWNINSHIELD 231
JONATHAN ELLIOT (EDITOR), DEBATES IN THE SEVERAL STATE CON-
  VENTIONS ON THE ADOPTION OF THE FEDERAL CONSTITUTION . 234

CHAPTER IV.—DEMOCRACY: JEFFERSONIAN, JACKSONIAN, INTEL-
          LECTUAL 244

ESSAY:

1. THE REVOLT AGAINST FEDERALIST COMMERCIALISM . . . 244
2. JEFFERSONIAN REPUBLICANISM 246
3. JEFFERSONIANISM AND JACKSONIANISM—A CONTRAST . . 254
4. JACKSONIAN DEMOCRACY 258
5. THE INTELLECTUAL DEMOCRATS 262

DOCUMENTS:

THOMAS JEFFERSON, LETTER TO JAMES MADISON, SEPT. 6, 1789 . 270
                NOTES ON VIRGINIA 273
                INAUGURAL ADDRESS, MARCH 4, 1801 . . 274
                LETTER TO SAMUEL KERCHIVAL, JULY 12, 1816 277
JOHN TAYLOR, AN INQUIRY INTO THE PRINCIPLES AND POLICY OF THE
                GOVERNMENT OF THE UNITED STATES . . . 283
                CONSTRUCTION CONSTRUED AND CONSTITUTIONS VIN-
                DICATED 286
                TYRANNY UNMASKED 297
ANDREW JACKSON, FIRST ANNUAL MESSAGE TO CONGRESS . . 301
DEBATES IN THE OHIO CONSTITUTIONAL CONVENTION, 1850–51 . 305
ROGER B. TANEY, THE CHARLES RIVER BRIDGE CASE . . 308
RALPH WALDO EMERSON, ESSAY ON POLITICS 310
HENRY DAVID THOREAU, CIVIL DISOBEDIENCE 319

CHAPTER V.—SLAVERY 325

ESSAY:

1. THE ECONOMICS OF THE SLAVERY CONTROVERSY . . . 325
2. THE ANTI-SLAVERY ATTACKS 329
3. THE DEFENSE OF SLAVEOCRACY 341

CONTENTS

DOCUMENTS:

    WILLIAM LLOYD GARRISON, DECLARATION OF SENTIMENTS OF THE
AMERICAN ANTI-SLAVERY CONVENTION, 1833 350

    WILLIAM ELLERY CHANNING, SLAVERY 354

    FRANCIS WAYLAND, THE ELEMENTS OF MORAL SCIENCE . . . 366

    ABRAHAM LINCOLN, SPEECH IN SPRINGFIELD, ILLINOIS, JUNE 26,
1857 376

    JOHN C. CALHOUN, A DISQUISITION ON GOVERNMENT . . . 384

    GEORGE FITZHUGH, CANNIBALS ALL; OR SLAVES WITHOUT MASTERS . 387

    WILLIAM HARPER, SLAVERY IN THE LIGHT OF SOCIAL ETHICS . . 394

CHAPTER VI.—PARTICULARISM VERSUS NATIONALISM 408

ESSAY:

    1. THE HISTORICAL BASIS FOR PARTICULARISM 408

    2. THE PARTICULARISTIC INTERPRETATIONS OF THE CONSTITUTION . 414

    3. THE EARLY NATIONALIST INTERPRETATIONS OF THE CONSTI-
TUTION 426

    4. POST-CIVIL WAR NATIONALISM 432

DOCUMENTS:

    JOHN C. CALHOUN, A DISQUISITION ON GOVERNMENT . . . 437

    ABEL P. UPSHUR, THE FEDERAL GOVERNMENT: ITS TRUE NATURE
AND CHARACTER 449

    ALEXANDER H. STEPHENS, A CONSTITUTIONAL VIEW OF THE LATE
WAR BETWEEN THE STATES 455

    JEFFERSON DAVIS, THE RISE AND FALL OF THE CONFEDERATE GOV-
ERNMENT 459

    JOSEPH STORY, COMMENTARIES ON THE CONSTITUTION OF THE
UNITED STATES 466

    DANIEL WEBSTER, SECOND SPEECH ON FOOT'S RESOLUTION, JANU-
ARY 26, 1830 479

    CHARLES SUMNER, OUR DOMESTIC RELATIONS; OR, HOW TO TREAT
THE REBEL STATES 487

    JOHN W. BURGESS, THE AMERICAN COMMONWEALTH: CHANGES IN ITS
RELATIONS TO THE NATION 489

CHAPTER VII.—GOVERNMENT AND ECONOMIC INSTITUTIONS . . 497

ESSAY:

    1. THE ECONOMIC AND SOCIAL REVOLUTION OF AMERICA . . 497

    2. THE RECRUDESCENCE OF INDIVIDUALISM 505

    3. THE PASSING OF LAISSEZ-FAIRE IN POLITICS . . . 517

    4. THE PASSING OF LAISSEZ-FAIRE IN POLITICAL THOUGHT—TRANSI-
TIONAL SCHOOL 520

    5. THE PASSING OF LAISSEZ-FAIRE IN POLITICAL THOUGHT—VIGOR-
OUS CRITICS 523

    6. THE PASSING OF LAISSEZ-FAIRE IN JURISPRUDENCE . . 539

DOCUMENTS:

    WILLIAM GRAHAM SUMNER, WHAT SOCIAL CLASSES OWE TO EACH
OTHER 546

    GEORGE SUTHERLAND, ADKINS V. CHILDREN'S HOSPITAL . . 549

CONTENTS

PAGE

HENRY D. LLOYD, WEALTH AGAINST COMMONWEALTH . . . 554
EDWARD BELLAMY, LOOKING BACKWARD: 2000–1887 . . . 562
EDWARD A. ROSS, SIN AND SOCIETY 572
WOODROW WILSON, THE NEW FREEDOM 577
ROBERT M. LA FOLLETTE, SPEECH DELIVERED AT THE ANNUAL
BANQUET OF THE PERIODICAL PUBLISHERS' ASSOCIATION, PHILA-
DELPHIA, FEBRUARY 2, 1912 581
ROSCOE POUND, THE SPIRIT OF THE COMMON LAW 589

CHAPTER VIII.—AMERICA COMES OF AGE 602

ESSAY:

1. THE UNITED STATES IN AN INTERDEPENDENT WORLD . . . 602
2. DISILLUSIONED DEMOCRACY 628
3. A CLASH OF CULTURES 638

DOCUMENTS:

WOODROW WILSON, THE FOURTEEN POINTS SPEECH, JANUARY 8, 1918 647
SPEECH PRESENTING THE VERSAILLES TREATY
FOR RATIFICATION, JULY 10, 1919 . . . 650
JAMES T. SHOTWELL, WAR AS AN INSTRUMENT OF NATIONAL POLICY 659
HENRY CABOT LODGE, OPENING ADDRESS IN THE LODGE-LOWELL
DEBATE ON THE PROPOSED LEAGUE OF NATIONS, MARCH 19, 1919 . 666
CHARLES K. LEITH, EXPLOITATION AND WORLD PROGRESS . . 672
EVERETT DEAN MARTIN, PSYCHOLOGY 681
ISAAC B. BERKSON, THEORIES OF AMERICANIZATION . . . 698

INDEX 717

THE DEVELOPMENT OF
AMERICAN POLITICAL THOUGHT

A DOCUMENTARY HISTORY

CHAPTER I

PURITANISM

I

Colonial Puritanism was the resultant of the old-world social and religious background of the New England settlers as modified by the environment confronting those pioneers in the New World. The Puritans did not spring full-born into life on the Massachusetts coast. They arrived only after spending half of their lives in old England. Consequently, the minds of the framers of the Puritan system in Massachusetts Bay were not totally barren of all social, political, or religious heritages. Nor is it in accordance with human experience to suppose that upon their arrival in America they consciously and deliberately erased from their memories all their previous social experiences. Inevitably, they erected a social system based upon that to which they were accustomed. To understand colonial Puritanism, therefore, we must first study its old world streams of thought and the new influences that played upon the movement.

Three important forces influenced colonial Puritanism: the social system of seventeenth-century England, Calvinism, and the New England environment. The first two demonstrated themselves immediately upon the arrival of the Puritans in America. The last acted more subtly and more indirectly. New England environment, however, ultimately caused the uprooting of the very foundations of the Puritan system.

Seventeenth-century England experienced the gradual breakdown of the old feudal system. The Wars of the Roses had decimated the ranks of the landed aristocracy. The conversion of the serfs into a free yeomanry had been gradually taking place. A capitalist trading class had risen during the Tudor reigns. The closed guild system was breathing its last in the cities. Nevertheless, the essentials of medieval feudalism still characterized the English social system of this age.

Society was still highly stratified. At the top rung of the social ladder stood royalty—the king, his family, and the princes of the royal blood. The high nobility, possessing important titles and large estates, and the high ecclesiastics, holding powerful bishoprics, came

3

next in the scale; beneath these were the lesser nobility and the lesser clergy of the established Church. At this point the social system diverged into two rather distinct lines—one based upon the country and the other on the town. In the country we find an increasingly important group, the untitled gentry; they possessed moderate-sized landed estates, and had by this time become important figures in parliamentary politics. Almost on a par with them stood the minor church ministers and parsons. A semi-feudal system still existed on the estates of the nobility and gentry; emancipated serfs, now called renters or laborers, tilled the soil for their masters. Between the group of large landlords and the class of agricultural laborers, how-ever, there had gradually evolved a number of yeoman freeholders, who possessed and tilled their own little plots of land. In the towns, despite the steady decline of the restricted artisan guilds, the masters of these organizations, together with the important merchants of the recently developed trading companies, constituted the leading citi-zens. These burghers of the cities had become outstanding figures in the turbulent politics of the Stuart régime. Below them stood the journeymen of the guilds and the increasingly large number of un-organized town laborers.

While this social system of the seventeenth century had lost some of the extreme caste characteristics of the rigid feudal system, class lines still severely separated one rung of the social ladder from the next. The history of the age records scarcely an instance of a yeoman rising to the nobility or even to the country gentry. Nor did the town laborer become a city burgher. The Puritans inherited this concept of a stratified class society.

Two other important social characteristics marked seventeenth-century England. The country's economic system was based on agriculture; and large landed estates predominated. Renters and laborers tilled the estates of the nobility and of the country gentry, while interspersed between these two classes stood a small group of yeoman freeholders. The established Church was the remaining important social feature of the century. Church and State were closely related. The king officially headed the Church; the State gave special concessions to its Church; and the Church in return supported the monarchy. This established Church, since the days of the later Tudors, was Anglican and Episcopalian in its organization. Within the Church, however, had grown up a group of dissenters who felt that the established Church should be purified in accordance with a more rigid Calvinism. The Puritans held that they must reform the Church dogma and ritual; they did not, however, with the exception of a few radical Separatists, demand the severing of Church and State. The goal of the English Puritans was their control and their purification of the established Church. This objective they temporarily achieved during the Cromwellian Commonwealth. The Puritan emigrants thus inherited the concept of an established State Church.

Upon the basis of our knowledge of the seventeenth-century English social system, let us attempt to envisage the institutions which the Puritan leaders desired to establish on the Massachusetts coast. The Puritan emigrants came from a stratified class society; this concept of class grouping they unconsciously accepted. It is important to note that the possessors of titles or of episcopates did not take passage to New England. The genealogies of the Puritan leaders indicate that they came from the middle class of English society— the country gentry, the town traders, and the lesser parish ministers. The rank and file of the New England Puritans came from the rural and urban laborers. The country gentry and the town burghers constituted the top rung of the social ladder transported to Massachusetts Bay. They had already developed a position of importance in the British House of Commons; they were accustomed to look down upon the classes beneath themselves. The representatives of these middle classes quite naturally assumed the rôle of leadership in the settlements. Had circumstances permitted, they would have transplanted their inherited social system and concepts. They desired to construct the old English arrangement of stratified classes, with, however, the rungs of the ladder above themselves cut off. The Puritan leaders had no intention of establishing a community based on democratic equality. They expected from the lower classes the same respect and deference accorded them in old England. Had circumstances not prevented, the Puritan leaders would have transplanted the English economic order of large landed estates. They would have continued the rôle of the country gentry. For them, renters and agricultural laborers would till the soil, and possibly a small group of yeoman freeholders would exist. Likewise, the Puritan fathers desired to carry over the concept of an established State Church. With the domination of the monarchy and of the Anglican ecclesiastics removed, they would now be free to reform and purify the official Church. The Puritans did not come to these shores to establish a doctrinaire freedom of worship; rather, they came to secure freedom for their particular brand of religion. Arriving upon virgin soil not already possessed of Christian churches, the Puritan leaders quite naturally expected to erect their own churches and to endow them with the same intimate relationship with the State that characterized the unpurified Anglican church in England. The concepts of social stratification, of landed estates, and of an established Church unconsciously but inevitably fashioned the thinking of the Puritans.

The second stream of thought that fed colonial Puritanism was Calvinism. Puritan religious thinking demonstrated a decided Calvinistic origin and influence. To understand Puritanism in colonial New England, therefore, we must turn to the Calvinist reformation of the sixteenth century.

John Calvin was by training and instinct a lawyer and a logician. His theological thinking was as legalistic as the law books of his day. This quality Calvin passed on to his new religious system. Calvinist doctrine became legalistic, logical, authoritative. No reservations, no exceptions, no gaps existed. An absolutist Sovereign of the universe prescribed for all men a universal moral code. Calvin held a monarchical conception of God; he portrayed Him as an oriental or French despot seated on a high throne and surrounded by a regular order of archangels, seraphim, saints, and elected souls. This heavenly order possessed all the rigidity of the European stratified society. An absolute, universal moral code guided the conduct of all men. All classes, all races, all civilizations owed allegiance to God's moral law. The absolute Sovereign of heaven and earth dictated His prescribed mode of conduct in the Hebraic Old Testament. Here, rather than in the New Testament, the Calvinists sought the irrevocable will of their Ruler.

Calvin expounded a doctrine of predestination. Certain individuals were preordained to salvation; others, to eternal damnation. While all men were sinners before God, an elect few were chosen through the grace of God to a place before His throne. In his *Institutes of the Christian Religion*, Calvin wrote:

"Predestination, by which God adopts some to the hope of life, and adjudges others to eternal death, no one, desirous of the credit of piety, dares absolutely to deny. . . . When we attribute foreknowledge to God, we mean that all things have ever been, and perpetually remain, before his eyes, so that to his knowledge nothing is future or past, but all things are present; and present in such a manner, that he does not merely conceive of them from ideas formed in his mind, as things remembered by us appear present to our minds, but really beholds and sees them as if actually placed before him. And this foreknowledge extends to the whole world, and to all the creatures. Predestination we call the eternal decree of God, by which he had determined in himself, what he would have to become of every individual of mankind. For they are not all created with a similar destiny; but eternal life is foreordained for some, and eternal damnation for others. Every man, therefore, being created for one or the other of these ends, we say, he is predestined either to life or to death." [1]

Democracy in the fall of man and aristocracy in his redemption characterized Calvinistic thought. This spiritual aristocracy constituted God's saints on earth. It was for them to exemplify the universal moral code; it was for them to lead the unredeemed to the divine light. The Calvinist discovered his predestined election to the spiritual aristocracy through an inward call and urge to service.

"Those whom Christ illuminates with the knowledge of his name, and introduces into the bosom of his Church, he is said to receive into his charge and protection. And all whom he receives are said to be committed and intrusted to him by the Father, to be kept to eternal life. . . . Now if we doubt whether Christ has received us into his charge and custody, he obviates this doubt, by freely offering himself as our Shepherd, and declaring that if we hear his voice, we shall be numbered among his sheep." [2]

It is interesting to note that the spiritual aristocracy among the colonial Puritans consisted of the identical individuals that constituted the social aristocracy among the emigrants. [3]

The old world background of the Puritan emigrants fashioned their thinking and molded their institutions. Their leaders confidently expected to transplant the English order of stratified classes and landed estates. They—the socially and spiritually elect—hoped to maintain a purified State Church. And through their domination of both Church and State, the elect intended to enforce the Calvinistic universal moral code. Turning to the Old Testament, they found in the *Book of Judges* adequate authority for their proposed theocracy.

The New England environment, however, played havoc with their best-laid plans. A social stratification, a State Church, and a theocratic domination of moral conduct—these they did immediately establish. Landed estates, however, proved impossible on New England soil. And ultimately the subtle influence of environment broke down the social scheme and its theocratic control.

---

[1] Calvin, *Institutes of the Christian Religion*, pp. 144–145.

[2] *Ibid.*, pp. 184–185.

[3] It is also interesting to note that the adoption of the strict Calvinist moral code assisted the adherents of this faith to rise in the economic scale. The strictness of Calvinist conduct produced those personal characteristics that make for a shrewd, hard, successful trader. Worldly success came to be considered as an earmark of divine election. See Tawney, *Religion and the Rise of Capitalism*.

New England environment did not permit the establishment of large landed estates lorded over by a country gentry. A landed estate system demands a limited amount of land or the ownership of land already in the hands of a few. In New England, land was plentiful. Whoever had the initiative and the courage to move beyond the pale of the already populated towns found ample land that he could till for himself. The would-be country gentry discovered a scarcity of laborers willing to be their serfs or renters. The fertile waters of Massachusetts and Cape Cod bays, moreover, invited the non-farmers to engage in fishing; the uncut forests encouraged ship-building; and the demands of England for fish, furs, and lumber prompted colonial trading. The opening of these unsuspected economic opportunities drained off the class that would otherwise have labored on the estates of the country gentry. The ruggedness of the New England country, the rockiness of the soil, and the intensive personal care necessary for the successful raising of a crop prevented any one from staking out a large claim. Freeholds became numerous and small. And the substitution of free alienation of property for the English system of entail discouraged the passing on of large estates. The New England environment thus prevented the transfer of the British order of concentrated land ownership. By the end of the seventeenth century, the opportunities for economic progress in this new country broke down even the barriers of class stratification. The spiritual aristocracy soon afterwards lost their grip upon political institutions. Environment transformed the Puritan into a Yankee.

II

Colonial Puritanism was a theocracy. The founders of Massachusetts Bay colony made no secret of their Calvinism. In Calvin's *Institutes*, and in the Old Testament, they discovered the foundations upon which their church and their polity should rest. From the Hebraic writings they deduced their system of law, their moral code, and the structure of their society. Their *Confession of Faith* of 1680 held that:

"God gave to Adam a law of universal obedience written in his heart, and a particular precept of not eating the fruit of the tree of knowledge of good and evil. . . . This law, so written in the heart, continued to be a perfect rule of righteousness after the fall of man, and was delivered by God on Mount Sinai in ten commandments, and written in two tables: the four first commandments containing our duty towards God, and the other six our duty to man." [4]

[4] *A Confession of Faith: Owned and Consented to by Elders and Messengers of the Churches, Assembled at Boston in New-England, May 12, 1680*, Ch. XIX, Nos. 1, 2. Cotton Mather, *Magnalia Christi Americana*, II, 196–197.

This Puritan theocracy manifested itself in three definite trends: (1) religious qualifications for political activity; (2) the predominant position of the clergy in public affairs; and (3) the employment of the civil arm of the state for the enforcement of church law.

The Puritan fathers were not democrats. They maintained no belief in the innate equality of men; only a godly few had been elected for salvation. They had no enthusiasm for political freedom; the unredeemed should play no rôle in guiding the conduct of the community. Orthodox Puritan settlements differentiated clearly between freemen and mere inhabitants. To the latter they granted certain civil rights; to the former, exclusive domination of public affairs. In Massachusetts Bay, during the first half of the seventeenth century, only one-fifth of the inhabitants were freemen. What, then, were the qualifications for political freedom? In Massachusetts Bay and in New Haven only members of the official Congregationalist church possessed the suffrage. Puritan communities differentiated between church-goers and church members. Everyone was compelled to attend services, but only the spiritual aristocrats could become members of the church congregations. The designation of an individual as one of the elect rested with those already church members. The Church was a closed, self-perpetuating corporation. The spiritual and social leaders had, upon their arrival in the new world, assumed control of the religious councils. Thereafter only those whom they approved could sit with the redeemed. And only the redeemed could guide public affairs. The spiritual aristocrats, God's saints on earth, were themselves to lead His flock and to enforce His commandments.

In 1635 a group of Puritan lords desired to emigrate from England to Massachusetts Bay, and made certain demands upon the governor of the colony as conditions for their settlement in the Bay communities. The reply drafted by the leading Puritans indicates the nature of their theocracy.

"None are admitted freemen of this commonwealth but such as are first admitted members of some church or other in this country, and, of such, none are excluded from the liberty of freemen. And out of such only, I mean the more eminent sort of such, it is that our magistrates are chosen. . . . It seemeth to . . . us to be a divine ordinance (and moral) that none should be appointed and chosen by the people of God, magistrates over them, but men fearing God chosen out of their brethren saints."

"The liberties of the freemen of this commonwealth are such, as require men of faithful integrity to God and the state, to preserve the same. Their liberties, among others, are chiefly these. 1. To chuse all magistrates, and to call them to account at their general courts. 2. To chuse such burgesses, every general court, as with the magistrates shall make or repeal all laws. Now both these liberties are such, as carry along much power with them, either to establish or subvert the commonwealth, and therewith the church, which power, if it be committed to men not according to their godliness, which maketh them fit for church fellowship, but according to their wealth, which, as such, makes them no better than wordly [sic] men, then, in case worldly men should prove the major part, as soon they might do, they would as readily set over us magistrates like themselves, such as might hate us according to the curse, and turn the edge of all authority and laws against the church and the members thereof, the maintenance of whose peace is the chief end which God aimed at in the institution of Magistracy." [5]

The closed, self-perpetuating nature of the church congregation is demonstrated in the *Platform of Church Discipline*, adopted in 1649 by a synod of the church elders and messengers held at Cambridge. The chapter dealing with "The Admission of Members into the Church" contains this interesting and enlightening provision:

"The doors of the churches of Christ upon earth do not by God's appointment stand so wide open, that all sorts of people, good and bad, may freely enter therein at their pleasure, but such as are admitted thereto, as members, ought to be examin'd and tryed first, whether they be fit and meet to be received into church-society or not. . . . The officers are charged with keeping of the door of the church, and therefore are in a special manner to make tryal of the fitness of such who enter." [6]

The Reverend John Cotton, the high priest of Puritan theocracy, employed his pulpit to attack any drifts toward democracy in Church or State.

"None are to be trusted with public permanent authority but godly men."
"It is better than the commonwealth be fashioned to the setting forth of God's house, which is his church: than to accommodate the church frame to the civill state. Democracy, I do not conceyve that ever God did ordeyne as a fitt government eyther for church or commonwealth. If the people be governors, who shall be governed? As for monarchy, and aristocracy, they are both of them clearly approved, and directed in scripture, yet so as referreth the soveraigntie to himselfe, and setteth up Theocracy in both, as the best forme of government in commonwealth, as well as in the church." [7]

Not only did the church group control political activity, but, in addition, the clergy assumed an eminent position of public influence. To speak ill of ministers was sedition. A citizen of Boston was in 1636 fined forty pounds and required to apologize publicly for saying that all except three ministers preached a covenant of works.[8] The

[5] Hutchinson, *History of Massachusetts Bay*, I, 493–495.
[6] *Platform of Church Discipline*, Ch. XII, No. 1. Mather, *Magnalia Christi Americana*, II, 225.
[7] Hutchinson, *History of Massachusetts Bay*, I, 497–498.
[8] Winthrop, *History of New England*, I, 98.

civil magistrates consulted the clergy upon all matters of public policy. Thus in 1632 when a dispute occurred between the deputy-governor, Thomas Dudley, and the governor, John Winthrop, a council of five ministers convened to settle the controversy. The clergy heard what the disputants had to say for themselves, then "went apart for one hour," and returned with their decision, to which the governor meekly submitted.[9] The Puritan ministers, moreover, employed their pulpits to expound their views on community problems. The seventeenth-century New England cleric did not restrict his preachings to salvation and damnation; as a leading member of the spiritually elect, he felt compelled to guide the application of the Calvinist universal moral code to everyday affairs. Early American novels concerning Puritan New England picture the important rôle of the ministry. Hawthorne's *The Scarlet Letter* clearly depicts the tremendous influence of the clergy upon public affairs. Hawthorne refers to an institution that throws light upon theocratic supremacy—the annual election sermons. Each year before the freemen held their civil elections the magistrates would select a prominent cleric to deliver a political sermon. This choice constituted an important honor for the favored minister; it became his rôle to apply the divine law to current problems.

The third phase of Puritan theocracy was probably of greater significance than the religious qualifications for suffrage or the ministerial predominance in politics. Long after the New England environment had broken down the strict social stratification, long after property ownership had superseded church membership as the suffrage qualification, long after the Yankee merchant had supplanted the Puritan cleric in political predominance, the civil arm of the state still enforced church law and dogma.

The Puritan fathers did not conceive of a separation of Church and State. Their social heritage from old England included the concept of an established State Church. They, as members of the spiritual aristocracy, were entrusted with the mission of enforcing the universal moral code ordained by their heavenly Sovereign. In the performance of this task, they could not exclude any effective methods, no matter how worldly. Civil magistrates, themselves members of the elect, were duty-bound to enforce the Hebraic moral code, to guarantee the observance of Church law and dogma, and to prevent heretical pollution of the Church. Calvin, a century before, had expounded this theocratic conception of the State;

[9] Hutchinson, *History of Massachusetts Bay*, I, 60.

among the objectives of the civil government, he included the following:

"That idolatry, sacrileges against the name of God, blasphemies against his truth, and other offences against religion, may not openly appear and be disseminated among the people. . . . I approve of civil government, which provides that the true religion which is contained in the law of God, be not violated, and polluted by public blasphemies, with impunity."

"These things evince the folly of those who would wish magistrates to neglect all thoughts of God, and to confine themselves entirely to the administration of justice among men; as though God appointed governors in his name to decide secular controversies, and disregard that which is of far greater importance—the pure worship of himself according to the rule of his law." [10]

In the same tenor wrote John Cotton: "It is a carnal and worldly, and, indeed, an ungodly imagination, to confine the magistrate's charge to the bodies and goods of the subjects, and to exclude them from the care of their soules." [11]

Civil authorities thus enforced sabbath-day laws and anti-heresy acts, compelled church attendance, and collected taxes for church support. In 1644 Massachusetts passed a law punishing with banishment any one who should openly or secretly speak against the orthodox doctrine regarding baptism. The close union of Church and State is illustrated by the attempts to enforce this and similar acts concerning religious dogma. Immediately three Baptists were arrested and heavily fined; in default of payment, they were to be whipped. One of the defendants asked by what law he was being punished, inasmuch as the penalty was not that prescribed by the ordinance of 1644. He related that Endicott "stept up to us, and told us we had denyed Infants Baptism, and being somewhat transported broke forth, and told me I had deserved death, and said he would not have such trash brought into this jurisdiction." [12]

The Platform of Church Discipline of 1649 codified the concepts of civil maintenance of church purity and magisterial enforcement of moral codes. In the chapter entitled "Of the Civil Magistrate's Power in Matters Ecclesiastical," we can note the close relationship of the Church and the State.

"It is the duty of the magistrate to take care of matters of religion, and to improve his civil authority for the observance of the duties commanded in the first as well as for observing of the duties commanded in the second table.

[10] Calvin, Institutes of the Christian Religion, pp. 635 and 641.
[11] Cotton, The Bloudy Tenent Washed and Made White, Ch. XXXIII.
[12] Adams, The Founding of New England, pp. 259–260.

They are called gods. The end of the magistrate's office is not only the quiet and peaceable life of the subject in matters of righteousness and honesty, but also in matters of godliness; yea, of all godliness.

"Idolatry, blasphemy, heresie, venting corrupt and pernicious opinions, that destroy the foundation, open contempt of the word preached, prophanation of the Lord's-Day, disturbing the peaceable administration and exercise of the worship and holy things of God, and the like, are to be restrained and punished by civil authority.

"If any church, one or more, shall grow schismatical, rendering itself from the communion of other churches, or shall walk incorrigibly and obstinately in any corrupt way of their own, contrary to the rule of the word; in such case, the magistrate is to put forth his coercive power, as the matter shall require." [13]

In recent years America has experienced a recrudescence of this militant Puritanism. Orthodox Protestant churches have endeavored again to secure civil sanction for their religious dogmas, now questioned by the new biological sciences. State legislatures have passed anti-evolution statutes in order to maintain the fundamentalist church interpretation of the Scriptures. And, in a way, the anti-Catholic opposition to Smith's candidacy for the presidency was in accord with Cotton's doctrine that only the godly should rule.

The Puritan theocracy was thus not in itself democratic. Religious qualifications for suffrage and office-holding denied political freedom to the great mass of colonists. Liberty existed only for those who traveled in the accepted light of the Lord. The founders were not interested in individual equality or liberty; their aspiration was for the independence of their communities from external domination and Anglican church control. They desired to establish a civil government under which they could best maintain their own religious system. In the achievement of that goal, they subordinated the individual to the group. They expelled the exponents of all other religious creeds. And among the adherents of the Puritan faith, the spiritually elect assumed religious and political domination.

III

And yet out of this oligarchic theocracy grew American democracy. Puritan institutions, even those of orthodox Massachusetts Bay, possessed the germs from which ultimately developed popular self-government. The democratic germs in seventeenth-century Puritanism were two: (1) the use of the social contract in the establishment

[13] *Platform of Church Discipline*, Ch. XVII, Nos. 6, 8, 9. Mather, *Magnalia Christi Americana*, II, 236.

of new communities, and (2) local self-government through the town meeting.

In the middle of the sixteenth century, at the time when the national states of western Europe were coming into existence, a group of writers developed the social contract theory to counter the doctrine of the divine right of kings to rule. George Buchanan in Scotland, Johannes Althusius in the Netherlands, Richard Hooker in England, and Francisco Suarez in Spain early expounded this new philosophy of the origin of the State. The doctrine of the divine right of kings and the force theory no longer satisfied these political philosophers. They pictured a pre-governmental state of nature; all men at that time were free from political restraints. Men possessed certain natural rights inherent in human beings; these rights they enforced by their own individual might. For various reasons, the state of nature became unbearable; consequently, individuals came together in order to establish civil government by means of a social contract. They agreed among themselves to surrender to the new civil government their individual enforcement of their natural rights. This civil authority might consist of one individual, of an oligarchic group, or of a representative assembly. There were almost as many variations of the social contract as there were theorists expounding the doctrine. But the important idea was that government, whatever its form, rested upon the individuals' consent expressed in a historical contract.

While the Puritans of Massachusetts Bay derived their theology from sixteenth-century Calvinism, their politics bore the earmarks of the seventeenth-century protest against Stuart autocracy. During the Stuart régime, the Puritan leaders in England drew heavily upon this social contract theory to undermine James I's claim to divine right to rule, and this democratic, anti-monarchical view of government gradually permeated through the Puritan ranks.

The main body of Puritan migration to the New World, it must be remembered, came during the two periods of Stuart supremacy and Anglican religious oppression—in 1630–1649, and in 1660–1688. In 1649 the Cromwellian Puritans beheaded Charles I and took over the reins of government. For two decades the Puritans were able to employ the civil arm of the government for their own religious purposes. There existed, then, no need for their escape to America. After the Restoration, however, the stream of Puritan migration again flowed westward. Many of the Cromwellian leaders now fled to Massachusetts Bay and assumed positions of prominence. Puritan emigrations thus came at times when the masses of English Puritans accepted the social contract philosophy. The colonial Puritans carried with them this political concept and made practical applications of it in their polity.

Before their landing in 1620, the Pilgrims drew up the Mayflower Compact. This brief document constituted an original social contract among its signatories for the establishment of a political community.

"We whose names are underwriten, ... haveing undertaken, for the glorie of God, and advancemente of the Christian faith, and honour of our king & countrie, a voyage to plant the first colonie in the Northerne parts of Virginia, doe by these presents solemnly & mutualy in the presence of God, and one of another, covenant & combine our selves togeather into a civill body politick, for our better ordering & preservation & furtherance of the ends aforesaid; and by vertue hearof to enacte, constitute, and frame such just & equall lawes, ordinances, acts, constitutions, & offices, from time to time, as shall be thought most meete & convenient for the generall good of the Colonie, unto which we promise all due submission and obedience." [14]

The orthodox Puritans, upon their arrival, followed the example of the earlier Pilgrims. As they established most of their new communities, they signed social contracts among themselves. Thus the Fundamental Orders of Connecticut provided:

"Forasmuch as it hath pleased the Allmighty God by the wise disposition of his divyne providence so to Order and dispose of things that we the Inhabitants and Residents of Windsor, Harteford and Wethersfield are now cohabiting and dwelling in and uppon the River of Conectecotte and the Lands thereunto adjoyneing; And well knowing a people are gathered togather the word of God requires that to mayntayne the peace and union of such a people there should be an orderly and decent Government established according to God, to order and dispose of the affayres of the people at all seasons as occation shall require; doe therefore associate and conjoyne our selves and our Successors and such as shall be adjoyned at us att any tyme hereafter, enter into Combination and Confederation togather, to mayntayne and presearve the liberty and purity of the gospell of our Lord Jesus which we now professe, as also the disciplyne of the Churches, which according to the truth of the said gospell is now practised amongst us; As also in our Civell Affaires to be guided and governed according to such Lawes, Rules, Orders, and decrees as shall be made, ordered & decreed." [15]

The Providence agreement (1636), the Portsmouth agreement (1636), the Newport Declaration (1641), and the Body of Liberties of Massachusetts (1641) are a few others of the more important contracts. This contract concept crept even into ecclesiastical institutions. Thus the orthodox Puritans, in the *Platform of Church*

[14] Bradford, *History of Plymouth Plantations*, Massachusetts Historical Collection, 4th series, III, 89–90.
[15] *Connecticut Colonial Records*, I, 20.

Discipline, defined a church as "a company of people combined together by covenant for the worship of God." [16] To be sure, these agreements gave political power only to the spiritually elect, who alone frequently signed these documents. Nevertheless, the use of the social contract became a practice from which a theory of democracy developed.

Regardless of the limited government that the contract might establish, the contract theory emphasized the importance of the individual as the basic unit in society. Neither force nor divine right brought government into being, but only the voluntary consent of the individual. This doctrine, because of its application in actual community contracts, permeated popular thinking in New England to a more marked degree than it ever did in England or on the Continent. The social contract, with its inherently democratic attributes, developed finally into the radical democratic thought of the Revolutionary period. An agreement among the spiritual aristocracy grew into an agreement among all men.

The contract for the establishment of a new community frequently contained a written enumeration of civil rights. The Body of Liberties of Massachusetts Bay illustrates this tendency. While we today would consider their enumerated civil rights as narrow and limited, these public documents, nevertheless, developed the concept of the written protection of rights. Out of this habit grew the bills of rights that characterize our present national and state constitutions.

The second germ from which grew American democracy can be found in the practice of local self-government by means of the town meeting. Through the town meeting the freemen maintained control of their local communities. Here they elected the magistrates, passed resolutions and ordinances, and criticized their officers. In Massachusetts Bay only about one-fifth of the inhabitants, however, were freemen. The Puritan leaders had created the town meeting as the governing organ of the spiritual aristocracy. Through this institution the elect could employ the civil arm of the State for the maintenance of their universal moral code. The town meeting of the seventeenth century was distinctly an undemocratic institution. By the end of the century, however, the subtle influence of New England environment had broken down the old social stratification. Property ownership superseded church membership as the suffrage qualification. Meanwhile, the old practice of local self-government through the

[16] *Platform of Church Discipline*, Ch. VI, No. 1. Mather, *Magnalia Christi Americana*, II, 217.

town meeting persisted. The widening of the suffrage thus made this institution an organ of democracy. The meeting of the spiritual aristocracy grew into a meeting of most of the men. Would that John Cotton could have peered through his grave at this revolution!

IV

Against the orthodox Puritan theocracy of Massachusetts Bay, several revolts occurred. Immediately they developed the democratic germs of Puritanism. The experiments of Roger Williams in Rhode Island, of Thomas Hooker in the Connecticut Valley, and of John Wise at Ipswich furnished examples for the later development of American democracy. They also stimulated a more rapid germination of the democratic seeds already existing in the older settlements. Williams, Hooker, and Wise clearly recognized the democratic implications of their social contract thinking, and fearlessly carried them to logical conclusions. The political system of Rhode Island contained institutions that many twentieth-century men would consider radical for to-day. While these new colonies were characterized by an increasingly popular participation in government, an important factor differentiated the three experiments. Hooker and Wise democratized the orthodox Puritan theocracy; they retained, however, the old Puritan forms and remained in an alliance with the orthodox churches of Massachusetts Bay. Roger Williams, on the other hand, broke entirely loose from Puritan theocracy; he refused to accept either its union of Church and State or its ecclesiastical dogma. While Hooker and Wise remolded the old institutions, Williams pulled up their roots. The first two reformed; the last revolted.

Three major ideas dominated the writings of Roger Williams: (1) an insistence upon religious toleration; (2) the doctrine of the complete separation of Church and State; and (3) the application of the social contract to the democratization of political institutions. His *The Bloudy Tenent of Persecution for Cause of Conscience* has long ranked among the world's outstanding works on religious toleration. Williams desired to develop a rôle of individual freedom, especially freedom of religion.

"It is the will and command of God, that (since the comming of his Sonne the Lord Jesus) a permission of the most Paganish, Jewish, Turkish, or Anti-christian consciences and worships, bee granted to all men in all Nations and Countries: and they are onely to bee fought against with that Sword which is only (in Soule matters) able to conquer, to wit, the Sword of God's Spirit, the Word of God. . . . God requireth not an uniformity of Religion to be inacted and inforced in any civill State; which inforced uniformity (sooner or later) is the greatest occasion of civill Warre, ravishing of conscience, persecution of Christ Jesus in his servants, and of the hypocrisie and destruction of millions of souls. . . . True civility and Christianity may both flourish in a State or Kingdome, notwithstanding the permission of divers and contrary consciences, either of Iew or Gentile."

The conclusion was that "persecution for cause of conscience is most evidently and lamentably contrary to the doctrine of Christ Jesus." Not only was the individual free to worship as he believed, but also he should not be bound to support a church against his own consent.[17]

Orthodox Puritanism employed the State for the maintenance of its religious law. Roger Williams revolted against this union of Church and State. The true Church is spiritual in its nature. The weapons for its defense must likewise be spiritual; worldly props would undermine the true Church of God's saints. The spiritual Church can, therefore, make no use of the secular State. Civil officers must not punish the disobedience of religious ordinances, must not seek out heretics, must not organize churches. While John Cotton endowed the magistrates with the care of the bodies, goods, and souls of the subjects, Williams placed stringent limitations upon the political arm of the community. "A Civill Government is an ordinance of God, to conserve the Civill peace of the people, so farre as concerns their Bodies and Goods," but not their souls.[18] The civil peace of a community is something entirely different from the religious peace; nor does civil peace depend upon religious uniformity.

"Hence it is that so many glorious and flourishing cities of the World maintaine their Civill peace, yea the very Americans and wildest Pagans keep the peace of their Towns or Cities; though neither in one nor the other can any man prove a true Church of God in those places, and consequently no spiritual heavenly peace: The Peace Spiritual (whether true or false) being of a higher and farre different nature from the Peace of the place or people, being meerly and essentially civill and humane.

"The Church or company of worshippers (whether true or false) is like unto a Body or Colledge of Physitians in a Citie; like unto a Corporation, Society, or Company of East-Indie or Turkie-Merchants, or any other Societie or Company in London: which Companies may hold their Courts, keep their Records, hold disputations; and in matters concerning their Societie, may dissent, divide, breake into Schismes and Factions, sue and implead each other at the Law, yea wholly breake and dissolve into pieces and nothing, and yet the peace of the Citie not be in the least measure impaired or disturbed; because of the essence or being of the Citie, and so the wellbeing and peace thereof is essentially distinct from those particular Societies; the Citie-Courts, Citie-Laws, Citie-punishments distinct from theirs. The

---

[17] Narragansett Club Publications, III. 3–4.   [18] Ibid., III, 349.

Citie was before them, and stands absolute and intire, when such a Corporation or Societie is taken down. For instance, further, The City or Civill State of Ephesus was essentially distinct from the worship of Diana in the Citie, or of the whole City. Againe, the Church of Christ in Ephesus (which were Gods people, converted and call'd out from the worship of that City unto Christianitie or worship of God in Christ) was distinct from both." [19]

The separation of Church and State demanded, in Williams's reasoning, not merely the employment of purely spiritual weapons for the maintenance of Church dogma and moral conduct, but also the abolition of religious qualifications for office-holding and suffrage. Choosing magistrates because of their church affiliations was as asinine as choosing pilots and physicians according to their schemes of salvation.

Williams aimed to avoid the coercive absolutism exercised by the spiritual aristocracy of Massachusetts Bay. Accepting fearlessly the democratic implications of the social contract system, he deliberately erected a government based on popular sovereignty. Nowhere does he develop a justification for this doctrine; nowhere does he attempt to demonstrate its validity as an explanation of the origin of government. He accepts the social contract theory as a major premise in his thinking and demonstrates the democratic consequences that must follow.

"The civill Magistrate, whether King or Parliaments, States, and Governours, can receive no more in justice than what the People give, and are therefore but the eyes and hands and instruments of the people." [20]

"Every lawful Magistrate, whether succeeding or elected, is not only the Minister of God, but the Minister or servant of the people also . . . and that Minister or Magistrate goes beyond his commission, who intermeddles with that which cannot be given him in commission from the people." [21]

"From this Grant I infer . . . that the Soveraigne, originall, and foundation of civill power lies in the people. . . . And if so, that a People may erect and establish what forme of Government seemes to them most meete for their civill condition: It is evident that such Governments as are by them erected and established, have no more power, nor for no longer time, then the civill power or people consenting and agreeing shall betrust them with." [22]

The mechanics of government instituted to achieve this democratic goal bore all the earmarks of modernity. By frequent elections the people sent representatives to a unicameral colonial legislature. A compulsory referendum, in turn, checked the popular assembly. Williams shunned a rigid constitution and opposed judicial interpretation of the fundamental laws. The people reserved the right of recall

---

[19] Narragansett Club Publications, III, 72–73.
[20] Ibid., III, 355.
[21] Ibid., IV, 187.
[22] Ibid., III, 249–250.

against all laws, including the constitution. The state thus became the expressor of the community will.

In many respects the political implications of the ecclesiastical writings of Hooker and Wise resembled those of Roger Williams. Hooker led his congregation from Newtown into the wilderness of the Connecticut Valley in order to escape the spiritual autocracy of the Boston magistrates. At Hartford he established a new settlement and persistently threw his influence in favor of democracy in political and religious institutions. Hooker was largely responsible for the Fundamental Orders of Connecticut of 1639. That document embodied much of his liberalism. It established no religious or property qualifications for voting; each town admitted whomsoever it willed as freemen. Some time before the establishment of the Fundamental Orders, Hooker preached a remarkable sermon on popular government. The foundation of authority, he said, rests in the free consent of the people.

"The choice of public magistrates belongs unto the people by God's own allowance.

"They who have the power to appoint officers and magistrates, it is in their power also, to set the bounds and limitations of the power and place unto which they call them." [23]

At the beginning of the next century, another revolt against orthodox Puritanism occurred. In 1705 the Boston Association of Ministers, under the leadership of Cotton Mather, drew up a series of *Proposals*, looking to a closer union of the churches and to a greater control of the separate congregations by the ministerial association. [24] John Wise, pastor of the Ipswich church, met this challenge of Presbyterianism. In 1710 he published his first reply under the title of *Churches Quarrel Espoused*, and in 1717 he brought forth his *Vindication of the Government of the New England Churches*.

While Wise wrote in defense of Congregationalism against Presbyterian centralization, his arguments had definite political applications. He attempted to justify local, democratic control in church organization by the application of the natural rights philosophy. He was thoroughly familiar with Pufendorf's *De Jure Naturæ et Gentium*, published in 1672, and drew heavily upon this textbook of natural rights. Wise held that man originally lived in a state of nature in which he was "a free-born subject under the crown of heaven, and owing homage to none but God himself." [25]

[23] Walker, *Thomas Hooker, Preacher, Founder, Democrat*, p. 125.
[24] Wise, *Vindication of New England Churches* (1860 edition), p. xv.
[25] *Ibid.*, p. 29.

"Man's external personal, natural liberty, antecedent to all human parts or alliances, must also be considered. And so every man must be conceived to be perfectly in his own power and disposal, and not to be controlled by the authority of any other. And thus every man must be acknowledged equal to every man, since all subjection and all command are equally banished on both sides; and considering all men thus at liberty, every man has a prerogative to judge for himself, namely, what shall be most his behoof, happiness, and well-being." [26]

The law of nature, dictated by man's rational nature, governed him.

"He is the favorite animal on earth; in that this part of God's image, namely, reason, is congenate with his nature, wherein by a law immutable, enstamped upon his frame, God has provided a rule for men in all their actions, obliging each one to the performance of that which is right, not only as to justice, but likewise as to all other moral virtues, the which is nothing but the dictates of right reason founded in the soul of man." [27]

The natural man had a sociable disposition and an affection or love for mankind in general; but the principle of self-love and self-preservation was predominant in every man's being.[28] Men formed civil government by means of a triple contract. They first covenanted among themselves to form a lasting society in order that they might "be capable to concert the measures of their safety, by a public vote." Next, they agreed to set up "some particular species of government over them." And finally, they contracted with their rulers "whereby those on whom sovereignty is conferred engage to take care of the common peace and welfare; and the subjects, on the other hand, to yield them faithful obedience." [29] Civil power originally rested with the people.

"As they have a power every man over himself in a natural state, so upon a combination they can and do bequeathe this power unto others, and settle it according as their united discretion shall determine. For that this is very plain, that when the subject of sovereign power is quite extinct, that power returns to the people again. And when they are free, they may set up what species of government they please." [30]

The chief end of civil communities, Wise held, is protection against the injuries men are liable to suffer from other men. "If every man could secure himself singly, it would be great folly for him to renounce his natural liberty, in which every man is his own king and protector." [31]

[26] Wise, *Vindication of New England Churches* (1860 edition) p. 34.
[27] *Ibid.*, p. 30.
[28] *Ibid.*, p. 31.
[29] *Ibid.*, p. 39.
[30] *Ibid.*, p. 38.
[31] *Ibid.*, p. 41.

Applying this natural rights reasoning to the problem of ecclesiastical organization, Wise attacked Presbyterianism and defended Congregationalism. The former he considered an aristocracy and a "dangerous constitution in the church of Christ." "It has no more barrier to it, against the ambition, insults, and arbitrary measures of men, than an absolute monarchy." [32] Wise favored democracy as the best government for the church of God.

"This is a form of government which the light of nature does highly value, and often directs to as most agreeable to the just and natural prerogatives of human beings."

"It is certainly a great truth, namely, that man's original liberty after it is resigned (yet under due restrictions) ought to be cherished in all wise governments; or otherwise a man in making himself a subject, he alters himself from a freeman into a slave, which to do is repugnant to the law of nature. Also the natural equality of men amongst men must be duly favored; in that government was never established by God or nature, to give one man a prerogative to insult over another, therefore, in a civil, as well as in a natural state of being, a just equality is to be indulged so far as that every man is bound to honor every man, which is agreeable both with nature and religion. . . . The end of all good government is to cultivate humanity, and promote the happiness of all, and the good of every man in all his rights, his life, liberty, estate, honor, etc., without injury or abuse done to any." [33]

In 1772, when the Revolutionary conflict over the bitter questions of home-rule and natural rights were stirring the minds of men, Wise's *Churches Quarrel Espoused* and his *Vindication of the Government of the New England Churches* were reprinted. The democratic teachings of these books, reappearing as they did at that critical period, influenced somewhat the leaders of the colonial defense against British imperial domination. [34]

[32] Wise, *Vindication of New England Churches* (1860 edition), pp. 53–54.

[33] *Ibid.*, pp. 54–55.

[34] Analysis of colonial political thought is in this volume deliberately restricted to orthodox Puritanism in Massachusetts Bay and to the revolts against this theocracy. The neglect of other colonial groups does not mean that the author considers them lacking in importance. The Pilgrims of Plymouth, the Quakers in Pennsylvania, the Cavaliers in the South, the Catholics in Maryland have made their contributions to the development of American political thinking and institutions. New England Puritanism, however, was more verbal in the exposition of its political attitudes. An even weightier reason for emphasizing this group is the fact that within the compass of a small area we find virtually all the problems of political philosophy and political development that characterized the colonial period; within this small area, too, are found nearly all of the various ideas from which later American thought developed.

JOHN CALVIN

Calvin, a native of northern France, became one of the leaders of the Reformation. He assumed a position of authority in Geneva and established there a theocratic system of government which he had devised. Calvin's views on church and state government are set forth in his *Institutes of the Christian Religion* (1535). This book and the Geneva experiment greatly influenced the Puritan emigrants to New England.

INSTITUTES OF THE CHRISTIAN RELIGION [35]

Book III

CHAPTER XXI

Eternal Election, or God's Predestination of Some to Salvation, and of Others to Destruction

. . . . . .

V. Predestination, by which God adopts some to the hope of life, and adjudges others to eternal death, no one, desirous of the credit of piety, dares absolutely to deny. But it is involved in many cavils, especially by those who make foreknowledge the cause of it. We maintain, that both belong to God; but it is preposterous to represent one as dependent on the other. When we attribute foreknowledge to God, we mean that all things have ever been, and perpetually remain, before his eyes, so that to his knowledge nothing is future or past, but all things are present; and present in such a manner, that he does not merely conceive of them from ideas formed in his mind, as things remembered by us appear present to our minds, but really beholds and sees them as if actually placed before him. And his foreknowledge extends to the whole world, and to all the creatures. Predestination we call the eternal decree of God, by which he has determined in himself, what he would have to become of every individual of mankind. For they are not all created with a similar destiny; but eternal life is foreordained for some, and eternal damnation for others. Every man, therefore, being created for one or the other of these ends, we say, he is predestined either to life or to death. This God has not only testified in particular persons, but has given a specimen of it in the whole posterity of Abraham, which should evidently show the future condition of every nation to depend upon his decision. "When the Most High divided the nations, when he separated the sons of Adam, the Lord's portion was his people; Jacob was the lot of his inheritance." (l) The separation is before the eyes of all: in the person of Abraham, as in the dry trunk of a tree, one people is peculiarly chosen to the rejection of others: no reason for this appears, except that Moses, to deprive their posterity of all occasion of glorying, teaches them that their exaltation is wholly from God's gratuitous love. He assigns this reason for their deliverance, that "he loved their fathers, and chose their seed after them." (m) More fully in another chapter: "The Lord did not set his love upon you, nor choose you, because you were more in number than any peo-

---

[35] John Calvin, *Institutes of the Christian Religion*, edited by J. Allen (Philadelphia: Presbyterian Board of Publication and Sabbath-School Work, 1813, 6th American edition, 1921), II, 144–146, 148–150, 184–186, 635–638, 641–643, 655–656, 662–663. (Reprinted by permission of the publishers.)

(l) Deut. xxxii. 8, 9.   (m) Deut. iv. 37.

ple; but because the Lord loved you." (n) He frequently repeats the same admonition: "Behold, the heaven is the Lord's thy God, the earth also, with all that therein is. Only the Lord had a delight in thy fathers to love them, and he chose their seed after them." (o) In another place, sanctification is enjoined upon them, because they were chosen to be a peculiar people. (p) And again, elsewhere, love is asserted to be the cause of their protection. It is declared by the united voice of the faithful, "He hath chosen our inheritance for us, the excellency of Jacob, whom he loved." (q) For the gifts conferred on them by God, they all ascribe to gratuitous love, not only from a consciousness that these were not obtained by any merit of theirs, but from a conviction, that the holy partriarch himself was not endued with such excellence as to acquire the privilege of so great an honour for himself and his posterity. And the more effectually to demolish all pride, he reproaches them with having deserved no favour, being "a stiff-necked and rebellious people." (r) The prophets also frequently reproach the Jews with the unwelcome mention of this election, because they had shamefully departed from it. . . .

VII. Though it is sufficiently clear, that God, in his secret counsel, freely chooses whom he will, and rejects others, his gratuitous election is but half displayed till we come to particular individuals, to whom God not only offers salvation, but assigns it in such a manner, that the certainty of the effect is liable to no suspense or doubt. These are included in that one seed mentioned by Paul; for though the adoption was deposited in the hand of Abraham, yet many of his posterity being cut off as putrid members, in order to maintain the efficacy and stability of election, it is necessary to ascend to the head, in whom their heavenly Father has bound his elect to each other, and united them to himself by an indissoluble bond. Thus the adoption of the family of Abraham displayed the favour of God, which he denied to others; but in the members of Christ there is a conspicuous exhibition of the superior efficacy of grace; because, being united to their head, they never fail of salvation. Paul, therefore, justly reasons from the passage of Malachi which I have just quoted, that where God, introducing the covenant of eternal life, invites any people to himself, there is a peculiar kind of election as to part of them, so that he does not efficaciously choose all with indiscriminate grace. The declaration, "Jacob have I loved," respects the whole posterity of the patriarch, whom the prophet there opposes to the descendants of Esau. Yet this is no objection to our having in the person of one individual a specimen of the election, which can never fail of attaining its full effect. These, who truly belong to Christ, Paul correctly observes, are called "a remnant;" for experience proves, that of a great multitude the most part fall away and disappear, so that often only a small portion remains. That the general election of a people is not always effectual and permanent, a reason readily presents itself, because, when God covenants with them, he does not also give them the spirit of regeneration to enable them to persevere in the covenant to the end; but the external call, without the internal efficacy of grace, which would be sufficient for their

(n) Deut. vii. 7, 8.
(o) Deut. x. 14, 15.
(p) Deut. xxiii.

(q) Psalms xlvii. 4.
(r) Deut. ix. 6, 7.

preservation, is a kind of medium between the rejection of all mankind and the election of the small number of believers. The whole nation of Israel was called "God's inheritance," though many of them were strangers; but God, having firmly covenanted to be their Father and Redeemer, regards that gratuitous favour rather than the defection of multitudes; by whom his truth was not violated, because his preservation of a certain remnant to himself, made it evident that his calling was without repentance. For God's collection of a Church for himself, from time to time, from the children to Abraham, rather than from the profane nations, was in consideration of his covenant, which, being violated by the multitude, he restricted to a few, to prevent its total failure. Lastly, the general adoption of the seed of Abraham was a visible representation of a greater blessing, which God conferred on a few out of the multitude. This is the reason that Paul so carefully distinguishes the descendants of Abraham according to the flesh, from his spiritual children called after the example of Isaac. Not that the mere descent from Abraham was a vain and unprofitable thing, which could not be asserted without depreciating the covenant; but because to the latter alone the immutable counsel of God, in which he predestinated whom he would, was of itself effectual to salvation. But I advise my readers to adopt no prejudice on either side, till it shall appear from adduced passages of Scripture what sentiments ought to be entertained. In conformity, therefore, to the clear doctrine of the Scripture, we assert, that by an eternal and immutable counsel, God has once for all determined, both whom he would admit to salvation, and whom he would condemn to destruction. We affirm that this counsel, as far as concerns the elect, is founded on his gratuitous mercy, totally irrespective of human merit; but that to those whom he devotes to condemnation, the gate of life is closed by a just and irreprehensible, but incomprehensible judgment. In the elect, we consider calling as an evidence of election, and justification as another token of its manifestation, till they arrive in glory, which constitutes its completion. As God seals his elect by vocation and justification, so by excluding the reprobate from the knowledge of his name and the sanctification of his Spirit, he affords an indication of the judgment that waits them. Here I shall pass over many fictions fabricated by foolish men to overthrow predestination. It is unnecessary to refute things which, as soon as they are advanced, sufficiently prove their own falsehood. I shall dwell only on those things which are subjects of controversy among the learned, or which may occasion difficulty to simple minds, or which impiety speciously pleads in order to stigmatize the Divine justice.

. . . . . .

CHAPTER XXIV

Election Confirmed by the Divine Call. The Destined Destruction of the Reprobate Procured by Themselves

. . . . . .

VI. For the establishment of our confidence, there is also another confirmation of election, which, we have said, is connected with our calling. For those whom Christ illuminates with the knowledge of his name, and introduces into the bosom of his Church, he is said to receive into his charge and protection. And all whom he receives are said to be committed and intrusted to him by the Father, to be kept to eternal life. What do we wish for ourselves? Christ loudly proclaims that all whose salvation was designed by the Father, had been delivered by him into his protection. (m) If, therefore, we want to ascertain whether God is concerned for our salvation, let us inquire whether he had committed us to Christ, whom he constituted the only Saviour of all his people. Now, if we doubt whether Christ has received us into his charge and custody, he obviates this doubt, by freely offering himself as our Shepherd, and declaring that if we hear his voice, we shall be numbered among his sheep. We therefore embrace Christ, thus kindly offered to us and advancing to meet us; and he will number us with his sheep, and preserve us enclosed in his fold. But yet we feel anxiety for our future state; for as Paul declares that "whom he predestinated, them he also called," (n) so Christ informs us that "many are called but few chosen." (o)

. . . . . .

Book IV

CHAPTER XX

On Civil Government

. . . . . .

III. But for speaking of the exercise of civil polity, there will be another place more suitable. At present we only wish it to be understood, that to entertain a thought of its extermination, is inhuman barbarism; it is equally as necessary to mankind as bread and water, light and air, and far more excellent. For it not only tends to secure the accommodations arising from all these things, that men may breathe, eat, drink, and be sustained in life, though it comprehends all these things while it causes them to live together, yet, I say, this is not its only tendency; its objects also are, that idolatry, sacrileges against the name of God, blasphemies against his truth, and other offences against religion, may not openly appear and be disseminated among the people; that the public tranquillity may not be disturbed; that every person may enjoy his property without molestation; that men may transact their business together without fraud or injustice; that integrity and modesty may be cultivated among them; in short, that there may be a public form of religion among Christians, and that humanity may be maintained among men. Nor let any one think it strange that I now refer to human polity the charge of the due maintenance of religion, which I may appear to have placed beyond the jurisdiction of men. For I do not allow men to make laws respecting religion and the worship of God now, any more than I did before; though I approve of civil government, which provides that the true religion which is contained in the law of God, be not violated, and pol- luted by public blasphemies, with impunity. But the perspicuity of order will assist the readers to attain a clearer understanding of what sentiments ought to be entertained respecting the whole system of civil administration, if we enter on a discussion of each branch of it. These are three: The magis- trate, who is the guardian and conservator of the laws: The laws, according to which he governs: The people, who are governed by the laws, and obey the magistrate. Let us, therefore, examine, first, the function of a magistrate,

(m) John vi. 37, 39; vii. 6, 12. (n) Rom. viii. 30. (o) Matt. xxii. 14.

whether it be a legitimate calling and approved by God, the nature of the duty, and the extent of the power; secondly, by what laws Christian government ought to be regulated; and lastly, what advantage the people derive from the laws, and what obedience they owe to the magistrate.

IV. The Lord has not only testified that the function of magistrates has his approbation and acceptance, but has eminently commended it to us, by dignifying it with the most honourable titles. We will mention a few of them. When all who sustain the magistracy are called "gods," (e) it ought not to be considered as an appellation of trivial importance; for it implies, that they have their command from God, that they are invested with his authority, and are altogether his representatives, and act as his vicegerents. This is not an invention of mine, but the interpretation of Christ, who says, "If he called them gods, unto whom the word of God came, and the Scripture cannot be broken." (f) What is the meaning of this, but that their commission has been given to them by God, to serve him in their office, and, as Moses and Jehoshaphat said to the judges whom they appointed, to "judge not for man, but for the Lord?" (g) To the same purpose is the declaration of the wisdom of God by the mouth of Solomon: "By me kings reign, and princes decree justice. By me princes rule, and nobles, even all the judges of the earth." (h) This is just as if it had been affirmed, that the authority possessed by kings and other governors over all things upon earth is not a consequence of the perverseness of men, but of the providence and holy ordinance of God, who has been pleased to regulate human affairs in this manner; for as much as he is present, and also presides among them, in making laws and in executing equitable judgments. This is clearly taught by Paul, when he enumerates governments (i) among the gifts of God, which, being variously distributed according to the diversity of grace, ought to be employed by the servants of Christ to the edification of the Church. For though in that place he is properly speaking of the council of elders, who were appointed in the primitive Church to preside over the regulation of the public discipline, the same office with which in writing to the Corinthians he calls "governments," (k) yet, as we see that civil government tends to promote the same object, there is no doubt that he recommends to us every kind of just authority. But he does this in a manner much more explicit, where he enters on a full discussion of that subject. For he says, "There is no power but of God; the powers that be are ordained of God. Rulers are ministers of God, revengers to execute wrath upon him that doeth evil. Do that which is good, and thou shalt have praise of the same." (l) This is corroborated by the examples of holy men; of whom some have been kings, as David, Josiah, Hezekiah; some have been viceroys, as Joseph and Daniel; some have held civil offices in a commonwealth, as Moses, Joshua, and the Judges; whose functions God declared to be approved by him. Wherefore no doubt ought now to be entertained by any person that civil magistracy is a calling not only holy and legitimate, but far the most sacred and honourable in human life. . . .

VI. This consideration ought continually to occupy the magistrates themselves, since it is calculated to furnish them with a powerful stimulus, by

(e) Psalm lxxxii. 1, 6.
(f) John x. 35.
(g) Deut. i. 16, 17. 2 Chron. xix. 6.
(h) Prov. viii. 15, 16.

(i) Rom. xii. 8.
(k) 1 Cor. xii. 28.
(l) Rom. xiii. 1, 3, 4.

which they may be excited to their duty, and to afford them peculiar consolation, by which the difficulties of their office, which certainly are many and arduous, may be alleviated. For what an ardent pursuit of integrity, prudence, clemency, moderation, and innocence ought they to prescribe to themselves, who are conscious of having been constituted ministers of the Divine justice! With what confidence will they admit iniquity to their tribunal, which they understand to be the throne of the living God? With what audacity will they pronounce an unjust sentence with that mouth which they know to be the destined organ of Divine truth? With what conscience will they subscribe to impious decrees with that hand which they know to be appointed to register the edicts of God? In short, if they remember that they are the vicegerents of God, it behoves them to watch with all care, earnestness, and diligence, that in their administration they may exhibit to men an image, as it were, of the providence, care, goodness, benevolence, and justice of God. And they must constantly bear this in mind, that if in all cases "he be cursed that doeth the work of the Lord deceitfully," (p) a far heavier curse awaits those who act fraudulently in a righteous calling. Therefore, when Moses and Jehoshaphat wished to exhort their judges to the discharge of their duty, they had nothing to suggest more efficacious than the principle which we have already mentioned. Moses says, "Judge righteously between every man and his brother, and the stranger that is with him. For the judgment is God's." (q) Jehoshaphat says, "Take heed what ye do; for ye judge not for man, but for the Lord, who is with you in the judgment. Wherefore now let the fear of the Lord be upon you: take heed and do it; for there is no iniquity with the Lord our God." (r) And in another place it is said, "God standeth in the congregation of the mighty: he judgeth among the gods;" (s) that they may be animated to their duty, when they understand that they are delegated by God, to whom they must one day render an account of their administration. And this admonition is entitled to have considerable weight with them; for if they fail in their duty, they not only injure men by criminally distressing them, but even offend God by polluting his sacred judgments. On the other hand, it opens a source of peculiar consolation to them to reflect, that they are not employed in profane things, or occupations unsuitable to a servant of God, but in a most sacred function, inasmuch as they execute a Divine commission. . . .

IX. Here it is necessary to state in a brief manner the nature of the office of magistracy, as described in the word of God, and wherein it consists. If the Scripture did not teach that this office extends to both tables of the law, we might learn it from heathen writers; for not one of them has treated of the office of magistrates, of legislation, and civil government, without beginning with religion and Divine worship. And thus they have all confessed that no government can be happily constituted, unless its first object be the promotion of piety and that all laws are preposterous which neglect the claims of God, and merely provide for the interests of men. Therefore, as religion holds the first place among all the philosophers, and as this has always been regarded by the universal consent of all nations, Christian princes and magistrates ought to be ashamed of their indolence, if they do not make it the

(p) Jer. xlviii. 10.　　　　　　　　　　(r) 2 Chron. xix. 6, 7.
(q) Deut. i. 16, 17.　　　　　　　　　　(s) Psalm lxxxii. 1.

object of their most serious care. We have already shown that this duty is particularly enjoined upon them by God; for it is reasonable that they should employ their utmost efforts in asserting and defending the honour of him, whose vicegerents they are, and by whose favour they govern. And the principal commendations given in the Scripture to the good kings are for having restored the worship of God when it had been corrupted or abolished, or for having devoted their attention to religion, that it might flourish in purity and safety under their reigns. On the contrary, the sacred history represents it as one of the evils arising from anarchy, or a want of good government, that when "there was no king in Israel, every man did that which was right in his own eyes." (x) These things evince the folly of those who would wish magistrates to neglect all thoughts of God, and to confine themselves entirely to the administration of justice among men; as though God appointed governors in his name to decide secular controversies, and disregarded that which is of far greater importance—the pure worship of himself according to the rule of his law. But a rage for universal innovation, and a desire to escape with impunity, instigate men of turbulent spirits to wish that all the avengers of violated piety were removed out of the world. With respect to the second table, Jeremiah admonishes kings in the following manner: "Execute ye judgment and righteousness, and deliver the spoiled out of the hand of the oppressor; and do no wrong, do no violence to the stranger, the fatherless, nor the widow, neither shed innocent blood." (y) To the same purpose is the exhortation in the eighty-second psalm: "Defend the poor and fatherless: do justice to the afflicted and needy: deliver the poor and needy: rid them out of the hand of the wicked." (z) And Moses "charged the judges" whom he appointed to supply his place, saying, "Hear the causes between your brethren, and judge righteously between every man and his brother, and the stranger that is with him: ye shall not respect persons in judgment; but ye shall hear the small as well as the great; ye shall not be afraid of the face of man; for the judgment is God's." (a) I forbear to remark the directions given by him in another place respecting their future kings: "He shall not multiply horses to himself; neither shall he greatly multiply to himself silver and gold; his heart shall not be lifted up above his brethren; he shall read in the law all the days of his life;" (b) also that judges show no partiality, nor take bribes, with similar injunctions, which abound in the Scriptures; because, in describing the office of magistrates in this treatise, my design is not so much to instruct magistrates themselves, as to show to others what magistrates are, and for what end God has appointed them. We see, therefore, that they are constituted the protectors and vindicators of the public innocence, modesty, probity, and tranquillity, whose sole object it ought to be to promote the common peace and security of all. Of these virtues, David declares that he will be an example, when he shall be exalted to the royal throne. "I will set no wicked thing before mine eyes. I will not know a wicked person. Whoso privily slandereth his neighbour, him will I cut off: him that hath a high look and a proud heart will I not suffer. Mine eyes shall be upon the faithful of the land, that they may dwell with

(x) Judges xxi. 25.
(y) Jer. xxii. 3.
(z) Psalm lxxxii, 3, 4.

(a) Deut. i. 16, 17.
(b) Deut. xvii. 16, 17, 19, 20.

me: he that walketh in a perfect way, he shall serve me." (c) But as they cannot do this, unless they defend good men from the injuries of the wicked, and aid the oppressed by their relief and protection, they are likewise armed with power for the suppression of crimes, and the severe punishment of malefactors, whose wickedness disturbs the public peace. For experience fully verifies the observation of Solon: "That all states are supported by reward and punishment; and that when these two things are removed, all the discipline of human societies is broken and destroyed." For the minds of many lose their regard for equity and justice, unless virtue be rewarded with due honour; nor can the violence of the wicked be restrained, unless crimes are followed by severe punishments. And these two parts are included in the injunction of the prophet to kings and other governors, to "execute judgment and righteousness." (d) *Righteousness* means the care, patronage, defence, vindication, and liberation of the innocent: *judgment* imports the repression of the audacity, the coercion of the violence, and the punishment of the crimes, of the impious. . . .

XXIII. Hence follows another duty, that, with minds disposed to honour and reverence magistrates, subjects approve their obedience to them, in submitting to their edicts, in paying taxes, in discharging public duties, and bearing burdens which relate to the common defence, and in fulfilling all their other commands. Paul says to the Roman, "Let every soul be subject unto the higher powers. Whosoever resisteth the power, resisteth the ordinance of God." (m) He writes to Titus, "Put them in mind to be subject to principalities and powers, to obey magistrates, to be ready to every good work." (n) Peter exhorts, "Submit yourselves to every ordinance of man for the Lord's sake; whether it be to the king, as supreme; or unto governors, as unto them that are sent by him for the punishment of evil-doers, and for the praise of them that do well." (o) Moreover, that subjects may testify that theirs is not a hypocritical but a sincere and cordial submission, Paul teaches, that they ought to pray to God for the safety and prosperity of those under whose government they live. "I exhort," he says, "that supplications, prayers, intercessions, and giving of thanks, be made for all men; for kings, and for all that are in authority; that we may lead a quiet and peaceable life in all godliness and honesty." (p) Here let no man deceive himself. For as it is impossible to resist the magistrate without, at the same time, resisting God himself; though an unarmed magistrate may seem to be despised with impunity, yet God is armed to inflict exemplary vengeance on the contempt offered to himself. Under this obedience I also include the moderation which private persons ought to prescribe to themselves in relation to public affairs, that they do not, without being called upon, intermeddle with affairs of state, or rashly intrude themselves into the office of magistrates, or undertake any thing of a public nature. If there be any thing in the public administration which requires to be corrected, let them not raise any tumults, or take the business into their own hands, which ought to be all bound in this respect, but let them refer it to the cognizance of the magistrate, who is alone authorized

(c) Psalm ci. 3–6.
(d) Jer. xxii. 3.
(m) Rom. xiii. 1, 2.

(n) Titus iii. 1.
(o) 1 Peter ii. 13, 14.
(p) 1 Tim. ii. 1, 2.

to regulate the concerns of the public. I mean, that they ought to attempt nothing without being commanded; for when they have the command of a governor, then they also are invested with public authority. For, as we are accustomed to call the counsellors of a prince *his eyes and ears,* so they may not unaptly be called *his hands* whom he has commissioned to execute his commands. . . .

XXXII. But in the obedience which we have shown to be due to the authority of governors, it is always necessary to make one exception, and that is entitled to our first attention,—that it do not seduce us from obedience to him, to whose will the desires of all kings ought to be subject, to whose decrees all their commands ought to yield, to whose majesty all their sceptres ought to submit. And, indeed, how preposterous it would be for us, with a view to satisfy men, to incur the displeasure of him on whose account we yield obedience to men! The Lord, therefore, is the King of kings; who, when he has opened his sacred mouth, is to be heard alone, above all, for all, and before all; in the next place, we are subject to those men who preside over us; but no otherwise than in him. If they command any thing against him, it ought not to have the least attention; nor, in this case, ought we to pay any regard to all the dignity attached to magistrates; to which no injury is done when it is subjected to the unrivalled and supreme power of God. On this principle Daniel denied that he had committed any crime against the king in disobeying his impious decree; (i) because the king had exceeded the limits of his office, and had not only done an injury to men, but, by raising his arm against God, had degraded his own authority. On the other hand, the Israelites are condemned for having been too submissive to the impious edicts of their king. For when Jeroboam had made his golden calves, in compliance with his will, they deserted the temple of God and revolted to new superstitions. Their posterity conformed to the decrees of their idolatrous kings with the same facility. The prophet severely condemns them for having "willingly walked after the commandment:" (k) so far is any praise from being due to the pretext of humility, with which courtly flatterers excuse themselves and deceive the unwary, when they deny that it is lawful for them to refuse compliance with any command of their king; as if God had resigned his right to mortal men when he made them rulers of mankind; or as if earthly power were diminished by being subordinated to its author, before whom even the principalities of heaven tremble with awe. I know what great and present dangers awaits this constancy, for kings cannot bear to be disregarded without the greatest indignation; and "the wrath of a king," says Solomon, "is as messengers of death." (l) But since this edict has been proclaimed by that celestial herald, Peter, "We ought to obey God rather than men," (m) —let us console ourselves with this thought, that we truly perform the obedience which God requires of us, when we suffer any thing rather than deviate from piety. And that our hearts may not fail us, Paul stimulates us with another consideration— that Christ has redeemed us at the immense price which our redemption cost him, that we may not be submissive to the corrupt desires of men, much less be slaves to their impiety. (n)

(i) Dan. vi. 22.   (l) Prov. xvi. 14.   (n) 1 Cor. vii. 23.
(k) Hos. v. 11.   (m) Acts v. 29.

JOHN COTTON

In 1635 a group of English nobles and gentry desired to settle in the colonies, but were undecided whether to go to Massachusetts Bay or to Connecticut, or to establish a new colony. They consequently made certain demands upon the governor of Massachusetts Bay as conditions of migrating there. These concerned the organization of the governmental system and the status that they might expect in the new communities. A group of colonial leaders, among whom was John Cotton, met and prepared an answer. Two replies were made: (1) a personal letter written by John Cotton to Lord Say and Seale, and (2) a document that answered the demands proposition by proposition. The answers proved unsatisfactory, and Lord Say and Seale and his followers did not migrate to Massachusetts Bay. These two communications clearly portray the political organization of Massachusetts Bay in 1636 and the theocratic nature of its polity.

John Cotton emigrated to Massachusetts Bay in 1633 and immediately became the leading minister of the colony. He assumed a rôle of prime importance in guiding its civil as well as its ecclesiastical affairs. As the arch-priest of orthodox Puritanism, he took the lead in the attack upon the radicalism and heresy of Roger Williams—a battle which continued after the expulsion of Williams from Massachusetts Bay. Cotton replied to Williams's plea for toleration with his book, *The Bloudy Tenent, Washed and Made White in the Blood of the Lambe* (1647).

COPY OF A LETTER FROM MR. COTTON TO LORD SAY AND SEALE IN THE YEAR 1636 [36]

Right honourable,

What your Lordship writeth of Dr. Twisse his works de *scientiâ mediâ*, and of the sabbath, it did refresh me to reade, that his labors of such arguments were like to come to light; and it would refresh me much more to see them here: though (for my owne particular) till I gett some release from some constant labors here (which the church is desirous to procure) I can get little, or noe oppertunity to reade any thing, or attend to any thing, but the dayly occurrences which presse in upon me continually, much beyond my strength either of body or minde. Your Lordships advertisement touching the civill state of this colony, as they doe breath forth your singular wisdome, and faithfulness, and tender care of the peace, so wee have noe reason to misinterprite, or undervalue your Lordships eyther directions, or intentions therein. I know noe man under heaven (I speake in Gods feare without flattery) whose counsell I should rather depend upon, for the wise administration of a civill state according to God, than upon your Lordship, and such confidence have I (not in you) but in the Lords presence in Christ with you, that I should never feare to betrust a greater commonwealth than this (as much as in us lyeth) under such a *perpetuâ dictaturâ* as your Lordship should prescribe. For I nothing doubt, but that eyther your Lordship would prescribe all things according to the rule, or be willing to examine againe, and againe, all things according to it. I am very apt to believe, what Mr. Perkins hath, in one of his prefatory pages to his golden chaine, that the word, and scriptures of God doe conteyne a short *upoluposis*, or platforme, not onely of theology, but also of other sacred sciences, (as he calleth them) at-

[36] Thomas Hutchinson, *History of the Colony of Massachusetts-Bay* (London 1760), I, 496–501.

tendants, and handmaids thereunto, which he maketh ethicks, eoconomicks, politicks, church-government, prophecy, academy.   It is very suitable to Gods all-sufficient wisdome, and to the fulnes and perfection of Holy Scriptures, not only to prescribe perfect rules for the right ordering of a private mans soule to everlasting blessednes with himselfe, but also for the right ordering of a mans family, yea, of the commonwealth too, so farre as both of them are subordinate to spiritual ends, and yet avoide both the churches usurpation upon civill jurisdictions, *in ordine ad spiritualia,* and the commonwealths invasion upon ecclesiasticall administrations, *in ordine* to civill peace, and conformity to the civill state.   Gods institutions (such as the government of church and of commonwealth be) may be close and compact, and coordinate one to another, and yet not confounded.   God hath so framed the state of church government and ordinances, that they may be compatible to any common-wealth, though never so much disordered in his frame.   But yet when a commonwealth hath liberty to mould his owne frame (*scripturæ plenitudinem adoro*) I conceyve the scripture hath given full direction for the right ordering of the same, and that, in such sort as best mainteyne the *euexia* of the church.   Mr. Hooker doth often quote a saying of our Mr. Cartwright (though I have not read it in him) that noe man fashioneth his house to his hangings, but his hangings to his house.   It is better that the commonwealth be fashioned to the setting forth of Gods house, which is his church: than to accommodate the church frame to the civill state.   Democracy, I do not conceyve that ever God did ordeyne as a fitt government eyther for church or commonwealth.   If the people be governors, who shall be governed? As for monarchy, and aristocracy, they are both of them clearly approved, and directed in scripture, yet so as referreth the soveraigntie to himselfe, and setteth up Theocracy in both, as the best forme of government in the commonwealth, as well as in the church.

The law, which your Lordship instanceth in (that none shall be chosen to magistracy among us but a church member) was made and enacted before I came into the country; but I have hitherto wanted sufficient light to plead against it.   1st. The rule that directeth the choice of supreame governors, is of like aequitie and weight in all magistrates, that one of their brethren (not a stranger) should be set over them, Deut. 17. 15. and Jethroes counsell to Moses was approved of God, that the judges, and officers to be set over the people, should be men fearing God, Exod. 18. 21. and Solomon maketh it the joy of a commonwealth, when the righteous are in authority, and their mourning when the wicked rule, Prov. 29. 21. Job 34. 30.   Your Lordship's feare, that this will bring in papal excommunication, is iust, and pious: but let your Lordship be pleased againe to consider whether the consequence be necessary.   *Turpius ejicitur quam non admittitur:* non-membership may be a just cause of non-admission to the place of magistracy, but yet, ejection out of his membership will not be a just cause of ejecting him out of his magistracy.   A godly woman, being to make choice of an husband, may justly refuse a man that is eyther cast out of church fellowship, or is not yet receyved into it, but yet, when shee is once given to him, shee may not reject him then, for such defect.   Mr. Humfrey was chosen for an assistant (as I heare) before the colony came over hither: and, though he be not as yet ioyned into church fellowship (by reason of the unsetlednes of the congregation where he liveth) yet the commonwealth doe still continue his magistracy to him, as knowing he waiteth for oppertunity of enioying church fellowship shortly.

When your Lordship doubteth, that this corse will draw all things under the determination of the church, *in ordine ad spiritualia* (seeing the church is to determine who shall be members, and none but a member may have to doe in the government of a commonwealth) be pleased (I pray you) to conceyve, that magistrates are neyther chosen to office in the church, nor doe governe by directions from the church, but by civill lawes, and those enacted in generall corts, and executed in corts of iustice, by the governors and assistants. In all which, the church (as the church) hath nothing to doe: onely, it prepareth fitt instruments both to rule, and to choose rulers, which is no ambition in the church, nor dishonor to the commonwealth, the apostle, on the contrary, thought it a great dishonor and reproach to the church of Christ, if it were not able to yield able judges to heare and determine all causes amongst their brethren, 1 Cor. 6. 1. to 5. which place alone seemeth to me fully to decide this question: for it plainely holdeth forth this argument: It is a shame to the church to want able judges of civill matters (as v. 5.) and an audacious act in any church member voluntarily to go for judgment, otherwise than before the saints (as v. 1.) then it will be noe arrogance nor folly in church members, nor prejudice to the commonwealth, if voluntarily they never choose any civill judges, but from amongst the saints, such as church members are called to be. But the former is cleare: and how then can the latter be avoyded. If this therefore be (as your Lordship rightely conceyveth one of the maine objections if not the onely one) which hindereth this commonwealth from the entertainment of the propositions of those worthy gentlemen, wee intreate them, in the name of the Lord Jesus, to consider, in meeknes of wisdome, it is not any conceite or will of ours, but the holy counsell and will of the Lord Jesus (whom they seeke to serve as well as wee) that overruleth us in this case: and we trust will overrule them also, that the Lord onely may be exalted amongst all his servants. What pittie and griefe were it, that the observance of the will of Christ should hinder good things from us!

But your Lordship doubteth, that if such a rule were necessary, then the church estate and the best ordered commonwealth in the world were not compatible. But let not your Lordship so conceyve. For, the church, submitteth itselfe to all the lawes and ordinances of men, in what commonwealth soever they come to dwell. But it is one thing, to submit unto what they have noe calling to reforme: another thing, voluntarily to ordeyne a forme of government, which is the best discerning of many of us (for I speake not of myselfe) is expressly contrary to rule. Nor neede your Lordship feare (which yet I speake with submission to your Lordships better judgment) that this corse will lay such a foundation, as nothing but a mere democracy can be built upon it. Bodine confesseth, that though it be *status popularis*, where a people choose their owne governors; yet the government is not a democracy, if it be administred, not by the people, but by the governors, whether one (for then it is a monarchy, though elective) or by many, for then (as you know) it is aristocracy. In which respect it is, that church government is iustly denyed (even by Mr. Robinson) to be democratical, though the people choose their owne officers and rulers.

Nor neede wee feare, that this course will, in time, cast the commonwealth into distractions, and popular confusions. For (under correction) these three things doe not undermine, but doe mutually and strongly mainteyne one another (even those three which wee principally aime at) authority in magistrates, liberty in people, purity in the church. Purity, preserved in the church, will preserve well ordered liberty in the people, and both of them establish well-balanced authority in the magistrates. God is the author of all these three, and neyther is himselfe the God of confusion, nor are his wayes the wayes of confusion, but of peace.

What our brethren (magistrates or ministers, or leading freeholders) will answer to the rest of the propositions, I shall better understand before the gentlemans returne from Connecticutt, who brought them over. Mean while two of the principall of them, the generall cort hath already condescended unto. 1. In establishing a standing councell, who, during their lives, should assist the governor in managing the chiefest affayres of this little state. They have chosen, for the present, onely two (Mr. Winthrope and Mr. Dudley) not willing to choose more, till they see what further better choyse the Lord will send over to them, that so they may keep an open doore, for such desireable gentlemen as your Lordship mentioneth. 2. They have graunted the governor and assistants a negative voyce, and reserved to the freemen the like liberty also. Touching other things, I hope to give your Lordship further account, when the gentleman returneth.

He being now returned, I have delivered to him an answer to the rest of your demands, according to the mindes of such leading men amongst us, as I thought meete to consult withall, concealing your name from any, except 2 or 3, who alike doe concurr in a joynt desire of yielding to any such propositions, as your Lordship demandeth, so farre as with allowance from the word they may, beyond which I know your Lordship would not require any thing.

Now the Lord Jesus Christ (the prince of peace) keepe and bless your Lordship, and dispose of all your times and talents to his best advantage: and let the covenant of his grace and peace rest upon your honourable family and posterity throughout all generations.

Thus, humbly craving pardon for my boldnesse and length, I take leave and rest,

Yours Honours to serve in Christ Jesus,

J. C.

CERTAIN PROPOSALS MADE BY LORD SAY, LORD BROOKE, AND OTHER PERSONS OF QUALITY, AS CONDITIONS OF THEIR REMOVING TO NEW-ENGLAND, WITH THE ANSWERS THERETO. (1636) [37]

Demand 1. That the common-wealth should consist of two distinct ranks of men, whereof the one should be for them and their heirs, gentlemen of the country, the other for them and their heirs, freeholders.

Answer. Two distinct ranks we willingly acknowledge, from the light of nature and scripture; the one of them called Princes, or Nobles, or Elders

[37] Thomas Hutchinson, *History of the Colony of Massachusetts-Bay* (London, 1760), I, 490–495.

(amongst whom gentlemen have their place) the other the people. Hereditary dignity or honours we willingly allow to the former, unless by the scandalous and base conversation of any of them, they become degenerate. Hereditary liberty, or estate of freemen, we willingly allow to the other, unless they also, by some unworthy and slavish carriage, do disfranchize themselves.

Dem. 2. That in these gentlemen and freeholders, assembled together, the chief power of the common-wealth shall be placed, both for making and repealing laws.

Ans. So it is with us.

Dem. 3. That each of these two ranks should, in all public assemblies, have a negative voice, so as without a mutual consent nothing should be established.

Ans. So it is agreed among us.

Dem. 4. That the first rank, consisting of gentlemen, should have power, for them and their heirs, to come to the parliaments or public assemblies, and there to give their free votes personally; the second rank of freeholders should have the same power for them and their heirs of meeting and voting, but by their deputies.

Ans. Thus far this demand is practised among us. The freemen meet and vote by their deputies; the other rank give their votes personally, only with this difference, there be no more of the gentlemen that give their votes personally, but such as are chosen to places of office, either governors, deputy governors, councellors, or assistants. All gentlemen in England have not that honour to meet and vote personally in Parliament, much less all their heirs. But of this more fully, in an answer to the ninth and tenth demand.

Dem. 5. That for facilitating and dispatch of business, and other reasons, the gentlemen and freeholders should sit and hold their meetings in two distinct houses.

Ans. We willingly approve the motion, only as yet it is not so practiced among us, but in time, the variety and discrepancy of sundry occurrences will put them upon a necessity of sitting apart.

Dem. 6. That there shall be set times for these meetings, annually or half yearly, or as shall be thought fit by common consent, which meetings should have a set time for their continuance, but should be adjourned or broken off at the discretion of both houses.

Ans. Public meetings, in general courts, are by charter appointed to be quarterly, which, in this infancy of the colony, wherein many things frequently occur which need settling, hath been of good use, but when things are more fully settled in due order, it is likely that yearly or half yearly meetings will be sufficient. For the continuance or breaking up of these courts, nothing is done but with the joint consent of both branches.

Dem. 7. That it shall be in the power of this parliament, thus constituted and assembled, to call the governor and all publick officers to account, to create new officers, and to determine them already set up: and, the better to stop the way to insolence and ambition, it may be ordered that all offices and fees of office shall, every parliament, determine, unless they be new confirmed the last day of every session.

Ans. This power to call governors and all officers to account, and to create new and determine the old, is settled already in the general court or parliament, only it is not put forth but once in the year, viz. at the great and general court in May, when the governor is chosen.

Dem. 8. That the governor shall ever be chosen out of the rank of gentlemen.

Ans. We never practice otherwise, chusing the governor either out of the assistants, which is our ordinary course, or out of approved known gentlemen, as this year Mr. Vane.

Dem. 9. That, for the present, the Right Honorable the Lord Viscount Say and Seale, the Lord Brooke, who have already been at great disbursements for the public works in New-England, and such other gentlemen of approved sincerity and worth, as they, before their personal remove, shall take into their number, should be admitted for them and their heirs, gentlemen of the country. But, for the future, none shall be admitted into this rank but by the consent of both houses.

Ans. The great disbursements of these noble personages and worthy gentlemen we thankfully acknowledge, because the safety and presence of our brethren at Connecticut is no small blessing and comfort to us. But, though that charge had never been disbursed, the worth of the honorable persons named is so well known to all, and our need of such supports and guides is so sensible to ourselves, that we do not doubt the country would thankfully accept it, as a singular favor from God and from them, if he should bow their hearts to come into this wilderness and help us. As for accepting them and their heirs into the number of gentlemen of the country, the custom of this country is, and readily would be, to receive and acknowledge, not only all such eminent persons as themselves and the gentlemen they speak of, but others of meaner estate, so be it is of some eminency, to be for them and their heirs, gentlemen of the country. Only, thus standeth our case. Though we receive them with honor and allow them pre-eminence and accommodations according to their condition, yet we do not, ordinarily, call them forth to the power of election, or administration of magistracy, until they be received as members into some of our churches, a privilege, which we doubt not religious gentlemen will willingly desire (as David did in Psal. xxvii. 4) and christian churches will as readily impart to such desirable persons. Hereditary honors both nature and scripture doth acknowledge (Eccles. xix. 17.) but hereditary authority and power standeth only by the civil laws of some commonwealths, and yet, even amongst them the authority and power of the father is no where communicated, together with his honors, unto all his posterity. Where God blesseth any branch of any noble or generous family, with a spirit and gifts fit for government, it would be a taking of God's name in vain to put such a talent under a bushel, and a sin against the honor of magistracy to neglect such in our public elections. But if God should not delight to furnish some of their posterity with gifts fit for magistracy, we should expose them rather to reproach and prejudice, and the commonwealth with them, than exalt them to honor, if we should call them forth, when God doth not, to public authority.

Dem. 10. That the rank of freeholders shall be made up of such, as shall have so much personal estate there, as shall be thought fit for men of that condition, and have contributed, some fit proportion, to the public charge of the country, either by their disbursements or labors.

Ans. We must confess our ordinary practice to be otherwise. For, excepting the old planters, i.e. Mr. Humphry, who himself was admitted an assistant at London, and all of them freemen, before the churches here were established, none are admitted freemen of this commonwealth but such as are first admitted members of some church or other in this country, and, of such, none are excluded from the liberty of freemen. And out of such only, I mean the more eminent sort of such, it is that our magistrates are chosen. Both which points we should willingly persuade our people to change, if we could make it appear to them, that such a change might be made according to God; for, to give you a true account of the grounds of our proceedings herein, it seemeth to them, and also to us, to be a divine ordinance (and moral) than none should be appointed and chosen by the people of God, magistrates over them, but men fearing God (Ex. xviii. 21) chosen out of their brethren (Deut. xvii. 15.) saints (1 Cor. vi. 1.) Yea, the apostle maketh it a shame to the church, if it be not able to afford wise men from out of themselves, which shall be able to judge all civil matters between their brethren (ver. 5.) And Solomon maketh it the joy of a commonwealth, when the righteous are in authority, and the calamity thereof, when the wicked bear rule. Prov. xxix. 2.

Obj. If it be said, there may be many carnal men whom God hath invested with sundry eminent gifts of wisdom, courage, justice, fit for government.

Ans. Such may be fit to be consulted with and employed by governors, according to the quality and use of their gifts and parts, but yet are men not fit to be trusted with place of standing power or settled authority. Ahitophel's wisdom may be fit to be heard (as an oracle of God) but not fit to be trusted with power of settled magistracy, lest he at last call for 12000 men to lead them forth against David, 2 Sam. xvii. 1, 2, 3. The best gifts and parts, under a covenant of works (under which all carnal men and hypocrites be) will at length turn aside by crooked ways, to depart from God, and, finally, to fight against God, and are therefore, herein, opposed to good men and upright in heart, Psal. cxxv. 4, 5.

Obj. If it be said again, that then the church estate could not be compatible with any commonwealth under heaven.

Ans. It is one thing for the church or members of the church, loyally to submit unto any form of government, when it is above their calling to reform it, another thing to chuse a form of government and governors discrepant from the rule. Now, if it be a divine truth, that none are to be trusted with public permanent authority but godly men, who are fit materials for church fellowship, then from the same grounds it will appear, that none are so fit to be trusted with the liberties of the commonwealth as church members. For, the liberties of the freemen of this commonwealth are such, as require men of faithful integrity to God and the state, to preserve the same. Their liberties, among others, are chiefly these. 1. To chuse all magistrates, and to call them to account at their general courts. 2. To chuse such burgesses, every general court, as with the magistrates shall make or repeal all laws. Now both these liberties are such, as carry along much power with them, either to establish or subvert the commonwealth, and therewith the church, which power, if it be committed to men not according to their godliness, which maketh them fit for church fellowship, but according to their wealth, which, as such, makes them no better than worldly men, then, in case worldly men should prove the major part, as soon they might do, they would as readily set over us magistrates like themselves, such as might hate us according to the curse, Levit. xxvi. 17. and turn the edge of all authority and laws against the church and the members thereof, the maintenance of whole peace is the chief end which God aimed at in the institution of Magistracy. 1 Tim. ii. 1. 2.

A PLATFORM OF CHURCH DISCIPLINE [38]

The Platform of Church Discipline was drawn up by a church synod meeting at Cambridge in 1649 and submitted to the General Court of Massachusetts Bay for its acceptance. Some of its provisions caused opposition, but the General Court finally accepted the Platform. The document is an exposition of church polity as it existed during the early period of Puritanism. It describes the nature, organization, and powers of the church and the relation of the church to the civil state.

A PLATFORM OF CHURCH DISCIPLINE
Gathered out of the Word of God
And Agreed upon by the Elders and Messengers of the Churches
Assembled in the Synod, at Cambridge, in New-England.
To be Presented to the Churches and General Court for
their Consideration and Acceptance in the Lord, the
8th Month, Anno 1649.

CHAPTER I
Of the Form of Church-Government; and that it is One, Immutable, and Prescribed in the Word.

1. Ecclesiastical polity, or church-government or discipline, is nothing else but that form and order that is to be observed in the church of Christ upon earth, both for the constitution of it, and all the administrations that herein are to be performed.

2. Church-government is considered in a double respect, either in regard of the parts of government themselves, or necessary circumstances thereof. The parts of government are prescribed in the word, because the Lord Jesus Christ, (Heb. iii. 5, 6; Exo. xxv. 40; 2 Tim. iii. 16,) the King and Law-giver in his Church, is no less faithful in the house of God, than was Moses, who from the Lord delivered a form and pattern of government to the children of Israel in the Old Testament; and the holy Scriptures are now also so perfect as they are able to make the man of God perfect, and thoroughly furnish unto every good work; and therefore doubtless to the well-ordering of the house of God.

3. The parts of church-government are all of them exactly described in the word of God, (1 Tim. iii. 15; 1 Chr. xv. 13; Exod. ii. 4; 1 Tim. vi. 13. 16; Heb. xii. 27, 28; 1 Cor. xv. 24,) being parts or means of instituted worship according to the second commandment, and therefore to continue one and the same unto the appearing of our Lord Jesus Christ, as a kingdom that cannot be shaken, until he shall deliver it up unto God, even to the Father.

[38] Cotton Mather, *Magnalia Christi Americana*. (Hartford, Connecticut, Silas Andrus & Son, 1855), II, 211-236.

(Deut. xii. 32; Ezek. xlv. 8; 1 Kin. xii. 31, 32, 33.) So that it is not left in the power of men, officers, churches or any state in the world, to add, or diminish, or alter any thing in the least measure therein.

4. The necessary circumstances, as time and place, &c., belonging unto order and decency, are not so left unto men, as that, under pretence of them, they may thrust their own inventions upon the churches, (2 Kin. xii.; Exo. xx. 19; Isa. xxviii. 13; Col. i. 22, 23,) being circumscribed in the word with many general limitations, where they are determined with respect to the matter to be neither worship it self, nor circumstances separable from worship. (Acts xv. 28; Mat. xv. 9; 1 Cor. xi. 23, and viii. 34.) In respect of their end, they must be done unto edification; in respect of the manner, decently and in order, according to the nature of the things themselves, and civil and church custom. Doth not even nature its self teach you? Yea, they are in some sort determined particularly—namely, that they be done in such a manner as, all circumstances considered, is most expedient for edification: (1 Cor. xiv. 26, and xiv. 40, and xi. 14. 16, and xiv. 12. 19; Acts xv. 28.) So as, if there be no error of man concerning their determination, the determining of them is to be accounted as if it were divine.

CHAPTER II

Of the Nature of the Catholick Church in General, and in Special of a Particular Visible Church.

1. The catholick church is the whole company of those that are elected, redeemed, and in time effectually called from the state of sin and death unto a state of grace and salvation in Jesus Christ.

2. This church is either triumphant or militant. Triumphant, the number of them who are glorified in heaven; militant, the number of them who are conflicting with their enemies upon earth.

3. This militant church is to be consider'd as invisible and visible. (2 Tim. ii. 19; Rev. ii. 17; 1 Cor. vi. 17; Eph. iii. 17; Rom. i. 8; 1 Thes. i. 8; Isa. ii. 2; 1 Tim. vi. 12.) Invisible, in respect to their relation, wherein they stand to Christ as a body unto the head, being united unto him by the Spirit of God and faith in their hearts. Visible, in respect of the profession of their faith, in their persons, and in particular churches. And so there may be acknowledged an universal visible church.

4. The members of the militant visible church, considered either as not yet in church order, or walking according to the church order of the gospel. (Acts xix. 1; Col. ii. 5; Mat. xviii. 17; 1 Cor. v. 12.) In order, and so besides the spiritual union and communion common to all believers, they enjoy moreover an union and communion ecclesiastical, political. So we deny an universal visible church.

5. The state of the members of the militant visible church, walking in order, was either before the law, (Gen. xviii. 19; Exod. xix. 6,) economical, that is, in families; or under the law, national; or since the coming of Christ, only congregational (the term *independent*, we approve not): therefore neither national, provincial, nor classical.

6. A congregational church is by the institution of Christ a part of the militant visible church, consisting of a company of saints by calling, united

into one body by an holy covenant, for the publique worship of God, and the mutual edification of one another in the fellowship of the Lord Jesus. (1 Cor. xiv. 23. 36, and 1. 2, and xii. 27; Ex. xix. 5, 6; Deut. xxix. 1, and 9 to 15; Acts ii. 42; 1 Cor. xiv. 26.)

CHAPTER III

Of the Matter of the Visible Church, both in Respect of Quality and Quantity.

1. The matter of the visible church are saints by calling.

2. By saints, we understand—1, Such as have not only attained the knowledge of the principles of religion, and are free from gross and open scandals, but also do, together with the profession of their faith and repentance, walk in blameless obedience to the word, so as that in charitable discretion they may be accounted saints by calling, (tho' perhaps some or more of them be unsound and hypocrites inwardly) because the members of such particular churches are commonly by the Holy Ghost called "saints and faithful brethren in Christ;" and sundry churches have been reproved for receiving, and suffering such persons to continue in fellowship among them, as have been offensive and scandalous; the name of God also, by this means, is blasphemed, and the holy things of God defiled and profaned, the hearts of the godly grieved, and the wicked themselves hardened and holpen forward to damnation. (1 Cor. i. 2; Eph. i. 1; Heb. vi. 1; 1 Cor. i. 5; Ro. xv. 14; Psalm l. 16, 17; Acts viii. 37; Mat. iii. 6; Ro. vi. 17; 1 Cor. i. 2; Phil. i. 2; Col. i. 2; Eph. i. 1; 1 Cor. v. 2. 13; Rev. ii. 14, 15. 20; Ezek. xliv. 7. 9, and xxiii. 38, 39; Numb. xix. 20; Hag. ii. 13, 14; 1 Cor. xi. 27. 29; Psa. xxxvii. 21; 1 Cor. v. 6; 2 Cor. vii. 14.) The example of such doth endanger the sanctity of others, a little leaven leaveneth the whole lump. 2, The children of such who are also holy.

3. The members of churches, tho' orderly constituted, may in time degenerate, and grow corrupt and scandalous, which, tho' they ought not to be tolerated in the church, yet their continuance therein, thro' the defect of the execution of discipline and just censures, doth not immediately dissolve the being of a church, as appears in the church of Israel, and the churches of Galatia and Corinth, Pergamos and Thyatira. (Rev. ii. 14, 15; and xxi. 21.)

4. The matter of the church, in respect of its quantity, ought not to be of greater number than may ordinarily meet together conveniently in one place; (1 Cor. xiv. 21; Mat. xviii. 17,) nor ordinarily fewer than may conveniently carry on church-work. Hence, when the holy Scripture makes mention of the saints combined into a church estate in a town or city, where was but one congregation, it usually calleth those saints ("the church") in the singular number, as "the church of the Thessalonians," "the church of Smyrna, Philadelphia," &c.; (Rom. xvi. 1; Thes. i. 1; Rev. ii. 28, and iii. 7,) but when it speaketh of the saints in a nation or province, wherein there were sundry congregations, it frequently and usually calleth them by the name of ["churches"] in the plural number, as the "churches of Asia, Galatia, Macedonia," and the like: (1 Cor. xvi. 1. 19; Gal. i. 2; 2 Cor. viii. 1; Thes. ii. 14,) which is further confirmed by what is written of sundry of those churches in particular, how they were assembled and met together the whole church in one place, as the church at Jerusalem, the church at Antioch, the church at Corinth and Cenchrea, tho' it were more near to Corinth, it being the port

thereof, and answerable to a village; yet being a distinct congregation from Corinth, it had a church of its own, as well as Corinth had. (Acts ii. 46, and v. 12, and vi. 2, and xiv. 27, and xv. 38; 1 Cor. v. 4, and xiv. 23; Rom. xvi. 1.)

5. Nor can it with reason be thought but that every church appointed and ordained by Christ, had a ministry appointed and ordained for the same, and yet plain it is that there were no ordinary officers appointed by Christ for any other than congregational churches; (Acts xx. 28,) elders being appointed to feed not all flocks, but the particular flock of God, over which the Holy Ghost had made them overseers, and that flock they must attend, even the whole flock: and one congregation being as much as any ordinary elders can attend, therefore there is no greater church than a congregation which may ordinarily meet in one place.

CHAPTER IV

Of the Form of the Visible Church, and of Church Covenant.

1. Saints by calling must have a visible political union among themselves, or else they are not yet a particular church, (1 Cor. xii. 27; 1 Tim. iii. 15; Eph. ii. 22; 1 Cor. xii. 15, 16, 17,) as those similitudes hold forth, which the Scripture makes use of to shew the nature of particular churches; as a *body*, a *building, house, hands, eyes, feet* and other members, must be united, or else (remaining separate) are not a body. Stones, timber, tho' squared, hewen and polished, are not an house until they are compacted and united: (Rev. ii.) so saints or believers in judgment of charity, are not a church unless orderly knit together.

2. Particular churches cannot be distinguished one from another but by their forms. Ephesus is not Smyrna, nor Pergamos Thyatira; but each one a distinct society of itself, having officers of their own, which had not the charge of others; virtues of their own, for which others are not praised; corruptions of their own, for which others are not blamed.

3. This form is the *visible covenant*, agreement or consent, whereby they give up themselves unto the Lord, to the observing of the ordinances of Christ together in the same society, which is usually call'd the "church covenant." (Ex. xix. 5. 8; Deut. xxix. 12, 13; Zec. xi. 14, and ix. 11,) for we see not otherwise how members can have church-power over one another mutually. The comparing of each particular church to a city, and unto a *spouse*, (Eph. ii. 19; 2 Cor. xi. 2,) seemeth to conclude not only a form, but that that form is by way of covenant. The covenant, as it was that which made the family of Abraham and children of Israel to be a church and people unto God, (Gen. xvii. 7; Eph. ii. 12. 18,) so is it that which now makes the several societies of Gentile believers to be churches in these days.

4. This voluntary agreement, consent or covenant—for all these are here taken for the same—altho' the more express and plain it is, the more fully it puts us in mind of our mutual duty; and stirreth us up to it, and leaveth less room for the questioning of the truth of the church-estate of a company of professors, and the truth of membership of particular persons; yet we conceive the substance of it is kept where there is real agreement and consent of a company of faithful persons to meet constantly together in one congregation, for the publick worship of God, and their mutual edification: which real agreement and consent they do express by their constant practice in coming to-

gether for the publick worship of God and by their religious subjection unto the ordinances of God there: (Exod. xix. 5, and xx. 8, and xxiv. 3. 17; Josh. xxiv. 18 to 24; Psal. l. 5; Neh. ix. 38, and x. 1; Gen. xvii.; Deut. xxix.) the rather, if we do consider how Scripture-covenants have been entred into, not only expressly by word of mouth, but by sacrifice, by hand-writing and seal; and also sometimes by silent consent, without any writing or expression of words at all.

5. This form being by mutual covenant, it followeth, it is not faith in the heart, nor the profession of that faith, nor cohabitation, nor baptism. 1, Not *faith in the heart*, because that is invisible. 2, Not *a bare profession*, because that declareth them no more to be members of one church than another. 3, Not *cohabitation:* Atheists or Infidels may dwell together with believers. 4, Not *Baptism*, because it presupposeth a church-estate, as circumcision in the Old Testament, which gave no being to the church, the church being before it, and in the wilderness without it. Seals presuppose a covenant already in being. One person is a compleat subject of baptism, but one person is uncapable of being a church.

6. All believers ought, as God giveth them opportunity thereunto, to endeavor to join themselves unto a particular church, and that in respect of the honour of Jesus Christ, in his example and institution, by the professed acknowledgment of and subjection unto the order and ordinances of the gospel: (Acts ii. 47, and ix. 26; Mat. iii. 13, 14, 15, and xxviii. 19, 20; Psa. cxxxiii. 2, 3, and lxxxvii. 7; Mat. xviii. 20; 1 John i. 3,) as also in respect of their good communion founded upon their visible union, and contained in the promises of Christ's special presence in the church; whence they have fellowship with him, and in him, one with another: also in the keeping of them in the way of God's commandments, and recovering of them in case of wandering, (which all Christ's sheep are subject to in this life,) being unable to return of themselves; together with the benefit of their mutual edification, and of their posterity, that they may not be cut off from the privilege of the covenant. (Psa. cxix. 176; 1 Pet. ii. 25; Eph. iv. 16; Job xxii. 24, 25; Mat. xviii. 15, 16, 17.) Otherwise, if a believer offends, he remains destitute of the remedy provided in that behalf. And should all believers neglect this duty of joining to all particular congregations, it might follow thereupon that Christ should have no visible, political churches upon earth.

CHAPTER V

Of the First Subject of Church-Power; or, To Whom Church-Power doth First Belong.

1. The first subject of church-power is either supreme, or subordinate and ministerial. The supreme (by way of gift from the Father) is the Lord Jesus Christ. (Mat. xviii. 18; Rev. iii. 7; Isa. ix. 6; Joh. xx. 21. 23; 1 Cor. xiv. 32; Tit. i. 5; 1 Cor. v. 12.) The ministerial is either extraordinary, as the apostles, prophets and evangelists; or ordinary, as every particular Congregational church.

2. Ordinary church power is either power of office—that is, such as is proper to the eldership—or power of privilege, such as belongs to the brotherhood. (Rom. xii. 4. 8; Acts i. 23, and vi. 3, and xiv. 23; 1 Cor. x. 29, 30.)

The latter is in the brethren formally and immediately from Christ—that is, so as it may be acted or exercised immediately by themselves; the former is not in them formally or immediately, and therefore cannot be acted or exercised immediately by them, but is said to be in them, in that they design the persons unto office, who only are to act or to exercise this power.

CHAPTER VI

Of the Officers of the Church, and Especially of Pastors and Teachers.

1. A church being a company of people combined together by covenant for the worship of God, it appeareth thereby that there may be the essence and being of a church without any officers, seeing there is both the form and matter of a church; which is implied when it is said, "the apostles ordained elders in every church." (Acts xiv. 23.)

2. Nevertheless, tho' officers be not absolutely necessary to the simple being of churches, when they be called; yet ordinarily to their calling they are, and to their well-being (Rom. x. 17; Jer. iii. 15; 1 Cor. xii. 28,) and therefore the Lord Jesus Christ, out of his tender compassion, hath appointed and ordained officers, which he would not have done, if they had not been useful and needful to the church; (Eph. iii. 11; Psa. lxviii. 18; Eph. iv. 8. 11,) yea, being ascended up to heaven, he received gifts for men; whereof officers for the church are justly accounted no small parts, they being to continue to the end of the world, and for the perfecting of all the saints.

3. These officers were either extraordinary or ordinary: extraordinary as apostles, prophets, evangelists; ordinary, as elders and deacons. The apostles, prophets, and evangelists, as they were called extraordinarily by Christ, so their office ended with themselves: (1 Cor. xii. 28; Eph. iv. 11; Acts viii. 6. 16. 19, and xi. 28; Rom. xi. 13; 1 Cor. iv. 9,) whence it is that Paul, directing Timothy how to carry along church-administration, giveth no direction about the choice or course of apostles, prophets or evangelists, but only of elders and deacons; and when Paul was to take his last leave of the church of Ephesus, he committed the care of feeding the church to no other, but unto the elders of that church. The like charge does Peter commit to the elders. (1 Tim. iii. 1, 2. 8 to 13; Tit. i. 5; Acts xx. 17. 28; 1 Pet. v. 1, 2, 3.)

4. Of elders (who are also in Scripture called *bishops*) some attend chiefly to the ministry of the word, as the pastors and teachers; (1 Tim. ii. 3; Phil. i. 1; Acts xx. 17. 28,) others attend especially unto rule, who are, therefore, called *ruling-elders*. (1 Tim. v. 17.)

5. The office of pastor and teacher appears to be distinct. The pastor's special work is, to attend to *exhortation*, and therein to administer a word of *wisdom:* (Eph. iv. 11; Rom. xii. 7, 8; 1 Cor. xii. 8,) the teacher is to attend to *doctrine*, and therein to administer a word of *knowledge:* (1 Tim. iv. 1, 2; Tit. i. 9,) and neither of them to administer the seals of that covenant, unto the dispensation whereof they are alike called; as also to execute the censures, being but a kind of application of the word: the preaching of which, together with the application thereof, they are alike charged withal.

6. Forasmuch as both pastors and teachers are given by Christ for the perfecting of the saints and edifying of his body; (Eph. iv. 11, 12, and i. 22,

23,) which saints and body of Christ is his church: and therefore we account pastors and teachers to be both of them church-officers, and not the pastor for the church, and the teacher only for the schools: (1 Sam. x. 12. 19, 20,) tho' this we gladly acknowledge, that schools are both lawful, profitable, and necessary, for the training up of such in good literature or learning as may afterwards be called for unto office of pastor or teacher in the church. (2 Kings ii. 3. 15.)

CHAPTER VII

Of Ruling Elders and Deacons.

1. The ruling elder's office is distinct from the office of pastor and teacher; (Rom. xii. 7, 8, 9; 1 Tim. v. 17; 1 Cor. xii. 28; Heb. xiii. 17; 1 Tim. v. 17,) the ruling elders are not so called to exclude the pastors and teachers from ruling, because ruling and governing is common to these with the other; whereas attending to teach and preach the word is peculiar unto the former.

2. The ruling elder's work is to join with the pastor and teacher in those acts of spiritual rule, which are distinct from the ministry of the word and sacraments committed to them: (1 Tim. v. 17; 2 Chron. xxiii. 19; Rev. xxi. 12; 1 Tim. iv. 14; Matth. xviii. 17; 2 Cor. ii. 7, 8; Acts ii. 6; Acts xxi. 18. 22, 23.) Of which sort these be as followeth: 1, To open and shut the doors of God's house, by the admission of members approved by the church; by ordination of officers chosen by the church, and by excommunication of notorious and obstinate offenders renounced by the church, and by restoring of penitents forgiven by the church. 2, To call the church together when there is occasion, (Acts vi. 2, 3; and xiii. 15,) and seasonably to dismiss them again. 3, To prepare matters in private, that in publick they may be carried an end with less trouble, and more speedy dispatch. (2 Cor. viii. 19; Heb. xiii. 7, 17; 2 Thess. ii. 10, 11, 12.) 4, To moderate the carriage of all matters in the church assembled, as to propound matters to the church. To order the season of speech and silence, and to pronounce sentence according to the mind of Christ, with the consent of the church. 5, To be guides and leaders to the church in all matters whatsoever pertaining to church-administrations and actions. 6, To see that none in the church live inordinately, out of rank and place without a *calling*, or idly in their calling. (Acts xx. 28. 32; 1 Thess. v. 12; Jam. v. 14; Acts xx. 20.) 7, To prevent and heal such offences in life or in doctrine as might corrupt the church. 8, To feed the flock of God with a word of admonition. 9, And, as they shall be sent for, to visit and pray over their sick brethren. 10, And at other times, as opportunity shall serve thereunto.

3. The office of a deacon is instituted in the church by the Lord Jesus: (Acts vi. 3, 6; Phil. i. 1; 1 Tim. iii. 8; 1. Cor. xii. 28; 1 Tim. iii. 8, 9; Acts iv. 35, and vi. 2, 3; Rom. xii. 8.) Sometimes they are called *helps*. The Scripture telleth us how they should be qualified: "Grave, not double-tongued, not given to much wine, not given to filthy lucre." They must first be proved, and then use the office of a deacon, being found blameless. The office and work of a deacon is to receive the offerings of the church, gifts given to the church, and to keep the treasury of the church, and therewith to serve the tables, which the church is to provide for; as the Lord's table,

the table of the ministers, and of such as are in necessity, to whom they are to distribute in simplicity.

4. The office, therefore, being limited unto the care of the temporal good things of the church, (1 Cor. vii. 17,) it extends not to the attendance upon, and administration of the spiritual things thereof, as the word, and sacraments, and the like.

5. The ordinance of the apostle, (1 Cor. xvi. 1, 2, 3,) and practice of the church, commends the Lord's-day as a fit time for the contributions of the saints.

6. The instituting of all these officers in the church is the work of God himself, of the Lord Jesus Christ, of the Holy Ghost: (1 Cor. xii. 28; Eph. iv. 8. 11; Acts xx. 28.) And therefore such officers as he hath not appointed, are altogether unlawful, either to be placed in the church or to be retained therein, and are to be looked at as humane creatures, meer inventions and appointments of man, to the great dishonour of Christ Jesus, the Lord of his, the King of his church, whether popes, cardinals, patriarchs, arch-bishops, lord-bishops, arch-deacons, officials, commissaries, and the like. These and the rest of that hierarchy and retinue, not being plants of the Lord's planting, shall all be certainly rooted out and cast forth. (Matth. xv. 13.)

7. The Lord hath appointed ancient widows (1 Tim. v. 9, 10,) (where they may be had) to minister in the church, in giving attendance to the sick, and to give succour unto them and others in the like necessities.

CHAPTER VIII

Of the Election of Church Officers.

1. No man may take the honour of a church-officer unto himself but he that was called of God, as was Aaron. (Heb. v. 4.)

2. Calling unto office is either *immediate*, by Christ himself—such was the *call* of the apostles and prophets; (Gal. i. 1; Acts xiv. 23, and vi. 3,) this manner of calling ended with them, as hath been said—or *mediate*, by the church.

3. It is meet that, before any be ordained or chosen officers, they should first be tried and proved, because hands are not suddenly to be laid upon any, and both elders and deacons must be of both honest and good report. (1 Tim. v. 22, and vii. 10; Acts xvi. 2, and vi. 3.)

4. The things in respect of which they are to be tried, are those gifts and vertues which the Scripture requireth in men that are to be elected unto such places, viz: That elders must be "blameless, sober, apt to teach," and endued with such other qualifications as are laid down: 1 Tim. iii. 2; Tit. i. 6 to 9. Deacons to be fitted as is directed: Acts vi. 3; 1 Tim. iii. 8 to 11.

5. Officers are to be called by such churches whereunto they are to minister. Of such moment is the preservation of this power, that the churches exercised it in the presence of the apostles. (Acts xiv. 23, and i. 23, and vi. 3, 4, 5.)

6. A church being free, cannot become subject to any but by a free election; yet when such a people do chuse any to be over them in the Lord, then do they become subject, and most willingly submit to their ministry in the Lord, whom they have chosen. (Gal. v. 13; Heb. xiii. 17.)

7. And if the church have power to chuse their officer and ministers, (Rom. xvi. 17,) then, in case of manifest unworthiness and delinquency, they have power also to depose them: for to open and shut, to chuse and refuse, to constitute in office, and to remove from office, are acts belonging to the same power.

8. We judge it much conducing to the well-being and communion of the churches, (Cant. viii. 8, 9,) that, where it may be conveniently done, neighbour churches be advised withal, and their help be made use of in trial of church-officers, in order to their choice.

9. The choice of such church-officers belongeth not to the civil magistrate as such, or diocesan bishops, or patrons: for of these, or any such like, the Scripture is wholly silent, as having any power therein.

CHAPTER IX
Of Ordination and Imposition of Hands.

1. Church-officers are not only to be chosen by the church, (Acts xiii. 3, and xiv. 23,) but also to be ordained by imposition of hands and prayer, with which at the ordination of elders, fasting also is to be joined. (1 Tim. v. 22.)

2. This ordination (Numb. viii. 10; Acts. vi. 5, 6, and xiii. 2, 3,) we account nothing else but the solemn putting a man into his place and office in the church, whereunto he had right before by election; being like the installing of a magistrate in the common-wealth. Ordination therefore is not to go before, but to follow election, (Acts vi. 5, 6, and xiv. 23.) The essence and substance of the outward calling of an ordinary officer in the church does not consist in his ordination, but in his voluntary and free election by the church, and his accepting of that election; whereupon is founded that relation between pastor and flock, between such a minister and such a people. Ordination does not constitute an officer, nor given him the essentials of his office. The apostles were elders, without imposition of hands by men: Paul and Barnabas were officers before that imposition of hands, (Acts xii. 3.) The posterity of Levi were priests and Levites before hands were laid on them by the children of Israel.

3. In such churches where there are elders, imposition of hands in ordination is to be performed by those elders. (1 Tim. iv. 10; Acts xiii. 3; 1 Tim. v. 22.)

4. In such churches where there are no elders, (Numb. iii. 10,) imposition of hands may be performed by some of the brethren orderly chosen by the *church* thereunto. For, if the people may elect officers, which is the greater, and wherein the substance of the office doth consist, they may much more (occasion and need so requiring) impose hands in ordination; which is less, and but the accomplishment of the other.

5. Nevertheless, in such churches where there are no elders, and the church so desire, we see not why imposition of hands may not be performed by the elders of other churches. Ordinary officers laid hands upon the officers of many churches: the presbytery at Ephesus laid hands upon Timothy an evangelist; (1 Tim. iv. 14; Acts xiii. 3,) the presbytery at Antioch laid hands upon Paul and Barnabas.

6. Church-officers are officers to one church, even that particular over which the Holy Ghost hath made them overseers. Insomuch as elders are commanded to feed not all flocks, but the flock which is committed to their faith and trust, and dependeth upon them. Nor can constant residence at one congregation be necessary for a minister—no, nor yet lawful—if he be not a minister to one congregation only, but to the church universal; (1 Pet. v. 2; Acts xx. 28,) because he may not attend one part only of the church to which he is a minister, but he is called to attend unto all the flock.

7. He that is clearly released from his office relation unto that church whereof he was a minister, cannot be looked at as an officer, nor perform any act of office in any other church, unless he be again orderly called unto office: which, when it shall be, we know nothing to hinder; but imposition of hands also in his ordination (Acts xx. 28,) ought to be used towards him again: for so Paul the apostle received imposition of hands twice at least from Ananias. (Acts ix. 17, and xiii. 3.)

CHAPTER X

Of the Power of the Church and its Presbytery.

1. Supreme and Lordly power over all the churches upon earth doth only belong to Jesus Christ, who is king of the church, and the head thereof (Ps. ii. 6; Eph. i. 21, 22; Isa. ix. 6; Mat. xxviii. 18.) He hath the government upon his shoulders, and hath all power given to him, both in heaven and earth.

2. A company of professed believers, ecclesiastically confederate, as they are a church before they have officers, and without them; so, even in that estate, subordinate church-power (Acts i. 23, and xiv. 23, and vi. 3, 4; Mat. xviii. 17; 1 Cor. v. 4, 5,) under Christ delegated to them by him, doth belong to them in such a manner as is before expressed, Chap. V. Sec. 2, and as flowing from the very nature and essence of a church; it being natural unto all bodies, and so unto a church-body, to be furnished with sufficient power for its own preservation and subsistence.

3. This government of the church (Rev. iii. 7; 1 Cor. v. 12,) is a mixt government (and so has been acknowledged, long before the term of *independency* was heard of); in respect of Christ, the head and king of the church, and the Sovereign Power residing in him, and exercised by him, it is a *monarchy;* in respect of the body or brotherhood of the church, and power from Christ granted unto them (1 Tim. v. 27,) it resembles a *democracy;* in respect of the presbytery and power committed unto them, it is an *aristocracy.*

4. The Sovereign Power, which is peculiar unto Christ, is exercised—1, In calling the church out of the world into an holy fellowship with himself. (Gal. i. 4; Rev. v. 8, 9; Mat. xxviii. 20; Eph. iv. 8. 11; Jam. iv. 12; Is. xxxiii. 22; 1 Tim. iii. 15; 2 Cor. x. 4, 5; Is. xxxii. 2; Luke i. 71.) 2, In instituting the ordinances of his worship, and appointing his ministers and officers for the dispensing of them. 3, In giving laws for the ordering of all our ways, and the ways of his house. 4, In giving power and life to all his institutions, and to his people by them. 5, In protecting and delivering his church against and from all the enemies of their peace.

5. The power granted by Christ unto the body of the church and brotherhood, is a *prerogative* or *priviledge* which the church doth exercise—1, In *choosing* their own officers, whether elders or deacons. (Acts vi. 3, 5, and xiv.

23, and ix. 26; Mat. xviii. 15, 16, 17.) 2, In *admission* of these members; and therefore there is great reason they should have power to remove any from their fellowship again. Hence, in case of offence, any brother hath power to convince and admonish an offending brother: and, in case of not hearing him, to take one or two more to set on the admonition: and in case of not hearing them, to proceed to tell the church: and as his offence may require, the whole church has power to proceed to the censure of him, whether by admonition or excommunication: (Tit. ii. 10; Col. iv. 17; Mat. xviii. 17; 2 Cor. ii. 7, 8,) and upon his repentance to restore him again unto his former communion.

6. In case an elder offend incorrigibly, the matter so requiring, as the church had power to call him to office, so they have power according to order (the counsel of other churches, where it may be had, directing thereto) to remove him from his office, and being now but a member, (Col. iv. 17; Ro. xvi. 17; Mat. xviii. 17,) in case he add contumacy to his sin, the church, that had power to receive him into their fellowship, hath also the same power to cast him out that they have concerning any other member.

7. Church-government or rule is placed by Christ in the officers of the church, (1 Tim. v. 17; Heb. xiii. 17; 1 Thes. v. 12,) who are therefore called *rulers*, while they rule with God: yet, in case of male-administration, they are subject to the power of the church, as hath been said before. (Rom. xii. 8; 1 Tim. v. 17; 1 Cor. xii. 28, 29; Heb. xiii. 7. 17.) The Holy Ghost frequently— yea always—where it mentioneth church-rule and church-government, ascribeth it to elders: whereas the work and duty of the people is expressed in the phrase of "obeying their elders," and "submitting themselves unto them in the Lord." So as it is manifest that an organick or compleat church is a body-politick, consisting of some that are governours and some that are governed in the Lord.

8. The power which Christ hath committed to the elders is to feed and rule the church of God, and accordingly to call the church together upon any weighty occasion; (Acts xx. 28, and vi. 2; Numb. xvi. 12; Ezek. xlvi. 10; Acts xiii. 15; Hos. iv. 4,) when the members so called, without just cause, may not refuse to come, nor when they are come, depart before they are dismissed, nor speak in the church, before they have leave from the elders, nor continue so doing when they require silence; nor may they oppose or contradict the judgment or sentence of the elders, without sufficient and weighty cause, because such practices are manifestly contrary unto order and government, and inlets of disturbance, and tend to confusion.

9. It belongs also unto the elders before to examine any officers or members before they be received of the church, (Rev. ii. 2; 1 Tim. v. 19; Acts xxi. 18. 22, 23; 1 Cor. v. 4, 5,) to receive the accusations brought to the church, and to prepare them for the churches hearing. In handling of offences and other matters before the church, they have power to declare and publish the will of God touching the same, and to pronounce sentence with the consent of the church. (Numb. vi. 23 to 26.) Lastly, They have power, when they dismiss the people, to bless them in the name of the Lord.

10. This power of government in the elders doth not any wise prejudice the power of privilege in the brotherhood; as neither the power of privilege in the brethren doth prejudice the power of government in the elders, (Acts

xiv. 15. 23, and vi. 2; 1 Cor. v. 4; 2 Cor. ii. 6, 7,) but they may sweetly agree together; as we may see in the example of the apostles, furnished with the greatest church-power, who took in the *concurrence* and *consent* of the brethren in church-administrations. Also that Scripture (2 Cor. ii. 9, and x. 6) doth declare that what the churches were to *act* and to *do* in these matters, they were to do in a way of obedience, and that not only to the direction of the apostles, but also of their ordinary elders. (Heb. xiii. 17.)

11. From the promises, namely, that the ordinary power of government belonging only to the elders, power of privilege remaining with the brotherhood, (as the power of judgment in matters of censure and power of liberty in matters of liberty,) it followeth that in an organick church and right administration, all church-acts proceed after the manner of a mixt administration, so as no church-act can be consummated or perfected without the consent of both.

CHAPTER XI

Of the Maintenance of Church-Officers.

1. The apostle concludes that necessary and sufficient maintenance is due unto the ministers of the word from the law of nature and nations, from the law of Moses, the equity thereof, as also the rule of common reason. Moreover, the Scripture doth not only call elders labourers and workmen, (Gal. vi. 6,) but also, speaking of them, doth say that "the labourer is worthy of his hire:" (1 Cor. ix. 9. 14; 1 Tim. v. 18,) and requires that he which is taught in the word, should communicate to him in all good things, and mention it, as an ordinance of the Lord, that they which preach the gospel, should live of the gospel, and forbiddeth the muzzling of the mouth of the ox that treadeth out the corn.

2. The Scripture alledged requiring this maintenance as a bounden duty, and due debt, and not as a matter of alms and free gift, therefore people are not at liberty to do or not to do, what and when they please in this matter, no more than in any other commanded duty and ordinance of the Lord; (Rom. xv. 27; 1 Cor. ix. 21,) but ought of duty to minister of their "carnal things" to them that labour among them in word and doctrine, as well as they ought to pay any other workmen their wages, and to discharge and satisfie their debts, or to submit themselves to observe any other ordinance of the Lord.

3. The apostle (Gal. vi. 6) enjoyning that he which is taught communicate to him that teacheth "in all good things," doth not leave it arbitrary, (1 Cor. xvi. 2,) what or how much a man shall give, or in what proportion, but even the latter, as well as the former, is prescribed and appointed by the Lord.

4. Not only members of churches, but "all that are taught in the word," are to contribute unto him that teacheth in all good things. In case that congregations are defective in their contributions, the deacons are to call upon them to do their duty: (Acts vi. 3, 4,) if their call sufficeth not, the church by her power is to require it of their members; and where church power, thro' the corruption of men, doth not or cannot attain the end, the magistrate is to see that the ministry be duly provided for, as appears from the commended example of Nehemiah. (Neh. xiii. 11; Isa. xliv. 23; 2 Cor. viii. 13, 14.) The

magistrates are nursing-fathers and nursing-mothers, and stand charged with the custody of both tables; because it is better to prevent a scandal, that it may not come, and easier also, than to remove it, when it is given. It's most suitable to rule, that by the church's care each man should know his proportion according to rule, what he should do before he do it, that so his judgment and heart may be satisfied in what he doth, and just offence prevented in what is done.

CHAPTER XII

Of the Admission of Members into the Church.

1. The doors of the churches of Christ upon earth do not by God's appointment stand so wide open, that all sorts of people, good and bad, may freely enter therein at their pleasure, (2 Chr. xxix. 19; Mat. xiii. 25, and xxii. 12,) but such as are admitted thereto, as members, ought to be examin'd and tryed first, whether they be fit and meet to be received into church-society or not. The Eunuch of Ethiopia, before his admission, was examined by Philip, (Acts viii. 37,) whether he did believe on Jesus Christ with all his heart. The angel of the church at Ephesus (Rev. ii. 2; Acts ix. 26,) is commended for trying such as said they were apostles, and were not. There is like reason for trying of them that profess themselves to be believers. The officers are charged with the keeping of the doors of the church, and therefore are in a special manner to make tryal of the fitness of such who enter. Twelve angels are set at the gates of the temple, (Rev. xxi. 12; 2 Chr. xxiii. 19,) lest such as were "ceremonially unclean" should enter thereunto.

2. The things which are requisite to be found in all church-members, are *repentance* from sin, and *faith* in Jesus Christ: (Acts ii. 38 to 42, and viii. 37,) and therefore these are the things whereof men are to be examined at their admission into the church, and which then they must profess and hold forth in such sort as may satisfie "rational charity" that the things are indeed. John Baptist admitted men to baptism confessing and bewailing their sins: (Mat. iii. 6; Acts xix. 18,) and of others it is said that "they came and confessed, and shewed their deeds."

3. The weakest measure of faith is to be accepted in those that desire to be admitted into the church, (Rom. xiv. 1,) if *sincere*, have the substance of that faith, repentance and holiness, which is required in church members; and such have most need of the ordinances for their confirmation and growth in grace. The Lord Jesus would not quench the smoaking flax, nor break the bruised reed, (Mat. xii. 20; Isa. xl. 11,) but gather the tender lambs in his arms, and carry them gently in his bosom. Such charity and tenderness is to be used, as the weakest Christian, if sincere, may not be excluded nor discouraged. Severity of examination is to be avoided.

4. In case any, thro' excessive fear or other infirmity, be unable to make their personal relation of their spiritual estate in publick, it is sufficient that the elders, having received private satisfaction, make relation thereof in publick before the church, they testify their assents thereunto: this being the way that tendeth most to edification. But whereas persons are of greater abilities, there it is most expedient that they make their relations and confessions personally with their own mouth, as David professeth of himself. (Psal. lxvi. 6.)

5. A personal and publick confession and declaring of God's manner of working upon the soul, is both lawful, expedient and useful, in sundry respects and upon sundry grounds. Those three thousand, (Acts ii. 37. 41,) before they were admitted by the apostles, did manifest that they were pricked at the heart by Peter's sermon, together with earnest desire to be delivered from their sins, which now wounded their consciences, and their ready receiving of the word of promise and exhortation. We are to be ready to "render a reason of the hope that is in us, to every one that asketh us;" (1 Pet. iii. 15; Heb. xi. 1; Eph. i. 18,) therefore we must be able and ready upon any occasion to declare and shew our *repentence* for sin, *faith* unfeigned, and *effectual calling*, because these are the *reason* of a well-grounded *hope*. "I have not hidden thy righteousness from the great congregation." (Psalm xl. 10.)

6. This profession of faith and repentance, as it must be made by such at their admission that were never in church society before; so nothing hindereth but the same way also be performed by such as have formerly been members of some other church, (Mat. iii. 5, 6; Gal. ii. 4; 1 Tim. v. 24,) and the church to which they now join themselves as members may lawfully require the same. Those three thousand (Acts ii.) which made their confession, were members of the church of the Jews before; so were those that were baptised by John. Churches may err in their admission; and persons regularly admitted may fall into offence. Otherwise, if churches might obtrude their members, or if church members might obtrude themselves upon other churches without due trial, the matter so requiring, both the liberty of the churches would thereby be infringed, in that they might not examine those, concerning whose fitness for communion they were unsatisfied; and besides the infringing of their liberty, the churches themselves would unavoidably be corrupted, and the ordinances defiled: whilst they might not refuse, but must receive the unworthy, which is contrary unto the Scripture, teaching that all churches are sisters, and therefore equal. (Cant. viii. 8.)

7. The like trial is to be required from such members of the church as were born in the same, or received their membership, or were baptised in their infancy or minority by virtue of the covenant of their parents, when being grown up into years of discretion, they shall desire to be made partakers of the Lord's Supper; unto which, because holy things must not be given unto the unworthy, therefore it is requisite (Mat. vii. 6; 1 Cor. xi. 27,) that these, as well as others, should come to their trial and examination, and manifest their faith and repentance by an open profession thereof, before they are received to the Lord's Supper, and otherwise not to be admitted thereunto. Yet these church members that were so born, or received in their childhood, before they are capable of being made partakers of full communion, have many privileges which others (not church members) have not; they are in covenant with God, have the seal thereof upon them, viz: baptism; and so, if not regenerated, yet are in a more hopeful way of attaining regenerating grace, and all the spiritual blessings, both of the covenant and seal; they are also under church-watch, and consequently subject to the reprehensions, admonitions and censures thereof, for their healing and amendment, as need shall require.

CHAPTER XIII

Of Church-Members, Their Removal from One Church to Another, and of Recommendation and Dismission.

1. Church-members may not remove or depart from the church, and so one from another as they please, nor without just and weighty cause, but ought to live and dwell together, (Heb. x. 25,) forasmuch as they are commanded not to forsake the assembling of themselves together. Such departure tends to the dissolution and ruine of the body, as the pulling of stones and pieces of timber from the building, and of members from the natural body, tend to the destruction of the whole.

2. It is, therefore, the duty of church-members, in such times and places, where counsel may be had, to consult with the church whereof they are members (Pro. xi. 16,) about their removal, that, accordingly, they having their approbation, may be encouraged, or otherwise desist. They who are joined with consent, should not depart without consent, except forced thereunto.

3. If a member's departure be manifestly unsafe and sinful, the church may not consent thereunto; for in so doing, (Ro. xiv. 23,) they should not act in faith, and should partake with him in his sin. (1 Tim. v. 22.) If the case be doubtful and the person not to be persuaded, (Acts xxi. 14,) it seemeth best to leave the matter unto God, and not forcibly to detain him.

4. Just reasons for a member's removal of himself from the church, are— 1, If a man cannot continue without partaking in sin. (Eph. v. 11.) 2, In case of personal persecution: (Acts ix. 25, 29, 30, and viii. 1,) so Paul departed from the disciples at Damascus; also, in case of general persecution, when all are scattered. In case of real, and not only pretended want of competent subsistence, a door being open for better supply in another place, (Neh. xiii. 20,) together with the means of spiritual edification. In these or like cases, a member may lawfully remove, and the church cannot lawfully detain him.

5. To separate from a church, either out of contempt of their holy fellowship, (2 Tim. iv. 10,) or out of covetousness, or for greater enlargements, with just grief to the church, or out of schism, or want of love, and out of a spirit of contention in respect of some unkindness, or some evil only *conceived* or *indeed* in the church, which might and should be tolerated and healed with a spirit of meekness, and of which evil the church is not yet convinced (tho' perhaps himself be) nor admonished; for these or the like reasons, to withdraw from publique communion in word or seals, or censures, is unlawful and sinful.

6. Such members as have orderly moved their habitation, ought to join themselves unto the church in order (Isa. lvi. 8,) where they do inhabit, (Acts ix. 26,) if it may be; otherwise, they can neither perform the duties nor receive the priviledges of members. Such an example, tolerated in some, is apt to corrupt others, which, if many should follow, would threaten the dissolution and confusion of churches, contrary to the Scripture. (1 Cor. xiv. 33.)

7. Order requires that a member thus removing, have letters testimonial and of dismission from the church (Acts xviii. 27,) whereof he yet

is, unto the church whereunto he desireth to be joined, lest the church should be deluded; that the church may receive him in faith, and not be corrupted in receiving deceivers and false brethren.   Until the person dismissed be received unto another church, he ceaseth not by his letters of dismission to be a member of the church whereof he was.   The church cannot make *a* member *no* member but by excommunication.

8. If a member be called to remove only for a time where a church is, (Rom. xvi. 1, 2,) letters of recommendation are requisite and sufficient for communion with that church (2 Cor. iii. 1) in the ordinances and in their watch; as Phoebe, a servant of the church at Cenchrea, had a letter written for her to the church at Rome, that she might be received as becometh saints.

9. Such letters of recommendations and dismission (Acts xviii. 27) were written for Apollos, for Marcus to the Colossians, (Col. iv. 10), for Phoebe to the Romans, (Rom. xvi. 1,) for sundry other churches.   (2 Cor. iii. 5.) And the apostle tells us that some persons, not sufficiently known otherwise, have special need of such letters, tho' he, for his part, had no need thereof.   The use of them is to be a benefit and help to the party for whom they are written, and for the furthering of his receiving among the saints, in the place whereto he goeth, and the due satisfaction of them in their receiving of him.

CHAPTER XIV

Of Excommunication and Other Censures.

1. The censures of the church are appointed by Christ for the preventing, removing and healing of offences in the church; (1 Tim. v. 20; Jude 19; Deu. xiii. 11; 1 Cor. v. 6; Rom. ii. 24; Rev. ii. 14, 15, 16. 20,) for the reclaiming and gaining of offending brethren; for the deterring others from the like offences; for purging out the leaven which may infect the whole lump; for vindicating the honour of Christ and of his church, and the holy profession of the gospel; and for preventing of the wrath of God, that may justly fall upon the church, if they should suffer his covenant and the seals thereof to be profaned by notorious and obstinate offenders.

2. If an offence be private, (Mat. v. 23, 24,) (one brother offending another) the offender is to go and acknowledge his repentance for it unto his offended brother, who is then to forgive him; but if the offender neglect or refuse to do it, the brother offended is to go, and convince and admonish him of it, between themselves privately: if therefore the offender be brought to repent of his offence, the admonisher has won his brother: but if the offender hear not his brother, the brother of the offended is to take with him one or two more, (verse 16,) that in the mouth of two or three witnesses every word may be established, (whether the word of admonition, if the offender receive it; or the word of complaint, if he refuse it,) for if he refuse it, (verse 17,) the offended brother is by the mouth of the elders to tell the church, and if he hear the church, and declare the same by penitent confession, he is recovered and gained: And if the church discern him to be willing to hear, yet not full convinced of his offence, as in case of heresie, they are to dispence to him a publick admonition; which, declaring the offender to lye under the publick offence of the church, doth thereby with-hold or suspend him from the holy fellowship of the Lord's Supper, till his offence be removed

by penitent confession. If he still continue obstinate, they are to cast him out by excommunication.

3. But if the offence be more publick at first, and of a more hainous and criminal nature, (1 Cor. v. 4. 8, 11,) to wit, such as are condemned by the light of nature; then the church, without such gradual proceeding, is to cast out the offender from their holy communion, for the further mortifying of his sin, and the healing of his soul in the day of the Lord Jesus.

4. In dealing with an offender, great care is to be taken that we be neither over-strict or rigorous, nor too indulgent or remiss: our proceeding herein ought to be with a spirit of meekness, considering ourselves, lest we also be tempted, (Gal. vi. 1,) and that the best of us have need of much forgiveness from the Lord. (Mat. xviii. 34, 35.) Yet the winning and healing of the offender's soul being the end of these endeavors, (Ezek. xiii. 10,) we must not daub with untempered mortar, nor heal the wounds of our brethren slightly. On some, have compassion; others, save with fear.

5. While the offender remains excommunicate, (Mat. xviii. 17,) the church is to refrain from all member-like communion with him in spiritual things, (1 Cor. v. 11,) and also from all familiar communion with him in civil things, (2 Thes. iii. 6. 14,) farther than the necessity of natural or domestical or civil relations do require; and are therefore to forbear to eat and drink with him, that he may be ashamed.

6. Excommunication being a spiritual punishment, it doth not prejudice the excommunicate in, or deprive him of his civil rights, and therefore toucheth not princes or magistrates in respect of their civil dignity or authority; (1 Cor. xiv. 24, 25,) and the excommunicate being but as a publican and a heathen, (2 Thes. iii. 14), heathens being lawfully permitted to hear the *word* in church-assemblies, we acknowledge therefore the like liberty of hearing the word may be permitted to persons excommunicate that is permitted unto heathens. And because we are not without hope of his recovery, we are not to account him as an enemy, but to admonish him as a brother.

7. If the Lord sanctifie the censure to the offender, so as by the grace of Christ, he doth testifie his repentence with humble confession of his sin, and judging of himself, giving glory unto God, (2 Cor. ii. 7, 8,) the church is then to forgive him, and to comfort him, and to restore him to the wonted brotherly communion, which he enjoyed with 'em.

8. The suffering of prophane or scandalous livers to continue in fellowship, and partake in the sacraments, (Rev. ii. 14, 15, 20,) is doubtless a great sin in those that have power in their hands to redress it, and do it not: Nevertheless, in so much as Christ, and his apostles in their times, and the prophets and other *godly men* in theirs, (Mat. xxiii. 3; Acts iii. 1,) did lawfully partake of the Lord's commanded ordinances in the Jewish church, and neither taught nor practised separation from the same, though unworthy ones were permitted therein: and inasmuch as the faithful in the church of Corinth, wherein were many unworthy persons and practises, (1 Cor. vi. and xv. 12,) are never commanded to absent themselves from the sacraments, because of the same; therefore the godly, in like cases, are not to separate.

9. As separation from such a church wherein profane and scandalous persons are tolerated, is not presently necessary; so for the members thereof, otherwise unworthy, hereupon to abstain from communicating with such a

church in the participation of the sacraments, is unlawful. (2 Chr. xxx. 18; Gen. xviii. 25.) For as it were unreasonable for an innocent person to be punished for the faults of others, wherein he hath no hand, and whereunto he gave no consent; so is it more unreasonable that a godly man should neglect duty, and punish himself, in not coming for his portion in the blessing of the seals, as he ought, because others are suffered to come that ought not; especially considering that himself doth neither consent to their sin, nor to their approaching to the ordinance in their sin, nor to the neglect of others, who should put them away, and do not, but, on the contrary, doth heartily mourn for these things, (Ezek. ix. 4,) modestly and seasonably stir up others to do their duty. If the church cannot be reformed, they may use their liberty, as is specified, Chap. XIII. Sect. 4. But this all the godly are bound unto, even every one to his endeavor, according to his power and place, that the unworthy may be duly proceeded against by the church, to whom this matter doth pertain.

CHAPTER XV

Of the Communion of Churches One With Another.

1. Altho' *churches* be distinct, and therefore may not be confounded one with another, and equal, and therefore have not dominion one over another; (Rev. i. 4; Cant. viii. 8; Rom. xvi. 16; 1 Cor. xvi. 19; Acts xv. 23; Rev. ii. 1,) yet all the churches ought to preserve *church-communion* one with another, because they are all united unto Christ, not only as a mystical, but as a political head: whence is derived a communion suitable thereunto.

2. The communion of churches is exercised several ways. (Cant. viii. 8.) 1, By way of *mutual care* in taking thought for one another's welfare. 2, By way of *consultation* one with another, when we have occasion to require the judgment and counsel of other churches, touching any person or cause, wherewith they may be better acquainted than our selves; (Acts xv. 2,) as the church of Antioch consulted with the Apostles and elders of the church at Jerusalem, about the question of circumcision of the Gentiles, and about the false teachers that broached that doctrine. In which case, when any church wanteth light or peace among themselves, it is a way of communion of the churches, according to the word, to meet together by their elders and other messengers in a synod, (ver. 22, 23,) to consider and argue the point in doubt or difference; and, having found out the way of truth and peace, to commend the same by their letters and messengers to the churches whom the same may concern. But if a church be rent with divisions among themselves, or lye under any open scandal, and yet refuse to consult with other churches for healing or removing of the same, it is matter of just offence, both to the Lord Jesus and to other churches, (Ezek. xxxiv. 4,) as bewraying too much want of mercy and faithfulness, not to seek to bind up the breaches and wounds of the church and brethren; And therefore the state of such a church calleth aloud upon other churches to exercise a fuller act of brotherly communion, to wit, by way of admonition. 3, A way, then, of communion of churches, is by way of *admonition;* to wit, in case any public offence be found in a church, which they either discern not, or are slow in proceeding to use the means for the removing and healing of. Paul had no authority over Peter, yet when he saw Peter not walking with a right foot, he publickly rebuked him before the

church. (Gal. ii. 11 to 14.) Tho' churches have no more authority one over another, than one apostle had over another, yet, as one apostle might admonish another, so may one church admonish another, and yet without usurpation. (Matth. xviii. 15, 16, 17, by proportion.) In which case, if the church that lieth under offence, do not hearken to the church that doth admonish her, the church is to acquaint other neighbour churches with that offence, which the offending church still lieth under, together with the neglect of their brotherly admonition given unto them: Whereupon those other churches are to join in seconding the admonition formerly given: and if still the offending church continue in obstinacy and impenitency, they may forbear communion with them, and are to proceed to make use of the help of a synod or counsel of neighbour churches, walking orderly (if a greater cannot conveniently be had) for their conviction. If they hear not the synod, the synod having declared them to be obstinate, particular churches accepting and approving of the judgment of the synod, are to declare the sentence of *non-communion* respectively concerning them; and thereupon, out of religious care to keep their own communion pure, they may justly withdraw themselves from participation with them at the Lord's table, and from such other acts of holy communion, as the communion of churches doth otherwise allow and require. Nevertheless, if any members of such a church as live under public offence, do not consent to the offence of the church, but do in due sort bear witness against it, (Gen. xviii. 25,) they are still to be received to wonted communion, for it is not equal that the innocent should suffer with the offensive. Yea, furthermore, if such innocent members, after due waiting in the use of all due means for the healing of the offence of their own church, shall at last (with the allowance of the counsel of neighbour churches,) withdraw from the fellowship of their own church, and offer themselves to the fellowship of another, we judge it lawful for the other church to receive them (being otherwise fit) as if they had been orderly dismissed to them from their own church. 4, A fourth way of communion with churches, is by way of *participation:* the members of one church occasionally coming to another, we willingly admit them to partake with them at the Lord's table, (1 Cor. xii. 13,) it being the seal of our communion not only with Christ, not only with the members of our own church, but also of all the churches of the saints: In which regard we refuse not to baptize their children presented to us, if either their own minister be absent, or such a fruit of holy fellowship be desired with us. In like cases, such churches as are furnished with more ministers than one, do willingly afford one of their own ministers to supply the absence or place of a sick minister of another church for a needful season. 5, A fifth way of church communion is by *recommendation*, (Rom. xvi. 1,) when the member of one church hath occasion to reside in another church, if but for a season, we commend him to their watchful fellowship by letters of recommendation: But if he be called to settle his abode there, we commit him, according to his desire, to the fellowship of their covenant by letters of dismission. 6, A sixth way of church communion, (Acts xviii. 27,) is in case of *need* to minister succour one unto another, (Acts xi. 22,) either of able members to furnish them with officers, or of outward support to the necessities of poorer churches, (verse 29,) as did the churches of the Gentiles contribute liberally to the poor saints at Jerusalem. (Rom. xiii. 26, 27.)

3. When a company of believers purpose to gather into church-fellowship, it is requisite for their safer proceeding and the mentioning of the communion of churches, that they signifie their intent unto the neighbouring churches, walking according to the order of the gospel, and desire their presence and help, and right hand of fellowship; (Gal. ii. 1, 2, and ix. by proportion,) which they ought readily to give unto them, when there is no just cause to except against their proceedings.

4. Besides these several ways of communion, there is also a way of *propagation of churches:* When a church shall grow too numerous, it is a way, and fit season to propagate one church out of another, by sending forth such of their members as are willing to remove, and to procure some officers to them, (Isa. xl. 20; Cant. viii. 8, 9,) as may enter with them into church estate among themselves. As bees, when the hive is too full, issue out by swarms, and are gathered into other hives, so the churches of Christ may do the same upon the like necessity; and therein hold forth to them the right hand of fellowship, both in their gathering into a church and in the ordination of their officers.

CHAPTER XVI

Of Synods.

1. Synods, orderly assembled, (Acts xv. 2 to 15,) and rightly proceeding according to the pattern, (Acts xv.) we acknowledge as the ordinance of Christ: and tho' not absolutely necessary to the being, yet many times, thro' the iniquity of men and perverseness of times, necessary to the wellbeing of churches, for the establishment of truth and peace therein.

2. Synods being spiritual and ecclesiastical assemblies, are therefore made up of spiritual and ecclesiastical causes. The next efficient cause of them, under Christ, is the power of the churches sending forth their elders and other messengers, (Acts xv. 2, 3,) who being met together in the name of Christ, are the matter of a synod; and they in arguing and debating and determining matters of religion, (verse 6,) according to the word, and publishing the same to the churches it concerneth, (verse 7 to 23,) do put forth the proper and formal acts of a synod, (verse 31,) to the conviction of errors, and heresies, and the establishment of truth and peace in the churches, which is the end of a synod. (Acts xvi. 4. 15.)

3. Magistrates have power to call a synod, by calling to the churches to send forth their elders and other messengers to counsel and assist them in matters of religion; (2 Chr. xxix. 4, 5 to 11,) but yet the constituting of a synod is a church-act, and may be transacted by the churches, (Acts xv.) even when civil magistrates may be enemies to churches and to church-assemblies.

4. It belongeth unto synods and councils to debate and determine controversies of faith and cases of conscience; (Acts xv. 1, 2. 6, 7; 1 Chr. xv. 13; 2 Chr. xxix. 6, 7; Acts xv. 24. 28, 29,) to clear from the word holy directions for the holy worship of God and good government of the church; to bear witness against maladministration and corruption in doctrine or manners, in any particular church, and to give directions for the reformation thereof; not to exercise church-censures in way of discipline, nor any other acts of church-authority or jurisdictiton which that presidential synod did forbear.

5. The synod's directions and determinations, so far as consonant to the word of God, are to be received with reverence and submission; not only for their agreement therewith, (Acts xv.) (which is the principal ground thereof, and without which they bind not at all,) but also, secondarily, for the power whereby they are made, as being an ordinance of God appointed thereunto in his word.

6. Because it is difficult, if not impossible, for many churches to come together in one place, in their members universally; therefore they may assemble by their delegates or messengers, as the church at Antioch went not all to Jerusalem, but some select men for that purpose. (Acts xv. 2.) Because none are or should be more fit to know the state of the churches, nor to advise of ways for the good thereof, than elders; therefore it is fit that, in the choice of the messengers for such assemblies, they have special respect unto such; yet, inasmuch as not only Paul and Barnabas, but certain others also, (Acts xv. 2. 22, 23,) were sent to Jerusalem from Antioch, (Acts xv.) and when they were come to Jerusalem, not only the apostle and elders, but other brethren, also do assemble and meet about the matter; therefore synods are to consist both of elders and other church-members, endued with gifts, and sent by the churches, not excluding the presence of any bretheren in the churches.

CHAPTER XVII
Of the Civil Magistrate's Power in Matters Ecclesiastical.

1. It is lawful, profitable and necessary for Christians to gather themselves together into church estate, and therein to exercise all the ordinances of Christ, according unto the word, (Acts ii. 41. 47, and iv. 1, 2, 3,) although the consent of the magistrate could not be had thereunto; because the apostles and Christians in their time did frequently thus practice, when the magistrates, being all of them Jewish and Pagan, and most persecuting enemies, would give no countenance or consent to such matters.

2. Church-government stands in no opposition to civil government of commonwealths, nor any way intrencheth upon the authority of civil magistrates in their jurisdictions; nor any whit weakeneth their hands in governing, but rather strengtheneth them, and furthereth the people in yielding more hearty and conscionable obedience to them, whatsoever some ill affected persons to the ways of Christ have suggested, to alienate the affections of kings and princes from the ordinances of Christ; as if the kingdom of Christ in his church could not rise and stand, without the falling and weakening of their government, which is also of Christ, (Isa. xlix. 23,) whereas the contrary is most true, that they may both stand together and flourish, the one being helpful unto the other, in their distinct and due administrations.

3. The power and authority of magistrates is not for the restraining of churches (Rom. xiii. 4; 1 Tim. ii. 2,) or any other good works, but for helping in and furthering thereof; and therefore the consent and countenance of magistrates, when it may be had, is not to be slighted, or lightly esteemed; but, on the contrary, it is part of that honor due to Christian magistrates to desire and crave their consent and approbation therein; which being obtained, the churches may then proceed in their way with much more encouragement and comfort.

4. It is not in the power of magistrates to compel their subjects to become church-members, and to partake of the Lord's Supper; (Ezek. xliv. 7. 9,) for the priests are reproved that brought unworthy ones into the sanctuary: (1 Cor. v. 11;) then it was unlawful for the priests, so it is as unlawful to be done by civil magistrates; those whom the church is to cast out, if they were in, the magistrate ought not to thrust them into the church, nor to hold them therein.

5. As it is unlawful for church-officers to meddle with the sword of the magistrate, (Mat. ii. 25, 26,) so it is unlawful for the magistrate to meddle with the work proper to church-officers. The acts of Moses and David, who were not only princes but prophets, were extraordinary, therefore not inimitable. Against such usurpation the Lord witnessed by smiting Uzziah with leprosie for presuming to offer incense. (2 Chr. xxvi. 16, 17.)

6. It is the duty of the magistrate to take care of matters of religion, and to improve his civil authority for the observing of the duties commanded in the first, as well as for observing of the duties commanded in the second table. They are called *gods*. (Psa. lxxxviii. 8.) The end of the magistrate's office is not only the quiet and peaceable life of the subject in matters of righteousness and honesty, but also in matters of godliness; yea, of all godliness. (1 Tim. ii. 1, 2; 1 Kings xv. 14, and xxii. 43; 2 Kings xii. 3, and xiv. 4, and xv. 35.) Moses, Joshua, David, Solomon, Asa, Jehoshaphat, Hezekiah, Josiah, are much commended by the Holy Ghost, for the putting forth their authority in matters of religion; on the contrary, such kings as have been failing this way, are frequently taxed and reproved by the Lord. (1 Kings xx. 42; Job xxxix. 25, and xxxi. 26. 28; Neh. xiii.; Jonah iii. 7; Ezra vii.; Dan. iii. 29.) And not only the kings of Juda, but also Job, Nehemiah, the king of Nineveh, Darius, Artaxerxes, Nebuchadnezzar, whom none looked at as types of Christ, (tho' were it so there were no place for any just objection) are commended in the books of God for exercising their authority this way.

7. The objects of the power of the magistrate are not things meerly inward, and so not subject to his cognizance and views: as unbelief, hardness of heart, erroneous opinions not vented, but only such things as are acted by the outward man: neither their power to be exercised in commanding such acts of the outward man, and punishing the neglect thereof, as are but meer inventions and devices of men, (1 Kings xx. 28. 42,) but about such acts as are commanded and forbidden in the word: yea, such as the word doth clearly determine, tho' not always clearly to the judgment of the magistrate or others, yet clearly in its self. In these he, of right, ought to put forth his authority, tho' oft-times actually he doth it not.

8. Idolatry, blasphemy, heresie, (Deut. xiii.; 1 Kings xx. 28. 42,) venting corrupt and pernicious opinions, that destroy the foundation, (Dan. iii. 29,) open contempt of the word preached, (Zech. xiii. 3,) prophanation of the Lord's-Day, (Neh. xiii. 31,) disturbing the peaceable administration and exercise of the worship and holy things of God, (1 Tim. ii. 2,) and the like, (Rom. xiii. 4,) are to be restrained and punished by civil authority.

9. If any church, one or more, shall grow schismatical, rending itself from the communion of other churches, or shall walk incorrigibly and obstinately in any corrupt way of their own, contrary to the rule of the word; in such case, the magistrate (Josh. xxii.) is to put forth his coercive power, as the

matter shall require. The tribes on this side Jordan intended to make war against the other tribes for building the altar of witness, whom they suspected to have turned away therein from following of the Lord.

MAYFLOWER COMPACT [39]

November 11/21, 1620

The Mayflower Compact was drawn up on shipboard before the Pilgrims landed. In his *History of Plymouth Plantation*, Bradford explains that it was signed in order to offset the "discontented and mutinous speeches" of some of the company to the effect that when they landed "they would use their own liberty; for none had power to command them, the patent they had being for Virginia, and not for New England, which belonged to another government, with which the Virginia Company had nothing to do." The signatories intended the Compact to serve as a basis for the government of the colony in the absence of a patent. The document thus constituted an original contract for the establishment of a new community. This example was followed in the establishment of many new colonies by the orthodox Puritans who followed the Pilgrim Separatists.

In the name of God, Amen. We whose names are underwriten, the loyall subjects of our dread soveraigne Lord, King James, by the grace of God, of Great Britaine, France, & Ireland king, defender of the faith, &c., haveing undertaken, for the glorie of God, and advancemente of the Christian faith, and honour of our king & countrie, a voyage to plant the first colonie in the Northerne parts of Virginia, doe by these presents solemnly & mutualy in the presence of God, and one of another, covenant & combine our selves togeather into a civill body politick, for our better ordering & preservation & furtherance of the ends aforesaid; and by vertue hearof to enacte, constitute, and frame such just & equall lawes, ordinances, acts, constitutions, & offices, from time to time, as shall be thought most meete & convenient for the generall good of the Colonie, unto which we promise all due submission and obedience. In witnes wherof we have hereunder subscribed our names at Cap-Codd the 11. of November, in the year of the raigne of our soveraigne lord, King James, of England, France, & Ireland the eighteenth, and of Scotland the fiftie fourth. Anno: Dom. 1620.

FUNDAMENTAL ORDERS OF CONNECTICUT [40]

January 14/24, 1638/9.

In 1635–1636 migrations took place from eastern communities in Massachusetts Bay to the Connecticut River valley. Thomas Hooker, minister at Newtown, removed his congregation to Hartford. In 1639, the three towns of Windsor, Wethersfield, and Hartford drew up the Fundamental Orders of Connecticut for their common government. In this work Hooker played an important rôle. The "Fundamental Orders" is the first written constitution that created a government. In this document

---

[39] W. Bradford, *History of Plymouth Plantation*, Massachusetts Historical Collection, 4th series, III, 89–90. (Boston, Massachusetts Historical Society. Reprinted by permission of the publishers.)

[40] *Public Records of the Colony of Connecticut.* (Hartford, Brown & Parsons, 1850.) I, 20–25.

we can notice the democratization of the orthodox Puritan theocracy. No property or religious qualifications for the franchise existed. American democracy can well be dated from Hooker's leadership in Hartford.

Forasmuch as it hath pleased the Allmighty God by the wise disposition of his divyne providence so to Order and dispose of things that we the Inhabitants and Residents of Windsor, Harteford and Wethersfield are now cohabiting and dwelling in and uppon the River of Conectecotte and the Lands thereunto adjoyneing; And well knowing a people are gathered togather the word of God requires that to mayntayne the peace and union of such a people there should be an orderly and decent Government established according to God, to order and dispose of the affayres of the people at all seasons as occation shall require; doe therefore assotiate and conjoyne our selves to be as one Publike State or Commonwealth; and doe, for our selves and our Successors and such as shall be adjoyned to us att any tyme hereafter, enter into Combination and Confederation togather, to mayntayne and presearve the liberty and purity of the gospell of our Lord Jesus which we now professe, as also the disciplyne of the Churches, which according to the truth of the said gospell is now practised amongst us; As also in our Civell Affaires to be guided and governed according to such Lawes, Rules, Orders and decrees as shall be made, ordered & decreed, as followeth:—

1. It is Ordered, sentenced and decreed, that there shall be yerely two generall Assemblies or Courts, the on [one] the second thursday in Aprill, the other the second thursday in September, following; the first shall be called the Courte of Election, wherein shall be yerely Chosen from tyme to tyme soe many Magestrats and other publike Officers as shall be found requisitte: Whereof one to be chosen Governour for the yeare ensueing and untill another be chosen, and noe other Magestrate to be chosen for more than one yeare; provided allwayes there be six chosen besids the Governour; which being chosen and sworne according to an Oath recorded for that purpose shall have power to administer justice according to the Lawes here established, and for want thereof according to the rule of the word of God; which choise shall be made by all that are admitted freemen and have taken the Oath of Fidellity, and doe cohabitte within this Jurisdiction, (having beene admitted Inhabitants by the major part of the Towne wherein they live.) or the major parte of such as shall be then present.

2. It is Ordered, sentensed and decreed, that the Election of the aforesaid Magestrats shall be on this manner: every person present and quallified for choyse shall bring in (to the persons deputed to receave them) one single paper with the name of him written in yt whom he desires to have Governour, and he that hath the greatest number of papers shall be Governor for that yeare. And the rest of the Magestrats or publike Officers to be chosen in this manner: The Secretary for the tyme being shall first read the names of all that are to be put to choise and then shall severally nominate them distinctly, and every one that would have the person nominated to be chosen shall bring in one single paper written uppon, and he that would not have him chosen shall bring in a blanke; and every one that hath more written papers then blanks shall be a Magistrat for that yeare; which papers shall be receaved and told by one or more that shall be then chosen by the court and sworne to be faythfull therein; but in case there should not be sixe chosen as aforesaid,

besides the Governor, out of those which are nominated, then he or they which have the most written papers shall be a Magestrate or Magestrats for the ensueing yeare, to make up the foresaid number.

3. It is Ordered, sentenced and decreed, that the Secretary shall not nominate any person, nor shall any person be chosen newly into the Magestracy which was not propownded in some Generall Courte before, to be nominated the next Election; and to that end yt shall be lawfull for ech of the Townes aforesaid by their deputyes to nominate any two whom they conceave fitte to be put to Election; and the Courte may ad so many more as they judge requisitt.

4. It is Ordered, sentenced and decreed that noe person be chosen Governor above once in two yeares, and that the Governor be alwayes a member of some approved congregation, and formerly of the Magestracy within this jurisdiction; and all the Magestrats Freemen of this Commonwelth: and that no Magestrate or other publike officer shall execute any parte of his or their Office before they are severally sworne, which shall be done in the face of the Courte if they be present, and in case of absence by some deputed for that purpose.

5. It is Ordered, sentenced and decreed, that to the aforesaid Courte of Election the severall Townes shall send their deputyes, and when the Elections are ended they may proceed in any publike searvice as at other Courts. Also the other Generall Courte in September shall be for the makeing of lawes, and any other publike occation, which conserns the good of the Commonwelth.

6. It is Ordered, sentenced and decreed, that the Governor shall, ether by himselfe or by the secretary, send out summons to the Constables of every Towne for the cauleing of these two standing Courts, on [one] month at lest before their severall tymes: And also if the Governor and the gretest parte of the Magestrats see cause uppon any spetiall occation to call a generall Courte, they may give order to the secretary soe to doe within fowerteene dayes worneing; and if urgent necessity so require, uppon a shorter notice, giveing sufficient grownds for yt to the deputyes when they meete, or els be questioned for the same; And if the Governor and Mayor [Major] parte of Magestrats shall ether neglect or refuse to call the two Generall standing Courts or ether of them, as also at other tymes when the occations of the Commonwelth require, the Freemen thereof, or the Mayor parte of them, shall petition to them soe to doe: if then yt be ether denyed or neglected the said Freemen or the Mayor parte of them shall have power to give order to the Constables of the severall Townes to doe the same, and so may meete togather, and chuse to themselves a Moderator, and may proceed to do any Acte of power, which any other Generall Courte may.

7. It is Ordered, sentenced and decreed that after there are warrants given out for any of the said Generall Courts, the Constable or Constables of ech Towne shall forthwith give notice distinctly to the inhabitants of the same, in some Publike Assembly or by goeing or sending from howse to howse, that at a place and tyme by him or them lymited and sett, they meet and assemble them selves togather to elect and chuse deputyes to be att the Generall Courte then following to agitate the afayres of the commonwelth; which said Deputyes shall be chosen by all that are admitted Inhabitants in

the severall Townes and have taken the oath of fidellity; provided that non be chosen a Deputy for any Generall Courte which is not a Freeman of this Commonwelth.

The foresaid deputyes shall be chosen in manner following: every person that is present and quallified as before expressed, shall bring the names of such, written in severall papers. as they desire to have chosen for that Imployment, and these 3 or 4, more or lesse, being the number agreed on to be chosen for that tyme, that have the greatest number of papers written for them shall be deputyes for that Courte; whose names shall be endorsed on the backe side of the warrant and returned into the Courte, with the Constable or Constables hand unto the same.

8. It is Ordered, sentenced and decreed, that Wyndsor, Hartford and Wethersfield shall have power, ech Towne, to send fower of their freemen as their deputyes to every Generall Courte; and whatsoever other Townes shall be hereafter added to this Jurisdiction, they shall send so many deputyes as the Courte shall judge meete, a resonable proportion to the number of Freemen that are in the said Townes being to be attended therein; which deputyes shall have the power of the whole Towne to give their voats and alowance to all such lawes and orders as may be for the publike good, and unto which the said Townes are to be bownd.

9. It is ordered and decreed, that the deputyes thus chosen shall have power and liberty to appoynt a tyme and a place of meeting togather before any Generall Courte to advise and consult of all such things as may concerne the good of the publike, as also to examine their owne Elections, whether according to the order, and if they or the gretest parte of them find any election to be illegall they may seclud such for the present from their meeting, and returne the same and their resons to the Courte; and if yt prove true, the Courte may fyne the party or partyes so intruding and the Towne, if they see cause, and give out a warrant to goe to a newe election in a legall way, either in parte or in whole. Also the said deputyes shall have power to fyne any that shall be disorderly at their meetings, or for not comming in due tyme or place according to appoyntment; and they may returne the said fynes into the Courte if yt be refused to be paid, and the Tresurer to take notice of yt, and to estreete or levy the same as he doth other fynes.

10. It is Ordered, sentenced and decreed, that every Generall Courte, except such as through neglecte of the Governor and the greatest parte of Magestrats the Freemen themselves doe call, shall consist of the Governor, or some one chosen to moderate the Court, and 4 other Magestrats at lest, with mayor parte of the deputyes of the severall Townes legally chosen; and in case the Freemen or mayor parte of the magestrats, shall call a Courte, it shall consist of the mayor parte of Freemen that are present or their deputyes, with a Moderator chosen by them: In which said Generall Courts shall consist the supreme power of the Commonwelth, and they only shall have power to make lawes or repeale them, to graunt levyes, to admitt of Freemen, dispose of lands undisposed of, to severall Townes or persons, and also shall have power to call ether Courte or Magestrate or any other person whatsoever into question for any misdemeanour, and may for just causes displace or deale otherwise according to the nature of the offence; and also may deale in any other matter that concerns the good of this commonwelth, ex-

cepte election of Magestrats, which shall be done by the whole boddy of Freemen.

In which Courte the Governor or Moderator shall have power to order the Courte to give liberty of spech, and silence unceasonable and disorderly speakeings, to put all things to voate, and in case the vote be equall to have the casting voice. But non of these Courts shall be adjorned or dissolved without the consent of the major parte of the Courte.

11. It is ordered, sentenced and decreed, that when any Generall Courte uppon the occasions of the Commonwelth have agreed uppon any summe or sommes of money to be levyed uppon the severall Townes within this Jurisdiction, that a Committee be chosen to sett out and appoynt what shall be the proportion of every Towne to pay of the said levy, provided the Committees be made up of an equall number out of each Towne.

THOMAS HOOKER

Before his migration to the colonies, Thomas Hooker was an English clergyman. He adhered steadfastly to the doctrine of the Church of England, but objected to its ceremonies. In 1630 Archbishop Laud silenced him. Hooker fled to Holland and in 1633 emigrated to New England. Upon his arrival in Massachusetts Bay, he became minister at Newtown (now Cambridge). He found himself out of sympathy with the authorities in both the church and the state; in 1636 he consequently removed his congregation to the Connecticut River valley and founded Hartford. Hooker played an important part in drafting the Fundamental Orders of Connecticut. He favored a democratization not only of the government but also of the church. His *Survey of the Summe of Church Discipline* is a defense of a democratized theocracy. Unlike Roger Williams, Hooker retained his Puritan theology and attempted to liberalize the church from within. The Preface to the *Survey of the Summe of Church Discipline* (1648) outlines the approach and the argument employed by Hooker in this book.

A SURVEY OF THE SUMME OF CHURCH DISCIPLINE

Preface [41]

. . . . . .

These two things seeming to be great reserved of inquiry, for this last age of the world.

1. Wherein the spirituall rule of Christs Kingdome consists, the manner how it is revealed and dispensed to the souls of his servants inwardly?

2. The order and manner how the government of his kingdome is managed outwardly in his Churches?

Vpon these two hinges the tedious agitations that are stirring in the earth turn: either having their first rise from hence directly, or by a secret influence, these fore-mentioned causes send in and insinuate their speciall interests indirectly, to make up that $\mu\epsilon\gamma\alpha\varsigma$ $\sigma\epsilon\iota\sigma\mu\grave{o}\varsigma$, to set forwards the shakings of heaven and earth, which are to be seen at this day.

This being the season, when all the kingdomes of the world, are becoming the Lords and his Christs: and to this purpose he is taking to himself his great might, which heretofore he seemed to lay aside and in silence, as him-

[41] *Old South Leaflets.* (Boston, Old South Association in Boston, 1896), No. 55, pp. 7–13. (Reprinted by permission of the publishers.)

self speaks in a like case. Psa, 50. to suffer wicked men to put forth their rage, according to their own pleasure, but he resolves by his Iron rod to dash those earthen vessels to peeces.

The first of these, to wit; The spiritual Kingdome of Christ, is most opposed by a generation of Enthusiasts; and Familists, who having refined the loathsome follies of their former predecessours, do adventure to set open their conceits, with greater insolency, to the view of the world, and under the pretence of free-grace, they destroy the grace of God in the power and operations of it, in the hearts and lives of men.

The other, which concerns the managing of the outward kingdome, unlesse my prospective much deceives me, is coming towards its last triall: because there is more liberty now given to each, to plead their own interests, when in former times the tyranny of Antichrist, and blinde obedience unto his dictates, turned the tomb stone of untimely silence upon all mens endeavors, buried all mens debates in their own bosomes, or else the unreasonable rigour of the prelates laboured to destroy the being of the defense as soon as it came to the birth.

This present term of Gods patience promiseth some allowance to his people, the distressed and despised ones of Christ, sub formâ pauperis, to take leave, to lay claim to the priviledges which they have conceived to be part of the legacy bequeathed unto them by the Lord Iesus, being estated and entitled members of the visible Kingdome of his Church.

To set out the bounds of these interests, worthy M. R. hath bestowed great labour, which I have again and again attended, and as I do freely acknowledge to have received light therefrom: so I do professe I do readily consent with him in many things.

In the number and nature of Officers, as Pastours, Teachers, Elders, &c. appointed by Christ and his Church.

That the people hath right to call their own officers, and that none must be imposed upon them by Patrons and Prelates.

That Scandalous persons are not fit to be members of a visible Church, nor should be admitted.

That the faithfull Congregations in England are true Churches: and therefore it is sinfull to separate from them as no Churches.

That the members which come commended from such Churches to ours here, so that it doth appear to the judgement of the Church, whence they come, that they are by them approved, and not scandalous, they ought to be received to Church communion with us, as members of other Churches with us in N. E. in like case so commended and approved.

To separate from Congregations for want of some Ordinances: Or,

To separate from the true worship of God, because of the sin of some worshippers, is unlawfull.

The Consociation of Churches is not only lawfull, but in some cases necessary.

That when causes are difficult, and particular Churches want light and help, they should crave the Assistance of such a consociation.

That Churches so meeting have right to counsell, rebuke, &c. as the case doth require.

In case any particular Church shall walk pertinaciously, either in the profession of errour, or sinfull practice, and will not hear their counsell, they may and should renounce the right hand of fellowship with them.

That Infants of visible Churches, born of wicked parents, being members of the Church, ought to be baptized.

In these and severall other particulars, we fully accord with M. R. and therefore no man in reason can conceive, that I write in opposition to his book; for then I should oppose my self, and mine own judgement: but for further disquisition and search into some particulars, which *pace tanti viri*, craves further and fuller discovery.

And hence, *this needs no toleration of religions*, or estrangement of affection, in tolerating the differences of such apprehensions, and that in some things, untill further light bring in further conviction and concurrence.

It is confessed by all the Casuists, I know, and that upon a rigid dispute, that longer time is to be allowed to two sorts of people, from whom consent is expected, then from others.

1. To some, who out of the strength of their judgement are able to oppose arguments, in case they come not so well guarded and pointed as they should.

2. To others, the like Indulgency is to be lent, who out of their weaknesse cannot so easily and readily perceive the valour and validity of an argument, to carry the cause, and win their assent thereunto.

Of this latter I profess my self, and therefore plead for allowance, and present Forbearance, especially considering, that modestly to inquire into, and for a time to dissent from the judgement of a generall counsell, hath been accounted tolerable.

He that will estrange his affection, because of the difference of apprehension in things difficult, he must be a stranger to himself one time or other. If men would be tender and carefull to keep off offenseive expressions, they might keep some distance in opinion, in some things, without hazard to truth or love. But when men set up their sheaves (though it be but in a dream, as Josephs was) and fall out with every one, that will not fall down and adore them, they will bring much trouble into the world, but little advantage to the truth, or peace.

Again, The Reader must know for his direction in this inquiry, my aim only was, and is, to lay down, and that briefly, the gounds of our practice, according to that measure of light I have received, and to give answer to such reasons, which might seem to weaken the evidence thereof: declining purposely, for the present, the examination of such answers, which are made to the arguments alledged by some of our Reverend Brethren, touching the same subject: because I would neither prejudice nor prevent their proper defense, which I do suppose in the fittest season, they will so present unto the world, as shall be fully satisfactory to such, as love and desire the knowledge of the truth.

The Summe is, we doubt not what we practise, but its beyond all doubt, that all men are liars, and we are in the number of those poor feeble men, either we do, or may erre, though we do not know it, what we have learned, we do professe, and yet professe still to live, that we may learn.

And therefore the errand upon which this present discourse is sent, is summarily to shew these two things unto the world,

1. That there must be more said (than yet it hath been my happinesse to see) before the principles we professe will be shaken, and consequently it cannot be expected, that we should be unsettled in our practice.

2. That I might occasion men eminently gifted to make further search, and to dig deeper, that if there be any vein of reason, which lies yet lower, it might be brought to light, and we professe and promise, not only a ready eare to hear it, but a heart willing to welcome it.

Its the perfection of a man, amidst these many weaknesses, we are surrounded withall, by many changes to come to perfection. Its the honour and conquest of a man truly wise to be conquered by the truth: and he hath attained the greatest liberty, that suffers himself to be led captive thereby.

That the discourse comes forth in such a homely dresse and course habit, the Reader must be desired to consider, It comes out of the wildernesse, where curiosity is not studied. Planters if they can provide cloth to go warm, they leave the cutts and lace to those that study to go fine.

As it is beyond my skill, so I professe it is beyond my care to please the nicenesse of mens palates, with any quaintnesse of language. They who covet more sauce then meat, they must provide cooks to their minde. It was a cavill cast upon Hierom, that in his writings he was *Ciceronianus non Christianus:* My rudeness frees me wholly from this exception, for being Λόγῳ Ἰδιώτης as the Apostle hath it, if I would, I could not lavish out in the loosenesse of language, and as the case stands, if I could answer any mans desire in that daintinesse of speech, I would not do the matter that Injury which is now under my hand: *Ornari res ipsa negat,* The substance and solidity of the frame is that, which pleaseth the builder, its the painters work to provide varnish.

If the manner of the discourse should occasion any disrellish in the apprehension of the weaker Reader, because it may seem too Logicall, or Scholasticall, in regard of the terms I use, or the way of dispute that I proceed in, in some places: I have these two tings to professe,

1. That plainesse and perspicuity, both for matter and manner of expression, are the things, that I have conscientiously indeavoured in the whole debate: for I have ever thought writings that come abroad, they are not to dazle, but direct the apprehension of the meanest, and I have accounted it the chiefest part of Iudicious learning, to make a hard point easy and familiar in explication. *Qui non vult intelligi, debet negligi.*

2. The nature of the subject that is under my hand, is such, that I was constrained to accommodate and conform my expressions more or lesse, in some kinde of sutablenesse thereunto: for in some passages of the dispute, the particulars in their very rise and foundation, border so neer upon the principles of Logick: (as whether *Ecclesia Catholica visibilis,* was to be attended, as a *Totum universale,* or *Integrale*) that either I must resolve to say nothing, or to speak (though as sparingly as I could of such things) as the quality of the things did require. And let any man make a triall, and I do much mistake my self, but he will be necessitated to take the same course, if he speaks to the cause. If the Reader shall demand how far this way of Church-proceeding receives approbation by any common concurrence amongst us: I shall plainly and punctually expresse my self in a word of truth, in these following points, viz.

Visible Saints are the only true and meet matter, whereof a visible Church should be gathered, and confoederation is the form.

The Church as *Totum essentiale*, is, and may be, before Officers.

There is no Presbyteriall Church (i.e., A Church made up of the Elders of many Congregations appointed Classickwise, to rule all those Congregations) in the N.T.

A Church Congregationall is the first subject of the keys.

Each Congregation compleatly constituted of all Officers, hath sufficient power in her self, to exercise the power of the keyes, and all Church discipline, in all the censures thereof.

Ordination is not before election.

There ought to be no ordination of a Minister at large, Namely, such as should make him Pastour without a People.

The election of the people hath an instrumentall casuall vertue under Christ, to give an outward call unto an Officer.

Ordination is only a solemn installing of an Officer into the Office, unto which he was formerly called.

Children of such, who are members of Congregations, ought only to be baptized.

The consent of the people gives a casuall vertue to the compleating of the sentence of excommunication.

Whilst the Church remains a true Church of Christ, it doth not loose this power, nor can it lawfully be taken away.

Consociation of Churches should be used, as occasion doth require.

Such consociation and Synods have allowance to counsell and admonish other Churches, as the case may require.

And if they grow obstinate in errour or sinfull miscarriages, they should renounce the right hand of fellowship with them.

But they have no power to excommunicate.

Nor do their constitutions binde *formalitèr* & *juridicè*.

In all these I have leave to professe the joint judgment of all the Elders upon the river: of New-haven, Guilford, Milford, Stratford, Fairfield: and of most of the Elders of the Churches in the Bay, to whom I did send in particular, and did receive approbation from them, under their hands: Of the rest (to whom I could not send) I cannot affirm; but this I can say, That at a common meeting, I was desired by them all, to publish what now I do.

Lastly, To ease the ordinary Reader, who happily is not acquainted with discourses of this kinde, I shall take leave to lend him this little advise.

The Treatise being divided into four parts, if he will be intreated to survey the Table set before the work, by a short and sudden cast of his eye, he shall presently perceive those particulars, which as so many pillars principall, bear up the whole frame.

1. Look at the Church in its first rise and essence, The causes of it, in the efficient, Matter and Form: The Qualifications of it, in its precedency, power, priviledges, make up the first part.

2. Look at the Church, as compleated with all her Officers, the number and nature of them, in her elections, and Ordinations, where the loathsome title of Independency is opened: these lay out the matter of the second part.

3. The Church thus constituted, The power that she exerciseth in admis-

sions, dispensations of Sacraments, and censures, especially that grand and great censure of excommunication, how it is to be managed, and the power of it lastly resolved. In these the third part is spent.

4. The consociation of Churches in Classes, Synods, and councels, is shortly discussed in the fourth part.

Let him be intreated to carry these along in this consideration, he will readily know, whether to refer any thing, and where to finde any thing; and as readily conceive the method and manner, both of the constitution of the Church, as the House of God, and the right managing of all the occasions and affairs thereof.

In the handling of all these particulars, so full of difficulty and of obscurity, I am not such a stranger at home, but that I am easily sensible of the weight of the matter and mine own weaknesse: and therefore I can professe in a word of truth, that against mine own inclination and affection, I was haled by importunity to this so hard a task, to kindle my rush candle, to joyn with the light of others, at least to occasion them to set up their lamps.

Now he that is the way, the truth, and the life, pave out all the waies of his people, and make their paths plain before them: Lead us all into that truth, which will lead us unto eternall life: bring us once unto that impotency and impossibility, that we can do nothing against truth, but for it, that so our Congregations may not only be stiled, as Ezekiels temple, but be really what was prophesied the Churches should be, in these last daies, Jehovah Shammah. In the Armes of his everlasing mercy I leave thee, but never cease to wish,

Spirituall welfare
in him,
THOMAS HOOKER.

ROGER WILLIAMS

Upon his arrival in Massachusetts Bay, Roger Williams immediately became an outstanding minister. However, he soon fell into disfavor because of his attacks upon the theocratic connection of Church and State, and because of his defense of Indian land claims. His teachings became so disturbing to the ruling oligarchy that they banished him from Massachusetts Bay in 1635. Shortly thereafter Williams founded a colony at Providence, Rhode Island. He became the leading influence in the colony of Rhode Island and Providence Plantations, where he secured the adoption of his theories of religious toleration and democratic government. After his banishment from Massachusetts Bay, Williams engaged in a sharp controversy with John Cotton, the exponent of Puritan theocracy. His two important treatises are *The Bloudy Tenent of Persecution for Cause of Conscience* and *The Bloudy Tenent yet More Bloudy*. These two works hold an important place in the world's literature in behalf of religious toleration.

THE BLOUDY TENENT, [42]

Of Persecution for Cause of
Conscience, discussed, in
A Conference *betweene*
Truth and Peace.
who
In all tender Affection, present to the High
Court of *Parliament,* (as the *Result* of their
Discourses) these, (amongst other *Passages*)
of *highest* consideration.

Printed in the Year 1644.

First, that the blood of *so* many hundred thousand soules of *Protestants* and *Papists,* spilt in the *Wars* of *present* and *former Ages,* for their respective *Consciences,* is not *required* nor *accepted* by *Jesus Christ* the *Prince* of *Peace.*

Secondly, Pregnant *Scripturs* and *Arguments* are throughout the Worke proposed against the *Doctrine* of *persecution* for *cause* of *Conscience.*

Thirdly, Satisfactorie Answers are given to *Scriptures,* and objections produced by Mr. *Calvin, Beza,* Mr. *Cotton,* and the Ministers of the New England Churches and others former and later, tending to prove the *Doctrine of persecution* for cause of *Conscience.*

Fourthly, The *Doctrine of persecution* for cause of *Conscience,* is proved guilty of all the *blood* of the *Soules* crying for *vengeance* under the *Altar.*

Fifthly, All *Civill States* with their *Officers* of *justice* in their respective *constitutions* and *administrations* are proved *essentially Civill,* and therefore not *Judges, Governours* or *Defendours* of the *Spirituall* or *Christian State* and *Worship.*

Sixtly, It is the will and command of *God,* that (since the comming of his Sonne the *Lord Jesus*) a *permission* of the most *Paganish, Jewish, Turkish,* or *Antichristian consciences* and *worships,* bee granted to *all* men in all *Nations* and *Countries:* and they are onely to bee *fought* against with that *Sword* which is only (in *Soule matters*) *able* to *conquer,* to wit, the *Sword of Gods Spirit,* the *Word* of *God.*

Seventhly, The *State* of the Land of *Israel,* the *Kings* and *people* thereof in *Peace* & *War,* is proved *figurative* and *ceremoniall,* and no *patterne* nor *president* for any *Kingdome* or *civill State* in the *world* to follow.

Eightly, *God* requireth not an *uniformity* of *Religion* to be *inacted* and *inforced* in any *civill State;* which inforced *uniformity* (sooner or later) is the greatest occasion of *civill Warre, ravishing* of *conscience, persecution* of *Christ Jesus* in his servants, and of the *hypocrisie* and *destruction* of *millions* of *souls.*

Ninthly, In holding an inforced *uniformity* of *Religion* in a *civill State,* wee must necessarily *disclaime* our desires and hopes of the *Iewes conversion* to *Christ.*

42 *Narragansett Club Publications.* (Providence: 1866–1870.) III, 3–4, 71–74, 126–128, 148–150, 202–204, 221, 247–250, 353–357.

Tenthly, An inforced *uniformity* of *Religion* throughout a *Nation* or *civill State*, confounds the *Civill* and *Religious*, denies the principles of Christianity and civility, and that *Jesus Christ* is come in the Flesh.

Eleventhly, The permission of other *consciences* and *worships* then a state professeth, only can (according to God) procure a firme and lasting *peace*, (good *assurance* being taken according to the *wisdome* of the *civill State* for *uniformity* of *civill obedience* from all sorts.)

Twelfthly, lastly, true *civility* and *Christianity* may both flourish in a *State* or *Kingdome*, notwithstanding the *permission* of divers and contrary *consciences*, either of *Iew* or *Gentile*.

. . . . . .

CHAP. VI

PEACE. The next *distinction* concerning the manner of *persons* holding the aforesaid *practices* (not onely the *waightier duties* of the *Law*, but points of *doctrine* and *worship* less principall.)

"Some (saith he) hold them forth in a *meeke* and *peaceable* way; some with "such *arrogance* and *impetuousnesse*, as of it selfe tendeth to the disturbance "of *civill peace.*

TRUTH. In the examination of this *distinction* we shall discusse,

First, what is *civill Peace*, (wherein we shall vindicate thy name the better.)

Secondly, what is to hold forth a Doctrine or Practice in this *impetuousnesse* or *arrogancy*.

First, for *civill peace*, what is it but *pax civitatis*, the peace of the Citie, whether an *English City*, *Scotch*, or *Irish* Citie, or further abroad, *French*, *Spanish*, *Turkish* City, &c.

Thus is pleased the Father of *Lights* to define it, *Ierem*. 29. 7. Pray for the *peace* of the *City*; which *peace* of the *City*, or *Citizens*, so compacted in a *civill* way of *union*, may be intire, unbroken, safe, &c. notwithstanding so many thousands of *Gods people* the *Jews*, were there in *bondage*, and would neither be *constrained* to the *worship* of the Citie *Babell*, nor restrained from so much of the *worship* of the true *God*, as they then could practice, as is plaine in the practice of the 3 Worthies, *Shadrack*, *Misach*, and *Abednego*, as also of *Daniel*, *Dan*. 3, & *Dan*. 6. (the peace of the *City* or *Kingdome*, being a far different Peace from the Peace of the *Religion* or Spiritual *Worship*, maintained & professed of the Citizens. This *Peace* of their *Worship* (which *worship* also in some Cities being various) being a false Peace, *Gods people* were and ought to be *Nonconformitants*, not daring either to be *restrained* from the *true*, or *constrained* to *false Worship*, and yet without *breach* of the Civill or *Citie-peace*, properly so called.

PEACE. Hence it is that so many glorious and flourishing *Cities* of the World maintaine their *Civill* peace, yea the very *Americans* & wildest *Pagans* keep the peace of their *Towns* or *Cities;* though neither in one nor the other can any man prove a true *Church* of God in those places, and consequently no spirituall and heavenly peace: The Peace *Spirituall* (whether true or false) being of a higher and farre different nature from the Peace of the place or people, being meerly and essentially *civill* and *humane*.

TRUTH. O how lost are the sonnes of men in this point? To illustrate this: The *Church* or *Company* of *worshippers* (whether true or false) is like

unto a Body or *Colledge* or *Physitians* in a *Citie;* like unto a *Corporation,
Society,* or *Company* of *East-Indie* or *Turkie-Merchants,* or any other *Societie*
or *Company* in *London:* which Companies may hold their *Courts,* keep their
Records, hold *disputations;* and in matters concerning their *Societie,* may dissent, divide, breake into *Schismes* and *Factions,* sue and implead each other
at the *Law,* yea wholly breake up and dissolve into pieces and nothing, and
yet the *peace* of the *Citie* not be in the least measure impaired or disturbed;
because the *essence* or being of the *Citie,* and so the *well-being* and *peace*
thereof is essentially distinct from those particular *Societies;* the *Citie-Courts,
Citie-Lawes, Citie-punishments* distinct from theirs. The *Citie* was before
them, and stands absolute and intire, when such a *Corporation* or *Societie* is
taken down. For instance, further, The *City* or *Civill State* of *Ephesus* was
essentially distinct from the *worship* of *Diana* in the Citie, or of the *whole
city.* Againe, the *Church* of *Christ* in *Ephesus* (which were Gods people,
converted and call'd out from the *worship* of that *City* unto *Christianitie* or
worship of *God* in *Christ*) was distinct from both.

Now suppose that *God* remove the *Candlestick* from *Ephesus,* yea though
the *whole Worship* of the *Citie of Ephesus* should be altered: yet (if men be
true and honestly ingenuous to *Citie-covenants, Combinations* and *Principles*)
all this might be without the least impeachment or infringement of the Peace
of the *City* of *Ephesus.*

Thus in the Citie of *Smirna* was the Citie it selfe or Civill estate one thing,
The Spirituall or Religious state of *Smirna,* another; The Church of *Christ* in
Smirna, distinct from them both; and the *Synagogue* of the *Jewes,* whether
literally *Jews* (so some thinke) or mystically, false *Christians,* (as others)
called the *Synagogue* of *Sathan, Reve.* 2. distinct from all these. And notwithstanding these spirituall oppositions in point of *Worship* and *Religion,*
yet heare we not the least noyse (nor need we, if Men keep but the Bond of
Civility) of any *Civil breach,* or *breach* of *Civill peace* amongst them: and to
persecute Gods people there for Religion, that only was a breach of Civilitie
it selfe.

. . . . . .

CHAP. XXXIV

PEACE. But it is said, be it granted that in a *common plague* or *infection*
none are smitten and dye but such as are appointed, yet it is not only every
mans duty, but the common duty of the Magistrate to prevent *infection,*
and to preserve the *common health* of the place; likewise though the number
of the *Elect* be sure, and *God* knowes who are His, yet hath He appointed
meanes for their *preservation* from *perdition,* and from *infection,* and therefore the *Angel* is blamed for *Balaams* doctrine, and *Jesabel* to seduce Christ
Jesus His servants, *Rev.* 2. *Tit.* 3. 10. *Rom.* 16. 17.

TRUTH. I answer, Let that Scripture and that of *Titus* reject an *Here-
ticke,* and *Rom.* 16. 17. avoid them that are *contentious,* &c. let them, and all
of like nature be axamined, and it will appeare that the great and good *Physi-
tian Christ Jesus,* the *Head* of the *Body,* and *King* of the *Church* hath not
been unfaithfull in providing spiritual *antidotes* and *preservatives* against
the spirituall *sicknesses, sores, weaknesses, dangers* of his *Church* and people;
but he never appointed the *civill Sword* for either *antidote* or *remedy,* as an

addition to those *Spiritualls*, which he hath left with his *wife*, his *Church* or People.

Hence how great is the *bondage*, the *captivity* of Gods owne People to *Babylonish* or *confused mixtures* in Worship, and unto worldly and earthly policies to uphold *State Religions* or *Worships*, since that which is written to the *Angel* and *Church* at *Pergamus*, shall be interpreted as sent to the Governour and City of *Pergamus*, and that which is sent to *Titus*, and the Church of Christ at *Creet* must be dilivered to the civill officers and City thereof.

But as the *Civill Magistrate* hath his charge of the *bodies* and *goods* of the *Subject:* So have the *Spirituall Officers*, *Governours* and *overseers* of *Christs City* or *Kingdome*, the charge of their *Souls*, and *Soule Safety;* Hence that charge of *Paul* to *Tim.* 1 *Tim.* 5. 20. Them that sinne *rebuke* before all, that others may learne to *fear*. This is in the Church of Christ a spirituall meanes for the *healing* of a *Soule* that hath sinned, or taken *infection*, and for the preventing of the infecting of others, that others may learne to feare, &c.

. . . . . .

CHAP. XLV

For (to keepe to the *similitude* which the *Spirit* useth, for instance) To batter downe a *strong hold*, *high wall*, *fort*, *tower* or *castle*, men bring not a first and second *Admonition*, and after obstinacie, *Excommunication*, which are *spirituall weapons* concerning them that be in the Church: not *exhortation* to *Repent* and be *baptized*, to beleeve in the Lord Jesus, &c. which are proper weapons to them that be without, &c. But to take a *strong hold*, men bring *Canons*, *Culverins*, *Saker*, *Bullets*, *Powder*, *Musquets*, *Swords*, *Pikes*, &c. and these to this end are weapons effectuall and proportionable.

On the other side, to batter downe *Idolatry*, *false worship*, *heresie*, *schisme*, *blindnesse*, *hardnesse*, out of the *soule* and *spirit*, it is vaine, improper, and unsutable to bring those *weapons* which are used by *persecutors*, *stocks*, *whips*, *prisons*, *swords*, *gibbets*, *stakes*, &c. (where these seem to prevaile with some Cities or Kingdomes, a stronger force sets up againe, what a weaker pull'd downe) but against these *spirituall strong holds* in the soules of men, *Spirituall Artillery* and *weapons* are proper, which are mighty through *God* to subdue and bring under the very *thought* to *obedience*, or else to binde fast the soule with *chaines* or *darknesse*, and locke it up in the *prison* of *unbeleefe* and hardnesse to *eternity*.

I observe that as *civill weapons* are improper in this businesse, and never able to effect ought in the *soule:* So (although they were proper, yet) they are *unnecessary*, for if as the *Spirit* here saith (and the *Answerer* grants) *spirituall weapons* in the hand of *Church officers* are able and ready to take *vengeance* on all disobedience, that is *able* and mighty, sufficient and ready for the *Lords* worke either to *save* the soule, or to *kill* the soule of whomsoever, be the party or parties opposite, in which respect I may againe remember that speech of *Job*, How hast thou helped him that hath no power? *Job* 26.

PEACE. Offer this (as *Malachie* once spake) to the Governours the *Kings* of the *Earth*, when they besiege, beleaguer, and assault great Cities, Castles, Forts, &c. should any subject pretending his service bring store of *pins*, *sticks*, *strawes*, *bulrushes*, to beat and batter downe *stone walls*, mighty

Bulwarkes, what might his expectation and reward be, but at least the censure of a man distract, beside himselfe? &c.

TRUTH. What shall we then conceive of His *displeasure*, (who is the *chiefe* or *Prince* of the *Kings* of the earth, and rides upon the *Word* of *Truth* and *meeknesse*, which is that *white Horse, Rev.* 6. and *Rev.* 19. with His holy *witnesses* the *white Troopers* upon *white horses*) when to His *helpe* and *aid* men bring and adde such *unnecessary, improper* and weake munition?

Will the *Lord Jesus* (did He ever in His owne Person practice, or did he appoint to) joyne to His *Breastplate* or *Righteousnesse*, the *breastplate* of *iron* and *steele?* to the *Helmet* of *righteousnesse* and *salvation* in *Christ*, an helmet and crest of *iron, brasse*, or *steel*, a target of wood to His shield of Faith? [to] His two *edged sword* comming forth of the mouth of *Jesus*, the *materiall sword*, the worke of Smiths and Cutlers? or a girdle of *shooes* leather to the girdle of truth, &c. Excellently fit and proper is that *alarme* and *item. Psal.* 2. Be *wise* therefore O ye *Kings* (especially those ten *Horns, Rev.* 17.) who under pretence of fighting for *Christ Jesus* give their power to the *Beast* against *Him*, and be warned ye *Judges* of the Earth: *Kisse the Son*, that is with *subjection* and *affection*, acknowledge Him only the *King* and *Judge* of *soules* (in that power bequeathed to His *Ministers* and *Churches*) lest if His wrath be kindled, yea but a little, then *blessed* are they that *trust* in Him.

CHAP. LXXIII

PEACE. The like answer (saith he) may bee returned to *Luther*, whom you next alledge.

First, that the *government* of the *civill Magistrate* extendeth no further then over the *bodies* and *goods* of their *subjects*, not over their *soules*, and therefore they may not undertake to give *Lawes* unto the *soules* and *consciences* of men.

Secondly, that the *Church* of *Christ* doth not use the Arme of *secular* power to compell men to the true profession of the *truth*, for this is to be done ·with *spirituall weapons*, whereby *Christians* are to be exhorted, not compelled. "But this (saith hee) hindreth not that *Christians* sinning against *light* of "*faith* and *conscience*, may justly be censured by the *Church* with *excommuni-* "*cation*, and by the *civill sword* also, in case they shall corrupt others to the "perdition of their soules.

TRUTH. I answer, in this joynt *confession* of the *Answerer* with *Luther*, to wit, that the *government* of the *civill Magistrate* extendeth no further then over the *bodies* and *goods* of their *subjects*, not over their *soules*: who sees not what a cleare *testimony* from his own mouth and pen is given, to wit, that either the *Spiritual* and *Church* estate, the preaching of the *Word*, and the gathering of the *Church*, the *Baptisme* of it, the *Ministry, Government* and *Administrations* thereof belong to the *civill* body of the Commonweale? that is, to the *bodies* and *goods* of men, which seemes monstrous to imagine: Or else that the *civill Magistrate* cannot (without exceeding the bounds of his office) meddle with those spirituall affaires.

Againe, necessarily must it follow, that these two are contradictory to themselves: to wit,

The *Magistrates* power extends no further then the *bodies* and *goods* of the subject, and yet

The *Magistrate* must punish *Christians* for sinning against the *light* of *faith* and *conscience*, and for *corrupting* the *soules* of men.

The Father of *Lights* make this worthy *Answerer* and all that feare him to see their wandring in this case, not only from his feare, but also from the light of *Reason* it selfe, their owne *convictions* and *confessions*.

Secondly, in his joint confession with *Luther*, that the *Church* doth not use the secular power to compell men to the Faith and Profession of the *truth*, he condemneth (as before I have observed).

First, his former *Implication, viz.* that they may bee compelled when they are convinced of the *truth* of it.

Secondly, their owne practice, who suffer no man of any different *conscience* and *worship* to live in their jurisdiction, except that he depart from his owne *exercise* of *Religion* and *Worship* differing from the *worship* allowed of in the *civill State*, yea and also actually submit to come to their *Church*.

Which howsoever it is coloured over with this varnish, *viz.* that men are *compelled* no further then unto the hearing of the *Word*, unto which all men are bound: yet it will appeare that *teaching* and being taught in a *Church* estate is a *Church* worship, as true and proper a *Church worship* as the Supper of the Lord, *Act.* 2. 46.

Secondly, all persons (*Papist* and *Protestant*) that are conscientious, have alwayes suffered upon this ground especially, that they have refused to come to each *others Church* or *Meeting*.

. . . . . .

The remaining chapters of *The Bloudy Tenent*, Ch. LXXXII on, which are introduced by the following title page, are an answer to Cotton's argument for the employment of civil power for the maintenance of church belief. The quotations that appear at the beginning of many chapters are from Cotton's argument.

A MODEL OF CHURCH AND CIVIL POWER

Composed by Mr. COTTON and
the MINISTERS of NEW-
ENGLAND,
And sent to the Church at Salem,
as a further Confirmation of the bloody
Doctrine of Persecution for cause
of Conscience.

Examined and Answered.

. . . . . .

CHAP. XCII

PEACE. The 4. head is, The proper meanes of both these Powers to attaine their ends.

"First, the proper meanes whereby the Civill Power may and should "attaine its end, are onely Politicall, and principally these Five.

"First the erecting and establishing what forme of Civill Government may "seeme in wisedome most meet, according to generall rules of the Word, and "state of the people.

"Secondly, the making, publishing, and establishing of the wholesome "Civill Lawes, not onely such as concerne Civill Justice, but also the free "passage of true Religion: for, outward Civill Peace ariseth and is maintained "from them both, from the latter as well as from the former:

"Civill peace cannot stand intire, where Religion is corrupted, 2 *Chron.* "15. 3. 5. 6. *Judg.* 8. And yet such Lawes, though conversant about Religion, "may still be counted Civill Lawes, as on the contrary, an Oath doth still "remaine Religious, though conversant about Civill Matters.

"Thirdly, Election and appointment of Civill officers, to see execution of "those Lawes.

"Fourthly, Civill Punishments and Rewards, of Transgressors and Ob- "servers of these Lawes.

"Fifthly, taking up Armes against the Enemies of Civill Peace.

"Secondly, the meanes whereby the Church may and should attaine her "ends, are only ecclesiasticall, which are chiefly five.

"First, setting up that forme of Church Government only, of which Christ "hath given them a pattern in his Word.

"Secondly, acknowledging and admitting of no Lawgiver in the Church, "but Christ, and the publishing of his Lawes.

"Thirdly, Electing and ordaining of such officers onely, as Christ hath "appointed in his Word.

"Fourthly, to receive into their fellowship them that are approved, "and inflicting Spirituall censures against them that offend.

"Fifthly, Prayer and patience in suffering any evill from them that be "without, who disturbe their peace.

"So that Magistrates, as Magistrates, have no power of setting up the "Forme of Church Government, electing Church officers, punishing with "Church censures, but to see that the Church doth her duty herein. And on "the other side, the Churches as Churches, have no power (though as mem- "bers of the Commonweale they may have power) of electing or altering "formes of Civill Government, electing of Civill officers, inflicting Civill "punishments (no not on persons excommunicate) as by deposing Magis- "trates from their Civill Authoritie, or withdrawing the hearts of the people "against them, to their Lawes, no more then to discharge wives, or children, "or servants, from due obedience to their husbands, parents, or masters: "or by taking up armes against their Magistrates, though he persecute them "for Conscience: for though members of Churches who are publique officers "also of the Civill State, may suppresse by force the violence of Usurpers, "as *Iehoiada* did *Athaliah,* yet this they doe not as members of the Church, "but as officers of the Civill State.

TRUTH. Here are divers considerable *passages* which I shall briefly examine, so far as concernes our *controversie.*

First, whereas they say, that the *Civill Power* may erect and establish what *forme* of *civill Government* may seeme in *wisedome* most meet, I acknowl-edge the *proposition* to be most true, both in it self, and also considered with the end of it, that a *civill Government* is an *Ordinance* of *God,* to conserve the *civill peace* of people, so farre as concernes their *Bodies* and *Goods,* as formerly hath beene said.

But from this Grant I infer, (as before hath been touched) that the *Sover-*

aigne, originall, and *foundation* of *civill power* lies in the *people*, (whom they must needs meane by the *civill power* distinct from the *Government* set up.) And if so, that a People may erect and establish what *forme* of *Government* seemes to them most meete for their *civill condition:* It is evident that such *Governments* as are by them erected and established, have no more *power*, nor for no longer time, then the *civill power* or people consenting and agreeing shall betrust them with. This is cleere not only in *Reason*, but in the experience of all *commonweales*, where the people are not deprived of their *naturall freedome* by the power of *Tyrants*.

And if so, that the Magistrates receive their power of governing the Church, from the People; undeniably it followes, that a *people*, as a *people*, naturally considered (of what *Nature* or *Nation* soever in *Europe, Asia, Africa* or *America*) have fundamentally and originally, as men, a power to governe the *Church*, to see her doe her *duty*, to correct her, fo redresse, reforme, establish, &c. And if this be not to pull *God* and *Christ*, and *Spirit* out of *Heaven* and subject them unto *naturall*, sinfull, inconstant men, and so consequently to *Sathan* himselfe, by whom all *people* naturally are guided, let *Heaven* and *Earth* judge.

PEACE. It cannot by their owne *Grant* be denied, but that the *wildest Indians* in *America* ought (and in their kind and severall degrees doe) to agree upon some *formes* of *Government*, some more *civill*, compact in Townes, &c. some lesse. As also that their *civill* and *earthly Governments* be as lawfull and true as any *Governments* in the *World*, and therefore consequently their *Governors* are *Keepers* of the *Church* or both *Tables*, (if any Church of Christ should arise or be amongst them:) and therefore lastly, (if *Christ* have betrusted and charged the *civill* Power with his *Church*) they must judge according to their *Indian* or *American consciences*, for other *consciences* it cannot be supposed they should have.

. . . . . .

CHAP. CXX

PEACE. Deare *Truth*, you have shewne me a little draught of Zions sorrowes, her children tearing out their mothers bowels: O when will Hee that stablisheth, comforteth, and builds up Zion, looke downe from Heaven, and have mercy on her? &c.

TRUTH. The Vision yet doth tarry (saith *Habacuk*) but will most surely come: and therefore the patient and believing must wait for it.

But to your last Proposition, whether the Kings of Israel and Judah were not types of Civill Magistrates? now I suppose by what hath been already spoken, these things will be evident.

First, that those former *types* of the *Land*, of the *People*, of their *Worships*, were *types* and *figures* of a *spirituall Land, spirituall People*, and *spirituall Worship* under *Christ*. Therefore consequently, their *Saviours, Redeemers, Deliverers, Judges, Kings*, must also have their *spirituall Antitypes*, and so consequently not *civill* but *spirituall Governours* and *Rulers;* lest the very *essential nature* of *Types, Figures* and Shadowes be overthrowue.

Secondly, although the Magistrate by a Civill sword might well compell that Nationall Church to the externall exercise of their Naturall Worship: yet it is not possible (according to the rule of the New Testament) to compell whole Nations to true Repentance and Regeneration, without which (so farre as may be discerned true) the Worship and holy Name of God is prophaned and blasphemed.

An Arme of Flesh, and Sword of Steele cannot reach to cut the darknesse of the Mind, the hardnesse and unbeleefe of the Heart, and kindely operate upon the Soules affections to forsake a long continued Fathers worship, and to imbrace a new, though the best and truest. This worke performes alone that sword out of the mouth of Christ, with two edges, *Rev.* 1. & 3.

Thirdly, we have not one tittle in the New Testament of *Christ Jesus* concerning such a *parallel,* neither from *Himselfe,* not from his *Ministers,* with whom he conversed fourty dayes after his *Resurrection,* instructing them in the matters of his *Kingdome, Acts* 1.

Neither find we any such *commission* or *direction* given to the *Civill Magistrate* to this purpose, nor to the *Saints* for their *submission* in matters spirituall, but the contrary, *Acts.* 4. & 5. 1 *Cor.* 7. 23. *Coloss.* 2. 18.

Fourthly, we have formerly viewed the very nature and essence of a *Civill Magistrate,* and find it the same in all parts of the *World,* where ever people live upon the face of the *Earth,* agreeing together in *Townes, Cities, Provinces, Kingdomes:* I say the same essentially Civill, both from, 1. the *rise* and *fountaine* whence it springs, to wit, the *peoples* choice and free consent. 2. The Object of it, viz. the *common-weale* or *safety* of such a *people* in their *bodies* and *goods,* as the *Authours* of this *Modell* have themselves confessed.

This *civill* Nature of the *Magistrate* we have proved to receive no *addition* of *power* from the *Magistrates* being a *Christian,* no more then it receives *diminution* from his not being a *Christian:* even as the *Commonweale* is a true *Common-weale,* although it have not heard of *Christianitie;* and *Christianitie* professed in it (as in *Pergamus, Ephesus, &c.*) makes it ne're no more a Commonweale, and *Christianitie* taken away, and the *candlestick* removed, makes it ne're the lesse a Commonweale.

Fifthly, the *Spirit* of *God* expresly relates the worke of the *civill Magistrate* under the *Gospel,* Rom. 13, expresly mentioning (as the *Magistrates* object) the duties of the *second Table,* concerning the *bodies* and *goods* of the *subject.* 2. The *reward* or *wages* which people owe for such a worke, to wit, (not the *contribution* of the *Church* for any *spirituall* work, but) *tribute, toll, custome* which are *wages* payable by all sorts of men, *Natives* and *Forreigners,* who enjoy the same benefit of *publick peace* and *commerce* in the *Nation.*

Sixthly, Since the *civill Magistrate,* whether *Kings* or *Parliaments, States,* and *Governours,* can receive no more in *justice* then what the People give, and are therefore but the *eyes* and *hands* and *instruments* of the people (simply considered, without respect to this or that *Religion*) it must inevitably follow (as formerly I have touched) that if *Magistrates* have received their power from the *people,* then the greatest number of the people of every Land have received from *Christ Iesus,* a power to *establish, correct, reforme* his *Saints* and *servants,* his *wife* and *spowse,* the *Church:* And she that by the expresse *word* of the *Lord* (*Psal.* 149.) binds *Kings* in *chaines,* and *Nobles* in *links* of *iron,* must her selfe be subject to the changeable pleasures of the people of the *World* (which lies in *wickednesse,* 1 *Iohn* 5.) even in matters of Heavenly and *spirituall* Nature.

Hence therefore in all controversies concerning the Church, Ministrie and worship, the last Appeale must come to the Bar of the People or Common-weal, where all may personally meet, as in some Commonweales of small number, or in greater by their Representatives.

Hence then no person esteemed a beleever, and added to the Church.

No Officer chosen and ordained.

No person cast forth and excommunicated, but as the Commonweale and people please, and in conclusion, no Church of Christ in this Land or World, and consequently no visible Christ the Head of it. Yea yet higher, consequently no God in the World worshipped according to the institutions of Christ Jesus, except the severall peoples of the Nations of the World shall give allowance.

PEACE. Deare Truth, Oh whither have our Forefathers and teachers led us? higher then to God himselfe (by these doctrines driven out of the World) you cannot rise: and yet so high must the inevitable and undeniable consequences of these their doctrines reach, if men walke by their owne common Principles.

TRUTH. I may therefore here seasonably adde a seventh, which is a necessary consequence of all the former *Arguments*, and an *Argument* it selfe: *viz.* we finde expresly a spirituall power of *Christ Jesus* in the hands of his *Saints, Ministers* and *Churches*, to bee the true *Antitype* of those former figures in all the *Prophecies* concerning *Christ* his *spirituall power*, Isa. 9. Dan. 5. Mich. 4. &c. compared with Luc. 1. 32. Act. 2. 30. 1 Cor. 5. Math. 18. Marc. 13. 34. &c.

THE
BLOODY TENENT
YET
MORE BLOODY:
by
Mr. *Cottons* endeavor to wash it white in the
Blood of the *Lambe;*

Of whose precious Blood spilt in the
Blood of his Servants; and

Of the blood of Millions spilt in former and
later Wars for Conscience sake,

That

Most Bloody Tenent of Persecution for cause of
Conscience, upon a second Tryal, is found now more
apparently and more notoriously guilty.

In this Rejoynder to Mr. *Cotton*, are principally

I.   *The Nature of Persecution,* ⎫
II. *The Power of the Civill Sword* ⎬ Examined;
     in Spirituals ⎭

III. *The Parliaments permission of* ⎫ Justified
     Dissenting Conciences ⎭

Also (as a Testimony to Mr *Clarks* Narrative) is added
a Letter to Mr. *Endicot* Governor of the *Massachusets* in N. E.

By R. Williams of *Providence* in *New-England.*

London, Printed for *Giles Calvert*, and are to be sold at the
black-spread-Eagle at the West-end of *Pauls*, 1652. [43]

[43] *Narragansett Club Publications.* (Providence: 1866-1870.) IV, 1, 68-80, 187-189.

EXAMINATION OF CHAP. VI

PEACE. But to proceed to the sixth Chapter, in which is handled that which more especially concerns my *self.* It is too lamentably known, how the furious *troopes* of *persecutors* in all *States, Cities, Towns,* &c. have ever marched under my name, the white colours of *peace, civil peace, publike peace.*

TRUTH. Yet Master *Cotton* confesseth, that the *Cities* peace is an *humane* and *civil peace,* as was further explained in many *instances* from *Babylon, Ephesus, Smyrna,* &c. against which Master *Cotton* excepts not.

PEACE. The difference or controversie in this Chapter lies in two things. First, In the *similitudes* used from *companies* and *societies,* voluntarily entering into *combinations,* which are distinct from the City.

2. In the nature of the *Church,* which he maintaines to be a *society,* whose *order* the City is bound to preserve, as well as any of their civil *orders* or *societies.*

TRUTH. To begin with the first, Master *Cotton* replies, "That although "such *societies* be not of the *essence* of the City, yet they are of the *integral* "and *conservant* causes of the City, and so the *disturbance* of any of those ".orders or *societies* in the City, disturbes the *City* it self.

But I answer, The *similitude* was used more especially from a *colledge* of *Physitians,* or a *society* of *Merchants, Turkish, East-Endies,* &c. and consequently any other of that kinde, voluntarily combining together for the better inriching of themselves in the improvement of their *faculties* for *publike* good (at least so pretended.) It was never intended, that if such necessary *Trades, Callings, &c.* as he mentioneth, be dissolved and ruined, that there would be no *disturbance* of the *peace* of the City: But that if such or such a way and *order* of men of those faculties I mentioned, voluntarily *combine,* and voluntarily also *dissolve;* yet all this may may be, without any breach of *civil* and *publike* peace.

PEACE. If so, much more the *church* of *Christ,* which is a *spiritual society* voluntarily uniting, may dissolve; I say, much more, without the breach of the *peace* of the *city,* which is of a *civil* and humane nature, as is confessed, and was urged in the instances of *Ephesus,* &c.

TRUTH. 2. We are wont when we speak of keeping or breaking the *Peace,* to speak of *Words* or *Actions* of *Violence, Sedition, Uproare,* &c. for, *Actions* of the *Cases, Pleas,* and *Traverses* may be, and yet no peace broken, when men submit to the *Rule* of *State,* for the composing of such *differences,* &c. Therefore it is that I affirme, that if any of *Christs Church* have difference with any other man in *civill* and *humane* things, he ought to be judged by the *Law:* But if the *Church* have *spiritual controversies* among themselves or with any other, or if *God* take away the *Candlestick* as he threatned the Church in *Ephesus,* all this may be, and yet no civil peace broken: Yea, amongst those that profess the same *God* and *Christ,* as the *Papists* and *Protestants,* or the same *Mahomet,* as the *Turks* and *Persians,* there would no civil *Peace* be broken, notwithstanding their *differences* in *Religion,* were it not for the bloody *Doctrine* of *Persecution,* which alone breaks the bounds of *civil* peace, and makes *Spiritual* causes the causes of their bloodie *dissentions.*

I observe therefore, a twofold *Fallacie* in Master *Cottons* reply. First, he fallaciously mingles *Peace* and *Prosperity* together: for though it be true, that under the termé *Peace* all good things are sometimes concluded, yet when we speak of *Hereticks* or *Schismaticks* breaking the *civil* peace, or strowing *Doctrines* tending to break the *civill peace*, we must understand some such words as acts of *violence*, wherein the *bounds* and *orders* of the *City, Laws*, and *Courts* are violated; taking it for granted (for this is the *Supposition*) that the *Lawes* of the *City* be meerely civil and humane, Hence then I affirme, that there is no *Doctrine*, no *Tenent* so directly tending to break the *Cities* peace, as this *Doctrine* of *persecuting* or *punishing* each other for the cause of *conscience* or *Religion*.

Againe, it is a second Fallacie to urge your order of the *Church*, and the *Excellency* thereof, and that therefore it is a Breach of the *civil peace*, when the *Order* of the *church* is not preserved: For although it is most true, that sooner or later the *God* of heaven punisheth the *nations* of the world, for their *Idolatries, Superstitions*, &c. yet Master *Cotton* himself acknowledgeth (as was affirmed) that many glorious flourishing *cities* there are all the world over, wherein no *church* of *Christ* is extant: Yea, that the *Commonweale of Rome* flourished five hundred years together, before ever the name of *Christ* was heard in it; which so great a *Glory* of so great a *continuance*, mightily evinceth the distinction of the *civill peace* of a *State* from that which is *Christian Religion*.

It is true (as Master *Cotton* tells us) that the Turks have plagued the *Antichristian* world, for their *Idolatries:* Yet *History* tells us, that one of their *Emperours* (*Mahomet*) was the man that first broke up and desolated two most glorious ancient *cities, Constantinople* (which had flourished 1120 yeares (since its first building by *Constantine*) and *Athens*, which from *Solons* giving of it *Laws*, had flourished two thousand yeares, notwithstanding their Idolatries, &c.

TRUTH. It is apparent that then the *Christian Religion* gloriously flourished (contrary to Master *Cottons* observation) when the *Roman Emperours* took not power to themselves to reform the *abuses* in the *Christian* Church, but persecuted it; and then the *church* was ruined and overwhelmed with *Apostacy* and *Antichristianism*, when the *Emperours* took that power unto themselves: And then it was (as Master *Cotton* elsewhere confesseth) that *Christianitie* lost more, even in *Constantines* time, then under bloody *Nero, Domitian*, &c.

PEACE. It cannot be denied (dear Truth) but that the *Peace* of a *civil State* (of all States, excepting that of typical *Israel*) was and is meerly and *essentially civil.* But Master *Cotton* saith further, Although the *Inward Peace* of a church is *Spiritual*, yet the *outward* Peace of it, *Magistrates* must keep in a way of *Godliness* and *Honestie*, 1 Tim. 2. 1.

TRUTH. The *Peace* of a *church* of *Christ* (the onely true *Christian State, Nation, Kingdom*, or *city*) is *Spiritual*, whether *internal* in the *Soul*, or *external* in the *administration* of it; as the peace of a *civil State* is *civil, internal* in the mindes of men, and *external* in the administration and conversation of it; and for that place of *Timothy*, it hath been fully spoken to in this *discourse*, and the Discusser hath as yet seen no *exception* against what hath been spoken.

PEACE. But further, saith Master *Cotton*, although the *peace* of a Country be *civil*, yet it is distracted by disturbing the peace of the *Church* for

God cut short the Coasts of the *civil State* when *Jehu* shortened his *Reformation*, 2 King. 10. 31. 32.

TRUTH. Master *Cotton* denies not (but confessed in his discourse concerning *Baptism*) that *Canaan* was *Typical*, and to be cast out of that *Land*, was to be cast out of *Gods sight:* which proves thus much, That the *church* of *Christ*, the *Israel* now, neglecting to reform, *God* will cut this *Israel* short. But what is this to a meerly *civil State*, which may flourish many hundreds, yea some thousands of yeers together (as I before instanced) when the Name of the true Lord *Jesus Christ* is not so much as heard of within it?

PEACE. Lastly, (saith he) the church is a *Society*, as well as the *Societies* of *Merchants*, *Drapers*, &c. and it is just to preserve the *Society* of the *church*, as well as any other *Society*.

TRUTH. When we speak of the *balances* of *Justice*, we must distinguish between the *Balances* of the *Sanctuary*, and the *Balances* of the *World* or *civil States*. It is *spiritual justice* to preserve *spiritual right;* and for that end, the *spiritual King* thereof hath taken care. It is *civil Justice* to preserve the *civil rights;* and the *Rights* of a *civil society* ought justly to be *preserved* by a *civil State:* (and yet if a *company* of men combine themselves into a *civil society* by voluntary agreement, and voluntarily dissolve it, it is not *justice* to enforce them to continue together.)

PEACE. The *church* can least of all be forced: for as it is a *spiritual society*, and not subject to any *civil Judicature;* (though some say that a *church* in *New England* was cited to appear before a *civil Court:*) so is the *combination* of it *voluntary*, and the *dissolution* of it in part or whole is voluntary, and endures no Civil violence, but as a *virgin* (in point of *marriage*) *nec cogit, nec cogitur*, she forceth not, nor can be forced by any *civil power.*

TRUTH. But lastly, if it be *justice* to preserve the Society of the *church*, is it not partiality in a meer *civil State* to preserve one onely *society*, and not the persons of other Religious societies and *consciences* also? But the Truth is, this mingling of the *church* and the *world* together, and their *orders* and *societies* together, doth plainly discover, that such *churches* were never called out from the *world*, and that this is only a secret *policy* of *flesh* and *blood*, to get *protection* from the *world*, and so to keep (with some little stilling of *conscience*) from the *Cross* or *Gallowes* of *Jesus Christ.*

TRUTH. Yea, but hear (saith Master *Cotton*) those *excellent penmen* of the *Spirit* (both the Father and the *Son*) *David* and *Solomon.* First *David* (Psalme 122) They shall prosper that love the peace of *Jerusalem:* and *Solomon*, Where the *righteous* rejoyce, there is great *glory*, *Prov.* 28. Now (saith he) what is the *church* but a *congregation* of *righteous* men? If the *rejoycing* of the *Church* be the *glory* of a *Nation*, surely the *disturbing*, and destroying, and dissolving the *church* is the *shame* and *confusion* of a *Nation.*

TRUTH. The outward *prosperity* of a *Nation*, was a typical figurative *blessing*, of that *national* and figurative *church* of *Israel* in *Canaan.* It is now made good spiritually to them that love the *spiritual Jerusalem:* for though godliness hath a promise of things of this life convenient; yet *persecution* is the common and ordinary position of the *Saints* under the *Gospel*, though that *cup* be infinitely sweetened also to them that drink of it with *Christ Jesus*, by the measure and increase of a hundred fold for one even with persecution in this life.

2. It is true, the *rejoycing* of a *Church* of *Christ*, is the *glory* of any *Nation*, and the contrary a shame: yet this proveth not that *God* vouchsafeth to no *state*, *civil peace*, and temporal *glory*, except it establish and keep up a Church of *Christ* by force of armes; for the contrary we have mentioned, and Master *Cotton* confesseth the flourishing of *States* ignorant of *Christ*, from *Age* to *Age*, yea, and as I have mentioned, even to two thousand yeers in *Athens;* six *generations* before it heard of *Christ*, and fourteen *generations* since, with the sprinking (for some time) of the knowledge of *Christ Jesus* in it.

PEACE. 2. But consider (saith Master *Cotton*) the *excellency* and *preheminence* of the *church*, that the *world* is for it, and would not subsist but for it, *&c.*

TRUTH. Tis true, *glorious* things are spoken of the *City* of *God*, &c. yet for many *Ages* together Master *Cotton* confesseth the *Nations* of the *world* may subsist & *flourish* without it; and though it be the *duty* of the *Nations* of the *world* to *countenance* and cherish the *church* of *Christ;* yet where is there any *commission*, either in the *New* or *Old Testament*, that the *Nations* of the *world* should be the *judges*, *governors*, and *defenders* of *Christ Iesus* his *spiritual kingdome*, and so bound to take up *Armes* and smite with the *civil sword* (among so many pretenders) for that which they believe to be the *church* of *Christ?*

PEACE. 3. (saith he) It is matter of just displeasure to *God*, and sad grief of *heart* to the *church*, when *civil states* looke at the *state* of the *church*, as of little or no concernment to themselves, *Zech.* 1. 19. *Lam.* 1. 13.

TRUTH. Grant this, and that the most jealous God will awake in his season, for these *sins*, and for the *persecutions*, *idolatries*, and *blasphemies;* which the *Nations* live in: yet what is this for warrant to the *Nations* (as before) to judge and rule the *church* of *Christ*, yea, and under the colour of defending *Christs* faith, and *preserving Christs church* pure, to tear *Christ* out of *heaven*, by *persecuting* of his *Saints* on *earth;* and to fire the *world* with devouring *flames* of bloody *wars*, and this onely for the *sweet sake* of the *prince* of *peace?*

PEACE. Dear *Truth*, we are now upon an high point, and that which neerly concerns my self, the *peace* of the *world*, and the *Nations* of it. Master *Cotton* saith further, *God* winketh at the *Nations* in the time of their *ignorance*, and suffers the *Nation* to flourish many hundred yeers together, as did the *Empire* of *Rome;* yet when the *church* of *Christ* comes to be planted amongst them, then, as he brought the *Turkes* upon the *Romans*, for their *persecuting* the *church*, and not preserving it in *purity;* so consequently will he do unto the *Nations* of the *world*.

TRUTH. I answer, the most righteous *Judge* of the whole world hath plauged the *Nations* of the *world*, both before *Christs coming*, and since, for their *pride* and *cruelty* against his people, for their *idolatries*, *blasphemies*, &c. Yet Master *Cotton* acknowledgeth that many *states* have flourished many hundred yeers together, when no true *church* of *Christ* hath been found in them: and Master *Cotton* will never prove, that *God* ever commanded the *Nations* and *governments* of the world, to gather or constitute his *churches*, and to preserve them in *purity:* For *God* gave his *ordinances*, both before and since *Christ*, to his *people* onely, whom he *chuseth* and calleth out of the *World*, and the *Nations* of it: and he hath punished and dissolved them for their obstinate *neglect* thereof. And for the *Roman Empire*, and the *Em-*

perors thereof, the *Christian Religion*, and the *purity* thereof, never lost so much, as when the *Emperors* were persuaded of Master *Cottons bloody Tenent*, as Master *Cotton* and all men seen in *History* and *Christianity* must confess.

PEACE. But further, although (saith Master *Cotton*) the peace of the *church* be a *spiritual inward* peace, yet there is an *outward peace* of the *church* due to them from *Princes* and *Magistrates*, in a way of *godliness* and *honesty*, 1 *Tim.* 2. (2.) But in a way of *ungodliness* and *idolatry*, it is an wholesome *faithfulness* to the *church*, if *Princes* trouble the *outward peace* of the *church*, that so the *church* finding themselves wounded, and pricked in the house of their *friends*, they may repent, and return to their first *husband, Zech.* 13. (6.) *Hos.* 2. (7.)

TRUTH. The peace of the Church is not only *inward*, between *God* and *themselves;* but as the *Argument* importeth, to which Master *Cotton* answereth, the peace of the Church *external* and *outward*, is *spiritual*, essentially differing from the *peace* of the *civil state*, which is meerly *civil* and *humane.* When the *peace* of the *churches, Antioch, Corinth, Galatia*, was disturbed by *spiritual oppositions*, the *Lord* never sent his *Saints* for *civil* help to maintaine their *spirituall* peace, though the *Lord* did send *Paul* to the higher *civill powers*, to preserve his *civill* peace, when he was molested and oppressed by the *Jews* and *Romans.*

2. For that place of *Timothy*, though I have fully spoken to it in this discourse elsewhere, yet this now: It proved not because the *church* must pray for *civil Rulers*, that so they may live a quiet and peaceable life in all *godliness* and *honesty*, that therefore *civil rulers* are *supream rulers* and *judges Ecclesiastical*, next unto *Christ Jesus*, of what is *godliness, holiness*, &c. since God hath chosen few *wise* or *noble*, to know *godliness:* And although it is true that Gods end of vouchsafing *peace* and *quietness*, is, that his *Churches* might walk in his fear, and in the wayes of *godliness;* yet it doth not hence follow, that *Magistrates* were the *causes* of the *Churches* walking in the fear of *God*, and being edified, but only of enjoying *Rest* from *Persecution, Act.* 9. (31.)

3. Although *Gods chastisement* call to *repentance*, and although the *false Prophet* in the *church* of *Israel* was to be wounded and slaine (as they are now to be cut off *spiritually* from the *church* of *spiritual Israel*) yet was it so in all the other *Nations* of the world? Or did *Christ Iesus* appoint it to be so in all the *Nations* of the *world*, since his coming, which is the great *question* in difference?

4. And indeed, what is this, but to add *coals* to *coals*, and *wood* to *fire*, to teach the *Nations* of the *world*, to be *briars* and *thorns*, *butchers* and *tormentors* to the *Lilies* and *Lambes* of the most holy and innocent *Lamb* of God *Christ Iesus?*

PEACE. But God (saith Master *Cotton*) cut *Israel* short in their *civil state* or *Nation* when they cut short their *reformation*, 1 (2) *King*, 10. (32.)

TRUTH. Master *Cotton* elswhere denying a *National church*, which is bounded with natural and earthly limits, it is a wonder how he can apply that instance of *National Israel*, to the now *spiritual Nation* and *Israel* of God? May he not as well promise earthly *peace* and prosperity then most to abound to *Gods people*, when they most prosper and flourish in *holiness, zeal*, &c. The contrary whereof, to wit, *persecution*, is most evident in all the New *Testament*, and all mens new and fresh *experience.*

PEACE. To end this Chapter, Master *Cotton* affirmes, that *civil* peace (to speak properly) is not only a *peace* in *civil* things for the *object*, but the peace of all the *persons* in the *City* for the *subject*. The *church* is one *society* in the *City*, as well as the *society* of *Merchants*, *Drapers*, &c. And if it be *civil justice* to protect one, then the other also.

TRUTH. *Civil peace* will never be proved to be the *peace* of all the subjects or *Citizens* of a City in *spiritual* Things: The *civil state* may bring into *order*, make *orders*, preserve in *civil order* all her members: But who ordained, that either the *spiritual estate* should bring in and force the *civil state* to keep *civil order*, or that the *civil state* should *sit*, *judge*, and force any of her subjects to keep *spiritual order*?

The true and *living God*, is the God of *order*, spiritual, civil and *natural*: *Natural* is the same ever and perpetual: *civil* alters according to the *constitutions* of *peoples* and *nations*: *spiritual* he hath changed from the *national* in one figurative land of *Canaan*, to *particular* and *congregational churches* all the world over; which *order spiritual*, *natural* or *civil*, to confound and abrogate, is to exalt mans *folly* against the most holy and incomprehensible *wisdome* of God. *&c.*

EXAMINATION OF CHAP. XXXIII

TRUTH. Every *lawful Magistrate*, whether succeeding or elected, is not only the *Minister* of *God*, but the *Minister* or servant of the people also (what *people* or *nation* soever they be all the world over) and that *Minister* or *Magistrate* goes beyond his *commission*, who intermeddles with that which cannot be given him in *commission* from the people, unless Master *Cotton* can prove that all the people and inhabitants of all *nations* in the *world* have *spiritual power*, *Christs power*, *naturally*, *fundamentally* and *originally* residing in them (as they are people and *inhabitants* of this world) to rule *Christs Spouse* the *church*, and to give spiritual power to their officers to exercise their *spiritual laws* and commands; otherwise it is but prophaning the holy name of the most *high*. It is but flattering of *Magistrates*, it is but the accursed trusting to an *arme* of *flesh*, to perswade the *rulers* of the *earth*, that they are *Kings* of the *Israel* or *church* of *God*, who were in their *institutions* and *government* immediately from *God*, the *rulers* and *governors* of his holy *church* and people.

PEACE. Grant (saith Master *Cotton*) that the *evil* be spiritual, and concern the inner man, and not the *civil state*, yet that evill will be destructive to such a City, it shall not rise up the second time, *Nahum*. 1. 9.

TRUTH. Although that it pleaseth *God* sometimes to bring a people to utter *destruction* for their *idolatry* against himself, and *cruelty* against his people; yet we see the Lord doth not presently and instantly do this, but after a long course of many *ages* and *generations*, as was seen in *Nineve* her self, and since in *Athens*, *Constantinople*, and *Rome* both *Pagan* and *Antichristian*. And therefore the example hereby Master *Cotton* produced, gives not the least colour of *warrant* for the *civil state* presently and immediately to execute vengeance for *idolatry* or *heresie* upon *persons* or *Cities* now all the world over, as he gave commandment to that *typical nation* of *Israel*, which is now also to be fulfilled spiritually upon the *spiritual Israelite*, or *Israelitish*

City, a *particular church* or people falling away from the *living God* in *Christ Jesus.*

PEACE. Whereas it was said by the discusser, that the *civil Magistrate* hath the charge of the *bodies* and *good* of the subjects, and the *spiritual officers* of the *church* or *kingdome* of *Christ,* the charge of their *souls* and soul safety. Master *Cotton* answers, First, If it were so that the *civil Magistrate* had charge of the *bodies* and *goods* onely of the subject, yet that might justly excite to watchfulness against such *pollution* of *religion* as tends to *apostacy,* for *God* will visit *city* and *country* with publike *calamity,* if not with *captivity,* for the *churches* sake. The *idolatry* and *worship* of *Christians* (saith he) brought the *Turkish captivity* upon the *citys* and *countries* of *Asia.*

TRUTH. By *soul* and *soul* safety, I think Master *Cotton* understands the same with the *discusser,* to wit, the *matters* of *religion* and *spiritual worship.* If the *Magistrate* hath received any such *charge* or *commission* from God in *spiritual* things, doubtless (as before) the people have received it *originally* and *fundamentally* as they are a people: But now if neither the *nations* of the *world,* as peoples and *nations,* have received this *power originally,* and *fundamentally;* nor can they derive it *Ministerially,* to their *civil officers* (by what name or *title,* high or low, soever they be distinguished) Oh what *presumption,* what *prophaning* of *Gods* most holy name, what *usurpation* over the *souls* and *consciences* of men, though it come under the *vaile* or *vizard* of saving the *City* or *kingdome,* yea of *saving* of *souls,* and honoring of *God* himself? . . .

SELECTED BIBLIOGRAPHY

J. T. Adams, *The Founding of New England* (1921).

J. Cotton, *The Bloudy Tenent Washed and Made White in the Bloud of the Lambe* (1647).

J. Davenport, *A Discourse about Civil Government* (1663).

J. E. Ernst, *Political Theory of Roger Williams* (1929).

J. Eliot, *The Christian Commonwealth or the Civil Policy of the Rising Kingdom of Jesus Christ* (1659), in Massachusetts Historical Collections, 3d series, Vol. IX.

T. Hooker, "Sermon before the General Court, May 31, 1638," in Connecticut Historical Society, Collections, Vol. I, No. 19.
　　A Survey of the Summe of Church Discipline (1648).

T. Hutchinson, *History of Massachusetts* (1828).
　　Diary and Letters of Thomas Hutchinson (1884).

C. Mather, *Magnalia Christi Americana* (1702).

V. L. Parrington, *The Colonial Mind* (1927).

G. L. Walker, *Thomas Hooker, Preacher, Founder, Democrat* (1891).

R. Williams, *The Bloudy Tenent of Persecution for Cause of Conscience* (1644), in Narragansett Club Publications, Vol. III.
　　The Bloudy Tenent Yet More Bloudy (1652), in Narragansett Club Publications, Vol. IV.

J. Winthrop, *History of New England* (1853).
　　Life and Letters of John Winthrop (1869).

J. Wise, *A Vindication of the Government of New England Churches* (1772).
　　Churches Quarrel Espoused (1772).

CHAPTER II

THE AMERICAN REVOLUTION

I

The American Revolution resulted from diverse causes. During the century before the Declaration of Independence there had arisen, imperceptibly but inevitably, a cleavage between the colonies and the mother country that spelled certain separation. The years after the French and Indian wars merely provided the incidents that led to a decisive clash. The Stamp Act, the Boston Massacre, the tea parties, were only the rapids that hastened the current to the sea.

The American scene of pre-Revolutionary days cannot be understood without considering the geographic separation of the colonies from Great Britain. The steamboat was an invention of a later century. There were no cable and radio to speed the communication of news. Individuals, news, and ideas traveled on slow, irregular, and uncertain packet ships. For over a century the vast expanse of ocean had caused the British ministry to neglect the American possessions; distance had made interference too difficult. Meanwhile, the colonists largely retained the political ideas current at the time of their migration. The new philosophies and the changing concepts of the British government hardly crossed the Atlantic.

This geographic separateness permitted the colonists to develop a distinct view-point. The absence of imperial control rendered possible the evolution of a colonial consciousness. Through their own initiative, the colonists provided for their internal order and security. Their own assemblies legislated for them; they carried on their own intercolonial relations and negotiated to solve their common difficulties. The New England Confederation of 1643 and the Albany Conference of 1754 were the forerunners of the later American union. The colonists also provided their own defense against Indian attacks; and colonial militia played a vital rôle in the wars against the French. The disastrous defeat, in 1755, of Braddock's crack British troops and the cool courage of Washington and his Virginia rangers stimulated colonial self-confidence. Thus "the psychology of the colonists in 1765 was, in an important degree, the imperceptible outgrowth of

many years of geographic separation. Such a people naturally regarded the new plan of imperial control, inaugurated by Grenville
in 1764–1765, as the unjustifiable interference of an 'alien' government." [1]

Coupled with this psychological cause of the Revolution was a
basic clash of economic interests. The survival of the mercantile
policy of England pitted the trader of America against the trader of
Britain. Mercantilism sought to increase wealth by enlarging the
quantity of precious metal in a country. Inasmuch as England did
not mine gold or silver, it could secure this sole criterion of wealth
only through trade. A favorable balance of trade—that is, an excess
of exports over imports—would mean an inflow of metallic currency.
The entire mercantile policy thus aimed at a restriction of imports
and an expansion of exports. The government encouraged native
shipping in order not to pay foreign freight bills; also, well-trained
seamen could win the commercial wars that accompanied mercantilistic competition. Agriculture, too, received active assistance, so
that the nation might produce for itself sufficient foodstuffs and raw
materials for manufacturing. Legislation protected and stimulated
home industry, lest imports become necessary. Complete domestic
self-sufficiency was the objective of mercantilism. For the success
of this system, colonial empires became essential. The mercantilistic
tariffs of other European states piled up the surplus manufactures of
the mother country; these the colonies could absorb. Colonies could
also supply those articles, as spices, lumber, or tobacco, not raised
at home. But imperial possessions must remain suppliers of raw
materials and purchasers of finished articles. Competition between
home and colonial traders would defeat the entire purpose of mercantilism—the increase of metallic wealth for the home country.
Mercantilistic ministers did not concern themselves with colonial
prosperity; imperial possessions were merely means toward the end
of domestic well-being.

The British government adopted this commercial system in the
middle of the seventeenth century. A series of navigation acts, beginning in 1651, placed stringent regulations on the economic activities
of the colonies. Parliament restricted to English markets the sale of
certain colonial products, as sugar, tobacco, cotton-wool, and naval

---

[1] A. M. Schlesinger, *New Viewpoints in American History* (New York, The Macmillan
Company), p. 25. Beveridge, in his *Life of John Marshall* (I, 1–6), and Benjamin
Franklin, in his *Autobiography* (pp. 186–195), point to Braddock's defeat as an important
factor in changing the psychology of the colonists and in fostering confidence in
themselves.

supplies. Thus, through lack of competition, the British dominated prices. On the other hand, trade between the colonies and foreign countries could be carried on only by way of England and in British or colonial ships; British merchants, consequently, dictated prices of colonial purchases. The imperial government even levied taxes on enumerated articles sent from one colony directly to another, in order to reimburse itself for the loss of revenue that it would have secured had the trade route been via England. Prohibitions and rigid regulations prevented the development of those colonial manufactures that competed with British industry.

Parliament passed the navigation acts in the middle of the seventeenth century; and yet the Revolution did not begin for another hundred years. Geographical separation and the general indifference of royal ministers toward the American colonies permitted these enactments to become dead letters. Colonial merchants constantly violated the navigation regulations. They carried their produce directly to the French West Indies and to the continents of Europe and Africa; likewise, they smuggled foreign articles into the colonies. But after the French and Indian wars, the Grenville ministry resurrected this dormant legislation. The Peace of 1763 had given England an unparalleled colonial empire. British troops had conquered Canada from the French and had snatched away India. But the costs of years of colonial and European wars had proved heavy. The Grenville ministry felt that the colonies should help pay for the defeat of the French and the resulting elimination of the constant fear of French and Indian ravages. The royal officers became imperial-minded. They felt that the time was ripe for the closer knitting together, militarily and economically, of the hitherto loose empire. They devised plans for colonial defense and sent troops across the Atlantic. The colonies, they argued, should help pay the bill of imperialism. The consequences of this new policy were the revival of the navigation acts and the taxation of the colonists. Admiralty enforcement of the navigation laws superseded civil enforcement. Writs of assistance and admiralty trials without juries made convictions possible and smuggling hazardous. Thus the efforts at law enforcement made these acts unpopular. Vital economic clashes resulted between colonial and British merchants. Added to this situation was an economic depression that marked the years before the Revolution.

The colonists, however, felt no need for imperial defense. With the French driven out of the New World, they no longer required protection; and they had learned to depend upon their own arms. They resented the quartering of British troops in the colonies, especially when they were required to pay the costs. The enforcement of the navigation restrictions, meanwhile, injured and angered the colonial merchants.

The development, as a result of the Peace of 1763, of these diametrically opposite attitudes led to irritations, misunderstandings, and clashes. The Boston Massacre, the burning of the Gaspee, the Boston Tea Party, were incidents that could well be expected to develop out of the existing psychological and economic situation. These incidents led to blunders by the British ministry, notably the closing of the port of Boston and the passage of the Quebec Act. By the latter law Parliament annexed to Quebec the territory between the Ohio River and the Great Lakes, thus extinguishing the claims of Virginia, New York, Connecticut, and Massachusetts to that region.

Certain other factors demand attention if we are to understand the American Revolution. The colonists were, on the whole, a frontier people; and frontier people have an aversion to taxation of any kind whatsoever and by whomsoever. British taxation they certainly did not welcome. A frontier people also are usually lacking in a supply of currency. Lack of money restricts economic activity and leads to agitation for "cheap" paper money. This demand for an artificial expansion of the currency—a movement that we shall encounter frequently in American politics—became articulate throughout the eighteenth century. The constant veto of such legislation by royal governors or by the crown became a source of bitterness.

Religion, too, played a rôle. Religious factors accentuated differences already flowing from economic, geographic, and psychological causes. The great majority of the colonists in most settlements belonged to dissenting sects and distrusted the Church of England. The royal governors and their retinues were Episcopalians. Disharmony and jealousy thus existed between governors and governed, between imperial representatives and popular delegates. The passage of the Quebec Act, which placed the Ohio Valley under the domination of Catholic Canada, naturally antagonized those Protestant communities that claimed that territory. Throughout the years preceding the Revolution, persistent rumors were current that the British government was planning to send Episcopal bishops to the colonies. The effect of these rumors resembled that of the story circulated in 1928 that upon the election of a Catholic President, the Pope would move into the White House. And, just as happened in this recent political battle, the Congregationalist ministers of New England employed their pulpits to preach against subjection to a foreign ecclesiastical power. They thus kept alive the fires of colonial discontent.

A social conflict within the colonies hastened the clash of arms. In most of them political and economic control rested in the hands of a narrow aristocracy along the seaboard. In the growing towns of Boston, Newport, New York, and Philadelphia, there labored a large, unenfranchised proletariat. Bitter political and economic struggles also occurred between the merchant aristocracy of the seaboard and the frontier agrarians of the western settlements. The latter charged discrimination against themselves in legislative representation, in taxation, in administration of justice. The agrarian and laboring groups gave impetus to the revolutionary movement in order to gain for themselves a more important rôle in government. The Revolution thus was not merely a question of "home rule" but also one of who should rule at home.

In order to comprehend the forces working for separation from England, we must turn our attention, not only to the fundamental causes of the conflict, but also to the social and economic groupings of the colonists. We must examine the grievances of each section and group. And we must note what regions and what groups tended most towards liberalism.

In the commercial colonies of the northern seaboard, ship-building and trading constituted the chief economic activities. A profitable carrying trade existed with Europe and the West Indies, often contrary to the navigation acts. Wholesale importers and exporters made up a wealthy and conservative minority; small tradesmen, mechanics, and yeomen, the great majority. The merchants, on the whole, and their allies, the lawyers, opposed the new imperial policy with its restrictions on their trade. To make effective their opposition to the stamp and tea taxes, they organized the mechanic and proletarian elements in the towns. Important Newport merchants, for example, led the attack upon the Gaspee. To this extent, liberalism and profits coincided. But at heart this commercial group was conservative. They fully recognized, despite the restrictions on their trade, the economic advantages of remaining within the British Empire and of keeping their English markets. They opposed independence and feared the loss of their power through the growth of domestic democracy. These early opponents of British taxation soon lost control of the movement to more radical leaders. In 1776 many of this group turned Tory and left the colonies; others gave lukewarm support to the cause; and only a few of the wealthy traders became enthusiastic exponents of independence.

The revolutionary leadership of the seaboard cities slipped into the hands of the small tradesmen and mechanics. The early agitation of the merchants had aroused them against British oppression and had stirred them into mob demonstrations. They, however, soon developed their own leaders. Such astute politicians as Samuel Adams came to the front and directed the group. With everything to gain in political influence and nothing to lose, the proletariat turned the protest against the British policy into a revolutionary channel.

In the agricultural colonies of the southern tide-water region, a large plantation system predominated. The planting aristocracy displayed the traditional independence of the English country gentry; they resented all outside interference. Their economic system caused a vital clash between them and the British. The plantations usually grew but one important crop—tobacco, rice, or cotton. This the planters sold to British trading companies, and from them they bought finished articles. The monopolistic domination of this trade by English concerns kept the farmers continually in debt. During the middle of the eighteenth century, the planters, through their provincial assemblies, attempted to escape from their crushing debts by the passage of lenient bankruptcy laws and by the establishment of restrictions on debt collections by non-resident creditors. Royal governors promptly vetoed these agrarian proposals. This political-economic conflict over debts made the planters resentful toward any attempts of the British authorities to exercise power over them.

The third important section constituted the indefinite hinterland west of the seaboard settlements. Here lived isolated small farmers. Difficulties in transportation forced them to become economically self-sufficient; and the hardships of the new country developed in them self-confidence. Frontier equalitarianism made them avowed democrats. The older settlements of the seaboard discriminated against them as to legislative representation and taxation. Thus they were already familiar with all the arguments against autocratic government, particularly against taxation without representation. They zealously fought for popular rights and self-government. Outside of New England, moreover, the majority of the hinterland settlers were dissenters in religion and racially of non-English stocks. Dutch, Germans, and Scotch-Irish inhabited this region; they had no inborn love for England as a motherland. Into their hands slipped much of the revolutionary leadership.

II

To an important degree, the political theory of the Revolution was a rationalization of the desires of the colonists. Their theory thus changed its form with the fluctuations of the British laws. When the admiralty began the enforcement of the navigation laws by juryless trials, Otis made his famous plea for the rights of Englishmen to trial by their peers. When Parliament passed the Stamp Act, John Dickinson differentiated between an imposition for the regulation of trade and an internal tax for revenue. The former fell within the purview of parliamentary authority; the latter was taxation without representation, and rendered private property insecure. When the British ministry accepted this argument and enforced only tariff imposts, John Adams and Alexander Hamilton flatly denied the jurisdiction of Parliament; they now claimed allegiance solely to the person of the king. When the armed conflict began and the king sent his troops to enforce allegiance, Thomas Paine attacked the "royal brute," and the Continental Congress declared independence.

The philosophical and historical foundations of the colonial arguments likewise shifted. During the early days of the controversy, Samuel Adams and others appealed to the charters granted to the colonies. When their demands became more radical, and when the British and Tory legalists smashed this attack, they argued from the nature of the British constitution and empire. Later they shifted to the natural rights of man. To a certain extent, all three of these rationalizations existed throughout the entire debate; however, a change of emphasis occurred. In the sixties, the charter-grant arguments predominated; while after Lexington and Concord, the natural rights philosophy became outstanding.

The colonial pamphleteers employed the charter-grant arguments to oppose such internal taxation as the Stamp Act. The charters given the colonists upon their migration to the New World usually entitled them to all the rights and privileges of native-born Englishmen. They were to be as free in their new settlements as they would have been had they remained at home. What were these rights of Englishmen? From the days of Magna Charta, argued the colonists, Englishmen claimed and enforced the right of taxation only by representation. Hence, since Parliament did not represent them, it could not tax them. With the exception of Benjamin Franklin, the opponents of imperial control did not, however, advocate the sending of American representatives to Westminster. The geographic separation rendered such a proposal chimerical. Rather, they claimed, their local assemblies alone could levy internal taxes. Samuel Adams made much of this type of reasoning. He argued:

"Thus we see that Whatever Governm^t in general may be founded in, Ours was manifestly founded in *Compact*. . . . By this Charter, we have an exclusive Right to make Laws for our own internal Government & Taxation: And indeed if the Inhabitants here are British Subjects . . . it seems necessary that they should exercise this Power themselves; for They are not represented in the British Parliam^t & their great Distance renders it impracticable: It is very probable that all the subordinate legislative Powers in America, were constituted upon the Apprehension of this Impracticability." [2]

The colonial argument of "no taxation without representation" was based on an entirely different conception of representation than the English held. Although they discriminated against their western communities, the colonists, nevertheless, attempted to apportion representation according to population; and the delegates lived in their own election districts. In England neither of these conditions existed. A parliamentary candidate could stand for any constituency. Nor did representation and population bear any necessary relations. The growing industrial cities of Manchester and Liverpool were quite as much without parliamentary representation as were the colonies. The "rotten borough" system persisted in England until the Reform Act of 1832. In the colonies, a legislator represented primarily his own district; in England, the entire kingdom. Thus Burke represented, not Bristol only, but the interests of the entire country.[3] A merchant in Parliament looked after the welfare of all merchants—English and colonial; a lawyer delegate, after the interests of all lawyers of the empire. Thus, according to the British view, Parliament represented the colonies and could, therefore, tax them as justly as it could tax Liverpool.

When Parliament embarked upon a policy of taxing only colonial imports, the exponents of home rule gradually shifted their own argument. They now denied completely all parliamentary authority. They owed allegiance, not to Parliament, but to the king. From him they had received their charters. The previous parliamentary regulation of colonial trade had not been by legal right, but only by their sufferance. They built up a concept of the British Empire, or the relationship of the colonies to Great Britain, remarkably like that of the present British Commonwealth of Nations.

[2] Samuel Adams, *Works*, I, 27–29.
[3] See Burke's "Speech to Electors of Bristol," *Works*, II, 89–98.

At the time of colonization the Stuart kings ruled supreme in England. They had granted the colonies royal charters in exactly the same manner as if they were giving away their private land. Parliament was weak and exercised but little control over the monarch. The king, not the legislature, controlled the country's colonies. Meanwhile, a political revolution had occurred in England. The execution of Charles I, the revolution of 1688, the enthronement of the Hanover princes—these and other events shifted power from king to Parliament. Parliamentary enactments superseded royal decrees.

Of this political revolution, the colonists refused to take cognizance. The king, not Parliament, had granted them their charters. To the king, not Parliament, therefore, they owed allegiance and obedience. It mattered not that in the seventeenth century Parliament had been powerless to charter colonies; nor did it concern the colonists that in the eighteenth century the king had become a political figure-head acquiescing in the decisions of "his" ministers, who were, in reality, responsible to Parliament. Thus, the opponents of imperial control looked back upon an abandoned political system. Undoubtedly, they swore allegiance to the king because it was now politically impossible for him to exercise those powers which the colonists attributed to him. This constitutional argument was thus a rationalization of colonial opposition to parliamentary legislation—in effect, to any imperial control whatsoever.

The argument from the nature of the British Empire found its clearest expositions in the writings of Alexander Hamilton and John Adams. Parliament, maintained Hamilton, has no power over colonial affairs. The House of Commons receives all its authority from its electors as a result of their right to a share in the legislature. Its electors, however, are freeholders, citizens, and others, in Great Britain. It follows, therefore, that all its authority is confined to Great Britain.

"The power which one society bestows upon any man, or body of men, can never extend beyond its own limits. The people of Great Britain may confer an authority over themselves, but they can never confer any over the people of America, because it is impossible for them to give *that* to another which they never possessed themselves." [4]

The House of Commons thus derives all its power from its real constituents only, who are the people of Great Britain.

Such a denial of parliamentary authority, Hamilton maintained, is not inconsistent with allegiance to the king.

[4] Hamilton, "Farmer Refuted," *Works* (Hamilton edition), II, 52.

"He is king of America by virtue of a compact between us and the kings of Great Britain. These colonies were planted and settled by the grants, and under the protection, of English kings, who entered into covenants with us, for themselves, their heirs, and successors; and it is from these covenants, that the duty of protection, on their part, and the duty of allegiance, on ours, arise."

The colonists owe loyalty—so ran the argument—to the king of Great Britain regardless of the manner of accession to the throne. The parliamentary act of succession is not the "efficient cause" of his being the sovereign over America; it is only the "occasion" of it.[5] The colonies hold their lands by virtue of charters from the British monarchs; and are under no obligations for them to the Lords or Commons. "Our title is similar, and equal, to that by which they possess their lands; and the king is the legal fountain of both." [6] This is one grand source of obligation to allegiance. The other is that allegiance is founded upon the principle of protection.

"Nothing is more common than to hear the votaries of Parliament urge the protection we have received from the mother country, as an argument for submission to its claims. But they entertain erroneous conceptions of the matter. The king himself, being the supreme executive magistrate, is regarded by the constitution as the supreme protector of the empire. For this purpose, he is the generalissimo, or first in military command. In him is vested the power of making war and peace; of raising armies, equipping fleets, and directing all their motions. He it is, that has defended us from our enemies; and to him alone we are obliged to render allegiance and submission." [7]

John Adams, likewise, differentiated between submission to Parliament and allegiance to the king. The provincial legislatures, he held, are the only supreme authorities in the colonies. The line of demarcation between parliamentary and colonial power may be fairly drawn at the banks of the ocean, or the low-water mark.

Parliament "may be allowed an authority supreme and sovereign over the ocean, which may be limited by the banks of the ocean, or the bounds of our charters; our charters give us no authority over the high seas. Parliament has our consent to assume a jurisdiction over them." [8]

Adams developed a conception of the British Empire remarkably like that, as has been suggested, of the present-day British Commonwealth of Nations. Under his theory, the relation of Massachusetts to Great Britain corresponded to that now existing between Canada

[5] Hamilton, "Farmer Refuted," *Works* (Hamilton edition), II, 46.
[6] *Ibid.*, II, 47.
[7] *Ibid.*, II, 47.
[8] John Adams, "Novanglus," *Works*, IV, 105–106.

and Great Britain. Each of the American colonies, he contended, was on a par with the mother country. Each was independent; each was governed by its own legislature; each owed allegiance to the same monarch. The British Parliament could exercise no more authority over Massachusetts than it now does over the self-governing dominions of the British Commonwealth of Nations. Adams visualized a group of virtually independent states loosely strung together by a common fealty. He pointed constantly to the relation of Scotland and England before the Act of Union in 1707. Both then had the same king, but Scotland possessed a parliament of its own. This same relationship, Adams maintained, exists between the colonies and Great Britain.

"That 'the colonies owe no allegiance to any imperial crown', provided such a crown involves in it a house of lords and a house of commons, is certain. Indeed, we owe no allegiance to any crown at all. We owe allegiance to the person of his majesty, King George III, whom God preserve. But allegiance is due universally, both from Britons and Americans to the person of the king, not to his crown; to his natural, not his politic capacity. . . . If his majesty's title to the crown is 'derived from an act of parliament, made since the settlement of these colonies,' it was not made since the date of our charter. Our charter was granted by King William and Queen Mary, three years after the revolution; and the oaths of allegiance are established by a law of the province. So that our allegiance to his majesty is not due by virtue of any act of a British parliament, but by our own charter and province laws. It ought to be remembered that there was a revolution here, as well as in England, and that we, as well as the people of England made an original, express contract with King William." [9]
"If it follows from thence, that he appears 'King of Massachusetts, King of Rhode Island, King of Connecticut, &c.' this is no absurdity at all. He will appear in this light, and does appear so, whether parliament has authority over us or not." [10]

The only alternative to such a loose union of coequal states, asserted Adams, is some scheme of Empire representation. If England with its six million people has five hundred members in the House of Commons, then America with its three million must have two hundred and fifty. Ireland, too, must be incorporated, and send another hundred or more members. The territory in the East and West Indies must send representatives. Further, the House of Lords must have American, African, and Indian, as well as English and Scottish, noblemen. After all this, every navigation act must be repealed, so that the colonies may have the same liberty to trade with all the world that the favored inhabitants of Great Britain have. If, in the

[9] John Adams, "Novanglus," *Works*, IV, 114.   [10] *Ibid.*, IV, 114-115.

course of years, America should outstrip Great Britain in population, it would have the right to transport Parliament and the crown to these shores. "Will the ministry thank Massachusettensis [11] for becoming an advocate for such a union, and incorporation of all the dominions of the King of Great Britain?" [12]

The third type of argument employed by the colonists was based on the natural rights philosophy. This philosophy, we have already noted, played a rôle in Puritan political thought. The establishment of New England communities on the basis of social contracts naturally gave emphasis to this doctrine.

Before civil governments came into existence, according to this philosophy, men lived in a state of nature. In this condition, each individual protected and defended himself. He was free and independent, and subject to no other man. Natural laws, rather than human laws, governed men; and all possessed the same natural rights. The Declaration of Independence declared that all men "are endowed by their Creator with certain inalienable rights: that among these are life, liberty, and the pursuit of happiness." Similarly, the Pennsylvania constitution of 1776 stated that all men "have certain natural, inherent and unalienable rights, amongst which are, the enjoying and defending life and liberty, acquiring, possessing, and protecting property, and pursuing and obtaining happiness and safety." [13] These natural rights antedate the existence of government and are superior to it; they form the real basis of political rights after the establishment of civil government. In the state of nature, each individual enforced his natural rights himself.

For various reasons, men found it expedient to escape from this state of nature. They, therefore, convened together and agreed to establish a civil state. They contracted with each other and devised machinery for political government. The only right, however, that the natural man surrendered by such a contract, argued the democratic thinkers, was his own individual enforcement of his other inherent rights. His right to life, liberty, property, and happiness he still retained; his defense of them he intrusted to the civil community. Natural rights thus formed the foundation of political rights. The

[11] Massachusettensis was the pen name of Daniel Leonard, a Boston Tory. He and John Adams engaged in a bitter newspaper debate. For Leonard's views, see below, pp. 106-107, 143-153.

[12] John Adams, "Novanglus," *Works*, IV, 101-102.

[13] Pennsylvania Constitution of 1776, Art. I. Isaac Newton's *Principia* had a subtle influence on the development of the natural rights philosophy. Newton deified nature and induced men to think in terms of natural laws. For his influence, see Becker, *The Declaration of Independence*, Ch. 2.

state acquired no powers not possessed by individuals in a state of nature. The Massachusetts Bill of Rights declared:

"The body politic is formed by a voluntary association of individuals; it is a social compact by which the whole people covenants with each citizen and each citizen with the whole people, that all shall be governed by certain laws for the common good." [14]

This social contract doctrine was capable of radical applications. Gradually, the colonial pamphleteers became bolder and more fearless in their development of its political corollaries. They carefully studied the contract theories of Milton, Harrington, Sydney, and Locke, expounded during the Puritan revolution; and they were familiar with the natural law of Blackstone. Vattel and Puffendorf also influenced a few colonial writers. Thomas Paine and the framers of the Declaration of Independence stated the extreme view of this philosophy.

The first important corollary of the social contract theory was the doctrine of the consent of the governed. The natural man established government by his contractual consent. Furthermore, he left the state of nature solely for the purpose of maintaining his natural rights more effectively. No government can continue to rule without his expressed or implied consent. "Governments derive their just powers," proclaimed the Declaration of Independence, "from the consent of the governed."

The doctrine of the consent of the governed had immediate application to the colonial conflict. If the colonists have any natural rights at all, they must possess that of defending their own property against confiscatory taxes. If a free political state rests solely on the foundation of the consent of the governed, then surely Parliament possesses no natural right to impose its will upon the colonists. Taxation without representation abridged their inherent rights. The right of the colonists to exercise legislative power, wrote Hamilton, is an inherent one. It is founded upon the rights of all men to freedom and happiness. Civil liberty cannot possibly have any existence where the society, for which laws are made, has no share in making them, and where the interests of its legislators is not inseparably interwoven with its own. [15] In a state of nature, he argued, no man had any moral power to deprive another of his life, limbs, property, or liberty; hence, the origin of all justly established civil governments must be a voluntary compact between the rulers and the ruled. To usurp

---

[14] Massachusetts Bill of Rights.
[15] Hamilton, "Farmer Refuted," *Works*, II, 62.

dominion over a people, or to grasp at a more extensive power than they are willing to intrust, is to violate that law of nature which gives every man a right to his personal liberty. Such usurpation can, therefore, confer no obligation to obedience.[16]   Judged by this criterion, the pretensions of Parliament over the colonies are eminently unjust.

"First, they are subversive of our natural liberty, because an authority is assumed over us, which we by no means assent to. And, secondly, they divest us of that moral security, for our lives and properties, which we are entitled to, and which it is the primary end of society to bestow. For such security can never exist, while we have no part in making the laws that are to bind us; and while it may be the interest of our uncontrolled legislators to oppress us as much as possible." [17]

A second important corollary of the social contract philosophy, and one closely allied to the doctrine of the consent of the governed, was the theory of popular sovereignty. This doctrine later played an important rôle in American political thought; its influence is still potent to-day. If the political state came into being by a contract of the people, and if just government continues only with the consent of the people, then behind the State looms the sovereignty of the people. The sovereign power, maintained the Massachusetts Proclamation of 1776, resides, always, in the body of the people; and it never was, or can be, delegated to one man or a few, the Creator having never given to men a right to vest others with authority over them unlimited either in duration or degree.[18] Despite monarchs and aristocrats, the inalienable and inherent sovereignty rested with the people. Exactly who constituted the people—this question remained for future discussion.

The third corollary of the social contract was the right of revolution. Irresistibly, this stream of reasoning fell into the rapids of rebellion. Although hints of armed resistance can be found before 1775, and although a year of fighting in defense of their "rights of Englishmen" had embittered the colonists, nevertheless, the first advocacy of independence came from the pen of Thomas Paine in January, 1776.

If the natural man established government by his own contract, if the operation of government rested on his sovereign consent, then he possessed the right to withdraw his consent. The right of revolution was thus not some frightful monster; it was an inalienable pos-

16 Hamilton, "Farmer Refuted," *Works*, II, 43-44.
17 *Ibid.*, II, 44.
18 Massachusetts Proclamation of 1776.

session of free men. The Declaration of Independence boldly proclaimed this doctrine. Whenever any form of government becomes destructive of the ends of political society, "it is the right of the people to alter or to abolish it, and to institute new government, laying its foundations on such principles and organizing its powers in such forms, as shall seem most likely to effect their safety and happiness." [19]

Two of the revolutionary political writers deserve added attention. Both were pamphleteers of considerable public influence. Both were forerunners of a democratic theory that later was to find wide acceptance in this country. Without them, the American Revolution might very possibly have slipped into quite a different channel. One, Samuel Adams, was a political organizer rather than an original thinker; the other, Thomas Paine, was one of the few theorists in world history who immediately influenced the course of events.

Samuel Adams was a poor Boston lawyer, more interested in politics than in a legal career. He successfully organized the mechanics and small tradesmen of Boston, and through the Caucus Club secured control of the Boston town meeting. An avowed democrat, he labored for the political education of the rank and file. His prime objective was the development of political machinery through which the mass of the people could control the practices of politics.

Adams and his group quite naturally became opponents of royal domination. He constantly attacked Governor Hutchinson of Massachusetts and his Tory adherents. The latter, through their snobbish disregard for the people, played into Adams's hand and subjected themselves to his effective ridicule. Adams questioned the integrity of the royal officials and assailed the judiciary, calling the courts mere tools of the ministers. In the agitation against imperial domination, he played a leading rôle through his writing and organizing. The general lines of his argument were not different from those of other writers. He built up his case on an appeal based (1) upon the express provisions of the royal charters, (2) upon the historical rights and privileges of Englishmen, and (3) upon the natural rights of man. His treatment of these theories was not novel; but the biting sarcasm that he heaped upon the Tory opponents of home rule opened a wide circulation for his writings. Adams's prime importance, however, was as the organizer of the Revolution. In Massachusetts, he developed a well-knit system of local patriotic committees, with which

---

[19] For a similar statement of this right of revolution see the Pennsylvania Constitution of 1776, Art. V.

he kept in constant touch; and thus he knew immediately the happenings and the sentiments in all parts of the province. Upon the
closing of the port of Boston in 1774, he succeeded in expanding this
information system into a set of inter-colonial committees of correspondence. From this developed the Continental Congress, and from
that body came the Declaration of Independence. When the fighting
began, the local committees seized the reins of politics and organized
the new state governments. Adams's organizing ability thus stimulated united action against England and provided the machinery
for colonial coöperation.

Certain of Adams's political views were destined to play a large
rôle in later American thinking. Hitherto, political writers had
talked loosely about the "people," about government by consent of
the "governed," about the sovereignty of the "people"; but they
had never defined their conception of the "people." At the most,
they would have included the middle class tradesman. Adams assumed a democratic view. By the "people" he did not mean a
wealthy minority, but the great mass of men.

"The multitude I am speaking of, is the *body of the people*—no *contemptible*
multitude—for whose sake government is instituted; or rather, who have
themselves erected it, solely for *their own* good—to whom even kings and all
in subordination to them, are strictly speaking, servants and not masters." [20]
"I am not of levelling principles: But I am apt to think, that constitution
of civil government which admits equality in the most extensive degree,
consistent with the true design of government, is the best." [21]

The people, having themselves instituted government, have the
fundamental right to change and interpret their constitutions. The
spirit, not the letter of the law, ought to rule. The opinion of judges
ought not to be final when they conflict with natural reason. The
referendum of judicial decisions thus became an attribute of popular
sovereignty.

The influence of Thomas Paine—but lately arrived from England—
upon the American Revolution is inestimable. Washington, Jefferson,
and other leaders of the movement attributed the independence
sentiment of 1776 to his *Common Sense*. During the long winter at
Valley Forge, Paine's issues of *The American Crisis* sustained the
courage of Washington's weary troops and stirred the patriotism of
the people.

Throughout the agitation against the imperial policy, the colonists
had made no demands for independence. While they denied parlia-

mentary authority, they avowed allegiance to the king. During the year 1775 much blood had been spilled in battles with the British troops; nevertheless, the colonists maintained that they were fighting only for their rights as British subjects. Thoughts of independence had not yet entered their minds. Upon this scene Paine's *Common Sense* appeared in January, 1776. Its influence was immediate and remarkable. His pamphlet attacked, not the authority of Parliament, but the pretensions of the king. He demanded, not dominion status, but independence. He exposed to ridicule the principle of hereditary rule and the doctrine of the divine right of kings, turning to Hebraic experience to demonstrate the unholy nature of this latter institution.[22]

Whence, asked Paine, did the "royal brute" of England get his divine right to rule? Upon usurpation only rests the British monarchy.

"England since the conquest hath known some few good monarchs, but groaned beneath a much larger number of bad ones: yet no man in his senses can say that their claim under William the Conqueror is a very honourable one. A French bastard landing with an armed Banditti and establishing himself king of England against the consent of the natives, is in plain terms a very paltry rascally original. It certainly hath no divinity in it." [23]

Having struck a fatal blow at royal allegiance, Paine demanded American independence. The time, he claimed, was ripe, and the prospects most favorable. Must we, after all this bloodshed, become reconciled with the beast that sits on the throne of Britain?

"I challenge the warmest advocate for reconciliation to show a single advantage that this continent can reap by being connected with Great Britain. . . . Our corn will fetch its price in any market in Europe, and our imported goods must be paid for buy them where we will." [24]

Much of his *Common Sense* Paine devoted to the natural rights philosophy. These ideas he developed even more fully in his *Rights of Man*, written in defense of the French Revolution. The origin of government, he held, rests on a social contract. The "inability of moral virtue to govern the world" caused men to leave the state of nature.[25] The end of government, consequently, is the freedom and security of the individual. And sovereignty resides in the majority will. In political communities, civil rights rest upon the rights of nature inherited from man's earlier state of being. Natural rights are those which appertain to man by fact of his existence. Of this

---

[22] Thomas Paine, *Common Sense* (Conway edition), pp. 77–78. (New York, G. P. Putnam's Sons.)

[23] *Ibid.*, p. 80.   [24] *Ibid.*, p 88.   [25] *Ibid.*, p. 71.

kind are all the intellectual rights, and also all those rights of acting for one's own comfort and happiness which are not injurious to the natural rights of others. Civil rights are those which appertain to man by right of his being a member of society. Every civil right has for its foundation some natural right preëxisting in the individual, but for the enjoyment of which his individual power is not in all cases sufficiently competent. Of this kind are all those rights which relate to security and protection. These civil rights should not be so applied as to invade the natural rights retained in the individual, and in which the power to execute is as perfect as the right itself.[26]

From his theory of social contract Paine developed a highly important corollary—the doctrine of the reaffirmation of natural rights. The natural man did not make his social contract for all time to come; rather each generation possesses the right of reaffirming it.

"The vanity and presumption of governing beyond the grave is the most ridiculous and insolent of all tyrannies. . . . Every age and generation must be free to act for itself *in all cases* as the ages and generations which preceded it. . . . It is the living, and not the dead, that are to be accommodated."[27]

Thus, the general body of the people may at any time remake its fundamental laws. "That which a whole nation chooses to do it has a right to do."[28]

Government, to Paine, was a necessary evil. While society is produced by our wants, government is due to our wickedness. Society promotes our happiness positively by uniting our affections; government, negatively by restraining our vices. "Government, like dress, is the badge of lost innocence." Were the impulses of conscience clear, uniform, and irresistibly obeyed, man would need no other law-giver; but that not being the case, he finds it necessary to surrender a part of his property to furnish means for the protection of the rest.[29] Since the end of government is freedom and security, it follows that whatever form of government appears most likely to insure these objectives, with the least expense and greatest benefit, is preferable to all others.[30]

"Formal government makes but a small part of civilised life; and when even the best that human wisdom can devise is established, it is a thing more in name and idea than in fact. . . . The more perfect civilization is,

[26] Paine, *Rights of Man*, Part I, pp. 306–307.
[27] *Ibid.*, p. 278. Compare with Jefferson's doctrine. See Chapter IV, pp. 249–250.
[28] *Ibid.*, p. 278.
[29] Paine, *Common Sense*, p. 69.
[30] *Ibid.*, p. 69.

the less occasion has it for government, because the more does it regulate its own affairs, and govern itself. . . . All the great laws of society are laws of nature." [31]

III

The political theory of the revolutionary group did not pass unchallenged. Many and skillful Tories answered their arguments point by point. Of this group, two stand out—Daniel Leonard, an aristocratic Boston lawyer, and Jonathan Boucher, an Episcopalian minister of Virginia.

Under the pen-name of "Massachusettensis," Leonard engaged in a lengthy and brilliant debate with John Adams. In his writings we find refutations of the leading arguments of the exponents of home rule. The colonial charters, he held, were given under the great seal of England. The king made the grants for himself, for his heirs and *successors*. Thus the king acted in his royal capacity as king of England. This "necessarily supposes the territory granted, to be part of the English dominions, holden of the crown of England." [32] The arguments from the nature of the British Empire were likewise attacked. Ireland, for example, has its own legislature and sends no members to the British Parliament; yet it is bound by parliamentary acts. Guernsey and Jersey similarly are not part of the realm of England, nor are they represented in Parliament, but are nevertheless subject to its authority. In the same status are the American colonies. [33]

Leonard was an exponent of Thomas Hobbes. Just as Hobbes, during the Puritan revolution, had employed the contract theory to support Stuart autocracy, Leonard now turned this doctrine against the American revolutionists. Men established civil government by social contracts, he argued, in order to escape from the state of nature. The state of nature he depicted as a reign of brute force, insecurity, and anarchy. The breaking of the social contract by revolution meant a return to such a condition of chaos. Obedience to authority is preferable.

"Rebellion is the most atrocious offence, that can be perpetrated by man, save those which are committed more immediately against the supreme Governor of the Universe, who is the avenger of his own cause. It dissolves the social band, annihilates the security resulting from law and government;

[31] Paine, *Rights of Man*, Part II, 408.
[32] Leonard, *Novanglus and Massachusettensis*, p. 174.
[33] *Ibid.*, p. 174. McIlvain, in *The American Revolution*, attacks this imperial argument. He presents evidence from British constitutional history to support the revolutionists' conception of the British Empire.

introduces fraud, violence, rapine, murder, sacrilege, and the long train of evils that riot, uncontrouled, in a state of nature. Allegiance and protection are reciprocal. The subject is bound by the compact to yield obedience .o government, and in return, is entitled to protection from it. . . . But when government is laid prostrate, a state of war, of all against all commences; might overcomes right; innocence itself has no security, unless the individual sequesters himself from his fellowmen, inhabits his own cave, and seeks his own prey. This is what is called a state of nature." [34]

Jonathan Boucher employed his pulpit to preach obedience to the king. His distrust of popular participation in government, and his association of democracy with anarchy, brought upon his head the hostility of his congregation. He preached his last sermons in this country, he tells us, with two pistols on the pulpit. Finally, the wrath of his pastorate drove him to England.

Boucher attacked the contract theory of government. Consent as the basis for the establishment and maintenance of government is utterly impracticable. If an individual gives his consent, he may at any time withdraw it. Chaos constantly results.

"If (according to the idea of the advocates of this chimerical scheme of equality) no man could rightfully *be compelled to come in* and be a member even of a government to be formed by a regular compact, but by his own individual consent; it clearly follows, from the same principles, that neither could he rightfully be made or compelled to submit to the ordinances of any government already formed, to which he has not individually or actually consented. On the principle of equality, neither his parents, nor even the vote of a majority of the society, (however virtuously and honourably that vote might be obtained,) can have any such authority over any man. Neither can it be maintained that acquiescence implies consent; because acquiescence may have been extorted from impotence or incapacity. Even an explicit consent can bind a man no longer than he chooses to be bound. The same principle of equality that exempts him from being governed without his consent, clearly entitles him to recall and resume that consent whenever he sees fit; and he alone has a right to judge when and for what reasons it may be resumed." [35]

Any attempt to put this fantastic system into practice would reduce the whole business of social life to the wearisome, confused, and useless task of making and remaking an endless succession of governments. "That which is now fixed might and would be soon unfixed." [36]

The social contract theory implies the inherent equality of men. The whole human race is born equal; no man is naturally inferior,

[34] Leonard, *Novanglus and Massachusettensis*, pp. 187–188.
[35] Boucher, *A View of the Causes and Consequences of the American Revolution*, pp. 515–516.
[36] *Ibid.*, p. 516.

and he can be made subject to another only by his own consent. But, argued Boucher, government cannot be founded upon equality. Governmental authority implies superiorities and inferiorities.

"By asking another to exercise jurisdiction over me, I clearly confess that I do not think myself his equal; and by his consenting to exercise such authority, he also virtually declares that he thinks himself superior." [37]

Inequality, not equality, is the order of nature. Man differs from man in everything that can be supposed to lead to supremacy and subjection. It was the purpose of the Creator that man should be a social creature; but without government there can be no society; nor without some relative inferiority and superiority can there be any government.

"A musical instrument composed of chords, keys, or pipes, all perfectly equal in size and power, might as well be expected to produce harmony, as a society composed of members all perfectly equal to be productive of order and peace." [38]

Unlike Paine, Boucher believed firmly in the value of government. To him it was not a necessary evil; rather, men owed to it some of the greatest blessings they enjoy.

"It is to government that mankind owe their having, after their fall and corruption, been again reclaimed, from a state of barbarity and war, to the conveniency and the safety of the social state: and it is by means of government that society is still preserved, the weak protected from the strong, and the artless and innocent from the wrongs of proud oppressors." [39]

All government, in its nature, is absolute and irresistible. It is not within the competency even of the supreme power to limit itself, because such limitation can emanate only from a superior. For any government to cease to be absolute, it must cease to be supreme; in other words, it must dissolve itself or be destroyed. If, then, to resist government be to destroy it, every man who is a subject must necessarily owe obedience to the government under which he lives. [40]

If government did not arise out of a social contract, how then did it come into being? For the answer to this query, Boucher turned to Filmer and his patriarchal defense of the Stuart autocracy. Government is God-given. All kings and princes derive their power from heaven; He only who gave life, can give the authority to take it away; and as such authority is essential to government, government

---

[37] Boucher, *A View of the Causes and Consequences of the American Revolution*, p. 520.
[38] *Ibid.*, pp. 514–515. [39] *Ibid.*, p. 519. [40] *Ibid.*, pp. 545–546.

must have originally come from God.[41] An all-wise and all-merciful Creator, having formed creatures capable of order and rule, would not turn them loose into the world under the guidance only of their own unruly wills, that, like so many wild beasts, they might worry and tear one another in their mad contest for preëminence. His purpose from the first was that men should live godly and sober lives. But ever since the Fall, men have been averse to good and prone to evil. Were it not for the restraints and the terrors of human laws, it would be impossible for men to dwell together. It is fair to infer, then, that government was also the original intention of God, who never decrees the end without also decreeing the means. Accordingly, when man was made, his Maker did not turn him adrift into a shoreless ocean without star or compass by which to steer. As soon as there were people to be governed, there were also people to govern. The first man, by virtue of his paternal claim, was the first king.[42] The glory of God is much concerned that there should be good government in the world; He, therefore, created and appointed kings, princes, and magistrates, not so much for their own sakes, as for the sake of the people committed to their charge. Rulers, therefore, are not the creatures of the people; they receive their commission from Heaven, the source and origin of all power.[43]

IV

After the Revolution began, the colonists, upon the advice of the Continental Congress, established their own state governments. The new political institutions showed the influence of two factors: (1) the revolutionary, democratic thinking, and (2) colonial experiences with royal governments. An individualistic conception of the purpose of government and a desire for weak government characterized the new revolutionary state constitutions.

The framers of these constitutions followed closely the political philosophy that government is a necessary evil. The contract theory, prevalent during the period, made government, not an original, but an acquired, habit of man. The natural rights philosophy stressed, not the community, but the individual. The political compact existed to enable the State to guard the other rights of the natural man; the State, then, could exercise no other functions. Colonial environment also made for individualism. The frontier struggle for existence

---

[41] Boucher, *A View of the Causes and Consequences of the American Revolution* p. 521.
[42] *Ibid.*, pp. 523–525.   [43] *Ibid.*, p. 534.

placed a high value upon the individual, upon his freedom and rights; the need for positive government did not exist in a country of pioneers. Consequently, the revolutionary constitutions reflected this rabid individualism. The contract reasoning and the frontier environment induced a heavy stress on the negative side of government. The chief end of government, to be sure, was the welfare of the people; government was to be the guardian of the general interests rather than of special privilege. But the framers interpreted the good of the people to mean merely the physical protection of property and person. Government was merely to be a big policeman. It was merely to enforce those natural rights which the individual could not maintain by his own power. The early constitutions also endeavored to prevent this policeman from infringing upon the natural rights of the people. They thus placed stringent limitations upon the powers of government. Officials must not deprive men of liberty or property, deny freedom of speech or religion, imprison any one without a jury trial, search a home or seize possessions without a warrant. It is interesting to note that the drafters of these documents adopted many of the prohibitions mentioned as a consequence of the abuses that they had experienced under the royal attempt to enforce the navigation acts.

Coupled with this individualistic conception of government was a desire for weak government. Under the doctrine of popular sovereignty, political power inhered in the people. The government was the servant or agent of its popular master. Not only that, but the people looked upon government as an untrustworthy and unreliable servant. They feared lest their agent usurp the authority belonging to them. Theory alone did not form the basis of this attitude; colonial experience with governments beyond popular control was responsible. Consequently, the framers devised means of holding in check their necessary but dangerous servant. First of all, they kept government close to the people; they opposed every kind of centralized administration. In local communities, the people could more readily watch their agents and detect any attempt upon their liberties. The farther government is removed from the local unit, the more danger of tyranny exists. This attitude formed one of the most powerful obstacles to the formation of the Constitution of 1787 and to national centralization. In the second place, by bills of rights the people informed their governors that thus far and no farther they might go. This idea of a bill of rights, the framers drew from their earlier colonial contracts, such as the Massachusetts Body of Liberties of 1641. In the third place, large standing armies were prohibited. With civil authority dominating military power, a popular militia could safely be employed to resist oppression. In the fourth place, the people granted only a short lease of power to their agents. And finally, they devised an elaborate system of checks and balances to prevent any one official or department from exercising too great an authority. The last two of these safeguards demand further examination.

The early state constitutions envisaged short terms of office. Governors and legislators were chosen usually for only one year; and there were stringent restrictions upon reëlection. The framers feared lest a longer lease of power might lead to an oligarchy, or even to a hereditary magistracy. Every officer was looked upon as a potential despot. Where annual elections end, they argued, tyranny begins.

The system of checks and balances was derived from the writings of Locke and Montesquieu. According to the theory underlying it, there are three important governmental divisions: (1) the legislative, which makes the laws; (2) the executive, which enforces the laws; and (3) the judiciary, which interprets the laws in cases presented to the courts. As long as these three powers remain in the hands of separate and independent officials, tyranny is impossible. But should the legislators enforce the laws or the executive interpret them, then liberty can no longer exist. The Massachusetts constitution declared this fear of political authority in capital letters:

"In the government of this commonwealth, the legislative department shall never exercise the executive and judicial powers or either of them; the executive shall never exercise the legislative and judicial powers or either of them; the judicial shall never exercise the legislative and executive powers or either of them—to the end that it may be a government of laws and not of men." [44]

Political theory thus called for an equilibrium of governmental powers. An exact balancing, however, is never possible. In their attempt to erect a check and balance system, framers of these early state constitutions were inevitably affected by their colonial experiences. In the days before the Revolution, bitter conflicts frequently occurred between the royal governors and the colonial assemblies. The governors, usually taking their orders from the king's ministers, became unpopular, while the people looked upon their own representatives as the guardians of their liberties. Monarchical connections also tainted the courts. It mattered not that royal governors and judges no longer ruled; prejudice remained ingrained against

[44] Massachusetts Constitution, Part I, Art. 30.

those offices. Consequently, in the attempt at a political equilibrium the scales were weighted in favor of the legislature and against the governor and the judiciary. In eight of the thirteen states the legislature elected the governor; [45] in nine, he had a one-year term of office. [46] He had very limited or no appointing power and lacked the veto. [47] An elected executive council checked the governor in the exercise of those powers that he did retain. The judiciary was subordinate to the legislature or to the governor and his elected council. The people thus placed their confidence in the legislative branch of government. In Pennsylvania, Vermont, and Georgia, they went so far as to establish unicameral legislatures. Constitutional amendments were usually intrusted to that department also. Massachusetts, Pennsylvania, and Georgia specifically provided for constitutional conventions, but the other state constitutions, when they mentioned amendment, vested the power in the legislature. In theory, a balance of powers existed; in practice, legislative supremacy.

The revolutionary movement inaugurated a democratic social campaign. The states attacked the very foundation of aristocracy— primogeniture and entail of estates. The fight against religious disabilities commenced at this time. An expansion of the suffrage likewise began. No one of these radical social changes was completed during the Revolutionary period. Limitations still remained upon the suffrage. Property qualifications, usually the holding of real estate, existed for voting and office-holding. It must, however, be remembered that in the existing agricultural civilization the great mass of farmers could qualify for voting. Religious restrictions on the suffrage and religious tests for public office still remained. Not until the advent of Jacksonian democracy did the eighteenth-century seeds of social revolution come to full bloom.

JOHN ADAMS

At the time of the Revolution, John Adams was already one of the leading members of the Boston bar. Under the pen name of Novanglus, he engaged in a long newspaper debate with Daniel Leonard. In his various articles, Adams presents a thorough history of the colonial dispute with Great Britain. Paper No. VII contains an interesting view of the nature of the British constitution and of the British Empire. This paper should be read in connection with Leonard's fifth article, to which it is an answer.

[45] New Jersey, Delaware, Maryland, Virginia, North Carolina, South Carolina, Pennsylvania, Georgia.
[46] Connecticut, Georgia, Maryland, Massachusetts, New Hampshire, North Carolina, Pennsylvania, Rhode Island, Virginia.
[47] The governors of Massachusetts and South Carolina had a veto power. In New York this power rested in a Council of Revision of which the governor was a member.

NOVANGLUS:

OR

A HISTORY OF THE DISPUTE WITH AMERICA,
FROM ITS ORIGIN IN 1754, TO THE PRESENT TIME [48]

Addressed to the Inhabitants of the Colony of Massachusetts Bay

No. VII

Our rhetorical magician, in his paper of January the 9th, continues to *wheedle:* You want nothing but "to know the true state of facts, to rectify whatever is amiss." He becomes an advocate for the poor of Boston! is for making great allowance for the whigs. "The whigs are too valuable a part of the community to lose. He would not draw down the vengeance of Great Britain. He shall become an advocate for the leading whigs," &c. It is in vain for us to inquire after the *sincerity* or *consistency* of all this. It is agreeable to the precept of Horace:

<blockquote>Irritat, mulcet, falsis terroribus implet,
    Ut magus,</blockquote>

And that is all he desires.

After a long discourse, which has nothing in it but what has been answered already, he comes to a great subject indeed, the British constitution; and undertakes to prove, that "the authority of parliament extends to the colonies."

Why will not this writer state the question fairly? The whigs allow that, from the necessity of a case not provided for by common law, and to supply a defect in the British dominions, which there undoubtedly is, if they are to be governed only by that law, America has all along consented, still consents, and ever will consent, that parliament, being the most powerful legislature in the dominions, should regulate the trade of the dominions. This is founding the authority of parliament to regulate our trade, upon *compact* and *consent* of the colonies, not upon any principle of common or statute law; not upon any original principle of the English constitution; not upon the principle that parliament is the supreme and sovereign legislature over them in all cases whatsoever. The question is not, therefore, whether the authority of parliament extends to the colonies in any case, for it is admitted by the whigs, that it does in that of commerce; but whether it extends in all cases.

We are then detained with a long account of the three simple forms of government; and are told, that "the British constitution, consisting of king, lords, and commons, is formed upon the principles of monarchy, aristocracy, and democracy, in due proportion; that it includes the principal excellences, and excludes the principal defects of the other kinds of government,—the most perfect system that the wisdom of ages has produced, and Englishmen glory in being subject to, and protected by it."

Then we are told, "that the colonies are a part of the British empire." But what are we to understand by this? Some of the colonies, most of them, indeed, were settled before the kingdom of Great Britain was brought into existence. The union of England and Scotland was made and established by

[48] C. F. Adams (editor), *The Works of John Adams* (Boston, Little, Brown & Company, 1851). IV. 99–102, 105–121.

act of parliament in the reign of Queen Anne, and it was this union and statute which erected the kingdom of Great Britain. The colonies were settled long before, in the reigns of the Jameses and Charleses. What authority over them had Scotland? Scotland, England, and the colonies were all under one king before that; the two crowns of England and Scotland united on the head of James I, and continued on that of Charles I, when our first charter was granted. Our charter, being granted by him, who was king of both nations, to our ancestors, most of whom were *post nati*, born after the union of the two crowns, and consequently, as was adjudged in Calvin's case, free, natural subjects of Scotland, as well as England,—had not the king as good a right to have governed the colonies by his Scottish, as by his English parliament, and to have granted our charters under the seal of Scotland, as well as that of England?

But to waive this. If the English parliament were to govern us, where did they get the right, without our consent, to take the Scottish parliament into a participation of the government over us? When this was done, was the American share of the democracy of the constitution consulted? If not, were not the Americans deprived of the benefit of the democratical part of the constitution? And is not the democracy as essential to the English constitution as the monarchy or aristocracy? Should we have been more effectually deprived of the benefit of the British or English constitution, if one or both houses of parliament, or if our houses and council, had made this union with the two houses of parliament in Scotland, without the king?

If a new constitution was to be formed for the whole British dominions, and a supreme legislature coextensive with it, upon the general principles of the English constitution, an equal mixture of monarchy, aristocracy, and democracy, let us see what would be necessary. England has six millions of of people, we will say; America has three. England has five hundred members in the house of commons, we will say; America must have two hundred and fifty. Is it possible she should maintain them there, or could they at such a distance know the state, the sense, or exigencies of their constituents? Ireland, too, must be incorporated, and send another hundred or two of members. The territory in the East Indies and West India Islands must send members. And after all this, every navigation act, every act of trade must be repealed. America, and the East and West Indies, and Africa too, must have equal liberty to trade with all the world, that the favored inhabitants of Great Britain have now. Will the ministry thank Massachusettensis for becoming an advocate for such a union, and incorporation of all the dominions of the King of Great Britain? Yet, without such a union, a legislature which shall be sovereign and supreme in all cases whatsoever, and coextensive with the empire, can never be established upon the general principles of the English constitution which Massachusettensis lays down, namely,—an equal mixture of monarchy, aristocracy, and democracy. Nay, further, in order to comply with this principle, this new government, this mighty colossus, which is to bestride the narrow world, must have a house of lords, consisting of Irish, East and West Indian, African, American, as well as English and Scottish noblemen; for the nobility ought to be scattered about all the dominions, as well as the representatives of the commons. If in twenty years more America should have six millions of inhabitants, as there is a boundless territory to fill up, she must have five hundred representatives. Upon these principles, if in forty years she should have twelve millions, a thousand; and if the inhabitants of the three kingdoms remain as they are, being already full of inhabitants, what will become of your supreme legislature? It will be translated, crown and all, to America. This is a sublime system for America. It will flatter those ideas of independency which the tories impute to them, if they have any such, more than any other plan of independency that I have ever heard projected.

"The best writers upon the law of nations tell us, that when a nation takes possession of a distant country, and settles there, that country, though separated from the principal establishment, or mother country, naturally becomes a part of the state, equal with its ancient possessions." We are not told who these "best writers" are. I think we ought to be introduced to them. But their meaning may be no more, than that it is best they should be incorporated with the ancient establishment by contract, or by some new law and institution, by which the new country shall have equal right, powers, and privileges, as well as equal protection, and be under equal obligations of obedience, with the old. Has there been any such contract between Britain and the colonies? Is America incorporated into the realm? Is it a part of the realm? Is it a part of the kingdom? Has it any share in the legislative of the realm? The constitution requires that every foot of land should be represented in the third estate, the democratical branch of the constitution. How many millions of acres in America, how many thousands of wealthy landholders, have no representatives there? . . .

I agree, that "two supreme and independent authorities cannot exist in the same state," any more than two supreme beings in one universe; and, therefore, I contend, that our provincial legislatures are the only supreme authorities in our colonies. Parliament, notwithstanding this, may be allowed an authority supreme and sovereign over the ocean, which may be limited by the banks of the ocean, or the bounds of our charters; our charters give us no authority over the high seas. Parliament has our consent to assume a jurisdiction over them. And here is a line fairly drawn between the rights of Britain and the rights of the colonies, namely, the banks of the ocean, or low-water mark; the line of division between common law, and civil or maritime law. If this is not sufficient,—if parliament are at a loss for any principle of natural, civil, maritime, moral, or common law, on which to ground any authority over the high seas, the Atlantic especially, let the colonies be treated like reasonable creatures, and they will discover great ingenuity and modesty. The acts of trade and navigation might be confirmed by provincial laws, and carried into execution by our own courts and juries, and in this case, illicit trade would be cut up by the roots forever. I knew the smuggling tories in New York and Boston would cry out against this, because it would not only destroy their profitable game of smuggling, but their whole place and pension system. But the whigs, that is, a vast majority of the whole continent, would not regard the smuggling tories. In one word, if public principles, and motives, and arguments were alone to determine this dispute between the two countries, it might be settled forever in a few hours; but the ever-lasting clamors of prejudice, passion, and private interest drown every consideration of that sort, and are precipitating us into a civil war.

"If, then, we are a part of the British empire, we must be subject to the supreme power of the state, which is vested in the estates in parliament."

Here, again, we are to be conjured out of our senses by the magic in the words "British empire," and "supreme power of the state." But, however it may sound, I say we are not a part of the British empire; because the British government is not an empire. The governments of France, Spain, &c. are not empires, but monarchies, supposed to be governed by fixed fundamental laws, though not really. The British government is still less entitled to the style of *an empire*. It is a limited monarchy. If Aristotle, Livy, and Harrington knew what a republic was, the British constitution is much more like a republic than an empire. They define a republic to be a *government of laws, and not of men*. If this definition be just, the British constitution is nothing more nor less than a republic, in which the king is first magistrate. This office being hereditary, and being possessed of such ample and splendid prerogatives, is no objection to the government's being a republic, as long as it is bound by fixed laws, which the people have a voice in making, and a right to defend. An empire is a despotism, and an emperor a despot, bound by no law or limitation but this own will; it is a stretch of tyranny beyond absolute monarchy. For, although the will of an absolute monarch is law, yet his edicts must be registered by parliaments. Even this formality is not necessary in an empire. There the maxim is *quod principi placuit legis habet rigorem*, even without having that will and pleasure recorded. There are but three empires now in Europe, the German or Holy Roman, the Russian, and the Ottoman.

There is another sense, indeed, in which the word *empire* is used, in which it may be applied to the government of Geneva, or any other republic, as well as to monarchy or despotism. In this sense it is synonymous with *government, rule,* or *dominion*. In this sense we are within the dominion, rule, or government of the King of Great Britain.

The question should be, whether we are a part of the kingdom of Great Britain. This is the only language known in English laws. We are not then a part of the British kingdom, realm, or state; and therefore the supreme power of the kingdom, realm, or state is not, upon these principles, the supreme power of us. That "supreme power over America is vested in the estates in parliament," is an affront to us; for there is not an acre of American land represented there; there are no American estates in parliament.

To say, that we "must be" subject, seems to betray a consciousness that we are not by any law, or upon any principles but those of mere power; and an opinion that we ought to be, or that it is necessary that we should be. But if this should be admitted for argument's sake only, what is the consequence? The consequences that may fairly be drawn are these; that Britain has been imprudent enough to let colonies be planted, until they are become numerous and important, without ever having wisdom enough to concert a plan for their government, consistent with her own welfare; that now it is necessary to make them submit to the authority of parliament; and, because there is no principle of law, or justice, or reason, by which she can effect it, therefore she will resort to war and conquest—to the maxim, *delenda est Carthago*. These are the consequences, according to this writer's idea. We think the consequences are, that she has, after one hundred and fifty years, discovered a defect in her government, which ought to be supplied by some just and reasonable means, that is, by the consent of the colonies; for metaphysicians and politicians may dispute forever, but they will never find any other moral principle or foundation of rule or obedience, than the consent of governors and governed. She has found out that the great machine will not go any longer without a new wheel. She will make this herself. We think she is making it of such materials and workmanship as will tear the whole machine to pieces. We are willing, if she can convince us of the necessity of such a wheel, to assist with artists and materials in making it, so that it may answer the end. But she says, we shall have no share in it; and if we will not let her patch it up as she pleases, her Massachusettensis and other advocates tell us, she will tear it to pieces herself, by cutting our throats. To this kind of reasoning, we can only answer, that we will not stand still to be butchered. We will defend our lives as long as Providence shall enable us.

"It is beyond doubt, that it was the sense both of the *parent country* and *our ancestors*, that they were to remain subject to parliament."

This has been often asserted, and as often contradicted and fully confuted. The confutation may not, however, have come to every eye which has read this newspaper.

The public acts of kings and ministers of state, in that age when our ancestors emigrated, which were not complained of, remonstrated and protested against by the commons, are looked upon as sufficient proof of the "sense" of the parent country.

The charter to the treasurer and company of Virginia, 23 May, 1609, grants ample powers of government, legislative, executive, and judicial, and then contains an express covenant, "to and with the said treasurer and company, their successors, factors, and assigns, that they, and every of them, shall be free from all taxes and impositions forever, upon any goods or merchandises, at any time or times hereafter, either upon importation thither, or exportation from thence, into our realm of England, or into any other of our realms or dominions."

I agree with this writer, that the authority of a supreme legislature includes the right of taxation. Is not this quotation, then, an irresistible proof, that it was not "the sense of King James or his ministers, or of the ancestors of the Virginians, that they were to remain subject to parliament as a supreme legislature"?

After this, James issued a proclamation recalling the patent, but this was never regarded. Then Charles issued another proclamation, which produced a remonstrance from Virginia, which was answered by a letter from the lords of the privy council, 22 July, 1634, containing the royal assurance, that "all their estates, trade, freedom, and privileges should be enjoyed by them in as extensive a manner as they enjoyed them before those proclamations."

Here is another evidence of the sense of the king and his ministers.

Afterwards, parliament sent a squadron of ships to Virginia; the colony rose in open resistance, until the parliamentary commissioners granted them conditions, that they should enjoy the privileges of Englishmen; that their assembly should transact the affairs of the colonies; that they should have a free trade to all places and nations, as the people of England; and fourthly, that "Virginia shall be free from all *taxes*, customs, and impositions whatever, and none to be imposed on them without consent of the grand assembly; and so that neither forts nor castles be erected, or garrisons maintained, without their consent."

One would think this was evidence enough of the sense both of the parent country and our ancestors.

After the acts of navigation were passed, Virginia sent agents to England, and a remonstrance against those acts. Charles, in answer, sent a declaration under the privy seal, 19 April, 1676, affirming "that taxes ought not to be laid upon the inhabitants and proprietors of the colony, but by the common consent of the general assembly; except such impositions as the parliament should lay on the commodities imported into England from the colony." And he ordered a charter under the great seal, to secure this right to the Virginians.

What becomes of the "sense of the parent country and our ancestors"? for the ancestors of the Virginians are our ancestors, when we speak of ourselves as Americans.

From Virginia let us pass to Maryland. Charles I, in 1633, gave a charter to the Baron of Baltimore, containing ample powers of government, and this express covenant: "to and with the said Lord Baltimore, his heirs and assigns, that we, our heirs and successors, shall at no time hereafter, set or make, or cause to be set, any imposition, custom, or other taxation, rate, or contribution whatsoever, in and upon the dwellings and inhabitants of the aforesaid province, for their lands, tenements, goods, or chattels within the said province; or to be laden or unladen within the ports or harbors of the said province."

What, then, was the "sense of the parent country and the ancestors" of Maryland? But if, by "our ancestors," he confines his idea to New England, or this province, let us consider. The first planters of Plymouth were "our ancestors" in the strictest sense. They had no charter or patent for the land they took possession of; and derived no authority from the English parliament or crown to set up their government. They purchased land of the Indians, and set up a government of their own, on the simple principle of nature; and afterwards purchased a patent for the land of the council at Plymouth; but never purchased any charter for government, of the crown or the king, and continued to exercise all the powers of government, legislative, executive, and judicial, upon the plain ground of an original contract among the independent individuals for sixty-eight years, that is until their incorporation with Massachusetts by our present charter. The same may be said of the colonies which emigrated to Say-Brook, New Haven, and other parts of Connecticut. They seem to have had no idea of dependence on parliament, any more than on the conclave. The Secretary of Connecticut has now in his possession an original letter from Charles II to that colony, in which he considers them rather as friendly allies, than as subjects to his English parliament; and even requests them to pass a law in their assembly relative to piracy.

The sentiments of your ancestors in the Massachusetts, may be learned from almost every ancient paper and record. It would be endless to recite all the passages, in which it appears that they thought themselves exempt from the authority of parliament, not only in the point of taxation, but in all cases whatsoever. Let me mention one. Randolph, one of the predecessors of Massachusettensis, in a representation to Charles II, dated 20 September, 1676, says, "I went to visit the governor at his house, and among other discourses, I told him, I took notice of several ships that were arrived at Boston, some since my being there, from Spain, France, Straits, Canaries, and other parts of Europe, contrary to your majesty's laws for encouraging navigation and regulating the trade of the plantations. He freely declared to me, that the law made by your majesty and your parliament, obligeth them in nothing but what consists with the interest of that colony; that the legislative power is and abides in them solely to act and make laws by virtue of a charter from your majesty's royal father." Here is a positive assertion of an exemption from the authority of parliament, even in the case of the regulation of trade.

Afterwards, in 1677, the general court passed a law which shows the sense of our ancestors in a very strong light. It is in these words:—

"This court being informed, by letters received this day from our messengers, of his majesty's expectation, that the acts of trade and navigation be exactly and punctually observed by this his majesty's colony, his pleasure therein not having before now been signified unto us, either by express from his majesty or any of his ministers of state:

"It is therefore hereby ordered, and by the authority of this court enacted, that henceforth, all masters of ships, ketches, or other vessels, of greater or lesser burthen, arriving in, or sailing from any of the ports in this jurisdiction, do, without coven or fraud, yield faithful and constant obedience unto, and observation of, all the said acts of navigation and trade, on penalty of suffering such forfeitures, loss, and damage, as in the said acts are particularly expressed. And the governor and council, and all officers commissionated and authorized by them, are hereby ordered and required to see to the strict observation of the said acts."

As soon as they had passed this law, they wrote a letter to their agent, in which they acknowledge they had not conformed to the acts of trade; and they say, they "apprehended them to be an invasion of the rights, liberties, and properties of the subjects of his majesty in the colony, they not being represented in parliament; and, according to the usual sayings of the learned in the law, *the laws of England were bounded within the four seas, and did not reach America*. However, as his majesty had signified his pleasure that these acts should be observed in the Massachusetts, they had made provision, by a law of the colony, that they should be strictly attended to from time to time, although it greatly discouraged trade, and was a great damage to his majesty's plantation."

Thus, it appears, that the ancient Massachusettensians and Virginians had precisely the same sense of the authority of parliament, namely,—that it had none at all; and the same sense of the necessity that, by the voluntary act of the colonies—their free, cheerful consent—it should be allowed the power of regulating trade; and this is precisely the idea of the late congress at Philadelphia, expressed in the fourth proposition of their Bill of Rights.

But this was the sense of the parent country, too, at that time; for King Charles II, in a letter to the Massachusetts, after this law had been laid before him, has these words: "We are informed that you have lately made *some good provision* for observing the acts of trade and navigation, which is well pleasing unto us." Had he or his ministers an idea that parliament was the sovereign legislative over the colony? If he had, would he not have censured this law, as an insult to that legislative?

I sincerely hope we shall see no more such round affirmations, that "it was the sense of the parent country and our ancestors, that they were to remain subject to parliament." So far from thinking themselves subject to parliament, it is clear that, during the interregnum, it was their desire and design to have been a free commonwealth, and independent republic; and after the restoration, it was with the utmost reluctance that, in the course of sixteen or seventeen years, they were brought to take the oaths of allegiance; and for some time after this, they insisted upon taking an oath of fidelity to the country, before that of allegiance to the king.

That "it is evident, from the charter itself, that they were to remain subject to parliament," is very unaccountable, when there is not one word in either charter concerning parliament.

That the authority of parliament "has been exercised almost ever since the first settlement of the country," is a mistake; for there is no instance, until the first Navigation Act, which was in 1660, more than forty years after the first settlement. This act was never executed nor regarded until seventeen years afterwards, and then it was not executed as an act of parliament, but as a law of the colony, to which the king agreed.

This "has been expressly acknowledged by our provincial legislatures." There is too much truth in this. It has been twice acknowledged by our house of representatives, that parliament, was the supreme legislative; but this was directly repugnant to a multitude of other votes, by which it was denied. This was in conformity to the distinction between taxation and legislation, which has since been found to be a distinction without a difference.

When a great question is first started, there are very few, even of the greatest minds, which suddenly and intuitively comprehend it, in all its consequences.

It is both "our interest and our duty to continue subject to the authority of parliament," as far as the regulation of our trade, if it will be content with that, but no longer.

"If the colonies are not subject to the authority of parliament, Great Britain and the colonies must be distinct states, as completely so as England and Scotland were before the union, or as Great Britain and Hanover are now." There is no need of being startled at this consequence. It is very harmless. There is no absurdity at all in it. Distinct states may be united under one king. And those states may be further cemented and united together by a treaty of commerce. This is the case. We have, by our own express consent, contracted to observe the Navigation Act, and by our implied consent, by long usage and uninterrupted acquiescence, have submitted to the other acts of trade, however grievous some of them may be. This may be compared to a treaty of commerce, by which those distinct states are cemented together, in perpetual league and amity. And if any further ratifications of this pact or treaty are necessary, the colonies would readily enter into them, provided their other liberties were inviolate.

That "the colonies owe no allegiance to any imperial crown," provided such a crown involves in it a house of lords and a house of commons, is certain. Indeed, we owe no allegiance to any crown at all. We owe allegiance to the person of his majesty, King George III, whom God preserve. But allegiance is due universally, both from Britons and Americans to the person of the king, not to his crown; to his natural, not his politic capacity, as I will undertake to prove hereafter, from the highest authorities, and the most solemn adjudications, which were ever made within any part of the British dominions.

If his majesty's title to the crown is "derived from an act of parliament, made since the settlement of these colonies," it was not made since the date of our charter. Our charter was granted by King William and Queen Mary, three years after the revolution; and the oaths of allegiance are established by a law of the province. So that our allegiance to his majesty is not due by virtue of any act of a British parliament, but by our own charter and province laws. It ought to be remembered that there was a revolution here, as well as in England, and that we, as well as the people of England, made an original, express contract with King William.

If it follows from thence, that he appears "King of Massachusetts, King of Rhode Island, King of Connecticut, &c." this is no absurdity at all. He will appear in this light, and does appear so, whether parliament has authority over us or not. He is King of Ireland, I suppose, although parliament is allowed to have authority there. As to giving his majesty those titles, I have no objection at all; I wish he would be graciously pleased to assume them.

The only proposition in all this writer's long string of pretended absurdities, which he says follows from the position that we are distinct states, is this:— That "as the king must govern each state by its parliament, those several parliaments would pursue the particular interest of its own state; and however well disposed the king might be to pursue a line of interest that was common to all, the checks and control that he would meet with would render it impossible." Every argument ought to be allowed its full weight; and therefore candor obliges me to acknowledge, that here lies all the difficulty that there is in this whole controversy. There has been, from first to last, on both sides of the Atlantic, an idea, an apprehension, that it was necessary there should be some superintending power, to draw together all the wills, and unite all the strength of the subjects in all the dominions, in case of war, and in the case of trade. The necessity of this, in case of war, has been so apparent, that, as has often been said, we have consented that parliament should exercise such a power. In case of war, it has by some been thought necessary. But in fact and experience, it has not been found so. What though the proprietary colonies, on account of disputes with the proprietors, did not come in so early to the assistance of the general cause in the last war as they ought, and perhaps one of them not at all? The inconveniences of this were small, in comparison of the absolute ruin to the liberties of all which must follow the submission to parliament, in all cases, which would be giving up all the popular limitations upon the government. These inconveniences fell chiefly upon New England. She was necessitated to greater exertions; but she had rather suffer these again and again than others infinitely greater.

However, this subject has been so long in contemplation, that it is fully understood now in all the colonies; so that there is no danger, in case of another war, of any colony's failing of its duty.

But, admitting the proposition in its full force, that it is absolutely necessary there should be a supreme power, coextensive with all the dominions, will it follow that parliament, as now constituted, has a right to assume this supreme jurisdiction? By no means.

A union of the colonies might be projected, and an American legislature; for, if America has three millions of people, and the whole dominions, twelve millions, she ought to send a quarter part of all the members to the house of commons; and, instead of holding parliaments always at Westminster, the haughty members for Great Britain must humble themselves, one session in four, to cross the Atlantic, and hold the parliament in America.

There is no avoiding all inconveniences in human affairs. The greatest possible, or conceivable, would arise from ceding to parliament power over us without a representation in it. The next greatest would accrue from any plan that can be devised for a representation there. The least of all would arise from going on as we began, and fared well for one hundred and fifty years, by letting parliament regulate trade, and our own assemblies all other matters.

As to "the prerogatives not being defined, or limited," it is as much so in the colonies as in Great Britain, and as well understood, and as cheerfully submitted to in the former as the latter.

But "where is the British constitution, that we all agree we are entitled to?" I answer, if we enjoy, and are entitled to more liberty than the British constitution allows, where is the harm? Or if we enjoy the British constitution in greater purity and perfection than they do in England, as is really the case, whose fault is this? Not ours.

We may find all the blessings of this constitution "in our provincial assemblies." Our houses of representatives have, and ought to exercise every power of the house of commons. The first charter to this colony is nothing to the present argument; but it did grant a power of taxing the people, implicitly, though not in express terms. It granted all the rights and liberties of Englishmen, which include the power of taxing the people.

"Our council boards" in the royal governments, "are destitute of the noble independence and splendid appendages of peerage." Most certainly, they are the meanest creatures and tools in the political creation, dependent every moment for their existence on the tainted breath of a prime minister. But they have the authority of the house of lords, in our little models of the English constitution; and it is this which makes them so great a grievance. The crown has really two branches of our legislature in its power. Let an act of parliament pass at home, putting it in the power of the king to remove any peer from the house of lords at his pleasure, and what will become of the British constitution? It will be overturned from the foundation. Yet we are perpetually insulted by being told, that making our council by mandamus brings us nearer to the British constitution. In this province, by charter, the council certainly hold their seats for the year, after being chosen and approved, independent of both the other branches. For their creation, they are equally obliged to both the other branches; so that there is little or no bias in favor of either; if any, it is in favor of the prerogative. In short, it is not easy, without an hereditary nobility, to constitute a council more independent, more nearly resembling the house of lords, than the council of this province has ever been by charter.

But perhaps it will be said, that we are to enjoy the British constitution in our supreme legislature, the parliament, not in our provincial legislatures. To this I answer, if parliament is to be our supreme legislature, we shall be under a complete oligarchy or aristocracy, not the British constitution, which this writer himself defines a mixture of monarchy, aristocracy, and democracy. For king, lords, and commons, will constitute one great oligarchy, as they will stand related to America, as much as the decemvirs did in Rome; with this difference for the worse, that our rulers are to be three thousand miles off. The definition of an oligarchy is a government by a number of grandees, over whom the people have no control. The States of Holland were once chosen by the people frequently, then chosen for life; now they are not chosen by the people at all. When a member dies, his place is filled up, not by the people he is to represent, but by the States. Is not this depriving the Hollanders of a free constitution, and subjecting them to an aristocracy, or oligarchy? Will not the government of America be like it? Will not representatives be chosen for them by others, whom they never saw nor heard of? If our provincial constitutions are in any respect imperfect, and want alteration, they have capacity enough to discern it, and power enough to affect it, without the interposition of parliament. There never was an American constitution attempted by parliament before the Quebec bill, and Massachusetts bill. These are such *samples* of what they may, and probably will be, that few Americans are in love with them. However, America will never allow that parliament has any authority to alter their constitutions at all. She is wholly penetrated with a sense of the necessity of resisting it at all hazards. And she would resist it, if the constitution of the Massachusetts had been altered as much for *the better* as it is for the worse. The question we insist on most is, not whether the alteration is for the better or not, but whether parliament has any right to make any alteration at all. And it is the universal sense of America, that it has none.

We are told, that "the provincial constitutions have no principle of stability within themselves." This is so great a mistake, that there is not more order or stability in any government upon the globe, than there ever has been in that of Connecticut. The same may be said of the Massachusetts and Pennsylvania; and, indeed of the others very nearly. "That these constitutions, in turbulent times, would become wholly monarchical, or wholly republican," they must be at such times as would have a similar effect upon the constitution at home. But in order to avoid the danger of this, what is to be done? Not give us an English constitution, it seems, but make sure of us at once, by giving us constitutions wholly monarchical, annihilating our houses of representatives first, by taking from them the support of government, &c., and then making the council and judges wholly dependent on the crown.

That a representation in parliament is impracticable, we all agree; but the consequence is, that we must have a representation in our supreme legislatures here. This was the consequence that was drawn by kings, ministers, our ancestors, and the whole nation, more than a century ago, when the colonies were first settled, and continued to be the general sense until the last peace; and it must be the general sense again soon, or Great Britain will lose her colonies.

"This is apparently the meaning of that celebrated passage in Governor Hutchinson's letter, that rung through the continent, namely,—'There must be an abridgment of what is called English liberties.' " But all the art and subtlety of Massachusettensis will never vindicate or excuse that expression. According to this writer, it should have been, "there is an abridgment of English liberties, and it cannot be otherwise." But every candid reader must see that the letter-writer had more than that in his *view* and in his *wishes*. In the same letter, a little before, he says, "what marks of resentment the parliament will show, whether they will be upon the province in general, or particular persons, is extremely uncertain; but that they will be placed somewhere is most certain; and I add, *because I think it ought to be so*." Is it possible to read this, without thinking of the Port Bill, the Charter Bill, and the resolves for sending persons to England, by the statute of Henry VIII, to be tried? But this is not all: "This is most certainly a crisis," says he, &c., "If no measure shall have been taken to secure this dependence, (that is, the dependence which a colony ought to have upon the parent state,) it is all over with us." "The friends of government will be utterly disheartened; and the friends of anarchy will be afraid of nothing, be it ever so extravagant." But this is not all: "I never think of the measures necessary for the peace and good order of the colonies without pain." "There must be an abridgment of what are called English liberties." What could he mean? Any thing less than depriving us of trial by jury? Perhaps he wanted an act of parliament to try persons here for treason, by a court of admiralty. Perhaps an act, that the province should be governed by a governor and a mandamus council, without a house of representatives. But to put it out of all doubt, that his meaning was much worse than Massachusettensis endeavors to make it, he explains himself in a subsequent part of the letter: "I wish," says he, "the good of the colony, *when I wish to see some further restraint of liberty*." Here it is rendered certain, that he is pleading for a further restraint of liberty, not explaining the restraint he apprehended the constitution had already laid us under.

My indignation at this letter has sometimes been softened by compassion. It carries on the face of it evident marks of *madness*. It was written in such a transport of passion, *ambition* and *revenge* chiefly, that his reason was manifestly overpowered. The vessel was tost in such a hurricane, that she could not feel her helm. Indeed, he seems to have had a confused consciousness of this himself. "Pardon me this excursion," says he; "it really proceeds from the state of mind into which our perplexed affairs often throw me."

"It is our highest interest to continue a part of the British empire; and equally our duty to remain subject to the authority of parliament," says Massachusettensis.

We are a part of the British dominions, that is, of the King of Great Britain, and it is our interest and duty to continue so. It is equally our interest and duty to continue subject to the authority of parliament, in the regulation of our trade, as long as she shall leave us to govern our internal policy, and to give and grant our own money, and no longer.

This letter concludes with an agreeable flight of fancy. The time may not be so fare off, however, as this writer imagines, when the colonies may have the balance of numbers and wealth in their favor. But when that shall happen, if we should attempt to rule her [Great Britain] by an American parliament, without an adequate representation in it, she will infallibly resist us by her arms.

ALEXANDER HAMILTON

Under the name of the "Westchester Farmer," Samuel Seabury wrote a series of vigorous articles against the colonial opposition to the British imperial policy. Alexander Hamilton replied with *The Farmer Refuted*. Hamilton was at that time still a college student. His reply to Seabury is one of the most cogent and systematic arguments on behalf of the colonial desire for home rule. In his later writings Hamilton dropped the natural rights philosophy that he employed so effectively in this revolutionary pamphlet.

THE FARMER REFUTED [49]
February 5, 1775

The Farmer Refuted; or, a more comprehensive and impartial View of the Disputes between Great Britain and the Colonies. Intended as a further Vindication of the Congress, in answer to a Letter from a Westchester Farmer, entitled a View of the Controversy between Great Britain and her Colonies, including a mode of determining the present disputes, finally and effectually, &c. By a sincere friend to America. Tituli remedia pollicentur, sed pixedes ipsæ venena continent—The title promises remedies, but the box itself poisons. Printed by James Rivington, 1775.

. . . . . .

As you sometimes swear *by him that made you*, I conclude your sentiments do not correspond with his, in that which is the basis of the doctrine you both agree in: and this makes it impossible to imagine whence this congruity between you arises. To grant, that there is a supreme intelligence, who rules the world, and has established laws to regulate the actions of his creatures; and, still, to assert that man, in a state of nature, may be considered as perfectly free from all restraints of *law* and *government*, appears, to a common understanding, altogether irreconcilable.

Good and wise men, in all ages, have embraced a very dissimilar theory. They have supposed, that the Deity, from the relations we stand in to Himself, and to each other, has constituted an eternal and immutable law, which is indispensably obligatory upon all mankind, prior to any human institutions whatever.

This is what is called the law of nature, "which, being coeval with mankind, and dictated by God himself, is, of course, superior in obligations to any other. It is binding over all the globe, in all countries, and at all times. No human laws are of any validity, if contrary to this; and such of them as are valid, derive all their authority, mediately, or immediately, from this original."—Blackstone.

Upon this law depend the natural rights of mankind: the Supreme Being gave existence to man, together with the means of preserving and beautify-

[49] J. C. Hamilton (editor), *The Works of Alexander Hamilton*. (New York, John F. Trow. 1850.) II, 43-53, 61-64, 79-80.

ing that existence. He endowed him with rational faculties, by the help of which, to discern and pursue such things as were consistent with his duty and interest; and invested him with an inviolable right to personal liberty and personal safety.

Hence, in a state of nature, no man had any *moral* power to deprive another of his life, limbs, property, or liberty; nor the least authority to command, or exact, obedience from him, except that which arose from the ties of consanguinity.

Hence, also, the origin of all civil government, justly established, must be a voluntary compact between the rulers and the ruled; and must be liable to such limitations, as are necessary for the security of the *absolute rights* of the latter: for what original title can any man, or set of men, have to govern others, except their own consent? To usurp dominion over a people, in their own despite; or to grasp at a more extensive power than they are willing to intrust; is to violate that law of nature, which gives every man a right to his personal liberty; and can, therefore, confer no obligation to obedience.

"The principal aim of society, is to protect individuals in the enjoyment of those absolute rights which were vested in them by the immutable laws of nature; but which could not be preserved, in peace, without that mutual assistance and intercourse, which is gained by the institution of friendly and social communities. Hence it follows, that the first and primary end of human laws, is to maintain and regulate these *absolute rights* of individuals."—Blackstone.

If we examine the pretensions of Parliament by this criterion, which is evidently a good one, we shall presently detect their injustice. First, they are subversive of our natural liberty, because an authority is assumed over us, which we by no means assent to. And, secondly, they divest us of that moral security, for our lives and properties, which we are entitled to, and which it is the primary end of society to bestow. For such security can never exist, while we have no part in making the laws that are to bind us; and while it may be the interest of our uncontrolled legislators to oppress us as much as possible.

To deny these principles, will be not less absurd, than to deny the plainest axioms. I shall not, therefore, attempt any further illustration of them.

You say, "When I assert, that since Americans have not, by any act of theirs, empowered the British Parliament to make laws for them, it follows they can have no just authority to do it; I advanced a position subversive of that dependence, which all colonies must, from their very nature, have on the mother country." The premises from which I drew this conclusion, are indisputable. You have not detected any fallacy in them; but endeavor to overthrow them by deducing a false and imaginary consequence. My principles admit the only dependence which can subsist, consistent with any idea of civil liberty, or with the future welfare of the British empire, as will appear hereafter.

"The dependence of the colonies on the mother country," you assert, "has ever been acknowledged. It is an impropriety of speech, to talk of an independent colony. The words independent and colony, convey contradictory ideas; much like *killing* and *sparing*. As soon as a colony becomes independent of the parent state, it ceases to be any longer a colony, just as when you *kill* a sheep, you cease to *spare* him."

In what sense the dependence of the colonies on the mother country, has been acknowledged, will appear from those circumstances of their political history, which I shall, by and by, recite. The term colony, signifies nothing more than a body of people drawn from the mother country, to inhabit some distant place, or the country itself so inhabited. As to the degrees and modifications of that subordination, which is due to the parent state, these must depend upon other things besides the mere act of emigration, to inhabit or settle a distant country. These must be ascertained by the spirit of the constitution of the mother country; by the compacts for the purpose of colonizing; and, more especially, by the law of nature, and that *supreme law* of every society—*its own happiness.*

The idea of colony does not involve the idea of slavery. There is a wide difference between the dependence of a free people, and the submission of slaves. The former I allow; the latter I reject with disdain. Nor does the notion of a colony imply any subordination to our fellow-subjects in the parent state, while there is one common sovereign established. The dependence of the colonies on Great Britain, is an ambiguous and equivocal phrase. It may either mean dependence on the people of Great Britain, or on the king. In the former sense, it is absurd and unaccountable. In the latter, it is just and rational. No person will affirm that a French colony is independent of the parent state, though it acknowledge the king of France as rightful sovereign. Nor can it, with any greater propriety, be said, that an English colony is independent, while it bears allegiance to the king of Great Britain. The difference between their dependence, is only that which distinguishes civil liberty from slavery; and results from the different genius of the French and English constitutions.

But you deny that "we can be liege subjects of the king of Great Britain, while we disavow the authority of Parliament." You endeavor to prove it thus: "The king of Great Britain was placed on the throne, by virtue of an act of Parliament: and he is king of America, by virtue of being king of Great Britain. He is, therefore, king of America by act of Parliament: and, if we disclaim that authority of Parliament which made him our king, we, in fact, reject him from being our king; for we disclaim that authority by which he is king at all."

Admitting that the king of Great Britain was enthroned by virtue of an act of Parliament; and that he is king of America, because he is king of Great Britain; yet, the act of Parliament is not the *efficient cause* of his being the king of America. It is only the *occasion* of it. He is king of America, by virtue of a compact between us and the kings of Great Britain. These colonies were planted and settled by the grants, and under the protection, of English kings, who entered into covenants with us, for themselves, their heirs, and successors; and it is from these covenants, that the duty of protection, on their part, and the duty of allegiance, on ours, arise.

So that, to disclaim the authority of a British Parliament over us, does by no means imply the dereliction of our allegiance to British monarchs. Our compact takes no cognizance of the manner of their accession to the throne. It is sufficient for us that they are kings of England.

The most valid reasons can be assigned for our allegiance to the king of Great Britain; but not one of the least force, or plausibility, for our subjection to parliamentary decrees.

We hold our lands in America by virtue of charters from British monarchs; and are under no obligations to the Lords or Commons for them. Our title is similar, and equal, to that by which they possess their lands; and the king is the legal fountain of both. This is one grand source of our obligation to allegiance.

Another, and the principal source, is, that protection which we have hitherto enjoyed from the kings of Great Britain. Nothing is more common than to hear the votaries of Parliament urge the protection we have received from the mother country, as an argument for submission to its claims. But they entertain erroneous conceptions of the matter. The king himself, being the supreme executive magistrate, is regarded by the constitution as the supreme protector of the empire. For this purpose, he is the generalissimo, or first in military command. In him is vested the power of making war and peace; of raising armies, equipping fleets, and directing all their motions. He it is, that has defended us from our enemies; and to him alone we are obliged to render allegiance and submission.

The laws of nature, and the British constitution, both confine allegiance to the person of the king; and found it upon the principle of protection. We may see the subject discussed at large, in the case of Calvin. The definition given of it by the learned Coke, is this: "Legiance is the mutual bond and obligation between the king and his subjects; whereby subjects are called his liege subjects, because they are bound to obey and serve him: and he is called their liege lord, because he is bound to maintain and defend them." Hence it is evident, that while we enjoy the protection of the king, it is incumbent upon us to obey and serve him, without the interposition of parliamentary supremacy.

The right of Parliament to legislate for us, cannot be accounted for upon any reasonable grounds. The constitution of Great Britain is very properly called a limited monarchy; the people having reserved to themselves a share in the legislature, as a check upon the regal authority, to prevent its degenerating into despotism and tyranny. The very aim and intention of the democratical part, or the House of Commons, is to secure the rights of the people. Its very being depends upon those rights. Its whole power is derived from them, and must be terminated by them.

It is the unalienable birth-right of every Englishman, who can be considered as a *free agent*, to participate in framing the laws which are to bind him, either as to his life or property. But, as many inconveniences would result from the exercise of this right in person, it is appointed by the constitution that he shall delegate it to another. Hence, he is to give his vote in the election of some person he chooses to confide in as his representative. This right no power on earth can divest him of. It was enjoyed by his ancestors time immemorial; recognized and established by Magna Charta; and is essential to the existence of the constitution. Abolish this privilege, and the House of Commons is annihilated.

But what was the use and design of this privilege? To secure his life and property from the attacks of exorbitant power. And in what manner is this done? By giving him the election of those who are to have the disposal and regulation of them, and whose interest is in every respect connected with him.

The representative, in this case, is bound, by every possible tie, to consult the advantage of his constituents. Gratitude for the high and honorable trust reposed in him, demands a return of attention, and regard to the advancement of his happiness. Self-interest, that most powerful incentive of human actions, points and attracts towards the same object.

The duration of his trust is not perpetual, but must expire in a few years: and if he is desirous of the future favor of his constituents, he must not abuse the present instance of it, but must pursue the end for which he enjoys it; otherwise he forfeits it, and defeats his own purpose. Besides, if he consent to any laws hurtful to his constituent, he is bound by the same, and must partake the disadvantage of them. His friends, relations, children, all whose ease and comfort are dear to him, will be in a like predicament. And should he concur in any flagrant acts of injustice or oppression, he will be within the reach of popular vengeance; and this will restrain him within due bounds.

To crown the whole; at the expiration of a few years, if their representatives have abused their trust, the people have it in their power to change them; and to elect others, who may be more faithful and more attached to their interest.

These securities, the most powerful that human affairs will admit of, have the people of Britain for the good deportment of their representatives towards them. They may have proved, at some times, and on some occasions, defective; but, upon the whole, they have been found sufficient.

When we ascribe to the British House of Commons a jurisdiction over the colonies, the scene is entirely reversed. All these kinds of security immediately disappear; no ties of gratitude or interest remain. Interest, indeed, may operate to our prejudice. To oppress us, may serve as a recommendation to their constituents, as well as an alleviation of their own incumbrances. The British patriots may, in time, be heard to court the gale of popular favor, by boasting their exploits in laying some new impositions on their American vassals; and, by that means, lessening the burthens of their friends and fellow-subjects.

But what merits still more serious attention is this: there seems to be already a jealousy of our dawning splendor. It is looked upon as portentous of approaching independence. This, we have reason to believe, is one of the principal incitements to the present rigorous and unconstitutional proceedings against us. And though it may have chiefly originated in the calumnies of designing men, yet it does not entirely depend upon adventitious or partial causes; but is also founded in the circumstances of our country and situation. The boundless extent of territory we possess; the wholesome temperment of our climate; the luxuriance and fertility of our soil; the variety of our products; the rapidity of our population; the industry of our countrymen; and the commodiousness of our ports; naturally lead to a suspicion of independence, and would always have an influence pernicious to us. Jealousy is a predominant passion of human nature, and is a source of the greatest evils. Whenever it takes place between rulers and their subjects, it proves the bane of civil society.

The experience of past ages may inform us, that when the circumstances of a people render them distressed, their rulers generally recur to severe, cruel, and oppressive measures. Instead of endeavoring to establish their authority in the *affection* of their subjects, they think they have no security but in their *fear*. They do not aim at gaining their fidelity and obedience, by making them flourishing, prosperous, and happy; but by rendering them abject and dispirited. They think it necessary to intimidate and awe them; to make every accession to their power, and to impair the people's as much as possible.

One great engine to effect this in America, would be a large standing army, maintained out of our own pockets, to be at the devotion of our oppressors. This would be introduced under pretext of defending us; but, in fact, to make our bondage and misery complete.

We might soon expect the martial law, universally prevalent to the abolition of trials by juries, the *Habeas Corpus* act, and every other bulwark of personal safety, in order to overawe the honest assertors of their country's cause. A numerous train of *court dependents* would be created and supported at our expense. The value of all our possessions, by a complication of extorsive measures, would be gradually depreciated, till it became a mere shadow.

This will be called too high wrought a picture, a phantom of my own deluded imagination. The highest eulogies will be lavished on the wisdom and justice of the British nation. But deplorable is the condition of that people, who have nothing else than the wisdom and justice of another to depend upon.

"Political writers," says a celebrated author (Hume, vol. 1, Essay 5.), "have established it as a maxim, that, in contriving any system of government, and fixing the several checks and controls of the constitution, *every man* ought to be supposed a *knave;* and to have no other end, in all his actions, but *private interest.* By this interest we must govern him; and, by means of it, *make him co-operate to public good,* notwithstanding his insatiable avarice and ambition. Without this, we shall in vain boast of the advantages of *any constitution;* and shall find, in the end, that we have no security for our liberties and possessions, except the *good will* of our rulers; that is, we should have *no security at all.*

"It is, therefore, a just *political* maxim, that *every man must be supposed a knave.* Though, at the same time, it appears somewhat strange, that a maxim should be true in politics which is false in fact. But to satisfy us on this head, we may consider that men are generally more honest in a private than in a public capacity; and will go greater lengths to serve a party than when their own private interest is alone concerned. Honor is a great check upon mankind. But, where a considerable body of men act together, this check is in a great measure removed, since a man is sure to be approved by his own party for what promotes the common interest; and he soon learns to despise the clamors of adversaries. To this we may add, that every court or senate is determined by the greater number of voices; so that, if self-interest influences only the majority (as it will always do), the whole senate follows the allurements of this separate interest; and acts as if it contained not one member who had any regard to public interest and liberty." What additional force do these observations acquire, when applied to the dominion of one community over another!

From what has been said, it is plain, that we are without those checks upon the representatives of Great Britain which alone can make them answer the end of their appointment to us; which is the preservation of the rights, and the advancement of the happiness of the governed. The direct and inevitable consequence is, *they have no right to govern us.*

Let us examine it in another light. The House of Commons receives all its authority from its electors, in consequence of the right they have to a share in the legislature. Its electors are freeholders, citizens, and others, in Great Britain. It follows, therefore, that all its authority is confined to Great Britain. This is demonstrative. Sophistry, by an artful play of ambiguous terms, may perplex and obscure it; but reason can never confute it. The power which one society bestows upon any man, or body of men, can never extend beyond its own limits. The people of Great Britain may confer an authority over themselves, but they can never confer any over the people of America, because it is impossible for them to give *that* to another which they never possessed themselves. Now, I should be glad to see an attempt to prove that a freeholder, citizen, or any other man in Great Britain, has any inherent right to the life, property, or liberty, of a freeholder, citizen, or any other man in America. He can have no original and intrinsic right, because nature has distributed an equality of rights to every man. He can have no secondary or derivative right, because, the only thing which could give him that is wanting—the consent of the natural proprietor. It is incumbent upon you to demonstrate the existence of such a right, or any thing else you may produce will be of little avail. I do not expect you will be discouraged at the apparent difficulty. It is the peculiar province of an enterprising genius to surmount the greatest obstacles, and you have discovered an admirable dexterity in this way. You have put to flight some of my best arguments, with no greater pains than a few positive assertions, and as many paltry witticisms; and you become altogether irresistible by adding, with a proper degree of confidence, *You know the case to be as I state it.*

When I say that the authority of Parliament is confined to Great Britain, I speak of it in its primitive and original state. Parliament may acquire an incidental influence over others, but this must be by their own free consent; for, without this, any power it might exercise would be mere usurpation, and by no means a just authority.

The best way of determining disputes, and of investigating truth, is by descending to elementary principles. Any other method may only bewilder and misguide the understanding, but this will soon lead to a convincing and satisfactory crisis. By observing this method, we shall learn the following truths.

That the existence of the House of Commons depends upon the people's right to a share in the legislature, which is exercised by means of electing the members of that house. That the end and intention of this right is to preserve the life, property, and liberty of the subject, from the encroachments of oppression and tyranny.

That this end is accomplished, by means of the *intimate connection* of interest, between those members and their constituents, the people of Great Britain.

That with respect to the people of America, there is no such *intimate con-*

nection of interest, but the contrary; and therefore that end could not be answered to them; consequently, the *end* ceasing, the *means* must cease also.

The House of Commons derives all its powers from its own real constituents, who are the people of Great Britain; and that, therefore, it has no power but what they *originally* had in themselves.

That they had no original right to the life, property, or liberty, of Americans; nor any acquired from their own consent; and of course could give no authority over them.

That, therefore, the House of Commons has no such authority. . . .

The fundamental source of all your errors, sophisms, and false reasonings, is a total ignorance of the natural rights of mankind. Were you once to become acquainted with these, you could never entertain a thought, that all men are not, by nature, entitled to a parity of privileges. You would be convinced, that natural liberty is a gift of the beneficent Creator, to the whole human race; and that civil liberty is founded in that; and cannot be wrested from any people, without the most manifest violation of justice. *Civil liberty is only natural liberty, modified and secured by the sanctions of civil society.* It is not a thing, in its own nature, precarious and dependent on human will and caprice; but it is conformable to the constitution of man, as well as necessary to the *well-being* of society.

Upon this principle, colonists, as well as other men, have a right to civil liberty. For, if it be conducive to the happiness of society (and reason and experience testify that it is), it is evident, that every society, of whatsoever kind, has an absolute and perfect right to it, which can never be withheld without cruelty and injustice. The practice of Rome towards her colonies, cannot afford the shadow of an argument against this. That mistress of the world was often unjust. And the treatment of her dependent provinces, is one of the greatest blemishes in her history. Through the want of that civil liberty for which we are so warmly contending, they groaned under every species of wanton oppression. If we are wise, we shall take warning from thence; and consider a like state of dependence, as more to be dreaded than pestilence and famine.

The right of colonists, therefore, to exercise a legislative power, is an inherent right. It is founded upon the rights of all men to freedom and happiness. For civil liberty cannot possibly have any existence, where the society, for whom laws are made, have no share in making them; and where the interest of their legislators is not inseparably interwoven with theirs. Before you asserted, that the right of legislation was derived "from the indulgence or grant of the parent state," you should have proved two things:— that all men have not a natural right to freedom; and that civil liberty is not advantageous to society.

"The position," you say, "that we are bound by no laws but those to which we have assented, either by ourselves, or by our representatives, is a novel position, unsupported by any authoritative record of the British constitution, ancient or modern. It is republican in its very nature; and tends to the utter subversion of the English monarchy.

"This position has arisen from an artful change of terms. To say, that an Englishman is not bound by any laws but those to which the representatives of the nation have given their consent, is to say what is true. But to say that an Englishman is bound by no laws but those to which he hath consented, in person, or by *his* representative, is saying what never was true, and never can be true. A great part of the people have no vote in the choice of representatives; and, therefore, are governed by laws to which they never consented, either by themselves, or by *their* representatives."

The foundation of the English constitution rests upon this principle; that no laws have any validity or binding force, without the consent and approbation of the *people*, given in the person of *their* representatives, periodically elected by *themselves*. This constitutes the democratical part of the government.

It is also undeniably certain, that no Englishman, who can be deemed *a free agent* in a *political* view, can be bound by laws, to which he has not consented, either in person, or by *his* representative. Or, in other words, every Englishman (exclusive of the mercantile and trading part of the nation) who possesses a freehold to the value of forty shillings per annum, has a right to share in the legislature; which he exercises, by giving his vote in the election of some person he approves of as his representative.

"The true reason," says Blackstone, "of requiring any qualification, with regard to property in voters, is to exclude such persons as are *in so mean a situation*, that they are esteemed to have *no will* of their own. If these persons had votes, they would be tempted to dispose of them, under some undue influence or other. This would give a great, an artful, or a wealthy man, a larger share in elections than is consistent with general liberty. If it were probable that every man would give his vote freely, and without influence of any kind; then, upon the true theory and genuine principles of liberty, every member of the community, however poor, should have a vote in electing those delegates, to whose charge is committed the disposal of his property, his liberty, and life. But since that can hardly be expected, in persons of indigent fortunes, or such as are under the immediate dominion of others; all popular States have been obliged to establish certain qualifications, whereby some, who are suspected to have no will of their own, are excluded from voting; in order to set other individuals, whose wills may be supposed independent, more thoroughly upon a level with each other."

Hence, it appears, that such "of the people as have no vote in the choice of representatives, and, therefore, are governed by laws to which they have not consented, either by themselves or by their representatives," are only those "persons who are *in so mean a situation*, that they are esteemed to have *no will* of their own." Every *free agent*, every free man, possessing a freehold of forty shillings per annum, is, by the British constitution, entitled to a vote in the election of those who are invested with the disposal of his life, his liberty, and property.

It is therefore evident, to a demonstration, that unless a *free agent* in America be permitted to enjoy the same privilege, we are entirely stripped of the benefits of the constitution, and precipitated into an abyss of slavery. For, we are deprived of that immunity which is the grand pillar and support of freedom. And this cannot be done without a direct violation of the constitution, which decrees to every *free agent*, a share in the legislature.

It deserves to be remarked here, that those very persons in Great Britain, who are *in so mean a situation* as to be excluded from a part in elections, are in more eligible circumstances than they would be in who have every necessary qualification.

They compose a part of that society to whose government they are subject. They are nourished and maintained by it; and partake in every other emolument for which they are qualified. They have, no doubt, most of them, relations and connections among those who are privileged to vote; and, by that means, are not entirely without influence in the appointment of their rulers. They are not governed by laws made expressly and exclusively for them; but by the general laws of their country, equally obligatory on the legal electors, and on the law makers themselves. So that they have nearly the same security against oppression, which the body of the people have.

To this we may add, that they are only under a conditional prohibition, which industry and good fortune may remove. They may, one day, accumulate a sufficient property to enable them to emerge out of their present state. Or, should they die in it, their situation is not entailed upon their posterity by a fixed and irremediable doom. They, agreeably to the ordinary vicissitudes of human affairs, may acquire what their parents were deficient in.

These considerations plainly show, that the people in America, of all ranks and conditions, opulent as well as indigent (if subjected to the British Parliament), would be upon a less favorable footing than that part of the people of Great Britain, who are *in so mean a situation*, that they are supposed to have no will of their own. The injustice of this, must be evident to every man of common sense. . . .

Thus, sir, I have taken a pretty general survey of the American charters, and proved, to the satisfaction of every unbiassed person, that they are entirely discordant with that sovereignty of Parliament for which you are an advocate. The disingenuity of your extracts (to give it no harsher name) merits the severest censure; and will, no doubt, serve to discredit all your former, as well as future, labors in your favorite cause of despotism.

It is true, that New-York has no charter. But if it could support its claim to liberty in no other way, it might, with justice, plead the common principles of colonization: for it would be unreasonable to exclude one colony from the enjoyment of the most important privileges of the rest. There is no need, however, of this plea. THE SACRED RIGHTS OF MANKIND ARE NOT TO BE RUMMAGED FOR AMONG OLD PARCHMENTS OR MUSTY RECORDS. THEY ARE WRITTEN, AS WITH A SUNBEAM, IN THE WHOLE VOLUME OF HUMAN NATURE, BY THE HAND OF THE DIVINITY ITSELF; AND CAN NEVER BE ERASED OR OBSCURED BY MORTAL POWER.

The nations of Turkey, Russia, France, Spain, and all other despotic kingdoms in the world, have an inherent right, whenever they please, to shake off the yoke of servitude (though sanctioned by the immemorial usage of their ancestors), and to model their government upon the principles of civil liberty. . . .

THOMAS PAINE

Thomas Paine was an English Quaker who migrated to Philadelphia in December, 1774. He immediately took an interest in the Revolutionary movement. In January, 1776, appeared *Common Sense;* the influence of this paper was immediately felt. During the Revolution, Paine also wrote *The Forester's Letters* and *The American Crisis.* Paine likewise played a rôle in the French Revolution. His most famous work, *The Rights of Man*, was a reply to Burke's conservative attack upon the French Revolution. *The Rights of Man* was widely read and had a great influence in this country during its early years.

COMMON SENSE [50]

On the Origin and Design of Government in General, with Concise Remarks on the English Constitution

Some writers have so confounded society with government, as to leave little or no distinction between them; whereas they are not only different, but have different origins. Society is produced by our wants, and government by our wickedness; the former promotes our happiness *positively* by uniting our affections, the latter *negatively* by restraining our vices. The one encourages intercourse, the other creates distinctions. The first is a patron, the last a punisher.

Society in every state is a blessing, but Government, even in its best state, is but a necessary evil; in its worst state an intolerable one: for when we suffer, or are exposed to the same miseries *by a Government*, which we might expect in a country *without Government*, our calamity is heightened by reflecting that we furnish the means by which we suffer. Government, like dress, is the badge of lost innocence; the palaces of kings are built upon the ruins of the bowers of paradise. For were the impulses of conscience clear, uniform and irresistibly obeyed, man would need no other law-giver; but that not being the case, he finds it necessary to surrender up a part of his property to furnish means for the protection of the rest; and this he is induced to do by the same prudence which in every other case advises him, out of two evils to choose the least. Wherefore, security being the true design and end of government, it unanswerably follows that whatever form thereof appears most likely to ensure it to us, with the least expence and greatest benefit, is preferable to all others.

In order to gain a clear and just idea of the design and end of government, let us suppose a small number of persons settled in some sequestered part of the earth, unconnected with the rest; they will then represent the first peopling of any country, or of the world. In this state of natural liberty, society will be their first thought. A thousand motives will excite them thereto; the strength of one man is so unequal to his wants, and his mind so unfitted for perpetual solitude, that he is soon obliged to seek assistance and relief of another, who in his turn requires the same. Four or five united would be able to raise a tolerable dwelling in the midst of a wilderness, but one man might labour out the common period of life without accomplishing any thing;

[50] M. D. Conway (editor), *The Writings of Thomas Paine.* (New York, G. P. Putnam's Sons, 1894), I, 69–73, 75–79, 80–82, 83–84, 88–91. (Reprinted by permission of the publishers.)

when he had felled his timber he could not remove it, nor erect it after it was removed; hunger in the mean time would urge him to quit his work, and every different want would call him a different way. Disease, nay even misfortune, would be death; for though neither might be mortal, yet either would disable him from living, and reduce him to a state in which he might rather be said to perish than to die.

Thus necessity, like a gravitating power, would soon form our newly arrived emigrants into society, the reciprocal blessings of which would supersede, and render the obligations of law and government unnecessary while they remained perfectly just to each other; but as nothing but Heaven is impregnable to vice, it will unavoidably happen that in proportion as they surmount the first difficulties of emigration, which bound them together in a common cause, they will begin to relax in their duty and attachment to each other: and this remissness will point out the necessity of establishing some form of government to supply the defect of moral virtue.

Some convenient tree will afford them a State House, under the branches of which the whole Colony may assemble to deliberate on public matters. It is more than probable that their first laws will have the title only of Regulations and be enforced by no other penalty than public disesteem. In this first parliament every man by natural right will have a seat.

But as the colony increases, the public concerns will increase likewise, and the distance at which the members may be separated, will render it too inconvenient for all of them to meet on every occasion as at first, when their number was small, their habitations near, and the public concerns few and trifling. This will point out the convenience of their consenting to leave the legislative part to be managed by a select number chosen from the whole body, who are supposed to have the same concerns at stake which those have who appointed them, and who will act in the same manner as the whole body would act were they present. If the colony continue increasing, it will become necessary to augment the number of representatives, and that the interest of every part of the colony may be attended to, it will be found best to divide the whole into convenient parts, each part sending its proper number: and that the *elected* might never form to themselves an interest separate from the *electors*, prudence will point out the propriety of having elections often: because as the *elected* might by that means return and mix again with the general body of the *electors* in a few months, their fidelity to the public will be secured by the prudent reflection of not making a rod for themselves. And as this frequent interchange will establish a common interest with every part of the community, they will mutually and naturally support each other, and on this, (not on the unmeaning name of king,) depends the *strength of government, and the happiness of the governed.*

Here then is the origin and rise of government; namely, a mode rendered necessary by the inability of moral virtue to govern the world; here too is the design and end of government, viz. Freedom and security. And however our eyes may be dazzled with show, or our ears deceived by sound; however prejudice may warp our wills, or interest darken our understanding, the simple voice of nature and reason will say, 'tis right.

I draw my idea of the form of government from a principle in nature which no art can overturn, viz. that the more simple any thing is, the less liable it is to be disordered, and the easier repaired when disordered; and with this maxim in view I offer a few remarks on the so much boasted Constitution of England. That it was noble for the dark and slavish times in which it was erected, is granted. When the world was overrun with tyranny the least remove therefrom was a glorious rescue. But that it is imperfect, subject to convulsions, and incapable of producing what it seems to promise, is easily demonstrated.

Absolute governments, (tho' the disgrace of human nature) have this advantage with them, they are simple; if the people suffer, they know the head from which their suffering springs; know likewise the remedy; and are not bewildered by a variety of causes and cures. But the Constitution of England is so exceedingly complex, that the nation may suffer for years together without being able to discover in which part the fault lies; some will say in one and some in another, and every political physician will advise a different medicine.

I know it is difficult to get over local or long standing prejudices, yet if we will suffer ourselves to examine the component parts of the English constitution, we shall find them to be the base remains of two ancient tyrannies, compounded with some new Republican materials.

First.—The remains of Monarchical tyranny in the person of the King.

Secondly.—The remains of Aristocratical tyranny in the persons of the Peers.

Thirdly.—The new Republican materials, in the persons of the Commons, on whose virtue depends the freedom of England.

The two first, by being hereditary, are independent of the People; wherefore in a *constitutional sense* they contribute nothing towards the freedom of the State.

To say that the Constitution of England is an *union* of three powers, reciprocally *checking* each other, is farcical; either the words have no meaning, or they are flat contradictions.

To say that the Commons is a check upon the King, presupposes two things.

First.—That the King is not to be trusted without being looked after; or in other words, that a thirst for absolute power is the natural disease of monarchy.

Secondly.—That the Commons, by being appointed for that purpose, are either wiser or more worthy of confidence than the Crown.

But as the same constitution which gives the Commons a power to check the King by withholding the supplies, gives afterwards the King a power to check the Commons, by empowering him to reject their other bills; it again supposes that the King is wiser than those whom it has already supposed to be wiser than him. A mere absurdity!

There is something exceedingly ridiculous in the composition of monarchy; it first excludes a man from the means of information, yet empowers him to act in cases where the highest judgment is required. The state of a King shuts him from the World, yet the business of a King requires him to know it thoroughly; wherefore the different parts, by unnaturally opposing and destroying each other, prove the whole character to be absurd and useless. . . .

OF MONARCHY AND HEREDITARY SUCCESSION

Mankind being originally equals in the order of creation, the equality could only be destroyed by some subsequent circumstance: the distinctions of rich and poor may in a great measure be accounted for, and that without having recourse to the harsh ill-sounding names of oppression and avarice. Oppression is often the *consequence*, but seldom or never the *means* of riches; and though avarice will preserve a man from being necessitously poor, it generally makes him too timorous to be wealthy.

But there is another and greater distinction for which no truly natural or religious reason can be assigned, and that is the distinction of men into KINGS and SUBJECTS. Male and female are the distinctions of nature, good and bad the distinctions of heaven; but how a race of men came into the world so exalted above the rest, and distinguished like some new species, is worth inquiring into, and whether they are the means of happiness or of misery to mankind.

In the early ages of the world, according to the scripture chronology there were no kings; the consequence of which was, there were no wars; it is the pride of kings which throws mankind into confusion. Holland, without a king hath enjoyed more peace for this last century than any of the monarchical governments in Europe. Antiquity favours the same remark; for the quiet and rural lives of the first Patriarchs have a happy something in them, which vanishes when we come to the history of Jewish royalty.

Government by kings was first introduced into the world by the Heathens, from whom the children of Israel copied the custom. It was the most prosperous invention the Devil ever set on foot for the promotion of idolatry. The Heathens paid honours to their deceased kings, and the Christian World hath improved on the plan by doing the same to their living ones. How impious is the title of sacred Majesty applied to a worm, who in the midst of his splendor is crumbling into dust.

As the exalting one man so greatly above the rest cannot be justified on the equal rights of nature, so neither can it be defended on the authority of scripture; for the will of the Almighty as declared by Gideon, and the prophet Samuel, expressly disapproves of government by Kings. All anti-monarchical parts of scripture, have been very smoothly glossed over in monarchical governments, but they undoubtedly merit the attention of countries which have their governments yet to form. *Render unto Cesar the things which are Cesar's*, is the scripture doctrine of courts, yet it is no support of monarchical government, for the Jews at that time were without a king, and in a state of vassalage to the Romans.

Near three thousand years passed away, from the Mosaic account of the creation, till the Jews under a national delusion requested a king. Till then their form of government (except in extraordinary cases where the Almighty interposed) was a kind of Republic, administered by a judge and the elders of the tribes. Kings they had none, and it was held sinful to acknowledge any being under that title but the Lord of Hosts. And when a man seriously reflects on the idolatrous homage which is paid to the persons of kings, he need not wonder that the Almighty, ever jealous of his honour, should disapprove a form of government which so impiously invades the prerogative of heaven.

Monarchy is ranked in scripture as one of the sins of the Jews, for which a curse in reserve is denounced against them. The history of that transaction is worth attending to.

The children of Israel being oppressed by the Midianites, Gideon marched against them with a small army, and victory thro' the divine interposition decided in his favour. The Jews, elated with success, and attributing it to the generalship of Gideon, proposed making him a king, saying, *Rule thou over us, thou and thy son, and thy son's son.* Here was temptation in the fullest extent; not a kingdom only, but an hereditary one; but Gideon in the piety of his soul replied, *I will not rule over you, neither shall my son rule over you.* THE LORD SHALL RULE OVER YOU. Words need not be more explicit; Gideon doth not decline the honour, but denieth their right to give it; neither doth he compliment them with invented declarations of his thanks, but in the positive style of a prophet charges them with disaffection to their proper Sovereign, the King of Heaven.

About one hundred and thirty years after this, they fell again into the same error. The hankering which the Jews had for the idolatrous customs of the Heathens, is something exceedingly unaccountable; but so it was, that laying hold of the misconduct of Samuel's two sons, who were intrusted with some secular concerns, they came in an abrupt and clamorous manner to Samuel, saying, *Behold thou art old, and thy sons walk not in thy ways, now make us a king to judge us like all the other nations.* And here we cannot but observe that their motives were bad, viz. that they might be *like* unto other nations, i.e. the Heathens, whereas their true glory lay in being as much *unlike* them as possible. *But the thing displeased Samuel when they said, give us a King to judge us; and Samuel prayed unto the Lord, and the Lord said unto Samuel, hearken unto the voice of the people in all that they say unto thee, for they have not rejected thee, but they have rejected me,* THAT I SHOULD NOT REIGN OVER THEM. *According to all the works which they have done since the day that I brought them up out of Egypt even unto this day, wherewith they have forsaken me, and served other Gods: so do they also unto thee.* Now therefore hearken unto their voice, howbeit, protest solemnly unto them and show them the manner of King that shall reign over them, i.e. not of any particular King, but the general manner of the Kings of the earth whom Israel was so eagerly copying after. And notwithstanding the great distance of time and difference of manners, the character is still in fashion. *And Samuel told all the words of the Lord unto the people, that asked of him a King. And he said, This shall be the manner of the King that shall reign over you. He will take your sons and appoint them for himself for his chariots and to be his horsemen, and some shall run before his chariots* (this description agrees with the present mode of impressing men) *and he will appoint him captains over thousands and captains over fifties, will set them to ear his ground and to reap his harvest, and to make his instruments of war, and instruments of his chariots. And he will take your daughters to be confectionaries, and to be cooks, and to be bakers* (this describes the expense and luxury as well as the oppression of Kings) *and he will take your fields and your vineyards, and your olive yards, even the best of them, and give them to his servants, and he will take the tenth of your seed, & of your vineyards, & give them to his officers & to his servants* (by which we see that bribery, corruption, and favouritism, are the standing vices of Kings) *and he will take the tenth of your men servants, and your maid servants, and your goodliest young men, and your asses, and put them to his work: and he will take the tenth of your sheep, and ye shall be his servants, and ye shall cry out in that day because of your king which ye shall have chosen,* AND THE LORD WILL NOT HEAR YOU IN THAT DAY. This accounts for the continuation of Monarchy; neither do the characters of the few good kings which have lived since, either sanctify the title, or blot out the sinfulness of the origin; the high encomium given of David takes no notice of him *officially as a King,* but only as a *Man* after God's own heart. *Nevertheless the people refused to obey the voice of Samuel, and they said, Nay but we will have a king over us, that we may be like all the nations, and that our king may judge us, and go out before us and fight our battles.* Samuel continued to reason with them but to no purpose; he set before them their ingratitude, but all would not avail; and seeing them fully bent on their folly, he cried out, *I will call unto the Lord, and he shall send thunder and rain* (which was then a punishment, being in the time of wheat harvest) *that ye may perceive and see that your wickedness is great which ye have done in the sight of the Lord,* IN ASKING YOU A KING. *So Samuel called unto the Lord, and the Lord sent thunder and rain that day, and all the people greatly feared the Lord and Samuel. And all the people said unto Samuel, Pray for thy servants unto the Lord thy God that we die not, for* WE HAVE ADDED UNTO OUR SINS THIS EVIL, TO ASK A KING. These portions of scripture are direct and positive. They admit of no equivocal construction. That the Almighty hath here entered his protest against monarchical government is true, or the scripture is false. And a man hath good reason to believe that there is as much of kingcraft as priestcraft in withholding the scripture from the public in popish countries. For monarchy in every instance is the popery of government. . . .

England since the conquest hath known some few good monarchs, but groaned beneath a much larger number of bad ones: yet no man in his senses can say that their claim under William the Conqueror is a very honourable one. A French bastard landing with an armed Banditti and establishing himself king of England against the consent of the natives, is in plain terms a very paltry rascally original. It certainly hath no divinity in it. However it is needless to spend much time in exposing the folly of hereditary right; if there are any so weak as to believe it, let them promiscuously worship the Ass and the Lion, and welcome. I shall neither copy their humility, nor disturb their devotion.

Yet I should be glad to ask how they suppose kings came at first? The question admits but of three answers, viz. either by lot, by election, or by usurpation. If the first king was taken by lot, it establishes a precedent for the next, which excludes hereditary succession. Saul was by lot, yet the succession was not hereditary, neither does it appear from that transaction that there was any intention it ever should. If the first king of any country was by election, that likewise establishes a precedent for the next; for to say, that the right of all future generations is taken away, by the act of the first electors, in their choice not only of a king but of a family of kings for ever, hath no parallel in or out of scripture but the doctrine of original sin, which supposes the free will of all men lost in Adam; and from such comparison, and it will admit of no other, hereditary succession can derive no glory. For as in

Adam all sinned, and as in the first electors all men obeyed; as in the one all mankind were subjected to Satan, and in the other to sovereignty; as our innocence was lost in the first, and our authority in the last; and as both disable us from re-assuming some former state and privilege, it unanswerably follows that original sin and hereditary succession are parallels. Dishonorable rank! inglorious connection! yet the must subtle sophist cannot produce a juster simile.

As to usurpation, no man will be so hardy as to defend it; and that William the Conqueror was an usurper is a fact not to be contradicted. The plain truth is, that the antiquity of English monarchy will not bear looking into.

But it is not so much the absurdity as the evil of hereditary succession which concerns mankind. Did it ensure a race of good and wise men it would have the seal of divine authority, but as it opens a door to the *foolish*, the *wicked*, and the *improper*, it has in it the nature of oppression. Men who look upon themselves born to reign, and others to obey, soon grow insolent. Selected from the rest of mankind, their minds are early poisoned by importance; and the world they act in differs so materially from the world at large, that they have but little opportunity of knowing its true interests, and when they succeed to the government are frequently the most ignorant and unfit of any throughout the dominions.

Another evil which attends hereditary succession is, that the throne is subject to be possessed by a minor at any age; all which time the regency acting under the cover of a king have every opportunity and inducement to betray their trust. The same national misfortune happens when a king worn out with age and infirmity enters the last stage of human weakness. In both these cases the public becomes a prey to every miscreant who can tamper successfully with the follies either of age or infancy.

The most plausible plea which hath ever been offered in favor of hereditary succession is, that it preserves a nation from civil wars; and were this true, it would be weighty; whereas it is the most bare-faced falsity ever imposed upon mankind. The whole history of England disowns the fact. Thirty kings and two minors have reigned in that distracted kingdom since the conquest, in which time there has been (including the revolution) no less than eight civil wars and nineteen Rebellions. Wherefore instead of making for peace, it makes against it, and destroys the very foundation it seems to stand upon. . . .

In England a King hath little more to do than to make war and give away places; which, in plain terms, is to impoverish the nation and set it together by the ears. A pretty business indeed for a man to be allowed eight hundred thousand sterling a year for, and worshipped into the bargain! Of more worth is one honest man to society, and in the sight of God, than all the crowned ruffians that ever lived.

Thoughts on the Present State of American Affairs

. . . . . .

I challenge the warmest advocate for reconciliation to show a single advantage that this continent can reap by being connected with Great Britain. I repeat the challenge; not a single advantage is derived. Our corn will fetch its price in any market in Europe, and our imported goods must be paid for buy them where we will.

But the injuries and disadvantages which we sustain by that connection, are without number; and our duty to mankind at large, as well as to ourselves, instructs us to renounce the alliance: because, any submission to, or dependence on, Great Britain, tends directly to involve this Continent in European wars and quarrels, and set us at variance with nations who would otherwise seek our friendship, and against whom we have neither anger nor complaint. As Europe is our market for trade, we ought to form no partial connection with any part of it. It is the true interest of America to steer clear of European contentions, which she never can do, while, by her dependence on Britain, she is made the make-weight in the scale of British politics.

Europe is too thickly planted with Kingdoms to be long at peace, and whenever a war breaks out between England and any foreign power, the trade of America goes to ruin, *because of her connection with Britain*. The next war may not turn out like the last, and should it not, the advocates for reconciliation now will be wishing for separation then, because neutrality in that case would be a safer convoy than a man of war. Every thing that is right or reasonable pleads for separation. The blood of the slain, the weeping voice of nature cries, 'TIS TIME TO PART. Even the distance at which the Almighty hath placed England and America is a strong and natural proof that the authority of the one over the other, was never the design of Heaven. The time likewise at which the Continent was discovered, adds weight to the argument, and the manner in which it was peopled, encreases the force of it. The Reformation was preceded by the discovery of America: As if the Almighty graciously meant to open a sanctuary to the persecuted in future years, when home should afford neither friendship nor safety.

The authority of Great Britain over this continent, is a form of government, which sooner or later must have an end: And a serious mind can draw no true pleasure by looking forward, under the painful and positive conviction that what he calls "the present constitution" is merely temporary. As parents, we can have no joy, knowing that this government is not sufficiently lasting to ensure any thing which we may bequeath to posterity: And by a plain method of argument, as we are running the next generation into debt, we ought to do the work of it, otherwise we use them meanly and pitifully. In order to discover the line of our duty rightly, we should take our children in our hand, and fix our station a few years farther into life; that eminence will present a prospect which a few present fears and prejudices conceal from our sight.

Thought I would carefully avoid giving unnecessary offence, yet I am inclined to believe, that all those who espouse the doctrine of reconciliation, may be included within the following descriptions.

Interested men, who are not to be trusted, weak men who *cannot* see, prejudiced men who will not see, and a certain set of moderate men who think better of the European world than it deserves; and this last class, by an ill-judged deliberation, will be the cause of more calamities to this Continent than all the other three.

It is the good fortune of many to live distant from the scene of present sorrow; the evil is not sufficiently brought to their doors to make them feel the precariousness with which all American property is possessed. But let our imaginations transport us a few moments to Boston; that seat of wretchedness

will teach us wisdom, and instruct us for ever to renounce a power in whom
we can have no trust. The inhabitants of that unfortunate city who but a
few months ago were in ease and affluence, have now no other alternative than
to stay and starve, or turn out to beg. Endangered by the fire of their friends
if they continue within the city, and plundered by the soldiery if they leave it,
in their present situation they are prisoners without the hope of redemption,
and in a general attack for their relief they would be exposed to the fury of
both armies.

Men of passive tempers look somewhat lightly over the offences of Great
Britain, and, still hoping for the best, are apt to call out, *Come, come, we shall
be friends again for all this.* But examine the passions and feelings of mankind:
bring the doctrine of reconciliation to the touchstone of nature, and then tell
me whether you can hereafter love, honour, and faithfully serve the power
that hath carried fire and sword into your land? If you cannot do all these,
then are you only deceiving yourselves, and by your delay bringing ruin upon
posterity. Your future connection with Britain, whom you can neither love
nor honour, will be forced and unnatural, and being formed only on the plan
of present convenience, will in a little time fall into a relapse more wretched
than the first. But if you say, you can still pass the violations over, then I
ask, hath your house been burnt? Hath your property been destroyed before
your face? Are your wife and children destitute of a bed to lie on, or bread to
live on? Have you lost a parent or a child by their hands, and yourself the
ruined and wretched survivor? If you have not, then are you not a judge of
those who have. But if you have, and can still shake hands with the murder-
ers, then are you unworthy the name of husband, father, friend, or lover, and
whatever may be your rank or title in life, you have the heart of a coward, and
the spirit of a sycophant.

DANIEL LEONARD

Daniel Leonard was an aristocratic Boston lawyer and one of the ablest exponents
of the Tory cause. Under the pen name of "Massachusettensis," he wrote weekly
letters addressed to "the Inhabitants of the Province of Massachusetts." These appeared from December 12, 1774, to April 3, 1775. It was in reply to these letters that
John Adams wrote as "Novanglus." A wide knowledge of English law and the influence of Hobbesian absolutism are conspicuous in Leonard's work.

MASSACHUSETTENSIS [51]

. . . . . .

No. 5

ADDRESSED

To the Inhabitants of the Province of Massachusetts,
January 9, 1775.

My Dear Countrymen,

Some of you may perhaps suspect that I have been wantonly scattering
firebrands, arrows, and death, to gratify a malicious and revengeful disposition. The truth is this. I had seen many excellent detached pieces, but could

[51] J. Adams and D. Leonard, *Novanglus and Massachusettensis.* (Boston, Hews and
Goss, 1819), pp. 168-173, 173-178, 187-188.

see no pen at work to trace our calamity to its source, and point out the many adventitious aids, that conspired to raise it to its present height, though I impatiently expected it, being fully convinced that you wait only to know the true state of facts, to rectify whatever is amiss in the province, without any foreign assistance. Others may be induced to think, that I grudge the industrious poor of Boston of their scantlings of charity. I will issue a brief in their favour. The opulent, be their political sentiments what they may, ought to relieve them from their sufferings, and those who, by former donations, have been the innocent cause of protracting their sufferings, are under a tenfold obligation to assist them now; and at the same time to make the most explicit declarations, that they did not intend to promote, nor ever will join in rebellion. Great allowances are to be made for the crossings, windings, and tergiversations of a politician; he is a cunning animal, and as government is said to be founded in opinion, his tricks may be a part of the *arcana imperii*. Had our politicians confined themselves within any reasonable bounds, I never should have molested them; but when I became satisfied, that many innocent, unsuspecting persons were in danger of being seduced to their utter ruin, and the province of Massachusetts Bay in danger of being drenched with blood and carnage, I could restrain my emotions no longer; and having once broke the bands of natural reserve, was determined to probe the sore to the bottom, though I was sure to touch the quick. It is very foreign from my intentions to draw down the vengeance of Great Britain upon the whigs; they are too valuable a part of the community to lose, if they will permit themselves to be saved. I wish nothing worse to the highest of them, than that they may be deprived of their influence, till such time as they shall have changed their sentiments, principles, and measures.

Sedition has already been marked through its zigzag path to the present times. When the statute for regulating the government arrived, a match was put to the train, and the mine, that had been long forming, sprung, and threw the whole province into confusion and anarchy. The occurrencies of the summer and autumn past are so recent and notorious, that a particular detail of them is unnecessary. Suffice it to say, that every barrier that civil government had erected for the security of property, liberty and life, was broken down, and law, constitution and government trampled under foot by the rudest invaders. I shall not dwell upon these harsh notes much longer. I shall yet become an advocate for the leading whigs; much must be allowed to men, in their situation, forcibly actuated by the chagrin of disappointment, the fear of punishment, and the fascination of hope at the same time.

Perhaps the whole story of empire does not furnish another instance of a forcible opposition to government, with so much apparent and little real cause, with such apparent probability without any possibility of success. The stamp-act gave the alarm. The instability of the public councils from the Greenvillian administration to the appointment of the Earl of Hillsborough to the American department, afforded as great a prospect of success, as the heavy duties imposed by the stamp-act, did a colour for the opposition. It was necessary to give the history of this matter in its course, offend who it would, because those acts of government, that are called the greatest grievances, became proper and necessary, through the misconduct of our politicians, and the justice of Great Britain towards us, could not be made apparent without first pointing out that. I intend to consider the acts of the British government, which are held up as the principal grievances, and inquire whether Great Britain is chargeable with injustice in any one of them; but must first ask your attention to the authority of parliament. I suspect many of our politicians are wrong in their first principle, in denying that the constitutional authority of parliament extends to the colonies; if so, it must not be wondered at, that their whole fabric is so ruinous. I shall not travel through all the arguments that have been adduced, for and against this question, but attempt to reduce the substance of them to a narrow compass, after having taken a cursory view of the British constitution.

The security of the people from internal rapacity and violence, and from foreign invasion, is the end and design of government. The simple forms of government are monarchy, aristocracy, and democracy; that is, where the authority of the state is vested in one, a few, or the many. Each of these species of government has advantages peculiar to itself, and would answer the ends of government, where the persons intrusted with the authority of the state, always guided, themselves, by unerring wisdom and public virtue; but rulers are not always exempt from the weakness and depravity which make government necessary to society. Thus monarchy is apt to rush headlong into tyranny, aristocracy to beget faction, and multiplied usurpation, and democracy, to degenerate into tumult, violence, and anarchy. A government formed upon these three principles, in due proportion, is the best calculated to answer the ends of government, and to endure. Such a government is the British constitution, consisting of king, lords and commons, which at once includes the principal excellencies, and excludes the principal defects of the other kinds of government. It is allowed, both by Englishmen and foreigners, to be the most perfect system that the wisdom of ages has produced. The distributions of power are so just, and the proportions so exact, as at once to support and controul each other. An Englishman glories in being subject to, and protected by such a government. The colonies are a part of the British empire. The best writers upon the law of nations tell us, that when a nation takes possession of a distant country, and settles there, that country, though separated from the principal establishment, or mother country, naturally becomes a part of the state, equal with its ancient possessions. Two supreme or independent authorities cannot exist in the same state. It would be what is called *imperium in imperio*, the height of political absurdity. The analogy between the political and human body is great. Two independent authorities in a state would be like two distinct principles of volition and action in the human body, dissenting, opposing, and destroying each other. If, then, we are a part of the British empire, we must be subject to the supreme power of the state, which is vested in the estates of parliament, notwithstanding each of the colonies have legislative and executive powers of their own, delegated, or granted to them for the purposes of regulating their own internal police, which are subordinate to, and must necessarily be subject to the checks, controul, and regulation of the supreme authority.

This doctrine is not new, but the denial of it is. It is beyond a doubt, that it was the sense both of the parent country, and our ancestors, that they were to remain subject to parliament. It is evident from the charter itself; and this authority has been exercised by parliament, from time to time, almost ever since the first settlement of the country, and has been expressly acknowledged by our provincial legislatures. It is not less our interest, than our duty, to continue subject to the authority of parliament, which will be more fully considered hereafter. The principal argument against the authority of parliament, is this; the Americans are entitled to all the privileges of an Englishman; it is the privilege of an Englishman to be exempt from all laws, that he does not consent to in person, or by representative. The Americans are not represented in parliament, and therefore are exempt from acts of parliament, or in other words, not subject to its authority. This appears specious; but leads to such absurdities as demonstrate its fallacy. If the colonies are not subject to the authority of parliament, Great Britain and the colonies must be distinct states, as completely so, as England and Scotland were before the union, or as Great Britain and Hanover are now. The colonies in that case will owe no allegiance to the imperial crown, and perhaps not to the person of the king, as the title to the crown is derived from an act of parliament, made since the settlement of this province, which act respects the imperial crown only. Let us waive this difficulty, and suppose allegiance due from the colonies to the person of the king of Great Britain. He then appears in a new capacity, of king of America, or rather in several new capacities, of king of Massachusetts, king of Rhode-Island, king of Connecticut, &c. &c. For if our connexion with Great Britain by the parliament be dissolved, we shall have none among ourselves, but each colony become as distinct from the others, as England was from Scotland, before the union. Some have supposed that each state, having one and the same person for its king, is a sufficient connection. Were he an absolute monarch, it might be; but in a mixed government, it is no union at all. For as the king must govern each state, by its parliament, those several parliaments would pursue the particular interest of its own state; and however well disposed the king might be to pursue a line of interest, that was common to all, the checks and controul that he would meet with, would render it impossible. If the king of Great Britain has really these new capacities, they ought to be added to his titles; and another difficulty will arise, the prerogatives of these new crowns have never been defined or limited. Is the monarchical part of the several provincial constitutions to be nearer or more remote from absolute monarchy, in an inverted ratio to each one's approaching to, or receding from a republic? But let us suppose the same prerogatives inherent in the several American crowns, as are in the imperial crown of Great Britain, where shall we find the British constitution, that we all agree we are entitled to? We shall seek for it in vain in our provincial assemblies. They are but faint sketches of the estates of parliament. The house of representatives, or Burgesses, have not all the powers of the house of commons; in the charter governments they have no more than what is expressly granted by their several charters. The first charters granted to this province did not empower the assembly to tax the people at all. Our council boards are as destitute of the constitutional authority of the house of lords, as their several members are of the noble independence, and splendid appendages of peerage. The house of peers is the bulwark of the British constitution, and through successive ages, has withstood the shocks of monarchy, and the sappings of democracy, and the constitution gained strength by the conflict. Thus the supposition of our being independent states, or exempt from the authority of parliament, destroys the very idea of our having a British constitution. The provincial constitutions, considered as subordinate, are generally well adapted to those purposes of government, for which they were intended; that is, to regulate the internal police of the several colonies; but have no principle of stability within themselves; they may support themselves in moderate times, but would be merged by the violence of turbulent ones, and the several colonies become wholly monarchical, or wholly republican, were it not for the checks, controuls, regulations, and supports of the supreme authority of the empire. Thus the argument, that is drawn from their first principle of our being entitled to English liberties, destroys the principle itself, it deprives us of the bill of rights, and all the benefits resulting from the revolution of English laws, and of the British constitution.

Our patriots have been so intent upon building up American rights, that they have overlooked the rights of Great Britain, and our own interest. Instead of proving that we were entitled to privileges, that our fathers knew our situation would not admit us to enjoy, they have been arguing away our most essential rights. If there be any grievance, it does not consist in our being subject to the authority of parliament, but in our not having an actual representation in it. Were it possible for the colonies to have an equal representation in parliament, and were refused it upon proper application, I confess I should think it a grievance; but at present it seems to be allowed, by all parties, to be impracticable, considering the colonies are distant from Great Britain a thousand transmarine leagues. If that be the case, the right or privilege, that we complain of being deprived of, is not withheld by Britain, but the first principles of government, and the immutable laws of nature, render it impossible for us to enjoy it. This is apparently the meaning of that celebrated passage in Governor Hutchinson's letter, that rang through the continent, viz: There must be an abridgment of what is called English liberties. He subjoins, that he had never yet seen the projection, whereby a colony, three thousand miles distant from the parent state, might enjoy all the privileges of the parent state, and remain subject to it, or in words to that effect. The obnoxious sentence, taken detached from the letter, appears very unfriendly to the colonies; but considered in connection with the other parts of the letter, is but a necessary result of our situation. Allegiance and protection are reciprocal. It is our highest interest to continue a part of the British empire; and equally our duty to remain subject to the authority of parliament. Our own internal police may generally be regulated by our provincial legislatures, but in national concerns, or where our own assemblies do not answer the ends of government with respect to ourselves, the ordinances or interposition of the great council of the nation is necessary. In this case, the major must rule the minor. After many more centuries shall have rolled away, long after we, who are now bustling upon the stage of life, shall have been received to the bosom of mother earth, and our names are forgotten, the colonies may be so far increased as to have the balance of wealth, numbers and power, in their favor, the good of the empire makes it necessary to fix the seat of government here; and some future George, equally the friend of mankind, with him that now sways the British sceptre, may cross the Atlantic, and rule Great Britain, by an American parliament.

MASSACHUSETTENSIS.

No. 6

ADDRESSED

To the Inhabitants of the Province of Massachusetts Bay, January 16, 1775.

My Dear Countrymen,

Had a person, some fifteen years ago, undertaken to prove that the colonies were a part of the British empire or dominion, and as such, subject to the authority of the British parliament, he would have acted as ridiculous a part, as to have undertaken to prove a self-evident proposition. Had any person denied it, he would have been called a fool or madman. At this wise period, individuals and bodies of men deny it, notwithstanding in doing it they subvert the fundamentals of government, deprive us of British liberties, and build up absolute monarchy in the colonies; for our charters suppose regal authority in the grantor; if that authority be derived from the British crown, it pre-supposes this territory to have been a part of the British dominion, and as such subject to the imperial sovereign; if that authority was vested in the person of the king, in a different capacity, the British constitution and laws are out of the question, and the king must be absolute as to us, as his prerogatives have never been circumscribed. Such must have been the sovereign authority of the several kings, who have granted American charters, previous to the several grants; there is nothing to detract from it, at this time, in those colonies that are destitute of charters, and the charter governments must severally revert to absolute monarchy, as their charters may happen to be forfeited by the grantees not fulfilling the conditions of them, as every charter contains an express or implied condition.

It is curious indeed to trace the denial and oppugnation to the supreme authority of the state. When the stamp-act was made, the authority of parliament to impose internal taxes was denied; but their right to impose external ones, or in other words, to lay duties upon goods and merchandize was admitted. When the act was made imposing duties upon tea, &c. a new distinction was set up, that the parliament had a right to lay duties upon merchandize for the purpose of regulating trade, but not for the purpose of raising a revenue: that is, the parliament had good right and lawful authority to lay the former duty of a shilling on the pound, but had none to lay the present duty of three pence. Having got thus far safe, it was only taking one step more to extricate ourselves entirely from their fangs, and become independent states, that our patriots most heroically resolved upon, and flatly denied that parliament had a right to make any laws whatever, that should be binding upon the colonies. There is no possible medium between absolute independence, and subjection to the authority of parliament. He must be blind indeed that cannot see our dearest interest in the latter, notwithstanding many pant after the former. Misguided men! could they once overtake their wish, they would be convinced of the madness of the pursuit.

My dear countrymen, it is of the last importance that we settle this point clearly in our minds; it will serve as a sure test, certain criterion and in-variable standard to distinquish the friends from the enemies of our country, patriotism from sedition, loyalty from rebellion. To deny the supreme authority of the state, is a high misdemeanor, to say no worse of it; to oppose it by force is an overt act of treason, punishable by confiscation of estate, and most ignominious death. The realm of England is an appropriate term for the ancient realm of England, in contradistinction to Wales and other territories, that have been annexed to it. These as they have been severally annexed to the crown, whether by conquest or otherwise, became a part of the empire, and subject to the authority of parliament, whether they send members to parlia-ment or not, and whether they have legislative powers of their own or not.

Thus Ireland, who has perhaps the greatest possible subordinate legisla-ture, and sends no members to the British parliament, is bound by its acts, when expressly named. Guernsey and Jersey are no part of the realm of England, nor are they represented in parliament, but are subject to its authority: and, in the same predicament are the American colonies, and all the other dispersions of the empire. Permit me to request your attention to this subject a little longer; I assure you it is as interesting and important, as it is dry and unentertaining.

Let us now recur to the first charter of this province, and we shall find irresistible evidence, that our being part of the empire, subject to the supreme authority of the state, bound by its laws and entitled to its protection, were the very terms and conditions by which our ancestors held their lands, and settled the province. Our charter, like all other American charters, is under the great seal of England; the grants are made by the king, for his heirs and *successors;* the several tenures to be of the king, his heirs and *successors;* in like manner are the reservations. It is apparent the king acted in his royal capacity, as king of England, which necessarily supposes the territory granted, to be a part of the English dominions, holden of the crown of England.

The charter, after reciting several grants of the territory to sir Henry Roswell and others, proceeds to incorporation in these words: "And of as much as the good and prosperous success of the plantations of the said parts of New England aforesaid, intended by the said sir Henry Roswell and others, to be speedily set upon, cannot but chiefly depend, next under the blessing of almighty God, and the support of our royal authority, upon the good govern-ment of the same, to the end that the *affairs of business,* which from time to time shall happen and arise concerning the said lands and the plantations of the same may be the better managed and ordered, we have further hereby, of our especial grace, certain knowledge and mere motion given, granted and confirmed, and for us, our heirs and successors, do give, grant and confirm unto our said trusty and well beloved subjects, sir Henry Roswell, &c. and all such others as shall hereafter be admitted and made free of *the company and society hereafter mentioned,* shall from time to time and at all times, forever hereafter, be by virtue of these presents, *one body corporate, politic in fact and name by the name of the governor and company of the Massachusetts Bay, in New England;* and them by the name of the governor and company of the Massachusetts Bay, in New England, one body politic and corporate in deed, fact and name. We do for us our heirs and successors make, ordain, constitute and confirm by these presents, and that by that name they and their successors shall be capable and enabled as well *to implead and to be implead, and to prosecute, demand and answer and be answered unto all and singular suits, causes, quarrels and actions of what kind or nature soever; and also to have, take, possess, acquire and purchase, any lands, tenements and hereditaments, or any goods or chattels, the same to lease, grant, demise, aleine, bargain, sell and dispose of as our liege people of this our realm of England, or any other corporation or body politic of the same may do."* I would beg leave to ask one simple question, whether this looks like a distinct state or independent empire? Provision is then made for electing a governor, deputy governor, and eighteen assistants. After which, is this clause: "We do for us, our heirs and successors, give and grant to the said governor and company, and their successors, that the governor or in his absense the deputy governor of the said company, for the time being, and such of the assistants or freemen of the said company as shall be present, or the great number of them so assembled, whereof the governor or deputy governor and six of the assistants, at the least to be seven, shall have full power and authority to choose, nominate and appoint such and so many others as they shall think fit, and shall be willing to accept the same, to be free of the said company and body, and them into the same to admit and elect and constitute such officers as they shall think fit and requisite for the ordering, managing and dispatching of the affairs of the said governor and company and their successors, and to make *laws and ordinances for the good and welfare of the said company,* and for the government and ordering of the said lands and plantations, and the people inhabiting and to inhabit the same, as to them from time to time shall be thought meet: *So as such laws and ordinances be not contrary or repugnant to the laws and statutes of this our realm of England."*

Another clause is this, "And for their further encouragement, of our especial grace and favor, we do by these presents, for us, our heirs, and successors, and every of them, their factors and assigns, that they and every of them shall be free and quit from all taxes, subsidies and customs in New England for the space of seven years, and from all taxes and impositions for the space of twenty-one years, upon all goods and merchandize, at any time or times hereafter, either upon importation thither, or exportation from thence into our realm of England, or into other of our dominions, by the said governor and company and their successors, their deputies, factors, and assigns, &c."

The exemption from taxes for seven years in one case, and twenty one years in the other, plainly indicates that after their expiration, this province would be liable to taxation. Now I would ask by what authority those taxes were to be imposed? It could not be by the governor and company, for no such power was delegated or granted to them; and besides it would have been absurd and nugatory to exempt them from their own taxation, supposing them to have had the power, for they might have exempted themselves. It must therefore be by the king or parliament; it could not be by the king alone, for as king of England, the political capacity in which he granted the charter, he had no such power, exclusive of the lords and commons, consequently it must have been by the parliament. This clause in the charter is as evident a recognition of the authority of the parliament over this province, as if the words, "acts of parliament," had been inserted, as they were in the Pennsylvania charter. There was no session of parliament after the grant of our charter until the year 1640. In 1642 the house of commons passed a resolve, "that for the better advancement of the plantations in New England, and the encouragement of the planters to proceed in their undertakings, their exports and imports should be freed and discharged from all customs, subsidies, taxations and duties until the further order of the house"; which was gratefully received and recorded in the archives of our predecessors. This transaction shews very clearly in what sense our connection with England was then understood. It is true, that in some arbitrary reigns, attempts were made by the servants of the crown to exclude the two houses of parliament, from any share of the authority over the colonies; they also attempted to render the king absolute in England; but the parliament always rescued the colonies, as well as England from such attempts.

I shall recite but one more clause of this charter, which is this, "And further our will and pleasure is, and we do hereby for us, our heirs and successors, ordain, declare and grant to the said governor and company, and their successors, that all and every of the subjects of us, our heirs and successors which shall go to and inhabit within the said land and premises hereby mentioned to be granted, and every of their children which shall happen to be born there, or on the seas in going thither, or returning from thence, shall have and enjoy *all liberties and immunities of free and natural subjects, within any of the dominions of us*, our heirs or successors, to all intents, constructions and purposes whatsoever, as if they and every of them were born within the realm of England." It is upon this, or a similar clause in the charter of William and Mary that our patriots have built up the stupendous fabric of American independence. They argue from it a total exemption from parliamentary authority, because we are not represented in parliament.

I have already shewn that the supposition of our being exempt from the authority of parliament, is pregnant with the grossest absurdities. Let us now consider this clause in connection with the other parts of the charter. It is a rule of law, founded in reason and common sense, to construe each part of an instrument, so as the whole may hang together, and be consistent with itself. If we suppose this clause to exempt us from the authority of parliament, we must throw away all the rest of the charter, for every other part indicates the contrary, as plainly as words can do it; and what is still worse, this clause becomes *felo de se*, and destroys itself; for if we are not annexed to the crown, we are aliens, and no charter, grant, or other act of the crown can naturalize us or entitle us to the liberties and immunities of Englishmen. It can be done only by act of parliament. An alien is one born in a strange country out of the allegiance of the king, and is under many disabilities though resident in the realm; as Wales, Jersey, Guernsey, Ireland, the foreign plantations, &c. were severally annexed to the crown, they became parts of one and the same empire, the natives of which are equally free as though they had been born in that territory which was the ancient realm. As our patriots depend upon this clause, detached from the charter, let us view it in that light. If a person born in England removes to Ireland and settles there, he is then no longer represented in the British parliament, but he and his posterity are, and will ever be subject to the authority of the British parliament. If he removes to Jersey, Guernsey, or any other parts of the

British dominions that send no members to parliament, he will still be in the same predicament. So that the inhabitants of the American colonies do in fact enjoy all the liberties and immunities of natural born subjects. We are entitled to no greater privileges than those that are born within the realm; and they can enjoy no other than we do, when they reside out of it. Thus, it is evident that this clause amounts to no more than the royal assurance, that we are a part of the British empire; are not aliens, but natural born subjects; and as such, bound to obey the supreme power of the state, and entitled to protection from it. To avoid prolixity, I shall not remark particularly upon other parts of this charter, but observe in general, that whoever reads it with attention, will meet with irresistible evidence in every part of it, that our being a part of the English dominions, subject to the English crown, and within the jurisdiction of parliament, were the terms upon which our ancestors settled this colony, and the very tenures by which they held their estates.

No lands within the British dominions are perfectly allodial; they are held mediately or immediately of the king, and upon forfeiture, revert to the crown. My dear countrymen, you have many of you been most falsely and wickedly told by our patriots, that Great Britain was meditating a land tax, and seeking to deprive us of our inheritance; but had all the malice and subtilty of men and devils been united, a readier method to effect it could not have been devised, than the late denials of the authority of parliament, and forcible oppositions to its acts. Yet, this has been planned and executed chiefly by persons of desperate fortunes.

MASSACHUSETTENSIS.

No. 9

ADDRESSED

TO THE INHABITANTS OF THE PROVINCE OF MASSACHUSETTS BAY,
February 6, 1775.

My Dear Countrymen,

When we reflect upon the constitutional connection between Great Britain and the colonies, view the reciprocation of interest, consider that the welfare of Britain, in some measure, and the prosperity of America wholly depends upon that connection; it is astonishing, indeed, almost incredible, that one person should be found on either side of the Atlantic, so base, and destitute of every sentiment of justice, as to attempt to destroy or weaken it. If there are none such, in the name of Almighty God, let me ask, wherefore is rebellion, that implacable fiend to society, suffered to rear its ghastly front among us, blasting, with haggard look, each social joy, and embittering every hour?

Rebellion is the most atrocious offence, that can be perpetrated by man, save those which are committed more immediately against the supreme Governor of the Universe, who is the avenger of his own cause. It dissolves the social band, annihilates the security resulting from law and government; introduces fraud, violence, rapine, murder, sacrilege, and the long train of evils, that riot, uncontrouled, in a state of nature. Allegiance and protection are reciprocal. The subject is bound by the compact to yield obedience to government, and in return, is entitled to protection from it; thus the poor are protected against the rich; the weak against the strong; the individual against the many; and this protection is guaranteed to each member, by the whole community. But when government is laid prostrate, a state of war, of all against all commences; might overcomes right; innocence itself has no security, unless the individual sequesters himself from his fellowmen, inhabits his own cave, and seeks his own prey. This is what is called a state of nature. I once thought it chimerical. . . .

JONATHAN BOUCHER

Jonathan Boucher came to Virginia in 1759 as a private tutor and later became an Anglican minister in Virginia and Maryland. From the first, he found the manners and conversation of the colonists distasteful. That he never found himself wholly at one with his associates in the colonies was, in a large measure, the cause of his later misfortunes. He was a firm supporter of established authority. He had no use for democracy and liberty; and he said so. He employed his pulpit to preach against the colonial demand for home rule. When the provincial convention proclaimed a solemn fast-day by way of protest against the British policy, he announced his intention of preaching against active resistance. A body of armed men, however, forbade him to enter his pulpit. From then on, believing his life in danger, he never preached without a pair of loaded pistols on the cushion. His popularity waned rapidly, until he was burned in effigy. In September, 1775, the hostility of his pastorate drove him out of the colonies. In 1797 he collected thirteen of the sermons that he had preached in America between 1763 and 1775. This work, *A View of the Causes and Consequences of the American Revolution*, is probably the best attack upon the revolutionary natural rights philosophy. Boucher derived his patriarchal theory of government from Filmer's *Patriarcha*, in which that writer had defended the Stuart autocracy against the Puritan revolution.

A VIEW OF THE CAUSES AND CONSEQUENCES OF THE AMERICAN REVOLUTION.[52]

Discourse XII

On Civil Liberty; Passive Obedience, and Non-Resistance
GALATIANS, CH. V. VER. I.

Stand Fast, Therefore, in the Liberty Wherewith Christ Hath Made Us Free.

. . . . . .

As the liberty here spoken of respected the Jews, it denoted an exemption from the burthersome services of the ceremonial law: as it respected the Gentiles, it meant a manumission from bondage under the *weak and beggarly elements of the world*, and an admission into the covenant of grace: and as it respected both in common, it meant a freedom from the servitude of sin. Every sinner is, literally, a slave; for, *his servants ye are, to whom ye obey:*— and the only true liberty is the liberty of being the servants of God; for, *his service is perfect freedom*. The passage cannot, without infinite perversion and torture, be made to refer to any other kind of liberty; much less to

[52] Jonathan Boucher, *A View of the Causes and Consequences of the American Revolution; in Thirteen Discourses Preached in North America between the Years 1763 and 1775.* (London, 1797), pp. 504–534, 545–546.

that liberty of which every man now talks, though few understand it. However common this term has been, or is, in the mouths chiefly of those persons who are as little distinguished for the accuracy as they are for the paucity of their words; and whatever influence it has had on the affairs of the world, it is remarkable that it is never used (at least not in any such sense as it is elsewhere used) in any of the laws either of God or men. Let a minister of God, then, stand excused if (taught by him who knoweth what is fit and good for us better than we ourselves, and is *wont also to give us more than either we desire or deserve*) he seeks not to amuse you by any flowery panegyrics on liberty. Such panegyrics are the productions of ancient heathens and modern patriots: nothing of the kind is to be met with in the Bible, nor in the Statute Book. The word *liberty*, as meaning civil liberty, does not, I believe, occur in all the Scriptures. With the aid of a concordance I find only two or three passages, in two apocryphal writers, that look at all like it. In the xivth chapter and 26th verse of the 1st Maccabees, the people are said to owe much gratitude to Simon, the high-priest, for having renewed a friendship and league with the Lacedemonians, confirmed the league with the Romans, established Israel, and *confirmed their liberty*. But it is evident that this expression means, not that the Jews were then to be exempted from any injunctions, or any restraints, imposed upon them by their own lawful government; but only that they were delivered from a foreign jurisdiction and from tributary payments, and left free to live under the law of Moses. The only circumstance relative to government, for which the Scriptures seem to be particularly solicitous, is in inculcating obedience to lawful governors, as well knowing where the true danger lies. Nevertheless, as occasion has lately been taken from this text, on which I am now to discourse, to treat largely on civil liberty and government, (though for no other reason that appears but that the word *liberty* happens to stand in the text,) I entreat your indulgence, whilst, without too nicely scrutinizing the propriety of deducing from a text a doctrine which it clearly does not suggest, I once more adopt a plan already chalked out for me, and deliver to you what occurs to me as proper for a Christian audience to attend to on the subject of Liberty.

It has just been observed, that liberty inculcated in the Scriptures, (and which alone the Apostle had in view in this text,) is wholly of the spiritual or religious kind. This liberty was the natural result of the new religion in which mankind were then instructed; which certainly gave them no new civil privileges. They remained subject to the governments under which they lived, just as they had been before they became Christians, and just as others were who never became Christians; with this difference only, that the duty of submission and obedience to Government was enjoined on the converts to Christianity with new and stronger sanctions. The doctrines of the Gospel make no manner of alteration in the nature or form of Civil Government; but enforce afresh, upon all Christians, that obedience which is due to the respective Constitutions of every nation in which they may happen to live. Be the supreme power lodged in one or in many, be the kind of government established in any country absolute or limited, this is not the concern of the Gospel. Its single object, with respect to these public duties, is to enjoin obedience to the laws of every country, in every kind or form of government.

The only liberty or freedom which converts to Christianity could hope to gain by becoming Christians, was the being exempted from sundry burthensome and servile Jewish ordinances, on the one hand and, on the other, from Gentile blindness and superstition. They were also in some measure perhaps made more *free* in the *inner man;* by being endowed with greater firmness of mind in the cause of truth, against the terrors and the allurements of the world; and with such additional strength and vigour as enabled them more effectually to resist the natural violence of their lust and passions. On all these accounts it was that our Saviour so emphatically told the Jews, that *the truth* (of which himself was now the preacher) would *make them free.* And on the same principle St. James terms the Gospel *the perfect law of liberty.*

In the infancy of Christianity, it would seem that some rumour had spread (probably by Judas of Galilee, who is mentioned in the Acts) that the Gospel was designed to undermine kingdoms and commonwealths; as if the intention of our Saviour's first coming had been the same with that which reserved for the second, viz. to *put down all rule, and all authority, and all power.* On this supposition the apparent solicitude of our Saviour and his Apostles, in their frequent and earnest recommendation of submission to *the higher powers,* is easily and naturally accounted for. Obedience to Government is every man's duty, because it is every man's interest: but it is particularly incumbent on Christians, because (in addition to its moral fitness) it is enjoined by the positive commands of God: and therefore, when Christians are disobedient to human ordinances, they are also disobedient to God. If the form of government under which the good providence of God has been pleased to place us be mild and free, it is our duty to enjoy it with gratitude and with thankfulness; and, in particular, to be careful not to abuse it by licentiousness. If it be less indulgent and less liberal than in reason it ought to be, still it is our duty not to disturb and destroy the peace of the community, by becoming refractory and rebellious subjects, and *resisting the ordinances of God.* However humiliating such acquiescence may seem to men of warm and eager minds, the wisdom of God in having made it our duty is manifest. For, as it is the natural temper and bias of the human mind to be impatient under restraint, it was wise and merciful in the blessed Author of our religion not to add any new impulse to the natural force of this prevailing propensity, but, with the whole weight of his authority, altogether to discountenance every tendency to disobedience.

If it were necessary to vindicate the Scriptures for this their total unconcern about a principle which so many other writings seem to regard as the first of all human considerations, it might be observed, that, avoiding the vague and declamatory manner of such writings, and avoiding also the useless and impracticable subtleties of metaphysical definitions, these Scriptures have better consulted the great general interests of mankind, by summarily recommending and enjoining a conscientious reverence for law whether human or divine. To respect the laws, is to respect liberty in the only rational sense in which the term can be used; for liberty consists in a subserviency to law. "Where there is no law," says Mr. Locke, "there is no freedom." The mere man of nature (if such an one there ever was) has no freedom: *all his lifetime he is subject to bondage.* It is by being included within the pale of civil polity and government that he takes his rank in society as a free man.

Hence it follows, that we are free, or otherwise, as we are governed by law, or by the mere arbitrary will, or wills, of any individual, or any number of individuals. And liberty is not the setting at nought and despising established laws—much less the making our own wills the rule of our own actions, or the actions of others—and not bearing (whilst yet we dictate to others) the being dictated to, even by the laws of the land; but it is the being governed by law, and by law only. The Greeks described Eleutheria, or Liberty, as the daughter of Jupiter, the supreme fountain of power and law. And the Romans, in like manner, always drew her with the pretor's wand, (the emblem of legal power and authority,) as well as with the cap. Their idea, no doubt, was, that liberty was the fair fruit of just authority, and that it consisted in men's being subjected to law. The more carefully well-devised restraints of law are enacted, and the more rigorously they are executed in any country; the greater degree of civil liberty does that country enjoy. To pursue liberty, then, in a manner not warranted by law, whatever the pretence may be, is clearly to be hostile to liberty: and those persons who thus *promise you liberty*, are themselves *the servants of corruption*.

"Civil liberty (says an excellent writer) is a severe and a restrained thing;
"implies, in the notion of it, authority, settled subordinations, subjection,
"and obedience; and is altogether as much hurt by too little of this kind,
"as by too much of it. And the love of liberty, when it is indeed the love
"of liberty, which carries us to withstand tyranny, will as much carry us to
"reverence authority, and to support it; for this most obvious reason, that
"one is as necessary to the being of liberty, as the other is destructive of
"it. And, therefore, the love of liberty which does not produce this effect,
"the love of liberty which is not a real principle of dutiful behavior towards
"authority, is as hypocritical as the religion which is not productive of a
"good life. Licentiousness is, in truth, such an excess of liberty as is of the
"same nature with tyranny. For, what is the difference betwixt them, but
"that one is lawless power exercised under the pretence of authority, or
"by persons vested with it; the other, lawless power exercised under pre-
"tence of liberty, or without any pretence at all? A people, then, must al-
"ways be less free in proportion as they are more licentious; licentiousness
"being not only different from liberty, but directly contrary to it—a direct
"breach upon it."

True liberty, then, is a liberty to do every thing that is right, and the being restrained from doing any thing that is wrong. So far from our having a right to do every thing that we please, under a notion of liberty, liberty itself is limited and confined—but limited and confined only by laws which are at the same time both its foundation and its support. It can, however, hardly be necessary to inform you, that ideas and notions respecting liberty, very different from these, are daily suggested in the speeches and the writings of the times; and also that some opinions on the subject of government at large, which appear to me to be particularly loose and dangerous, are advanced in the sermon now under consideration; and that, therefore, you will acknowledge the propriety of my bestowing some farther notice on them both.

It is laid down in this sermon, as a settled maxim, that the end of government is "the common good of mankind." I am not sure that the position itself is indisputable; but, if it were, it would by no means follow that, "this common good being matter of common feeling, government must therefore have been instituted by common consent." There is an appearance of logical accuracy and precision in this statement; but it is only an appearance. The position is vague and loose; and the assertion is made without an attempt to prove it. If by men's "common feelings" we are to understand that principle in the human mind called common sense, the assertion is either unmeaning and insignificant, or it is false. In no instance have mankind ever yet agreed as to what is, or is not, "the common good." A form or mode of government cannot be named, which these "common feelings" and "common consent," the sole arbiters, as it seems, of "common good," have not, at one time or another, set up and established, and again pulled down and reprobated. What one people in one age have concurred in establishing as the "common good," another in another age have voted to be mischievous and big with ruin. The premises, therefore, that "the common good is matter of common feeling," being false, the consequence drawn from it, viz. that government was instituted by "common consent," is of course equally false.

This popular notion, that government was originally formed by the consent or by a compact of the people, rests on, and is supported by, another similar notion, not less popular, nor better founded. This other notion is, that the whole human race is born equal; and that no man is naturally inferior, or, in any respect, subjected to another; and that he can be made subject to another only by his own consent. The position is equally ill-founded and false both in its premises and conclusions. In hardly any sense that can be imagined is the position strictly true; but, as applied to the case under consideration, it is demonstrably not true. Man differs from man in every thing that can be supposed to lead to supremacy and subjection, *as one star differs from another star in glory*. It was the purpose of the Creator, that man should be social: but, without government, there can be no society; nor, without some relative inferiority and superiority, can there be any government. A musical instrument composed of chords, keys, or pipes, all perfectly equal in size and power, might as well be expected to produce harmony, as a society composed of members all perfectly equal to be productive of order and peace. If (according to the idea of the advocates of this chimerical scheme of equality) no man could rightfully *be compelled to come in* and be a member even of a government to be formed by a regular compact, but by his own individual consent; it clearly follows, from the same principles, that neither could he rightfully be made or compelled to submit to the ordinances of any government already formed, to which he has not individually or actually consented. On the principle of equality, neither his parents, nor even the vote of a majority of the society, (however virtuously and honourably that vote might be obtained,) can have any such authority over any man. Neither can it be maintained that acquiescence implies consent; because acquiescence may have been extorted from impotence or incapacity. Even an explicit consent can bind a man no longer than he chooses to be bound. The same principle of equality that exempts him from being governed without his own consent, clearly entitles him to recall and resume that consent whenever he sees fit; and he alone has a right to judge when and for what reasons it may be resumed.

Any attempt, therefore, to introduce this fantastic system into practice, would reduce the whole business of social life to the wearisome, confused, and useless task of mankind's first expressing, and then withdrawing, their consent to an endless succession of schemes of government. Governments, though always forming, would never be completely formed: for, the majority to-day, might be the minority to-morrow; and, of course, that which is now fixed might and would be soon unfixed. Mr. Locke indeed says, that, "by con-"senting with others to make one body-politic under government, a man "puts himself under an obligation to every one of that society to submit to "the determination of the majority, and to be concluded by it." For the sake of the peace of society, it is undoubtedly reasonable and necessary that this should be the case: but, on the principles of the system now under consideration, before Mr. Locke or any of his followers can have authority to say that it actually is the case, it must be stated and proved that every individual man, on entering into the social compact, did first consent, and declare his consent, to be concluded and bound in all cases by the vote of the majority. In making such a declaration, he would certainly consult both his interest and his duty; but at the same time he would also completely relinquish the principle of equality, and eventually subject himself to the possibility of being governed by ignorant and corrupt tyrants. Mr. Locke himself afterwards disproves his own position respecting this supposed obligation to submit to the "determination of the majority," when he argues that a right of resistance still exists in the governed: for, what is resistance but a recalling and resuming the consent heretofore supposed to have been given, and in fact refusing to submit to the "determination of the majority"? It does not clearly appear what Mr. Locke exactly meant by what he calls "the determination of the majority": but the only rational and practical public manner of declaring "the determination of the majority," is by law: the laws, therefore, in all countries, even in those that are despotically governed, are to be regarded as the declared "determination of a majority" of the members of that community; because, in such cases, even acquiescence only must be looked upon as equivalent to a declaration. A right of resistance, therefore, for which Mr. Locke contends, is incompatible with the duty of submitting to the determination of "the majority," for which he also contends.

It is indeed impossible to carry into effect any government which, even by compact, might be framed with this reserved right of resistance. Accordingly there is no record that any such government ever was so formed. If there had, it must have carried the seeds of its decay in its very constitution. For, as those men who make a government (certain that they have the power) can have no hesitation to vote that they also have the right to unmake it; and as the people, in all circumstances, but more especially when trained to make and unmake governments, are at least as well disposed to do the latter as the former, it is morally impossible that there should be any thing like permanency or stability in a government so formed. Such a system, therefore, can produce only perpetual dissensions and contests, and bring back mankind to a supposed state of nature; arming every man's hand, like Ishmael's, against every man, and rendering the world an *aceldama*, or field of blood.—Such theories of government seem to give something like plausibility to the notions of those other modern theorists, who regard all governments as invasions of the natural rights of men, usurpations, and tyranny. On this principle it would follow, and could not be denied, that government was indeed fundamentally, as our people are sedulously taught it still is, an evil. Yet it is to government that mankind owe their having, after their fall and corruption, been again reclaimed, from a state of barbarity and war, to the conveniency and the safety of the social state: and it is by means of government that society is still preserved, the weak protected from the strong, and the artless and innocent from the wrongs of proud oppressors. It was not without reason, then, that Mr. Locke asserted, that a greater wrong cannot be done to prince and people, than is done by "propagating wrong notions concerning government."

Ashamed of this shallow device, that government originated in superior strength and violence, another party, hardly less numerous, and certainly not less confident than the former, fondly deduce it from some imaginary compact. They suppose that, in the decline perhaps of some fabulous age of gold, a multitude of human beings, who, like their brother beasts, had hitherto ranged the forests, *without guide, overseer, or ruler*—at length convinced, by experience, or the impossibility of living either alone with any degree of comfort or security, or together in society, with peace, without government, had (in some lucid interval of reason and reflection) met together in a spacious plain, for the express purpose of framing a government. Their first step must have been the transferring to some individual, or individuals, some of those rights which are supposed to have been inherent in each of them: of these it is essential to government that they should be divested; yet can they not, rightfully, be deprived of them, otherwise than by their own consent. Now, admitting this whole supposed assembly to be perfectly equal as to rights, yet all agreed as to the propriety of ceding some of them, on what principles of equality is it possible to determine, either who shall relinquish such a portion of his rights, or who shall be invested with such new accessory rights? By asking another to exercise jurisdiction over me, I clearly confess that I do not think myself his equal; and by his consenting to exercise such authority, he also virtually declares that he thinks himself superior. And, to establish this hypothesis of a compact, it is farther necessary that the whole assembly should concur in this opinion—a concurrence so extremely improbable, that it seems to be barely possible. The supposition that a large concourse of people, in a rude and imperfect state of society, or even a majority of them, should thus rationally and unanimously concur to subject themselves to various restrictions, many of them irksome and unpleasant, and all of them contrary to all their former habits, is to suppose them possessed of more wisdom and virtue than multitudes in any instance in real life have ever shewn. Another difficulty respecting this notion may yet be mentioned. Without a power of life and death, it will, I presume, be readily admitted that there could be no government. Now, admitting it to be possible that men, from motives of public and private utility, may be induced to submit to many heavy penalties, and even to corporal punishment, inflicted by the sentence of the law, there is an insuperable objection to any man's giving to another a power over his life: this objection is, that no man had such a power over his own life; and cannot therefore transfer to another, or to others, be they few or many, on any condition, a right which he does not himself possess. He only who gave life, can give the authority to take it away: and as such authority is essential to government, this argument seems very decidedly to prove, not only that government did not originate in any compact, but also that it was originally from God.

This visionary idea of a government by compact was, as Filmer says, "first hatched in the schools; and hath, ever since, been fostered by "Papists, for good divinity." For some time, the world seemed to regard it merely as another Utopian fiction; and it was long confined to the disciples of Rome and Geneva, who, agreeing in nothing else, yet agreed in this. In an evil hour it gained admittance into the Church of England; being first patronized by her during the civil wars, by "a few miscreants, who were as far from being true Protestants, as true Subjects." Mankind have listened, and continue to listen to it with a predilection and partiality, just as they do to various other exceptionable notions, which are unfavourable to true religion and sound morals; merely from imagining, that if such doctrines be true, they shall no longer be subjected to sundry restraints, which, however wholesome and proper, are too often unpalatable to our corrupt natures. What we wish to be true, we easily persuade ourselves is true. On this principle it is not difficult to account for our thus eagerly following these *ignes fatui* of our own fancies or "feelings," rather than the sober steady light of the word of God; which (in this instance as well as in others) lies under this single disadvantage, that it proposes no doctrines which may conciliate our regards by flattering our pride.

If, however, we can even resolve no longer to be bewildered by these vain imaginations, still the interesting question presses on us, "Where," in the words of Plato, "where shall we look for the origin of government?" Let Plato himself instruct us. Taught then by this oracle of Heathen wisdom, "we will take our stations there, where the prospect of it is most easy and most beautiful." Of all their theories respecting the origin of government with which the world has ever been either puzzled, amused, or instructed, that of the Scriptures alone is accompanied by no insuperable difficulties.

It was not to be expected from an all-wise and all-merciful Creator, that, having formed creatures capable of order and rule, he should turn them loose into the world under the guidance only of their own unruly wills; that, like so many wild beasts, they might tear and worry one another in their mad contests for preëminence. His purpose from the first, no doubt, was, that men should *live godly and sober lives*. But, such is the sad estate of our corrupted nature, that, ever since the Fall, we have been averse from good, and prone to evil. We are, indeed, so disorderly and unmanageable, that, were it not for the restraints and the terrors of human laws, it would not be possible for us to dwell together. But as men were clearly formed for society, and to dwell together, which yet they cannot do without the restraints of law, or, in other words, without government, it is fair to infer that government was also the original intention of God, who never decrees the end, without also decreeing the means. Accordingly, when man was made, his Maker did not turn him adrift into a shoreless ocean, without star or compass to steer by. As soon as there were some to be governed, there were also some to govern: and the first man, by virtue of that paternal claim, on which all subsequent governments have been founded, was first invested with the power of government. For, we are not to judge the Scriptures of God, as we do of some other writings; and so, where no express precept appears, hastily to conclude that none was given. On the contrary, in commenting on the Scriptures, we are frequently called upon to find out the precept from the practice. Taking this rule, then, for our direction in the present instance, we find, that, copying after the fair model of heaven itself, wherein there was government even among the angels, the families of the earth were subjected to rulers; at first set over them by God: *for, there is no power, but of God; the powers that be are ordained of God.* The first father was the first king: and if (according to the rule just laid down) the law may be inferred from the practice, it was thus that all government originated; and monarchy is its most ancient form.

Little risque is run in affirming, that this idea of the patriarchal origin of government has not only the most and best authority of history, as far as history goes, to support it; but that it is also by far the most natural, most consistent, and most rational idea. Had it pleased God not to have interfered at all in the case, neither directly nor indirectly, and to have left mankind to be guided only by their own uninfluenced judgments, they would naturally have been led to the government of a community, or a nation, from the natural and obvious precedent of the government of a family. In confirmation of this opinion, it may be observed, that the patriarchal scheme is that which always has prevailed, and still does prevail, among the most enlightened people: and (what is no slight attestation of its truth) it has also prevailed, and still does prevail, among the most unenlightened. According to Vitruvius, the rudiments of architecture are to be found in the cottage: and, according to Aristotle, the first principles of government are to be traced to private families. Kingdoms and empires are but so many larger families: and hence it is that our Church, in perfect conformity with the doctrine here inculcated, in her explication of the fifth commandment, from the obedience due to parents, wisely derives the congenial duty of *honouring the king and all that are put in authority under him.*

It is from other passages of Scripture, from the nature of the thing, from the practice of Adam, and from the practice of all nations (derived from and founded on this precedent) that we infer that Adam had and exercised sovereign power over all his issue. But the first instance of power exercised by one human being over another is in the subjection of Eve to her husband. This circumstance suggests sundry reflections, of some moment in this argument. In the first place, it shews that power is not a natural right. Adam could not have assumed, nor could Eve have submitted to it, had it not been so ordained of God. It is, therefore, equally an argument against the domineering claims of despotism, and the fantastic notion of a compact. It proves too, that there is a sense in which it may, with truth, be asserted, that government was originally founded in weakness and in guilt: that it may and must be submitted to by a fallen creature, even when exercised by a fallen creature, lost both to wisdom and goodness. The equality of nature (which, merely as it respects an ability to govern, may be admitted, only because God, had he so seen fit, might have ordained that the man should be subjected to the woman) was superseded by the actual interference of the Almighty, to whom alone original underived power can be said to belong.

Even where the Scriptures are silent, they instruct: for, in general, whatever is not therein commanded is actually forbidden. Now, it is certain that mankind are no where in the Scriptures commanded to resist authority; and no less certain that, either by direct injunction, or clear implication, they are commanded to *be subject to the higher powers:* and this subjection is said to be enjoined, not for our sakes only, but also *for the Lord's sake.* The glory of God is much concerned, that there should be good government in the world: it is, therefore, the uniform doctrine of the Scriptures, that it is under the deputation and authority of God alone that *kings reign and princes decree justice.* Kings and princes (which are only other words for supreme magistrates) were doubtless created and appointed, not so much for their own sakes, as for the sake of the people committed to their charge: yet are they not, therefore, the creatures of the people. So far from deriving their authority from any supposed consent or suffrage of men, they receive their commission from Heaven; they receive it from God, the source and original of all power. However obsolete, therefore, either the sentiment or the language may now be deemed, it is with the most perfect propriety that the supreme magistrate, whether consisting of one or of many, and whether denominated an emperor, a king, an archon, a dictator, a consul, or a senate, is to be regarded and venerated as the vicegerent of God. . . .

All government, whether lodged in one or in many, is, in its nature absolute and irresistible. It is not within the competency even of the supreme power to limit itself; because such limitation can emanate only from a superior. For any government to make itself irresistible, and to cease to be absolute, it must cease to be supreme; which is but saying, in other words, that it must dissolve itself, or be destroyed. If, then, to resist government be to destroy it, every man who is a subject must necessarily owe to the government under which he lives an obedience either active or passive: active, where the duty enjoined may be performed without offending God; and passive, (that is to say, patiently to submit to the penalties annexed to disobedience,) where that which is commanded by man is forbidden by God. No government upon earth can rightfully compel any one of its subjects to an active compliance with any thing that is, or that appears to his conscience to be, inconsistent with, or contradictory to, the known laws of God: because every man is under a prior and superior obligation to *obey God in all things.* When such cases of incompatible demands of duty occur, every well-informed person knows what he is to do; and every well-principled person will do what he ought, viz. he will submit to the ordinances of God, rather than comply with the commandments of men. In thus acting he cannot err and this alone is "passive obedience"; which I entreat you to observe is so far from being "unlimited obedience," (as its enemies wilfully persist to miscall it,) that it is the direct contrary. Resolute not to disobey God, a man of good principles determines, in case of competition, as the lesser evil, to disobey man: but he knows that he should also disobey God, were he not, at the same time, patiently to submit to any penalties incurred by his disobedience to man. . . .

SELECTED BIBLIOGRAPHY

J. ADAMS, *Novanglus* (1774–1775).
    Thoughts on Government (1776).
S. ADAMS, *The Rights of the Colonists* (1772), in *Writings*, Vol. II.
C. BECKER, *The Declaration of Independence* (1922).
J. BOUCHER, *A View of the Causes and Consequences of the American Revolution* (1797).

A. HAMILTON, *The Farmer Refuted* (1775), in *Works*, Vol. II.

J. F. JAMESON, *The American Revolution Considered as a Social Movement* (1926).

C. H. McILWAIN, *The American Revolution* (1923).

J. OTIS, *A Vindication of the Conduct of the House of Representatives* (1762).
   The Rights of British Colonists Asserted and Proved (1764).

T. PAINE, *Works*, edited by M. D. Conway (1894), especially: *Common Sense* (1776)
   American Crisis (1776–1783), and *Rights of Man* (1792).

V. L. PARRINGTON, *The Colonial Mind* (1927).

C. H. VAN TYNE, *The Causes of the War of Independence* (1922).
   The Loyalists in the American Revolution (1902).

CHAPTER III

FEDERALISM

I

We cannot hope to understand the political theory underlying the framing of the Constitution without an analysis of the conditions existing between the battle of Yorktown and the calling of the Philadelphia convention. No movement in world history is a better illustration of social and economic determinism; no accomplishment, a more complete rebound of the pendulum.

During the Revolution democratic political ideas had run rampant. The social contract theory, especially that of Paine, had glorified the "people." And under the leadership of such men as Samuel Adams in Massachusetts and Patrick Henry in Virginia, political control had passed from the aristocratic merchants and plantation owners to the petty traders and small farmers. In the struggle to determine who should rule at home, the conservative elements had lost ground. Revolutionary thought had looked upon government as a necessary evil. Government consequently became weak and decentralized. State governments had powerless executives and omnipotent legislatures. The central government under the Articles of Confederation was almost non-existent. Congress could act only through the states; it possessed no authority over individuals. It could raise no taxes; it could only request requisitions from the states. The Articles endowed Congress with authority over foreign affairs, but granted it no power to enforce treaties. The Continental Congress had carried the Revolution to a successful conclusion, but before long some states refused to send delegates or to pay their quotas. Congress remained only an ineffective symbol of a loose union.

As a consequence of this political disorganization, and as an aftermath of the war, economic chaos set in. Colonial independence from Great Britain meant withdrawal from the British mercantile system. The American merchants found the ports of England and the West Indies closed against them; and the impotent central government could not negotiate favorable trade agreements with other European powers. The loss of foreign trade threatened to wipe out those merchants who had cast their lot with the Revolutionists. Interstate trade became even more chaotic; jealousies developed among the states; each desired to keep money from going beyond its boundaries. Like modern nations, they endeavored to build up their own business prosperity at the expense of their neighbors. Thus New York taxed the produce of Connecticut farmers and destroyed their only profitable market. The seaport states financed their governments through imposts on European goods passing through their harbors, but destined for consumption in neighboring states. Madison thus picturesquely depicted the unhappy plight of those states not having seaports: "New Jersey placed between Phil^a & N. York, was likened to a cask tapped at both ends; And N. Carolina, between Virg^a & S. Carolina to a patient bleeding at both Arms." [1] The existence of different currencies in each of the thirteen states likewise hampered interstate trade. A Rhode Island merchant could not trade in Massachusetts without first exchanging his money into the currency of Massachusetts. The financial mechanism of present-day foreign trade did not then exist; even if the value of money had remained stable, the necessity of exchange would have discouraged trading. The continuous fluctuation of the depreciated state currencies, however, made commerce so hazardous as to be almost impossible. Furthermore, the attitude of the state courts toward non-resident creditors frequently prevented the collection of debts contracted in inter-state trade. Truly, Madison wrote: "Most of our political evils may be traced to our commercial ones." [2]

Chaotic finances likewise characterized the post-Revolutionary period. In an effort to finance the Revolution, the Continental Congress and each of the states had floated large bond issues and had printed much paper money. Both the securities and the money, unsupported save by the hope of victory and of possible repayment, depreciated rapidly in value. In Virginia by 1781 the Continental notes "fell to 1000 for 1," wrote Jefferson, "and then expired, as it had done in other States, without a single groan." [3] Jefferson records that he sold some land before the issuance of paper currency, but that he "did not receive the money till it was not worth Oak leaves." [4]

The depreciation of money resulted in an interesting and important

---

[1] Madison, *Writings*, II, 395. See II, 361–369, for Madison's analysis of the weakness of the state governments.
[2] *Ibid.*, II, 228, Letter to Jefferson, March 18, 1786.
[3] Jefferson, *Works* (Ford edition), V, 27, Letter to Meusnier, January 24, 1786.
[4] *Ibid.*, V. 90, Letter to McCaul, April 19, 1786.

class struggle. The creditor groups suffered greatly. The merchants who sold on credit received upon payment a greatly decreased purchasing power; meanwhile, they had to pay their European creditors in gold or silver. The debtor groups, on the other hand, benefited from this situation. In the spring the farmer bought seed and provisions for repayment at harvest season; also, his farm usually had a heavy, long-term mortgage. With the declining value of money and the corresponding increase in farm prices, the farmer could repay his debts with fewer bushels of wheat or corn. Paper money thus proved valuable to him. It supplied the frontier communities for the first time with a sufficient medium of exchange. Consequently, the debtor groups opposed a stabilization in currency and favored further operation of the money presses.

The debtor-creditor conflict, which, as we have noted, began in the pre-Revolutionary days, now took an acute form. Constant agitation in favor of fiat money, lax bankruptcy acts, and installment laws punctuated politics. In some states, as Rhode Island, the agrarians dominated the legislature and enacted debtor laws. In Massachusetts the attempt of the courts to enforce debts and foreclose on mortgages led to a violent reaction on the part of the agrarian debtors. Led by Shays, the farmers of western Massachusetts rose in revolt. By armed opposition, they shut the courts—those pernicious institutions of aristocracy—and prevented the legal collection of debts. The militia, financed by the private subscriptions of Boston merchants, put down the rebellion. But the memory of Shays's attack struck terror into the conservative hearts of the commercial and financial class. This incident, more than any other, brought about the Constitutional Convention of 1787.

The depreciation of public securities and paper currency led to another important phenomenon. Just as after the World War heavy speculation occurred in the depreciated German mark and Russian ruble, so during and after the Revolution speculation took place in bonds, money, and land certificates.[5] The moneyed men gambled on the possibility of repayment. But as long as the central government could not raise revenues, it could not redeem its issues. As long as agrarian debtors controlled the state legislatures, the value of their securities declined. And until the central government was sufficiently strong to build roads to the West and to afford protection against

---

[5] The central and state governments paid their soldiers in certificates of ownership of western lands. Also, some of the states sold portions of their public lands to land companies.

Indian attacks, settlers would move there in but small numbers, and the value of land certificates would not rise. The immediate outlook for the speculators was thus dark and uncertain.

These political and economic factors characterized the post-Revolutionary period and produced the American Constitution. The principal purposes to be served by the new government, according to *The Federalist*, were:

"The common defence of the members; the preservation of the public peace, as well against internal convulsions as external attacks; the regulation of commerce with other nations, and between the states; the superintendence of our intercourse political and commercial, with foreign countries." [6]

Edmund Randolph, in the opening address of the Constitutional Convention, expressed a similar view of the needs of the existing situation. Commercial chaos, depreciated currency, Shays's rebellion, loomed large in his mind.

"The character of such a governme(nt) ought to secure 1. against foreign invasion: 2. against dissentions between members of the Union, or seditions in particular states: 3. to p(ro)cure to the several States various blessings, of which an isolated situation was i(n)capable: 4. to be able to defend itself against incroachment: & 5. to be paramount to the state constitutions."

In speaking of the defects of the Confederation, Randolph professed

"A high respect for its authors, and considered them as having done all that patriots could do, in the then infancy of the science of constitutions, & of confederacies,—when the inefficiency of requisitions was unknown—no commercial discord had arisen among any states—no rebellion had appeared as in Massts.—foreign debts had not become urgent—the havoc of paper money had not been foreseen—treaties had not been violated—and perhaps nothing better could be obtained from the jealousy of the states with regard to their sovereignty." [7]

The existing political and economic conditions injured the large property groups. The merchants and manufacturers [8] suffered through the loss of foreign trade and the chaotic obstacles against interstate commerce. The creditor class, in general, lost through the constant decline in the value of money. Speculators in securities, currency, and land desired a rise in values. A swing of the pendulum in that direction was impossible under the political situation of a weak central

[6] *Federalist* (Lodge Edition), No. 23, p. 136. (New York, G. P. Putnam's Sons.)

[7] M. Farrand, *Record of the Federal Convention*, I, 18-19. (New Haven, Yale University Press.)

[8] At this time manufacturing on a small scale, especially the making of iron products, began in the states. See Faulkner, *American Economic History*, pp. 170-172. (New York, Harper & Bros.)

government and agrarian and popular control in the state legislatures. At this time, too, the large plantation owners of the South feared slave uprisings and preferred a strong central government for defense. And finally, possible repetition of Shays's rebellion of agrarian debtors frightened the conservative lovers of law, order, and security.

II

It was the representatives of these economic and social groups that convened in Philadelphia in May, 1787. They framed the American Constitution. Not one member represented, in his immediate personal economic interests, the small farming or mechanic classes.[9] The agrarian legislature of Rhode Island refused to send delegates to such a capitalistic gathering. Patrick Henry, the populist leader of Virginia and a delegate from that state, "smellt a rat" and refused to attend.[10] A majority of the delegates were lawyers by profession, and most of them came from towns, on or near the coast, where property was largely concentrated. Forty of the fifty-five members were public security holders. With the exception of New York and possibly Delaware, each state had one or more prominent representatives who held large amounts of securities. At least fourteen members held lands for speculation, and twenty-four had property in the form of money loaned at interest. Eleven delegates were interested in mercantile, manufacturing, and shipping lines. And fifteen were slave-owners.[11] Beard, in his *Economic Interpretation of the Constitution*, has declared that:

"The overwhelming majority of members, at least five-sixths, were immediately, directly, and personally interested in the outcome of their labors at Philadelphia, and were to a greater or less extent economic beneficiaries from the adoption of the Constitution." [12]

Beveridge, in his monumental study of Federalism, *The Life of John Marshall*, writes:

"Too much emphasis cannot be put upon the fact that the mercantile and financial interests were the weightiest of all the influences for the Constitution; the debtor and agricultural interests the strongest groups against it. It deserves repetition, for a proper understanding of the craft and force practiced by both sides in the battle over ratification, that those who owed

---

[9] Beard, *Economic Interpretation of the Constitution*, p. 149. (New York, The Macmillan Co.)
[10] Beard, *Rise of American Civilization*, I, 311. (New York, The Macmillan Co.)
[11] Beard, *Economic Interpretation of the Constitution*, pp. 149-151.
[12] *Ibid.*, p. 149.

debts were generally against the Constitution and practically all to whom debts were due were for the new Government." [13]

The experiences and the economic needs of the conservative propertied group that met at Philadelphia fashioned their attitudes. The delegates distrusted popular democracy and state legislatures, frequently agrarian in composition. Their main desire was for stability. Beveridge thus cogently depicts their mental state:

"Since the victory at Yorktown a serious alteration had taken place in the views of many who had fought hardest for Independence and popular government. These men were as strong as ever for the building of a separate and distinct National entity; but they no longer believed in the wisdom or virtue of democracy without extensive restrictions. They had come to think that, at the very best, the crude ore of popular judgment could be made to enrich sound counsels only when passed through many screens that would rid it of the crudities of passion, whimsicality, interest, ignorance, and dishonesty which, they believed, inhered in it. Such men esteemed less and less a people's government and valued more and more a good government. And the idea grew that this meant a government the principal purpose of which was to enforce order, facilitate business, and safeguard property." [14]

American historians have long written the story of the Constitutional Convention as an epic of conflict and compromise. They have devoted much attention to the struggle between the large and small states, with the resulting equal representation in the Senate. Attention, too, has been paid to the battle between the commercial North and the agricultural South, and to the compromises over the slave trade and the counting of slaves in connection with representation. But an examination of the realities of the proceedings at Philadelphia reveals, amidst the discord, a fundamental harmony. In the essential objectives of the Convention, virtual unanimity existed. The delegates differed only in the means of achieving their common ends. Not the conflicts and compromises, but the uniform distrust of democracy and the universal desire for stability, stand out in clear perspective.

The secret sessions of the Convention permitted the members utter freedom of expression. No speeches to the gallery, no orations for popular consumption, marked the meetings. With brutal frankness, the delegates passed judgment on the demerits of government by the people. Randolph of Virginia struck the keynote in the opening speech of the Convention:

[13] Beveridge, *Life of John Marshall*, I, 312. (Boston, Houghton Mifflin Company.)
[14] *Ibid.*, I, 252.

"Our chief danger arises from the democratic parts of our constitutions. It is a maxim which I hold incontrovertible, that the powers of government exercised by the people swallow up the other branches. None of the constitutions have provided sufficient checks against the democracy. The feeble Senate of Virginia is a phantom. Maryland has a more powerful senate, but the late distractions in that State, have discovered that it is not powerful enough. The check established in the constitution of New York and Massachusetts is yet a stronger barrier against democracy, but they all seem insufficient." [15]

Alexander Hamilton, a leader at the Convention and later the moving spirit in Washington's administration, "acknowledged himself not to think favorably of Republican Government." He addressed his remarks to "those who did think favorably of it, in order to prevail on them to tone their Government as high as possible." [16] An economic determinism characterized Hamilton's speeches. In every community where industry is encouraged, he maintained, there will be a division into the few and the many, into creditors and debtors; hence separate interests will arise. If you give all the power to the many, they will oppress the few.

"To the want of this check we owe our paper money—instalment laws &c. To the proper adjustment of it the British owe the excellence of their Constitution. Their house of Lords is a most noble institution. Having nothing to hope for by a change, and a sufficient interest by means of their property, in being faithful to the National interest, they form a permanent barrier agst. every pernicious innovation, whether attempted on the part of the Crown or of the Commons. No temporary Senate will have firmness en'o' to answer the purpose." [17]

Inequality of property would, he felt, exist as long as liberty lasted, and would unavoidably result from that very liberty itself. This inequality of property constituted the great and fundamental distinction in society.[18]

"All communities divide themselves into the few and the many. The first are the rich and well born, the other the mass of the people. The voice of the people has been said to be the voice of God; and however generally this maxim has been quoted and believed, it is not true in fact. The people are turbulent and changing; they seldom judge or determine right. Give therefore to the first class a distinct, permanent share in the government. They will check the unsteadiness of the second, and as they cannot receive any advantage by a change, they will ever maintain good government. Can a democratic assembly who annually revolve in the mass of the people, be supposed steadily to pursue the public good? Nothing but a permanent body can check the imprudence of democracy." [19]

---

[15] Farrand, *Records of the Federal Convention*, I, 26–27.
[16] *Ibid.*, I, 424.
[17] *Ibid.*, I, 288.
[18] *Ibid.*, I, 424.
[19] *Ibid.*, I, 298.

What is the remedy? "We ought to go as far in order to attain stability and permanency, as republican principles will admit." [20] Hamilton was willing to grant life tenures to the senators and the President. At the very least, the Constitution should, he said, provide a seven-year term for the Senate in order that the upper chamber might have "a permanent will, a weighty interest, which would answer essential purposes." [21] Thus did Hamilton express his distrust of democracy and his desire for stability.

James Madison played a leading rôle at the Convention; his influence was such that historians have labeled him "the Father of the Constitution." While he later became a follower of Jefferson, at this time he was an ardent nationalist and conservative. Madison frequently rose to demonstrate the necessity of checks upon the propertyless classes. In a speech on the suffrage, he felt that the freeholders of the country would be the safest depositories of "Republican liberty." In future times, he feared, a great majority of the people would be not only without land, but without any sort of property. These would either combine under the influence of their common situation, in which case the rights of property and the public liberty would not be secure, or they would become the tools of opulence and ambition. [22] In discussing the Senate, Madison's anti-democratic attitude again found expression. He argued that a limited number of enlightened citizens was a necessary defense against the impetuous counsel, fickleness, and passion of a numerous popular assembly. Like Hamilton, he held that in all civilized countries the people fall into different classes having a real or supposed difference of interests. Creditors and debtors, farmers, merchants and manufacturers, rich and poor—these classes divide society. In time, a growth of population would of necessity increase the proportion of those who labor under all the hardships of life. While no agrarian attempt at a more equal distribution of property had as yet been made in this country, symptoms of a leveling spirit had, he claimed, appeared sufficiently in certain quarters to give warning of the future danger. [23]

"The government we mean to erect is intended to last for ages. The landed interest, at present, is prevalent; but in process of time, when we approximate to the states and kingdoms of Europe; when the number of land-holders shall be comparatively small, through the various means of trade and manufactures, will not the landed interests be overbalanced in future elections, and unless wisely provided against, what will become of your government? In

---

[20] Farrand, *Records of the Federal Convention*, I, 289.
[21] *Ibid.*, I, 289–290.
[22] *Ibid.*, II, 203–204.
[23] *Ibid.*, I, 422–423.

England, at this day, if elections were open to all classes of people, the property of the landed proprietors would be insecure. An agrarian law would soon take place. If these observations be just, our government ought to secure the permanent interests of the country against innovation. Landholders ought to have a share in the government, to support these invaluable interests and to balance and check the other. They ought to be so constituted as to protect the minority of the opulent against the majority. The senate, therefore, ought to be this body; and to answer these purposes, they ought to have permanency and stability. Various have been the propositions; but my opinion is, the longer they continue in office, the better will these views be answered." [24]

A few other statements will indicate the existing distrust of democracy and the prevalent desire for stability. Elbridge Gerry was a leading Massachusetts merchant; a decade later he turned against the Federalists, and even in 1788 he found the Constitution drawn up by the Convention too aristocratic for his support. Yet, even Gerry admitted that heretofore he had been too republican; he had, he said, been taught by experience the danger of the leveling spirit. "The evils we experience flow from the excess of democracy. The people do not want virtue; they are the dupes of pretended patriots." [25]

Gouverneur Morris of Pennsylvania held that there was as much reason to intrust the suffrage to children as to the ignorant and the dependent.

"Give the votes to people who have no property, and they will sell them to the rich who will be able to buy them."

"The time is not distant when this Country will abound with mechanics and manufacturers who will receive their bread from their employers. Will such men be the secure & faithful Guardians of liberty? Will they be the impregnable barrier agst. aristocracy?" [26]

Roger Sherman of Connecticut was one of the few delegates who had risen from poverty through his own efforts; but with his rise in the economic scale, he had left behind all sympathy for the masses. The people, he held, should have as little as may be to do about the government. "They want information and are constantly liable to be misled." [27]

John Dickinson of Delaware had written learned dissertations against British taxation of the colonies; at the Convention, however, he argued for vesting the rights of suffrage in the freeholders of the country. He considered them the best guardians of liberty, and felt that to restrict the suffrage to them was a necessary defense against "the dangerous influence of those multitudes without property &

[24] Farrand, *Records of the Federal Convention*, I, 431.
[25] *Ibid.*, I, 48.
[26] *Ibid.*, II, 202.
[27] *Ibid.*, I, 48.

without principle, with which our country like all others, will in time abound." [28]

Thus spoke the framers of the Constitution. Distrust of democracy, acquired through a decade of proletariat-agrarian-debtor control in local politics, dominated their thinking. A desire for stability, developed through commercial and fiscal chaos, directed their construction of the new governmental system. Benjamin Franklin, an aged delegate at the Convention, cynically remarked:

"Few men in public affairs act from a mere view of the good of their country, whatever they may pretend; and though their activity may bring real good to their country, they do not act from a spirit of benevolence." [29]

III

The American Constitution is the resultant of two important factors: the economic and political situation after the Revolution, and the attitude which this situation inspired in the delegates at Philadelphia. The framers of the Constitution were not visionary idealists; they were practical men of affairs. They opposed popular democracy and desired upper class control in government. Naturally, they wrote their economic and social views into the document.

The Revolutionary theorists had glorified the "people"; the Convention delegates considered the masses, "turbulent and changing." The early state constitutions had trusted the legislature as the safest agent of the sovereign people; the Constitution of 1787 placed checks on the fickleness and passion of popular assemblies. Just as the Revolutionary state constitutions had accepted the thesis of the separation of powers, so likewise did the framers at Philadelphia; but in their equilibrium of departments, the scales weighed heavily against the legislature.

The Constitution minimized the rôle of the legislature and endeavored to prevent that organ from coming under popular domination. The Convention encountered considerable difficulty in framing the suffrage restrictions to operate in electing members of the House of Representatives. Finally, they adopted the provision that: "The Electors in each State shall have the Qualifications requisite for Electors of the most numerous Branch of the State Legislature." [30] On its face, this section appears extremely liberal. But we must remember that almost every state had at this time property qualifica-

---

[28] Farrand *Records of the Federal Convention,* II, 202.
[29] Quoted, W. B. Munro, *Invisible Government,* p. 113.
[30] Art. I, section 2.

tions for voting. The turbulent masses were to play no rôle in the new régime.

Even after such restriction, the framers still distrusted the legislature. They adopted a bicameral system so that the permanency of the Senate might check the impetuous counsels of the lower chamber. Furthermore, to the independent executive they gave a strong veto; and no elected council shared the power with the executive, as was the case in several of the states. Congress could override a presidential veto only by a two-thirds vote of each house; and at the end of a congressional session the legislature could not check the President at all. Finally, the framers subjected Congress to judicial control. Critics of the Supreme Court frequently accuse Marshall of usurping the power of judicial review in the case of *Marbury v. Madison*. A careful analysis, however, of the debates at Philadelphia, of the proceedings of the state ratifying conventions, and of the *Federalist Papers*, shows that the framers of the Constitution intended that the Supreme Court should act as a check on Congress. Suffrage restrictions, bicameralism, executive veto, judicial review—all were brought into play to guard against the dangers of populist or debtor legislation.

The Constitution-makers not only feared democracy, but also desired stability. Above all, the new government must render their property and social system secure. Consequently, they constructed a government of balances devised to prevent the majority from ever dominating "the minority of the opulent." They erected four separate units of government: a House of Representatives, a Senate, a President, and a Supreme Court. For each they provided a distinct method of selection. The qualified voters of each state were to elect the representatives; both branches of the legislature were to choose a state's senators. A specially constructed and entirely independent electoral college was to select the chief magistrate. The framers wanted no popular participation. Each state, through either its legislature or its electorate, was to choose a body of men; these colleges, each meeting in its own state, were to be uninstructed; they were to deliberate, to nominate, and to elect the President and Vice-President. Should this scheme fail, then the choice was to fall to the House of Representatives—the House, however, elected two years previously. And finally, the President was to appoint the justices of the Supreme Court, subject to senatorial confirmation. Similarly, the framers established a different time-schedule of election for each unit. To the House of Representatives they gave a two-year term.

The Senate was to stay in office for six years, one-third retiring biennially. The President's tenure was made four years; and the Supreme Court justices were to hold office during good behavior.

This scheme of balances, with its different methods and time-schedules of election, rendered the new government virtually safe from the dangers of popular, agrarian domination. In order for the debtor class to bring about issues of fiat paper money, they must now so dominate the state electorates as to win the House of Representatives, the state legislatures for a period of years as to win the Senate, and the electoral colleges as to win the presidency. Should the agrarians or the propertyless townspeople, by any chance, break through this carefully arranged system of different methods and times of election, the Supreme Court would still stand intact as the bulwark of property. The life tenure of the judges would render them independent and fearless in their opposition to the legislature. Later events actually demonstrated the foresight of the framers in this important matter. In 1800 the Jeffersonian Republicans captured the national government; but the judiciary, entrenched with staunch, conservative Federalists, acted as an effective check. Marshall and his associates, as we shall see, safeguarded the propertied classes.

A popular majority, during a period of temporary control, might, however, contrive to subvert this carefully arranged scheme. Against even this exigency the framers provided. They established a difficult method of constitutional amendment. A constitutional revolution must secure the sanction of two-thirds of the House of Representatives, two-thirds of the state-controlled Senate, and both legislative branches, or special conventions, in three-fourths of the states. The framers built well. Thus far only nineteen amendments have run this difficult gauntlet. Of these, the first ten, or the Bill of Rights, became law immediately as part of the bargain of ratification. The thirteenth, fourteenth, and fifteenth amendments were the aftermath of civil war. And the last two amendments passed Congress during the upheaval of the World War. Thus, only four constitutional changes have occurred during periods of normal political functioning. Truly, said Madison, "The government we mean to erect is intended to last for ages."

The powers granted to the federal government reflect the economic and political needs of the framers. The old Confederation acted only through the states; the new government could act directly upon the individual. The federal government was to have its own tax collectors, its own attorneys, its own marshals, its own criminal courts, its own army. The Constitution empowered Congress to lay and collect its own "Taxes, Duties, Imposts, and Excises";[31] no longer need it beg requisitions from the states. Direct taxes, however, Congress must apportion according to population—a provision included with a view to reconciling the rural interests. The taxing power and the immediate control over individuals formed the basis for all the other powers granted to the federal government.

Congress was given authority "to regulate Commerce with foreign Nations, and among the several States, and with the Indian Tribes."[32] No longer was a labyrinth of state regulations to render trade chaotic. National commerce demanded national uniformity. The power "to coin Money, regulate the Value thereof, . . . and fix the Standard of Weights and Measures"[33] likewise eliminated the previous obstacles to profitable interstate commerce. Thus did the mercantile and manufacturing groups at the Convention guard their interests.

Speculators, too, found protection. The Constitution provided: "All Debts contracted and Engagements entered into, before the Adoption of this Constitution, shall be as valid against the United States under this Constitution, as under the Confederation."[34] This section guaranteed the repayment of the securities issued by the Continental Congress. To Congress the framers gave power "To dispose of and make all needful Rules and Regulations respecting the Territory or other Property belonging to the United States."[35] Congress could admit new states into the union[36] and could establish post roads.[37] By the exercise of these powers, the western lands would be opened, migration encouraged, and land certificates increased in value.

Still further, the framers provided for national peace and domestic security. Congress could raise and support an army,[38] provide and maintain a navy,[39] call forth the militia "to execute the Laws of the Union, suppress Insurrections and repel Invasions."[40] These military provisions would enable the federal government to defend itself against foreign and domestic foes. The navy would defend our commerce, and the President might threaten its use to secure favorable trade treaties.[41] The army and militia would put down class uprisings and slave revolts. The framers had not forgotten Shays's rebellion.

[31] Art. I, section 8, paragraph 1.
[32] Art. I, section 8, paragraph 3.
[33] Art. I, section 8, paragraph 5.
[34] Art. VI, paragraph 1.
[35] Art. IV, section 3, paragraph 2.
[36] Art. IV, section 3, paragraph 1.
[37] Art. I, section 8, paragraph 7.
[38] Art. I, section 8, paragraph 12.
[39] Art. I, section 8, paragraph 13.
[40] Art. I, section 8, paragraph 15.
[41] See *Federalist*, No. 11.

Shortly afterwards, the propertied Federalists were to use military force against a second agrarian revolt—the Whiskey Rebellion of the Pennsylvania corn growers.

In establishing the federal judiciary, the delegates at Philadelphia wrote into the Constitution safeguards for their commercial interests. Under the Articles of Confederation, New York merchants, for example, had experienced considerable difficulty in collecting debts in Connecticut; the state courts, often popularly controlled, had discriminated against non-resident creditors. To the new federal courts the framers granted jurisdiction in controversies between citizens of different states.[42] Collection of interstate debts now rested in impartial courts. The federal judiciary also heard cases between a state and citizens of another state.[43] Holders of state securities and land grants could now sue for the collection of their claims. All such grants of power to the federal government tended to eliminate those political and economic ills that had plagued the propertied classes. The new régime could maintain domestic peace and security, develop commerce and industry, and repay public security holders in full.

The framers, however, did not stop here. The populist state legislatures had attacked their property. This danger, too, they must eliminate. Article I, section 10, of the Constitution placed rigid restrictions on the states. No state hereafter should coin money, emit bills of credit, make anything but gold and silver legal tender in payment of debts, pass any *ex post facto* acts or laws impairing the obligation of contracts, or, without the consent of Congress, lay any taxes on imports or exports, or collect tonnage duties. Thus the Constitution-makers ruled out paper money, installment acts, lenient bankruptcy laws, repudiation of securities, and interstate tariff barriers. Thus they prevented any direct attack upon property. It is instructive to note that the Convention adopted these prohibitions with virtually no debate.

The framers of the Constitution distrusted popular democracy and desired stability. They built with their eyes well trained on their economic and political experiences. The structure of the new government eliminated popular rule and emphasized stability. The powers granted to the central government permitted it to eradicate the economic evils that oppressed the propertied groups. And the restrictions upon the states prevented future agrarian attacks.

The framers of this economic and social document naturally faced a serious problem in its ratification. In the first place, the state leg-

[42] Art. III, section 2, paragraph 1.   [43] Art. III, section 2, paragraph 1.

islatures had authorized their delegates merely to amend the Articles of Confederation; the Convention, however, had drawn up a new document. In the second place, the Articles of Confederation had provided for amendment only by the unanimous consent of all thirteen state legislatures; and Rhode Island had refused to send delegates. And finally, the agrarians and urban wage-earners controlled some of the state legislatures; they would surely resent the restrictions on their authority. The Convention took the bull by the horns and engineered a peaceful revolution. It provided for ratification by nine states only and by special conventions. To the election of these conventions, the framers could more successfully devote their efforts.[44]

Almost everywhere the people distrusted the new Constitution. They feared lest the new government would overawe the state sovereignties; they suspected that the new régime, being beyond their reach, would prove subversive of their liberties. Four groups, in the main, were in opposition: the small farmers, the town mechanics, the petty traders, and the politicians at the state capitals. The latter feared the decline of their importance and influence through the enlargement of the political pond; and they frequently became the leaders in expressing the more genuine popular fear of federal centralization. Amos Singletary, a rural member of the Massachusetts convention, typified the populist distrust of the new Constitution.

"These lawyers, and men of learning, and monied men, that talk so finely and gloss over matters so smoothly, to make us, poor illiterate people, swallow down the pill, expect to get into Congress themselves; they expect to be the managers of this constitution, and get all the power and all the money into their own hands, and then they will swallow up all us little folks, like the great *Leviathan*, Mr. President; yes, just as the whale swallowed up *Jonah*." [45]

The speeches of Patrick Henry and George Mason at the Virginia convention likewise voice the popular fear of the political and economic domination of the propertied groups.[46] Only through the superior ability of the Federalist leaders and the promise of numerous amendments—but ten of which later prevailed—could the supporters of the Constitution secure its ratification. The Bill of Rights thus resulted from the populist fears of the new oligarchic centralization.

[44] See speeches of Randolph, Gorham, and Madison on the ratification clauses of the Constitution. Farrand, *Records of the Federal Convention*, II, 88–93.

[45] J. Elliot, *Debates of the Several State Conventions on the Adoption of the Federal Constitution*, II, 117–118.

[46] *Ibid.*, III, 410–414, 435–437, 478–483.

Rhode Island and North Carolina did not join their sister states until after the new government began operation.[47]

At the outset of the new régime, the Federalists were in control. Alexander Hamilton, as secretary of the treasury, became the leader of Washington's administration. The propertied classes now wrote into law their own economic ideas. Congress established a tariff to raise revenue and to protect manufacturers. It chartered a bank and gave financial control to the moneyed group. In the United States Bank the government deposited its revenue, thus providing much of the bank's resources; from the bank, it borrowed money at interest, thus giving the bank a profit. The bank profited also by the issuance of notes, and by the expansion and contraction of such currency. The centralization of the credit institutions, meanwhile, benefited the national commercial interests. And finally, Congress refunded at par value both the Continental and the state debts. The security speculators, many of whom were then in Congress, collected on their gamble.[48]

IV

The clearest and most concise statement of the political ideas underlying the Constitution of 1787 may be found in *The Federalist*. During the conflict over ratification, many pamphlets favored and attacked the proposed system. Of them all, *The Federalist* alone has retained the interest of later generations. Hamilton, Madison, and Jay coöperated in writing a series of articles for New York papers in an effort to win over that state to the new Constitution. Their efforts produced probably the best sugar-coating of economic self-interest that this country has ever seen. R. G. Adams characterizes these papers in the following manner:

"Too often has the 'propaganda' of one generation become the classic of the next. . . . So the work of ratifying our Federal Constitution produced a work of propaganda which is a classic. *The Federalist* is itself the frankest, the baldest and boldest propaganda ever penned—but what of it?" [49]

Throughout its numbers, we find stability emphasized and change deplored. *The Federalist* wanted not a high-compression motor, but

[47] For an interesting account of the struggle over ratification, see Beveridge, *Life of John Marshall*, I, Chs. 8–12; also, Beard, *Economic Interpretation of the Constitution*, Ch. 8.

[48] See Beard, *Economic Origins of Jeffersonian Democracy*, Chs. 4–6. (New York, The Macmillan Company.)

[49] R. G. Adams, *Selected Political Essays of James Wilson*, p. 24. (New York, Alfred A. Knopf, Inc.)

four-wheel brakes. Four major theses run through the papers: (1) a conception of human corruptibility and the consequent necessity of strong government; (2) a reconciliation of territorial expansion with democratic liberties; (3) a doctrine of government as a protector of property; and (4) a theory of checks and balances.

The Revolutionary political thought, which was still current among the rank and file, had viewed government as an evil. The less government, the better—argued the natural rights school. The Constitutional Convention proposed, however, a strong government. The authors of *The Federalist* thus faced the task of overcoming the popular prejudice against such a government. Government, argued Madison, is necessary because the passions of men are so unruly as to require restraint. Coercive authority must reënforce pure reason. "What is government itself, but the greatest of all reflections on human nature? If men were angels, no government would be necessary." [50] Above all, *The Federalist* feared "faction"—the euphemistic term for agrarianism. Madison defined a faction as "a number of citizens, whether amounting to a majority or minority of the whole, who are united and actuated by some common impulse of passion, or of interest, adverse to the rights of other citizens, or to the permanent and aggregate interests of the community." [51] Human nature is such that factions inevitably develop.

"The friend of popular government never finds himself so much alarmed for their character and fate, as when he contemplates their propensity to this dangerous vice. . . . The instability, injustice, and confusion introduced into the public councils, have, in truth, been the mortal diseases under which popular governments have everywhere perished; as they continue to be the favorite and fruitful topics from which the adversaries to liberty derive their most specious declamations." [52]

As long as the reason of man continues fallible, and he is at liberty to exercise it, factions will exist. "As long as the connection subsists between his reason and his self-love, his opinions and his passions will have a reciprocal influence on each other; and the former will be objects to which the latter will attach themselves." [53]

The writers of *The Federalist* faced a second task of probably even greater difficulty. In the popular mind, liberty and local rule were synonymous. The farther removed government was from the people, the more tyrannical they feared it would become. The Revolutionists had fought against the despotism of British imperial centralization.

[50] *Federalist*, No. 51, p. 323.
[51] *Ibid.*, No. 10, p. 52.
[52] *Ibid.*, No. 10, pp. 51–52.
[53] *Ibid.*, No. 10, p. 53.

Why, they now asked, should they permit the erection of another centralized autocracy? The new national government ran counter to the inherited conception of direct democracy through the town meeting. *The Federalist* attempted to reconcile government over a large area with popular liberties.

Madison's effort in the tenth paper constitutes one of the world's classics in political literature. A large republic, he argued, will minimize the dangers of faction. Society divides itself into factious groups—creditors against debtors, manufacturers against farmers, etc. Suppose a law is proposed concerning the payment of private debts, or the restriction of foreign manufactures, or the apportionment of taxes. These are all vital economic problems. Justice, not numerical supremacy, ought to hold the balance between the conflicting groups. But under the existing American system, the most powerful faction prevails. Every shilling with which the predominant party overburdens the inferior number is a shilling saved to their own pockets. How can we secure relief from this pernicious vice? How can we insure the victory of "justice"? If a faction consists of less than a majority, the republican principle supplies relief. But when a majority constitutes a faction, the form of popular government, on the other hand, enables it to sacrifice to its ruling passion or interest both the public good and the private rights of other citizens. To eliminate this danger, and at the same time to preserve the spirit and form of popular government—this task deserves serious attention. Only two methods exist: either prevent the existence of the same interest or passion in a majority at the same time or, if the majority have such coexistent interest or passion, render it by its numbers and local situation unable to concert and carry out its schemes of oppression. How can this be done? Republican government must supersede direct democracy. A pure democracy—a society consisting of a small number of citizens, who assemble and administer the government in person—can admit of no cure for the mischiefs of faction. A majority of the people, in almost every case, will feel a common passion or interest. Nothing can here check the inducements to sacrifice the weaker party. Hence it is that such democracies have ever been spectacles of turbulence and contention, have ever been incompatible with personal security or the rights of property. They have been as short in their lives as they have been violent in their deaths.

A republic—a government based on representation—promises the cure for faction. A republican government can encompass a greater number of citizens and a larger extent of territory than can a democracy. This circumstance renders factious combinations less dangerous in a republic. The smaller the society, the fewer probably will be the distinct parties and interests composing it; the fewer the distinct parties and interests, the more frequently will a majority exist; and the smaller the number of individuals composing the majority and the smaller the area within which they live, the more easily will they concert and execute their plans of oppression. Extend the sphere, and you take in a greater variety of parties and interests; you make it thus less probable that a majority of the whole will have a common motive to invade the rights of other citizens; or if such a common motive does exist, you render it more difficult for all who feel it to discover their own strength and to act in unison with each other. The influence of a factious leader may kindle a flame within his particular state, but he will be unable to spread a general conflagration through the other states. A rage for paper money, for an abolition of debts, for an equal division of property, or for any other "improper or wicked project," has less danger of pervading the whole union than a particular commonwealth. A large republic will thus minimize the dangers of faction.[54]

A large republic possesses certain other advantages. In the first place, however small a republic may be, it must have a large enough representative assembly to guard against the cabals of a few. On the other hand, however large, it must limit its legislature to a certain size to prevent the confusion of a multitude. Hence, the number of representatives in the two cases is not in proportion to the number of constituents. Since the appropriate size of a legislative body remains fixed, a large republic possesses a greater number of able men from which to choose its assembly. In the second place, in a large republic worthy candidates can win elections more readily than in a small one. Cheap politicians will experience greater difficulty in successfully practicing the vicious arts which too often carry elections. Men of attractive merit and established characters will thus win legislative seats.[55] Possibly in Madison's time this contention was sound. The modern newspaper, the radio, the barnstorming trip, were not yet developed. Inventions have indefinitely expanded the area for the "vicious arts" of electioneering.

The third major thesis of *The Federalist* was that government should act as a protector of property. The rights of property originate in the differences in the faculties of men. The protection of these

[54] *Federalist*, No. 10, pp. 53–60.   [55] *Ibid.*, No. 10, pp. 57–58.

faculties is the first object of government. The various and unequal distribution of property divides society into different interests and parties. Those who hold and those who are without property have ever formed distinct groups. Those who are creditors and those who are debtors divide similarly. Of necessity, a landed interest, a manufacturing interest, a moneyed interest, with many lesser interests, grow up in civilized nations. The regulation of these various and conflicting interests forms the principal task of modern legislation.[56]

The framers of the Constitution had placed prohibitions against the states in the interest of private property. These restrictions *The Federalist* supported.

"The extension of the prohibition to bills of credit must give pleasure to every citizen, in proportion to his love of justice and his knowledge of the true springs of public prosperity. The loss which America has sustained since the peace, from the pestilent effects of paper money on the necessary confidence between man and man, on the necessary confidence in the public councils, on the industry and morals of the people, and on the character of republican government, constitutes an enormous debt against the States chargeable with this unadvised measure, which must long remain unsatisfied; or rather an accumulation of guilt, which can be expiated no otherwise than by a voluntary sacrifice on the altar of justice, of the power which has been the instrument of it." [57]

Similarly, *ex post facto* laws and laws impairing the obligation of contracts are contrary to "the first principles of the social compact, and to every principle of sound legislation." This attack upon populism demanded further sugar-coating. "The sober people of America are weary of the fluctuating policy which has directed the public councils." [58]

The fourth thesis of *The Federalist* was the theory of checks and balances. Like the makers of the Revolutionary state constitutions, its authors accepted, as an axiom of political science, the division of government into legislative, executive, and judicial departments. But unlike the former, in its equilibrium of powers *The Federalist* weighed down the scales heavily against the legislature.

The drafters of these earlier constitutions, complained Madison, "seem never for a moment to have turned their eyes from the danger to liberty, from the overgrown and all-grasping prerogative of an hereditary magistracy, supported and fortified by an hereditary branch of the legislative authority. They seem never to have recollected the danger from legislative usurpation, which, by assembling

[56] *Federalist*, No. 10, pp. 53–54.
[57] *Ibid.*, No. 44, p. 278.
[58] *Ibid.*, No. 44, p. 279.

all power in the same hands, must lead to the same tyranny as is threatened by executive usurpations." [59]   But in a representative republic the executive magistracy is carefully limited both in the extent and the duration of its power.   Here the legislative power rests in an assembly, which is sufficiently numerous to feel all the passions that actuate a multitude, and yet not so numerous as to be incapable of pursuing the objects of its passions.   It is against the enterprising ambition of this department that the people ought to indulge all their jealousy and exhaust all their precautions.[60]

All single legislative bodies are apt to be impulsive, passionate, and violent. A bicameral system is thus essential.

" The necessity of a senate is not less indicated by the propensity of all single and numerous assemblies, to yield to the impulse of sudden and violent passions, and to be seduced by factious leaders into intemperate and pernicious resolutions." [61]

In order to correct this infirmity, the Senate ought to be small in size and stable in its membership. "It ought to possess great firmness, and consequently ought to hold its authority by a tenure of considerable duration." [62]   The overlapping terms of office of the senators is another safeguard.

"The mutability in the public councils arising from a rapid succession of new members, however qualified they may be, points out, in the strongest manner, the necessity of some stable institution in the government. Every new election in the States is found to change one half of the representatives. From this change of men must proceed a change of opinions; and from a change of opinions, a change of measures. But a continual change even of good measures is inconsistent with every rule of prudence and every prospect of success." [63]

The Federalist defended the small size of the proposed legislative houses. A small assembly more faithfully represents the true interests of the people than a large one. The more numerous any body becomes, the greater is the ascendancy of passion over reason. The larger the number, the greater is the proportion of members of limited information and of weak capacities. In a large legislative machine, only a few actually direct the proceedings, and through secret channels. "The countenance of the government may become more democratic; but the soul that animates it will be more oligarchic." [64] The later history of the House of Representatives cogently illustrates the truth of this last argument.

[59] *Federalist*, No. 48, p. 309.
[60] *Ibid.*, No. 48, p. 309.
[61] *Ibid.*, No. 62, pp. 387–388.
[62] *Ibid.*, No. 62, p. 388.
[63] *Ibid.*, No. 62, p. 389.
[64] *Ibid.*, No. 58, pp. 366–367.

While the Revolutionary leaders placed their confidence in the legislature, *The Federalist* trusted the executive. An energetic executive, its authors argued, is essential to efficient government. Independence is one attribute of strength. The Constitution, therefore, did not vest the choice of the President in the legislature or in the people; rather it empowered an electoral college to choose him. This method would not only grant him political independence but also check the people and prevent the election of a factious leader.

"It was also peculiarly desirable to afford as little opportunity as possible to tumult and disorder. This evil was not least to be dreaded in the election of a magistrate, who was to have so important an agency in the administration of the government." [65]

The veto likewise strengthens the President. It shields him from the encroachments of the legislature. But the veto power has an even greater significance: it maintains the *status quo* and prevents the enactment of improper laws.

"It establishes a salutary check upon the legislative body, calculated to guard the community against the effects of faction, precipitancy, or of any impulse unfriendly to the public good, which may happen to influence a majority of that body."
"It may perhaps be said that the power of preventing bad laws included that of preventing good ones; and may be used to the one purpose as well as to the other. But this objection will have little weight with those who can properly estimate the mischiefs of that inconstancy and mutability in the laws, which form the greatest blemish in the character and genius of our governments. They will consider every institution calculated to restrain the excess of law-making, and to keep things in the same state in which they happen to be at any given period, as much more likely to do good than harm; because it is favorable to greater stability in the system of legislation. The injury which may possibly be done by defeating a few good laws, will be amply compensated by the advantage of preventing a number of bad ones." [66]

The Federalist placed confidence in the judiciary, as well as in the presidency. The new Constitution proposed a powerful and independent court system. The people, wrote Hamilton, ought never to fear the judges. This department is the least dangerous to liberty. While the executive dispenses honors and wields the sword, while the legislature commands the purse and regulates our duties and rights, the judiciary has neither force nor will, but merely judgment. Without a union with the legislature or the executive, the courts cannot imperil liberty.[67]

[66] *Federalist*, No. 68, p. 424.   [67] *Ibid.*, No. 78, pp. 483-484.
[66] *Ibid.*, No. 73, pp. 458, 459.

One of the important functions of the judiciary is to check the legislature. The Constitution forbids bills of attainder, *ex post facto* laws, and the like. Only the courts can enforce these limitations. It is their duty "to declare all acts contrary to the manifest tenor of the Constitution void." They must guard the rights of individuals "from the effects of those ill humors, which the arts of designing men, or the influence of particular conjunctures, sometimes disseminate among the people themselves, and which, though they speedily give place to better information, and more deliberate reflection, have a tendency, in the meantime, to occasion dangerous innovations in the government, and serious oppressions of the minor party in the community." [68]

If, then, the courts are the bulwarks of a limited constitution against legislative encroachments, the independence of the judges is important. Their permanent tenure will contribute to the desired independent spirit. In a monarchy, the term of good behavior is an excellent barrier to the despotism of the prince; in a republic, it is a no less excellent barrier to the encroachments and oppressions of the representative body. "It is the best expedient which can be devised in any government, to secure a steady, upright, and impartial administration of the laws." [69]

V

The writings of John Adams constitute the second main contribution of this period to political philosophy. His *Defence of the Constitutions of Government of the United States* was published a year before the Philadelphia Convention. Adams envisaged the underlying concepts of the new government; and the members of the Convention were acquainted with his work. Throughout his writings runs a decided thread of economic interpretation of politics, and a desire for the *status quo* characterizes his philosophy. To demonstrate his contentions, he drew upon his extensive historical knowledge; he repeatedly illustrated his points by reference to the experiences of the Italian republics. Three major aspects of his work are significant: (1) his distrust of unlimited democracy, (2) his theory of aristocracy, and (3) his doctrine of balanced government.

In his earlier writings against the British imperial system, Adams had leaned toward liberalism. The post-Revolutionary days, however, produced a sharp reaction. He now attacked the view that the

---

[68] *Federalist*, No. 78, pp. 484–485, 487–488. [69] *Ibid.*, No. 78, p. 483.

people are incapable of tyrannical and oppressive rule.[70]   Rather, they are jealous, exacting, and suspicious. No stable government can exist on the foundation of unlimited democracy. Of all governmental forms, simple democracy is the most exposed to tumult. The histories of the Italian city states demonstrate that popular disorders inevitably destroy democracies.[71] Adams held that there is no such thing as an abstract love of democracy or equality. Men favor these conditions only in so far as they bring an advancement of individual interest or personal welfare. Mankind in general had rather be rich under a simple monarchy than poor under a democracy.[72]

Adams's distrust of democracy had a realistic economic basis. Suppose, he said, a nation composed of rich and poor, high and low, all assembled together. Of ten million individuals, not more than one or two million would have lands, houses, or personal property. A great majority of every nation is wholly destitute of property, except a small quantity of clothes and few other trifling movables. Perhaps, at first, prejudice, habit, shame, or fear, principle or religion, would restrain the poor from attacking the rich, and the idle from usurping on the industrious. But the time would not be long before courage would develop, and pretexts be invented by degrees, to justify the majority in dividing all the property among themselves. They would abolish debts first, lay heavy taxes on the rich, and at last vote a downright equal division of everything. Then the idle, the vicious, the intemperate would rush into the utmost extravagance of debauchery, sell and spend all their share, and once more demand a division of wealth.

"The moment the idea is admitted into society, that property is not as sacred as the laws of God, and that there is not a force of law and public justice to protect it, anarchy and tyranny commence."

"Property is surely a right of mankind as really as liberty." [73]

Adams vigorously attacked the Revolutionary doctrine that "all men are created equal." "No two men are perfectly equal in person, property, or understanding, activity, and virtue." [74] If you take a hundred men at random, you will find an aristocracy of thirty. There will be six wealthy, six eloquent, six learned, six fortunate, and six artful and cunning.[75] The inequalities of wealth, birth, and education are most important; they are, in the main, based upon property.[76]

[70] John Adams, *Works*, VI, 10.
[71] *Ibid.*, VI, 166.
[72] *Ibid.*, VI, 210–211.
[73] *Ibid.*, VI, 8–9.

[74] *Ibid.*, VI, 286.
[75] *Ibid.*, VI, 456.
[76] *Ibid.*, VI, 185.

No well-ordered commonwealth, his historical studies taught him, has ever existed without aristocracy and hereditary nobility. A system of hereditary honors is the surest way to attract talent.[77] Hereditary or life tenure of office, Adams. commended. He thus traveled a long way from his previous view that "where annual elections end, there tyranny begins." Adams's attack upon the masses and his advocacy of aristocracy received wide circulation. Certainly the frankness of his views did not add to his popularity as President, and undoubtedly they lost him many votes in his unsuccessful campaign for reëlection.

Adams's third major contribution was his conception of a balanced government. In every free state there must be a chief magistrate, a small council, and a larger assembly; the government will thus combine the monarchical, aristocratic, and democratic elements in society.[78] Only such a mixed form of government can survive. The entire legislative power cannot be intrusted to the people with a moment's safety. The poor and the vicious would instantly rob the rich and virtuous, spend their plunder in debauchery, or confer it upon some idol, who would become a despot; or the rich, by debauching the vicious to their corrupt interest, would plunder the virtuous and become richer, until they acquired all the property in their own hands and domineered as despots in an oligarchy.[79] The rich are people as well as the poor. They have rights as well as others; they have as sacred a right to their large property as others have to theirs which is smaller. Oppression of them is as possible and as wicked as of others.

"The rich, therefore, ought to have an effectual barrier in the constitution against being robbed, plundered, and murdered, as well as the poor; and this can never be without an independent senate. The poor should have a bulwark against the same dangers and oppressions; and this can never be without a house of representatives of the people. But neither the rich nor the poor can be defended by their respective guardians in the constitution, without an executive power, vested with a negative, equal to either, to hold the balance even between them, and decide when they cannot agree." [80]

Exactly why he is so certain that the executive will act as an impartial balancer, Adams does not explain.

In his later writings, Adams discovered to his satisfaction eight distinct checks and balances in the federal system: (1) the states and territories against the central government; (2) the House of Repre-

---

[77] John Adams, *Works*, VI, 250–251.
[78] *Ibid.*, IV, 378–382.

[79] *Ibid.*, VI, 66.
[80] *Ibid.*, VI, 65.

sentatives against the Senate; (3) the President against Congress; (4) the judiciary against Congress, the President, and the state governments; (5) the Senate against the President in respect to appointments and treaties; (6) the people against their representatives; (7) the state legislatures against the Senate; and (8) the electoral college against the people.[81] This multiplicity of balances ought to have produced the stability so much desired.

VI

The election of 1800 fulfilled the worst fears of the Federalists. A Republican "faction" won control of the national government. The agrarians and urban mechanics elected to the presidency their idol— Thomas Jefferson. To the staunch conservatives, the deluge had come. Their political and economic schemes for the strengthening of their property would now crumble in a flood of populism. Before Adams left office, however, the Federalists entrenched themselves within their last remaining stronghold. Congress immediately increased the size of the judiciary, and Adams appointed conservatives for life terms. Thus John Marshall, an outstanding Federalist politician, became chief justice of the Supreme Court.

Marshall was frankly a politician, rather than a jurist. His great decisions embodied Federalist philosophy and supported Federalist institutions. Through his efforts, the major tenets of conservative Federalism passed into the Supreme Court's precedents, and have become part of the fundamental law of the land. The framers of the Constitution had feared the possibility of an agrarian legislature; to this end, they had established an independent judiciary. They had experienced the discord of state supremacy, and had strengthened the central government. And finally, they had desired security in property, and had restricted the power of the states to adopt an agrarian program. These political-economic objectives of Federalism, Marshall now embodied in his decisions. His three outstanding theses were: (1) the supremacy of the judiciary over Congress, (2) the sovereignty of the federal state, and (3) the sanctity of private property, or the irrevocable nature of contracts.

In *Marbury v. Madison*,[82] Marshall announced to the Jeffersonians that the Supreme Court would restrain any agrarian excesses. At this time the Republicans were engaged in an effort to cleanse the judiciary of Federalists. Marshall employed an unimportant case to

[81] John Adams, *Works*, VI, 467–468.   [82] 1 Cranch 137.

lecture his political opponents. Adams had made a large number of "midnight appointments"; Marshall, then secretary of state, had neglected to deliver some of the commissions. Marbury, appointed a justice of the peace, applied directly to the Supreme Court for a writ of mandamus to compel the new administration to deliver his commission. Marshall, although he agreed that Marbury legally deserved his commission, refused to grant the writ on the ground that that section of the Judiciary Act of 1789 which granted the Supreme Court original jurisdiction in such cases was unconstitutional. This contention was novel and daring. The framers of the Constitution had supported the bill; and the Supreme Court had previously acted under the condemned section.[83] But for this decision, the Federalist doctrine of judicial supremacy might have died a quiet death. Until then, the court had not declared void a single act of Congress; and during the next fifty-two years no case came before the court in which an act of Congress was overthrown. Had Marshall not taken this stand, nearly seventy years would have passed without any question arising as to the omnipotence of Congress. After so long a period of judicial acquiescence, it seems likely that opposition to congressional supremacy would have been futile.[84]

In a series of important decisions, Marshall expounded the Federalist doctrine of national sovereignty. In the cases of *McCulloch v. Maryland*[85] and *Osborn v. the Bank*,[86] he defended the Hamiltonian bank against state attack. The constitutionality of the bank act had always been questioned; and the economic opposition to the second United States Bank became so bitter that several states laid heavy taxes on its branches. Marshall declared that the financial powers given to Congress were broad enough to cover the bank act. The doctrine of implied powers passed into the court precedents and vastly expanded the authority of the national government. The bank thus was an agency of the central government; and the states could not tax a federal instrumentality. Thus at one blow Marshall pronounced national supremacy and saved a Federalist institution. In *Gibbons v. Ogden*,[87] Marshall declared void a New York act that granted to Livingston and Fulton an exclusive monopoly over the steamboat navigation of that state's waters. He thus supported against state attacks the commercial institution of free interstate trade.

In three remarkable decisions, Marshall declared the irrevocable

---

[83] Beveridge, *Life of John Marshall*, III, 127–130.
[84] *Ibid.*, III, 131–132.
[85] 4 Wheaton 316.

[86] 9 Wheaton 738.
[87] 9 Wheaton 1.

nature of contracts.   In *Sturges v. Crowninshield*,[88] he announced that he would declare void any state bankruptcy act that released a debtor from the obligations of his contracts.   In *Fletcher v. Peck* [89] he declared that a grant made by a state is a contract regardless of fraud.   Land speculating companies had corrupted the Georgia legislature to secure from the state large tracts of valuable land.   At the next election the people "turned the rascals out," and the new legislature repealed the grant.   Two speculators arranged a dummy case, and Marshall held that the motives of the grantor did not destroy the sanctity of the contract.   In the *Dartmouth College Case*,[90] Marshall held that a charter given to the trustees of Dartmouth College in 1769 by the royal governor of the colony of New Hampshire constituted an irrevocable contract, and placed that educational institution of the state beyond public control.   In this manner, the major tenets of conservative Federalism survived the Jeffersonian assault.   They became the precedents of the Supreme Court, and thus the key to the interpretation of the fundamental law of the land.

JOHN ADAMS

John Adams published his *Defence of the Constitutions of Government of the United States of America* in 1786 in reply to an attack by M. Turgot of France. Adams devotes considerable attention to a refutation of a radical English work by Marchamont Nedham, *The Excellency of a Free State*, which was written in 1656 and republished in 1767.   In his work Adams swings away from his earlier liberalism of the Revolutionary period and adopts an aristocratic tone.   Many delegates at the Constitutional Convention of 1787 read his *Defence*.   To a remarkable degree, Adams envisaged the system of government that the Convention set up.

DEFENCE OF THE CONSTITUTIONS OF GOVERNMENT OF THE UNITED STATES OF AMERICA [91]

VOL. III., CHAP. I.

The Right Constitution of a Commonwealth Examined.

. . . . . .

Our first attention should be turned to the proposition itself,—"The people are the best keepers of their own liberties."

But who are the people?

"Such as shall be successively chosen to represent them."

Here is a confusion both of words and ideas, which, though it may pass with the generality of readers in a fugitive pamphlet, or with a majority of

[88] 4 Wheaton 122. In this particular case Marshall did uphold the state act because it did not release the debtor from his obligations.

[89] 6 Cranch 87.

[90] 4 Wheaton 518.

[91] C. F. Adams (editor), *The Works of John Adams*. (Boston, Little, Brown & Company, 1851.) VI, 6–9, 57–59, 64–68, 115–118.

auditors in a popular harangue, ought, for that very reason, to be as carefully avoided in politics as it is in philosophy or mathematics. If by *the people* is meant the whole body of a great nation, it should never be forgotten, that they can never act, consult, or reason together, because they cannot march five hundred miles, nor spare the time, nor find a space to meet; and, therefore, the proposition, that they are the best keepers of their own liberties, is not true. They are the worst conceivable; they are no keepers at all. They can neither act, judge, think, or will, as a body politic or corporation. If by *the people* is meant all the inhabitants of a single city, they are not in a general assembly, at all times, the best keepers of their own liberties, nor perhaps at any time, unless you separate from them the executive and judicial power, and temper their authority in legislation with the maturer counsels of the one and the few. If it is meant by *the people*, as our author explains himself, a representative assembly, "such as shall be successively chosen to represent the people," still they are not the best keepers of the people's liberties or their own, if you give them all the power, legislative, executive, and judicial. They would invade the liberties of the people, at least the majority of them would invade the liberties of the minority, sooner and oftener than an absolute monarchy, such as that of France, Spain, or Russia, or then a well-checked aristocracy, like Venice, Bern, or Holland.

An excellent writer has said, somewhat incautiously, that "a people will never oppress themselves, or invade their own rights." This compliment, if applied to human nature, or to mankind, or to any nation or people in being or in memory, is more than has been merited. If it should be admitted that a people will not unanimously agree to oppress themselves, it is as much as is ever, and more than is always, true. All kinds of experience show, that great numbers of individuals do oppress great numbers of other individuals; that parties often, if not always, oppress other parties; and majorities almost universally minorities. All that this observation can mean then, consistently with any color of fact, is, that the people will never unanimously agree to oppress themselves. But if one party agrees to oppress another, or the majority the minority, the people still oppress themselves, for one part of them oppress another.

"The people never think of usurping over other men's rights."

What can this mean? Does it mean that the people never *unanimously* think of usurping over other men's rights? This would be trifling; for there would, by the supposition, be no other men's rights to usurp. But if the people never, jointly nor severally, think of usurping the rights of others, what occasion can there be for any government at all? Are there no robberies, burglaries, murders, adulteries, thefts, nor cheats? Is not every crime a usurpation over other men's rights? Is not a great part, I will not say the greatest part, of men detected every day in some disposition or other, stronger or weaker, more or less, to usurp over other men's rights? There are some few, indeed, whose whole lives and conversations show that, in every thought, word, and action, they conscientiously respect the rights of others. There is a larger body still, who, in the general tenor of their thoughts and actions, discover similar principles and feelings, yet frequently err. If we should extend our candor so far as to own, that the majority of men are generally under the dominion of benevolence and good intentions, yet, it must be confessed, that a vast majority frequently transgress; and, what is more directly to the point, not only a majority, but almost all, confine their benevolence to their families, relations, personal friends, parish, village, city, country, province, and that very few, indeed, extend it impartially to the whole community. Now, grant but this truth, and the question is decided. If a majority are capable of preferring their own private interest, or that of their families, counties, and party, to that of the nation collectively, some provision must be made in the constitution, in favor of justice, to compel all to respect the common right, the public good, the universal law, in preference to all private considerations.

The proposition of our author, then, should be reversed, and it should have been said, that they mind so much their own, that they never think enough of others. Suppose a nation, rich and poor, high and low, ten millions in number, all assembled together; not more than one or two millions will have lands, houses, or any personal property; if we take into the account the women and children, or even if we leave them out of the question, a great majority of every nation is wholly destitute of property, except a small quantity of clothes, and a few trifles of other movables. Would Mr. Nedham be responsible that, if all were to be decided by a vote of the majority, the eight or nine millions who have no property, would not think of usurping over the rights of the one or two millions who have? Property is surely a right of mankind as really as liberty. Perhaps, at first, prejudice, habit, shame or fear, principle or religion, would restrain the poor from attacking the rich, and the idle from usurping on the industrious; but the time would not be long before courage and enterprise would come, and pretexts be invented by degrees, to counterance the majority in dividing all the property among them, or at least, in sharing it equally with its present possessors. Debts would be abolished first; taxes laid heavy on the rich, and not at all on the others; and at last a downright equal division of every thing be demanded, and voted. What would be the consequences of this? The idle, the vicious, the intemperate, would rush into the utmost extravagance of debauchery, sell and spend all their share, and then demand a new division of those who purchased from them. The moment the idea is admitted into society, that property is not as sacred as the laws of God, and that there is not a force of law and public justice to protect it, anarchy and tyranny commence. If "THOU SHALT NOT COVET," and "THOU SHALT NOT STEAL," were not commandments of Heaven, they must be made inviolable precepts in every society, before it can be civilized or made free.

If the first part of the proposition, namely, that "the people never think of usurping over other men's rights," cannot be admitted, is the second, namely, "they mind which way to preserve their own," better founded?

There is in every nation and people under heaven a large proportion of persons who take no rational and prudent precautions to preserve what they have, much less to acquire more. Indolence is the natural character of man, to such a degree that nothing but the necessities of hunger, thirst, and other wants equally pressing, can stimulate him to action, until education is introduced in civilized societies, and the strongest motives of ambition to excel in arts, trades, and professions, are established in the minds of all men. Until this emulation is introduced, the lazy savage holds property in too little estimation to give himself trouble for the preservation or acquisition of it. In societies the most cultivated and polished, vanity, fashion, and folly prevail over every thought of ways to preserve their own. They seem rather to study what means of luxury, dissipation, and extravagance they can invent to get rid of it. . . .

Though we allow benevolence and generous affections to exist in the human breast, yet every moral theorist will admit the selfish passions in the generality of men to be the strongest. There are few who love the public better than themselves, though all may have some affection for the public. We are not, indeed, commanded to love our neighbor better than ourselves. Self-interest, private avidity, ambition, and avarice, will exist in every state of society, and under every form of government. A succession of powers and persons, by frequent elections, will not lessen these passions in any case, in a governor, senator, or representative; nor will the apprehension of an approaching election restrain them from indulgence if they have the power. The only remedy is to take away the power, by controlling the selfish avidity of the governor, by the senate and house; of the senate, by the governor and house; and of the house, by the governor and senate. Of all possible forms of government, a sovereignty in one assembly, successively chosen by the people, is perhaps the best calculated to facilitate the gratification of self-love, and the pursuit of the private interest of a few individuals; a few eminent conspicuous characters will be continued in their seats in the sovereign assembly, from one election to another, whatever changes are made in the seats around them; by superior art, address, and opulence, by more splendid birth, reputation, and connections, they will be able to intrigue with the people and their leaders, out of doors, until they worm out most of their opposers, and introduce their friends; to this end, they will bestow all offices, contracts, privileges in commerce, and other emoluments, on the latter and their connections, and throw every vexation and disappointment in the way of the former, until they establish such a system of hopes and fears throughout the state, as shall enable them to carry a majority in every fresh election of the house. The judges will be appointed by them and their party, and of consequence, will be obsequious enough to their inclinations. The whole judicial authority, as well as the executive, will be employed, perverted and prostituted to the purposes of electioneering. No justice will be attainable, nor will innocence or virtue be safe, in the judicial courts, but for the friends of the prevailing leaders; legal prosecutions will be instituted and carried on against opposers, to their vexation and ruin; and as they have the public purse at command, as well as the executive and judicial power, the public money will be expended in the same way. No favors will be attainable but by those who will court the ruling demagogues in the house, by voting for their friends and instruments; and pensions and pecuniary rewards and gratifications, as well as honors and offices of every kind, will be voted to friends and partisans. The leading minds and most influential characters among the clergy will be courted, and the views of the youth in this department will be turned upon those men, and the road to promotion and employment in the church will be obstructed against such as will not worship the general idol. Capital characters among the physicians will not be forgotten, and the means of acquiring reputation and practice in the healing art will be to get the state trumpeters on the side of youth. The bar, too, will be made so subservient, that a young gentleman will have no chance to obtain a character or clients, but by falling in with the views of the judges and their creators. Even the theatres, and actors and actresses, must become politicians, and convert the public pleasures into engines of popularity for the governing members of the house. The press, that great barrier and bulwark of the rights of mankind, when it is protected in its freedom by law, can now no longer be free; if the authors, writers, and printers, will not accept the hire that will be offered them, they must submit to the ruin that will be denounced against them. The presses, with much secrecy and concealment, will be made the vehicles of calumny against the minority, and of panegyric and empirical applauses of the leaders of the majority, and no remedy can possibly be obtained. In one word, the whole system of affairs, and every conceivable motive of hope and fear, will be employed to promote the private interests of a few, and their obsequious majority; and there is no remedy but in arms. Accordingly we find in all the Italian republics the minority always were driven to arms in despair. . . .

It is agreed that the people are the best keepers of their own liberties, and the only keepers who can be always trusted; and, therefore, the people's fair, full, and honest consent, to every law, by their representatives, must be made an essential part of the constitution; but it is denied that they are the best keepers, or any keepers at all, of their own liberties, when they hold collectively, or by representation, the executive and judicial power, or the whole and uncontrolled legislative; on the contrary, the experience of all ages has proved, that they instantly give away their liberties into the hand of grandees, or kings, idols of their own creation. The management of the executive and judicial powers together always corrupts them, and throws the whole power into the hands of the most profligate and abandoned among themselves. The honest men are generally nearly equally divided in sentiment, and, therefore, the vicious and unprincipled, by joining one party, carry the majority; and the vicious and unprincipled always follow the most profligate leader, him who bribes the highest, and sets all decency and shame at defiance. It becomes more profitable, and reputable too, except with a very few, to be a party man than a public-spirited one.

It is agreed that "the end of all government is the good and ease of the people, in a secure enjoyment of their rights, without oppression"; but it must be remembered, that the rich are *people* as well as the poor; that they have rights as well as others; that they have as clear and as *sacred* a right to their large property as others have to theirs which is smaller; that oppression to them is as possible and as wicked as to others; that stealing, robbing, cheating, are the same crimes and sins, whether committed against them or others. The rich, therefore, ought to have an effectual barrier in the constitution against being robbed, plundered, and murdered, as well as the poor; and this can never be without an independent senate. The poor should have a bulwark against the same dangers and oppressions; and this can never be without a house of representatives of the people. But neither the rich nor the poor can be defended by their respective guardians in the constitution, without an executive power, vested with a negative, equal to either, to hold the balance even between them, and decide when they cannot agree. If it is asked, When will this negative be used? it may be answered,

Perhaps never. The known existence of it will prevent all occasion to exercise it; but if it has not a being, the want of it will be felt every day. If it has not been used in England for a long time past, it by no means follows that there have not been occasions when it might have been employed with propriety. But one thing is very certain, that there have been many occasions since the Revolution, when the constitution would have been overturned if the negative had not been an indubitable prerogative of the crown.

It is agreed that the people are "most sensible of their own burdens; and being once put into a capacity and freedom of acting, are the most likely to provide remedies for their own relief." For this reason they are an essential branch of the legislature, and have a negative on all laws, an absolute control over every grant of money, and an unlimited right to accuse their enemies before an impartial tribunal. Thus far they are most sensible of their burdens, and are most likely to provide remedies. But it is affirmed that they are not only incapable of managing the executive power, but would be instantly corrupted by it in such numbers, as would destroy the integrity of all elections. It is denied that the legislative power can be wholly intrusted in their hands with a moment's safety. The poor and the vicious would instantly rob the rich and virtuous, spend their plunder in debauchery, or confer it upon some idol, who would become the despot; or, to speak more intelligibly, if not more accurately, some of the rich, by debauching the vicious to their corrupt interest, would plunder the virtuous, and become more rich, until they acquired all the property, or a balance of property and of power, in their own hands, and domineered as despots in an oligarchy.

It is agreed that the "people know where the shoe wrings, what grievances are most heavy," and, therefore, they should always hold an independent and essential part in the legislature, and be always able to prevent the shoe from wringing more, and the grievances from being made more heavy; they should have a full hearing of all their arguments, and a full share of all consultations, for easing the foot where it is in pain, and for lessening the weight of grievances or annihilating them. But it is denied that they have right, or that they should have power to take from one man his property to make another easy, and that they *only* know "what fences they stand in need of to shelter them from the injurious assaults of those powers that are above them"; meaning, by the powers above them, senators and magistrates, though, properly speaking, there are no powers above them but the law, which is above all men, governors and senators, kings, and nobles, as well as commons.

The Americans have agreed with this writer in the sentiment, that "it is but reason that the people should see that none be interested in the supreme authority but persons of their own election, and such as must, in a short time, return again into the same condition with themselves." This hazardous experiment they have tried, and, if elections are soberly made, it may answer very well; but if parties, factions, drunkenness, bribes, armies, and delirium come in, as they always have done sooner or later, to embroil and decide every thing, the people must again have recourse to conventions and find a remedy. Neither philosophy nor policy has yet discovered any other cure, than by prolonging the duration of the first magistrate and senators. The evil may be lessened and postponed, by elections for longer periods of years, till they become for life; and if this is not found an adequate remedy, there will remain no other but to make them hereditary. The delicacy or the dread of unpopularity that should induce any man to conceal this important truth from the full view and comtemplation of the people, would be a weakness, if not a vice. As to "reaping the same benefit or burden, by the laws enacted, that befalls the rest of the people," this will be secured, whether the first magistrate and senate be elective or hereditary, so long as the people are an integral branch of the legislature, can be bound by no laws to which they have not consented, and can be subjected to no tax which they have not agreed to lay. It is agreed that the "issue of such a constitution," whether the governor and senate be hereditary or elective, must be this, "that no load be laid upon any, but what is common to all, and that always by common consent; not to serve the lusts of any, but only to supply the necessities of their country."

The next paragraph is a figurative flourish, calculated to amuse a populace without informing their understandings. Poetry and mystics will answer no good end in discussing the questions of this nature. The simplest style, the most mathematical precision of words and ideas, is best adapted to discover truth, and to convey it to others, in reasoning on this subject. There is here a confusion that is more than accidental—it is artful. The author purposely states the question, and makes the comparison only between simple forms of government, and carefully keeps out of sight the idea of a judicious mixture of them all. He seems to suppose, that the supreme power must be wholly in the hands of a simple monarch, or of a single senate, or of the people, and studiously avoids considering the sovereignty lodged in a composition of all three. "When a supreme power long continues in the hands of any person or persons, they, by greatness of place, being seated above the middle region of the people, sit secure from all winds and weathers, and from those storms of violence that nip and terrify the inferior part of the world." If this is popular poetry, it is not philosophical reasoning. It may be made a question, whether it is true in fact, that persons in the higher ranks of life are more exempted from dangers and evils that threaten the commonwealth than those in the middle or lower rank? But if it were true, the United States of America have established their governments upon a principle to guard against it; and, "by a successive revolution of authority, they come to be degraded of their earthly godheads, and return into the same condition with other mortals"; and, therefore, "they must needs be the more sensible and tender of what it laid upon them." . . .

Even in our author's "Right Constitution," every man would have an equal right to be representative, chosen or not. The reason why one man is content to submit to the government of another, as assigned by our author, namely,—"not because he conceives himself to have less right than another to govern, but either because he finds himself less able, or else because he judgeth it will be more convenient for himself and the community, if he submits to another's government," is a proof of this; because, the moment it is allowed that some are more able than others, and that the community are judges who the most able are, you take away the right to rule, derived from the nobleness of each man's individual nature, from his affections to rule rather than obey, or from his natural appetite or desire of principality, and give the right of conferring the power to rule to the community. As a share in the appointment of deputies is all that our author can with any color infer from this noble nature of man, his nature will be gratified and his dignity supported as well, if you divide his deputies into three orders,—of governor for the executive and an integral share in the legislative, of senators for another independent part of the legislative, and of representatives for a third;—and if you introduce a judicious balance between them, as if you huddle them into one assembly, where they will soon disgrace their own nature and that of their constituents, by ambition, avarice, jealousy, envy, faction, division, sedition, and rebellion. Nay, if it should be found that annual elections of governors and senators cannot be supported without introducing venality and convulsions, as is very possible, the people will consult the dignity of their nature better by appointing a standing executive and senate, than by insisting on elections, or at least by prolonging the duration of those high trusts, and making elections less frequent.

It is indeed a "most excellent maxim, that the original and fountain of all just power and government is in the people"; and if ever this maxim was fully demonstrated and exemplified among men, it was in the late American Revolution, where thirteen governments were taken down from the foundation, and new ones elected wholly by the people, as an architect would pull down an old building and erect a new one. There will be no dispute, then, with Cicero, when he says, "A mind well instructed by the light of nature, will pay obedience," willingly "to none but such as command, direct, or govern for its good or benefit"; nor will our author's inferences from these passages from that oracle of human wisdom be denied:

"1. That by the light of nature people are taught to be their own carvers and contrivers in the framing of that government under which they mean to live.

"2. That none are to preside in government, or sit at the helm, but such as shall be judged fit, and chosen by the people.

"3. That the people are the only proper judges of the convenience or inconvenience of a government when it is erected, and of the behavior of governors after they are chosen."

But then it is insisted, that rational and regular means shall be used that the whole people may be their own carvers, that they may judge and choose who shall preside, and that they may determine on the convenience or inconvenience of government, and the behavior of governors. But then it is insisted, that the town of Berwick upon Tweed shall not carve, judge, choose, and determine for the whole kingdom of Great Britain, nor the county of Berkshire for the Massachusetts; much less that a lawless tyrannical rabble shall do all this for the state, or even for the county of Berkshire.

It may be, and is admitted, that a free government is most natural, and only suitable to the reason of mankind; but it by no means follows "that the other forms, as of a standing power in the hands of a particular person, as a king; or of a set number of great ones, as in a senate," much less that a mixture of the three simple forms "are beside the dictates of nature, and mere artificial devices of great men, squared out only to serve the ends and interests of avarice, pride, and ambition of a few, to a vassalizing of the community." If the original and fountain of all power and government is in the people, as undoubtedly it is, the people have as clear a right to erect a simple monarchy, aristocracy, or democracy, or an equal mixture, or any other mixture of all three, if they judge it for their liberty, happiness, and prosperity, as they have to erect a democracy; and infinitely greater and better men than Marchamont Nedham, and the wisest nations that ever lived, have preferred such mixtures, and even with such standing powers as ingredients in their compositions. But even those nations who choose to reserve in their own hands the periodical choice of the first magistrate, senate, and assembly, at certain stated periods, have as clear a right to appoint a first magistrate for life as for years, and for perpetuity in his descendants as for life.

When I say for perpetuity or for life, it is always meant to imply, that the same people have at all times a right to interpose, and to depose for maladministration—to appoint anew. No appointment of a king or senate, or any standing power, can be, in the nature of things, for a longer period than *quam diu se bene gesserit*, the whole nation being judge. An appointment for life or perpetuity can be no more than an appointment until further order; but further order can only be given by the nation. And, until the nation shall have given the order, an estate for life or in fee is held in the office. It must be a great occasion which can induce a nation to take such a subject into consideration, and make a change. Until a change is made, an hereditary limited monarch is the representative of the whole nation, for the management of the executive power, as much as a house of representatives is, as one branch of the legislature, and as guardian of the public purse; and a house of lords, too, or a standing senate, represents the nation for other purposes, namely, as a watch set upon both the representatives and the executive power. The people are the fountain and original of the power of kings and lords, governors and senates, as well as the house of commons, or assembly of representatives. And if the people are sufficiently enlightened to see all the dangers that surround them, they will always be represented by a distinct personage to manage the whole executive power; a distinct senate, to be guardians of property against levellers for the purposes of plunder, to be a repository of the national tradition of public maxims, customs, and manners, and to be controllers, in turn, both of kings and their ministers on one side, and the representatives of the people on the other, when either discover a disposition to do wrong; and a distinct house of representatives, to be the guardians of the public purse, and to protect the people, in their turn, against both king and nobles.

A science certainly comprehends all the principles in nature which belong to the subject. The principles in nature which relate to government cannot all be known, without a knowledge of the history of mankind. The English constitution is the only one which has considered and provided for all cases that are known to have generally, indeed to have always, happened in the progress of every nation; it is, therefore, the only scientifical government. To say, then, that standing powers have been erected, as "mere artificial devices of great men, to serve the ends of avarice, pride, and ambition of a few, to the vassalizing of the community," is to declaim and abuse. Standing powers have been instituted to avoid greater evils,—corruption, sedition, war, and bloodshed, in elections; it is the people's business, therefore, to find out some method of avoiding them, without standing powers. The Americans flatter themselves they have hit upon it; and no doubt they have for a time, perhaps a long one; but this remains to be proved by experience.

THE CONSTITUTIONAL CONVENTION [92]

The Constitutional Convention convened in Philadelphia in May, 1787; delegates from every state except Rhode Island were present. To understand these debates properly, we must read them in the light of the post-Revolutionary conditions in the thirteen states. Farrand's *Records of the Federal Convention of 1787* were compiled from the notes made by several of the delegates. The most complete of these notes were those of James Madison. The following abstracts from the Convention debates are taken from Madison's minutes.

TUESDAY MAY 29

. . . . . .
Mr. Randolph (then) opened the main business. He expressed his regret, that it should fall to him, rather than those, who were of longer standing in life and political experience, to open the great subject of their mission. But, as the convention had originated from Virginia, and his colleagues supposed, that some proposition was expected from them, they had imposed this task on him.

He then commented on the difficulty of the crisis, and the necessity of preventing the fulfilment of the prophecies of the American downfal.

He observed that in revising the foederal system we ought to inquire 1. into the properties, which such a government ought to possess, 2. the defects of the confederation, 3. the danger of our situation &. 4. the remedy.

1. The character of such a governme[nt] ought to secure 1. against foreign invasion: 2. against dissentions between members of the Union, or seditions in particular states: 3. to p[ro]cure to the several States various blessings, of which an isolated situation was i[n]capable: 4. to be able to defend itself against incroachment: & 5. to be paramount to the state constitutions.

2. In speaking of the defects of the confederation he professed a high respect for its authors, and considered, them as having done all that patriots could do, in the then infancy of the science, of constitutions, & of confederacies,—when the inefficiency of requisitions was unknown—no commercial discord had arisen among any states—no rebellion had appeared as in Massts. —foreign debts had not become urgent—the havoc of paper money had not been foreseen—treaties had not been violated—and perhaps nothing better could be obtained from the jealousy of the states with regard to their sovereignty.

He then proceeded to enumerate the defects: 1. that the confederation produced no security agai[nst] foreign invasion; congress not being permitted to prevent a war nor to support it by th[eir] own authority.—Of this he cited many examples; most of whi[ch] tended to shew, that they could not cause infractions of treaties or of the law of nations, to be punished: that particular states might by their conduct provoke war without controul; and that neither militia nor draughts being fit for defence on such occasions, enlistments only could be successful, and these could not be executed without money.

[92] Max Farrand (editor), *The Records of the Federal Convention of 1787*. (Yale University Press, 1911.) I, 18–23, 132–137, 421–425; II, 88–90, 92–93, 202–204. (Reprinted by permission of the publishers.)

2. that the foederal government could not check the quarrels between states, nor a rebellion in any not having constitutional power Nor means to interpose according to the exigency:

3. that there were many advantages, which the U. S. might acquire, which were not attainable under the confederation—such as a productive impost—counteraction of the commercial regulations of other nations—pushing of commerce ad libitum—&c &c.

4. that the foederal government could not defend itself against the incroachments from the states:

5. that it was not even paramount to the state constitutions, ratified as it was in may of the states.

3. He next reviewed the danger of our situation appealed to the sense of the best friends of the U. S.—the prospect of anarchy from the laxity of government every where; and to other considerations.

4. He then proceeded to the remedy; the basis of which he said, must be the republican principle.

He proposed as conformable to his ideas the following resolutions, which he explained one by one.

RESOLUTIONS PROPOSED BY MR. RANDOLPH IN CONVENTION.
May 29, 1787.

1. Resolved that the articles of Confederation ought to be so corrected & enlarged as to accomplish the objects proposed by their institution; namely, "common defence, security of liberty and general welfare."

2. Resd. therefore that the rights of suffrage in the National Legislature ought to be proportioned to the Quotas of contribution, or to the number of free inhabitants, as the one or the other rule may seem best in different cases.

3. Resd. that the National Legislature ought to consist of two branches.

4. Resd. that the members of the first branch of the National Legislature ought to be elected by the people of the several States every for the term of   ; to be of the age of   years at least, to receive liberal stipends by which they may be compensated for the devotion of their time to public service; to be ineligible to any office established by a particular State, or under the authority of the United States, except those peculiarly belonging to the functions of the first branch, during the term of service, and for the space of   after its expiration; to be incapable of re-election for the space of   after the expiration of their term of service, and to be subject to recall.

5. Resold. that the members of the second branch of the National Legislature ought to be elected by those of the first, out of a proper number of persons nominated by the individual Legislatures, to be of the age of   years at least; to hold their offices for a term sufficient to ensure their independency, to receive liberal stipends, by which they may be compensated for the devotion of their time to public service; and to be ineligible to any office established by a particular State, or under the authority of the United States, except those peculiarly belonging to the functions of the second branch, during the term of service, and for the space of   after the expiration thereof.

6. Resolved that each branch ought to possess the right of originating

Acts; that the National Legislature ought to be impowered to enjoy the Legislative Rights vested in Congress by the Confederation & moreover to legislate in all cases to which the separate States are incompetent, or in which the harmony of the United States may be interrupted by the exercise of individual Legislation; to negative all laws passed by the several States, contravening in the opinions of the National Legislature the articles of Union; and to call forth the force of the Union agst. any member of the Union failing to fulfill its duty under the articles thereof.

7. Resd. that a National Executive be instituted; to be chosen by the National Legislature for the term of   years, to receive punctually at stated times, a fixed compensation for the services rendered, in which no increase or diminution shall be made so as to affect the Magistracy, existing at the time of increase or diminution, and to be ineligible a second time; and that besides a general authority to execute the National laws, it ought to enjoy the Executive rights vested in Congress by the Confederation.

8. Resd. that the Executive and a convenient number of the National Judiciary, ought to compose a council of revision with authority to examine every act of the National Legislature before it shall operate, & every act of a particular Legislature before a Negative thereon shall be final; and that dissent of the said Council shall amount to a rejection, unless the Act of the National Legislature be again passed, or that of a particular Legislature be again negatived by   of the members of each branch.

9. Resd. that a National Judiciary be established to consist of one or more supreme tribunals, and of inferior tribunals to be chosen by the National Legislature, to hold their offices during good behaviour; and to receive punctually at stated times fixed compensation for their services, in which no increase or diminution shall be made so as to affect the persons actually in office at the time of such increase or diminution. that the jurisdiction of the inferior tribunals shall be to hear & determine in the first instance, and of the supreme tribunal to hear and determine in the dernier resort, all piracies & felonies on the high seas, captures from an enemy; cases in which foreigners or citizens of other States applying to such jurisdictions may be interested, or which respect the collection of the National revenue; impeachments of any National officers, and questions which may involve the national peace and harmony.

10. Resolvd. that provision ought to be made for the admission of States lawfully arising within the limits of the United States, whether from a voluntary junction of Government & Territory or otherwise, with the consent of a number of voices in the National legislature less than the whole.

11. Resd. that a Republican Government & the territory of each State, except in the instance of a voluntary junction of Government & territory, ought to be guaranteed by the United States to each State.

12. Resd. that provision ought to be made for the continuance of Congress and their authorities and privileges, until a given day after the reform of the articles of Union shall be adopted, and for the completion of all their engagements.

13. Resd. that provision ought to be made for the amendment of the Articles of Union whensoever it shall seem necessary, and that the assent of the National Legislature ought not to be required thereto.

14. Resd. that the Legislative Executive & Judiciary powers within the several States ought to be bound by oath to support the articles of Union.

15. Resd. that the amendments which shall be offered to the Confederation, by the Convention ought at a proper time, or times, after the approbation of Congress to be submitted to an assembly or assemblies of Representatives, recommended by the several Legislatures to be expressly chosen by the people, to consider & decide thereon.

He concluded with an exhortation, not to suffer the present opportunity of establishing general peace, harmony, happiness and liberty in the U. S. to pass away unimproved. . . .

WEDNESDAY JUNE 6TH. IN COMMITTEE OF THE WHOLE

. . . . .

Mr. Pinkney according to previous notice & rule obtained, moved "that the first branch of the national Legislature be elected by the State Legislatures, and not by the people." contending that the people were less fit Judges (in such a case,) and that the Legislatures would be less likely to promote the adoption of the new Government, if they were to be excluded from all share in it.

Mr. Rutlidge 2ded. the motion.

Mr. Gerry. Much depends on the mode of election. In England, the people will probably lose their liberty from the smallness of the proportion having a right of suffrage. Our danger arises from the opposite extreme: hence in Massts. the worst men get into the Legislature. Several members of that Body had lately been convicted of infamous crimes. Men of indigence, ignorance & baseness, spare no pains however dirty to carry their point agst. men who are superior to the artifices practiced. He was not disposed to run into extremes. He was as much principled as ever agst. aristocracy and monarchy. It was necessary on the one hand that the people should appoint one branch of the Govt. in order to inspire them with the necessary confidence. But he wished the election on the other to be so modified as to secure more effectually a just preference of merit. His idea was that the people should nominate certain persons in certain districts, out of whom the State Legislatures shd. make the appointment.

Mr. Wilson. He wished for vigor in the Govt. but he wished that vigorous authority to flow immediately from the legitimate source of all authority. The Govt. ought to possess not only 1st. the *force* but 2ndly. the *mind or sense* of the people at large. The Legislature ought to be the most exact transcript of the whole Society. Representation is made necessary only because it is impossible for the people to act collectively. The opposition was to be expected he said from the *Governments*, not from the Citizens of the States. The latter had parted as was observed (by Mr. King) with all the necessary powers; and it was immaterial to them, by whom they were exercised, if well exercised. The State officers were to be losers of power. The people he supposed would be rather more attached to the national Govt. than to the State Govts. as being more important in itself, and more flattering to their pride. There is no danger of improper elections if made by *large* districts. Bad elections proceed from the smallness of the districts which give an opportunity to bad men to intrigue themselves into office.

Mr. Sherman. If it were in view to abolish the State Govts. the elections ought to be by the people. If the State Govts. are to be continued, it is necessary in order to preserve harmony between the national & State Govts. that the elections to the former shd. be made by the latter. The right of participating in the National Govt. would be sufficiently secured to the people by their election of the State Legislatures. The objects of the Union, he thought were few. 1. defence agst. foreign dangers. 2. agst. internal disputes & a resort to force. 3. Treaties with foreign nations 4. regulating foreign commerce, & drawing revenue from it. These & perhaps a few lesser objects alone rendered a Confederation of the States necessary. All other matters civil & criminal would be much better in the hands of the States. The people are more happy in small than large States. States may indeed be too small as Rhode Island, & thereby be too subject to faction. Some others were perhaps too large, the powers of Govt not being able to pervade them. He was for giving the General Govt. power to legislate and execute within a defined province.

Col. Mason. Under the existing Confederacy, Congs. represents the *States* not the *people* of the States: their acts operate on the *States* not on the individuals. The case will be changed in the new plan of Govt. The people will be represented; they ought therefore to choose the Representatives. The requisites in actual representation are that the Reps. should sympathize with their constituents; shd. think as they think, & feel as they feel; and that for these purposes shd. even be residents among them. Much he sd. had been alledged agst. democratic elections. He admitted that much might be said; but it was to be considered that no Govts. was free from imperfections & evils; and that improper elections in many instances, were inseparable from Republican Govts. But compare these with the advantage of this Form in favor of the rights of the people, in favor of human nature. He was persuaded there was a better chance for proper elections by the people, if divided into large districts, than by the State Legislatures. Paper money had been issued by the latter when the former were against it. Was it to be supposed that the State Legislatures then wd. not send to the Natl. legislature patrons of such projects, if the choice depended on them.

Mr. Madison considered an election of one branch at least of the Legislature by the people immediately, as a clear principle of free Govt. and that this mode under proper regulations had the additional advantage of securing better representatives, as well as of avoiding too great an agency of the State Governments in the General one.—He differed from the member from Connecticut (Mr. Sherman) in thinking the objects mentioned to be all the principal ones that required a National Govt. Those were certainly important and necessary objects; but he combined with them the necessity, of providing more effectually for the security of private rights, and the steady dispensation of Justice. Interferences with these were evils which had more perhaps than any thing else, produced this convention. Was it to be supposed that republican liberty could long exist under the abuses of it practiced in (some of) the States? The gentleman (Mr. Sherman) had admitted that in a very small State, faction & oppression wd. prevail. It was to be inferred then that wherever these prevailed the State was too small. Had they not prevailed in the largest as well as the smallest tho' less than in the smallest; and were we not thence admonished to enlarge the sphere as far as the nature of the Govt. would admit. This was the only defence agst. the inconveniences of democracy consistent with the democratic form of Govt. All civilized Societies would be divided into different Sects, Factions, & interests, as they happened to consist of rich & poor, debtors & creditors, the landed the manufacturing, the commercial interests, the inhabitants of this district, or that district, the followers of this political leader or that political leader, the disciples of this religious sect or that religious sect. In all cases where a majority are united by a common interest or passion, the rights of the minority are in danger. What motives are to restrain them? A prudent regard to the maxim that honesty is the best policy is found by experience to be as little regarded by bodies of men as by individuals. Respect for character is always diminished in proportion to the number among whom the blame or praise is to be divided. Conscience, the only remaining tie is known to be inadequate in individuals: In large numbers, little is to be expected from it. Besides, Religion itself may become a motive to persecution & oppression.—These observations are verified by the Histories of every Country antient & modern. In Greece & Rome the rich & poor, the creditors & debtors, as well as the patricians & plebeians alternately oppressed each other with equal unmercifulness. What a source of oppression was the relation between the parent Cities of Rome, Athens & Carthage, & their respective provinces: the former possessing the power & the latter being sufficiently distinguished to be separate objects of it? Why was America so justly apprehensive of Parliamentary injustice? Because G. Britain had a separate interest real or supposed, & if her authority had been admitted, could have pursued that interest at our expense. We have seen the mere distinction of colour made in the most enlightened period of time, a ground of the most oppressive dominion ever exercised by man over man. What has been the source of those unjust laws complained of among ourselves? Has it not been the real or supposed interest of the major number? Debtors have defrauded their creditors. The landed interest has borne hard on the mercantile interest. The Holders of one species of property have thrown a disproportion of taxes on the holders of another species. The lesson we are to draw from the whole is that where a majority are united by a common sentiment and have an opportunity, the rights of the minor party become insecure. In a Republican Govt. the Majority if united have always an opportunity. The only remedy is to enlarge the sphere, & thereby divide the community into so great a number of interests & parties, that in the 1st. place a majority will not be likely at the same moment to have a common interest separate from that of the whole or of the minority; and in the 2d. place, that in case they shd. have such an interest, they may not be apt to unite in the pursuit of it. It was incumbent on us then to try this remedy, and with that view to frame a republican system on such a scale & in such a form as will controul all the evils wch. have been experienced.

Mr. Dickinson considered it as essential that one branch of the Legislature shd. be drawn immediately from the people; and as expedient that the other shd. be chosen by the Legislatures of the States. This combination of the State Govts. with the National Govt. was as politic as it was unavoidable. In the formation of the Senate we ought to carry it through such a refining process as will assimilate it as near as may be to the House of Lords in England. He repeated his warm eulogiums on the British Constitution. He was for a strong National Govt. but for leaving the States a considerable agency in the System. The objection agst. making the former dependent on the latter might be obviated by giving to the Senate an authority permanent & irrevocable for three, five or seven years. Being thus independent they will speak & decide with becoming freedom.

Mr. Read. Too much attachment is betrayed to the State Govermts. We must look beyond their continuance. A national Govt. must soon of necessity swallow all of them up. They will soon be reduced to the mere office of electing the national Senate. He was agst. patching up the old federal System: he hoped the idea wd. be dismissed. It would be like putting new cloth on an old garment. The confederation was founded on temporary principles. It cannot last: it cannot be amended. If we do not establish a good Govt. on new principles, we must either go to ruin, or have the work to do over again. The people at large are wrongly suspected of being averse to a Genl. Govt. The aversion lies among interested men who possess their confidence.

Mr. Pierce was for an election by the people as to the 1st. branch & by the States as to the 2d. branch; by which means the Citizens of the States wd. be represented both *individually* & *collectively*.

General Pinkney wished to have a good national Govt. & at the same time to leave a considerable share of power in the States. An election of either branch by the people scattered as they are in many States, particularly in S. Carolina was totally impracticable. He differed from gentlemen who thought that a choice by the people wd. be a better guard agst. bad measures, than by the Legislatures. A majority of the people in S. Carolina were notoriously for paper money as a legal tender; the Legislature had refused to make it a legal tender. The reason was that the latter had some sense of character and were restrained by that consideration. The State Legislatures also he said would be more jealous, & more ready to thwart the National Govt. if excluded from a participation in it. The Idea of abolishing these Legislatures wd. never go down.

Mr. Wilson, would not have spoken again, but for what had fallen from Mr. Read; namely, that the idea of preserving the State Govts. ought to be abandoned. He saw no incompatibility between the *national & State* Govts. provided the latter were restrained to certain local purposes; nor any probability of their being devoured by the former. In all confederated systems antient & modern the reverse had happened; the Generality being destroyed gradually by the usurpation of the parts composing it.

On the question for electing the 1st. branch by the State Legislatures as moved by Mr. Pinkney; (it was negatived;) . . .

TUESDAY. JUNE 26. IN CONVENTION

The duration of the 2d. branch under consideration.

Mr. Ghorum moved to fill the blank with "six years." (One third of the members to go out every second year.)

Mr. Wilson 2ded. the motion.

Genl. Pinkney opposed six years in favor of four years. The States he said had different interests. Those of the Southern, and of S. Carolina in particular were different from the Northern. If the Senators should be appointed for a long term, they wd. settle in the State where they exercised their functions; and would in a little time be rather the representatives of that than of the State appoint'g them.

Mr. Read movd. that the term be nine years. This wd. admit of a very convenient rotation, one third going out triennially. He wd. still prefer "during good behaviour," but being little supported in that idea, he was willing to take the longest term that could be obtained.

Mr. Broome 2ded. the motion.

Mr. Madison. In order to judge of the form to be given to this institution, it will be proper to take a view of the ends to be served by it. These were first to protect the people agst. their rulers: secondly to protect (the people) agst. the transient impressions into which they themselves might be led. A people deliberating in a temperate moment, and with the experience of other nations before them, on the plan of govt. most likely to secure their happiness, would first be aware, that those chargd. with the public happiness, might betray their trust. An obvious precaution agst. this danger wd. be to divide the trust between different bodies of men, who might watch & check each other. In this they wd. be governed by the same prudence which has prevailed in organizing the subordinate departments' of Govt. where all business liable to abuses is made to pass thro' separate hands, the one being a check on the other. It wd. next occur to such a people, that they themselves were liable to temporary errors, thro' want of information as to their true interest, and that men chosen for a short term, & employed but a small portion of that in public affairs, might err from the same cause. This reflection wd. naturally suggest that the Govt. be so constituted, as that one of its branches might have an oppy. of acquiring a competent knowledge of the public interests. Another reflection equally becoming a people on such an occasion, wd. be that they themselves, as well as a numerous body of Representatives, were liable to err also, from fickleness and passion. A necessary fence agst. this danger would be to select a portion of enlightened citizens, whose limited number, and firmness might seasonably interpose agst. impetuous counsels. It ought finally to occur to a people deliberating on a Govt. for themselves, that as different interests necessarily result from the liberty meant to be secured, the major interests might under sudden impulses be tempted to commit injustice on the minority. In all civilized Countries the people fall into different classes havg. a real or supposed difference of interests. There will be creditors & debtors, farmers, merchts. & manufacturers. There will be particularly the distinction of rich & poor. It was true as had been observd. (by Mr Pinkney) we had not among us those hereditary distinctions, of rank which were a great source of the contests in the ancient Govts. as well as the modern States of Europe, nor those extremes of wealth or poverty which characterize the latter. We cannot however be regarded even at this time, as one homogeneous mass, in which every thing that affects a part will affect in the same manner the whole. In framing a system which we wish to last for ages, we shd. not lose sight of the changes which ages will produce. An increase of population will of necessity increase the proportion of those who will labour under all the hardships of life, & secretly sigh for a more equal distribution of its blessings. These may in time outnumber those who are placed above the feelings of indigence. According to the equal laws of suffrage, the power will slide into the hands of the former. No agrarian attempts have yet been made in this Country, but symptoms of a leveling spirit, as we have understood, have sufficiently appeared in a certain quarters to give notice of the future danger. How is this danger to be guarded agst. on republican principles? How is the danger in all cases of interested coalitions to oppress the minority to be guarded agst.? Among other means by the establishment of a body in the Govt. sufficiently respectable for its wisdom & virtue, to aid on such emergencies, the preponderance of justice by throwing its weight into that scale. Such being the objects of the second branch in the proposed Govt. he thought a considerable duration ought to be given to it. He did not conceive that the term of nine years could threaten any real danger; but in pursuing his particular ideas on the subject, he should require that the long term allowed to the 2d. branch should not commence till such a period of life as would render a perpetual disqualification to be re-elected little inconvenient either in a public or private view. He observed that as it was more than probable we were now digesting a plan which in its operation wd. decide forever the fate of Republican Govt we ought not only to provide every guard to liberty that its preservation cd. require, but be equally careful to supply the defects which our own experience had particularly pointed out.

Mr. Sherman. Govt. is instituted for those who live under it. It ought therefore to be so constituted as not to be dangerous to their liberties. The more permanency it has the worse if it be a bad Govt. Frequent elections are necessary to preserve the good behavior of rulers. They also tend to give permanency to the Government, by preserving that good behavior, because it ensures their re-election. In Connecticut elections have been very frequent, yet great stability & uniformity both as to persons & measures have been experienced from its original establishmt. to the present time; a period of more than 130 years. He wished to have provision made for steadiness & wisdom in the system to be adopted; but he thought six or (four) years would be sufficient. He shd. be content with either.

Mr. Read wished it to be considered by the small States that it was their interest that we should become one people as much as possible, that State attachments shd. be extinguished as much as possible, that the Senate shd. be so constituted as to have the feelings of citizens of the whole.

Mr. Hamilton. He did not mean to enter particularly into the subject. He concurred with Mr. Madison in thinking we were now to decide for ever the fate of Republican Government; and that if we did not give to that form due stability and wisdom, it would be disgraced & lost among ourselves, disgraced & lost to mankind for ever. He acknowledged himself not to think favorably of Republican Government; but addressed his remarks to those who did think favorably of it, in order to prevail on them to tone their Government as high as possible. He professed himself to be as zealous an advocate for liberty as any man whatever, and trusted he should be as willing a martyr to it though he differed as to the form in which it was most eligible.—He concurred also in the general observations of (Mr. Madison) on the subject, which might be supported by others if it were necessary. It was certainly true that nothing like an equality of property existed: that an inequality would exist as long as liberty existed, and that it would unavoidably result from that very liberty itself. This inequality of property constituted the great & fundamental distinction in Society. When the Tribunitial power had levelled the boundary between the *patricians* & *plebeians* what followed? The distinction between rich & poor was substituted. He meant not however to enlarge on the subject. He rose principally to remark that (Mr. Sherman) seemed not to recollect that one branch of the proposed Govt. was so formed, as to render it particularly the guardians of the poorer orders of citizens; nor to have adverted to the true causes of the stability which had been exemplified in Cont. Under the British system as well as the federal, many of the great powers appertaining to Govt. particularly all those relating to foreign Nations were not in the hands of the Govt there. Their internal affairs also were extremely simple, owing to sundry causes many of which were peculiar to that Country. Of late the Governmt. had entirely given way to the people, and had in fact suspended many of its ordinary functions in order to prevent those turbulent scenes which had appeared elsewhere. (He asks Mr. S. whether the State at this time, dare impose & collect a tax on ye people?) To those causes & not to the frequency of elections, the effect, as far as it existed ought to be chiefly ascribed. . . .

MONDAY. JULY. 23. IN CONVENTION.

. . . . . .

Resol: 19. referring the new Constitution to Assemblies to be chosen by the people for the express purpose of ratifying it" was next taken into consideration.

Mr. Elseworth moved that it be referred to the Legislatures of the States for ratification. Mr. Patterson 2ded. the motion.

Col. Mason considered a reference of the plan to the authority of the people as one of the most important and essential of the Resolutions. The Legislatures have no power to ratify it. They are the mere creatures of the State Constitutions, and cannot be greater than their creators. And he knew of no power in any of the Constitutions, he knew there was no power in some of them, that could be competent to this object. Whither then must we resort? To the people with whom all power remains that has not been given up in the Constitutions derived from them. It was of great moment he observed that this doctrine should be cherished as the basis of free Government. Another strong reason was that admitting the Legislatures to have a competent authority, it would be wrong to refer the plan to them, because succeeding Legislatures having equal authority could undo the acts of their predecessors; and the National Govt. would stand in each State on the weak and tottering foundation of an Act of Assembly. There was a remaining consideration of some weight. In some of the States the Govts. were (not) derived from the clear & undisputed authority of the people. This was the case in Virginia. Some of the best & wisest citizens considered the Constitution as established by an assumed authority. A National Constitution derived from such a source would be exposed to the severest criticism.

Mr. Randolph. One idea has pervaded all (our) proceedings, to wit, that opposition as well from the States as from individuals, will be made to the

System to be proposed. Will it not then be highly imprudent, to furnish any unnecessary pretext by the mode of ratifying it. Added to other objections agst. a ratification by Legislative authority only, it may be remarked that there have been instances in which the authority of the Common law has been set up in particular States agst. that of the Confederation which has had no higher sanction than Legislative ratification.—Whose opposition will be most likely to be excited agst. the System? That of the local demogagues who will be degraded by it from the importance they now hold. These will spare no efforts to impede that progress in the popular mind which will be necessary to the adoption of the plan, and which every member will find to have taken place in his own, if he will compare his present opinions with those brought with him into the Convention. It is of great importance therefore that the consideration of this subject should be transferred from the Legislatures where this class of men have their full influence to a field in which their efforts can be less mischievous. It is moreover worthy of consideration that some of the States are averse to any change in their Constitution, and will not take the requisite steps, unless expressly called upon to refer the question to the people.

Mr. Gerry. The arguments of Col. Mason & Mr. Randolph prove too much, they prove an unconstitutionality in the present federal (system) & even in some of the State Govts. Inferences drawn from such a source must be inadmissable. Both the State Govts. & the federal Govt. have been too long acquiesced in, to be now shaken. He considered the Confederation to be paramount to any State Constitution. The last article of it authorizing alterations must consequently be so as well as the others, and everything done in pursuance of the article must have the same high authority with the article. —Great confusion he was confident would result from a recurrence to the people. They would never agree on any thing. He could not see any ground to suppose that the people will do what their rulers will not. The rulers will either conform to, or influence the sense of the people.

Mr. Ghorum was agst. referring the plan to the Legislatures. 1. Men chosen by the people for the particular purpose, will discuss the subject more candidly than members of the Legislature who are to lose the power which is to be given up to the Genl. Govt. 2. Some of the Legislatures are composed of several branches. It will consequently be more difficult in these cases to get the plan through the Legislatures, than thro' a Convention. 3. in the States many of the ablest men are excluded from the Legislatures, but may be elected into a Convention. Among these may be ranked many of the Clergy who are generally friends to good Government. Their services were found to be valuable in the formation & establishment of the Constitution of Massachts. 4. the Legislatures will be interrupted with a variety of little business, by artfully pressing which, designing men will find means to delay from year to year, if not to frustrate altogether the national system. 5. If the last art: of the Confederation is to be pursued the unanimous concurrence of the States will be necessary. But will any one say. that all the States are to suffer themselves to be ruined, if Rho. Island should persist in her opposition to general measures. Some other States might also tread in her steps. The present advantage which N. York seems to be so much attached to, of taxing her neighbours (by the regulation of her trade), makes it very probable, that she will be of the number. It would therefore deserve serious consideration whether provision ought not to be made for giving effect to the System without waiting for the unanimous concurrence of the States. . . .

Mr. (Madison) thought it clear that the Legislatures were incompetent to the proposed changes. These changes would make essential inroads on the State Constitutions, and it would be a novel & dangerous doctrine that a Legislature could change the Constitution under which it held its existence. There might indeed be some Constitutions within the Union, which had given a power to the Legislature to concur in alterations of the federal Compact. But there were certainly some which had not; and in the case of these, a ratification must of necessity be obtained from the people. He considered the difference between a system founded on the Legislatures only, and one founded on the people, to be the true difference between a *league* or *treaty*, and a *Constitution*. The former in point of *moral obligation* might be as inviolable as the latter. In point of *political operation*, there were two important distinctions in favor of the latter. 1. A law violating a treaty ratified by a preëxisting law, might be respected by the Judges as a law, though an unwise or perfidious one. A law violating a constitution established by the people themselves, would be considered by the Judges as null & void. 2. The doctrine laid down by the law of Nations in the case of treaties is that a breach of any one article by any of the parties, frees the other parties from their engagements. In the case of a union of people under one Constitution, the nature of the pact has always been understood to exclude such an interpretation. Comparing the two modes in point of expediency he thought all the considerations which recommended this Convention in preference to Congress for proposing the reform were in favor of State Conventions in preference to the Legislatures for examining and adopting it. . . .

TEUSDAY [*sic*] AUGUST 7TH. IN CONVENTION

Mr. Govr. Morris. He had long learned not to be the dupe of words. The sound of Aristocracy therefore, had no effect on him. It was the thing, not the name, to which he was opposed, and one of his principal objections to the Constitution as it is now before us, is that it threatens this Country with an Aristocracy. The aristocracy will grow out of the House of Representatives. Give the votes to people who have no property, and they will sell them to the rich who will be able to buy them. We should not confine our attention to the present moment. The time is not distant when this Country will abound with mechanics & manufacturers who will receive their bread from their employers. Will such men be the secure & faithful Guardians of liberty? Will they be the impregnable barrier agst. aristocracy?—He was as little duped by the association of the words, "taxation & Representation"—The man who does not give his vote freely is not represented. It is the man who dictates the vote. Children do not vote. Why? because they want prudence, because they have no will of their own. The ignorant & the dependent can be as little trusted with the public interest. He did not conceive the difficulty of defining "freeholders" to be insuperable. Still less that the restriction could be unpopular. 9/10 of the people are at present freeholders and these will certainly be pleased with it. As to Merchts. &c. if they have wealth & value the right they can acquire it. If not they don't deserve it.

Col. Mason. We all feel too strongly the remains of antient prejudices, and view things too much through a British Medium. A Freehold is the qualification in England, & hence it is imagined to be the only proper one. The true idea in his opinion was that every man having evidence of attachment to & permanent common interest with the Society ought to share in all its rights & privileges. Was this qualification restrained to freeholders? Does no other kind of property but land evidence a common interest in the proprietor? does nothing besides property mark a permanent attachment? Ought the merchant, the monied man, the parent of a number of children whose fortunes are to be pursued in their own (Country), to be viewed as suspicious characters, and unworthy to be trusted with the common rights of their fellow Citizens.

Mr. (Madison.) the right of suffrage is certainly one of the fundamental articles of republican Government, and ought not to be left to be regulated by the Legislature. A gradual abridgment of this right has been the mode in which Aristocracies have been built on the ruins of popular forms. Whether the Constitutional qualification ought to be a freehold, would with him depend much on the probable reception such a change would meet with in States where the right was now exercised by every description of people. In several of the States a freehold was now the qualification. Viewing the subject in its merits alone, the freeholders of the Country would be the safest depositories of Republican liberty. In future times a great majority of the people will not only be without landed, but any other sort of, property. These will either combine under the influence of their common situation; in which case, the rights of property & the public liberty, (will not be secure in their hands;) or which is more probable, they will become the tools of opulence & ambition, in which case there will be equal danger on another side. The example of England has been misconceived (Col. Mason). A very small proportion of the Representatives are there chosen by freeholders. The greatest part are chosen by the Cities & boroughs, in many of which the qualification of suffrage is as low as it is in any one of the U. S. and it was in (the boroughs & Cities) rather than the Counties, that bribery most prevailed, & the influence of the Crown on elections was most dangerously exerted. . . .

THE FEDERALIST PAPERS [93]

Alexander Hamilton, James Madison, and John Jay coöperated in writing a series of articles for New York newspapers in order to win the support of that state for the new Constitution. These essays expound and defend the various provisions of the Constitution. While the same distrust of democracy and desire for stability that permeated the debates of the Constitutional Convention are present in *The Federalist*, its authors carefully sugar-coated their work for popular consumption.

[93] Alexander Hamilton, John Jay, and James Madison, *The Federalist—a Commentary on the Constitution of the United States—Being a Collection of Essays Written in Support of the Constitution Agreed upon September 17, 1787, by the Federal Convention*, edited by H. C. Lodge. (New York: G. P. Putnam's Sons, 1889), pp. 51–60, 277–280, 387–389, 457–459, 482–491. (Reprinted by permission of the publishers.)

THE FEDERALIST NO. X

(Madison)

To the People of the State of New York:

Among the numerous advantages promised by a well-constructed Union, none deserves to be more accurately developed than its tendency to break and control the violence of faction. The friend of popular governments never finds himself so much alarmed for their character and fate, as when he contemplates their propensity to this dangerous vice. He will not fail, therefore, to set a due value on any plan which, without violating the principles to which he is attached, provides a proper cure for it. The instability, injustice, and confusion introduced into the public councils, have, in truth, been the mortal diseases under which popular governments have everywhere perished; as they continue to be the favorite and fruitful topics from which the adversaries to liberty derive their most specious declamations. The valuable improvements made by the American constitutions on the popular models, both ancient and modern, cannot certainly be too much admired; but it would be an unwarrantable partiality, to contend that they have as effectually obviated the danger on this side, as was wished and expected. Complaints are everywhere heard from our most considerate and virtuous citizens, equally the friends of public and private faith, and of public and personal liberty, that our governments are too unstable, that the public good is disregarded in the conflicts of rival parties, and that measures are too often decided, not according to the rules of justice and the rights of the minor party, but by the superior force of an interested and overbearing majority. However anxiously we may wish that these complaints had no foundation, the evidence of known facts will not permit us to deny that they are in some degree true. It will be found, indeed, on a candid review of our situation, that some of the distresses under which we labor have been erroneously charged on the operation of our governments; but it will be found, at the same time, that other causes will not alone account for many of our heaviest misfortunes; and, particularly, for that prevailing and increasing distrust of public engagements, and alarm for private rights, which are echoed from one end of the continent to the other. These must be chiefly, if not wholly, effects of the unsteadiness and injustice with which a factious spirit has tainted our public administrations.

By a faction, I understand a number of citizens, whether amounting to a majority or minority of the whole, who are united and actuated by some common impulse of passion, or of interest, adverse to the rights of other citizens, or to the permanent and aggregate interests of the community.

There are two methods of curing the mischiefs of faction: the one, by removing its causes; the other, by controlling its effects.

There are again two methods of removing the causes of faction: the one, by destroying the liberty which is essential to its existence; the other, by giving to every citizen the same opinions, the same passions, and the same interests.

It could never be more truly said than of the first remedy, that it was worse than the disease. Liberty is to faction what air is to fire, an ailment without which it instantly expires. But it could not be less folly to abolish liberty, which is essential to political life, because it nourishes faction, than it would be to wish the annihilation of air, which is essential to animal life, because it imparts to fire its destructive agency.

The second expedient is as impracticable as the first would be unwise. As long as the reason of man continues fallible, and he is at liberty to exercise it, different opinions will be formed. As long as the connection subsists between his reason and his self-love, his opinions and his passions will have a reciprocal influence on each other; and the former will be objects to which the latter will attach themselves. The diversity in the faculties of men, from which the rights of property originate, is not less an insuperable obstacle to a uniformity of interests. The protection of these faculties is the first object of government. From the protection of different and unequal faculties of acquiring property, the possession of different degrees and kinds of property immediately results; and from the influence of these on the sentiments and views of the respective proprietors, ensues a division of the society into different interests and parties.

The latent causes of faction are thus sown in the nature of man; and we see them everywhere brought into different degrees of activity, according to the different circumstances of civil society. A zeal for different opinions concerning religion, concerning government, and many other points, as well of speculation as of practice; an attachment to different leaders ambitiously contending for pre-eminence and power; or to persons of other descriptions whose fortunes have been interesting to the human passions, have, in turn, divided mankind into parties, inflamed them with mutual animosity, and rendered them much more disposed to vex and oppress each other than to co-operate for their common good. So strong is this propensity of mankind to fall into mutual animosities, that where no substantial occasion presents itself, the most frivolous and fanciful distinctions have been sufficient to kindle their unfriendly passions and excite their most violent conflicts. But the most common and durable source of factions has been the various and unequal distribution of property. Those who hold and those who are without property have ever formed distinct interests in society. Those who are creditors, and those who are debtors, fall under a like discrimination. A landed interest, a manufacturing interest, a mercantile interest, a moneyed interest, with many lesser interests, grow up of necessity in civilized nations, and divide them into different classes, actuated by different sentiments and views. The regulation of these various and interfering interests forms the principal task of modern legislation, and involves the spirit of party and faction in the necessary and ordinary operations of the government.

No man is allowed to be a judge in his own cause, because his interest would certainly bias his judgment, and, not improbably, corrupt his integrity. With equal, nay with greater reason, a body of men are unfit to be both judges and parties at the same time; yet what are many of the most important acts of legislation, but so many judicial determinations, not indeed concerning the rights of single persons but concerning the rights of large bodies of citizens? And what are the different classes of legislators but advocates and parties to the causes which they determine? Is a law proposed concerning private debts? It is a question to which the creditors are parties on one side and the debtors on the other. Justice ought to hold the balance between them. Yet the parties are, and must be, themselves the judges; and the most numerous party, or, in other words, the most powerful faction must be expected to prevail. Shall domestic manufactures be encouraged, and in what degree, by restrictions on foreign manufactures? are questions which would be differently decided by the landed and the manufacturing classes, and probably by neither with a sole regard to justice and the public good. The apportionment of taxes on the various descriptions of property is an act which seems to require the most exact impartiality; yet there is, perhaps, no legislative act in which greater opportunity and temptation are given to a predominant party to trample on the rules of justice. Every shilling with which they overburden the inferior number, is a shilling saved to their own pockets.

It is in vain to say that enlightened statesmen will be able to adjust these clashing interests, and render them all subservient to the public good. Enlightened statesmen will not always be at the helm. Nor, in many cases, can such an adjustment be made at all without taking into view indirect and remote considerations, which will rarely prevail over the immediate interest which one party may find in disregarding the rights of another or the good of the whole.

The inference to which we are brought is, that the *causes* of faction cannot be removed, and that relief is only to be sought in the means of controlling its *effects*.

If a faction consists of less than a majority, relief is supplied by the republican principle, which enables the majority to defeat its sinister views by regular vote. It may clog the administration, it may convulse the society; but it will be unable to execute and mask its violence under the forms of the Constitution. When a majority is included in a faction, the form of popular government, on the other hand, enables it to sacrifice to its ruling passion or interest both the public good and the rights of other citizens. To secure the public good and private rights against the danger of such a faction, and at the same time to preserve the spirit and the form of popular government, is then the great object to which our inquiries are directed. Let me add that it is the great desideratum by which this form of government can be rescued from the opprobrium under which it has so long labored, and be recommended to the esteem and adoption of mankind.

By what means is this object attainable? Evidently by one of two only. Either the existence of the same passion or interest in a majority at the same time must be prevented, or the majority, having such coexistent passion or interest, must be rendered, by their number and local situation, unable to concert and carry into effect schemes of oppression. If the impulse and the opportunity be suffered to coincide, we well know that neither moral nor religious motives can be relied on as an adequate control. They are not found to be such on the injustice and violence of individuals, and lose their efficacy in proportion to the number combined together, that is, in proportion as their efficacy becomes needful.

From this view of the subject it may be concluded that a pure democracy, by which I mean a society consisting of a small number of citizens, who assemble and administer the government in person, can admit of no cure for the mischiefs of faction. A common passion or interest will, in almost every case, be felt by a majority of the whole; a communication and concert result from the form of government itself; and there is nothing to check the inducements to sacrifice the weaker party or an obnoxious individual. Hence it is that such democracies have ever been spectacles of turbulence and contention; have ever been found incompatible with personal security or the rights of property; and have in general been as short in their lives as they have been violent in their deaths. Theoretic politicians, who have patronized this species of government, have erroneously supposed that by reducing mankind to a perfect equality in their political rights, they would, at the same time, be perfectly equalized and assimilated in their possessions, their opinions, and their passions.

A republic, by which I mean a government in which the scheme of representation takes place, opens a different prospect, and promises the cure for which we are seeking. Let us examine the points in which it varies from pure democracy, and we shall comprehend both the nature of the cure and the efficacy which it must derive from the Union.

The two great points of difference between a democracy and a republic are; first, the delegation of the government, in the latter, to a small number of citizens elected by the rest; secondly, the greater number of citizens, and greater sphere of country, over which the latter may be extended.

The effect of the first difference is, on the one hand, to refine and enlarge the public views, by passing them through the medium of a chosen body of citizens, whose wisdom may best discern the true interest of their country, and whose patriotism and love of justice will be least likely to sacrifice it to temporary or partial considerations. Under such a regulation, it may well happen that the public voice, pronounced by the representatives of the people, will be more consonant to the public good than if pronounced by the people themselves, convened for the purpose. On the other hand, the effect may be inverted. Men of factious tempers, of local prejudices, or of sinister designs, may, by intrigue, by corruption, or by other means, first obtain the suffrages, and then betray the interests, of the people. The question resulting is, whether small or extensive republics are more favorable to the election of proper guardians of the public weal; and it is clearly decided in favor of the latter by two obvious considerations:

In the first place, it is to be remarked that, however small the republic may be, the representatives must be raised to a certain number, in order to guard against the cabals of a few; and that, however large it may be, they must be limited to a certain number, in order to guard against the confusion of a multitude. Hence, the number of representatives in the two cases not being in proportion to that of the two constituents, and being proportionally greater in the small republic, it follows that, if the proportion of fit characters be not less in the large than in the small republic, the former will present a greater option, and consequently a greater probability of a fit choice.

In the next place, as each representative will be chosen by a greater number of citizens in the large than in the small republic it will be more difficult, for unworthy candidates to practise with success the vicious arts by which elections are too often carried; and the suffrages of the people being more free, will be more likely to centre in men who possess the most attractive merit and the most diffusive and established characters.

It must be confessed that in this, as in most other cases, there is a mean, on both sides of which inconveniences will be found to lie. By enlarging too

much the number of electors, you render the representative too little acquainted with all their local circumstances and lesser interests; as by reducing it too much, you render him unduly attached to these, and too little
fit to comprehend and pursue great and national objects. The federal Constitution forms a happy combination in this respect; the great and aggregate interests being referred to the national, the local and particular to the
State legislatures.

The other point of difference is, the greater number of citizens and extent
of territory which may be brought within the compass of republican than
of democratic government; and it is this circumstance principally which renders factious combinations less to be dreaded in the former than in the latter.
The smaller the society, the fewer probably will be the distinct parties and
interests composing it; the fewer the distinct parties and interests, the more
frequently will a majority be found of the same party; and the smaller the
number of individuals composing a majority, and the smaller the compass
within which they are placed, the more easily will they concert and execute
their plans of oppression. Extend the sphere, and you take in a greater variety
of parties and interests; you make it less probable that a majority of the whole
will have a common motive to invade the rights of other citizens; or if such a
common motive exists, it will be more difficult for all who feel it to discover their
own strength, and to act in unison with each other. Besides other impediments, it may be remarked that, where there is a consciousness of unjust or
dishonorable purposes, communication is always checked by distrust in
proportion to the number whose concurrence is necessary.

Hence, it clearly appears, that the same advantage which a republic has
over a democracy, in controlling the effects of faction, is enjoyed by a large
over a small republic,—is enjoyed by the Union over the States composing
it. Does the advantage consist in the substitution of representatives whose
enlightened views and virtuous sentiments render them superior to local
prejudices and to schemes of injustice? It will not be denied that the representation of the Union will be most likely to possess these requisite endowments. Does it consist in the greater security afforded by a greater variety
of parties, against the event of any one party being able to outnumber and
oppress the rest? In an equal degree does the increased variety of parties
comprised within the Union, increase this security. Does it, in fine, consist
in the greater obstacles opposed to the concert and accomplishment of the
secret wishes of an unjust and interested majority? Here, again, the extent
of the Union gives it the most palpable advantage.

The influence of factious leaders may kindle a flame within their particular
States, but will be unable to spread a general conflagration through the other
States. A religious sect may degenerate into a political faction in a part of
the Confederacy; but the variety of sects dispersed over the entire face of
it must secure the national councils against any danger from that source.
A rage for paper money, for an abolition of debts, for an equal division of
property, or for any other improper or wicked project, will be less apt to
pervade the whole body of the Union than a particular member of it; in
the same proportion as such a malady is more likely to taint a particular
county or district, than an entire State.

In the extent and proper structure of the Union, therefore, we behold a republican remedy for the diseases most incident to republican government. And according to the degree of pleasure and pride we feel in being republicans, ought to be our zeal in cherishing the spirit and supporting the character of Federalists.

PUBLIUS.

THE FEDERALIST NO. XLIV

(Madison)

To the People of the State of New York:

A *fifth* class of provisions in favor of the federal authority consists of the following restrictions on the authority of the several States.

1. "No State shall enter into any treaty, alliance, or confederation; grant letters of marque and reprisal; coin money; emit bills of credit; make any thing but gold and silver a legal tender in payment of debts; pass any bills of attainder, *ex-post facto* law, or law impairing the obligation of contracts; or grant any title of nobility."

The prohibition against treaties, alliances, and confederations makes a part of the existing articles of Union; and for reasons which need no explanation, is copied into the new Constitution. The prohibition of letters of marque is another part of the old system, but is somewhat extended in the new. According to the former, letters of marque could be granted by the States after a declaration of war; according to the latter, these licenses must be obtained, as well during war as previous to its declaration, from the government of the United States. This alteration is fully justified by the advantage of uniformity in all points which relate to foreign powers; and of immediate responsibility to the nation in all those for whose conduct the nation itself is to be responsible.

The right of coining money, which is here taken from the States, was left in their hands by the Confederation, as a concurrent right with that of Congress, under an exception in favor of the exclusive right of Congress to regulate the alloy and value. In this instance, also, the new provision is an improvement on the old. Whilst the alloy and value depended on the general authority, a right of coinage in the particular States could have no other effect than to multiply expensive mints and diversify the forms and weights of the circulating pieces. The latter inconveniency defeats one purpose for which the power was originally submitted to the federal head; and as far as the former might prevent an inconvenient remittance of gold and silver to the central mint for recoinage, the end can be as well attained by local mints established under the general authority.

The extension of the prohibition to bills of credit must give pleasure to every citizen, in proportion to his love of justice and his knowledge of the true springs of public prosperity. The loss which America has sustained since the peace, from the pestilent effects of paper money on the necessary confidence between man and man, on the necessary confidence in the public councils, on the industry and morals of the people, and on the character of republican government, constitutes an enormous debt against the States chargeable with this unadvised measure, which must long remain unsatisfied; or rather an accumulation of guilt, which can be expiated no otherwise than by a voluntary sacrifice on the altar of justice, of the power which has been the instrument of it. In addition to these persuasive considerations, it may be observed, that the same reasons which show the necessity of denying to the States the power of regulating coin, prove with equal force that they ought not to be at liberty to substitute a paper medium in the place of coin. Had every State a right to regulate the value of its coin, there might be as many different currencies as States, and thus the intercourse among them would be impeded; retrospective alterations in its value might be made, and thus the citizens of other States be injured, and animosities be kindled among the States themselves. The subjects of foreign powers might suffer from the same cause, and hence the Union be discredited and embroiled by the indiscretion of a single member. No one of these mischiefs is less incident to a power in the States to emit paper money, than to coin gold and silver. The power to make any thing but gold and silver a tender in payment of debts, is withdrawn from the States, on the same principle with that of issuing a paper currency.

Bills of attainder, *ex-post-facto* laws, and laws impairing the obligation of contracts, are contrary to the first principles of the social compact, and to every principle of sound legislation. The two former are expressly prohibited by the declarations prefixed to some of the State constitutions, and all of them are prohibited by the spirit and scope of these fundamental charters. Our own experience has taught us, nevertheless, that additional fences against these dangers ought not to be omitted. Very properly, therefore, have the convention added this constitutional bulwark in favor of personal security and private rights; and I am much deceived if they have not, in so doing, as faithfully consulted the genuine sentiments as the undoubted interests of their constituents. The sober people of America are weary of the fluctuating policy which has directed the public councils. They have seen with regret and indignation that sudden changes and legislative interferences, in cases affecting personal rights, become jobs in the hands of enterprising and influential speculators, and snares to the more-industrious and less-informed part of the community. They have seen too, that one legislative interference is but the first link of a long chain of repetitions, every subsequent interference being naturally produced by the effects of the preceding. They very rightly infer, therefore, that some thorough reform is wanting, which will banish speculations on public measures, inspire a general prudence and industry, and give a regular course to the business of society. The prohibition with respect to titles of nobility is copied from the articles of Confederation, and needs no comment.

2. "No State shall, without the consent of the Congress, lay any imposts or duties on imports or exports, except what may be absolutely necessary for executing its inspection laws, and the net produce of all duties and imposts laid by any State on imports or exports, shall be for the use of the treasury of the United States; and all such laws shall be subject to the revision and control of the Congress. No State shall, without the consent of Congress, lay any duty on tonnage, keep troops or ships of war in time of peace, enter into any agreement or compact with another State, or with a foreign power, or engage in war unless actually invaded, or in such imminent danger as will not admit of delay."

The restraint on the power of the States over imports and exports is enforced by all the arguments which prove the necessity of submitting the regulation of trade to the federal councils. It is needless, therefore, to remark further on this head, than that the manner in which the restraint is qualified seems well calculated at once to secure to the States a reasonable discretion in providing for the conveniency of their imports and exports, and to the United States a reasonable check against the abuse of this discretion. The remaining particulars of this clause fall within reasonings which are either so obvious, or have been so fully developed, that they may be passed over without remark. . . .

PUBLIUS.

THE FEDERALIST. NO. LXII

(Hamilton or Madison)

To the People of the State of New York:

. . . . . .

IV. The number of senators, and the duration of their appointment, come next to be considered. In order to form an accurate judgment on both these points, it will be proper to inquire into the purposes which are to be answered by a senate; and in order to ascertain these, it will be necessary to review the inconveniences which a republic must suffer from the want of such an institution.

First. It is a misfortune incident to republican government, though in a less degree than to other governments, that those who administer it may forget their obligations to their constituents, and prove unfaithful to their important trust. In this point of view, a senate, as a second branch of the legislative assembly, distinct from, and dividing the power with, a first, must be in all cases a salutary check on the government. It doubles the security to the people, by requiring the concurrence of two distinct bodies in schemes of usurpation or perfidy, where the ambition or corruption of one would otherwise be sufficient. This is a precaution founded on such clear principles, and now so well understood in the United States, that it would be more than superfluous to enlarge on it. I will barely remark, that as the improbability of sinister combinations will be in proportion to the dissimilarity in the genius of the two bodies, it must be politic to distinguish them from each other by every circumstance which will consist with a due harmony in all proper measures, and with genuine principles of republican government.

Secondly. The necessity of a senate is not less indicated by the propensity of all single and numerous assemblies to yield to the impulse of sudden and violent passions, and to be seduced by factious leaders into intemperate and pernicious resolutions. Examples on this subject might be cited without number; and from proceedings within the United States, as well as from the history of other nations. But a position that will not be contradicted, need not be proved. All that need be remarked is, that a body which is to correct this infirmity ought itself to be free from it, and consequently ought to be less numerous. It ought, moreover, to possess great firmness, and consequently ought to hold its authority by a tenure of considerable duration.

Thirdly. Another defect to be supplied by a senate lies in a want of due acquaintance with the objects and principles of legislation. It is not possible that an assembly of men called for the most part from pursuits of a private nature, continued in appointment for a short time, and led by no permanent motive to devote the intervals of public occupation to a study of the laws, the affairs, and the comprehensive interests of their country, should, if left wholly to themselves, escape a variety of important errors in the exercise of their legislative trust. It may be affirmed, on the best grounds, that no small share of the present embarrassments of America is to be charged on the blunders of our governments; and that these have proceeded from the heads rather than the hearts of most of the authors of them. What indeed are all the repealing, explaining, and amending laws, which fill and disgrace our voluminous codes, but so many monuments of deficient wisdom; so many impeachments exhibited by each succeeding against each preceding session; so many admonitions to the people, of the value of those aids which may be expected from a well-constituted senate?

A good government implies two things: first, fidelity to the object of government, which is the happiness of the people; secondly, a knowledge of the means by which that object can be best attained. Some governments are deficient in both these qualities; most governments are deficient in the first. I scruple not to assert, that in American governments too little attention has been paid to the last. The federal Constitution avoids this error; and what merits particular notice, it provides for the last in a mode which increases the security for the first.

Fourthly. The mutability in the public councils arising from a rapid succession of new members, however qualified they may be, points out, in the strongest manner, the necessity of some stable institution in the government. Every new election in the States is found to change one half of the representatives. From this change of men must proceed a change of opinions: and from a change of opinions, a change of measures. But a continual change even of good measures is inconsistent with every rule of prudence and every prospect of success. The remark is verified in private life, and becomes more just, as well as more important, in national transactions. . . .

PUBLIUS.

THE FEDERALIST. NO. LXXIII

(Hamilton)

To the People of the State of New York:

. . . . . .

The last of the requisites to energy, which have been enumerated, are competent powers. Let us proceed to consider those which are proposed to be vested in the President of the United States.

The first thing that offers itself to our observation, is the qualified negative of the President upon the acts or resolutions of the two houses of the legislature; or, in other words, this power of reurning all bills with objections, to have the effect of preventing their becoming laws, unless they should afterwards be ratified by two thirds of each of the component members of the legislative body.

The propensity of the legislative department to intrude upon the rights, and to absorb the powers, of the other departments, has been already suggested and repeated; the insufficiency of a mere parchment delineation of the boundaries of each, has also been remarked upon; and the necessity of furnishing each with constitutional arms for its own defence, has been inferred and proved. From these clear and indubitable principles results the propriety of a negative, either absolute or qualified, in the Executive, upon the acts of the legislative branches. Without the one or the other, the former would be absolutely unable to defend himself against the depredations of the latter. He might gradually be stripped of his authorities by successive resolutions, or annihilated by a single vote. And in the one mode or the other, the legislative and executive powers might speedily come to be blended in the same hands. If even no propensity had ever discovered itself in the legislative body to invade the rights of the Executive, the rules of just reasoning and theoretic propriety would of themselves teach us, that the one ought not to be left to the mercy of the other, but ought to possess a constitutional and effectual power of self-defence.

But the power in question has a further use. It not only serves as a shield to the Executive, but it furnishes an additional security against the enaction of improper laws. It establishes a salutary check upon the legislative body, calculated to guard the community against the effects of faction, precipitancy, or of any impulse unfriendly to the public good, which may happen to influence a majority of that body.

The propriety of a negative has, upon some occasions, been combated by an observation, that it was not to be presumed a single man would possess more virtue and wisdom than a number of men; and that unless this presumption should be entertained, it would be improper to give the executive magistrate any species of control over the legislative body.

But this observation, when examined, will appear rather specious than solid. The propriety of the thing does not turn upon the supposition of superior wisdom or virtue in the Executive, but upon the supposition that the legislature will not be infallible; that the love of power may sometimes betray it into a disposition to encroach upon the rights of other members of the government; that a spirit of faction may sometimes pervert its deliberations; that impressions of the moment may sometimes hurry it into measures which itself, on maturer reflection, would condemn. The primary inducement to conferring the power in question upon the Executive is, to enable him to defend himself; the secondary one is to increase the chances in favor of the community against the passing of bad laws, through haste, inadvertence, or design. The oftener the measure is brought under examination, the greater the diversity in the situations of those who are to examine it, the less must be the danger of those errors which flow from want of due deliberation, or of those missteps which proceed from the contagion of some common passion or interest. It is far less probable, that culpable views of any kind should infect all the parts of the government at the same moment and in relation to the object, than that they should by turns govern and mislead every one of them.

It may perhaps be said that the power of preventing bad laws includes that of preventing good ones; and may be used to the one purpose as well as to the other. But this objection will have little weight with those who can properly estimate the mischiefs of that inconstancy and mutability in the laws, which form the greatest blemish in the character and genius of our

governments. They will consider every institution calculated to restrain the
excess of law-making, and to keep things in the same state in which they
happen to be at any given period, as much more likely to do good than harm;
because it is favorable to greater stability in the system of legislation. The
injury which may possibly be done by defeating a few good laws, will be amply
compensated by the advantage of preventing a number of bad ones. . . .

PUBLIUS.

THE FEDERALIST. NO. LXXVIII

(Hamilton)

To the People of the State of New York:

We proceed now to an examination of the judiciary department of the
proposed government.

In unfolding the defects of the existing Confederation, the utility and
necessity of a federal judicature have been clearly pointed out. It is the less
necessary to recapitulate the considerations there urged, as the propriety of
the institution in the abstract is not disputed; the only questions which have
been raised being relative to the manner of constituting it, and to its extent.
To these points, therefore, our observations shall be confined.

The manner of constituting it seems to embrace these several objects:
1st. The mode of appointing the judges. 2d. The tenure by which they are
to hold their places. 3d. The partition of the judiciary authority between
different courts, and their relation to each other.

First. As to the mode of appointing the judges; this is the same with that
of appointing the officers of the Union in general, and has been so fully discussed in the two last numbers, that nothing can be said here which would not
be useless repetition.

Second. As to the tenure by which the judges are to hold their places: this
chiefly concerns their duration in office; the provisions for their support; the
precautions for their responsibility.

According to the plan of the convention, all judges who may be appointed
by the United States are to hold their offices *during good behavior;* which is
conformable to the most approved of the State constitutions, and among the
rest, to that of this State. Its propriety having been drawn into question by
the adversaries of that plan, is no light symptom of the rage for objection,
which disorders their imaginations and judgments. The standard of good
behavior for the continuance in office of the judicial magistracy, is certainly
one of the most valuable of the modern improvements in the practice of
government. In a monarchy it is an excellent barrier to the despotism of the
prince; in a republic it is a no less excellent barrier to the encroachments and
oppressions of the representative body. And it is the best expedient which
can be devised in any government, to secure a steady, upright, and impartial
administration of the laws.

Whoever attentively considers the different departments of power must
perceive, that, in a government in which they are separated from each other,
the judiciary, from the nature of its functions, will always be the least dangerous to the political rights of the Constitution; because it will be least in a
capacity to annoy or injure them. The Executive not only dispenses the

honors, but holds the sword of the community. The legislature not only commands the purse, but prescribes the rules by which the duties and rights of every citizen are to be regulated. The judiciary, on the contrary, has no influence over either the sword or the purse; no direction either of the strength or of the wealth of the society; and can take no active resolution whatever. It may truly be said to have neither FORCE nor WILL, but merely judgment; and must ultimately depend upon the aid of the executive arm even for the efficacy of its judgments.

This simple view of the matter suggests several important consequences. It proves incontestably, that the judiciary is beyond comparison the weakest of the three departments of power; that it can never attack with success either of the other two; and that all possible care is requisite to enable it to defend itself against their attacks. It equally proves, that though individual oppression may now and then proceed from the courts of justice, the general liberty of the people can never be endangered from that quarter; I mean so long as the judiciary remains truly distinct from both the legislature and the Executive. For I agree, that "there is no liberty, if the power of judging be not separated from the legislative and executive powers." And it proves, in the last place, that as liberty can have nothing to fear from the judiciary alone, but would have every thing to fear from its union with either of the other departments; that as all the effects of such a union must ensue from a dependence of the former on the latter, notwithstanding a nominal and apparent separation: that as, from the natural feebleness of the judiciary, it is in continual jeopardy of being overpowered, awed, or influenced by its coördinate branches; and that as nothing can contribute so much to its firmness and independence as permanency in office, this quality may therefore be justly regarded as an indispensable ingredient in its constitution, and, in a great measure, as the citadel of the public justice and the public security.

The complete independence of the courts of justice is peculiarly essential in a limited Constitution. By a limited Constitution, I understand one which contains certain specified exceptions to the legislative authority; such, for instance, as that it shall pass no bills of attainder, no *ex-post-facto* laws, and the like. Limitations of this kind can be preserved in practice no other way than through the medium of courts of justice, whose duty it must be to declare all acts contrary to the manifest tenor of the Constitution void. Without this, all the reservations of particular rights or privileges would amount to nothing.

Some perplexity respecting the rights of the courts to pronounce legislative acts void, because contrary to the Constitution, has arisen from an imagination that the doctrine would imply a superiority of the judiciary to the legislative power. It is urged that the authority which can declare the acts of another void, must necessarily be superior to the one whose acts may be declared void. As this doctrine is of great importance in all the American constitutions, a brief discussion of the ground on which it rests cannot be unacceptable.

There is no position which depends on clearer principles, than that every act of a delegated authority, contrary to the tenor of the commission under which it is exercised, is void. No legislative act, therefore, contrary to the Constitution, can be valid. To deny this, would be to affirm, that the deputy is greater than his principal; that the servant is above his master; that the representatives of the people are superior to the people themselves; that men acting by virtue of powers, may do not only what their powers do not authorize, but what they forbid.

If it be said that the legislative body are themselves the constitutional judges of their own powers, and that the construction they put upon them is conclusive upon the other departments, it may be answered, that this cannot be the natural presumption, where it is not to be collected from any particular provisions in the Constitution. It is not otherwise to be supposed, that the Constitution could intend to enable the representatives of the people to substitute their *will* to that of their constituents. It is far more rational to suppose, that the courts were designed to be an intermediate body between the people and the legislature, in order, among other things, to keep the latter within the limits assigned to their authority. The interpretation of the laws is the proper and peculiar province of the courts. A constitution is, in fact, and must be regarded by the judges, as a fundamental law. It therefore belongs to them to ascertain its meaning, as well as the meaning of any particular act proceeding from the legislative body. If there should happen to be an irreconcilable variance between the two, that which has the superior obligation and validity ought, of course, to be preferred; or, in other words, the Constitution ought to be preferred to the statute, the intention of the people to the intention of their agents.

Nor does this conclusion by any means suppose a superiority of the judicial to the legislative power. It only supposes that the power of the people is superior to both; and that where the will of the legislature, declared in its statutes, stands in opposition to that of the people, declared in the Constitution, the judges ought to be governed by the latter rather than the former. They ought to regulate their decisions by the fundamental laws, rather than by those which are not fundamental.

This exercise of judicial discretion, in determining between two contradictory laws, is exemplified in a familiar instance. It not uncommonly happens, that there are two statutes existing at one time, clashing in whole or in part with each other, and neither of them containing any repealing clause or expression. In such a case, it is the province of the courts to liquidate and fix their meaning and operation. So far as they can, by any fair construction, be reconciled to each other, reason and law conspire to dictate that this should be done; where this is impracticable, it becomes a matter of necessity to give effect to one, in exclusion of the other. The rule which has obtained in the courts for determining their relative validity is, that the last in order of time shall be preferred to the first. But this is a mere rule of construction, not derived from any positive law, but from the nature and reason of the thing. It is a rule not enjoined upon the courts by legislative provision, but adopted by themselves, as consonant to truth and propriety, for the direction of their conduct as interpreters of the law. They thought it reasonable, that between the interfering acts of an *equal* authority, that which was the last indication of its will should have the preference.

But in regard to the interfering acts of a superior and subordinate authority, of an original and derivative power, the nature and reason of the thing indicate the converse of that rule as proper to be followed. They teach us that the prior act of a superior ought to be preferred to the subsequent act of an inferior and subordinate authority; and that accordingly, whenever a particular statute contravenes the Constitution, it will be the duty of the judicial tribunals to adhere to the latter and disregard the former.

It can be of no weight to say that the courts, on the pretence of a repugnancy, may substitute their own pleasure to the constitutional intentions of the legislature. This might as well happen in the case of two contradictory statutes; or it might as well happen in every adjudication upon any single statute. The courts must declare the sense of the law; and if they should be disposed to exercise WILL instead of JUDGMENT, the consequences would equally be the substitution of their pleasure to that of the legislative body. The observation, if it prove any thing, would prove that there ought to be no judges distinct from that body.

If, then, the courts of justice are to be considered as the bulwarks of a limited Constitution against legislative encroachments, this consideration will afford a strong argument for the permanent tenure of judicial offices, since nothing will contribute so much as this to that independent spirit in the judges which must be essential to the faithful performance of so arduous a duty.

This independence of the judges is equally requisite to guard the Constitution and the rights of individuals from the effects of those ill humors, which the arts of designing men, or the influence of particular conjunctures, sometimes disseminate among the people themselves, and which, though they speedily give place to better information, and more deliberate reflection, have a tendency, in the meantine, to occasion dangerous innovations in the government, and serious oppressions of the minor party in the community. Though I trust the friends of the proposed Constitution will never concur with its enemies, in questioning that fundamental principle of republican government, which admits the rights of the people to alter or abolish the established Constitution, whenever they find it inconsistent with their happiness, yet it is not to be inferred from this principle, that the representatives of the people, whenever a momentary inclination happens to lay hold of a majority of their constituents, incompatible with the provisions in the existing Constitution, would, on that account, be justifiable in a violation of those provisions; or that the courts would be under a greater obligation to connive at infractions in this shape, than when they had proceeded wholly from the cabals of the representative body. Until the people have, by some solemn and authoritative act, annulled or changed the established form, it is binding upon themselves collectively, as well as individually; and no presumption, or even knowledge, of their sentiments, can warrant their representatives in a departure from it, prior to such an act. But it is easy to see, that it would require an uncommon portion of fortitude in the judges to do their duty as faithful guardians of the Constitution, where legislative invasions of it had been instigated by the major voice of the community.

But it is not with a view to infractions of the Constitution only, that the independence of the judges may be an essential safeguard against the effects of occasional ill humors in the society. These sometimes extend no farther than to the injury of the private rights of particular classes of citizens, by unjust and partial laws. Here also the firmness of the judicial magistracy is of vast importance in mitigating the severity and confining the operation of such laws. It not only serves to moderate the immediate mischiefs of those which may have been passed, but it operates as a check upon the legislative body in passing them; who, perceiving that obstacles to the success of iniquitous intention are to be expected from the scruples of the courts, are in a manner compelled, by the very motives of the injustice they meditate, to qualify their attempts. This is a circumstance calculated to have more influence upon the character of our governments, than but few may be aware of. The benefits of the integrity and moderation of the judiciary have already been felt in more States than one; and though they may have displeased those whose sinister expectations they may have disappointed, they must have commanded the esteem and applause of all the virtuous and disinterested. Considerate men, of every description, ought to prize whatever will tend to beget or fortify that temper in the courts; as no man can be sure that he may not be to-morrow the victim of a spirit of injustice, by which he may be a gainer to-day. And every man must now feel, that the inevitable tendency of such a spirit is to sap the foundations of public and private confidence, and to introduce in its stead universal distrust and distress.

That inflexible and uniform adherence to the rights of the Constitution, and of individuals, which we perceive to be indispensable in the courts of justice, can certainly not be expected from judges who hold their offices by a temporary commission. Periodical appointments, however regulated, or by whomsoever made, would, in some way or other, be fatal to their necessary independence. If the power of making them was committed either to the Executive or legislature, there would be danger of an improper complaisance to the branch which possessed it; if to both, there would be an unwillingness to hazard the displeasure of either; if to the people, or to persons chosen by them for the special purpose, there would be too great a disposition to consult popularity, to justify a reliance that nothing would be consulted but the Constitution and the laws.

There is yet a further and a weightier reason for the permanency of the judicial offices, which is deducible from the nature of the qualifications they require. It has been frequently remarked, with great propriety, that a voluminous code of laws is one of the inconveniences necessarily connected with advantages of a free government. To avoid an arbitrary discretion in the courts, it is indispensable that they should be bound down by strict rules and precedents, which serve to define and point out their duty in every particular case that comes before them; and it will readily be conceived from the variety of controversies which grow out of the folly and wickedness of mankind, that the records of those precedents must unavoidably swell to a very considerable bulk, and must demand long and laborious study to acquire a competent knowledge of them. Hence it is, that there can be but a few men in the society who will have sufficient skill in the laws to qualify them for the stations of judges. And making the proper deductions for the ordinary depravity of human nature, the number must be still smaller of those who unite the requisite integrity with the requisite knowledge. These considerations apprise us, that the government can have no great option between fit character; and that a temporary duration in office, which would naturally discourage such characters from quitting a lucrative line of practice to accept a seat on the bench, would have a tendency to throw the administration of justice into hands less able, and less well qualified, to conduct it with utility and dignity. In the present circumstances of this country, and in those in which it is likely to be for a long time to come, the disadvantages on this score would be greater than they may at first sight appear; but it must be confessed, that they are far inferior to those which present themselves under the other aspects of the subject.

Upon the whole, there can be no room to doubt that the convention acted wisely in copying from the models of those constitutions which have established *good behavior* as the tenure of their judicial offices, in point of duration; and that so far from being blamable on this account, their plan would have been inexcusably defective, if it had wanted this important feature of good government. The experience of Great Britain affords an illustrious comment on the excellence of the institution.

PUBLIUS.

JOHN MARSHALL

In 1800, when the Jeffersonian Republicans defeated the Federalists, the latter entrenched themselves in the judiciary. John Marshall, then secretary of state, received appointment as Chief Justice of the Supreme Court. A staunch Federalist politician, he translated into court decisions those fundamental ideas of the Federalists that the people had repudiated at the polls.

In *Marbury v. Madison*, Marshall expounded the Federalist principle of judicial supremacy. Among his "midnight appointments" Adams had appointed Marbury as a justice of the peace; Marshall, as secretary of state, had failed to deliver the commission. Marbury appealed to the Supreme Court for a writ of *mandamus* to compel the new secretary of state to deliver the commission. Marshall seized this unimportant case to lecture the Jeffersonians. He declared that the section of the judiciary act that gave the Supreme Court original jurisdiction in such a case was unconstitutional.

In *Sturges v. Crowninshield*, Marshall expounded the Federalist principle of irrevocable contracts. The state of New York had passed a bankruptcy act discharging the person of the debtor. Marshall held that this law came within the Constitution, since it did not destroy the debtor's obligation to pay in full, but merely abolished imprisonment for debt. Marshall, however, employed this case to warn the states against the passage of acts that impaired the obligation of contracts.

WILLIAM MARBURY V. JAMES MADISON [94]

. . . . . .

The authority, therefore, given to the Supreme Court by the act establishing the judicial courts of the United States to issue writs of *mandamus* to public officers appears not to be warranted by the Constitution; and it becomes necessary to inquire whether a jurisdiction so conferred can be exercised.

The question whether an act repugnant to the Constitution can become the law of the land is a question deeply interesting to the United States; but, happily, not of an intricacy proportioned to its interest. It seems only necessary to recognize certain principles supposed to have been long and well established to decide it.

[94] 1 Cranch's Reports, 137, 176–180 (1803).

That the people have an original right to establish for their future government such principles as in their opinion shall most conduce to their own happiness is the basis on which the whole American fabric has been erected. The exercise of this original right is a very great exertion, nor can it, nor ought it to be frequently repeated. The principles, therefore, so established are deemed fundamental. And as the authority from which they proceed is supreme and can seldom act, they are designed to be permanent.

This original and supreme will organizes the government, and assigns to different departments their respective powers. It may either stop here or establish certain limits not to be transcended by those departments.

The government of the United States is of the latter description. The powers of the Legislature are defined and limited; and that those limits may not be mistaken or forgotten the Constitution is written. To what purpose are powers limited and to what purpose is that limitation committed to writing, if these limits may at any time be passed by those intended to be restrained? The distinction between a government with limited and unlimited powers is abolished if those limits do not confine the persons on whom they are imposed and if acts prohibited and acts allowed are of equal obligation. It is a proposition too plain to be contested, that the Constitution controls any legislative act repugnant to it; or that the Legislature may alter the Constitution by an ordinary act.

Between these alternatives there is no middle ground. The Constitution is either a superior, paramount law, unchangeable by ordinary means, or it is on a level with ordinary legislative acts, and like other acts is alterable when the Legislature shall please to alter it.

If the former part of the alternative be true, then a legislative act contrary to the Constitution is not law; if the latter part be true, then written Constitutions are absurd attempts on the part of the people to limit a power in its own nature illimitable.

Certainly all those who have framed written Constitutions contemplate them as forming the fundamental and paramount law of the nation, and consequently the theory of every such government must be that an act of the Legislature repugnant to the Constitution is void.

This theory is essentially attached to a written Constitution, and is consequently to be considered by this court as one of the fundamental principles of our society. It is not, therefore, to be lost sight of in the further consideration of this subject.

If an act of the Legislature repugnant to the Constitution is void, does it, notwithstanding its invalidity, bind the courts and oblige them to give it effect? Or, in other words, though it be not law, does it constitute a rule as operative as if it was a law? This would be to overthrow in fact what was established in theory, and would seem, at first view, an absurdity too gross to be insisted on. It shall, however, receive a more attentive consideration.

It is emphatically the province and duty of the judicial department to say what the law is. Those who apply the rule to particular cases must of necessity expound and interpret that rule. If two laws conflict with each other the courts must decide on the operation of each.

So, if a law be in opposition to the Constitution; if both the law and the Constitution apply to a particular case, so that the court must either decide that case conformably to the law, disregarding the Constitution, or conformably to the Constitution, disregarding the law, the court must determine which of these conflicting rules governs the case. This is of the very essence of judicial duty.

If, then, the courts are to regard the Constitution, and the Constitution is superior to any ordinary act of the Legislature, the Constitution, and not such ordinary act, must govern the case to which they both apply.

Those, then, who controvert the principle that the Constitution is to be considered in court as a paramount law are reduced to the necessity of maintaining that courts must close their eyes on the Constitution and see only the law.

This doctrine would subvert the very foundation of all written Constitutions. It would declare that an act which, according to the principles and theory of our government, is entirely void, is yet, in practice, completely obligatory. It would declare that, if the Legislature shall do what is expressly forbidden, such act, notwithstanding the express prohibition, is in reality effectual. It would be giving to the Legislature a practical and real omnipotence with the same breath which professes to restrict their powers within narrow limits. It is prescribing limits and declaring that those limits may be passed at pleasure.

That it thus reduces to nothing what we have deemed the greatest improvement on political institutions, a written Constitution, would of itself be sufficient in America, where written Constitutions have been viewed with so much reverence, for rejecting the construction. But the peculiar expressions of the Constitution of the United States furnish additional arguments in favor of its rejection.

The judicial power of the United States is extended to all cases arising under the Constitution.

Could it be the intention of those who gave this power to say that in using it the Constitution should not be looked into? That a case arising under the Constitution should be decided without examining the instrument under which it arises?

This is too extravagant to be maintained.

In some cases, then the Constitution must be looked into by the judges, and, if they can open it at all, what part of it are they forbidden to read or to obey?

There are many other parts of the Constitution which serve to illustrate this subject.

It is declared that "no tax or duty shall be laid on articles exported from any State." Suppose a duty on the export of cotton, of tobacco, or of flour, and a suit instituted to recover it, ought judgment to be rendered in such a case? Ought the judges to close their eyes on the Constitution and only see the law?

The Constitution declares "that no bill of attainder or *ex post facto* law shall be passed."

If, however, such a bill should be passed, and a person should be prosecuted under it, must the court condemn to death those victims whom the Constitution endeavors to preserve?

"No person," says the Constitution, "shall be convicted of treason, unless on the testimony of two witnesses to the same overt act, or on confession in open court."

Here the language of the Constitution is addressed especially to the courts. It prescribes directly for them a rule of evidence not to be departed from. If the Legislature should change that rule, and declare *one* witness, or a confession *out* of court, sufficient for conviction, must the constitutional principle yield to the legislative act?

From these and many other selections which might be made, it is apparent that the framers of the Constitution contemplated that instrument as a rule for the government of *courts*, as well as of the Legislature.

Why otherwise does it direct the judges to take an oath to support it? This oath certainly applies in an especial manner to their conduct in their official character. How immoral to impose it on them if they were to be used as the instruments, and the knowing instruments, for violating what they swear to support!

The oath of office, too, imposed by the Legislature, is completely demonstrative of the legislative opinion on this subject. It is in these words: "I do solemnly swear that I will administer justice without respect to persons and do equal right to the poor and to the rich; and that, I will faithfully and impartially discharge all the duties incumbent on me as————, according to the best of my abilities and understanding, agreeably to the *Constitution* and laws of the United States."

Why does a judge swear to discharge his duties agreeably to the Constitution of the United States, if that Constitution forms no rule for his government? if it is closed upon him, and cannot be inspected by him?

If such be the real state of things, this is worse than solemn mockery. To prescribe, or to take this oath, becomes equally a crime.

It is also not entirely unworthy of observation, that, in declaring what shall be the *supreme* law of the land, the *Constitution* itself is first mentioned, and not the laws of the United States generally, but those only which shall be made in *pursuance* of the Constitution, have that rank.

Thus the particular phraseology of the Constitution of the United States confirms and strengthens the principle supposed to be essential to all written Constitutions that a law repugnant to the Constitution is void, and that *courts*, as well as other departments, are bound by that instrument.

STURGES V. CROWINSHIELD [95]

The Constitution does not grant to the States the power of passing bankrupt laws, or any other power; but finds them in possession of it, and may either prohibit its future exercise entirely, or restrain it so far as national policy may require. It has so far restrained it as to prohibit the passage of any law impairing the obligation of contracts. Although, then, the States may, until that power shall be exercised by Congress, pass laws concerning bankrupts, yet they cannot constitutionally introduce into such laws a clause which discharges the obligations the bankrupt has entered into. It is not admitted that, without this principle, an act cannot be a bankrupt law; and

[95] 4 Wheaton, 122, 199-201, 203-206 (1819).

if it were, that admission would not change the Constitution, nor exempt such acts from its prohibitions.

The argument drawn from the omission in the Constitution to prohibit the States from passing insolvent laws admits of several satisfactory answers. It was not necessary, nor would it have been safe, had it even been the intention of the framers of the Constitution to prohibit the passage of all insolvent laws, to enumerate particular subjects to which the principle they intended to establish should apply. The principle was the inviolability of contracts. This principle was to be protected in whatsoever form it might be assailed. To what purpose enumerate the particular modes of violation which should be forbidden, when it was intended to forbid all? Had an enumeration of all the laws which might violate contracts been attempted, the provision must have been less complete and involved in more perplexity than it now is. The plain and simple declaration, that no State shall pass any law impairing the obligation of contracts, includes insolvent laws, and all other laws, so far as they infringe the principle the convention intended to hold sacred, and no farther.

But a still more satisfactory answer to this argument is that the convention did not intend to prohibit the passage of all insolvent laws. To punish honest insolvency by imprisonment for life, and to make this a constitutional principle, would be an excess of inhumanity which will not readily be imputed to the illustrious patriots who framed our Constitution, nor to the people who adopted it. The distinction between the obligation of a contract and the remedy given by the Legislature to enforce that obligation has been taken at the bar, and exists in the nature of things. Without impairing the obligation of the contract, the remedy may certainly be modified as the wisdom of the Nation shall direct. Confinement of the debtor may be a punishment for not performing his contract, or may be allowed as a means of inducing him to perform it. But the State may refuse to inflict this punishment, or may withhold this means, and leave the contract in full force. Imprisonment is no part of the contract, and simply to release the prisoner does not impair its obligation. No argument can be fairly drawn from the sixty-first section of the act for establishing a uniform system of bankruptcy, which militates against this reasoning. That section declares that the act shall not be construed to repeal or annul the laws of any State *then in force* for the relief of insolvent debtors, except so far as may respect persons and cases clearly within its purview; and in such cases it affords its sanction to the relief given by the insolvent laws of the State, if the creditor of the prisoner shall not, within three months, proceed against him as a bankrupt. . . .

The fact is too broadly stated. The insolvent laws of many, indeed of by far the greater number, of the States do not contain this principle. They discharge the person of the debtor, but leave his obligation to pay in full force. To this the Constitution is not opposed.

But were it even true that this principle has been introduced generally into those laws, it would not justify our varying the construction of the section. Every State in the Union, both while a colony and after becoming independent, had been in the practice of issuing paper money; yet this practice is in terms prohibited. If the long exercise of the power to emit bills of credit did not restrain the convention from prohibiting its future exercise, neither can it be said that the long exercise of the power to impair the obligation of contracts should prevent a similar prohibition. It is not admitted that the prohibition is more express in the one case than in the other. It does not, indeed, extend to insolvent laws by name, because it is not a law by name, but a principle, which is to be forbidden; and this principle is described in as appropriate terms as our language affords.

Neither, as we conceive, will any admissible rule of construction justify us in limiting the prohibition under consideration to the particular laws which have been described at the bar, and which furnished such cause for general alarm. What were those laws?

We are told they were such as grew out of the general distress following the war in which our independence was established. To relieve this distress, paper money was issued; worthless lands, and other property of no use to the creditor, were made a tender in payment of debts; and the time of payment stipulated in the contract was extended by law. These were the peculiar evils of the day. So much mischief was done, and so much more was apprehended, that general distrust prevailed, and all confidence between man and man was destroyed. To laws of this description, therefore, it is said, the prohibition to pass laws impairing the obligation of contracts ought to be confined.

Let this argument be tried by the words of the section under consideration.

Was this general prohibition intended to prevent paper money? We are not allowed to say so, because it is expressly provided that no State shall "emit bills of credit." Neither could these words be intended to restrain the States from enabling debtors to discharge their debts by the tender of property of no real value to the creditor, because for that subject also particular provision is made. Nothing but gold and silver coin can be made a tender in payment of debts.

It remains to inquire whether the prohibition under consideration could be intended for the single case of a law directing that judgments should be carried into execution by instalments?

This question will scarcely admit of discussion. If this was the only remaining mischief against which the Constitution intended to provide, it would undoubtedly have been, like paper money and tender laws, expressly forbidden. At any rate, terms more directly applicable to the subject, more appropriately expressing the intention of the Convention, would have been used. It seems scarcely possible to suppose that the framers of the Constitution, if intending to prohibit only laws authorizing the payment of debts by instalment, would have expressed that intention by saying, "No State shall pass any law impairing the obligation of contracts." No men would so express such an intention. No men would use terms embracing a whole class of laws, for the purpose of designating a single individual of that class. No court can be justified in restricting such comprehensive words to a particular mischief to which no allusion is made.

The fair and, we think, the necessary, construction of the sentence requires that we should give these words their full and obvious meaning. A general dissatisfaction with that lax system of legislation which followed the war of our revolution undoubtedly directed the mind of the convention to this subject. It is probable that laws, such as those which have been stated in argument, produced the loudest complaints, were most immediately felt. The attention of the convention, therefore, was particularly directed to paper money, and to acts which enabled the debtor to discharge his debt otherwise than was stipulated in the contract. Had nothing more been intended, nothing more would have been expressed. But, in the opinion of the convention, much more remained to be done. The same mischief might be effected by other means. To restore public confidence completely, it was necessary not only to prohibit the use of particular means by which it might be effected, but to prohibit the use of any means by which the same mischief might be produced. The convention appears to have intended to establish a great principle, that contracts should be inviolable. The Constitution therefore declares that no State shall pass "any law impairing the obligation of contracts." . . .

STATE RATIFYING CONVENTIONS [96]

The Constitution drawn up at the Philadelphia Convention generated considerable popular antagonism. The people feared a centralized government and a loss of their liberties. This attitude was well expressed in the debates of the state ratifying conventions. The following speeches by Singletary, Henry, and Mason are typical of the popular and agrarian distrust of the new Constitution.

MASSACHUSETTS—FRIDAY, JANUARY 25.

. . . .

Hon. Mr. Singletary.—Mr. President, I should not have troubled the convention again, if some gentlemen had not called on them that were on the stage in the beginning of our troubles, in the year 1775. I was one of them. I have had the honor to be a member of the Court all the time, Mr. President, and I say, that if any body had proposed such a constitution as this, in that day it would have been thrown away at once. It would not have been looked at. We contended with Great Britain—some said for a threepenny duty on tea; but it was not that—it was because they claimed a right to tax us and bind us in all cases whatever. And does not this constitution do the same? does it not take away all we have—all our property? does it not lay *all* taxes, duties, imposts and excises? and what more have we to give? They tell us congress won't lay dry taxes upon us, but collect all the money they want by impost. I say, there has always been a difficulty about impost. Whenever the general court was going to lay an impost, they would tell us it was more than trade could bear, that it hurt the fair trader and encouraged smuggling; and there will always be the same objection; they wont be able to raise money enough by impost, and then they will lay it on the land and take all we have got. These lawyers, and men of learning, and monied men, that talk so finely and gloss over matters so smoothly, to make us, poor illiterate people, swallow down the pill, expect to get into Congress themselves; they expect to be the managers of this constitution, and get all the power and all the money into their own hands, and then they will swallow up all us little folks, like the great *Leviathan*, Mr. President; yes, just as the whale swallowed up *Jonah*. This is what I am afraid of; but I won't say any more at present, but reserve the rest to another opportunity. . . .

VIRGINIA—MONDAY, THE 14th OF JUNE, 1788

. . . . . .

Mr. Henry.—Mr. Chairman, the necessity of a bill of rights appears to me to be greater in this government, than ever it was in any government, before. I observe already, that the sense of the European nations, and particularly Great Britain, is against the construction of rights being retained, which are not expressly relinquished. I repeat, that all nations have adopted this construction—that all rights not expressly and unequivocally reserved to the people, are impliedly and incidentally relinquished to rulers; as necessarily inseparable from the delegated powers. It is so in Great Britain; for every possible right which is not reserved to the people by some express provision or compact, is within the king's prerogative. It is so in that country which is said to be in such full possession of freedom. It is so in Spain, Germany, and other parts of the world. Let us consider the sentiments which have been entertained by the people of America on this subject. At the revolution it must be admitted, that it was their sense to put down those great rights which ought in all countries to be held inviolable and sacred. Virginia did so, we all remember. She made a compact to reserve, expressly, certain rights.

When fortified with full, adequate and abundant representation, was she satisfied with that representation? No. She most cautiously and guardedly reserved and secured those invaluable, inestimable rights and privileges, which no people, inspired with the least glow of the patriotic liberty, ever did inspire or ever can, abandon. She is called upon now to abandon them, and dissolve that compact which secured them to her. She is called upon to accede to another compact which most infallibly supersedes and annihilates her present one. Will she do it? This is the question. If you intend to reserve your unalienable rights, you must have the most express stipulation. For if implication be allowed, you are ousted of those rights. If the people do not think it necessary to reserve them they will be supposed to be given up. How were the congressional rights defined when the people of America united under a confederacy to defend their liberties and rights against the tyrannical attempts of Great Britain? The states were not then contented with implied reservation. No, Mr. Chairman. It was expressly declared in our confederation that every right was retained by the states respectively, which was not given up to the government of the United States. But there is no such thing here. You therefore, by a natural and unavoidable implication, give up your rights to the general government.

Your own example furnishes an argument against it. If you give up these powers, without a bill of rights, you will exhibit the most absurd thing to mankind that ever the world saw—a government that has abandoned all its powers—the powers of a direct taxation, the sword and the purse. You have disposed of them to congress, without a bill of rights—without check, limitation, or control. And still you have checks and guards—still you keep barriers—pointed where? Pointed against your weakened, prostrated, enervated state government! You have a bill of rights to defend you against the state government, which is bereaved of all power; and yet you have none against congress, though in full and exclusive possession of all power! You arm yourselves against the weak and defenceless, and expose yourselves naked to the armed and powerful. Is not this a conduct of unexampled absurdity? What barriers have you to oppose to this most energetic government? To that government, you have nothing to oppose. All your defence is given up. This is a real actual defect. It must strike the mind of every gentleman. When our government was first instituted in Virginia, we declared the common law of England to be in force.

That system of law which has been admired, and has protected us and our ancestors is excluded by that system. Added to this, we adopted a bill of rights. By this constitution, some of the best barriers of human rights are thrown away. Is there not an additional reason to have a bill of rights? By the ancient common law, the trial of all facts is decided by a jury of impartial men from the immediate vicinage. This paper speaks of different juries from the common law, in criminal cases; and in civil controversies excludes trial by jury altogether.—There is therefore more occasion for the supplementary check of a bill of rights now, than then. Congress from their general powers may fully go into business of human legislation. They may legislate in criminal cases from treason to the lowest offence, petty larceny. They may define crimes and prescribe punishments. In the definition of crimes, I trust they will be directed by what wise representatives ought to be governed by. But when we come to punishments, no latitude ought to be left, nor dependence put on the virtue of representatives. What say our bill of rights? "That excessive bail ought not to be required, nor excessive fines imposed, nor cruel and unusual punishments inflicted." Are you not therefore now calling on those gentlemen who are to compose congress, to prescribe trials and define punishments without this control? Will they find sentiments there similar to this bill of rights? You let them loose—you do more—you depart from the genius of your country. That paper tells you, that the trial of crimes shall be by jury, and held in the state where the crime shall have been committed. Under this extensive provision they may proceed in a manner extremely dangerous to liberty—persons accused may be carried from one extremity of the state to another, and be tried, not by an impartial jury of the vicinage, acquainted with his character, and the circumstances of the fact, but by a jury unacquainted with both, and who may be biassed against him. Is not this sufficient to alarm men?—How different is this from the immemorial practice of your British ancestors, and your own? I need not tell you, that by the common law a number of hundredors were required on a jury, and that afterwards it was sufficient if the jurors came from the same county. With less than this, the people of England have never been satisfied. That paper ought to have declared the common law in force.

In this business of legislation, your members of congress will loose the restriction of not imposing excessive fines, demanding excessive bail, and inflicting cruel and unusual punishments. These are prohibited by your declaration of rights. What has distinguished our ancestors?—That they would not admit of tortures, or cruel and barbarous punishment. But congress may introduce the practice of the civil law, in preference to that of the common law. They may introduce the practice of France, Spain, and Germany—of torturing to extort a confession of the crime. They will say that they might as well draw examples from those countries as from Great Britain, and they will tell you, that there is such a necessity of strengthening the arm of government, that they must have a criminal equity, and extort confession by torture, in order to punish with still more relentless severity. We are then lost and undone. And can any man think it troublesome, when we can by a small interference prevent our rights from being lost?—If you will, like the Virginian government, give them knowledge of the extent of the rights retained by the people, and the powers themselves, they will, if they be honest men, thank you for it. Will they not wish to go on sure grounds?—But if you leave them otherwise, they will not know how to proceed; and being in a state of uncertainty, they will assume rather than give up powers by implication.

A bill of rights may be summed up in a few words. What do they tell us?— That our rights are reserved. Why not say so? Is it because it will consume too much paper? Gentlemen's reasoning against a bill of rights, do not satisfy me. Without saying which has the right side, it remains doubtful. A bill of rights is a favorite thing with the Virginians, and the people of the other states likewise. It may be their prejudice, but the government ought to suit their geniuses, otherwise its operation will be unhappy. A bill of rights, even if its necessity be doubtful, will exclude the possibility of dispute; and with great submission, I think the best way is to have no dispute. In the present constitution, they are restrained from issuing general warrants to search suspected places, or seize persons not named, without evidence of the commission of a fact, &c. There was certainly some celestial influence governing those who deliberated on that constitution.—For they have with the most cautious and enlightened circumspection, guarded those indefeasible rights, which ought ever to be held sacred. The officers of congress may come upon you, fortified with all the terrors of paramount federal authority. Excisemen may come in multitudes.—For the limitation of their numbers no man knows. They may, unless the general government be restrained by a bill of rights, or some similar restriction, go into your cellars and rooms, and search, ransack and measure, every thing you eat, drink and wear. They ought to be restrained within proper bounds. With respect to the freedom of the press, I need say nothing; for it is hoped that the gentlemen who shall compose congress, will take care as little as possible to infringe the rights of human nature. This will result from their integrity. They should from prudence, abstain from violating the rights of their constituents. They are not however expressly restrained. But whether they will intermeddle with that palladium of our liberties or not, I leave you to determine. . . .

VIRGINIA—TUESDAY, THE 15TH OF JUNE, 1788

Mr. Henry.—Mr. Chairman—I am convinced, and I see clearly that this paper money must be discharged, shilling for shilling. The honorable gentleman must see better than I can, from his particular situation and judgment, but this has certainly escaped his attention. The question arising on the clause before you, is, whether an act of the legislature of this state, for scaling money, will be of sufficient validity to exonerate you from paying the nominal value, when such a law, called *ex post facto*, and impairing the obligation of contracts, are expressly interdicted by it? Your hands are tied up by this clause, and you must pay shilling for shilling; and, in the last section, there is a clause that prohibits the general legislature from passing any *ex post facto* law—so that the hands of congress are tied up, as well as the hands of the state legislatures.

How will this thing operate, when ten or twenty millions are demanded as the quota of this state? You will cry out that speculators have got it at one for a thousand, and that they ought to be paid so. Will you then have recourse for relief, to legislative interference? They cannot relieve you because of that clause. The expression includes public contracts, as well as private contracts between individuals. Notwithstanding the sagacity of the gentleman, he cannot prove its exclusive relation to private contracts. Here is an enormous demand, which your children to the tenth generation will not be able to pay. Should we ask, if there be any obligation in justice to pay more than the depreciated value, we shall be told that contracts must not be impaired. Justice may make a demand of millions, but the people cannot pay them.

I remember the clamors and public uneasiness concerning the payment of British debts, put into the treasury. Was not the alarm great and general lest these payments should be laid on the people at large? Did not the legislature interfere and pass a law to prevent it? Was it not re-echoed every where, that the people of this country ought not to pay the debts of their great ones? And though some urged their patriotism, and merits in putting money on the faith of the public into the treasury, yet the outcry was so great, that it required legislative interference. Should these enormous demands be made upon us, would not legislative interference be more necessary than it was in that case? Let us not run the risk of being charged with carelessness, and neglect of the interests of our constituents and posterity. I would ask the number of millions! It is without exaggeration, immense. I ask gentlemen if they can pay one hundred millions, or two hundred millions? Where have they the means of paying it? Still they would make us proceed to tie the hands of the states and of congress.

A gentleman has said with great force, that there is a contest for empire. There is also a contest for money. The states of the north wish to secure a superiority of interest and influence. In one part their deliberation is marked with wisdom, and in the other with the most liberal generosity. When we have paid all the gold and silver we could to replenish the congressional coffers, here they ask for confidence. Their hands will be tied up. They cannot merit confidence. Here is a transfer from the old to the new government, without the means of relieving the greatest distresses which can befall the people. This money might be scaled, sir, but the exclusion of *ex post facto* laws, and laws impairing the obligation of contracts, steps in and prevents it. These were admitted by the old confederation. There is a contest for money as well as empire, as I have said before. The eastern states have speculated chiefly in this money. As there can be no congressional scale, their speculations will be extremely profitable. Not satisfied with a majority in the legislative councils, they must have all our property. I wish the southern genius of America had been more watchful.

This state may be sued in the federal courts, for those enormous demands; and judgment may be obtained, unless *ex post facto* laws be passed. To benefit whom are we to run this risk? I have heard there were vast quantities of that money packed up in barrels—those formidable millions are deposited in the northern states, and whether in public or private hands, makes no odds. They have acquired it for the most inconsiderable trifle. If you accord to this part, you are bound hand and foot. Judgment must be rendered against you for the whole. Throw all pride out of the question, this is a most nefarious business. Your property will be taken from you to satisfy this most infamous speculation. It will destroy your public peace, and establish the ruin of your citizens. Only general resistance will remedy. You will shut the door against every ray of hope, if you allow the holders of this money, by this clause, to recover their formidable demands. I hope gentlemen will see the absolute necessity of amending it, by enabling the state legislatures to relieve their people from such nefarious oppressions. . . .

VIRGINIA—WEDNESDAY, THE 18TH OF JUNE, 1788

. . . . . .

Mr. Mason replied that if he recollected rightly, the propriety of the power as explained by him, had been contended for, but that as his memory had never been good, and was now impaired much from his age, he would not insist on that interpretation. He then proceeded:—Give me leave to advert to the operation of this judicial power. Its jurisdiction in the first case will extend to all cases affecting revenue, excise, and custom house officers. If I am mistaken I will retract. "All cases in law and equity arising under this constitution, and the laws of the United States, take in all the officers of the government. They comprehend all those who act as collectors of taxes, excisemen, &c. It will take in of course what others do to them, and what is done by them to others. In what predicament will our citizens then be? We know the difficulty we are put in by our own courts, and how hard it is to bring officers to justice even in them. If any of the federal officers should be guilty of the greatest oppressions, or behave with the most insolent and wanton brutality to a man's wife or daughter, where is this man to get relief? If you suppose in the inferior courts, they are not appointed by the states. They are not men in whom the community can place confidence. It will be decided by federal judges. Even suppose the poor man should be able to obtain judgment in the inferior court, for the greatest injury, what justice can he get on appeal? Can he go 400 or 500 miles? Can he stand the expense attending it? On this occasion they are to judge of fact as well as law. He must bring his witnesses where he is not known, where a new evidence may be brought against him, of which he never heard before, and which he cannot contradict.

The honorable gentleman, who presides here, has told us, that the supreme court of appeals must embrace every object of maritime, chancery, and common law controversy. In the two first, the indiscriminate appellate jurisdiction as to fact, must be generally granted; because otherwise it could exclude appeals in those cases. But why not discriminate as to matters of fact as to common law controversies? The honorable gentleman has allowed that it was dangerous, but hopes regulations will be made to suit the convenience of the people. But mere hope is not a sufficient security. I have said that it appears to me (though I am no lawyer) to be very dangerous. Give me leave to lay before the committee an amendment, which I think convenient, easy, and proper.

(Here Mr. Mason proposed an alteration nearly the same as the first part of the fourteenth amendment recommended by the convention, which see at the conclusion.)

Thus, Sir, said Mr. Mason, after limiting the cases in which the federal judiciary could interpose, I would confine the appellate jurisdiction to matters of law only, in common law controversies.

It appears to me that this will remove oppressions, and answer every purpose of an appellate power.

A discrimination arises between common law trials and trials in courts of equity and admiralty. In these two last, depositions are committed to record, and therefore on an appeal the whole fact goes up; the equity of the whole case, comprehending fact and law, is considered, and no new evidence requisite. Is it so in courts of common law? There evidence is only given *viva voce*. I know not a single case, where there is an appeal of fact as to common law. But I may be mistaken. Where there is an appeal from an inferior to a superior court, with respect to matters of fact, a new witness may be introduced, who is perhaps suborned by the other party, a thousand miles from the place where the first trial was had. These are some of the inconveniences and insurmountable objections against this general power being given to the federal courts. Gentlemen will perhaps say, there will be no occasion to carry up the evidence by *viva voce* testimony, because congress may order it to be committed to writing, and transmitted in that manner with the rest of the record. It is true they may, but it is as true that they may not. But suppose they do, little conversant as I am in this subject, I know there is a great difference between *viva voce* evidence given at the bar, and testimony given in writing. I leave it to gentlemen more conversant in these matters to discuss it. They are also to have cognizance in controversies to which the United States shall be a party. This power is superadded, that there might be no doubt, and that all cases arising under the government might be brought before the federal court. Gentlemen will not, I presume, deny that all revenue and excise controversies, and all proceedings relative to the duties of the officers of government, from the highest to the lowest, may, and must be brought by these means to the federal courts; in the first instance, to the inferior federal court, and afterwards to the superior court. Every fact proved with respect to these, in the court below, may be revived in the superior court. But this appellate jurisdiction is to be under the regulations of congress. What these regulations may be, God only knows.

Their *jurisdiction* further extends to controversies between citizens of different states. Can we not trust our state courts with the decision of these? If I have a controversy with a man in Maryland—if a man in Maryland has my bond for £100, are not the state courts competent to try it? Is it suspected that they would enforce the payment if unjust, or refuse to enforce it if just? The very idea is ridiculous. What, carry me a thousand miles from home—from my family and business, where, perhaps, it will be impos-

sible for me to prove that I paid it? Perhaps I have a respectable witness
who saw me pay the money, but I must carry him one thousand miles to
prove it, or be compelled to pay it again. Is there any necessity for this
power? It ought to have no unnecessary or dangerous power. Why should
the federal courts have this cognizance? Is it because one lives on one side
of the Potomac, and the other on the other? Suppose I have your bond for
£1000—if I have any wish to harass you, or if I be of a ligitious disposition, I
have only to assign it to a gentleman in Maryland. This assignment will involve
you in trouble and expense. What effect will this power have between British
creditors and the citizens of this state? This is a ground on which I shall
speak with confidence. Every one who heard me speak on the subject, knows,
that I always spoke for the payment of the British debts. I wish every honest
debt to be paid. Though I would wish to pay the British creditor, yet I
would not put it in his power to gratify private malice to our injury. Let
me be put right if I be mistaken. But there is not, in my opinion, a single
British creditor, but who can bring his debtors to the federal court.

There are a thousand instances where debts have been paid, and yet must
by this appellate cognizance be paid again. Are these imaginary cases? Are
they only possible cases, or are they certain and inevitable? "To controversies between a state, and the citizens of another state." How will their jurisdiction in this case do? Let gentlemen look at the westward. Claims respecting those lands, every liquidated account, or other claim against this state,
will be tried before the federal court. Is not this disgraceful? Is this state
to be brought to the bar of justice like a delinquent individual? Is the sovereignty of the state to be arraigned like a culprit, or private offender? Will
the states undergo this mortification? I think this power perfectly unnecessary. But let us pursue this subject further. What is to be done if a judgment be obtained against a state? Will you issue a *fieri facias*? It would
be ludicrous to say, that you could put the state's body in jail. How is the
judgment then to be enforced? A power which cannot be executed, ought
not to be granted.

Let us consider the operation of the last subject of its *cognizance*. Controversies between a state, or the citizens thereof, and foreign states, citizens
or subjects. There is a confusion in this case. This much, however, may be
raised out of it—that a suit will be brought against Virginia. She may be
sued by a foreign state. What reciprocity is there in it? In a suit between
Virginia and a foreign state, is the foreign state to be bound by the decision? Is there a similar privilege given to us in foreign states? Where will
you find a parallel regulation? How will the decision be enforced? Only by
the *ultima ratio regum*. A dispute between a foreign citizen or subject, and a
Virginian, cannot be tried in our own courts, but must be decided in the
federal court. Is this the case in any other country? Are not men obliged to
stand by the laws of the country where the disputes are? This is an innovation which is utterly unprecedented and unheard of. Cannot we trust the
state courts with disputes between a Frenchman, or an Englishman, and a
citizen; or with disputes between two Frenchmen? This is disgraceful: it
will annihilate your state judiciary: it will prostrate your legislature.

Thus, sir, it appears to me that the greater part of these powers are unnecessary, and dangerous, as tending to impair and ultimately destroy the

state judiciaries, and by the same principle, the legislation of the state governments. To render it safe there must be an amendment, such as I have pointed out. After mentioning the original jurisdiction of the supreme court, which extends to but three cases, it gives its appellate jurisdiction in all other cases mentioned, both as to law and fact, indiscriminately and without limitation. Why not remove the cause of fear and danger? But it is said that the regulations of congress will remove these. I say, that in my opinion they will have a contrary effect, and will utterly annihilate your state courts. Who are the court? The judges. It is a familiar distinction. We frequently speak of a court in contradiction to a jury. I think the court are to be judges of this. The judges on the bench, are to be judges of fact and law, with such exceptions, &c. as congress shall make. Now give me leave to ask, is not a jury excluded absolutely? By way of illustration, were congress to say that a jury, instead of a court, should judge the fact, will not the court be still judges of the fact consistently with this constitution? Congress may make such a regulation, or may not. But suppose they do, what sort of a jury would they have in the ten miles square? I would rather a thousand times be tried by a court than by such a jury. This great palladium of national safety, which is secured to us by our own government, will be taken from us in those courts; or if it be reserved, it will be but in name, and not in substance. In the government of Virginia we have secured an impartial jury of the vicinage. We can except to jurors and peremptorily challenge them in criminal trials. If I be tried in the federal court for a crime which may affect my life, have I a right of challenging or excepting to the jury? Have not the best men suffered by weak and partial juries? This sacred right ought therefore, to be secured. I dread the ruin that will be brought on thirty thousand of our people, with respect to disputed lands. I am personally endangered as an inhabitant of the Northern Neck. The people of that part will be obliged, by the operation of this power, to pay the quit rent of their land. Whatever other gentlemen may think, I consider this as a most serious alarm. It will little avail a man to make a profession of his candour. It is to his character and reputation they will appeal. Let gentlemen consider my public and private character. To these I wish gentlemen to appeal for an interpretation of my motives and views. Lord Fairfax's title was clear and undisputed. After the revolution, we taxed his lands as private property. After his death, an act of assembly was made, in 1782, to sequester the quit rents due at his death, in the hands of his debtors. Next year an act was made restoring them to the executor of the proprietor. Subsequent to this the treaty of peace was made, by which it was agreed, that there should be no further confiscations. But after this an act of assembly passed, confiscating this whole property. As Lord Fairfax's title was indisputably good, and as treaties are to be the supreme law of the land, will not his representatives be able to recover all in the federal court? How will gentlemen like to pay additional tax on lands in the Northern Neck? This the operation of this system will compel them to do. They now are subject to the same tax that other citizens are, and if the quit rents be recovered in the federal court, they are doubly taxed. This may be called an assertion, but were I going to my grave, I would appeal to heaven that I think it true. How will a poor man, who is injured or dispossessed unjustly, get a remedy? Is he to go to the federal court, seven or eight hundred miles? He might as well give his claim up. He may grumble, but finding no relief, he will be contented.

Again, all that tract of country between the Blue Ridge and the Alleghany Mountains, will be claimed, and probably recovered in the federal court, from the present possessors, by those companies who have a title to them. These *lands* have been sold to a great number of people. Many settled on them, on terms which were advertised. How will this be with respect to *ex post facto* laws? We have not only confirmed the title of those who made the contract, but those who did not, by a law in 1799, on their paying the original price. Much was paid in a depreciated value, and much was not paid at all. Again, the great Indiana purchase which was made to the westward, will by this judicial power, be rendered a cause of dispute. The possessors may be ejected from those lands. That company paid a consideration of ten thousand pounds to the crown, before the lands were taken up. I have heard gentlemen of the law say, (and I believe it is right) that after the consideration was paid to the crown, the purchase was legally made, and ought to be valid. That company may come in, and shew that they have paid the money, and have a full right to the land. Of the Indiana company I need not say much. It is well known that their claims will be brought before these courts. Three or four counties are settled on the lands to which that company claims a title, and have long enjoyed it peaceably. All these claims before those courts, if they succeed, will introduce a scene of distress and confusion never heard of before. Our peasants will be like those mentioned by *Virgil* reduced to ruin and misery; driven from their farms, and obliged to leave their country.—

Nos patriam fugimus—et dulcia linquimus arva.

Having mentioned these things, give me leave to submit an amendment, which I think would be proper and safe, and would render our citizens secure in their possessions justly held. I mean, sir, "that the judicial power shall extend to no case where the cause of action shall have originated before the ratification of this constitution, except in suits due for debts due to the United States; disputes between states about their territory; and disputes between persons claiming lands under the grants of different states." In these cases there is an obvious necessity for giving it a retrospective power. I have laid before you my idea on the subject, and expressed my fears, which I most conscientiously believe to be well founded. . . .

SELECTED BIBLIOGRAPHY

J. ADAMS, *A Defense of the Constitutions of Government of the United States* (1787-1788).
    Discourses on Davila (1790).
C. A. BEARD, *Economic Interpretation of the Constitution* (1913).
    Economic Origins of Jeffersonian Democracy (1915).
A. J. BEVERIDGE, *The Life of John Marshall* (4 vols., 1916-1919).
J. ELLIOT (ed.), *Debates of the Several State Conventions on the Adoption of the Federal Constitution* (5 vols., 1836).
M. FARRAND (ed.), *The Records of the Federal Convention* (3 vols., 1911).
P. L. FORD (ed.), *Pamphlets on the Constitution* (1888).
V. L. PARRINGTON, *The Colonial Mind* (1927).
J. WILSON, *Works* (edited by J. D. Andrews, 1896)
Documentary History of the Constitution of the United States of America (3 vols., 1894).
The Federalist (edited by H. C. Lodge, 1888).

CHAPTER IV

DEMOCRACY—JEFFERSONIAN, JACKSONIAN, INTELLECTUAL

I

Hamilton's fiscal schemes brought into clear relief a fundamental conflict that had smoldered since colonial days—the clash between commerce and agriculture. The conservative merchants, bankers, and speculators had organized the new government. Under the leadership of Hamilton, they employed it for their own economic aggrandizement. The agrarian groups had, with varying degrees of intensity and skill, fought the proposed constitution; during the Hamiltonian régime their wrath against the commercial autocracy knew no bounds. The farmers of all parts of the country began to coalesce; in this movement of agrarian protest, Thomas Jefferson assumed the pivotal position. The leaders of Jeffersonian Republicanism were, in the main, southern plantation owners. To the South, then, we must turn to understand the causes and nature of this force that was destined to play so important a rôle in American life.

The large plantations of the southern Piedmont were still frontier settlements. Great distances and impassable forest trails separated them. The farmer, his sons, and possibly a few slaves wrested their existence from the wilderness. Their combat with nature developed self-reliance and stimulated social equality among the planters.

Their economic system rendered these agrarians independent of external governmental aid. In the main, the plantations produced single crops of tobacco, cotton, or rice. These were floated down the many rivers that cut the south Atlantic coast—the Potomac, the James, the Savannah—and reshipped to European markets. From England chiefly the planters imported their finished products. This simple economic life lessened their need for government; their problems were primarily individual, or, at the most, local; the new central government could benefit only through its stimulation of foreign trade and its added protection against slave uprisings. The day had not yet arrived when a department of agriculture could teach farmers scientific methods of raising more wheat or fatter hogs; nor could a farm board then control surpluses and stabilize prices. The farmers of the Jeffersonian period had little need for government. The cheaper the administration, the less taxes they would have to pay.

The Hamiltonian system of commercial assistance thus ran counter to the economic needs of the agrarian group. The new administration added to the total cost of government. The maintenance of the federal departments, the training of an army, and the construction of a navy proved expensive. Congress redeemed the Continental securities at full value and took over the state debts. The great bulk of these bonds had found their way into the vaults of northern speculators. Several of the southern states had already refunded their own debts. Hamilton's debt policy thus proved of little positive value to the agrarians, and at the same time it greatly increased the cost of government. The United States Bank centralized credit control and, to a certain degree, made it more difficult for farmers to secure loans on easy terms. The bank directors also could expand and contract the issue of notes, and thus control price trends.

All these schemes adopted by the new government were costly, and yet the farmers throughout the country had to pay their share of taxes. In one instance, an agrarian revolution actually occurred. The corn-growers of eastern Pennsylvania, lacking transportation facilities for the marketing of their crops, found it more profitable to distill their corn into whiskey, which they could ship more readily. In his plan of federal finance, Hamilton placed an internal revenue tax upon whiskey. This whiskey tax threatened the economic existence of the farmers, and they rose in armed opposition. The Hamiltonian tariff, furthermore, bore down upon agriculture, especially upon the southern plantations. The tobacco and cotton growers feared lest foreign states retaliate and destroy their European markets; the duties also increased the prices on their imports. The agrarians thus paid for a government which could do nothing for them. The revolt against commercial Federalism was fundamentally economic.

Into this economic conflict an extraneous force of immeasurable significance thrust itself. The French Revolution widened the split in American politics. The Jeffersonian agrarians and the urban mechanics looked upon the Revolution as a repetition of the American struggle against England. The French were battling for political freedom, for the rights of man. To the Jeffersonians, the Allied attempt to crush the Revolution seemed to parallel the British efforts to stifle American liberties. The conservative merchants of the Federalist party, however, saw only the destruction of law, order, and security of property. They feared lest the French enthusiasm for equality and fraternity—lest the devastating attack upon aristocracy —sweep across the Atlantic. For a time, American politics consisted of a "French party" and a "British party." Jacobin clubs sprang up everywhere and attacked the anti-French members of the government. In this crisis, the Federalists lost their heads. Congress passed the Alien and Sedition Acts to stifle freedom of the press and of discussion; and partisan judges sent Republican politicians and editors to prison for petty criticisms. The autocracy of the commercial group strengthened the Republican agrarians. Under the influence of Jefferson and Madison, Virginia and Kentucky passed resolutions declaring the Alien and Sedition Acts null and void. A quarrel, meanwhile, broke out within the Federalist ranks between Hamilton and John Adams, and in the election of 1800 Jefferson's agrarians swept into power.

II

Just as the motivating force of Hamiltonian Federalism was commercial, so Jeffersonian democracy was fundamentally agrarian. Until Jefferson was eighteen years old, he had never seen a hamlet of twenty houses. His neighbors "were capable and vigorous frontier democrats, who managed the affairs of local government with the same homespun skill that went to their farming." [1]

In his *Notes on Virginia*, Jefferson early expounded his agrarian doctrines and his hostility toward other economic systems. In Europe, he held, manufacturing was necessary because all of the lands were either in cultivation or locked up in large estates. But America had an immensity of land inviting the industry of the husbandman. It was better that all our people be employed in its improvement than that half be drawn off to handicraft arts. Those who labor in the earth were the chosen people of God, "whose breasts He has made His peculiar deposit for substantial and genuine virtue."

"Corruption of morals in the mass of cultivators is a phenomenon of which no age nor nation has furnished an example. It is the mark set on those, who, not looking up to heaven, to their own soil and industry, as does the husbandman, for their subsistence, depend for it on casualties and caprice of customers. Dependence begets subservience and venality, suffocates the germ of virtue, and prepares fit tools for the designs of ambition."

Speaking generally, the proportion of artisans and tradesmen to farmers was the proportion of the unsound to the healthy parts of

[1] Parrington, *Main Currents in American Thought*, I, 345. (New York, Harcourt, Brace and Company.)

the state, and "is a good enough barometer whereby to measure its degree of corruption." "While we have land to labor, then, let us never wish to see our citizens occupied at a work-bench, or twirling a distaff." For the general operations of manufacture, it was better that we carry provisions and materials to Europe than to bring foreign workmen here, and with them their manners and principles. "The mobs of great cities add just so much to the support of pure government, as sores do to the strength of the human body." [2] In 1785 Jefferson wrote to John Jay in a similar vein:

"We have now lands enough to employ an infinite number of people in their cultivation. Cultivators of the earth are the most valuable citizens. They are the most vigorous, the most independent, the most virtuous, and they are tied to their country, and wedded to its liberty and interests, by the most lasting bonds. As long, therefore, as they can find employment in this line, I would not convert them into mariners, artisans, or any thing else. But our citizens will find employment in this line, till their numbers, and of course their production, become too great for the demand, both internal and foreign. This is not the case as yet, and probably will not be for a considerable time. As soon as it is, the surplus of hands must be turned to something else. I should then, perhaps, wish to turn them to the sea in preference to manufactures; because, comparing the characters of the two classes, I find the former the most valuable citizens. I consider the class of artificers as the panders of vice, and the instruments by which the liberties of a country are generally overturned." [3]

"When we get piled upon one another in large cities, as in Europe, we shall become corrupt as in Europe, and go to eating one another as they do there." [4]

Jefferson's bitter experience as President during the Napoleonic wars, however, somewhat tempered his hostility toward industry. The British and French attacks upon American commerce and the necessary embargo upon foreign shipping impelled him to "place the manufacturer by the side of the agriculturalist." Economic independence was his new objective. But he was still skeptical as to the value of an extended foreign trade. He still felt that surplus labor would be more beneficially employed in the "culture of the earth" than in the "fabrications of art." [5] Throughout his life, he remained an agrarian; and his agrarianism permeated his entire philosophy.

Jeffersonian democracy made three vital contributions to American political thought: (1) a confidence in majority rule; (2) the theory of natural rights, with its corollaries, the right of revolution and the

[2] Jefferson, *Works* (Washington edition), VIII, 405–406.
[3] *Ibid.* (Washington edition), I, 403–404.
[4] *Ibid.* (Washington edition), II, 332.
[5] *Ibid.* (Washington edition), VI, 521.

periodic revision of the fundamental laws; and (3) a scheme of gradation in governmental units with its emphasis on localism and *laissez-
faire*.

Jefferson's confidence in majority rule had a double origin. On the
one hand, it was the philosophical product of the Revolutionary social
contract theory; his reading of the British and French natural rights
philosophers influenced him somewhat. On the other hand, it was the
consequence of agrarianism; the frontier struggle had created a spirit
of equalitarianism. William E. Dodd gives the following explanation
of Jefferson's democratic attitude:

"It is not difficult to see how the great principle of Jefferson's life—absolute
faith in democracy—came to him. He was the product of the first West in
American hsitory; he grew up with men who ruled their country well, who
fought the Indians valiantly." [6]

Majority rule, too, proved itself a powerful political weapon for agrarianism. The great majority of the Americans of 1800 were farmers;
the establishment of majority control would overthrow commercialism
and perpetuate agrarianism. It is curious, however, that Jefferson
never took active steps toward the expansion of the suffrage. Possibly
his distrust of the "mobs of great cities" explains this discrepancy
between his teachings and his practice.

Jefferson defined a republic as "a government by its citizens in
mass, acting directly and personally, according to rules established
by the majority." [7] The essence of a republic consists in "action by
the citizens in person, in affairs within their reach and competence; in
all others by representatives chosen immediately, and removable
by themselves." [8] In his first inaugural address, Jefferson asserted
as an essential principle of the American government the doctrine
of "absolute acquiescence in the decisions of the majority—the vital
principle of republics, from which there is no appeal but to force." [9]
His confidence in majority rule led to his biting attack upon Marshall,
and upon the Supreme Court's review of majority legislation.[10] If
government is to rest upon the people, then we must enlighten public
opinion.[11] Freedom of the press and public education, he felt, are
vital to the life of a republic.

[6] W. E. Dodd, *Statesmen of the Old South* (New York, The Macmillan Company),
p. 23. Chinard in *Thomas Jefferson—Apostle of Americanism* maintains that Jefferson
was influenced intellectually most by Kames.
[7] Jefferson, *Works* (Washington edition), VI, 605.
[8] *Ibid.* (Washington edition), VI, 591.
[9] *Ibid.* (Washington edition), VIII, 4.
[10] *Ibid.* (Washington edition), VI, 177-179.
[11] *Ibid.* (Ford edition), IV, 360.

Jefferson carried on the natural rights philosophy that had dominated the political thought of the Revolution, and which he himself had written into the Declaration of Independence. All men possess certain inalienable, natural rights. These they did not surrender upon their entrance into the social contract; rather, they provided a more effective method of enforcing their rights. The consent of men originally created government; and a just government ought to continue only on this basis.

Government is created for the benefit of the governed. When it fails to fulfill this end, the people may withdraw their consent to the social contract and overthrow the government. Jefferson did not look askance at revolution. He felt that armed resistance to oppression is bitter but wholesome; it clears the air like a thunderstorm.[12] Shays's Rebellion did not disturb him as it did his commercial contemporaries.

"God forbid! we should ever be 20 years without such a rebellion. . . . What country can preserve its liberties, if their rulers are not warned from time to time that this people preserve the spirit of resistance? Let them take arms! . . . What signify a few lives lost in a century or two? The tree of liberty must be refreshed from time to time with the blood of patriots & tyrants. It is its natural manure." [13]

The establishment of free institutions and the rule of the majority make it possible to provide methods of peaceful revolution. Periodical constitutional conventions can take the place of force in the renewal or revision of the social contract. The provisions in many state constitutions for the calling of constitutional conventions date from the Jeffersonian period.

Each generation has a right to establish its own laws. "The earth belongs in usufruct to the living." The dead have neither powers nor rights over it.[14] By examining De Buffon's tables of mortality, Jefferson learned that every nineteen years a new generation constitutes the majority of living individuals.[15] The earth belongs always to the living generation. "They may manage it then, and what proceeds from it, as they please, during their usufruct." But no society can make a perpetual constitution, or even a perpetual law. Every constitution and every law naturally expires at the end of nineteen years. To apply it longer is an act of force and not of right.[16]

[12] Jefferson, *Works* (Washington edition), II, 105.
[13] *Ibid.* (Washington edition), II, 318–319.
[14] *Ibid.* (Washington edition), III, 103.
[15] *Ibid.* (Ford edition), V, 117–120.
[16] *Ibid.* (Washington edition), III, 106.

"I am certainly not an advocate for frequent and untried changes in laws and constitutions. I think moderate imperfections had better be borne with; because, when once known, we accommodate ourselves to them, and find practical means of correcting their ill effects. But I know also, that laws and institutions must go hand in hand with the progress of the human mind. As that becomes more developed, more enlightened, as new discoveries are made, new truths disclosed, and manners and opinions change with the change of circumstances, institutions must advance also, and keep pace with the times. We might as well require a man to wear still the coat which fitted him when a boy, as civilized society to remain ever under the regimen of their barbarous ancestors. It is this preposterous idea which has lately deluged Europe in blood. Their monarchs, instead of wisely yielding to the gradual change of circumstances, of favoring progressive accommodation to progressive improvement, have clung to old abuses, entrenched themselves behind steady habits, and obliged their subjects to seek through blood and violence rash and ruinous innovations, which, had they been referred to the peaceful deliberation and collected wisdom of the nation, would have been put into acceptable and salutary forms." [17]

Since each generation is as independent of the one preceding as that one was of all which had gone before, like them it has a right to choose for itself the form of government that it believes most conducive to its own happiness. The constitution ought, therefore, to provide for revision every nineteen or twenty years.[18] It is interesting to note that Jefferson's thesis that no society can make a perpetual constitution formed the philosophical origin of the later secession movement; the exponents of particularism accepted the doctrine of the terminable nature of the social contract.

Present-day opponents of federal centralization find support in Jefferson's advocacy of localism. His doctrine of local supremacy was part of a general scheme of gradation in governmental units. America, he felt, was too large to have all its affairs directed by a single government. Public servants, removed from under the eyes of their constituents, are unable to administer all the details necessary for good government. And the same circumstance of distance, by rendering detection impossible to their constituents, invites the public agents to corruption, plunder, and waste.[19] Rather, authority should be delegated "by a synthetic process to higher and higher orders of functionaries, so as to trust fewer and fewer powers in proportion as the trustees become more and more oligarchical." [20] We should marshal our government into the following units:

[17] Jefferson, *Works* (Washington edition), VII, 15.
[18] *Ibid.* (Washington edition), VII, 16.
[19] *Ibid.* (Washington edition), IV, 331.
[20] *Ibid.* (Washington edition), VI, 543.

"1. The general federal republic, for all concerns foreign and federal; 2. that of the State, for what relates to our own citizens exclusively; 3. the county republics, for the duties and concerns of the county; and 4. the ward republics, for the small, and yet numerous and interesting concerns of the neighborhood." [21]

In government, as well as in every other business of life, it is by division and subdivision of duties alone that all matters, great and small, can be managed to perfection.[22]

"Let the general government be reduced to foreign concerns only, and let our affairs be disentangled from those of all other nations, except as to commerce, which the merchants will manage the better, the more they are left to manage for themselves, and our General Government may be reduced to a very simple organization, and a very inexpensive one." [23]

Let the counties, it was further argued, be divided into wards of such size that every citizen can attend, when called on, and act in person. The ward will relieve the county administration of nearly all its business, will do it better, and, by making every citizen an acting member of the government, will increase his interest in community affairs.

"These wards, called townships in New England, are the vital principle of their government, and have proved themselves the wisest invention ever devised by the wit of man for the perfect exercise of self-government, and for its preservation." [24]

"It is not by the consolidation, or concentration of powers, but by their distribution, that good government is effected. Were not this country already divided into States, that division must be made, that each might do for itself what concerns itself directly, and what it can so much better do than a distant authority. Each State again is divided into counties, each to take care of what lies within its local bounds; each county again into townships or wards, to manage minuter details; and every ward into farms, to be governed each by its individual proprietor. Were we directed from Washington when to sow, and when to reap, we should soon want bread. It is by this partition of cares, descending in gradation from general to particular, that the mass of human affairs may be best managed for the good and prosperity of all." [25]

Jefferson's thesis of decentralization grew out of his agrarian environment. The political needs of a plantation farmer were few. The central government could render no aid save in the emergency of a slave uprising or in the negotiation of new trade treaties. These

[21] Jefferson, *Works* (Washington edition), VII, 13.
[22] *Ibid.* (Washington edition), VII, 13.
[23] *Ibid.* (Washington edition), IV, 331.
[24] *Ibid.* (Washington edition), VII, 13.
[25] *Ibid.* (Washington edition), I, 82.

frontiersmen, accustomed to depend upon their own arms, could not tolerate a government removed from their sight and reach.

Jefferson's agrarianism induced him to attach to his scheme of governmental gradation a theory of *laissez-faire*. If government could not benefit the farmer, then it should be as inexpensive as possible. And if government performed but a few simple tasks, its costs would be low. "We must make our election between *economy and liberty*, or *profusion and servitude*." If the government runs into heavy debt, it must tax our necessities and our comforts, our meat and our drink, our labors and our amusements. Then, like the people of England, we must labor sixteen hours a day and give the earnings of fifteen of these to the government for its debts and daily expenses. Public extravagance thus destroys private fortunes.[26] In his first inaugural address, Jefferson described the sum of good government in the following terms:

"A wise and frugal government, which shall restrain men from injuring one another, which shall leave them otherwise free to regulate their own pursuits of industry and improvement, and shall not take from the mouth of labor the bread it has earned." [27]

No better statement of the policeman concept of government can be found.

Jefferson nowhere presented his political philosophy in correlated form. His ideas are scattered throughout his public papers, letters, and articles. It remained for John Taylor of Virginia to write a systematic treatise on Jeffersonian agrarianism. Among this author's many works, three stand out: *An Inquiry into the Principles and Policy of the Government of the United States, Construction Construed and Constitutions Vindicated,* and *Tyranny Unmasked.* They constitute a deadly attack upon Adams's theory of aristocracy, upon the Hamiltonian fiscal system, and upon Marshall's decisions in favor of irrevocable contracts.

In his attack upon Adams, Taylor argued that biological inequality among individuals cannot explain social classes. Accidental opportunity, brute force, or unscrupulousness—these are the historical origins of aristocracies. All property is founded in social theft.[28] Throughout history, the ruling classes—royal, ecclesiastical, or feudal —have always exploited the masses. In their efforts at domination,

[26] Jefferson, *Works*, (Washington edition), VII, 14.
[27] *Ibid.* (Washington edition), VIII, 3–4.
[28] Taylor, *An Inquiry into the Principles and Policy of the Government of the United States,* p. 28.

the aristocrats have employed symbols. As Walter Lippmann would put it, they created pictures in the minds of the people in order to fashion their vision of the world outside.[29]

"Superstition and noble orders were defended by the strongest sanctions within the scope of human invention. Penalties, temporal and eternal; splendour, pomp and honour; united to terrify, to dazzle, to awe and to flatter the human mind: and the real or external virtues of charity and meekness, hostility and nobleness of mind, induced some to love that, which most hated, and all feared." [30]

America, said Taylor, abandoned these old hierarchies, but has accepted a new class, capitalistic in nature. The Hamiltonian schemes of tariff, banking, and debt assumption created this new aristocracy of wealth. Like other hierarchies, this one, too, robs productive labor. Like other noble orders, it, too, employs psychological devices. The symbol of "public faith and national credit" fascinates us, Taylor feared, into an opinion that fraud, corruption, and oppressions constitute national credit; and debt and slavery, public faith.[31]

"We pity the ancients for their dullness in discovering oppressions, so clearly seen by ourselves now that they are exploded. We moderns; we enlightened Americans; we who are submitting to be taxed and enslaved by patronage and paper, without being deluded or terrified by the promise of heaven, the denunciation of hell, the penalties of law, the brilliancy and generosity of nobility, or the pageantry and charity of superstition." [32]

The Hamiltonian system, wrote Taylor, introduced into this country a vital class conflict and economic struggle. The five million must ally themselves against the five thousand. Of what avail was the abolition of the clerical and noble orders? Of what value is an exchange of one system of monopoly for another? The combination of "exclusive pecuniary privileges" outruns in its consequences all former aristocracies.

"The encroachments upon property by noble and clerical combinations, once fixed by law, remained stationary; and each individual could calculate his fate with some certainty: but pecuniary combinations, once sanctioned as constitutional, will perpetually open new channels, and breed new invaders, whose whole business it will be, to make inroads upon the territories of industry. Legislatures will become colleges for teaching the science of getting money by monopolies or favours; and the deluge of laws will become as great

[29] W. Lippmann, *Public Opinion* (New York, The Macmillan Company), Ch. I.
[30] Taylor, *An Inquiry into the Principles and Policy of the Government of the United States*, p. 60.
[31] *Ibid.*, p. 61.   [32] *Ibid.*, pp. 60–61.

in the United States, as was once the deluge of papal indulgences in Europe for effecting the same object." [33]

"To define the nature of a government truly, I would say, that a power of distributing property, able to gratify avarice and monopoly, designated a bad one; and that the absence of every such power, designated a good one." [34]

Taylor's attack upon Marshall's thesis of the irrevocable nature of contracts was able and biting. A law enacted for the benefit of a nation, he complained, is repealable; but a law passed for the benefit of private individuals, though oppressive to the nation, is a charter and irrepealable. Posterity is bound by the contracts of its ancestors in every case which diminishes its rights. A government intrusted with the administration of public affairs for the good of a nation may deed away that nation for the good of itself or its partisans; and these deeds bind posterity.[35]

"A law or a contract, prescribing an immoral action is void. No sanction can justify murder, perjury or theft. Yet the murder of national liberty, the perjury of a traitorous government, and the theft of national wealth, by the gradual introduction of the aristocracy of the third age, are varnished into a gloss by a cunning dogma, capable even of dazzling men, so excessively honest as to put other men to death for petty thefts, committed to appease hunger or cover nakedness." [36]

III

During the second quarter of the nineteenth century a second populist movement dominated American politics and thought. Jacksonianism, it is interesting to note, entirely repudiated the leadership of Jeffersonian democracy. These two populist attacks upon commercial capitalism—these two movements toward democracy—could not combine. The election of Andrew Jackson in 1828 marked the decline of Jeffersonianism and the rise to supremacy of the new democracy. To a certain extent, party politics explains this shift. The Jeffersonian Republicans, after the War of 1812, became the dominant party. The old Federalist group disappeared, save in New England. The lack of an effective opposition caused disputes within the former party and finally produced its split. But there are more fundamental causes of this interesting phenomenon.

Vital differences in economic and social composition separated Jeffersonian and Jacksonian agrarianism. By 1828, the old South,

---

[33] Taylor, *Construction Construed and the Constitutions Vindicated*, p. 15.
[34] *Ibid.*, p. 15.
[35] Taylor, *An Inquiry into the Principles and Policy of the Government of the United States*, p. 61.
[36] *Ibid.*, p. 63.

the stronghold of Jefferson's party, had passed from the frontier stage. The economic system of the old plantations had become thoroughly static. No great increases in property values occurred. The agrarians of this district, as typified by John Taylor, discounted the possibility of an expansion of wealth in land. Jeffersonianism was the philosophy of a static agrarianism. Not so Jacksonianism. After the formation of the Union, population gradually migrated into the Northwest Territory; the purchase of Louisiana in 1803 stimulated this population movement. As emigrants moved into the new districts, land values jumped. Eager to amass fortunes, speculators bought up vast tracks, and organized land companies. Everywhere the settlers were intent upon selling their holdings to the newer comers. A general land hunger produced a vast unearned increment. Jacksonianism thus was a dynamic agrarianism. In his biography, *Meet General Grant*, W. E. Woodward well describes the psychology of the New West. In discussing Ohio in 1830, he says:

"It was a land of calloused hands, of lean and muscular men, of canvas-covered wagons with mud flaking from their wheels, of shot-guns and hunting dogs, of silent women bending over the fires of cooking, with the smoke blowing in their eyes, of log-houses, of wheat growing boisterously in fields full of stumps, of Bibles and poor liquor, of sharp trades, of illiterate lawyers, of hell-fire preachers and innumerable quacks. Everything was new. . . . The country was not yet settled down. Every farm was simply an experiment in soil and muscle, with the farmer looking wistfully toward the next county, where, he thought, the land might be cheaper and more fertile. This flood of newcomers, paid little attention to comfort, to the building of houses, to the laying of walls or fences, because nearly everybody expected either to move on to a better place or to be in such a position, within a few years, that he could build himself a really fine house. Coarse and heavy-handed as these people were . . . they were buoyant with the high tension of adventure. They were not looking merely for a home. They wanted land, money and power, and their energies fell instinctively into a social pattern that expressed these aspirations." [37]

Thus the psychology of Jacksonian agrarianism differed diametrically from that of the static Jeffersonian democracy.

In the second place, geography lent a fundamentally different tone to Jacksonian agrarianism. Numerous rivers cut the south Atlantic coastline; the cotton and tobacco raisers loaded river boats at their plantation docks and floated their crops down stream to such ports as Norfolk, Charlestown, or Savannah; from there they easily re-shipped their products to northern and European markets. The

[37] W. E. Woodward, *Meet General Grant* (New York, Horace Liveright, Inc.), p. 19.

southern agrarians felt no crying need for artificial methods of transportation. Roads and canals, moreover, were costly. Nature provided
the South with a convenient and cheap system of communication.
But nature, in the form of the Alleghenies, cut the western farmer
from his eastern markets. The wheat raiser of the Ohio Valley could
send his surplus to New York or Philadelphia by only two tedious
and disadvantageous routes: either by wagon across the roadless
expanse of wooded mountains, or by boat down the endless Ohio
and Mississippi rivers to New Orleans and then through the Gulf of
Mexico and up the Atlantic coast. He consequently raised his voice
in behalf of internal improvements. The era became one of large-
scale construction of turnpikes and canals. A national highway was
pushed across the Alleghenies into Ohio; and the Erie Canal linked
the Great Lakes with the Hudson. Jackson, in his first message to
Congress, advocated federal aid for internal improvements, and the
national government shortly afterwards "loaned" the states large
sums of surplus money. Thus while Jeffersonianism emphasized
laissez-faire, Jacksonianism, to a certain degree, abandoned that
doctrine. While government could scarcely benefit the static agrarianism of the South, it could immeasurably foster the prosperity of
the dynamic West. The construction of transportation systems would
provide ready markets for surplus crops. The new ease of travel, together with a liberal land policy, would increase population and raise
property values. The Jacksonian farmer thus looked upon the state
as more than a big policeman.

And finally, the historical antecedents of these two democratic
movements differed. The southern states, prior to their acceptance
of the Constitution, had been free, independent, sovereign commonwealths. State pride made a man a Virginian first and an American
afterwards. The agrarians of this section were accustomed to look to
their state governments rather than to Washington. Consequently,
they developed a concept of decentralization and localism. The new
western states, however, prior to their entrance into the Union, had
been federal territories. The laws for their regulation had emanated
from the federal Congress. The national government had sent governors into these regions; and in their frequent squabbles with these
governors, the westerners had appealed to the federal administration. They were thus accustomed to look upon the national government as a parent. They were not, therefore, advocates of state supremacy. From the central government, as well as from the states,
they would accept internal improvements and land grants.

Jacksonian democracy was an agrarian movement. It emanated, in the main, from the new states of the West. From this region it acquired its primary characteristics. The frontier struggle for existence made for equalitarianism. Blue blood, education, or even wealth, counted for nothing in the clearing of a claim, the building of a hut, or the harvesting of a crop. Individual ability alone counted. To the strong and skillful went the rewards. Thus, on the frontier, class lines vanished. Equalitarianism, not aristocracy, ruled.

While the leadership and characteristics of Jacksonianism came from the West, two eastern groups aligned themselves with the movement. The farmers of the eastern states recognized the fundamental conflict between farm and factory, and joined in the new agrarian attack upon the second United States Bank and other institutions of commercial capitalism. The laboring class of the rapidly growing seaboard cities also coöperated with the agrarians.

The Jacksonian period witnessed a remarkable growth of labor organizations. The new mechanic and factory groups utilized the democratic movement to demonstrate their hostility against the reigning economic hierarchy and to secure for themselves political privileges and power. The concentration of population in the new and growing industrial centers fostered labor organization. By 1828 city craft unions had sprung up, and labor had founded national trade unions. The Philadelphia Mechanics' Trade Association, founded in 1828, stood for free schools, abolition of imprisonment for debt, mechanics' lien laws, direct election of officials, shorter hours, and better working conditions. In ten years, five national trade unions were organized. In 1835 the newly created Workingmen's Party, or the "Locofocos," won control of the New York Democratic convention. This political labor movement was not aimed against the evils of the Industrial Revolution; the factory system had not yet become a serious problem. Rather it was, on the one hand, a conflict of the mechanics against the capitalist system which was gradually reducing them to a status of wage slavery, and, on the other, a demand of the workers for a larger share in the political and economic life of the nation. Into this battle against aristocracy and privilege, the immigrants from Europe, now arriving in increasing numbers, entered with all the vigor of the native rebels. This new labor movement joined forces with the democratic agrarians of the West. Together, they attacked their common enemy—the commercial aristocracy. Together, they fought for equalitarian democracy and economic opportunity.

IV

Jacksonian democracy boasted no philosophers. The builders of a new country cannot find time for writing. For the ideals of the movement we must examine the political institutions that went with it.

An abolition of suffrage restrictions constituted one of the principal tendencies of the period. The new state constitutions abolished property and religious qualifications for voting. If, as the frontiersman felt, one man was as good as another, the denial of the ballot was unjustifiable. The agrarians and laborers of the east coast, as well, gradually secured suffrage expansion; and in time the electorate rested on a manhood basis for whites. At this time the movement for women suffrage began in the West; and some sentiment existed also for free negro suffrage. Likewise, property qualifications for office-holding lost favor; the new states imposed none, and between 1810 and 1852, eight of the original commonwealths dropped their restrictions.[38]

A second characteristic of Jacksonianism was an increased popular participation in politics. Many of the early state constitutions had vested the choice of governor, judges, and other officers in the legislature. The new constitutions, in both new and old states, removed the election of officials from the legislature and placed it directly in the popular electorate.[39] Not only the governorship, but the offices of judges and administrators were democratized. Secretaries of state, treasurers, auditors, attorneys-general, superintendents of public education—the election of all now rested with the people. The present long ballot in state politics dates back to the second quarter of the nineteenth century. The new constitutions accomplished the democratization of the judiciary by shortening the term of office and by popular election.[40] Democratic control extended even to the adoption of constitutions. By 1830, popular ratification of new constitutions became the usual thing; only the constitution of Delaware in 1831 and that of Arkansas in 1836 went into effect without the sanction of the electorate.

The framers of the federal Constitution had intended largely to

[38] Maryland 1810, Pennsylvania 1838, Massachusetts (except for governor) 1840, New Jersey 1844, Connecticut 1845, Georgia 1847, Virginia 1850, New Hampshire 1852.

[39] Constitutional changes in the original states: Pennsylvania 1790, Georgia 1824, Delaware 1793, North Carolina 1835, Maryland 1837, New Jersey 1844, Virginia 1850.

[40] Between 1846 and 1853, thirteen states provided for direct election of judges: California, Iowa, Kentucky, Maryland, Michigan, Missouri, New York, Ohio, Pennsylvania, Tennessee, Virginia, Wisconsin, Louisiana.

eliminate the people from the choice of the President. According to their scheme, the nomination as well as the election of the chief magistrate was to rest with the electoral college. But in 1831 the Anti-Masonic Party set a new example by calling a national nominat- ing convention. The other parties soon followed suit. Representa- tives of the rank and file, rather than the hierarchy of party officials, now nominated candidates and drafted platforms. To-day the na- tional conventions of the major parties are cloaks from behind which a few political bosses pull their puppets; in the thirties, however, the convention system was a democratization of the party machinery. The convention, rather than the electoral college, nominated the presidential candidates. And the electors, now chosen by the people rather than the state legislatures, merely rubber-stamped the pop- ular choice of each state. Jackson in 1829 even advocated direct popular election of the President.

With the democratization of elections, we find a third major char- acteristic of Jacksonian populism—the expansion of executive power. The President of the country and the governors of the states were now nominated and elected directly by the people. They came to look upon themselves as the representatives of the nation or of the commonwealth; they championed the rights of the people against the representatives of the "special interests" entrenched in the leg- islature. The new constitutions materially lengthened the governor's term of office,[41] increased his appointing power, and vested him with a veto.[42] The energetic executive leadership of Jackson would not have been possible without this changed attitude toward the chief executive.

And finally, a system of spoils and rotation in office marked Jack- sonian democracy. Rotation in office grew out of frontier equalitarian- ism. If one man is as good as another, then no persons, or class of persons, should have an exclusive claim to office. Experience, it was felt, was not important for good administration. In fact, a long term of office, by destroying an officer's sympathy with the people and by making him a devotee of officialism and bureaucracy, might actually prove detrimental to the public service. The spoils system quite naturally developed out of this idea of rotation. The new political

[41] Seven of the original states changed the governor's term of office: Georgia 1789, Pennsylvania 1790, Virginia 1830, Delaware 1831, North Carolina 1835, Maryland 1837, New Jersey 1844.
[42] Five of the original states changed their constitutional provisions concerning the veto power. Georgia 1789, Pennsylvania 1790, New Hampshire 1792, Connecticut 1818, New Jersey 1844.

machines adopted this equalitarian principle and for practical political purposes turned it into the spoils system. In his first message to Congress, Jackson clearly expressed the philosophy of rotation.

"There are, perhaps, few men who can for any great length of time enjoy office and power without being more or less under the influence of feelings unfavorable to the faithful discharge of their public duties. Their integrity may be proof against improper considerations immediately addressed to themselves, but they are apt to acquire a habit of looking with indifference upon the public interests and of tolerating conduct from which an unpracticed man would revolt. Office is considered as a species of property, and government rather as a means of promoting individual interests than as an instrument created solely for the service of the people. . . . The duties of all public officers are, or at least admit of being made, so plain and simple that men of intelligence may readily qualify themselves for their performance; and I can not but believe that more is lost by the long continuance of men in office than is generally to be gained by their experience. . . . In a country where offices are created solely for the benefit of the people no one man has any more intrinsic right to official station than another. Offices were not established to give support to particular men at the public expense. No individual wrong is, therefore, done by removal, since neither appointment to nor continuance in office is a matter of right. The incumbent became an officer with a view to public benefits, and when these require his removal they are not to be sacrificed to private interests. . . . He who is removed has the same means of obtaining a living that are enjoyed by the millions who never held office. The proposed limitation would destroy the idea of property now so generally connected with official station, and although individual distress may be sometimes produced, it would, by promoting that rotation which constitutes a leading principle in the republican creed, give healthful action to the system." [43]

Upon the death of Marshall in 1835, the Supreme Court at last felt the force of the new democracy. Under the leadership of Roger Taney, it repudiated Marshall's decisions on national supremacy and irrevocable contracts. In *City of New York v. Miln*,[44] it upheld a New York statute that required the masters of ships arriving in the city of New York to report to the mayor all facts concerning passengers and to remove all those whom the mayor decided to be undesirable. The object of this act was to prevent the influx of pauper immigrants, who were becoming a charge upon the city. According to a strict interpretation of the Constitution, such as Marshall had desired to render in this very case, this first law against unrestricted immigration violated the commerce clause. However, in the view of

[43] J. D. Richardson, *A Compilation of the Messages and Papers of the Presidents*, Vol. II, pp. 448–449.
[44] 11 Peters 102.

the new judges, the complete, unqualified, and exclusive right of the state to exercise its own internal police powers took precedence over national control of commerce.

The decision in *Briscoe v. The Commonwealth's Bank of the State of Kentucky* [45] overthrew Marshall's conservative precedents against state bills of credit. The state legislature had authorized the Kentucky Bank, owned by the state, to issue bills which were made receivable for taxes and other public dues; it furthermore had directed that an endorsement and tender of these state bank notes should, in general, satisfy any judgment against a debtor. The Supreme Court now held that the constitutional prohibition against state bills of credit did not apply to a state-owned bank.

Taney's famous decision in the *Charles River Bridge Case* [46] deserves a place in judicial annals alongside the Dartmouth College decision. In it Taney abandoned Marshall's theory of the permanent, irrevocable nature of a charter grant. In 1785 the Massachusetts legislature incorporated the "Proprietors of the Charles River Bridge," and authorized the company to construct a bridge from Charlestown to Boston. In 1828 the legislature, feeling the need of additional transportation facilities, incorporated the "Proprietors of the Warren Bridge" and authorized this new company to build another bridge next to the old structure. By the terms of its charter, the Warren Bridge company was to surrender the new bridge to the state as soon as the tolls had reimbursed it for the costs of building and maintaining the structure. The old company attempted to enjoin the building of the new bridge, on the ground that the act of 1828 impaired the obligation of its contract of 1785. Legislation, held Taney, must be progressive. The internal improvements of a state must take precedence over an implied contract to a private company. A state contract, he maintained, must be construed strictly; unless it specifically granted a monopoly, the government reserved the right to charter competing companies. The contention of the Charles River Bridge company would enable the proprietors of every turnpike to prevent the construction of competing canals and railroads.

"We shall be thrown back to the improvements of the last century, and obliged to stand still, until the claims of the old turnpike corporations shall be satisfied; and they shall consent to permit these states to avail themselves of the lights of modern science, and to partake of the benefits of those improvements which are now adding to the wealth and prosperity, and the convenience and comfort, of every other part of the civilized world." [47]

[45] 11 Peters 257.   [46] 11 Peters 420.   [47] 11 Peters 553.

V

During the second quarter of the nineteenth century a third phase of the democratic movement developed. In its literary consequences, the new intellectual democracy proved more prolific and more profound than did Jeffersonian and Jacksonian democracies. A humanitarian wave struck the intellectual circles of the country, especially in Massachusetts. To a certain degree, the Jacksonian struggle for human betterment through majority rule generated this new liberalism; but to a more important extent, the stimuli came from Europe. The radical writings of Rousseau and William Godwin, in the previous century, brought forth fruit on this continent. The humanitarianism of Robert Owen stirred the imagination. Under the impetus of Owen of England and Charles Fourier of France, numerous Utopian communities were started in this country. The New England intellectuals set up a coöperative settlement at Brook Farm. The writings of Emerson, Thoreau, Holmes, Hawthorne, Channing, and Whitman reflected the new democratic spirit. "Plays written around the theme of the revolt of the masses against the classes were also popular, especially R. M. Bird's *The Gladiator,* and R. T. Conrad's *Jack Cade.*" [48] Throughout this intellectual movement runs a definite thread of individualism. "Utopian dreams for an ebullient democratic faith" [49] characterized its literature. The glorification of the individual and his elevation above society meant a minimized importance for the state.

The leading exponent of this intellectual democracy was Ralph Waldo Emerson. "Stripped of its idealistic phraseology, of its beauty and fervor, the master idea of the Emersonian philosophy is the divine sufficiency of the individual." [50] The root and seed of democracy, Emerson felt, is the doctrine, "Judge for yourself. Reverence thyself." "How is the King greater than I, if he is not more just?" [51]

"Democracy, Freedom, has its root in the sacred truth that every man hath in him the divine Reason, or that, though few men since the creation of the world live according to the dictates of Reason, yet all men are capable of so doing. That is the equality and the only equality of all men." [52]

[48] Gettell, *History of American Political Thought* (New York, The Century Co.), p. 242, footnote.
[49] Parrington, *Main Currents in American Thought*, II, 390.
[50] *Ibid.*, II, 390.
[51] Emerson, *Journals* (Boston, Houghton Mifflin Company, 1834), III, 369–370.
[52] *Ibid.*, III, 390.

We Americans, said Emerson, are vain of our political institutions, which are singular in this, that they sprang, within the memory of living men, from the character and condition of the people, which they still express with sufficient fidelity. Democracy is better for us than other forms of government. The religious sentiments of the time accord better with it.[53] Property restrictions upon the suffrage Emerson attacked because they minimize the importance of persons. Doubts have arisen, he said, whether the laws had not hitherto granted too much weight to property and whether such restrictions on the franchise had not allowed the rich to encroach upon the poor, and to keep them poor. "There is an instinctive sense, however obscure and yet inarticulate, that the whole constitution of property, on its present tenures, is injurious, and its influence on persons deteriorating and degrading." Truly, the only interest for the consideration of the state is persons. The highest end of government is the culture of men.[54]

No glorification of the state creeps into Emerson's individualism. Political institutions are not aboriginal nor superior to the citizen. We must remember that every one of them was once the act of a single man; every law and usage was a man's expedient to meet a particular case. "They are all imitable, all alterable; we may make as good, we may make better." Legislation must conform to the temper of the times. The state must follow, and not lead, the character and progress of the citizen. The form of government which prevails at any time is the expression of that cultivation which exists in the population permitting it.

"The law is only a memorandum."
"The statute stands there to say, Yesterday we agreed so and so, but how feel ye this article to-day? Our statute is a currency which we stamp with our own portrait: it soon becomes unrecognizable, and in process of time will return to the mint."
"Foolish legislation is a rope of sand which perishes in the twisting."[55]

The less government, the fewer laws, the less confided power we have the better. The antidote for the abuse of normal government is the influence of private character, the growth of the individual, the appearance of the principal to supersede the proxy. The object of the state is the education of the wise man. Yet existing governments are but shabby imitations of this goal. With the appearance of the wise

[53] Emerson, *Essay on Politics, Essays, second series*, p. 201.
[54] *Ibid.*, pp. 197–198.   [55] *Ibid.*, p. 194.

man, the State expires. The introduction of character makes the State unnecessary.[56]

Emerson well depicted the plight of the liberal of his time. Of the two great parties which shared the nation between them, one, Emerson complained, has the best cause and the other contains the best men. The philosopher, the poet, or the religious man desires to cast his vote with the democrat, for free-trade, for wide suffrage, for the abolition of legal cruelties in the penal code, and for facilitating in every manner the access of the young and the poor to the sources of wealth and power. But these liberals can rarely accept the persons whom the so-called popular party propose to them as representatives of these measures. They have not at heart the ends which give the name of democracy what hope and virtue are in it.[57] By democracy Emerson does not mean "that ill thing, vain and loud, which writes lying newspapers, spouts at caucuses, and sells its lies for gold; but that spirit of love for the general good whose name this assumes. There is nothing of the true democratic element in what is called Democracy."[58] The spirit of American radicalism is destructive and aimless. It has no divine ends, but is destructive out of hatred and selfishness. On the other side, the conservative party, composed of the most moderate, able, and cultivated part of the population, is timid and merely defensive of property. It vindicates no right and aspires to no real good. It brands no crime and proposes no generous policy.

"It does not build, nor write, nor cherish the arts, nor foster religion, nor establish schools, nor encourage science, nor emancipate the slave, nor befriend the poor, or the Indian, or the immigrant."

"From neither party, when in power, has the world any benefit to expect in science, art, or humanity, at all commensurate with the resources of the nation."[59]

William Ellery Channing, the guiding spirit of Unitarianism, voiced a similar concept of democracy. The influence of Rousseau's *Social Contract* and Godwin's *Political Justice* loom large upon his every page. Like Emerson, Channing glorified the individual. Man is "a Rational, Moral, Immortal Being," created in God's image and as His child. Every human being has in him the germ of the greatest idea in the universe, the idea of God; and to unfold this is the end of his existence. He has in his breast the elements of that divine,

[56] Emerson, *Essay on Politics, Essays, second series*, pp. 208–209.
[57] *Ibid.*, pp. 202–203.
[58] Emerson, *Journals* (1836), IV, 95.
[59] Emerson, *Essay on Politics*, p. 203.

everlasting law which the highest orders of creation obey. Man is an end in himself.[60]

Out of this religious conception of man, Channing constructs a minimized State. The State, to be sure, possesses authority to impose laws on its members; but the progress of moral science proportionally narrows the limits of State authority. Moral law restrains the State as well as the individual. The idea of rights should be fundamental and supreme in civil institutions. Government becomes a nuisance and scourge in proportion as it sacrifices these to the many or the few.

"Right is older than human law. Law ought to be its voice."

"That government is most perfect, in which Policy is most entirely subjected to Justice, or in which the supreme and constant aim is to secure the rights of every human being."

"Justice is a greater good than property, not greater in degree, but in kind."

Moral good, not national wealth, is the supreme end to which states are bound to subject all their legislation. The good of the individual is more important than the outward prosperity of the State.[61]

Strangely enough, behind Channing's attack upon the State lies a distrust of the masses.

"I have thought it right to recommend restrictions on power and a simplicity in government beyond what most approve. Power, I apprehend, should not be suffered to run into great masses. No more of it should be confided to rulers than is absolutely necessary to repress crime and preserve public order. A purer age may warrant larger trusts; but the less of government now the better, if society be kept in peace."

There should exist no office to madden ambition. Is any man pure enough to be trusted with an accumulation of power? "Can we wonder at the shameless profligacy, intrigue, and the base sacrifice of public interests by which it is sought, and, when gained, held fast?" Government is at best a rude machinery which can accomplish but very limited good, and which, when strained to accomplish what individuals should do for themselves, is sure to be perverted by selfishness to narrow purposes, or to defeat through ignorance its own ends. "Man is too ignorant to govern much, to form vast plans for states and empires." Human policy has almost always clashed with the great laws of social well-being. "The less power given to man over man the better."[62] Of all powers, the last to be intrusted to the multitude of men is that of determining the questions for public discussion. Free speech is a necessary safeguard.

[60] Channing, *Works*, II, 26–27.   [61] *Ibid.*, II, 37–43.   [62] *Ibid.*, I, xxii–xxiii.

"The greatest truths are often the most unpopular and exasperating; and were they to be denied discussion, till the many should be ready to accept them, they would never establish themselves in the general mind. The progress of society depends on nothing more, than on the exposure of time-honored abuses, which cannot be touched without offending multitudes, than on the promulgation of principles, which are in advance of public sentiment and practice, and which are constantly at war with the habits, prejudices, and immediate interests of large classes of the community."

The multitude, if once allowed to dictate or proscribe subjects of discussion, would strike society with spiritual blindness and death. The right of free discussion is at once the most sacred and the most endangered of all our rights. "He who would rob his neighbour of it, should have a mark set on him as the worst enemy of freedom." [63]

Henry Thoreau was the arch-individualist of the intellectual democrats. His early hostility to political compulsion increased with his experiences as an ardent Abolitionist. His opposition to the State led him to suffer prison rather than support that nefarious institution with his taxes.

"I heartily accept the motto,—'That government is best which governs least;' and I should like to see it acted up to more rapidly and systematically. Carried out, it finally amounts to this, which also I believe,—'That government is best which governs not at all;' and when men are prepared for it, that will be the kind of government which they will have."

Government is an expedient by which "men would fain succeed in letting one another alone." When it is most expedient, the governed are most let alone by it. Most governments are usually, and all governments are sometimes, inexpedient. The objections against a standing army are valid against a standing government. The government, "which is only the mode which the people have chosen to execute their will," is, like a standing army, liable to be abused and perverted before the people can act through it.[64]

Participation in government is futile. Voting is "a sort of gaming, like checkers or backgammon, with a slight moral tinge to it, a playing with right and wrong, with moral questions; and betting naturally accompanies it." The voter is not vitally concerned that right should prevail; he is willing to leave it to the majority. "Even voting *for the right* is *doing* nothing for it. It is only expressing to men feebly your desire that it should prevail." [65] Thus spoke America's philosophical anarchist.

[63] Channing, *Works*, II, 161.
[64] Thoreau, *A Yankee in Canada, with Anti-Slavery and Reform Papers*, p. 123.
[65] *Ibid.*, p. 130.

The high-water mark of American intellectual democracy came with Walt Whitman. From almost the beginning of his career, Whitman preached the religion of democracy. The fervor of the Jacksonian movement caught his fancy, and he became closely connected with the New York Democratic organization. During the years 1846 and 1847 he edited the Brooklyn *Daily Eagle*. In his editorials we can find the beginnings of those democratic ideas that he immortally expressed in his *Leaves of Grass* (1855) and *Democratic Vistas* (1870).

Whitman early proclaimed that democracy is primarily of the spirit. His religion demanded faith in the potentialities of the common man. While government may fail, while existing politics may prove discouraging, confidence in progress must, nevertheless, be paramount. To Whitman, democracy meant more than a political system. It must not depend merely on political means, superficial suffrage, and legislation. Democracy must go deeper and get a firm and warm hold in men's hearts, emotions, and beliefs.

"My comrade!
 For you, to share with me, two greatnesses—and a third one, rising
   inclusive and more resplendent,
 The greatness of Love and Democracy—and the greatness of Religion." [66]

Whitman recognized the crudities of his contemporaries, but these did not shake his faith in the common man. The very turbulence of the democratic spirit guaranteed the political progress of his people. A quiet, contented race sooner or later becomes a race of slaves— "and when so become, there are always among them *still worse* slaves, bound mentally, who argue that it is better so, than to rise and destroy that tyranny that galls them." But endowed with the democratic spirit, even accompanied by its fantasies and excesses, no people can ever become enslaved. The noisy tempestuous scenes of politics evince that the people act; "they are the discipline of the young giant, getting his maturer strength." [67]

"Other states indicate themselves in their deputies: but the genius of the United States is not best or most in its executives or legislatures, nor in its ambassadors or authors or colleges, or churches, or parlours, nor even in its newspapers or inventors, but always most in the common people. Their manners, speech, dress, friendships,—the freshness and candour of their physiognomy—the picturesque looseness of their carriage—their deathless attachment to freedom—their aversion to anything indecorous or soft or mean—the practical acknowledgment of the citizens of one state by the citizens of all other states—the fierceness of their roused resentment—their

[66] Walt Whitman, *Leaves of Grass*, "Starting from Paumanok."
[67] C. Rodgers and J. Black, *The Gathering of the Forces*, I, 3–4.

curiosity and welcome of novelty—their self-esteem and wonderful sympathy—their susceptibility to a slight—the air they have of persons who never knew how it felt to stand in the presence of superiors—the fluency of their speech—their delight in music, the sure symptom of manly tenderness and native elegance of soul—their good temper and openhandedness—the terrible significance of their elections, the President's taking off his hat to them, not they to him—these too are unrhymed poetry." [68]

In his religion of democracy, Whitman preached two highly significant doctrines: liberty and individualism. The idea of political liberty he considered indispensable to literature.

"Liberty takes the adherence of heroes wherever men and women exist; but never takes any adherence or welcome from the rest more than from poets. They are the voice and exposition of liberty. . . . The attitude of great poets is to cheer up slaves and horrify despots." [69]

There is no greater fallacy on earth than the doctrine of force as applied in government.[70] Whitman conceived of liberty as freedom from restraint. His doctrine became that of *laissez-faire*. He maintained that, although government can do little positive good to the people, it may do an immense deal of harm. Democracy would prevent all this harm: it would have no man's benefit achieved at the expense of his neighbors. "It would have no one's rights infringed upon, and that, after all, is pretty much the sum and substance of the prerogatives of government." One single rule is enough to form the starting point of all that is necessary in government: to make no more laws than those useful for preventing a man or body of men from infringing on the rights of other men.[71] Above all, it is folly to expect from law the popular virtues, worth, and self-denial which must come from the influence of the home, from well-rooted principles, from a habit of morality. Laws cannot make men good.[72]

"Where outside authority enters always after the precedence of inside authority;
Where the citizen is always the head and ideal—and President, Mayor, Governor, and what not, are agents for pay;
Where children are taught to be laws to themselves, and to depend on themselves;
Where equanimity is illustrated in affairs;
. . . .
There the great city stands." [73]

[68] Whitman, *Leaves of Grass*, "Preface to 1855 edition."
[69] *Ibid.*
[70] Rodgers and Black, *op. cit.*, I, 54.
[71] *Ibid.*, pp. 52–53.
[72] *Ibid.*, p. 59.
[73] Whitman, *Leaves of Grass*, "Song of the Broad Axe."

Individualism was the second foundation stone of Whitman's religion of democracy. He demanded the full development of one's personality. More precious than all worldly riches is freedom from the painful constipation and tyranny of convention. His was a philosophy of revolt. His was a yearning for even more democratic America.

"I am for those that have never been master'd,
   For men and women whose tempers have never been master'd,
   For those whom laws, theories, conventions can never master."
"I swear I begin to see the meaning of these things,
   It is not the earth, it is not America who is so great,
   It is I who am great or to be great, it is You up there, or any one,
   It is to walk rapidly through civilizations, governments, theories,
   Through poems, pageants, shows, to form individuals.
   Underneath all, individuals,
   I swear nothing is good to me now that ignores individuals,
   The American compact is altogether with individuals,
   The only government is that which makes minute of individuals,
   The whole theory of the universe is directed unerringly to one single individual—namely to You." [74]

The Jeffersonian, Jacksonian, and intellectual movements of democracy had certain common attributes. They emphasized the value of the individual, and demanded for him equality of opportunity in the economic as well as the political life of the nation. Individualism meant freedom from restraint. The less power given to man over man the better. On the whole, these populist movements favored a minimized state. Only two important exceptions to the *laissez-faire* doctrine developed. The western agrarian demanded governmental aid in road and canal construction; and the eastern laborers desired legislation establishing a ten-hour day and mechanics' liens. These populist movements naturally ran up against the stone wall of conservatism. The banking, merchant, and industrial groups entrenched themselves against these attacks upon their economic and political supremacy. Fortunately for them, the spot-light of national politics soon turned upon the slavery and secession controversies. Not until the Granger movement of the 'seventies did the agrarian-labor attack upon capitalism again dominate the scene.

[74] Whitman, *Leaves of Grass*, "By Blue Ontario's Shore."

THOMAS JEFFERSON

Thomas Jefferson played a rôle of outstanding importance in American politics and political thought. The Declaration of Independence was largely his work. After the Revolution, he was the American minister at Paris; while there, he developed a wide acquaintanceship in the intellectual circles of Europe. Throughout his writings a democratic, agrarian outlook is conspicuous. Nowhere, however, did Jefferson assemble his political ideas; they are scattered throughout his letters, addresses, and articles.

Jefferson wrote the *Notes on Virginia* in reply to a questionnaire on Virginia by the secretary of the French legation in 1781. His answers were not published until 1787.

TO JAMES MADISON. [75]

Paris, September 6, 1789.

DEAR SIR,—I sit down to write to you without knowing by what occasion I shall send my letter. I do it, because a subject comes into my head, which I would wish to develop a little more than is practicable in the hurry of the moment of making up general despatches.

The question, whether one generation of men has a right to bind another, seems never to have been started either on this or our side of the water. Yet it is a question of such consequences as not only to merit decision, but place also among the fundamental principles of every government. The course of reflection in which we are immersed here, on the elementary principles of society, has presented this question to my mind; and that no such obligation can be transmitted, I think very capable of proof. I set out on this ground, which I suppose to be self-evident, that the *earth belongs in usufruct to the living;* that the dead have neither powers nor rights over it. The portion occupied by any individual ceases to be his when himself ceases to be, and reverts to the society. If the society has formed no rules for the appropriation of its lands in severalty, it will be taken by the first occupants, and these will generally be the wife and children of the decedent. If they have formed rules of appropriation, those rules may give it to the wife and children, or to some one of them, or to the legatee of the deceased. So they may give it to its creditor. But the child, the legatee or creditor, takes it, not by natural right, but by a law of the society of which he is a member, and to which he is subject. Then, no man can, by *natural right*, oblige the lands he occupied, or the persons who succeed him in that occupation, to the payment of debts contracted by him. For if he could, he might during his own life, eat up the usufruct of the lands for several generations to come; and then the lands would belong to the dead, and not to the living, which is the reverse of our principle.

What is true of every member of the society, individually, is true of them all collectively; since the rights of the whole can be no more than the sum of the rights of the individuals. To keep our ideas clear when applying them to a multitude, let us suppose a whole generation of men to be born on the same day, to attain mature age on the same day, and to die on the same day, leaving a succeeding generation in the moment of attaining their

---

[75] H. A. Washington (editor), *The Writings of Thomas Jefferson.* (Washington, Taylor and Maury, 1853.) III, 102–108.

mature age, all together. Let the ripe age be supposed of twenty-one years, and their period of life thirty-four years more, that being the average term given by the bills of mortality to persons of twenty-one years of age. Each successive generation would, in this way, come and go off the stage at a fixed moment, as individuals do now. Then I say, the earth belongs to each of these generations during its course, fully and in its own right. The second generation receives it clear of the debts and incumbrances of the first, the third of the second, and so on. For if the first could charge it with a debt, then the earth would belong to the dead and not to the living generation. Then, no generation can contract debts greater than may be paid during the course of its own existence. At twenty-one years of age, they may bind themselves and their lands for thirty-four years to come; at twenty-two, for thirty-three; at twenty-three, for thirty-two; and at fifty-four, for one year only; because these are the terms of life which remain to them at the respective epochs. But a material difference must be noted, between the succession of an individual and that of a whole generation. Individuals are parts only of a society, subject to the laws of a whole. These laws may appropriate the portion of land occupied by a decedent, to his creditor, rather than to any other, or to his child, on condition he satisfies the creditor. But when a whole generation, that is, the whole society, dies, as in the case we have supposed, and another generation or society succeeds, this forms a whole, and there is no superior who can give their territory to a third society, who may have lent money to their predecessors, beyond their faculties of paying.

What is true of generations succeeding one another at fixed epochs, as has been supposed for clearer conception, is true for those renewed daily, as in the actual course of nature. As a majority of the contracting generation will continue in being thirty-four years, and a new majority will then come into possession, the former may extend their engagements to that term, and no longer. The conclusion then, is, that neither the representatives of a nation, nor the whole nation itself assembled, can validly engage debts beyond what they may pay in their own time, that is to say, within thirty-four years of the date of the engagement.

To render this conclusion palpable, suppose that Louis the XIV and XV had contracted debts in the name of the French nation, to the amount of ten thousand milliards, and that the whole had been contracted in Holland. The interest of this sum would be five hundred milliards, which is the whole rent-roll or net proceeds of the territory of France. Must the present generation of men have retired from the territory in which nature produces them, and ceded it to the Dutch creditors? No; they have the same rights over the soil on which they were produced, as the preceding generations had. They derive these rights not from them, but from nature. They, then, and their soil are, by nature, clear of the debts of their predecessors. To present this in another point of view, suppose Louis XV and his contemporary generation, had said to the money lenders of Holland, give us money, that we may eat, drink, and be merry in our day; and on condition you will demand no interest till the end of thirty-four years, you shall then, forever after, receive an annual interest of fifteen per cent. The money is lent on these conditions, is divided among the people, eaten, drunk, and squandered. Would the present generation be obliged to apply the produce of the earth and of their labor, to replace their dissipations? Not at all.

I suppose that the received opinion, that the public debts of one generation devolve on the next, has been suggested by our seeing, habitually, in private life, that he who succeeds to lands is required to pay the debts of his predecessor; without considering that this requisition is municipal only, not moral, flowing from the will of the society, which has found it convenient to appropriate the lands of a decedent on the condition of a payment of his debts; but that between society and society, or generation and generation, there is no municipal obligation, no umpire but the law of nature.

The interest of the national debt of France being, in fact, but a two thousandth part of its rent-roll, the payment of it is practicable enough; and so becomes a question merely of honor or of expediency. But with respect to future debts, would it not be wise and just for that nation to declare in the constitution they are forming, that neither the legislature nor the nation itself, can validly contract more debt than they may pay within their own age, or within the term of thirty-four years? And that all future contracts shall be deemed void, as to what shall remain unpaid at the end of thirty-four years from their date? This would put the lenders, and the borrowers also, on their guard. By reducing, too, the faculty of borrowing within its natural limits, it would bridle the spirit of war, to which too free a course has been procured by the inattention of money lenders to this law of nature, that succeeding generations are not responsible for the preceding.

On similar ground it may be proved, that no society can make a perpetual constitution, or even a perpetual law. The earth belongs always to the living generation: they may manage it, then, and what proceeds from it, as they please, during their usufruct. They are masters, too, of their own persons, and consequently may govern them as they please. But persons and property make the sum of the objects of government. The constitution and the laws of their predecessors are extinguished then, in their natural course, with those whose will gave them being. This could preserve that being, till it ceased to be itself, and no longer. Every constitution, then, and every law, naturally expires at the end of thirty-four years. If it be enforced longer, it is an act of force, and not of right. It may be said, that the succeeding generation exercising, in fact, the power of repeal, this leaves them as free as if the constitution or law had been expressly limited to thirty-four years only. In the first place, this objection admits the right, in proposing an equivalent. But the power of repeal is not an equivalent. It might be, indeed, if every form of government were so perfectly contrived, that the will of the majority could always be obtained, fairly and without impediment. But this is true of no form. The people cannot assemble themselves; their representation is unequal and vicious. Various checks are opposed to every legislative proposition. Factions get possession of the public councils, bribery corrupts them, personal interests lead them astray from the general interests of their constituents; and other impediments arise, so as to prove to every practical man, that a law of limited duration is much more manageable than one which needs a repeal.

This principle, that the earth belongs to the living and not to the dead, is of very extensive application and consequences in every country, and most especially in France. It enters into the resolution of the questions, whether the nation may change the descent of lands holden in tail; whether they may change the appropriation of lands given anciently to the church, to hospitals, colleges, orders of chivalry, and otherwise in perpetuity; whether they may abolish the charges and privileges attached on lands, including the whole catalogue, ecclesiastical and feudal; it goes to hereditary offices, authorities and jurisdictions, to hereditary orders, distinctions and appellations, to perpetual monopolies in commerce, the arts or sciences, with a long train of *et ceteras;* and it renders the question of reimbursement, a question of generosity and not of right. In all these cases, the legislature of the day could authorize such appropriations and establishments for their own time, but no longer; and the present holders, even where they or their ancestors have purchased, are in the case of *bona fide* purchasers of what the seller had no right convey.

Turn this subject in your mind, my dear Sir, and particularly as to the power of contracting debts, and develop it with that cogent logic which is so peculiarly yours. Your station in the councils of our country gives you an opportunity of producing it to public consideration, of forcing it into discussion. At first blush it may be laughed at, as the dream of a theorist; but examination will prove it to be solid and salutary. It would furnish matter for a fine preamble to our first law for appropriating the public revenue; and it will exclude, at the threshold of our new government, the ruinous and contagious errors of this quarter of the globe, which have armed despots with means which nature does not sanction, for binding in chains their fellow-men. We have already given, in example, one effectual check to the dog of war, by transferring the power of declaring war from the executive to the legislative body, from those who are to spend, to those who are to pay. I should be pleased to see this second obstacle held out by us also, in the first instance. No nation can make a declaration against the validity of long-contracted debts, so disinterestedly as we, since we do not own a shilling which will not be paid, principal and interest, by the measures you have taken, within the time of our own lives. I write you no news, because when an occasion occurs, I shall write a separate letter for that.

I am always, with great and sincere esteem, dear Sir, your affectionate friend and servant.[76]

Notes on Virginia [77]

QUERY XIX

The present state of manufactures, commerce, interior and exterior trade?

We never had an interior trade of any importance. Our exterior commerce has suffered very much from the beginning of the present contest. During this time we have manufactured within our families the most necessary articles of clothing. Those of cotton will bear some comparison with the same kinds of manufacture in Europe; but those of wool, flax and hemp are

[76] Jefferson later, upon a more detailed analysis of De Buffon's tables of mortality, changed the span of a generation from thirty-four years to nineteen years. *Writings of Thomas Jefferson* (Ford edition), V, 117–120.
[77] H. A. Washington, *op. cit.*, VIII, 404–406.

very coarse, unsightly, and unpleasant; and such is our attachment to agriculture, and such our preference for foreign manufactures, that be it wise or unwise, our people will certainly return as soon as they can, to the raising raw materials, and exchanging them for finer manufactures than they are able to execute themselves.

The political economists of Europe have established it as a principle, that every State should endeavor to manufacture for itself; and this principle, like many others, we transfer to America, without calculating the difference of circumstance which should often produce a difference of result. In Europe the lands are either cultivated, or locked up against the cultivator. Manufacture must therefore be resorted to of necessity not of choice, to support the surplus of their people. But we have an immensity of land courting the industry of the husbandman. Is it best then that all our citizens should be employed in its improvement, or that one half should be called off from that to exercise manufactures and handicraft arts for the other? Those who labor in the earth are the chosen people of God, if ever He had a chosen people, whose breasts He has made His peculiar deposit for substantial and genuine virtue. It is the focus in which he keeps alive that sacred fire, which otherwise might escape from the face of the earth. Corruption of morals in the mass of cultivators is a phenomenon of which no age nor nation has furnished an example. It is the mark set on those, who, not looking up to heaven, to their own soil and industry, as does the husbandman, for their subsistence, depend for it on casualties and caprice of customers. Dependence begets subservience and venality, suffocates the germ of virtue, and prepares fit tools for the designs of ambition. This, the natural progress and consequence of the arts, has sometimes perhaps been retarded by accidental circumstances; but, generally speaking, the proportion which the aggregate of the other classes of citizens bears in any State to that of its husbandmen, is the proportion of its unsound to its healthy parts, and is a good enough barometer whereby to measure its degree of corruption. While we have land to labor then, let us never wish to see our citizens occupied at a work-bench, or twirling a distaff. Carpenters, masons, smiths, are wanting in husbandry; but, for the general operations of manufacture, let our workships remain in Europe. It is better to carry provisions and materials to workmen there, than bring them to the provisions and materials, and with them their manners and principles. The loss by the transportation of commodities across the Atlantic will be made up in happiness and permanence of government. The mobs of great cities add just so much to the support of pure government, as sores do to the strength of the human body. It is the manners and spirit of a people which preserve a republic in vigor. A degeneracy in these is a canker which soon eats to the heart of its laws and constitution.

INAUGURAL ADDRESS.—MARCH 4, 1801 [78]

Friends and Fellow Citizens:—

Called upon to undertake the duties of the first executive office of our country, I avail myself of the presence of that portion of my fellow citizens which is here assembled, to express my grateful thanks for the favor with

[78] H. A. Washington, *op. cit.*, VIII, 1–5.

which they have been pleased to look toward me, to declare a sincere consciousness that the task is above my talents, and that I approach it with those anxious and awful presentiments which the greatness of the charge and the weakness of my powers so justly inspire. A rising nation, spread over a wide and fruitful land, traversing all the seas with the rich productions of their industry, engaged in commerce with nations who feel power and forget right, advancing rapidly to destinies beyond the reach of mortal eye—when I contemplate these transcendent objects, and see the honor, the happiness, and the hopes of this beloved country committed to the issue and the auspices of this day, I shrink from the contemplation, and humble myself before the magnitude of the undertaking. Utterly indeed, should I despair, did not the presence of many whom I here see remind me, that in the other high authorities provided by our constitution, I shall find resources of wisdom, of virtue, and of zeal on which to rely under all difficulties. To you, then, gentlemen, who are charged with the sovereign functions of legislation, and to those associated with you, I look with encouragement for that guidance and support which may enable us to steer with safety the vessel in which we are all embarked amid the conflicting elements of a troubled world.

During the contest of opinion through which we have passed, the animation of discussion and of exertions has sometimes worn an aspect which might impose on strangers unused to think freely and to speak and to write what they think; but this being now decided by the voice of the nation, announced according to the rules of the constitution, all will, of course, arrange themselves under the will of the law, and unite in common efforts for the common good. All, too, will bear in mind this sacred principle, that though the will of the majority is in all cases to prevail, that will, to be rightful, must be reasonable; that the minority possess their equal rights, which equal laws must protect, and to violate which would be oppression. Let us, then, fellow citizens, unite with one heart and one mind. Let us restore to social intercourse that harmony and affection without which liberty and even life itself are but dreary things. And let us reflect that having banished from our land that religious intolerance under which mankind so long bled and suffered, we have yet gained little if we countenance a political intolerance as despotic, as wicked, and capable of as bitter and bloody persecutions. During the throes and convulsions of the ancient world, during the agonizing spasms of infuriated man, seeking through blood and slaughter his long-lost liberty, it was not wonderful that the agitation of the billows should reach even this distant and peaceful shore; that this should be more felt and feared by some and less by others; that this should divide opinions as to measures of safety. But every difference of opinion is not a difference of principle. We have called by different names brethren of the same principle. We are all republicans—we are federalists. If there be any among us who would wish to dissolve this Union or to change its republican form, let them stand undisturbed as monuments of the safety with which error of opinion may be tolerated where reason is left free to combat it. I know, indeed, that some honest men fear that a republican government cannot be strong; that this government is not strong enough. But would the honest patriot, in the full tide of successful experiment, abandon a government which has so far kept us free and firm, on the theoretic and visionary fear that this government, the best world's hope, may by possibility want energy to preserve itself? I trust not. I believe this, on the contrary, the strongest government on earth. I believe it is the only one where every man, at the call of the laws, would fly to the standard of the law, and would meet invasions of the public order as his own personal concern. Sometimes it is said that man cannot be trusted with the government of himself. Can he, then, be trusted with the government of others? Or have we found angels in the forms of kings to govern him? Let history answer this question.

Let us, then, with courage and confidence pursue our own federal and republican principles, our attachment to our union and representative government. Kindly separated by nature and a wide ocean from the exterminating havoc of one quarter of the globe; too high-minded to endure the degradations of the others; possessing a chosen country, with room enough for our descendants to the hundredth and thousandth generation; entertaining a due sense of our equal right to the use of our own faculties, to the acquisitions of our industry, to honor and confidence from our fellow citizens, resulting not from birth but from our actions and their sense of them; enlightened by a benign religion, professed, indeed, and practiced in various forms, yet all of them including honesty, truth, temperance, gratitude, and the love of man; acknowledging and adoring an overruling Providence, which by all its dispensations proves that it delights in the happiness of man here and his greater happiness hereafter; with all these blessings, what more is necessary to make us a happy and prosperous people? Still one thing more, fellow citizens—a wise and frugal government, which shall restrain men from injuring one another, which shall leave them otherwise free to regulate their own pursuits of industry and improvement, and shall not take from the mouth of labor the bread it has earned. This is the sum of good government, and this is necessary to close the circle of our felicities.

About to enter, fellow citizens, on the exercise of duties which comprehend everything dear and valuable to you, it is proper that you should understand what I deem the essential principles of our government, and consequently those which ought to shape its administration. I will compress them within the narrowest compass they will bear, stating the general principle, but not all its limitations. Equal and exact justice to all men, of whatever state or persuasion, religious or political; peace, commerce, and honest friendship, with all nations—entangling alliances with none; the support of the state governments in all their rights, as the most competent administrations for our domestic concerns and the surest bulwarks against anti-republican tendencies; the preservation of the general government in its whole constitutional vigor, as the sheet anchor of our peace at home and safety abroad; a jealous care of the right of election by the people—a mild and safe corrective of abuses which are lopped by the sword of the revolution where peaceable remedies are unprovided; absolute acquiescence in the decisions of the majority—the vital principle of republics, from which there is no appeal but to force, the vital principle and immediate parent of despotism; a well-disciplined militia— our best reliance in peace and for the first moments of war, till regulars may relieve them; the supremacy of the civil over the military authority; economy in the public expense, that labor may be lightly burdened; the honest payment of our debts and sacred preservation of the public faith; encouragement of agriculture, and of commerce as its handmaid; the diffusion of information and the arraignment of all abuses at the bar of public reason; freedom of religion; freedom of the press; freedom of persons under the protection of the *habeas corpus;* and trial by juries impartially selected—these principles form the bright constellation which has gone before us, and guided our steps through an age of revolution and reformation. The wisdom of our sages and the blood of our heroes have been devoted to their attainment. They should be the creed of our political faith—the text of civil instruction—the touchstone by which to try the services of those we trust; and should we wander from them in moments of error or alarm, let us hasten to retrace our steps and to regain the road which alone leads to peace, liberty, and safety.

I repair, then, fellow citizens, to the post you have assigned me. With experience enough in subordinate offices to have seen the difficulties of this, the greatest of all, I have learned to expect that it will rarely fall to the lot of imperfect man to retire from this station with the reputation and the favor which bring him into it. Without pretensions to that high confidence reposed in our first and great revolutionary character, whose preëminent services had entitled him to the first place in his country's love, and destined for him the fairest page in the volume of faithful history, I ask so much confidence only as may give firmness and effect to the legal administration of your affairs. I shall often go wrong through defect of judgment. When right, I shall often be thought wrong by those whose position will not command a view of the whole ground. I ask your indulgence for my own errors, which will never be intentional; and your support against the errors of others, who may condemn what they would not if seen in all its parts. The approbation implied by your suffrage is a consolation to me for the past; and my future solicitude will be to retain the good opinion of those who have bestowed it in advance, to conciliate that of others by doing them all the good in my power, and to be instrumental to the happiness and freedom of all.

Relying, then, on the patronage of your good will, I advance with obedience to the work, ready to retire from it whenever you become sensible how much better choice it is in your power to make. And may that Infinite Power which rules the destinies of the universe, lead our councils to what is best, and give them a favorable issue for your peace and prosperity.

To Samuel Kerchival [79]

Monticello, July 12, 1816.

Sir,—I duly received your favor of June the 13th, with the copy of the letters on the calling a convention, on which you are pleased to ask my opinion. I have not been in the habit of mysterious reserve on any subject, nor of buttoning up my opinions within my own doublet. On the contrary, while in public service especially, I thought the public entitled to frankness, and intimately to know whom they employed. But I am now retired: I resign myself, as a passenger, with confidence to those at present at the helm, and ask but for rest, peace and good will. The question you propose, on equal representation, has become a party one, in which I wish to take no public share. Yet, if it be asked for your own satisfaction only, and not to be quoted before the public, I have no motive to withhold it, and the less from you, as it coincides

[79] H. A. Washington, *op. cit.*, VII, 9-17.

with your own. At the birth of our republic, I committed that opinion to the world, in the draught of a constitution annexed to the "Notes on Virginia," in which a provision was inserted for a representation permanently equal. The infancy of the subject at that moment, and our inexperience of self-government, occasioned gross departures in that draught from genuine republican canons. In truth, the abuses of monarchy had so much filled all the space of political contemplation, that we imagined everything republican which was not monarchy. We had not yet penetrated to the mother principle, that "governments are republican only in proportion as they embody the will of their people, and execute it." Hence, our first constitutions had really no leading principles in them. But experience and reflection have but more and more confirmed me in the particular importance of the equal representation then proposed. On that point, then, I am entirely in sentiment with your letters; and only lament that a copy-right of your pamphlet prevents their appearance in the newspapers, where alone they would be generally read, and produce general effect. The present vacancy too, of other matter, would give them place in every paper, and bring the question home to every man's conscience.

But inequality of representation in both Houses of our legislature, is not the only republican heresy in this first essay of our revolutionary patriots at forming a constitution. For let it be agreed that a government is republican in proportion as every member composing it has his equal voice in the direction of its concerns, (not indeed in person, which would be impracticable beyond the limits of a city, or small township, but) by representatives chosen by himself, and responsible to him at short periods, and let us bring to the test of this canon every branch of our constitution.

In the legislature, the House of Representatives is chosen by less than half the people, and not at all in proportion to those who do choose. The Senate are still more disproportionate, and for long terms of irresponsibility. In the Executive, the Governor is entirely independent of the choice of the people, and of their control; his Council equally so, and at best but a fifth wheel to a wagon. In the Judiciary, the judges of the highest courts are dependent on none but themselves. In England, where judges were named and removable at the will of an hereditary executive, from which branch most misrule was feared, and has flowed, it was a great point gained, by fixing them for life, to make them independent of that executive. But in a government founded on the public will, this principle operates in an opposite direction, and against that will. There, too, they were still removable on a concurrence of the executive and legislative branches. But we have made them independent of the nation itself. They are irremovable, but by their own body, for any depravities of conduct, and even by their own body for the imbecilities of dotage. The justices of the inferior courts are self-chosen, are for life, and perpetuate their own body in succession forever, so that a faction once possessing themselves of the bench of a county, can never be broken up, but hold their county in chains, forever indissoluble. Yet these justices are the real executive as well as judiciary, in all our minor and most ordinary concerns. They tax us at will; fill the office of sheriff, the most important of all the executive officers of the county; name nearly all our military leaders, which leaders, once named, are removable but by themselves. The juries, our judges of all fact, and of law when they choose it, are not selected by the people, nor amenable to them. They are chosen by an officer named by the court and executive. Chosen, did I say? Picked up by the sheriff from the loungings of the court yard, after everything respectable has retired from it. Where then is our republicanism to be found? Not in our constitution certainly, but merely in the spirit of our people. That would oblige even a despot to govern us republicanly. Owing to this spirit, and to nothing in the form of our constitution, all things have gone well. But this fact, so triumphantly misquoted by the enemies of reformation, is not the fruit of our constitution, but has prevailed in spite of it. Our functionaries have done well, because generally honest men. If any were not so, they feared to show it.

But it will be said, it is easier to find faults than to amend them. I do not think their amendment so difficult as is pretended. Only lay down true principles, and adhere to them inflexibly. Do not be frightened into their surrender by the alarms of the timid, or the croakings of wealth against the ascendency of the people. If experience be called for, appeal to that of our fifteen or twenty governments for forty years, and show me where the people have done half the mischief in these forty years, that a single despot would have done in a single year; or show half the riots and rebellions, the crimes and the punishments, which have taken place in any single nation, under kingly government, during the same period. The true foundation of republican government is the equal right of every citizen, in his person and property, and in their management. Try by this, as a tally, every provision of our constitution, and see if it hangs directly on the will of the people. Reduce your legislature to a convenient number for full, but orderly discussion. Let every man who fights or pays, exercise his just and equal right in their election. Submit them to approbation or rejection at short intervals. Let the executive be chosen in the same way, and for the same term, by those whose agent he is to be; and leave no screen of a council behind which to skulk from responsibility. It has been thought that the people are not competent electors of judges *learned in the law*. But I do not know that this is true, and, if doubtful, we should follow principle. In this, as in many other elections, they would be guided by reputation, which would not err oftener, perhaps, than the present mode of appointment. In one State of the Union, at least, it has long been tried, and with the most satisfactory success. The judges of Connecticut have been chosen by the people every six months, for nearly two centuries, and I believe there has hardly ever been an instance of change; so powerful is the curb of incessant responsibility. If prejudice, however, derived from a monarchical institution, is still to prevail against the vital elective principle of our own, and if the existing example among ourselves of periodical election of judges by the people be still mistrusted, let us at least not adopt the evil, and reject the good, of the English precedent; let us retain amovability on the concurrence of the executive and legislative branches, and nomination by the executive alone. Nomination to office is an executive function. To give it to the legislature, as we do, is a violation of the principle of the separation of powers. It swerves the members from correctness, by temptations to intrigue for office themselves, and to a corrupt barter of votes; and destroys responsibility by dividing it among a multitude. By leaving nomination in its proper place, among executive functions, the principle in the distribution of power is preserved, and responsibility weighs with its heaviest force on a single head.

The organization of our county administrations may be thought more difficult. But follow principle, and the knot unties itself. Divide the counties into wards of such size as that every citizen can attend, when called on, and act in person. Ascribe to them the government of their wards in all things relating to themselves exclusively. A justice, chosen by themselves, in each, a constable, a military company, a patrol, a school, the care of their own poor, their portion of the public roads, the choice of one or more jurors to serve in some court, and the delivery within their own wards, of their own votes for all elective officers of higher sphere, will relieve the county administration of nearly all its business, will have it better done, and by making every citizen an acting member of the government, and in the offices nearest and most interesting to him, will attach him by his strongest feelings to the independence of his country, and its republican constitution. The justices thus chosen by every ward, would constitute the county court, would do its judiciary business, direct roads and bridges, levy county and poor rates, and administer all the matters of common interest to the whole country. These wards, called townships in New England, are the vital principle of their government, and have proved themselves the wisest invention ever devised by the wit of man for the perfect exercise of self-government, and for its preservation. We should thus marshal our government into, 1, the general federal republic, for all concerns foreign and federal; 2, that of the State, for what relates to our own citizens exclusively; 3, the county republics, for the duties and concerns of the county; and 4, the ward republics, for the small, and yet numerous and interesting concerns of the neighborhood; and in government, as well as in every other business of life, it is by division and subdivision of duties alone, that all matters, great and small, can be managed to perfection. And the whole is cemented by giving to every citizen, personally, a part in the administration of the public affairs.

The sum of these amendments is, 1. General suffrage. 2. Equal representation in the legislature. 3. An executive chosen by the people. 4. Judges elective or amovable. 5. Justices, jurors, and sheriffs elective. 6. Ward divisions. And 7. Periodical amendments of the constitution.

I have thrown out these as loose heads of amendment, for consideration and correction; and their object is to secure self-government by the republicanism of our constitution, as well as by the spirit of the people; and to nourish and perpetuate that spirit. I am not among those who fear the people. They, and not the rich, are our dependence for continued freedom. And to preserve their independence, we must not let our rulers load us with perpetual debt. We must make our election between *economy and liberty, or profusion and servitude.* If we run into such debts, as that we must be taxed in our meat and in our drink, in our necessaries and our comforts, in our labors and our amusements, for our callings and our creeds, as the people of England are, our people, like them, must come to labor sixteen hours in the twenty-four, give the earnings of fifteen of these to the government for their debts and daily expenses; and the sixteenth being insufficient to afford us bread, we must live, as they now do, on oatmeal and potatoes; have no time to think, no means of calling the mismanagers to account; but be glad to obtain subsistence by hiring ourselves to rivet their chains on the necks of our fellow-sufferers. Our land-holders, too, like theirs, retaining indeed the title and stewardship of estates called theirs, but held really in trust for the treasury, must wander, like theirs, in foreign countries, and be contented with penury, obscurity, exile, and the glory of the nation. This example reads to us the salutary lesson, that private fortunes are destroyed by public as well as by private extravagance. And this is the tendency of all human governments. A departure from principle in one instance becomes a precedent for a second; that second for a third; and so on, till the bulk of the society is reduced to be mere automatons of misery, to have no sensibilities left but for sinning and suffering. Then begins, indeed, the *bellum omnium in omnia*, which some philosophers observing to be so general in this world, have mistaken it for the natural, instead of the abusive state of man. And the fore horse of this frightful team is public debt. Taxation follows that, and in its train wretchedness and oppression.

Some men look at constitutions with sanctimonious reverence, and deem them like the ark of the covenant, too sacred to be touched. They ascribe to the men of the preceding age a wisdom more than human, and suppose what they did to be beyond amendment. I knew that age well; I belonged to it, and labored with it. It deserved well of its country. It was very like the present, but without the experience of the present; and forty years of experience in government is worth a century of book-reading; and this they would say themselves, were they to rise from the dead. I am certainly not an advocate for frequent and untried changes in laws and constitutions. I think moderate imperfections had better be borne with; because, when once known, we accommodate ourselves to them, and find practical means of correcting their ill effects. But I know also, that laws and institutions must go hand in hand with the progress of the human mind. As that becomes more developed, more enlightened, as new discoveries are made, new truths disclosed, and manners and opinions change with the change of circumstances, institutions must advance also, and keep pace with the times. We might as well require a man to wear still the coat which fitted him when a boy, as civilized society to remain ever under the regimen of their barbarous ancestors. It is this preposterous idea which has lately deluged Europe in blood. Their monarchs, instead of wisely yielding to the gradual change of circumstances, of favoring progressive accommodation to progressive improvement, have clung to old abuses, entrenched themselves behind steady habits, and obliged their subjects to seek through blood and violence rash and ruinous innovations, which, they had been referred to the peaceful deliberations and collected wisdom of the nation, would have been put into acceptable and salutary forms. Let us follow no such examples, nor weakly believe that one generation is not as capable as another of taking care of itself, and of ordering its own affairs. Let us, as our sister States have done, avail ourselves of our reason and experience, to correct the crude essays of our first and unexperienced, although wise, virtuous, and well-meaning councils. And lastly, let us provide in our constitution for its revision at stated periods. What these periods should be, nature herself indicates. By the European tables of mortality, of the adults living at any one moment of time, a majority will be dead in about nineteen years. At the end of that period then, a new majority is come into place; or, in other words, a new generation. Each generation is as independent of the one preceding, as that was of all which had gone before. It has then, like them, a right to choose for itself the form of government it believes most promotive of its own happiness; consequently, to accommodate to the circumstances in which it finds itself, that received from its predecessors; and it is for the peace and good of mankind, that a solemn opportunity of doing this every nineteen or twenty years, should be provided by the constitution; so that it may be handed on, with periodical repairs, from generation to generation, to the end of time, if anything human can so long endure. It is now forty years since the constitution of Virginia was formed. The same tables inform us, that, within that period two-thirds of the adults then living are now dead. Have then the remaining third, even if they had the wish, the right to hold in obedience to their will, and to laws heretofore made by them, the other two-thirds, who, with themselves, compose the present mass of adults? If they have not, who has? The dead? But the dead have no rights. They are nothing; and nothing cannot own something. Where there is no substance, there can be no accident. This corporeal globe, and everything upon it, belong to the present corporeal inhabitants, during their generation. They alone have a right to direct what is the concern of themselves alone, and to declaré the law of that direction; and this declaration can only be made by their majority. That majority, then, has a right to depute representatives to a convention, and to make the constitution what they think will be the best for themselves. But how collect their voice? This is the real difficulty. If invited by private authority, or county or district meetings, these divisions are so large that few will attend; and their voice will be imperfectly, or falsely pronounced. Here, then, would be one of the advantages of the ward divisions I have proposed. The mayor of every ward, on a question like the present, would call his ward together, take the simple yea or nay of its members, convey these to the county court, who would hand on those of all its wards to the proper general authority; and the voice of the whole people would be thus fairly, fully, and peaceably expressed, discussed, and decided by the common reason of the society. If this ayenue be shut to the call of sufferance, it will make itself heard through that of force, and we shall go on, as other nations are doing, in the endless circle of oppression, rebellion, reformation; and oppression, rebellion, reformation, again; and so on forever.

These, Sir, are my opinions of the government we see among men, and of the principles by which alone we may prevent our own from falling into the same dreadful track. I have given them a greater length than your letter called for. But I cannot say things by halves; and I confide them to your honor, so to use them as to preserve me from the gridiron of the public papers. If you shall approve and enforce them, as you have done that of equal representation, they may do some good. If not, keep them to yourself as the effusions of withered age and useless time. I shall, with not the less truth, assure you of my great respect and consideration.

JOHN TAYLOR

John Taylor of Virginia was the theorist of Jeffersonian democracy. A fear of aristocracy and commercial autocracy permeates his writings. He looked upon politics from an economic point of view. His *Inquiry into the Principles and Policy of the Government of the United States* is an attack upon the Hamiltonian fiscal system and upon John Adams's theory of aristocracy. In *Construction Construed and Constitutions Vindicated*, he presents the agrarian reply to Marshall's decisions. *Tyranny Unmasked* he wrote by way of attack upon a report of a congressional committee on manufactures which recommended the enactment of high protective tariffs in order to establish industry in this country.

INQUIRY INTO THE PRINCIPLES AND POLICY OF THE GOVERNMENT OF THE UNITED STATES.[80]

Section the First

ARISTOCRACY

. . . . . .

Superstition and noble orders were defended by the strongest sanctions within the scope of human invention. Penalties, temporal and eternal; splendour, pomp and honour; united to terrify, to dazzle, to awe and to flatter the human mind; and the real or external virtues of charity and meekness, hospitality and nobleness of mind, induced some to love that, which most hated, and all feared. Yet the intellect of the last age pierced through the delusions, behind which the oppressions of hierarchy and nobility had taken shelter.

We pity the ancients for their dullness in discovering oppressions, so clearly seen by ourselves now that they are exploded. We moderns; we enlightened Americans; we who have abolished hierarchy and title; and we who are submitting to be taxed and enslaved by patronage and paper, without being deluded or terrified by the promise of heaven, the denunciation of hell, the penalties of law, the brilliancy and generosity of nobility, or the pageantry and charity of superstition.

A spell is put upon our understandings by the words "publick faith and national credit," which fascinates us into an opinion, that fraud, corruption and oppressions, constitute national credit; and debt and slavery, publick faith. This delusion of the aristocracy of the present age, is not less apparent, than the ancient divinity of kings, and yet it required the labours of Locke and Sidney to detect that ridiculous imposture.

Publick faith is made with great solemnity to mount the rostrum, and to pronounce the following lecture:

"Law enacted for the benefit of a nation, is repealable; but law enacted "for the benefit of individuals, though oppressive to a nation, is a charter, "and irrepealable. The existing generation is under the tutelage of all past "generations, and must rely upon the responsibility of the grave for the "preservation of its liberty. Posterity, being bound by the contracts of its "ancestry, in every case which diminishes its rights, man is daily growing less

[80] John Taylor, *Inquiry into the Principles and Policy of the Government of the United States*. (Fredericksburg, Green and Cady, 1814), pp. 60–64.

"free by a doctrine which never increases them. A government intrusted "with the administration of public affairs for the good of a nation, has a "right to deed away that nation for the good of itself or its partisans, by law "charters for monopolies or sinecures; and posterity is bound by these deeds. "But although an existing generation can never reassume the liberty or "property held by its ancestors, it may recompense itself by abridging or "abolishing the rights of its descendants."

Such is the doctrine which has prevented the eye of investigation from penetrating the recesses of the aristocracy of the present age. It simply offers the consolation of softening injuries to ourselves by adding to the wretchedness of our descendants. By this artifice, (the offspring of interest and cunning,) whenever men cut off their shackles with the sword, they are riveted on again by the pen. A successful war, to avenge a small and temporary injury, is made to gain a great and lasting calamity. Victory over enemies is followed by defeat from friends. And an enemy destroyed abroad, is only the head of an hydra, which produces two at home. This is not exaggeration, if the idea of the aristocracy of paper and patronage is not chimerical. And hence occur these curious questions: Can the United States kill one Englishman or Frenchman, without converting two at least of their own citizens, into members of this aristocracy? Which would be most dangerous and burdensome to the union, one of these foreigners abroad, or two of these aristocratic at home?

The best argument in favour of the mortgage of a nation to a faction, is, that it is a purchase; an argument however, which does not extend to the family of law charters in general. A few of a nation, have bought the nation. Cæsar by plunder and rapine, amassed the means by buying or corrupting the Roman government; was his title to despotism over the Roman people therefore sound? If Jugurtha had been rich enough to buy Rome, ought the nation to have submitted to the sale, because the bargain was made with the government? If a freeman has no right to enslave his child by selling him, can one generation sell another? And if one generation has no right to sell another, can a government which exercises the double character of seller and buyer, in erecting the aristocracy of the present age, transform the most atrocious iniquity into political or moral rectitude, by writing in its forehead "publick faith"? Then let us acquit every thief, who assumes for his motto the words "honest man."

This kind of faith and honesty, have invented the opinion "that policy and "justice require a law, beneficial to individuals at the expense of a nation, to "exist for the period prescribed;" to sustain which, it is necessary to reverse the elemental political maxim "that the good of the whole, ought to be pre-"ferred to the good of a few." Government is erected for the purpose of carrying this maxim into execution, by passing laws for the benefit of a nation; and shall a violation of the purpose of its institution, by passing laws injurious to a nation, in creating or fostering the aristocracy of paper and patronage, be cleansed of its guiltiness, because individuals have become the accomplices of the government?

A law or a contract, prescribing an immoral action, is void. No sanction can justify murder, perjury or theft. Yet the murder of national liberty, the perjury of a traitorous government, and the theft of national wealth, by the gradual introduction of the aristocracy of the third age, are varnished into a gloss by a cunning dogma, capable even of dazzling men, so excessively honest as to put other men to death for petty thefts, committed to appease hunger or cover nakedness.

The same mouth will solemnly assert, that the principles of equity annul every contract, which defrauds an individual; and that justice or policy requires a catalogue of law charters which defraud a nation, to exist and have their effect.

This is owing to the artful conversion of good words, into knavish dogmas. It is not new, to see errour take refuge under the garb of truth. Superstition has in all ages called itself religion. Thus law charters, with the faithless design of enslaving a nation by the introduction of the aristocracy of the present age, crouch behind the good and honest words "publick faith and national credit," to prevent a nation from destroying that, which is destroying it. And they succeed; because we are as unsuspicious that a false and fraudulent dogma, is hidden under fair language, as that a well dressed gentleman indicates a thief.

To come at truth, we ought not to stop at a verbal investigation. We must consider whether the effects of every law and every measure, by whatever names the law or measure are called, are on the side of virtue or vice.

An irrepealable law charter is a standing temptation to governments to do evil, and an invitation to individuals to become their accessories; by its hold, a predominant party may use temporary power, to enact corporate or individual emoluments for itself, at the national expense. Successive parties will repeat the same iniquity; and even the outs or opposition will be corrupted, to do obeisance at the shrine of the dogma, that they also may reap of the fruit it bestows, when a nation shall fall into their hands; which upon every change of administration, will have its hopes of reform gratified, by new pillages under the sanction of publick faith and national credit.

This modern system of law charters, is founded in the same design, with the ancient system of a social compact. Under the sanction of social compact, governments have formerly tyrannised over nations. Under the sanction of law charters, governments now buy a faction, rob nations of enormous wealth, and soar beyond responsibility. The inviolability of a social compact was the old dogma; the inviolability of law charters is the new; for effecting the same end. The last is however an engine in the hands of avarice and ambition, of power far superior to the first. It is able to corrupt and pillage a nation without limit. The first was an opinion unable to purchase partisans; the last offers every thing to its disciples, which can gratify pernicious passions, and meets arguments with bribes. Thus a nation, which won self-government by exploding the doctrine of the antiquated compact dogma, may lose it again in the modern law charter dogma; and thus a nation, which thought it morally wrong to suffer slavery from troops hired by clothes, pay and rations, may be persuaded that it is morally right to suffer slavery from troops hired by dividends, interest upon stock, and protecting duty bounties. . . .

CONSTRUCTION CONSTRUED AND CONSTITUTIONS VINDICATED [81]

SECTION I

THE PRINCIPLES OF OUR REVOLUTION

. . . . . .

No form of government can foster a fanaticism for wealth, without being corrupted. The courtiers of republicks, able to exercise an absolute power over the national property, are more numerous and more vicious than the courtiers of kings, because access to patrons is easier; they have more occasion for partisans, and a multiplication of despots over property multiplies the channels of fraud. New ones also are frequently opened by a revolution of parties, and of patrons, who with their favorites and dependents, are in haste to bolster power or amass wealth, during the continuance of a fleeting authority. Against a propensity so mischievous, and so fatal to republicks, there seems to be no resource, but a constitutional prohibition of the power by which it is nurtured; and a rejection of precedents, by which infringements of so wholesome a prohibition are usually justified. Both reason and morality unite to impress upon nations, a necessity for imposing restraints upon a propensity, which may so easily be concealed under the most glittering robes of patriotism. What real patriot would feel himself molested, by restraints upon avarice and ambition? Are not both unfriendly to human happiness? Some patriots have sacrificed their lives for the happiness of their country. Is the sacrifice of an error, by which fraud and avarice are nurtured, too much to expect of ours?

A love of wealth, fostered by honest industry, is an ally both of moral rectitude, and national happiness, because it can only be gratified by increasing the fund for national subsistence, comfort, strength and prosperity; but a love of wealth, fostered by partial laws for enriching corporations and individuals, is allied to immorality and oppression, because it is gratified at the expense of industry, and diminishes its ability to work out national blessings.

Look for a moment at Congress, as a power for creating pecuniary inequalities, or for striking balances between favours to states, combinations and individuals. If it could even distribute wealth and poverty, by some just scale, which has never yet been discovered, justice itself would beget discontent, and sow among its medley of courtiers, a mass of discord, not more propitious to the safety of the union, than to the happiness of the people. All would weigh their own merits, and none would be convinced that they were light. Even the distribution of those preferences, necessary to civil government, is liable to defects and productive of inconveniences. Where then is the wisdom of extending the power beyond the limits of social necessity, to the despotick principle of a gratuitous distribution of wealth and poverty by law; and of converting a small evil, abundantly counterbalanced by the blessings of government, into a calamity by which these blessings are diminished or destroyed?

To answer this question, turn your eyes towards a government accoutred

[81] John Taylor, *Construction Construed and Constitutions Vindicated.* (Richmond, Shepard and Pollard, 1820), pp. 11–18, 317–325.

in the complete panoply of fleets, armies, banks, funding systems, pensions, bounties, corporations, exclusive privileges; and in short, possessing an absolute power to distribute property, according to the pleasure, the pride, the interest, the ambition, and the avarice of its administrators; and consider whether such a government is the servant or the master of the nation. However oppressive, is it not able to defy, to deride and to punish the complaints of the people? Partisans, purchased and made powerful by their wealth, zealously sustained the abuses by which their own passions are gratified. I discern no reason in the principles of our revolution, for investing our governments with such of these instruments for oppression, as were both unnecessary for the end in view, and even inimical to its attainment; and no such reason existing, it is more difficult to discern the propriety of investing our governments with these superfluous and pernicious powers, by inference and construction. Would liberty be well established in England, if her hierarchy was destroyed, whilst the government retained the absolute power of distributing wealth and poverty? Is not that establishment merely one of the modes for exercising this species of despotism; and what substantial or lasting remedy could arise from abolishing one mode, whilst others remained amply sufficient to establish the same pernicious principle? Is not a power of transferring property by pensions, bounties, corporations and exclusive privileges; and even of bestowing publick money by the unlimited will of legislative bodies, as dangerous to liberty, as a power of doing the same thing by the instrumentality of a privileged church? Is the casuistry consistent, which denied to a government the power of infringing the freedom of religion, and yet invests it with a despotism over the freedom of property? A corporation, combination, or chartered church for one purpose, in its pecuniary effects, is analogous to corporations for effecting the other. It has been said, that government in its best form is an evil. This absurd idea seems to have been suggested, by its being usually invested with an army of supernumerary powers wholly unnecessary for effecting the end of preserving social tranquillity and safety. Against these supernumerary powers, the United States waged a long war, upon the ground, that governments are instituted to secure, and not to bestow the freedom of property; and it would be highly absurd to suppose, that having established their great principle, they directly became contented with an unfruitful theory, and surrendered the idea of its application. It was tyrannical in the English government, said the colonies, to insist upon taking away their property, and giving it to placemen and pensioners; and they very justly considered life and liberty as so intimately connected with property, that the rights of the latter could not be invaded, without invading the other rights also. They fought for a revolution, and established governments to secure all three of these natural rights, because a loss of one was equivalent to a loss of all, in a national view.

I see no infallible criterion for defining the nature of a government, except its acts. If the acts of a monarchy, aristocracy and democracy are the same, these forms of government are to a nation essentially the same also. To contend for forms only, is to fight for shadows. The United States did not go to war for nothing but forms. A government is substantially good or bad, in the degree that it produces the happiness or misery of a nation; and I see but little difficulty in finding a mode of detecting the fallacy of form, and the frauds of profession. If we can ascertain the quality in human nature, from which political evil has chiefly proceeded under every form of government, this quality is the cause which can corrupt any form; and instead of amusing ourselves with these new forms, not to be confided in, it behooves us to search for a remedy, able to remove or control the cause itself.

Cupidity, avarice or monopoly, both in the savage and civilized state, is the quality of human nature, always requiring control, and always striving to break down the restraints imposed upon it. To resist this quality, the United States endured the evils of a long war with a powerful nation. They had seen a limited monarchy tried in the parent country, as a remedy for this bad quality of human nature; but ineffectually; because a considerable power remained with the king, and an absolute power was conceded to or usurped by the government, of distributing property. The hostile principles, of leaving men to be enriched by their own industry, or of enriching them by the favours of the government, were to be weighed against each other; that which made many poor to enrich a few was rejected, and that which encouraged industry was preferred, in the most distinct manner, as I shall hereafter endeavour to prove.

Almost all governments have espoused and nourished the spirit of avarice, which they were instituted to discipline by justice; and have betrayed the weak, whom it was their duty to protect. In assuming a power of distributing property by law, they have reduced it in a great degree to a destiny, approximating to its savage destiny, when subjected to force. From this cause have arisen the most pernicious imperfections of society. Aristocracies and democracies, by usurping this despotick power, in imitation of monarchs, have driven nations into a circle of forms, through which they have perpetually returned to the oppression they intended to escape. Had the essentials, rather than the structure of governments, attracted the attention of mankind, they would not have trusted to any theory, however excellent, asserting it to be the duty of a government to protect rights; under a system of legislation, by which governments of the worst form destroy them. They would have discovered, that a power of distributing property, according to its pleasure, has made governments of the best forms, bad; and that a remedy for an evil, poisonous to the best theories, ought to awaken their solicitude and ingenuity. For want of this remedy, republicks, of the finest theoretical structure, have universally died more prematurely, even than absolute monarchies; because, the more numerous the depositaries of an absolute power over property have become, the more widely has the spirit of avarice or monopoly been excited. If this universal cause of oppression must exist, that government which afforded the most channels for its operation, is the worst; and hence has arisen the general perference of mankind for monarchy. Governments of all forms having exercised an absolute power over property, they have experimentally ascertained, that the oppression derived from this source was the most tolerable, when the tyrannts were the least numerous.

If the age has at length arrived, in which knowledge is able to break the fetters forged by fraud and credulity, political enquiry, as in other sciences, may take its stand on the eminence of truth, hail with exultation the happy advent, and direct its arrows straight forward against an error fraught with plagues to mankind.

To define the nature of a government truly, I would say, that a power of distributing property, able to gratify avarice and monopoly, designated a bad one; and that the absence of every such power, designated a good one.

Of what value is an exchange of one system of monopoly for another? How shall we estimate the difference between noble and clerical orders, and between combinations of exclusive pecuniary privileges? Is pure avarice better than some honour and some sanctity? The encroachments upon property by noble and clerical combinations, once fixed by law, remained stationary; and each individual could calculate his fate with some certainty: but pecuniary combinations, once sanctioned as constitutional, will perpetually open new channels, and breed new invaders, whose whole business it will be, to make inroads upon the territories of industry. Legislatures will become colleges for teaching the science of getting money by monopolies or favours; and the deluge of laws will become as great in the United States, as was once the deluge of papal indulgences in Europe for effecting the same object. What an unaccountable feature of the human character it is, that it should exert so much ingenuity to get the property of others, and be so dull finding out means for the preservation of its own?

The morality of the gospel and that of monopoly, seem to me, not to bear the least resemblance to each other. A christian "loves man. His light must "shine before men. He keeps judgment and does justice. He trusts in the "Lord and does good. He lives in goodness and honesty. He is a doer and "not a hearer only of the divine law. Whoever doeth not right, is not of God, "neither he that loveth not his brother. Repentance and an avoidance of "sin, constitute the claim to the atonement of a saviour. By their works ye "shall know them." The pope of Rome for many centuries persuaded the people of Europe, that he fulfilled all these texts of scripture, by uttering annually a great number of indulgences, to cheat the people of money.

Is there a man who could be so infatuated, as to foster zealously both bible and missionary societies, and also a spirit of avarice and monopoly? Geographical malice, combined frauds, individual deceit, and civil commotion, some of the effects of this latter policy, suggest the idea, that the same person is equally zealous to convert the heathens to christianity, and the christians to heathenism. This ideal character may be also a philosopher, who ridicules the notion of being saved by faith without works; and yet contends that the people ought to confide in forms without acts, and take it for granted that their property will be safe under a theory, which exercises an absolute power over it. If he should make an eloquent speech, one half in favour of the theory of equal laws, and the other half in favour of actual exclusive privileges, what should we think? that it was like placing Christ on the care of Juggernaut, and dressing the United States in British regimentals.

There are sundry points of resemblance between the English revolution in the time of Charles the first, and ours, replete with edification. Let us go into a comparison. The English reformation of religion, by compromising with the rapaciousness of individuals, and by retaining sundry of the principles and habits of popery, inoculated the government with a poison, which diffused its virulence throughout the body politick, and contaminated the blessings promised by the experiment. Those who resisted the frauds of selfishness, and the artifices of ambition, were called puritans; and the derision of a nickname, united with the excesses produced by oppression, to render the doctrine of a freedom of religion, both ridiculous and detestable. Those who contended for it, were successfully represented as wild visionaries, whose views were unnatural and impracticable. Yet to these puritans the United States are indebted for the religious freedom they enjoy; and the whole world, for a refutation of the arguments advanced by ambition and avarice, to obstruct the progress of political improvement, and the advancement of human happiness.

The same contrivances practised in England to destroy religious freedom, are using in the United States to defeat civil liberty. The puritanism of republican principles is ridiculed; it is called democracy; and violations of the freedom of property (an important principle of our civil puritanism) are providing combustibles for some calamitous explosion. Our political reformation is daily corrupted by the principles and habits of the English system, as was the English religious reformation, by the principles and habits of popery; and we are exchanging the pure principles of the revolution, for the garbage of aristocracy, and compromises with venality. By disregarding these principles, our fluctuations of parties invested with power, have been made to resemble the bauble called a Kaleidescope, which at each revolution exhibits new scenes of glittering delusions, whilst the pebbles from which they are reflected, remain substantially the same. The remedy for an evil so mischievous, is that by which religious freedom has been established. Freedom of property will beget civil liberty, as freedom of conscience has begotten religious. The success of one experiment proves the other to be practicable. Every man, except he belongs to a privileged combination, is as much interested to effect a freedom of property, as he is to maintain a freedom of religion, except he could become a priest of an established and endowed hierarchy.

The English protestants had adopted a variety of imaginary habits and opinions. The several American States also entertained a variety of opinions and habits, fixed by real interest, more reasonable and more stubborn, as being derived from natural and unconquerable circumstances. Each of the sects in England, after the religious revolution was established, as power fluctuated among them, endeavoured when uppermost, to impose its own opinions and habits upon the others. The apparel of the clergy, surplices, tippets, caps, hoods and crosiers; and ceremonies; such as the sign of the cross in baptism, the ring in marriage, the mode of administering the sacrament, and the consecration and powers of bishops; all inconsiderable compared with the cardinal end of religious freedom; became subjects of controversy in England. The endowment of certificate holders, banking corporations, exclusive privileges, compulsory laws over free will in the employment of the earnings of industry, and violations of the local interests and habits of States, more materially affecting the cardinal end of civil liberty, have become subjects of controversy in the United States. In England, the force of opinions, less substantial, produced a frightful civil war. In the United States, opinions, better founded, have already produced awful ideas of dissolving the union. In England, the religious controversies terminated in an act of uniformity, by which a majority of the people are cruelly oppressed; there are more meeting-houses than churches, and more dissenters than conformists; yet by bribery with publick money, so as exorbitantly to increase taxation, the majority are both excluded from civil offices, and subjected to the payment of tithes for the suppression of their own opinions and interests. In the United States, the majority of the people of each state, are subjected to the payment of more than tithes, to deprive themselves of free will as to their own interest, and to foster exclusive privileges. Our division into state governments of great extent, and embracing a great variety of local circumstances, will render a compulsory uniformity of temporal interests, habits and opinions infinitely more difficult, than a religious uniformity in England; and require means, more coercive and severe to effect it. A very powerful standing army, so necessary in England for one purpose, would be more indispensable here for the other. Whole states will more sensibly feel, and be more able to resist burdens, inflicted to enrich privileged civil sects, bearing heavily on their local interests and habits, than individuals only combined by the slight threads of ceremonials and speculative prejudices. Had the freedom of religion been established in England at the Reformation, a mass of civil war, national inquietude and oppression would have been avoided. A greater mass of these evils was foreseen by the farmers of the Union, and attempted to be avoided, by restricting the powers given to Congress, and by retaining to the states those powers united with the local interests, habits and opinions of each state; in fact, by securing the freedom of property. . . .

SECTION 16

THE DISTRESSES OF THE UNITED STATES

. . . .

It is really wonderful that the most lively imagination should be persuaded, that our distresses have been produced by what we have not done; or that the effect has preceded the cause. This, however, is the doctrine of the protecting-duty panacea. We are ruined, it says, for want of more protecting duties and obstructions to commerce: but as causes precede effects, it is more probable that we have had too many. Instead, therefore, of ascribing the distresses of the United States to things which they have not done, I shall look for them in things which they have done; to which I am induced by considering, that the national distresses of Britain and of the United States could not both have been caused by the manufacturing occupation, because abundance and scarcity could not have produced the same effects; and a similarity in the distresses does not indicate a contrariety in their causes.

The creation of a nest-egg for rearing an eleemosynary family was almost the first act of the federal government. It received the people of the states with the pre-existing relations produced by a paper-currency intercourse, prescribed by unavoidable necessity. This currency was called by two names, "certificates" and "paper money," both offsprings of the same necessity, both sanctioned by publick faith, and both transferable; but one species had been collected into a few hands, and the other was more equally distributed among the people. These currencies, whilst passing, had gradually depreciated; and each temporary occupant had sustained the losses thereby occasioned during his occupation. In this state of things, justice called for some consistent remedy, equally applicable to all the currency and to all the sufferers. Either all the intermediate losses sustained between the emission and termination of the whole currency, or none, should have been reimbursed. Both the currencies should have been redeemed at their nominal value, or neither; or both should have been redeemed at their depreciated value. The last rule would have perfectly corresponded with the right of free will in contracts or exchanges, to risque gain or loss; but it was directly adverse to legislative interferences with this right, for the introduction of the eleemosynary system, to get rid of which the states had recently passed through a long war. Instead of an equal and consistent rule, according with the publick interest, and recommended by justice, an exclusive eleemosynary capitalist interest was created by a partiality, unjust as it regarded individuals, and highly impolitick as it regarded the United States, if such an interest be oppressive and dangerous to liberty. No recompense was made to those who had sustained losses of property and labour by depreciation, during the circulation of these credit papers. If the right of free will in exchanges be sound, no recompense was due or practicable, and each individual ought to sustain its consequences; but by no principle could it be right, that these losses, instead of being thus merged into the national capital, should have been seized by law, and bestowed upon a selected class, in order to introduce the eleemosynary system. The losses inflicted upon individuals by depreciation, during the circulation of these currencies, were either property or not property. As property, they were either transferred, they passed with both the paper certificates and the paper money, to the last holder of each species of credit paper; and the right of all such holders to the value of the paper, when issued, was the same. But if these intermediate losses did neither pass, nor constitute a just claim to compensation on the part of the last holders, both the certificate and paper-money holders were equally excluded from advancing such a demand against the publick. However, disregarding consistency, the partiality was committed, of considering certificates as carrying to the last holder all intermediate losses, and paper money as carrying none. One sect of holders being a minority and influential, obtained the value of its paper when issued, with interest; and the other sect, including the body of the people, was put off with depreciated value without interest. This was the more glaringly unjust, as the receipt of depreciated paper money was enforced by tender laws highly penal, and the receipt of depreciated certificates was free and voluntary. By this management, a certificate which had passed from A to Z, depreciating as it travelled, and purchased by Z for a twentieth part of its nominal value, resuscitated the intermediate losses for the benefit of Z, and subjected the actual sufferers to taxes for paying to Z what they had themselves lost, with interest; whilst the certificate holders escaped the burden of contributing for making good to the paper money holder a claim of the same nature with his own. This exclusive partiality transferred about one hundred millions of capital, from the people of the United States to a capitalist sect artificially created, and became the source of a stream of taxation, which may perhaps run and increase down to another revolution. The wealth of this sect was not derived from fair industry, but from an unfair law [for what law can be fair which creates what industry never does, a rich eleemosynary sect?] which, under cover of a sovereign legislative power over property, contrived to gratify the personal interest of a few members of congress, and a sect of certificate holders, by slicing off one hundred millions from the national capital; a paltry sum indeed compared with subsequent speculations, but at that time considered as so very formidable, that it generated two animated parties. The certificate sect happened chiefly to reside in particular states, and had the address to persuade these states, that the trivial and transitory circumstance of personal residence was a sufficient reason to induce them to put upon their own necks an interminable eleemosynary system, to be transmitted with their other legacies to their children.

A greater speculation upon the national capital soon grew out of the hundred millions of capital thus created by law. The artificial sect wanted more profit than funding interest, and taking into partnership members of legislative bodies, it convinced the states collectively and individually, that they would be enriched, by enabling certificate, now funded debt holders, to convert their fictitious capital into bank stock, without changing its capacity as funded stock. Thus, the same paper transferred national capital to an eleemosynary sect, in two characters; and the first acquisition of one hundred millions became comparatively inconsiderable. The locality of artificial capital soon disappeared, as if providence designed to give all the states a taste of the eleemosynary policy, to enable them to decide, whether the residence of its disciples would make that policy a publick good. Let us consider whether it can be so in the form of banking.

To determine this question, I shall urge a new argument to prove, that banks, both state and federal, destroy a principle essential to all our constitutions, and essential also to every conceivable free form of government; and that this vital desolation has caused many of the publick distresses. The people, by all our constitutions, have delegated to their representatives a power of legislation; but by none have they delegated to their representatives a power to delegate legislative powers to persons, not elected by the people, nor indeed by themselves. Legitimate legislatures have no power to appoint deputy or attorney legislatures, and if they had, they must do it themselves, and not depute others to do it both for their constituents and themselves. These positions bring to a fair test the doctrine of legislative sovereignty. If it be true, I admit that our legislatures may create deputy legislatures, or enable stockholders or whomsoever they please to elect deputy legislatures, and invest them when elected with legislative powers; but if it be not true, then our legislatures cannot directly or indirectly invest bank directors with legislative power, formal or substantial. Now I ask, if a power of regulating the national currency, and increasing or diminishing its quantity at pleasure, is not both a formal and substantial legislative power? What is legislative power? Something able to dispense good or harm to a community. Cannot bank directors do this? Somebody has said that money *governs* the world. Have those who govern money no governing powers? If they have any, are they legislative, executive or judicial? The idea, that banking was an aristocratical institution, has been hitherto inferred from its privilege of getting money in an exclusive mode; but it is far better founded. It established a great body of directors, invested with an absolute power of pecuniary legislation, and in no degree responsible to the people. If this be not a formal and complete aristocratical power, I am unable to conceive one. The house of lords in England is an imperfect aristocratical power, because it can pass no law without the concurrence of the commons; but if it could regulate the currency of the country without the concurrence of the representatives of the people, is there any one who can believe, that it would be less aristocratical and less legislative than it now is? In that case it would be an exact portrait of our bank directors.

I ask every candid man, whether the community has not suffered a great variety of calamities from the doings of bank directors, in the exercise of their powers over currency. What are these doings? Are they not powers, able to hurt very materially the whole United States? If they are powers, do they belong neither to the civil nor political classes of powers? But if they belong to either, is not a body of men constituted as bank directors are, and exercising powers either civil or political, affecting a whole community, an aristocratical department, as formal and as complete as can be imagined, and infinitely more so than the British house of lords?

Need we go searching about for the causes of the publick distress, after we have found a perfect aristocracy, exercising an absolute power over the national currency? If there be an object of legislation, through which a nation can receive deeper wounds, I hope it will never be discovered; as those which this can inflict, seem sufficient to punish us for all our political sins. The secret, as to the distresses of the United States, lies in the difference between republican and aristocratical legislation, upon the important subject of money. It is a power probably equal in its capacity of doing harm, to all other legislative powers united. It can derange the fairness of all exchanges between man and man; it can tempt by legislating an abundance of currency, and ruin by legislating a scarcity; it can raise and diminish prices according to its interest, its caprices or its partialities, without controul, detection or responsibility; it can refuse when it suits its interest, to redeem its own paper, and terrify the people and the government into acquiescence, by a fear of losing their debts and salaries, and by the inconveniences of wanting a circulating medium; and when it does not choose to pay its debts, it can put its funds in its pocket, say that it has got nothing, and enjoy the fruits of fraud beyond the reach of justice. Can any republican legislature remedy these evils except by removing the cause? Dare any republican legislature to produce the distresses, which have for years been mere sport, however cruel, in the hands of their aristocratical deputies? It is wonderful, after mankind have discovered the folly and mischief of a single legislative maximum price, to see them quietly submit to an eternal alternation between maximum and minimum, and bear injuries from the aristocracy by which they are imposed, which would be indignantly resisted if imposed by a republican legislature. I do not compute the power of an aristocratical legislature, without reponsibility, over national morals; it is sufficiently seen and felt, and it unfortunately operates most upon those classes of society, whose integrity and patriotism are perhaps the only hostages for the continuance of a republican form of government. These aristocratical legislatures have even been able to prescribe, not a test oath, but a test of honesty, to most or all of our republican legislatures, by furnishing them first with a pretext for raising their salaries, and then with a correspondent reason for reducing them; thus directly legislating upon that whole order of men, upon whose honesty and patriotism a free and fair government immediately depends.

For this aristocratical legislation, the state and federal governments have appropriated a portion of the capital of the community, far exceeding that appropriated for all our republican legislatures. It is probable, that the dividends of banks have sometimes amounted to twelve millions of dollars annually, requiring a capital of four hundred millions to supply; but as these dividends have sustained an occasional diminution preparatory to an augmentation, nine millions only may now constitute the total of the dividends received by all the banks; yet in contemplation of a prospective augmentation, twelve may be assumed as a future probable amount, and four hundred millions of national capital as appropriated to the use of bankers. It would have been correct to have charged banking with a great augmentation of salaries, expenses and taxation, which it has bestowed upon the community, but this enormous item is left out, because the community possess the means of throwing it off; until it does so, however, it ought to be considered as nearly or quite equal to the other.

The third eleemosynary appropriation of national capital was effected by the protecting-duty laws. There is more difficulty in computing its amount, than in the similar instances of the same system we have passed over, because we cannot ascertain the portion of the tax they inflict, which gets into the pockets of owners of manufactories. But, as these laws create a species of aristocratical legislatures over manufactures, exactly of the same character with that created to regulate currency, there will undoubtedly be a great similitude in their proceedings. Behold then a great community, industrious, at peace, and in distress. What an enigma? But behold its currency consigned to the regulation of bank directors, and its consumptions to the regulation of manufacturing capitalists, and you will confess that there is no enigma in the case.

The corn laws of England are equivalent to our protecting-duty laws, with respect to that portion of the tax, which goes into the pockets of capitalists. The prohibition of the importation of grain, until wheat gets to the price of eighty shillings sterling a quarter, is a tax upon the nation for augmenting the rents of landed capitalists. Whatever is carried by our protecting-duty laws into the pockets of manufacturing capitalists, is a tax upon the community for augmenting their wealth. Bread and manufactures being both necessaries, both these taxes are direct and unavoidable. By the corn laws of England, the manufacturers are compelled to pay about one-third more for home made bread, than they would have paid, if importation had been free. At this time, the price of wheat in England is about nine shillings sterling, and about eighty cents here. By our protecting-duty laws, agriculturalists and all other occupations are compelled to pay for home made manufactures, about one third more, than if importations were free. The corn law tax falls most heavily on the poor, whence arises much of the distress of the working manufacturers. Our protecting-duty tax must also fall most heavily on the poor, because every tax upon necessary consumptions operates as a poll tax. A protecting-duty system exists in England in favour of manufacturing, but it inflicts no tax upon the nation, because the surplus of manufactures, beyond the wants of home consumption, renders their monopoly impossible, and makes the law internally, nominal; but the land capitalists have used this inoperative law as a pretext, to inflict an impoverishing tax upon manufacturers by the corn laws. Protecting-duty laws have been passed here in favour of several agricultural manufactures, but they are wholly unbeneficial to agriculturists, and inflict no tax upon any other occupation, because of the abundance of agricultural manufactures beyond the home demand. Yet the manufacturing capitalists here, in imitation of the land capitalists in England, have seized upon these inert laws as a pretext, for inflicting an impoverishing tax upon all other occupations for their own benefit. The appropriation of English national capital to the use of land capitalists is a heavy item of an eleemosynary system in favour of the rich, which requires a great standing army to maintain. The appropriation of a large portion of the capital of the United States to the use of the same system, has only caused hitherto such distresses, as suggested a necessity for the English army. An important distinction, however, exists between their corn laws, and our protecting-duty laws. Corn possesses few or none of the qualities of a general or universal currency. Being too perishable to bear repeated voyages, and of universal growth, it is unsuitable for a re-exportation and exchange; and would not act as circulating currency upon English manufactures, or increase their value in any considerable degree. But manufactures possess most of the qualities of an universal currency. They are susceptible of long preservation, and can endure repeated voyages, and are every where in demand. They are in short a better currency than any local paper. A surplus imported, beyond the wants of internal consumption, is therefore an accession of mercantile currency as valuable as coin, and will have a similar effect in raising the value of products in the country so fortunate as to obtain it. We hear continually of the balance of trade; but we err, if we compute this balance only by money, and reject those things which money represents. A nation would have the balance of trade in its favour if it never brought home money, and only more valuable things than it carried out; nor would it be difficult to prove, that it would be better to receive a balance of trade in commodities, than in coin. Many cities have derived great prosperity from being depots of commodities, because they are the most valuable species of universal currency; and if all the manufactures of England could be circulated by way of the United States, it would undoubtedly add to our wealth. Whatever portion can be so circulated, will have a comparative effect. Nor is it a sufficient answer to this observation to say, that protecting-duties do not prohibit importations for exportation, because by diminishing the home market, and changing an alluring invitation into a scowling prohibition, the adventures of commerce will be dispirited, and the sources of a surplus for re-exportation dried up. However this may be, it is evident that the English corn laws, bad as they are, may be defended by one argument, of which our protecting-duty laws cannot avail themselves; namely, that an importation of corn is not an acquisition of an universal currency, and an accession of wealth.

But there is another material distinction between corn, and the whole compass of manufactures. The consumption of manufactures excites the effort and industry, which are better sources of national wealth, than exclusive privileges and commercial prohibitions. It converts numberless feelings of human nature into productive labourers, and contructs comfort, taste, pride, luxury and self-love into a machinery, worked by the steam of our passions, which compared with the sluggishness caused by suppressing gratifications, or with the animation inspired by consuming corn, will manifest the true character of the intervening gradations. Freedom in the enjoyment of the comforts and elegancies of life is the parent of that activity which reimburses a nation, both with intelligence and re-productions for its consumptions by enlarging the capacities of the mind and body. By copying the English corn laws, we are therefore cultivating two supernumerary evils, with which those laws are not chargeable, in expelling from our shores a general and valuable currency, and in suppressing some of the strongest motives for bodily industry and mental improvement.

TYRANNY UNMASKED [82]

9. DESTROY AGRICULTURE

Neither ambition nor avarice could ever succeed in depriving nations of their liberty and property, if they did not by some artifice enlist the services of a body of men, numerically powerful. The general promises the plunder of a town to his soldiers; they take it; and he keeps most of it for himself and his officers. These are enriched, and the soldiers remain poor. The demagogue promises liberty to a rabble, and by their help makes himself their tyrant. And capitalists, by promising wealth to mechanicks, accumulate it for themselves, and become their masters. The Committee disclaim a predilection for factory capitalists, and an enmity towards agriculture. I balance this argument by disclaiming also a predilection for agriculturalists, and an enmity towards mechanicks; but I avow an enmity against all modes for transferring property by exclusive privileges. As no man, however, can find the seeds from which his opinions have germinated, such protestations are frivolous, and they are also unworthy of weight; because the consequences, and not the origin of opinions, constitute their materiality. If it was important to decide, whether the policy proposed by the Committee or its competitor, could be convicted of foreign origin, the difficulty of the subject would not be increased; but I wave the unedifying enquiry, and proceed to the substantial part of the question, whether it will be most injurious to agriculturalists or mechanicks. At the threshold of this enquiry, I have changed a term by substituting mechanicks for manufacturers, to display truth more clearly. The term agriculture needs no such correction, because we have not the two conflicting classes of landlords and tenants, as we have of capitalists and mechanicks. Where the land of a country is owned by landlords, and worked by tenants, the phrase "landed interest" refers to the landlords, who may enjoy exclusive privileges of which the tenants do not partake; and the impoverishment of one interest may contribute to the enrichment of the other. In like manner, where the factories belong to capitalists, and are worked by mechanicks, the phrase "manufacturing interest" refers to the capitalists, who may enjoy exclusive privileges of which the workmen do not partake; and their impoverishment may contribute to the enrichment of the capitalists, as the impoverishment of tenants may enrich landlords. In deciding the questions, therefore, by the test of friendship or enmity, we ought to exhibit persons, and not confound distinct interests,

[82] John Taylor, *Tyranny Unmasked*. (Fredericksburg, Green and Cady, 1822), pp. 194–201.

as the objects of these passions. A cold calculation of the profit to be made by factories, may be a vice of avarice, but a friendly sympathy for the calamities of workmen, arising from the policy of making laws to accumulate this profit, can only flow from good will towards them.

The interest of mechanicks against the factory policy, advocated by the Committee, is infinitely stronger than that of farmers, because, they may more easily be swept into factories, and the profits of their labour be more completely carried into the pockets of the capitalists, than can be effected in the case of land-owners. These are so powerful as to be able, when they feel a loss, to give themselves a compensation, as the English landlords have done by the corn laws; and between the capitalists and landlords in that country, the mechanicks find poverty. A keen sense of misery fraudulently inflicted, is the cause of their frequent insurrections, and fixed hatred of the government. Why are soldiers necessary to protect their masters, their work-houses and their looms, against the mechanicks themselves? The great lexicographer Johnson, in defining the condition and character of an English mechinick, has called him "mean and servile." The definition is justified by the fact, that his best resource against ending his days in a hospital or poor house, is the shortness of his life. A mechanick employed in a factory rarely acquires a competence; opulence is out of the question; and he is completely excluded from publick employments, by being doomed to a situation in which he can never acquire a capacity for them. He can hardly be considered as a citizen. A code of laws draws around him a magick circle, by making mechanical combinations punishable, lest they should check capitalist combinations; and he is re-imbursed by penalties for the loss of hope.

The condition of the mechanick in the United States has hitherto been extremely different. It neither excites insurrections, nor inculcates a hatred of the government. It does not require a regular army to cure the agonies of misery. It neither shortens life, nor devotes old age to an hospital. It never fails to acquire a competency by industry and good conduct; sometimes rises to opulence; and receives its due share of publick employments. Instead of being deemed mean and servile, it is capable of respectability, and the whole magistracy is open to it. I have heard that the son of a mechanick has been a President; and I know that a weaver, a carpenter, and a carriage-maker, (the two first from Pennsylvania, and the last from Virginia,) were at one time for a long period, worthy members of Congress. Probably there have been many other similar instances. In State legislatures mechanicks are often seen, and as magistrates and militia officers, they abound. They are real, and not nominal citizens. How often do the hirelings of a factory in England, become members of Parliament, magistrates, or militia officers?

For these enormous differences between the condition of the mechanicks in England and the United States, there must be some cause. What can it be, except that the factory and capitalist policy, deprives them of the erect attitude in society inspired by the freedom of industry, and bears hardest upon them, as the chief objects of its gripe? Has this policy bettered the condition of mechanicks, even whilst it was creating enormous fortunes for their masters? If not, the strongest motive for resisting it, is the happiness and prosperity of the mechanicks themselves; though the success of this resistance will also contribute towards the happiness and prosperity of all other useful occupations, because the freedom of talents and industry, and the absence of a system for making both subservient to the interest of avarice, is the principle which must operate beneficially to all, though most so to that occupation most immediately assailed.

To counteract facts established by a double example, the same bribe is offered to land-owners here, which has created in England, a conspiracy between landlords and capitalists against mechanicks, by which they have been reduced to perpetual labour and perpetual poverty.—The land-owners are told, that by coercing mechanicks into factories, the prices of their manufactures will be reduced, and that the land-owners will then be reimbursed for the bounties now paid to capitalists, by a future cheapness to be effected at the expense of mechanicks, thus coerced into factories. I do not deny that such would be the case, if the factory scheme could be carried to the same extent here as in England. This could not be effected, even if our populousness could furnish the materials, except by the English system of legislation to prevent mechanicks from breaking their factory chains, and compelling them to labour hard for low wages to supply the conspirators cheaply. But is not this coerced cheapness evidently imposed upon the mechanical occupation? If it could be effected in the United States, the first class of valuable and respectable citizens which would be ruined by it, would be the great body of mechanicks scattered throughout the country, who would be undersold by the factory capitalists, and compelled to relinquish their free occupations, and become hirelings at the factories. The promised consummation of the factory project, therefore, however tempting to farmers, would be a complete degradation of mechanicks from the equal and comfortable station they hold in society, to one much less desirable. Every present fraud offers a future bribe. The future cheapness offered to land-holders is too distant and uncertain, to induce them to enter into this conspiracy with the capitalists against the mechanicks; and besides, why should they get less than the English landlords for doing so? These have had their rents, and of course the value of their lands doubled or trebled into the bargain, and if without this additional bribe, cheapness would have been insufficient to compensate them for the evils of the capitalist-policy, the land-owners here may safely conclude that they will not be compensated by this promise alone, for co-operating in the conspiracy; and that to make a good bargain, they ought to have the price of their lands doubled or trebled, like the English landlords.

The solitary promise of future cheapness to farmers, to arise from the factory policy, is met by many formidable considerations: If it could be fulfilled at some distant period, the great injury to society from reducing the respectable and numerous class of mechanicks down to Johnson's definition of them; for creating a moneyed aristocracy; and from establishing the policy of exclusive privileges, in which few or no farmers can ever share, would alone suffice to prove that the bribe, if received, would bring along with it a far greater cargo of evils than of benefits.

The prices paid by farmers to the great number of free mechanicks, scattered throughout the country, and by these mechanicks to farmers, promote neighbourhood consumptions; create much domestick commerce regulated by free exchanges, and not by a fraudulent monopoly; stimulate mutual industry, and increase the value of property; but the prices paid to factory capitalists, so long as their monopoly operates, will to a great extent be employed in transferring and accumulating capital. A transfer of profit from industry to the accumulation of capital, whether the profit is agricultural or mechanical, is a mutual diminution of the fund, acting and reacting between industrious occupations, and begetting mutual prosperity. The more of his profits the agriculturist can save from the capitalist, the more employment he will give to his friend and neighbour, the mechanick; and the more of his are retained by the mechanick, the more he will consume of agricultural products, or enhance by his savings, the value of land.—In either case would domestick commerce be rendered more beneficial to the society, by diverting these funds from this intercourse, to the accumulation of pecuniary capitals?

Monopoly is a word sufficiently indefinite, to enable ingenuity to obscure its malignity, by extending it to property acquired by industry and free exchanges; and though private property begets civilization, society, and happiness, it is made, by calling it monopoly, to supply arguments for its own invasion. If monopoly, like money, does really reach every species of acquisition, yet it may also possess good and evil qualities; and a discrimination between them is necessary, to reap the good and avoid the evil. The monopolies obtained by industry, admitting the phrase to be correct, are, like earning money, beneficial to society; those obtained by exclusive privileges, like stealing money, are pernicious.—These qualities of monopoly are hostile to each other. The latter species of monopoly takes away the acquisition of the former. The most enormous monopoly is that of monarchs of all the land within their territories, once established in Europe by the feudal system, and still subsisting in Turkey and some Asiatic countries.—This deprives industry of its power to acquire, to a great extent. Of the same nature is the protecting-duty monopoly. A monopoly of land, enables the monopolist to extract wealth from the produce of land; and a monopoly of mechanicks, enables the monopolist to extract wealth from the produce of mechanicks. The monopolist in both cases is able to enhance the price of land or its produce, or the produce of his mechanicks, at the expense of buyers. Land was monopolized by the feudal system, incidentally to monopolize labour; by the factory system, the labour itself is directly monopolized. Next to that of land, a monopoly of manufacturing is the most extensive and oppressive of which we can have a conception. It even appears to operate more widely than a monopoly of land, because all are consumers of manufactures. It does not indeed take away the land itself of agriculturists, but it effects the same end which the feudal monopoly effected; it obtains a portion of its profits. If a law was made to bestow all the land of the United States upon a few persons, it would be equivalent to a policy for enabling capitalists to build factories, and monopolize mechanicks. We should then have the English policy complete; landlords and tenants, capitalists and mechanicks. I know but of two modes of ascertaining whether a monopoly exists. One consists of appropriations without compensation, the other of an appropriation obtained by compensation. The latter is only called a monopoly, in attempting to confound it with the former. Loss and gain without equivalent determined by free commerce, is established between farmers and capitalists by legal coercion, and if this does not constitute the former species of monopoly, the Committee may be right in denying its existence. . . .

ANDREW JACKSON

Nowhere is the philosophy of Jacksonian democracy systematized. The major tenets of Jacksonianism can be found only through an examination of its political institutions.

In his first message to Congress Jackson expresses some of the new agrarian attitudes, notably the desire for internal improvements and the advocacy of rotation in office.

FIRST ANNUAL MESSAGE [83]

Fellow-Citizens of the Senate and House of Representatives:

. . . . . .

In this as in all other matters of public concern policy requires that as few impediments as possible should exist to the free operation of the public will. Let us, then, endeavor so to amend our system that the office of Chief Magistrate may not be conferred upon any citizen but in pursuance of a fair expression of the will of the majority.

I would therefore recommend such an amendment of the Constitution as may remove all intermediate agency in the election of the President and Vice-President. The mode may be so regulated as to preserve to each State its present relative weight in the election, and a failure in the first attempt may be provided for by confining the second to a choice between the two highest candidates. In connection with such an amendment it would seem advisable to limit the service of the chief magistrate to a single term of either four or six years. If, however, it should not be adopted, it is worthy of consideration whether a provision disqualifying for office the Representatives in Congress on whom such an election may have devolved would not be proper.

While members of Congress can be constitutionally appointed to offices of trust and profit it will be the practice, even under the most conscientious adherence to duty, to select them for such stations as they are believed to be better qualified to fill than other citizens; but the purity of our Government would doubtless be promoted by their exclusion from all appointments in the gift of the President, in whose election they may have been officially concerned. The nature of the judicial office and the necessity of securing in the Cabinet and in diplomatic stations of the highest rank the best talents and political experience should, perhaps, except these from the exclusion.

There are, perhaps, few men who can for any great length of time enjoy office and power without being more or less under the influence of feelings unfavorable to the faithful discharge of their public duties. Their integrity may be proof against improper considerations immediately addressed to themselves, but they are apt to acquire a habit of looking with indifference upon the public interests and of tolerating conduct from which an unpracticed man would revolt. Office is considered as a species of property, and government rather as a means of promoting individual interests than as an instrument created solely for the service of the people. Corruption in some and in others a perversion of correct feelings and principles divert government from its legitimate ends and make it an engine for the support of the few at the

[83] J. D. Richardson, *A Compilation of the Messages and Papers of the Presidents.* (Washington, Government Printing Office, 1896), II, 448-452.

expense of the many. The duties of all public officers are, or at least admit of being made, so plain and simple that men of intelligence may readily qualify themselves for their performance; and I can not but believe that more is lost by the long continuance of men in office than is generally to be gained by their experience. I submit, therefore, to your consideration whether the efficiency of the Government would not be promoted and official industry and integrity better secured by a general extension of the law which limits appointments to four years.

In a country where offices are created solely for the benefit of the people no one man has any more intrinsic right to official station than another. Offices were not established to give support to particular men at the public expense. No individual wrong is, therefore, done by removal, since neither appointment to nor continuance in office is matter of right. The incumbent became an officer with a view to public benefits, and when these require his removal they are not to be sacrificed to private interests. It is the people, and they alone, who have a right to complain when a bad officer is substituted for a good one. He who is removed has the same means of obtaining a living that are enjoyed by the millions who never held office. The proposed limitation would destroy the idea of property now so generally connected with official station, and although individual distress may be sometimes produced, it would, by promoting that rotation which constitutes a leading principle in the republican creed, give healthful action to the system.

No very considerable change has occurred during the recess of Congress in the condition of either our agriculture, commerce, or manufactures. The operation of the tariff has not proved so injurious to the two former or as beneficial to the latter as was anticipated. Importations of foreign goods have not been sensibly diminished, while domestic competition, under an illusive excitement, has increased the production much beyond the demand for home consumption. The consequences have been low prices, temporary embarrassment, and partial loss. That such of our manufacturing establishments as are based upon capital and are prudently managed will survive the shock and be ultimately profitable there is no good reason to doubt.

To regulate its conduct so as to promote equally the prosperity of these three cardinal interests is one of the most difficult tasks of Government; and it may be regretted that the complicated restrictions which now embarrass the intercourse of nations could not by common consent be abolished, and commerce allowed to flow in those channels to which individual enterprise, always its surest guide, might direct it. But we must ever expect selfish legislation in other nations, and are therefore compelled to adapt our own to their regulations in the manner best calculated to avoid serious injury and to harmonize the conflicting interests of our agriculture, our commerce, and our manufactures. Under these impressions I invite your attention to the existing tariff, believing that some of its provisions require modification.

The general rule to be applied in graduating the duties upon articles of foreign growth or manufacture is that which will place our own in fair competition with those of other countries; and the inducements to advance even a step beyond this point are controlling in regard to those articles which are of primary necessity in time of war. When we reflect upon the difficulty and delicacy of this operation, it is important that it should never be attempted but with the utmost caution. Frequent legislation in regard to any branch of industry, affecting its value, and by which its capital may be transferred to new channels, must always be productive of hazardous speculation and loss.

In deliberating, therefore, on these interesting subjects local feelings and prejudices should be merged in the patriotic determination to promote the great interests of the whole. All attempts to connect them with the party conflicts of the day are necessarily injurious, and should be discountenanced. Our action upon them should be under the control of higher and purer motives. Legislation subjected to such influences can never be just, and will not long retain the sanction of a people whose active patriotism is not bound by sectional limits nor insensible to that spirit of concession and forbearance which gave life to our political ascendency, the North, the South, the East, and the West should unite in diminishing any burthen of which either may justly complain.

The agricultural interest of our country is so essentially connected with every other and so superior in importance to them all that it is scarcely necessary to invite to it your particular attention. It is principally as manufactures and commerce tend to increase the value of agricultural productions and to extend their application to the wants and comforts of society that they deserve the fostering care of Government.

Looking forward to the period, not far distant, when a sinking fund will no longer be required, the duties on those articles of importation which cannot come in competition with our own productions are the first that should engage the attention of Congress in the modification of the tariff. Of these, tea and coffee are the most prominent. They enter largely into the consumption of the country, and have become articles of necessity to all classes. A reduction, therefore, of the existing duties will be felt as a common benefit, but like all other legislation connected with commerce, to be efficacious and not injurious it should be gradual and certain.

The public prosperity is evinced in the increased revenue arising from the sale of the public lands and in the steady maintenance of that produced by imposts and tonnage, notwithstanding the additional duties imposed by the act of 19th May, 1828, and the unusual importations in the early part of that year.

The balance in the Treasury on January 1, 1829, was $5,972,435.81. The receipts of the current year are estimated at $24,602,230 and the expenditures for the same time at $26,164,595, leaving a balance in the Treasury on the 1st of January next of $4,410,070.81.

There will have been paid on account of the public debt during the present year the sum of $12,405,005.80, reducing the whole debt of the Government on the 1st of January next to $48,565,406.50, including seven millions of 5 per cent stock subscribed to the Bank of the United States. The payment on account of public debt made on the 1st of July last was $8,715,462.87. It was apprehended that the sudden withdrawal of so large a sum from the banks in which it was deposited, at a time of unusual pressure in the money market, might cause much injury to the interests dependent on bank accommodations. But this evil was wholly averted by an early anticipation of it at the Treasury, aided by the judicious arrangements of the officers of the Bank of the United States.

This state of the finances exhibits the resources of the nation in an aspect highly flattering to its industry and auspicious of the ability of Government in a very short time to extinguish the public debt. When this shall be done our population will be relieved from a considerable portion of its present burthens, and will find not only new motives to patriotic affection, but additional means for the display of individual enterprise. The fiscal power of the States will also be increased, and may be more extensively exerted in favor of education and other public objects, while ample means will remain in the Federal Government to promote the general weal in all the modes permitted to this authority.

After the extinction of the public debt it is not probable that any adjustment of the tariff upon principles satisfactory to the people of the Union will until a remote period, if ever, leave the Government without a considerable surplus in the Treasury beyond what may be required for its current service. As, then, the period approaches when the application of the revenue to the payment of debt will cease, the disposition of the surplus will present a subject for the serious deliberation of Congress; and it may be fortunate for the country that it is yet to be decided. Considered in connection with the difficulties which have heretofore attended appropriations for purposes of internal improvement, and with those which this experience tells us will certainly arise whenever power over such subjects may be exercised by the General Government, it is hoped that it may lead to the adoption of some plan which will reconcile the diversified interests of the States and strengthen the bonds which unite them. Every member of the Union, in peace and in war, will be benefited by the improvement of inland navigation and the construction of highways in the several States. Let us, then, endeavor to attain this benefit in a mode which will be satisfactory to all. That hitherto adopted has by many of our fellow-citizens been deprecated as an infraction of the Constitution, while by others it has been viewed as inexpedient. All feel that it has been employed at the expense of harmony in the legislative councils.

To avoid these evils it appears to me that the most safe, just, and federal disposition which could be made of the surplus revenue would be its apportionment among the several States according to their ratio of representation, and should this measure not be found warranted by the Constitution that it would be expedient to propose to the States an amendment authorizing it. I regard an appeal to the source of power in cases of real doubt, and where its exercise is deemed indispensable to the general welfare, as among the most sacred of all our obligations. Upon this country more than any other has, in the providence of God, been cast the special guardianship of the great principle of adherence to written constitutions. If it fail here, all hope in regard to it will be extinguished. That this was intended to be a government of limited and specific, and not general, powers must be admitted by all, and it is our duty to preserve for it the character intended by its framers. If experience points out the necessity for an enlargement of these powers, let us apply for it to those for whose benefit it is to be exercised, and not undermine the whole system by a resort to overstrained constructions. The scheme has worked well. It has exceeded the hopes of those who devised it, and become an object of admiration to the world. We are responsible to our country and to the glorious cause of self-government for the preservation of so great a good. The great mass of legislation relating to our internal affairs was intended to be left where the Federal Convention found it—in the State governments. Nothing is clearer, in my view, than that we are chiefly indebted for the success of the Constitution under which we are now acting to the watchful and auxiliary operation of the State authorities. This is not the reflection of a day, but belongs to the most deeply rooted convictions of my mind. I can not, therefore, too strongly or too earnestly, for my own sense of its importance, warn you against all encroachments upon the legitimate sphere of State sovereignty. Sustained by its healthful and invigorating influence the federal system can never fall. . . .

OHIO CONSTITUTIONAL CONVENTION [84]

1850–1851.

The convention adopted the following provision concerning suffrage: "Every white male citizen of the United States, of the age of twenty-one years, who shall have been a resident of the State one year next preceding the election, and of the county, township, or ward, in which he resides, such time as may be provided by law, shall have the qualifications of an elector, and be entitled to a vote at all elections." (Article V, Section 1.)

The extreme democrats were not satisfied with this provision and fought for the extension of the suffrage to women and free negroes. In the debates on this subject are found the culmination of western equalitarianism. The speech of Mr. Townshend is typical of the then radical democratic view-point.

ONE HUNDRED AND TENTH DAY

Saturday, February 8, 1851,
9 o'clock, A.M.

. . . . . .
EXTENSION OF THE ELECTIVE FRANCHISE

. . . . . .
MR. TOWNSHEND. . . .

I am opposed, Mr. President to the insertion of the word *white* in this Report. The first reason I have to offer for my opposition is the belief that the intended restriction of the right of suffrage is *unjust*.

Sir, I not only say, but I believe that "*all* men are created equal," that is they are equally endowed by their Creator with certain inherent rights. These rights are essential to our existence, they spring from the necessities of our being. In order to live we must have a place somewhere, we must have air and food, and each of these and every other necessity imposed on us by our maker, involves a corresponding right whether it pertain to our physical or to our intellectual or moral nature. Some of our rights grow directly out of the relations we sustain, such as husbands or fathers, &c., each of these relations imposing certain obligations or duties, and these involving corresponding rights. All men have by nature the same necessities, and may sustain the same or equal relations, consequently all men must

[84] *Report of the Debates and Proceedings of the Convention for the Revision of the Constitution of the State of Ohio, 1850–1851.* (Columbus, 1851), II, 550–551.

have the same natural rights. For the protection of these natural rights governments are instituted among men, and this single purpose of protection is the only legitimate function of government. All the human governments on earth cannot create a right, nor can they take a right away, and the idea that man on entering into jural or civil relations with these, surrenders any part of his natural rights, is only one of the grand but mischievous blunders of the past. Human governments derive all their just authority from the consent of the governed; all persons have the same rights to protect, and are therefore equally interested, and equally entitled to share as principals in government, and the consent of one person is just as necessary as the consent of another person, in order to constitute just authority.

To attempt to govern men without seeking their consent is usurpation and tyranny, whether in Ohio or in Austria. There is a portion of the people of this State who have the same right to stand upon this part of God's earth, and to breathe this free air, that you or I have, and yet you seek to impose a government upon them without consulting them. I can only say that they are under no obligation to obey your laws or to submit to your authority. You burthen them with taxation without representation, and thus inflict upon them the identical wrong for which the thirteen United Colonies threw off the yoke of the mother country. To establish a government over them, not based on their consent; to subject them to laws they have had no voice in framing; to tax them while you deny them representation is clearly and manifestly unjust; and I might stop here without urging any futher objections to the Report, for with governments there should be really but one enquiry, what is just?

Another objection I have to this limitation of the right of suffrage, I believe it is *anti-democratic*. I desire to speak on this point with becoming modesty, for I am but a young man, while I see around me many whose hair has grown gray in the study of democratic principles. One of these gentlemen has said with Jefferson that democracy consists in doing "equal and exact justice to all men," another gentleman has said that democracy concedes to others all it demands for itself, and demands for itself all it concedes to others. If the restriction of the elective franchise is tested by either of these rules it will be found anti-democratic. To justify the practice the report recommends, Jefferson's rule should be amended so as to read "equal and exact justice to all *white* men—or to all men *except negroes*." If I understand genuine democracy it is neither more nor less than the golden rule of christianity applied to politics, or to our civil relations—that is doing unto others as we would have others to do unto us, and I see no reason why democracy is not like christianity, comprehensive enough to embrace the whole family of man. I was looking the other day, Mr. President, into Noah Webster's Dictionary for the meaning of democracy, and I found as I expected that he defines a democrat to be "one who favors universal suffrage." Now some of our friends here have been busy of late in reading out of the democratic party all who did not come up to their standard of democracy. If they were justified in that proceeding I suppose I shall be equally justified in reading them out if they do not come up to this, the true authoritative standard. I should regret to do it, for some of these gentlemen consider themselves pretty good democrats, although in this particular, they are, as I think, behind the times. Nothing is clearer than that genuine democracy must ever be progressive. The rule "equal and exact justice to all men," perhaps, can never be amended, but in its application our measures will change from year to year. The evils and abuses to which this rule was first applied, have now, many of them, passed away, but every succeeding age develops abuses requiring new applications of the same rule, and he only is a genuine democrat who faithfully applies this good democratic rule to any new species of abuse or injustice that appears, and not he who having used it once or twice throws it away and uses it no further. I believe it to be our duty here to erect a civil platform upon which the foot of every person in the State may stand and on exactly the same level. I have not intentionally given in this body, one vote, nor do I intend to give one vote, to place any man, or set of men, above the common level. I will vote for no franchise, if by that is meant a something which makes one man free to do what may not be done by others. I will vote for no privilege, if by that is meant a private law for the benefit of the few over the many. I will vote for no charters, because I will not by my vote, give to a part by a special grant, what belongs alike to all, and none of these things have any sacredness for me, I will not give the benefit of my vote. I will not give the benefit of holy rood to any hoary abuse, but right the wrong wherever given. But sir, the same sense of justice, which will not permit me to place another man's foot higher than my own, will also prevent me from consenting to place any man a hair's breadth below the common level. If the government of Ohio is to be in the hands of a privileged class, whether that class be large or small, it will be an aristocracy, a form of government for which I have no partiality; this government ought to be democratic—a government shared by all, for the good of all. Let us then have no limitations of suffrage—for who does not know that all such limitations are anti-democratic?

Another reason for opposing this restriction of what is called the elective franchise, I believe it is *impolitic.*

We have already stated that the true function of government is to protect rights, or in other words, to prevent wrongs. Experience has taught us that ignorance is one of the most fruitful sources of crime, and it has therefore been found to be good policy to secure the education of the whole people, as a means of preventing crime, which it does at less expense and more effectually than all the jails or penitentiaries, or scaffolds, that were ever erected. I was surprised, when we were considering the subject of education, to hear some gentleman propose to exclude the children of colored persons from the benefits of our common school system. Surely, after what we know of the good influences of education, to provide for keeping one class of our inhabitants in ignorance, would be most miserable policy. But it is not enough that all should have the means of education; we ought to give to all the inhabitants of the State the full benefit of the powerful stimulus of hope and ambition. Let no man feel that the law which ought to be his protector, interposes a barrier to his progress, by saying to him, "thus far shalt thou come, but no farther." Rather let us offer the strongest inducements to the intellectual and moral elevation of every person, of whatever class or condition, by opening the race and offering every prize of wealth, or honor, or usefulness, alike to all. If, on the other hand, we make it impossible for any class of our people to rise—if we consign them to ignorance, and want, and degradation, we ought to consider ourselves responsible for whatever invasion of our rights may be the consequence; we shall reap exactly what we sow. To my view, the political degradation of any portion of our people is in the highest degree impolitic.

I object also to inserting the word "white," because for the purpose employed, it is indefinite and ambiguous, and therefore improper. . . .

ROGER B. TANEY

Jackson appointed Taney as Chief Justice of the Supreme Court after the death of Marshall. Being of democratic attitude, Taney proceeded to reverse many of Marshall's decisions.

The decision in the *Charles River Bridge case* is an interesting contrast to Marshall's decision on irrevocable contracts and the sacredness of private property. In 1785 the legislature of Massachusetts incorporated "The Proprietors of the Charles River Bridge" and authorized them to construct a bridge from Boston to Charlestown. In 1828 the legislature incorporated another bridge company, "The Proprietors of the Warren Bridge," and authorized it to build a second bridge close to the first structure. By the terms of its charter, the second company was to surrender its bridge as soon as the tolls had reimbursed it for its construction and maintenance. The Charles River Bridge Company sought to enjoin the construction of the second bridge on the ground that its erection impaired the obligation of its contract of 1785. Taney stressed progress where Marshall would undoubtedly have emphasized property rights.

THE PROPRIETORS OF THE CHARLES RIVER BRIDGE v. THE PROPRIETORS OF THE WARREN BRIDGE AND OTHERS [85]

. . . . . .

Adopting the rule of construction above stated as the settled one, we proceed to apply it to the charter of 1785 to the proprietors of the Charles River bridge. This act of incorporation is in the usual form, and the privileges such as are commonly given to corporations of that kind. It confers on them the ordinary faculties of a corporation, for the purpose of building the bridge; and establishes certain rates of toll, which the company are authorized to take: this is the whole grant. There is no exclusive privilege given to them over the waters of Charles river, above or below their bridge; no right to erect another bridge themselves, nor to prevent other persons from erecting one, no engagement from the state, that another shall not be erected; and no undertaking not to sanction competition, not to make improvements that may diminish the amount of its income. Upon all these subjects, the charter is silent; and nothing is said in it about a line of travel, so much insisted on in the argument, in which they are to have exclusive privileges. No words are used from which an intention to grant any of these rights can be inferred; if the plaintiff is entitled to them, it must be implied, simply, from the nature of the grant; and cannot be inferred, from the words by which the grant is made.

The relative position of the Warren bridge has already been described. It does not interrupt the passage over the Charles River bridge, nor make the way to it, or from it, less convenient. None of the faculties or franchises granted to that corporation, have been revoked by the legislature; and its right to take the tolls granted by the charter remains unaltered. In short, all

[85] 11 Peters, 420, 548–550, 551–553 (1837).

the franchises and rights of property, enumerated in the charter, and there mentioned to have been granted to it, remain unimpaired. But its income is destroyed by the Warren bridge; which, being free, draws off the passengers and property which would have gone over it, and renders their franchise of no value. This is the gist of the complaint. For it is not pretended, that the erection of the Warren bridge would have done them any injury, or in any degree affected their right of property, if it had not diminished the amount of their tolls. In order, then, to entitle themselves to relief, it is necessary to show, that the legislature contracted not to do the act of which they complain; and that they impaired, or in other words, violated, that contract by the erection of the Warren bridge.

The inquiry, then, is, does the charter contain such a contract on the part of the state? Is there any such stipulation to be found in that instrument? It must be admitted on all hands, that there is none; no words that even relate to another bridge, or to the diminution of their tolls, or to the line of travel. If a contract on that subject can be gathered from the charter, it must be by implication; and cannot be found in the words used. Can such an agreement be implied? The rule of construction before stated is an answer to the question; in charters of this description, no rights are taken from the public, or given to the corporation, beyond those which the words of the charter, by their natural and proper construction, purport to convey. There are no words which import such a contract as the plaintiff in error contend for, and none can be implied; and the same answer must be given to them that was given by this court to Providence Bank. The whole community are interested in this inquiry, and they have a right to require that the power of promoting their comfort and convenience, and of advancing the public prosperity, by providing safe, convenient and cheap ways for the transportation of produce, and the purposes of travel shall not be construed to have been surrendered or diminished by the state, unless it shall appear by plain words, that it was intended to be done. . . .

Indeed, the practice and usage of almost every state in the Union, old enough to have commenced the work of internal improvement, is opposed to the doctrine contended for on the part of the plaintiffs in error. Turnpike roads have been made in succession, on the same line of travel; the later ones interfering materially with the profits of the first. These corporations have, in some instances, been utterly ruined by the introduction of newer and better modes of transportation and travelling. In some cases, railroads have rendered the turnpike roads on the same line of travel so entirely useless, that the franchise of the turnpike corporation is not worth preserving. Yet in none of these cases have the corporations supposed that their privileges were invaded, or any contract violated on the part of the state. Amid the multitude of cases which have occurred, and have been daily occurring for the last forty or fifty years, this is the first instance in which such an implied contract has been contended for, and this court called upon to infer it, from an ordinary act of incorporation, containing nothing more than the usual stipulations and provisions to be found in every such law. The absence of any such controversy, when there must have been so many occasions to give rise to it, proves, that neither states, nor individuals, nor corporations, ever imagined that such a contract could be implied from such charters. It shows, that the men who voted for these laws never imagined that they were forming such a contract; and if we maintain that they have made it, we must create it by a legal fiction, in opposition to the truth of the fact, and the obvious intention of the party. We cannot deal thus with the rights reserved to the states; and by legal intendments and mere technical reasoning, take away from them any portion of that power over their own internal police and improvement, which is so necessary to their well-being and prosperity.

And what would be the fruits of this doctrine of implied contracts, on the part of the states, and of property in a line of travel by a corporation, if it should now be sanctioned by this court? To what results would it lead us? If it is to be found in the charter to this bridge, the same process of reasoning must discover it, in the various acts which have been passed, within the last forty years, for turnpike companies. And what is to be the extent of the privileges of exclusion on the different sides of the road? The counsel who have so ably argued this case, have not attempted to define it by any certain boundaries. How far must the new improvement be distant from the old? How near may you approach, without invading its rights in the privileged line? If this court should establish the principles now contended for, what is to become of the numerous railroads established on the same line of travel with turnpike companies; and which have rendered the franchises of the turnpike companies of no value? Let it once be understood, that such charters carry with them these implied contracts, and give this unknown and undefined property in a line of travelling; and you will soon find the old turnpike corporations awakening from their sleep and calling upon this court to put down the improvements which have taken their place. The millions of property which have been invested in railroads and canals, upon lines of travel which had been before occupied by turnpike corporations, will be put in jeopardy. We shall be thrown back to the improvements of the last century, and obliged to stand still, until the claims of the old turnpike corporations shall be satisfied; and they shall consent to permit these states to avail themselves of the lights of modern science, and to partake of the benefit of those improvements which are now adding to the wealth and prosperity, and the convenience and comfort, of every other part of the civilized world. Nor is this all. This court will find itself compelled to fix, by some arbitrary rule, the width of this new kind of property in a line of travel; for if such a right of property exists, we have no lights to guide us in marking out its extent, unless, indeed, we resort to the old feudal grants, and to the exclusive rights of ferries, by prescription, between towns; and are prepared to decide that when a turnpike road from one town to another, had been made, no railroad or canal, between these two points, could afterwards be established. This court are not prepared to sanction principles which must lead to such results. . . .

RALPH WALDO EMERSON

After Emerson's graduation from Harvard University he studied theology under William E. Channing, by whose liberalism in religious and ethical thinking he was greatly influenced. Emerson was ordained in 1829, but he stayed in the ministry only three years. Differences with his congregation over matters of theology led him to resign. He thereafter devoted his attention to a literary career. Emerson was influenced by Channing and by Goethe's deep love of nature as a companion of man.

He maintained that natural laws, when applied to man, become moral laws. While he was an individualist and an exponent of natural laws, he nevertheless emphasized discipline. Self-discipline, he held, trains the reason, develops the intellect, and becomes the means of moral culture.

Emerson's writings represent the intellectual democracy that developed during the second quarter of the nineteenth century. In his *Essay on Politics*, the influence of humanitarianism is conspicuous. In it he elevated the individual above the State. Emerson played a rôle in the intellectual attack upon slavery.

ESSAY ON POLITICS [86]

(1842)

VII

Politics

In dealing with the State, we ought to remember that its institutions are not aboriginal, though they existed before we were born: that they are not superior to the citizen: that every one of them was once the act of a single man: every law and usage was a man's expedient to meet a particular case: that they all are imitable, all alterable; we may make as good; we may make better. Society is an illusion to the young citizen. It lies before him in rigid repose, with certain names, men and institutions rooted like oak-trees to the centre, round which all arrange themselves the best they can. But the old statesman knows that society is fluid; there are no such roots and centres, but any particle may suddenly become the centre of the movement, and compel the system to gyrate round it, as every man of strong will, like Pisistratus or Cromwell, does for a time, and every man of truth, like Plato or Paul, does forever. But politics rest on necessary foundations, and cannot be treated with levity. Republics abound in young civilisans, who believe that the laws make the city, that grave modifications of the policy and modes of living, and employments of the population, that commerce, education, and religion, may be voted in or out; and that any measure, though it were absurd, may be imposed on a people, if only you can get sufficient voices to make it a law. But the wise know that foolish legislation is a rope of sand, which perishes in the twisting; that the State must follow and not lead the character and progress of the citizen; the strongest usurper is quickly got rid of; and they only who build on Ideas, build for eternity; and that the form of government which prevails, is the expression of what cultivation exists in the population which permits it. The law is only a memorandum. We are superstitious, and esteem the statute somewhat: so much life as it has in the character of living men is its force. The statute stands there to say, yesterday we agreed so and so, but how feel ye this article to-day? Our statute is a currency, which we stamp with our own portrait: it soon becomes unrecognizable, and in process of time will return to the mint. Nature is not democratic, nor limited monarchical, but despotic, and will not be fooled or abated of any jot of her authority, by the protest of her sons: and as fast as the public mind is opened to more intelligence, the code is seen to be brute and stammering. It speaks not articulately, and

[86] R. W. Emerson, *Essays, Second Series.* (Boston, Phillips, Sampson & Company, 1855), pp. 193-214.

must be made to. Meantime the education of the general mind never stops. The reveries of the true and simple are prophetic. What the tender poetic youth dreams, and prays, and paints to-day, but shuns the ridicule of saying aloud, shall presently be the resolutions of public bodies, then shall be carried as grievance and bill of rights through conflict and war, and then shall be triumphant law and establishment for a hundred years, until it gives place in turn to new prayers and pictures. The history of the State sketches in coarse outline the progress of thought, and follows at a distance the delicacy of culture and of aspiration.

The theory of politics, which has possessed the mind of men, and which they have expressed the best they could in their laws and in their revolutions, considers persons and property as the two objects for whose protection government exists. Of persons, all have equal rights, in virtue of being identical in nature. This interest, of course, with its whole power demands a democracy. Whilst the rights of all as persons are equal, in virtue of their access to reason, their rights in property are very unequal. One man owns his clothes, and another owns a county. This accident, depending, primarily, on the skill and virtue of the parties, of which there is every degree, and, secondarily, on patrimony, falls unequally, and its rights, of course, are unequal. Personal rights, universally the same, demand a government framed on the ratio of the census: property demands a government framed on the ratio of owners and of owning. Laban, who has flocks and herds, wishes them looked after by an officer on the frontiers, lest the Midianites shall drive them off, and pays a tax to that end. Jacob has no flocks or herds, and no fear of the Midianites, and pays no tax to the officer. It seemed fit that Laban and Jacob should have equal rights to elect the officer, who is to defend their persons, but that Laban and not Jacob should elect the officer who is to guard the sheep and cattle. And, if question arise whether additional officers or watch-towers should be provided, must not Laban and Isaac, and those who must sell part of their herds to buy protection for the rest, judge better of this, and with more right, than Jacob, who, because he is a youth and a traveller, eats their bread and not his own?

In the earliest society the proprietors made their own wealth, and so long as it comes to the owners in the direct way, no other opinion would arise in any equitable community, than that property should make the law for property, and persons the law for persons.

But property passes through donation or inheritance to those who do not create it. Gift, in one case, makes it as really the new owner's, as labor made it the first owner's: in the other case, of patrimony, the law makes an ownership, which will be valid in each man's view according to the estimate which he sets on the public tranquillity.

It was not, however, found easy to embody the readily admitted principle, that property should make law for property, and persons for persons: since persons and property mixed themselves in every transaction. At last it seemed settled, that the rightful distinction was, that the proprietors should have more elective franchise than non-proprietors, on the Spartan principle of "calling that which is just, equal; not that which is equal, just."

That principle no longer looks so self-evident as it appeared in former times, partly because doubts have arisen whether too much weight had not been allowed in the laws, to property, and such a structure given to our usages, as allowed the rich to encroach on the poor, and to keep them poor; but mainly, because there is an instinctive sense, however obscure and yet inarticulate, that the whole constitution of property, on its present tenures, is injurious, and its influence on persons deteriorating and degrading; that truly, the only interest for the consideration of the State is persons; that property will always follow persons; that the highest end of government is the culture of men; and that if men can be educated, the institutions will share their improvement, and the moral sentiment will write the law of the land.

If it be not easy to settle the equity of this question, the peril is less when we take note of our natural defences. We are kept by better guards than the vigilance of such magistrates as we commonly elect. Society always consists, in greatest part, of young and foolish persons. The old, who have seen through the hypocrisy of courts and statesmen, die and leave no wisdom to their sons. They believe their own newspaper, as their fathers did at their age. With such an ignorant and deceivable majority, States would soon run to ruin, but that there are limitations beyond which the folly and ambition of governors cannot go. Things have their laws, as well as men; and things refuse to be trifled with. Property will be protected. Corn will not grow, unless it is planted and manured; but the farmer will not plant or hoe it, unless the chances are a hundred to one that he will cut and harvest it. Under any forms, persons and property must and will have their just sway. They exert their power, as steadily as matter its attraction. Cover up a pound of earth never so cunningly, divide and subdivide it; melt it to liquid, convert it to gas; it will always weigh a pound: it will always attract and resist other matter, by the full virtue of one pound weight;—and the attributes of a person, his wit and his moral energy, will exercise, under any law or extinguishing tyranny, their proper force,—if not overtly, then covertly; if not for the law, then against it; if not wholesomely, then poisonously; with right, or by might.

The boundaries of personal influence it is impossible to fix, as persons are organs of moral or supernatural force. Under the dominion of an idea, which possesses the minds of multitudes, as civil freedom, or the religious sentiment, the powers of persons are no longer subjects of calculation. A nation of men unanimously bent on freedom, or conquest, can easily confound the arithmetic of statists, and achieve extravagant actions, out of all proportion to their means; as the Greeks, the Saracens, the Swiss, the Americans, and the French have done.

In like manner, to every particle of property belongs its own attraction. A cent is the representative of a certain quantity of corn or other commodity. Its value is in the necessities of the animal man. It is so much warmth, so much bread, so much water, so much land. The law may do what it will with the owner of property, its just power will still attach to the cent. The law may in a mad freak say, that all shall have power except the owners of property; they shall have no vote. Nevertheless, by a higher law, the property will, year after year, write every statute that respects property. The non-proprietor will be the scribe of the proprietor. What the owners wish to do, the whole power of property will do, either through the law or else in defiance of it. Of course, I speak of all the property, not merely of the great estates. When the rich are out-voted, as frequently happens, it is the joint treasury of the poor which exceeds their accumulations. Every man owns something, if it is only a cow, or a wheel-barrow, or his arms, and so has that property to dispose of.

The same necessity which secures the rights of persons and property against the malignity or folly of the magistrate, determines the form and method of governing, which are proper to each nation and to its habits of thought, and nowise transferable to other states of society. In this country, we are very vain of our political institutions, which are singular in this, that they sprung, within the memory of living men, from the character and condition of the people, which they still express with sufficient fidelity,—and we ostentatiously prefer them to any other in history. They are not better, but only fitter for us. We may be wise in asserting the advantage in modern times of the democratic form, but to other states of society, in which religion consecrated the monarchical, that and not this was expedient. Democracy is better for us, because the religious sentiment of the present time accords better with it. Born democrats, we are nowise qualified to judge of monarchy, which, to our fathers living in the monarchical idea, was also relatively right. But our institutions, though in coincidence with the spirit of the age, have not any exemption from the practical defects which have discredited other forms. Every actual State is corrupt. Good men must not obey the laws too well. What satire on government can equal the severity of censure conveyed in the word *politic*, which now for ages has signified *cunning*, intimating that the State is a trick?

The same benign necessity and the same practical abuse appear in the parties into which each State divides itself, of opponents and defenders of the administration of the government. Parties are also founded on instincts, and have better guides to their own humble aims than the sagacity of their leaders. They have nothing perverse in their origin, but rudely mark some real and lasting relation. We might as wisely reprove the east wind, or the frost, as a political party, whose members, for the most part, could give no account of their position, but stand for the defence of those interests in which they find themselves. Our quarrel with them begins, when they quit this deep natural ground at the bidding of some leader, and obeying personal considerations, throw themselves into the maintenance and defence of points nowise belonging to their system. A party is perpetually corrupted by personality. Whilst we absolve the association from dishonesty, we cannot extend the same charity to their leaders. They reap the rewards of the docility and zeal of the masses which they direct. Ordinarily, our parties are parties of circumstance, and not of principle; as, the planting interest in conflict with the commercial; the party of capitalists, and that of operatives; parties which are identical in their moral character, and which can easily change ground with each other, in the support of many of their measures. Parties of principle, as, religious sects, or the party of free-trade, of universal suffrage, of abolition of slavery, of abolition of capital punishment, degenerate into personalities, or would inspire enthusiasm. The vice of our leading parties in this country (which may be cited as a fair specimen of these societies of opinion) is, that they do not plant themselves on the deep and necessary grounds to which they are respectively entitled, but lash themselves to fury in the carrying of some local and momentary measure, nowise useful to the commonwealth. Of the two great parties, which at this hour almost share the nation between them, I should say that one has the best cause, and the other contains the best men. The philosopher, the poet, or the religious man, will, of course, wish to cast his vote with the democrat, for free-trade, for wide suffrage, for the abolition of legal cruelties in the penal code, and for facilitating in every manner the access of the young and the poor to the sources of wealth and power. But he can rarely accept the persons whom the so-called popular party propose to him as representatives of these liberalities. They have not at heart the ends which give to the name of democracy what hope and virtue are in it. The spirit of our American radicalism is destructive and aimless: it is not loving; it has no ulterior and divine ends; but is destructive only out of hatred and selfishness. On the other side, the conservative party, composed of the most moderate, able, and cultivated part of the population, is timid, and merely defensive of property. It vindicates no right, it aspires to no real good, it brands no crime, it proposes no generous policy; it does not build, nor write, nor cherish the arts, nor foster religion, nor establish schools, nor encourage science, nor emancipate the slave, nor befriend the poor, or the Indian, or the immigrant. From neither party, when in power, has the world any benefit to expect in science, art, or humanity, at all commensurate with the resources of the nation.

I do not for these defects despair of our republic. We are not at the mercy of any waves of chance. In the strife of ferocious parties, human nature always finds itself cherished, as the children of the convicts at Botany Bay are found to have as healthy a moral sentiment as other children. Citizens of feudal states are alarmed at our democratic institutions lapsing into anarchy; and the older and more cautious among ourselves are learning from Europeans to look with some terror at our turbulent freedom. It is said that in our license of construing the Constitution, and in the despotism of public opinion, we have no anchor; and one foreign observer thinks he has found the safeguard in the sanctity of Marriage among us; and another thinks he has found it in our Calvinism. Fisher Ames expressed the popular security more wisely, when he compared a monarchy and a republic, saying, "that a monarchy is a merchantman, which sails well, but will sometimes strike on a rock, and go to the bottom; whilst a republic is a raft, which would never sink, but then your feet are always in water." No forms can have any dangerous importance, whilst we are befriended by the laws of things. It makes no difference how many tons weight of atmosphere presses on our heads, so long as the same pressure resists it within the lungs. Augment the mass a thousand fold, it cannot begin to crush us, as long as reaction is equal to action. The fact of two poles, of two forces, centripetal and centrifugal, is universal, and each force by its own activity develops the other. Wild liberty develops iron conscience. Want of liberty, by strengthening law and decorum, stupefies conscience. 'Lynch law' prevails only where there is greater hardihood and self-subsistency in the leaders. A mob cannot be a permanency: everybody's interest requires that it should not exist, and only justice satisfies all.

We must trust infinitely to the beneficent necessity which shines through all laws. Human nature expresses itself in them as characteristically as in statues, or songs, or railroads, and an abstract of the codes of nations would be a transcript of the common conscience. Governments have their origin in the moral identity of men. Reason for one is seen to be reason for another, and for every other. There is a middle measure which satisfies all parties, be they never so many or so resolute for their own. Every man finds a sanction for his simplest claims and deeds, in decisions of his own mind, which he calls Truth and Holiness. In these decisions all the citizens find a perfect agreement, and only in these; not in what is good to eat, good to wear, good use of time, or what amount of land or of public aid, each is entitled to claim. This truth and justice men presently endeavor to make application of to the measuring of land, the apportionment of service, the protection of life and property. Their first endeavors, no doubt, are very awkward. Yet absolute right is the first governor; or, every government is an impure theocracy. The idea, after which each community is aiming to make and mend its law, is the will of the wise man. The wise man, it cannot find in nature, and it makes awkward but earnest efforts to secure his government by contrivance; as, by causing the entire people to give their voices on every measure; or by a double choice to get the representation of the whole; or, by a selection of the best citizens; or, to secure the advantages of efficiency and internal peace, by confiding the government to one, who may himself select his agents. All forms of government symbolize an immortal government, common to all dynasties and independent of numbers, perfect where two men exist, perfect where there is only one man.

Every man's nature is a sufficient advertisement to him of the character of his fellows. My right and my wrong, is their right and their wrong. Whilst I do what is fit for me, and abstain from what is unfit, my neighbor and I shall often agree in our means, and work together for a time to one end. But whenever I find my dominion over myself not sufficient for me, and undertake the direction of him also, I overstep the truth, and come into false relations to him. I may have so much more skill or strength than he, that he cannot express adequately his sense of wrong, but it is a lie, and hurts like a lie both him and me. Love and nature cannot maintain the assumption: it must be executed by a practical lie, namely, by force. This undertaking for another, is the blunder which stands in colossal ugliness in the governments of the world. It is the same thing in numbers, as in a pair, only not quite so intelligible. I can see well enough a great difference between my setting myself down to a self-control, and my going to make somebody else act after my views: but when a quarter of the human race assume to tell me what I must do, I may be too much disturbed by the circumstances to see so clearly the absurdity of their command. Therefore, all public ends look vague and quixotic beside private ones. For, any laws but those which men make for themselves, are laughable. If I put myself in the place of my child, and we stand in one thought, and see that things are thus or thus, that perception is law for him and me. We are both there, both act. But if, without carrying him into the thought, I look over into his plot, and, guessing how it is with him, ordain this or that, he will never obey me. This is the history of governments,— one man does something which is to bind another. A man who cannot be acquainted with me, taxes me; looking from afar at me, ordains that a part of my labor shall go to this or that whimsical end, not as I, but as he happens to fancy. Behold the consequence. Of all debts men are least willing to pay the taxes. What a satire is this on government! Everywhere they think they get their money's worth, except for these.

Hence the less government we have the better,—the fewer laws, and the less confided power. The antidote to this abuse of formal Government, is, the influence of private character, the growth of the Individual; the appearance of the principal to supersede the proxy; the appearance of the wise man, of whom the existing government is, it must be owned, but a shabby imitation. That which all things tend to educe, which freedom, cultivation, intercourse, revolutions, go to form and deliver, is character; that is the end of nature, to reach unto this coronation of her king. To educate the wise man, the State exists, and with the appearance of the wise man the State expires. The appearance of character makes the State unnecessary. The wise man is the State. He needs no army, fort, or navy,—he loves men too well; no bribe, or feast, or palace, to draw friends to him; no vantage ground, no favorable circumstance. He needs no library, for he has not done thinking; no church, for he is a prophet; no statute book, for he has the lawgiver; no money, for he is value; no road, for he is at home where he is; no experience, for the life of the creator shoots through him, and looks from his eyes. He has no personal friends, for he who has the spell to draw the prayer and piety of all men unto him, needs not husband and educate a few, to share with him a select and poetic life. His relation to men is angelic; his memory is myrrh to them; his presence, frankincense and flowers.

We think our civilization near its meridian, but we are yet only at the cock-crowing and the morning star. In our barbarous society the influence of character is in its infancy. As a political power, as the rightful lord who is to tumble all rulers from their chairs, its presence is hardly yet suspected. Malthus and Ricardo quite omit it; the Annual Register is silent; in the Conversations' Lexicon it is not set down; the President's Message, the Queen's Speech, have not mentioned it; and yet it is never nothing. Every thought which genius and piety throw into the world, alters the world. The gladiators in the lists of power feel, through all their frocks of force and simulation, the presence of worth. I think the very strife of trade and ambition is confession of this divinity; and successes in those fields are the poor amends, the fig-leaf with which the shamed soul attempts to hide its nakedness. I find the like unwilling homage in all quarters. It is because we know how much is due from us, that we are impatient to show some petty talent as a substitute for worth. We are haunted by a conscience of this right to grandeur of character, and are false to it. But each of us has some talent, can do somewhat useful, or graceful, or formidable, or amusing, or lucrative. That we do, as an apology to others and to ourselves for not reaching the mark of a good and equal life. But it does not satisfy *us*, whilst we thrust it on the notice of our companions. It may throw dust in their eyes, but does not smooth our own brow, or give us the tranquillity of the strong when we walk abroad. We do penance as we go. Our talent is a sort of expiation, and we are constrained to reflect on our splendid moment, with a certain humiliation, as somewhat too fine, and not as one act of many acts, a fair expression of our permanent energy. Most persons of ability meet in society with a kind of tacit appeal. Each seems to say, 'I am not all here.' Senators and presidents have climbed so high with pain enough, not because they think the place specially agreeable, but as an apology for real worth, and to vindicate their manhood in our eyes. This conspicuous chair is their compensation to themselves for being of a poor, cold, hard nature. They must do what they can. Like one class of forest animals, they have nothing but a prehensile tail: climb they must, or crawl. If a man found himself so rich-natured that he could enter into strict relations with the best persons, and make life serene around him by the dignity and sweetness of his behavior, could he afford to circumvent the favor of the caucus and the press, and covet relations so hollow and pompous, as those of a politician? Surely nobody would be a charlatan, who could afford to be sincere.

The tendencies of the times favor the idea of self-government, and leave the individual, for all code, to the rewards and penalties of his own constitution, which work with more energy than we believe, whilst we depend on artificial restraints. The movement in this direction has been very marked in modern history. Much has been blind and discreditable, but the nature of the revolution is not affected by the vices of the revolters; for this is a purely moral force. It was never adopted by any party in history, neither can be. It separates the individual from all party, and unites him, at the same time, to the race. It promises a recognition of higher rights than those of personal freedom, or the security of property. A man has a right to be employed, to be trusted, to be loved, to be revered. The power of love, as the basis of a State, has never been tried. We must not imagine that all things are lapsing into confusion, if every tender protestant be not compelled to bear his part in certain social conventions: nor doubt that roads can be built, letters carried, and the fruit of labor secured, when the government of force is at an end. Are our methods now so excellent that all competition is hopeless? could not a nation of friends even devise better ways? On the other hand, let not the most conservative and timid fear anything from a premature surrender of the bayonet, and the system of force. For, according to the order of nature, which is quite superior to our will, it stands thus; there will always be a government of force, where men are selfish; and when they are pure enough to abjure the code of force, they will be wise enough to see how these public ends of the post-office, of the highway, of commerce and the exchange of property, of museums and libraries, of institutions of art and science, can be answered.

We live in a very low state of the world, and pay unwilling tribute to governments founded on force. There is not, among the most religious and instructed men of the most religious and civil nations, a reliance on the moral sentiment, and a sufficient belief in the unity of things, to persuade them that society can be maintained without artificial restraints, as well as the solar system; or that the private citizen might be reasonable, and a good neighbor, without the hint of a jail or a confiscation. What is strange too, there never was in any man sufficient faith in the power of rectitude, to inspire him with the broad design of renovating the State on the principle of right and love. All those who have pretended this design, have been partial reformers, and have admitted in some manner the supremacy of the bad State. I do not call to mind a single human being who has steadily denied the authority of the laws, on the simple ground of his own moral nature. Such designs, full of genius and full of faith as they are, are not entertained except avowedly as air-pictures. If the individual who exhibits them, dares to think them practicable, he disgusts scholars and churchmen; and men of talent, and women of superior sentiments, cannot hide their contempt. Not the less does nature continue to fill the heart of youth with suggestions of this enthusiasm, and there are now men,—if indeed I can speak in the plural number,—more exactly, I will say, I have just been conversing with one man, to whom no weight of adverse experience will make it for a moment appear impossible, that thousands of human beings might exercise towards each other the grandest and simplest sentiments, as well as a knot of friends, or a pair of lovers.

HENRY DAVID THOREAU

The guiding passion in the life of Thoreau was nature. He disliked civilization and cities, and consequently secluded himself at his Walden hut. Like Garrison, he was a radical abolitionist. Slavery he considered to be contrary to nature and individualism. He carried his hostility against slavery over to the State, which he felt made slavery possible and stifled individualism. His essay on *Civil Disobedience* is a masterpiece of philosophical anarchism. Thoreau practiced what he preached. At one time he went to prison rather than pay taxes to the State. He advocated passive resistance rather than violent opposition to government.

CIVIL DISOBEDIENCE [87]

(1849)

I heartily accept the motto,—"That government is best which governs least"; and I should like to see it acted up to more rapidly and systematically. Carried out, it finally amounts to this, which also I believe,—"That government is best which governs not at all"; and when men are prepared for it, that will be the kind of government which they will have. Government is at best but an expedient; but most governments are usually, and all governments are sometimes, inexpedient. The objections which have been brought against a standing army, and they are many and weighty, and deserve to prevail, may also at last be brought against a standing government. The standing army is only an arm of the standing government. The government itself, which is only the mode which the people have chosen to execute their will, is equally liable to be abused and perverted before the people can act through it. Witness the present Mexican war, the work of comparatively a few individuals using the standing government as their tool; for, in the outset, the people would not have consented to this measure.

This American government,—what is it but a tradition, though a recent one, endeavoring to transmit itself unimpaired to posterity, but each instant losing some of its integrity? It has not the vitality and force of a single living man; for a single man can bend it to his will. It is a sort of wooden gun to the people themselves. But it is not the less necessary for this; for the people must have some complicated machinery or other, and hear its din, to satisfy that idea of government which they have. Governments

[87] H. D. Thoreau, *A Yankee in Canada, with Anti-Slavery and Reform Papers*. (Boston, Ticknor and Fields, 1866), pp. 123–124, 127–130, 135–139.

show thus how successfully men can be imposed on, even impose on themselves, for their own advantage. It is excellent, we must all allow. Yet this government never of itself furthered any enterprise, but by the alacrity with which it got out of its way. *It* does not keep the country free. *It* does not settle the West. *It* does not educate. The character inherent in the American people has done all that has been accomplished; and it would have done somewhat more, if the government had not sometimes got in its way. For government is an expedient by which men would fain succeed in letting one another alone; and, as has been said, when it is most expedient, the governed are most let alone by it. Trade and commerce, if they were not made of India-rubber, would never manage to bounce over the obstacles which legislators are continually putting in their way; and, if one were to judge these men wholly by the effects of their actions and not partly by their intentions, they would deserve to be classed and punished with those mischievous persons who put obstructions on the railroads. . . .

How does it become a man to behave toward this American government to-day? I answer, that he cannot without disgrace be associated with it. I cannot for an instant recognize that political organization as *my* government which is the *slave's* government also.

All men recognize the right of revolution; that is, the right to refuse allegiance to, and to resist, the government, when its tyranny or its inefficiency are great and unendurable. But almost all say that such is not the case now. But such was the case, they think, in the Revolution of '75. If one were to tell me that this was a bad government because it taxed certain foreign commodities brought to its ports, it is most probable that I should not make an ado about it, for I can do without them. All machines have their friction; and possibly this does enough good to counterbalance the evil. At any rate, it is a great evil to make a stir about it. But when the friction comes to have its machine, and oppression and robbery are organized, I say, let us not have such a machine any longer. In other words, when a sixth of the population of a nation which has undertaken to be the refuge of liberty are slaves, and a whole country is unjustly overrun and conquered by a foreign army, and subjected to military law, I think that it is not too soon for honest men to rebel and revolutionize. What makes this duty the most urgent is the fact that the country so overrun is not our own, but ours is the invading army.

Paley, a common authority with many on moral questions, in his chapter on the "Duty of Submission to Civil Government," resolves all civil obligation into expediency; and he proceeds to say, "that so long as the interest of the whole society requires it, that is, so long as the established government cannot be resisted or changed without public inconveniency, it is the will of God that the established government be obeyed, and no longer. . . . This principle being admitted, the justice of every particular case of resistance is reduced to a computation of the quantity of the danger and grievance on the one side, and of the probability and expense of redressing it on the other." Of this, he says, every man shall judge for himself. But Paley appears never to have contemplated those cases to which the rule of expediency does not apply, in which a people, as well as an individual, must do justice, cost what it may. If I have unjustly wrested a plank from a drowning man,

I must restore it to him though I drown myself. This, according to Paley, would be inconvenient. But he that would save his life, in such a case, shall lose it. This people must cease to hold slaves, and to make war on Mexico, though it cost them their existence as a people.

In their practice, nations agree with Paley; but does any one think that Massachusetts does exactly what is right at the present crisis?

"A drab of state, a cloth-o'-silver slut,
To have her train borne up, and her soul trail in the dirt."

Practically speaking, the opponents to a reform in Massachusetts are not a hundred thousand politicians at the South, but a hundred thousand merchants and farmers here, who are more interested in commerce and agriculture than they are in humanity, and are not prepared to do justice to the slave and to Mexico, *cost what it may*. I quarrel not with far-off foes, but with those who, near home, coöperate with, and do the bidding of, those far away, and without whom the latter would be harmless. We are accustomed to say, that the mass of men are unprepared; but improvement is slow, because the few are not materially wiser or better that the many. It is not so important that many should be as good as you, as that there be some absolute goodness somewhere; for that will leaven the whole lump. There are thousands who are *in opinion* opposed to slavery and to the war, who yet in effect do nothing to put an end to them; who, esteeming themselves the children of Washington and Franklin, sit down with their hands in their pockets, and say that they know not what to do, and do nothing; who even postpone the question of freedom to the question of free-trade, and quietly read the prices-current along with the latest advices from Mexico, after dinner, and, it may be, fall asleep over them both. What is the price-current of an honest man and patriot to-day? They hesitate, and they regret, and sometimes they petition; but they do nothing in earnest and with effect. They will wait, well disposed, for others to remedy the evil, that they may no longer have it to regret. At most, they give only a cheap vote, and a feeble countenance and God-speed, to the right, as it goes by them. There are nine hundred and ninety-nine patrons of virtue to one virtuous man. But it is easier to deal with the real possessor of a thing than with the temporary guardian of it.

All voting is a sort of gaming, like checkers or backgammon, with a slight moral tinge to it, a playing with right and wrong, with moral questions; and betting naturally accompanies it. The character of the voters is not staked. I cast my vote, perchance, as I think right; but I am not vitally concerned that right should prevail. I am willing to leave it to the majority. Its obligation, therefore, never exceeds that of expediency. Even voting *for the right* is *doing* nothing for it. It is only expressing to men feebly your desire that it should prevail. A wise man will not leave the right to the mercy of chance, nor wish it to prevail through the power of the majority. There is but little virtue in the action of masses of men. When the majority shall at length vote for the abolition of slavery, it will be because they are indifferent to slavery, or because there is but little slavery left to be abolished by their vote. *They* will then be the only slaves. Only *his* vote can hasten the abolition of slavery who asserts his own freedom by his vote. . . .

I meet this American government, or its representative, the state government, directly, and face to face, once a year—no more—in the person of its tax-gatherer; this is the only mode in which a man situated as I am neces-sarily meets it; and it then says distinctly, Recognize me; and the simplest, the most effectual, and, in the present posture of affairs, the indispensablest mode of treating with it on this head, of expressing your little satisfaction with and love for it, is to deny it then. My civil neighbor, the tax-gatherer, is the very man I have to deal with,—for it is, after all, with men and not with parchment that I quarrel,—and he has voluntarily chosen to be an agent of the government. How shall he ever know well what he is and does as an officer of the government, or as a man, until he is obliged to consider whether he shall treat me, his neighbor, for whom he has respect, as a neigh-bor and well-disposed man, or as a maniac and disturber of the peace, and see if he can get over this obstruction to his neighborliness without a ruder and more impetuous thought or speech corresponding with his action. I know this well, that if one thousand, if one hundred, if ten men whom I could name,—if ten *honest* men only,—ay, if *one* HONEST man, in this State of Massachusetts, *ceasing to hold slaves*, were actually to withdraw from this copartnership, and be locked up in the county jail therefor, it would be the abolition of slavery in America. For it matters not how small the beginning may seem to be: what is once well done is done forever. But we love better to talk about it: that we say is our mission. Reform keeps many scores of newspapers in its service, but not one man. If my esteemed neighbor, the State's ambassador, who will devote his days to the settlement of the ques-tion of human rights in the Council Chamber, instead of being threatened with the prisons of Carolina, were to sit down the prisoner of Massachusetts, that State which is so anxious to foist the sin of slavery upon her sister,— though at present she can discover only an act of inhospitality to be the ground of a quarrel with her,—the Legislature would not wholly waive the subject the following winter.

Under a government which imprisons any unjustly, the true place for a just man is also a prison. The proper place to-day, the only place which Massachusetts has provided for her freer and less desponding spirits, is in her prisons, to be put out and locked out of the State by her own act, as they have already put themselves out by their principles. It is there that the fugitive slave, and the Mexican prisoner on parole, and the Indian come to plead the wrongs of his race should find them; on that separate, but more free and honorable ground, where the State places those who are not *with* her, but *against* her,—the only house in a slave State in which a free man can abide with honor. If any think that their influence would be lost there, and their voices no longer afflict the ear of the State, that they would not be as an enemy within its walls, they do not know by how much truth is stronger than error, nor how much more eloquently and effectively he can combat injustice who has experienced a little in his own person. Cast your whole vote, not a strip of paper merely, but your whole influence. A minority is powerless while it conforms to the majority; it is not even a minority then; but it is irresistible when it clogs by its whole weight. If the alternative is to keep all just men in prison, or give up war and slavery, the State will not hesitate which to choose. If a thousand men were not to pay their tax-bills this year, that would not be a violent and bloody measure, as it would be to pay them, and enable the State to commit violence and shed innocent blood. This is, in fact, the definition of a peaceable revolution, if any such is possible. If the tax-gatherer, or any other public officer, asks me, as one has done, "But what shall I do?" my answer is, "If you really wish to do anything, resign your office." When the subject has refused allegiance, and the officer has resigned his office, then the revolution is accomplished. But even suppose blood should flow. Is there not a sort of blood shed when the conscience is wounded? Through this wound a man's real manhood and immortality flow out, and he bleeds to an everlasting death. I see this blood flowing now.

I have contemplated the imprisonment of the offender, rather than the seizure of his goods,—though both will serve the same purpose,—because they who assert the purest right, and consequently are most dangerous to a corrupt State, commonly have not spent much time in accumulating property. To such the State renders comparatively small service, and a slight tax is wont to appear exorbitant, particularly if they are obliged to earn it by special labor with their hands. If there were one who lived wholly without the use of money, the State itself would hesitate to demand it of him. But the rich man—not to make any invidious comparison—is always sold to the institution which makes him rich. Absolutely speaking, the more money, the less virtue; for money comes between a man and his objects, and obtains them for him; and it was certainly no great virtue to obtain it. It puts to rest many questions which he would otherwise be taxed to answer; while the only new question which it puts is the hard but superfluous one, how to spend it. Thus his moral ground is taken from under his feet. The opportunities of living are diminished in proportion as what are called the "means" are increased. The best thing a man can do for his culture when he is rich is to endeavor to carry out those schemes which he entertained when he was poor. Christ answered the Herodians according to their condition. "Show me the tribute-money," said he;—and one took a penny out of his pocket;—if you use money which has the image of Caesar on it, and which he has made current and valuable, that is, *if you are men of the State*, and gladly enjoy the advantages of Caesar's government, then pay him back some of his own when he demands it. "Render therefore to Caesar that which is Caesar's, and to God those things which are God's,"—leaving them no wiser than before as to which was which; for they did not wish to know.

When I converse with the freest of my neighbors, I perceive that, whatever they may say about the magnitude and seriousness of the question, and their regard for the public tranquillity, the long and the short of the matter is, that they cannot spare the protection of the existing government, and they dread the consequences to their property and families of disobedience to it. For my own part, I should not like to think that I ever rely on the protection of the State. But, if I deny the authority of the State when it presents its tax-bill, it will soon take and waste all my property, and so harass me and my children without end. This is hard. This makes it impossible for a man to live honestly, and at the same time comfortably, in outward respects. It will not be worth the while to accumulate property; that would be sure to go again. You must hire or squat somewhere, and raise but a small crop, and eat that soon. You must live within yourself, and depend upon yourself always tucked up and ready for a start, and not have many affairs. A man may grow rich in Turkey even, if he will be in all respects a good subject of the Turkish government. Confucius said: "If a state is governed by the principles of reason, poverty and misery are subjects of shame; if a state is not governed by the principles of reason, riches and honors are the subjects of shame." No: until I want the protection of Massachusetts to be extended to me in some distant Southern port, where my liberty is endangered, or until I am bent solely on building up an estate at home by peaceful enterprise, I can afford to refuse allegiance to Massachusetts, and her right to my property and life. It costs me less in every sense to incur the penalty of disobedience to the State than it would to obey. I should feel as if I were worth less in that case. . . .

SELECTED BIBLIOGRAPHY

T. H. Benton, *Thirty Years' View* (2 vols., 1854–1857).

G. Chinard, *Thomas Jefferson: Apostle of Americanism* (1929).

R. W. Emerson, *Essays* (1855).

T. Jefferson, *Works* (edited by H. A. Washington, 1861).

J. Taylor, *An Inquiry into the Principles and Policy of the Government of U. S.* (1814).
    Construction Construed and Constitution Vindicated (1820).
    Tyranny Unmasked (1922).
    New Views on the Constitution (1823).

H. D. Thoreau, *Civil Disobedience* (1849).

F. J. Turner, *The Frontier in American History* (1920).

W. Whitman, *Leaves of Grass* (1855).
    Democratic Vistas (1870).

B. F. Wright, Jr., "The Philosopher of Jeffersonian Democracy," *American Political Science Review*, 22: 870–892, November, 1928.

CHAPTER V

SLAVERY

I

Not until after 1830 did the slavery controversy come into the foreground of American politics. At the end of the eighteenth century, there had been a decided sentiment in the South against slavery. The representatives from that section had permitted Congress to prohibit the importation of negroes, and a movement for manumission had gained headway. Washington and Jefferson had freed their slaves. The economic unprofitableness of slave labor seemed likely to bring the institution to an end. The Missouri Compromise of 1820, thought the politicians and the people, had settled the dispute for all time to come. Nevertheless, in the second quarter of the nineteenth century slavery became, as it long remained, a vital political issue. What caused this new situation?

In the first place, an economic revolution made slavery profitable. During the eighteenth century the principal problem of cotton culture had been the removal of the seed from the fiber. The slaves could at that time perform this operation only by hand. The slowness of the task cut into the profits of the plantation owners and discouraged extensive cultivation. Furthermore, hand picking of the seed, slow as it was, was possible only on the long-fibered or sea-island cotton. The inland, short-fibered variety remained unprofitable. Sea-island cotton, however, grew only upon a narrow stretch of the Atlantic coast. Nature thus placed a definite limitation upon the expansion of cotton culture. But an ingenious Yankee broke down this barrier; in 1793 Ely Whitney invented a mechanical cotton gin. Not only did his machine greatly speed the process of removing seed from fiber, but it could also gin the short-fibered cotton. The latter variety now became profitable. And, as it could be grown remote from the coast, Whitney's invention led to a rapid extension of cotton cultivation into the uplands of the South and Southwest.

Meanwhile, another economic change augmented the demand for raw cotton. At the end of the eighteenth century a series of mechanical devices revolutionized the textile industry of England. The application of power to machinery speeded the production and cheapened the price of cotton cloth. The demand for such cloth grew by leaps and bounds. By 1815 this same industrial revolution reached New England. The new factories demanded larger supplies of raw cotton. Whitney's cotton gin made possible the satisfaction of this demand. As more mills raised their walls in Manchester and Lowell, more cotton pushed itself out of the soil of the new South. In the years of 1791–1795 the South produced annually only slightly over five million pounds of cotton. In the period 1800–1805 the effect of the cotton gin was conspicuous; the annual yield averaged almost sixty million pounds. By 1835, production amounted to four hundred million; and by 1856, to one and a third billion pounds.[1] Truly, cotton was king.

With the revitalization of the cotton industry, slavery became profitable. It was, indeed, admirably adapted to cotton cultivation. The raising of cotton called for no complicated or difficult technique; it demanded few tools and little equipment. The simplicity of operation suited slave mentality. Once the negro learned the easy methods of planting and picking cotton, he merely repeated them mechanically year after year. The plantations, moreover, specialized in a single crop; the slave need not bother with the technique of raising different plants, as is necessary in truck farming. The southern climate, finally, made the maintenance of slave labor inexpensive. The cost of negro subsistence ranged from fifteen to forty dollars a year. With the expansion of cotton cultivation, a remarkable increase in slave population occurred. Although Congress in 1807 prohibited further importation of slaves, their numbers continued to grow. The border states, especially Virginia and Maryland, had exhausted the fertility of their soil; they now undertook the breeding of negroes. Their surplus supply they sold at high prices to the cotton planters further south and west. In 1800 the negro population totaled only one million. By 1820 the number had increased by three-quarters of a million. The census of 1840 showed a growth of over another million; and in 1860 almost four and a half million negroes lived in the United States.[2]

The second important explanation for the new rôle of slavery in politics is the humanitarian movement of the thirties. The widespread European revolutions of 1830, with their emphasis upon the rights of man and human brotherhood, produced a repercussion on these shores almost as sharp as did the first French Revolution. Men became interested in human values and rights. All the leaders

[1] Faulkner, *American Economic History*, p. 223.   [2] *Ibid.*, p. 225.

of the intellectual democracy were ardent in their opposition to slavery. Northern writers now turned their attention toward the slave institution and aroused a certain mild hostility against it. As a result of the new humanitarianism, the rabid abolition movement gained considerable headway. The bitter attacks of Garrison's speeches, *The Liberator*, and the National Anti-Slavery Society aroused the South. The plantation owners had discovered profit in slavery. The agitation against their labor system frightened them, lest they lose their property. Southern presses worked overtime to print counter-propaganda. And southern politicians resented and resisted the slightest attack upon their peculiar institution. Just as the Federalists under Adams had erred in enacting the stifling Alien and Sedition Acts, the southern politicians erred in foisting stringent fugitive slave laws upon the North. The capture and rendition of escaped negroes drove the problem of slavery home to the northerners and directed the existing humanitarian sentiment toward the slave.

In the third place, the territorial expansion of the United States made slavery the vital issue. Had the territory of the country remained that of the original thirteen states, no problem would have developed. In 1787 a political equilibrium had existed between the North and South. Neither could control the councils of the federal government. Such a limitation of territory would also have prevented the expansion of cotton cultivation, and the exhaustion of the soil by cheap slave labor would soon have rendered slavery unprofitable. The purchase of Louisiana in 1803 and the invention of the cotton gin, however, opened a vast, fertile territory for cotton and slavery. As the planters of the old South exhausted their soil by unscientific methods, they moved to the virgin lands of the Southwest. In their hunger for land, the southern leaders became imperialists. They won the independence of Texas from Mexico and, aided by speculators in Texan securities, secured its annexation to the Union. They compelled the federal government to fight the Mexican War and to wrest a vast territory from that country. Had they secured their way entirely, the southern leaders would have taken all of Mexico. Southern imperialists turned their eyes towards the Caribbean, and under their stimuli filibustering expeditions set out for Cuba and Central America. In the famous Ostend Manifesto of 1854, three American ministers abroad threatened seizure of Cuba from Spain. This territorial expansion destroyed the original political equilibrium between the North and the South.

A conflict of economic systems now occurred. While the South expanded its cotton culture, the North grew industrially. The War of 1812 had turned capital from commerce to manufacturing. The textile mills of New England and the iron foundries of Pennsylvania increased rapidly. The new industries demanded tariff protection against European competition. But the agricultural South had no desire to pay duties. Its principal market for cotton was England, and from England the planters imported cheap clothing for their slaves. A clash of economic interests thus occurred. So bitter did the conflict become that South Carolina threatened armed nullification against the tariff acts of 1828 and 1832.

The territorial expansion of the country vitally affected this farm-factory conflict. The admission of each new state into the Union tended to upset the original political equilibrium. Each new slave state certainly meant two additional votes in the Senate and at least one more seat in the House of Representatives in favor of free trade. The addition of a free state might possibly mean more tariff support. Thus the slavery question was irretrievably entangled in the net of a tariff controversy. The intelligent political leaders well understood this economic connection. In a speech in the Senate, Jefferson Davis turned to the northerners and free-soil advocates and asked:

"Do you propose to better the conditions of the slave? Not at all. What then do you propose? You say you are opposed to the expansion of slavery. . . . Is the slave to be benefited by it? Not at all. It is not humanity that influences you in the position which you now occupy before the country. . . . It is that you may have an opportunity of cheating us that you want to limit slave territory within circumscribed bounds. It is that you may have a majority in the Congress of the United States and convert the Government into an engine of northern aggrandizement. It is that your section may grow in power and prosperity upon treasures unjustly taken from the South, like the vampire bloated and gorged with the blood which it has secretly sucked from its victim. . . . You desire to weaken the political power of the southern states; and why? Because you want, by an unjust system of legislation, to promote the industry of the New England states, at the expense of the people of the South and their industry." [3]

Similarly, an economic conflict between two incompatible labor systems occurred in the West. The free farmers of the Ohio Valley constantly looked westward to the more fertile lands of Nebraska and Kansas. Much to their anguish, they saw the new territories filling up with cotton and slaves. The free farmers could not afford slaves; nor could they adapt wheat and corn raising to such cheap labor. They thus could not and did not desire to adopt the southern

[3] Quoted: Beard, *Rise of American Civilization*, II, 5–6.

economic system. And, on the other hand, they refused to work beside negroes and to suffer that loss of dignity in labor that characterizes a slave society. They wanted land, but land exclusively for their
own economic and social institutions. Thus the agrarian Northwest
joined with the industrial Northeast in attacking the spread of
slavery and cotton. The bitter political controversy over slavery was
the consequence of the territorial growth of the United States and
the resulting breakdown of the political equilibrium. An economic
war existed between cotton culture, on the one hand, and industrialism and free agriculture, on the other.

II

In the fight against slavery, three schools of thought grew up:
(1) a radical abolitionism under Garrison's leadership, (2) a free-
soilism, typified by Lincoln, and (3) a philosophical attack led by
Channing and Wayland. The abolitionists and the philosophers felt
the force of humanitarianism; free-soilism was predominantly economic and social. The Garrison and Lincoln groups made no attempts
to get at basic premises; they felt instinctively that slavery was an
evil. Channing and Wayland attacked slavery with a thoroughgoing
analysis of its logical fallacies and consequential dangers; they supplied the arguments for the propagandists of the other two groups.

The radical abolitionists demanded the immediate emancipation
of the negro. They looked upon liberty as an innate faculty and birth-
right of man. It is not a privilege to be enjoyed under favorable
conditions, nor does it require training for its effective exercise.

"Liberty being the birthright of every man, the natural and normal condition of his existence, all the preparation he needs for its enjoyment is born
with him. He gets his fitness for liberty as he gets his hands and feet—not
by education, but by inheritance." [4]

The National Anti-Slavery Society, in its platform of 1833, held
that no man has a right to enslave his brother, to hold or acknowledge
him for one moment as a piece of merchandise. No man may morally
brutalize the mind of another by denying him the means of intellectual, social, and moral improvement. "The right to enjoy liberty is
inalienable. To invade it is to usurp the prerogative of Jehovah."
Every man possesses a right to his own body, to the products of his
own labor, to the protection of law, and to the common advantages
of society. If it is piracy to buy or steal a native African, then the

[4] W. Hosmer, *The Higher Law*, pp. 149–150.

sin is as great to enslave an American negro.[5] All persons of color, who possess the qualifications which are demanded of others, ought to be admitted to the enjoyment of the same privileges and the exercise of the same prerogatives as others.[6]

The abolitionists made effective use of the preamble to the Declaration of Independence. The National Anti-Slavery Convention in Philadelphia struck this keynote:

"More than fifty-seven years have elapsed, since a band of patriots convened in this place, to devise measures for the deliverance of this country from a foreign yoke. The corner-stone upon which they founded the Temple of Freedom was broadly this—'that all men are created equal; that they are endowed by their Creator with certain inalienable rights; that among these are life, LIBERTY, and the pursuit of happiness.' At the sound of their trumpet-call, three millions of people rose up as from the sleep of death, and rushed to the strife of blood; deeming it more glorious to die instantly as freemen, than desirable to live one hour as slaves."[7]

Garrison, in his opening issue of *The Liberator*, was equally vigorous.

"Assenting to the 'self-evident truth' maintained in the American Declaration of Independence, 'that all men are created equal, and endowed by their Creator with certain inalienable rights—among which are life, liberty, and the pursuit of happiness,' I shall strenuously contend for the immediate enfranchisement of our slave population. . . . I am aware that many object to the severity of my language; but is there not cause for severity? I will be as harsh as truth, and as uncompromising as justice. On this subject, I do not wish to think, or speak, or write, with moderation. . . . Urge me not to use moderation in a cause like the present! I am in earnest. I will not equivocate—I will not excuse—I will not retreat a single inch—AND I WILL BE HEARD."[8]

The abolitionists advocated immediate emancipation of all slaves. Garrison refused to countenance delay.

"Gradualism in theory is perpetuality in practice."
"There must be no compromise with slavery—none whatever. Nothing is gained, every thing is lost, by subordinating principle to expediency. The spirit of freedom must be inexorable in its demand for the instant release of all who are sighing in bondage, nor abate one jot or tittle of its righteous claims."[9]

Nor would the abolitionists compensate the planters for their slaves; that would be a surrender of the great fundamental principle that man cannot hold property in man. Since the slave-holders are not the just proprietors of what they claim, freeing the slaves does not deprive them of property; rather it restores property to its rightful

[5] Garrison, *Selections from the Writings and Speeches of W. L. Garrison*, p. 68.
[6] *Ibid.*, p. 69.
[7] *Ibid.*, p. 66.
[8] *Ibid.*, pp. 62–63.
[9] *Ibid.*, p. 140.

owner by returning the negro to himself. "If compensation is to be given at all, it should be given to the outraged and guiltless slaves, and not to those who have plundered and abused them." [10]

The harshness of the abolitionists led to public hostility against them. Garrison attacked all who opposed immediate and unconditional emancipation. The keenness of his darts pierced the complacency of the comfortable bourgeoisie. Never has a radical agitator received enthusiastic support; he is too disturbing to men's peace of mind. Garrison and his colleagues met violent opposition and attack. Mobs, in many cases engineered by northerners who were profiting from slavery, broke up his meetings. His enemies wrecked the office of *The Liberator*, and only police intervention saved Garrison from a lynching. The authorities of Boston threw him into prison to preserve the public peace. These experiences naturally engendered hostility among the abolitionists against the political state. Furthermore, they clearly saw that government maintained slavery. The force of its army prevented the negroes from freeing themselves; its police captured and returned escaped slaves; its agents hampered the activities of the abolition organizations. Garrison and his group became virtual anarchists. They attacked government in general, and the federal Union in particular.

Human governments, held Garrison, result from disobedience to the requirements of heaven.

"They are better than anarchy just as a hail-storm is preferable to an earthquake, or the small-pox to the Asiatic cholera."
"Shall we, *as Christians*, applaud and do homage to human government? or shall we not rather lay the axe at the root of the tree, and attempt to destroy both cause and effect together?" [11]

The Peace Convention of 1838 declared that every human government is upheld by physical strength, and its laws enforced virtually at the point of the bayonet.

"We therefore voluntarily exclude ourselves from every legislative and judicial body, and repudiate all human politics, worldly honors, and stations of authority. If *we* cannot occupy a seat in the legislature, or on the bench, neither can we elect *others* to act as our substitutes in any such capacity."

They refused to sue any man at law or to compel him by force to restore anything that he might wrongfully have taken. "If he has seized our coat, we shall surrender up our cloak, rather than subject

[10] Garrison, *Selections from the Writings of W. L. Garrison*, p. 69, Platform of National Anti-Slavery Society, 1833.
[11] *Life of W. L. Garrison, by His Children*, II, 150–151.

him to punishment." The convention went on record for non-resistance and passive submission.[12]

The abolitionists were by no means indefinite in their attack upon government; rather they demanded the dissolution of the Union and the destruction of the Constitution that sanctioned slavery.

"To say that this 'covenant with death' shall not be annulled—that this 'agreement with hell' shall continue to stand—that this 'refuge of lies' shall not be swept away—is to hurl defiance at the eternal throne, and to give the lie to Him who sits thereon." [13]

"The people of this country have bound themselves by an oath to have no other God before them than a CONSTITUTIONAL GOD, which their own hands have made, and to which they demand homage of every one born or resident on the American soil, on peril of imprisonment or death! His fiat is 'the supreme law of the land.'" [14]

Slavery, wrote Garrison, must be overthrown. No matter how numerous the difficulties, how formidable the obstacles, how strong the foes to be vanquished, slavery must cease to pollute the land. No matter whether by a peaceful or a bloody process, slavery must die. No matter if to effect it, every party should be torn by dissension, every sect dashed into fragments, the national compact dissolved,—still slavery must be buried in the grave of infamy beyond the possibility of a resurrection. If the state cannot survive the antislavery agitation, then let the state perish. If the American Union cannot be maintained save by sacrificing human freedom on the altar of tyranny, then let the American Union be consumed by a living thunderbolt, and no tear be shed over its ashes.

"If the Republic must be blotted out from the roll of nations, by proclaiming liberty to the captives, then let the Republic sink beneath the waves of oblivion, and a shout of joy, louder than the voice of many waters, fill the universe at its extinction." [15]

"Let the American Union perish; let these allied States be torn with factions, or drenched in blood; let this republic realize the fate of Rome and Carthage, or Babylon and Tyre." [16]

Man is superior to all political compacts and governmental arrangements. The freedom and happiness of the individual are the ends of human activity. The public good can never require the violent sacrifice of even the humblest citizen. To do evil that good may come, is absurd and criminal. If nations perish, it is not because of their devotion to liberty, but because of their disregard of its requirements.[17]

[12] Garrison, *Selections*, pp. 74, 75.
[13] *Ibid.*, p. 118.
[14] *Ibid.*, p. 304.

[15] *Ibid.*, pp. 138-139.
[16] *Ibid.*, p. 116.
[17] *Ibid.*, p. 117.

Under Garrison's influence, the National Anti-Slavery Society adopted a similar attitude. The highest obligations, they argued, rest upon the people of the free states to remove slavery by moral and political action. The people of the North are liable to be called at any moment to suppress a general insurrection of the slaves. They enable the slave owners to perpetuate their oppression by permitting them to count three-fifths of their slaves for national representation. Northern taxes support a standing army in the South; and their agents seize the slave who has escaped into their territories, and send him back to an enraged master or a brutal driver. "This relation to slavery is criminal, and full of danger. IT MUST BE BROKEN UP." [18]

Thoreau probably went furthest in his antagonism to government. "That government is best which governs not at all." [19] He asked:

"How does it become a man to behave toward this American government to-day? I answer, that he cannot without disgrace be associated with it. I cannot for an instant recognize that political organization as *my* government which is the slave's government also." [20]

Thoreau advanced an anarchist solution of the slavery problem—the non-participation in government. He argued:

"If one thousand, if one hundred, if ten men whom I could name,—if ten *honest* men only,—ay, if *one* HONEST man, in this State of Massachusetts, *ceasing to hold slaves*, were actually to withdraw from this copartnership, and be locked up in the county jail therefor, it would be the abolition of slavery in America." [21]

No such religious fervor characterized the free-soil attack upon slavery. Its origin and impetus were economic. The small farmers of the Northwest feared lest the expansion of slave territory cut them off from the fertile plains upon which they had set their hearts. The black cloud from the South threatened their economic future. Their frontier equalitarianism also produced a prejudice against slavery; the simplicity and freedom of their social life prevented that stratification of classes that underlies a slaveocracy. The free-soilers at first entertained no humanitarian regard for the negro. The Topeka Constitution of Kansas went so far as to bar all negroes, free as well as slave, from the new state. In their struggle for economic existence the small white farmer wanted no competition. Slavery must halt its march at its existing confines. As the conflict progressed, how-

[18] Garrison, *Selections*, p. 70.
[19] Thoreau, *A Yankee in Canada, with Anti-Slavery and Reform Papers*, p. 123.
[20] *Ibid.*, p. 127.   [21] *Ibid.*, p. 136.

ever, a spark of humanitarianism did light. The Congregationalist and Baptist ministers of the West, taught by Channing and Wayland, aroused resentment against the moral injustice of slavery. But until the eve of the Civil War, the free-soil arguments against slavery were but rationalizations of the western economic demands and social attitudes.

The Dred Scott decision had destroyed the possibility of a free-soil solution of the slavery problem on the basis of "squatter sovereignty." Under the leadership of Lincoln, the free-soilers developed an increasingly nationalist, and yet non-economic, attack upon slavery. Like the abolitionists, Lincoln and his followers turned to the Declaration of Independence. He would not grant Douglas's contention that the Declaration of 1776 applied only to the British colonists or, at the most, to white men. "The authors of that notable instrument, declared Lincoln, intended to include *all* men." They meant to set up a standard maxim for free society, which should be familiar to all and revered by all. They set up a goal which, though never perfectly attained, society would constantly approximate. The assertion that "all men are created equal" was of no practical use in effecting our separation from Great Britain. The framers placed it in the Declaration not for that purpose, but for future use. They meant it to be a stumbling-block to all those who in after times might seek to turn a free people back into the hateful paths of despotism.[22] That document declared that governments derive "their just powers from the consent of the governed." No man is good enough to govern another without his consent. This is the sheet-anchor of American republicanism.[23]

"In those days our Declaration of Independence was held sacred by all, and thought to include all; but now, to aid in making the bondage of the negro universal and eternal, it is assailed and sneered at and construed, and hawked at and torn, till, if its framers could rise from their graves, they would not recognize it." [24]

Lincoln did not demand for the negro entire equality with the white. The authors of the Declaration of Independence, he held, did not intend to declare all men equal in all respects. They did not mean to say that all were equal in color, size, intellect, moral development, or social capacity. They defined with tolerable distinctness in what respects they considered all men created equal: all men are

[22] Lincoln, *Works* (edited by Nicolay and Hay), I, 232. (New York, The Century Company.)

[23] *Ibid.*, I, 195.   [24] *Ibid.*, I, 231.

equal in the possession of "certain inalienable rights, among which
are life, liberty, and the pursuit of happiness." They did not mean
to assert the obvious untruth that all men were then actually enjoying that equality; they meant simply to declare the right, so that enforcement of it might follow as fast as circumstances should permit.[25]

Despite the application of this attack to the entire institution of
slavery, Lincoln demanded only that slavery be restricted to its
existing limits. The farmers of the West must have free scope in
their exploitation of the new territories. Not until the Civil War was
well under way did Lincoln change his attitude. Only once did he
make a speech that might be interpreted otherwise; even then he qualified his remarks; speaking in Springfield, on June 16, 1858, he said:

> "In my opinion it [agitation] will not cease until a crisis shall have been
> reached and passed. 'A house divided against itself cannot stand.' I believe
> this government cannot endure permanently half slave and half free. I
> do not expect the Union to be dissolved—I do not expect the house to fall—
> but I do expect it will cease to be divided. It will become all one thing, or
> all the other. Either the opponents of slavery will arrest the further spread
> of it, and place it where the public mind shall rest in the belief that it is in the
> course of ultimate extinction; or its advocates will push it forward till it
> shall become alike lawful in all the States, old as well as new, North as well
> as South." [26]

Until his election to the presidency, Lincoln was not an ardent abolitionist; rather he represented the economic interests and the social
equalitarianism of the western agrarian.

Of the three anti-slavery groups, the philosophical school alone
attempted to get at fundamental premises. They examined carefully
into the nature of man and society in order to ascertain whether
slavery was a proper institution. William Ellery Channing, a Unitarian divine, and Francis Wayland, a Baptist minister and president
of Brown University, led the mild opponents of slavery. Their
influence as leading clergymen and educators was immeasurable.
The churches of the North and the West felt the force of their teachings. While they differed in the development of their argument,
Channing and Wayland agreed in their general approach.

The starting point of Channing's attack was the proposition that
man is "a Rational, Moral, Immortal Being . . . created in God's
image, and therefore in the highest sense his child." No earthly or
celestial language can exaggerate the worth of a human being. In

[25] Lincoln, *Works*, I, 232.
[26] *Ibid.*, I, 240.

every human being, no matter how obscure, God has breathed an immortal spirit, "more precious than the whole outward creation."

"Thought, Reason, Conscience, the capacity of Virtue, the capacity of Christian Love, an immortal Destiny, an intimate connection with God,— here are attributes of our common humanity which reduce to insignificance all outward distinctions, and make every human being unspeakably dear to his Maker."

"Every human being has in him the germ of the greatest idea in the universe, the idea of God; and to unfold this is the end of his existence."

Every human being has in his breast the idea of duty and truth. He sees, however dimly, the great object of Divine intelligence and is capable of an ever-enlarging perception of duty and truth. "Every human being has affections, which may be purified and expanded into a Sublime Love." He has, too, the idea of happiness. Such is our nature. "Wherever we see a man, we see the possessor of these great capacities." [27] Such a being God made as an end in himself. He is a person, not a thing. He was made for his own virtues and happiness. He is an end in himself, not a mere instrument or means for the furtherance of the ends of others. The sacrifice of a person to another's will, "to another's present, outward, ill-comprehended good," is the greatest violence possible to any creature of God. "It is to degrade him from his rank in the universe, to make him a means, not an end, to cast him out from God's spiritual family into the brutal herd." [28] The end of man's existence is improvement. Action is the indispensable condition of progress to the intellect, conscience, and heart.[29]

Wayland, in his *Elements of Moral Science*, likewise depicted man as a moral being. "Every human being is a distinct and separate accountable individual." To each man God has given just such means of happiness and placed him under just such circumstances for improving these means of happiness as it has pleased him. So far as natural advantages are concerned, we can scarcely find two individuals who are not created under circumstances widely dissimilar. But, viewed in another light, all men possess perfect equality. The Creator fashioned each separate individual with precisely the same right as every other individual to use his advantages. The relation in which men stand to each other is essentially that of equality of rights.[30]

[27] Channing, *Works*, II, 26–27.
[28] *Ibid.*, II, 27–28.
[29] *Ibid.*, II, 28.
[30] Wayland, *Elements of Moral Science*, pp. 190–191.

Since man is a moral being, he possesses certain rights. Channing argued that every man has a right to exercise and invigorate his intellect or the power of knowledge, "for knowledge is the essential condition of successful effort for every good; and whoever obstructs or quenches the intellectual life in another, inflicts a grievous and irreparable wrong." Every man has a right to inquire into his duty, and to conform himself to what he learns of it. Every man has a right to use all the means sanctioned by virtue for bettering his condition. He has a right to be respected according to his moral worth, a right to be regarded as a member of the community to which he belongs. He has a right to protection by impartial laws and to exemption from coercion and punishment as long as he respects the rights of others. He has a right to his labor and to domestic relations.[31]

Wayland based his concept of rights upon the duty of reciprocity. Every man is under obligation to pursue his own happiness in such a manner only as will leave his neighbor in the undisturbed exercise of his rights. He must restrain his physical power of gratifying his desires within such limits that he shall interfere with the rights of no other being.[32] The simple fact that a being is a man places him within the reach of these obligations and of their protection.[33] All men are created with an equal right to employ their unequal faculties of body or mind in such manner as will promote their own happiness, provided they do not use them in such manner as to interfere with the rights of their neighbors.[34]

If man is a moral being, and if man, therefore, possesses rights, slavery obviously is wrong. It is plain that a human being cannot rightfully be owned by another, who claims, as proprietor, the right to repress the power of his slaves, to withhold from them the means of development, to keep them within the limits which are necessary to contentment in chains, to shut out every ray of light and every generous sentiment which may interfere with entire subjection to his will.[35]

Slavery is property in a human being. But the very concept of property runs counter to that of man as a moral being, as an end in himself. Property is an exclusive right; it shuts out all claims but that of the possessor. What one owns cannot belong to another. The consequence of holding a human being as property is that he can have no right to himself. His limbs are not his own.

[31] Channing, *Works*, II, 35.
[32] Wayland, *Elements of Moral Science*, p. 193.
[33] *Ibid.*, pp. 193–194.
[34] *Ibid.*, p. 204.
[35] Channing, *Works*, II, 28.

"His will, intellect, and muscles, all the powers of body and mind which are exercised in labor, he is bound to regard as another's. Now, if there be property in any thing, it is that of a man in his own person, mind, and strength." [36]

The very idea of a slave is that he belongs to another, that he is bound to live and labor for another, to be another's instrument, and to make another's will his habitual law. Another owns him and has a right to his time and strength, a right to the fruits of his labor. The master claims a right to work him without his consent, to determine the kind and duration of his toil, to confine him to any bounds, to extort the required work by stripes. In a word, a slave-holder uses a person as a tool, without contract, against his will, and in denial of his right to dispose of himself or to use his powers for his own good. [37] The very essence of slavery is to put a man defenseless into the hands of another.

"The right claimed by the master, to task, to force, to imprison, to whip, and to punish the slave, at discretion, and especially to prevent the least resistance to his will, is a virtual denial and subversion of all the rights of the victim of his power. The two cannot stand together." [38]

Slavery, wrote Wayland similarly, violates the personal liberty of man as a physical, intellectual, and moral being. Slavery proceeds upon the principle that the master has a right to control the actions, physical and intellectual, of the slave for the master's benefit. The happiness of the master, when it comes into conflict with that of the slave, extinguishes the rights of the latter. The slave has no rights at all over the means of happiness.

"Slavery purports to give to the master a right to control the physical labor of the slave, not for the sake of the happiness of the slave, nor upon terms mutually satisfactory to the parties, but for the sake of the happiness of the master. It subjects the amount of labor, and the kind of labor, and the remuneration for labor, entirely to the will of the one party, to the entire exclusion of the will of the other party."

If we concede this right in the master over the slave, then, of course, we must concede with it all other rights necessary to insure its possession. Hence, inasmuch as the slave can be held in servitude only while he remains in a state of comparative mental imbecility, the master has a right to control his intellectual development. Thus the slave has no right to use his intellect for the production of his own happiness. [39]

[36] Channing, *Works*, II, 22-23.
[37] *Ibid.*, II, 17.
[38] *Ibid.*, II, 20.
[39] Wayland, *Elements of Moral Science*, pp. 206-207.

Slavery thus violates the fundamental nature of man. It denies
that man is a rational and moral being, that he is a person, an end
in himself, that he possesses rights for the furtherance of his own
happiness. Slavery makes man property, an instrument to accomplish
the ends of others. Out of this corruption of man's nature, grow the
evils of slavery.

The first rank among the evils of slavery we must give to its moral
influence. Its effects are disastrous upon the morals of both parties.
By accustoming the slave to subject his moral principles to the will
of another, argued Wayland, slavery tends to abolish in him all moral
distinctions. It thus fosters lying, deceit, hypocrisy, dishonesty, and
a willingness to yield himself up to minister to the appetites of his
master.[40] Slavery, said Channing, destroys the proper consciousness
and spirit of a man. The extinction of his personality degrades the
slave from a man into a brute. The violation of his own rights, to
which the slave is inured from birth, throws confusion over his idea
of all human rights. He faintly apprehends the most common distinctions of morality. Respect for property can hardly be instilled
into him; his dishonesty is proverbial. Idleness, to his mind, is paradise, for he works always without hope of reward. Slavery thus
robs him of moral force and prepares him to fall prey to appetite and
passion. That the slave should yield himself to intemperance, licentiousness, and, in general, to sensual excess inevitably follows.[41]

By presenting objects on whom passion may be satiated without
resistance and without redress, slavery tends to cultivate in the
master pride, anger, cruelty, selfishness, and licentiousness.[42] Men's
worst crimes, maintained Channing, have sprung from the desire of
being masters, of bending others to their yoke.

"The natural tendency of bringing others into subjection to our absolute
will, is to quicken into fearful activity the imperious, haughty, proud, self-
seeking propensities of our nature." [43]

"To own the persons of others, to hold females in slavery, is necessarily
fatal to the purity of a people. That unprotected females, stripped by their
degraded condition of woman's self-respect, should be used to minister to
other passions in men than the love of gain, is next to inevitable. Accordingly, in such a community, the reins are given to youthful licentiousness.
. . . And the evil cannot stop at youth. . . . Domestic happiness is not
blighted in the slave's hut alone." [44]

[40] Wayland, *Elements of Moral Science*, pp. 207-208.
[41] Channing, *Works*, II, 60-63.
[42] Wayland, *Elements of Moral Science*, p. 207.
[43] Channing, *Works*, II, 79.
[44] *Ibid.*, II, 80-81.

Slavery, in the second place, is injurious to national wealth. Instead of imposing upon all the necessity of labor, it restricts the number of producers by rendering work disgraceful. It takes from the slave the natural stimulus to labor, namely, the desire to improve his condition, and substitutes that motive which is the least effective and the least constant—the fear of punishment, without the consciousness of moral delinquency. Slavery removes from both parties the disposition and the motives to frugality. The master does not learn frugality from the necessity of labor, nor the slave from the benefits which it confers. One party wastes from ignorance of the laws of acquisition and the other because he can have no motive to economy. Capital under such a system accumulates slowly, if at all. No country, unless of great fertility, can long sustain a large slave population. Slavery in this country has impoverished the soil; hence the migrations from the older settlements "to those new and untilled regions, where the accumulated manure of centuries of vegetation has formed a soil, whose productiveness may, for a while, sustain a system at variance with the laws of nature." [45]

And, in the third place, slavery is destructive to democracy. Free institutions rest on two great political virtues, the love of liberty and the love of order. The slave-holder is of necessity more or less wanting in both. "How plain is it, that no man can love liberty with a true love, who have the heart to wrest it from others!" Attachment to freedom does not consist in rejecting a yoke prepared for our own necks; rather it is a moral sentiment that others as well as ourselves may be protected from every unjust restraint. Slavery is at open war with this principle. Its habitual contempt for human rights impairs the sense of their sacredness. "It offers, every day and hour, a precedent of usurpation to the ambitious." It creates a caste with despotic powers and ignites a burning zeal not for the rights of man but for the privileges of class. Force, accustomed to triumph over right, is prone to leap every bound and to lead to a universal contempt for all human rights. Slavery is also hostile to the love of order. Slave-holding tends directly to lawlessness; it gives the habit of command, but not of obedience. The absolute master is not likely to subject himself to civil authority. The substitution of passion and self-will for law is nowhere so common as in the slave states. There it is thought honorable to rely on one's own arm, rather than on the magistrate, for the defense of rights. In many districts

[45] Wayland, *Elements of Moral Science*, p. 208.

"the chief peace-officer seems to be the weapon worn as part of the common dress." Such communities offer no pledge of stable liberty.[46]

III

In their defense of slavery the southern writers faced a difficult task. They encountered, even in their own territory, serious obstacles in the current social and political philosophy. They had to destroy the fundamental concepts of Jeffersonian democracy, which had dominated the old South for almost a half century. Jefferson had epitomized his ideas in the Declaration of Independence:

"That all men are created equal; that they are endowed by their Creator with certain inalienable rights; that among these are life, liberty, and the pursuit of happiness. That to secure these rights, governments are instituted among men, deriving their just powers from the consent of the governed."

This natural rights philosophy, with its emphasis on liberty and equality, was a stumbling-block to the exponents of slaveocracy. They had to remove the débris of the old order before they could construct their own positive social philosophy. To this difficult task the southern writers were, however, more than equal.

In their desire for the perpetuation of their social system, the southern leaders did not trust their pens alone. There were only ten thousand large slave owners; and over six million whites in the South owned no slaves at all. The upper class feared the propaganda of the abolitionists and took strong measures to keep out their literature. Southern postmasters destroyed abolition pamphlets sent through the mails. A number of states forbade the printing and distribution of attacks upon slavery. A Louisiana statute punished persons guilty of this heinous offense with life imprisonment or death. Everywhere there was a price on Garrison's head. With an eye to protecting the young, the guardians of the established order scrutinized school text-books that came from the North, and established their own intellectual center at Charleston. To warn the unsophisticated, they indexed the dangerous books.[47]

The intellectual leaders of the South turned their pens to an attack upon Jeffersonianism. Men, they held, are not created equal. Calhoun ridiculed the Declaration of Independence:

"Taking the proposition literally, there is not a word of truth in it. It begins with, 'all men are born,' which is utterly untrue. Men are not born. Infants are born. They grow to be men." [48]

[46] Channing, *Works*, II, 85–86.   [48] Calhoun, *Works*, IV, 507.
[47] Beard, *Rise of American Civilization*, I, 707.

The exponents of slavery looked about themselves and saw inequalities of all sorts. Some men are rich and others poor; some strong and others weak; some geniuses and others morons; some white and others black. Surely, the framers of the Declaration could not have meant what they said. Chancellor Harper was emphatic on this point. He asked:

"Is it not palpably nearer the truth to say that no man was ever born free, and that no two men were ever born equal? Man is born in a state of the most helpless dependence on others. He continues subject to the absolute control of others, and remains without many of the civil and all of the political privileges of his society, until the period which the laws have fixed as that at which he is supposed to have attained the maturity of his faculties. Then inequality is further developed, and becomes infinite in every society, and under whatever form of government. Wealth and poverty, fame or obscurity, strength or weakness, knowledge or ignorance, ease or labor, power or subjection, mark the endless diversity in the condition of men." [49]

Not only are men born unequal, but this very inequality is the essential condition for human progress. Calhoun, in his *Disquisition on Government*, made out a strong case for human inequality. While inequality of condition is a necessary consequence of liberty, it is, at the same time, indispensable to progress. The mainspring to progress is the desire of individuals to better their condition. The strongest impulse which we can give to progress is to leave individuals free to exert themselves in the manner they may deem best for that purpose and to secure the fruits of their exertions. Individuals differ greatly from each other in intelligence, sagacity, energy, perseverance, skill, habits of industry and economy, physical power, position, and opportunity. The necessary effect of leaving men free to exert themselves to better their conditions must be a corresponding inequality between those who possess these qualities and advantages in a high degree, and those who are deficient in them.

"It is, indeed, this inequality of condition between the front and rear ranks, in the march of progress, which gives so strong an impulse to the former to maintain their position, and to the latter to press forward into their files. This gives to progress its greatest impulse. To force the front ranks back to the rear, or attempt to push forward the rear into line with the front, by the interposition of the government, would put an end to the impulse, and effectually arrest the march of progress." [50]

---

[49] Chancellor Harper, *Slavery in the Light of Social Ethics;* in E. N. Elliott, *Cotton is King, and Pro-Slavery Arguments*, pp. 553–554.

[50] Calhoun, *Works*, I, 56–57.

The exponents of slavery similarly undermined the second prop of Jeffersonianism, the concept of liberty. Men are not born free; liberty is not a natural inheritance granted to every man. Rather, liberty is a condition dependent upon human development; it is a goal toward which men must struggle, and which only the most highly endowed can reach. It is a great and dangerous error, wrote Calhoun, to suppose that all people are equally entitled to liberty.

"It is a reward to be earned, not a blessing to be gratuitously lavished on all alike;—a reward reserved for the intelligent, the patriotic, the virtuous and deserving;—and not a boon to be bestowed on a people too ignorant, degraded and vicious, to be capable either of appreciating or of enjoying it. Nor is it any disparagement to liberty, that such is, and ought to be the case. On the contrary, its greatest praise,—its proudest distinction is, that an all-wise Providence has reserved it, as the noblest and highest reward for the development of our faculties, moral and intellectual. A reward more appropriate than liberty could not be conferred on the deserving;—nor a punishment inflicted on the undeserving more just, than to be subject to lawless and depotic rule. This dispensation seems to be the result of some fixed law;—and every effort to disturb or defeat it, by attempting to elevate a people in the scale of liberty, above the point to which they are entitled to rise, must ever prove abortive, and end in disappointment. The progress of a people rising from a lower to a higher point in the scale of liberty, is necessarily slow;—and by attempting to precipitate, we either retard, or permanently defeat it." [51]

Liberty, thus, when forced upon a people unfit for it, would prove a curse and not a blessing. Its reaction would lead directly to anarchy. Although it may possibly be true that a people may not have as much liberty as they are fairly entitled to and are capable of enjoying, yet the reverse is unquestionably true—that no people can long possess more liberty than they deserve. Moreover, while liberty is among the great blessings, it is not so great a blessing as protection. The end of liberty is the progress and improvement of the race; but the end of protection is preservation and perpetuation. Hence, when the two come into conflict, liberty must yield to protection, as the existence of the race is of greater moment than its improvement. [52]

Finally, the southern writers demolished the entire natural rights and social contract foundation of Jeffersonian democracy. This theory held that men had created government by their voluntary consent. They brought with them upon their entrance into civil society certain unimpaired rights that they had derived from the state of nature. These rights were independent of government, and government could not justly deprive men of them. George Fitzhugh

[51] Calhoun, *Works*, I, 55–56.   [52] *Ibid.*, I, 54–55.

refused to agree with the authors of the Declaration of Independence that "governments derive their just powers from the consent of the governed." He was a realist; no romanticism tinged his writings. The women, the children, the negroes, and but few of the non-property holders were consulted or consented to the Revolution and to the governments that followed from its success. As to them, the new governments originated in force and have been continued by force. Force is the basis of all government. The very term government implies that it is carried on against the consent of the governed. Fathers do not derive their authority, as heads of families, from the consent of their wives and children. Captains of ships are not appointed by the consent of the crew and never take their vote, even in "doubling Cape Horn." If they did, the crew would vote to get drunk. Not even in the most democratic countries are soldiers governed by their consent, nor is their vote taken on the eve of battle. They have somehow lost or never had the "inalienable rights of life, liberty, and the pursuit of happiness." Likewise, masters dare not take the vote of slaves as to their government; if they did, constant holiday, dissipation, and extravagance would result.[53] Physical force, not moral suasion, governs the world. Fitzhugh argued:

"The negro sees the driver's lash, becomes accustomed to obedient, cheerful industry, and is not aware that the lash is the force that impels him. The free citizen fulfills, 'con amore,' his round of social, political and domestic duties, and never dreams that the Law, with its fines and jails, penitentiaries and halters, or Public Opinion, with its ostracism, its mobs, and its tar and feathers, help to keep him revolving in his orbit. Yet, remove these physical forces, and how many good citizens would shoot like fiery comets, from their spheres, and disturb society with their eccentricities and their crimes."[54]

Similarly, Thomas Cooper argued that force is the basis of all rights. "The universal law of nature is force. By this law the lower animals are subdued to man, and the same law governs the relations between men."[55]

Chancellor Harper argued that society, not nature, grants human rights. He ridiculed the contention that society is guilty of violating God's moral law when it deprives men of life or liberty or restrains them in the pursuit of happiness. All the laws of society are intended for nothing else but to restrain men from the pursuit of happiness, according to their own ideas of happiness or advantage.

[53] Fitzhugh, *Cannibals All, or Slaves without Masters*, pp. 353–354.
[54] *Ibid.*, pp. 361–362.
[55] Thomas Cooper, *Lectures on the Elements of Political Economy*, p. 65.

"By what right does society punish by the loss of life or liberty? Not on account of the moral guilt of the criminal—not by impiously and arrogantly assuming the prerogative of the Almighty, to dispense justice or suffering, according to moral desert. It is for its own protection—it is the right of self-defense. . . . If an action, the most harmless in its moral character, could be dangerous to the security of society, society would have the perfect right to punish it. If the possession of a black skin would be otherwise dangerous to society, society has the same right to protect itself by disenfranchising the possessor of civil privileges, and to continue the disability to his posterity, if the same danger would be incurred by its removal. Society inflicts these forfeitures for the security of the lives of its members; it inflicts them for the security of their property, the great essential of civilization; it inflicts them also for the protection of its political institutions, the forcible attempt to overturn which, has always been justly regarded as the greatest crime; and who has questioned its right so to inflict?" [56]

The South possesses, he said, the same right to subject the negro as a people would have against a barbarian tribe on its borders, whom no treaties or faith could bind and whose attacks constantly endangered their security.[57]

Calhoun carefully analyzed the fundamental bases of society and government, and arrived at the conclusion that the state of nature is purely hypothetical and fictitious. Man is a social being. His inclinations and wants, physical and moral, irresistibly impel him to associate with other men. While man's social instincts demand human society, nevertheless, his selfish instincts predominate. Each has a greater regard for his own safety or happiness than for that of others. When these come into conflict, he is ready to sacrifice the interests of others to his own. Suspicion, jealousy, anger, revenge, fraud, and cruelty occur. Government is consequently necessary to enable men to live in society. Government is the natural consequence of man's character; it grows out of the clash between his social and selfish feelings.[58] Government did not originate artificially. A pregovernmental state of nature never did, nor can exist.

"Instead of being the natural state of man, it is, of all conceivable states, the most opposed to his nature—most repugnant to his feelings, and most incompatible with his wants. His natural state is, the social and political—the one for which his Creator made him, and the only one in which he can preserve and perfect his race."

Men are born in the social and political state and, instead of being born free and equal, are born subject, not only to parental authority, but also to the laws and institutions of their country.[59]

[56] Harper: in Elliott, *Cotton is King*, pp. 557–558.
[57] *Ibid.*, p. 558.
[58] Calhoun, *Works*, I, 1–5.
[59] *Ibid.*, I, 58–59.

Having removed the débris of Jeffersonianism, the exponents of slavery turned their attention to the construction of a new social philosophy. They were no longer apologetic toward slavery, but emphatic in their insistence upon its superiority. They drew heavily upon the old Greek experiences and writers. Athenian society, they knew, had been a slaveocracy; and Plato had founded his *Republic* upon servitude. They believed that they were establishing in the South the Greek ideal.

The first constructive argument of the southern writers was a thesis on the relationship of superior and inferior races. All men are not born equal, and liberty is "a reward reserved for the intelligent, the patriotic, the virtuous and deserving." The negroes, they held, are an inferior people too ignorant, degraded, and vicious to be capable of enjoying or appreciating liberty. J. C. Nott argued that the black man stands at the lowest point in the scale of human beings. He is essentially inferior in body and mind.[60] John Campbell quoted contemporary authorities in the scientific world to show that the racial characteristics of the negro stamped him as an inferior species.[61] De Bow contended that "the negro cannot be schooled, nor argued, nor driven into a love of freedom." [62] Thus the negro is unworthy of liberty and incapable of self-government. To rule him without his consent is no more an injustice than to govern a child.

Slavery, held the southern writers, is beneficial to the slave. The relationship between the white and black people is not that of master and slave, of oppressor and victim. Rather it is that of guardian and ward. The whites have a definite obligation toward the inferior race within their midst; they must do for the negro what he cannot do for himself. Laws of the state protect the slave and restrain the master so that he will truly be a guardian. Governor Hammond of South Carolina argued that "Providence has placed him in our hands for his good, and has paid us from his labor for our guardianship." [63]

[60] J. C. Nott, *Nature and Destiny of the Negro;* in J. D. B. De Bow, *The Industrial Resources of the Southern and Western States*, II, 308–310.

[61] In De Bow, *Industrial Resources*, II, 196. See also S. A. Cartwright, *Slavery in the Light of Ethnology*, in Elliott, *Cotton is King*.

[62] De Bow, *Industrial Resources*, II, 204.

[63] J. H. Hammond, *Slavery in the Light of Political Science;* in Elliott, *Cotton is King*, p. 638. It is interesting to note that this same principle forms the basis for the rationalization of modern imperialism. The American people are superior; we know the principles of order and government. Our neighbors in the Caribbean are incapable of peaceful government; they are an inferior people. Consequently, it is our divine duty to send marines there to instruct them and to raise their standards. Intervention is entirely magnanimous. Civilized states are charged with the "white men's burden"; their mission is that of the good samaritan. On this thesis the western nations have divided among themselves the "backward" countries of the world. The League of

The slave is not a victim of oppression; this guardianship is for his benefit. If the negro does not recognize the value of slavery to himself, that merely proves more conclusively his inferior intelligence.

Not only is slavery of benefit to the negro, argued the southern writers, but this social system is also invaluable for human progress. They turned their eyes back to the glorious days of Athenian culture. Slavery and a stratified society produced there a high degree of human development. The exponents of slavery looked into the works of Plato and Aristotle, and found a philosophical justification for stratification and slavery. In his Utopian *Republic*, Plato had divided society into four distinct classes: the guardians to rule the community, the warriors to protect it, the merchants and artisans to carry on its economic activities, and the slaves to do the menial labor. Such a division of labor, he argued, would produce the greatest economy of effort and lead to the maximum cultural growth.

The supporters of slaveocracy intended to construct a similar stratified society in the South. If society were organized on this basis, there would be three classes with well defined rank and standing: the highest, or the guiding and teaching group; the traders and free laborers, and perhaps small landowners from whom the skilled labor necessary to all groups would come; and the slaves at the bottom of the social ladder. Society would recruit professional men— lawyers, physicians, preachers, and teachers—from the small farmers, and even from the wealthier class. If every man remained in his place and performed the tasks expected from him, the greatest economy of effort and the highest possible civilization would result.[64]

In all social systems, argued Governor Hammond, there must be a class to do the mean duties, to perform the drudgery of life. Such a class you must have or you cannot have that other class which leads to progress, refinement, and civilization.[65] Harper contended that slavery anticipates the benefits of civilization. Property, or the accumulation of capital, is the first element of civilization. But to accumulate, or to use, capital to any considerable extent, combination of labor is necessary. In early stages of society, when people are thinly scattered over an extensive territory, men cannot command the labor necessary to extensive operations. Men are independent

Nations mandate system is rationalized on a similar conception of trusteeship. The "inferior people" now are those with a low culture rather than with poor biological equipment.

[64] W. E. Dodd, *The Cotton Kingdom*, p. 52. (Yale University Press.)

[65] Quoted: Beard, *Rise of American Civilization*, I, 693.

of each other. Having the command of abundant land, no one will labor for his neighbor. No one, therefore, can employ more capital than he can use with his own hands, or those of his family, nor have an income much beyond the necessaries of life. There can thus be little leisure for intellectual pursuits or means of acquiring the comforts or elegancies of life. But if a man commands slaves, he may combine labor and use capital to any required extent and therefore accumulate wealth.[66] Slavery thus produces leisure, and leisure makes for cultural progress.

There has never yet existed a wealthy and civilized society, asserted Calhoun in the Senate, in which one portion of the community did not, in point of fact, live on the labor of another.[67] Slavery is the most solid foundation for a sound society.

"Many in the South once believed that it was a moral and political evil. That folly and delusion are gone. We see it now in its true light, and regard it as the most safe and stable basis for free institutions in the world." [68]

Having demonstrated that social stratification is essential for progress, the slavery supporters convinced themselves that some sort of stratification always exists in civilized communities. All that then remained necessary was to contrast the class system of slave and free societies. They contrasted the conditions of the plantations with those of northern and British industrial cities, and much to the advantage of the former. Fitzhugh pointed out that all society is based upon exploitation. We are "cannibals all." The white slavery of the North is even worse than the black slavery of the South. Free laborers have not a thousandth part of the rights and liberties of the negro. The latter are the happiest and, in a sense, the freest people of the world. The children, the aged, and the infirm do not work at all, and yet have all the comforts and necessaries of life provided for them; women do little hard work, and their masters protect them against the despotism of their husbands. The men and stout boys work, on the average, in good weather not more than nine hours a day; the balance of their time and their sabbaths and holidays they spend in perfect abandon. The free laborer, on the other hand, must work or starve. He works longer and harder for less allowance. The cares of life with him begin when its labors end.[69] Governor Hammond claimed that even the North had a slave class.

[66] Harper; in Elliott, *Cotton is King*, pp. 563–565. Harper here expanded the argument of F. R. Dew.
[67] Calhoun, *Works*, II, 631.
[68] *Ibid.*, III, 180.
[69] Fitzhugh, *Cannibals All*, Ch. I.

"We call them slaves. We are old-fashioned at the South yet."

"The difference between us is that our slaves are hired for life and well compensated; there is no starvation, no begging, no want of employment among our people, and not too much employment either. Yours are hired by the day, not cared for, and scantily compensated, which may be proved in the most deplorable manner, at any hour in any street of your large towns. . . . Our slaves do not vote. We give them no political power. Yours do vote and being the majority, they are the depositaries of all your political power. If they knew the tremendous secret that the ballot box is stronger than any army with bayonets, and could combine, where would you be? Your society would be reconstructed, your property divided." [70]

Harper compared the stratification in slave and free societies, and contended that slavery is essential to retard the evils of civilization. The intense competition of civilized life gives rise to an excessive cheapness of labor, and this, in turn, causes serious evils. Where competition is intense, men will labor for a bare subsistence. In periods of commercial depression, the distress, in countries of free labor, falls principally on the laborers; in those of slave labor, it falls almost exclusively on the employer. The employer of free labor dismisses his workers or reduces their wages; as far as he is concerned, they may starve. But the holder of slaves cannot do so; in order to receive the full benefit of their services, he must maintain their health and vigor.[71]

Not only is the guardianship of the master invaluable to the inferior race, not only is a social stratification based on slavery conducive to human progress and culture, but, in the third place, slavery is essential to democracy and free government. Here, again, the southern writers pointed to the Athenian example. In a free society, all men share in its political life. But many of its citizens are necessarily occupied in the drudgery of making a living; they lack the leisure necessary for devotion to public affairs; they cannot afford the time for intellectual development and political reflection. Consequently, the average intelligence of such a political society is low. In a slave society, on the other hand, the disenfranchised negroes perform the menial labor and permit leisure to their masters. Thus the upper class can devote itself to intellectual improvement and political participation. The level of politics is kept high by the absence of unintelligent groups.

Slave-holding, moreover, infuses an indomitable spirit that is a

[70] Quoted: Beard, *Rise of American Civilization*, I, 693–694. Hammond developed a similar argument in his *Slavery in the Light of Political Science;* in Elliott, *Cotton is King*, pp. 637–639.

[71] Harper; in Elliott, *Cotton is King*, pp. 569–570.

pledge against tyranny. The leaders of a slave society are invariably men of great capacity for self-government. A perfect equality among them is possible.[72] Within such a class, democracy may safely be established.

Finally, a slave society does not suffer the turbulence that marks other communities. There never was and never can be, said Fitzhugh, an old society in which the immediate interests of a majority of its members do not conflict with all established order, all rights of property, and all existing institutions. If the interests of the governing class are not conservative, then the governors will not protect those institutions that are injurious to their interests. In the North, consequently, government, with its wide suffrage, "vibrates and oscillates between Radicalism and Conservatism; at present, Radicalism or Black Republicanism is in the ascendant." In the South, however, the interests of the governing class are eminently conservative.[73] The exclusion from power of all who might attack the established order renders a slave society free from turbulence. Security to order, property, and institutions is the essential attribute of free government. Thus did Calhoun lecture the Senate:

"It is impossible with us that the conflict can take place between labor and capital, which makes it so difficult to establish and maintain free institutions in all wealthy and highly civilized nations where such institutions as ours do not exist. The Southern States are an aggregate, in fact, of communities, not of individuals. Every plantation is a little community, with the master at its head, who concentrates in himself the united interests of capital and labor, of which he is the common representative. These small communities in the aggregate make the State in all, whose action, labor, and capital is equally represented and perfectly harmonized. Hence the harmony, the union, the stability of that section, which is rarely disturbed, except through the action of this Government. The blessing of this state of things extends beyond the limits of the South. It makes that section the balance of the system; the great conservative power which prevents other portions, less fortunately constituted, from rushing into conflict." [74]

WILLIAM LLOYD GARRISON

Garrison received his training for his life work as a printer's apprentice at the age of fourteen. From this position he graduated to the editorship of a small newspaper. Benjamin Lundy, the Quaker abolitionist, stirred his moral enthusiasm. Garrison joined him in the publication of *The Genius of Universal Emancipation* in Baltimore. As a result of his rabid editorial attacks upon the Baltimore slave trade and slave traders, Garrison found himself in jail. In 1831 he established the *Liberator* and as-

[72] Hammond and Bledsoe, in Elliott, *Cotton is King*, pp. 639, 289.
[73] Fitzhugh, *Cannibals All*, pp. 356-357.
[74] Calhoun, *Works*, III, 180.

sumed the rôle of the leading and most outspoken abolitionist. He was instrumental in organizing various anti-slavery societies, including the American Anti-Slavery Society in 1833. In 1835 he was mobbed and almost lynched in Boston. A rabid hatred of slavery and a hostility against the State marked his work. The following Declaration of Sentiments of the American Anti-Slavery Convention of 1833 was largely his work.

DECLARATION OF SENTIMENTS OF THE AMERICAN ANTI-SLAVERY CONVENTION. (1833) [75]

The Convention assembled in the city of Philadelphia, to organize a National Anti-Slavery Society, promptly seized the opportunity to promulgate the following Declaration of Sentiments, as cherished by them in relation to the enslavement of one-sixth portion of the American people.

More than fifty-seven years have elapsed, since a band of patriots convened in this place, to devise measures for the deliverance of this country from a foreign yoke. The corner-stone upon which they founded the Temple of Freedom was broadly this—'That all men are created equal; that they are endowed by their Creator with certain inalienable rights; that among these are life, LIBERTY, and the pursuit of happiness.' At the sound of their trumpet-call, three millions of people rose up as from the sleep of death, and rushed to the strife of blood; deeming it more glorious to die instantly as freemen, than desirable to live one hour as slaves. They were few in number—poor in resources; but the honest conviction that Truth, Justice and Right were on their side, made them invincible.

We have met together for the achievement of an enterprise, without which that of our fathers is incomplete; and which, for its magnitude, solemnity, and probable results upon the destiny of the world, as far transcends theirs as moral truth does physical force.

In purity of motive, in earnestness of zeal, in decision of purpose, in intrepidity of action, in steadfastness of faith, in sincerity of spirit, we would not be inferior to them.

Their principles led them to wage war against their oppressors, and to spill human blood like water, in order to be free. Ours forbids the doing of evil that good may come, and leads us to reject, and to entreat the oppressed to reject, the use of all carnal weapons for deliverance from bondage; relying solely upon those which are spiritual, and mighty through God to the pulling down of strongholds.

Their measures were physical resistance—the marshalling in arms—the hostile array—the mortal encounter. Ours shall be such only as the opposition of moral purity to moral corruption—the destruction of error by the potency of truth—the overthrow of prejudice by the power of love—and the abolition of slavery by the spirit of repentance.

Their grievances, great as they were, were trifling in comparison with the wrongs and sufferings of those for whom we plead. Our fathers were never slaves—never bought and sold like cattle—never shut out from the light of knowledge and religion—never subjected to the lash of brutal taskmasters.

[75] *Selections from the Writings and Speeches of William L. Garrison.* (Boston, R. F. Wallcut, 1852), pp. 66–71.

But those, for whose emancipation we are striving—constituting at the present time at least one-sixth part of our countrymen—are recognized by law, and treated by their fellow-beings, as marketable commodities, as goods and chattels, as brute beasts; are plundered daily of the fruits of their toil without redress; really enjoy no constitutional nor legal protection from licentious and murderous outrages upon their persons; and are ruthlessly torn asunder—the tender babe from the arms of its frantic mother—the heart-broken wife from her weeping husband—at the caprice or pleasure of irresponsible tyrants. For the crime of having a dark complexion, they suffer the pangs of hunger, the infliction of stripes, the ignominy of brutal servitude. They are kept in heathenish darkness by laws expressly enacted to make their instruction a criminal offence.

These are the prominent circumstances in the condition of more than two millions of our people, the proof of which may be found in thousands of indisputable facts, and in the laws of the slaveholding States.

Hence we maintain—that, in view of the civil and religious privileges of this nation, the guilt of its oppression is unequalled by any other on the face of the earth; and, therefore, that it is bound to repent instantly, to undo the heavy burdens, and to let the oppressed go free.

We further maintain—that no man has a right to enslave or imbrute his brother—to hold or acknowledge him, for one moment, as a piece of merchandize—to keep back his hire by fraud—or to brutalize his mind, by denying him the means of intellectual, social and moral improvement.

The right to enjoy liberty is inalienable. To invade it is to usurp the prerogative of Jehovah. Every man has a right to his own body—to the products of his own labor—to the protection of law—and to the common advantages of society. It is piracy to buy or steal a native African, and subject him to servitude. Surely, the sin is as great to enslave an American as an African.

Therefore we believe and affirm—that there is no difference, in principle, between the African slave trade and American slavery:

That every American citizen, who detains a human being in involuntary bondage as his property, is, according to Scripture, (Ex. xxi. 16,) a man-stealer:

That the slaves ought instantly to be set free, and brought under the protection of law:

That if they had lived from the time of Pharaoh down to the present period, and had been entailed through successive generations, their right to be free could never have been alienated, but their claims would have constantly risen in solemnity:

That all those laws which are now in force, admitting the right of slavery, are therefore, before God, utterly null and void; being an audacious usurpation of the Divine prerogative, a daring infringement on the law of nature, a base overthrow of the very foundations of the social compact, a complete extinction of all the relations, endearments and obligations of mankind, and a presumptuous transgression of all the holy commandments; and that therefore they ought instantly to be abrogated.

We further believe and affirm—that all persons of color, who possess the qualifications which are demanded of others, ought to be admitted forthwith

to the enjoyment of the same privileges, and the exercise of the same prerogatives, as others; and that the paths of preferment, of wealth, and of
intelligence, should be opened as widely to them as to persons of a white
complexion.

We maintain that no compensation should be given to the planters emancipating their slaves:

Because it would be a surrender of the great fundamental principle, that
man cannot hold property in man:

Because slavery is a crime, and therefore is not an article to be sold:

Because the holders of slaves are not the just proprietors of what they
claim; freeing the slaves is not depriving them of property, but restoring
it to its rightful owner; it is not wronging the master, but righting the slave—
restoring him to himself:

Because immediate and general emancipation would only destroy nominal, not real property; it would not amputate a limb or break a bone of
the slaves, but by infusing motives into their breasts, would make them
doubly valuable to the masters as free laborers; and

Because, if compensation is to be given at all, it should be given to the
outraged and guiltless slaves, and not to those who have plundered and abused
them.

We regard as delusive, cruel and dangerous, any scheme of expatriation
which pretends to aid, either directly or indirectly, in the emancipation of
the slaves, or to be a substitute for the immediate and total abolition of
slavery.

We fully and unanimously recognize the sovereignty of each State, to
legislate exclusively on the subject of the slavery which is tolerated within
its limits; we concede that Congress, under the present national compact,
has no right to interfere with any of the slave States, in relation to this momen-
tous subject:

But we maintain that Congress has a right, and is solemnly bound, to
suppress the domestic slave trade between the several States, and to abolish
slavery in those portions of our territory which the Constitution has placed
under its exclusive jurisdiction.

We also maintain that there are, at the present time, the highest obligations resting upon the people of the free States to remove slavery by moral
and political action, as prescribed in the Constitution of the United States.
They are now living under a pledge of their tremendous physical force, to
fasten the galling fetters of tyranny upon the limbs of millions in the Southern States; they are liable to be called at any moment to suppress a general
insurrection of the slaves; they authorize the slave owners to vote for three-
fifths of his slaves as property, and thus enable him to perpetuate his oppression; they support a standing army at the South for its protection; and they
seize the slave, who has escaped into their territories, and send him back to
be tortured by an enraged master or a brutal driver. This relation to slavery
is criminal, and full of danger: IT MUST BE BROKEN UP.

These are our views and principles—these our designs and measures.
With entire confidence in the overruling justice of God, we plant ourselves
upon the Declaration of our Independence and the truths of Divine Revelation, as upon the Everlasting Rock.

We shall organize Anti-Slavery Societies, if possible, in every city, town and village in our land.

We shall send forth agents to lift up the voice of remonstance, of warning, of entreaty, and of rebuke.

We shall circulate, unsparingly and extensively, anti-slavery tracts and periodicals.

We shall enlist the pulpit and the press in the cause of the suffering and the dumb.

We shall aim at a purification of the churches from all participation in the guilt of slavery.

We shall encourage the labor of freemen rather than that of slaves, by giving a preference to their productions: and

We shall spare no exertions nor means to bring the whole nation to speedy repentance.

Our trust for victory is solely in God. We may be personally defeated, but our principles never! Truth, Justice, Reason, Humanity, must and will gloriously triumph. Already a host is coming up to the help of the Lord against the mighty, and the prospect before us is full of encouragement.

Submitting this Declaration to the candid examination of the people of this country, and of the friends of liberty throughout the world, we hereby affix our signatures to it; pledging ourselves that, under the guidance and by the help of Almighty God, we will do all that in us lies, consistently with this Declaration of our principles, to overthrow the most execrable system of slavery that has ever been witnessed upon earth; to deliver our land from its deadliest curse; to wipe out the foulest stain which rests upon our national escutcheon; and to secure to the colored population of the United States, all the rights and privileges which belong to them as men, and as Americans— come what may to our persons, our interests, or our reputation—whether we live to witness the triumph of Liberty, Justice and Humanity, or perish untimely as martyrs in this great, benevolent, and holy cause.

Done at Philadelphia, December 6th, A.D. 1833.

WILLIAM ELLERY CHANNING

Channing, upon graduation from Harvard College in 1798, became a private tutor in Virginia. During his two-year stay in the South he developed an abhorrence for slavery. At this same time he came under the intellectual influence of the writings of Rousseau, Godwin, and Mary Wollstonecraft. He returned to New England and entered the ministry in 1803. By 1819 he had become the leader of the Unitarian faction of the Congregationalist church. Channing represents the philosophical attack upon slavery. He had but little sympathy for the rabid abolitionists, and he felt that the cure for slavery must come from the South. His *Essay on Slavery* (1835) is the most thorough attack upon the ethical foundations of slavery. Among his other anti-slavery writings are *The Abolitionists* (1836), *Emancipation* (1840), and *The Duty of the Free States* (1842). In addition to his attack upon slavery, Channing was also interested in many domestic social problems. He was an outstanding exponent of the intellectual democracy.

SLAVERY [76]

(1841)

CHAPTER I

Property

The slave-holder claims the slave as his Property. The very idea of a slave is, that he belongs to another, that he is bound to live and labor for another, to be another's instrument, and to make another's will his habitual law, however adverse to his own. Another owns him, and, of course, has a right to his time and strength, a right to the fruits of his labor, a right to task him without his consent, and to determine the kind and duration of his toil, a right to confine him to any bounds, a right to extort the required work by stripes, a right, in a word, to use him as a tool, without contract, against his will, and in denial of his right to dispose of himself, or to use his power for his own good. "A slave," says the Louisiana code, "is in the power of the master to whom he belongs. The master may sell him, dispose of his person, his industry, his labor; he can do nothing, possess nothing, nor acquire any thing, but which must belong to his master." "Slaves shall be deemed, taken, reputed, and adjudged," says the South-Carolina laws, "to be chattels personal in the hands of their masters, and possessions to all intents and purposes whatsoever." Such is slavery, a claim to man as property.

Now this claim of property in a human being is altogether false, groundless. No such right of man in man can exist. A human being cannot be justly owned. To hold and treat him as property is to inflict a great wrong, to incur the guilt of oppression.

This position there is a difficulty in maintaining, on account of its exceeding obviousness. It is too plain for proof. To defend it is like trying to confirm a self-evident truth. To find arguments is not easy, because an argument is something clearer than the proposition to be sustained. The man who, on hearing the claim to property in man, does not see and feel distinctly that it is a cruel usurpation, is hardly to be reached by reasoning, for it is hard to find any plainer principles than what he begins with denying. I will endeavor, however, to illustrate the truth which I have stated.

1. It is plain, that, if one man may be held as property, then every other man may be so held. If there be nothing in human nature, in our common nature, which excludes and forbids the conversion of him who possesses it into an article of property; if the right of the free to liberty is founded, not on their essential attributes as rational and moral beings, but on certain adventitious, accidental circumstances, into which they have been thrown; then every human being, by a change of circumstances, may justly be held and treated by another as property. If one man may be rightfully reduced to slavery, then there is not a human being on whom the same chain may not be imposed. Now let every reader ask himself this plain question: Could I, can I, be rightfully seized, and made an article of property; be made a passive instrument of another's will and pleasure; be subjected to another's

[76] *Works of William E. Channing.* (Boston, American Unitarian Association, 1871) II, 17–29, 31–36, 82–87.

irresponsible power; be subjected to stripes at another's will; be denied the control and use of my own limbs and faculties for my own good? Does any man, so questioned, doubt, waver, look about him for an answer? Is not the reply given immediately, intuitively, by his whole inward being? Does not an unhesitating, unerring conviction spring up in my breast, that no other man can acquire such a right in myself? Do we not repel, indignantly and with horror, the thought of being reduced to the condition of tools and chattels to a fellow-creature? Is there any moral truth more deeply rooted in us, than that such a degradation would be an infinite wrong? And, if this impression be a delusion, on what single moral conviction can we rely? This deep assurance, that we cannot be rightfully made another's property, does not rest on the hue of our skins, or the place of our birth, or our strength, or wealth. These things do not enter our thoughts. The consciousness of indestructible rights is a part of our moral being. The consciousness of our humanity involves the persuasion, that we cannot be owned as a tree or a brute. As men, we cannot justly be made slaves. Then no man can be rightfully enslaved. In casting the yoke from ourselves as an unspeakable wrong, we condemn ourselves as wrong-doers and oppressors in laying it on any who share our nature.—It is not necessary to inquire whether a man, by extreme guilt, may not forfeit the rights of his nature, and be justly punished with slavery. On this point crude notions prevail. But the discussion would be foreign to the present subject. We are now not speaking of criminals. We speak of innocent men, who have given us no hold on them by guilt; and our own consciousness is a proof that such cannot rightfully be seized as property by a fellow-creature.

2. A man cannot be seized and held as property, because he has Rights. What these rights are, whether few or many, or whether all men have the same, are questions for future discussion. All that is assumed now is, that every human being has *some* rights. This truth cannot be denied, but by denying to a portion of the race that moral nature which is the sure and only foundation of rights. This truth has never, I believe, been disputed. It is even recognized in the very codes of slave legislation, which, while they strip a man of liberty, affirm his right to life, and threaten his murderer with punishment. Now, I say, a being having rights cannot justly be made property; for this claim over him virtually annuls all his rights. It strips him of all power to assert them. It makes it a crime to assert them. The very essence of slavery is, to put a man defenceless into the hands of another. The right claimed by the master, to task, to force, to imprison, to whip, and to punish the slave, at discretion, and especially to prevent the least resistance to his will, is a virtual denial and subversion of all the rights of the victim of his power. The two cannot stand together. Can we doubt which of them ought to fall?

3. Another argument against property is to be found in the Essential Equality of men. I know that this doctrine, so venerable in the eyes of our fathers, has lately been denied. Verbal logicians, have told us that men are "born equal" only in the sense of being equally born. They have asked whether all are equally tall, strong, or beautiful; or whether nature, Procrustes-like, reduces all her children to one standard of intellect and virtue. By such arguments it is attempted to set aside the principle of equality, on which

the soundest moralists have reared the structure of social duty; and in these ways the old foundations of despotic power, which our fathers in their simplicity thought they had subverted, are laid again by their sons.

It is freely granted, that there are innumerable diversities among men; but be it remembered, they are ordained to bind men together, and not to subdue one to the other; ordained to give means and occasions of mutual aid, and to carry forward each and all, so that the good of all is equally intended in this distribution of various gifts. Be it also remembered, that these diversities among men are as nothing in comparison with the attributes in which they agree; and it is this which constitutes their essential equality. All men have the same rational nature and the same power of conscience, and all are equally made for indefinite improvement of these divine faculties, and for the happiness to be found in their virtuous use. Who, that comprehends these gifts, does not see the diversities of the race vanish before them? Let it be added, that the natural advantages, which distinguish one man from another, are so bestowed as to counterbalance one another, and bestowed without regard to rank or condition in life. Whoever surpasses in one endowment is inferior in others. Even genius, the greatest gift, is found in union with strange infirmities, and often places its possessors below ordinary men in the conduct of life. Great learning is often put to shame by the mother-wit and keen good sense of uneducated men. Nature, indeed, pays no heed to birth or condition in bestowing her favors. The noblest spirits sometimes grow up in the obscurest spheres. Thus equal are men; and among these equals, who can substantiate his claim to make others his property, his tools, the mere instruments of his private interest and gratification? Let this claim begin, and where will it stop? If one may assert it, why not all? Among these partakers of the same rational and moral nature, who can make good a right over others, which others may not establish over himself? Does he insist on superior strength of body or mind? Who of us has no superior in one or the other of these endowments? Is it sure that the slave or the slave's child may not surpass his master in intellectual energy, or in moral worth? Has nature conferred distinctions, which tell us plainly who shall be owners and who be owned? Who of us can unblushingly lift his head and say, that God has written "Master" there? or who can show the word "Slave" engraven on his brother's brow? The equality of nature makes slavery wrong. Nature's seal is affixed to no instrument by which property in a single human being is conveyed.

4. That a human being cannot be justly held and used as property, is apparent from the very nature of property. Property is an exclusive right. It shuts out all claim but that of the possessor. What one man owns, cannot belong to another. What, then, is the consequence of holding a human being as property? Plainly this. He can have no right to himself. His limbs are, in truth, not morally his own. He has not a right to his own strength. It belongs to another. His will, intellect, and muscles, all the powers of body and mind which are exercised in labor, he is bound to regard as another's. Now, if there be property in any thing, it is that of a man in his own person, mind, and strength. All other rights are weak, unmeaning, compared with this, and, in denying this, all right is denied. It is true, that an individual may forfeit by crime his right to the use of his limbs, perhaps to his limbs,

and even to life. But the very idea of forfeiture implies, that the right was originally possessed. It is true, that a man may by contract give to another a limited right to his strength. But he gives only because he possesses it, and gives it for considerations which he deems beneficial to himself; and the right conferred ceases at once on violation of the conditions on which it was bestowed. To deny the right of a human being to himself, to his own limbs and faculties, to his energy of body and mind, is an absurdity too gross to be confuted by any thing but a simple statement. Yet this absurdity is involved in the idea of his belonging to another.

5. We have a plain recognition of the principle now laid down, in the universal indignation excited towards a man who makes another his slave. Our laws know no higher crime than than of reducing a man to slavery. To steal or to buy an African on his own shores, is piracy. In this act the greatest wrong is inflicted, the most sacred right violated. But if a human being cannot without infinite injustice be seized as property, then he cannot without equal wrong be held and used as such. The wrong in the first seizure lies in the destination of a human being to future bondage, to the criminal use of him as a chattel or brute. Can that very use, which makes the original seizure an enormous wrong, become gradually innocent? If the slave receive injury without measure at the first moment of the outrage, is he less injured by being held fast the second or the third? Does the duration of wrong, the increase of it by continuance, convert it into right? Is it true, in many cases, that length of possession is considered as giving a right, where the good were acquired by unlawful means? But in these cases, the goods were such as might justly be appropriated to individual use. They were intended by the Creator to be owned. They fulfill their purpose by passing into the hands of an exclusive possessor. It is essential to rightful property in a thing, that the thing from its nature may be rightfully appropriated. If it cannot originally be made one's own without crime, it certainly cannot be continued as such without guilt. Now the ground, on which the seizure of the African on his own shore is condemned, is, that he is a man, who has by his nature a right to be free. Ought not, then, the same condemnation to light on the continuance of his yoke? Still more. Whence is it, that length of possession is considered by the laws as conferring a right? I answer, from the difficulty of determining the original proprietor, and from the apprehension of unsettling all property by carrying back inquiry beyond a certain time. Suppose, however, an article of property to be of such a nature that it could bear the name of the true original owner stamped on it in bright and indelible characters. In this case, the whole ground, on which length of possession bars other claims, would fail. The proprietor would not be concealed, or rendered doubtful by the lapse of time. Would not he, who should receive such an article from the robber or a succession of robbers, be involved in their guilt? Now the true owner of a human being is made manifest to all. It is Himself. No brand on the slave was ever so conspicuous as the mark of property which God has set on him. God, in making him a rational and moral being, has put a glorious stamp on him, which all the slave legislation and slave-markets of worlds cannot efface. Hence, no right accrues to the master from the length of the wrong which has been done to the slave.

6. Another argument against the right of property in man, may be drawn

from a very obvious principle of moral science. It is a plain truth, universally received, that every right supposes or involves a corresponding obligation. If, then, a man has a right to another's person or powers, the latter is under obligation to give himself up as a chattel to the former. This is his duty. He is bound to be a slave; and bound not merely by the Christian law, which enjoins submission to injury, not merely by prudential considerations, or by the claims of public order and peace; but bound because another has a right of ownership, has a moral claim to him, so that he would be guilty of dishonesty, of robbery, in withdrawing himself from this other's service. It is his duty to work for his master, though all compulsion were withdrawn; and in deserting him he would commit the crime of taking away another man's property, as truly as if he were to carry off his owner's purse. Now do we not instantly feel, can we help feeling, that this is false? Is the slave thus morally bound? When the African was first brought to these shores, would he have violated a solemn obligation by slipping his chain, and flying back to his native home? Would he not have been bound to seize the precious opportunity of escape? Is the slave under a moral obligation to confine himself, his wife, and children, to a spot where their union in a moment may be forcibly dissolved? Ought he not, if he can, to place himself and his family under the guardianship of equal laws? Should we blame him for leaving his yoke? Do we not feel, that, in the same condition, a sense of duty would quicken our flying steps? Where, then, is the obligation which would necessarily be imposed, if the right existed which the master claims? The absence of obligation proves the want of the right. The claim is groundless. It is a cruel wrong.

7. I come now to what is to my own mind the great argument against seizing and using a man as property. He cannot be property in the sight of God and justice, because he is a Rational, Moral, Immortal Being; because created in God's image, and therefore in the highest sense his child; because created to unfold godlike faculties, and to govern himself by a Divine Law written on his heart, and republished in God's Word. His whole nature forbids that he should be seized as property. From his very nature it follows, that so to seize him is to offer an insult to his Maker, and to inflict aggravated social wrong. Into every human being God has breathed an immortal spirit, more precious than the whole outward creation. No earthly or celestial language can exaggerate the worth of a human being. No matter how obscure his condition. Thought, Reason, Conscience, the capacity of Virtue, the capacity of Christian Love, an immortal Destiny, an intimate moral connection with God,—here are attributes of our common humanity which reduce to insignificance all outward distinctions, and make every human being unspeakably dear to his Maker. No matter how ignorant he may be. The capacity of Improvement allies him to the more instructed of his race, and places within his reach the knowledge and happiness of higher worlds. Every human being has in him the germ of the greatest idea in the universe, the idea of God; and to unfold this is the end of his existence. Every human being has in his breast the elements of that Divine, Everlasting Law, which the highest orders of the creation obey. He has the idea of Duty; and to unfold, revere, obey this, is the very purpose for which life was given. Every human being has the idea of what is meant by that word, Truth; that is,

he sees, however dimly, the great object of Divine and created intelligence, and is capable of ever-enlarging perceptions of truth. Every human being has affections, which may be purified and expanded into a Sublime Love. He has, too, the idea of Happiness, and a thirst for it which cannot be appeased. Such is our nature. Wherever we see a man, we see the possessor of these great capacities. Did God make such a being to be owned as a tree or a brute? How plainly was he made to exercise, unfold, improve his highest powers, made for a moral, spiritual good! and how is he wronged, and his Creator opposed, when he is forced and broken into a tool to another's physical enjoyment!

Such a being was plainly made for an End in Himself. He is a Person, not a Thing. He is an End, not a mere Instrument or Means. He was made for his own virtue and happiness. Is this end reconcilable with his being held and used as a chattel? The sacrifice of such a being to another's will, to another's present, outward, ill-comprehended good, is the greatest violence which can be offered to any creature of God. It is to degrade him from his rank in the universe, to make him a means, not an end, to cast him out from God's spiritual family into the brutal herd.

Such a being was plainly made to obey a Law within Himself. This is the essence of a moral being. He possesses, as a part of his nature, and the most essential part, a sense of Duty, which he is to reverence and follow, in opposition to all pleasure or pain, to all interfering human wills. The great purpose of all good education and discipline is, to make a man Master of Himself, to excite him to act from a principle in his own mind, to lead him to propose his own perfection as his supreme law and end. And is this highest purpose of man's nature to be reconciled with entire subjection to a foreign will, to an outward, overwhelming force, which is satisfied with nothing but complete submission?

The end of such a being as we have described, is, manifestly, Improvement. Now it is the fundamental law of our nature, that all our powers are to improve by free exertion. Action is the indispensable condition of progress to the intellect, conscience, and heart. Is it not plain, then, that a human being cannot, without wrong, be owned by another, who claims, as proprietor, the right to repress the powers of his slaves, to withold from them the means, of development, to keep them within the limits which are necessary to contentment in chains, to shut out every ray of light and every generous sentiment, which may interfere with entire subjection to his will?

No man, who seriously considers what human nature is, and what it was made for, can think of setting up a claim to a fellow-creature. What! own a spiritual being, a being made to know and adore God, and who is to outlive the sun and stars! What! chain to our lowest uses a being made for truth and virtue! convert into a brute instrument that intelligent nature, on which the idea of Duty has dawned, and which is a nobler type of God than all outward creation! Should we not deem it a wrong which no punishment could expiate, were one of our children seized as property, and driven by the whip to toil? And shall God's child, dearer to him than an only son to a human parent, be thus degraded? Every thing else may be owned in the universe; but a moral, rational being cannot be property. Suns and stars may be owned, but not the lowest spirit. Touch any thing but this. Lay not your hands on God's rational offspring. The whole spiritual world cries out, Forbear! The highest intelligences recognize their own nature, their own rights, in the humblest human being. By that priceless, immortal spirit which dwells in him, by that likeness of God which he wears, tread him not in the dust, confound him not with the brute. . . . .

CHAPTER II

Rights

I now proceed to the second division of the subject. I am to show, that man has sacred Rights, the gifts of God, and inseparable from human nature, which are violated by slavery. Some important principles, which belong to this head, were necessarily anticipated under the preceding; but they need a fuller exposition. The whole subject of Rights needs to be reconsidered. Speculations and reasonings about it have lately been given to the public, not only false, but dangerous to freedom, and there is a strong tendency to injurious views. Rights are made to depend on circumstances, so that pretences may easily be made or created for violating them successively, till none shall remain. Human rights have been represented as so modified and circumscribed by men's entrance into the social state, that only the shadows of them are left. They have been spoken of as absorbed in the public good; so that a man may be innocently enslaved, if the public good shall so require. To meet fully all these errors, for such I hold them, a larger work than the present is required. The nature of man, his relations to the state, the limits of civil government, the elements of the public good, and the degree to which the individual must be surrendered to this good, these are topics which the present subject involves. I cannot enter into them particularly, but shall lay down what seem to me the great and true principles in regard to them. I shall show, that man has rights from his very nature, not the gifts of society, but of God; that they are not surrendered on entering the social state; that they must not be taken away under the plea of public good; that the Individual is never to be sacrificed to the Community; that the idea of Rights is to prevail above all the interests of the state.

Man has rights by nature. The disposition of some to deride abstract rights, as if all rights were uncertain, mutable, and conceded by society, shows a lamentable ignorance of human nature. Whoever understands this must see in it an immovable foundation of rights. These are gifts of the Creator, bound up indissolubly with our moral constitution. In the order of things, they precede society, lie at its foundation, constitute man's capacity for it, and are the great objects of social institutions. The consciousness of rights is not a creation of human art, a conventional sentiment, but essential to and inseparable from the human soul.

Man's rights belong to him as a Moral Being, as capable of perceiving moral distinctions, as a subject of moral obligation. As soon as he becomes conscious of Duty, a kindred consciousness springs up, that he has a Right to do what the sense of duty enjoins, and that no foreign will or power can obstruct his moral action without crime. He feels, that the sense of duty was given to him as a Law, that it makes him responsible for himself, that to exercise, unfold, and obey it is the end of his being, and that he has a right to exercise and obey it without hindrance or opposition. A consciousness of dignity, however obscure, belongs also to this divine principle; and, though he may want words to do justice to his thoughts, he feels that he has that within him which makes him essentially equal to all around him.

The sense of duty is the foundation of human rights. In other words, the same inward principle, which teaches the former, bears witness to the latter. Duties and Rights must stand or fall together. It has been too common to oppose them to one another; but they are indissolubly joined together. That same inward principle, which teaches a man what he is bound to do to others, teaches equally, and at the same instant, what others are bound to do to *him*. That same voice, which forbids him to injure a single fellow-creature, forbids every fellow-creature to do *him* harm. His conscience, in revealing the moral law, does not reveal a law for himself only, but speaks as a Universal Legislator. He has an intuitive conviction, that the obligations of this divine code press on others as truly as on himself. That principle, which teaches him that he sustains the relation of brotherhood to all human beings, teaches him that this relation is reciprocal, that it gives indestructible claims, as well as imposes solemn duties, and that what he owes to the members of this vast family, they owe to him in return. Thus the moral nature involves rights. These enter into its very essence. They are taught by the very voice which enjoins duty. Accordingly there is no deeper principle in human nature, than the consciousness of rights. So profound, so ineradicable is this sentiment, that the oppressions of ages have nowhere wholly stifled it.

Having shown the foundation of human rights in human nature, it may be asked what they are. Perhaps they do not admit very accurate definition, any more than human duties; for the Spiritual cannot be weighed and measured like the Material. Perhaps a minute criticism may find fault with the most guarded exposition of them; but they may easily be stated in language which the unsophisticated mind will recognize as the truth. Volumes could not do justice to them; and yet, perhaps they may be comprehended in one sentence. They may all be comprised in the right, which belongs to every rational being, to exercise his powers for the promotion of his own and others' Happiness and Virtue. These are the great purposes of his existence. For these his powers were given, and to these he is bound to devote them. He is bound to make himself and others better and happier, according to his ability. His ability for this work is a sacred trust from God, the greatest of all trusts. He must answer for the waste or abuse of it. He consequently suffers an unspeakable wrong, when stripped of it by others, or forbidden to employ it for the ends for which it is given; when the powers, which God has given for such generous uses, are impaired or destroyed by others, or the means for their action and growth are forcibly withheld. As every human being is bound to employ his faculties for his own and others' good, there is an obligation on each to leave all free for the accomplishment of this end; and whoever respects this obligation, whoever uses his own, without invading others' powers, or obstructing others' duties, has a sacred, indefeasible right to be unassailed, unobstructed, unharmed by all with whom he may be connected. Here is the grand, all-comprehending right of human nature. Every man should revere it, should assert it for himself and for all, and should bear solemn testimony against every infraction of it, by whomsoever made or endured.

Having considered the great fundamental right of human nature, particular rights may easily be deduced. Every man has a right to exercise and invigorate his intellect or the power of knowledge, for knowledge is the essential condition of successful effort for every good; and whoever obstructs or quenches the intellectual life in another, inflicts a grievous and irreparable wrong. Every man has a right to inquire into his duty, and to conform himself to what he learns of it. Every man has a right to use the means, given by God and sanctioned by virtue, for bettering his condition. He has a right to be respected according to his moral worth; a right to be regarded as a member of the community to which he belongs, and to be protected by impartial laws; and a right to be exempted from coercion, stripes, and punishment, as long as he respects the rights of others. He has a right to an equivalent for his labor. He has a right to sustain domestic relations, to discharge their duties, and to enjoy the happiness which flows from fidelity in these and other domestic relations. Such are a few of human rights; and if so, what a grievous wrong is slavery!

Perhaps nothing has done more to impair the sense of the reality and sacredness of human rights, and to sanction oppression, than loose ideas as to the change made in man's natural rights by his entrance into civil society. It is commonly said, that men part with a portion of these by becoming a community, a body politic; that government consists of powers surrendered by the individual; and it is said, "If certain rights and powers may be surrendered, why not others? why not all? what limit is to be set? The good of the community, to which a part is given up, may demand the whole; and in this good, all private rights are merged." This is the logic of despotism. We are grieved that it finds its way into republics, and that it sets down the great principles of freedom as abstractions and metaphysical theories, good enough for the cloister, but too refined for practical and real life.

Human rights, however, are not to be so reasoned away. They belong, as we have seen, to man as a moral being, and nothing can divest him of them but the destruction of his nature. They are not to be given up to society as a prey. On the contrary, the great end of civil society is to secure them. The great end of government is to repress *all wrong*. Its highest function is to protect the weak against the powerful, so that the obscurest human being may enjoy his rights in peace. Strange that an institution, built on the idea of Rights, should be used to unsettle this idea, to confuse our moral perceptions, to sanctify wrongs as means of general good! . . .

CHAPTER IV

The Evils of Slavery

. . . . . .

6. I cannot leave the subject of the evils of slavery, without saying a word of its Political influence. Under this head, I shall not engage in discussions which belong to the economists. I shall not repeat, what has been often proved, that slave-labor is less productive than free; nor shall I show, how the ability of a community to unfold its resources in peace, and to defend itself in war, must be impaired, by degrading the laboring population to a state, which takes from them motives to toil, and renders them objects of suspicion or dread. I wish only to speak of the influence of slavery on Free

Institutions. This influence, we are gravely told, is favorable, and therefore I am bound to give it a brief notice. Political liberty is said to find strength and security in domestic servitude. Strange mode, indeed, of ensuring freedom to ourselves, to violate it in the persons of others! Among the new lights of the age, the most wonderful discovery is, that to spoil others of their rights is the way to assert the sacredness of our ow .

And now is slavery proved to support free institutions? Slave-holding, we are told, infuses an indomitable spirit, and this is a pledge against tyranny. But do we not know that Asia and Africa, slave-holding countries from the earliest date of history, have been paralyzed for ages and robbed of all manly force by despotism? In the feudal ages, the baron, surrounded by his serfs, had undoubtedly enough of a fiery spirit to keep him free, if this were the true defense of freedom; but gradually his pride was curbed, his power broken; a greater tyrant swallowed him up; and the descendants of nobles, who would have died sooner than brooked a master, were turned into courtiers, as pliant as their fathers had been ferocious.

But "the free states of antiquity," we are told, "had slaves." So had the monarchies of the same periods. With which of these institutions was slavery most congenial? To which did it most probably give support? Besides, it is only by courtesy that we call the ancient republics free. Rome in her best days was an aristocracy; nor were private rights, which it is the chief office of liberty to protect, rendered a whit more secure by the gradual triumphs of the people over patrician power. Slavery was at all periods the curse of Rome. The great mass of her free population, throwing almost every laborious occupation on the slaves, became an idle, licentious rabble; and this unprincipled populace, together with the slaves, furnished ready instruments for every private and public crime. When Clodius prowled the streets of Rome for the murder of Cicero and the best citizens, his train was composed in part of slaves, fit bloodhounds for his nefarious work. The Republic in its proudest days was desolated and convulsed by servile wars. Imperial Rome was overwhelmed by savage hordes, for this among other reasons, that her whole peasantry consisted either of slaves, or of nominal freemen degraded to a servile condition, so that the legions could be recruited only from tribes of barbarians whom she had formerly subdued.

But the great argument in favor of the political benefits of slavery, remains to be stated. In plain language it amounts to this, that slavery excludes the laboring or poorer classes from the elective franchise, from political power; and it is the turbulence of these classes which is supposed to constitute the chief peril of liberty. But in slave-holding communities, are there no distinctions of condition among the free? Are none comparatively poor? Is there no democracy? Was not Athens, crowded as she was with slaves, the most turbulent of democracies? And further, do not the idleness and impatience of restraint, into which the free of a slave-holding community naturally fall, generate an intenser party-spirit, fiercer political passions, and more desperate instruments of ambition, than can be found among the laboring classes in a community where slavery is unknown? In which of the two great divisions of our own country are political strifes most likely to be settled by the sword? In the Slave-holding States, or the Free? The laboring classes, when brought up under free institutions and equal laws, are not necessarily or peculiarly disposed to abuse the elective franchise. Their daily toil, often exhausting, secures them from habitual political excitement. The most powerful spirits among them are continually rising to a prosperity, which gives them an interest in public order. There is also a general diffusion of property, the result of unfettered industry, which forms a general motive to the support of the laws. It should be added, that the domestic virtues and religious sentiments, which in a Christian country spread through all ranks, and spread more widely among the industrious than the idle, are powerful checks on the passions, strong barriers against civil convulsion. Idleness, rather than toil, makes the turbulent partisan. Whoever knows the state of society in the Free States, can testify, that the love of liberty, pride in our free institutions, and jealousy of rights, are nowhere more active than in those very classes which in a slave-holding country are reduced to servitude. Undoubtedly the jealousies, passions, and prejudices of the laboring portion of the community may work evil, and even ruin to the state; and so may the luxury, the political venality, the gambling spirit of trade, and the cupidity, to be found in other ranks or conditions. If freedom must be denied wherever it will be endangered, then every class in society must be reduced to slavery.

Free institutions rest on two great political virtues, the love of liberty and the love of order. The slave-holder (I mean the slave-holder by choice) is of necessity more or less wanting in both. How plain is it, that no man can love liberty with a true love, who has the heart to wrest it from others! Attachment to freedom does not consist in spurning indignantly a yoke prepared for our own necks; for this is done even by the savage and the beast of prey. It is a moral sentiment, an impartial desire and choice, that others as well as ourselves may be protected from every wrong, may be exempted from every unjust restraint. Slave-holding, when perpetuated selfishly and from choice, is at open war with this generous principle. It is a plain, habitual contempt of human rights, and of course impairs that sense of their sanctity, which is their best protection. It offers, every day and hour, a precedent of usurpation to the ambitious. It creates a caste with despotic powers; and under such guardians is liberty peculiarly secure? It creates a burning zeal for the rights of a privileged class, but not for the Rights of Men. These the voluntary slave-holder casts down by force; and, in the changes of human affairs, the time may not be distant, when he will learn, that force, accustomed to triumph over right, is prone to leap every bound, and to make the proud as well as abject stoop to its sway.

Slavery is also hostile to the love of order, which, in union with the love of liberty, is the great support of free institutions. Slave-holding in a republic tends directly to lawlessness. It gives the habit of command, not of obedience. The absolute master is not likely to distinguish himself by subjection to the civil power. The substitution of passion and self-will for law, is nowhere so common as in the Slave-holding States. In these it is thought honorable to rely on one's own arm, rather than on the magistrate, for the defence of many rights. In some, perhaps many, districts, the chief peace-officer seems to be the weapon worn as part of the common dress; and the multitude seem to be more awed by one another's passions, than by the authority of the state. Such communities have no pledge of stable liberty. Reverence for the laws, as manifestations of the public will, is the very spirit of free institutions.

Does this spirit find its best nutriment in the habits and feelings generated by slavery?

Slavery is a strange element to mix with free institutions. It cannot but endanger them. It is a pattern for every kind of wrong. The slave brings insecurity on the free. Whoever holds one human being in bondage, invites others to plant the foot on his own neck. Thanks to God, not one human being can be wronged with impunity. The liberties of a people ought to tremble, until every man is free. Tremble they will. Their true foundation is sapped by the legalized degradation of a single innocent man to slavery. That foundation is impartial justice, is respect for human nature, is respect for the rights of every human being.

I have endeavoured, in these remarks, to show the hostility between slavery and free institutions. If, however, I err, if these institutions cannot stand without slavery for their foundation, then I say, Let them fall. Then they ought to be buried in perpetual ruins. Then the name of republicanism ought to become a by-word and reproach among the nations. Then monarchy, limited as it is in England, is incomparably better and happier than our more popular forms. Then despotism, as it exists in Prussia, where equal laws are in the main administered with impartiality, ought to be preferred. A republican government, bought by the sacrifice of half or more than half of a people, by stripping them of their most sacred rights, by degrading them to a brutal condition, would cost too much. A freedom so tainted with wrong ought to be our abhorrence. They, who tell us that slavery is a necessary condition of a republic, do not justify the former, but pronounce a sentence of reprobation on the latter. If they speak truth, we are bound as a people to seek more just and generous institutions, under which the rights of all will be secure. . . .

FRANCIS WAYLAND

Wayland was graduated from Union College in 1813, where he had come under the influence of Dr. Eliphalet Nott. In 1821 he became a Baptist minister, and soon rose to a prominent position within his church. For over two decades he was president of Brown University. Like Channing, he attacked slavery because he felt it to be contrary to his conception of human values. Like Channing also, he influenced many of the next generation of preachers. *The Elements of Moral Science* was a textbook on philosophy and ethics; the attack upon slavery was incidental to his general development of moral philosophy.

THE ELEMENTS OF MORAL SCIENCE [77]

(1835)

PART II

DUTIES TO MAN.—RECIPROCITY AND BENEVOLENCE

DIVISION I

THE DUTY OF RECIPROCITY.—GENERAL PRINCIPLE ILLUSTRATED, AND THE DUTIES OF RECIPROCITY CLASSIFIED.

It has been already observed, that our duties, to both God and man, are all enforced by the obligation of love to God. By this we mean, that, in

[77] Francis Wayland, *The Elements of Moral Science*. (Boston, Gould and Lincoln, 1863), pp. 190–194, 200–209, 214–216.

consequence of our moral constitution, we are under obligation to love our fellow-men, because they are our fellow-men; and we are also under obligation to love them, because we have been commanded to love them by our Father who is in heaven. The nature of this obligation may be illustrated by a familiar example. Every child in a family is under obligation to love its parent. And every child is bound to love its brother, both because *he is its brother*, and, also, because this love is a duty enforced by the relation in *which they both stand to their common parent.*

The relation in which men stand to each other, is essentially the relation of *equality;* not *equality of condition,* but *equality of right.*

Every human being is a distinct and separate accountable individual. To each one, God has given just such means of happiness, and placed him under just such circumstances for improving those means of happiness, as it has pleased him. To one he has given wealth; to another, intellect; to another, physical strength; to another, health; and to all in different degrees. In all these respects, the human race presents a scene of the greatest possible diversity. So far as natural advantages are concerned, we can scarcely find two individuals, who are not created under circumstances widely dissimilar.

But, viewed in another light, all men are placed under circumstances of *perfect equality.* Each separate individual is created with precisely *the same right to use* the advantages with which God has endowed him, as every other individual. This proposition seems to me in its nature so self-evident, as almost to preclude the possibility of argument. The only reason that I can conceive, on which any one could found a plea for *inequality of right,* must be *inequality of condition.* But this can manifestly create no diversity of *right.* I may have been endowed with better eye-sight than my neighbor; but this evidently gives me no right to put out his eyes, or to interfere with his right to derive from them whatever of happiness the Creator has placed within his power. I may have greater muscular strength than my neighbor; but this gives me no right to break his arms, or to diminish, in any manner, his ability to use them for the production of his own happiness. Besides, this supposition involves direct and manifest contradiction. For the principle asserted is, that superiority of condition confers superiority of right. But if this be true, then every kind of superiority of condition must confer correspondent superiority of right. Superiority in muscular strength must confer it, as much as superiority of intellect, or of wealth; and must confer it in the ratio of that superiority. In that case, if A, on the ground of intellectual superiority, have a right to improve his own means of happiness, by diminishing those which the Creator has given to B, B would have the same right over A, on the ground of superiority of muscular strength; while C would have a correspondent right over both, on the ground of superiority of wealth; and so on indefinitely; and these rights would change every day, according to the relative situation of the respective parties. That is to say, as right is, in its nature, exclusive, all the men in the universe have an exclusive right to the same thing; while the right of every one absolutely annihilates that of every other. What is the meaning of such an assertion, I leave it for others to determine.

But let us look at man in another point of light.

1. We find all men possessed of the same appetites and passions, that is,

of the same desire for external objects, and the same capacity for receiving happiness from the gratification of these desires. We do not say that all men possess them all in an equal degree; but only that all men actually possess them all, and that their happiness depends upon the gratification of them.

2. These appetites and passions are created, so far as they themselves are exclusively concerned, without limit. Gratification generally renders them both more intense and more numerous. Such is the case with the love of wealth, the love of power, the love of sensual pleasure, or with any of the others.

3. These desires *may be* gratified in such a manner, as *not to interfere* with the right which every other man has over his own means of happiness. Thus, I may gratify my love of wealth, by industry and frugality, while I conduct myself towards every other man with entire honesty. I may gratify my love of science, without diminishing, in any respect, the means of knowledge possessed by another. And, on the other hand, I am created with the *physical power* to gratify my desires, in such a *manner as to interfere* with the right which another has over the means of happiness which God has given him. Thus, I have a physical power to gratify my love of property, by stealing the property of another, as well as to gratify it by earning property for myself. I have, by the gift of speech, the physical power to ruin the reputation of another, for the sake of gratifying my own love of approbation. I have the physical power to murder a man, for the sake of using his body to gratify my love of anatomical knowledge. And so of a thousand cases.

4. And, hence, we see that the relation in which human beings stand to each other, is the following: Every individual is created with a desire to use the means of happiness which God has given him, in such a manner as he thinks will best promote that happiness; and of this manner he is the sole judge. Every individual is endowed with the same desires, which he *may gratify* in such a manner as will *not* interfere with his neighbor's means of happiness; but each individual has, also, the *physical power* of so gratifying his desires, as *will* interfere with the means of happiness which God has granted to his neighbor.

5. From this relation, it is manifest that every man is under obligation to pursue his own happiness, in such manner *only* as will leave his neighbor in the undisturbed exercise of that common right which the creator has equally conferred upon both, that is, to restrain his physical power of gratifying his desires within such limits that he shall interfere with the rights of no other being; because in no other manner can the evident design of the Creator, the common happiness of all, be promoted.

That this is the law of our being, may be shown from several considerations:

1. By violating it, the happiness of the aggressor is not increased, while that of the sufferer is diminished; while, by obeying it, the greatest amount of happiness of which our condition is susceptible, is secured; because, by obeying it, every one derives the greatest possible advantage from the gifts bestowed upon him by the Creator.

2. Suppose any other rule of obligation; that is, that a man is not under obligation to observe, with this exactitude, the rights of his neighbor. Where

shall the limit be fixed? If violation be allowed in a small degree, why not in a great degree? and if he may interfere with one right, why not with all? And, as all men come under the same law, this principle would lead to the same absurdity as that of which we have before spoken; that is, it would abolish the very idea of right; and, as every one has an equal liberty of violation, would surrender the whole race to the dominion of unrestrained desire.

3. If it be said that one class of men is not under the obligation to observe this rule in its conduct towards another class of men, then it will be necessary to show that the second class are not men, that is, human beings; for these principles apply to men, as men; and the simple fact, that a being is a man, places him within the reach of these obligations, and of their protection. Nay, more, suppose the inferior class of beings were not *truly men;* if they were intelligent moral agents, I suppose that we should be under the same obligation to conduct ourselves towards them upon the principle of reciprocity. I see no reason why an angel would have a right, by virtue of his superior nature, to interfere with the means of happiness which God has conferred upon man. By parity of reasoning, therefore, superiority of rank would give to man no such power over an inferior species of moral an intelligent beings.

And, lastly, if it be true that the Creator has given to every separate individual, control over those means of happiness which He has bestowed upon him, then the simple question is, Which is the highest authority, this grant of the Creator, or the desires and passions of the creature? for these are really the notions which are brought into collision. That is to say, ought the grant of God, and the will of God, to limit my desires; or ought my desires to vitiate the grant, and set at definace the will of God? On this question, a moral and intelligent creature can entertain but one opinion. . . .

CHAPTER FIRST

PERSONAL LIBERTY

Section I

Of the Nature of Personal Liberty

Every human being is, by his constitution, a separate, and distinct, and complete system, adapted to all the purposes of self-government, and responsible, separately, to God, for the manner in which his powers are employed. Thus, every individual possesses a body, by which he is connected with the physical universe, and by which that universe is modified for the supply of his wants; an understanding, by which truth is discovered, and by which means are adapted to their appropriate ends; passions and desires, by which he is excited to action, and in the gratification of which his happiness consists; conscience, to point out the limit within which these desires may be rightfully gratified; and a will, which determines him to action. The possession of these is necessary to a human nature, and it also renders every being so constituted, a distinct and independent individual. He may need society, but every *one* needs it equally with *every other one;* and, hence, all enter into it upon terms of strict and evident reciprocity. If the individua!

use these powers according to the laws imposed by his Creator, his Creator holds him guiltless. If he use them in such manner as not to interfere with the use of the same powers which God has bestowed upon his neighbor, he is, as it respects his neighbor, whether that neighbor be an individual or the community, to be held guiltless. So long as he uses them within this limit, he has a right, so far as his fellowmen are concerned, to use them, in the most unlimited sense, *suo arbitrio*, at his own discretion. His will is his sufficient and ultimate reason. He need assign no other reason for his conduct, than his own free choice. Within this limit, he is still responsible to God; but, within this limit, he is not responsible *to man*, nor *is man responsible for him.*

1. Thus, a man has an entire right to use his own *body* as he will, provided he do not so use it as to interfere with the rights of his neighbor. He may go where he will, and stay where he pleases; he may work, or be idle; he may pursue one occupation, or another, or no occupation at all; and it is the concern of no one else, if he leave inviolate the rights of every one else; that is, if he leave every one else in the undisturbed enjoyment of those means of happiness bestowed upon him by the Creator.

It seems almost trifling to argue a point, which is, in its nature, so evident upon inspection. If, however, any additional proof be required, the following considerations will readily suggest themselves. It is asserted that every individual has an equal and ultimate right with every other individual, to the use of his body, his mind, and all the other means of happiness with which God has endowed him. But suppose it otherwise. Suppose that one individual has a right to the body, or mind, or means of happiness, of another. That is, suppose that A has a right to use the body of B according to his, that is, A's, *will*. Now, if this be true, it is true universally; hence, A has the control over the body of B, and B has control over the body of C, C of that of D, &c., and Z again over the body of A; that is, every separate will has the right of control over some other body or intellect besides its own, and has no right of control over its own body or intellect. Whether such is the constitution of human nature, or, if it be not, whether it would be an improvement upon the present constitution, may be easily decided.

And, if it be said, that, to control one man's body by another man's will is impossible, for that every man acts as he will, since he cannot do any thing unless he *will* do it, it may be answered, that the term *will* is used here in a different sense from that intended in the preceding paragraph. Every one must see, that a man, who, out of the various ways of employing his body, set *before him by his Creator*, chooses that which he prefers, is in a very different condition from him who is debarred from all choice, excepting that he may do what his fellow-man appoints, or else must suffer what his fellow-man chooses to inflict. Now, the true condition of a human being is that in which his will is influenced by no other circumstances that those which arise from the constitution under which his Creator has placed him. And he who for his own pleasure places his fellow-man under any other conditions of existence, is guilty of the most odious tyranny, and seems to me to arrogate to himself the authority of the Most High God.

But it may be said that, in this case, the individual may become chargeable to the community. To this I answer, not unless the community *assume* the charge. If every man be left to himself, but is obliged to respect the rights of others; if he do not labor, a remedy is provided in the laws of the system,—he will very soon starve; and, if he prefer starvation to labor, he has no one to blame but himself. While the law of reciprocity frees him from the control of society, it discharges society from any responsibility for the result of his actions upon himself. I know that society undertakes to support the indigent and helpless, and to relieve men in extreme necessity. This, however, is a conventional arrangement, into which men, who choose, have a right to enter; and, having entered into it, they are bound by its provisions. If they become responsible for the support of the individual's life, they have a right over his power of labor to an extent sufficient to cover that responsibility. And he who has become a member of such a society, has surrendered voluntarily his control over his body, *to this amount*. But as he has done it *voluntarily*, such a convention proceeds upon the concession, that the *original right* vests in the individual.

2. The same remarks apply to the use of the *intellect*.

If the preceding observations are just, it will follow, that every man, within the limit before suggested, has a right to use his intellect as he will. He may investigate whatever subjects he will, and in what manner soever he will, and may come to such conclusions as his investigations may teach, and may publish those conclusions to those who are willing to hear them, provided he interfere with the happiness of no other human being. The denial of this right would lead to the same absurdities as in the former case.

If it be said that the individual may, by so doing, involve himself in error, and thus diminish his own happiness, the answer is at hand, namely, for this the constitution of things provides its appropriate and adquate punishment. He who imbibes error, suffers, in his own person, the consequences of error, which are misfortune and loss of respect. And, besides, as, for his happiness, society is not in this case responsible: there can be no reason, derived from the consideration of *his happiness*, why society should interfere with the free use of this instrument of happiness, which the Creator has intrusted solely to the individual himself.

But, it may be asked, has not society a right to oblige men to acquire a certain amount of intellectual cultivation? I answer, men have a right to form a society upon such conditions as they please; and, of course, so to form it, that it shall be necessary, in order to enjoy its privileges, for the individual to possess a certain amount of knowledge. Having formed such a society, every one is bound by its provisions, so long as he remains a member of it; and the enforcing of its provisions upon the individual, is no more than obliging him to do what he, for a sufficient consideration, voluntarily contracted to do. And society may rightfully enforce this provision in either of two ways: it may either withhold from every man who neglects to acquire this knowledge, the benefits of citizenship; or else it may grant these benefits to every one, and oblige every one to possess the assigned amount of knowledge. In this case, there is no violation of reciprocity; for the same requirements are made of all, and every one receives his full equivalent, in the results of the same law upon others. More than this, the individual could not justly require. He could not justly demand to be admitted to rights which presuppose certain intellectual attainments, and which can only be, safety to others, enjoyed by those who have made these attainments, unless he be willing to conform to the condition necessary to that enjoyment.

3. I have thus far considered man only in his relations to the present life. So far as I have gone, I have endeavored to show that, provided the individual interfere not with the rights of others, he has a right to use his own body and mind as he thinks will best promote his own happiness; that is, as he will. But, if he have this right, within these limits, to pursue his *present happiness*, how much more incontrovertible must be his right to use his body and mind in such manner, as he supposes will best promote his eternal happiness! And, besides, if, for the sake of his own happiness, he have a right to the unmolested enjoyment of whatever God has given him, how much more is he entitled to the same unmolested enjoyment, for the sake of obeying God, and fulfilling the highest obligation of which he is susceptible!

We say, then, that every man, provided he does not interfere with the rights of his neighbor, has a right, so far as his neighbor is concerned, to worship God, or not to worship him; and to worship him in any manner that he will, and that, for the abuse of this liberty, he is accountable only to God.

If it be said, that, by so doing, a man may ruin his own soul, the answer is obvious; for this ruin, the individual himself, and not *society*, is responsible. And, moreover, as religion consists in the temper of heart, which force cannot affect,—and not in external observance, which is all that force can affect, —no application of force can change our relations to God, or prevent the ruin in question. All application of force must then be gratuitous mischief.

To sum up what has been said,—all men are created with an equal right to employ their faculties, of body or of mind, in such manner as will promote their own happiness, either here or hereafter; or, which is the same thing, every man has a right to use his own powers, of body or of mind, in such manner as he will; provided he do not use them in such manner as to interfere with the rights of his neighbor.

The exceptions to this law are easily defined.

1. The first exception is in the case of infancy. By the law of nature a parent is under obligation to support his child, and is responsible for his actions. He had, therefore, a right to control the actions of the child, so long as this responsibility exists. He is under obligation to render that child a suitable member of the community; and this obligation he could not discharge, unless the physical and intellectual liberty of the child were placed within his power.

2. As the parent has supported the child during infancy, he has, probably, by the law of nature, a right to his services during youth, or for so long a period as may be sufficient to insure an adequate remuneration. When, however, this remuneration is received, the right of the parent over the child ceases for ever.

3. This right he may, if he sees fit, transfer to another, as in the case of apprenticeship. But he can transfer the right for no longer time than he holds it. He can, therefore, negotiate it away for no period beyond that of the child's minority.

4. A man may transfer his right over his own labor for a limited time, and for a satisfactory equivalent. But this transfer proceeds upon the principle that the original right vests in himself, and it is, therefore, no violation of

that right. He has, however, no right to transfer the services of any other person except his child; nor of his child, except under the limitations above specified.

In strict accordance with these remarks, is the memorable senteↄce in the commencement of the Declaration of Independence, "We hold these truths to be self-evident: that all men are created equal; that they are endowed by their Creator with certain inalienable rights; that among these are life, liberty, and the pursuit of happiness." That the equality here spoken of is not of the means of happiness, but in the right to use them as we will, is too evident to need illustration.

Section II

Modes in which Personal Liberty may be Violated

Personal liberty may be violated in two ways: 1. By the individual; 2. By society.

PART FIRST. *Of the violation of personal liberty by the* INDIVIDUAL. The most common violation of personal liberty, under this head, is that which exists in the case of *Domestic Slavery*.

Domestic slavery proceeds upon the principle that the master has a right to control the actions, physical and intellectual, of the slave, for his own, that is, the master's, individual benefit; and, of course, that the happiness of the master, when it comes in competition with the happiness of the slave, extinguishes in the latter the right to pursue it. It supposes, at best, that the relation between master and slave, is not that which exists between man and man, but is a modification at least, of that which exists between man and the brutes.

Now, this manifestly supposes that the two classes of beings are created with dissimilar rights: that the master possesses rights which have never been conceded by the slave; and that the slave has no rights at all over the means of happiness which God has given him, whenever these means of happiness can be rendered available to the service of the master. It supposes that the Creator intended one human being to govern the physical, intellectual and moral actions of as many other human beings as by purchase he can bring within his physical power; and that one human being may thus acquire a right to sacrifice the happiness of any number of other human beings, for the purpose of promoting his own.

Slavery thus violates the personal liberty of man as a *physical, intellectual,* and *moral being.*

1. It purports to give to the master a right to control the *physical* labor of the slave, not for the sake of the happiness of the slave, nor upon terms mutually satisfactory to the parties, but for the sake of the happiness of the master. It subjects the amount of labor, and the kind of labor, and the remuneration for labor, entirely to the will of the one party, to the entire exclusion of the will of the other party.

2. But if this right in the master over the slave be conceded, there are of course conceded with it all other rights necessary to insure its possession. Hence, inasmuch as the slave can be held in this condition only while he remains in a state of comparative mental imbecility, it supposes the master

to have the right to control his intellectual development, just as far as may be necessary to secure entire subjection. Thus, it supposes the slave to have no right to use his intellect for the production of his own happiness; but, only to use it in such manner as may be consistent with his master's profit.

3. And, moreover, inasmuch as the acquisition of the knowledge of his duty to God could not be freely made without the acquisition of other knowledge, which might, if universally diffused, endanger the control of the master, slavery supposes the master to have the right to determine how much knowledge of his duty a slave shall obtain, the manner in which he shall obtain it, and the manner in which he shall discharge that duty after he shall have obtained a knowledge of it. It thus subjects the duty of man to God, entirely to the will of man; and this for the sake of pecuniary profit. It renders the eternal happiness of the one party subservient to the temporal happiness of the other. And this principle is commonly recognized by the laws of all slave-holding countries.

If argument were necessary to show that such a system as this must be at variance with the ordinance of God, it might be easily drawn from the effects which it produces both upon *morals* and upon *national wealth*,

1. Its effects must be disastrous upon the *morals* of both parties. By presenting objects on whom passion may be satiated without resistance and without redress, it tends to cultivate in the master, pride, anger, cruelty, selfishness and licentiousness. By accustoming the slave to subject his moral principles to the will of another, it tends to abolish in him all moral distinctions; and thus fosters in him lying, deceit, hypocrisy, dishonesty, and a willingness to yield himself up to minister to the appetites of his master. That in all slave-holding countries there are exceptions to this remark, and that there are principles in human nature which, in many cases, limit the effects of these tendencies, may be gladly admitted. Yet, that such is the *tendency of slavery, as slavery*, we think no reflecting person can for a moment hesitate to allow.

2. The effects of slavery on *national wealth*, may be easily seen from the following considerations:

1. Instead of imposing upon *all* the necessity of labor, it restricts the number of laborers, that is, of producers, within the smallest possible limit, by rendering labor disgraceful.

2. It takes from the laborers the *natural stimulus* to labor, namely, the desire in the individual of improving his condition; and substitutes, in the place of it, that motive which is the least operative and the least constant, namely, the fear of punishment without the consciousness of moral delinquency.

3. It removes, as far as possible, from both parties, the disposition and the motives to *frugality*. Neither the master learns frugality from the necessity of labor, nor the slave from the benefits which it confers. And hence, while the one party wastes from ignorance of the laws of acquisition, and the other because he can have no motive to economy, capital must accumulate but slowly, if indeed it accumulate at all.

And that such are the tendencies of slavery, is manifest from observation. No country, not of great fertility, can long sustain a large slave population. Soils of more than ordinary fertility cannot sustain it long, after the first richness of the soil has been exhausted. Hence, slavery in this country is acknowledged to have impoverished many of our most valuable districts; and, hence, it is continually migrating from the older settlements, to those new and untilled regions, where the accumulated manure of centuries of vegetation has formed a soil, whose productiveness may, for a while, sustain a system at variance with the laws of nature. Many of our free and of our slave-holding States were peopled at about the same time. The slave-holding States had every advantage, both in soil and climate, over their neighbors. And yet the accumulation of capital has been greatly in favor of the latter. If any one doubt whether this difference be owing to the use of slave labor, let him ask himself what would have been the condition of the slave-holding States, at this moment, if they had been inhabited, from the beginning, by an industrious yeomanry; each one holding his own land, and each one tilling it with the labor of his own hands. . . .

Before closing this part of the subject, it may be proper to consider the question, What is the duty of masters and slaves, under a condition of society in which slavery now exists?

I. As to masters.

If the system be wrong, as we have endeavored to show, if it be at variance with our duty both to God and to man, it must be abandoned. If it be asked, When? I ask again, When shall a man begin to cease doing wrong? Is not the answer always, *Immediately?* If a man is injuring *us*, do we ever doubt as to the time when *he* ought to cease? There is then no doubt in respect to the time when we ought to cease inflicting injury upon others.

But it may be said, immediate abolition would be the greatest possible injury to the slaves themselves. They are not competent to self-government. This is a question of fact, which it is not within the province of moral philosophy to decide. It very likely may be so. So far as I know, the facts are not sufficiently known to warrant a full opinion on the subject. We will, therefore, suppose it to be the case, and ask, What is the duty of masters *under these circumstances?*

1. The situation of the slaves, in which this obstacle to their emancipation consists, is not by their *own act,* but by the *act of their masters;* and, therefore, the *masters are bound to remove it.* The slaves were brought here without their own consent, they have been continued in their present state of degradation without their own consent, and *they* are not responsible for the consequences. If a man have done injustice to his neighbor, and have also placed impediments in the way of remedying that injustice, he is as much under obligation to remove the impediments in the way of justice, as he is to do justice. Were it otherwise, a man might, by the accumulation of injury, at last render the most atrocious injury innocent and right.

2. But it may be said, this cannot be done, unless the slave is held in bondage until the object be accomplished. This is also a question of fact, on which I will not pretend to decide. But suppose it to be so, the question returns, What then is the duty of the master? I answer, supposing such to be the fact, it may be the duty of the master to hold the slave; not, however, *on the ground of right over him* but of *obligation to him,* and of obligation *to him* for the *purpose of accomplishing a particular and specific good.* And, of course, he who holds him for any other purpose, holds him wrongfully,

and is guilty of the sin of slavery. In the mean while, he is innocent *in just so far as* he, in the fear of God, holds the slave, not for the good of the master, but for the good of the slave, and with the entire and honest intention of accomplishing the object as soon as he can, and of liberating the slave as soon as the object is accomplished. He thus admits the slave to equality of right. He does unto another as he would that another should do unto him; and, thus acting, though he may *in form* hold a fellow-creature in bondage, he is *in fact* innocent of the crime of violation of liberty. This opinion, however, proceeds upon the supposition that the facts are as above stated. As to the question of fact, I do not feel competent to a decision.

II. The *duty of slaves* is also explicitly made known in the Bible. They are bound to obedience, fidelity, submission, and respect to their masters, not only to the good and kind, but also to the unkind and froward; not, however, on the ground of *duty to man*, but on the ground of *duty to God*. This obligation extends to every thing but matters of conscience. When a master commands a slave to do wrong, the slave ought not to obey. The Bible does not, as I suppose, authorize resistance to injury; but it commands us to refuse obedience in such a case, and suffer the consequences, looking to God alone, to whom vengeance belongeth. Acting upon these principles, the slave may attain to the highest grade of virtue, and may exhibit a sublimity and purity of moral character, which, in the condition of the master, is absolutely unattainable.

Thus we see that the Christian religion not only forbids slavery, but that it also provides the only method in which, after it has once been established, it may be abolished, and that with entire safety and benefit to both parties. By instilling the right moral dispositions into the bosom of the master and of the slave, it teaches the one the duty of reciprocity, and the other the duty of submission; and thus, without tumult, without disorder, without revenge, but, by the real moral improvement of both parties, restores both to the relation towards each other intended by their Creator.

Hence, if any one will reflect on these facts, and remember the moral law of the Creator, and the terrible sanctions by which his laws are sustained, and also the provision which in the gospel of reconciliation, He has made for removing this evil after it has once been established; he must, I think, be convinced of the imperative obligation which rests upon him to remove it without the delay of a moment. The Judge of the whole earth will do justice. He hears the cry of the oppressed, and he will, in the end, terribly vindicate right. And, on the other hand, let those who suffer wrongfully, bear their sufferings with patience, committing their souls unto him as unto a *faithful Creator*. . . .

ABRAHAM LINCOLN

Lincoln, before his election to the Presidency, was a representative of the free-soil attack upon slavery. The western agrarians opposed the extension of slavery into the new territories in order that those fertile lands might be free for their own exploitation. Their frontier equalitarianism also made them instinctively hostile to the social caste system that accompanied slavery. Lincoln rationalized this economic hostility and this conflict of culture patterns; he based his arguments primarily upon the Declaration of Independence.

SPEECH IN SPRINGFIELD, ILLINOIS, JUNE 26, 1857.[78]

. . . . . .
And now as to the Dred Scott decision. That decision declares two propositions—first, that a negro cannot sue in the United States courts; and
secondly, that Congress cannot prohibit slavery in the Territories. It was
made by a divided court—dividing differently on the different points. Judge
Douglas does not discuss the merits of the decision, and in that respect I
shall follow his example, believing I could no more improve on McLean and
Curtis than he could on Taney.

He denounces all who question the correctness of that decision, as offering
violent resistance to it. But who resists it? Who has, in spite of the decision,
declared Dred Scott free, and resisted the authority of his master over him?

Judicial decisions have two uses—first, to absolutely determine the case
decided; and secondly, to indicate to the public how other similar cases will
be decided when they arise. For the latter use, they are called "precedents"
and "authorities."

We believe as much as Judge Douglas (perhaps more) in obedience to,
and respect for, the judicial department of government. We think its decisions on constitutional questions, when fully settled, should control not
only the particular cases decided, but the general policy of the country,
subject to be disturbed only by amendments of the Constitution as provided
in that instrument itself. More than this would be revolution. But we think
the Dred Scott decision is erroneous. We know the court that made it has
often overruled its own decisions, and we shall do what we can to have it to
overrule this. We offer no resistance to it.

Judicial decisions are of greater or less authority as precedents according
to circumstances. That this should be so accords both with common sense
and the customary understanding of the legal profession.

If this important decision had been made by the unanimous concurrence
of the judges, and without any apparent partizan bias, and in accordance
with legal public expectation and with the steady practice of the departments throughout our history, and had been in no part based on assumed
historical facts which are not really true; or, if wanting in some of these,
it had been before the court more than once, and had there been affirmed and
reaffirmed through a course of years, it then might be, perhaps would be,
factious, nay, even revolutionary, not to acquiesce in it as a precedent.

But when, as is true, we find it wanting in all these claims to the public
confidence, it is not resistance, it is not factious, it is not even disrespectful,
to treat it as not having yet quite established a settled doctrine for the country. But Judge Douglas considers this view awful. Hear him:

"The courts are the tribunals prescribed by the Constitution and created
by the authority of the people to determine, expound, and enforce the law.
Hence, whoever resists the final decision of the highest judicial tribunal
aims a deadly blow at our whole republican system of government—a blow
which, if successful, would place all our rights and liberties at the mercy of
passion, anarchy, and violence. I repeat, therefore, that if resistance to the

---

[78] J. G. Nicolay and J. Hay (editors), *Abraham Lincoln, Complete Works.* (New York,
The Century Co., 1920), I, 228-235. (Reprinted by permission of the publishers.)

decisions of the Supreme Court of the United States, in a matter like the points decided in the Dred Scott case, clearly within their jurisdiction as defined by the Constitution, shall be forced upon the country as a political issue, it will become a distinct and naked issue between the friends and enemies of the Constitution—the friends and the enemies of the supremacy of the laws."

Why, this same Supreme Court once decided a national bank to be constitutional; but General Jackson, as President of the United States, disregarded the decision, and vetoed a bill for a recharter, partly on constitutional ground declaring that each public functionary must support the Constitution, "as he understands it." But hear the general's own words. Here they are, taken from his veto message:

"It is maintained by the advocates of the bank, that its constitutionality, in all its features, ought to be considered as settled by precedent, and by the decision of the Supreme Court. To this conclusion I cannot assent. Mere precedent is a dangerous source of authority, and should not be regarded as deciding questions of constitutional power, except where the acquiescence of the people and the States can be considered as well settled. So far from this being the case on this subject, an argument against the bank might be based on precedent. One Congress, in 1791, decided in favor of a bank; another, in 1811, decided against it. One Congress, in 1815, decided against a bank; another, in 1816, decided in its favor. Prior to the present Congress, therefore, the precedents drawn from that source were equal. If we resort to the States, the expressions of legislative, judicial, and executive opinions against the bank have been probably to those in favor as four to one. There is nothing in precedent, therefore, which, if its authority were admitted, ought to weigh in favor of the act before me."

I drop the quotations merely to remark that all there ever was in the way of precedent up to the Dred Scott decision, on the points therein decided, had been against that decision. But hear General Jackson further:

"If the opinion of the Supreme Court covered the whole ground of this act, it ought not to control the coördinate authorities of this government. The Congress, the executive, and the court must, each for itself, be guided by its own opinion of the Constitution. Each public officer who takes an oath to support the Constitution swears that he will support it as he understands it, and not as it is understood by others."

Again and again I have heard Judge Douglas denounce that bank decision and applaud General Jackson for disregarding it. It would be interesting for him to look over his recent speech, and see how exactly his fierce philippics against us for resisting Supreme Court decisions fall upon his own head. It will call to mind a long and fierce political war in this country, upon an issue which, in his own language, and, of course, in his own changeless estimation, was "a distinct issue between the friends and the enemies of the Constitution," and in which war he fought in the ranks of the enemies of the Constitution.

I have said, in substance, that the Dred Scott decision was in part based on assumed historical facts which were not really true, and I ought not to leave the subject without giving some reasons for saying this; I therefore give an instance or two, which I think fully sustain me. Chief Justice Taney, in delivering the opinion of the majority of the court, insists at great length that negroes were no part of the people who made, or for whom was made the Declaration of Independence, or the Constitution of the United States.

On the contrary, Judge Curtis, in his dissenting opinion, shows that in five of the then thirteen States—to wit, New Hampshire, Massachusetts, New York, New Jersey, and North Carolina—free negroes were voters, and in proportion to their numbers had the same part in making the Constitution that the white people had. He shows this with so much particularity as to leave no doubt of its truth; and as a sort of conclusion on that point, holds the following language:

"The Constitution was ordained and established by the people of the United States, through the action, in each State, of those persons who were qualified by its laws to act thereon in behalf of themselves and all other citizens of the State. In some of the States, as we have seen, colored persons were among those qualified by law to act on the subject. These colored persons were not only included in the body of 'the people of the United States' by whom the Constitution was ordained and established; but in at least five of the States they had the power to act, and doubtless did act, by their suffrages, upon the question of its adoption."

Again, Chief Justice Taney says:

"It is difficult at this day to realize the state of public opinion, in relation to that unfortunate race, which prevailed in the civilized and enlightened portions of the world at the time of the Declaration of Independence, and when the Constitution of the United States was framed and adopted."

And again, after quoting from the Declaration, he says:

"The general words above quoted would seem to include the whole human family, and if they were used in a similar instrument at this day, would be so understood."

In these the Chief Justice does not directly assert, but plainly assumed, as a fact, that the public estimate of the black man is more favorable now than it was in the days of the Revolution. This assumption is a mistake. In some trifling particulars the condition of that race has been ameliorated; but as a whole, in this country, the change between then and now is decided the other way; and their ultimate destiny has never appeared so hopeless as in the last three or four years. In two of the five States—New Jersey and North Carolina—that then gave the free negro the right of voting, the right has since been taken away, and in a third—New York—it has been greatly abridged; while it has not been extended, so far as I know, to a single additional State, though the number of the States has more than doubled. In those days, as I understand, masters could, at their own pleasure, emancipate their slaves; but since then such legal restraints have been made upon emancipation as to amount almost to prohibition. In those days legislatures held the unquestioned power to abolish slavery in their respective States, but now it is becoming quite fashionable for State constitutions to withhold that power from the legislatures. In those days, by common consent, the spread of the black man's bondage to the new countries was prohibited, but now Congress decides that it will not continue the prohibition, and the Supreme Court decides that it could not if it would. In those days our Declaration of Independence was held sacred by all, and thought to include all;

but now, to aid in making the bondage of the negro universal and eternal, it is assailed and sneered at and construed, and hawked at and torn, till, if its framers could rise from their graves, they could not at all recognize it. All the powers of earth seem rapidly combining against him. Mammon is after him, ambition follows, philosophy follows, and the theology of the day is fast joining the cry. They have him in his prison-house; they have searched his person, and left no prying instrument with him. One after another they have closed the heavy iron doors upon him; and now they have him, as it were, bolted in with a lock of a hundred keys, which can never be unlocked without the concurrence of every key—the keys in the hands of a hundred different men, and they scattered to a hundred different and distant places; and they stand musing as to what invention, in all the dominions of mind and matter, can be produced to make the impossibility of his escape more complete than it is.

It is grossly incorrect to say or assume that the public estimate of the negro is more favorable now than it was at the origin of the government.

Three years and a half ago, Judge Douglas brought forward his famous Nebraska bill. The country was at once in a blaze. He scorned all opposition, and carried it through Congress. Since then he has seen himself superseded in a presidential nomination by one indorsing the general doctrine of his measure, but at the same time standing clear of the odium of its untimely agitation and its gross breach of national faith; and he has seen that successful rival constitutionally elected, not by the strength of friends, but by the division of adversaries, being in a popular minority of nearly four hundred thousand votes. He has seen his chief aids in his own State, Shields and Richardson, politically speaking, successively tried, convicted, and executed for an offense not their own, but his. And now he sees his own case standing next on the docket for trial.

There is a natural disgust in the minds of nearly all white people at the idea of an indiscriminate amalgamation of the white and black races; and Judge Douglas evidently is basing his chief hope upon the chances of his being able to appropriate the benefit of his disgust to himself. If he can, by much drumming and repeating, fasten the odium of that idea upon his adversaries, he thinks he can struggle through the storm. He therefore clings to this hope, as a drowning man to the last plank. He makes an occasion for lugging it in from the opposition to the Dred Scott decision. He finds the Republicans insisting that the Declaration of Independence includes *all* men, black as well as white, and forthwith be boldly denies that it includes negroes at all, and proceeds to argue gravely that all who contend it does, do so only because they want to vote, and eat, and sleep, and marry with negroes! He will have it that they cannot be consistent else. Now I protest against the counterfeit logic which concludes that, because I do not want a black woman for a slave I must necessarily want her for a wife. I need not have her for either. I can just leave her alone. In some respects she certainly is not my equal; but in her natural right to eat the bread she earns with her own hands without asking leave of any one else, she is my equal, and the equal of all others.

Chief Justice Taney, in his opinion in the Dred Scott case, admits that the language of the Declaration is broad enough to include the whole human family, but he and Judge Douglas argue that the authors of that instrument did not intend to include negroes, by the fact that they did not at once actually place them on an equality with the whites. Now this grave argument comes to just nothing at all, by the other fact that they did not at once, or ever afterward, actually place all white people on an equality with one another. And this is the staple argument of both the chief justice and the senator for doing this obvious violence to the plain, unmistakable language of the Declaration.

I think the authors of that notable instrument intended to include *all* men, but they did not intend to declare all men equal *in all respects*. They did not mean to say all were equal in color, size, intellect, moral developments, or social capacity. They defined with tolerable distinctness in what respects they did consider all men created equal—equal with "certain inalienable rights, among which are life, liberty, and the pursuit of happiness." This they said, and this they meant. They did not mean to assert the obvious untruth that all were then actually enjoying that equality, nor yet that they were about to confer it immediately upon them. In fact, they had no power to confer such a boon. They meant simply to declare the right, so that enforcement of it might follow as fast as circumstances should permit.

They meant to set up a standard maxim for free society, which should be familiar to all, and revered by all; constantly looked to, constantly labored for, and even though never perfectly attained, constantly approximated, and thereby constantly spreading and deepening its influence and augmenting the happiness and value of life to all people of all colors everywhere. The assertion that "all men are created equal" was of no practical use in effecting our separation from Great Britain; and it was placed in the Declaration not for that, but for future use. Its authors meant it to be—as, thank God, it is now proving itself—a stumbling-block to all those who in after times might seek to turn a free people back into the hateful paths of despotism. They knew the proneness of prosperity to breed tyrants, and they meant when such should reappear in this fair land and commence their vocation, they should find left for them at least one hard nut to crack.

I have now briefly expressed my view of the meaning and object of that part of the Declaration of Independence which declares that "all men are created equal."

Now let us hear Judge Douglas's view of the same subject, as I find it in the printed report of his late speech. Here it is:

"No man can vindicate the character, motives, and conduct of the signers of the Declaration of Independence, except upon the hypothesis that they referred to the white race alone, and not to the African, when they declared all men to have been created equal; that they were speaking of British subjects on this continent being equal to British subjects born and residing in Great Britain; that they were entitled to the same inalienable rights, and among them were enumerated life, liberty, and the pursuit of happiness. The Declaration was adopted for the purpose of justifying the colonists in the eyes of the civilized world in withdrawing their allegiance from the British crown, and dissolving their connection with the mother country."

My good friends, read that carefully over some leisure hour, and ponder well upon it; see what a mere wreck—mangled ruin—it makes of our once glorious Declaration.

"They were speaking of British subjects on this continent being equal to British subjects born and residing in Great Britain!" Why, according to this, not only negroes but white people outside of Great Britain and America were not spoken of in that instrument. The English, Irish, and Scotch, along with white Americans, were included, to be sure, but the French, Germans, and other white people of the world are all gone to pot along with the judge's inferior races!

I had thought the Declaration promised something better than the condition of British subjects; but no, it only meant that we should be equal to them in their own oppressed and unequal condition. According to that, it gave no promise that, having kicked off the king and lords of Great Britain, we should not at once be saddled with a king and lords of our own.

I had thought the Declaration contemplated the progressive improvement in the condition of all men everywhere; but no, it merely "was adopted for the purpose of justifying the colonists in the eyes of the civilized world in withdrawing their allegiance from the British crown, and dissolving their connection with the mother country." Why, that object having been effected some eighty years ago, the Declaration is of no practical use now—mere rubbish—old wadding left to rot on the battle-field after the victory is won.

I understand you are preparing to celebrate the "Fourth," to-morrow week. What for? The doings of that day had no reference to the present; and quite half of you are not even descendants of those who were referred to at that day. But I suppose you will celebrate, and even go so far as to read the Declaration. Suppose, after you read it once in the old-fashioned way, you read it once more with Judge Douglas's version. It will then run thus: "We hold these truths to be self-evident, that all British subjects who were on this continent eighty-one years ago, were created equal to all British subjects born and then residing in Great Britain."

And now I appeal to all—to Democrats as well as others—are you really willing that the Declaration shall thus be frittered away?—thus left no more, at most, than an interesting memorial of the dead past?—thus shorn of its vitality and practical value, and left without the germ or even the suggestion of the individual rights of man in it?

But Judge Douglas is especially horrified at the thought of the mixing of blood by the white and black races. Agreed for once—a thousand times agreed. There are white men enough to marry all the white women, and black men enough to marry all the black women; and so let them be married. On this point we fully agree with the judge, and when he shall show that his policy is better adapted to prevent amalgamation than ours, we shall drop ours and adopt his. Let us see. In 1850 there were in the United States 405,751 mulattos. Very few of these are the offspring of whites and free blacks; nearly all have sprung from black slaves and white masters. A separation of the races is the only perfect preventive of amalgamation; but as an immediate separation is impossible, the next best thing is to keep them apart where they are not already together. If white and black people never get together in Kansas, they will never mix blood in Kansas. That is at least one self-evident truth. A few free colored persons may get into the free States, in any event; but their number is too insignificant to amount to much in the way of mixing blood. In 1850 there were in the free States 56,649 mulattos; but for the most part they were not born there—they came from the slave States, ready made up. In the same year the slave States had 348,874 mulattos, all of home production. The proportion of free mulattos to free blacks—the only colored classes in the free States—is much greater in the slave than in the free States. It is worthy of note, too, that among the free States those which make the colored man the nearest equal to the white have proportionably the fewest mulattos, the least amalgamation. In New Hampshire, the State which goes farthest toward equality between the races, there are just 184 mulattos, while there are in Virginia—how many do you think?—79,775, being 23,126 more than in all the free States together.

These statistics show that slavery is the greatest source of amalgamation, and next to it, not the elevation, but the degradation of the free blacks. Yet Judge Douglas dreads the slightest restraints on the spread of slavery, and the slightest human recognition of the negro, as tending horribly to amalgamation.

The very Dred Scott case affords a strong test as to which party most favors amalgamation, the Republicans or the dear Union-saving Democracy. Dred Scott, his wife, and two daughters were all involved in the suit. We desired the court to have held that they were citizens so far at least as to entitle them to a hearing as to whether they were free or not; and then, also, that they were in fact and in law really free. Could we have had our way, the chances of these black girls ever mixing their blood with that of white people would have been diminished at least to the extent that it could not have been without their consent. But Judge Douglas is delighted to have them decided to be slaves, and not human enough to have a hearing, even if they were free, and thus left subject to the forced concubinage of their masters, and liable to become the mothers of mulattos in spite of themselves: the very state of case that produces nine tenths of all the mulattos—all the mixing of blood in the nation.

Of course, I state this case as an illustration only, not meaning to say or intimate that the master of Dred Scott and his family, or any more than a percentage of masters generally, are inclined to exercise this particular power which they hold over their female slaves.

I have said that the separation of the races is the only perfect preventive of amalgamation. I have no right to say all the members of the Republican party are in favor of this, not to say that as a party they are in favor of it. There is nothing in their platform directly on the subject. But I can say a very large proportion of its members are for it, and that the chief plank in their platform—opposition to the spread of slavery—is most favorable to that separation.

Such separation, if ever effected at all, must be effected by colonization; and no political party, as such, is now doing anything directly for colonization. Party operations at present only favor or retard colonization incidentally. The enterprise is a difficult one; but "where there is a will there is a way," and what colonization needs most is a hearty will. Will springs from the two elements of moral sense and self-interest. Let us be brought to believe it is morally right, and at the same time favorable to, or at least not against, our interest to transfer the African to his native clime, and we shall find a way to do it, however great the task may be. The children of Israel, to such numbers as to include four hundred thousand fighting men, went out of Egyptian bondage in a body.

How differently the respective courses of the Democratic and Republican parties incidentally bear on the question of forming a will—a public sentiment —for colonization, is easy to see. The Republicans inculcate, with whatever of ability they can, that the negro is a man, that his bondage is cruelly wrong, and that the field of his oppression ought not to be enlarged. The Democrats deny his manhood; deny, or dwarf to insignificance, the wrong of his bondage; so far as possible, crush all sympathy for him, and cultivate and excite hatred and disgust against him; compliment themselves as Union-savers for doing so; and call the indefinite outspreading of his bondage "a sacred right of self-government."

The plainest print cannot be read through a gold eagle; and it will be ever hard to find many men who will send a slave to Liberia, and pay his passage, while they can send him to a new country—Kansas, for instance —and sell him for fifteen hundred dollars, and the rise.

JOHN C. CALHOUN

Calhoun entered politics in 1811 as a young nationalist. He aided Henry Clay in forcing the War of 1812; he favored the tariff act of 1816, the United States Bank, and building of roads and canals. Then he changed to a particularist and a free-trader. During his political career, he served as United States senator from South Carolina, secretary of war, secretary of state, and vice-president of the United States. While he held the latter office, he fought against the tariff of 1828 and drew up the *South Carolina Exposition of 1828* to demonstrate the unconstitutionality of protective tariff legislation. This document formed the basis of the South Carolina ordinance of nullification four years later, and it became one of the bibles of the particularist school. In the Senate, Calhoun frequently defended slaveocracy as the highest social system developed by man. His *Disquisition on Government* and his *Discourse on the Constitution and Government of the United States* were published after his death in 1850. The following selection from the *Disquisition* is an attack upon the natural rights philosophy of liberty and equality.

A DISQUISITION ON GOVERNMENT [79]

. . . . . .

The principle, in all communities, according to these numerous and various causes, assigns to power and liberty their proper spheres. To allow to liberty, in any case, a sphere of action more extended than this assigns, would lead to anarchy; and this, probably, in the end, to a contraction instead of an enlargement of its sphere. Liberty, then, when forced on a people unfit for it, would, instead of a blessing, be a curse; as it would, in its reaction, lead directly to anarchy,—the greatest of all curses. No people, indeed, can long enjoy more liberty than that to which their situation and advanced intelligence and morals fairly entitle them. If more than this be allowed,

[79] R. K. Cralle (editor), *Works of John C. Calhoun*. (New York, D. Appleton and Company, 1863), I, 54–59.

they must soon fall into confusion and disorder,—to be followed, if not by anarchy and despotism, by a change to a form of government more simple and absolute; and, therefore, better suited to their condition. And hence, although it may be true, that a people may not have as much liberty as they are fairly entitled to, and are capable of enjoying,—yet the reverse is unquestionably true,—that no people can long possess more than they are fairly entitled to.

Liberty, indeed, though among the greatest blessings, is not so great as that of protection; inasmuch, as the end of the former is the progress and improvement of the race,—while that of the latter is its preservation and perpetuation. And hence, when the two come into conflict, liberty must, and ever ought, to yield to protection; as the existence of the race is of greater moment than its improvement.

It follows, from what has been stated, that it is a great and dangerous error to suppose that all people are equally entitled to liberty. It is a reward to be earned, not a blessing to be gratuitously lavished on all alike;—a reward reserved for the intelligent, the patriotic, the virtuous and deserving;—and not a boon to be bestowed on a people too ignorant, degraded and vicious, to be capable either of appreciating or of enjoying it. Nor is it any disparagement to liberty, that such is, and ought to be the case. On the contrary, its greatest praise,—its proudest distinction is, that an all-wise Providence has reserved it, as the noblest and highest reward for the development of our faculties, moral and intellectual. A reward more appropriate than liberty could not be conferred on the deserving;—nor a punishment inflicted on the undeserving more just, than to be subject to lawless and despotic rule. This dispensation seems to be the result of some fixed law;—and every effort to disturb or defeat it, by attempting to elevate a people in the scale of liberty, above the point to which they are entitled to rise, must ever prove abortive, and end in disappointment. The progress of a people rising from a lower to a higher point in the scale of liberty, is necessarily slow;—and by attempting to precipitate, we either retard, or permanently defeat it.

There is another error, not less great and dangerous, usually associated with the one which has just been considered. I refer to the opinion, that liberty and equality are so intimately united, that liberty cannot be perfect without perfect equality.

That they are united to a certain extent,—and that equality of citizens, in the eyes of the law, is essential to liberty in a popular government, is conceded. But to go further, and make equality of *condition* essential to liberty, would be to destroy both liberty and progress. The reason is, that inequality of condition, while it is a necessary consequence of liberty, is, at the same time, indispensable to progress. In order to understand why this is so, it is necessary to bear in mind, that the main spring to progress is, the desire of individuals to better their condition; and that the strongest impulse which can be given to it is, to leave individuals free to exert themselves in the manner they may deem best for that purpose, as far at least as it can be done consistently with the ends for which government is ordained, —and to secure to all the fruits of their exertions. Now, as individuals differ greatly from each other, in intelligence, sagacity, energy, perseverance, skill, habits of industry and economy, physical power, position and opportunity,—the necessary effect of leaving all free to exert themselves to better their condition, must be a corresponding inequality between those who may possess these qualities and advantages in a high degree, and those who may be deficient in them. The only means by which this result can be prevented are, either to impose such restrictions on the exertions of those who may possess them in a high degree, as will place them on a level with those who do not; or to deprive them of the fruits of their exertions. But to impose such restrictions on them would be destructive of liberty,—while, to deprive them of the fruits of their exertions, would be to destroy the desire of bettering their condition. It is, indeed, this equality of condition between the front and rear ranks, in the march of progress, which gives so strong an impulse to the former to maintain their position, and to the latter to press forward into their files. This gives to progress its greatest impulse. To force the front rank back to the rear, or attempt to push forward the rear into line with the front, by the interposition of the government, would put an end to the impulse, and effectually arrest the march of progress.

These great and dangerous errors have their origin in the prevalent opinion that all men are born free and equal;—than which nothing can be more unfounded and false. It rests upon the assumption of a fact, which is contrary to universal observation, in whatever light it may be regarded. It is, indeed, difficult to explain how an opinion so destitute of all sound reason, ever could have been so extensively entertained, unless we regard it as being confounded with another, which has some semblance of truth;—but which, when properly understood, is not less false and dangerous. I refer to the assertion, that all men are equal in the state of nature; meaning, by a state of nature, a state of individuality, suppposed to have existed prior to the social and political state; and in which men lived apart and independent of each other. If such a state ever did exist, all men would have been, indeed, free and equal in it; that is, free to do as they pleased, and exempt from the authority or control of others—as, by supposition, it existed anterior to society and government. But such a state is purely hypothetical. It never did, nor can exist; as it is inconsistent with the preservation and perpetuation of the race. It is, therefore, a great misnomer to call it *the state of nature*. Instead of being the natural state of man, it is, of all conceivable states, the most opposed to his nature—most repugnant to his feelings, and most incompatible with his wants. His natural state is, the social and political—the one for which his Creator made him, and the only one in which he can preserve and perfect his race. As, then, there never was such a state as the, so called, state of nature, and never can be, it follows, that men, instead of being born in it, are born in the social and political state; and of course instead of being born free and equal, are born subject, not only to parental authority, but to the laws and institutions of the country where born, and under whose protection they draw their first breath. With these remarks, I return from this digression, to resume the thread of the discourse. . . .

GEORGE FITZHUGH

Fitzhugh was a Virginia lawyer and sociologist. He was one of the outstanding southern defenders of slavery. His two books, *Sociology for the South, or the Failure of Free Society* (1854) and *Cannibals All; or Slaves without Masters* (1856), are probably the clearest exposition of the southern view on slavery during the decade before the Civil War. He did not apologize for slavery, but rather attacked the labor system of the free North. He sought to demonstrate that slavery was a superior social and economic system. He attacked the principles of liberty and *laissez-faire* in order to preserve social institutions against their threatened subversion by the socialists and other radicals of his day.

CANNIBALS ALL; OR SLAVES WITHOUT MASTERS [80]

CHAPTER I

The Universal Trade

We are, all, North and South, engaged in the White Slave Trade, and he who succeeds best, is esteemed most respectable. It is far more cruel than the Black Slave Trade, because it exacts more of its slaves, and neither protects nor governs them. We boast, that it exacts more, when we say, "that the *profits* made from employing free labor are greater than those from slave labor." The profits, made from free labor, are the amount of the products of such labor, which the employer, by means of the command which capital or skill gives him, takes away, exacts or "exploitates" from the free laborer. The profits of slave labor are that portion of the products of such labor which the power of the master enables to appropriate. These profits are less, because the master allows the slave to retain a larger share of the results of his own labor, than do the employers of free labor. But we not only boast that the White Slave Trade is more exacting and fraudulent (in fact, though not in intention,) than Black Slavery; but we also boast, that it is more cruel, in leaving the laborer to take care of himself and family out of the pittance which skill or capital have allowed him to retain. When the day's labor is ended, he is free, but is overburdened with the cares of family and household, which make his freedom an empty and delusive mockery. But his employer is really free, and may enjoy the profits made by others' labor, without a care, or a trouble, as to their well-being. The negro slave is free, too, when the labors of the day are over, and free in mind as well as body; for the master provides food, raiment, house, fuel, and everything else necessary to the physical well-being of himself and family. The master's labors commence just when the slave's end. No wonder men should prefer white slavery to capital, to negro slavery, since it is more profitable, and is free from all the cares and labors of black slave-holding.

Now, reader, if you wish to know yourself—to "descant on your deformity" —read on. But if you would cherish self-conceit, self-esteem, or self-appreciation, throw down our book; for we will dispel illusions which have promoted your happiness, and shew you that what you have considered and practiced as virtue, is little better than moral Cannibalism. But you will

[80] George Fitzhugh, *Cannibals All; or Slaves Without Masters*. (Richmond, A. Morris, 1857), pp. 25–32, 353–362.

find yourself in numerous and respectable company; for all good and respectable people are "Cannibals all," who do not labor, or who are successfully trying to live without labor, on the unrequited labor of other people:— Whilst low, bad, and disreputable people, are those who labor to support themselves, and to support said respectable people besides. Throwing the negro slaves out of the account, and society is divided in Christendom into four classes: The rich, or independent respectable people, who live well and labor not at all; the professional and skillful respectable people, who do a little light work, for enormous wages; the poor hard-working people, who support every body, and starve themselves; and the poor thieves, swindlers and sturdy beggars, who live like gentlemen, without labor, on the labor of other people. The gentlemen exploitate, which being done on a large scale, and requiring a great many victims, is highly respectable—whilst the rogues and beggars take so little from others, that they fare little better than those who labor.

But, reader, we do not wish to fire into the flock. "Thou art the man!" You are a Cannibal! and if a successful one, pride yourself on the number of your victims, quite as much as any Feejee chieftain, who breakfasts, dines and sups on human flesh.—And your conscience smites you, if you have failed to succeed, quite as much as his, when he returns from an unsuccessful foray.

Probably, you are a lawyer, or a merchant, or a doctor, who have made by your business fifty thousand dollars, and retired to live on your capital. But, mark! not to spend your capital. That would be vulgar, disreputable, criminal. That would be, to live by your own labor; for your capital is your amassed labor. That would be, to do as common working men do; for they take the pittance which their employers leave them, to live on. They live by labor; for they exchange the results of their own labor for the products of other people's labor. It is, no doubt, an honest, vulgar way of living; but not at all a respectable way. The respectable way of living is, to make other people work for you, and to pay them nothing for so doing—and to have no concern about them after their work is done. Hence, white slaveholding is much more respectable than negro slavery—for the master works nearly as hard for the negro, as he for the master. But you, my virtuous, respectable reader, exact three thousand dollars per annum from white labor, (for your income is the product of white labor) and make not one cent of return in any form. You retain your capital, and never labor, and yet live in luxury on the labor of others. Capital commands labor, as the master does the slave. Neither pays for labor; but the master permits the slave to retain a larger allowance from the proceeds of his own labor, and hence "free labor is cheaper than slave labor." You, with the command over labor which your capital gives you, are a slave owner—a master, without the obligations of a master. They who work for you, who create your income, are slaves, without the rights of slaves. Slaves without a master! Whilst you were engaged in amassing your capital, in seeking to become independent, you were in the White Slave Trade. To become independent, is to be able to make other people support you, without being obliged to labor for *them*. Now, what man in society is not seeking to attain this situation? He who attains it, is a slave owner, in the worst sense. He who is in pursuit of it, is engaged in the slave trade. You, reader, belong to the one or other class. The men without property, in free society, are theoretically in a worse condition than slaves. Practically, their condition corresponds with this theory, as history and statistics every where demonstrate. The capitalists, in free society, live in ten times the luxury and show that Southern masters do, because the slaves to capital work harder and cost less, than negro slaves.

The negro slaves of the South are the happiest, and, in some sense, the freest people in the world. The children and the aged and infirm work not at all, and yet have all the comforts and necessaries of life provided for them. They enjoy liberty, because they are oppressed neither by care nor labor. The women do little hard work, and are protected from the despotism of their husbands by their masters. The negro men and stout boys work, on the average, in good weather, not more than nine hours a day. The balance of their time is spent in perfect abandon. Besides, they have their Sabbaths and holidays. White men, with so much of license and liberty, would die of ennui; but negroes luxuriate in corporeal and mental repose. With their faces upturned to the sun, they can sleep at any hour; and quiet sleep is the greatest of human enjoyments. "Blessed be the man who invented sleep." 'Tis happiness in itself—and results from contentment with the present, and confident assurance of the future. We do not know whether free laborers ever sleep. They are fools to do so; for, whilst they sleep, the wily and watchful capitalist is devising means to ensnare and exploitate them. The free laborer must work or starve. He is more of a slave than the negro, because he works longer and harder for less allowance than the slave, and has no holiday, because the cares of life with him begin when its labors end. He has no liberty, and not a single right. We know, 'tis often said, air and water, are common property, which all have equal right to participate and enjoy; but this is utterly false. The appropriation of the lands carries with it the appropriation of all on or above the lands, *usque ad caelum, aut ad inferos*. A man cannot breathe the air, without a place to breathe it from, and all places are appropriated. All water is private property "to the middle of the stream," except the ocean, and that is not fit to drink.

Free laborers have not a thousandth part of the rights and liberties of negro slaves. Indeed, they have not a single right or a single liberty, unless it be the right or liberty to die. But the reader may think that he and other capitalists and employers are freer than negro slaves. Your capital would soon vanish, if you dared indulge in the liberty and abandon of negroes. You hold your wealth and position by the tenure of constant watchfulness, care and circumspection. You never labor; but you are never free.

Where a few own the soil, they have unlimited power over the balance of society, until domestic slavery comes in, to compel them to permit this balance of society to draw a sufficient and comfortable living from "cerra mater." Free society, asserts the right of a few to the earth—slavery maintains that it belongs, in different degrees, to all.

But, reader, well may you follow the slave trade. It is the only trade worth following, and slaves the only property worth owning. All other is worthless, a mere *caput mortuum*, except in so far as it vests the owner with the power to command the labors of others—to enslave them. Give you a palace, ten thousand acres of land, sumptuous clothes, equippage and every other luxury;

and with your artificial wants, you are poorer than Robinson Crusoe, or the lowest working man, if you have no slaves to capital, or domestic slaves. Your capital will not bring you an income of a cent, nor supply one of your wants, without labor. Labor is indispensable to give value to property, and if you owned everything else, and did not own labor, you would be poor. But fifty thousand dollars means, and is, fifty thousand dollars worth of slaves. You can command, without touching on that capital, three thousand dollars' worth of labor per annum. You could do no more were you to buy slaves with it, and then you would be cumbered with the cares of governing and providing for them. You are a slaveholder now, to the amount of fifty thousand dollars, with all the advantages, and none of the cares and responsibilities of a master.

"Property in man" is what all are struggling to obtain. Why should they not be obliged to take care of man, their property, as they do of their horses and their hounds, their cattle and their sheep. Now, under the delusive name of liberty, you work him, "from morn to dewy eve"—from infancy to old age—then turn him out to starve. You treat your horses and hounds better. Capital is a cruel master. The free slave trade, the commonest, yet the cruellest of trades.

CHAPTER XXXV

Government a Thing of Force, Not of Consent

We do not agree with the authors of the Declaration of Independence, that governments "derive their just powers from the consent of the governed." The women, the children, the negroes, and but few of the non-property holders were consulted, or consented to the Revolution, or the governments that ensued from its success. As to these, the new governments originated in force, and have been continued by force. All governments must originate in force, and be continued by force. The very term, government, implies that it is carried on against the consent of the governed. Fathers do not derive their authority, as heads of families, from the consent of wife and children, nor do they govern their families by their consent. They never take the vote of the family as to the labors to be performed, the moneys to be expended, or as to anything else. Masters dare not take the vote of slaves, as to their government. If they did, constant holiday, dissipation and extravagance would be the result. Captains of ships are not appointed by the consent of the crew, and never take their vote, even in "doubling Cape Horn." If they did, the crew would generally vote to get drunk, and the ship would never weather the cape. Not even in the most democratic countries are soldiers governed by their consent, nor is their vote taken on the eve of battle. They have somehow lost (or never had) the "inalienable rights of life, liberty and the pursuit of happiness"; and, whether Americans or Russians, are forced into battle, without and often against their consent. The ancient republics were governed by a small class of adult male citizens, who assumed and exercised the government, without the consent of the governed. The South is governed just as those ancient republics were. In the county in which we live, there are eighteen thousand souls, and only twelve hundred voters. But we twelve hundred, the governors, never asked and never intend to ask the consent of the sixteen thousand eight hundred whom we govern. Were we to do so, we should soon have an "organized anarchy." The governments of Europe could not exist a week without the positive force of standing armies. They are all governments of force, not of consent. Even in our North, the women, children, and free negroes, constitute four-fifths of the population; and they are all governed without their consent. But they mean to correct this gross and glaring iniquity at the North. They hold that all men, women, and negroes, and smart children, are equals, and entitled to equal rights. The widows and free negroes begin to vote in some of those States, and they will have to let all colors and sexes and ages vote soon, or give up the glorious principles of human equality and universal emancipation.

The experiment which they will make, we fear, is absurd in theory, and the symptoms of approaching anarchy and agrarianism among them, leave no doubt that its practical operation will be no better than its theory. Antirentism, "vote-myself-a-farm"-ism, and all the other isms, are but the spattering drops that precede a social deluge.

Abolition ultimates in "Consent Government"; Consent Government in Anarchy, Free Love, Agrarianism, &c., &c., and "Self-elected despotism," winds up the play.

If the interests of the governors, or governing class, be not conservative, they will not conserve institutions injurious to their interests. There never was and never can be an old society, in which the immediate interests of a majority of human souls do not conflict with all established order, all right of property, and all existing institutions. Immediate interest is all the mass look to; and they would be sure to revolutionize government, as often as the situation of the majority was worse than that of the minority. Divide all property to-day, and a year hence the inequalities of property would provoke a re-division.

In the South, the interest of the governing class is eminently conservative, and the South is fast becoming the most conservative of nations.

Already, at the North, government vibrates and oscillates between Radicalism and Conservatism; at present, Radicalism or Black Republicanism is in the ascendant.

The number of paupers is rapidly increasing; radical and agrarian doctrines are spreading; the women and children, and the negroes, will soon be let in to vote; and then they will try the experiment of "Consent Government and Constituted Anarchy."

It is falsely said, that revolutions never go backwards. They always go backwards, and generally farther back than where they started. The Social Revolution now going on at the North, must some day go backwards. Shall it do so now, ere it has perpetrated an infinitude of mischief, shed oceans of blood, and occasioned endless human misery; or will the Conservatives of the North let it run the length of its leather, inflict all these evils, and then rectify itself by issuing into military despotism? We think that by a kind of alliance, offensive and defensive, with the South, Northern Conservatism may now arrest and turn back the tide of Radicalism and Agrarianism. We will not presume to point out the whole means and *modus operandi*. They on the field of action will best see what is necessary to be done.

Whilst we hold that all government is a matter of force, we yet think the governing class should be numerous enough to understand, and so situated as to represent fairly, all interests. The Greek and Roman masters were thus situated; so were the old Barons of England, and so are the white citizens of the South. If not all masters, like Greek and Roman citizens, they all belong to the master race, have exclusive rights and privileges of citizenship, and an interest not to see this right of citizenship extended, disturbed, and rendered worthless and contemptible.

Whilst the governments of Europe are more obviously kept alive and conducted by force than at any other period, yet are they all from necessity, watchful and regardful of Public Opinion. Opinion now rules the world, but not as expressed through the ballot-box. Governments become more popular as they become more forcible. A large governing class is not apt to mistake or disregard opinion; and, therefore, Republican institutions are best adapted to the times. Under Monarchical forms, the governments of Europe are daily becoming more Republican. The fatal error committed in Western Europe is, the wielding of government by a class who govern but do not represent, the masses. Their interests and those of the masses are antagonistic, whilst those of masters and slaves are identical.

Looking to theory, to the examples of the Ancient Republics, and to England under the Plantaganets, we shall find that Southern institutions are far the best now existing in the world.

We think speculations as to constructing governments are little worth; for all government is the gradual accretion of Nature, time and circumstances. Yet these theories have occurred to us, and, as they are conservative, we will suggest them. In slave-holding countries all freemen should vote and govern, because their interests are conservative. In free states, the government should be in the hands of the land-owners, who are also conservative. A system of primogeniture, and entails of small parcels of land, might, in a great measure, identify the interests of all; or, at least, those who held no lands would generally be the children and kinsmen of those who did, and be taken care of by them. The frequent accumulation of large fortunes, and consequent pauperism of the masses, is the greatest evil of modern society. Would not small entails prevent this? All cannot own lands, but as many should own them as is consistent with good farming and advanced civilization. The social institutions of the Jews, as established by Moses and Joshua, most nearly fulfill our ideas of perfect government.

A word, at parting, to Northern Conservatives. A like danger threatens North and South, proceeding from the same source. Abolitionism is maturing what Political Economy began. With inexorable sequence "Let Alone" is made to usher in No-Government. North and South our danger is the same, and our remedies, though differing in degree, must in character be the same. "Let Alone" must be repudiated, if we would have any Government. We must, in all sections, act upon the principle that the world is "too little governed." You of the North need not institute negro slavery. But the masses require more of protection, and the masses and philosophers equally require more of control. Leave it to time and circumstances to suggest the necessary legislation; but, rely upon it, "Anarchy, plus the street constable," won't answer any longer. The Vigilance Committee of California is but a mob, rendered necessary by the inadequacy of the regular government. It is the "vis medicatrix naturae," vainly attempting to discharge the office of physician. That country is "too little governed," where the best and most conservative citizens have to resolve themselves into mobs and vigilance committees to protect rights which government should, but does not, protect.

The element of force exists probably in too small a degree in our Federal Government. It has neither territory nor subjects. Kansas is better off; for she has a few citizens and a large and fertile territory. She is backing the Government out, if not whipping her. Massachusetts, too, has nullified her laws. Utah contemns her authority, and the Vigilance Committee of California sets her at successful defiance. She is an attempt at a *paper consent* government, without territory or citizens. Considered and treated as a league or treaty between *separate States or Nations*, she may yet have a long and useful existence; for then those *Nations* or *States*, seeing that she has no means of self-enforcement, self-support, or self-conservation, may, for their mutual interests, combine to sustain and defend her. Heretofore, domestic weakness and danger from foreign foes has combined the States in sustaining the Union. Hereafter, the great advantages of friendly and mutual intercourse, trade and exchanges, may continue to produce a like result. But the prospects are alarming, and it is well that all patriots should know that the Union has little power to sustain and perpetuate itself.

There are three kinds of force that occur to us will sustain a government. First, "inside necessity," such as slavery, that occasions a few to usurp power, and to hold it forcibly, without consulting the many; secondly, the force of foreign pressure or aggression, which combines men and States together for common defence; and thirdly, the inherent force of a prescriptive or usurpative government, which sustains itself by standing armies. Such are all the governments of Western Europe. Not one of them could exist forty-eight hours, but for the standing armies. These standing armies became necessary and grew up as slavery disappeared. The old Barons kept the Canaille, the Proletariat, the Sans Culottes, the Nomadic Beggars, in order, by lashing their backs and supplying their wants. They must be fed and kept at work. Modern society tries to effect this (but in vain) by moral suasion and standing armies. Riots, mobs, strikes and revolutions are daily occurring. The mass of mankind cannot be governed by Law. More of despotic discretion, and less of Law, is what the world wants. We take our leave by saying, "THERE IS TOO MUCH LAW AND TOO LITTLE OF GOVERNMENT IN THIS WORLD."

Physical force, not moral suasion, governs the world. The negro sees the driver's lash, becomes accustomed to obedient, cheerful industry, and is not aware that the lash is the force that impels him. The free citizen fulfills, "con amore," his round of social, political and domestic duties, and never dreams that the Law, with its fines and jails, penitentiaries and halters, or Public Opinion, with its ostracism, it mobs, and its tar and feathers, help to keep him revolving in his orbit. Yet, remove these physical forces, and how many good citizens would shoot, like fiery comets, from their spheres, and disturb society with their eccentricities and their crimes.

Government is the life of a nation, and as no one can foresee the various future circumstances of social, any more than of individual life, it is absurd to define on paper, at the birth of either the nation or individual, what they shall do and what not do. Broad construction of constitutions is as good as no constitution, for it leaves the nation to adapt itself to circumstances; but strict construction will destroy any nation, for action is necessary to national conservation, and constitution-makers cannot foresee what action will be necessary. If individual or social life were passed in mere passivity, constitutions might answer. Not in a changing and active world. Louisiana, Florida and Texas would have been denied to the South under strict construction, and she would have been ruined. A constitution, strictly construed, is absolutely inconsistent with permanent national existence.

WILLIAM HARPER

William Harper was a prominent figure in South Carolina politics during the thirties and forties of the last century, holding various legislative and judicial positions. He was a member of the South Carolina constitutional convention of 1832 and voted for the nullification of the tariff act of that year. He wrote several articles and delivered addresses on the questions of nullification, states' rights, and slavery. In his article, *Slavery in the Light of Social Ethics*, Harper attempted to demonstrate that human progress and culture became possible through the institution of slavery.

SLAVERY IN THE LIGHT OF SOCIAL ETHICS [81]

INFLUENCE OF SLAVERY ON SOCIAL LIFE

. . . . . .

President Dew has shown that the institution of slavery is a principal cause of civilization. Perhaps nothing can be more evident than that it is the sole cause. If any thing can be predicated as universally true of uncultivated man, it is that he will not labor beyond what is absolutely necessary to maintain his existence. Labor is pain to those who are unaccustomed to it, and the nature of man is averse to pain. Even with all the training, the helps, and motives of civilization, we find that this aversion can not be overcome in many individuals of the most cultivated societies. The coercion of slavery alone is adequate to form man to habits of labor. Without it, there can be no accumulation of property, no providence for the future, no tastes for comfort or elegancies, which are the characteristics and essentials of civilization. He who has obtained the command of another's labor, first begins to accumulate and provide for the future, and the foundations of civilization are laid. We find confirmed by experience that which is so evident in theory. Since the existence of man upon the earth, with no exception whatever, either of ancient or modern times, every society which has attained civilization, has advanced to it through this process.

Will those who regard slavery as immoral, or crime in itself, tell us that man was not intended for civilization, but to roam the earth as a biped brute? That he was not to raise his eyes to Heaven, or be conformed in his nobler faculties to the image of his Maker? Or will they say that the Judge of all the earth has done wrong in ordaining the means by which alone that end can be obtained? It is true that the Creator can make the wickedness as

[81] E. N. Elliott (editor), *Cotton is King, and Pro-Slavery Arguments*. (Augusta, Pritchard, Abbott and Loomis, 1860), pp. 551-571.

well as the wrath of man to praise him, and bring forth the most benevolent results from the most atrocious actions. But in such cases, it is the motive of the actor alone which condemns the action. The act itself is good, if it promotes the good purposes of God, and would be approved by him, if that result only were intended. Do they not blaspheme the providence of God who denounce as wickedness and outrage, that which is rendered indispensable to his purposes in the government of the world? Or at what stage of the progress of society will they say that slavery ceases to be necessary, and its very existence becomes sin and crime? I am aware that such argument would have little effect on those with whom it would be degrading to contend—who pervert the inspired writings—which in some parts expressly sanction slavery, and throughout indicate most clearly that it is a civil institution, with which religion has no concern—with a shallowness and presumption not less flagrant and shameless than his, who would justify murder from the text, "and Pineas arose and executed judgment."

There seems to be something in this subject which blunts the perceptions, and darkens and confuses the understandings and moral feelings of men. Tell them that, of necessity, in every civilized society, there must be an infinite variety of conditions and employments, from the most eminent and intellectual, to the most servile and laborious; that the negro race, from their temperament and capacity, are peculiarly suited to the situation which they occupy, and not less happy in it than any corresponding class to be found in the world; prove incontestably that no scheme of emancipation could be carried into effect without the most intolerable mischiefs and calamities to both master and slave, or without probably throwing a large and fertile portion of the earth's surface out of the pale of civilization—and you have done nothing. They reply, that whatever may be the consequence, you are bound to do *right;* that man has a right to himself, and man cannot have property in man; that if the negro race be naturally inferior in mind and character, they are not less entitled to the rights of humanity; that if they are happy in their condition, it affords but the stronger evidence of their degradation, and renders them still more objects of commiseration. They repeat, as the fundamental maxim of our civil policy, that all men are born free and equal, and quote from our Declaration of Independence, "that men are endowed by their Creator with certain inalienable *rights*, among which are life, liberty, and the pursuit of happiness."

It is not the first time that I have had occasion to observe that men may repeat with the utmost confidence, some maxim or sentimental phrase, as self-evident or admitted truth, which is either palpably false, or to which, upon examination, it will be found that they attach no definite idea. Notwithstanding our respect for the important document which declared our independence, yet if any thing be found in it, and especially in what may be regarded rather as its ornament than its substance—false, sophistical or unmeaning, that respect should not screen it from the freest examination.

All men are born free and equal. Is it not palpably nearer the truth to say that no man was ever born free, and that no two men were ever born equal? Man is born in a state of the most helpless dependence on others. He continues subject to the absolute control of others, and remains without many of the civil and all of the political privileges of his society, until the period which the laws have fixed as that at which he is supposed to have attained the maturity of his faculties. Then inequality is further developed, and becomes infinite in every society, and under whatever form of government. Wealth and poverty, fame or obscurity, strength or weakness, knowledge or ignorance, ease or labor, power or subjection, mark the endless diversity in the condition of men.

But we have not arrived at the profundity of the maxim. This inequality is, in a great measure, the result of abuses in the institutions of society. They do not speak of what exists, but of what ought to exist. Every one should be left at liberty to obtain all the advantages of society which he can compass, by the free exertion of his faculties, unimpeded by civil restraints. It may be said that this would not remedy the evils of society which are complained of. The inequalities to which I have referred, with the misery resulting from them, would exist in fact under the freest and most popular form of government that man could devise. But what is the foundation of the bold dogma so confidently announced? Females are human and rational beings. They may be found of better faculties, and better qualified to exercise political privileges, and to attain the distinctions of society, than many men; yet who complains of the order of society by which they are excluded from them? For I do not speak of the few who would desecrate them; do violence to the nature which their Creator has impressed upon them; drag them from the position which they necessarily occupy for the existence of civilized society, and in which they constitute its blessing and ornament—the only position which they have ever occupied in any human society—to place them in a situation in which they would be alike miserable and degraded. Low as we descend in combating the theories of presumptuous dogmatists, it cannot be necessary to stoop to this. A youth of eighteen may have powers which cast into the shade those of any of his more advanced contemporaries. He may be capable of serving or saving his country, and if not permitted to do so now, the occasion may have been lost forever. But he can exercise no political privilege, or aspire to any political distinction. It is said that, of necessity, society must exclude from some civil and political privileges those who are unfitted to exercise them, by infirmity, unsuitableness of character, or defect of discretion; that of necessity there must be some general rule on the subject, and that any rule which can be devised will operate with hardship and injustice on individuals. This is all that can be said, and all that need be said. It is saying, in other words, that the privileges in question are no matter of natural rights, but to be settled by convention, as the good and safety of society may require. If society should disfranchise individuals convicted of infamous crimes, would this be an invasion of natural rights? Yet this would not be justified on the score of their moral guilt, but that the good of society required or would be promoted by it. We admit the existence of a moral law, binding on societies as on individuals. Society must act in good faith. No man, or body of men, has a right to inflict pain or privation on others, unless with a view, after full and impartial deliberation, to prevent a greater evil. If this deliberation be had, and the decision made in good faith, there can be no imputation of moral guilt. Has any politician contended that the very existence of governments in which there are orders privileged by law, constitutes a violation of morality; that their continuance is a crime, which men are bound to put an end to, without any consideration of the good or evil to result from the change? Yet this is the natural inference from the dogma of the natural equality of men as applied to our institution of slavery—an equality not to be invaded without injustice and wrong, and requiring to be restored instantly, unqualified, and without reference to consequences.

This is sufficiently common-place, but we are sometimes driven to common-place. It is no less a false and shallow, than a presumptuous philosophy, which theorizes on the affairs of men as a problem to be solved by some unerring rule of human reason, without reference to the designs of a superior intelligence, so far as he has been placed to indicate them, in their creation and destiny. Man is born to subjection. Not only during infancy is he dependent, and under the control of others; at all ages, it is the very bias of his nature, that the strong and the wise should control the weak and ignorant. So it has been since the days of Nimrod. The existence of some form of slavery in all ages and countries, is proof enough of this. He is born to subjection as he is born in sin and ignorance. To make any considerable progress in knowledge, the continued efforts of successive generations, and the diligent training and unwearied exertions of the individual, are requisite. To make progress in moral virtue, not less time and effort, aided by superior help, are necessary; and it is only by the matured exercise of his knowledge and his virtue, that he can attain to civil freedom. Of all things, the existence of civil liberty is most the result of artificial institution. The proclivity of the natural man is to domineer or to be subservient. A noble result, indeed, but in the attaining of which, as in the instances of knowledge and virtue, the Creator, for his own purposes, has set a limit beyond which we cannot go.

But he who is most advanced in knowledge, is most sensible of his own ignorance, and how much must forever be unknown to man in his present condition. As I have heard it expressed, the further you extend the circle of light, the wider is the horizon of darkness. He who has made the greatest progress in moral purity, is most sensible of the depravity, not only of the world around him, but of his own heart, and the imperfection of his best motives; and this he knows that men must feel and lament so long as they continue men. So when the greatest progress in civil liberty has been made, the enlightened lover of liberty will know that there must remain much inequality, much injustice, much *slavery*, which no human wisdom or virtue will ever be able wholly to prevent or redress. As I have before had the honor to say to this Society, the condition of our whole existence is but to struggle with evils—to compare them—to choose between them, and, so far as can, to mitigate them. To say that there is evil in any institution, is only to say that it is human.

And can we doubt but that this long discipline and laborious process, by which men are required to work out the elevation and improvement of their individual nature and their social condition, is imposed for a great and benevolent end? Our faculties are not adequate to the solution of the mystery, why it should be so; but the truth is clear, that the world was not intended for the seat of universal knowledge, or goodness, or happiness, or freedom.

Man has been endowed by his Creator with certain inalienable rights, among which are life, liberty, and the pursuit of happiness. What is meant by the *inalienable* right of liberty? Has any one who has used the words ever asked himself this question? Does it mean that a man has no right to alienate his own liberty—to sell himself and his posterity for slaves? This would seem to be the more obvious meaning. When the word *right* is used, it has reference to some law which sanctions it, and would be violated by its invasion. It must refer either to the general law of morality, or the law of the country— the law of God or the law of man. If the law of any country permitted it, it would of course be absurd to say that the law of that country was violated by such alienation. If it have any meaning in this respect, it must mean that though the law of the country permitted it, the man would be guilty of an immoral act who should thus alienate his liberty. A fit question for schoolmen to discuss, and the consequences resulting from its decision as important as from any of theirs. Yet who will say that the man pressed by famine, and in prospect of death, would be criminal for such an act? Self-preservation, as is truly said, is the first law of nature. High and peculiar characters, by elaborate cultivation, may be taught to prefer death to slavery, but it would be folly to prescribe this as a duty to the mass of mankind.

If any rational meaning can be attributed to the sentence I have quoted, it is this: That the society, or the individuals who exercise the powers of government, are guilty of a violation of the law of God or of morality, when, by any law or public act, they deprive men of life or liberty, or restrain them in the pursuit of happiness. Yet every government does, and of necessity must, deprive men of life and liberty for offenses against society. Restrain them in the pursuit of happiness! Why all the laws of society are intended for nothing else but to restrain men from the pursuit of happiness, according to their own ideas of happiness or advantage—which the phrase must mean if it means any thing. And by what right does society punish by the loss of life or liberty? Not on account of the moral guilt of the criminal—not by impiously and arrogantly assuming the prerogative of the Almighty, to dispense justice or suffering, according to moral desert. It is for its own protection—it is the right of self-defense. If there existed the blackest moral turpitude, which by its example or consequences, could be of no evil to society, government would have nothing to do with that. If an action, the most harmless in its moral character, could be dangerous to the security of society, society would have the perfect right to punish it. If the possession of a black skin would be otherwise dangerous to society, society has the same right to protect itself by disfranchising the possessor of civil privileges, and to continue the disability to his posterity, if the same danger would be incurred by its removal. Society inflicts these forfeitures for the security of the lives of its members; it inflicts them for the security of their property, the great essential of civilization; it inflicts them also for the protection of its political institutions, the forcible attempt to overturn which, has always been justly regarded as the greatest crime; and who has questioned its right so to inflict? "Man can not have property in man"—a phrase as full of meaning as, "who slays fat oxen should himself be fat." Certainly he may, if the laws of society allow it, and if it be on sufficient grounds, neither he nor society do wrong.

And is it by this—as we must call it, however recommended to our higher feelings by its association—well-sounding, but unmeaning verbiage of natural equality and inalienable rights, that our lives are to be put in jeopardy, our property destroyed, and our political institutions overturned or endangered? If a people had on its borders a tribe of barbarians, whom no treaties or faith could bind, and by whose attacks they were constantly endangered, against whom they could devise no security, but that they should be exterminated or enslaved; would they not have the right to enslave them, and keep them in slavery so long as the same danger would be incurred by their manumission? If a civilized man and a savage were by chance placed together on a desolate island, and the former, by the superior power of civilization, would reduce the latter to subjection, would he not have the same right? Would this not be the strictest self-defense? I do not now consider, how far we can make out a similar case to justify our enslaving of the negroes. I speak to those who contend for inalienable rights, and that the existence of slavery always, and under all circumstances, involves injustice and crime.

As I have said, we acknowledge the existence of a moral law. It is not necessary for us to resort to the theory which resolves all right into force. The existence of such a law is imprinted on the hearts of all human beings. But though its existence be acknowledged, the mind of man has hitherto been tasked in vain to discover an unerring standard of morality. It is a common and undoubted maxim of morality, that you shall not do evil that good may come. You shall not do injustice or commit an invasion of the rights of others, for the sake of a greater ulterior good. But what is injustice, and what are the rights of others? And why are we not to commit the one or invade the other? It is because it inflicts pain or suffering, present or prospective, or cuts them off from enjoyment which they might otherwise attain. The Creator has sufficiently revealed to us that *happiness* is the great end, the sole object of all animated and sentient beings. To this he has directed their aspirations and efforts, and we feel that we thwart his benevolent purposes when we destroy or impede that happiness. This is the only *natural* right of man. All other rights result from the conventions of society, and these, to be sure, we are not to invade, whatever good may appear to us likely to follow. Yet are we in no instance to inflict pain or suffering, or disturb enjoyment, for the sake of producing a greater good? Is the madman not to be restrained who would bring destruction on himself or others? Is pain not to be inflicted on the child, when it is the only means by which he can be effectually instructed to provide for his own future happiness? Is the surgeon guilty of wrong who amputates a limb to preserve life? Is not the object of all penal legislation, to inflict suffering for the sake of greater good to be secured to society?

By what right is it that man exercises dominion over the beasts of the field; subdues them to painful labor, or deprives them of life for his sustenance or enjoyment? They are not rational beings. No, but they are the creatures of God, sentient beings, capable of suffering and enjoyment, and entitled to enjoy according to the measure of their capacities. Does not the voice of nature inform every one, that he is guilty of wrong when he inflicts on them pain without necessity or object? If their existence be limited to the present life, it affords the stronger argument for affording them the brief enjoyment of which it is capable. It is because the greater good is effected; not only to man but to the inferior animals themselves. The care of man gives the boon of existence to myriads who would never otherwise have enjoyed it, and the enjoyment of their existence is better provided for while it lasts. It belongs to the being of superior faculties to judge of the relations which shall subsist between himself and inferior animals, and the use he shall make of them; and he may justly consider himself, who has the greater capacity of enjoyment, in the first instance. Yet he must do this conscientiously, and no doubt, moral guilt has been incurred by the infliction of pain on these animals, with no adequate benefit to be expected. I do no disparagement to the dignity of human nature, even in its humblest form, when I say that on the very same foundation, with the difference only of circumstances and degree, rests the right of the civilized and cultivated man, over the savage and ignorant. It is the order of nature and of God, that the being of superior faculties and knowledge, and therefore of superior power, should control and dispose of those who are inferior. It is as much in the order of nature, that men should enslave each other, as that other animals should prey upon each other. I admit that he does this under the highest moral responsibility, and is most guilty if he wantonly inflicts misery or privation on beings more capable of enjoyment or suffering than brutes, without necessity or any view to the greater good which is to result. If we conceive of society existing without government, and that one man by his superior strength, courage or wisdom, could obtain the mastery of his fellows, he would have a perfect right to do so. He would be morally responsible for the use of his power, and guilty if he failed to direct them so as to promote their happiness as well as his own. Moralists have denounced the injustice and cruelty which have been practiced towards our aboriginal Indians, by which they have been driven from their native seats and exterminated, and no doubt with much justice. No doubt, much fraud and injustice has been practiced in the circumstances and the manner of their removal. Yet who has contended that civilized man had no moral right to possess himself of the country? That he was bound to leave this wide and fertile continent, which is capable of sustaining uncounted myriads of a civilized race, to a few roving and ignorant barbarians? Yet if any thing is certain, it is certain that there were no means by which he could possess the country, without exterminating or enslaving them. Savage and civilized man cannot live together, and the savage can be tamed only by being enslaved or by having slaves. By enslaving alone could he have preserved them. And who shall take upon himself to decide that the more benevolent course, and more pleasing to God, was pursued towards them, or that it would not have been better that they had been enslaved generally, as they were in particular instances? It is a refined philosophy, and utterly false in its application to general nature, or the mass of human kind, which teaches that existence is not the greatest of all boons, and worthy of being preserved even under the most adverse circumstances. The strongest instinct of all animated beings sufficiently proclaims this. When the last red man shall have vanished from our forests, the sole remaining traces of his blood will be found among our enslaved population. The African slave trade has given, and will give, the boon of existence to millions and millions in our country, who would otherwise never have enjoyed it, and the enjoyment of their existence is better provided for while it lasts. Or if, for the rights of man over inferior animals, we are referred to revelation, which pronounces—"ye shall have dominion over the beasts of the field, and over the fowls of the air," we refer to the same, which declares not the less explicitly—

"Both the bond-man and bond-maids which thou shalt have, shall be of the heathen that are among you. Of them shall you buy bond-men and bond-maids."

"Moreover of the children of strangers that do sojourn among you, of them shall ye buy, and of their families that are with you, which they begot in your land, and they shall be your possession. And ye shall take them as an inheritance for your children after you, to inherit them by possession. They shall be your bond-men forever."

In moral investigations, ambiguity is often occasioned by confounding the intrinsic nature of an action, as determined by its consequence, with the motive of the actor, involving moral guilt or innocence. If poison be given with a view to destroy another, and it cures him of disease, the poisoner is guilty, but the act is beneficent in its results. If medicine be given with a view to heal, and it happens to kill, he who administered it is innocent, but the act is a noxious one. If they who begun and prosecuted the slave trade, practiced horrible cruelties and inflicted much suffering—as no doubt they did, though these have been much exaggerated—for merely selfish purposes, and with no view to future good, they were morally most guilty. So far as unnecessary cruelty was practiced, the motive and the act were alike bad. But if we could be sure that the entire effect of the trade has been to produce more happiness than would otherwise have existed, we must pronounce it good, and that it has happened in the ordering of God's providence, to whom evil cannot be imputed. Moral guilt has not been imputed to Las Casas, and if the importation of African slaves into America, had the effect of preventing more suffering than it inflicted, it was good, both in the motive and the result. I freely admit that, it is hardly possible to justify morally, those who begun and carried on the slave trade. No speculation of future good to be brought about, could compensate the enormous amount of evil it occasioned.

If we should refer to the common moral sense of mankind, as determined by their conduct in all ages and countries, for a standard of morality, it would seem to be in favor of slavery. The will of God, as determined by utility, would be an infallible standard, if we had an unerring measure of utility. The utilitarian philosophy, as it is commonly understood, referring only to the animal wants and employments, and physical condition of man, is utterly false and degrading. If a sufficiently extended definition be given to utility, so as to include every thing that may be a source of enjoyment or suffering, it is for the most part useless. How can you compare the pleasures resulting from the exercise of the understanding, the taste and the imagination, with the animal enjoyments of the senses—the gratification derived from a fine poem with that from a rich banquet? How are we to weigh the pains and enjoyments of one man highly cultivated and of great sensibility, against those of many men of blunter capacity for enjoyment or suffering? And if we could determine with certainty in what utility consists, we are so short-sighted with respect to consequences—the remote results of our best considered actions are so often wide of our anticipations, or contrary to them, that we should still be very much in the dark. But though we cannot arrive at absolute certainty with respect to the utility of actions, it is always fairly matter of argument. Though an imperfect standard, it is the best we have, and perhaps the Creator did not intend that we should arrive at perfect certainty with regard to the morality of many actions. If, after the most careful examination of consequences that we are able to make, with due distrust of ourselves, we impartially, and in good faith, decide for that which appears likely to produce the greatest good, we are free from moral guilt. And I would impress most earnestly, that with our imperfect and limited faculties, and short-sighted as we are to the future, we can rarely, very rarely indeed, be justified in producing considerable present evil or suffering, in the expectation of remote future good—if indeed this can ever be justified.

In considering this subject, I shall not regard it in the first instance in reference to the present position of the slaveholding States, or the difficulties which lie in the way of their emancipating their slaves, but as a naked, abstract question—whether it is better that the institution of praedial and domestic slavery should, or should not, exist in civilized society. And though some of my remarks may seem to have such a tendency, let me not be understood as taking upon myself to determine that it is better that it should exist. God forbid that the responsibility of deciding such a question should ever be thrown on me or my countrymen. But this I will say, and not without confidence, that it is in the power of no human intellect to establish the contrary proposition—that it is better it should not exist. This is probably known but to one being, and concealed from human sagacity.

There have existed in various ages, and we now see existing in the world, people in every stage of civilization, from the most barbarous to the most refined. Man, as I have said, is not born to civilization. He is born rude and ignorant. But it will be, I suppose, admitted that it is the design of his Creator that he should attain to civilization: that religion should be known, that the comforts and elegancies of life should be enjoyed, that letters and arts should be cultivated; in short, that there should be the greatest possible development of moral and intellectual excellence. It can hardly be necessary to say any thing of those who have extolled the superior virtues and enjoyments of savage life—a life of physical wants and sufferings, of continual insecurity. of furious passions and depraved vices. Those who have praised savage life, are those who have known nothing of it, or who have become savages themselves. But as I have said, so far as reason or universal experience instruct us, the institution of slavery is an essential process in emerging from savage life. It must then produce good, and promote the designs of the Creator.

I add further, *that slavery anticipates the benefits of civilization, and retards the evils of civilization.* The former part of this proposition has been so fully established by a writer of great power of thought—though I fear his practical conclusions will be found of little value—that it is hardly necessary to urge it. Property—the accumulation of capital, as it is commonly called—is the first element of civilization. But to accumulate, or to use capital to any considerable extent, the combination of labor is necessary. In early stages of society, when people are thinly scattered over an extensive territory, the labor necessary to extensive works cannot be commanded. Men are independent of each other. Having the command of abundance of land, no one will submit to be employed in the service of his neighbor. No one, therefore, can employ more capital than he can use with his own hands, or those of his family, nor have an income much beyond the necessaries of life. There can, therefore, be little leisure for intellectual pursuits, or means of acquiring the comforts or elegancies of life. It is hardly necessary to say, however, that if a man has the command of slaves, he may combine labor, and use capital to any required extent, and therefore accumulate wealth. He shows that no colonies have been successfully planted without some sort of slavery. So we find the fact to be. It is only in the slaveholding States of our Confederacy, that wealth can be acquired by agriculture—which is the general employment of our whole country. Among us, we know that there is no one, however humble his beginning, who, with persevering industry, intelligence, and orderly and virtuous habits, may not attain to considerable opulence. So far as wealth has been accumulated in the States which do not possess slaves, it has been in cities by the pursuit of commerce, or lately, by manufactures. But the products of slave labor furnish more than two-thirds of the materials of our foreign commerce, which the industry of those States is employed in transporting and exchanging; and among the slaveholding States is to be found the great market for all the productions of their industry, of whatever kind. The prosperity of those States, therefore, and the civilization of their cities, have been for the most part created by the existence of slavery. Even in the cities, but for a class of population, which our institutions have marked as servile, it would be scarcely possible to preserve the ordinary habitudes of civilized life, by commanding the necessary menial and domestic service.

Every stage of human society, from the most barbarous to the most refined, has its own peculiar evils to mark it as the condition of mortality; and perhaps there is none but omnipotence who can say in which the scale of good or evil most preponderates. We need say nothing of the evils of savage life. There is a state of society elevated somewhat above it, which is to be found in some of the more thinly peopled portions of our own country—the rudest agricultural state—which is thus characterized by the author to whom I have referred: "The American of our back woods has often been described to the English as grossly ignorant, dirty, unsocial, delighting in rum and tobacco, attached to nothing but his rifle, adventurous, restless, more than half savage. Deprived of social enjoyments or excitements, he has recourse to those of savage life, and becomes (for in this respect the Americans degenerate) unfit for society." This is no very inviting picture, which, though exaggerated, we know not to be without likeness. The evils of such a state, I suppose, will hardly be thought compensated by unbounded freedom, perfect equality, and ample means of subsistence.

But let us take another stage in the progress—which to many will appear to offer all that is desirable in existence, and realize another Utopia. Let us suppose a state of society in which all shall have property, and there shall be no great inequality of property—in which society shall be so much condensed as to afford the means of social intercourse, without being crowded, so as to create difficulty in obtaining the means of subsistence—in which every family that chooses may have as much land as will employ its own hands, while others may employ their industry in forming such products as it may be desirable to exchange with them. Schools are generally established, and the rudiments of education universally diffused. Religion is taught, and every village has its church, neat, though humble, lifting its spire to heaven. Here is a situation apparently the most favorable to happiness. I say *apparently*, for the greatest source of human misery is not in external circumstances, but in men themselves—in their depraved inclinations, their wayward passions and perverse wills. Here is room for all the petty competition, the envy, hatred, malice and dissimulation that torture the heart in what may be supposed the most sophisticated states of society; and though less marked and offensive, there may be much of the licentiousness.

But apart from this, in such a condition of society, if there is little suffering, there is little high enjoyment. The even flow of life forbids the high excitement which is necessary for it. If there is little vice, there is little place for the eminent virtues, which employ themselves in controlling the disorders and remedying the evils of society, which, like war and revolution, call forth the highest powers of man, whether for good or for evil. If there is little misery, there is little room for benevolence. Useful public institutions we may suppose to be created, but not such as are merely ornamental. Elegant arts can be little cultivated, for there are no means to reward the artists; nor the higher literature, for no one will have leisure or means to cultivate it for its own sake. Those who acquire what may be called liberal education, will do so in order to employ it as the means of their own subsistence or advancement in a profession, and literature itself will partake of the sordidness of trade. In short, it is plain that in such a state of society, the moral and intellectual faculties cannot be cultivated to their highest perfection.

But whether that which I have described be the most desirable state of society or no, it is certain that it can not continue. Mutation and progress is the condition of human affairs. Though retarded for a time by extraneous or accidental circumstances, the wheel must roll on. The tendency of population is to become crowded, increasing the difficulty of obtaining subsistence. There will be some without any property except the capacity of labor. This they must sell to those who have the means of employing them, thereby swelling the amount of their capital, and increasing inequality. The process still goes on. The number of laborers increases until there is a difficulty in obtaining employment. Then competition is established. The remuneration of the laborer becomes gradually less and less; a larger and larger proportion of the product of his labor goes to swell the fortune of the capitalist; inequality becomes still greater and more invidious, until the process ends in the establishment of just such a state of things, as the same author describes as now existing in England. After a most imposing picture of her greatness and resources; of her superabounding capital, and all pervading industry and enterprise; of her public institutions for purposes of art, learning and benevolence; her public improvements, by which intercourse is facilitated, and the convenience of man subserved; the conveniences and luxuries of life enjoyed by those who are in possession of fortune, or have profitable employments; of all, in short, that places her at the head of modern civilization, he proceeds to give the reverse of the picture. And here I shall use his own words: "The laboring class compose the bulk of the people; the great body of the people; the vast majority of the people—these are the terms by which English writers and speakers usually describe those whose only property is their labor."

"Of comprehensive words, the two most frequently used in English politics, are distress and pauperism. After these, of expressions applied to the state of the poor, the most common are vice and misery, wretchedness, suffering, ignorance, degradation, discontent, depravity, drunkenness, and the increase of crime; with many more of the like nature."

He goes on to give the details of this inequality and wretchedness, in terms calculated to sicken and appall one to whom the picture is new. That he has painted strongly we may suppose; but there is ample corroborating testimony, if such were needed, that the representation 'is substantially just. Where so much misery exists, there must of course be much discontent, and many have been disposed to trace the source of the former in vicious legislation, or the structure of government; and the author gives the various schemes, sometimes contradictory, sometimes ludicrous, which projectors have devised as a remedy for all this evil to which flesh is heir. That ill-judged legislation may have sometimes aggravated the general suffering, or that its extremity may be mitigated by the well-directed efforts of the wise and virtuous, there can be no doubt. One purpose for which it has been permitted to exist is, that it may call forth such efforts, and awaken powers and virtues which would otherwise have slumbered for want of object. But remedy there is none, unless it be to abandon their civilization. This inequality, this vice, this misery, this *slavery*, is the price of England's civilization. They suffer the lot of humanity. But perhaps we may be permitted humbly to hope, that great, intense and widely spread as this misery undoubtedly is in reality, it may yet be less so than in appearance. We can estimate but very, very imperfectly the good and evil of individual condition, as of different states of society. Some unexpected solace arises to alleviate the severest calamity. Wonderful is the power of custom, in making the hardest condition tolerable; the most generally wretched life has circumstances of mitigation, and moments of vivid enjoyment, of which the more seemingly happy can scarcely conceive; though the lives of individuals be shortened, the aggregate of existence is increased; even the various forms of death accelerated by want, familiarized to the contemplation, like death to the soldier on the field of battle, may become scarcely more formidable than what we are accustomed to regard as nature's ordinary outlets of existence. If we could perfectly analyze the enjoyments and sufferings of the most happy, and the most miserable man, we should perhaps be startled to find the difference so much less than our previous impressions had led us to conceive. But it is not for us to assume the province of omniscience. The particular theory of the author quoted, seems to be founded on an assumption of this sort—that there is a certain stage in the progress, when there is a certain balance between the demand for labor, and the supply of it, which is more desirable than any other—when the territory is so thickly peopled that all can not own land and cultivate the soil for themselves, but a portion will be compelled to sell their labor to others; still leaving, however, the wages of labor high, and the laborer independent. It is plain, however, that this would in like manner partake of the good and the evil of other states of society. There would be less of equality and less rudeness, than in the early stages; less civilization, and less suffering, than in the latter.

It is the competition for employment, which is the source of this misery of society, that gives rise to all excellence in art and knowledge. When the demand for labor exceeds the supply, the services of the most ordinarily qualified laborer will be eagerly retained. When the supply begins to exceed, and competition is established, higher and higher qualifications will be required, until at length when it becomes very intense, none but the most consummately skillful can be sure to be employed. Nothing but necessity can drive men to the exertions which are necessary so to qualify themselves. But it is not in arts, merely mechanical alone, that this superior excellence will be required. It will be extended to every intellectual employment; and though this may not be the effect in the instance of every individual, yet it will fix the habits and character of the society, and prescribe everywhere, and in every department, the highest possible standard of attainment.

But how is it that the existence of slavery, as with us, will retard the evils of civilization? Very obviously. It is the intense competition of civilized life, that gives rise to the excessive cheapness of labor, and the excessive cheapness of labor is the cause of the evils in question. Slave labor can never be so cheap as what is called free labor. Political economists have established as the natural standard of wages in a fully peopled country, the value of the laborer's existence. I shall not stop to inquire into the precise truth of this proposition. It certainly approximates the truth. Where competition is intense, men will labor for a bare subsistence, and less than a competent subsistence. The employer of free laborers obtains their services during the time of their health and vigor, without the charge of rearing them from infancy, or supporting them in sickness or old age. This charge is imposed on the employer of slave labor, who, therefore, pays higher wages, and cuts off the principal source of misery—the wants and sufferings of infancy, sickness, and old age. Laborers too will be less skillful, and perform less work—enhancing the price of that sort of labor. The poor laws of England are an attempt—but an awkward and empirical attempt—to supply the place of that which we should suppose the feelings of every human heart would declare to be a natural obligation—that he who has received the benefit of the laborer's services during his health and vigor, should maintain him when he becomes unable to provide for his own support. They answer their purpose, however, very imperfectly, and are unjustly and unequally imposed. There is no attempt to apportion the burden according to the benefit received—and perhaps there could be none. This is one of the evils of their condition.

In periods of commercial revulsion and distress, like the present, the distress, in countries of free labor, falls principally on the laborers. In those of slave labor, it falls almost exclusively on the employer. In the former, when a business becomes unprofitable, the employer dismisses his laborers or lowers their wages. But with us, it is the very period at which we are least able to dismiss our laborers; and if we would not suffer a further loss, we can not reduce their wages. To receive the benefit of the services of which they are capable, we must provide for maintaining their health and vigor. In point of fact, we know that this is accounted among the necessary expenses of management. If the income of every planter of the Southern States were permanently reduced one-half, or even much more than that, it would not take one jot from the support and comforts of the slaves. And this can never be materially altered, until they shall become so unprofitable that slavery must be of necessity abandoned. It is probable that the accumulation of individual wealth will never be carried to quite so great an extent in a slaveholding country, as in one of free labor; but a consequence will be, that there will be less inequality and less suffering.

Servitude is the condition of civilization. It was decreed, when the command was given, "be fruitful, and multiply and replenish the earth, and subdue it," and when it was added, "in the sweat of thy face shalt thou eat bread." And what human being shall arrogate to himself the authority to pronounce that our form of it is worse in itself, or more displeasing to God, than that which exists elsewhere? Shall it be said that the servitude of other countries grows out of the exigencies of their circumstances, and therefore society is not responsible for it? But if we know that in the progress of things it is to come, would not it seem the part of wisdom and foresight, to make provision for it, and thereby, if we can, mitigate the severity of its evils? But the fact is not so. Let any one who doubts, read the book to which I have several times referred, and he may be satisfied that it was forced upon us by the extremest exigency of circumstances, in a struggle for very existence. Without it, it is doubtful whether a white man would be now existing on this continent—certain, that if there were, they would be in a state of the utmost destitution, weakness, and misery. It was forced on us by necessity, and further fastened upon us by the superior authority of the mother country. I, for one, neither deprecate nor resent the gift. Nor did we institute slavery. The Africans brought to us had been, speaking in the general, slaves in their own country, and only underwent a change of masters. In the countries of Europe, and the States of our Confederacy, in which slavery has ceased to exist, it was abolished by positive legislation. If the order of nature has been departed from, and a forced and artificial state of things introduced, it has been, as the experience of all the world declares, by them and not by us. . . .

SELECTED BIBLIOGRAPHY

A. T. Bledsoe, *An Essay on Liberty and Slavery* (1856).

W. E. Channing, *Essay on Slavery* (1835).

J. D. B. De Bow, *The Industrial Resources of the Southern and Western States* (3 vols., 1852–1853).

F. R. Dew, *An Essay on Slavery* (1849).

W. E. Dodd, *The Cotton Kingdom* (1911).

E. N. Elliott (ed.), *Cotton is King and Pro-Slavery Arguments* (1860).

G. Fitzhugh, *Sociology for the South, or the Failure of Free Society* (1854).
    Cannibals All, or Slaves Without Masters (1857).

W. L. Garrison, *Selections from the Writings and Speeches of W. L. Garrison* (1852).
    Life of W. L. Garrison (by his sons, 3 vols., 1889).

H. R. Helper, *The Impending Crisis* (1859).

W. Hosmer, *The Higher Law in its Relation to Civil Government* (1852).

A. Lincoln, *Works* (edited by Nicolay and Hay, 2 vols., 1894).

J. R. Lowell, *Anti-Slavery Papers* (1902)

W. S. Simms, *The Morals of Slavery* (1837).

F. Wayland, *Elements of Moral Science* (1835).

CHAPTER VI

PARTICULARISM VERSUS NATIONALISM

I

The conflict between the economic and social system of the North and that of the South did more than develop theories of slavery. It brought into sharp relief diametrically opposite views on the nature of the Union. In the battle between industrial capitalism and slave agrarianism, the stakes were high. Political dominance of the central government would enable the North to impose heavy tariffs upon the South; the victory of the South would result in free trade and imperialistic expansion. Neither could permit the success of the other group. Already in 1832 South Carolina had attempted to nullify a tariff law. During the next thirty years the controversy grew increasingly bitter. Both contestants attempted to control the federal government by the admission of additional free or slave states. But the South before long realized that in this game the North held trumps. The South managed to hold its own in the fight for the Senate; but the rapidly increasing population of the industrial North and free West doomed the South to a decided inferiority in the House of Representatives. The growth of the railroad system and the economic tying up of the East and the Northwest spelled political disaster to the South. This union of interests finally led to the success of the new Republican party in 1860; its leaders advocated homesteads for the West and protective tariffs for the East. The southern leaders foresaw the eventual decline of the South in national councils. The natural tendency, therefore, was for them to minimize the powers of the national government and to expand the authority of the states. Moreover, the central, not the state, government passed tariff laws. Decentralization would be synonymous with free trade and *laissez-faire*. The adoption of local autonomy, on the other hand, would prevent the northern industrialists from employing the government for their economic aggrandizement. The growth of manufacturing and commerce demanded federal aid in the form of tariffs, trade treaties, naval protection, and other similar measures that could emanate only from the central government. Thus their respective

economic systems drove the South to particularism and the North
to nationalism.

Fortunately for the disputants, unfortunately for the peace of the
nation, the framers of the Constitution had been practical men, not
political philosophers. In 1787 serious problems of economic chaos,
domestic dissension, and personal financial loss confronted them. In
a purely pragmatic fashion they constructed a new central government in order to eliminate the then pressing evils. But not being
theorists, they did not bother themselves as to the exact nature of
the new government. They granted it those powers that would
enable them to solve the existing economic problems; they denied
to the states those powers which, as they felt, the states had abused.
No philosophical excursions into the allocation or the nature of sovereignty disturbed these pragmatists. The framers of the Constitution thus left the southern particularists and the northern nationalists
unhampered in their conflicting contentions.

Even when the framers of the new government did temporarily
desert the realm of pure pragmatism, they expounded a theory of the
nature of the Union that was sufficiently indefinite not to affect the
later controversy. They felt that somehow they were dividing sovereignty between the federal and state governments. The new government, they said, was neither a confederation nor a "consolidated
republic." Rather it was a new mixed form. The states did not believe that they were surrendering all of their sovereignty; on the
other hand, they thought that they were renouncing some of their
previous supreme authority. The *Federalist* asserted that the states
will retain "all the rights of sovereignty which were not by that act
exclusively delegated to the United States." [1] The structure of the
new government was a happy union of national and confederate
characteristics. The organization of the legislature, the election of
the President, the delegation of powers, the ratification and amendment provisions—all called for the combination of national and state
units. James Madison, "the Father of the Constitution," expounded
most staunchly this concept of divided sovereignty. Writing in his
later years, and looking back upon the framing of the Constitution,
he said:

"It has hitherto been understood that the supreme power, that is, the
sovereignty of the people of the States, was in its nature divisible, and was,
in fact, divided, according to the Constitution of the United States, between
the States in their united and the States in their individual capacities, and

[1] *Federalist* No. 32, p. 186.

so viewed by the Convention in transmitting the Constitution to the Congress of the Confederation; so viewed and called in official, in controversial, and in popular language; that as the States, in their highest sovereign character, were competent to surrender the whole sovereignty and form themselves into a consolidated State, so they might surrender a part and retain, as they have done, the other part, forming a mixed Government, with a division of its authority as marked out in the Constitution." [2]

This same idea of divided sovereignty crept into the federal courts. As early as 1792 the Supreme Court, in the case of *Chisholm v. Georgia,* pronounced this dictum: "The United States are sovereign as to all the powers of government actually surrendered. Each state in the Union is sovereign as to all the powers reserved." [3]

This theory of divided sovereignty settled nothing. It satisfied neither the particularists nor the nationalists. It did not determine who should decide the exact line of division between state and federal authority. It provided the states with no machinery for checking any excess of sovereignty by the central government. It, moreover, ran afoul of the later more philosophical demonstration that sovereignty, as the ultimate and supreme power, is indivisible by its very nature. The particularists completely abandoned divided sovereignty and expounded undiluted state supremacy. And, while the phraseology of divided sovereignty crept occasionally into the speech of the nationalists, they too dropped this theory.

No sooner had the new government begun operation than a conflict occurred between the exponents of centralization and decentralization. The Federalist party favored the strengthening of the national government; the Jeffersonians advocated localism. In order to win the ratification of the Constitution, the Federalists made concessions to the opponents of that document. Among these was the Tenth Amendment, providing that: "The powers not delegated to the United States by the Constitution, nor prohibited by it to the States, are reserved to the States respectively, or to the people." In 1792 the Supreme Court upheld the right of one Chisholm to sue in the federal courts the sovereign state of Georgia. The anti-nationalists rose in an uproar. Within six years they pushed through the Eleventh Amendment to the effect that:

"The Judicial power of the United States shall not be construed to extend to any suit in law or equity, commenced or prosecuted against one of the United States by Citizens of another State, or by Citizens or Subjects of any Foreign State."

[2] Madison, *Works*, IV, 390–391 (1835).   [3] 2 Dallas 435.

From the formation of the Union to the Civil War, almost every one of the states at one time or another expounded the doctrine of states' rights. Whenever the shoe pinched a state, it temporarily joined the particularistic camp. During John Adams's administration the Federalists, in order to stifle the bitter criticisms of their administration, passed the Alien and Sedition Acts. These stringent restrictions upon public discussion and their energetic enforcement by Federalist judges enraged the Jeffersonian democrats. John Taylor suggested to Jefferson that:

"The right of the State governments to expound the constitution might possibly be made the basis of a movement towards its amendment. If this is insufficient the people in state conventions are incontrovertibly the contracting parties and, possessing the infringing rights, may proceed by orderly steps to attain the object." [4]

Jefferson was then Vice-President of the United States. He, nevertheless, took active steps against the Alien and Sedition Acts. Under his and Madison's leadership, the legislatures of Virginia and Kentucky passed resolutions against their constitutionality. The Kentucky Resolution of November 22, 1799, went so far as to declare:

"That the several states who formed that instrument [the constitution] being sovereign and independent, have the unquestionable right to judge of the infraction; and, That a Nullification by those sovereignties, of all unauthorized acts done under color of that instrument is the rightful remedy." [5]

The election of Jefferson in 1800 quieted this agitation.

After the victory of Jefferson's agrarians, however, commercial New England looked with suspicion upon the central government. Previously, the Federalists had been ardent nationalists; now they talked of secession. They opposed the purchase of Louisiana; and, when, in 1811, Congress was considering the admission of Louisiana as a state, Quincy of Massachusetts threatened the dissolution of the Union.[6] Commercial New England also opposed the War of 1812. During the heat of that conflict the Hartford Convention met; and to it the New England governments sent delegates. The "free, sovereign and independent State of Massachusetts" declared: "Whenever the national compact is violated, . . . this legislature is bound to interpose its power, and wrest from the oppressor his victim." The Connecticut legislature resolved that: "The state of Connecticut is a Free Sovereign and Independent state; that the United States

[4] Quoted: Beveridge, *Life of John Marshall*, II, 397.
[5] MacDonald, *Documentary Source Book, 1606-1926*, p. 278.
[6] Ames, *State Documents on Federal Relations*, p. 65.

are a confederacy of states; that we are a confederated and not a consolidated republic." [7] The Convention discussed the alleged violation of the Constitution by the federal government, and considered the secession of New England and its annexation to Canada. The sudden end of the war caused the Convention's adjournment; and the passage of a protective tariff act temporarily pacified New England. The annexation of Texas in 1845 again disturbed that section, which feared that Texas would be broken up into several slave states. Its political leaders again threatened secession.[8] Only a compromise under which Texas was admitted as a single state averted a serious crisis.

During Jackson's administration, Georgia had an interesting conflict with the United States Supreme Court. The state attempted to oust from its territory certain Indian tribes under the protection of the federal government. The Indians appealed to the courts. Before Marshall could hand down a decision in the case of *The Cherokee Nation v. The State of Georgia*,[9] Georgia asserted her sovereignty. In December, 1827, the legislature recorded its approval of a statement made by Governor Troup to the secretary of war to the effect that he felt it "to be his duty to resist to the utmost any military attack which the Government of the United States shall think proper to make on the territory, the People or the sovereignty of Georgia." [10] Shortly afterwards, the state court convicted a Cherokee, George Tassels, of murder and sentenced him to death; the federal Supreme Court issued a writ of error and ordered Georgia to appear before it to defend the judgment of its state court. The Georgia legislature enjoined the state officers to ignore "every mandate and process" issued by the Supreme Court and ordered the governor to defend the rights of the state "with all the force and means placed at his command by the Constitution and laws of this state." Under instructions from the legislature, the sheriff hanged Tassels while the Supreme Court looked on helpless and humiliated.[11] When the case of *The Cherokee Nation* finally reached the Supreme Court, Georgia disdained to appear. In *Worcester v. Georgia*,[12] Marshall declared the state's legislation unconstitutional. Georgia ignored the court. President Jackson, a bitter enemy of the Chief Justice, declared, "John

---

[7] A. N. Schlesinger, *New Viewpoints in American History*, p. 225.
[8] Ames, *State Documents on Federal Relations*, pp. 229–232.
[9] 5 Peters 1.
[10] Schlesinger, *New Viewpoints in American History*, p. 227.
[11] Beveridge, *Life of John Marshall*, IV, 542–543. Also Schlesinger, p. 227.
[12] 6 Peters 515.

Marshall has made his decision:—*now let him enforce it!*" [13] Georgia never obeyed the court's mandate. A state had successfully asserted its sovereignty.

In 1828 and 1832 Congress passed high tariff laws. The southern states, especially South Carolina, objected. The agitation became intense. In 1828 Calhoun, on behalf of the legislature, drafted the "South Carolina Exposition," in which he argued the supremacy of the state over the federal government. When Congress passed another tariff act in 1832, a state convention met in South Carolina and nullified the tariff laws. The Nullification Ordinance directed the government to take measures to prevent the enforcement of those acts within the state, forbade appeals to the United States Supreme Court from the state courts in any case where the tariff law was involved, and required all state officers to take an oath to "obey, execute and enforce this Ordinance, and such act or acts of the Legislature as may be passed in pursuance thereof." The Ordinance set forth that:

"We, the People of South Carolina, . . . *Do further Declare*, that we will not submit to the application of force, on the part of the Federal Government, to reduce this State to obedience; but that we will consider . . . [any act of the national government to enforce the tariff laws] as inconsistent with the longer continuance of South Carolina in the Union." [14]

Jackson, who hated Calhoun as much as he hated Marshall, attacked the South Carolina Ordinance; but it was not so much his proclamation as the passage of a lower tariff act that kept South Carolina in the Union. South Carolina achieved her purpose—the repeal of the tariff laws. Again a state had defied the federal government successfully.

Space permits mention of but one other instance of a state standing immovably upon its own sovereignty. This case is especially interesting because it occurred on the eve of the Civil War in a state that later opposed southern secession. Congress had passed a stringent fugitive slave law. In 1854 the federal attorney, acting under this statute, charged the editor of a Wisconsin newspaper with violating the statutes. The accused appealed to the state court for a writ of habeas corpus; and the state judges released him, on the ground that the fugitive slave law was unconstitutional. The federal attorney appealed; and the United States Supreme Court over-ruled the state decision; and in 1859 the federal court convicted the defendant.

[13] Beveridge, *Life of John Marshall*, IV, 547–551.
[14] *Ibid.*, IV, 560–561. Also Ames, *State Documents on Federal Relations*, pp. 40–41.

Immediately, Wisconsin was in an uproar. The legislature passed a "personal liberty" act and adopted a resolution censuring the Supreme Court of the United States for "abridging the right of habeas corpus." The legislature claimed that the federal government is not "the exclusive or final judge of the extent of the powers delegated to itself"; each sovereign state has the right to judge for itself.[15] Two years later, Wisconsin troops helped prevent the southern states from enforcing a similar construction of the Constitution.

II

The antecedents of particularism are strange and interesting. Most of the states' rights advocates were also exponents of slavery, and in their defense of that institution they repudiated Jeffersonian natural rights. But in their attack upon nationalism they turned to Jefferson. Jefferson's thesis that no society can make a perpetual law, and that each generation may terminate its social contract, formed the philosophical foundation of particularism. Jefferson had applied his concepts in the Virginia and Kentucky resolutions against the Alien and Sedition Acts, and the exponents of decentralization now adopted these resolutions of nullification as precedents for their actions. They also turned to John Taylor, the philosopher of Jeffersonianism. He had suggested to Jefferson the plan of state attack upon the Alien and Sedition Acts. His book, *New Views of the Constitution,* written in 1823, became the text of the particularists. Calhoun, the intellectual and political leader of the South, early formulated the general particularistic attack. His "South Carolina Exposition" of 1828 formed the basis of that state's Ordinance of Nullification four years later. Senator Hayne drew heavily upon this argument in his famous debate with Webster.

The particularistic school employed three approaches in its attack upon national centralization: (1) an historical argument, that the states had originally been sovereign and had never surrendered their sovereignty; (2) a constitutional or legal argument based upon an examination of the governmental structure and on the law of partnerships; and (3) a philosophical argument, that sovereignty is indivisible and that minority groups must have protection against the tyranny of the majority.

John Calhoun, in his *Discourse on the Constitution and Government of the United States,* and Jefferson Davis, in his *Rise and Fall of the Confederate Government,* presented in a most thorough fashion the

15 Ames, *State Documents on Federal Relations,* pp. 303–305.

history of the Union. Their historical data convinced them that before the formation of the Constitution in 1787 the thirteen states had been free, sovereign, and independent units, and that in ratifying that document they had not intended to renounce their sovereignty. They thus continued to retain political supremacy. In the last analysis, sovereignty rested with the people organized in separate states, not in the people of the nation as a single unit.

In 1776 the thirteen colonies, each acting for itself, although in concert with the others, determined to dissolve their political connection with the mother-country. They sent their representatives to a general congress of the colonies and through them declared that the colonies were, and of right ought to be, "free and independent States." As such, they contracted an alliance for their "common defense," successfully resisted the British efforts to reduce them to submission, and secured the recognition of their separate independence. The peace treaty distinctly recognized the independence of each state under its own name, not as one of a group or nation. The Articles of Confederation, adopted after the Declaration of Independence, similarly recognized the sovereignty of each state. It declared that:

"Each State retains its sovereignty, freedom, and independence and every power, jurisdiction, and right, which is not by this Constitution expressly delegated to the United States in Congress assembled."

During the period in which the Articles of Confederation remained in force, the general government rested in Congress alone. In this body each state, through its representatives, had an equal vote in the determination of all questions whatever. When Congress was not in session the general management of affairs remained in a "Committee of the States," consisting of one delegate from each state. Various exigencies led to a movement for a change in the central government. A meeting at Annapolis in 1786, which the representatives of only five states attended, unanimously believed that:

"It may essentially tend to advance the interests of the Union, if the States . . . would themselves concur, and use their endeavors to procure the concurrence of the other States, in the appointment of commissioners, to meet at Philadelphia on the second Monday in May next, to take into consideration the situation of the United States, to devise such further provisions as shall appear to them necessary to render the Constitution of the Federal Government adequate to the exigencies of the Union, and to report such an act for that purpose to the United States in Congress assembled, as, when agreed to by them, and afterward confirmed by the Legislatures of every State, will effectually provide for the same."

Following this suggestion, Congress adopted a similar resolution. Indeed, the legislature of every state, with the exception of Rhode Island, adopted the suggestions and appointed delegates to the Constitutional Convention. In all cases, however, the states restricted their delegates and provided for state ratification of the constitutional changes proposed.[16]

This historical data indicates, according to the particularistic interpretation, that the delegates to the Philadelphia Convention represented, not the people of the United States in mass, but the people of the several states, as states. Delaware with her sixty thousand inhabitants had entire equality with Virginia with her three-quarters of a million people. In the second place, the object for which the states appointed their delegates was not the organization of a new government, but solely and expressly the amendment of the federal Constitution already existing. They instructed their representatives to revise the Articles of Confederation and to suggest such alterations or additional provisions as they should deem necessary to render that document "adequate to the exigencies of the Union." And in the third place, the only functions of the delegates were to devise, deliberate, and discuss. No validity could attach to any action taken unless and until ratified by the several states.[17]

The ratification process likewise demonstrates that the people of each state, rather than the people of the entire country, established the Constitution. The deputies of the state ratifying conventions adopted it in the name of the people of their own states.[18] Rhode Island and North Carolina at first refused to ratify. The new government consequently regarded them as free and sovereign foreign states.[19] Not content with the new document, the states passed the Tenth Amendment specifically limiting the power of the central government and guarding against the presumption of a surrender of anything by implication.[20]

Not the people of the United States, but the people of the several states, ordained and established the Constitution. The process and acts of ratification prove this conclusively. The first draft of the preamble read, "We, the people of New Hampshire, Massachusetts, etc.," as did the Articles of Confederation. Thus originally the Con-

---

[16] Jefferson Davis, *The Rise and Fall of the Confederate Government* (New York, D. Appleton and Company), I, 86–90. Also Calhoun, *Works*, I, 111–118.

[17] Davis, *The Rise and Fall of the Confederate Government*, I, 93–94.

[18] *Ibid.*, I, 104–105.

[19] Calhoun, *Works*, I, 120.

[20] Davis, *Rise and Fall of the Confederate Government*, I, 157. A. H. Stephens, *A Constitutional View of the Late War between the States*, I, 490–491.

stitution specifically named each of the thirteen states. The later provision for ratification by only nine states, however, made this draft preamble impossible. Not knowing what states would ratify, the framers substituted "We, the people of the United States," meaning the people of the several states united. Thus an historical analysis of the preamble demonstrates the particularistic intent of the framers.[21]

In adopting the Constitution the states created a new government but no new people, and consequently no new sovereignty—"for sovereignty in an American republic can belong only to a people, never to a government."

"No such political community or corporate unit as one people of the United States existed then [in 1787], has ever been organized, or yet exists.

"No political action by the people of the United States in the aggregate has ever taken place, or ever can take place, under the Constitution." [22]

The legal approach of particularism examined the organization and powers of the central government. That unit is merely an agent for the states, which possess full sovereignty. The federal government acts as a sovereign, but is not a sovereign. The legitimate owners of sovereignty, the states, merely permit it to wear certain robes of authority. The states delegated to the central government certain attributes of sovereignty, as the war power, the taxing power, the commerce power. The states did not, however, surrender their sovereignty: they merely loaned the exercise of certain sovereign powers, and these they may recall at any time. Since the federal government is the agent of the states, it is not the final judge of its delegated powers in either the legislative or the judicial branch. The principal retains always the right to review and annul the actions of the agent.

A. P. Upshur contended that the Union is, in its structure, "a federative and not a consolidated government." [23] The legislature consists of two houses. The Senate is composed of two members from each state, chosen by its own legislature, whatever be the state's size or population. The Senate is universally admitted to be strictly federative in its structure. The House of Representatives, too, presents federative characteristics. Each state, regardless of its size, is entitled to at least one congressman. Each state votes for its

[21] Calhoun, *Works*, I, 128, 132–134.
[22] Davis, *Rise and Fall of the Confederate Government*, I, 158. Also Calhoun, *Works*, I, 162.
[23] Upshur, *A Brief Inquiry into the True Nature and Character of our Federal Government*, p. 143.

own representatives—by itself, not in connection with any other state, and not for the representatives of any other state. Each state prescribes the qualifications of its own voters. The federal government has no rôle in the choice of representatives, except only that it may prescribe the "times, places, and manner of holding elections." A state may withdraw its representation altogether, and Congress has no power to prevent it, nor to fill the vacancy thus created. In the election of the President and Vice-President, the Constitution preserves with equal distinction the exclusive agency of the states, as such. The people of each state, acting by and for itself and in such mode as itself may prescribe, choose the electors. Each state has a number equal to the sum of its representatives and senators. The electors, when chosen, give their votes within their respective states, and at such times and places as the states may respectively prescribe. The federal government can exercise no rightful power in the choice of its own executive. The electoral college, representing the states, may choose a President with a decided majority of the people against him. If no candidate receives a majority in the electoral college, the House of Representatives elects the President. In doing so, two-thirds of the states must be present through their representatives. The House then votes by states, all the members of each state giving but one vote. And a majority of all the states is necessary for a choice. This is precisely the same rule which prevailed in the congress under the Articles of Confederation. The President is thus a federative officer. He, with the approval of the Senate, chooses the judges.[24]

If the Constitution is federative in the structure of all three of its great departments, it is equally so in the power of amendment. The people at large cannot alter the Constitution. Congress may propose amendments whenever two-thirds of each house agree. And such action becomes part of the Constitution upon the ratification of three-fourths of the states through their legislatures or conventions. No form of words could more distinctly convey the idea of separate and independent political corporations. To alter or amend a government requires the same extent of power as to form one. And of all political acts, the formation of a constitution is that which admits and implies to the fullest extent the existence of absolute, unqualified, unconditional and unlimited sovereignty. So long as the power of amendment rests exclusively with the states, it is idle to contend that they are less sovereign now than they were before the adoption of the

[24] Upshur, *A Brief Inquiry into the True Nature and Character of our Federal Government*, pp. 144–154.

Constitution.   Moreover, no amendment may deprive any state, without its consent, of equal suffrage in the Senate.[25]

The Constitution delegates certain authority to Congress and denies certain powers to the states. The people of the several states thus imposed restrictions on the exercise of their own sovereign powers by entering into a solemn obligation to do no act inconsistent with its provisions and to uphold and support it within their respective limits. To this extent, but no further, the restrictions go. As parties to the constitutional compact, the people of each state retain the unrestricted right to judge as to the extent of the obligation imposed by the agreement. The right to judge as to the extent of the obligation imposed necessarily involves the right of pronouncing whether an act of the federal government is in conformity with the provisions of the constitutional compact. If not, the parties to the agreement may pronounce it null, void, and of no effect. Calhoun declared, "If the constitution be a compact, and the several States, regarded in their sovereign character, be parties to it, all the rest follows as necessary consequences." [26]

If the states in their sovereign capacity loaned a few powers to the central government, and if, in the new government, they still retained their own identities, then they may recall the loan and secede from the Union. In 1788 the states *acceded* to the Constitution as sovereign states; they could, therefore, maintained Stephens, *secede* and resume the full exercise of their sovereign powers. Each state need merely repeal the ordinance by which it ratified and agreed to the Constitution. It has a perfect right to do so, "subject to no authority, but the great moral law which governs the intercourse between Independent Sovereign Powers, Peoples, or Nations." It is the inherent right of nations—subject to this law alone—to disregard the obligations of their compacts whenever their own preservation demands it. By universal consent, abrogation of agreements is justifiable when there has been a breach by the other party or parties. It was on this principle that the United States abrogated the treaty with France in 1798.[27]

The compact among the states which formed the Union, argued Davis, is in the nature of a partnership between individuals without limitation of time. The recognized law of such partnerships provides that if the contract between the partners does not specify a definite

[25] Upshur, *A Brief Inquiry into the True Nature and Character of our Federal Government*, pp. 154–157.

[26] Calhoun, *Works*, I, pp. 277–278.

[27] Stephens, *A Constitutional View of the Late War between the States*, I, 495–497.

period of duration; either partner may dissolve the agreement. During the Revolution, a number of sovereign, free, and independent states entered into a partnership with one another. This agreement not only was unlimited in duration but was expressly declared to be a "perpetual union." Yet, when that union failed to accomplish the purposes for which it was formed, the parties withdrew, separately and independently, one after another, without any question asked of their right to do so, and formed a new association. The states merely established a new agent, who, however enlarged its powers might be, would remain subordinate and responsible to them. The Constitution of 1787 created another partnership without a specific time limit; the partners, therefore, may withdraw at any time.[28]

In delegating powers to their common agency, the states did not leave without ample assertion their right to resume the delegated authority. In its ratification of the Constitution, Virginia expressly declared that "the powers granted under the Constitution, being derived from the people of the United States, may be resumed by them, whensoever the same shall be perverted to their injury or oppression." New York and Rhode Island were no less explicit. Both declared that "the powers of government may be reassumed by the people whenever it shall become necessary to their happiness." By inserting these declarations in their ordinances of ratification, Virginia, New York, and Rhode Island, formally, officially, and permanently declared their interpretation of the Constitution as recognizing the right of secession by the resumption of their grants. By accepting the ratifications with these declarations, the other states formally approved the principle which they asserted.[29]

The philosophical approach to particularism aimed at accomplishing two objectives. It attacked as a fallacy in logic the earlier theory of divided sovereignty, and it provided a justification for state nullification. Calhoun demonstrated that by its very nature sovereignty is indivisible. Sovereignty is the highest political power in a community, the power above which there can be no other. It must be a unity or it does not exist. "To divide it is to destroy it." Within the same geographical territory there cannot be two sovereigns; nor can a State surrender only a portion of its supreme power. There can be no State partly sovereign and partly non-sovereign. Sovereignty is the vital principle of statehood; no State can surrender it and still remain a state. The American states thus must be fully sovereign or

<hr>

[28] Davis, *Rise and Fall of the Confederate Government*, I, 168–170.
[29] *Ibid.*, I, 173.

fully subject. From the very nature of sovereignty, they could not have surrendered a part and retained another part of a unity; they must either have given it all up or have retained it all. The states originally were sovereign, and they have never yielded their supremacy.[30] Thus if the state of South Carolina is sovereign, then the federal government cannot likewise be supreme over that same territory.

Stephens followed the lead of Calhoun. Sovereignty, he said, must reside with the people somewhere. But does it rest with the people, in mass, of all the states together, or with the people of the several states separately? "Where, in this country, resides that Paramount authority that can rightfully make and unmake Constitutions?" There can be no such thing as a perfect state without sovereignty. Sovereignty is the highest and greatest of all political powers. "It is itself the source as well as the embodiment of all political powers, both great and small. All proceed and emanate from it." Nowhere in the Constitution did the states specifically surrender their sovereignty. If sovereignty be surrendered, it must be by implication only.

"If carried by implication, it must be on the strange assumption that it is an incident only of some one or all of those specific and specially enumerated powers expressly delegated. This cannot be, as that would be making the incident greater than the object, the shadow more solid than the substance."

All the great powers specifically and expressly delegated in the Constitution, such as the power to declare war and make peace, to raise and support armies, to tax and lay excise duties, are but the incidents of sovereignty. "If this great embodiment of all powers was parted with, why were any minor specifications made? Why any enumeration? Was not such specification or enumeration both useless and absurd?" All the implications are in favor of the retention of sovereignty by the states. The bare fact that the states merely delegated all these powers necessarily implies that the greater power, sovereignty, still continued with them.[31]

In his masterpiece of political theory, *A Disquisition on Government*, Calhoun presents in cogent logic the second objective of the philosophical attack upon nationalism—a rationalization of nullification. Beneath his argument lie two basic premises: (1) that the political state is partisan to those who administer it, and (2) that the majority, if unchecked, will oppress the minority.

[30] Calhoun, *Works*, II, 231–233.
[31] Stephens, *A Constitutional View of the Late War*, I, 487–489.

Calhoun, we have already noted, maintained that government is natural to man. It inevitably develops out of the clash between our social and selfish instincts. Man cannot live without the society of his fellow beings; and without governmental restraint society is impossible. But although government is intended to protect and preserve society, it has in itself a strong tendency to disorder and abuse of power. The cause of this phenomenon is to be found in the same constitution of our nature which makes government indispensable. The powers which government must possess in order to repress violence and preserve order cannot execute themselves. Men must administer government. In them, as in others, "the individual are stronger than the social feelings." Hence, the powers vested in the governors to prevent injustice and oppression on the part of others will, if unchecked, be converted into instruments to oppress the rest of the community.[32]

How can we counteract this tendency? How can we prevent those invested with the powers of government from employing their authority to aggrandize themselves, instead of protecting and preserving society? We cannot do this by so limiting the powers of government as to make it too feeble to be an instrument of abuse. This would defeat the end for which government is ordained; it would make government too feeble to protect and preserve society. In estimating what amount of power is requisite to secure the objects of government, we must take into the reckoning what is necessary to defend the community against external as well as internal dangers. We must not overlook the fact that the human race is not comprehended in a single community.

"The limited reason and faculties of man, the great diversity of language, customs, pursuits, situation and complexion, and the difficulty of intercourse, with various other causes, have, by their operation, formed a great many separate communities, acting independently of each other. Between these there is the same tendency to conflict,—and from the same constitution of our nature,—as between men individually."

This state of things indicates the danger of withholding from government the full command of the power and resources of the state.[33]

How, then, can we prevent government from abusing its powers without divesting it of the full command of the community resources? How can we construct a strong, yet safe, government? The right of suffrage is a partial safeguard; it gives the electors complete control over the conduct of those whom they have elected and converts the

[32] Calhoun, *Works*, I, 7.   [33] *Ibid.*, I, 9–10.

governors into faithful representatives instead of irresponsible rulers. The right of suffrage, in reality, transfers the actual control over the government from those who make and execute the laws to the body of the community itself.

If the whole community had the same interests, then the right of suffrage by itself would be all-sufficient to counteract the tendency of government to oppression. If the action of the government so affected the interests of each and every portion that the laws which impoverished one portion would necessarily impoverish all others, then the right of suffrage would of itself form a perfect constitutional government. But such is not the case.

"On the contrary, nothing is more difficult than to equalize the action of the government in reference to the various and diversified interests of the community; and nothing more easy than to pervert its powers into instruments to aggrandize and enrich one or more interests by oppressing and impoverishing the others; and this too, under the operation of laws, couched in general terms;—and which, on their face, appear fair and equal. . . . The more extensive and populous the country, the more diversified the condition and pursuits of its population, and the richer, more luxurious, and dissimilar the people, the more difficult it is to equalize the action of the government,—and the more easy for one portion of the community to pervert its powers to oppress and plunder the other." [34]

If then the right of suffrage, without some other provision, cannot counteract the tendency of government to oppression, what will? What will prevent the majority from tyrannizing over the interests of the minority? Since government is partisan to those who administer it, some device is essential to prevent any one interest, or combination of interests, from using the powers of government to aggrandize itself at the expense of the others. For example, some constitutional provision must prevent the manufacturing interest from enriching itself through tariffs at the expense of the agricultural groups. It is necessary that each interest have either a concurrent voice in making the laws or a veto on their execution. Only thus can the different interests, orders, classes, or portions, into which the community may divide itself, protect themselves against the oppressions of any one group. The concurrent consent of all would thus be necessary for political action.[35]

"It results, from what has been said, that there are two different modes in which the sense of the community may be taken: one, simply, by the right of suffrage, unaided; the other, by the right through a proper organism. Each

[34] Calhoun, *Works*, I, 13-16.   [35] *Ibid.*, I, 25-28.

collects the sense of the majority. But one regards numbers only, and considers the whole community as a unit, having but one common interest throughout; and collects the sense of the greater number of the whole, as that of the community. The other regards interests as well as number;—considering the community as made up of different and conflicting interests, as far as the action of the government is concerned; and takes the sense of each, through its majority or appropriate organ, and the united sense of all, as the sense of the entire community. The former of these I shall call the numerical, or absolute majority; and the latter, the concurrent, or constitutional majority." [36]

In Calhoun's day, economic interests, on the whole, coincided with state lines. In South Carolina, for example, the most important interest was that of cotton cultivation. He thus proposed that upon the indiscriminate numerical majority there be superimposed the will of geographical units. The consent of a majority of the various sections or interests, not merely the consent of a majority of individuals, would condition governmental action. Compromise would supersede majority tyranny.

"The necessary consequence of taking the sense of the community by the concurrent majority is . . . to give to each interest or portion of the community a negative on the others. It is this mutual negative among its various conflicting interests, which invests each with the power of protecting itself;—and places the rights and safety of each, where only they can be securely placed, under its own guardianship. Without this there can be no systematic, peaceful, or effective resistance to the natural tendency of each to come into conflict with the others, and without this there can be no constitution. It is this negative,—the power of preventing or arresting the action of the government,—be it called by what term it may,—veto, interposition, nullification, check, or balance of power,—which, in fact, forms the constitution. . . . It is, indeed, the negative which makes the constitution,—and the positive which makes the government. The one is the power of acting;—and the other the power of preventing or arresting action. The two, combined, make constitutional governments." [37]

Just as the right of suffrage is necessary to prevent rulers from abusing their authority, so is the concurrent majority, or sectional referendum, essential to compel the parts of society to be just to one another.[38]

Calhoun's theory of concurrent majorities antedated the later proposals for functional representation. The functionalists maintain that each economic group within the country must be able to defend itself against the selfish attacks of other economic groups. Thus the wheat farmers must possess political weapons to prevent high tariffs upon agricultural implements for the benefit of machine manu-

[36] Calhoun, *Works*, I, 28.   [37] *Ibid.*, I, 35–36.   [38] *Ibid.*, VI, 189–190.

facturers. Likewise coal miners should be able to check legislation hostile to their wage level and social institutions. Progress for one group must not be at the expense of another. Compromise and mutual gain must guide society. To provide the necessary instruments for group vetoes, the present-day functionalists propose a congress of industry. Occupation, not geography, would form the basis of representation. Calhoun's doctrine aimed at the same goal. The greater simplicity of economic groupings in his day, however, meant that this objective could, to a large measure, be attained by state nullification.

In his later work, *A Discourse on the Constitution and Government of the United States*, Calhoun demonstrated clearly the application of his doctrine of concurrent majority. Should the numerical majority of the federal government enact any law oppressive to any interest or portion of the country, that interest, through its state government, could veto or nullify the act. If three-fourths of the interests or states should uphold the action of Congress, then the opposing state would have the choice of yielding or withdrawing from the Union.[39] In his desire to guard against majority tyranny, Calhoun went so far as to suggest a plural executive.[40] He did not contemplate frequent use of this right of nullification or secession; its very existence would compel the federal government to respect the various interest groups. And should a crisis actually arise, the minority state would weigh in the balance of expediency the loss through the proposed legislation against the disadvantages of secession.

Calhoun's thesis of the concurrent majority was not the result of sequestered philosophical exploration. It was rather the consequence of his practical observations as the political leader of the South. With the rapid expansion of the country westward, he feared the increase in hostile free-soil power. With the dynamic growth of population in the industrial Northeast, he foresaw that the South was doomed to a steadily diminishing voice in the national councils. The relatively static life of the South thus threatened the destruction of slavery and the imposition of tariffs. Calhoun, therefore, opposed a numerical democracy and advocated a sectional referendum. His system of concurrent majorities would enable the cotton interest to protect itself against the tyranny of a sheer mathematical majority, which would inevitably prove partisan to the growing industrial interest. The particularistic bias of Calhoun's writings rose directly out of sectional interests.

[39] Calhoun, *Works*, I, 300–301, 396.   [40] *Ibid.*, I, 394.

III

Economic and social factors, likewise, fashioned nationalism. With the growth of industrialism, the capitalists and laborers of the Northeast began to look beyond their local confines to a national market. They, moreover, desired protective tariffs; and these they could secure only from Congress. The West similarly turned to the central government with its demands for internal improvements and more land. The development of rapid means of transportation, especially the railroad, knit the country together. A rail system soon tied up the granaries of the West with the markets of the East. Economic interdependence destroyed localism. And finally, this new economic order lessened the earlier fear of a strong and centralized government. The popular antagonism against centralization that had marked the political history of the first two decades of the new Constitution gradually disappeared.

Daniel Webster and Joseph Story led the pre-Civil War nationalists. Unlike the particularistic school, they did not approach the basic problem of centralization versus decentralization from a philosophical or historical outlook. They employed only constitutional arguments. Throughout, a narrow legalism marks the work of Webster and Story. Webster certainly realized the economic clash that underlay the conflict over states' rights. In his earlier political career, he had advocated free trade; the Yankee merchant at that time dominated Massachusetts politics. After the War of 1812, the economic and political balance in that state shifted to the new industrialists. Webster reversed his view and now became an exponent of high protective tariffs. Thus, while he understood the economics of nationalism, he never allowed an inkling of this knowledge to permeate his speeches. He based his entire case upon a strict interpretation of legal phraseology. Webster and Story examined only the actual words of the Constitution; they did not study the debates of the Constitutional Convention in order to trace the historical evolution of the peculiar phraseology employed by the framers. As guides, they employed law dictionaries, not history books. From the language of the Constitution, they attempted to prove that the Union was an agreement among individuals to form a national government, with the states as such playing no rôle. From this agreement among individuals there resulted a constitution, or fundamental law, operative immediately upon individuals. A state, accordingly, has no more right to question the authority of the national Constitution than has a citizen of South Carolina to question the fundamental law of that state.

In their proof by words, these nationalists turned first to the preamble of the Constitution. The preamble reads: "We the people of the United States . . . do ordain and establish this Constitution for the United States of America." The Constitution, argued Webster, is established by the people of the United States. The preamble does not say by the people of the several states. It is as the people of the United States that they established the Constitution.

"How can any man get over the words of the Constitution itself?—'We, the People of the United States do ordain and establish this Constitution.' These words must cease to be a part of the Constitution, they must be obliterated from the parchment on which they are written, before any human ingenuity or human agreement can remove the popular basis on which the Constitution rests, and turn the instrument into a mere compact between sovereign States." [41]

"So far from saying that it is established by the governments of the several States, it does not even say that it is established by *the people of the several States*. But it pronounces that it is established by the people of the United States in the aggregate. Doubtless the people of the several States, taken collectively, constitute the people of the United States. But it is in this their collective capacity, it is as all the people of the United States, that they established the Constitution." [42]

Story reasoned in the same manner.[43] He likewise placed emphasis on the preamble.

"It is an admitted maxim in the ordinary course of the administration of justice, that the preamble of a statute is a key to open the mind of the makers, as to the mischiefs which are to be remedied and the objects which are to be accomplished by the provisions of the statute." [44]

This argument based upon the peculiar phraseology of the Constitution differs radically in its conclusion from the historical approach of Calhoun and Davis. Webster and Story proved by the preamble that this is a people's Constitution, nationalistic in its intent. Calhoun, we have noted, traced the history of the preamble through the debates of the Philadelphia Convention. In its original form, it read "We, the people of New Hampshire, Massachusetts," etc. The later agreement upon ratification by nine instead of all thirteen states rendered this original draft impossible. The Convention consequently substituted "We, the people of the United States." Thus through a historical analysis Calhoun demonstrated that the states,

<hr>

[41] Webster, *Works*, III, 477.   [43] Story, *Commentaries on the Constitution*, I, 255.
[42] *Ibid.*, III, 346.   [44] *Ibid.*, I, 338.

not the people, made the Constitution, that it is particularistic and not nationalistic in its intent.

By again employing the phraseology of the Constitution, Webster and Story sought to prove that the Constitution is the organic law of the land, not a mere covenant among sovereign states. It is, argued Story, an ordinance or establishment of government, and not a compact. The language is: "We the *people* of the United States . . . do *ordain* and *establish* this *Constitution*," not "We the *States* do *contract* and enter into a *treaty* with each other." The obvious object was to substitute a government of the people for a confederacy of states, a constitution for a compact.[45] The framers thus distinguished carefully between a constitution and a confederation. A confederation is a mere treaty or league between independent states, and binds no longer than during the good pleasure of each. It rests forever in articles of compact, where each is or may be the supreme judge of its own legal rights and duties. A constitution, on the other hand, is a permanent form of government, where the powers, once given, are irrevocable and cannot be resumed or withdrawn at pleasure. Whether formed by a single people, or by different societies of people, a constitution, upon ratification, becomes obligatory as a fundamental law.[46] A constitution is a rule of action prescribed by the supreme power in a state, regulating the rights and duties of the whole community.

"It is a *rule*, as contradistinguished from a temporary or sudden order; permanent, uniform, and universal. . . . Like the ordinary municipal laws, it may be founded upon our consent or that of our representatives; but it derives its ultimate obligatory force as a law, and not as a compact." [47]

The Constitution itself declares that it shall be the fundamental law of the land. Article six provides that "This Constitution . . . shall be the supreme law of the land; and the judges in every State shall be bound thereby, anything in the Constitution or laws of any State to the contrary notwithstanding." Story concluded from this provision that "If it is the supreme law, how can the people of any State, either by any form of its own constitution or laws or other proceedings, repeal or abrogate or suspend it?" [48]

Webster similarly demonstrated that the Constitution is an organic law and not a state compact. In his attack upon Calhoun's contention on behalf of nullification and secession, Webster pointed to the words of the preamble.

[45] Story, *Commentaries on the Constitution*, I, 340.
[46] *Ibid.*, I, 244.
[47] *Ibid.*, I, 236.
[48] *Ibid.*, I, 246.

"Therefore, Sir, since any State, before she can prove her right to dissolve the Union, must show her authority to undo what has been done, no State is at liberty to *secede*, on the ground that she and other States have done nothing but *accede*. She must show that she has a right to *reverse* what has been or-dained, to *unsettle* and *overthrow* what has been *established*, to *reject* what the people have *adopted*, and to *break up* what they have *ratified;* because these are the terms which express the transactions which have actually taken place." [49]

To strengthen his contention that the Constitution is an organic law, Webster resorted to legal terminology. The Constitution, he claimed, is the result of an "executed contract." It is, therefore, final and irrevocable. An executed contract, as distinguished from an executory contract, is an agreement in which nothing remains to be done by either party, in which the transaction is completed at the moment that the arrangement is made. An illustration of such a contract is the case where an automobile or a book is sold and de-livered, and complete payment is made on the spot. An executory contract, on the other hand, is an agreement in which some future act remains to be done, as a contract to build a house in six months. The Constitution, maintained Webster, is the result of an executed contract. Upon ratification, nothing further remained to be done. It is, therefore, as binding and irrevocable as an executed contract in private law.

"The Constitution, Sir, is not a contract, but the result of a contract; meaning by contract no more than assent. Founded on consent, it is a govern-ment proper. Adopted by the agreement of the people of the United States, when adopted, it has become a Constitution. The people have agreed to make it a Constitution; but when made, that Constitution becomes what its name imports. It is no longer a mere agreement. . . . When the people agree to erect a government, and actually erect it, the thing is done; and the agreement is at an end. The compact is executed, and the end designed by it attained. Henceforth, the fruit of the agreement exists, but the agreement itself is merged in its own accomplishment; since there can be no longer a subsisting agreement or compact *to form* a constitution or government, after that constitution or government has been actually formed and established." [50]

This fundamental law, established by the sovereign people, pro-vides, argued Webster and Story, its own organ of interpretation. The Constitution itself refutes the thesis of state nullification. The people wisely provided therein "a proper suitable mode and tribunal for settling questions of constitutional law." [51] Article six provides that:

[49] Webster, *Works*, III, 455.   [50] *Ibid.*, III, 468.   [51] *Ibid.*, III, 334.

"This Constitution, and the laws of the United States which shall be made, . . . under the authority of the United States, shall be the supreme law of the land, anything in the constitution or laws of any State to the contrary notwithstanding."

The people willed the supremacy of the Constitution. No state law is valid which comes into conflict with the Constitution, or any law of the United States passed in pursuance thereof. The Constitution also determines the method of settling disputes by declaring that:

"The judicial power shall extend to all cases, in law and equity, arising under the Constitution, and laws of the United States, and treaties made, or which shall be made, under their authority."

Nothing is left to implication.[52] In pursuance of these clear and express provisions, Congress at its very first session passed a judiciary act in which it established a mode for bringing all questions of constitutional power to the final decision of the Supreme Court. "It then, Sir, became a government. It then had the means of self-protection; and but for this, it would, in all probability, have been now among things which are past." [53]

Again by turning to the words of the Constitution, Webster attacked the proposition of state sovereignty. The people, who alone are sovereign, chose to impose restraints upon the states. Calhoun saw in the delegation of powers merely a loan by the states of a few sovereign powers; Webster saw a total denial of sovereignty to the states. To make war, for instance, is an exercise of sovereignty; but the Constitution declares that no state shall make war. To coin money is another exercise of sovereignty; but no state is at liberty to do so. Again, no state is so sovereign as to make a treaty.[54]

"This government, Sir, is the independent offspring of the popular will. It is not the creature of State legislatures; nay, more, if the whole truth must be told, the people brought it into existence, established it, and have hitherto supported it, for the very purpose, amongst others, of imposing certain salutary restraints on State sovereignties. The States cannot make war; they cannot contract alliances; they cannot make, each for itself, separate regulations of commerce; they cannot lay imposts; they cannot coin money. If this Constitution, Sir, be the creature of State legislatures, it must be admitted that it has obtained a strange control over the volition of its creators." [55]

And finally, the express phraseology of the Constitution disputes the thesis of state nullification. Under that doctrine, argued Webster,

[52] Story, *Commentaries*, I, 269; Webster, *Works*, III, 335. [54] *Ibid.*, III, 322.
[53] Webster, *Works*, III, 335. [55] *Ibid.*, III, 333.

the tariff in South Carolina becomes "a palpable, deliberate usurpation." That state may, therefore, nullify it and refuse to pay the duties. Pennsylvania, on the other hand, may regard the tariff as clearly constitutional and highly expedient; there the duties are to be paid.

"And yet we live under a government of uniform laws, and under a constitution too, which contains an express provision, as it happens, that all duties shall be equal in all the States. Does not this approach absurdity?"

The doctrine of nullification makes the Union "a rope of sand." [56] The result of nullification is that no act of Congress can bind all the states if its constitutionality is not admitted by all. No single state is bound, against its own dissent, by a law of imposts. Yet this is precisely the evil experienced under the old Confederation, and for remedy of which the Constitution was adopted.

"The leading object in establishing this government, an object forced on the country by the condition of the times and the absolute necessity of the law, was to give to Congress power to lay and collect imposts *without the consent of particular States*. The Revolutionary debt remained unpaid; the national treasury was bankrupt; the country was destitute of credit; Congress issued its requisitions on the States, and the States neglected them; there was no power of coercion but war; Congress could not lay imposts, or other taxes, by its own authority; the whole general government, therefore, was little more than a name." [57]

"Four-and-twenty interpreters of constitutional law, each with a power to decide for itself, and none with authority to bind any body else, and this constitutional law the only bond of their union! What is such a state of things but a mere connection during pleasure, or, to use the phraseology of the times, *during feeling?*" [58]

The particularistic and nationalistic approaches offer some interesting contrasts. Calhoun and his colleagues employed historical, philosophical, and legal arguments; Webster and Story resorted only to constitutional law, and looked merely at the express terms of the Constitution. The particularists located sovereignty in the people of the states; they recognized no composite people of the United States. The nationalists, on the other hand, located sovereignty in the people of the United States; they, not the states, ordained and established the Constitution. Calhoun held that the sovereign states had merely formed a partnership among themselves and had loaned certain attributes of sovereignty to their new agent. Webster and Story insisted that the people had created an organic law operative

---

[56] Webster, *Works*, III, 323–324.   [57] *Ibid.*, III, 461–462.   [58] *Ibid.*, III, 324.

directly upon the individual; this was as fundamental as the state constitutions. Both schools agreed that the central government possessed only limited powers; but they differed as to the means of determining when it exceeded these powers. The particularists asserted that the sovereign states should determine whether or not their agent had exceeded its authority. The nationalists claimed that the central government was the final and conclusive judge of its own powers. Calhoun feared lest federal interpretation should lead to centralization; Webster feared that state nullification would result in decentralization. Calhoun realized that majority tyranny in a centralized government would prove destructive to minority interest groups, such as the cotton growers. Webster and Story dreaded a return to the evils of decentralization that the country had experienced under the Articles of Confederation.[59] The particularists interpreted the Constitution from the viewpoint of international law; secession they compared to the abrogation of a treaty. The nationalists viewed the Union through the eyes of constitutional lawyers; secession to them was revolution. In the last analysis, the conflict was one of decentralization against centralization.

IV

A contrast equally instructive differentiated the pre-Civil War and the later schools of nationalism. The newer nationalist doctrine was less legal and constitutional in form than that of Webster and Story. It adopted rather an evolutionary and philosophical approach. No longer satisfied merely to construe the language of the Constitution, the new nationalists went back to the power that makes and unmakes government. They were no longer interpreters of law, but observers of the forces that create law. They examined those factors—political, social, and economic—that mold the life of a people.

In the fashioning of this new school of nationalism, Francis Lieber played a major rôle. Lieber came to the United States from Germany in 1827. Like many other German liberals, he fled from the reaction that followed the fall of Napoleon. The rising spirit of nationalism that developed in Germany, and that found its way into the writings of Hegel and Fichte, influenced Lieber. He brought to this country a more thorough knowledge of world history and political institutions than most American writers then possessed. Unlike the American political theorists, Lieber was a student of, and not a participant

---

[59] Story, *Commentaries*, Bk. III, Ch. VI.—"The Preamble"; also Webster, *Works*, III, 461–462.

in, politics.   He agreed with Calhoun in rejecting the doctrine of natural rights and social contract.   A state of nature never had existed and never could do so, since man was a social being.   The political state developed spontaneously from man's needs and from the necessity that individuals recognize mutual rights and duties.[60] Lieber did not, however, entirely abandon the doctrine of natural rights.   While he rejected the eighteenth-century romanticism, he held that since man is a human being, he possesses such inalienable rights as are inherent in his nature.   Natural rights thus come not from a vague state of nature but from the essential make-up of man.[61] "I exist as a human being; therefore, I have a right to exist as a human being." [62]

Lieber's doctrine of nationalism glorified the nation as a real entity.   It is an actual being to which supreme power can be attributed. He defined a nation as a homogeneous population, inhabiting a coherent territory, with a common language, literature, institutions, and consciousness of a common destiny.[63]   To the nation belongs sovereignty.   Not contract, but the gradual and unconscious growth of the national spirit created the Union.[64]   An evolutionary, not a legalistic, approach characterized Lieber's nationalism.

While Lieber's teachings, to an important degree, influenced the newer school of nationalism, four years of fierce civil war played a rôle of probably greater significance.   The clash of arms stirred a patriotic fervor in the North and generated a more intense love of the Union.   The nation must be saved.   Thus Lincoln declared that "Measures otherwise unconstitutional might become lawful by becoming indispensable to the preservation of the nation." [65]   In his *The Trial of the Constitution*, Sidney Fisher announced: "If *the* Union and *the* government cannot be saved out of this terrible shock of war constitutionally, *a* Union and *a* government must be saved unconstitutionally." [66]

After the war ended, the nationalist school continued along the lines indicated by Lieber.   Its exponents keenly felt that the nation's existence was more important than the interpretation of a written constitution.   Their philosophy was organic and evolutionary.   They laid constant stress on the "unwritten constitution."

[60] Lieber, *Political Ethics*, I, 104–107.
[61] *Ibid.*, I, 383–411.
[62] *Ibid.*, I, 68.
[63] Lieber, *Miscellaneous Writings*, II, 227–228.
[64] *Ibid.*, II, 228–239.
[65] Lincoln, *Works*, II, 508.
[66] S. Fisher, *The Trial of the Constitution* (1862), p. 199.

The political exponents of nationalism now vented their hostility upon the particularists. Senator Charles Sumner held that the seceding states had committed treason against the Union and, therefore, had forfeited their constitutional rights. They had "vacated" their territory and no longer existed as states. They had returned to a territorial status under which Congress could exercise complete control over them.[67] Similarly, Congressman Thaddeus Stevens, the leader of the lower house, agreed that the southern states, as such, had ceased to exist. They were now "conquered provinces."

The philosophers of nationalism were equally zealous on behalf of the nation. In his *Constitutional Conventions*, Jameson held that: "Back of all the states, and of all forms of government either the states or the Union, we are to conceive of the nation, a political body, one and indivisible." [68] Brownson, in his *American Republic*, distinguished between the constitution of a government, which rests merely upon a particular legal document, and the more fundamental constitution of a nation, which rests on "the genius, the character, the habits, customs, and wants of the people." [69] Similarly, Mulford differentiated between the "enacted constitution," which is the particular statement of the political organization at a given time, and the "historical constitution," which results from the nation's development.[70] Hurd declared that political facts must yield to those social, political, and economic forces that demand the existence of a nation. If the United States under the Constitution is not legally a nation, it ought to be one and has actually become one. Sovereignty is a matter not of law, but of fact. It does not proceed from or depend upon constitutions or laws, but itself creates them. We cannot, therefore, determine the location of sovereignty in the United States by a study of the Constitution, but only by an examination of facts. These prove the sovereignty of the nation.[71]

John W. Burgess was the high priest of American nationalism. As a Tennessee lad, he had fought in the Union army and had experienced the intense feeling toward the war that characterized the border states. Like Lieber, he studied in Germany, and came under the influence of Hegel's and Bluntschli's teachings. Like Lieber, too, he brought back to this country the evolutionary philosophy of

---

[67] C. Sumner, "Our Domestic Relations," *Atlantic Monthly*, October, 1863.
[68] J. A. Jameson, *The Constitutional Convention* (1866), p. 54.
[69] O. A. Brownson, *The American Republic* (1866), pp. 185–186.
[70] E. Mulford, *The Nation* (1870), p. 144.
[71] J. C. Hurd, *The Theory of Our National Existence* (1881), pp. 523–538.

politics. And he taught in American universities rather than participated in practical politics.

Like Lieber and Calhoun, Burgess rejected the natural rights and
social contract theories. He looked upon the State as the natural
consequence of evolutionary development. Just as the human body
had evolved from some single-celled organism, so the State had evolved
from a simpler form of political life. Just as we look upon man as
the climax of biological evolution, so in the process of political evolution the nation is the highest product. It is "for the present and discernible future, the organ of interpretation in last instance of the
order of life for its subjects." [72] The national State possesses sovereignty. This he defined as the "original, absolute, unlimited, universal power over the individual subject, and all associations of
subjects." Sovereignty is the essential, indispensable mark of statehood. We cannot, he said, conceive of a state without unlimited
power over its subjects.[73] In the United States such sovereignty rests
with the people as organized into the nation. The commonwealths
he considered merely organs of government whose relative importance
was gradually declining. Since they do not possess sovereignty, we
should not even call them states.[74]

Despite his absolutist conception of sovereignty, Burgess did not
look upon the State as destructive of liberty. The national State is
"the human organ least likely to do wrong." [75] Liberty can exist
only under law and within political society. "There never was, and
there never can be any liberty upon this earth and among human
beings, outside of state organization." [76] Rights have no political
force whatever, unless recognized and enforced by the State. The
State is the source of individual liberty. Men obtained liberty only
through the organization of political institutions. The State does
not take away rights, but creates them.[77]

The Civil War and Reconstruction have passed. But the basic
conflict of particularism versus nationalism persists. The four years
of armed combat and the decade of military control over the South
decided only one immediate issue in this controversy—that the

---

[72] *Political Science Quarterly*, I, 13–14. In 1886 this doctrine of nationalism emphasized centralization. In his writings after the World War, Burgess opposed the League
of Nations because it minimized the importance of nationality. His theory of nationality, although unchanged, was now one of world decentralization. Burgess stood
still while the world moved on.

[73] Burgess, *Political Science and Comparative Constitutional Law* (1891), I, 52.

[74] *Political Science Quarterly*, I, 22–23.

[75] Burgess, *Political Science and Comparative Constitutional Law*, I, 53–58.

[76] *Ibid.*, I, 88.

[77] *Ibid.*, I, 175–177.

southern states could not secede from the Union. The fundamental choice between centralization and decentralization remains unsolved. This issue recurs periodically in new forms. The clash between Wilson and California over Japanese land restrictions indicated that the old battle of states' rights was still alive at that time.

With the important changes in our social and economic institutions, new problems concerning areas of government develop. The issue is .no longer restricted to a clash between central and state governments. New areas now exist. Regionalism introduces a new phase to the controversy over centralization. Thus, the urbanization of New York City and its neighboring New Jersey communities has produced problems of transportation peculiar to that metropolitan area. The states of New York and New Jersey have accordingly set up a Commission for the Port of New York. This body builds bridges and tunnels, plans future projects, and issues bonds. Plans are now under way for the establishment of a New York metropolitan area, including parts of New Jersey and Connecticut and providing a unified plan of economic, social, and recreational development. New problems of governmental areas similarly arise out of the Boulder Dam project on the Colorado River. The states of the Southwest are now attempting to attack their common problems of water-power and irrigation through the device of an interstate compact.

Since the World War, the clash over particularism has spread beyond our national boundaries. The new problems of world economic interdependence have slowly developed a movement toward international government. The war and the enforced coöperation among the Entente Powers speeded this tendency. Centralization of national units into a world community is a vital current problem. The Senate debates over the League of Nations and the World Court are a repetition of the Webster-Calhoun clash over the American Constitution. A legalistic interpretation of phraseology characterizes the present-day analyses of the League Covenant and the Court Protocol.[78] The nationalists have become exponents of world decentralization.

[78] See Lodge's speech on the League of Nations, Chapter 8.

JOHN C. CALHOUN

Calhoun was the outstanding exponent of states' rights before the Civil War. His *South Carolina Exposition* of 1828 formed the basis for that state's Ordinance of Nullification four years later. In *A Disquisition on Government*, he develops a theory of concurrent majority as a philosophical rationalization for state nullification of congressional legislation. In his *Discourse on the Constitution and Government of the United States*, he presents a historical and constitutional analysis of the federal government in favor of particularism.

A DISQUISITION ON GOVERNMENT [79]

In order to have a clear and just conception of the nature and object of government, it is indispensable to understand correctly what that constitution or law of our nature is, in which government originates; or, to express it more fully and accurately,—that law, without which government would not, and with which, it must necessarily exist. Without this, it is as impossible to lay any solid foundation for the science of government, as it would be to lay one for that of astronomy, without a like understanding of that constitution or law of·the material world, according to which the several bodies composing the solar system mutually act on each other, and by which they are kept in their relative spheres. The first question, accordingly, to be considered is,—What is that constitution or law of our nature, without which government would not exist, and with which its existence is necessary?

In considering this, I assume, as an incontestable fact, that man is so constituted as to be a social being. His inclinations and wants, physical and moral, irresistibly impel him to associate with his kind; and he has, accordingly, never been found, in any age or country, in any state other than the social. In no other, indeed, could he exist; and in no other,—were it possible for him to exist,—could he attain to a full development of his moral and intellectual faculties, or raise himself, in the scale of being, much above the level of the brute creation.

I next assume, also, as a fact not less incontestable, that, while man is so constituted as to make the social state necessary to his existence and the full development of his faculties, this state itself cannot exist without government. The assumption rests on universal experience. In no age or country has any society or community ever been found, whether enlightened or savage, without government of some description.

Having assumed these, as unquestionable phenomena of our nature, I shall, without further remark, proceed to the investigation of the primary and important question,—What is that constitution of our nature, which, while it impels man to associate with his kind, renders it impossible for society to exist without government?

The answer will be found in the fact, (not less incontestable than either of the others,) that, while man is created for the social state, and is accordingly so formed as to feel what affects others, as well as what affects himself, he is, at the same time, so constituted as to feel more intensely what affects him directly, than what affects him indirectly through others; or, to express

[79] R. K. Cralle (editor), *Works of John C. Calhoun*. (New York, D. Appleton and Company, 1863), I, 1–10, 13–17, 24–38.

it differently, he is so constituted, that his direct or individual affections are stronger than his sympathetic or social feelings. I intentionally avoid the expression, *selfish* feelings, as applicable to the former; because, as commonly used, it implies an unusual excess of the individual over the social feelings, in the person to whom it is applied; and, consequently, something depraved and vicious. My object is, to exclude such inference, and to restrict the inquiry exclusively to facts in their bearings on the subject under consideration, viewed as mere phenomena appertaining to our nature,—constituted as it is; and which are as unquestionable as is that of gravitation, or any other phenomenon of the material world.

In asserting that our individual are stronger than our social feelings, it is not intended to deny that there are instances, growing out of peculiar relations,—as that of a mother and her infant,—or resulting from the force of education and habit over peculiar constitutions, in which the latter have overpowered the former; but these instances are few, and always regarded as something extraordinary. The deep impression they make, whenever they occur, is the strongest proof that they are regarded as exceptions to some general and well understood law of our nature; just as some of the minor powers of the material world are apparently to gravitation.

I might go farther, and assert this to be a phenomenon, not of our nature only, but of all animated existence, throughout its entire range, so far as our knowledge extends. It would, indeed, seem to be essentially connected with the great law of self-preservation which pervades all that feels, from man down to the lowest and most insignificant reptile or insect. In none is it stronger than in man. His social feelings may, indeed, in a state of safety and abundance, combined with high intellectual and moral culture, acquire great expansion and force; but not so great as to overpower this all-pervading and essential law of animated existence.

But that constitution of our nature which makes us feel more intensely what affects us directly than what affects us indirectly through others, necessarily leads to conflict between individuals. Each, in consequence, has a greater regard for his own safety or happiness, than for the safety or happiness of others; and, where these come in opposition, is ready to sacrifice the interests of others to his own. And hence, the tendency to a universal state of conflict, between individual and individual; accompanied by the connected passions of suspicion, jealousy, anger and revenge,—followed by insolence, fraud and cruelty;—and, if not prevented by some controlling power, ending in a state of universal discord and confusion, destructive of the social state and the ends for which it is ordained. This controlling power, wherever vested, or by whomsoever exercised, is GOVERNMENT.

It follows, then, that man is so constituted, that government is necessary to the existence of society, and society to his existence, and the perfection of his faculties. It follows, also, that government has its origin in this twofold constitution of his nature; the sympathetic or social feelings constituting the remote,—and the individual or direct, the proximate cause.

If man had been differently constituted in either particular;—if, instead of being social in his nature, he had been created without sympathy for his kind, and independent of others for his safety and existence; or if, on the other hand, he had been so created, as to feel more intensely what affected others than what affected himself, (if that were possible,) or, even, had this supposed interest been equal,—it is manifest that, in either case, there would have been no necessity for government, and that none would ever have existed. But, although society and government are thus intimately connected with and dependent on each other,—of the two society is the greater. It is the first in the order of things, and in the dignity of its object; that of society being primary,—to preserve and perfect our race; and that of government secondary and subordinate, to preserve and perfect society. Both are, however, necessary to the existence and well-being of our race, and equally of Divine ordination.

I have said,—if it were possible for man to be so constituted, as to feel what affects others more strongly than what affects himself, or even as strongly,—because, it may be well doubted, whether the stronger feeling or affection of individuals for themselves, combined with a feebler and subordinate feeling of affection for others, is not, in beings of limited reason and faculties, a constitution necessary to their preservation and existence. If reversed,—if their feelings and affections were stronger for others than for themselves, or even as strong, the necessary result would seem to be, that all individuality would be lost; and boundless and remediless disorder and confusion would ensue. For each, at the same moment intensely participating in all the conflicting emotions of those around him, would, of course, forget himself and all that concerned him immediately, in his officious intermeddling with the affairs of all others; which, from his limited reason and faculties, he could neither properly understand nor manage. Such a state of things would, as far as we can see, lead to endless disorder and confusion, not less destructive to our race than a state of anarchy. It would, besides, be remediless,—for government would be impossible; or, if it could by possibility exist, its object would be reversed. Selfishness would have to be encouraged, and benevolence discouraged. Individuals would have to be encouraged, by rewards, to become more selfish, and deterred, by punishments, from being too benevolent; and this, too, by a government, administered by those who, on the supposition, would have the greatest aversion for selfishness and the highest admiration for benevolence.

To the Infinite Being, the Creator of all, belongs exclusively the care and superintendence of the whole. He, in his infinite wisdom and goodness, has allotted to every class of animated beings its condition and appropriate functions; and has endowed each with feelings, instincts, capacities, and faculties, best adapted to its allotted condition. To man, he has assigned the social and political state, as best adapted to develop the great capacities and faculties, intellectual and moral, with which he has endowed him; and has, accordingly, constituted him so as not only to impel him into the social state, but to make government necessary for his preservation and well-being.

But government, although intended to protect and preserve society, has itself a strong tendency to disorder and abuse of its powers, as all experience and almost every page of history testify. The cause is to be found in the same constitution of our nature which makes government indispensable. The powers which it is necessary for government to possess, in order to repress violence and preserve order, cannot execute themselves. They must be administered by men in whom, like others, the individual are stronger than the social feelings. And hence, the powers vested in them to prevent injustice and oppression on the part of others, will, if left unguarded, be by them converted into instruments to oppress the rest of the community. That, by which this is prevented, by whatever name called, is what is meant by CONSTITUTION, in its most comprehensive sense, when applied to GOVERNMENT.

Having its origin in the same principle of our nature, *constitution* stands to *government*, as *government* stands to *society;* and, as the end for which society is ordained, would be defeated without government, so that for which government is ordained would, in a great measure, be defeated without constitution. But they differ in this striking particular. There is no difficulty in forming government. It is not even a matter of choice, whether there shall be one or not. Like breathing, it is not permitted to depend on our volition. Necessity will force it on all communities in some one form or another. Very different is the case as to constitution. Instead of a matter of necessity, it is one of the most difficult tasks imposed on man to form a constitution worthy of the name; while, to form a perfect one,—one that would completely counteract the tendency of government to oppression and abuse, and hold it strictly to the great ends for which it is ordained,—has thus far exceeded human wisdom, and possibly ever will. From this, another striking difference results. Constitution is the contrivance of man, while government is of Divine ordination. Man is left to perfect what the wisdom of the Infinite ordained, as necessary to preserve the race.

With these remarks, I proceed to the consideration of the important and difficult question: How is this tendency of government to be counteracted? Or, to express it more fully,—How can those who are invested with the powers of government be prevented from employing them, as the means of aggrandizing themselves, instead of using them to protect and preserve society? It cannot be done by instituting a higher power to control the government, and those who administer it. This would be but to change the seat of authority, and to make this higher power, in reality, the government; with the same tendency, on the part of those who might control its powers, to pervert them into instruments of aggrandizement. Nor can it be done by limiting the powers of government, so as to make it too feeble to be made an instrument of abuse; for, passing by the difficulty of so limiting its powers, without creating a power higher than the government itself to enforce the observance of the limitations, it is a sufficient objection that it would, if practicable, defeat the end for which government is ordained, by making it too feeble to protect and preserve society. The powers necessary for this purpose will ever prove sufficient to aggrandize those who control it, at the expense of the rest of the community.

In estimating what amount of power would be requisite to secure the objects of government, we must take into the reckoning, what would be necessary to defend the community against external, as well as internal dangers. Government must be able to repel assaults from abroad, as well as to repress violence and disorders within. It must not be overlooked, that the human race is not comprehended in a single society or community. The limited reason and faculties of man, the great diversity of language, customs, pursuits, situation and complexion, and the difficulty of intercourse, with various other causes, have, by their operation, formed a great many separate communities, acting independently of each other. Between these there is the same tendency to conflict,—and from the same constitution of our nature,—as between men individually; and even stronger,—because the sympathetic or social feelings are not so strong between different communities, as between individuals of the same community. So powerful, indeed, is this tendency, that it has led to almost incessant wars between contiguous communities for plunder and conquest, or to avenge injuries, real or supposed.

So long as this state of things continues, exigencies will occur, in which the entire powers and resources of the community will be needed to defend its existence. When this is at stake, every other consideration must yield to it. Self-preservation is the supreme law, as well with communities as individuals. And hence the danger of withholding from government the full command of the power and resources of the state; and the great difficulty of limiting its powers consistently with the protection and preservation of the community. And hence the question recurs,—By what means can government, without being divested of the full command of the resources of the community, be prevented from abusing its powers? . . .

I call the right of suffrage the indispensable and primary principle; for it would be a great and dangerous mistake to suppose, as many do, that it is, of itself, sufficient to form constitutional governments. To this erroneous opinion may be traced one of the causes, why so few attempts to form constitutional governments have succeeded; and why, of the few which have, so small a number have had durable existence. It has led, not only to mistakes in the attempts to form such governments, but to their overthrow, when they have, by some good fortune, been correctly formed. So far from being, of itself, sufficient,—however well guarded it might be, and however enlightened the people,—it would, unaided by other provisions, leave the government as absolute, as it would be in the hands of irresponsible rulers; and with a tendency, at least as strong, towards oppression and abuse of its powers; as I shall next proceed to explain.

The right of suffrage, of itself, can do no more than give complete control to those who elect, over the conduct of those they have elected. In doing this, it accomplishes all it possibly can accomplish. This is its aim,—and when this is attained, its end is fulfilled. It can do no more, however enlightened the people, or however widely extended or well guarded the right may be. The sum total, then, of its effects, when most successful, is, to make those elected, the true and faithful representatives of those who elected them,— instead of irresponsible rulers,—as they would be without it; and thus, by converting it into an agency, and the rulers into agents, to divest government of all claims to sovereignty, and to retain it unimpaired to the community. But it is manifest that the right of suffrage, in making these changes, transfers, in reality, the actual control over the government, from those who make and execute the laws, to the body of the community; and, thereby, places the powers of the government as fully in the mass of the community, as they would be if they, in fact, had assembled, made, and executed the laws themselves, without the intervention of representatives or agents. The more perfectly it does this, the more perfectly it accomplishes its ends; but in doing so, it only changes the seat of authority, without counteracting, in the least, the tendency of the government to oppression and abuse of its powers.

If the whole community had the same interests, so that the interests of each and every portion would be so affected by the action of the government, that the laws which oppressed or impoverished one portion, would necessarily oppress and impoverish all others,—or the reverse,—then the right of suffrage, of itself, would be all-sufficient to counteract the tendency of the government to oppression and abuse of its powers; and, of course, would form, of itself, a perfect constitutional government. The interest of all being the same, by supposition, as far as the action of the government was concerned, all would have like interests as to what laws should be made, and how they should be executed. All strife and struggle would cease as to who should be elected to make and execute them. The only question would be, who was most fit; who the wisest and most capable of understanding the common interest of the whole. This decided, the election would pass off quietly, and without party discord; as no one portion could advance its own peculiar interest without regard to the rest, by electing a favorite candidate.

But such is not the case. On the contrary, nothing is more difficult than to equalize the action of the government, in reference to the various and diversified interests of the community; and nothing more easy than to pervert its powers into instruments to aggrandize and enrich one or more interests by oppressing and impoverishing the others; and this too, under the operation of laws, couched in general terms;—and which, on their face, appear fair and equal. Nor is this the case in some particular communities only. It is so in all; the small and the great,—the poor and the rich,—irrespective of pursuits, productions, or degrees of civilization;—with, however, this difference, that the more extensive and populous the country, the more diversified the condition and pursuits of its population, and the richer, more luxurious, and dissimilar the people, the more difficult is it to equalize the action of the government,—and the more easy for one portion of the community to pervert its powers to oppress and plunder the other.

Such being the case, it necessarily results, that the right of suffrage, by placing the control of the government in the community must, from the same constitution of our nature which makes government necessary to preserve society, lead to conflict among its different interests,—each striving to obtain possession of its powers, as the means of protecting itself against the others;—or of advancing its respective interests, regardless of the interests of others. For this purpose, a struggle will take place between the various interests to obtain a majority, in order to control the government. If no one interest be strong enough, of itself, to obtain it, a combination will be formed between those whose interests are most alike;—each conceding something to the others, until a sufficient number is obtained to make a majority. The process may be slow, and much time may be required before a compact, organized majority can be thus formed; but formed it will be in time, even without preconcert or design, by the sure workings of that principle or constitution of our nature in which government itself originates. When once formed, the community will be divided into two great parties,—a major and minor,—between which there will be incessant struggles on the one side to retain, and on the other to obtain the majority,—and, thereby, the control of the government and the advantages it confers.

So deeply seated, indeed, is this tendency to conflict between the different interests or portions of the community, that it would result from the action of the government itself, even though it were possible to find a community, where the people were all of the same pursuits, placed in the same condition of life, and in every respect, so situated, as to be without inequality of condition or diversity of interests. The advantages of possessing the control of the powers of the government, and, thereby, of its honors and emoluments, are, of themselves, exclusive of all other considerations, ample to divide even such a community into two great hostile parties. . . .

As, then, the right of suffrage, without some other provision, cannot counteract this tendency of government, the next question for consideration is— What is that other provision? This demands the most serious consideration; for of all the questions embraced in the science of government, it involves a principle, the most important, and the least understood; and when understood, the most difficult of application in practice. It is, indeed, emphatically, that principle which *makes* the constitution, in its strict and limited sense.

From what has been said, it is manifest, that this provision must be of a character calculated to prevent any one interest, or combination of interests, from using the powers of government to aggrandize itself at the expense of the others. Here lies the evil: and just in proportion as it shall prevent, or fail to prevent it, in the same degree it will effect, or fail to effect the end intended to be accomplished. There is but one certain mode in which this result can be secured; and that is, by the adoption of some restriction or limitation, which shall so effectually prevent any one interest, or combination of interests, from obtaining the exclusive control of the government, as to render hopeless all attempts directed to that end. There is, again, but one mode in which this can be effected; and that is, by taking the sense of each interest or portion of the community, which may be unequally and injuriously affected by the action of the government, separately, through its own majority, or in some other way by which its voice may be fairly expressed; and to require the consent of each interest, either to put or to keep the government in action. This, too, can be accomplished only in one way,—and that is, by such an organism of the government,—and, if necessary for the purpose, of the community also,—as will, by dividing and distributing the powers of government, give to each division or interest, through its appropriate organ, either a concurrent voice in making and executing the laws, or a veto on their execution. It is only by such an organism, that the assent of each can be made necessary to put the government in motion; or the power made effectual to arrest its action, when put in motion;—and it is only by the one or the other that the different interests, orders, classes, or portions, into which the community may be divided, can be protected, and all conflict and struggle between them prevented,—by rendering it impossible to put or to keep in it action, without the concurrent consent of all.

Such an organism as this, combined with the right of suffrage, constitutes, in fact, the elements of constitutional government. The one, by rendering those who make and execute the laws responsible to those on whom they operate, prevents the rulers from oppressing the ruled; and the other, by making it impossible for any one interest or combination of interests or class, or order, or portion of the community, to obtain exclusive control, prevents any one of them from oppressing the other. It is clear, that oppression and abuse of power must come, if at all, from the one or the other quarter. From no other can they come. It follows, that the two, suffrage and proper organism combined, are sufficient to counteract the tendency of government to oppression and abuse of power; and to restrict it to the fulfillment of the great ends for which it is ordained.

In coming to this conclusion, I have assumed the organism to be perfect, and the different interests, portions, or classes of the community, to be sufficiently enlightened to understand its character and object, and to exercise, with due intelligence, the right of suffrage. To the extent that either may be defective, to the same extent the government would fall short of fulfilling its end. But this does not impeach the truth of the principles on which it rests. In reducing them to proper form, in applying them to practical uses, all elementary principles are liable to difficulties; but they are not, on this account, the less true, or valuable. Where the organism is perfect, every interest will be truly and fully represented, and of course the whole community must be so. It may be difficult, or even impossible, to make a perfect organism,—but, although this be true, yet even when, instead of the sense of each and of all, it takes that of a few great and prominent interests only, it would still, in a great measure, if not altogether, fulfill the end intended by a constitution. For, in such case, it would require so large a portion of the community, compared with the whole, to concur, or acquiesce in the action of the government, that the number to be plundered would be too few, and the number to be aggrandized too many, to afford adequate motives to oppression and the abuse of its powers. Indeed, however imperfect the organism, it must have more or less effect in diminishing such tendency.

It may be readily inferred, from what has been stated, that the effect of organism is neither to supersede nor diminish the importance of the right of suffrage; but to aid and perfect it. The object of the latter is, to collect the sense of the community. The more fully and perfectly it accomplishes this, the more fully and perfectly it fulfils its end. But the most it can do, of itself, is to collect the sense of the greater number; that is, of the stronger interests, or combination of interests; and to assume this to be the sense of the community. It is only when aided by a proper organism, that it can collect the sense of the entire community,—of each and all its interest; of each, through its appropriate organ, and of the whole, through all of them united. This would truly be the sense of the entire community; for whatever diversity each interest might have within itself,—as all would have the same interest in reference to the action of the government, the individuals composing each would be fully and truly represented by its own majority or appropriate organ, regarded in reference to the other interests. In brief, every individual of every interest might trust with confidence, its majority or appropriate organ, against that of every other interest.

It results, from what has been said, that there are two different modes in which the sense of the community may be taken; one, simply by the right of suffrage, unaided; the other, by the right through a proper organism. Each collects the sense of the majority. But one regards numbers only, and considers the whole community as a unit, having but one common interest through-out; and collects the sense of the greater number of the whole, as that of the community. The other, on the contrary, regards interests as well as num-bers;—considering the community as made up of different and conflicting interests, as far as the action of the government is concerned; and takes the sense of each, through its majority or appropriate organ, and the united sense of all, as the sense of the entire community. The former of these I shall call the numerical, or absolute majority; and the latter, the concurrent, or constitutional majority. I call it the constitutional majority, because it is an essential element in every constitutional government,—be its form what it may. So great is the difference, politically speaking, between the two ma-jorities, that they cannot be confounded, without leading to great and fatal errors; and yet the distinction between them has been so entirely overlooked, that when the term *majority* is used in political discussions, it is applied ex-clusively to designate the numerical,—as if there were no other. Until this distinction is recognized, and better understood, there will continue to be great liability to error in properly constructing constitutional governments, especially of the popular form, and of preserving them when properly con-structed. Until then, the latter will have a strong tendency to slide, first, into the government of the numerical majority, and, finally, into absolute govern-ment of some other form. To show that such must be the case, and at the same time to mark more strongly the difference between the two, in order to guard against the danger of overlooking it, I propose to consider the subject more at length.

The first and leading error which naturally arises from overlooking the distinction referred to, is, to confound the numerical majority with the people; and this so completely as to regard them as identical. This is a consequence that necessarily results from considering the numerical as the only majority. All admit, that a popular government, or democracy, is the government of the people; for the terms imply this. A perfect government of the kind would be one which would embrace the consent of every citizen or member of the community; but as this is impracticable, in the opinion of those who regard the numerical as the only majority, and who can perceive no other way by which the sense of the people can be taken,—they are compelled to adopt this as the only true basis of popular government, in contradistinction to govern-ments of the aristocratical or monarchical form. Being thus constrained, they are, in the next place, forced to regard the numerical majority, as, in effect, the entire people; that is, the greater part as the whole; and the govern-ment of the greater part as the government of the whole. It is thus the two come to be confounded, and a part made identical with the whole. And it is thus, also, that all the rights, powers, and immunities of the whole people come to be attributed to the numerical majority; and, among others, the supreme, sovereign authority of establishing and abolishing governments at pleasure.

This radical error, the consequence of confounding the two, and of regard-ing the numerical as the only majority, has contributed more than any other cause, to prevent the formation of popular constitutional governments,—and to destroy them even when they have been formed. It leads to the con-clusion that, in their formation and establishment nothing more is necessary than the right of suffrage,—and the allotment to each division of the community a representation in the government, in proportion to numbers. If the numerical majority were really the people; and if, to take its sense truly, were to take the sense of the people truly, a government so constituted would be a true and perfect model of a popular constitutional government; and every departure from it would detract from its excellence. But, as such is not the case,—as the numerical majority, instead of being the people, is only a portion of them,—such a government, instead of being a true and perfect model of the people's government, that is, a people self-governed, is but the government of a part, over a part,—the major over the minor portion.

But this misconception of the true elements of constitutional government does not stop here. It leads to others equally false and fatal, in reference to the best means of preserving and perpetuating them, when, from some fortunate combination of circumstances, they are correctly formed. For they who fall into these errors regard the restrictions which organism imposes on the will of the numerical majority as restrictions on the will of the people, and, therefore, as not only useless, but wrongful and mischievous. And hence they endeavor to destroy organism, under the delusive hope of making government more democratic.

Such are some of the consequences of confounding the two, and of regarding the numerical as the only majority. And in this may be found the reason why so few popular governments have been properly constructed, and why, of these few, so small a number have proved durable. Such must continue to be the result, so long as these errors continue to be prevalent.

There is another error, of a kindred character, whose influence contributes much to the same results: I refer to the prevalent opinion, that a written constitution, containing suitable restrictions on the powers of government, is sufficient, of itself, without the aid of any organism,—except such as is necessary to separate its several departments, and render them independent of each other,—to counteract the tendency of the numerical majority to oppression and the abuse of power.

A written constitution certainly has many and considerable advantages; but it is a great mistake to suppose, that the mere insertion of provisions to restrict and limit the powers of the government, without investing those for whose protection they are inserted with the means of enforcing their observance, will be sufficient to prevent the major and dominant party from abusing its powers. Being the party in possession of the government, they will, from the same constitution of man which makes government necessary to protect society, be in favor of the powers granted by the constitution, and opposed to the restrictions intended to limit them. As the major and dominant party, they will have no need of these restrictions for their protection. The ballot-box, of itself, would be ample protection to them. Needing no other, they would come, in time, to regard these limitations as unnecessary and improper restrains;—and endeavor to elude them, with the view of increasing their power and influence.

The minor, or weaker party, on the contrary, would take the opposite direction;—and regard them as essential to their protection against the dominant party. And, hence, they would endeavor to defend and enlarge the restrictions, and to limit and contract the powers. But where there are no means by which they could compel the major party to observe the restrictions, the only resort left them would be, a strict construction of the constitution,—that is, a construction which would confine these powers to the narrowest limits which the meaning of the words used in the grant would admit.

To this the major party would oppose a liberal construction,—one which would give to the words of the grant the broadest meaning of which they were susceptible. It would then be construction against construction; the one to contract, and the other to enlarge the powers of the government to the utmost. But of what possible avail could the strict construction of the minor party be, against the liberal interpretation of the major, when the one would have all the powers of the government to carry its construction into effect,—and the other be deprived of all means of enforcing its construction? In a contest so unequal, the result would not be doubtful. The party in favor of the restrictions would be overpowered. At first, they might command some respect, and do something to stay the march of encroachment; but they would, in the progress of the contest, be regarded as mere abstractionists; and, indeed, deservedly, if they should indulge the folly of supposing that the party in possession of the ballot-box and the physical force of the country, could be successfully resisted by an appeal to reason, truth, justice, or the obligations imposed by the constitution. For when these, of themselves, shall exert sufficient influence to stay the hand of power, then government will be no longer necessary to protect society, nor constitutions needed to prevent government from abusing its powers. The end of the contest would be the subversion of the constitution, either by the undermining process of construction,—where its meaning would admit of possible doubt,—or by substituting in practice what is called party-usage, in place of its provisions; —or, finally, when no other contrivance would subserve the purpose, by openly and boldly setting them aside. By the one or the other, the restrictions would ultimately be annulled, and the government be converted into one of unlimited powers.

Nor would the division of government into separate, and, as it regards each other, independent departments, prevent this result. Such a division may do much to facilitate its operations, and to secure to its administration greater caution and deliberation; but as each and all the departments,—and, of course, the entire government,—would be under the control of the numerical majority, it is too clear to require explanation, that a mere distribution of its powers among its agents or representatives, could do little or nothing to counteract its tendency to oppression and abuse of power. To effect this, it would be necessary to go one step further, and make the several departments the organs of the distinct interests or portions of the community; and to clothe each with a negative on the others. But the effect of this would be to change the government from the numerical into the concurrent majority.

Having now explained the reasons why it is so difficult to form and preserve popular constitutional government, so long as the distinction between the two majorities is overlooked, and the opinion prevails that a written constitution, with suitable restrictions and a proper division of its powers, is sufficient to counteract the tendency of the numerical majority to the abuse of its power,—I shall next proceed to explain, more fully, why the concurrent majority is an indispensable element in forming constitutional governments; and why the numerical majority, of itself, must, in all cases make governments absolute.

The necessary consequence of taking the sense of the community by the concurrent majority is, as has been explained, to give to each interest or portion of the community a negative on the others. It is this mutual negative among its various conflicting interests, which invests each with the power of protecting itself;—and places the rights and safety of each, where only they can be securely placed, under its own guardianship. Without this there can be no systematic, peaceful, or effective resistance to the natural tendency of each to come into conflict with the others: and without this there can be no constitution. It is this negative power,—the power of preventing or arresting the action of the government,—be it called by what term it may,— veto, interposition, nullification, check, or balance of power,—which, in fact, forms the constitution. They are all but different names for the negative power. In all its forms, and under all its names, it results from the concurrent majority. Without this there can be no negative; and, without a negative, no constitution. The assertion is true in reference to all constitutional governments, be their forms what they may. It is, indeed, the negative power which makes the constitution,—and the positive which makes the government. The one is the power of acting;—and the other the power of preventing or arresting action. The two, combined, make constitutional governments.

But, as there can be no constitution without the negative power, and no negative power without the concurrent majority;—it follows, necessarily, that where the numerical majority has the sole control of the government, there can be no constitution; as constitution implies limitation or restriction,—and, of course, is inconsistent with the idea of sole or exclusive power. And hence, the numerical, unmixed with the concurrent majority, necessarily forms, in all cases, absolute government.

It is, indeed, the single, or *one power*, which excludes the negative, and constitutes absolute government; and not the *number* in whom the power is vested. The numerical majority is as truly a *single power*, and excludes the negative as completely as the absolute government of one, or of the few. The former is as much the absolute government of the democratic, or popular form, as the latter of the monarchical or aristocratical. It has, accordingly, in common with them, the same tendency to oppression and abuse of power.

Constitutional governments, of whatever form, are, indeed, much more similar to each other, in their structure and character, than they are, respectively, to the absolute governments, even of their own class. All constitutional governments, of whatever class they may be, take the sense of the community by its parts,—each through its appropriate organ; and regard the sense of all its parts, as the sense of the whole. They all rest on the right of suffrage, and the responsibility of rulers, directly or indirectly. On the contrary, all absolute governments, of whatever form, concentrate power in one uncontrolled and irresponsible individual or body, whose will is regarded as the sense of the community. And, hence, the great and broad distinction between governments is,—not that of the one, the few, or the many,—but of the constitutional and the absolute.

From this there results another distinction, which, although secondary in its character, very strongly marks the difference between these forms of government. I refer to their respective conservative principle;—that is, the principle by which they are upheld and preserved. This principle, in constitutional governments, is *compromise;*—and in absolute governments, is *force;*—as will be next explained.

It has been already shown, that the same constitution of man which leads those who govern to oppress the governed,—if not prevented,—will, with equal force and certainty, lead the latter to resist oppression, when possessed of the means of doing so peaceably and successfully. But absolute governments, of all forms, exclude all other means of resistance to their authority, than that of force; and, of course, leave no other alternative to the governed, but to acquiesce in oppression, however great it may be, or to resort to force to put down the government. But the dread of such a resort must necessarily lead the government to prepare to meet force in order to protect itself; and hence, of necessity, force becomes the conservative principle of all such governments.

On the contrary, the government of the concurrent majority, where the organism is perfect, excludes the possibility of oppression, by giving to each interest, or portion, or order,—where there are established classes,—the means of protecting itself, by its negative, against all measures calculated to advance the peculiar interests of others at its expense. Its effect, then, is, to cause the different interests, portions, or orders,—as the case may be,—to desist from attempting to adopt any measure calculated to promote the prosperity of one, or more, by sacrificing that of others; and thus to force them to unite in such measures only as would promote the prosperity of all, as the only means to prevent the suspension of the action of the government;—and, thereby, to avoid anarchy, the greatest of all evils. It is by means of such authorized and effectual resistance, that oppression is prevented, and the necessity of resorting to force superseded, in governments of the concurrent majority;—and, hence, compromise, instead of force, becomes their conservative principle. . . .

ABEL P. UPSHUR

Abel P. Upshur was a Virginia lawyer. He early entered politics and became a state legislator and judge. During Tyler's administration, he served as Secretary of the Navy and then as Secretary of State. He died while in the latter office. Upshur was an extreme exponent of slavery and states' rights. In 1840 he wrote his *Brief Inquiry into the True Nature and Character of our Federal Government*. This volume was a particularistic reply to Joseph Story's nationalist *Commentaries on the Constitution*.

THE FEDERAL GOVERNMENT: ITS TRUE NATURE AND CHARACTER[80]

CHAPTER VIII

The Union a Federative and Not a National Government

Having disposed of this preliminary question, we now approach the Constitution itself. I affirm that it is, in its structure, a federative and not a

[80] A. P. Upshur, *The Federal Government: Its True Nature and Character; being a Review of Judge Story's Commentaries on the Constitution of the United States*. (New York, Van Evrie, Horton and Company, 1868), pp. 143–159.

consolidated government; that it is so in all its departments, and in all its leading and distinguishing provisions; and, of course, that it is to be interpreted, *by force of its own terms*, apart from any influence to be derived from that rule of construction which has just been laid down. We will first examine it in the structure of its several departments.

The Legislature.—This consists of two houses. The Senate is composed of two members from each State, chosen by its own legislature, whatever be its size or population, and is universally admitted to be strictly federative in its structure. The House of Representatives consists of members chosen in each State, and is regulated in its numbers according to a prescribed ratio of representation. The number to which each State is entitled is proportioned to its own population, and not to the population of the United States; and if there happen to be a surplus in any State less than the established ratio, the surplus is not added to the surplus or population of any other State, in order to make up the requisite number for a representative, but is wholly unrepresented. In the choice of representatives, each State votes by itself, and for its own representatives, and not in connection with any other State, nor for the representatives of any other State. Each State prescribes the qualifications of its own voters, the Constitution only provides that they shall have the qualifications which such State may have prescribed for the voters for the most numerous branch of its own legislature. And, as the *right* to vote is prescribed by the State, the *duty* of doing so cannot be enforced, except by the authority of the State. No one can be elected to represent any State, except a citizen thereof. Vacancies in the representation of any State are to be supplied under writs of election, issued by the Executive of such State. In all this, there is not one feature of nationality. The whole arrangement has reference to the State as such, and is carried into effect solely by their authority. The Federal Government has no agency in the choice of representatives, except only that it may prescribe the "times, places and manner of holding elections." It can neither prescribe the qualifications of the electors, nor impose any penalty upon them, for refusing to elect. The States alone can do these things; and, of course, the very existence of the House of Representatives depends, as much as does that of the Senate, upon the action of the States. A State may withdraw its representation altogether, and Congress has no power to prevent it, nor to supply the vacancy thus created. If the House of Representatives were national, in any practical sense of the term, the "nation" would have authority to provide for the appointment of its members, to prescribe the qualifications of voters, and to enforce the performance of that duty. All these things the State legislature can do, within their respective States, and it is obvious that they are strictly national. In order to make the House of Representatives equally so, the people of the United States must be so consolidated that the Federal Government may distribute them, without regard to State boundaries, into numbers according to the prescribed ratio; so that *all* the people may be represented, and no unrepresented surplus be left in any State. If these things could be done under the Federal Constitution, there would then be a strict analogy between the popular branches of the federal and State legislatures, and the former might, with propriety, be considered "national." But it is difficult to imagine a national legislature which does not exist under the authority of the nation, and over the very appointment of which the nation, as such, can exert no effective control.

There are only two reasons which I have ever heard assigned for the opinion that the House of Representatives is national, and not federative. The first is, that its measures are carried by the votes of a majority of the *whole number*, and not by those of a majority of the States. It would be easy to demonstrate that this fact does not warrant such a conclusion; but all reasoning is unnecessary, since the conclusion is disproved by the example of the other branch of the federal legislature. The Senate, which is strictly federative, votes in the same way. The argument, therefore, proves nothing, because it proves too much.

The second argument is, that the States are not *equally* represented, but each one has a representation proportioned to its population. There is no reason, apparent to me, why a league may not be formed among independent sovereignties, giving to each an influence in the management of their common concerns, proportioned to its strength, its wealth, or the interest which it has at stake. This is but simple justice, and the rule ought to prevail in all cases, except where higher considerations disallow it. History abounds with examples of such confederations, one of which I will cite. The States General of the United Provinces were strictly a federal body. The Council of State had almost exclusively the management and control of all their military and financial concerns; and in that body, Holland and some other provinces had three votes each, whilst some had two, and others only one vote each. Yet it never was supposed that for this reason the United Provinces were a consolidated nation. A single example of this sort affords a full illustration of the subject, and renders all farther argument superfluous.

It is not, however, from the apportionment of its powers, not from the modes in which these powers are exercised, that we can determine the true character of a legislative body, in the particular now under consideration. The true rule of decision is found in the manner in which the body is constituted, and that, we have already seen, is, in the case before us, federative, and not national.

We may safely admit, however, that the House of Representatives is not federative, and yet contend, with perfect security, that *the legislative department* is so. Congress consists of the House of Representatives and Senate. Neither is a complete legislature in itself, and neither can pass any law without the concurrence of the other. And, as the Senate is the peculiar representative of the States, no act of legislation whatever can be performed without the consent of the States. They hold, therefore, a complete check and control over the powers of the people in this respect, even admitting that those powers are truly and strictly represented in the other branch. It is true that the check is mutual; but if the legislative department were national, there would be no federative feature in it. The question is, whether or not the States have preserved their distinct sovereign characters, in this feature of the Constitution. If they have done so in any part of it, the whole must be considered federative; because national legislation implies a *unity*, which is absolutely inconsistent with all idea of a confederation; whereas, there is nothing to prevent the members of a confederation from exerting their several powers, in any form of *joint action* which may seem to them proper.

But there is one other provision of the Constitution which appears to me to be altogether decisive upon this point. Each State, whatever be its population, is entitled to at least one representative. It may so happen that the unrepresented surplus, in some one State, may be greater than the whole population of some other State; and yet such latter State would be entitled to a representative. Upon what principle is this? Surely, if the House of Representatives were national, something like *equality* would be found in the constitution of it. Large surpluses would be arbitrarily rejected in some places, and smaller numbers, not equal to the general ratio, be represented in others. There can be but one reason for this: As the Constitution was made by the States, the true principles of the confederation could not be preserved, without giving to each party to the compact a place and influence in each branch of the common legislature. This was due to their perfect *equality* as sovereign States.

The Executive.—In the election of the President and Vice-President, the exclusive agency of the States, as such, is preserved with equal distinction. These officers are chosen by electors, who are themselves chosen by the people of each State, acting by and for itself, and in such mode as itself may prescribe. The number of electors to which each State is entitled is equal to the whole number of its representatives *and senators*. This provision is even more federative than that which apportions representation in the House of Representatives; because it adds two to the electors of each State, and, so far, places them on an equality, whatever be their comparative population. The people of each State vote *within* the State, and not elsewhere; and for their own electors, and for no others. Each State prescribes the qualifications of its own electors, and can alone compel them to vote. The electors, when chosen, give their votes within their respective States, and at such times and places as the States may respectively prescribe.

There is not the least trace of national agency, in any part of this proceeding. The Federal Government can exercise no rightful power in the choice of its own Executive. "The people of the United States" are equally unseen in that important measure. Neither a majority, nor the whole of them together, can choose a President, except in their character as citizens of the several States. Nay, a President may be constitutionally elected, *with a decided majority of the people against him*. For example, New York has forty-two votes, Pennsylvania thirty, Virginia twenty-three, Ohio twenty-one, North Carolina fifteen. These seven States can give a majority of all the votes, and each may elect its own electors by a majority of only one vote. If we add their minorities to the votes of the other States, (supposing those States to be unanimous against the candidate,) we may have a President constitutionally elected, with less than half—perhaps with little more than a fourth—of the people in his favor. It is true that he may also be constitutionally elected with a majority of the *States*, as such, against him, as the above example shows; because the States may, as before remarked, properly agree, by the provisions of their compact, that they shall possess influence, in this respect, proportioned to their population. But there is no mode, consistent with the true principles of free representative government, by which a minority of those to whom, *en masse*, the elective franchise is confided, can countervail the concurrent and opposing action of the majority. If the

President could be chosen by the people of the "United States" in the aggregate, instead of by the States, it is difficult to imagine a case in which a majority of those people, concurring in the same vote, could be overbalanced by a minority.

All doubt upon this point, however, is removed by another provision of the Constitution touching this subject. If no candidate should receive a majority of votes in the Electoral College, the House of Representatives elects the President, from the three candidates which have received the largest electoral vote. In doing this, two-thirds of the States must be present by their representatives, or one of them, and then *they vote by States, all the members of each State giving one vote, and a majority of all the States being necessary to a choice.* This is precisely the rule which prevailed in the ordinary legislature of that body, under the Articles of Confederation, and which proved its federative character as strongly as any other provision of those articles. Why, then, should this federative principle be preserved, in the election of the President by the House of Representatives, if it was designed to abandon it, in the election of some officer by the Electoral College? No good reason for it has yet been assigned, so far as I am informed. On the contrary, there is every just reason to suppose, that those who considered the principle safe and necessary in one form of election, would adhere to it as equally safe and necessary in every other, with respect to the same public trust. And this is still farther proved by the provision of the Constitution relating to the election of the Vice-President. In case of the death or constitutional disability of the President, every executive trust devolves on him; and, of course, the same general principle should be applied, in the election of both of them. This is done in express terms, so far as the action of the Electoral College is contemplated. But if those Colleges should fail to elect a Vice-President, that trust devolves on the *Senate*, who are to choose from the two highest candidates. Here the federative principle is distinctly seen, for the Senate is the representative of the States.

This view of the subject is still farther confirmed by the clause of the Constitution relating to impeachments. The power to try the President is vested in the Senate alone, that is, in the representatives of the States. There is a strict fitness and propriety in this; for those only, whose office the President is, should be entrusted with the power to remove him.

It is believed to be neither a forced nor an unreasonable conclusion from all this, that the Executive Department is, in its structure, strictly federative.

The Judiciary.—The Judges are nominated by the President, and approved by the Senate. Thus the nominations are made by a federative officer, and the approval and confirmation of them depend on those who are the exclusive representatives of the States. This agency is manifestly federative, and "the people of the United States" cannot mingle in it, in any form whatever.

As the Constitution is federative in the structure of all three of its great departments, it is equally so *in the power of amendment.*

Congress may *propose* amendments, "whenever two-thirds of both houses shall deem it necessary." This secures the States against any action upon the subject by the people at large. In like manner, Congress may call a convention for proposing amendments, "on the application of the legislatures of two-thirds of the several States." It is remarkable that, whether Congress or the States act upon the subject, the *same proportion* is required; not less than two-thirds of either being authorized to act. From this, it is not unreasonable to conclude, that the convention considered that the *same power* would act in both cases; to wit: the power of the States, who might effect their object either by their separate action as States, or by the action of Congress, their common federative agent; but, whether they adopted the one mode or the other, not less than two-thirds of them should be authorized to act efficiently.

The amendments thus proposed "shall be valid to all intents and purposes, as part of this Constitution, *when ratified by the legislatures of three-fourths of the several States, or by conventions in three-fourths thereof*, as the one or the other mode of ratification may be proposed by Congress." It is the act of adoption or ratification alone which makes a constitution. In the case before us, the States alone can perform that act. The language of the Constitution admits of no doubt, and gives no pretext for double construction. It is not the people of the United States in the aggregate, merely *acting* in their several States, who can ratify amendments. *Three-fourths of the several States* can alone do this. The idea of separate and independent political corporations could not be more distinctly conveyed, by any form of words. If the people of the United States, as one people, but acting in their several States, could ratify amendments, then the very language of the Constitution requires that *three-fourths of them* shall concur therein. Is it not, then, truly wonderful that no mode has yet been prescribed to ascertain, whether three-fourths of them do concur or not? By what power can the necessary arrangement have already been made, in strict conformity with this provision of the Constitution? We ask our author, whether three-fourths of the people of the United States concurred in those amendments or not; and if they did, whence does he derive the proof of it?

If Judge Story, and the politicians of his school, be correct in the idea, that the Constitution was formed by "the people of the United States," and not by the States, as such, this clause relating to amendments presents a singular anomaly in politics. Their idea is that the State sovereignties were merged, to a certain extent, in that act, and that the government established was emphatically the government of the people of the United States. And yet, those same people can neither alter nor amend that government. In order to perform this essential function, it is necessary to call again into life and action those very State sovereignties which were supposed to be merged and dead, by the very act of *creating* the instrument which they are required to amend. To alter or amend a government requires the same extent of power which is required to *form* one; for every alteration or amendment is, as to so much, a new government. And, of all political acts, the formation of a constitution of government is that which admits and implies, the most distinctly and to the fullest extent, the existence of absolute, unqualified, unconditional, and unlimited sovereignty. So long, therefore, as the power of amending the Constitution rests exclusively with the States, it is idle to contend that they are less sovereign now than they were before the adoption of that instrument.

The idea which I am endeavoring to enforce, of the federative character of the Constitution, is still farther confirmed by that clause of the article under consideration, which provides that no amendment shall be made to deprive any State of its equal suffrage in the Senate, without its own consent. So strongly were the States attached to that perfect equality which their perfect sovereignty implied, and so jealous were they of every attack upon it, that they guarded it, by an express provision of the Constitution, against the possibility of overthrow. All other rights they confided to that power of amendment which they reposed in three-fourths of all the States; but *this* they refused to entrust, except to the separate, independent and sovereign will of each State; giving to each, in its own case, an absolute negative upon all the rest.

The object of the preceding pages has been to show that the Constitution is federative, in the power which framed it; federative in the power which adopted and ratified it; federative in the power which sustains and keeps it alive; federative in the power by which alone it can be altered or amended; and federative in the structure of all its departments. In what respect, then, can it justly be called a consolidated or national government? Certainly, the mere fact that, in particular cases, it is authorized to act directly on the people, does not disprove its federative character, since that very sovereignty in the States, which a confederation implies, includes within it the right of the State to subject its own citizens to the action of the common authority of the confederated States, in any form which may seem proper to itself. Neither is our Constitution to be deemed the less federative, because it was the object of those who formed it to establish "a government," and one effective for the legitimate purposes of government. Much emphasis has been laid upon this word, and it even has been thought, by one distinguished statesman of Judge Story's school, that ours is "*a government proper*," which I presume implies that it is a government in a peculiarly emphatic sense. I confess that I do not very clearly discern the difference between a government and a government proper. Nothing is a government which is not *properly* so; and whatever is properly a government is a government proper. But whether ours is a "government proper," or only a simple government, does not prove that it is not a confederation, unless it be true that a confederation cannot be a government.

For myself, I am unable to discover why States, absolutely sovereign, may not create for themselves, by compact, a common government, with powers as extensive and supreme as any sovereign people can confer on a government established by themselves. In what other particular ours is a consolidated or national government, I leave it to the advocates of that doctrine to show.

ALEXANDER H. STEPHENS

Alexander H. Stephens entered Georgia politics while he was still in his twenties, and rose to a position of prominence in the South. Throughout his political career he fought for the principles of individual liberty and local supremacy. He opposed the Mexican War as an imperialistic enterprise, but when the war ended he accepted its results as a godsend of valuable territory for the South. In the fifties he opposed the growing secession movement as politically inexpedient, although he firmly believed in States' Rights. He became vice-president of the Confederacy. Even during the darkest days of the Civil War, he continued to fight for constitutional liberties, freedom of speech, and States' Rights within the Confederacy. After the Civil War, he reëntered politics as a Georgia representative in Congress, and became governor of his state. During the period of reconstruction, he collected his notes on the nature of the union in a masterpiece of historical information, *A Constitutional View of the Late War between the States.*

A CONSTITUTIONAL VIEW OF THE LATE WAR BETWEEN THE STATES[81]

COLLOQUY XI

THE GREAT TRUTH ESTABLISHES THAT THE CONSTITUTION IS A COMPACT BETWEEN SOVEREIGN STATES—THE GOVERNMENT OF THE UNITED STATES IS STRICTLY A FEDERAL GOVERNMENT—EACH STATE FOR ITSELF HAS THE RIGHT TO JUDGE OF INFRACTIONS AS WELL AS THE MODE AND MEASURE OF REDRESS—THE RIGHT OF A STATE TO WITHDRAW FROM THE UNION UPON BREACH OF THE COMPACT BY OTHER PARTIES TO ITS PRINGS FROM THE VERY NATURE OF THE GOVERNMENT—THE COMPACT BROKEN BY THIRTEEN STATES OF THE UNION—WEBSTER, STORY, TUCKER, RAWLE, DE TOCQUEVILLE, WADE, GREELEY AND LINCOLN UPON THIS RIGHT TO WITHDRAW OR SECEDE IN SUCH CASE.

. . . .

Where, under the system so constituted, does Sovereignty reside? This is now the great and last question. It must reside somewhere. It must reside, as all admit, with the people somewhere. Does it reside with the whole people in mass of all the States together, or with the people of the several States separately? That is the only question. The whole subject is narrowed down to this: Where, in this country, resides that Paramount authority that can rightfully make and unmake Constitutions? In all Confederated Republics, according to Montesquieu, Vattel, and Burlamaqui, it remains with the Sovereign States so Confederated. Is our Confederated Republic an exception to this rule? If so, how does it appear? Is there any thing in its history, anterior to the present Compact of Union, that shows it to be an exception? Certainly not; for the Sovereignty of each State was expressly retained in the first Articles of Union. Is there then any thing in the present compact itself that shows that it was surrendered by them in that? If so, where is the clause bearing that import? None can be found! Again: if it was thereby surrendered, to whom was it surrendered? to whom did it pass? Did it pass to all the people of the United States? Of course not; for not one particle of power of any sort, much less Sovereignty, is delegated in the Constitution to the people of the United States. All powers therein delegated are to the States in their Sovereign character, under the designation of United States. Is it then surrendered to the United States jointly? Certainly not, for one of the main objects in forming the Compact, as before stated, and as clearly appears from the instrument itself, was, to preserve and perpetuate separate State existence. The guarantee to this effect, from the very words used, implies their Sovereignty. There can be no such thing as a *perfect State* without Sovereignty. It certainly is not parted with by any express terms in that instrument. If it be surrendered thereby it must be by implication only. But how can it be implied from any words or phrases in that instru-

[81] A. H. Stephens, *A Constitutional View of the Late War between the States.* (Philadelphia, National Publishing Company, 1867), I, 487–491, 495–497.

ment? If carried by implication, it must be on the strange assumption that it is an incident only of some one or all of those specific and specially enumerated powers expressly delegated. This cannot be, as that would be making the incident greater than the object, the shadow more solid than the substance. For Sovereignty is the highest and greatest of all political powers. It is itself the source as well as embodiment of all political powers, both great and small. All proceed and emanate from it. All the great powers specifically and expressly delegated in the Constitution, such as the power to declare war and make peace; to raise and support armies, to tax and lay excise duties, etc., are themselves but the incidents of Sovereignty. If this great embodiment of all powers was parted with, why were any minor specifications made? Why any enumeration? Was not such specification or enumeration both useless and absurd?

All the implications are the other way. The bare fact that all the powers parted with by the States were delegated only, as all admit, necessarily implies that the greater power delegating still continued to exist.

If, then, this ultimate absolute Sovereignty did reside with the several States separately, as without question it did, up to the formation of the Constitution; and if, in the Constitution, Sovereignty is not parted with by the States in express terms; if, as Mr. Webster said, in 1839, there is not a word about Sovereignty in it, and if, further, this greatest of all political powers cannot justly be claimed as an incident to lesser ones, and thereby carried by implication; then, of course, was it not, most clearly, still retained and reserved to the people of the several States in that mass of residuary rights, in the language of Mr. Jefferson, which was expressly reserved in the Constitution itself?

It is true it was not so expressly reserved in the Constitution at first, because it was deemed, as the debates in the Federal Convention, as well as the State Conventions, clearly show, wholly unnecessary; so general was the understanding that it could not go, by inference or implication, from any thing in the Constitution; or in other words, that it could not be surrendered without express terms to that effect. The general understanding was the universally acknowledged principle in public law, that nothing is held good against Sovereignty by implication. But to quiet the apprehensions of Patrick Henry, Samuel Adams, and the Conventions of a majority of the States, this reservation of Sovereignty was soon after put in the Constitution amongst other amendments, in plain and unequivocal language. So cautious and guarded were the men of that day that the Government had hardly commenced operations before all inferences that had been drawn against the reserved Sovereignty of the States, from the silence of the Constitution, in this particular and some others, were fully rebutted by several amendments, proposed by the States, in Congress assembled, at their first session. These amendments were preceded by a preamble, which shows that they were both declaratory and restrictive in their object. Here is what was done:—

"The Conventions of a number of the States, having, at the time of their adoption of the Constitution, expressed a desire, in order to prevent misconstruction or abuse of its powers, that further declaratory and restrictive clauses should be added: And as extending the ground of public confidence in the Government, will best insure the beneficent ends of its institution;

"*Resolved, by the Senate and House of Representatives of the United States of America, in Congress assembled,* two thirds of both Houses concurring, That the following Articles be proposed to the Legislatures of the several States, as amendments to the Constitution of the United States, all, or any of which Articles, when ratified by three fourths of the said Legislatures, to be valid to all intents and purposes, as part of the said Constitution."

The language of one of the amendments then proposed, on the subject we are now upon, is as follows: "The powers not *delegated* to the *United States* by the Constitution, nor prohibited by it to the States, are reserved to the States, respectively, or to the people."

This amendment, which was promptly agreed to by the States unanimously, declares that *all powers* not *delegated* were reserved to the States respectively; this, of course, includes, in the reservation, Sovereignty, which is the source of all powers, those delegated as well as those reserved. This reservation Mr. Samuel Adams said, we have seen in the Massachusetts Convention, was consonant with the like reservation in the first Articles of Confederation. And such was the universal understanding at the time. Most of the other amendments, then proposed, were likewise agreed to by the States, but not unanimously.

Can any proposition within the domain of reason be clearer, from all these facts, than that the Sovereignty of the States, that great Paramount authority which can rightfully make and unmake Constitutions, resides still with the States? Does not this declaratory amendment, added to the original covenant in the Constitution, which provides for its own amendment, show this beyond all doubt or question? Why were further amendments to it to be submitted to the States for their ratification before they could be binding, but upon the indisputable principle or postulate that Sovereignty, which alone has control of all such matters, still resides with the States severally? There is, my dear sirs, no answer to this. . . .

Now as to the *rightfulness* of the State's thus resuming her Sovereign powers! In doing it she *seceded* from that Union, to which, in the language of Mr. Jefferson, as well as General Washington, she had *acceded* as a Sovereign State. She repealed her ordinance by which she ratified and agreed to the Constitution and became a party to the Compact under it. She declared herself no longer bound by that Compact, and dissolved her alliance with the other parties to it. The Constitution of the United States, and the laws passed in pursuance of it, were no longer the supreme law of the people of Georgia, any more than the treaty with France was the supreme law of both countries, after its abrogation, in 1798, by the same rightful authority which had made it in the beginning.

In answer to your question, whether she could do this without a breach of her solemn obligations, under the Compact, I give this full and direct answer: she had a perfect right so to do, subject to no authority, but the great moral law which governs the intercourse between Independent Sovereign Powers, Peoples, or Nations. Her action was subject to the authority of that law and none other. It is the inherent right of Nations, subject to this law alone, to disregard the obligations of Compacts of all sorts, by declaring themselves no longer bound in any way by them. This, by universal consent, may be rightfully done, when there has been a breach of the Compact by the other party or parties. It was on this principle, that the United States abrogated their treaty with France, in 1798. The justifiableness of the act depends, in every instance, upon the circumstances of the case. The general rule is, if all the other States—the Parties to the Confederation—faithfully comply with their obligations, under the Compact of Union, no State would be morally justified in withdrawing from a Union so formed, unless it were necessary for her own preservation. Self-preservation is the first law of nature, with States or Nations, as it is with individuals.

But in this case the breach of plighted faith was not on the part of Georgia, or those States which withdrew or attempted to withdraw from the Union. Thirteen of their Confederates had openly and avowedly disregarded their obligations under that clause of the Constitution which covenanted for the rendition of the fugitives from service, to say nothing of the acts of several of them, in a like open and palpable breach of faith, in the matter of the rendition of fugitives from justice. These are facts about which there can be no dispute. Then, by universal law, as recognized by all Nations, savage as well as civilized, the Compact, thus broken by some of the Parties, was no longer binding upon the others. The breach was not made by the seceding States. Under the circumstances, *and the facts* of this case, therefore, the legal as well as moral right, on the part of Georgia, according to the laws of Nations and nature, to declare herself no longer bound by the Compact, and to withdraw from the Union under it, was perfect and complete. These principles are too incontestably established to be questioned, much less denied, in the forum of reason and justice. . . .

JEFFERSON DAVIS

For many years Jefferson Davis represented Mississippi in the United States Senate. Later he became the President of the Confederacy. After the war he wrote a history of the "lost cause"—*The Rise and Fall of the Confederate Government*. In this work he devotes considerable space justifying particularism and secession.

THE RISE AND FALL OF THE CONFEDERATE GOVERNMENT [82]

PART II

THE CONSTITUTION

CHAPTER I

When certain American colonies of Great Britain, each acting for itself, although in concert with the others, determined to dissolve their political connection with the mother-country, they sent their representatives to a general Congress of those colonies, and through them made a declaration that the colonies were, and of right ought to be, "free and independent States." As such they contracted an alliance for their "common defence,"

[82] Jefferson Davis, *The Rise and Fall of the Confederate Government*. (New York, D. Appleton and Company, 1881), I, 86–90, 103–105, 157–159, 168–170, 173. (Reprinted by permission of the publishers.)

successfully resisted the efforts to reduce them to submission, and secured the recognition by Great Britain of their separate independence; each State being distinctly recognized under its own name—not as one of a group or nation. That this was not merely a foreign view is evident from the second of the "Articles of Confederation" between the States, adopted subsequently to the Declaration of Independence, which is in these words: "Each State retains its sovereignty, freedom, and independence, and every power, jurisdiction, and right, which is not by this Constitution expressly delegated to the United States in Congress assembled."

These "Articles of Confederation and Perpetual Union between the States," as they were styled in their title, were adopted by eleven of the original States in 1778, and by the other two in the course of the three years next ensuing, and continued in force until 1789. During this period the General Government was vested in the Congress alone, in which each State, through its representatives, had an equal vote in the determination of all questions whatever. The Congress exercised all the executive as well as legislative powers delegated by the States. When not in session the general management of affairs was intrusted to a "Committee of the States," consisting of one delegate from each State. Provision was made for the creation, by the Congress, of courts having a certain specified jurisdiction in admiralty and maritime cases, and for the settlement of controversies between two or more States in a mode specifically prescribed.

The Government thus constituted was found inadequate for some necessary purposes, and it became requisite to reorganize it. The first idea of such reorganization arose from the necessity of regulating the commercial intercourse of the States with one another and with foreign countries, and also of making some provision for payment of the debt contracted during the war for independence. These exigencies led to a proposition for a meeting of commissioners from the various States to consider the subject. Such a meeting was held at Annapolis in September, 1786; but, as only five States (New York, New Jersey, Delaware, Pennsylvania, and Virginia) were represented, the Commissioners declined to take any action further than to recommend another Convention, with a wider scope for consideration. As they expressed it, it was their "unanimous conviction that it may essentially tend to advance the interests of the Union, if the States, by whom they have been respectively delegated, would themselves concur, and use their endeavors to procure the concurrence of the other States, in the appointment of commissioners, to meet at Philadelphia on the second Monday in May next, to take into consideration the situation of the United States, to devise such further provisions as shall appear to them necessary to render the Constitution of the Federal Government adequate to the exigencies of the Union, and to report such an act for that purpose to the United States in Congress assembled, as, when agreed to by them, and afterward confirmed by the Legislatures of every State, will effectually provide for the same."

It is scarcely necessary to remind the well-informed reader that the terms, "Constitution of the Federal Government," employed above, and "Federal Constitution," as used in other proceedings of that period, do not mean the instrument to which we now apply them, and which was not then in existence. They were applied to the system of government formulated in the Articles of Confederation. This is in strict accord with the definition of the word constitution, given by an eminent lexicographer: "The body of fundamental laws, as contained in written documents or prescriptive usage, which constitute the form of government for a nation, state, community, association, or society." Thus we speak of the British Constitution, which is an unwritten system of "prescriptive usage"; of the Constitution of Massachusetts or of Mississippi, which is the fundamental or organic law of a particular State embodied in a written instrument; and of the Federal Constitution of the United States, which is the fundamental law of an association of States, at first embraced in the Articles of Confederation, and afterward as revised, amended, enlarged, and embodied in the instrument framed in 1787, and subsequently adopted by the various States. The manner in which this revision was effected was as follows. Acting on the suggestion of the Annapolis Convention, the Congress, on the 21st of the ensuing February (1787), adopted the following resolution:

"*Resolved*, That, in the opinion of Congress, it is expedient that, on the second Monday in May next, a convention of delegates, who shall have been appointed by the several States, be held at Philadelphia, for the sole and express purpose of revising the Articles of Confederation, and reporting to Congress and the several Legislatures such alterations and provisions therein as shall, when agreed to in Congress and confirmed by the States, render the Federal Constitution adequate to the exigencies of Government and the preservation of the Union."

The language of this resolution, substantially according with that of the recommendation made by the commissioners at Annapolis a few months before, very clearly defines the objects of the proposed Convention and the powers which it was thought advisable that the States should confer upon their delegates. These were, "solely and expressly," as follows:

1. "To revise the Articles of Confederation with reference to the 'situation of the United States';

2. "To devise such alterations and provisions therein as should seem to them requisite in order to render 'the Federal Constitution,' or 'Constitution of the Federal Government,' adequate to 'the exigencies of the Union,' or 'the exigencies of the government and the preservation of the Union';

3. "To report the result of their deliberations—that is, the 'alterations and provisions' which they should agree to recommend—to Congress and the Legislatures of the several States."

Of course, their action could be only advisory until ratified by the States. The "Articles of Confederation and Perpetual Union," under which the States were already united, provided that no alteration should be made in any of them, "unless such alteration be agreed to in a Congress of the United States, and afterward confirmed by the Legislatures of every State."

The Legislatures of the various States, with the exception of Rhode Island, adopted and proceeded to act upon these suggestions by the appointment of delegates—some of them immediately upon the recommendation of the Annapolis Commissioners in advance of that of the Congress, and the others in the course of a few months after the resolution adopted by Congress. The instructions given to these delegates in all cases conformed to the recommendations which have been quoted, and in one case imposed an additional restriction or limitation. As this is a matter of much importance, in order to a right understanding of what follows, it may be advisable to cite in detail the action of the several States, italicizing such passages as are specially significant of the duties and powers of the delegates to the Convention.

The General Assembly of Virginia, after reciting the recommendation made at Annapolis, enacted: "That seven commissioners be appointed by joint ballot of both Houses of Assembly, who, or any three of them, are hereby authorized, as deputies from this Commonwealth, to meet such deputies as may be appointed and authorized by other States, to assemble in convention at Philadelphia, as above recommended, and to join with them in devising and discussing *all such alterations and further provisions as may be necessary to render the Federal Constitution adequate to the exigencies of the Union, and in reporting such an act for that purpose to the United States in Congress, as, when agreed to by them, and duly confirmed by the several States,* will effectually provide for the same."

The Council and Assembly of New Jersey issued commissions to their delegates to meet such commissioners as have been, or may be, appointed *by the other States of the Union,* at the city of Philadelphia, in the commonwealth of Pennsylvania on the second Monday in May next, *for the purpose of taking into consideration the state of the Union as to trade and other important objects, and of devising such other provisions as shall appear to be necessary to render the Constitution of the Federal Government adequate to the exigencies thereof."* . . .

CHAPTER III

The amended system of union, or confederation (the terms are employed indiscriminately and interchangeably by the statesmen of that period), devised by the Convention of 1787, and embodied, as we have seen, in the Constitution which they framed and have set forth, was now to be considered and acted on by the people of the several States. This they did in the highest and most majestic form in which the sanction of organized communities could be given or withheld—not through ambassadors, nor Legislatures, or deputies with limited powers, but through conventions of delegates chosen expressly for the purpose and clothed with the plenary authority of sovereign people. The action of these conventions was deliberate, cautious, and careful. There was much debate, and no little opposition to be conciliated. Eleven States, however, ratified and adopted the new Constitution within the twelve months immediately following its submission to them. Two of them positively rejected it, and, although they afterward acceded to it, remained outside of the Union in the exercise of their sovereign right, which nobody then denied—North Carolina for nine months, Rhode Island for nearly fifteen, after the new Government was organized and went into operation. In several of the other States the ratification was effected only by small majorities.

The terms in which this action was expressed by the several States and the declarations with which it was accompanied by some of them are worthy of attention.

Delaware was the first to act. Her Convention met on December 3, 1787, and ratified the Constitution on the 7th. The readiness of this least in population, and next to the least in territorial extent, of all the States, to accept that instrument, is a very significant fact when we remember the jealous care with which she had guarded against any infringement of her sovereign Statehood. Delaware alone had given special instructions to her deputies in the Convention not to consent to any sacrifice of the principle of equal representation in Congress. The promptness and unanimity of her people in adopting the new Constitution prove very clearly, not only that they were satisfied with the preservation of that principle in the Federal Senate, but that they did not understand the Constitution, in any of its features, as compromising the "sovereignty, freedom, and independence" which she had so especially cherished. The ratification of their Convention is expressed in these words:

"We, the deputies *of the people of the Delaware State*, in convention met, having taken into our serious consideration the Federal Constitution proposed and agreed upon by the deputies of the United States as a General Convention held at the city of Philadelphia on the 17th day of September, A.D. 1787, have *approved of, assented to, and ratified and confirmed,* and by these presents do, in virtue of the powers and authority to us given for that purpose, for and in behalf of ourselves and our constituents, fully, freely, and entirely, *approve of, assent to, ratify, and confirm* the said Constitution.

"Done in convention at Dover, December 7, 1787."

This, and twelve other like acts, gave to the Constitution "all the life and validity it ever had, or could have, as to the thirteen united or associated States." . . .

CHAPTER X

Looking back for a moment at the ground over which we have gone, I think it may be fairly asserted that the following propositions have been clearly and full established:

1. That the States of which the American Union was formed, from the moment when they emerged from their colonial or provincial condition, became severally sovereign, free, and independent States—not one State, or nation.

2. That the union formed under the Articles of Confederation was a compact between the States, in which these attributes of "sovereignty, freedom, and independence," were expressly asserted and guaranteed.

3. That, in forming the "more perfect union" of the Constitution, afterward adopted, the same contracting powers formed an *amended compact*, without any surrender of these attributes of sovereignty, freedom, and independence, either expressed or implied: on the contrary, that, by the tenth amendment to the Constitution, limiting the power of the Government to its express grants, they distinctly guarded against the presumption of a surrender of anything by implication.

4. That political sovereignty resides, neither in individual citizens, nor in unorganized masses, nor in fractional subdivisions of a community, but in the people of an organized political body.

5. That no "republican form of government," in the sense in which that expression is used in the Constitution, and was generally understood by the founders of the Union—whether it be the government of a State or of a confederation of States—is possessed of any sovereignty whatever, but merely

exercises certain powers delegated by the sovereign authority of the people, and subject to recall and reassumption by the same authority that conferred them.

6. That the "people" who organized the first confederation, the people who dissolved it, the people who ordained and established the Constitution which succeeded it, the only people, in fine, known or referred to in the phraseology of that period—whether the term was used collectively or distributively—were the people of the respective States, each acting separately and with absolute independence of the others.

7. That, in forming and adopting the Constitution, the States, or the people of the States—terms which, when used with reference to acts performed in a sovereign capacity, are precisely equivalent to each other—formed a new *Government*, but no new *people;* and that, consequently, no new sovereignty was created—for sovereignty in an American republic can belong only to a people, never to a government—and that the Federal Government is entitled to exercise only the powers delegated to it by the people of the respective States.

8. That the term "people," in the preamble to the Constitution and in the tenth amendment, is used distributively; that the only "people of the United States" known to the Constitution are the people of each State in the Union; that no such political community or corporate unit as one people of the United States then existed, has even been organized, or yet exists; and that no political action by the people of the United States in the aggregate has ever taken place, or ever can take place, under the Constitution.

The fictitious idea of *one* people of the United States, contradicted in the last paragraph, has been so impressed upon the popular mind by false teaching, by careless and vicious phraseology, and by the ever-present spectacle of a great Government, with its army and navy, its custom-houses and post-offices, its multitude of office-holders, and the splendid prizes which it offers to political ambition, that the tearing away of these illusions and presentation of the original fabric, which they have overgrown and hidden from view, have no doubt been unwelcome, distasteful, and even repellent to some of my readers. The artificial splendor which makes the deception attractive is even employed as an argument to prove its reality.

The glitter of the powers delegated to the agent serves to obscure the perception of the sovereign power of the principal by whom they are conferred, as, by the unpracticed eye, the showy costume and conspicuous functions of the drum-major are mistaken for emblems of chieftaincy—while the misuse or ambiguous use of the term "Union" and its congeners contributes to increase the confusion.

So much the more need for insisting upon the elementary truths which have been obscured by these specious sophistries. The reader really desirous of ascertaining truth is, therefore, again cautioned against confounding two ideas so essentially distinct as that of *government*, which is derivative, dependent, and subordinate, with that of the *people*, as an organized political community, which is sovereign, without any other than self-imposed limitations, and such as proceed from the general principles of the personal rights of man. . . .

CHAPTER XI

THE RIGHT OF SECESSION—that subject which, beyond all others, ignorance, prejudice, and political rancor have combined to cloud with misstatements and misapprehensions—is a question easily to be determined in the light of what has already been established with regard to the history and principles of the Constitution. It is not something standing apart by itself—a factious creation, outside of and antagonistic to the Constitution—as might be imagined by one deriving his ideas from the political literature most current of late years. So far from being against the Constitution or incompatible with it, we contend that, if the right to secede is not prohibited to the States, and no power to prevent it expressly delegated to the United States, it remains as reserved to the States or the people, from whom all the powers of the General Government were derived

The compact between the States which formed the Union was in the nature of a partnership between individuals without limitation of time, and the recognized law of such partnerships is thus stated by an eminent lawyer of Massachusetts in a work intended for popular use:

"If the articles between the partners do not contain an agreement that the partnership shall continue for a specified time, it may be dissolved at the pleasure of either partner. But no partner can exercise this power wantonly and injuriously to the other partners, without making himself responsible for the damages he thus causes. If there be a provision that the partnership shall continue a certain time, this is binding."

We have seen that a number of "sovereign, free, and independent" States, during the war of the Revolution, entered into a partnership with one another, which was not only unlimited in duration, but expressly declared to be a "perpetual union." Yet, when that Union failed to accomplish the purposes for which it was formed, the parties withdrew, separately and independently, one after another, without any question made of their right to do so, and formed a new association. One of the declared objects of this new partnership was to form "a more perfect union." This certainly did not mean more perfect in respect of duration; for the former union had been declared perpetual, and perpetuity admits of no addition. It did not mean that it was to be more indissoluble; for the delegates of the States, in ratifying the former compact of union, had expressed themselves in terms that could scarcely be made more stringent. They then said:

"And we do further *solemnly plight and engage the faith of our respective constituents*, that they shall abide by the determinations of the United States in Congress assembled, on all questions which, by the said confederation, are submitted to them; and that the articles thereof shall be *inviolably observed* by the States we respectively represent; and that *the Union shall be perpetual*."

The formation of a "more perfect union" was accomplished by the organization of a government more complete in its various branches, legislative, executive, and judicial, and by the delegation to this Government of certain additional powers or functions which had previously been exercised by the Governments of the respective States—especially in providing the means of operating directly upon individuals for the enforcement of its legitimately delegated authority. There was no abandonment nor modification of the essential principle of a *compact* between sovereigns, which applied to the one case as fully as to the other. There was not the slightest intimation of so radical a revolution as the surrender of the sovereignty of the contracting parties would have been. The additional powers conferred upon the Federal Government by the Constitution were merely transfers of some of those possessed by the State governments—not subtractions from the reserved and inalienable sovereignty of the political communities which conferred them. It was merely the institution of a new agent who, however enlarged his powers might be, would still remain subordinate and responsible to the source from which they were derived—that of the sovereign people of each State. It was an amended Union, not a consolidation. . . .

The right of the people of the several States to resume the powers delegated by them to the common agency, was not left without positive and ample assertion, even at a period when it had never been denied. The ratification of the Constitution by Virginia has already been quoted, in which the people of that State, through their Convention, did expressly "declare and make known that the powers granted under the Constitution, being derived from the people of the United States, *may be resumed by them*, whensoever the same shall be perverted to their injury or oppression, and that every power not granted thereby remains with them and at their will."

New York and Rhode Island were no less explicit, both declaring that "the powers of government *may be reassumed by the people* whenever it shall become necessary to their happiness."

These expressions are not mere *obiter dicta*, thrown out incidentally, and entitled only to be regarded as an expression of opinion by their authors. Even if only such, they would carry great weight as the deliberately expressed judgment of enlightened contemporaries, but they are more: they are parts of the very acts or ordinances by which these States ratified the Constitution and acceded to the Union, and can not be detached from them. If they are invalid, the ratification itself was invalid, for they are inseparable. By inserting these declarations in their ordinances, Virginia, New York, and Rhode Island, formally, officially, and permanently, declared their interpretation of the Constitution as recognizing the right of secession by the resumption of their grants. By accepting the ratifications with this declaration incorporated, the other States as formally accepted the principle which it asserted. . . .

JOSEPH STORY

Joseph Story was a Massachusetts lawyer. Early in his career he affiliated himself with the Jeffersonian Republicans and in 1811 was appointed by Madison to the United States Supreme Court. He came under the intellectual influence of John Marshall and adopted a nationalist and conservative view of the Constitution. In 1833 he published his *Commentaries on the Constitution*. This three-volume study analyzed the various phases of American constitutional law as it then existed and presented a survey of the constitutional history of the colonies and the states before the adoption of the Constitution.

COMMENTARIES ON THE CONSTITUTION OF THE UNITED STATES [83]

Book III

CHAPTER VI

The Preamble

§ 457. Having disposed of these preliminary inquiries, we are now arrived at that part of our labors which involves a commentary upon the actual provisions of the Constitution of the United States. It is proposed to take up the successive clauses in the order in which they stand in the instrument itself, so that the exposition may naturally flow from the terms of the text.

§ 458. We begin then with the preamble of the Constitution. It is in the following words:—

"We, the people of the United States, in order to form a more perfect union, establish justice, insure domestic tranquillity, provide for the common defence, promote the general welfare, and secure the blessings of liberty to ourselves and our posterity, do ordain and establish this Constitution for the United States of America."

§ 459. The importance of examining the preamble, for the purpose of expounding the language of a statute, has been long felt, and universally conceded in all juridical discussions. It is an admitted maxim in the ordinary course of the administration of justice, that the preamble of a statute is a key to open the mind of the makers, as to the mischiefs which are to be remedied and the objects which are to be accomplished by the provisions of the statute. We find it laid down in some of our earliest authorities in the common law, and civilians are accustomed to a similar expression, *cessante legis praemio, cessat et ipsa lex.* Probably it has a foundation in the expression of every code of written law, from the universal principle of interpretation, that the will and intention of the legislature are to be regarded and followed. It is properly resorted to where doubts or ambiguities arise upon the words of the enacting part; for if they are clear and unambiguous, there seems little room for interpretation, except in cases leading to an obvious absurdity, or to a direct overthrow of the intention expressed in the preamble.

§ 460. There does not seem any reason why, in a fundamental law or constitution of government, an equal attention should not be given to the intention of the framers, as stated in the preamble. And accordingly we find that it has been constantly referred to by statesmen and jurists to aid them in the exposition of its provisions.

§ 461. The language of the preamble of the Constitution was probably in a good measure drawn from that of the third article of the confederation, which declared that "The said States hereby severally enter into a firm *league* of friendship with each other, for their common defence, the security of their liberties, and their mutual and general welfare." And we accordingly

---

[83] Joseph Story, *Commentaries on the Constitution of the United States: with a Preliminary Review of the Constitutional History of the Colonies and States before the Adoption of the Constitution.* (Boston, Little, Brown and Company, 1873), I, 338–341, 347–357, 366–371.

find that the first resolution proposed in the convention which framed the Constitution was, that the Articles of the Confederation ought to be so corrected and enlarged as to accomplish the objects proposed by their institution, namely, common defence, security of liberty, and general welfare.

§ 462. And here we must guard ourselves against an error which is too often allowed to creep into the discussions upon this subject. The preamble never can be resorted to to enlarge the powers confided to the general government or any of its departments. It cannot confer any power *per se;* it can never amount, by implication, to an enlargement of any power expressly given. It can never be the legitimate source of any implied power, when otherwise withdrawn from the Constitution. Its true office is to expound the nature and extent and application of the powers actually conferred by the Constitution, and not substantively to create them. For example, the preamble declares one object to be, "to provide for the common defence." No one can doubt that this does not enlarge the powers of Congress to pass any measures which they may deem useful for the common defence. But suppose the terms of a given power admit of two constructions, the one more restrictive, the other more liberal, and each of them is consistent with the words, but is, and ought to be, governed by the intent of the power; if one would promote and the other defeat the common defence, ought not the former, upon the soundest principles of interpretation, to be adopted? Are we at liberty, upon any principles of reason or common-sense, to adopt a restrictive meaning which will defeat an avowed object of the Constitution, when another equally natural and more appropriate to the object is before us? Would not this be to destroy an instrument by a measure of its words, which that instrument itself repudiates?

§ 463. We have already had occasion, in considering the nature of the Constitution, to dwell upon the terms in which the preamble is conceived, and the proper conclusion deducible from it. It is an act of the people, and not the States in their political capacities. It is an ordinance or establishment of government, and not a compact, though originating in consent; and it binds as a fundamental law promulgated by the sovereign authority, and not as a compact or treaty entered into and *in fieri,* between each and all the citizens of the United States as distinct parties. The language is: "We, the *people* of the United States," (not, We, the *States,*) "do *ordain* and *establish*" (not, do *contract* and enter into a *treaty* with each other) "this *Constitution* for the United States of America" (not this *treaty* between the several States). And it is, therefore, an unwarrantable assumption, not to call it a most extravagant stretch of interpretation, wholly at variance with the language, to substitute other words and other senses for the words and senses incorporated, in this solemn manner, into the substance of the instrument itself. We have the strongest assurances that this preamble was not adopted as a mere formulary, but as a solemn promulgation of a fundamental fact, vital to the character and operations of the government. The obvious object was to substitute a government of the people for a confederacy of States; a constitution for a compact. The difficulties arising from this source were not slight; for a notion commonly enough, however incorrectly, prevailed, that, as it was ratified by the States only, the States respectively at their pleasure might repeal it; and this, of itself, proved the necessity of

laying the foundations of a national government deeper than in the mere
sanction of delegated power. The convention determined that the fabric
of American empire ought to rest and should rest on the solid basis of the
consent of the people. The streams of national power ought to flow and
should flow immediately from the highest original fountain of all legitimate
authority. And, accordingly, the advocates of the Constitution so treated
it in their reasoning in favor of its adoption. "The Constitution," said the
Federalist, "is to be founded on the assent and ratification of the people of
America, given by deputies elected for that purpose; but this assent and
ratification is to be given by the people, not as individuals composing a whole
nation, but as composing the distinct and independent States to which they
belong." And the uniform doctrine of the highest judicial authority has
accordingly been, that it was the act of the people, and not of the States;
and that it bound the latter as subordinate to the people. "Let us turn,"
said Mr. Chief Justice Jay, "to the Constitution. The people therein
declare that their design in establishing it comprehended six objects: 1. to
form a more perfect union; 2. to establish justice; 3. to insure domestic
tranquillity; 4. to provide for the common defence; 5. to promote the general welfare; 6. to secure the blessings of liberty to themselves and their
posterity. It would," he added, "be pleasing and useful to consider and trace
the relations which each of these objects bears to the others, and to show
that, collectively they comprise everything requisite, with the blessing of
Divine Providence, to render a people prosperous and happy." In *Martin v.
Hunter's Lessee*, the Supreme Court say, (as we have seen,) "The Constitution of the United States was ordained and established, not by the States
in their sovereign capacities, but emphatically, as the preamble of the Constitution declares, by the people of the United States"; and language still
more expressive will be found used on other solemn occasions. . . .

§ 474. In the mean time, the following considerations may serve to cheer
our hopes and dispel our fears: first, 1. the extent of territory is not incompatible with a just spirit of patriotism; 2. nor with a general representation of
all the interests and population with it; 3. nor with a due regard to the peculiar
local advantages or disadvantages of any part; 4. nor with a rapid and convenient circulation of information useful to all, whether they are rulers or
people. On the other hand, it has some advantages of a very important nature.
1. It can afford greater protection against foreign enemies. 2. It can give a
wider range to enterprise and commerce. 3. It can secure more thoroughly
national independence to all the great interests of society, agriculture, commerce, manufactures, literature, learning, religion. 4. It can more readily
disarm and tranquillize domestic factions in a single State. 5. It can administer justice more completely and perfectly. 6. It can command larger revenues for public objects without oppression or heavy taxation. 7. It can
economize more in all its internal arrangements, whenever necessary. In
short, as has been said with equal truth and force, "One government can
collect and avail itself of the talents and experience of the ablest men, in
whatever part of the Union they may be found. It can move on uniform
principles of policy. It can harmonize, assimilate, and protect the several
parts and members, and extend the benefit of its foresight and precautions
to each. In the formation of treaties, it will regard the interests of the whole,

and the particular interests of the parts as connected with that of the whole. It can apply the revenues of the whole to the defence of any particular part, and that more easily and expeditiously than State governments or separate confederacies can possibly do, for want of concert and unity of system." Upon some of these topics we may enlarge hereafter.

§ 475. The union of these States, "the more perfect union," is, then, and must forever be, invaluable to all, in respect both to foreign and domestic concerns. It will prevent some of the causes of war, that scourge of the human race, by enabling the general government, not only to negotiate suitable treaties for the protection of the rights and interests of all, but by compelling a general obedience to them, and a general respect for the obligations of the law of nations. It is notorious that, even under the confederation, the obligations of treaty stipulations were openly violated or silently disregarded; and the peace of the whole confederacy was at the mercy of the majority of any single State. If the States were separated, they would, or might, form separate and independent treaties with different nations, according to their peculiar interests. These treaties would, or might, involve jealousies and rivalries at home as well as abroad, and introduce conflicts between nations struggling for a monopoly of the trade with each State. Retaliatory or evasive stipulations would be made, to counteract the injurious system of a neighboring or distant State, and thus the scene be again acted over with renewed violence which succeeded the peace of 1783, when the common interests were forgotten in the general struggle for superiority. It would manifestly be the interest of foreign nations to promote these animosities and jealousies, that, in the general weakness, the States might seek their protection by an undue sacrifice of their interests, or fall an easy prey to their arms.

§ 476. The dangers, too, to all the States in case of division, from foreign wars and invasion, must be imminent, independent of those from the neighborhood of the colonies and dependencies of other governments on this continent. Their very weakness would invite aggression. The ambition of the European governments to obtain a mastery of power in colonies and distant possessions would be perpetually involving them in embarrassing negotiations or conflicts, however peaceable might be their own conduct, and however inoffensive their own pursuits and objects. America, as of old, would become the theatre of warlike operations in which she had no interests; and, with a view to their own security, the States would be compelled to fall back into a general colonial submission, or sink into dependencies of such of the great European powers as might be most favorable to their interests, or most commanding over their resources.

§ 477. There are also peculiar interests of some of the States, which would, upon a separation, be wholly sacrificed, or become the source of immeasurable calamities. The New England States have a vital interest in the fisheries with their rivals, England and France; and how could New England resist either of these powers in a struggle for the common right, if attempted to be restrained or abolished? What would become of Maryland and Virginia, if the Chesapeake were under the dominion of different powers *de facto*, though not in form? The free navigation of the Mississippi and the lakes, and, it may be added, the exclusive navigation of them, seems indispensable to the security as well as the prosperity of the Western States. How, otherwise than by a general union, could this be maintained or guaranteed?

§ 478. And again, as to commerce, so important to the navigating States, and so productive to the agricultural States, it must be at once perceived that no adequate protection could be given to either, unless by the strong and uniform operations of a general government. Each State by its own regulations would seek to promote its own interests, to the ruin or injury of those of others. The relative situation of these States; the number of rivers by which they are intersected, and of bays that wash their shores; the facility of communication in every direction; the affinity of language and manners; the familiar habits of intercourse,—all these circumstances would conspire to render an illicit trade between them matter of little difficulty, and would insure frequent evasions of the commercial regulations of each other. All foreign nations would have a common interest in crippling us; and all the evils of colonial servitude and commercial monopoly would be inflicted upon us by the hands of our own kindred and neighbors. But this topic, though capable of being presented in detail from our past experience in such glowing colors as to startle the most incredulous into a conviction of the ultimate poverty, wretchedness, and distress which would overwhelm every State does not require to be more than hinted at. We have already seen, in our former examination of the defects of the confederation, that every State was ruined in its revenues, as well as in its commerce, by the want of a more efficient government.

§ 479. Nor should it be imagined that, however injurious to commerce, the evils would be less in respect to domestic manufactures and agriculture. In respect to manufactures, the truth is so obvious that it requires no argument to illustrate it. In relation to the agricultural States, however, an opinion has, at some times and in some sections of the country, been prevalent, that the agricultural interests would be equally safe without any general government. The following, among other considerations, may serve to show the fallacy of all such suggestions. A large and uniform market at home for native productions has a tendency to prevent those sudden rises and falls in prices which are so deeply injurious to the farmer and the planter. The exclusive possession of the home market against all foreign competition gives a permanent security to investments which slowly yield their returns, and encourages the laying out of capital in agricultural improvements. Suppose cotton, tobacco, and wheat were at all times admissible from foreign states without duty, would not the effect be permanently to check any cultivation beyond what at the moment seems sure of a safe sale? Would not foreign nations be perpetually tempted to send their surplus here, and thus, from time to time, depress or glut the home market?

§ 480. Again, the neighboring States would often engage in the same species of cultivation, and yet with very different natural or artificial means of making the products equally cheap. This inequality would immediately give rise to legislative measures to correct the evil, and to secure, if possible, superior advantages over the rival State. This would introduce endless crimination and retaliation, laws for defence and laws for offence. Smuggling would be everywhere openly encouraged or secretly connived at. The vital interests of a State would lie in many instances at the mercy of its neighbors, who might, at the same time, feel that their own interests were promoted by the ruin of their neighbors. And the distant States, knowing that their own wants and pursuits were wholly disregarded, would become willing auxiliaries in any plans to encourage cultivation and consumption elsewhere. Such is human nature! Such are the infirmities which history severely instructs us belong to neighbors and rivals; to those who navigate, and those who plant; to those who desire, and those who repine at the prosperity of surrounding States.

§ 481. Again, foreign nations, under such circumstances, must have a common interest, as carriers, to bring to the agricultural States their own manufactures at as dear a rate as possible, and to depress the market of the domestic products to the minimum price of competition. They must have a common interest to stimulate the neighboring States to a ruinous jealousy; or, by fostering the interests of one with whom they can deal upon more advantageous terms, or over whom they have acquired a decisive influence, to subject to a corresponding influence others which struggle for an independent existence. This is not merely theory. Examples, and successful examples, of this policy may be traced through the period between the peace of 1783 and the adoption of the Constitution.

§ 482. But not to dwell further on these important inducements "to form a more perfect union," let us pass to the next object, which is to "establish justice." This must forever be one of the great ends of every wise government; and even in arbitrary governments it must, to a great extent, be practised, at least in respect to private persons, as the only security against rebellion, private vengeance, and popular cruelty. But in a free government it lies at the very basis of all its institutions. Without justice being freely, fully, and impartially administered, neither our persons, nor our rights, nor our property, can be protected. And if these, or either of them, are regulated by no certain laws, and are subject to no certain principles, and are held by no certain tenure, and are redressed, when violated, by no certain remedies, society fails of all its value; and men may as well return to a state of savage and barbarous independence. No one can doubt, therefore, that the establishment of justice must be one main object of all our State governments. Why, then, may it be asked, should it form so prominent a motive in the establishment of the national government.

§ 483. This is now proposed to be shown in a concise manner. In the administration of justice, foreign nations and foreign individuals, as well as citizens, have a deep stake; but the former have not always as complete means of redress as the latter; for it may be presumed, that the State laws will always provide adequate tribunals to redress the grievances and sustain the rights of their own citizens. But this would be a very imperfect view of the subject. Citizens of contiguous States have a very deep interest in the administration of justice in each State; and even those which are most distant, but belonging to the same confederacy, cannot but be affected by every inequality in the provisions or the actual operations of the laws of each other. While every State remains at full liberty to legislate upon the subject of rights, privileges, contracts, and remedies, as it may please, it is scarcely to be expected that they will with all concur in the same general system of policy. The natural tendency of every government is to favor its own citizens;

and unjust preferences, not only in the administration of justice, but in the very structure of the laws, may reasonably be expected to arise. Popular prejudices, or passions, supposed or real injuries, the predominance of home pursuits and feelings over the comprehensive view of a liberal jurisprudence, will readily achieve the most mischievous projects for this purpose. And these, again, by a natural reaction, will introduce correspondent regulations and retaliatory measures in other States.

§ 484. Now, exactly what this course of reasoning has led us to presume as probable, has been demonstrated by experience to be true in respect to our own confederacy during the short period of its existence, and under circumstances well calculated to induce each State to sacrifice many of its own objects for the general good. Nay, even when we were colonies, dependent upon the authority of the mother country, these inequalities were observable in the local legislation of several of the States, and produced heartburnings and discontents, which were not easily appeased.

§ 485. First, in respect to foreign nations. After the confederacy was formed, and we had assumed the general rights of war as a sovereign, belligerent nation, authority to make captures and to bring in ships and cargoes for adjudication naturally flowed from the proper exercise of these rights by the law of nations. The States respectively retained the power of appointing prize tribunals, to take cognizance of these matters in the first instance; and thus thirteen distinct jurisdictions were established, which acted entirely independent of each other. It is true that the Articles of Confederation had delegated to the general government the authority of establishing courts for receiving and determining, finally, appeals in all cases of captures. Congress according instituted proper appellate tribunals, to which the State courts were subordinate, and, upon constitutional principles, were bound to yield obedience. But it is notorious, that the decisions of the appellate tribunals were disregarded, and treated as mere nullities, for no power to enforce them was lodged in Congress. They operated, therefore, merely by moral influence and requisition, and as such, soon sank into insignificance. Neutral individuals, as well as neutral nations, were left wholly without any adequate redress for the most inexcusable injustice, and the confederacy subjected to imminent hazards. And until the Constitution of the United States was established, no remedy was ever effectually administered. Treaties, too, were formed by Congress with various nations; and above all, the treaty of peace of 1783, which gave complete stability to our independence against Great Britain. These treaties were, by the theory of the confederation, absolutely obligatory upon all the States. Yet their provisions were notoriously violated both by State legislation and State judicial tribunals. The non-fulfilment of the stipulations of the British treaty on our part more than once threatened to involve the whole country again in war. And the provision in that treaty for the payment of British debts was practically disregarded in many, if not in all, the State courts. These debts never were enforced until the Constitution gave them a direct and adequate sanction, independently of State legislation and State courts.

§ 486. Besides the debts due to foreigners, and the obligations to pay the same, the public debt of the United States was left utterly unprovided for; and the officers and soldiers of the Revolution, who had achieved our independence, were, as we have had occasion to notice, suffered to languish in want, and their just demands evaded, or passed by with indifference. No efficient system to pay the public creditors was ever carried into operation, until the Constitution was adopted; and, notwithstanding the increase of the public debt, occasioned by intermediate wars, it is now on the very eve of a total extinguishment.

§ 487. These evils, whatever might be their magnitude, did not create so universal a distress, or so much private discontent, as others of a more domestic nature, which were subversive of the first principles of justice. Independent of the unjustifiable preferences, which were fostered, in favor of citizens of the State over those belonging to other States, which were not few nor slight, there were certain calamities inflicted by the common course of legislation in most of the States, which went to the prostration of all public faith and all private credit. Laws were constantly made by the State legislatures violating, with more or less degrees of aggravation, the sacredness of private contracts. Laws compelling the receipt of a depreciated and depreciating paper currency in payment of debts were generally, if not universally, prevalent. Laws authorizing the payment of debts by instalments, at periods differing entirely from the original terms of the contract; laws suspending, for a limited or uncertain period, the remedies to recover debts in the ordinary course of legal proceedings; laws authorizing the delivery of any sort of property, however unproductive or undesirable, in payment of debts upon an arbitrary or friendly appraisement; laws shutting up the courts for certain periods and under certain circumstances,—were not infrequent upon the statute-books of many of the States now composing the Union. In the rear of all these came the systems of general insolvent laws, some of which were of a permanent nature, and others again were adopted upon the spur of the occasion, like a sort of gaol delivery under the lords' acts in England, which had so few guards against frauds of every kind by the debtor, that in practice they amounted to an absolute discharge from any debt, without anything more than a nominal dividend; and sometimes even this vain mockery was dispensed with. In short, by the operations of proper currency, tender laws, instalment laws, suspension laws, appraisement laws, and insolvent laws, contrived with all the dexterous ingenuity of men oppressed by debt, and popular by the very extent of private embarrassments, the States were almost universally plunged into a ruinous poverty, distrust, debility, and indifference to justice. The local tribunals were bound to obey the legislative will; and in the few instances in which it was resisted, the independence of the judges was sacrificed to the temper of the times. It is well known, that Shay's rebellion in Massachusetts took its origin from this source. The object was to prostrate the regular administration of justice by a system of terror, which would prevent the recovery of debts and taxes.

§ 488. The Federalist speaks on this subject with unusual emphasis. "The loss which America has sustained from the pestilent effects of paper-money on the necessary confidence between man and man, on the necessary confidence in the public councils, on the industry and morals of the people, and on the character of republican government, constitutes an enormous debt against the States, chargeable with this unadvisable measure, which must long remain unsatisfied; or rather an accumulation of guilt, which can be expiated no otherwise than by a voluntary sacrifice on the altar of justice of the power which has been the instrument of it." "Laws impairing the obligation of contracts are contrary to the first principles of the social compact, and to every principle of sound legislation." And the Federalist dwells on the suggestion, that as such laws amount to an aggression on the rights of the citizens of those States, whose citizens are injured by them, they must necessarily form a probable source of hostilities among the States. Connecticut retaliated in an exemplary manner upon enormities of this sort, which she thought had been perpetrated by a neighboring State upon the just rights of her citizens. Indeed, war constitutes almost the only remedy to chastise atrocious breaches of moral obligations and social justice in respect to debts and other contracts."

§ 489. So, that we see completely demonstrated by our history the importance of a more effectual establishment of justice under the auspices of a national government. . . .

§ 503. Passing from these general considerations to those of a direct practical nature, let us see how far certain measures, confessedly promotive of the general welfare, have been, or would be, affected by a disunion of the States. Take, for example, the post-office establishment, the benefits of which can scarcely be too strongly stated in respect to the public interests or to private convenience. With what a wonderful facility it now communicates intelligence, and transmits orders and directions, and money and negotiable paper, to every extremity of the Union. The government is enabled to give the most prompt notice of approaching dangers, of its commands, its wishes, its interests, its duties, its laws, and its policy, to the most distant functionaries, with incredible speed. Compare this with the old course of private posts and special expresses. Look to the extensive advantages to trade, navigation, and commerce, to agriculture and manufactures, in the ready distribution of news, of knowledge of markets, and of transfer of funds, independent of the inestimable blessings of communication between distant friends, to relieve the heart from its oppressive anxieties. In our colonial state it took almost as long a period of time to convey a letter (independent of the insecurity and uncertainty of its transmission) from Philadelphia to Boston, as it now takes to pass from the seat of government to the farthest limits of any of the States. Even under the confederation, from the want of efficient funds and an efficient government, the post moved on with a tardy indifference and delay, which made it almost useless. We now communicate with England and the continent of Europe, within periods not essentially different from those which were then consumed in passing from the centre to the eastern and southern limits of the Union. Suppose the national government were now dissolved, how difficult would it be to get the twenty-four States to agree upon any uniform system of operations, or proper apportionment of the postage to be paid on the transmission of the mail. Each State must act continually by a separate legislation; and the least change by any one would disturb the harmony of the whole system. It is not at all improbable that before a single letter could reach New Orleans from Eastport, it would have to pay a distinct postage in sixteen independent States, subject to no common control or appointment of officers. The very statement of such a case amounts to a positive prohibition upon any extensive internal intercourse by the mail, as the burdens and the insecurity of the establishment would render it intolerable. With what admirable ease and expedition, and noiseless uniformity of movement, is the whole now accomplished through the instrumentality of the national government!

§ 504. Let us take another example, drawn from the perils of navigation, and ask ourselves how it would be possible, without an efficient national government, to provide adequately for the erection and support of lighthouses, monuments, buoys, and other guards against shipwreck. Many of these are maintained at an expense wholly disproportionate to their advantage to the State in which they are situated. Many of them never would be maintained, except for the provident forecast of a national government intent on the good of the whole, and possessing powers adequate to secure it. The same considerations apply to all measures of internal improvement, either to navigation by removing obstructions in rivers and inlets, or by erecting fortifications for purposes of defence and to guard our harbors against the inroads of enemies.

§ 505. Independent of these means of promoting the general welfare, we shall at once see, in our negotiations with foreign powers, the vast superiority of a nation combining numbers and resources over States of small extent and divided by different interests. If we are to negotiate for commercial or other advantages, the national government has more authority to speak, as well as more power to influence, than can belong to a single State. It has more valuable privileges to give in exchange, and more means of making those privileges felt by prohibitions or relaxations of its commercial legislation. Is money wanted; how much more easy and cheap to borrow upon the faith of a nation competent to pay, than of a single State of fluctuating policy. Is confidence asked for the faithful fulfilment of treaty stipulations; how much more strong the guaranty of the Union with suitable authorities, than any pledge of an individual State. Is a currency wanted at once fixed on a solid basis, and sustained by adequate sanctions to enlarge public or private credit; how much more decisive is the legislation of the Union, than of a single State with a view to extent or uniformity of operations.

§ 506. Thus we see that the national government, suitably organized, has more efficient means and more extensive jurisdiction to promote the general welfare, than can belong to any single State of the confederacy. And there is much truth in the suggestion that it will generally be directed by a more enlightened policy, a more liberal justice, and more comprehensive wisdom, in the application of its means and its powers to their appropriate end. Generally speaking, it will be better administered, because it will command higher talents, more extensive experience, more practical knowledge, and more various information of the wants of the whole community, than can belong to smaller societies. The wider the sphere of action, the less reason there is to presume that narrow views or local prejudices will prevail in the public councils. The very diversities of opinion in the different representatives of distant regions will have a tendency, not only to introduce mutual concession and conciliation, but to elevate the policy and instruct the judgment of those who are to direct the public measures.

§ 507. The last clause in the preamble is to "secure the blessings of liberty to ourselves and our posterity." And surely no object could be more worthy of the wisdom and ambition of the best men in any age. If there be anything which may justly challenge the admiration of all mankind, it is that sublime patriotism which, looking beyond its own times and its own fleeting pursuits, aims to secure the permanent happiness of posterity by laying the broad foundations of government upon immovable principles of justice. Our affections, indeed, may naturally be presumed to outlive the brief limits of our own lives, and to repose with deep sensibility upon our own immediate descendants. But there is a noble disinterestedness in that forecast which disregards present objections for the sake of all mankind, and erects structures to protect, support, and bless the most distant generations. He who founds a hospital, a college, or even a more private and limited charity, is justly esteemed a benefactor of the human race. How much more do they deserve our reverence and praise, whose lives are devoted to the formation of institutions which, when they and their children are mingled in the common dust, may continue to cherish the principles and the practice of liberty in perpetual freshness and vigor!

§ 508. The grand design of the State governments is, doubtless, to accomplish this important purpose; and there can be no doubt that they are, when well administered, well adapted to the end. But the question is not so much whether they conduce to the preservation of the blessings of liberty, as whether they of themselves furnish a complete and satisfactory security. If the remarks which have been already offered are founded in sound reasoning and human experience, they establish the position that the State governments, *per se*, are incompetent and inadequate to furnish such guards and guaranties as a free people have a right to require for the maintenance of their vital interests, and especially of their liberty. The inquiry then naturally presents itself whether the establishment of a national government will afford more effectual and adequate securities.

§ 509. The fact has been already adverted to that when the Constitution was before the people for adoption, it was generally represented by its opponents that its obvious tendency to a consolidation of the powers of government would subvert the State sovereignties, and thus prove dangerous to the liberties of the people. This indeed was a topic dwelt on with peculiar emphasis; and it produced so general an alarm and terror that it came very nigh accomplishing the rejection of the Constitution. And yet the reasoning by which it was supported was so vague and unsatisfactory, and the reasoning on the other side was so cogent and just, that it seems difficult to conceive how, at that time or at any later time (for it has often been resorted to for the same purpose), the suggestion could have had any substantial influence upon the public opinion.

§ 510. Let us glance at a few considerations (some of which have been already hinted at) which are calculated to suppress all alarm upon this subject. In the first place, the government of the United States is one of limited powers, leaving all residuary general powers in the State governments, or in the people thereof. The jurisdiction of the general government is confined to a few enumerated objects which concern the common welfare of all the States. The State governments have a full superintendence and control over the immense mass of local interests of their respective States, which connect themselves with the feelings, the affections, the municipal institutions, and the internal arrangements of the whole population. They possess, too, the immediate administration of justice in all cases, civil and criminal, which concern the property, personal rights, and peaceful pursuits of their own citizens. They must of course possess a large share of influence; and, being independent of each other, will have many opportunities to interpose checks, as well as to combine a common resistance to any undue exercise of power by the general government, independent of direct force.

§ 511. In the next place, the State governments are, by the very theory of the Constitution, essential constituent parts of the general government. They can exist without the latter, but the latter cannot exist without them. Without the intervention of the State legislatures, the President of the United States cannot be elected at all; and the Senate is exclusively and absolutely under the choice of the State legislatures. The Representatives are chosen by the people of the States. So that the executive and legislative branches of the national government depend upon, and emanate from the States. Everywhere the State sovereignties are represented; and the national sovereignty, as such, has no representation. How is it possible under such circumstances, that the national government can be dangerous to the liberties of the people, unless the States, and the people of the States, conspire together for their overthrow? If there should be such a conspiracy, is not this more justly to be deemed an act of the States through their own agents, and by their own choice, rather than a corrupt usurpation by the general government?

§ 512. Besides, the perpetual organization of the State governments, in all their departments, executive, legislative, and judicial; their natural tendency to co-operate in cases of threatened danger to their common liberties; the perpetually recurring right of the elective franchise, at short intervals,— must present the most formidable barriers against any deliberate usurpation, which does not arise from the hearty co-operation of the people of the States. And when such a general co-operation for usurpation shall exist, it is obvious that neither the general nor the State governments can interpose any permanent protection. Each must submit to that public will which created and may destroy them.

§ 513. Another not unimportant consideration is, that the powers of the general government will be, and indeed must be, principally employed upon external objects, such as war, peace, negotiations with foreign powers, and foreign commerce. In its internal operations it can touch but few objects, except to introduce regulations beneficial to the commerce, intercourse, and other relations between the States, and to lay taxes for the common good. The powers of the States, on the other hand, extend to all objects which, in the ordinary course of affairs, concern the lives and liberties and property of the people, and the internal order, improvement, and prosperity of the State. The operations of the general government will be most extensive and important in times of war and danger; those of the State governments, in times of peace and security. Independent of all other considerations, the fact that the States possess a concurrent power of taxation, and an exclusive power to regulate the descent, devise, and distribution of estates, (a power the most formidable to despotism, and the most indispensable in its right exercise to republicanism,) will forever give them an influence which will be as commanding as, with reference to the safety of the Union, they could deliberately desire. . . .

DANIEL WEBSTER

Daniel Webster was one of the outstanding lawyers of his day. His legal activities associated him with the propertied groups, and he was a retainer for such important business organizations as the second United States Bank. He entered Massachusetts politics and represented that state in the House of Representatives and later in the Senate. In the early years of his career he was a free-trader. The predominant group in Massachusetts at that time was the merchant, shipping class. After the War of 1812, however, the economic and political balance shifted to the new industrialists; and Webster became an exponent of protective tariffs. His nationalism is entangled with his desire for tariff protection for New England industries. He was opposed to an extension of slavery, but he supported the Compromise of 1850 in order to preserve the Union. In his debates with Hayne and Calhoun in the Senate, Webster presented a legalistic interpretation of the Constitution.

In 1830 Senator Foot introduced a resolution concerning the restriction of public land sales. The debate soon turned into one between the North and the South over the question of State nullification of congressional acts. Webster's second speech on the resolution was a reply to Senator Hayne of South Carolina.

SECOND SPEECH ON FOOT'S RESOLUTION

Delivered in the U. S. Senate on the 26th of January, 1830.[84]

There yet remains to be performed, Mr. President, by far the most grave and important duty, which I feel to be devolved on me by this occasion. It is to state, and to defend, what I conceive to be the true principles of the Constitution under which we are here assembled. I might well have desired that so weighty a task should have fallen into other and abler hands. I could have wished that it should have been executed by those whose character and experience give weight and influence to their opinions, such as cannot possibly belong to mine. But, Sir, I have met the occasion, not sought it; and I shall proceed to state my own sentiments, without challenging for them any particular regard, with studied plainness, and as much precision as possible.

I understand the honorable gentleman from South Carolina to maintain, that it is a right of the State legislatures to interfere, whenever, in their judgment, this government transcends its constitutional limits, and to arrest the operation of its laws.

I understand him to maintain this right, as a right existing *under* the Constitution, not as a right to overthrow it on the ground of extreme necessity, such as would justify violent revolution.

I understand him to maintain an authority, on the part of the States, thus to interfere, for the purpose of correcting the exercise of power by the general government, of checking it, and of compelling it to conform to their opinion of the extent of its powers.

I understand him to maintain, that the ultimate power of judging of the constitutional extent of its own authority is not lodged exclusively in the general government, or any branch of it; but that, on the contrary, the States may lawfully decide for themselves, and each State for itself, whether, in a given case, the act of the general government transcends its power.

I understand him to insist, that, if the exigency of the case, in the opinion

[84] Daniel Webster, *Works*. (Boston, Little, Brown and Company, 1872), III, 317–322, 323–324, 332–337.

of any State government, require it, such State government may, by its own sovereign authority, annul an act of the general government which it deems plainly and palpably unconstitutional.

This is the sum of what I understand from him to be the South Carolina doctrine, and the doctrine which he maintains. I propose to consider it, and compare it with the Constitution. Allow me to say, as a preliminary remark, that I call this the South Carolina doctrine only because the gentleman himself has so denominated it. I do not feel at liberty to say that South Carolina, as a State, has ever advanced these sentiments. I hope she has not, and never may. That a great majority of her people are opposed to the tariff laws, is doubtless true. That a majority, somewhat less than that just mentioned, conscientiously believe these laws unconstitutional, may probably also be true. But that any majority holds to the right of direct State interference at State discretion, the right of nullifying acts of Congress by acts of State legislation, is more than I know, and what I shall be slow to believe.

That there are individuals besides the honorable gentleman who do maintain these opinions, is quite certain. I recollect the recent expression of a sentiment, which circumstances attending its utterance and publication justify us in supposing was not unpremeditated. "The sovereignty of the State, —never to be controlled, construed, or decided on, but by her own feelings of honorable justice."

Mr. Hayne here rose and said, that, for the purpose of being clearly understood, he would state that his proposition was in the words of the Virginia resolution, as follows:—

"That this assembly doth explicitly and peremptorily declare, that it views the powers of the federal government, as resulting from the compact to which the States are parties, as limited by the plain sense and intention of the instrument constituting that compact, as no farther valid than they are authorized by the grants enumerated in that compact; and that, in case of a deliberate, palpable, and dangerous exercise of other powers, not granted by the said compact, the States who are parties thereto have the right, and are in duty bound, to interpose, for arresting the progress of the evil, and for maintaining within their respective limits the authorities, rights, and liberties appertaining to them."

Mr. Webster resumed:—

I am quite aware, Mr. President, of the existence of the resolution which the gentleman read, and has now repeated, and that he relies on it as his authority. I know the source, too, from which it is understood to have proceeded. I need not say that I have much respect for the constitutional opinions of Mr. Madison; they would weigh greatly with me always. But before the authority of his opinion be vouched for the gentleman's proposition, it will be proper to consider what is the fair interpretation of that resolution, to which Mr. Madison is understood to have given his sanction. As the gentleman construes it, it is an authority for him. Possibly, he may not have adopted the right construction. That resolution declares, that, *in the case of the dangerous exercise of powers not granted by the general government, the States may interpose to arrest the progress of the evil.* But how interpose, and what does this declaration purport? Does it mean no more than that there may be extreme cases, in which the people, in any mode of assembling, may resist usurpation, and relieve themselves from a tyrannical government? No one will deny this. Such resistance is not only acknowledged to be just in America, but in England also Blackstone admits as much, in the theory and practice, too, of the English constitution. We, Sir, who oppose the Carolina doctrine, do not deny that the people may, if they choose, throw off any government when it becomes oppressive and intolerable, and erect a better in its stead. We all know that civil institutions are established for the public benefit, and that when they cease to answer the ends of their existence they may be changed. But I do not understand the doctrine now contended for to be that, which, for the sake of distinction, we may call the right of revolution. I understand the gentleman to maintain, that, without revolution, without civil commotion, without rebellion, a remedy for supposed abuse and transgression of the powers of the general government lies in a direct appeal to the interference of the State governments.

Mr. Hayne here rose and said: He did not contend for the mere right of revolution, but for the right of constitutional resistance. What he maintained was, that in case of a plain, palpable violation of the Constitution by the general government, a State may interpose; and that this interposition is constitutional.

Mr. Webster resumed:—

So, Sir, I understood the gentleman, and am happy to find that I did not misunderstand him. What he contends for is, that it is constitutional to interrupt the administration of the Constitution itself, in the hands of those who are chosen and sworn to administer it, by the direct interference, in form of law, of the States, in virtue of their sovereign capacity. The inherent right in the people to reform their government I do not deny; and they have another right, and that is, to resist unconstitutional laws, without overturning the government. It is no doctrine of mine that unconstitutional laws bind the people. The great question is, Whose prerogative is it to decide on the constitutionality or unconstitutionality of the laws? On that, the main debate hinges. The proposition, that, in case of a supposed violation of the Constitution by Congress, the States have a constitutional right to interfere and annul the law of Congress, is the proposition of the gentleman. I do not admit it. If the gentleman had intended no more than to assert the right of revolution for justifiable cause, he would have said only what all agree to. But I cannot conceive that there can be a middle course, between submission to the laws, when regularly pronounced constitutional, on the one hand, and open resistance, which is revolution or rebellion, on the other. I say, the right of a State to annul a law of Congress cannot be maintained, but on the ground of the inalienable right of man to resist oppression; that is to say, upon the ground of revolution. I admit that there is an ultimate violent remedy, above the Constitution and in defiance of the Constitution, which may be resorted to when a revolution is to be justified. But I do not admit, that, under the Constitution and in conformity with it, there is any mode in which a State government, as a member of the Union, can interfere and stop the progress of the general government, by force of her own laws, under any circumstances whatever.

This leads us to inquire into the origin of this government and the source of its power. Whose agent is it? Is it the creature of the State legislatures, or the creature of the people? If the government of the United States be the agent of the State governments, then they may control it, provided they can agree in the manner of controlling it; if it be the agent of the people, then the people alone can control it, restrain it, modify, or reform it. It is observable enough, that the doctrine for which the honorable gentleman contends leads him to the necessity of maintaining, not only that this general government is the creature of the States, but that it is the creature of each of the States severally, so that each may assert the power for itself of determining whether it acts within the limits of its authority. It is the servant of four-and-twenty masters, of different wills and different purposes, and yet bound to obey all. This absurdity (for it seems no less) arises from a misconception as to the origin of this government and its true character. It is, Sir, the people's Constitution, the people's government, made for the people, made by the people, and answerable to the people. The people of the United States have declared that this Constitution shall be the supreme law. We must either admit the proposition, or dispute their authority. The States are, unquestionably sovereign, so far as their sovereignty is not affected by this supreme law. But the State legislatures, as political bodies, however sovereign, are yet not sovereign over the people. So far the people have given power to the general government, so far the grant is unquestionably good, and the government holds of the people, and not of the State governments. We are all agents of the same supreme power, the people. The general government and the State governments derive their authority from the same source. Neither can, in relation to the other, be called primary, though one is definite and restricted, and the other general and residuary. The national government possesses those powers which it can be shown the people have conferred on it, and no more. All the rest belongs to the State governments, or to the people themselves. So far as the people have restrained State sovereignty, by the expression of their will, in the Constitution of the United States, so far, it must be admitted, State sovereignty is effectually controlled. I do not contend that it is, or ought to be, controlled farther. The sentiment to which I have referred propounds that State sovereignty is only to be controlled by its own "feeling of justice"; that is to say, it is not to be controlled at all, for one who is to follow his own feelings is under no legal control. Now, however men may think this ought to be, the fact is, that the people of the United States have chosen to impose control on State sovereignties. There are those, doubtless, who wish they had been left without restraint; but the Constitution has ordered the matter differently. To make war, for instance, is an exercise of sovereignty; but the Constitution declares that no State shall make war. To coin money is another exercise of sovereign power; but no State is at liberty to coin money. Again, the Constitution says that no sovereign State shall be so sovereign as to make a treaty. These prohibitions, it must be confessed, are a control on the State sovereignty of South Carolina, as well as of the other States, which does not arise "from her own feelings of honorable justice." The opinion referred to, therefore, is in defiance of the plainest provisions of the Constitution. . . .

In Carolina, the tariff is a palpable, deliberate usurpation; Carolina, therefore, may nullify it, and refuse to pay the duties. In Pennsylvania, it is both clearly constitutional and highly expedient; and there the duties are to be paid. And yet we live under a government of uniform laws, and under a Constitution too, which contains an express provision, as it happens, that all duties shall be equal in all the States. Does not this approach absurdity?

If there be no power to settle such questions, independent of either of the States, is not the whole Union a rope of sand? Are we not thrown back again, precisely, upon the old Confederation?

It is too plain to be argued. Four-and-twenty interpreters of constitutional law, each with a power to decide for itself, and none with authority to bind any body else, and this constitutional law the only bond of their union! What is such a state of things but a mere connection during pleasure, or, to use the phraseology of the times, *during feeling?* And that feeling, too, not the feeling of the people, who established the Constitution, but the feeling of the State governments.

In another of the South Carolina addresses, having premised that the crisis requires "all the concentrated energy of passion," an attitude of open resistance to the laws of the Union is advised. Open resistance to the laws, then, is the constitutional remedy, the conservative power of the State, which the South Carolina doctrines teach for the redress of political evils, real or imaginary. And its authors further say, that, appealing with confidence to the Constitution itself, to justify their opinions, they cannot consent to try their accuracy by the courts of justice. In one sense, indeed, Sir, this is assuming an attitude of open resistance in favor of liberty. But what sort of liberty? The liberty of establishing their own opinions, in defiance of the opinions of all others; the liberty of judging and of deciding exclusively themselves, in a matter in which others have as much right to judge and decide as they; the liberty of placing their own opinions above the judgment of all others, above the laws, and above the Constitution. This is their liberty, and this is the fair result of the proposition contended for by the honorable gentleman. Or, it may be properly said, it is identical with it, rather than a result from it. . . .

I must now beg to ask, Sir, Whence is this supposed right of the States derived? Where do they find the power to interfere with the laws of the Union? Sir, the opinion which the honorable gentleman maintains is a notion founded in a total misapprehension, in my judgment, of the origin of this government, and of the foundation on which it stands. I hold it to be a popular government, erected by the people; those who administer it, responsible to the people; and itself capable of being amended and modified, just as the people may choose it should be. It is as popular, just as truly emanating from the people, as the State governments. It is created for one purpose; the State governments for another. It has its own powers; they have theirs. There is no more authority with them to arrest the operation of a law of Congress, than with Congress to arrest the operation of their laws. We are here to administer a Constitution emanating immediately from the people, and trusted by them to our administration. It is not the creature of the State governments. It is of no moment to the argument, that certain acts of the State legislatures are necessary to fill our seats in this body. That is not one of their original State powers, a part of the sovereignty of the State. It is a duty which the people, by the Constitution itself, have imposed on the State legislatures; and which they might have left to be performed elsewhere, if they had seen fit. So they have left the choice of President with electors; but all this does not affect the proposition that this whole government, President, Senate, and House of Representatives, is a popular government. It leaves it still all its popular character. The governor of a State (in some of the States) is chosen, not directly by the people, but by those who are chosen by the people, for the purpose of performing, among other duties, that of electing a governor. Is the government of the State, on that account, not a popular government? This government, Sir, is the independent offspring of the popular will. It is not the creature of State legislatures; nay, more, if the whole truth must be told, the people brought it into existence, established it, and have hitherto supported it, for the very purpose, amongst other, of imposing certain salutary restraints on State sovereignties. The States cannot now make war; they cannot contract alliances; they cannot make, each for itself, separate regulations of commerce; they cannot lay imposts; they cannot coin money. If this Constitution, Sir, be the creature of State legislatures, it must be admitted that it has obtained a strange control over the volitions of its creators.

The people, then, Sir, erected this government. They gave it a Constitution, and in that Constitution they have enumerated the powers which they bestow on it. They have made it a limited government. They have defined its authority. They have restrained it to the exercise of such powers as are granted; and all others, they declare, are reserved to the States or the people. But, Sir, they have not stopped here. If they had, they would have accomplished but half their work. No definition can be so clear, as to avoid possibility of doubt; no limitation so precise, as to exclude all uncertainty. Who, then, shall construe this grant of the people? Who shall interpret their will, where it may be supposed they have left it doubtful? With whom do they repose this ultimate right of deciding on the powers of the government? Sir, they have settled all this in the fullest manner. They have left it with the government itself, in its appropriate branches. Sir, the very chief end, the main design, for which the whole Constitution was framed and adopted, was to establish a government that should not be obliged to act through State agency, or depend on State opinion and State discretion. The people had had quite enough of that kind of government under the Confederation. Under that system, the legal action, the application of law to individuals, belonged exclusively to the States. Congress could only recommend; their acts were not of binding force, till the States had adopted and sanctioned them. Are we in that condition still? Are we yet at the mercy of State discretion and State construction? Sir, if we are, then vain will be our attempt to maintain the Constitution under which we sit.

But, Sir, the people have wisely provided, in the Constitution itself, a proper suitable mode and tribunal for settling questions of constitutional law. There are in the Constitution grants of powers to Congress, and restrictions on these powers. There are, also, prohibitions on the States. Some authority must, therefore, necessarily exist, having the ultimate jurisdiction to fix and ascertain the interpretation of these grants, restrictions, and prohibitions. The Constitution has itself pointed out, ordained, and established that authority. How has it accomplished this great and essential end? By declaring, Sir, that "*the Constitution, and the laws of the United States made in pursuance thereof, shall be the supreme law of the land, any thing in the constitution or laws of any State to the contrary notwithstanding.*"

This, Sir, was the first great step. By this the supremacy of the Constitution and laws of the United States is declared. The people so will it. No State law is to be valid which comes in conflict with the Constitution, or any law of the United States passed in pursuance of it. But who shall decide this question of interference? To whom lies the last appeal? This, Sir, the Constitution itself decides also, by declaring, "*that the judicial power shall extend to all cases arising under the Constitution and laws of the United States.*" These two provisions cover the whole ground. They are, in truth, the keystone of the arch! With these it is a government; without them it is a confederation. In pursuance of these clear and express provisions, Congress established, at its very first session, in the judicial act, a mode for carrying them into full effect, and for bringing all questions of constitutional power to the final decision of the Supreme Court. It then, Sir, became a government. It then had the means of self-protection; and but for this, it would, in all probability, have been now among things which are past. Having constituted the government, and declared its powers, the people have further said, that, since somebody must decide on the extent of these powers, the government shall itself decide; subject, always, like other popular governments, to its responsibility to the people. And now, Sir, I repeat, how is it that a State legislature acquires any power to interfere? Who, or what, gives them the right to say to the people, "We, who are your agents and servants for one purpose, will undertake to decide, that your agents and servants, appointed by you for another purpose, have transcended the authority you gave them!" The reply would be, I think, not impertinent,—"Who made you a judge over another's servants? To their own masters they stand or fall."

Sir, I deny this power of State legislatures altogether. It cannot stand the test of examination. Gentlemen may say, that, in an extreme case, a State government might protect the people from intolerable oppression. Sir, in such a case, the people might protect themselves, without the aid of the State governments. Such a case warrants revolution. It must make, when it comes, a law for itself. A nullifying act of a State legislature cannot alter the case, nor make resistance any more lawful. In maintaining these sentiments, Sir, I am but asserting the rights of the people. I state what they have declared, and insist on their right to declare it. They have chosen to repose this power in the general government, and I think it my duty to support it, like other constitutional powers.

For myself, Sir, I do not admit the competency of South Carolina, or any other State, to prescribe my constitutional duty; or to settle, between me and the people, the validity of laws of Congress, for which I have voted. I decline her umpirage. I have not sworn to support the Constitution according to her construction of its clauses. I have not stipulated, by my oath of office or otherwise, to come under any responsibility, except to the people, and those whom they have appointed to pass upon the question, whether laws, supported by my votes, conform to the Constitution of the country. And, Sir, if we look to the general nature of the case, could any thing have been more preposterous, than to make a government for the whole Union, and yet leave its powers subject, not to one interpretation, but to thirteen or twenty-four interpretations? Instead of one tribunal, established by all, responsible to all, with power to decide for all, shall constitutional questions be left to four-and-twenty popular bodies, each at liberty to decide for itself, and none bound to respect the decisions of others; and each at liberty, too, to give a new construction on every new election of its own members? Would any thing, with such a principle in it, or rather with such a destitution of all principle, be fit to be called a government? No, Sir. It should not be denominated a Constitution. It should be called, rather, a collection of topics for everlasting controversy; heads of debate for a disputatious people. It would not be a government. It would not be adequate to any practical good, or fit for any country to live under.

To avoid all possibility of being misunderstood, allow me to repeat again, in the fullest manner, that I claim no powers for the government by forced or unfair construction. I admit that it is a government of strictly limited powers; and that whatsoever is not granted, is withheld. But notwithstanding all this, and however the grant of powers may be expressed, its limit and extent may yet, in some cases admit of doubt; and the general government would be good for nothing, it would be incapable of long existing, if some mode had not been provided in which those doubts, as they should arise, might be peaceably, but authoritatively, solved.

And now, Mr. President, let me run the honorable gentleman's doctrine a little into its practical application. Let us look at his probable *modus operandi*. If a thing can be done, an ingenious man can tell *how* it is to be done, and I wish to be informed *how* this State interference is to be put in practice, without violence, bloodshed, and rebellion. We will take the existing case of the tariff law. South Carolina is said to have made up her opinion upon it. If we do not repeal it (as we probably shall not), she will then apply to the case the remedy of her doctrine. She will, we must suppose, pass a law of her legislature, declaring the several acts of Congress, usually called the tariff laws, null and void, so far as they respect South Carolina, or the citizens thereof. So far, all is a paper transaction, and easy enough. But the collector at Charleston is collecting the duties imposed by these tariff laws. He, therefore, must be stopped. The collector will seize the goods if the tariff duties are not paid. The State authorities will undertake their rescue, the marshal, with his posse, will come to the collector's aid, and here the contest begins. The militia of the State will be called out to sustain the nullifying act. They will march, Sir, under a very gallant leader; for I believe the honorable member himself commands the militia of that part of the State. He will raise the NULLIFYING ACT on his standard, and spread it out as his banner! It will have a preamble, setting forth, that the tariff laws are palpable, deliberate, and dangerous violations of the Constitution! He will proceed, with this banner flying, to the custom-house of Charleston,

> "All the while,
> Sonorous metal blowing martial sounds."

Arrived at the custom-house, he will tell the collector that he must collect no more duties under any of the tariff laws. This he will be somewhat puzzled to say, by the way, with a grave countenance, considering what hand South

Carolina herself had in that of 1816. But, Sir, the collector would not, probably, desist, at his bidding. He would show him the law of Congress, the treasury instruction, and his own oath of office. He would say, he should perform his duty, come what come might. . . .

CHARLES SUMNER

Charles Sumner studied at the Harvard Law School under Joseph Story, who was a professor of law during the last half of his term on the Supreme Court Bench. While Sumner early became interested in the anti-slavery movement, he did not enter politics until the decade before the Civil War. In 1851 Massachusetts sent him to the United States Senate. There he was as uncompromising a representative of freedom and northern interests as Calhoun was of slavery and the South. During the Civil War he opposed compromise, and during the reconstruction period he stood for the rights of the negroes and against the early return of the South to a position of national power.

OUR DOMESTIC RELATIONS
OR, HOW TO TREAT THE REBEL STATES [85]

. . . .
It only remains that we should see things as they are, and not seek to substitute theory for fact. On this important question I discard all theory, whether it be of State suicide or State forfeiture or State abdication, on the one side, or of State rights, immortal and unimpeachable, on the other side. Such discussions are only endless mazes in which a whole senate may be lost. And in discarding all theory, I discard also the question of *de jure*,—whether, for instance, the Rebel States, while the Rebellion is flagrant, are *de jure* States of the Union, with all the rights of States. It is enough, that, for the time being, and *in the absence of a loyal government*, they can take no part and perform no function in the Union, *so that they cannot be recognized by the National Government*. The reason is plain. There are in these States no local functionaries bound by constitutional oaths, so that, in fact, there are no constitutional functionaries; and since the State government is necessarily composed of such functionaries, there can be no State government. Thus, for instance, in South Carolina, Pickens and his associates may call themselves the governor and legislature, and in Virginia, Letcher and his associates may call themselves governor and legislature; but we cannot recognize them as such. Therefore to all pretensions in behalf of State governments in the Rebel States I oppose the simple FACT, that for the time being no such governments exist. The broad spaces once occupied by those governments are now abandoned and vacated.

That patriot Senator, Andrew Johnson,—faithful among the faithless, the Abdiel of the South,—began his attempt to reorganize Tennessee by an Address, as early as the 18th of March, 1862, in which he made use of these words:—

"I find most, if not all, of the offices, both State and Federal, *vacated, either by actual abandonment, or by the action of the incumbents in attempting to subordinate their functions* to a power in hostility to the fundamental law of the State and subversive of her national allegiance."

[85] *The Atlantic Monthly*, October, 1863, XII, 521-522, 523-524.

In employing the word "vacated," Mr. Johnson hit upon the very term which, in the famous resolution of 1688, was held to be most effective in dethroning King James. After declaring that he had abdicated the government, it was added, "that the throne had thereby become *vacant*," on which Macaulay happily remarks:—

"The word *abdication* conciliated politicians of a more timid school. To the real statesman the simple important clause was that *which declared the throne vacant;* and if that clause could be carried, he cared little by what preamble it might be introduced."

And the same simple principle is now in issue. It is enough that the Rebel States be declared *vacated*, as *in fact* they are, by all local government which are bound to recognize, so that the way is open to the exercise of a rightful jurisdiction.

And here the question occurs, How shall this rightful jurisdiction be established in the vacated States? Some there are, so impassioned for State rights, and so anxious for forms even at the expense of substance, that they insist upon the instant restoration of the old State governments in all their parts, through the agency of loyal citizens, who meanwhile must be protected in this work of restoration. But, assuming that all this is practicable, as it clearly is not, it attributes to the loyal citizens of a Rebel State, however few in numbers,—it may be an insignificant minority,—a power clearly inconsistent with the received principles of popular government, that the majority must rule. The seven voters of Old Sarum were allowed to return two members of Parliament, because this place,—once a Roman fort, and afterwards a sheepwalk,—many generations before, at the early casting of the House of Commons, had been entitled to this representation; but the argument for State Rights assumes that all these rights may be lodged in voters as few in number as ever controlled a rotten borough of England.

Pray, admitting that an insignificant minority is to organize the new government, how shall it be done? and by whom shall it be set in motion? In putting these questions I open the difficulties. As the original government has ceased to exist, and there are none who can be its legal successors, so as to administer the requisite oaths, it is not easy to see how the new government can be set in motion without a resort to some revolutionary proceeding, instituted either by the citizens or by the military power,—unless Congress, in the exercise of its plenary powers, should undertake to organize the new jurisdiction. . . .

But, happily, we are not constrained to any such revolutionary proceeding. The new governments can all be organized by Congress, which is the natural guardian of people without any immediate government, and within the jurisdiction of the Constitution of the United States. Indeed, with the State governments already *vacated* by rebellion, the Constitution becomes, for the time, the supreme and only law, binding alike on President and Congress, so that neither can establish any law or institution incompatible with it. And the whole Rebel region, deprived of all local government, lapses under the exclusive jurisdiction of Congress, precisely as any other territory; or, in other words, the lifting of the local governments leaves the whole vast region without any other government than Congress unless the President should undertake to govern it by military power. Startling as this proposition may seem, especially to all who believe that "there is a divinity that doth hedge" a State, hardly less than a king, it will appear, on careful consideration, to be as well founded in the Constitution as it is simple and natural, while it affords an easy and constitutional solution to our present embarrassments. . . .

JOHN W. BURGESS

John W. Burgess was born in Tennessee and while only eighteen years of age served in the Union army against the South. He thus early absorbed the bitter border-state feeling during the Civil War and became an intense nationalist. After the war he returned to his collegiate studies, entered the Massachusetts bar, taught for a while, and then studied in Germany, 1871–1873. There he came under the influence of the organic school of nationalism. The philosophy of Bluntschli especially impressed him. He returned to the United States and shortly became professor of political science at Columbia University. His many books and articles on American political institutions and history reflect the influence of his early nationalism and of his German philosophical training.

THE AMERICAN COMMONWEALTH: CHANGES IN ITS RELATION TO THE NATION[86]

. . . . . .

Now it seems to me that the great vitiating principles of the most of our political and judicial reasoning is this dogma that our political system is an indestructible union of immutable states; and it is in reference to this dogma that I shall endeavor to excite skepticism. I shall undertake to show, in the first place, that the perpetuity of our Union depends primarily upon the existence of certain geographical relations and ethnical conditions; and, in the second place, that the doctrine of the indestructibility and immutability of the states in an abstraction which has no warrant either in history or present fact or tendency.

The volumes which have been written and spoken upon these two cardinal doctrines view the subject almost exclusively from the standpoint of the constitution. The *constitution* sets no period to the existence of the Union— therefore it is perpetual; the *constitution* reserves the rights of the states— therefore they are indestructible and immutable. The fundamental fallacy in such reasoning springs from regarding the constitution as the *creator* of these relations instead of as an attempt to express them in human speech and legitimize them by common consent. The constitution of the old Confederation of 1781 used stronger language in reference to the perpetuity of the Union than our present instrument, and yet in less than a decade it was laid with the things of the past. The Union Act for the German states of 1815 declared indissolubility as the first principle of the system; and yet, after forty years of impotence, the Union thus nominally created fell asunder, and the system it expressed disappeared in the smoke of the Seven Days' War. I might easily occupy the entire space assigned to this paper in citing the instances of history which show that a political system cannot be perpetuated simply through the guaranty contained in its written constitution.

[86] *Political Science Quarterly*, March, 1886, I, pp. 12–13, 15–23, 25–26, 34–35. (Reprinted by permission of the publishers.)

We must go back of the constitution into the domain of geography and ethnography, the womb of constitutions and of revolutions, and ask there for the principle of perpetuity in any political union. The answer comes to us, if we have but the ear to catch it, quick and sharp and decisive: that a population of an ethnic unity inhabiting a territory of a geographic unity constitutes a distinct nationality, and *nationality* is the condition of political perpetuity; more fully, that a population, speaking a common language and having common ideas as to the fundamental principles of rights and wrongs, and resident upon a territory separated by high mountain-ranges or broad bodies of water or by climatic differences from other territory, presents us with the natural basis of a true and permanent political establishment; and the further the departure from these conditions, the greater is the danger of ultimate dissolution. . . .

Now *we* do not live under any other heavens, nor are we directed by any other providence or nature; and the question of the perpetuity of our Union is the question as to the natural unity of our territory, and the homogeneity of our people. Is our population substantially one in language and in the fundamental ideas of rights and wrongs? and is our territory substantially a geographic unity? The answer to these inquiries is neither easy nor certain. Take the last first. This side of the Rocky Mountains, it would seem that our territory satisfies the physical requirements of political unity. The mass of it is the great valley of the Mississippi and its tributaries. But how is it in reference to that which lies beyond the great chain. Mr. Webster regarded it, at the time of its connection with us, as the Asia of our territory; and so it is. Its formation, climate, and scenery favor the pastoral economy and the patriarchal politic; and the perpetuity of its connection with the great empire on the east depends upon the power of the eastern civilization to overcome those physical influences. Now take the other question: Is our population substantially one in language and in the fundamental ideas of rights and wrongs? We can say in reply, that we are substantially though not exclusively an English-speaking people; and this, with freedom and facility of intercourse, is the mightiest force in producing unity of nationality; but are we one in our philosophy of rights and wrongs? It is here that the variety of race seems to have produced the greatest aberration. We all know that the slavery of the African race occasioned the development of a view of civil rights and of government altogether contradictory to that held where this relation between the superior race and the inferior did not exist. And now the appearance of the Mongol in the far west threatens the repetition, in some degree, of that same experience. In addition to race differences, there are other things which have become, and threaten to become still more, disturbing elements in the development of a national consciousness of rights and wrongs, *e. g.*, the silver mines and the Mormonism of our Asia. The influences exerted by both are confusing and corrupting forces, and enemies dire to honor in both man and woman. Shall we be able now to expel these powers of dissolution and decay through the development of a powerful national morality, and thus solve successfully and completely the great ethnical question upon which our national perpetuity depends? I hope so; I believe so; but I do not know. Of one thing I feel certain, however, that if we would accomplish this great end surely and speedily, we must not be in a hurry about erecting any more of that territory into commonwealths or, as the common parlance would have it, states.

To bestow upon the residents of a territory, no matter how numerous they may be, the powers of local self-government and of participation in the national government, before they have the moral and intellectual qualities which warrant it, is in my opinion a political crime. It is not only the right, but the duty of the Congress, as the interpreter of the Nation's political consciousness, to withhold such powers until it is clearly manifest that their bestowal will not result in unrepublicanism and unnationalism. The claim of a *right* by the population of any part of our territory to become a commonwealth or state rests upon a vicious doctrine in regard to the origin of rights. The right of government over such populations is wholly in the Nation; and what they may receive from time to time of governmental powers is derived from the Nation's grant through the Congress; and the Congress is bound to take care in the making of such grants not to denationalize the Nation. Every student of political and legal science should divest himself, at the outset, of this pernicious doctrine of natural rights, according to which each individual or the population of any section is practically authorized to determine in what his or its rights consist. Natural rights are at best but the ethical feeling as to what rights should be, and the more individual or particularistic that feeling is, the less, as a rule, is it to be trusted; while the more general it is, the more is it to be relied upon; and when it originates in the Nation's consciousness, it has the moral persuasiveness behind it which influences the Nation's *will* to transform it into rights. Until this happens, however, the assertion of rights is but an ignorant boast or a disloyal threat.

It was not, whoever, the doctrine of rights, nor principally that of the indissolubility of the Union, that I propose to expound or criticise, but the dogma of the indestructibility and immutability of the commonwealths under this Union. The special purpose with which I started out, and to which I shall now return, was to indicate the present position of the commonwealths in our system, and their probable position in the near future; and I know of no other way to accomplish this purpose than to review the history of their relation to the Nation from the beginning, and see if, instead of immutability, there has not been constant mutability and general tendency towards a certain end. The great mistake usually made in the presentation of our constitutional history is beginning at too recent a date. The formation of the constitution of 1787 is commonly regarded as the starting-point, and all that went before is generally not counted for much, or ignored altogether. This has a reason, of course, and I think it is the confused idea of the American mind that the government of the English crown over the colonies was all usurpation, and therefore not to be taken into account; but this is *borné*, not to say silly. We must begin with the beginning, whatever and wherever that may be, if we would attain a proper comprehension of any subject. The beginning, in this case, is the act of the English King issuing patents to certain combinations of individuals, making them corporations, granting to them the property in loosely-defined savage territory, and vesting in them certain limited powers of local government over the population which they might induce to settle upon it. The *crown* was, therefore, the centre of unity, from which the colonial establishments all proceeded, and to which they were all subject; and they were provinces whose boundaries were lines of property grants and administrative convenience, and in which such powers of local self-government were exercised as the crown was pleased to confer in the patents, and through such organs as were constituted thereby. This was all regular and legitimate. It corresponded to the political consciousness and the political system of the age, and to the universally recognized prerogatives of the English crown. There is no fault to find with it, therefore, from a true historical and cosmopolitan standpoint, and we should not regard it from any other standpoint.

Now the next step. The impatient commentator answers, rebellion, revolution. No, it was not. It was the development of a sentiment of national unity and independence throughout the population resident within the thirteen colonies along the Atlantic coast, from New Hampshire to Georgia; then the assembly in Philadelphia of the representatives of this entire population for consultation in regard to the wrongs which they fancied the central government had perpetrated, or was about to perpetrate, upon them—wrongs which appear so doubtful, in themselves considered, that an unprejudiced mind feels forced to look deeper for the cause of the disaffection, and does not fail to find it, either, in the growing consciousness of nationality. The great Frenchmen, Turgot and Choiseul, had it right, twenty years before the declaration of '76, when they argued, no matter what might be the attitude of Great Britain toward her North American colonists, the result would be the same. They were one whole and separate nation, fast becoming adult, and no matter how mild the government of the crown over them, it would soon be felt to be foreign rule. But I must not lose the point of significance to our question; viz., that this assembly of the young Nation's representatives it was which protested first, then waged war against the royal sovereignty and government; and, finally, after two years of existence, declared, as the representatives of the whole People, and by the authority of the whole People, the independence of the *United Colonies*. What now was the relation of the individual colony to the Nation, and to the Nation's representative—the Continental Congress? The united People had, through the Continental Congress, asserted their sovereignty. They were organized only in that Congress. They had not as yet made any constitution vesting powers or reserving powers or withholding powers. We must, therefore, determine the powers of the Continental Congress by regarding it as the organization of the People, and the successor to the British government. In the former capacity it was sovereign constituting power. In the latter it was central government, authorized by the general principles of the devolution of powers to succeed to all of the powers exercised by the King and Parliament over and in the colonies: viz., the functions of international government; of inter-colonial government; and the right of participation in the purely internal government of most of the colonies, through the veto power upon the acts of their legislatures, the ultimate revision of the decisions of their higher courts, and the appointment of their governors and chief judicial officers. In the former capacity, it might and should have constituted a new system of governmental organs, both central and local, with such reservations of rights and distributions of powers as it judged conducive to the welfare of the whole people; while in the latter it should have governed with all the powers of both crown and Parliament until the new system was ready. By all the reasons of political science and the natural devolution of powers, this was the position of the Nation and its representative, the Continental Congress, on the one side, and the commonwealths and their local governmental establishments on the other; and there were at the moment no other reasons and norms by which to measure these relations. Such was the general feeling during the first moments subsequent to the "Declaration." This was manifest from the appeals of the existing authorities of the old establishment in the colonies to the Continental Congress for direction in regard to how their local governments should be re-organized after the expulsion of the royal supremacy—in reality, for authority to re-organize them—and from the acts of the Congress authorizing them to proceed, upon the basis of the widest possible suffrage, to a provisional re-organization. Under this permission and advice, conventions of the people resident within the several colonies began the work of framing paper constitutions, for their local governments, while the Continental Congress, busy with the waging of the war to maintain the declared independence, delayed the construction of a constitution for a permanent central government which should define the relation of the Nation and its general representative to the states and the state-governments. This was the fatal error. All powers were, so to speak, in the air; and the state conventions, by proceeding first to the formation of written constitutions, got the pick, and in half a decade the leavings were few enough; so that when the plan of the new central government, drafted by the Continental Congress itself, came to be established in 1781, it presented the system of separately sovereign and independent states—sovereign and independent now as against *each other*, and not, as the Declaration had it, *unitedly* sovereign and independent as against *Great Britain*—and connected with each other by a league of friendship. According to this system, there was no Nation, and the government which it established was no representative of the Nation; it was but a congress of joint commissioners. From provinces of the British crown, these colonial establishments had now become, in name and theory at least, sovereign and independent States. Here certainly was mutability, construction and destruction. No one can possibly claim that the relation of local to central power in our system had not undergone within less than a decade a complete transformation. The constitution declared the relation now unchangeable save by the consent of every state given through its legislature. So far as the paper constitution was concerned, this system of sovereign states in league was made immutable. In fact, it lasted just eight years, and was then overthrown by revolution. The states had usurped the powers of the Nation. They had planted themselves upon ground false to philosophy, false to history, and false to physical and ethnical relations. These powers must be wrenched from them, and they forced back into their proper subordination. But how could it be done? The existing law provided: Only upon proposition of the Congress ratified by each and every state through its legislature. This method was tried in modest demands, and failed every time.

At length two far-seeing spirits divined the means of escape from the unbearable situation. These two were Bowdoin and Hamilton; and their argument was: The states have usurped the sovereignty of the *people of the*

Nation, and the *People* must reassert their sovereign power. But this was revolution—revolution against usurpation. Bowdoin boldly proclaimed it by securing from the Massachusetts legislature an instruction to the delegates sent by it to the Confederate Congress to move in that body for the summoning of a convention of the people of the whole Confederacy to revise the constitution. But these delegates were so frightened at the revolutionary character of the proposition, that they disobeyed the command of the legislature which sent and instructed them, and never presented the project at all. On the other hand, the more politic Hamilton had recourse to one subterfuge and another; until at last, chiefly through his shrewd manipulation of opportunities, the best talent of the Nation was brought together in secret convention, and persuaded to frame a constitution withdrawing from the states the greater part of the usurped powers, and to make appeal to the people of the Nation to establish it. The People answered with sufficient unanimity, Yea, and the Nation reasserted its sovereignty. What now was the relation between the states and the Nation in the new system? The most superficial comparison of the new constitution with its predecessor manifests the immense change which had been wrought in this respect.

In the first place, *sovereignty* could no longer be claimed as a state attribute, nor *separate* independence. Sovereignty resided alone in the *people* of the whole Nation, and a state could be legally bound in organic changes against its will. In the second place, it withdrew all of the really political functions from the states, and vested them in the Nation's governmental representative, *viz.*, the powers of war and peace, of diplomacy and commerce, the regulation of internal intercourse, of finance and the monetary system, of the military system, and of the local governmental system. It left to the states thus mainly jural and police functions. So thorough-going was the change which the relation between state and Nation now suffered, that we cannot longer properly speak of our local organizations as states, but as commonwealths, *i. e.*, local governments containing, under the sovereignty of the Nation and the supremacy of the Nation's general governmental representative, a large element of self-government. . . .

But this is not yet all. There is still another standpoint from which to view the rapid and constant changes in the constitution of our "indestructible and immutable states." We have been considering what the people of the Nation have been doing to the commonwealth; let us now contemplate the changes which the people resident within the limits of the particular commonwealth have been imposing upon its governmental organization. And right here let me point out the fact that there is no true parallelism in the relation of the Nation and the commonwealth to their respective governmental organizations. The commonwealth really exists only in its governmental organization, while the Nation has a physical and an ethnical existence as well as a governmental. There is really no such thing as the people *of* a commonwealth, in a sound view of our political and social system; there is only the people of the Nation resident *within* the commonwealth. The People is a national conception, and preserves its integrity against government only as Nation. Blot out the national government, and you still have the Nation physically and ethnically, which, by its own innate owner, will restore its political organization; but blot out the government of the commonwealth, and you have a territory measured by the chain of the surveyor, with a population governed exclusively by the Nation's organs, and restored to local self-government only by the Nation's act. This is really, though probably not consciously, what every judge means when he says: "To the government of the United States that which has not been granted is denied; but to the governments of the states that which has not been denied is granted." The commonwealth is purely a creation of law, and is identical with its political organization. I am endeavoring by this analysis to lead the mind of the reader up to the proposition that, when the people resident within a commonwealth withdraw powers from the government of the commonwealth, the result is practically a change in the position of the commonwealth, and not simply a redistribution of powers between different organs of the commonwealth. . . .

The two natural elements in our system are now the Community and the Nation. The former is the point of real local self-government; the latter that of general self-government; and in the adjustments of the future these are the forces which will carry with them the determining power. The commonwealth government is now but a sort of middle instance. Too large for local government, too small for general, it is beginning to be regarded as a meddlesome intruder in both spheres—the tool of the strongest interest, the oppressor of the individual. This has been its history in other lands and other times; and the mere fact that it professes to be popular here, while it has been princely or aristocratic elsewhere, will not save it from the same fate.

Putting together all these principles, facts and tendencies—physical, ethnological, historical, legal, and political—how can we any longer declare the cardinal doctrine of our system to be "an indestructible union of indestructible and immutable states"? Are we not dealing in mere abstractions when we say so? Are we not giving way to an exaggerated Platonism in our political philosophy—attempting to substitute ideas *for* things, instead of seeking to find ideas *in* things? Are we not grinding out an old tune, from which the melody has long since departed? In a word, have we not completed our Federal era and attained the natural condition of a real national system—conditions which not only permit it but require it? And if this be true, in any degree, with regard to our present status, will it not be so in a much higher degree fifty years from now? It seems to me that it must. It seems to me that, in the twentieth century, the commonwealth will occupy a much lower place in our political system, the Nation a much higher, and the municipalities a much more distinct and independent sphere. It seems to me that we shall then, if not before, be compelled to reformulate our cardinal doctrine, and that it will read: the Nation, sole and exclusive sovereign, distributing the powers and functions of government between central organs, commonwealths and municipality; and defining, guaranteeing, and defending the fundamental principles of the civil right—in accordance with the dictates of the Nation's political and juristic policy. This sounds rather jejune, I confess, when compared with the grandiloquence of the other statement; and I have no expectation that the view thus expressed will meet with any general acceptance at this moment. As I said at the outset, I have not proposed to play the rôle of the propagandist. My object is not, at this time, to inspire belief, but to excite skepticism; and if I have accomplished this in a single mind, I am content: for I shall have aroused in that mind the spirit of independent research in politics; and, according to my scholastic arithmetic, one capable and conscientious inquirer counts for more than a hundred disciples.

SELECTED BIBLIOGRAPHY

H. V. Ames, *State Documents on Federal Relations* (1906).

J. W. Burgess, *Political Science and Comparative Constitutional Law* (1890).
  The Middle Period (1904).
  Civil War and the Constitution (1901).
  "The American Commonwealth," *Political Science Quarterly* 1: 9–35, March, 1886.

O. A. Brownson, *The American Republic* (1866).

J. C. Calhoun, *Works* (edited by R. K. Cralle, 6 vols., 1863), especially:
  A Disquisition on Government, Vol. I.
  A Discourse on the Constitution and Government of U. S., Vol. I.
  "Letter to General Hamilton," Vol. VI.

J. Davis, *The Rise and Fall of the Confederate Government* (1881).

S. G. Fisher, *The Trial of the Constitution* (1862).

J. C. Hurd, *The Theory of our National Existence* (1881).

J. A. Jameson, *The Constitutional Convention* (1886).

F. Lieber, *Political Ethics* (2 vols., 1838–1839).
  Civil Liberty and Self-Government (1853).
  Miscellaneous Writings (2 vols., 1881).

A. Lincoln, *Works* (edited by Nicolay and Hay, 2 vols., 1894).

C. S. Phinney, *Francis Lieber's Influence on American Thought* (1918).

E. P. Powell, *Nullification and Secession in the United States* (1898).

A. H. Stephens, *A Constitutional View of the Late War between the States* (1867).

J. Story, *Commentaries on the Constitution* (1833).

A. P. Upshur, *A Brief Inquiry into the True Nature and Character of our Federal Government* (1840).

D. Webster, *Works* (6 vols., 1851), especially:
  "Constitution not a Compact between Sovereign States," Vol. III.
  "Speeches on the Foot Resolution," Vol. III.
  "The Constitution and the Union," Vol. V.

CHAPTER VII

GOVERNMENT AND ECONOMIC INSTITUTIONS

I

Since the Civil War, the most outstanding problem in American political history has been the relationship of government to the individual in the realm of economics. A renewed class conflict has developed between industry and agriculture. The exigencies of the Civil War and the loss of southern agrarian votes in Congress gave the industrialists a strangle hold upon the national government. They converted it into an instrument for their economic aggrandizement. For them Congress raised the tariff and centralized the banking system. Under the guise of protecting the negro, the Fourteenth Amendment granted capitalism immunity from all state attacks upon property and from state interference with the liberty to do business as one saw fit. The Republican party, born in the agricultural West, became the guardian angel of capitalism in its conflict with agrarianism. The last quarter of the nineteenth century saw the golden age of free business expansion and of governmental *laissez-faire*. Agriculture, however, was not entirely silent. The Granger movement of the seventies was the vanguard of its coming offensive. The munitions of the war upon business were, on the one hand, the grievances of the farmer against the mortgage-holding capitalist and the railroad that overcharged and discriminated against him, and, on the other hand, the distrust of the average citizen toward the stifling consolidation of industry and capital. The Greenback and free-silver movements manifested the agrarian unrest. The same demand for cheap money that punctuated post-Revolutionary politics, again emanated from the agricultural West. The farmers, being debtors, desired to repay their capitalistic creditors with easy money and less purchasing power. However, big business, through its domination of the "party of Lincoln" and by waving the "bloody flag of rebellion" against the Democratic party, maintained for a long time control of the organs of government and withstood the onrush of agrarianism.

Within its own geographical domain, capitalistic industrialism has fought a second class conflict. The concomitant of expanding industry has naturally been the growth of the laboring class. The proletariat of congested factory cities has developed a group consciousness. Organized in trade unions, labor has endeavored to wrest from the owners of industry an increasing share of the financial returns. The skilled crafts, notably those among the railroad workers, have conspicuously succeeded. Labor unions have employed with increasing frequency the economic weapons of the strike and the boycott. Nor have the workers been adverse to using the State in their class battle. Maximum hours of work, child labor, accident compensation, and other similar laws, have found their way into the statute-books. On the other hand, business, too, has employed political agencies in its defense against the assault of labor. The judicial weapon of the injunction has mowed down many an attack upon the stronghold of industrial capitalism. Both contestants learned the value of a governmental alliance.

In order to understand properly the new rôle of government in economic life, we must first appreciate the economic institutions that have developed during the last quarter of the nineteenth century and that characterize the contemporary scene. Probably the best method of understanding America of to-day is to contrast it with America of 1800.

The outstanding characteristic in our picture of early American life is its agricultural basis. Manufacturing and commerce played a minor rôle; the great mass of inhabitants were farmers. The farms of 1800 were, on the whole, isolated, self-sustaining communities consisting of economically independent individuals. With the exception of the tobacco and cotton plantations of the South, the essence of this old agricultural system was production for use rather than for exchange or profit. The farmer of that day did not depend upon distant markets and market prices; nor did he employ expensive farm implements that necessitated heavy bank borrowings. In those pioneering days, moreover, the science of agriculture had not yet developed; and scientific education of farmers by government employees was consequently impossible. The farmer of one hundred years ago was independent of the outside world. On his plot of land he grew his own grains, cultivated his own vegetables, raised his own cattle. For only two important items was he at all dependent upon the world outside: salt for preserving meat and iron for tipping ploughs.

A second characteristic of life in 1800 was the slow and difficult transportation system. The steamboat, the railroad, the airplane were inventions of the future. The principal methods of communication were the rivers and the ocean. Until the second quarter of the last century, but few roads were built. Bridle paths followed the old Indian trails, and occasionally the forest would be sufficiently cleared to permit, with difficulty, a wagon or a coach. When Washington, as President, was on his way to meet Congress, his carriage stuck in the mud, and only after it had been pried up with poles and pulled out by ropes could he proceed on his journey. Only in the immediate neighborhood of Philadelphia, Boston, and New York were highways good, even from the point of view of the eighteenth century. Elsewhere roads did not exist at all. Very often such trails as had been made were hard to find, and harder to keep after they had been found. Farmers only a short distance from New York City could not bring their surplus produce to that market in the winter because the roads were impassable. The best road in the entire country was the post-road between Boston and New York. Yet the public conveyance which made regular trips took, in the most favorable season of the year, usually an entire week for the journey. Passengers often had to help the coachman lift the coach out of a quagmire. The length of the trip—now made in five hours—was not due to lazy traveling. Frequent relays of horses speeded the coach on its way, and the daily drive lasted from 2.30 A.M. to 10.00 P.M. Mail from New York to Boston took six days; and from Richmond, Virginia, to New York, two months.[1] In terms of transportation, New York was further away from Boston than it now is from Los Angeles.

The difficulty of transportation helped to fashion the economic and social life. Communities were isolated and consequently grew up economically self-dependent. Those industries that did exist were naturally organized for local markets. Knowledge of outside events and new ideas in the world of thought permeated very slowly beyond the narrow seaboard fringe. Economic problems, as a result, were of local and not national concern.

A third characteristic of economic life in the early eighteen-hundreds was the simple division of labor within communities. The industrial revolution did not reach these shores until the War of 1812 cut off the United States from British products and induced New England merchants to shift their capital from ships to factories. As far as possible, each farmer attempted to perform for himself those activities necessary for his economic existence. In the village community, to a certain degree, and in the larger towns, a few crafts did develop. Thus the blacksmith shod the horses of his neighbors, built

[1] A. J. Beveridge, *Life of John Marshall*, I, 255–265.

their ploughs, and repaired their wagons. The shoemaker made the boots for the countryside. In parts of Pennsylvania metal crafts grew up. But in all these industries no minute, complex division of labor took place. The shoemaker himself cut the leather, fashioned the last, and sewed the shoe. All told, he employed only four processes and eight tools in shoemaking.[2] Thus the craftsman controlled his job. He sold a finished product, not his time. He himself performed all the steps in production; he was not a mere cog in a labor machine.

A fourth characteristic was the existence of cheap western lands. The fertile prairies of the Ohio Valley and the Louisiana Territory invited the tiller of worn-out lands in the East. During the second decade of the century the construction of canals and roads across the Alleghenies encouraged migration away from the more populated sections of the country. All those dissatisfied with their economic and social status and possessing the necessary initiative could and did move west, clear a farm, and become economically self-sufficient. The abundance of cheap, fertile lands tended to produce a substantial equality of wealth. Even those who remained on the Atlantic sea-board benefited. The western lands drained off the surplus labor from the eastern cities and enabled the new labor organizations to secure substantial increases in wages. Economic opportunity broadened; and individualism was the result.

Our picture of twentieth-century America is vitally different. No longer do agricultural self-sufficiency, rural isolation, difficult transportation, simple division of labor, abundant western lands, and substantial equality of wealth loom in bright colors in the panorama of modern life. The industrial revolution with its resulting mechanization of production, transportation, and leisure has eliminated the previous simplicity of economic and social institutions. The outstanding characteristic of present-day society is not the self-sufficiency of the individual, but his interdependence. Every detail in the new portrait of America manifests this changed relationship.

In the first place, the United States has become increasingly urbanized. One hundred years ago, the vast majority of Americans lived on farms; to-day over 50 per cent dwell in cities. In the first quarter of the nineteenth century, New York was a city of but eighty thousand people; now over six million human beings crowd together in that metropolis. There are now over eighty cities having a population of one hundred thousand. In the formative period of

[2] B. E. Hazard, *The Organization of the Boot and Shoe Industry in Massachusetts before 1875*, pp. 3-4.

American history, city life was simple and leisurely. People lived in individual houses with large yards. Frequently, they planted their own vegetables, milked their own cows, pumped their own drinking water. To-day dozens, sometimes hundreds, of families live piled up upon each other in modern apartment houses. To-day city dwellers buy their food supplies. Their meat comes from the packing houses of Chicago, their milk from the great dairy companies, their vegetables from the canneries, their water from the city reservoir. The relation of individual to individual has necessarily changed. In the old days, a garbage pile in the back-yard affected the health of the inhabitants of that property; to-day it may spread disease to a thousand families of a congested section. In the days of the family cow, tubercular milk killed off the farmer's family; now tens of thousands of customers buy the diseased milk of a dairy dealer. Formerly, a polluted well sickened only the users of it; to-day pollution of a city reservoir means a typhoid epidemic. In 1800, an individual's negligence or thoughtlessness boomeranged immediately and convincingly upon himself, and himself primarily; in 1931, one's carelessness vitally affects the well-being of others. No longer does our health and safety depend upon our own vigilance; we are now dependent upon the efficient and honest team-work of vast numbers of producers, distributors, apartment owners, transportation companies, and inspectors. New problems of urban transportation, congestion in slums, public health, sanitation, food supplies, pure water, and the like, are constantly rising.

A second characteristic of contemporary America is its industrialization. The industrial revolution reached this country during the second quarter of the last century. Power—water, then steam, and now electricity—was applied to machinery. The complexity of modern engines would astound Watt, Cartwright, or Stephenson. This industrialization has affected the division of labor, created the factory system, introduced a new interdependence of individuals, revolutionized transportation, and produced a concentration of financial control unparalleled in American history.

The first result of the industrial revolution has been the destruction of the old simple division of labor and the creation of the factory system. A minute, complex division of labor has superseded the earlier economic system. The handicraft system of a master and a few journeymen has given way to vast buildings housing hundreds of workers. To-day, one hundred operations change leather into boots; one hundred individuals and over fifty machines perform these operations.[3] To-day, a carriage maker does not construct the entire carriage by himself; rather an employee in a Ford factory stands all day long beside a moving belt and tightens bolt no. 235 on every car that passes by him. He cannot work at whatever speed pleases him; he must adjust his body to the speed of the moving belt. He no longer owns his own tools, but employs those of the management. His safety from accident depends but partially upon his own vigilance; the speeding up of the machinery by an engineer or the snapping of an overhead belt might snuff out his life. He no longer sells a finished product, but only his time. The new economic system has demolished his individual self-dependence. The new division of labor and the complicated machinery demand the team-work of labor squads and encourage large scale, mass production. The size of factories has grown steadily. In 1859 the average factory employed 9.34 men and its annual product was valued at $13,429.[4] In 1925 the average number of men employed in a factory had increased to 44.16 and the value of its product to $334,616.[5] In 1925 only 5.6 per cent of the factories in the United States produced an annual product of $1,000,000; yet these 5.6 per cent plants employed 56.8 per cent of the industrial wage-earners and manufactured 67.6 per cent of the total value of industrial products.[6]

The second result of industrialization has been a revolution in transportation. In 1800 the fastest coaches spent six days *en route* between New York and Boston. To-day the Yankee Clipper speeds over the rails in less than five hours. Steamboats cross the Atlantic in five days; passenger planes fly between New York and Chicago in seven hours. The Erie Canal of Clinton, the steamboat of Fulton, the railroad of Stephenson, the airplane of Wright have revolutionized transportation. The telegraph, telephone, and radio have done the same for communication. The new transportation system has destroyed the economic independence of localities. Not only has the division of labor become complex and minute, but it has also become geographical. For example, New Bedford, Massachusetts, manufactures cotton cloth and sells its products throughout the United States, and throughout the world as well. However, New Bedford is dependent upon Alabama and Mississippi for raw cotton, upon Pennsylvania and West Virginia for coal, upon Pittsburgh for its

[3] B. E. Hazard, *The Organization of the Boot and Shoe Industry in Massachusetts before 1875*, pp. 159–160.

[4] H. U. Faulkner, *American Economic History*, p. 517.

[5] *Statistical Abstract of U. S.*, 1928, p. 780.

[6] *Ibid.*, p. 750.

iron and machinery, upon the Dakotas for its wheat and flour. A business depression in Chicago or in Rio de Janeiro may slow up the spindles in a New Bedford mill. A strike in the coal mines of Pennsylvania may compel a shut-down of the factories. The devastation of the boll-weevil in Alabama may increase cotton prices and affect profits in New Bedford. A successful railroad strike would soon starve the city. This geographical division of labor has destroyed sectional, as well as individual, self-dependence. New Bedford, Pittsburgh, Natchez, Fargo, Scranton are now interdependent. The revolution in transportation has resulted not only in a sectional interdependence for raw materials, but also in sectional competition for markets. The ease and rapidity of transportation have widened markets. New Bedford cotton mills send their cloth over the entire United States. But so do the textile plants of Gastonia, North Carolina. Massachusetts, being an old manufacturing state, has already passed through the adolescent stage of the industrial revolution; it is vitally concerned with the well-being of its workers. Child labor laws, minimum wage acts for women, accident compensation legislation, and the like, fill its statute-books. North Carolina, on the other hand, is a new industrial state, and has not yet enacted protective labor legislation. The state regulations of Massachusetts somewhat increase the labor costs of production of the New Bedford textile plants above those of Gastonia. And yet they must compete for the same markets. The new transportation system has resulted in a situation wherein a backward community injures economically the more progressive states.

The third result of the industrial revolution has been a profound change in our financial institutions. Paralleling the remarkable growth in the scale of industry, there has developed a similar concentration of financial power. The Pujo committee of Congress in 1913 found that four allied financial institutions in New York City held 341 directorships in banks, transportation, public utility, and insurance companies, whose aggregate resources were $22,245,000,-000.[7] The factory system quite naturally places emphasis upon capital, and consequently results in a concentration of wealth. The United States Commission on Industrial Relations reported in 1915 that 2 per cent of all the people in the United States owned 60 per cent of the national wealth, while 65 per cent of the people owned only 5 per cent of the national wealth.[8] The federal income tax re-

[7] Faulkner, op. cit., p. 543.
[8] Final Report of the U. S. Commission on Industrial Relations (1915), p. 28.

turns for 1920 indicate that less than 1 per cent of the people with incomes received close to 12 per cent of the sum total of incomes in the United States, and that 10 per cent received 34 per cent.[9] The substantial equality of wealth existing in 1800 has disappeared. The industrialization of the country has resulted in extremes of fortune and poverty.

A third major characteristic of contemporary America is the changed nature of agriculture. The introduction of machine production and of crop specialization has produced a revolution as vital and as real as that caused in industry by the invention of the steam engine. Production now is not chiefly for use; it is for exchange and profit. The agricultural revolution has swept the former isolated, economic independence of the farmer into the limbo of a discarded past. The economic existence of the present-day agrarian depends upon distant markets and upon market-controlled prices. The dairy farmers of Wisconsin now compete with the dairy farmers of New York. The modern farmer has been compelled to develop a market psychology. The high cost of land and of complicated farm machinery has resulted in the financial subservience of the agrarian. His prosperity is no longer dependent solely upon his success in raising crops, but upon the interplay of economic factors beyond his individual control.

A fourth characteristic of the new economic order is the passing of cheap western lands. The homesteading movement of the sixties and seventies rapidly filled in the public domain of the United States. Little land suited for farming now remains unoccupied. The social results of this factor are only now being realized. No escape now exists for the tillers of outworn farms. No escape exists for the economically oppressed and socially dissatisfied dwellers of congested industrial centers. A permanent laboring class is the consequence. The closing of this safety valve inevitably has stimulated labor agitation. In the America of the past century, the presence of inviting western homesteads kept class lines fluid and maintained a substantial equality of wealth. The closing of this avenue of escape probably means the further concentration of wealth and economic power. The ideal of America as a land of opportunity is gradually fading. Fewer and fewer stories will henceforth be written of the rise from factory hand to bank president.

This contrast of contemporary life with that of one hundred years ago reveals two significant facts. The new complexity of society has

[9] Faulkner, *op. cit.*, p. 671.

altered the relation of individual to individual.   Interdependence characterizes every aspect of our life. Our jobs, our health, our comfort are affected by others. The selling of diseased meat by a Chicago packing house and the howls of our neighbor's radio alike destroy our self-sufficiency. Nor are geographical localities now independent units. Sectional interdependence for supplies and competition for markets have nationalized our economic problems.

II

During the last quarter of the nineteenth century the doctrine of individualism and governmental *laissez-faire* flourished with renewed vigor. The concept of government as "anarchy plus the street constable" had developed during the period of Jeffersonian agrarianism. The capitalist group, however, soon discovered that it admirably suited the needs of a growing industrialism. If individual initiative were stressed, if government assumed merely the rôle of policeman, if government kept its hands off the economic conflict, then the financiers and industrialists would undoubtedly be more successful in the race for economic domination. After the Civil War, with the agrarian votes of the South missing from Congress, the capitalist group assumed control of legislation. Under the guise of protecting the emancipated negro, they slipped through the Fourteenth Amendment providing that "no state shall deprive any person of life, liberty, or property without due process of law." During the same period the federal judiciary, influenced by this business individualism, resurrected and reinterpreted the Fifth Amendment, placing a similar restriction upon the national government, and likewise the contract clause of Article I, section 10, prohibiting states from passing any law impairing the obligation of contracts.

This business individualism found vigorous support in the writings of the intellectuals. The Jeffersonian concept of "a wise and frugal government" influenced many scholars. The *laissez-faire* teachings of Adam Smith's *The Wealth of Nations* found its counterpart in the economic books of the past fifty years. In 1776 Smith had written: "Let each man, each employer of labor, each seller of merchandise follow his own personal interest without let or hindrance, for in so doing he is led by an invisible hand to promote the good of all." This philosophy was reflected in the economic studies of J. B. Clarke and other orthodox economists. A more recent influence on intellectual individualism in America was the evolutionary, sociological works of Herbert Spencer in England. Spencer applied the Darwinian thesis of the survival of the fittest to social evolution. He maintained that society has evolved through immutable, unalterable, natural laws. He traced the changes in social institutions and concluded therefrom that man was gradually becoming a freer individual. Human interference with these natural laws invariably retarded social progress. It resulted in the survival of the unfit and the weighting down of society with dead timber. Governmental action subordinated the individual to the state and destroyed his true freedom.

The leading American exponent of Spencerian individualism was William Graham Sumner. From his chair of sociology at Yale University, Sumner argued for *laissez-faire* and personal liberty. He became the most conspicuous antagonist of governmental activity. His little book, *What Social Classes Owe to Each Other*,[10] became the bible of the individualists. With logical consistency, he attacked tariff protection. The business group did not, however, carry individualism to that extent; and Sumner became the object of their attacks.

Sumner held that the social order is fixed by laws of nature precisely analogous to those of the physical order. The most that man can do is to mar the operation of the social laws by his own ignorance and conceit. In this social order, freedom of contract plays a major rôle. In the Middle Ages, men were united by custom and prescription into associations, ranks, guilds, and communities of various kinds. These ties endured as long as life lasted. Consequently, society was dependent, throughout all its details, on status; and the tie or bond was sentimental. In our modern State, and in the United States more than anywhere else, the social structure is based on contract, and status is of the least importance.[11] Especially in the field of labor and social relations was Sumner insistent upon freedom of contract.

"If a man, in the organization of labor, employs other men to assist in an industrial enterprise, it was formerly thought that the rights and duties of the parties were defined by the contract which they made with each other. The new doctrine is that the employer becomes responsible for the welfare of the employees in a number of respects. They do not each remain what they were before this contract, independent members of society, each pursuing happiness in his own way according to his own ideas of it. The employee is not held to any new responsibility for the welfare of the employer; the duties are all held to lie on the other side." [12]

[10] New York, Harper & Brothers, 1884.
[11] *Ibid.*, pp. 24–25. Contrast this view of contract and status with that of Roscoe Pound, *The Spirit of the Common Law*.
[12] Sumner, *The Challenge of Facts*, pp. 195–196. (Yale University Press.)

In this social order based on freedom of contract, government can very well afford to offer protection to property. The safeguarding of property is not hostile to the interests of the individual. The popular antithesis between persons and capital, Sumner claimed, is fallacious. Every law or institution which protects persons at the expense of capital makes it easier for persons to live and to increase the number of consumers of capital, while at the same time lowering all the motives to prudence and frugality by which capital is created. Hence every such law or institution tends to produce a large population, sunk in misery. All poor laws and all eleemosynary institutions and expenditures have this tendency. On the other hand, all laws and institutions which give security to capital against the interests of other persons than its owners restrict numbers while preserving the means of subsistence. Hence such laws or institutions tend to produce a small society on a high stage of comfort and well-being. "It follows that the antithesis commonly thought to exist between the protection of persons and the protection of property is in reality only an antithesis between numbers and quality." [13] All the institutions which we have inherited were invented to guard liberty against the encroachments of a powerful monarch or aristocracy, when these classes possessed land and the possession of land was the greatest social power. Now, argued Sumner, we must devise institutions to guard civil liberty against popular majorities. The protection of property is the first function of government and the chief element in civil liberty.[14]

Underlying Sumner's analysis of the social order is the assumption that the individual is a free member of society. His status depends upon himself. He need but possess the will and the initiative, and he can rise in the economic scale. Class lines, Sumner believed, are fluid. Social evolution and personal betterment result from individual effort.

"Not even in the slums of great modern cities, is there any class of persons who could be called proletarians and yet be distinguished from the dangerous and criminal class; for any honest man who finds himself there and is discontented can make his way, by moderate effort, to other places where the conditions are easier." [15]

Governmental interference is robbing Peter to pay Paul. Political questions resolve themselves into struggles of individuals and groups for larger margins of the product of industry. The "Forgotten Man,"

[13] Sumner, *The Challenge of Facts*, pp. 27–28. (Yale University Press.)
[14] *Ibid.*, pp. 49–50.   [15] *Ibid.*, p. 169.

the private citizen who minds his own business and pays his taxes, is the victim of governmental interference. The opponents of *laissez-faire*, complained Sumner, invite us to accept a policy in which every duty a man performs is made the basis, not for rights and rewards, but for new duties and subjection to new demands. Every duty which is neglected becomes a ground for new rights and claims. The well-to-do man is to do without things which his means might buy for himself in order that he may pay taxes to provide those same things in a public way for people who have not earned them.[16] "Poverty is the best policy. If you get wealth, you will have to support other people; if you do not get wealth, it will be the duty of other people to support you." [17] "We are constantly preached at by our public teachers, as if respectable people were to blame because some people are not respectable—as if the man who has done his duty in his own sphere was responsible in some way for another man who has not done his duty in his sphere." [18] For example, there are relations of employer and employee which need to be regulated by compromise and treaty. Sanitary precautions need to be taken in factories and houses; precautions against fire are necessary; care is needed that children be not employed too young, and that they have an education; care is needed too that banks, insurance companies, and railroads be well managed, and that officers do not abuse their trusts. In each case, however, the interested parties have the duty of defending their own interests. The penalty of neglect is suffering. The system of providing for these things by boards and inspectors throws the cost, not on the interested parties, but on the tax-payers. Some of them, no doubt, are the interested parties, and they may consider that they are exercising the proper care by paying taxes to support an inspector. If so, they only get their fair deserts when the railroad inspector finds out that a bridge is not safe after it has broken down, or when a bank examiner comes in to find out why a bank failed after the cashier has stolen all the funds. The real victim is the "Forgotten Man"—the man who has watched his own investments, made his own machinery safe, attended to his own plumbing, and educated his own children, and "who, just when he wants to enjoy the fruits of his care, is told that it is his duty to go and take care of some of his negligent neighbors, or, if he does not go, to pay an inspector to go." [19]

An immoral political system is created whenever there are priv-

---

[16] Sumner, *The Challenge of Facts*, p. 197.
[17] Sumner, *Social Classes*, p. 24.   [18] *Ibid.*, p. 136.   [19] *Ibid.*, pp. 137–138.

ileged classes—that is, "classes who have arrogated to themselves rights while throwing the duties upon others." The real danger of democracy is that the classes which possess the political power will assume all the rights and reject all the duties. They will plunder "those who have." Any scheme for coddling and helping the wage-earners, for making the rich pay for whatever the poor want, is immoral to the very last degree and opposed to the simplest common sense.[20]

"The most specious application of the dogma of rights is to labor. It is said that every man has a right to work. The world is full of work to be done. Those who are willing to work find that they have three days' work to do in every day that comes. Work is the necessity to which we are born. It is not a right, but an irksome necessity, and men escape it whenever they can get the fruits of labor without it. What they want is the fruits, or wages, not work. But wages are capital which some one has earned and saved. If he and the workman can agree on the terms on which he will part with his capital, there is no more to be said. If not, then the right must be set up in a new form. It is not now a right to work, nor even a right to wages, but a right to a certain rate of wages, and we have simply returned to the old doctrine of spoliation again. It is immaterial whether the demand for wages be addressed to an individual capitalist or to a civil body, for the latter can give no wages which it does not collect by taxes out of the capital of those who have labored and saved." [21]

Sumner concludes that government must vigorously adhere to the doctrine of *laissez-faire*. Society does not need supervision. Governmental control is corrupting to free institutions, because men who are taught to expect government inspectors to come and take care of them lose all true education in liberty.[22]

"If we can acquire a science of society, based on observation of phenomena and study of forces, we may hope to gain some ground slowly toward the elimination of old errors and the re-establishment of a sound and natural social order. Whatever we gain that way will be by growth, never in the world by any reconstruction of society on the plan of some enthusiastic social architect. The latter is only repeating the old error over again, and postponing all our chances of real improvement. Society needs first of all to be freed from these meddlers—that is, to be let alone. Here we are, then, once more back at the old doctrine—*Laissez faire*. Let us translate it into blunt English, and it will read, Mind your own business. It is nothing but the doctrine of liberty. Let every man be happy in his own way. If his sphere of action and interest impinges on that of any other man, there will have to be compromise and adjustment." [23]

[20] Sumner, *Social Classes*, pp. 36–37.
[21] Sumner, *Challenge of Facts*, pp. 34–35.
[22] Sumner, *Social Classes*, p. 98.
[23] *Ibid.*, pp. 119–120.

Government is notoriously corrupt and inefficient. Political interference in economic matters results from the selfish desire of individuals to get something for which others must pay. The less government there is, the better off will society be.

"Jobbery is the vice of plutocracy, and it is the especial form under which
plutocracy corrupts a democratic and republican form of government. The
United States is deeply afflicted with it, and the problem of civil liberty here
is to conquer it. It affects everything which we really need to have done to
such an extent that we have to do without public objects which we need
through fear of jobbery. Our public buildings are jobs—not always, but
often. They are not needed, or are costly beyond all necessity or even decent
luxury. Internal improvements are jobs. They are not made because they
are needed to meet needs which have been experienced. They are made to
serve private ends, often incidentally the political interests of the persons
who vote the appropriations. Pensions have become jobs. In England pensions used to be given to aristocrats, because aristocrats had political influence, in order to corrupt them. Here pensions are given to the great
democratic mass, because they have political power, to corrupt them. Instead of going out where there is plenty of land and making a farm there,
some people go down under the Mississippi River to make a farm, and then
they want to tax all the people in the United States to make dikes to keep
the river off their farms. The California gold-miners have washed out gold,
and have washed the dirt down into the rivers and on the farms below. They
want the Federal Government to now clean out the rivers and restore the
farms. The silver-miners found their product declining in value, and they
got the Federal Government to go into the market and buy what the public
did not want, in order to sustain (as they hoped) the price of silver. The
Federal Government is called upon to buy or hire unsalable ships, to build
canals which will not pay, to furnish capital for all sorts of experiments, and
to provide capital for enterprises of which private individuals will win the
profits. All this is called 'developing our resources,' but it is, in truth, the
great plan of all living on each other." [24]

Sumner realized that in modern society there are some problems
which the individual, acting by himself, cannot solve. The solution
of these problems does not, however, fall to the political State. The
individual must coöperate with other individuals in non-governmental
organizations. If laborers want to be protected, they must protect
themselves. They ought to protect their own children and women;
their own class opinion ought to secure the education of their children.
Trade-unions ought to be perfected so as to undertake a great range
of important duties for which we now rely on government inspection.

"The safety of workmen from machinery, the ventilation and sanitary
arrangements required by factories, the special precautions of certain proc-

[24] Sumner, *Social Classes*, pp. 141–143.

esses, the hours of labor of women and children, the schooling of children, the limits of age for employed children, Sunday work, hours of labor—these and other like matters ought to be controlled by the men themselves through their organizations." [25]

Directly, and through Sumner, Herbert Spencer influenced American individualism. In 1915 Truxton Beale conceived the idea of publishing a special American edition of Spencer's masterpiece of *laissez-faire*, *The Man versus The State*. Prefacing each chapter was a short essay by some prominent contemporary individualist.[26] Here we can find in concise form the doctrines of conservative leaders relating to the problem of governmental activity. David J. Hill introduced this collection of essays by questioning the positive value of the State. If the State were a wise institution, exercising always beneficent, parental care over its people, then, argued Hill, the only important evil developing from its unlimited authority would be the destruction of individual self-reliance, initiative, and responsibility; but, he asserted, the State possesses none of these fine qualities. Rather, it is a means whereby some human beings control the activities of their fellows.[27]

E. H. Gary cogently summarized the *laissez-faire* doctrine. The continued development of America, with its freedom for the individual, depends, he held, upon the life and power of the Constitution. That instrument warns government to keep its hands off, to let men work, to protect and encourage, but not to interfere with individual enterprise.[28] That government which governs least governs best. This does not, however, mean that men are happy when they do as they please; rather it means that the best father brings up his children with the least possible nagging and scolding and with the fewest regulations. Likewise, the best government is that which maintains order, protects the rights, and promotes the prosperity of the people with the least possible amount of law-writing, interference, and control of the individual. Nothing is more dangerous than hampering

[25] Sumner, *Social Classes*, pp. 94–95.

[26] T. Beale, *The Man versus the State in America* (M. Kennerley), containing: Elihu Root, "The New Toryism;" H. C. Lodge, "The Coming Slavery; " E. H. Gary, "Overlegislation;" A. P. Gardner, "From Freedom to Bondage;" N. M. Butler, "The Great Political Superstition;" D. J. Hill, "The Man versus the State;" Harlan F. Stone, "The Sins of Legislators;" Charles W. Eliot, "Specialized Administration;" W. H. Taft, "The Duty of the State." It is interesting to note the change that has occurred in the viewpoint of Harlan F. Stone since his appointment to the U. S. Supreme Court. His decisions evidence the influence of Holmes or Brandeis rather than of the individualists on the bench.

[27] H. Spencer, *The Man versus The State* (Beale edition), pp. ix–x.

[28] *Ibid.*, p. 72.

the power of the human mind or limiting the enterprise of man.[29] In looking about for methods of preventing governmental interference with free individual initiative, Gary placed considerable emphasis upon the judiciary. The chief work of the Supreme Court, he maintained, is to prevent over-legislation. Over and over again the learned judges have laid down the rule that excessive lawmaking is in itself a crime against law and the rights of every American citizen. The constant admonition of the Supreme Court is that you cannot make laws that are excessive; you cannot twist or write new meanings into old laws.[30]

J. W. Burgess, the high priest of American nationalism, likewise expounded the doctrine of individualism. The national State may possess sovereignty over the commonwealths, but it is to give free reins to the individual. Burgess feared that we were swaying from the path of true progress. That path, he held, must lead ever to the better and more perfect reconciliation of government and individual liberty. This signifies, in the ultimate analysis, four things:

(1) "A true and correct organization of the sovereign power as the basis of all Government and Liberty, so as to give every element and every force within the state its proper value and open the way for its legitimate activity and for the exercise of its natural weight."

(2) "A Government of conservative structure and limited power, a Government which will not only be proof against the usurpation of a despot, but which cannot be adapted to further the rôle of class interests."

(3) "A fully rounded, well-defined sphere of Individual Immunity from governmental power, such as will liberate the physical, intellectual, and moral capacity of the Individual, stimulate it to the fullest development and encourage its service to the advancement of civilization."

(4) "A learned, experienced, impartial, unprejudiced, upright organ for maintaining in detail, through its interpretations and judgments, the constitutional balance between Government and Liberty." [31]

Burgess feared that we are having too much government. A republic which makes its government the arbiter of business is, of all forms of State, the most universally corrupt; a republic which undertakes to do its cultural work through governmental force is the most demoralizing.[32] Before we attempt to solve our new problems by appealing to government, we ought, Burgess insisted, to consider whether a revival of religion and morals, a reëstablishment of the

---

[29] Spencer, *The Man versus The State* (Beale edition), p. 78.
[30] *Ibid.*, p. 76.
[31] J. W. Burgess, *Reconciliation of Government with Liberty* (New York, Charles Scribner's Sons, 1915), p. 379.
[32] *Ibid.*, p. 382.

functions and influence of the churches, and an improvement of our system of education may not better subserve the social uplift and still preserve our liberty.[33]

This philosophy of individualism and minimized government has survived the days of Spencer and Sumner. Recently it has found its way afresh into political literature. In his presidential campaign speech at New York on October 22, 1928, Herbert Hoover voiced the Spencerian and Jeffersonian doctrines of *laissez-faire* and local decentralization. During the past one hundred and fifty years, he argued, we have built up a form of self-government and a social system peculiarly our own. It is founded upon a particular conception of self-government in which decentralized local responsibility is the very base. "Further than this, it is founded upon the conception that only through ordered liberty, freedom and equal opportunity to the individual will his initiative and enterprise spur on the march of progress. And in our insistence upon equality of opportunity has our system advanced beyond all the world." During the war, Hoover declared, we necessarily turned to the government to solve every difficult economic problem. The government having absorbed every energy of our people for war, there was no other solution. For the preservation of the country, the federal government became a centralized despotism; it undertook unprecedented responsibilities, assumed autocratic powers, and took over the business of citizens. "To a large degree we regimented our whole people temporarily into a socialistic state. However justified in time of war, if continued in peace time it would destroy not only our American system but with it our progress and freedom as well." When the war closed we were challenged with a peace-time choice between "the American system of rugged individualism and a European philosophy of diametrically opposed doctrines—doctrines of paternalism and state socialism. The acceptance of these ideas would have meant the destruction of self-government through centralization of government. It would have meant the undermining of the individual initiative and enterprise through which our people have grown to unparalleled greatness." [34]

This philosophy of individualism and *laissez-faire* has been widely accepted by the United States Supreme Court. The due process clauses of the Fifth and Fourteenth Amendments and the contract

[33] J. W. Burgess, *Reconciliation of Government with Liberty*, p. 381.
[34] New York *Times*, October 23, 1928, p. 2. See also Hoover's veto of the Muscle Shoals Bill, New York *Times*, March 4, 1931, p. 16.

clause of Article I, section 10, of the federal Constitution are now the safeguards of business against governmental regulations that reduce profits, limit the liberty to do business as the management sees fit, or restrict the freedom of contract with individual employees.

In the case of *Coppage v. Kansas*, the Supreme Court declared void a state act prohibiting "yellow-dog contracts." In 1903 the legislature of Kansas passed a statute making it unlawful for any individual, firm, or corporation "to coerce, require, demand or influence any person or persons to enter into any agreement . . . not to join or become or remain a member of any labor organization or association, as a condition of such person or persons securing employment, or continuing in the employment of such individual, firm or corporation." Justice Pitney, delivering the opinion of the court, held that this statute interfered with freedom of contract.

"Included in the right of personal liberty and the right of private property —partaking of the nature of each—is the right to make contracts for acquisition of property. Chief among such contracts is that of personal employment, by which labor and other services are exchanged for money or other forms of property. If this right be struck down or arbitrarily interfered with there is a substantial impairment of liberty in the long-established constitutional sense. The right is as essential to labor as to the capitalist, to the poor as to the rich; for the vast majority of persons have no other honest way to begin to acquire property, save by working for money. An interference with this liberty so serious as that now under consideration, and so disturbing of equality of right, must be deemed to be arbitrary, unless it be supported as a reasonable exercise of the police power of the State." [35]

In *Adair v. U. S.*, the court declared unconstitutional a similar federal act directed against interstate carriers. In this case Justice Harlan maintained that the right of a person to sell his labor upon such terms as he deems proper is, in its essence, the same as the right of the purchaser to prescribe the conditions upon which he will accept such labor from the person offering to sell. In all such particulars the employer and employee have equality of right, and any legislation that disturbs that equality is an arbitrary interference with liberty of contract which no government can legally justify in a free land. [36]

In a series of important cases the Supreme Court has denied the state and federal governments the right to pass various forms of protective labor legislation. Laws regulating hours of work, wages for women, and methods of wage payment, the court has held, deprive a person of his property, his liberty, or his freedom of contract. In 1897 the legislature of New York enacted a statute limiting work

[35] 236 U. S. 1, 14 (1915).   [36] 208 U. S. 161, 174 (1907).

in bakery or confectionary establishments to not more than sixty hours a week or ten hours a day. Justice Peckham, in the case of *Lochner v. New York*, declared that this labor law was unconstitutional, on the ground that it necessarily interfered with the right of contract between the employer and employees concerning the number of hours of work.

"The general right to make a contract in relation to his business is part of the liberty of the individual protected by the Fourteenth Amendment of the federal Constitution."

"When the State, by its legislature, in the assumed exercise of its police powers, has passed an act which seriously limits the right to labor or the right of contract in regard to their means of livelihood between persons who are *sui juris* (both employer and employe), it becomes of great importance to determine which shall prevail—the right of the individual to labor for such time as he may choose, or the right of the State to prevent the individual from laboring or from entering into contract to labor, beyond a certain time prescribed by the State."

"Statutes of the nature of that under review, limiting the hours in which grown and intelligent men may labor to earn their living, are mere meddlesome interferences with the rights of the individual, and they are not saved from condemnation by the claim that they are passed in the exercise of the police power and upon the subject of the health of the individual whose rights are interfered with, unless there be some fair ground, reasonable in and of itself, to say that there is material danger to the public health or to the health of the employes, if the hours of labor are not curtailed. If this be not clearly the case the individuals whose rights are thus made the subject of legislative interference, are under the protection of the Federal Constitution regarding their liberty of contract as well as of person; and the legislature of the State has no power to limit their right as proposed in this statute." [37]

In the case of *Adkins v. Children's Hospital*, the Supreme Court declared void a congressional statute establishing a minimum wage for women in the District of Columbia, upon the ground that it was an unconstitutional interference with the freedom of contract. Justice Sutherland, delivering the majority opinion, recognized that there is no such thing as absolute freedom of contract; he held, however, that freedom of contract is the general rule and restraint the exception. The exercise of legislative authority to abridge such liberty can be justified only by the existence of exceptional circumstances. Sutherland pictured individual women workers as being on the same bargaining level as their employers. He complained, consequently, that the statute exacts from the employer an arbitrary payment for a purpose and upon a basis having no causal connection with his business, or the contract, or the work the employee engages

[37] 198 U. S. 45, 53, 54, 61 (1905).

to do. The declared basis is not the value of the services rendered, but the extraneous circumstance that the employee needs to get a prescribed sum of money to insure her subsistence, health, and morals.

"In principle, there can be no difference between the case of selling labor and the case of selling goods. If one goes to the butcher, the baker or grocer to buy food, he is morally entitled to obtain the worth of his money but he is not entitled to more. If what he gets is worth what he pays he is not justified in demanding more simply because he needs more; and the shopkeeper, having dealt fairly and honestly in that transaction, is not concerned in any peculiar sense with the question of his customer's necessities." [38]

Underlying this individualistic philosophy and jurisprudence are certain basic assumptions that demand examination. The *laissez-faire* school posits a free individual in a free society. It assumes that the individual, possessed of the required initiative, can find his place in the economic order. The mechanization of industry, the emphasis upon capital and credit, the recurring cycles of overproduction and unemployment—these and other phases of the machine age, however, render the individual a virtual cog in an economic machine. The new interdependence that characterizes the twentieth century has destroyed the free society and the free individual. The *laissez-faire* exponents assumed, in the second place, that all men are substantially equal in economic and political power, or that through their own efforts they can attain such equality. For example, they visualize the bargaining power of individual, unorganized female workers as being on the same level with that of large corporations. Fair wages and working conditions, accordingly, result out of this even process of give and take. No consideration, however, is taken of the unequal waiting ability of the employee and the capitalist. Another basic assumption of the individualistic school is that whenever free competition exists, society has a guarantee that goods will be produced at the lowest possible cost, since the hope of personal gain will lead to the best disposal of labor, to invention, and the adoption of the best machinery; society also has a guarantee that the goods produced will be placed upon the market at fair prices. The validity of this assumption depends upon the possibility of free competition in an economic system that emphasizes large-scale production, consolidation of financial control, and concentration of national wealth.

[38] 261 U. S. 525, 558–559 (1922).

III

A half century ago saw the first political attack upon governmental do-nothingism. The Granger movement of the seventies was its vanguard. The grievances of the farmer against the discriminating, exorbitant rate-charging railroad and mortgage-holding capitalist, coupled with the distrust of the average citizen toward the stifling consolidation of industry and finance, were the munitions of this attack. The nation could not long turn a deaf ear to the demands of its middle class, and regulation became the order of the day. National legislation in the form of the Interstate Commerce Act of 1887 and a half-dozen other important measures sought to end railroad abuses— arbitrary rates, pools, rebates, dicrimination. The Sherman Anti-Trust Law of 1890 forbade "big business" to form combinations in restraint of trade. The administration of President Roosevelt became the heyday of "trust busting"; the prosecution of the oil, sugar, and tobacco monopolies clearly indicated that government had abandoned pure *laissez-faire*.

The victory of Wilsonian liberalism in 1912 introduced a new chapter in the repudiation of *laissez-faire* principles. The Federal Farm Loan system, with its easy credits, was established to ease the financial worries of the farmer. The interest rate on farm loans fell from 10 or 12 per cent to 5 or 6 per cent. Congress gave the Federal Trade Commission powers to prevent unfair methods in competition and commerce. The Clayton Act forbade price discriminations, consolidations, combinations, and interlocking directorates; it also exempted labor organizations and agricultural coöperatives from the restraints of the anti-trust laws. The Wilsonian administration set up the Federal Reserve Board to control banking and finance through its domination of the rediscount rate. The La Follette Seamen's Act provided a Magna Carta for the rights of American sailors. The Adamson Act gave railroad employees a coveted eight-hour day. Then came the World War and our participation; victory demanded teamwork in industry. Through the War Labor Board and the War Labor Policies Board, the federal government recognized labor, encouraged its fight for living wages, and pushed the establishment of workers' shop committees in industrial plants.

The states, even more than the federal government, were responsible for the passing of *laissez-faire*. Under the influence of the Adamses and the compulsion of urbanization, Massachusetts set up a railroad commission in 1869 and endowed it with power to investigate, issue reports, and make recommendations. The Massachusetts gas and electric lighting commissioners of 1885 were authorized to issue orders to the utilities under their jurisdiction, to regulate rates, conditions of service, and the issuance of new securities, and to forbid the construction of unnecessary competitive plants. Wisconsin, under the drive of La Follette Progressivism, became a veritable laboratory for social legislation. Workmen's compensation acts abolished the old common-law defenses of the employer against accidents to his workers; the framers of these acts insisted that industrial accidents be charged to the costs of production. Minimum wage and maximum hour legislation protected women in industry. And safety codes and child labor laws found their way into the statute books of many states. Income taxes—first established in Wisconsin in 1910 and adopted by the federal government in 1913—together with inheritance taxes, sought to nationalize great fortunes and gradually to end the growing menace of multimillionaires.

In the realm of practical party politics, this revolt against *laissez-faire* repeatedly threatened the supremacy of the Republican and Democratic parties. Both were slow to abandon the old individualism; the Republican party, especially, was tied up with large-scale business, which was benefiting from the policy of do-nothingism. The main cry of protest arose from the farmers of the Northwest. In the seventies the Liberal Republican, the Granger, and the Greenback parties clamored against the domination of big business. The Populist party of the nineties, under the influence of Bryan, for a time threatened the domination of the older groups. Consolidation with the Democratic party in 1896, however, soon buried the Populist movement in a quagmire of conservatism. The Roosevelt Progressive split from the Republican ranks of 1912 spelled the defeat of that organization and the election of Woodrow Wilson. During the War the farmers of North Dakota organized the Non-Partisan League and captured the state government. For a while, the movement spread in the wheat belt, though within a few years the League's political power disappeared. In 1920 a Farmer-Labor party was organized, and in 1924 La Follette threatened the security of the older machines with a new Progressive party. While these protest movements failed to capture the national government, they nevertheless served a useful purpose. Under the spur of their attack, the Republican and Democratic parties felt compelled to adopt policies that pointed toward complete abandonment of doctrinaire *laissez-faire*.

Since 1870, the legislative and philosophical revolt against governmental non-interference and against the new industrial capitalism has taken four forms. Frequently, a confusion of objectives clouds the minds of the reformers; occasionally, two approaches to the problem find their way into a single legislative act. One school of thought desires a return to the good old days of individual enterprise. Its proponents consider that business and financial consolidation has destroyed this individualism; and they are confident that competition, if it can be restored, will solve the problem. Their program, therefore, is the break-up of large business organizations and the enforcement of competition. The legislative results of this type of thinking have been the Sherman Anti-Trust Act of 1890 and the Clayton Anti-Trust Act of 1914. The present-day attacks upon chain stores and chain banks typify this approach. A second school of thought holds that consolidations cannot be broken, or that large-scale enterprise is more economical than the previous economic system. Do not attempt, therefore, to enforce competition, it argues; rather regulate these large organizations to eliminate their evils. Thus the Hepburn Act of 1909 regulated railroad rates and services, prohibited pools, and forbade rebates; the Federal Trade Commission regulates business methods to eliminate unfair trade practices; and the Federal Reserve Board keeps an eye upon banking methods. A third school of thought holds that government inevitably is a participant in the existing economic struggles. Conflicts occur between capital and labor, or between industry and agriculture. Governmental action or inaction invariably benefits one of the conflicting groups; if government deliberately adopts a policy of do-nothingism, then organized capital can more easily win over poorly organized labor, or industry and finance over agriculture. Consequently, maintain these writers, government should deliberately interfere on behalf of the underdog in this economic conflict; government should attempt to make the battle more equal. This philosophy has led to labor legislation—minimum wages, eight-hour days, factory inspection, workmen's compensation. Similarly, various farm relief statutes resulted from this point of view, as the Federal Farm Loan Act of 1916 and the Federal Farm Board of 1929. Finally, a fourth school feels that there are certain basic economic institutions, as railroads, banks, grain warehouses, water power, public utilities, etc; although these may be privately owned, they have become vested with a public interest. Such institutions, because of the complexity of our economic interdependence, can no longer be operated purely for private profit; rather their influence upon the economic life of the nation must be considered. Some form of public control or direction is, therefore, essential. In accordance with this viewpoint, the federal government took over the parcel post system in 1912, and in 1910 established the postal savings banks. The Transportation Act of 1920 treated railroads as a basic economic institution. Through the recapture of excess profits, the more prosperous roads are supposed to aid the weaker but, nevertheless, essential links in the railroad chain. And the Interstate Commerce Commission may now require the consolidation of railroads into unified systems. The establishment by federal and state governments of marketing agencies for agriculture is another instance of this philosophy in operation.

IV

In political philosophy, the attack upon *laissez-faire* has made gradual headway. During the last quarter of the nineteenth century, many writers began to realize the necessity of some expansion of governmental activities; some, however, felt that governmental functions should be kept at the lowest possible minimum. This hesitant attitude characterizes even some present-day thinkers. Before we examine the more vigorous critics of *laissez-faire*, we may profitably take note of a few members of this transitional group.

Theodore Woolsey, in his *Political Science* (1877), analyzed the functions of government. Government has four duties: (1) the redress of wrongs; (2) the prevention of wrongs; (3) care of the welfare of citizens, as in industry, highways, and health; and (4) care of spiritual matters. In all cases of proposed expansion of governmental functions, especially in the third group of duties, the burden of proof rests upon those who propose the new activities.[39]

W. W. Willoughby held that government exercised functions relating to the life of the state and the preservation of internal order, the maintenance of human liberty, and the safeguarding of the general welfare. He divided these functions into the essential and the non-essential. He viewed as essential the defense of the State against external attack, the maintenance of internal order, and the preservation of the national life. Activities relating to the economic, industrial, and moral interests of the people he considered as non-essential. The State should undertake them only upon proof of their utility. In view of the tendencies of modern life, he predicted the expansion of political activities.[40]

[39] Woolsey, *Political Science* (1877), pp. 209–211.
[40] Willoughby, *The Nature of the State* (1896); *Social Justice* (1900).

Woodrow Wilson, in his earlier writings,[41] was identified with this transitional school. Government, he held, is the organ of society, "its only potent and universal instrument." The objects of government must consequently be the objects of society. Society is an organic association of individuals for mutual aid to self-development. "The hope of society lies in an infinite individual variety, in the freest possible play of individual forces: only in that can it find that wealth of resource which constitutes civilization, with all its appliances for satisfying human wants and mitigating human sufferings, all its incitements to thought and spurs to action." It should be the end of government to assist in accomplishing these objects of society. Through regulation rather than interference, government should attempt, so far as possible, the equalization of conditions in all branches of endeavor.[42] Thus all combinations which necessarily create monopoly and necessarily put and keep indispensable means of industrial and social development in the hands of a few must be under the direct or indirect control of society. "To society alone can the power of dominating by combination belong."[43] However, there are natural and imperative limits to State action.

"The limit of state functions is the limit of necessary coöperation on the part of Society as a whole, the limit beyond which such combination ceases to be imperative for the public good and becomes merely convenient for industrial or social enterprise. Coöperation is necessary in the sense here intended when it is indispensable to the equalization of the conditions of endeavor, indispensable to the maintenance of uniform rules of individual rights and relationships, indispensable because to omit it would inevitably be to hamper or degrade some for the advancement of others in the scale of wealth and social advancement."[44]

As a rule, the State should do nothing which is "equally possible under equitable conditions to optional associations."[45]

Elihu Root was throughout his earlier career a staunch exponent of individualism. In his later writings, however, he has begun to realize the necessity of some abandonment of the *laissez-faire* doctrine. Root surveyed the relationship of recent economic changes to legal institutions and concluded that we are now in the midst of a process of rapid change in the conditions to which the principles of law are to be applied. If we are to have a consistent legal system, that change must be met, not by haphazard, but by constructive development.

[41] *The State* (1889). In his *New Freedom* Wilson left this transitional school. See Part V, below.
[42] Wilson, *The State* (Boston, D. C. Heath & Company), p. 633.
[43] *Ibid.*, pp. 633-634.   [44] *Ibid.*, pp. 636-637.   [45] *Ibid.*, p. 637.

"We have only just begun to realize the transformation in industrial and social conditions produced by the wonderful inventions and discoveries of the past century. The vast increase of wealth resulting from the increased power of production is still in the first stages of the inevitable processes of distribution. The power of organization for the application of capital and labor in the broadest sense to production and commerce has materially changed the practical effects of the system of free contract to the protection of which our law has been largely addressed. The interdependence of modern life, extending not merely to the massed city community but to the farm and mine and isolated factory, which depend for their markets and their supplies upon far distant regions and upon complicated processes of transportation and exchange, has deprived the individual largely of his power of self-protection, and has opened new avenues through which, by means unknown to the ancient law, fatal injuries may be inflicted upon his rights, his property, his health, his liberty of action, his life itself." [46]

In the field of labor activity, Root feared that the new economic order has reduced freedom of contract to an ironic misnomer. The power of organization has massed both capital and labor in such vast operations that in many directions the right of contract can no longer be at once individual and free. In the great massed industries the free give and take of industrial demand and supply does not apply to the individual.

"Nor does the right of free contract protect the individual under those conditions of complicated interdependence which make so large a part of the community dependent for their food, their clothing, their health and means of continuing life itself, upon the service of a multitude of people with whom they have no direct relations whatever, contract or otherwise." [47]

Root recognized the new interdependence of modern economic life. He realized, accordingly, that "democracy turns again to government to furnish by law the protection which the individual can no longer secure through his freedom of contract and to compel the vast multitude on whose coöperation all of us are dependent to do their necessary part in the life of the community." [48] Nevertheless, Root was loath to abandon *laissez-faire* individualism. In some directions and to some extent governmental control is necessary, he admitted; but we should not forget, he insisted, that every increase of governmental power to control the conduct of life is to some extent a surrender of individual freedom and "a step backward toward that social condition in which men's lives are determined by status rather than by their own free will." [49]

[46] E. Root, *Addresses on Government and Citizenship*, pp. 532–533: "Public Service at the Bar," address as President of American Bar Association, August 30, 1916 (Harvard University Press).
[47] *Ibid.*, p. 539.   [48] *Ibid.*, p. 539.   [49] *Ibid.*, pp. 539–540.

Another important representative of this transition attitude is Nicholas Murray Butler, president of Columbia University. Butler recognized that the era of unrestricted individual competition has gone forever. "There is no power in Presidents, there is no power in Attorneys-General, there is no power in Supreme Courts, there is no power in Congress, there is no power in political platforms, there is no power in oratory to restore it." Coöperation as a substitute for unlimited, unrestricted, individual competition has come to stay as an economic fact. It cannot, it ought not, to be stopped. The public interest demands that legal institutions be adjusted to it.[50] Our economic system has changed radically.

"The rapid growth and steady concentration of population, the annihilation of distance and time by steam and electricity, the swift rise of the factory system and the phenomenal success of that form of coöperative industry known as the corporation, have all tended to bring about a real, though invisible, business partnership between the individual and the community, and both partners must be heard in respect to the policies which the partnership wishes to pursue."

The industrial history of the past hundred years offers an immediate and conclusive answer to the defender of strict *laissez-faire*.

"The community's contribution to property values, the community's grant of individual monopoly, of patent rights and of corporate privileges, the community's protection of individual obligations and responsibilities through its enforcement of contracts, and the easily demonstrated moral evils of unrestricted and unsupervised competition, make it plain that whatever may have been the advantage of a policy of *laissez-faire* earlier in the world's history, the time for it is now passed." [51]

Butler, however, refused to sanction any important expansion of State functions. The remedy for our present ills can be found, not in political action, but rather in morality and education. Public control through the enforcement of moral standards and through the approval or disapproval of public opinion is far more effective, Butler felt, than governmental control through penal statute and police regulation.[52]

V

Just as Herbert Spencer and William G. Sumner were the teachers of the new individualism, so Lester F. Ward heads the attack upon

[50] N. M. Butler, *Why Should We Change Our Form of Government?* (New York, C. Scribner's Sons), pp. 81–82.
[51] *Ibid.*, pp. 57–58.
[52] H. Spencer, *The Man versus The State* (Beale edition), p. 180.

laissez-faire. Trained as a geologist, paleontologist, and botanist, Ward, in the last half of his life, turned to sociology. His *Dynamic Sociology*, written in 1883, was Ward's reply to Spencer's *Social Statics*. The very difference in the titles of their books indicate the diametrically opposite points of approach.

The Spencerian individualists had urged social evolution by individual effort; the struggle for survival would eliminate the unfit and in time produce a society of superior beings. Ward, on the other hand, emphasized the superiority of teleological over genetic evolution. He considered the "efficacy of effort" a cardinal principle of progress. The defenders of *laissez-faire*, Ward argued, almost uniformly fall into a fallacy fatal to their fundamental position. They insist that governmental interference is injurious and pernicious in preventing the successful operation of the benign tendencies of spontaneous natural law; this, Ward asserted, involves the admission of the efficacy of effort and reduces the individualists to demonstrating that the admitted effects must necessarily be injurious. "The main and really difficult task of proving the efficacy of effort is therefore already performed by the *laissez-faire* school. It is not difficult to prove that social effort may have beneficial as well as injurious effects." [53]

Ward severely criticized the Spencerian thesis of progress through competition and the survival of the fittest. The effect of competition, he pointed out, is to prevent any form from attaining its maximum development and to maintain a certain comparatively low level of development for all forms that succeed in surviving. Whenever competition is wholly removed, as through the agency of man in the interest of any one form, great strides are immediately made by the form thus protected, and it soon outstrips all those that depend upon competition for their motive to advancement. All the forms of life that man has excepted from the biologic law and has subjected to the law of mind demonstrate their unquestionable superiority. The method of man must differ from that of nature, which is intrinsically wasteful. Competition involves nature's enormous waste, and thus prevents the maximum development. The whole upward struggle of rational man has been against this tyrant of nature—the law of competition. Ward viewed all human institutions as so many ways of meeting and checkmating the principle of competition.[54]

[53] L. F. Ward, *Applied Sociology*, p. 14.
[54] Ward, *Psychic Factors of Civilization*, pp. 245–263.

Society, Ward insisted, must adopt a policy of coöperation. Paradoxical as it may sound, individual freedom can come only through social regulation.[55] The objects of government are three: protection, accommodation, and melioration. Legislation is progressing from primitive prohibitory statutes, "Thou shalt nots," to attractive regulation which offers a social reward for favored conduct.[56] Ward proposed that in addition to democracy we must establish a sociocracy, the rule of society itself. Government now finds itself in the toils of plutocracy, the rule of great organized wealth; yet he felt confident that the rule of plutocracy was nearing its last black hour before a real dawn of constructive social government.[57]

Quite different from Ward in their attack upon *laissez-faire* individualism was a group of outspoken social economists. Henry D. Lloyd, Edward Bellamy, Henry George, Thorstein Veblen, Richard T. Ely, and Henry C. Adams—all attacked the new economic order. Their analyses, unlike Ward's, did not search into the basic laws of social evolution; their approaches were not sociological. Rather, they examined the existing economic institutions in order to ascertain to what degree they were conducive to human happiness, security, and comfort.

Henry D. Lloyd's prime attack was upon large-scale business. He feared the growth of consolidation with its stifling disregard of the consumer and the small proprietor. His *Wealth Against Commonwealth* was an indictment of the methods employed by large corporations to stifle competition. Nature is rich, but, complained Lloyd, man everywhere is poor. The world enriched by thousands of generations of toilers has reached a fertility which can give every human being a plenty undreamed of even in the Utopias. But between this plenty ripening on the boughs of our civilization and the people hungering for it step the "cornerers," the syndicates, the trusts, with their cry of over-production. They hold back the riches of earth and sea from their fellows who famish and freeze. They assert the right, for their private profit, to regulate the consumption of the necessaries of life and to control their production. The majority have never been able to buy enough of anything. But the coal syndicate thinks there is too much coal; there is too much iron, too much lumber, too much flour—for this or that syndicate.[58]

[55] Ward, *Pure Sociology*, pp. 549–551.
[56] *Ibid.*, pp. 569–570.
[57] Ward, *Psychic Factors of Civilization*, pp. 323–327.
[58] H. D. Lloyd, *Wealth Against Commonwealth* (New York, Harper & Brothers), pp. 1–2.

"Rome banished those who had been found to be public enemies by forbidding every one to give them fire and water. That was done by all to a few. In America it is done by a few to all. A small number of men are obtaining the power to forbid any but themselves to supply the people with fire in nearly every form known to modern life and industry, from matches to locomotives and electricity. They control our hard coal and much of the soft, the stoves, furnaces, and steam and hot-water heaters; the governors on steam-boilers and the boilers; gas and gas-fixtures; natural gas and gas pipes; electric lighting, and all the appurtenances. You cannot free yourself by changing from electricity to gas, or from gas of the city to the gas of the fields. If you fly from kerosene to candles, you are still under the ban." [59]

Our industry, as Lloyd portrayed it, is a fight of every man for himself. "The prize we give the fittest is monopoly of the necessaries of life, and we leave these winners of the powers of life and death to wield them over us by the same 'self-interest' with which they took them from us." The main doctrine of industry since Adam Smith has been the fallacy that the self-interest of the individual was a sufficient guide to the welfare of the individual and society.[60] The results have been disastrous: the filling up of the Mississippi by the forest-destroying, self-seeking lumber companies; the disintegration of the American family—among the rich by too little poverty, and among the poor by too much; the embezzlement of public highways and public franchises into private property; the devolution of the American merchants and manufacturers into the business dependents of a few men in each great department of trade; the devolution of the free farmer into a tenant, and of the working-man into a fixture of the factory; and "that mêlée of injunctions, bayonets, idle men and idle machinery, rich man's fear of poor man and poor man's fear of starvation, we call trade and industry." [61] Where the self-interest of the individual is allowed to rule social and personal action, the level of all is forced down to that of the lowest.

"Business excuses itself for the things it does—cuts in wages, exactions in hours, tricks of competition—on the plea that the merciful are compelled to follow the cruel." [62]

"The philosophy of self-interest as the social solution was a good living and working synthesis in the days when civilization was advancing its frontiers twenty miles a day across the American continent, and every man for himself was the best social mobilisation possible. But to-day it is a belated ghost that has overstayed the cock-crow. These were frontier morals. But this same, everyone for himself, becomes most immoral when the frontier is abolished and the pioneer becomes the fellow-citizen, and these frontier morals are most

[59] H. D. Lloyd, *Wealth Against Commonwealth*, pp. 9–10.   [61] *Ibid.*, p. 498.
[60] *Ibid.*, p. 494.   [62] *Ibid.*, p. 498.

uneconomic when labour can be divided and the product multiplied. Most uneconomic, for they make closure the rule of industry, leading not to wealth but to that awful waste of wealth which is made visible to every eye in our unemployed—not hands alone, but land, machinery, and, most of all, hearts." [63]

Lloyd optimistically prophesied that society was on the verge of an important social transformation. Social coöperation would soon take the place of individual self-interest and would remold our institutions of wealth into the Commonwealth. Lloyd's optimism rested largely upon his confidence in the inherent goodness of men. Men have become so intelligent, so responsive and responsible, so coöperative, that they can be intrusted in great masses with the care of vast properties owned entirely by others and with the operation of complicated processes, although but a slender subsistence wage is awarded them out of fabulous profits.

"The spectacle of the million or more employes of the railroads of this country despatching trains, maintaining tracks, collecting fares and freights, and turning over hundreds of millions of net profits to the owners, not one in a thousand of whom would know how to do the simplest of these things for himself, is possible only where civilization has reached a high average of morals and culture. More and more the mills and mines and stores, and even the farms and forests, are being administered by others than the owners. The virtue of the people is taking the place Poor Richard thought only the eye of the owner could fill. If mankind, driven by their fears and the greed of others, can do so well, what will be their productivity and cheer when the 'interest of all' sings them to their work?" [64]

"'Love thy neighbor as thyself' is not the phrase of a ritual of sentiment for the unapplied emotion of pious hours; it is the exact formula of the force today operating the greatest institutions man has established. It is as secular as sacred." [65]

While Lloyd was concerned about industrial consolidation, Henry George described the existing economic ills in terms of land monopoly. In the new West, land speculation was rampant and unearned increment was often the readiest means to wealth. Consequently, to frontier folk land monopoly was the prime source of social injustice. The monopolization of natural resources produces a static society and economic exploitation. In his *Progress and Poverty*,[66] George defines rent as the difference between the income value of a given plot of land and that of the least valuable land in use in the neighbor-

[63] Lloyd, *Man, the Social Creator* (Garden City, N. Y., Doubleday, Doran & Co.), p. 83.
[64] Lloyd, *Wealth Against Commonwealth*, p. 505.
[65] *Ibid.*, p. 503.   [66] Published in 1879.

hood; rent measures the difference between the yields per acre on the richest and the poorest soils with a like outlay of labor and capital. In an urban community, rent results likewise from the difference between the income value of two plots of land. This difference is not based upon soil fertility but upon monopoly value arising from strategic location, from the number of people passing a plot of land, from its access to docks, railroads, or markets, or its desirability for a residence. The rent increases, not because of the individual's efforts, but because of the community's growth. The increment is unearned. Thus the progress of society profits the landlord monopolist. George proposed as the economic solution of this basic evil the taxation of this unearned increment. This proposal of a single tax would return to the community the land values created by society and expropriated by the private owners of land. The recapture of these society-created land values would permit the removal of taxes from improvements on land and from productive labor. This scheme, George believed, would make impossible the acquisition of large fortunes through the increase in the value of the land held. It would reduce the congestion in large cities by compelling building upon vacant lots. Labor and productive enterprise would be free from the millstone of parasitic landlordship. The taxation of the unearned increment would give these economic groups the just rewards of their efforts. This single tax movement, irrevocably interwoven as it was with the frontier emphasis upon land, may be described as "a sort of agrarian socialism—the product of conditions peculiar to the undeveloped capitalism of the West and—a distinctly American contribution to economic thought." [67]

Edward Bellamy, in 1888, published his novel *Looking Backward: 2000–1887* and expounded by means of a dream narrative his thesis of national socialism. His work is probably the outstanding American contribution to socialist literature. The narrator, a Mr. West, is put to sleep in 1887 by a "magnetic physician" and does not awake until the year 2000. His conversations with his host, Dr. Leete, disclose the radical transformations that had occurred in economic institutions. The Utopian conditions described by Dr. Leete indicate by contrast the fundamental weaknesses of society in the eighties. By 2000 all problems of labor, of industrial organization, of adjustment of production to consumption had been satisfactorily solved.

Bellamy looked upon the consolidation of corporations in his day as the stepping-stone to the new economic order. Dr. Leete explained

[67] Macy, *Socialism in America*, p. 63.

that the absorption of business by ever larger monopolies continued, despite popular clamor against it. Soon no opportunity whatever for individual enterprise in any important field of industry remained, unless backed by a great capital. "Small businesses, as far as they still remained, were reduced to the condition of rats and mice, living in holes and corners, and counting on evading notice for the enjoyment of existence." Syndicates, pools, or trusts fixed prices and crushed all competition except when combinations as vast as themselves arose. Having no business of his own to put his money in, the small capitalist, at the same time that he took service under the corporation, found no investment for his money except its stocks and bonds, thus becoming doubly dependent upon it. Early in the twentieth century, narrated Dr. Leete, the evolution was completed by the final consolidation of the entire capital of the nation.

"The industry and commerce of the country, ceasing to be conducted by a set of irresponsible corporations and syndicates of private persons at their caprice and for their profits, were intrusted to a single syndicate representing the people, to be conducted in the common interest for the common profit. The nation, that is to say, organized as the one great business corporation in which all other corporations were absorbed; it became the one capitalist in the place of all other capitalists, the sole employer, the final monopoly in which all previous and lesser monopolies were swallowed up, a monopoly in the profits and economies of which all citizens shared. The epoch of trusts ended in The Great Trust." [68]

The labor problem disappeared the moment the nation assumed the responsibilities of capital. When the nation became the sole employer, all the citizens, by virtue of their citizenship, became employees, to be distributed according to the needs of industry. The principles of universal military service were applied to the labor question. It became the duty of every citizen to contribute his quota of industrial or intellectual services to the maintenance of the nation. The period of industrial service was twenty-four years, beginning at the close of education at twenty-one and terminating at forty-five.[69] This industrial army was divided into ten great departments, each of which had a chief. The President was the head of the army, and these ten chiefs formed his council. Promotion to rank of officer was based upon excellence as a worker.[70]

Money, Dr. Leete explained, had become unknown. The machinery of money and credit in the past had often produced, and always ag-

[68] E. Bellamy, *Looking Backward* (Boston, Houghton Mifflin Company), Ch. 5.
[69] *Ibid.*, Ch. 6.   [70] *Ibid.*, Ch. 17.

gravated, economic crises. Since the nation was the sole producer and the sole employer, buying and selling became antiquated processes. Credit-cards, issued to all persons, secured for them, at the nation's distributing shops, whatever they needed. The yearly allowance was the same for all persons. Public opinion compelled all to exert themselves.[71]

The new economic order functioned without waste. The wastes which in the nineteenth century had resulted from leaving the conduct of industry to irresponsible individuals, Dr. Leete enumerated as: (1) the waste from mistaken undertakings; (2) the waste from the competition and mutual hostility of those engaged in industry; (3) the waste from periodical gluts and crises, with the consequent interruptions of industry; and (4) the waste at all times from idle capital and labor. The new national socialism eliminated these wastes through the coördination of production and consumption and through the unified planning of industrial projects. The total product, consequently, multiplied greatly.

"The effectiveness of the working force of a nation, under the myriad-headed leadership of private capital, even if the leaders were not mutual enemies, as compared with that which it attains under a single head, may be likened to the military efficiency of a mob, or a horde of barbarians with a thousand petty chiefs, as compared with that of a disciplined army under one general—such a fighting machine, for example, as the German army in the time of Von Moltke." [72]

Through this method of conversation between a representative of his own age and a spokesman of the Utopian future, Bellamy analyzed in a searching fashion the fundamental weaknesses of American economic life. His solution in the form of a Prussianized socialism is unimportant in comparison with his description of the consequences of free competition and the growth of industrial monopoly. The influence of Bellamy was immediate, although temporary. Within two years, over a third of a million copies of *Looking Backward* were sold. Nationalist clubs sprang up and entered politics. In 1891 this movement merged with the new Populist party and lost its identity; and the vague enthusiasm for a Utopian social order, generated by Bellamy, naturally had only a passing influence.

In his attack upon *laissez-faire* individualism, Thorstein Veblen likewise criticized the existing socio-economic order. In his earliest and most significant work, *The Theory of the Leisure Class*,[73] Veblen

[71] E. Bellamy, *Looking Backward*, Ch. 9.
[72] *Ibid.*, Ch. 22.
[73] Published in 1899.

analyzed the development of social distinctions and the growth of "conspicuous consumption." The upper social and economic groups, he found, lavishly waste our economic goods in their desire to demon-strate their freedom from financial cares. In *The Theory of Business Enterprise*,[74] Veblen pointed out that present-day business is organized on the profit motive. Social efficiency does not count. The quality or quantity of the services rendered to society does not concern the controllers of business. Usually, their pecuniary rewards are increased through the cornering or destruction of a part of the marketable supply. The teamwork of the financial managers of different industries permits the fixing of prices at the point conducive to the greatest profits. The hierarchy of business men, Veblen claimed, controls and manipulates government for its own ends.[75]

In 1885 the American Economic Association was founded. Under the influence of Richard T. Ely, the preliminary platform of the organization sharply attacked the *laissez-faire* doctrine. It read:

"We regard the state as an educational and ethical agency whose positive aid is an indispensable condition of human progress. While we recognize the necessity of individual initiative in industrial life, we hold that the doctrine of *laissez-faire* is unsafe in politics and unsound in morals; and that it suggests an inadequate explanation of the relations between the state and the citizens." [76]

Professor E. J. James of the University of Pennsylvania spoke in defense of this platform at the first meeting of the association. His attack upon governmental individualism was unmistakable.

"On one point we certainly all differ from the general tone of Adam Smith and some of his so-called orthodox followers of the early half of this century, and that is as to his conception of the state. We do not regard it as a merely negative factor, the influence of which is most happy when it is smallest, but we recognize that some of the most necessary functions of a civilized society can be performed only by the state, and some others most efficiently by the state; that the state, in a word, is a permanent category of economic life, and not merely a temporary crutch which may be cast away when society becomes more perfect." [77]

Professor Henry C. Adams, in his article, *Relation of the State to Industrial Action*,[78] expounded further the platform of the American Economic Association. Unrestrained competition results in serious evils. In the first place, the free play of individual interests tends to

---

[74] Published in 1904.
[75] This thesis is further developed in *Vested Interests, Absentee Ownership, The Engineers and the Price System*.
[76] Publications of American Economic Association, I, 6–7.
[77] *Ibid.*, I, 24.   [78] *Ibid.*, I.

force the moral sentiment pervading any trade down to the level of that which characterizes the worst man who can maintain himself in it. So far as morals are concerned, it is the character of the worst men and not of the best men that gives color to business society.[79] An isolated man is powerless to stem the tide of prevalent custom, and in many lines of business those men whose moral sensibilities are the most blunt exercise an influence in determining custom altogether out of proportion to their importance as industrial agents.

"Suppose that of ten manufacturers nine have a keen appreciation of the evils that flow from protracted labor on the part of women and children; and, were it in their power, would gladly produce cottons without destroying family life, and without setting in motion those forces that must ultimately result in race-deterioration. But the tenth man has no such appreciations. The claims of family life, the rights of childhood, and the maintenance of social well-being are but words to him. He measures success wholly by the rate of profit and controls his business solely with a view to grand sales. If now the state stands as an unconcerned spectator, whose only duty is to put down a riot when a strike occurs (a duty which government in this country is giving up to private management), the nine men will be forced to conform to the methods adopted by the one. Their goods come into competition with his goods, and we who purchase do not inquire under what conditions they were manufactured. In this manner it is that men of the lowest character have it in their power to give the moral tone to the entire business community." [80]

Adams suggested that when the large body of competitors agree respecting some given method of procedure, but are powerless to follow it because a few men engaged in the same line of business refuse to conform to the proposed regulations, it becomes the province of the State to incorporate the wish of the majority in some practical law. In this manner there is established a legal plane of competition higher than that which could be maintained in the absence of legal enactment. "This is no curtailment of competitive action, but a determination of the manner in which it shall take place." [81]

The application of the rule of governmental non-interference, Adams argues in the second place, renders it impossible for men to realize the benefits that arise in certain lines of business from organization in the form of monopoly. "The theory of *laissez-faire* sees clearly the beneficent principle in free competition, but fails wholly to recognize a beneficent principle in monopoly." [82] And finally, the policy of restricting public powers within the narrowest possible limits tends to render government weak and inefficient; and a weak

[79] Publications of American Economic Association, I, 502.
[80] *Ibid.*, I, 505–506.
[81] *Ibid.*, I, 507–508.
[82] *Ibid.*, I, 502.

government placed in the midst of a society controlled by the commercial spirit will quickly become a corrupt government; this in its turn reacts upon commercial society by encouraging private corporations to adopt bold measures for gaining control of governmental machinery.[83]

E. A. Ross examined the social changes of industrialism from the viewpoint of the new relationship of individuals to each other. The new economic order, he found, produced an interdependence inconceivable in the days of the old individualism. The water main supersedes the well; the trolley car, the carriage; the banker's safe, the old stocking. Our own eyes and nose and judgment defer to the inspector of food, or drugs, or gas, or factories, or tenements, or insurance companies. We let the meat trust butcher our pigs, the oil trust mold our candles, the sugar trust boil our sorghum, the coal trust chop our wood. But this spread-out manner of life lays snares for the weak and opens doors to the wicked. "Interdependence puts us, as it were, at one another's mercy, and so ushers in a multitude of new forms of wrong-doing." [84] The new sin consequently is the sin against society. The new sinner is the one who takes unfair advantage of the new interdependence of individuals.

"The mob lynches the red-handed slayer, when it ought to keep a gallows Haman-high for the venal mine inspector, the seller of infected milk, the maintainer of a fire-trap theatre. The child-beater is forever blasted in reputation, but the exploiter of infant toil, or the concocter of a soothing syrup for the drugging of babies, stands a pillar of society. The petty shoplifter is more abhorred than the stealer of a franchise, and the wife-whipper is outcast long before the man who sends his over-insured ship to founder with its crew." [85]

In the realm of politics, Woodrow Wilson's *The New Freedom* [86] definitely abandoned the philosophy of governmental do-nothingism. Wilson advanced far from his hesitating, transitional stand in *The State*. His experience as governor of New Jersey gave him a realistic contact with modern economic institutions. In the old-fashioned days when life was very simple, Wilson now argued, we used to think, that all government had to do was to put on a policemen's uniform; we used to say that the ideal of government was for every man to be left alone and that the best government was the government that did as little governing as possible. But now, said Wilson, we are

[83] Publications of American Economic Association, I, 502.
[84] E. A. Ross, *Sin and Society* (Boston, Houghton Mifflin Company), pp. 3-4.
[85] *Ibid.*, pp. 15-16.   [86] Published in 1913.

coming to realize that life is so complicated that we are not dealing with the old conditions, and that the law has to step in and create new conditions under which we may live, the conditions which will make it tolerable for us to live.[87]

Above all social changes, Wilson feared the growth of trusts. These have been artificially created by the deliberate planning of men who are more powerful than their neighbors in the business world and who wish to make their power secure against competition.[88] The proper economic policy of the State, therefore, is the elimination of artificial barriers to free competition, the "hindrance of hindrances." Wilson's attack upon *laissez-faire* thus falls into that school of thought that desires the return of the old days of individual enterprise and is confident that the restoration of competition will solve our economic ills.

In surveying the new social order, Wilson found that our laws regarding the relationship of employer and employee are in many respects wholly antiquated. The employer is now generally a large corporation; the employee is one of hundreds or of thousands brought together, not by individual masters whom they knew and with whom they have personal relations, but by agents of one sort or another. Workingmen are now marshaled in great numbers for the performance of a multitude of particular tasks under a common discipline. They generally use dangerous and powerful machinery, over whose repair and renewal they have no control. New rules, Wilson insisted, must be devised with regard to their obligations and their rights. Likewise, the law must be modernized in order to equalize bargaining power. "We must not pit power against weakness." [89]

Unfair trade methods that stifle competition and permit monopoly must come under the purview of government. American industry is not free, as once it was free. The man with only a little capital, Wilson complained, is finding it harder to get into the field, and "more and more impossible to compete with the big fellow." The lines of endeavor have more and more narrowed and stiffened. The strong have crushed the weak and now dominate the economic life of the nation. Why? Because the laws of the country permit the strong to crush the weak. No one can get large amounts of credit except upon the terms of uniting his efforts with those who already control the industries of the country. "Any man who tries to set himself up in

[87] Wilson, *The New Freedom* (Garden City, N. Y., Doubleday, Doran & Company), pp. 19–20.

[88] *Ibid.*, pp. 164–165.   [89] *Ibid.*, pp. 7–8.

competition with any process of manufacture which has been taken under the control of large combinations of capital will presently find himself either squeezed out or obliged to sell and allow himself to be absorbed." [90] In the readjustments that Wilson included in his program, not one single legitimate or honest arrangement, he promised, would be disturbed; but every impediment to business would be removed and every illegitimate kind of control destroyed. "Every man who wants an opportunity and has the energy to seize it, is going to be given a chance." [91]

It is interesting to note that the second important political attack upon *laissez-faire* belonged to this same school of thought. La Follette Progressivism has been primarily concerned with the destruction of trusts. Economic freedom means opportunity for the small farmer and the man with little capital. The legal enforcement of competition will, La Follette maintained, destroy monopoly and restore individual enterprise. Formerly, the Progressive movement emphasized "trust-busting"; now it is devoting its attention to monopolistic utilities, chain stores, and chain banks.

Robert La Follette maintained that the great issue before the American people is the control of their government. In recent years, he asserted, a mighty power has grown up, so strong, so insidious, and so far-reaching in its influence that he feared lest its iron grip on government and business might never be broken. The trust, La Follette maintained, has crippled competition. It has stifled individual initiative. It has fixed limitations on production. It makes prices and imposes its burdens upon the consuming public at will. In the field of finance its power is unlimited. It gives or withholds credit. From time to time it contracts or inflates the volume of the money required for the transaction of the business of the country, regardless of everything excepting its own profits. It has acquired vast areas of the public domain, and is rapidly monopolizing the natural resources—timber, iron, coal, oil.[92]

The method of solving this vital economic problem, urged La Follette, is the dissolution of combinations in restraint of trade. He outlined specific prohibitions against well-known practices employed by trusts, as price-cutting in order to kill off a local competitor, or restraining jobbers from buying from a competitor by denying them the goods necessary to the successful conduct of their business. His

[90] Wilson, *The New Freedom*, pp. 15–16.
[91] *Ibid.*, p. 257.
[92] La Follette, *Autobiography* (Madison, Wis., R. N. La Follette Co.), pp. 762–764.

proposed remedy was the legal prohibition of these and other obviously unreasonable restraints of trade; it also placed the burden of proof on the trust to show that any restraint of trade it practices is reasonable—that is, that it benefits the community. La Follette also proposed that when the court has once entered its final decree and has declared a trust illegal, any person who has suffered damages may come in under that decree and simply petition that his damages be paid without proving anything except the amount of the damages. Finally, the Progressive attack upon the problem of business consolidation called for the establishment of a commission to investigate the facts and to prohibit all unreasonable restraints not specifically described in the law.

"This commission should have full power to ascertain the actual cost of reproduction, or physical value of the property; the reasonable value that the intangible property, such as good will, would have under conditions of fair competition, and to distinguish this from the illegal values that have been built up in violation of law. It should ascertain the values that depend on patents, monopoly of natural resources and all other forms of special privilege; the amount of property that has been paid for out of illegal profits taken from the public, distinguished from the property paid for out of legitimate profits and true investment. It should in this way ascertain the true cost of production and whether the prices charged are yielding extortionate profits or only reasonable profits that competitors could earn. These are the facts that the people must know before they will consent to any legislation that treats illegal values as though they were legal." [93]

The attack upon *laissez-faire* individualism comes from one other important source, the socialists. The best contemporary representative of this group is Norman Thomas, Socialist candidate for President in 1928 and author of a stimulating program for democracy, *America's Way Out*. Thomas analyzes the consequences of our machine civilization and indicts the planlessness and chaos of the capitalistic organization of society. When private profit is the primary test of what shall be done and what left undone, wastes inevitably result. Society suffers from the wastes of idle men, the wastes in the production of illth rather than true wealth, the wastes in lack of social planning, and the wastes in reckless exploitation of raw materials.[94] In his examination and evaluation of the present capitalistic organization of society, Thomas levies five significant charges. In the first place, the whole system is planless and chaotic; employers cannot

---

[93] La Follette, *Autobiography*, pp. 787–789.
[94] Norman Thomas, *America's Way Out* (New York, The Macmillan Company), p. 31. Thomas is here quoting from Stuart Chase's *The Tragedy of Waste*.

forecast the market for their own products or prevent recurring depressions. In the second place, shifts in the value system give wealth, without any effort on their own part, to those who are fortunate enough to get in on the ground floor; changes in wants and in industrial processes capriciously bestow vast riches on the men who are in the right spot at the right time, with corresponding losses to others. In the third place, the capitalist system rewards people in favored positions irrespective of their ability; this is true concerning the rent of land, and is almost equally true of the marginal advantage which other forms of ownership give. In the fourth place, the extraordinary disparity of income not only is unjust in itself but also is demoralizing and socially wasteful because of the emphasis that it gives to luxury and competitive spending; a false standard of values poisons society. And finally, this planless, wasteful profit system produces poverty and unemployment in the midst of potential plenty; "overproduction" results from a tragic under-consumption by the mass of workers who cannot buy back the equivalent of what they produce.[95] The earlier days of pioneering and individualism are gone; while we still talk that language, the machine has driven us to a collectivism of great mergers and standardized men. The old dogma of the economic man who knew and served his own interests, the doctrine of the survival of the fittest through competition, and the automatic, infallible, and foolproof law of supply and demand—these have been exploded.[96]

While Thomas opposes the continuation of the present capitalistic order, he attacks with equal vehemence communism as it exists in Russia. Its stopping of the economic wheels during the revolution, its demand for a long period of dictatorship, and its denial of civil liberties render communism an inadequate solution for the problems confronting us.[97] The only remaining solution is socialism. Thomas does not, however, accept in full the Marxian doctrines; he looks upon socialism not as a dogmatic creed but as a living philosophy of "coöperating in owning and managing the things necessary for our common life, a philosophy of the dignity of work and the shame of shirking, a philosophy made beautiful by the hope of plenty, peace and freedom in an interdependent world."[98]

The first and most important problem of socialism, Thomas argues, is the actual shift of property and of economic power over the necessities for our common life from private ownership and management

[95] Norman Thomas, *America's Way Out*, pp. 35–37.
[96] *Ibid.*, p. 305.
[97] *Ibid.*, Ch. 6.
[98] *Ibid.*, p. 307.

for profit to social control for use. Society must control the "key industries"—those industries and services already recognized as public utilities and others which by monopolistic nature and by their importance should be treated as public utilities. We must begin, he maintains, with those industries and services in which already the engineer is more important than the *entrepreneur;* here the demand is or may be fairly constant.[99] Next, society should control through public representation on their directorates those industries which it finds impossible or undesirable immediately to operate itself. But in the long run, the coupling of public control and private ownership is a psychological and practical impossibility.[100] To be sure, the purchase of great industries will cost money; but, Thomas argues, it will result in an immediate public saving. Society can well afford to substitute its bonds for the swelling amount of outstanding securities under private ownership. These public industries should be self-supporting and self-administering. Thomas does not propose an "omnicompetent state" which tries through elected officials to do everything; rather he proposes to set up industrial boards removed as far as possible from partisan politics.[101]

Thomas's ultimate objective is thus a socialization of industry. The nation will become a convenient trustee of society in acquiring ownership and setting up controls. However, his immediate, practical program, curiously enough, is non-socialistic. To relieve human misery, he proposes the accurate compilation of unemployment statistics, public employment agencies, long-range planning of public works, unemployment insurance as part of a comprehensive scheme of social insurance, control of the rate of the introduction of machinery to give time to plan for the absorption of displaced workers by increased demand for goods and by a decrease in the length of the working week, a rigid prohibition of child labor under sixteen, and the reëducation of older workers for other jobs when the progress of machinery and technique or the shift of demand renders them superfluous in their former trades.[102]

Although the opponents of *laissez-faire* differed in their solutions of the economic and political ills confronting the country, they agreed in many essential respects in their analyses of the existing problem of the relation of government to economic institutions. All saw the machine revolution that had changed the individual from an independent being into an interdependent cell of a complex social organ-

[99] Norman Thomas, *America's Way Out*, pp. 154–155.   [101] *Ibid.*, pp. 164–165.
[100] *Ibid.*, p. 163.   [102] *Ibid.*, p. 197.

ism; they realized that society, acting through government, must tackle these new problems. In their solutions, however, they did not agree. They ranged from individualists to socialists. Wilson and La Follette desired the aid of government in order to kill the trend toward large-scale business that destroyed individual enterprise. Lloyd, Bellamy, Ward, and Thomas, on the other hand, envisaged the growth of social and economic coöperation. The last three especially minimized the significance of competition in human progress. Regardless of their ideal of social organization, however, the individualists and the socialists looked upon government as an essential instrument for the achievement of their goals. All proposed the abandonment of *laissez-faire;* all believed in the "efficacy of effort."

VI

The changing economic order and the consequent changing rôle of the individual have had their repercussion in the field of law. Gradually judges and jurists have abandoned the nineteenth century concept of law as the absolute expression of the eternal verities. At the end of the last century, many American judges insisted—and many insist to-day—upon a legal theory of equality of rights and liberty of contract in the face of notorious social and economic facts. These absolutists lived in von Jhering's heaven of juristic conceptions, and sat before a celestial machine that brought out of each conception its 999,999 logical results. The new jurisprudence, however, is slowly but surely substituting a relativist view of law as an institution of society that must necessarily change to accommodate itself to the changes in economic institutions. Law is now being viewed as a means toward an end.

The new philosophy of law has found expression in the Supreme Court of the United States. There Justices Oliver Wendell Holmes and Louis D. Brandeis, usually speaking through the medium of dissenting opinions, have demanded the adaptation of court precedents to new economic realities. The New York Court of Appeals, through the influence of Justice Benjamin N. Cardozo, has in important instances succeeded in the modernization of law in fields where the supreme courts of the nation and of the other states have continued to speak in terms of free individuals in a free society.

Justice Holmes has bitterly attacked the application to law of Spencerian individualism. He has taken a sharp stand against the interpretation of the Fifth and Fourteenth Amendments adopted by the court. The Fourteenth Amendment, he protests, "does not enact Mr. Herbert Spencer's *Social Statics*." "The liberty of a citizen to do as he likes as long as he does not interfere with the liberty of others to do the same, which has been a shibboleth for some well-known writers, is interfered with by school laws, by the Post Office, by every State or municipal institution which takes his money for purposes thought desirable, whether he likes it or not." [103] Holmes frequently points out the dangers of "a delusive exactness in the application of the Fourteenth Amendment." By calling a business "property," he complains, we make it seem like land, and lead up to the conclusion that a statute cannot substantially cut down the advantages of ownership existing before the statute was passed. Business is a course of conduct, and like other conduct is subject to substantial modification according to time and circumstances, both in itself and in regard to what shall justify doing it a harm.

"There is nothing I more deprecate than the use of the Fourteenth Amendment beyond the absolute compulsion of its words to prevent the making of social experiments that an important part of the community desires, in the insulated chambers afforded by the several States, even though the experiments may seem futile or even noxious to me and to those whose judgment I most respect." [104]

In general, Holmes holds that the legislature, federal or state, should be permitted to prescribe for the economic and social ills of the country. The strict and literal application of the due process and contract clauses means the substitution of judicial attitudes for that of the legislature. "The criterion of constitutionality is not whether we believe the law to be for the public good." [105]

The legal philosophy of Justice Brandeis likewise takes cognizance of the fundamental revolution in social institutions. Practically every change in the law governing the relation of employer and employee, he holds, must in some respect abridge the liberty or property of one of the parties, if liberty and property be measured by the standard of the law previously prevailing. Although the change may involve interference with existing liberty or property of individuals, the court should not declare the statute a violation of the due process clause, unless it finds that the interference is arbitrary or unreasonable, or that, "considered as a means, the measure has no real or

[103] *Lochner v. N. Y.*, 198 U. S. 45, 75 (1904).
[104] *Truax v. Corrigan*, 257 U. S. 312, 342–344 (1921).
[105] *Adkins v. Children's Hospital*, 261 U. S. 525, 567, 570 (1922).

substantial relation of cause to a permissible end." Nor should the court hold such an act to be violative of the equal protection clause merely because the liberty or property of individuals in other relations to each other—as competitors in trade or as vendor and purchaser—would not, under similar circumstances, be subject to a like abridgment. "Few laws are of universal application. It is of the nature of our law that it has dealt not with man in general, but with him in relationships." Whether a law enacted in the exercise of the police power is justly subject to the charge of being unreasonable or arbitrary, Brandeis maintains, can ordinarily be determined only by a consideration of the contemporary conditions, social, industrial, and political, of the community to be affected thereby. Resort to such facts is necessary, in order to appreciate the evils sought to be remedied and the possible effects of the remedy proposed. Nearly all legislation involves a weighing of public needs as against private desires, and likewise a weighing of relative social values. Since government is not an exact science, prevailing public opinion concerning the evils and the remedy is among the important facts deserving consideration. What, at any particular time, is the paramount public need is necessarily largely a matter of judgment. Hence, in passing upon the validity of a law challenged as being unreasonable, the court may profitably derive aid from the experience of other countries and of the several states in the Union.[106]

Ernst Freund has developed in a systematic form the theory of police power. The principles of justice ordinarily are based on the common sense of right and wrong and on the faith of obligations. The public welfare, however, is determined more immediately by economic and social conditions. In order to protect the public welfare, the state prescribes rules of conduct. The characteristic methods of the police power are restraint and compulsion. The common welfare demands that the State provide for safety, order, morals, the care of dependents, and now the economic protection of the individual and the promotion of the public good.[107]

In the field of jurisprudence, the outstanding exponent of this new legal outlook is Roscoe Pound, dean of the Harvard Law School. Pound is the most severe critic of the individualistic, or "mechanical,"

---

[106] *Truax v. Corrigan*, 257 U. S. 312, 354–357 (1921). Brandeis, in his decisions, followed this procedure: he collected and presented vast amounts of factual detail concerning the evils that the statute aimed to remedy and the operation of similar laws elsewhere. A good example of this method can be found in his dissenting opinion in *Adams v. Tanner*, 244 U. S. 590, 597 (1916).
[107] *Police Power* (1904); *Standards of American Legislation* (1917).

school of jurisprudence. In the last century, he stated, men thought of law as involving a restraint on liberty which might be justified only so far as it was necessary to maintain liberty. "Hence they conceived that law was to be held down to the minimum which was required to protect the individual against aggression and to secure the harmonious coexistence of the free will of each and the free will of all." However, this, Pound holds, was only a way of stating a paramount social interest in the general security in traditional terms of individual liberty. During the last century men also strove zealously to insure complete security through absolute certainty and uniformity in judicial administration. When the eighteenth-century idea that these things might be achieved through a complete and perfect code broke down, they sought to achieve it through a method of mechanical, logical deductions from fixed legal conceptions. These attempts to frame and administer the law with an eye solely to that one social interest have broken down because of the pressure of other social interests which could not possibly be ignored.[108]

Pound looks upon law as "an attempt to reconcile, to harmonize, to compromise" the overlapping or conflicting social interests or needs of the community. Law achieves this end "either through securing them directly and immediately, or through securing certain individual interests or delimitations or compromises of individual interests, so as to give effect to the greatest number of interests or to the interests that weigh most in our civilization, with the least sacrifice of other interests." [109]

Historically, this conception of social interests has varied. Since the seventeenth century, juristic thought has sought to state all interests in terms of individual natural rights. The nineteenth century, under the influence of Hegel, wrote legal history as the unfolding in human experience of an idea of individual liberty, which was the outcome of the clash of individual free wills leading to the discovery of the invisible bounds within which each might realize a maximum of self-assertion. Thus for a season, social interests were pushed into the background. Courts were slow and cautious in taking "public policy" into account. This attitude resulted from a weighing of the social interest in the general security against other social interests which men sought to maintain.[110] However, at the end of the last and the beginning of the present century, a new way of thinking

---

[108] "A Theory of Social Interests," *Proceedings* of American Sociological Society (1920), XV, 23–27.
[109] *Ibid.*, p. 44.
[110] *Ibid.*, pp. 21–22.

developed. Jurists began to think in terms of human wants or desires rather than of human wills.

"They began to think that what they had to do was not simply to equalize or harmonize wills, but, if not to equalize, at least to harmonize the satisfaction of wants. They began to weigh or balance and reconcile claims or wants or desires, as formerly they had balanced or reconciled wills. They began to think of the end of law not as a maximum of self-assertion, but as a maximum satisfaction of wants. Hence for a time they thought of the problem of ethics, of jurisprudence, and of politics as chiefly one of valuing; as a problem of finding criteria of the relative value of interests. In jurisprudence and politics they saw that we must add practical problems of the possibility of making interests effective through governmental action, judicial or administrative. But the first question was one of the wants to be recognized—of the interests to be recognized and secured. Having inventoried the wants or claims or interests which are asserting and for which legal security is sought, we were to value them, select those to be recognized, determine the limits within which they were to be given effect in view of other recognized interests, and ascertain how far we might give them effect by law in view of the inherent limitations upon effective legal action." [111]

Pound reduces the purpose of law to the problem of eliminating friction and precluding waste in human enjoyment of the goods of existence and of the legal order. The function of the jurist is to discover and survey our wants, to perceive when and where they conflict or overlap, to observe how friction and waste result, and to study how the existing social and legal machinery may be improved or new machinery devised to obviate the friction, preclude the waste, and insure the best possible social engineering.[112]

In the support of his thesis that law necessitates the balancing of social interests, Pound inventories the various social interests of which law has taken account. First, there is the social interest in the general security—"the claim or want or demand of the social group to be secured against these forms of action and courses of conduct that threaten its existence." General safety, peace, public order, health, security of acquisitions, security of transaction—these are important forms of the general security. Second, there is the social interest in the security of social institutions—"the claim or want or demand of civilized society that its fundamental institutions be secure from those forms of action and courses of conduct which threaten their existence or impair their effective functioning." Domestic, religious, and political institutions come under this category. Third, there is the social interest in the general morality—"the claim

[111] *An Introduction to the Philosophy of Law* (Yale University Press), pp. 89-90.
[112] *Proceedings* of American Sociological Society, XV, 45.

or want or demand of society to be secured against acts or courses of conduct offensive to the moral sentiments of the general body of individuals therein for the time being." Fourth, there is the social interest in the conservation of social resources—"the claim or want or demand of society that the goods of existence shall not be wasted, that where all human wants may not be satisfied, in view of infinite individual desires and limited natural means of satisfying them, the latter be made to go as far as possible, and to that end that acts or courses of conduct which tend needlessly to impair these goods shall be restrained." Fifth, there is the social interest in general progress— "the claim or want or demand of society that the development of human powers and of human control over nature for the satisfaction of human wants go forward; the demand that social engineering be increasingly and continually improved; as it were, the self-assertion of the group toward higher and more complete development of human powers." And lastly, there is the social interest in the individual life—"the claim or want or demand of society that each individual be able to live a human life according to the standards of society; that if all individual wants may not be satisfied, they be satisfied at least so far as is reasonably possible and to the extent of a human minimum." [113] Thus, in general, two needs have determined philosophical thinking about law. On the one hand, the paramount social interest in the general security has led men to seek some fixed basis of a certain ordering of human action which should restrain magisterial as well as individual willfulness and assure a firm and stable social order. On the other hand, the pressure of less immediate social interests, and the need of reconciling them with the exigencies of the general security and of making continual new compromises because of continual changes in society, has called even for readjustment at least of the details of the social order. It has called for continuous overhauling of legal precepts and refitting them to unexpected situations. [114]

In his exposition of law as the balancing of social interests, Pound follows closely in the footsteps of the German jurist, von Jhering. [115] He considers von Jhering's work to be of enduring value for legal science. The older juristic theory of law as a means to individual liberty, and of laws as limitations upon individual wills, divorced the jurist from the actual life of to-day. On the other hand, Pound argues,

[113] *Proceedings* of American Sociological Society, XV, pp. 33–41.
[114] *An Introduction to the Philosophy of Law*, p. 18.
[115] Von Jhering, *Law as a Means to an End.*

von Jhering's concept of law as a means toward social ends requires the jurist to keep in touch with life. Under such a theory wholly abstract considerations do not suffice to justify legal rules.[116]

Pound confidently predicts that the American courts will adopt this new social philosophy of law.

"When once the current of juristic thought and judicial decision is turned into the new course our Anglo-American method of judicial empiricism has always proved adequate. Given new premises, our common law has the means of developing them to meet the exigencies of justice and of molding the results into a scientific system." [117]

Indeed, Pound points out, fundamental changes have already been taking place in our legal system almost unnoticed. The law of to-day is imposing social limitations upon the use of property.

"It is endeavoring to delimit the individual interest better with respect to social interests and to confine the legal rights to the bounds so delimited. More and more the tendency is to hold that what the law should secure is satisfaction of the owner's reasonable wants with respect to the property— that is those which consist with the like wants of his neighbors and the interests of society." [118]

Thus, to the nineteenth-century way of thinking, the dominion of a property owner was complete within the physical boundaries of his property. The end of law was then taken to be a maximum of self-assertion by each individual, limited only by the possibility of a like self-assertion by all. Present-day jurists, on the other hand, are coming more and more to regard law as a social institution existing for social ends. They now say that there is a social interest in the security of acquisitions, on which our economic order rests, and a social interest in the individual life, but that security of acquisition can be satisfied by use of property for the satisfaction of wants of the owner which are consistent with social life. The social interest does not extend to the exercise of individual faculties for anti-social purposes. Likewise, social limitations upon freedom of contract are developing. Gradually the courts have been resolving contracts between employer and employee into terms of social interests. The point of view taken is that, since all demands cannot be satisfied, we should aim to satisfy as many as we can with the least sacrifice of other demands.[119]

116 Pound, *Spirit of the Common Law* (Marshall Jones Company), p. 205.
117 *Ibid.*, pp. 184–185.
118 *Ibid.*, p. 186.
119 *Ibid.*, pp. 196–199. Pound catalogues the various points at which the courts have socialized the common law; see *Spirit of the Common Law*, pp. 196–203, or 27 *Harvard Law Review*, 195, 285.

WILLIAM GRAHAM SUMNER

After graduation fromYale University, Sumner spent three years studying in Switzerland, Germany, and England. He returned for another year of study at Yale and then entered the ministry. During his five years in the ministry, he came under the influence of Herbert Spencer's sociological writings, and decided that his real interest was in the field of social studies. In 1872 he returned to Yale as a professor of Sociology and became the leading American exponent of Spencerian philosophy. His outstanding sociological work was *Folkways* (1907). Sumner wrote numerous essays and short books on the *laissez-faire* theory of government; among these were *What Social Classes Owe to Each Other*. He attempted to be consistent in his political philosophy, and therefore sharply attacked the American protective tariff policy; this brought upon him many uncomfortable assaults from industrial groups influential at Yale.

WHAT SOCIAL CLASSES OWE TO EACH OTHER [120]

CHAPTER X

The Case of the Forgotten Man Farther Considered

There is a beautiful notion afloat in our literature and in the minds of our people that men are born to certain "natural rights." If that were true, there would be something on earth which was got for nothing, and this world would not be the place it is at all. The fact is, that there is no right whatever inherited by man which has not an equivalent and corresponding duty by the side of it, as the price of it. The rights, advantages, capital, knowledge, and all other goods which we inherit from past generations have been won by the struggles and sufferings of past generations; and the fact that the race lives, though men die, and that the race can by heredity accumulate within some cycle its victories over Nature, is one of the facts which make civilization possible. The struggles of the race as a whole produce the possessions of the race as a whole. Something for nothing is not to be found on earth.

If there were such things as natural rights, the question would arise, Against whom are they good? Who has the corresponding obligation to satisfy these rights? There can be no rights against Nature, except to get out of her whatever we can, which is only the fact of the struggle for existence stated over again. The common assertion is, that the rights are good against society; that is, that society is bound to obtain and secure them for the persons interested. Society, however, is only the persons interested plus some other persons; and as the persons interested have by the hypothesis failed to win the rights, we come to this, that natural rights are the claims which certain persons have by prerogative against some other persons. Such is the actual interpretation in practice of natural rights—claims which some people have by prerogative on other people.

This theory is a very far-reaching one, and of course it is adequate to furnish a foundation for a whole social philosophy. In its widest extension it comes to mean that if any man finds himself uncomfortable in this world, it must be somebody's else's fault, and that somebody is bound to come and make him comfortable. Now, the people who are most uncomfortable in this

[120] W. G. Sumner, *What Social Classes Owe to Each Other* (New York, Harper & Brothers, 1884), pp. 134–143. (Reprinted by permission of Mr. Graham Sumner.)

world (for if we should tell all our troubles it would not be found to be a very comfortable world for anybody) are those who have neglected their duties, and consequently have failed to get their rights. The people who can be called upon to serve the uncomfortable must be those who have done their duty, as the world goes, tolerably well. Consequently the doctrine which we are discussing turns out to be in practice only a scheme for making injustice prevail in human society by reversing the distribution of rewards and punishments between those who have done their duty and those who have not.

We are constantly preached at by our public teachers, as if respectable people were to blame because some people are not respectable—as if the man who has done his duty in his own sphere was responsible in some way for another man who has not done his duty in his sphere. There are relations of employer and employe which need to be regulated by compromise and treaty. There are sanitary precautions which need to be taken in factories and houses. There are precautions against fire which are necessary. There is care needed that children be not employed too young, and that they have an education. There is care needed that banks, insurance companies, and railroads be well managed, and that officers do not abuse their trusts. There is a duty in each case on the interested parties to defend their own interest. The penalty of neglect is suffering. The system of providing for these things by boards and inspectors throws the cost of it, not on the interested parties, but on the tax-payers. Some of them, no doubt, are the interested parties, and they may consider that they are exercising the proper care by paying taxes to support an inspector. If so, they only get their fair deserts when the railroad inspector finds out that a bridge is not safe after it is broken down, or when the bank examiner comes in to find out why a bank failed after the cashier has stolen all the funds. The real victim is the Forgotten Man again— the man who has watched his own investments, made his own machinery safe, attended to his own plumbing, and educated his own children, and who, just when he wants to enjoy the fruits of his care, is told that it is his duty to go and take care of some of his negligent neighbors, or, if he does not go, to pay an inspector to go. No doubt it is often his interest to go or to send, rather than to have the matter neglected, on account of his own connection with the thing neglected, and his own secondary peril; but the point now is, that if preaching and philosophizing can do any good in the premises, it is all wrong to preach to the Forgotten Man that it is his duty to go and remedy other people's neglect. It is not his duty. It is a harsh and unjust burden which is laid upon him, and it is only the more unjust because no one thinks of him when laying the burden so that it falls on him. The exhortations ought to be expended on the negligent—that they take care of themselves.

It is an especially vicious extension of the false doctrine above mentioned that criminals have some sort of a right against or claim on society. Many reformatory plans are based on a doctrine of this kind when they are urged upon the public conscience. A criminal is a man who, instead of working with and for the society, has turned against it, and become destructive and injurious. His punishment means that society rules him out of its membership, and separates him from its association, by execution or imprisonment, according to the gravity of his offence. He has no claims against society at all. What shall be done with him is a question of expediency to be settled in view of the interests of society—that is, of the non-criminals. The French writers of the school of '48 used to represent the badness of the bad men as the fault of "society." As the object of this statement was to show that the badness of the bad men was not the fault of the bad men, and as society contains only good men and bad men, it followed that the badness of the bad men was the fault of the good men. On that theory, of course the good men owed a great deal to the bad men who were in prison and at the galleys on their account. If we do not admit that theory, it behooves us to remember that any claim which we allow to the criminal against the "State" is only so much burden laid upon those who have never cost the State anything for discipline or correction. The punishments of society are just like those of God and Nature—they are warnings to the wrong-doer to reform himself.

When public offices are to be filled numerous candidates at once appear. Some are urged on the ground that they are poor, or cannot earn a living, or want support while getting an education, or have female relatives dependent on them, or are in poor health, or belong to a particular district, or are related to certain persons, or have done meritorious service in some other line of work than that which they apply to do. The abuses of the public service are to be condemned on account of the harm to the public interest, but there is an incidental injustice of the same general character with that which we are discussing. If an office is granted by favoritism or for any personal reason to A, it cannot be given to B. If an office is filled by a person who is unfit for it, he always keeps out somebody somewhere who is fit for it; that is, the social injustice has a victim in an unknown person—the Forgotten Man— and he is some person who has no political influence, and who has known no way in which to secure the chances of life except to deserve them. He is passed by for the noisy, pushing, importunate, and incompetent.

I have said something disparagingly in a previous chapter about the popular rage against combined capital, corporations, corners, selling futures, etc., etc. The popular rage is not without reason, but it is sadly misdirected, and the real things which deserve attack are thriving all the time. The greatest social evil with which we have to contend is jobbery. Whatever there is in legislative charters, watering stocks, etc., etc., which is objectionable, comes under the head of jobbery. Jobbery is any scheme which aims to gain, not by the legitimate fruits of industry and enterprise, but by extorting from somebody a part of his product under guise of some pretended industrial undertaking. Of course it is only a modification when the undertaking in question has some legitimate character, but the occasion is used to graft upon it devices for obtaining what has not been earned. Jobbery is the vice of plutocracy, and it is the especial form under which plutocracy corrupts a democratic and republican form of government. The United States is deeply afflicted with it, and the problem of civil liberty here is to conquer it. It affects everything which we really need to have done to such an extent that we have to do without public objects which we need through fear of jobbery. Our public buildings are jobs—not always, but often. They are not needed, or are costly beyond all necessity or even decent luxury. Internal improvements are jobs. They are not made because they are needed to meet needs which have been experienced. They are made to serve private ends, often incidentally the political interests of the persons who vote the appropriations. Pensions have become jobs. In England pensions used to be given to aristocrats, because aristocrats had political influence, in order to corrupt them. Here pensions are given to the great democratic mass, because they have political power, to corrupt them. Instead of going out where there is plenty of land and making a farm there, some people go down under the Mississippi River to make a farm, and then they want to tax all the people in the United States to make dikes to keep the river off their farms. The California gold-miners have washed out gold, and have washed the dirt down into the rivers and on the farms below. They want the Federal Government to now clean out the rivers and restore the farms. The silver-miners found their product declining in value, and they got the Federal Government to go into the market and buy what the public did not want, in order to sustain (as they hoped) the price of silver. The Federal Government is called upon to buy or hire unsalable ships, to build canals which will not pay, to furnish capital for all sorts of experiments, and to provide capital for enterprises of which private individuals will win the profits. All this is called "developing our resources," but it is, in truth, the great plan of all living on each other. . . .

ADKINS v. CHILDREN'S HOSPITAL [121]

In 1918 Congress passed a minimum wage act for the District of Columbia. This statute created a minimum wage board and authorized it to investigate the wages of women and minors and, in the case of women, to determine what wages were necessary to supply the necessary cost of living in order to maintain them in good health and to protect their morals. The board was authorized to fix minimum standards of wage payments and to prohibit employers in the District of Columbia to pay less than the rates set by the board. The Children's Hospital brought action to restrain the board from enforcing its orders concerning female wages. An unemployed female worker also petitioned the court for a restraining order, on the ground that the enforcement of the act had caused her to lose her job. Justice Sutherland, writing the majority opinion, declared the act unconstitutional as contrary to the due process clause of the Fifth Amendment. This case is typical of the attitude frequently taken by the United States Supreme Court on questions that involve a conflict between property rights and social welfare.

SUTHERLAND, J.

. . . .

The statute now under consideration is attacked upon the ground that it authorized an unconstitutional interference with the freedom of contract included within the guaranties of the due process clause of the Fifth Amendment. That the right to contract about one's affairs is a part of the liberty of the individual protected by this clause, is settled by the decisions of this Court and is no longer open to question. . . . Within this liberty are contracts of employment of labor. In making such contracts, generally speaking, the parties have an equal right to obtain from each other the best terms they can as the result of private bargaining.

[121] 261 U. S. 525, 545–546, 554–562 (1923).

In *Adair v. United States, supra,* Mr. Justice Harlan (pp. 174, 175), speaking for the Court, said:

"The right of a person to sell his labor upon such terms as he deems proper is, in its essence, the same as the right of the purchaser to prescribe the conditions upon which we will accept such labor from the person offering to sell. . . . In all such particulars the employer and employe have equality of right, and any legislation that disturbs that equality is an arbitrary interference with the liberty of contract which no government can legally justify in a free land."

In *Coppage v. Kansas, supra* (p. 14), this Court, speaking through Mr. Justice Pitney, said:

"Included in the right of personal liberty and the right of private property —partaking of the nature of each—is the right to make contracts for acquisition of property. Chief among such contracts is that of personal employment, by which labor and other services are exchanged for money or other forms of property. If this right be struck down or arbitrarily interfered with there is a substantial impairment of liberty in the long established constitutional sense. The right is as essential to the laborer as to the capitalist, to the poor as to the rich; for the vast majority of persons have no other honest way to begin to acquire property, save by working for money.

"An interference with this liberty so serious as that now under consideration, and so disturbing of equality of right, must be deemed to be arbitrary, unless it be supportable as a reasonable exercise of the police power of the State."

There is, of course, no such thing as absolute freedom of contract. It is subject to a great variety of restraints. But freedom of contract is, nevertheless, the general rule and restraint the exception; and the exercise of legislative authority to abridge it can be justified only by the existence of exceptional circumstances. Whether these circumstances exist in the present case constitutes the question to be answered. It will be helpful to this end to review some of the decisions where the interference has been upheld and consider the grounds upon which they rest. . . .

If, now, in the light furnished by the foregoing exceptions to the general rule forbidding legislative interference with freedom of contract, we examine and analyze the statute in question, we shall see that it differs from them in every material respect. It is not a law dealing with any business charged with a public interest, or with public work, or to meet and tide over a temporary emergency. It has nothing to do with the character, method or periods of wage payments. It does not prescribe hours of labor or conditions under which labor is to be done. It is not for the protection of persons under legal disability or for the prevention of fraud. It is simply and exclusively a price-fixing law, confined to adult women (for we are not now considering the provisions relating to minors), who are legally as capable of contracting for themselves as men. It forbids two parties having lawful capacity—under penalties as to the employer—to freely contract with one another in respect of the price for which one shall render service to the other in a purely private employment where both are willing, perhaps anxious, to agree, even though the consequence may be to oblige one to surrender a desirable engagement and the other to dispense with the services of a desirable employee. The price fixed by the board need have no relation to the capacity or earning power of the employee, the number of hours which may happen to constitute the day's work, the character of the place where the work is to be done, or the circumstances or surroundings of the employment; and, while it has no other basis to support its validity than the assumed necessities of the employee, it takes no account of any independent resources she may have. It is based wholly on the opinions of the members of the board and their advisers—perhaps an average of their opinions, if they do not precisely agree—as to what will be necessary to provide a living for a woman, keep her in health and preserve her morals. It applies to any and every occupation in the District, without regard to its nature or the character of the work.

The standard furnished by the statute for the guidance of the board is so vague as to be impossible of practical application with any reasonable degree of accuracy. What is sufficient to supply the necessary cost of living for a woman worker and maintain her in good health and protect her morals is obviously not a precise or unvarying sum—not even approximately so. The amount will depend upon a variety of circumstances: the individual temperament, habits of thrift, care, ability to buy necessaries intelligently, and whether the woman live alone or with her family. Those who practice economies of the family group are not taken into account though they constitute an important consideration in estimating the cost of living, for it is obvious that the individual expense will be less in the case of a member of a family than in the case of one living alone. The relation between earnings and morals is not capable of standardization. It cannot be shown that well paid women safeguard their morals more carefully than those who are poorly paid. Morality rests upon other considerations than wages; and there is, certainly, no such prevalent connection between the two as to justify a broad attempt to adjust the latter with reference to the former. As a means of safeguarding morals the attempted classification, in our opinion, is without reasonable basis. No distinction can be made between women who work for others and those who do not; nor is there ground for distinction between women and men, for certainly, if women require a minimum wage to preserve their morals men require it to preserve their honesty. For these reasons, and others which might be stated, the inquiry in respect of the necessary cost of living and of the income necessary to preserve health and morals, presents an individual and not a composite question, and must be answered for each individual considered by herself and not by a general formula prescribed by a statutory bureau.

This uncertainty of the statutory standard is demonstrated by a consideration of certain orders of the board already made. These orders fix the sum to be paid to a woman employed in a place where food is served or in a mercantile establishment, at $16.50 per week; in a printing establishment, at $15.50 per week; and in a laundry, at $15 per week, with a provision reducing this to $9 in the case of a beginner. If a woman employed to serve food requires a minimum of $16.50 per week, it is hard to understand how the same woman working in a printing establishment or in a laundry is to get on with an income lessened by from $1 to $7.50 per week. The board probably found it impossible to follow the indefinite standard of the statute, and brought other and different factors into the problem; and this goes far in the direction of demonstrating the fatal uncertainty of the act, an infirmity which, in our opinion, plainly exists.

This law takes account of the necessities of only one party to the contract. It ignores the necessities of the employer by compelling him to pay not less than a certain sum, not only whether the employee is capable of earning it, but irrespective of the ability of his business to sustain the burden, generously leaving him, of course, the privilege of abandoning his business as an alternative for going on at a loss. Within the limits of the minimum sun, he is precluded, under penalty of fine and imprisonment, from adjusting compensation to the differing merits of his employees. It compels him to pay at least the sum fixed in any event, because the employee needs it, but requires no service of equivalent value from the employee. It therefore undertakes to solve but one-half of the problem. The other half is the establishment of a corresponding standard of efficiency, and this forms no part of the policy of the legislation, although in practice the former half without the latter must lead to ultimate failure, in accordance with the inexorable law that no one can continue indefinitely to take out more than he puts in without ultimately exhausting the supply. The law is not confined to the great and powerful employers but embraces those whose bargaining power may be as weak as that of the employee. It takes no account of periods of stress and business depression, of crippling losses, which may leave the employer himself without adequate means of livelihood. To the extent that the sum fixed exceeds the fair value of the services rendered, it amounts to a compulsory exaction from the employer for the support of a partially indigent person, for whose condition there rests upon him no peculiar responsibility, and therefore, in effect, arbitrarily shifts to his shoulders a burden which, if it belongs to anybody, belongs to society as a whole.

The feature of this statute which, perhaps more than any other, puts upon it the stamp of invalidity is that it exacts from the employer an arbitrary payment for a purpose and upon a basis having no causal connection with his business, or the contract or the work the employee engages to do. The declared basis, as already pointed out, is not the value of the service rendered, but the extraneous circumstance that the employee needs to get a prescribed sum of money to insure her subsistence, health and morals. The ethical right of every worker, man or woman, to a living wage may be conceded. One of the declared and important purposes of trade organizations is to secure it. And with that principle and with every legitimate effort to realize it in fact, no one can quarrel; but the fallacy of the proposed method of attaining it is that it assumes that every employer is bound at all events to furnish it. The moral requirement implicit in every contract of employment, viz., that the amount to be paid and the service to be rendered shall bear to each other some relation of just equivalence, is completely ignored. The necessities of the employee are alone considered and these arise outside of the employment, are the same when there is no employment, and as great in one occupation as in another. Certainly the employer by paying a fair equivalent for the service rendered, though not sufficient to support the employee, has neither caused nor contributed to her poverty. On the contrary, to the extent of what he pays he has relieved it. In principle, there can be no difference between the case of selling labor and the case of selling goods.

If one goes to the butcher, the baker or grocer to buy food, he is morally entitled to obtain the worth of his money but he is not entitled to more. If what he gets is worth what he pays he is not justified in demanding more simply because he needs more; and the shopkeeper, having dealt fairly and honestly in that transaction, is not concerned in any peculiar sense with the question of his customer's necessities. Should a statute undertake to vest in a commission power to determine the quantity of food necessary for individual support and require the shopkeeper, if he sell to the individual at all, to furnish that quantity at not more than a fixed maximum, it would undoubtedly fall before the constitutional test. The fallacy of any argument in support of the validity of such a statute would be quickly exposed. The argument in support of that now being considered is equally fallacious, though the weakness of it may not be so plain. A statute requiring an employer to pay in money, to pay at prescribed and regular intervals, to pay the value of the services rendered, even to pay with fair relation to the extent of the benefit obtained from the service, would be understandable. But a statute which prescribes payment without regard to any of these things and solely with relation to circumstances apart from the contract of employment, the business affected by it and the work done under it, is so clearly the product of a naked, arbitrary exercise of power that it cannot be allowed to stand under the Constitution of the United States.

We are asked, upon the one hand, to consider the fact that several States have adopted similar statutes, and we are invited, upon the other hand, to give weight to the fact that three times as many States, presumably as well informed and as anxious to promote the health and morals of their people, have refrained from enacting such legislation. We have also been furnished with a large number of printed opinions approving the policy of the minimum wage, and our own reading has disclosed a large number to the contrary. These are all proper enough for the consideration of the lawmaking bodies, since their tendency is to establish the desirability or undesirability of the legislation; but they reflect no legitimate light upon the question of its validity, and that is what we are called upon to decide. The elucidation of that question cannot be aided by counting heads.

It is said that great benefits have resulted from the operation of such statutes, not alone in the District of Columbia but in the several States, where they have been in force. A mass of reports, opinions of special observers and students of the subject, and the like, has been brought before us in support of this statement, all of which we have found interesting but only mildly persuasive. That the earnings of women now are greater than they were formerly and that conditions affecting women have become better in other respects may be conceded, but convincing indications of the logical relation of these desirable changes to the law in question are significantly lacking. They may be, and quite probably are, due to other causes. We cannot close our eyes to the notorious fact that earnings everywhere in all occupations have greatly increased—not alone in States where the minimum wage law obtains but in the country generally—quite as much or more among men as among women and in occupations outside the reach of the law as in those governed by it. No real test of the economic value of the law can be had during periods of maximum employment, when general causes keep wages up to or above the minimum; that will come in periods of depression and struggle for employment when the efficient will be employed at the minimum rate while the less capable may not be employed at all.

Finally, it may be said that if, in the interest of the public welfare, the police power may be invoked to justify the fixing of a minimum wage, it may, when the public welfare is thought to require it, be invoked to justify a maximum wage. The power to fix high wages connotes, by like course of reasoning, the power to fix low wages. If, in the face of the guaranties of the Fifth Amendment, this form of legislation shall be legally justified, the field for the operation of the police power will have been widened to a great and dangerous degree. If, for example, in the opinion of future lawmakers, wages in the building trades shall become so high as to preclude people of ordinary means from building and owning homes, an authority which sustains the minimum wage will be invoked to support a maximum wage for building laborers and artisans, and the same argument which has been here urged to strip the employer of his constitutional liberty of contract in one direction will be utilized to strip the employee of his constitutional liberty of contract in the opposite direction. A wrong decision does not end with itself: it is a precedent, and, with the swing of sentiment, its bad influence may run from one extremity of the arc to the other.

It has been said that legislation of the kind now under review is required in the interest of social justice, for whose ends freedom of contract may lawfully be subjected to restraint. The liberty of the individual to do as he pleases, even in innocent matters, is not absolute. It must frequently yield to the common good, and the line beyond which the power of interference may not be pressed is neither definite nor unalterable but may be made to move, within limits not well defined, with changing need and circumstance. Any attempt to fix a rigid boundary would be unwise as well as futile. But, nevertheless, there are limits to the power, and when these have been passed, it becomes the plain duty of the court in the proper exercise of their authority to so declare. To sustain the individual freedom of action contemplated by the Constitution, is not to strike down the common good but to exalt it; for surely the good of society as a whole cannot be better served than by the preservation against arbitrary restraint of the liberties of its constituent members.

It follows from what has been said that the act in question passes the limit prescribed by the Constitution, and, accordingly, the decrees of the court below are

Affirmed.

HENRY DEMAREST LLOYD

By profession, Lloyd was a journalist. He early became interested in economic problems and wrote a number of articles on monopolies and their threat to American institutions. He covered the important labor strikes of the eighties and nineties for newspapers and periodicals. His interest was so aroused that he lectured on behalf of the working class and helped to organize labor. His *Wealth against Commonwealth* (1894) is his description of how trusts develop and function and operate against the well-being of the common man. His concern for labor induced him to travel abroad and study new labor movements. In 1897 he went to Europe to get facts about the coöperative movements there; his *Labor Copartnership* (1898) presented his findings. In 1899 he visited New Zealand and wrote *A Country Without Strikes* (1900). This last book was influential in the American movement for industrial arbitration.

WEALTH AGAINST COMMONWEALTH [122]

CHAPTER I

"There are None"—"They are Legion"

Nature is rich; but everywhere man, the heir of nature, is poor. Never in this happy country or elsewhere—except in the Land of Miracle, where "they did all eat and were filled"—has there been enough of anything for the people. Never since time began have all the sons and daughters of men been all warm, and all filled, and all shod and roofed. Never yet have all the virgins, wise or foolish, been able to fill their lamps with oil.

The world, enriched by thousands of generations of toilers and thinkers, has reached a fertility which can give every human being a plenty undreamed of even in the Utopias. But between this plenty ripening on the boughs of our civilization and the people hungering for it step the "cornerers," the syndicates, trusts, combinations, with the cry of "overproduction"—too much of everything. Holding back the riches of earth, sea, and sky from their fellows who famish and freeze in the dark, they declare to them that there is too much light and warmth and food. They assert the right, for their private profit, to regulate the consumption by the people of the necessaries of life, and to control production, not by the needs of humanity, but by the desires of a few for dividends. The coal syndicate thinks there is too much coal. There is too much iron, too much lumber, too much flour—for this or that syndicate.

The majority have never been able to buy enough of anything; but this minority have too much of everything to sell.

Liberty produces wealth, and wealth destroys liberty. "The splendid empire of Charles V," says Motley, "was erected upon the grave of liberty." Our bignesses—cities, factories, monopolies, fortunes, which are our empires, are the obesities of an age gluttonous beyond its powers of digestion. Mankind are crowding upon each other in the centers, and struggling to keep each other out of the feast set by the new sciences and the new fellowships. Our size has got beyond both our science and our conscience. The vision of the railroad stock-holder is not far-sighted enough to see into the office of the General Manager; the people cannot reach across even a ward of a city to rule their rulers; Captains of Industry "do not know" whether the men in the ranks are dying from lack of food and shelter; we cannot clean our cities nor our politics; the locomotive has more man-power than all the ballot-boxes, and mill-wheels wear out the hearts of workers unable to keep up beating time to their whirl. If mankind had gone on pursuing the ideals of the fighter, the time would necessarily have come when there would have been only a few, then only one, and then none left. This is what we are witnessing in the world of livelihoods. Our ideals of livelihood are ideals of mutual deglutition. We are rapidly reaching the stage where in each province

[122] Henry D. Lloyd, *Wealth Against Commonwealth* (New York, Harper & Brothers, 1898), pp. 1–7, 516–521. (Reprinted by permission of Mr. William Bross Lloyd.)

only a few are left; that is the key to our times. Beyond the deep is another deep. This era is but a passing phase in the evolution of industrial Cæsars, and there Cæsars will be of a new type—corporate Cæsars.

For those who like the perpetual motion of a debate in which neither of the disputants is looking at the same side of the shield, there are infinite satisfactions in the current controversy as to whether there is any such thing as "monopoly." "There are none," says one side. "They are legion," says the other. "The idea that there can be such a thing is absurd," says one, who with half a dozen associates controls the source, the price, the quality, the quantity of nine-tenths of a great necessity of life. But "There will soon be a trust for every production, and a master to fix the price for every necessity of life," said the Senator who framed the United States Anti-Trust Law. This difference as to facts is due to a difference in the definitions through which the facts are regarded. Those who say "there are none" hold with the Attorney-General of the United States and the decision he quotes from the highest Federal court which had then passed on this question that no one has a monopoly unless there is a "disability" or "restriction" imposed by law on all who would compete. A syndicate that had succeeded in bottling for sale all the air of the earth would not have a monopoly in this view, unless there were on the statute-books a law forbidding every one else from selling air. No others could get air to sell; the people could not get air to breathe, but there would be no monopoly because there is no "legal restriction" on breathing or selling the atmosphere.

Excepting in the manufacture of postage-stamps, gold dollars, and a few other such cases of a "legal restriction," there are no monopolies according to this definition. It excludes the whole body of facts which the people include in their definition, and dismisses a great public question by a mere play on words. The other side of the shield was described by Judge Barrett, of the Supreme Court of New York. A monopoly he declared to be "any combination the tendency of which is to prevent competition in its broad and general sense, and to control and thus at will enhance prices to the detriment of the public. . . . Nor need it be permanent or complete. It is enough that it may be even temporarily and partially successful. The question in the end is, Does it inevitably tend to public injury?"

Those who insist that "there are none" are the fortunate ones who came up to the shield on its golden side. But common usage agrees with the language of Judge Barrett, because it exactly fits a fact which presses on common people heavily, and will grow heavier before it grows lighter.

The committee of Congress investigating trusts in 1889 did not report any list of these combinations to control markets, "for the reason that new ones are constantly forming, and that old ones are constantly extending their relations so as to cover new branches of the business and invade new territories."

It is true that such a list, like a dictionary, would begin to be wrong the moment it began to appear. But though only an instantaneous photograph of the whirlwind, it would give an idea, to be gained in no other way, of a movement shadowing two hemispheres. In an incredible number of the necessaries and luxuries of life, from meat to tombstones, some inner circle of the "fittest" has sought, and very often obtained, the sweet power which

Judge Barrett found the sugar trust had. It "can close every refinery at will, close some and open others, limit the purchases of raw material (thus jeopardizing, and in a considerable degree controlling, its production), artificially limit the production of refined sugar, enhance the price to enrich themselves and their associates at the public expense, and depress the price when necessary to crush out and impoverish a foolhardy rival."

Corners are "acute" attacks of that which combinations exhibit as chronic. First a corner, then a pool, then a trust, has often been the genesis. The last stage, when the trust throws off the forms of combination and returns to the simpler dress of corporations, is already well along. Some of the "sympathetical co-operations" on record have no doubt ceased to exist. But that they should have been attempted is one of the signs of the time, and these attempts are repeated again and again until success is reached.

The line of development is from local to national, and from national to international. The amount of capital changes continually with the recrystallizations in progress. Not less than five hundred million dollars is in the coal combination, which our evidence shows to have flourished twenty-two years; that in oil has nearly if not quite two hundred millions; and the other combinations in which its members are leaders foot up hundreds of millions more. Hundreds of millions of dollars are united in the railroads and elevators of the Northwest against the wheat-growers. In cattle and meat there are not less than one hundred millions; in whiskey, thirty-five millions; and in beer a great deal more than that; in sugar, seventy-five millions; in leather, over a hundred millions; in gas, hundreds of millions. At this writing a union is being negotiated of all the piano-makers in the United States, to have a capital of fifty millions. Quite beyond ordinary comprehension is the magnitude of the syndicates, if there is more than one, which are going from city to city, consolidating all the gas-works, electric-lighting companies, street-railways in each into single properties, and consolidating these into vast estates for central corporations of capitalists, controlling from metropolitan offices the transportation of the people of scores of cities. Such a syndicate negotiating in December, 1892, for the control of the street-railways of Brooklyn, was said by the New York *Times*, "on absolute authority, to have subscribed $23,000,000 towards that end, before a single move had been made or a price set on a single share of stock." It was in the same hands as those busy later in gathering together the coal-mines of Nova Scotia and putting them under American control. There are in round numbers ten thousand millions of dollars claiming dividends and interest in the railroads of the United States. Every year they are more closely pooled. The public saw them marshalled, as by one hand, in the maintenance of the high passenger rates to the World's Fair in the summer of 1893. Many rates are higher than thirty years ago.

Many thousands of millions of dollars are represented in these centralizations. It is a vast sum, and yet is but a minority of our wealth.

Laws against these combinations have been passed by Congress and by many of the States. There have been prosecutions under them by the State and Federal governments. The laws and the lawsuits have alike been futile.

In a few cases names and form of organization have been changed, in consequence of legal pursuit. The whiskey, sugar, and oil trusts had to hang out new signs. But the thing itself, the will and the power to control markets, livelihoods, and liberties, and the toleration of this by the public—this remains unimpaired; in truth, facilitated by the greater secrecy and compactness which have been the only results of the appeal to law.

The Attorney-General of the national government gives a large part of his annual report for 1893 to showing "what small basis there is for the popular impression" "that the aim and effect of this statute" (the Anti-Trust Law) "are to prohibit and prevent those aggregations of capital which are so common at the present day, and which sometimes are on so large a scale as to practically control all the branches of an extensive industry." This executive says of the actions of the "co-ordinate" Legislature: "It would not be useful, even if it were possible, to ascertain the precise purposes of the framers of the statute." He is the officer charged with the duty of directing the prosecutions to enforce the law; but he declares that since, among other reasons, "all ownership of property is a monopoly, . . . any literal application of the provisions of the statute is out of the question." Nothing has been accomplished by all these appeals to the legislature and the courts, except to prove that the evil lies deeper than any public sentiment or public intelligence yet existent, and is stronger than any public power yet at call.

What we call Monopoly is Business at the end of its journey. The concentration of wealth, the wiping out of the middle classes, are other names for it. To get it is, in the world of affairs, the chief end of man.

There are no solitary truths, Goethe says, and monopoly—as the greatest business fact of our civilization, which gives to business what other ages gave to war and religion—is our greatest social, political, and moral fact.

The men and women who do the work of the world have the right to the floor. Everywhere they are rising to "a point of information." They want to know how our labor and the gifts of nature are being ordered by those whom our ideals and consent have made Captains of Industry over us; how it is that we, who profess the religion of the Golden Rule and the political economy of service for service, come to divide our produce into incalculable power and pleasure for a few, and partial existence for the many who are the fountains of these powers and pleasures. This book is an attempt to help people answer these questions. It has been quarried out of official records, and it is a venture in realism in the world of realities. Decisions of courts and of special tribunals like the Interstate Commerce Commission, verdicts of juries in civil and criminal cases, reports of committees of the State Legislatures and of Congress, oath-sworn testimony given in legal proceedings and in official inquiries, corrected by rebutting testimony and by cross-examination—such are the sources of information.

. . . . . .

CHAPTER XXXV

The New Self-Interest

We have given the prize of power to the strong, the cunning, the arithmetical, and we must expect nothing else but that they will use it cunningly and arithmetically. For what else can they suppose we gave it to them? If the power really flows from the people, and should be used for them; if its best administration can be got, as in government, only by the participation in it of men of all views and interests; if in the collision of all these, as in democracy, the better policy is progressively preponderant; if this is a policy which, with whatever defects, is better than that which can be evolved by narrower or more selfish or less multitudinous influences of persons or classes, then this power should be taken up by the people. "The mere conflict of private interests will never produce a well-ordered commonwealth of labor," says the author of the article on political economy in the *Encyclopædia Britannica*. The failure of monarchy and feudalism and the visibly impending failure of our business system all reveal a law of nature. The harmony of things insists that that which is the source of power, wealth, and delight shall also be the ruler of it. That which is must also seem. It is the people from whom come the forces with which kings and millionaires ride the world, and until the people take their proper place in the seat of sovereignty, these pseudo owners—mere claimants and usurpers—will, by the very falsity and iniquity of their position, be pushed into deceit, tyranny, and cruelty, ending in downfall.

Thousands of years' experience has proved that government must begin where it ends—with the people; that the general welfare demands that they who exercise the powers and they upon whom these are exercised must be the same, and that higher political ideals can be realized only through higher political forms. Myriads of experiments to get the substance of liberty out of the forms of tyranny, to believe in princes, to trust good men to do good as kings, have taught the inexorable truth that, in the economy of nature, form and substance must move together, and are as inextricably interdependent as are, within our experience, what we call matter and spirit. Identical is the lesson we are learning with regard to industrial power and property. We are calling upon their owners, as mankind called upon kings in their day, to be good and kind, wise and sweet, and we are calling in vain. We are asking them not to be what we have made them to be. We put power into their hands and ask them not to use it as power. If the spirit of power is to change, institutions must change as much. Liberty recast the old forms of government into the Republic, and it must remould our institutions of wealth into the Commonwealth.

The question is not whether monopoly is to continue. The sun sets every night on a greater majority against it. We are face to face with the practical issue: Is it to go through ruin or reform? Can we forestall ruin by reform? If we wait to be forced by events we shall be astounded to find how much more radical they are than our utopias. Louis XVI waited until 1793, and gave his head and all his investitures to the people who in 1789 asked only to sit at his feet and speak their mind. Unless we reform of our own free will, nature will reform us by force, as nature does. Our evil courses have already gone too far in producing misery, plagues, hatreds, national enervation. Already the leader is unable to lead, and has begun to drive with judges armed with bayonets and Gatling guns. History is the serial obituary of the men who thought they could drive men.

Reform is the science and conscience with which mankind in its manhood overcomes temptations and escapes consequences by killing the germs. Ruin is already hard at work among us. Our libraries are full of the official inquiries and scientific interpretations which show how our master-motive is working decay in all our parts. The family crumbles into a competition between the father and the children whom he breeds to take his place in the factory, to unfit themselves to be fathers in their turn. A thorough, stalwart resimplification, a life governed by simple needs and loves, is the imperative want of the world. It will be accomplished: either self-conscious volition does it, or the slow wreck and decay of superfluous and unwholesome men and matters. The latter is the method of brutes and brute civilizations. The other is the method of man, so far as he is divine. Has not man, who has in personal reform risen above the brute method, come to the height at which he can achieve social reform in masses and by nations? We must learn; we can learn by reason. Why wait for the crueler teacher?

We have a people like which none has ever existed before. We have millions capable of conscious co-operation. The time must come in social evolution when the people can organize the free-will to choose salvation which the individual has been cultivating for 1900 years, and can adopt a policy more dignified and more effective than leaving themselves to be kicked along the path of reform by the recoil of their own vices. We must bring the size of our morality up to the size of our cities, corporations, and combinations, or these will be brought down to fit our half-grown virtue.

Industry and monopoly cannot live together. Our modern perfection of exchange and division of labor cannot last without equal perfection of morals and sympathy. Every one is living at the mercy of every one else in a way entirely peculiar to our times. Nothing is any longer made by a man; parts of things are made by parts of men, and become wholes by the luck of a good-humor which so far keeps men from flying asunder. It takes a whole company to make a match. A hundred men will easily produce a hundred million matches, but not one of them could make one match. No farm gets its plough from the cross-roads blacksmith, and no one in the chilled-steel factory knows the whole of the plough. The life of Boston hangs on a procession of reciprocities which must move, as steadily and sweetly as the roll of the planets, between its bakeries, the Falls of St. Anthony, and the valley of the Red River. Never was there a social machinery so delicate. Only on terms of love and justice can men endure contact so close.

The break-down of all other civilizations has been a slow decay. It took the Northerners hundreds of years to march to the Tiber. They grew their way through the old society as the tree planting itself on a grave is found to have sent its roots along every fibre and muscle of the dead. Our world is not the simple thing theirs was, of little groups sufficient to themselves, if need be. New York would begin to die to-morrow if it were not for Illinois and Dakota. We cannot afford a revulsion in the hearts by whose union locomotives run, mills grind, factories make. Practical men are speculating to-day on the possibility that our civilization may some afternoon be flashed away by the tick of a telegraph. All these co-operations can be scattered by a word of hate too many, and be left, with no one who knows how to make a plough or a match, a civilization cut off as by the Roman curse from food and fire. Less sensitive civilizations than ours have burst apart.

Liberty and monopoly cannot live together. What chance have we against the persistent coming and the easy coalescence of the confederated cliques, which aspire to say of all business, "This belongs to us," and whose members, though moving among us as brothers, are using against us, through the corporate forms we have given them, powers of invisibility, of entail and accumulation, unprecedented because impersonal and immortal, and, most peculiar of all, power to act as persons, as in the commission of crimes, with exemption from punishment as persons? Two classes study and practise politics and government: place hunters and privilege hunters. In a world of relativities like ours, size of area has a great deal to do with the truth of principles. America has grown so big—and the tickets to be voted, and the powers of government, and the duties of citizens, and the profits of personal use of public functions have all grown so big—that the average citizen has broken down. No man can half understand or half operate the fulness of this big citizenship, except by giving his whole time to it. This the place hunter can do, and the privilege hunter. Government, therefore—municipal, State, national—is passing into the hands of these two classes, especialized for the functions of power by their appetite for the fruits of power. The power of citizenship is relinquished by those who do not and cannot know how to exercise it to those who can and do—by those who have a livelihood to make to those who make politics their livelihood.

These specialists of the ward club, the primary, the campaign, the election, and office unite, by a law as irresistible as that of the sexes, with those who want all the goods of government—charters, contracts, rulings, permits. From this marriage it is easy to imagine that among some other people than ourselves, and in some other century than this, the off-spring might be the most formidable, elusive, unrestrained, impersonal, and cruel tyranny the world has yet seen. There might come a time when the policeman and the railroad president would equally show that they cared nothing for the citizen, individually or collectively, because aware that they and not he were the government. Certainly such an attempt to corner "the dear people" and the earth and the fulness thereof will break down. It is for us to decide whether we will let it go on till it breaks down of itself, dragging down to die, as a savage dies of his vice, the civilization it has gripped with its hundred hands; or whether, while we are still young, still virtuous, we will break it down, self-consciously, as the civilized man, reforming, crushes down the evil. If we cannot find a remedy, all that we love in the word America must die. It will be an awful price to pay if this attempt at government of the people, by the people, for the people must perish from off the face of the earth to prove to mankind that political brotherhood cannot survive where industrial brotherhood is denied. But the demonstration is worth even that.

Aristotle's lost books of the Republics told the story of two hundred and fifty attempts at free government, and these were but some of the many that had to be melted down in the crucible of fate to teach Hamilton and Jefferson what they knew. Perhaps we must be melted by the same fierce flames to be a light to the feet of those who come after us. For as true as that a house divided against itself cannot stand, and that a nation half slave and half free cannot permanently endure, is it true that a people who are slaves to market-tyrants will surely come to be their slaves in all else, that all liberty begins to be lost when one liberty is lost, that a people half democratic and half plutocratic cannot permanently endure.

The secret of the history we are about to make is not that the world is poorer or worse. It is richer and better. Its new wealth is too great for the old forms. The success and beauties of our old mutualities have made us ready for new mutualities. The wonder of to-day is the modern multiplication of products by the union of forces; the marvel of to-morrow will be the greater product which will follow when that which is co-operatively produced is co-operatively enjoyed. It is the spectacle of its concentration in the private fortunes of our day which reveals this wealth to its real makers— the whole people—and summons them to extend the manners and institutions of civilization to this new tribal relation. . . .

EDWARD BELLAMY

When Bellamy was only eighteen years old he spent a year in Europe and was impressed with man's inhumanity to man. He returned to this country and engaged for a while in newspaper work. Dissatisfied with this career, he turned to novel writing. In 1888 he published *Looking Backward: 2000–1887*, in which he presented a utopian solution of the economic and social ills of his day. He continued his attack upon social injustice in *Equality* (1897). The success of *Looking Backward* was immediate, and numerous nationalist clubs were established to propagate Bellamy's philosophy of national socialism. This movement induced him to found the *New Nation*, a weekly periodical; but the enthusiasm died down, and both the clubs and the periodical disappeared. Bellamy's nationalists joined the Populist party and lost their political identity.

LOOKING BACKWARD: 2000–1887 [123]

CHAPTER V

. . . .

"And what was the motive of these great organizations?"

"The workingmen claimed they had to organize to get their rights from the big corporations," I replied.

"That is just it," said Dr. Leete; "the organization of labor and the strikes were an effect, merely, of the concentration of capital in greater masses than had ever been known before. Before this concentration began, while as yet commerce and industry were conducted by innumerable petty concerns with small capital, instead of a small number of great concerns with vast capital, the individual workman was relatively important and independent in his relations to the employer. Moreover, when a little capital or a new idea was enough to start a man in business for himself, workingmen were constantly becoming employers and there was no hard and fast line between the two classes. Labor unions were needless then, and general strikes out of the question. But when the era of small concerns with small capital was succeeded by that of the great aggregations of capital, all this was changed. The individual laborer, who had been relatively important to the small employer, was reduced to insignificance and powerlessness over against the great corporation, while at the same time the way upward to the grade of employer was closed to him. Self-defense drove him to union with his fellows.

"The records of the period show that the outcry against the concentration

[123] Edward Bellamy, *Looking Backward: 2000–1887* (Boston, Houghton Mifflin Company, 1888), pp. 52–58, 60–64, 229–243. (Reprinted by permission of the publishers.)

of capital was furious. Men believed that it threatened society with a form of tyranny more abhorrent than it had ever endured. They believed that the great corporations were preparing for them the yoke of a baser servitude than had ever been imposed on the race, servitude not to men but to soulless machines incapable of any motive but insatiable greed. Looking back, we cannot wonder at their desperation, for certainly humanity was never confronted with a fate more sordid and hideous than would have been the era of corporate tyranny which they anticipated.

Meanwhile, without being in the smallest degree checked by the clamor against it, the absorption of business by ever larger monopolies continued. In the United States there was not, after the beginning of the last quarter of the century, any opportunity whatever for individual enterprise in any important field of industry, unless backed by a great capital. During the last decade of the century, such small businesses as still remained were fast-failing survivals of a past epoch, or mere parasites on the great corporations, or else existed in fields too small to attract the great capitalists. Small businesses, as far as they still remained, were reduced to the condition of rats and mice, living in holes and corners, and counting on evading notice for the enjoyment of existence. The railroads had gone on combining till a few great syndicates controlled every rail in the land. In manufactories, every important staple was controlled by a syndicate. These syndicates, pools, trusts, or whatever their name, fixed prices and crushed all competition except when combinations as vast as themselves arose. Then a struggle, resulting in a still greater consolidation, ensued. The great city bazar crushed its country rivals with branch stores, and in the city itself absorbed its smaller rivals till the business of a whole quarter was concentrated under one roof, with a hundred former proprietors of shops serving as clerks. Having no business of his own to put his money in, the small capitalist, at the same time that he took service under the corporation, found no other investment for his money buys its stocks and bonds, thus becoming doubly dependent upon it.

"The fact that the desperate popular opposition to the consolidation of business in a few powerful hands had no effect to check it proves that there must have been a strong economical reason for it. The small capitalists, with their innumerable petty concerns, had in fact yielded the field to the great aggregations of capital, because they belonged to a day of small things and were totally incompetent to the demands of an age of steam and telegraphs and the gigantic scale of its enterprises. To restore the former order of things, even if possible, would have involved returning to the day of stage-coaches. Oppressive and intolerable as was the régime of the great consolidations of capital, even its victims, while they cursed it, were forced to admit the prodigious increase of efficiency which had been imparted to the national industries, the vast economies effected by concentration of management and unity of organization, and to confess that since the new system had taken the place of the old the wealth of the world had increased at a rate before undreamed of. To be sure this vast increase had gone chiefly to make the rich richer, increasing the gap between them and the poor; but the fact remained that, as a means merely of producing wealth, capital had been proved efficient in proportion to its consolidation. The restoration of the old system with the subdivision of capital, if it were possible, might indeed bring back a greater equality of conditions, with more individual dignity and freedom, but it would be at the price of general poverty and the arrest of material progress.

"Was there, then, no way of commanding the services of the mighty wealth-producing principle of consolidated capital without bowing down to a plutocracy like that of Carthage? As soon as men began to ask themselves these questions, they found the answer ready for them. The movement toward the conduct of business by larger and larger aggregations of capital, the tendency toward monopolies, which had been so desperately and vainly resisted, was recognized at last, in its true significance, as a process which only needed to complete its logical evolution to open a golden future to humanity.

"Early in the last century the evolution was completed by the final consolidation of the entire capital of the nation. The industry and commerce of the country, ceasing to be conducted by a set of irresponsible corporations and syndicates of private persons at their caprice and for their profits, were intrusted to a single syndicate representing the people, to be conducted in the common interest for the common profit. The nation, that is to say, organized as the one great business corporation in which all other corporations were absorbed; it became the one capitalist in the place of all other capitalists, the sole employer, the final monopoly in which all previous and lesser monopolies were swallowed up, a monopoly in the profits and economies of which all citizens shared. The epoch of trusts had ended in The Great Trust. In a word, the people of the United States concluded to assume the conduct of their own business, just as one hundred odd years before they had assumed the conduct of their own government, organizing now for industrial purposes on precisely the same grounds that they had then organized for political purposes. At last, strangely late in the world's history, the obvious fact was perceived that no business is so essentially the public business as the industry and commerce on which the people's livelihood depends, and that to entrust it to private persons to be managed for private profit is a folly similar in kind, though vastly greater in magnitude, to that of surrendering the functions of political government to kings and nobles to be conducted for their personal glorification."

"Such a stupendous change as you describe," said I, "did not, of course, take place without great bloodshed and terrible convulsions."

"On the contrary," replied Dr. Leete, "there was absolutely no violence. The change had been long foreseen. Public opinion had become fully ripe for it, and the whole mass of the people was behind it. There was no more possibility of opposing it by force than by argument. On the other hand the popular sentiment toward the great corporations and those identified with them had ceased to be one of bitterness, as they came to realize their necessity as a link, a transition phase, in the evolution of the true industrial system. The most violent foes of the great private monopolies were now forced to recognize how invaluable and indispensable had been their office in educating the people up to the point of assuming control of their own business. Fifty years before, the consolidation of the industries of the country under national control would have seemed a very daring experiment to the most sanguine. But by a series of object lessons, seen and studied by all men, the great corporations had taught the people an entirely new set of ideas on this subject. They had seen for many years syndicates handling revenues greater than those of states, and directing the labors of hundreds of thousands of men with an efficiency and economy unattainable in smaller operations. It had come to be recognized as an axiom that the larger the business the simpler the principles that can be applied to it; that, as the machine is truer than the hand, so the system, which in a great concern does the work of the master's eye in a small business, turns out more accurate results. Thus it came about that, thanks to the corporations themselves, when it was proposed that the nation should assume their functions, the suggestion implied nothing which seemed impracticable even to the timid. To be sure it was a step beyond any yet taken, a broader generalization, but the very fact that the nation would be the sole corporation in the field would, it was seen, relieve the undertaking of many difficulties with which the partial monopolies had contended."

CHAPTER VI

. . . . . .

"Human nature itself must have changed very much," I said.

"Not at all," was Dr. Leete's reply, "but the conditions of human life have changed, and with them the motives of human action. The organization of society with you was such that officials were under a constant temptation to misuse their power for the private profit of themselves or others. Under such circumstances it seems almost strange that you dared entrust them with any of your affairs. Nowadays, on the contrary, society is so constituted that there is absolutely no way in which an official, however illdisposed, could possibly make any profit for himself or any one else by a misuse of his power. Let him be as bad an official as you please, he cannot be a corrupt one. There is no motive to be. The social system no longer offers a premium on dishonesty. But these are matters which you can understand as you come, with time, to know us better."

"But you have not yet told me how you have settled the labor problem. It is the problem of capital which we have been discussing," I said. "After the nation had assumed conduct of the mills, machinery, railroads, farms, mines, and capital in general of the country, the labor question still remained. In assuming the responsibilities of capital the nation had assumed the difficulties of the capitalist's position."

"The moment the nation assumed the responsibilities of capital those difficulties vanished," replied Dr. Leete. "The national organization of labor under one direction was the complete solution of what was, in your day and under your system, justly regarded as the insoluble labor problem. When the nation became the sole employer, all the citizens, by virtue of their citizenship, became employees, to be distributed according to the needs of industry."

"That is," I suggested, "you have simply applied the principles of universal military service, as it was understood in our day, to the labor question."

"Yes," said Dr. Leete, "that was something which followed as a matter of course as soon as the nation had become the sole capitalist. The people were already accustomed to the idea that the obligation of every citizen, not physically disabled, to contribute his military services to the defense of the nation was equal and absolute. That it was equally the duty of every citizen to contribute his quota of industrial or intellectual services to the maintenance of the nation was equally evident, though it was not until the nation became the employer of labor that citizens were able to render this sort of service with any pretense either of universality or equity. No organization of labor was possible when the employing power was divided among hundreds or thousands of individuals and corporations, between which concert of any kind was neither desired, nor indeed feasible. It constantly happened then that vast numbers who desired to labor could find no opportunity, and on the other hand, those who desired to evade a part or all of their debt could easily do so."

"Service, now, I suppose, is compulsory upon all," I suggested.

"It is rather a matter of course than of compulsion," replied Dr. Leete. "It is regarded as so absolutely natural and reasonable that the idea of its being compulsory has ceased to be thought of. He would be thought to be an incredibly contemptible person who should need compulsion in such a case. Nevertheless, to speak of service being compulsory would be a weak way to state its absolute inevitableness. Our entire social order is so wholly based upon and deduced from it that if it were conceivable that a man could escape it, he would be left with no possible way to provide for his existence. He would have excluded himself from the world, cut himself off from his kind, in a word, committed suicide."

"Is the term of service in this industrial army for life?"

"Oh, no; it both begins later and ends earlier than the average working period in your day. Your workshops were filled with children and old men, but we hold the period of youth sacred to education, and the period of maturity, when the physical forces begin to flag, equally sacred to ease and agreeable relaxation. The period of industrial service is twenty-four years, beginning at the close of the course of education at twenty-one and terminating at forty-five. After forty-five, while discharged from labor, the citizen still remains liable to special calls, in case of emergencies causing a sudden great increase in the demand for labor, till he reaches the age of fifty-five, but such calls are rarely, in fact almost never, made. The fifteenth day of October of every year is what we call Muster Day, because those who have reached the age of twenty-one are then mustered into the industrial service, and at the same time those who, after twenty-four years' service, have reached the age of forty-five, are honorably mustered out. It is the great day of the year with us, whence we reckon all other events our Olympiad, save that it is annual." . . .

CHAPTER XXII

. . . . . .

"As I said," responded the doctor, "the subject is too large to discuss at length now, but if you are really interested to know the main criticisms which we moderns make on your industrial system as compared with our own, I can touch briefly on some of them.

"The wastes which resulted from leaving the conduct of industry to irresponsible individuals, wholly without mutual understanding or concert, were mainly four: first, the waste by mistaken undertakings; second, the waste from the competition and mutual hostility of those engaged in industry;

third, the waste by periodical gluts and crises, with the consequent interruptions of industry; fourth, the waste from idle capital and labor, at all times. Any one of these four great leaks, were all the others stopped, would suffice to make the difference between wealth and poverty on the part of a nation.

"Take the waste by mistaken undertakings, to begin with. In your day the production of commodities being without concert or organization, there was no means of knowing just what demand there was for any class of products, or what was the rate of supply. Therefore, any enterprise by a private capitalist was always a doubtful experiment. The projector having no general view of the field of industry and consumption, such as our government has, could never be sure either what the people wanted, or what arrangements other capitalists were making to supply them. In view of this, we are not surprised to learn that the chances were considered several to one in favor of the failure of any given business enterprise, and that it was common for persons who at last succeeded in making a hit to have failed repeatedly. If a shoemaker, for every pair of shoes he succeeded in completing, spoiled the leather of four or five pair, besides losing the time spent on them, he would stand about the same chance of getting rich as your contemporaries did with their system of private enterprise, and its average of four or five failures to one success.

"The next of the great wastes was that from competition. The field of industry was a battlefield as wide as the world, in which the workers wasted, in assailing one another, energies which, if expended in concerted effort, as to-day, would have enriched all. As for mercy or quarter in this warfare, there was absolutely no suggestion of it. To deliberately enter a field of business and destroy the enterprises of those who had occupied it previously, in order to plant one's own enterprise on their ruins, was an achievement which never failed to command popular admiration. Nor is there any stretch of fancy in comparing this sort of struggle with actual warfare, so far as concerns the mental agony and physical suffering which attended the struggle, and the misery which overwhelmed the defeated and those dependent on them. Now nothing about your age is, at first sight, more astounding to a man of modern times than the fact that men engaged in the same industry, instead of fraternizing as comrades and co-laborers to a common end, should have regarded each other as rivals and enemies to be throttled and overthrown. This certainly seems like sheer madness, a scene from bedlam. But more closely regarded, it is seen to be no such thing. Your contemporaries, with their mutual throat-cutting, knew very well what they were at. The producers of the nineteenth century were not, like ours, working together for the maintenance of the community, but each solely for his own maintenance at the expense of the community. If, in working to this end, he at the same time increased the aggregate wealth, that was merely incidental. It was just as feasible and as common to increase one's private hoard by practices injurious to the general welfare. One's worst enemies were necessarily those of his own trade, for, under your plan of making private profit the motive of production, a scarcity of the article he produced was what each particular producer desired. It was for his interest that no more of it should be produced than he himself could produce. To secure this consummation as far as circumstances permitted, by killing off and discouraging those engaged in his line of industry, was his constant effort. When he had killed off all he could, his policy was to combine with those he could not kill, and convert their mutual warfare into a warfare upon the public at large by cornering the market, as I believe you used to call it, and putting up prices to the highest point people would stand before going without the goods. The day dream of the nineteenth century producer was to gain absolute control of the supply of some necessity of life, so that he might keep the public at the verge of starvation, and always command famine prices for what he supplied. This, Mr. West, is what was called in the nineteenth century a system of production. I will leave it to you if it does not seem, in some of its aspects, a great deal more like a system for preventing production. Some time when we have plenty of leisure I am going to ask you to sit down with me and try to make me comprehend, as I never yet could, though I have studied the matter a great deal, how such shrewd fellows as your contemporaries appear to have been in many respects ever came to entrust the business of providing for the community to a class whose interest it was to starve it. I assure you that the wonder with us is, not that the world did not get rich under such a system, but that it did not perish outright from want. This wonder increases as we go on to consider some of the other prodigious wastes that characterized it.

"Apart from the waste of labor and capital by misdirected industry, and that from the constant bloodletting of your industrial warfare, your system was liable to periodical convulsions, overwhelming alike the wise and unwise, the successful cut-throat as well as his victim. I refer to the business crises at intervals of five to ten years, which wrecked the industries of the nation, prostrating all weak enterprises and crippling the strongest, and were followed by long periods, often of many years, of so-called dull times, during which the capitalists slowly regathered their dissipated strength while the laboring classes starved and rioted. Then would ensue another brief season of prosperity, followed in turn by another crisis and the ensuing years of exhaustion. As commerce developed, making the nations mutually dependent, these crises became world-wide, while the obstinacy of the ensuing state of collapse increased with the area affected by the convulsions, and the consequent lack of rallying centres. In proportion as the industries of the world multipled and became complex, and the volume of capital involved was increased, these business cataclysms became more frequent, till, in the latter part of the nineteenth century, there were two years of bad times to one of good, and the system of industry, never before so extended or so imposing, seemed in danger of collapsing by its own weight. After endless discussions, your economists appear by that time to have settled down to the despairing conclusion that there was no more possibility of preventing or controlling these crises than if they had been drouths or hurricanes. It only remained to endure them as necessary evils, and when they had passed over to build up again the shattered structure of industry, as dwellers in an earthquake country keep on rebuilding their cities on the same site.

"So far as considering the causes of the trouble inherent in their industrial system, your contemporaries were certainly correct. They were in its very basis, and must needs become more and more maleficent as the business fabric grew in size and complexity. One of these causes was the lack of any common control of the different industries, and the consequent impossibility of their orderly and coördinate development. It inevitably resulted from this lack that they were continually getting out of step with one another and out of relation with the demand.

"Of the latter there was no criterion such as organized distribution gives us, and the first notice that it had been exceeded in any group of industries was a crash of prices, bankruptcy of producers, stoppage of production, reduction of wages, or discharge of workmen. This process was constantly going on in many industries, even in what were called good times, but a crisis took place only when the industries affected were extensive. The markets then were glutted with goods, of which nobody wanted beyond a sufficiency at any price. The wages and profits of those making the glutted classes of goods being reduced or wholly stopped, their purchasing power as consumers of other classes of goods, of which there was no natural glut, was taken away, and, as a consequence, goods of which there was no natural glut became artificially glutted, till their prices also were broken down, and their makers thrown out of work and deprived of income. The crisis was by this time fairly under way, and nothing could check it till a nation's ransom had been wasted.

"A cause, also inherent in your system, which often produced and always terribly aggravated crises, was the machinery of money and credit. Money was essential when production was in many private hands, and buying and selling was necessary to secure what one wanted. It was, however, open to the obvious objection of substituting for food, clothing, and other things a merely conventional representative of them. The confusion of mind which this favored, between goods and their representative, led the way to the credit system and its prodigious illusions. Already accustomed to accept money for commodities, the people next accepted promises for money, and ceased to look at all behind the representative for the thing represented. Money was a sign of real commodities, but credit was but the sign of a sign. There was a natural limit to gold and silver, that is, money proper, but none to credit, and the result was that the volume of credit, that is, the promises of money, ceased to bear any ascertainable proportion to the money, still less to the commodities, actually in existence. Under such a system, frequent and periodical crises were necessitated by a law as absolute as that which brings to the ground a structure overhanging its centre of gravity. It was one of your fictions that the government and the banks authorized by it alone issued money; but everybody who gave a dollar's credit issued money to that extent, which was as good as any to swell the circulation till the next crises. The great extension of the credit system was a characteristic of the latter part of the nineteenth century, and accounts largely for the almost incessant business crises which marked that period. Perilous as credit was, you could not dispense with its use, for, lacking any national or other public organization of the capital of the country, it was the only means you had for concentrating and directing it upon industrial enterprises. It was in this way a most potent means for exaggerating the chief peril of the private enterprise system of industry by enabling particular industries to absorb disproportionate amounts of the disposable capital of the country, and thus prepare disaster. Business enterprises were always vastly in debt for advances of credit, both to one another and to the banks and capitalists, and the prompt withdrawal of this credit at the first sign of a crisis was generally the precipitating cause of it.

"It was the misfortune of your contemporaries that they had to cement their business fabric with a material which an accident might at any moment turn into an explosive. They were in the plight of a man building a house with dynamite for mortar, for credit can be compared with nothing else.

"If you would see how needless were these convulsions of business which I have been speaking of, and how entirely they resulted from leaving industry to private and unorganized management, just consider the working of our system. Over-production in special lines, which was the great hobgoblin of your day, is impossible now, for by the connection between distribution and production supply is geared to demand like an engine to the governor which regulates its speed. Even suppose by an error of judgment an excessive production of some commodity. The consequent slackening or cessation of production in that line throws nobody out of employment. The suspended workers are at once found occupation in some other department of the vast workshop and lose only the time spent in changing, while, as for the glut, the business of the nation is large enough to carry any amount of product manufactured in excess of demand till the latter overtakes it. In such a case of over-production, as I have supposed, there is not with us, as with you, any complex machinery to get out of order and magnify a thousand times the original mistake. Of course, having not even money, we still less have credit. All estimates deal directly with the real things, the flour, iron, wood, wool, and labor, of which money and credit were for you the very misleading representatives. In our calculations of cost there can be no mistakes. Out of the annual product the amount necessary for the support of the people is taken, and the requisite labor to produce the next year's consumption provided for. The residue of the material and labor represents what can be safely expended in improvements. If the crops are bad, the surplus for that year is less than usual, that is all. Except for slight occasional effects of such natural causes, there are no fluctuations of business; the material prosperity of the nation flows on uninterruptedly from generation to generation, like an ever broadening and deepening river.

"Your business crises, Mr. West," continued the doctor, "like either of the great wastes I mentioned before, were enough, alone, to have kept your nose to the grindstone forever; but I have still to speak of one other great cause of your poverty, and that was the idleness of a great part of your capital and labor. With us it is the business of the administration to keep in constant employment every ounce of available capital and labor in the country. In your day there was no general control of either capital or labor, and a large part of both failed to find employment. 'Capital,' you used to say, 'is naturally timid,' and it would certainly have been reckless if it had not been timid in an epoch when there was a large preponderance of probability that any particular business venture would end in failure. There was no time when, if security could have been guaranteed it, the amount of capital devoted to productive industry could not have been greatly increased. The proportion of it so employed underwent constant extraordinary fluctuations, according to the greater or less feeling of uncertainty as to the stability of the industrial situation, so that the output of the national industries greatly varied in different years. But for the same reason that the amount of capital employed at times of special insecurity was far less than at times of somewhat greater security, a very large proportion was never employed at all, because the hazard of business was always very great in the best of times.

"It should be also noted that the great amount of capital always seeking employment where tolerable safety could be insured terribly embittered the competition between capitalists when a promising opening presented itself. The idleness of capital, the result of its timidity, of course meant the idleness of labor in corresponding degree. Moreover, every change in the adjustment in the condition of commerce or manufactures, not to speak of the innumerable business failures that took place yearly, even in the best of times, were constantly throwing a multitude of men out of employment for periods of weeks or months, or even years. A great number of these seekers after employment were constantly traversing the country, becoming in time professional vagabonds, then criminals. 'Give us work!' was the cry of an army of the unemployed at nearly all seasons, and in seasons of dullness in business this army swelled to a host so vast and desperate as to threaten the stability of the government. Could there conceivably be a more conclusive demonstration of the imbecility of the system of private enterprise as a method for enriching a nation than the fact that, in an age of such general poverty and want of everything, capitalists had to throttle one another to find a safe chance to invest their capital and workmen rioted and burned because they could find no work to do?

"Now, Mr. West," continued Dr. Leete, "I want you to bear in mind that these points of which I have been speaking indicate only negatively the advantages of the national organization of industry by showing certain fatal defects and prodigious imbecilities of the systems of private enterprise which are not found in it. These alone, you must admit, would pretty well explain why the nation is so much richer than in your day. But the larger half of our advantage over you, the positive side of it, I have yet barely spoken of. Supposing the system of private enterprise in industry were without any of the great leaks I have mentioned; that there were no wastes on account of misdirected effort growing out of mistakes as to the demand, and inability to command a general view of the industrial field. Suppose, also, there were no neutralizing and duplicating of effort from competition. Suppose, also, there were no waste from business panics and crises through bankruptcy and long interruptions of industry, and also none from the idleness of capital and labor. Supposing these evils, which are essential to the conduct of industry by capital in private hands, could all be miraculously prevented, and the system yet retained; even then the superiority of the results attained by the modern industrial system of national control would remain overwhelming.

"You used to have some pretty large textile manufacturing establishments, even in your day, although not comparable with ours. No doubt you have visited these great mills in your time, covering acres of ground, employing thousands of hands, and combining under one roof, under one control, the hundred distinct processes between, say, the cotton bale and the bale of glossy calicoes. You have admired the vast economy of labor as of mechanical force resulting from the perfect interworking with the rest of every wheel

and every hand. No doubt you have reflected how much less the same force of workers employed in that factory would accomplish if they were scattered, each man working independently. Would you think it an exaggeration to say that the utmost product of those workers, working thus apart, however amicable their relations might be, was increased not merely by a percentage, but many fold, when their efforts were organized under one control? Well now, Mr. West, the organization of the industry of the nation under a single control, so that all its processes interlock, has multiplied the total product over the utmost that could be done under the former system, even leaving out of account the four great wastes mentioned, in the same proportion that the product of these mill-workers was increased by coöperation. The effectiveness of the working force of a nation, under the myriad-headed leadership of private capital, even if the leaders were not mutual enemies, as compared with that which it attains under a single head, may be likened to the military efficiency of a mob, or a horde of barbarians with a thousand petty chiefs, as compared with that of a disciplined army under one general—such a fighting machine, for example, as the German army in the time of Von Moltke."
. . .

EDWARD ALSWORTH ROSS

E. A. Ross has been a professor of sociology at the University of Wisconsin since 1906 and has written a number of books in that field. *Sin and Society: An Analysis of Latter-Day Iniquity*, published in 1907, presents one of the many phases of the new problem of social interdependence that characterizes contemporary life. Sins against society have, from Ross's viewpoint, become more important than the old sins against an individual. Theodore Roosevelt said that this book influenced his thinking to an important degree.

SIN AND SOCIETY:
AN ANALYSIS OF LATTER-DAY INIQUITY.[124]

CHAPTER I
New Varieties of Sin

The sinful heart is ever the same, but sin changes its quality as society develops. Modern sin takes its character from the mutualism of our time. Under our present manner of living, how many of my vital interests I must trust to others! Nowadays the water main is my well, the trolley car my carriage, the banker's safe my old stocking, the policeman's billy my fist. My own eyes and nose and judgment defer to the inspector of food, or drugs, or gas, or factories, or tenements, or insurance companies. I rely upon others to look after my drains, invest my savings, nurse my sick, and teach my children. I let the meat trust butcher my pig, the oil trust mould my candles, the sugar trust boil my sorghum, the coal trust chop my wood, the barb wire company split my rails.

But this spread-out manner of life lays snares for the weak and opens doors to the wicked. Interdependence puts us, as it were, at one another's mercy, and so ushers in a multitude of new forms of wrong-doing. The practice of mutualism has always worked this way. Most sin is preying, and

[124] E. A. Ross, *Sin and Society: An Analysis of Latter-Day Iniquity* (Boston, Houghton Mifflin Company, 1907), pp. 3-19. (Reprinted by permission of the publishers.)

every new social relation begets its cannibalism. No one will "make the ephah small" or "falsify the balances" until there is buying and selling, "withhold the pledge" until there is loaning, "keep back the hire of the laborers" until there is a wage system, "justify the wicked for a reward" until men submit their disputes to a judge. The rise of the state makes possible counterfeiting, smuggling, peculation, and treason. Commerce tempts the pirate, the forger, and the embezzler. Every new fiduciary relation is a fresh opportunity for breach of trust. To-day the factory system makes it possible to work children to death or the double-quick speculative building gives the jerry-builder his chance, long-range investment spawns the get-rich-quick concern, and the trust movement opens the door to the bubble promoter.

The springs of the older sin seem to be drying up. Our forced-draught pace relieves us of the superabundance of energy that demands an explosive outlet. Spasms of violent feeling go with a sluggish habit of life, and are as out of place to-day as are the hard-drinking habits of our Saxon ancestors. We are too busy to give rein to spite. The stresses and lures of civilized life leave slender margin for the gratification of animosities. In quiet, side-tracked communities there is still much old-fashioned hatred, leading to personal clash, but elsewhere the cherishing of malice is felt to be an expensive luxury. Moreover, brutality, lust, and cruelty are on the wane. In this country, it is true, statistics show a widening torrent of bloody crime, but the cause is the weakening of law rather than an excess of bile. Other civilized people seem to be turning away from the sins of passion.

The daring sins that are blackening the face of our time are incidental to the ruthless pursuit of private ends, and hence quite "without prejudice." The victims are used or sacrificed not at all from personal ill-will, but because they can serve as pawns in somebody's little game. Like the way-farers run down by the automobilist, they are offered up to the God of Speed. The essence of the wrongs that infest our articulated society is betrayal rather than aggression. Having perforce to build men of willow into a social fabric that calls for oak, we see on all hands monstrous treacheries,—adulterators, peculators, boodlers, grafters, violating the trust others have placed in them. The little finger of Chicane has come to be thicker than the loins of Violence.

The sinister opportunities presented in this webbed social life have been seized unhesitatingly, because such treasons have not yet become infamous. The man who picks pockets with a railway rebate, murders with an adulterant instead of a bludgeon, burglarizes with a "rake-off" instead of a jimmy, cheats with a company prospectus instead of a deck of cards, or scuttles his town instead of his ship, does not feel on his brow the brand of a malefactor. The shedder of blood, the oppressor of the widow and the fatherless, long ago became odious, but latter-day treacheries fly no skull-and-crossbones flag at the masthead. The qualities which differentiate them from primitive sin and procure them such indulgence may be clearly defined.

Modern Sin is Not Superficially Repulsive

To-day the sacrifice of life incidental to quick success rarely calls for the actual spilling of blood. How decent are the pale slayings of the quack, the adulterator, and the purveyor of polluted water, compared with the red slayings of the vulgar bandit or assassin! Even if there is blood-letting, the long-range, tentacular nature of modern homicide eliminates all personal collision. What an abyss between the knife-play of brawlers and the law-defying neglect to fence dangerous machinery in a mill, or to furnish cars with safety couplers! The providing of unsuspecting passengers with "cork" life-preservers secretly loaded with bars of iron to make up for their deficiency in weight of cork, is spiritually akin to the treachery of Joab, who, taking Amasa by the beard "to kiss him" smote Amasa "in the fifth rib"; but it wears a very different aspect. The current methods of annexing the property of others are characterized by a pleasing indirectness and refinement. The furtive, apprehensive manner of the till-tapper or the porch-climber would jar disagreeably upon the tax-dodger "swearing off" his property, or the city official concealing a "rake-off" in his specifications for a public building. The work of the card-shark and the thimblerigger shocks a type of man that will not stick at the massive "artistic swindling" of the contemporary pro-moter. A taint of unworthiness, indeed, always attaches to transactions that force the person into humiliating postures. Your pretty parasite or your minor delinquent inspires the contempt that used to be felt for the retailer. The confidence man is to the promoter what the small shopkeeper was to the merchant prince.

Modern Sin Lacks the Familiar Tokens of Guilt

The stealings and slayings that lurk in the complexities of our social re-lations are not deeds of the dive, the dark alley, the lonely road, and the midnight hour. They require no nocturnal prowling with muffled step and bated breath, no weapon or offer of violence. Unlike the old-time villain, the latter-day malefactor does not wear a slouch hat and a comforter, breathe forth curses and an odor of gin, go about his nefarious work with clenched teeth and an evil scowl. In the supreme moment his lineaments are not distorted with rage, or lust, or malevolence. One misses the dramatic setting, the time-honored insignia of turpitude. Fagin and Bill Sykes and Simon Legree are vanishing types. Gamester, murderer, body-snatcher, and kidnap-per may appeal to a Hogarth, but what challenge finds his pencil in the coun-tenance of the boodler, the savings-bank wrecker, or the ballot-box stuffer? Among our criminals of greed, one begins to meet the "grand style" of the great criminals of ambition, Macbeth or Richard III. The modern high-power dealer of woe wears immaculate linen, carries a silk hat and a lighted cigar, sins with a calm countenance and a serene soul, leagues or months from the evil he causes. Upon his gentlemanly presence the eventual blood and tears do not obtrude themselves.

This is why good, kindly men let the wheels of commerce and of industry redden and redden, rather than pare or lose their dividend. This is why our railroads yearly injure one employee in twenty-six, and we look in vain for that promised "day of the Lord" that "will make a man more precious than fine gold."

Modern Sins Are Impersonal

The covenant breaker, the suborned witness, the corrupt judge, the op-pressor of the fatherless,—the old-fashioned sinner, in short,—knows his vic-tim, must hearken, perhaps, to bitter upbraidings. But the tropical belt of sin we are sweeping into is largely impersonal. Our iniquity is wireless, and we know not whose withers are wrung by it. The hurt passes into that vague mass, the "public," and is there lost to view. Hence it does not take a Borgia to knead "chalk and alum and plaster" into the loaf, seeing one cannot know just who will eat that loaf, or what gripe it will give him. The purveyor of spurious life-preservers need not be a Cain. The owner of rotten tenement houses, whose "pull" enables him to ignore the orders of the health department, foredooms babies, it is true, but for all that he is no Herod.

Often there are no victims. If the crazy hulk sent out for "just one more trip" meets with fair weather, all is well. If no fire breaks out in the theatre, the sham "emergency exits" are blameless. The corrupt inspector who O. K.'s low-grade kerosene is chancing it, that is all. Many sins, in fact, simply augment risk. Evil does not dog their footsteps with relentless and heart-shaking certainty. When the catastrophe does come, the sinner salves his conscience by blasphemously calling it an "accident" or an "act of God."

Still more impersonal is sin when the immediate harm touches beneficent institutions rather than individuals, when, following his vein of private profit, the sinner drives a gallery under some pillar upholding our civilization. The blackguarding editor is really undermining the freedom of the press. The policy kings and saloon keepers, who get out to the polls the last vote of the vicious and criminal classes, are sapping manhood suffrage. Striking engineers who spitefully desert passenger trains in mid-career are jeopardizing the right of a man to work only when he pleases. The real victim of a lynching mob is not the malefactor, but the law-abiding spirit. School-board grafters who blackmail applicants for a teacher's position are stabbing the free public school. The corrupt bosses and "combines" are murdering representative government. The perpetrators of election frauds unwittingly assail the institution of the ballot. Rarely, however, are such transgressions abominated as are offenses against persons.

Because of the special qualities of the Newer Unrighteousness, because these devastating latter-day wrongs, being comely of look, do not advertise their vileness, and are without the ulcerous hag-visage of the primitive sins, it is possible for iniquity to flourish greatly, even while men are getting better. Briber and boodler and grafter are often "good men," judged by the old tests, and would have passed for virtuous in the American community of seventy years ago. Among the chiefest sinners are now enrolled men who are pure and kind-hearted, loving in their families, faithful to their friends, and generous to the needy.

One might suppose that an exasperated public would sternly castigate these modern sins. But the fact is, the very qualities that lull the conscience of the sinner blind the eyes of the onlookers. People are sentimental, and bastinado wrong-doing not according to its harmfulness, but according to the infamy that has come to attach to it. Undiscerning, they chastise with scorpions the old authentic sins, but spare the new. They do not see that boodling is treason, that blackmail is piracy, that embezzlement is theft, that speculation is gambling, that tax-dodging is larceny, that railroad discrimination is treachery, that the factory labor of children is slavery, that deleterious adulteration is murder. It has not come home to them that the fraudulent promoter "devours widows' houses," that the monopolist "grinds the faces of the poor," that mercenary editors and spellbinds "put bitter for sweet and sweet for bitter." The cloven hoof hides in patent leather; and to-day, as in Hosea's time, the people "are destroyed for lack of knowledge." The mob lynches the red-handed slayer, when it ought to keep a gallows Haman-high for the venal mine-inspector, the seller of infected milk, the maintainer of a fire-trap theatre. The child-beater is forever blasted in reputation, but the exploiter of infant toil, or the concocter of a soothing syrup for the drugging of babies, stands a pillar of society. The petty shop-lifter is more abhorred than the stealer of a franchise, and the wife-whipper is outcast long before the man who sends his over-insured ship to founder with its crew.

There is a special cause for the condoning of sins committed in the way of business and without personal malice. Business men, as a rule, insist upon a free hand in their dealings, and, since they are conspicuous and influential in the community, they carry with them a considerable part of the non-business world. The leisured, the non-industrial employees, the bulk of professional men, and many public servants, hold to the unmitigated maxim of *caveat emptor*, and accept the chicane of trade as reasonable and legitimate. In England till 1487 any one who knew how to read might commit murder with impunity by claiming "benefit of clergy." There is something like this in the way we have granted quack and fakir and mine operator and railroad company indulgence to commit manslaughter in the name of business.

On the other hand, the active producers, such as farmers and workingmen, think in terms of livelihood rather than of profit, and tend therefore to consider the social bearings of conduct. Intent on well-being rather than on pecuniary success, they are shocked at the lenient judgment of the commercial world. Although they have hitherto deferred to the traders, the producers are losing faith in business men's standards, and may yet pluck up the courage to validate their own ethics against the individualistic, anti-social ethics of commerce.

Still, even if the mass turns vehement, it is not certain the lash of its censure can reach the cuticle of the sinner. A differentiated society abounds in closed doors and curtained recesses. The murmurs of the alley do not penetrate to the boulevard. The shrieks from the blazing excursion steamer do not invade the distant yacht of her owners. If the curses of tricked depositors never rise to the circles of "high finance" that keep the conscience of the savings-bank wrecker, why should the popular hiss stay the commercial buccaneer? All turns on the power of the greater public to astringe the flaccid conscience of business men until they become stern judges of one another. If we have really entered upon the era of jangling classes, it is, of course, idle to hope for a truly public sentiment upon such matters. Nevertheless, in the past, antiseptic currents of opinion have mounted from the healthy base to the yellowing top of the social tree, and they may do so again.

While idealists are dipping their brushes into the sunset for colors bright enough to paint the Utopias that might be if society were quite made over, one may be pardoned for dreaming of what would be possible, even on the plane of existing institutions, if only in this highly articulated society of ours every one were required to act in good faith, and to do what he had deliberately led others to expect of him.

WOODROW WILSON

While still a college student, Wilson became interested in political problems. In 1885 he published his *Congressional Government,* and in 1889 *The State.* He taught at Princeton University and became president of the institution. During this period of his life, Wilson believed in a rigid restriction of state functions. He became governor of New Jersey and was confronted with new problems of business, labor, and social welfare. Contact with these pressing issues compelled him to alter his political philosophy. In 1912 he was elected President of the United States. His campaign and the legislative program of his first administration were based upon the new political outlook that he had developed as governor. He abandoned *laissez-faire* and induced Congress to pass a series of significant bills that expanded the functions of the federal government. His later outlook is presented in *The New Freedom* (1913).

THE NEW FREEDOM [125]

CHAPTER I

The Old Order Changeth

There is one great basic fact which underlies all the questions that are discussed on the political platform at the present moment. That singular fact is that nothing is done in this country as it was done twenty years ago.

We are in the presence of a new organization of society. Our life has broken away from the past. The life of America is not the life that it was twenty years ago; it is not the life that it was ten years ago. We have changed our economic conditions, absolutely, from top to bottom; and, with our economic society, the organization of our life. The old political formulas do not fit the present problems; they read now like documents taken out of a forgotten age. The older cries sound as if they belonged to a past age which men have almost forgotten. Things which used to be put into the party platforms of ten years ago would sound antiquated if put into a platform now. We are facing the necessity of fitting a new social organization, as we did once fit the old organization, to the happiness and prosperity of the great body of citizens; for we are conscious that the new order of society has not been made to fit and provide the convenience or prosperity of the average man. The life of the nation has grown infinitely varied. It does not center now upon questions of governmental structure or of the distribution of governmental powers. It centers upon questions of the very structure and operation of society itself, of which government is only the instrument. Our development has run so fast and so far along the lines sketched in the earlier day of constitutional definition, has so crossed and interlaced those lines, has piled upon them such novel structures of trust and combination, has elaborated within them a life so manifold, so full of forces which transcend the boundaries of the country itself and fill the eyes of the world, that a new nation seems to have been created which the old formulas do not fit or afford a vital interpretation of.

We have come upon a very different age from any that preceded us. We have come upon an age when we do not do business in the way in which we

[125] Woodrow Wilson, *The New Freedom* (Garden City, N. Y., Doubleday, Doran Company, 1913), pp. 3–5, 7–13, 19–24. (Reprinted by permission of the publishers.)

used to do business,—when we do not carry on any of the operations of manufacture, sale, transportation, or communication as men used to carry them on. There is a sense in which in our day the individual has been submerged. In most parts of our country men work, not for themselves, not as partners in the old way in which they used to work, but generally as employees,—in a higher or lower grade,—of great corporations. There was a time when corporations played a very minor part in our business affairs, but now they play the chief part, and most men are the servants of corporations. . . .

In this new age we find, for instance, that our laws with regard to the relations of employer and employee are in many respects wholly antiquated and impossible. They were framed for another age, which nobody now living remembers, which is, indeed, so remote from our life that it would be difficult for many of us to understand it if it were described to us. The employer is now generally a corporation or a huge company of some kind; the employee is one of hundreds or of thousands brought together, not by individual masters whom they know and with whom they have personal relations, but by agents of one sort or another. Workingmen are marshaled in great numbers for the performance of a multitude of particular tasks under a common discipline. They generally use dangerous and powerful machinery, over whose repair and renewal they have no control. New rules must be devised with regard to their obligations and their rights, their obligations to their employers and their responsibilities to one another. Rules must be devised for their protection, for their compensation when injured, for their support when disabled.

There is something very new and very big and very complex about these new relations of capital and labor. A new economic society has sprung up, and we must effect a new set of adjustments. We must not pit power against weakness. The employer is generally, in our day, as I have said, not an individual, but a powerful group; and yet the workingman when dealing with his employer is still, under our existing law, an individual.

Why is it that we have a labor question at all? It is for the simple and very sufficient reason that the laboring man and the employer are not intimate associates now as they used to be in time past. Most of our laws were formed in the age when employer and employees knew each other, knew each other's characters, were associates with each other, dealt with each other as man with man. That is no longer the case. You not only do not come into personal contact with the men who have the supreme command in those corporations, but it would be out of the question for you to do it. Our modern corporations employ thousands, and in some instances hundreds of thousands, of men. The only persons whom you see or deal with are local superintendents or local representatives of a vast organization, which is not like anything that the workingmen of the time in which our laws were framed knew anything about. A little group of workingmen, seeing their employer every day, dealing with him in a personal way, is one thing, and the modern body of labor engaged as employees of the huge enterprises that spread all over the country, dealing with men of whom they can form no personal conception, is another thing, A very different thing. You never saw a corporation, any more than you ever saw a government. Many a workingman to-day never saw the body of men who are conducting the industry in which he is employed. And they never saw him. What they know about him is written in ledgers and books and letters, in the correspondence of the office, in the reports of the superintendents. He is a long way off from them.

So what we have to discuss is, not wrongs which individuals intentionally do,—I do not believe there are a great many of those,—but the wrongs of a system. I want to record my protest against any discussion of this matter which would seem to indicate that there are bodies of our fellow-citizens who are trying to grind us down and do us injustice. There are some men of that sort. I don't know how they sleep o' nights, but there are men of that kind. Thank God, they are not numerous. The truth is, we are all caught in a great economic system which is heartless. The modern corporation is not engaged in business as an individual. When we deal with it, we deal with an impersonal element, an immaterial piece of society. A modern corporation is a means of co-operation in the conduct of an enterprise which is so big that no one man can conduct it, and which the resources of no one man are sufficient to finance. A company is formed; that company puts out a prospectus; the promoters expect to raise a certain fund as capital stock. Well, how are they going to raise it? They are going to raise it from the public in general, some of whom will buy their stock. The moment that begins, there is formed—what? A joint stock corporation. Men begin to pool their earnings, little piles, big piles. A certain number of men are elected by the stockholders to be directors, and these directors elect a president. This president is the head of the undertaking, and the directors are its managers.

Now, do the workingmen employed by that stock corporation deal with that president and those directors? Not at all. Does the public deal with that president and that board of directors? It does not. Can anybody bring them to account? It is next to impossible to do so. If you undertake it you will find it a game of hide and seek, with the objects of your search taking refuge now behind the tree of their individual personality, now behind that of their corporate irresponsibility.

And do our laws take note of this curious state of things? Do they even attempt to distinguish between a man's act as a corporation director and as an individual? They do not. Our laws still deal with us on the basis of the old system. The law is still living in the dead past which we have left behind. This is evident, for instance, with regard to the matter of employers' liability for workingmen's injuries. Suppose that a superintendent wants a workman to use a certain piece of machinery which it is not safe for him to use, and that workman is injured by that piece of machinery. Some of our courts have held that the superintendent is a fellow-servant, or, as the law states it, a fellow-employee, and that, therefore, the man cannot recover damages for his injury. The superintendent who probably engaged the man is not his employer. Who is his employer? And whose negligence could conceivably come in there? The board of directors did not tell the employee to use that piece of machinery; and the president of the corporation did not tell him to use that piece of machinery. And so forth. Don't you see by that theory that a man never can get redress for negligence on the part of the employer? When I hear judges reason upon the analogy of the relationships that used to exist between workmen and their employers a generation ago, I wonder if they have not opened their eyes to the modern world. You know, we have a right to expect that judges will have their eyes open, even though the law which they administer hasn't awakened.

Yet that is but a single small detail illustrative of the difficulties we are in because we have not adjusted the law to the facts of the new order. . . .

We used to think in the old-fashioned days when life was very simple that all that government had to do was to put on a policeman's uniform and say, "Now don't anybody hurt anybody else." We used to say that the ideal of government was for every man to be left alone and not interfered with, except when he interfered with somebody else; and that the best government was the government that did as little as possible. That was the idea that obtained in Jefferson's time. But we are coming now to realize that life is so complicated that we are not dealing with the old conditions, and that the law has to step in and create new conditions under which we may live, the conditions which will make it tolerable for us to live.

Let me illustrate what I mean: It used to be true in our cities that every family occupied a separate house of its own, that every family had its own little premises, that every family was separated in its life from every other family. That is no longer the case in our great cities. Families live in tenements, they live in flats, they live on floors; they are piled layer upon layer in the great tenement houses of our crowded districts, and not only are they piled layer upon layer, but they are associated room by room, so that there is in every room, sometimes, in our congested districts, a separate family. In some foreign countries they have made much more progress than we in handling these things. In the city of Glasgow, for example (Glasgow is one of the model cities of the world), they have made up their minds that the entries and the hallways of great tenements are public streets. Therefore, the policeman goes up the stairway, and patrols the corridors; the lighting department of the city sees to it that the halls are abundantly lighted. The city does not deceive itself into supposing that a great building is a unit from which the police are to keep out and the civic authority to be excluded, but it says: "These are public highways, and light is needed in them, and control by the authority of the city."

I liken that to our great modern industrial enterprises. A corporation is very like a large tenement house; it isn't the premises of a single commercial family; it is just as much a public affair as a tenement house is a network of public highways.

When you offer the securities of a great corporation to anybody who wishes to purchase them, you must open that corporation to the inspection of everybody who wants to purchase. There must, to follow out the figure of the tenement house, be lights along the corridors, there must be police patrolling the openings, there must be inspection wherever it is known that men may be deceived with regard to the contents of the premises. If we believe that fraud lies in wait for us, we must have the means of determining whether our suspicions are well founded or not. Similarly, the treatment of labor by the great corporations is not what it was in Jefferson's time. Whenever bodies of men employ bodies of men, it ceases to be a private relationship. So that when courts hold that workingmen cannot peaceably dissuade other workingmen from taking employment, as was held in a notable case in New Jersey, they simply show that their minds and understandings are lingering in an age which has passed away. This dealing of great bodies of men with other bodies of men is a matter of public scrutiny, and should be a matter of public regulation.

Similarly, it was no business of the law in the time of Jefferson to come into my house and see how I kept house! But when my house, when my so-called private property, became a great mine, and men went along dark corridors amidst every kind of danger in order to dig out of the bowels of the earth things necessary for the industries of a whole nation, and when it came about that no individual owned these mines, that they were owned by great stock companies, then all the old analogies absolutely collapsed and it became the right of the government to go down into these mines to see whether human beings were properly treated in them or not; to see whether accidents were properly safe-guarded against; to see whether modern economical methods of using these inestimable riches of the earth were followed or were not followed. If somebody puts a derrick improperly secured on top of a building or over-topping the street, then the government of the city has the right to see that that derrick is so secured that you and I can walk under it and not be afraid that the heavens are going to fall on us. Likewise, in these great beehives where in every corridor swarm men of flesh and blood, it is the privilege of the government, whether of the State or of the United States, as the case may be, to see that human life is protected, that human lungs have something to breathe.

These, again, are merely illustrations of conditions. We are in a new world, struggling under old laws. As we go inspecting our lives to-day, surveying this new scene of centralized and complex society, we shall find many more things out of joint. . . .

ROBERT M. LA FOLLETTE

Robert M. La Follette was one of the outstanding figures in recent American politics. Early in life he entered Wisconsin politics as an opponent of the then existing party machine and of the vested interests. He became the champion of the farmer, the laborer, and small middle class, rising rapidly to the positions of governor and United States senator. Throughout his career he fought against "big business." Disgusted with the conservatism of the major parties, he organized a new Progressive party in 1924 and ran for the presidency.

SPEECH DELIVERED AT THE ANNUAL BANQUET OF THE PERIODICAL PUBLISHERS' ASSOCIATION, PHILADELPHIA, FEBRUARY 2, 1912. [126]

The great issue before the American people to-day is the control of their own government. In the midst of political struggle, it is not easy to see the historical relations of the present Progressive movement. But it represents a conflict as old as the history of man—the fight to maintain human liberty, the right of all the people.

[126] R. M. La Follette, *Autobiography* (Madison, Wisconsin, R. M. La Follette Company, 1912), pp. 762-769, 771-774, 776-777, 781-782, 783-785, 787-793. (Reprinted by permission of the publishers.)

A mighty power has been builded up in this country in recent years, so strong, yet so insidious and far-reaching in its influence, that men are gravely inquiring whether its iron grip on government and business can ever be broken. Again and again it has proved strong enough to nominate the candidates of both political parties. It rules in the organization of legislative bodies, state and national, and of the committees which frame legislation. Its influence is felt in cabinets and in the policies of administrations, and is clearly seen in the appointment of prosecuting officers and the selection of judges upon the Bench.

In business it has crippled or destroyed competition. It is stifled individual initiative. It has fixed limitations in the field of production. It makes prices and imposes its burdens upon the consuming public at will.

In transportation, after a prolonged struggle for government control, it is, with only slight check upon its great power, still master of the highways of commerce.

In finance its power is unlimited. In large affairs it gives or withholds credit, and from time to time contracts or inflates the volume of the money required for the transaction of the business of the country, regardless of everything excepting its own profits.

It has acquired vast areas of the public domain, and is rapidly monopolizing the natural resources—timber, iron, coal, oil.

And this THING has grown up in a country where, under the Constitution and the law, the citizen is sovereign!

The related events which led to this centralized control are essential to a clear understanding of the real danger—the magnitude of this danger now menacing the very existence of every independent concern remaining in the field of business enterprise.

The First Period—The Individual and the Partnership.—For nearly a century after Jefferson declared for a government of "equal rights for all, and special privileges for none," the business of the country was conducted by individuals and partnerships. During this first period business methods were simple, its proportions modest, and there was little call for larger capital than could be readily furnished by the individual or, in the most extreme cases, a partnership of fair size.

From the beginning, when men bartered their products in exchange, down through all the ages, the business of the world had been conducted under the natural laws of trade—demand, supply, competition. Like all natural laws, they were fair and impartial; they favored neither the producer nor the consumer. They had ruled the market and made the prices when the individual and the partnership conducted substantially all commercial enterprises during the first period of our business life.

But as the country developed, as the population poured over the Alleghenies, occupied the Mississippi Valley, pushed on to the Rocky Mountains and down the western slope to California, discovering the boundless wealth of our natural resources—the fields and forests, the mountains of iron and coal and precious metals, there was a pressing call on every hand for larger capital beyond the power of any individual or any partnership to supply. We had outgrown the simple methods; there was a demand for a new business device strong enough to unlock the treasure house of the new world.

The Second Period—The Private Corporation.—The modern corporation was invented to meet that demand, and general statutes for incorporation were soon upon the statute books of every state. Their adoption marked the beginning of the second period of our business life. It was the best machine ever invented for the purpose; simple in organization, effective in operation.

A hundred, a thousand, any number of men could associate their capital, and employing the representative principle upon which our country was based, vote for and elect a president, a general manager, a board of directors, a body of men, no larger than an ordinary partnership, and clothe them with power to conduct the business to the success of which the aggregate capital was contributed.

Men no longer stood baffled by the magnitude of any undertaking, but promptly enlisted an army of contributors, large or small, massed together the required capital and under the direction of the officers and directors of the corporation, a small executive body, seized upon these waiting opportunities, and this second period marked a material development, surpassing anything in the world's history. It was not the era of greatest individual fortune building, but it was the period of greatest general prosperity. And why?

The natural laws of trade—demand, supply and competition—still ruled the market and made the prices in the second period of our business life. The private corporation, in a large measure, supplanted the individual, and the partnership in mining, manufacturing and large commercial enterprises, but each corporation competed with every other in the same line of business. Production was larger, development more rapid, but, under the free play of competition, the resulting prosperity was fairly distributed between the producer and the consumer, the seller and the buyer, because profits and prices were reasonable.

Big capital behind the private corporations drove business at a pace and upon a scale never before witnessed. Competition was at once the spur to the highest efficiency and the check against waste and abuse of power.

In this period of our industrial and commercial progress, America amazed and alarmed our business rivals of the old world. We were soon foremost among the nations of the earth in agriculture, in mines and mining, in manufactures and in commerce as well.

The American market became the greatest thing in all the material world. Its control became the one thing coveted.

The Third Period—The Combination of Corporations.—The evil hour was come upon us. Daring, unscrupulous men plotted in violation of the common law, the criminal statutes and against public right to become masters of that market and take what toll they pleased. To do this thing it was necessary to set aside, abrogate, nullify the natural laws of trade that had ruled in business for centuries. Production was to be limited, competition stifled and prices arbitrarily fixed by selfish decree. And thus we entered upon the third period of our business and commercial life—the period of a combination of the corporations under a single control in each line of business. It was not an evolution; it was a revolution.

And yet certain economists set it down in the literature of the day that the Supreme Ruler of the universe reserved in His great plan a divinely appointed place and time for a Rockefeller, a Morgan, a Carnegie, a Baer, to evolve this new law, which should enable them to appropriate the wealth of the country and Mexicanize its business and its people.

The combination became supreme in each important line, controlling the markets for the raw material and the finished product, largely dictating the price of everything we sell and the price of everything we buy—beef, sugar, woolens, cottons, coal, oil, copper, zinc, iron, steel, agricultural implements, hardware, gas, electric light, food supplies.

Monopoly acquired dominion everywhere.

It brought with it the inevitable results of monopoly—extortionate prices, inferior products. We soon found shoddy in everything we wear, and adulteration in everything we eat.

Did these masters of business stop there? By no means! "Increase of appetite had grown by what it fed on." The floodgates of fictitious capitalization were thrown wide open. These organizations of combinations overcapitalized for a double purpose. The issue of bonds and stocks in excess of investment covered up the exaction of their immense profits, and likewise offered an unlimited field for promotion and speculation.

The establishment of this third period was the beginning of rapidly advancing prices, increasing the cost of living upon people of average earning power until the burden is greater than they can bear.

The Fourth Period—The Combination of Combinations.—The strife for more money, more power—more power, more money—swept everything before it.

It remained only to bring together into a community of interest or ownership the great combinations which controlled, each in its own field—in short, to combine these combinations.

One needs but to study the directory of directories of the great business concerns of the country to determine the extent to which this combination of combinations has been successfully accomplished, thus carrying us over into the fourth period of our industrial and commercial life—the period of complete industrial and commercial servitude in which we now unhappily find ourselves. And this supreme control of the business of the country is the triumph of men who have at every step defied public opinion, the common law and criminal statutes.

This condition is intolerable. It is hostile to every principle of democracy. If maintained it is the end of democracy. We may preserve the form of our representative government and lose the soul, the spirit of our free institutions. . . .

The Centralization of Railroad Control.—In the meantime what were the powers doing in the great field of transportation? A swift backward glance reveals the fact that the same system of consolidation, centralized control and suppressed competition had been forced through in violation of law and public right.

The vital interests of organized society in commerce and the public nature of transportation impose upon government the duty to establish and maintain control over common carriers.

To discharge this obligation the government must exact from the common carrier:

(1) Reasonable rates, (2) impartial rates, (3) adequate and impartial services.

The public is interested in adequate and impartial services. The shipper is especially interested in equal and impartial rates. The consumer is especially interested in reasonable rates.

For forty years after railroads were established there was no attempt to invoke government control. The public depended solely upon competition between railroads for the protection of public interests.

Finally it learned the elementary lesson that the railroad is a natural monopoly; that there can be no competition excepting at common points, and that at common points the railroads were destroying all competition by pooling agreements.

Then came the demand in 1870 for governmental control—in order to secure reasonable rates. It originated in the upper Mississippi Valley—in Wisconsin, Iowa, Minnesota, and Illinois, for a control of rates within the state.

It spread east and west and became a national movement for controlling interstate commerce.

The supreme courts of the middle western states sustained the state legislation. The Supreme Court of the United States sustained the state courts, and the power of the state and federal governments to control and fix reasonable transportation rates, each in its own sphere, was adjudicated as a public right thirty-eight years ago.

For a generation of time since those decisions the people have struggled to secure an interstate commerce law which would establish and enforce reasonable rates. That was the relief which the consumer, the great body of the people, demanded—reasonable rates.

The shippers have no interest in reasonable rates. They do not pay the freight. The consumer pays the freight. But the shipper is at a disadvantage in supplying his trade unless he has rates relatively equal to those given to other shippers engaged in the same business.

Shippers could easily present concrete cases of injustice. They could readily organize and appear before committees and make their representatives feel their power.

Not so with the consumer, who, in the end, pays all the freight, as a part of the purchase price of everything he buys. He cannot identify the freight charge, because it is a part of the price he pays when he purchases supplies. However small the item, in the aggregate it is important to him. He cannot maintain a lobby. If his United States Senators and his Congressmen do not represent him, he is helpless.

What is the net result of thirty-eight years' struggle with the railroads? Congress enacted the interstate commerce law of 1887; the Elkins law of 1903; the Hepburn law of 1906; and the recent law of 1910.

Out of all this legislation the shippers have been able to secure a partial enforcement of their contention for an equalization of rates.

The consumers have lost in their long fight for reasonable rates.

After all these years it is not to-day within the power of the interstate commerce commission to take the first step to ascertain a reasonable rate. There is a vast difference between equal rates and reasonable rates.

The consumers are no nearer to securing reasonable rates than they were thirty-eight years ago. . . .

The Centralized Control of Banking, Capital, and Credits.—The country is just beginning to understand how completely great banking institutions in the principal money centres have become bound up with the control of industrial institutions, the railroads and franchise combinations.

That there was a tendency on the part of great banking associations to merge and combine could not be overlooked. But while financial and economic writers had directed public attention to the fact, and had even pointed out the opportunity and temptation for the use of this augmented power, in connection with the promotion of the speculative side of business organization, they were slow to believe that banking institutions could be so prostituted. Certain critical observers had, however, as long as five or six years ago, suggested the dangerous tendencies in this direction. . . .

The centralization of the banking power in New York City would not only open the way for financing the reorganization and consolidation of industrial enterprises and of public utilities throughout the country, but would place those in authority where they could control the markets on stocks and bonds almost at will.

With this enormous concentration of business it is possible to create artificially, periods of prosperity and periods of panic. Prices can be lowered or advanced at the will of the "System." When the farmer must move his crops a scarcity of money may be created and prices lowered. When the crop passes into the control of the speculator the artificial stringency may be relieved and prices advanced, and the illegitimate profit raked off the agricultural industry may be pocketed in Wall Street.

If an effort is made to compel any one of these great "Interests" to obey the law, it is easy for them to enter into a conspiracy to destroy whoever may be responsible for the undertaking.

The bare names of the directors of two great bank groups—the Standard Oil group and the Morgan group—given in connection with their other business associations is all the evidence that need be offered of the absolute community of interest between banks, railroads, and all the great industries. . . .

The ability of these group banks of New York through their connected interests to engage in underwriting, to finance promotion schemes, where the profits resulting from overcapitalization represent hundreds of millions of dollars, places them beyond let or hindrance from competitors elsewhere in the country. Their ability to take advantage of conditions in Wall Street, even if they did not create these conditions, forcing interest rates on call loans as high as 150 per cent., would enable them to command, almost at will, the capital of the country for these speculative purposes.

But one result could follow. Floating the stocks and bonds in overcapitalized transportation, traction, mining and industrial organizations does not create wealth, but it does absorb capital. Through the agency of these great groups hundreds of millions of dollars of the wealth of the country have been tied up. Other hundreds of millions have been drawn upon to supply these great speculating groups in their steadily increasing Wall Street business.

I would not unjustly decry Wall Street or ignore the necessity of a great central market to provide capital for the large business undertakings of this country. I recognize the rights of capital and the service which capital can render to a great producing nation such as ours. But this government guarantees equality of opportunity for all men, and it likewise guarantees equality of opportunity for all capital. And corporations and combinations of corporations, with their centralized banking and extending branch connections from state to state, are not entitled to special favors in legislation.

The whole course of banking and currency legislation has steadily favored the great banking institutions, especially those having community of interest with the industrial and transportation companies of the country. . . .

Amend the Sherman law by enacting specific prohibitions against well-known practices that constitute unreasonable restraints of trade. One of these is the brutal method of the Standard Oil Company of cutting prices in any place where there is a competitor in order to kill him off, while keeping up prices in other places. Another is the club wielded by the tobacco trust, which put the jobbers in a position where, unless they refrained from buying of a competitor, they could not get from the trust the brands which were indispensable to the successful conduct of their business. These and several other obviously unreasonable restraints of trade are definitely prohibited in the bill which I have introduced in the Senate.

The bill also places the burden of proof on the trust to show that any restraint of trade which it practices is reasonable—that is, that it benefits the community.

It also provides that when the court has once entered its final decree and declared a trust illegal, any person who has suffered damages may come in under that decree and simply petition that his damages be paid without proving anything except the amount of the damages. If this had been law when the Standard Oil and Tobacco decisions were rendered, those decisions would have meant something more than mere victories on paper.

In addition to these amendments to the anti-trust law, there is need of a commission to stand between the people and the courts in order to investigate the facts and to prohibit all unreasonable restraints not specifically described in the law. This commission should have full power to ascertain the actual cost of reproduction, or physical value of the property; the reasonable value that the intangible property, such as good will, would have under conditions of fair competition, and to distinguish this from the illegal values that have been built up in violation of law. It should ascertain the values that depend on patents, monopoly of natural resources and all other forms of special privilege; the amount of property that has been paid for out of illegal profits taken from the public, distinguished from the property paid for out of legitimate profits and true investment. It should in this way ascertain the true cost of production and whether the prices charged are yielding extortionate profits or only the reasonable profits that competitors could earn. These are the facts that the people must know before they will consent to any legislation that treats illegal values as though they were legal.

With these facts ascertained and made *prima facie* evidence in court, these illegal values cannot be permanently fastened on the American people. It will take time to pull down this false structure of illegal capitalization of the trusts, but it is now the greatest menace to prosperity.

If these laws are adopted, then every business man, as well as the courts, will know definitely what is meant by the "rule of reason." Legitimate business will have its course laid out clear and certain before it, and every investor will know precisely what the law allows and what it prohibits.

The trust problem has become so interwoven in our legal and industrial system that no single measure or group of measures can reach all of it. It must be picked off at every point where it shows its head.

Every combination of a manufacturing business with the control of transportation, including pipe lines, should be prohibited, in order that competitors may have equal facilities for reaching markets.

The control of limited sources of raw material, like coal, iron ore, or timber, by a manufacturing corporation, should be broken up and these resources should be opened to all manufacturers on equal terms.

It is claimed on all sides that competition has failed. I deny it. Fair competition has not failed. It has been suppressed. When competitors are shut out from markets by discrimination, and denied either transportation, raw material or credit on equal terms, we do not have competition. We have the modern form of highway robbery. The great problem of legislation before us is first for the people to resume control of their government, and then to protect themselves against those who are throttling competition by the aid of government.

I do not say that competition does not have its evils. Labor organizations are the struggling protest against cut-throat competition. The anti-trust law was not intended or understood to apply to them. They should be exempt from its operation.

The tariff should be brought down to the difference in labor cost of the more efficient plants and the foreign competitor, and where there is no difference the tariff should be removed. Where the protective tariff is retained its advantages must be passed along to labor, for whose benefit the manufacturer contends it is necessary.

The patent laws should be so amended that the owners of patents will be compelled to develop them fully or permit their use on equal terms by others.

More vital and menacing than any other power that supports trusts is the control of credit through the control of the people's savings and deposits. When the Emergency Currency Bill was before Congress in 1908, Senator Aldrich slipped into the conference report certain provisions which he had withdrawn in the Senate, and withdrew provisions which he had first included. He eliminated protection against promotion schemes, excluded penalties for false reporting, dropped provisions for safe-guarding reserves, inserted provisions for accepting railroad bonds as security. Now he comes with another plausible measure to remedy the admitted evils of our inelastic banking system.

When we realize that the control of credit and banking is the greatest power that the trusts possess to keep out competitors, we may well question their sincerity in offering a patriotic measure to dispossess themselves of that power. It is the people's money that is expected to give security to this plan and the people must and shall control it.

The proposed Aldrich Currency plan is the product of a commission composed of men who are or have been members of Congress, which have controlled all legislation relating to currency and banking. With such a record it behooves the public to examine with the utmost care any plan which they recommend, however plausible it may appear upon its face. A critical study of the scheme of this commission will convince any student of government finance, that under the guise of providing elasticity to our currency system, it is in reality an adroit means of further concentration and control of the money and credits of the United States under a fifty-year franchise, augmenting the power of those who already dominate the banking and insurance resources of the country.

Our National Banking Law is a patchwork of legislation. It should be thoroughly revised. And all authorities agree that a comprehensive plan for an emergency currency is vitally important. When the basic principle of such a plan is once determined, when it is settled that government controlled banks are to be, *in fact*, controlled by the government *in the public interest*, the details can easily be worked out.

An emergency currency circulation should be backed by proper reserves, issued only against commercial paper that represents actual and legitimate business transactions. No plan should be adopted which admits of control by banking interests which, under existing conditions, means, in the end, control by the great speculative banking groups.

In all our plans for progressive legislation, it must not be forgotten that we are only just beginning to get control of the railroads. The present law is an improvement, but the Interstate Commerce Commission requires to be greatly strengthened. It should have a much larger appropriation, enabling it to prosecute investigations in all parts of the country. It should make physical valuations of the railroads, eliminating watered stock, monopoly values and the unwarranted inflation of railway terminals to conceal monopoly values. And the Commerce Court should be abolished as a mere subterfuge interposed to handicap the commission.

As a first necessary step for the regulation of interstate commerce, we *must* ascertain the reasonable value of the physical property of railroads, justly inventoried, upon a sound economic basis, distinguishing *actual* values from *monopoly* values derived from violations of law, and must make such discriminating values the *base line* for determining rates. The country should know how much of the eighteen billions of capitalization was contributed by those who own the railroads, and how much by the people themselves. We should also provide for the extension of the powers and the administrative control of the Interstate Commerce Commission. . . .

ROSCOE POUND

Roscoe Pound has been the dean of the Harvard Law School since 1916, and is one of the outstanding contemporary legal philosophers. In addition to numerous law review articles on sociological jurisprudence, he has written several important books on jurisprudence. Among these are: *The Spirit of the Common Law* (1921), *Introduction to the Philosophy of Law* (1922), and *Interpretations of Legal History* (1923). Pound looks upon law as a changing set of concepts, and maintains that it should keep pace with changing economic institutions and social systems. The job of the jurist should be that of "social engineering."

THE SPIRIT OF THE COMMON LAW. [127]

CHAPTER VIII

Legal Reason

William James tells a story which he attributes to the Danish philosopher Höffding, about a small boy who asked his mother if it were really true that God had made the whole world in six days. "Oh yes," she answered, "it was quite true." "Did he make it *all* in six days," asked the boy? "Oh yes," she said, "it's all done." "Well then," said he, "mamma, what is God doing now?" Höffding considered that the mother ought to have explained to him that God was now sitting for His portrait to the metaphysicians. In truth all attempt to give a philosophical account of some section of recorded human conduct is on a smaller scale very like the attempt of the professional philosopher to make God sit for His portrait. Moreover, if we are to make an adequate picture of a stage of legal development, the picture must be taken after the period has definitely come to an end so that we may view its phenomena, as it were, under the aspect of eternity. It is, therefore, a rash undertaking to essay even a snapshot photograph of the stage of legal development into which we are passing. But without some such attempt we shall fail to understand one of the chief instruments by which the traditional materials of our legal system are kept in touch with reality and are made available for a changed and changing society.

In a former lecture I sought to show that the process of judicial lawmaking consisted in development of the materials of the common-law tradition and of the new premises provided, largely on the basis of that tradition by jurist and legislator, by means of a known technique—the "artificial reason and judgment of the law" of which Lord Coke told his indignant sovereign. For whether working upon the materials of the tradition with the case-knife or pickax of the beginnings of legal science or with the more complicated instruments of the modern legal armory, judicial activity must be directed consciously or unconsciously to some end. In the beginnings of law this end was simply a peaceable ordering. In Roman law and in the Middle Ages it was the maintenance of the social *status quo*. From the seventeenth century until our own day it has been the promotion of a maximum of individual self-assertion. Assuming some one of these as the end of the legal ordering of society, the jurist works out an elaborate critique on the basis thereof, the legislator provides new premises for judicial decision more or less expressing the principles of this critique, and the judge applies it in his choice of analogies when called upon to deal with questions of first impression and uses it to measure existing rules or doctrines in passing upon variant states of fact and thus to shape these rules and doctrines by extending or limiting them in different directions. The basis of all these operations is some theory as to what law is for. What, then, is the theory of the new stage of legal development upon which we seem to be entering?

Those who conceive that the law is entering upon such a new stage of development—and this category includes the professor of jurisprudence at

[127] Roscoe Pound, *The Spirit of the Common Law* (Boston, Marshall Jones Company, 1921), pp. 193–216. (Reprinted by permission of the publishers.)

as conservative an institution as the University of Oxford—speak of that stage, in contrast with the nineteenth century, as a stage of socialization of law. For in contrast with the nineteenth century it appears to put the emphasis upon social interests; upon the demands or claims or desires involved in social life rather than upon the qualities of the abstract man *in vacuo* or upon the freedom of will of the isolated individual. But if the term "socialization of law" has alarming implications for any of you, if like the Russian censor who blocked out the words "dynamic" and "sociology" in Ward's Dynamic Sociology wherever they occurred—not that he knew what they meant, but because they sounded too suspiciously like dynamite and socialism—or like the president of one of our universities to whom the word sociological, when used in connection with jurisprudence suggests a professorial masseur massaging a *corpus juris* which is safe only in the hands of regular practitioners—if like either of these you are in fear of mere names, it is possible to put the matter in wholly innocuous phrases and in terms of the modes of thought of the moment. Let us put the new point of view in terms of engineering; let us speak of a change from a political or ethical idealistic interpretation to an engineering interpretation. Let us think of the problem of the end of law in terms of a great task or great series of tasks of social engineering. Let us say that the change consists in thinking not of an abstract harmonizing of human wills but of a concrete securing or realizing of human interests. From an earthly standpoint the central tragedy of existence is that there are not enough of the material goods of existence, as it were, to go round; that while individual claims and wants and desires are infinite, the material means of satisfying them are finite; that while, in common phrase, we all want the earth, there are many of us but there is only one earth. Thus we may think of the task of the legal order as one of precluding friction and eliminating waste; as one of conserving the goods of existence in order to make them go as far as possible, and of precluding friction and eliminating waste in the human use and enjoyment of them, so that where each may not have all that he claims, he may at least have all that is possible. Put in this way, we are seeking to secure as much of human claims and desires—that is as much of the whole scheme of interests—as possible, with the least sacrifice of such interests. Let us apply this engineering interpretation to the eight phenomena in American law of the present of which I spoke in the last lecture.

First we noted the growth of limitations on the use of property, of limitations on exercise of the incident of ownership. To the nineteenth-century way of thinking the question was simply one of the right of the owner and of the right of his neighbor. Within his physical boundaries the dominion of each was complete. So long as he kept within them and what he did within them was consistent with an equally absolute dominion of the neighbor within his boundaries, the law was to keep its hands off. For the end of law was taken to be a maximum of self-assertion by each, limited only by the possibility of a like self-assertion by all. If, therefore, he built a fence eight feet high cutting off light and air from his neighbor and painted the fence on the side toward his neighbor in stripes of hideous colors, this was consistent with his neighbor's doing the same; it was an exercise of his incidental *jus utendi,* and the mere circumstance that he did it out of unmixed malice was quite immaterial since it in no way infringed the liberty or invaded the property of the neighbor. But suppose we think of law not negatively as a system of hands off while individuals assert themselves freely, but positively as a social institution existing for social ends. Thinking thus, what claims or demands or wants of society are involved in such a controversy? There is an individual interest of substance on the part of each. Each asserts a claim to use, enjoy and get the benefit of the land of which the law recognizes him as the owner. Also the one asserts an individual interest of personality, a claim to exert his will and exercise his faculties freely and hence to employ them in such building operations upon his land as he thinks proper. What shall society say to these claims? If we think in terms of social interests and of giving effect to individual claims to the extent that they coincide with or may be identified with a social interest, we shall say that there is a social interest in the security of acquisitions, on which our economic order rests, and a social interest in the individual life. But that security of acquisitions is satisfied by use of property for the satisfaction of wants of the owner which are consistent with social life; or at least it is not seriously impaired by so limiting it in order to give effect to other wants which are consistent with social life. And the individual life, in which there is a social interest, is a moral and social life. Hence the social interest does not extend to exercise of individual faculties for anti-social purposes of gratifying malice. The moment we put the matter in terms of social life rather than of abstract individual will, we come to the result to which the law has been coming more and more of late thoughout the world.

Take our second case, the rise of limitations upon freedom of contract. In a case of 1886, which was the starting point of a long line of cases in the last century, a mining company paid wages in orders on a company store. The legislature forbade this, and the question was whether the statute forbidding it and enacting that persons employing more than a certain number of employees should pay wages in cash was an arbitrary interference with free contract, an unreasonable restriction of the power of free men to make such contracts as they pleased, and so unconstitutional and void. Looking at the matter simply as between the abstract individual mining operator and the abstract individual miner, and this was the way in which the nineteenth century looked at such things, we should probably say something like the following: The legislative restriction does not promote a maximum of free individual self-assertion but on the contrary restrains such self-assertion and does not do this in order that others may have a like freedom of self-assertion. Hence it is an unjustifiable interference with a natural right. And this is exactly what the court said in the actual case. But suppose we think in terms of the interest of society in the individual moral and social life, the interest of society in the human life of the individuals therein. It is no infringement of the human dignity and no considerable interference with the full human life of the operator to say to him that he shall pay wages only in cash, while only by some compromise of conflicting claims which imposes such a limitation may we secure the human dignity of the employees and enable them to live human lives in a civilized society. The criterion actually employed is the one proposed by William James as a principle of ethical philosophy—"since all demands conjointly cannot be satisfied in this poor world," our aim should be "to satisfy as many as we can with the least sacrifice of other demands." Tried by a social-utilitarian criterion of securing as many interests or as much of interests as we may with the least sacrifice of other interests, the restriction upon free contract is justified, and the courts of today have come to the conclusion.

Turn now to the third case, namely, imposition of limitations upon the power of an owner to dispose of property. A husband earns one hundred dollars in wages and is about to assign this product of his toil to a "loan shark." The legislature steps in and says to him: You shall not exercise this incident of your ownership of this claim for wages unless your wife is willing to join in the assignment. The nineteenth century would have thought at once of an abstract free man of full age and sound mind, possessed of a claim for wages as part of his substance, and would have asked: How does this restriction of the power of the owner of a claim to assign it promote a maximum of abstract individual self-assertion? Is such a restriction in any way required to secure some liberty to all by which we may justify restraint of the liberty of this one? The answer must be in the negative, and if such a statute had been enacted in the eighties of the last century instead of the second decade of the present century, it would have fared hard in the courts. But let us look at it from the standpoint of the social interests involved. The husband's claim is to be subsumed under a social interest in the security of acquisitions, the wife's under social interest in the security of domestic institutions, the chiefest of social institutions. The infringement of the general security of acquisitions involved in such a restriction is negligible. The control of men in general over their property is scarcely affected thereby. On the other hand the most important of social institutions is secured and protected against practices that solely threaten its existence in crowded, urban, industrial communities.

Or take the limitations upon the power of creditors to exact satisfaction which have become so common and were denounced so extravagantly by courts when first they were enacted. These courts thought wholly in terms of an abstract individual debtor and an abstract individual creditor, and so the case against such restrictions seemed simple and clear. But if we ask how far we may trench upon the social interest in the security of transactions, a fundamental form of the general security in a commercial and industrial society based upon credit—if we ask how far we may impair this interest to secure the social interest in the individual life to the extent of preserving a minimum human life to the debtor, our question becomes one of a compromise that will secure as much as possible of each with the least sacrifice of either, and we obtain a rational basis for legislation which when enacted more or less on instinct in the immediate past, has been governed too often merely by sentiment or by pressure from class-conscious persons "actually engaged in the business of agriculture."

Just now few things excite more vigorous judicial dissent than new examples of the notable tendency in recent decisions and in recent legislation to impose liability in the absence of fault. A minority of the highest courts in the land see in decisions upholding legislative imposition of such liability "a menace to all rights, subjecting them unreservedly to considerations of policy." But new cases are adding continually. Let us take an example from legislation. In more than one jurisdiction if the owner of an automobile allows the machine to go out upon the highway in control of a person who is not licensed to operate a car he is liable at his peril both penally and in damages if some injury occurs, although he is wholly free from want of care and has taken all reasonable precautions. If an unauthorized person took the machine out without his knowledge he is none the less held to answer for resulting injuries. How may we justify the imposition of such a liability? If we think only in terms of the individual owner and the individual pedestrian who is run over it is not easy to do so. But if we think on the one hand of the security of acquisitions and the individual life of the owner, with its incident of free exercise of his faculties by owning a car, and on the other hand of the general security of life and limb, and ask what rule will secure the most with the least sacrifice, the matter looks very different. The whole course of the law today is palpably a result of the latter way of looking at such questions.

Another change in the judicial and legislative attitude in the last thirty years has taken the form of change of *res communes* and *res nullius* into *res publicæ*. As we used to think, certain things were *res communes*. Although, following the language of Roman law they were said to be incapable of ownership by any one and their use was said to be common to all, we had come to think rather of individual rights of using these things and of the persons in whom these rights resided. The law ascertained the persons who might use these things, attributed to them individual rights of property and fixed the extent of such rights. Other things were *res nullius*. No one owned them for the time being, but any one who took possession of them intending to make them his own might become owner by so doing. Of late there has been an increasing tendency to treat both as *res publicæ;* to hold, as some have put it, that both are "owned by the state in trust for the people"; to hold that conservation and socially advantageous use of these things, regarded as natural resources of society, requires that no one be suffered to acquire any property in them or any property right in the use of them, but that they be administered by the state so as to secure the largest and widest and most beneficial use of them consistent with conserving them. Here the social interest in the conservation of natural resources has come to be recognized and a compromise is sought not between the wills of conflicting individual claimants to control over them but between the exigencies of that interest and those of the interest in free exercise of individual powers and the interest in security of acquisitions.

But enough of these illustrations. For by this time you will have perceived the method. The jurisprudence of today catalogues or inventories individual claims, individual wants, individual desires, as did the jurisprudence of the nineteenth century. Only it does not stop there and assume that these claims inevitably call for legal recognition and legal securing in and of themselves. It goes on to ask: What claims, what demands are involved in the existence of the society in which these individual demands are put forward; how far may these individual demands be put in terms of those social interests or identified with them, and when so subsumed under social interests, in so far as they may be treated, what will give the fullest effect to those social interests with the least sacrifice? We owe this way of thinking to Rudolf von Jhering who was the first to insist upon the interests which the legal order secures rather than the legal rights by which it secures them.

Law begins by granting remedies; by allowing actions. In time we generalize from these actions and perceive rights behind them. But as the actions are means for vindicating rights, so the rights are means conferred by law for securing the interests which it recognizes. Accordingly the scheme of natural rights, to be secured at all hazards, becomes a scheme of interests— of human claims or wants or demands—which we may think the law ought to protect and secure so far as they may be protected and secured; it becomes something for the lawmaker to take account of as of moral and political significance rather than something for the judge to consider as of *legal* significance. As was pointed out in the lecture on the philosophy of law in the nineteenth century, prior to Jhering all theories of laws were individualist. The purpose of law was held to be a harmonizing of individual wills in such a way as to leave to each the greatest possible scope for free action. Such, we say, was the view both of philosophical and of historical jurists. On the other hand, Jhering's is a social theory of law. Whereas the eighteenth century conceived of law as something which the individual invoked against society, the idea of our American bills of rights, Jhering taught that it was something created by society, through which the individual found a means of securing his interests, so far as society recognized them. Although much ingenious philosophical criticism has been directed against this theory, it has not affected the central point. The conception of law as a securing of interests or a protecting of relations has all but universally superseded the individualist theory.

Jhering's work is of enduring value for legal science. The older juristic theory of law as a means to individual liberty and of laws as limitations upon individual wills to secure individual liberty, divorced the jurist from the actual life of today. The jurists of whom Jhering made fun, translated to a heaven of juristic conceptions and seated before a machine which brought out of each conception its nine hundred and ninety-nine thousand nine hundred and ninety-nine logical results, have their counterpart in American judges of the end of the last century who insisted upon a legal theory of equality of rights and liberty of contract in the face of notorious social and economic facts. On the other hand, the conception of law as a means toward social ends, the doctrine that law exists to secure interests, social, public and individual, requires the jurists to keep in touch with life. Wholly abstract considerations do not suffice to justify legal rules under such a theory. The function of legal history comes to be one of illustrating how rules and principles have met concrete situations in the past and of enabling us to judge how we may deal with such situations in the present rather than one of furnishing self-sufficient premises from which rules are to be obtained by rigid deduction.

Three features of this social utilitarianism are significant for our task of shaping the materials of the common-law tradition to meet the purposes of today and of tomorrow. One is the light which it throws on legal history. Nineteenth-century individualism wrote legal history as the record of a continually strengthening and increasing securing of the logical deductions from individual freedom in the form of individual rights, and hence as a product of the pressure of individual claims or wants or desires. But this is just what it is not. It is not too much to say that the social interest in the general security, in its lowest terms of an interest in peace and order, dictated the very beginnings of law. Take, for example, the truce or peace, the most fruitful of the institutions of Germanic law. As we find this institution in Anglo-Saxon law, one type comprises the church peace and the peace of festivals and holy-days—the exemption of the church and of these days from prosecution of the feud or seeking of redress by means of private war. What is behind this exemption, the pressure of individual interests calling for public recognition and security or the social interest in social performance of the duties of religion in a Christian society? Another type comprises the peace of the walled town to which the country people had fled when the kingdom was invaded and the peace of the time when the king summoned the host to gather under his leadership in event of war. Here also the feud and private vengeance were suspended. Why? Is it because of the pressure of individual rights, or is it because of a social interest in the performance of military duties essential to maintenance of society, to which the individual claims to redress must for the time being give way? Still another type comprises the peace of the market, the peace of forest and the peace of the great highways. These places also were exempted from violent prosecution of claims to redress. Is it not clear that the basis of this exemption is to be found not in the pressure of individual interests but in the social interest in the social performance of the economic functions on which society rested? Again the peace of the *gemot* or assembly of the free men for political and judicial purposes rests upon the social interest in the unimpeded functioning of the political institutions by which the social order was maintained, and, without going into more detail, the other phases of the truce or peace are expressions or recognitions of the paramount social interest in the general security.

Secondly, from a social-utilitarian standpoint the history of law is a record of continually wider recognition and more efficacious securing of social interests. This may be seen in the development of legal rules and doctrines, but it appears also in the development of juristic thought as to the end of the legal order. Hippodamus of Miletus, a writer on law and politics in the fifth century B.C., proposed a threefold classification of law because, he said, there were but three possible subjects of legal proceedings, namely, insult, injury and homicide. In this statement of the scope of law the general security is the only interest taken into account and only the simplest phases of that interest are regarded. More than a thousand years later the Institutes of Justinian sought to reduce the whole law to three precepts: To live honorably, not to insure another, and to give to each his own. In this statement of the scope and subject matter of law the general security is conceived more widely, the security of acquisitions if recognized as such, and a social interest in the general morals is added. Still a thousand years later Bacon, if indeed the treatise on the Use of the Law is his, could not find as much as this in the English law of the sixteenth century. He put the ends of the legal order as three: To secure us in property, to secure us in life and to secure us in our reputations. Here the general security is conceived narrowly in terms of individual substance and of individual personality in the two simple forms of life and reputation. In the nineteenth century Bentham stated the ends of law as four: To provide subsistence, to maintain security, to promote abundance and to favor equality. Here the second of the four includes two of Justinian's three and much besides.

But even Bentham's comprehensive statement is inadequate to the multitude of claims which the law of today recognizes and seeks to secure. For if we look only at social interests, we may see that the legal order endeavors to give effect to at least six groups of claims or demands involved in the existence of civilized society. First we may put the general security, the claim or want of civilized society to be secure from those acts or courses of conduct that threaten its existence. This paramount social interest includes (1) peace and order, the first interest to receive legal recognition, (2) the general health, recognition whereof by means of sanitary legislation was objected to by the positivists a generation ago, (3) the security of acquisitions and (4) the security of transactions. The security of acquisitions was recognized in Justinian's three precepts and has been emphasized ever since. The security of transactions is no less important in an economic order resting upon credit, and the last century insisted upon these two phases of the general security at the expense of the individual life. Second, there is the security of social institutions, the claim or want of civilized society to be secure from those acts or course of conduct which threaten or impede the functioning of its fundamental institutions, domestic, religious and political. Third, we may put the conservation of social resources, the claim or want of civilized society that the natural media of civilized human existence and means of satisfying human wants in such a society shall not be wasted and shall be used and enjoyed in a manner consistent with the widest and most beneficial application of them to human purposes. In a world of discovery and colonizing activity, in a society of pioneers engaged in discovering, appropriating and exploiting the resources of nature, this interest seemed negligible. In the crowded world of today the law is constantly taking account of it and the *jus abutendi* as an incident of ownership is becoming obsolete. Fourth, we may put the general morals, the claim or want of civilized society to be secure against those acts and courses of conduct which run counter to the moral sentiment of the general body of those who live therein for the time being. In primitive society this interest is secured through organized religion. But the law soon takes it over. In our law today it is secured through the common law as to misdemeanors, by definition of a multitude of statutory offences and by the doctrine of a public policy against things of immoral tendency. Fifth, there is the interest in general progress, the claim or want of civilized society to be secure against those acts and courses of conduct that interfere with economic, political and cultural progress and the claim that so far as possible individual conduct be so shaped as to conduce to these forms of progress. The law is coming to be full of recognition of this interest. Lastly, sixth, we may put the social interest in the individual human life, the claim or want of civilized society that each individual therein be able to live a human life according to the standards of the society, and to be secure against those acts and courses of conduct which interfere with the possibility of each individual's living such a life. Recognition of this interest as such is characteristic of the law of the present, and the twentieth century is insisting upon it as strongly as the seventeenth century upon the security of acquisitions and the security of transactions.

Finally as a result of social utilitarianism the legal reason of today in shaping rules and developing traditional premises of the legal system in order to give effect to social interests, looks at them in terms of the concrete situation, not in terms of the abstract claims of abstract human beings. The purely abstract legal reason of the nineteenth century was set forth satirically by an English judge who, in the old days before the divorce court, was called on to sentence a workingman convicted of bigamy. On being asked what he had to say why sentence should not be pronounced, the accused told a moving story of how his wife had run away with another man and left him with a number of small children to look after while barely earning a living by hard labor. After waiting several years he remarried in order to provide a proper home for the children. Mr. Justice Maule shook his head. "My good man," said he, "the law did not in any wise leave you without a sufficient remedy. You should first have brought an action in Her Majesty's Court of Common Pleas against this man with whom, as you say, your wife went away. In that action, after two or three years and the expenditure of two or three hundred pounds you would have obtained a judgment against him which very likely would have been uncollectible. You should then have brought a suit against your wife in the ecclesiastical court for a divorce from bed and board, which you might have obtained in two or three years after expenditure of two or three hundred pounds. You would then have been able to apply to Parliament for an absolute divorce, which you might have obtained in four or five years more after spending four or five hundred pounds. And," he continued, for he saw the accused impatiently seeking to interpose and to say something, "if you tell me that you never had and never in your life expect to have so many pennies at one time, my answer must be that it hath ever been the glory of England not to have one law for the rich and another for the poor." Accordingly, he imposed a sentence of imprisonment for one day. But Maule, J., was ahead of his time. Even down to the end of the last century, lawyers took seriously the existence of theoretical remedies which in practice were unavailable and regarded the abstract justice of abstract rules as quite enough, be the concrete results what they might. This attitude was a natural result of measuring the law solely by standards drawn from the law itself.

In the past century we studied law from within. The jurists of today are studying it from without. The past century sought to develop completely and harmoniously the fundamental principles which jurists discovered by metaphysics or by history. The jurists of today seek to enable and to compel lawmaking and also the interpretation and application of legal rules, to take more account and more intelligent account, of the social facts upon which law must proceed and to which it is to be applied. Where the last century studied law in the abstract, they insist upon study of the actual social effects of legal institutions and legal doctrines. Where the last century prepared for legislation by study of other legislation analytically, they insist on sociological study in connection with legal study in preparation for legislation. Where the last century held comparative law the best foundation for wise lawmaking, they hold it not enough to compare the laws themselves, but that even more their social operation must be studied and the effects which they produce, if any, when put in action. Where the last century studied only the making of law, they hold it necessary to study as well the means of making legal rules effective. Where the last century made the legal history merely a study of how doctrines have evolved and developed considered solely as jural materials, they call for a sociological legal history, a study of the social effects which the doctrines of the law have produced in the past and of how they have produced them. They call for a legal history which shall not deal with rules and doctrines apart from the economic and social history of their time, as if the causes of change in the law were always to be found in the legal phenomena of the past; a legal history that shall not try to show that the law of the past can give us an answer to every question by systematic deductions as if it were a system without hiatus and without antinomies. They call for a legal history which is to show us how the law of the past grew out of social, economic and psychological conditions, how it accommodated itself to them, and how far we may proceed upon that law as a basis, or in disregard of it, with well-grounded expectations of producing the results desired. In these ways they strive to make effort more effective in achieving the purposes of law. Such is the spirit of twentieth-century jurisprudence. Such is the spirit in which legal reason is to be employed upon our received jural materials in order to make of them instruments for realizing justice in the world of today.

But a new theory of lawmaking as a social function is not the whole of our task. Before we can have sound theories here we need facts on which to build them. Even after we get sound theories, we shall need facts to enable us to apply them. Hard as it is for legislators to ascertain social facts, it is even more difficult for courts with the machinery which our judicial organization affords. As a general proposition, courts have no adequate machinery for getting at the facts required for the exercise of their necessary lawmaking function. As things are, our courts must decide on the basis of matters of general knowledge and on supposed accepted principles of uniform application. Except as counsel furnish material in their printed arguments, a court has no facilities for obtaining knowledge of social facts comparable to hearings before committees, testimony of specialists who have conducted detailed investigations, and other means of the sort available to the legislature. Yet judges must make law as well as apply it, and judicial reference bureaus not remotely unlike Dr. McCarthy's epoch-making contribution to practical legislative lawmaking are not unlikely to develop. The laboratories and staffs of experts which are coming to be attached to some tribunals strongly suggest this. But before we can do anything in this direction, we must provide a more flexible judicial organization. We must give our courts power to organize such administrative agencies as the business before them may require. The present system, in which in many of our jurisdictions the judges are at the mercy of elective administrative officers over whom they have no control, is compatible with effective handling of social facts in our tribunals. We must abandon to some extent the hard and fast line between the judicial and the administrative involved in our legal tradition. We must recognize that not a little of the administrative is involved in and necessary to the effective working of the judicial and must make a court within its proper scope a bureau of justice, not merely a machine for grinding out judgments and written opinions. Only by a gradual process did our law evolve a rational mode of trial for ascertainment of the facts of particular controversies. There may be an analogy here. Starting with purely mechanical modes of trying facts, the law developed rational methods. In the immediate past the social facts required for exercise of the judicial function of lawmaking have been arrived at by means which may fairly be called mechanical. In a transition from the mechanical law making of the past century to rational lawmaking, not the least problem is to discover a rational mode of advising the court of facts of which it is supposed to take judicial notice.

What will be the effect of all these changes upon the spirit of our legal tradition—upon the spirit of the common law? They are so at variance with the course of our legal thought since the end of the seventeenth century that some fear our whole juristic edifice is about to be subverted. Yet the change of front today is no more radical than that which took place in the rise of the court of chancery, the development of equity and the consequent making over the strict law by an infusion of morals. And the nineteenth century, after equity had been absorbed, could look back into the Year Books and recognize Choke and Brian and Fortescue, the worthies of our medieval law, as lights of the same system under which it was living. For through all vicissitudes the supremacy of law, the insistence upon law as reason to be developed by judicial experience in the decision of causes and the refusal to take the burden of upholding right from the concrete each and put it wholly upon the abstract all have survived. These ideas are realities in comparison whereof rules and dogmas are ephemeral appearances. They are so much a part of the mental and moral makeup of our race, that much more than legal and political revolutions will be required to uproot them.

SELECTED BIBLIOGRAPHY

H. C. Adams, *Relation of the State to Industrial Action*, in *Publications of American Economic Association*, Vol. I (1887).

E. Bellamy, *Looking Backward: 2000–1887* (1888).

S. J. Buck, *The Agrarian Crusade* (1920).

B. N. Cardozo, *The Nature of the Judicial Process* (1921).
 The Paradoxes of Legal Science (1928).
 Law and Literature (1931).

J. M. Clarke, *Social Control of Business* (1926).

E. W. Crecraft. *Government and Business* (1928).

H. Croly, *Progressive Democracy* (1912).

J. Dewey, *Individualism New and Old* (1930).

W. Fite, *Individualism* (1911).

F. Frankfurter, *The People and its Government* (1930).

F. Frankfurter and J. M. Landis, *The Business of the Supreme Court* (1928).

H. George, *Progress and Poverty* (1879).

F. E. Haynes, *Third Party Movements since the Civil War* (1916).
 Social Politics in the United States (1924).

M. Hillquit, *History of Socialism in the United States* (1910).

O. W. Holmes, *Collected Legal Papers* (1921).

R. M. La Follette, *Autobiography* (1913).

H. LAIDLER, *History of Socialist Thought* (1927).
   Socialism in Thought and Action (1920).
A. LIEF, *Dissenting Opinions of Mr. Justice Holmes* (1929).
   Social and Economic Views of Mr. Justice Brandeis (1930).
H. D. LLOYD, *Wealth Against Commonwealth* (1898).
R. S. LYND and H. M. LYND, *Middletown: A Study in Contemporary American Culture* (1929).
W. MACDONALD, *A New Constitution for a New America* (1921).
S. P. ORTH, *Readings on the Relation of Government to Property and Industry* (1915).
R. POUND, *The Spirit of the Common Law* (1921).
   Introduction to the Philosophy of Law (1922).
   Interpretations of Legal History (1923).
   "A Theory of Social Interests," *Proceedings of American Sociological Society*, Vol. XV (1920).
D. RICHARDSON, *Constitutional Doctrines of Justice O. W. Holmes*, in Johns Hopkins University Studies in Historical and Political Science, Series XLII, No. 3 (1924).
E. A. ROSS, *Sin and Society: An Analysis of Latter-Day Iniquity* (1907).
W. G. SUMNER, *What Social Classes Owe Each Other* (1884).
N. THOMAS, *America's Way Out* (1931).
W. THOMPSON, *Federal Centralization* (1923).
T. VEBLEN, *Theory of the Leisure Class* (1899).
   Theory of Business Enterprise (1910).
L. F. WARD, *Dynamic Sociology* (1883).
   Applied Sociology (1906).
   Psychic Factors in Civilization (1893).
W. WEYL, *The New Democracy* (1912).
W. WILSON, *The State* (1889).
   New Freedom (1913).

CHAPTER VIII

"AMERICA COMES OF AGE"

The turn of the century marked the passing of American adolescence. American litterateurs and European lecturers are still fond of calling this a young nation; but we are no longer a growing, swaddling youngster. Our ailments are not now those of growing pains; they are the problems of adjustment that confront maturity. The filling up of the Mississippi Valley and the Pacific coast, the piling up of human beings in metropolitan centers, the massing of labor within factory walls, the concentration of financial control, the lessening of individual opportunity, the presence of large immigrant groups —these are problems that cannot be solved merely by outgrowing them. They are the ailments that afflict our maturity. They are conditions to which we must adjust ourselves. America has come of age and has inherited the responsibilities of manhood.

The problems of our contemporary life are too numerous and complex to permit all to be included in this volume; selection, however difficult, is imperative. The historian of the next century may be able to look back upon our age and easily discern our contributions to thought. Time solves many conflicts, and the moving finger erases many a line. In the whirl of our present complexities, an Olympian survey of ourselves is too prophetic for human endeavor. The worm's eye view of the life rushing on about us, however, may prove of some value. It indicates four phases of political thought that are of increasing significance. One, the new relationship of government to our complicated economic institutions, we have already discussed. Three others remain for analysis: (1) the United States in an interdependent world, (2) democratic disillusionment, and (3) the clash of cultures.

The United States in an Interdependent World

The end of the nineteenth century found the United States forced into a new rôle in world politics. Theretofore, our problems were those of domestic expansion. Up to 1890 there had been free land suitable for settlement, and abundant opportunities for capital seek-

ing investment. In fact, the usual scarcity of capital that characterizes a new country was so acute that European wealth to the extent
of $6,000,000,000 was still invested here in 1910. The last three
decades of the nineteenth century produced a remarkable change
and advanced us to a position of world economic importance. Between 1870 and 1900 population increased 97 per cent; the annual
production of wheat increased from 236,000,000 to 522,000,000 bushels, corn from 1,094,000,000 to 2,105,000,000 bushels, cotton from
4,352,000 to 10,100,000 bales, petroleum from 221,000,000 to 2,672,-
000,000 gallons, coal from 29,000,000 to 241,000,000 tons, and pig
iron from 1,665,000 to 13,789,000 tons.[1] Foreign markets for surplus
products and capital became imperative. The Spanish-American
War, hastened by our investments in and commerce with Cuba,
marked a turning point in our world position. The war left us possessing the Philippines and Porto Rico. The "Platt Amendment"
to the Cuban constitution gave us a protectorate over that island.
During the present century we have continued to expand beyond our
national boundaries. The Panama Canal not only speeded commercial communication between our Atlantic and Pacific ports, but
also gave us new interests in the Caribbean. The republics of that
region have come under the economic influence and the military
policing of the United States. Our possessions in Hawaii, Guam, and
the Philippines have opened an increasingly profitable trade route
to the Orient. In order to prevent the disintegration of China through
European aggrandizement and to protect America's growing commerce, Secretary of State John Hay promulgated the "open door"
policy. Thus the United States was gradually assuming a significant
rôle in world trade and politics.

The outbreak of the World War in August, 1914, compelled American leaders and lay public to realize for the first time that we had
become a unit of a highly interdependent world. The clash of arms
in western and central Europe seriously affected our markets there.
Allied loans from American financiers and purchases of American
munitions and materials gave us an economic interest in the conflict.
British and the German interference with American shipping threatened our prosperity. The war thus multiplied our commercial and
diplomatic relations. The reports of German atrocities in Belgium
and of submarine attacks upon vessels carrying defenseless women
and children aroused the moral sentiments of the average American.
The execution of Edith Cavell and the sinking of the *Lusitania*

[1] Faulkner, *American Economic History*, pp. 621–622.

produced a high moral tension. Wilson's attempts to induce Germany to accept humanitarian methods of warfare fostered this idealism. America began to think in international terms to a degree greater than ever before in our history. A spirit of moral leadership and the enthusiasm of participation in the great experiment of world coöperation characterized the Wilsonian era. Despite the post-war reaction and disillusionment, this sentiment still motivates many of our intellectual leaders.

America's entrance into the war in April, 1917, was partially due to the government's fear that the German submarine warfare would ruin our shipping and deprive us of the economic fruits of the European demands for foods and war supplies. Fear of a German victory and the consequent destruction of the world balance of power also played an important rôle. The Wilsonian régime, however, rationalized our participation on high moral grounds. The American troops died in France, the American people bought liberty bonds and ate meatless dinners—all to "make the world safe for democracy." Wilson announced that Germany was committing a crime against humanity, that if she triumphed she would set back the civilization of the world a hundred years. America's mission was to punish one of the greatest wrongs in history. Thus, our entrance into the World War was justified, not on grounds of economic necessity or military fear, but on grounds of morality and humanity.

In his now famous speech presenting the Treaty of Versailles to the Senate,[2] Wilson stated that the United States entered the war upon a different footing from every other nation except our associates on this side of the Atlantic. We entered it, he said, not because our material interests were directly threatened or because any special treaty obligations to which we were parties had been violated. Rather we saw the supremacy, and even the validity, of right everywhere put in jeopardy and free government likely to be everywhere imperiled by the intolerable aggression of a power which respected neither right nor obligation.[3] In his speech before Congress on April 2, 1917, recommending the declaration of war against Germany, Wilson declared that the chief objective of America was to make "the world safe for democracy."

"We are accepting this challenge of hostile purpose because we know that in such a government, following such methods, we can never have a

[2] July 10, 1919.
[3] Baker and Dodd, *Public Papers of Woodrow Wilson: War and Peace* (New York, Harper & Brothers), I, 538.

friend; and that in the presence of its organized power, always lying in wait to accomplish we know not what purpose, there can be no assured security for the democratic governments of the world. We are now about to accept the gage of battle with this natural foe to liberty and shall, if necessary, spend the whole force of the nation to check and nullify its pretensions and its powers. We are glad, now that we see the facts with no veil of false pretence about them, to fight thus for the ultimate peace of the world and for the liberation of its people, the German people included: for the rights of nations great and small and the privilege of men everywhere to choose their way of life and of obedience. The world must be made safe for democracy. Its peace must be planted upon the tested foundations of political liberty. We have no selfish ends to serve. We desire no conquest, no dominion. We seek no indemnities for ourselves, no material compensation for the sacrifices we shall freely make. We are but one of the champions of the rights of mankind. We shall be satisfied when those rights have been made as secure as the faith and the freedom of nations can make them." [4]

Wilson further expressed this idealistic rationalization of our entrance into the war in his exposition of the "Fourteen Points." We entered the war because violations of right had occurred that touched us to the quick and made the life of our people impossible unless they were corrected and the world secured once for all against their recurrence. Wilson demanded that the world be made fit and safe to live in: and "particularly that it be made safe for every peace-loving nation which, like our own, wishes to live its own life, determine its own institutions, be assured of justice and fair dealing by the other peoples of the world as against force and selfish aggression." His program of world peace included: open covenants openly arrived at, freedom of the seas, removal of hampering trade barriers, reduction of armaments, adjustment of colonial claims in the interest of the populations concerned, fair treatment of Russia, evacuation of Belgium, restoration of Alsace-Lorraine to France, adjustment of Italian frontiers on the principle of nationality, autonomy for the peoples of Austria-Hungary, evacuation of Rumania, Serbia, and Montenegro, reorganization of the Ottoman Empire, the reëstablishment of Poland, and an association of nations to maintain world peace. Such were the ideals of the American "crusade." [5]

Upon the successful termination of the war, Wilson and a corps of assistants journeyed to Paris to draft the Versailles Treaty. The peace settlement redrew the map of Europe and established a new world order. Wilson promised the continued and increased participation of the United States in world affairs. From the American point

---

[4] Baker and Dodd, *Public Papers of Woodrow Wilson: War and Peace*, I, pp. 13–14.
[5] *Ibid.*, pp. 158–161.

of view, the Covenant of the League of Nations constituted the most significant phase of the treaty. It created three international agencies: an Assembly of deputies from each nation, dominion, and self-governing colony; a Council of representatives from the United States, Great Britain, France, Italy, and Japan, and four other countries selected and rotated periodically by the Assembly; and a Secretariat, or an international civil service, to administer the routine affairs of the world community. The members of the League agreed not to resort to arms, but to arbitrate every dispute which they could not settle by diplomacy. They guaranteed to respect and preserve the territorial integrity of one another against external aggression.[6] The Covenant set up a scheme of diplomatic, economic, and, if necessary, military reprisals to punish states that resorted to war.

The new plan of world order contemplated increased American participation in European and world affairs. It consequently became Wilson's duty to justify the abandonment of the traditional American isolation. His entire approach to this problem and to the League rested primarily upon the desire for peace. The need for the coöperation of nations to solve their common difficulties played a minor rôle; Wilson rather looked upon the League and American participation as essential to preserve and enforce peace.

American isolation, Wilson argued upon his return to this country, is no longer possible. The isolation of the United States is at an end, not because we chose to go into the politics of the world, but because by the sheer genius of our people and the growth of our power we have become a determining factor in the history of mankind. America is growing more powerful, and the more powerful she is the more inevitable it is that she should be the trustee of the world's peace. The United States has greater material wealth and greater physical power than any other nation. We are the only nation in the world that has sufficient moral influence with the rest of the world; while old rivalries and old jealousies and "many of the intricate threads of history woven in unhappy patterns" have made the other nations suspect one another, nobody doubts America.[7] In respect to the much contested Article X, Wilson insisted that we are partners with the rest of the world in guaranteeing the territorial integrity and political independence of others. Only by that article can we under-

[6] This provision of Article X has been a subject of controversy ever since its drafting. The nature and extent of this "guarantee" has been debated frequently by French and British statesmen and publicists.

[7] H. Foley, *Woodrow Wilson's Case for the League of Nations*, pp. 185-186.

write civilization. America alone cannot do this; all the great free peoples of the world must coöperate.[8]

Wilson conceived of the League as an instrument to guarantee peace to a troubled world. It is the only thing that can prevent the recurrence of the dreadful catastrophe of war.

"That is what the League of Nations is for, to end this war justly, and then not merely to serve notice on governments which would contemplate the same things that Germany contemplated that they will do it at their peril, but also concerning the combination of power which will prove to them that they will do it at their peril. It is idle to say the world *will* combine against you, because it may not, but it is persuasive to say that the world *is* combined against you, and will remain combined against the things that Germany attempted."[9]

Wilson stated that at first the statesmen of Europe felt that the formation of a League was a "council of perfection" which practical men of world affairs must agree to very cautiously and with many misgivings.

"It was only as the difficult work of arranging an all but universal adjustment of the world's affairs advanced from day to day from one stage of conference to another that it became evident to them that what they were seeking would be little more than something written upon paper, to be interpreted and applied by such methods as the chances of politics might make available if they did not provide a means of common counsel which all were obliged to accept, a common authority whose decisions would be recognized as decisions which all must respect. And so the most practical, the most skeptical among them turned more and more to the League as the authority through which international action was to be secured, the authority without which, as they had come to see it, it would be difficult to give assured effect either to this treaty or to any other international understanding upon which they were to depend for the maintenance of peace."[10]

The League, however, was not merely an instrument to adjust and remedy old wrongs under a new treaty of peace; it was, argued Wilson, the only hope of mankind.

"Again and again had the demon of war been cast out of the house of the people and the house swept clean by a treaty of peace; only to prepare a time when he would enter it again with spirits worse than himself. The house must now be given a new tenant who could hold it against all such. Convenient, indeed, indispensable, as statesmen found the newly planned League of Nations to be for the execution of present plans of peace and rep-

[8] H. Foley, *Woodrow Wilson's Case for the League of Nations*, p. 77.
[9] Baker and Dodd, *op. cit.*, I, 593.
[10] *Ibid.*, p. 546.

aration, they saw it in a new aspect before their work was finished. They saw it as the main object of the peace, as the only thing that could complete it or make it worth while. They saw it as the hope of the world, and that hope they did not dare to disappoint." [11]

Wilsonian internationalism thus rested on high moral idealism. America entered the war to prevent a potent threat to humanity and civilization. America should continue its rôle of world moral leadership to preserve peace. The United States was to receive no material reward for its efforts; it was not to share in the distribution of German colonies or the spoils of victory. Wilson did not, moreover, fully envisage the problem of coöperation as aimed, not directly at the maintenance of peace, but at a common attack upon common economic and social diseases. His was an idealistic, a moralistic, desire to crush the demon of war.

Wilsonian internationalism has survived his political collapse and his death. His high moral enthusiasm and the new contact of America with the world outside have stimulated an interest in the world community. One of the several evidences of the continuation of Wilsonian internationalism is the maintenance of pro-League agitation in the United States. The League of Nations Non-Partisan Association and the Bok peace award have done much to sustain interest in the League Covenant. The advocates of American entrance into the League have, in the main, been university teachers closely connected with the study of history, foreign affairs, and international law. Of this group Manley O. Hudson of the Harvard Law School, Pitman B. Potter of the University of Wisconsin, and James T. Shotwell of Columbia University and the Carnegie Peace Foundation have been the most vocal in their demands that the United States play a larger rôle in world affairs.

Probably the most influential exponent of the League since Wilson has been John H. Clarke, who resigned from the United States Supreme Court to lecture on behalf of the League and to head the League of Nations Association. America, Clarke demonstrated, has a vital interest in world peace. Our country really touched only the fringe of the Great War. We engaged in it for only a year and seven months, and against an already greatly exhausted foe. And yet the war costs us more than one hundred thousand precious young lives and twenty-five billions of dollars. Our government spent money at the rate of more than one million dollars an hour. The total amount, Clarke pointed out, is equal to the entire cost of our gov-

[11] Baker and Dodd, *op. cit.*, I, p. 548.

ernment for the one hundred and twenty-five years from the organization of it in 1789 to the outbreak of the war. It is a sum sufficient to pay the cost of such a war as that of the American Revolution for just about one thousand years. A child born in our country to-day, though he live to extreme old age, must contribute a large part of his earnings to the day of his death toward the payment of the costs of the World War.[12] Clarke gave statistics to indicate that seven and a half million young men were killed in battle, that five and a half million more died of their wounds almost immediately after battle, and that twenty million more were wounded severely. Thus thirty-three million of the youth of the world were killed and wounded in four years of war. Nothing that any man in this world can say, he concludes, can add to the impressiveness of this plain statement of plain facts as a measure of the importance of world peace to America.[13]

Clarke did not stop with pointing out the direct costs of the war. He went on to indicate its lasting economic and moral effects. Promptly upon its outbreak, the World War deprived us of a large part of our foreign market, with the result that millions of American farmers in a half dozen of our northwestern states were thrown into unprecedented financial distress. Then came the years of feverish war markets, and later the after-effects of the war which have steadily and resistlessly been destroying our domestic markets by depriving millions of our own people of the power to purchase. Almost every one of the banks in four or five states, he pointed out, have failed or voluntarily closed; thousands of farmers are abandoning their lands to their creditors; and great districts are being practically depopulated, the after effects of the Great War driving out the inhabitants precisely as the onrush of advancing armies scattered the farmers of northern France and Poland. Meanwhile, ever since the war ended, millions of men, women, and children in Europe have been hungry, cold, and perishing. They need the food and clothing which we desire to sell; but, impoverished by the war, they cannot buy. Unless some means are devised for restoring the European market to our farmers, Clarke predicted, 30 per cent of our wheat and cotton lands and 20 per cent of our corn lands must go out of cultivation. While such a process of readjustment is going on, sustained business prosperity is impossible.[14]

[12] J. H. Clarke, *America and World Peace* (New York, Henry Holt and Company, 1925), pp. 15–16.

[13] *Ibid.*, p. 32. [14] *Ibid.*, pp. 18–20.

America thus has an interest in world peace. But permanent peace cannot be obtained by prayer; neither can it be accomplished by carrying banners declaring "There shall be no more war," nor by passing resolutions in favor of the outlawing of war. The one way of achieving this great result is by setting up some permanent political institutions, comprehensive enough, powerful enough, and moral enough to substitute reason and discussion, justice and law for war—civilization's way of settling disputes for the savage way.[15] Our remaining outside the League is not only making it impossible for us to share in the leadership of "this greatest experiment of all times," but it is resulting in misunderstanding and misrepresentation of our motives. It is believed abroad that we entertain imperialistic designs against Mexico and Latin-America.[16]

To an important degree, the focus of agitation in the past few years has shifted from the League of Nations to the Permanent Court of International Justice. This institution was drafted, in accordance with Article XIV of the League Covenant, by a commission of jurists, including Elihu Root. Three Republican presidents—Harding, Coolidge, and Hoover—have advocated American adherence to the court protocol. Among its leading exponents are Root and Hudson. Hudson believes that the World Court will contribute to the maintenance of peace in three ways: (1) by its decision of disputes and vexed questions as they arise; (2) by building a cumulating body of international law; and (3) by facilitating the settlement of problems directly handled by the foreign offices.[17]

A third example of the continuation in this country of Wilsonian internationalism has been the movement for disarmament and the outlawry of war. The maintenance of large navies and the competitive building of battleships, it is felt, results in a psychology of distrust. There develops a vicious circle—the building of American ships; Japanese fear that we are building against her; increase in the Japanese navy; American apprehension that Japan is planning to attack us; further expansion of our navy; increased Japanese fear of American aggression; and so on until an explosion occurs. One nation builds for defense; another invariably regards the new ships as instruments of potential aggression. The proposals for disarmament aim to cut this vicious circle and allay international distrust. The Washington conference of 1921 and the London conference

[15] J. H. Clarke, *America and World Peace*, p. 34.
[16] *Ibid.*, pp. 83–84.
[17] M. O. Hudson, *The Permanent Court of International Justice*, p. 281.

of 1930 succeeded to a slight degree in slowing up the race for armaments.

Closely allied with this movement has been one for the outlawry of war. In 1923 Senator Borah introduced a resolution in the Senate based upon this point of view. He suggested: (1) that by a universal treaty the nations of the world declare war to be a public crime under international law and agree to indict and punish their own "international war breeders or instigators and war profiteers"; (2) that there be created a code of international law of peace based upon equality and justice between nations, "amplified and expanded and adapted and brought down to date"; (3) that there be created a judicial substitute for war. In 1928 the United States signed the multilateral Kellogg-Briand Pact outlawing war. This brief document provided: (1) "The high contracting parties solemnly declare . . . that they condemn recourse to war for the solution of international controversies, and renounce it as an instrument of national policy in their relations with one another"; and (2) they "agree that the settlement or solution of all disputes or conflicts of whatever nature or of whatever origin they may be, which may arise among them, shall never be sought except by pacific means."

The leading advocate of the outlawry of war school is James T. Shotwell, professor of history at Columbia University and an official of the Carnegie Foundation for the Advancement of Peace. Shotwell's thesis is that war in the new world era is no longer a satisfactory state instrument. In the pre-scientific age, war, like industry, was localized. War was then primarily a question of man-power. A nation which went to war simply called upon its nationals and each came with his own arms and accoutrements. The advancing armies lived off the supplies of the countryside through which they marched. A nation which did not wish to fight could remain aloof from the conflict by simply keeping its armies from the field. But in the industrial and financial era of to-day the nature of war has utterly changed. Not only does war now involve the entire economic structure of the belligerent nations, but it also spreads like a contagion throughout all other countries whose economic life has become involved with that of the nations at war.

"As the armies advance in one direction, the ships go out in another for the raw materials of war, and the more the conflagration grows the more the belligerent becomes dependent on ever new supplies, and so, when the war is over, finds that the territory covered by the advance of its armies is perhaps of far less value to it than the wealth which it has sacrificed to win the victory. In other words, the direction of war in the modern world of industry and finance does not wholly follow that of military strategy; it follows rather that of economic needs satisfied only at the ruinous cost of war-time prices." [18]

Modern war not only involves so many people but it involves them so completely. "The shifting map of economic interests was invaded to a far greater degree than the march of armies invaded any country on the geographic map." The industry of war combines two techniques: the technique of destruction and the technique of peace which supplies war with its resources. Since each new scientific invention progressively modifies both of these techniques, war is as uncertain in its direction as in its intensity or its spread. It is now too dangerous an instrument for statesmen to employ.

"It is no longer an *ultima ratio*, for it has lost its *raison d'être*. Victor and victim may suffer a common disaster. Its effects reach even into the unformed future and rob the savings of generations yet unborn. Time, as well as peace, levels its barriers to the march of destruction. This new dynamic world, the creation of human intelligence, containing as it does the most precious things in our heritage, has no other defense against it, once it is loosed, than that which endangers it as well. Such are the phenomena of war as revealed by a study of the tragic years 1914 to 1918. Moreover, it is equally clear from this analysis, that these phenomena are not merely incidental and temporary. They are typical and more and more true as civilization develops. In short, war which was once a directable instrument of policy has now changed its nature with the nature of modern society and ceases to be controllable and directable in the hands of statesmen. By reason of its all-embracing needs, it becomes a contagion among the nations; and one cannot safely use a contagion as an instrument." [19]

Shotwell believes that the Kellogg-Briand treaty will form a sound basis for increased American participation in world affairs. The preamble of the pact states that "any signatory Power which shall hereafter seek to promote its national interests by resort to war should be denied the benefits furnished by this treaty." Thus, instead of enumerating the duties of the law-abiding states, the treaty denies the aggressor the right to calculate upon the continuance of friendly relations. The pact does not guarantee that those relations will be broken, but, in leaving the signatories free to take this step, Shotwell argues, it points to this action as a moral duty. Consequently, the aggressor states should receive no aid or comfort from the co-signatories. Modern warfare has become industrialized. The

---

[18] J. T. Shotwell, *War as an Instrument of National Policy* (New York, Harcourt, Brace and Company), pp. 32–33. See also C. C. Morrison, *The Outlawry of War.*
[19] *Ibid.*, pp. 35–36.

arsenals of the European belligerents before we entered the World War were in Pittsburgh and Bridgeport as well as at Woolwich and Creusot. We must consequently change the conception of neutrality to fit the conditions of modern warfare.

"If the United States is unwilling to go to the extent of dissociating itself from a nation which goes to war in violation of its pledge of peace in a treaty to which the United States is a co-signatory, when that treaty leaves the United States its own judge as to whether the violation has actually occurred or not, then the United States has really put itself on the side of the aggressor. For to supply such a belligerent with the resources of war and to insist upon our right to do so would be making ourselves the accomplices in the aggression. The article in the preamble goes no farther than to warn a nation planning such aggression that it cannot calculate upon our joining it in this way. Our own good faith would count for little if we were to give it aid and comfort in such a violation of the peace. The treaty indicates that once convinced of the nature of the violation we could notify it that we recover full liberty of action with reference to it, and in view of the financial power and the control of resources at the command of the United States, a notification of this kind, that we regarded its act as canceling our obligation to remain at peace, would make any adventurous state pause on the threshold of its adventure. It is a way of using the influence of the United States for peace without any obligations to join in positive measures of suppression." [20]

A fourth manifestation of Wilsonian internationalism is the increasingly accepted philosophy that world economic interdependence must develop an international point of view, and ultimately a world community. To an important degree, this new outlook upon American participation in world affairs differs from Wilsonianism. Its impelling motive is not that of moral leadership for the United States. Rather, a greater realism underlies this school of thought—the realization that economic interdependence has irrevocably destroyed political isolation, that this country is an organic cell in the economic physiology of the world.

The use of steam and electricity has worked the mightiest revolution that has so far taken place. The Industrial Revolution has brought the civilized nations into closer contact with each other than were our thirteen colonies a century and a half ago when they struggled for independence. The Industrial Revolution has brought with itself the economic interdependence of the nations.[21] The development of the steamboat, the railroad, and now the airplane, has knit the once isolated corners of the planet into a single system.

[20] J. T. Shotwel, *War as an Instrument of National Policy*, pp. 221–223.
[21] H. F. Fraser, *Foreign Trade and World Politics* (F. S. Crofts & Company), p. 158.

Three hundred years ago, it took the Puritans a month to cross the Atlantic; to-day the *Bremen* makes the trip in five days, and by ship-plane service American mail reaches England in three days. One hundred years ago, news traveled no faster than man; to-day by the radio the voice of the Pope at Rome reaches simultaneously listeners in America, England, and Australia. The unit of measure to-day is not space, but time. During the past fifty years the world has shrunk from the size of a football to that of an English walnut.[22]

The consequence of this diminished size of the globe is an economic interdependence of nations inconceivable a century ago. We Americans like to think of ourselves as an economically self-sufficient nation. Despite our continental area and our wide range of natural resources, our economic life is interwoven with that of the other countries. Raymond B. Fosdick picturesquely depicts this interdependence. Our machine civilization, he says, has "wired the world together in a vast, intricate circuit; the electric spark that starts anywhere on the line will travel to the end." [23] Industrial nations, including the United States, are dependent upon the outside world for the satisfaction of four basic needs: (1) raw materials, (2) foodstuffs, (3) markets for surplus commodities, and (4) markets for surplus capital.

The dependence of the United States upon raw materials from abroad can readily be noted when we examine the basic industrial needs of the country. The twentieth century is a steel age; the products of our Pittsburgh and Youngstown plants are in use all over the United States and the world. In the making of steel, iron ore and coal are prime requisites; and we produce 60 per cent of the world's pig iron and 43 per cent of the world's coal. Nevertheless, our steel industry rests upon contributions from the other side of the globe. Manganese and vanadium ore come from South America, and tungsten from China. Without these minerals we could not produce a steel tool. The rubber industry, whose rapid rise coincides with the growth of the automobile industry, depends completely upon Brazil and the Malay Archipelago for its raw supplies. Our tinplate manufacturers import their tin from Bolivia and the Malay States. Our leather industry secures its hides from Argentina. The raw products for our silk mills come from China and Japan. During the fiscal year 1923 we imported crude materials for use in manufacturing

[22] J. A. Randall, *A World Community* (New York, Frederick A. Stokes Company), p. 22.

[23] R. Fosdick, *The Old Savage in the New Civilization* (Garden City, N. Y., Doubleday, Doran & Company), p. 143.

to the amount of $1,475,941,029, and partially manufactured goods for further use in manufacturing to the amount of $711,358,726.[24]

All industrial countries are, in the second place, dependent upon other lands for food supplies. Great Britain is the most cogent illustration of this statement. Despite our own expanse of territory and diversity of climate, the United States also imports important items in our bill of fare. Coffee comes from Brazil; tea from China, Ceylon, and Japan; cocoa from Venezuela and the Caribbean; sugar from Cuba and the Philippines; spices from the East Indies; fruit and nuts from the tropics; meat from South America. During the fiscal year 1925 the total value of our imported foodstuffs, in crude or manufactured form, amounted to almost one billion dollars.[25]

In the third place, industrial countries need foreign markets for their surplus products. The modern factory system has grown so efficient in its application of mass production that any well developed industry in the United States can easily produce more than the domestic market can absorb. The full-time operation of the automobile plants can assemble more automobiles than we can buy; the Pittsburgh mills roll out more steel than American building and shipping companies need; New England textile factories weave more fine cotton cloths than we can wear. Our industries must thus choose between the alternatives of reducing uneconomically their rate of production or selling to foreign markets. Naturally, they have chosen the latter. During the fiscal year 1927 the United States exported industrial machinery to the value of $192,300,000, agricultural machinery amounting to $79,700,000, lumber and related products valued at $101,000,000, copper products worth $136,900,000. These few items are indicative of our dependence upon foreign markets.

Finally, all industrial countries, and especially the United States, need foreign markets for surplus capital. Sooner or later, the developing industrial state produces a surplus of capital beyond that which can profitably be invested in home industries. This surplus seeks investment in all parts of the world, wherever there is an opportunity to build railroads, construct docks, develop mines, grow rubber, or bore oil wells. The foreign investments of the United States, exclusive of the Allied indebtedness, amount to-day to fourteen billion dollars, and are increasing at the rate of a billion a year.[26] J. H. Randall cogently depicts the growth of American financial interdependence. The American oil industry, he demonstrates, is increasing its operations in Europe and throughout the world; everywhere we

[24] Fraser, *op. cit.*, pp. 85–86.   [25] *Ibid.*, pp. 86–87.   [26] Randall, *op. cit.*, p. 27.

can find its refineries, factories, tank wagons, pumps, drills, engineers, and experts. General Electric, Westinghouse, and Western Electric have vast interests and powerful alliances abroad. The moving picture industry exports over two hundred thousand dollars worth of films a year and maintains a large distributing machine in Europe. From the time that the American tourist awakes in his European hotel until he retires, he uses American products manufactured in European branch plants. Randall's list includes razor blades, Palmolive soap, Quaker oats, National cash registers, and coco-cola.[27]

This analysis of the economic interdependence of the world—so this new school of thought points out—demonstrates how economic considerations are cutting across all boundary lines and disregarding national political barriers. We are weaving around ourselves as nations an intricate network of industrial interests where ruthless competition is suicidal. If the war spirit should lift its ugly head again and beckon the nations to slaughter, we may find ourselves hopelessly entrapped through the growing up of these mutual economic interests.[28] W. S. Culbertson likewise points to the dangers of this new economic interdependence.

"Nations which are at peace today can argue themselves into a false security through peace societies, and through pleasant references to their past relations, but if economic rivalry is permitted to go on unrestricted, unsuspecting people will awake some morning and find themselves at war. War is not a necessary accompaniment of human relationships, but the causes of war are imbedded in our economic life and, if they are not removed, war follows inevitably upon them." [29]

Fosdick indicates clearly the economic significance of this new interdependence. The very compactness of our machine civilization is its greatest weakness. It is fast developing a unity, an organic body. The cells that compose it are no longer independent, rather they are now woven together like the cells of the human body, each highly specialized, each performing its own functions, each essential to the health and life of the whole. Thus, if one group of cells be damaged, the whole body of cells is injured, and this whole body can be killed by a single vital wound.

"Each factory, each area, each nation, is part of a vast living body. The cells have united in an organism in which lack of harmony, or the disease

[27] Randall *op. cit.*, pp. 252–253.
[28] *Ibid.*, p. 254.
[29] *American Academy of Political and Social Science* 112: 2, March, 1924.

or disuse of any of its members, may imperil not only the health of the other members but the health of the whole." [30]

"In brief, our machine civilization is a vast nervous system. When shock comes it grows in the process of transmission, carrying its reactions to all the cells of the body—a body into which modern science has breathed the breath of life. It is this unity, this solidarity, that threatens the future. If the wheels of our machines ever stop, it will be because some disease, originating perhaps in a remote part of the organism, blocks a commercial vein or artery, or exerts some pressure upon an industrial nerve, finally bringing an irresistible paralysis to the whole body of our civilization." [31]

Fraser analyzes in a like fashion the economic consequences of American dependence upon the outside world. Let us imagine, he argues, that by some strange freak of nature the waters of the flood were again to cover the earth, and we were left "a nation of Noahs in the ark of the good old U. S. A." We should then have real isolation, and the political independence and freedom of action that goes with it. But we should also have the greatest industrial depression that this country ever passed through! One-half of our cotton crop would rot on the plantations; one-fourth of the wheat crop would find no market; one-third of the tobacco crop would go to waste; two-thirds of our copper would remain in the mines. Such is the nonsense advocated in the name of independence and isolation. [32]

The new world economic organism, of which the United States is an important cell, necessitates an international outlook. The exponents of internationalism insist that economic realities demand the abandonment of our political isolation, and our participation in a world organization. Fraser insists that the Monroe Doctrine of American isolation must be relegated to the scrap-heap of worn-out doctrines. Our commerce makes us interested, for example, in the freedom of the seas. From its very nature, this is an international political question, and its solution requires concerted action. The American people, with their eight billion dollars' worth of commerce a year on the high seas, will not be content to sit back while other nations formulate the law on this important question. [33] Nor can we stand aside and permit that uncontrolled economic conflict that invariably leads to war. In an interdependent world, victor, vanquished, and non-belligerent alike emerge from such an ordeal with their economic life badly wrecked. [34] From the economic standpoint, world organization is now a necessity for all of the highly organized industrial nations. The progress of the last hundred years has made

[30] Fosdick, op. cit., pp. 130–131.
[31] Ibid., pp. 145–146.
[32] Fraser, op. cit., pp. 89–90.
[33] Ibid., p. 85.
[34] Ibid., p. 157.

the nation a part of a still wider community, the community of the civilized world. It is to this larger social unit that the beginning of political organization must now be imparted. An organized association of states, Fraser argues, will supplant the struggle for empire and trade by coöperation in the development of backward lands. National security will be found in association under law; and with national security assured, preparedness will cease and the resources now wasted on armanents will be put to the service of education and other civilized arts. A world parliament, with open discussion, will supersede the old secret diplomacy that sent men to death on behalf of policies of which they knew nothing.[35]

Fosdick is another contemporary American who bases his demand for American participation in world affairs, not upon the Wilsonian desire for moral leadership, but upon the exigencies of economic interdependence. "Nations to-day are roped like Alpine climbers crossing a glacier: they survive or perish together." [36] The decreasing size of the globe and the closer knitting of economic interests demand international teamwork. "The League of Nations was foreshadowed from the day that Robert Fulton ran his steamboat, the *Clermont*, up the Hudson River, and George Stephenson induced the projectors of the Stockton and Darlington Railroad to substitute steam for horses." [37] Fosdick does not view the League of Nations as an Utopian institution, nor as the expression of moral idealism. To him it is the natural and essential outgrowth of the world economic organism. The League is a new technique for handling international affairs. It is a means of getting people together, an agency for conference and consultation, a method of international life. It is developing new habits of thought and establishing a fresh method of approach. The nations of the League are gradually learning the technique of teamwork.

"Through practice with less important issues, they are beginning slowly to see that when men get together about a table, thorny historic situations and pressing international difficulties often yield more fairly and more sensibly to conciliation and compromise than to nationalistic or obscurantist claims. The hope of the situation lies at this point: with this habit of teamwork more thoroughly interwoven into the life of the world, with the technique of coöperation more completely understood, perhaps when the next great test comes, and another 1914 throws down its ugly challenge to mankind, there will be a better chance for sanity and self-control and a larger hope of escape from a world wreck of untold proportions." [38]

[35] Fraser, *op. cit.*, pp. 244–245.
[36] Fosdick, *op. cit.*, p. 204.
[37] *Ibid.*, pp. 205–206.
[38] *Ibid.*, pp. 202–204.

The League Council meets at least every three months and the Assembly every year. Also a steady succession of international bodies and committees has met under the auspices of the League, dealing with many kinds of human problems—passports, freedom of transit, public health, and so on.[39] In place of diplomatic notes and memoranda and all the shop-worn paraphernalia of foreign-office routine, the world, except the United States, has begun to employ the town-meeting idea, the system of open conference, with the entire family of nations participating in the discussion.[40]

Despite the enthusiasm generated by Wilson's idealism, and despite the growth in recent years of a more realistic approach to the problem of world organization, a pessimism born of disillusionment characterizes the great body of American international thought. Contemporary American opinion, to a large degree, discounts the possibility of establishing an Utopian community based upon peace and brotherly love. The great American public looks with suspicious eyes upon what it believes to be European pretensions against American prosperity. Disillusionment regarding international coöperation and government has set in. Often this reaction against Wilsonianism finds no expression in the field of letters; often it comes to light only in newspaper editorials, American Legion speeches, or private conversations. There has, however, developed a decided tone of cynicism toward world affairs.

This disillusionment goes back to the days of the Peace Conference of 1919. In the congressional elections of 1918, the Republicans won control of the Senate; and in 1919 they dominated the Committee on Foreign Affairs. Wilson failed to take this situation into consideration. Furthermore, his personal tactics did not mollify the partisan bias of his political adversaries. Wilson himself represented the United States at the Versailles Conference. He took with him not a single member of the Senate; and while aiding in drafting the peace treaty, he quite neglected that body. He sent back a few messages; but, on the whole, he ignored political sentiment at home. When the negotiators completed their task, Wilson permitted American bankers and journalists to examine copies of the treaty before the senators saw it. In his dealings with the Senate during the hectic days of ratification, he was quite as stubborn as the "irreconcilable" Republicans. His air of finality did not assuage the antagonism of his opponents. He would permit no important changes in the treaty or in the League Covenant. The result of this political and personal clash is now

[39] Fosdick, op. cit., pp. 208–209.   [40] Ibid., p. 217.

history. Wilson stumped the country; the Senate refused ratification; the Republicans swept into power in 1920; and America returned to its political isolation.

The first manifestation of the reaction against Wilsonian internationalism came as a result of the political and personal animus against Wilson. The immediate object of the attack was to defeat America's entrance into the League of Nations. For the benefit of the impressible voter, the Republican Senate, with deft strokes of the brush, pictured the League as an ugly monster. Article X—the guarantee of territorial integrity and political independence of League members—would involve America in petty Balkan quarrels. American troops would fight the battles of Europe; European powers, at the same time, would concern themselves with the peculiar American concerns of the western hemisphere. Washington, Jefferson, and Monroe worked overtime in their graves in order to reëstablish the stereotype of European pretensions to the new world. And, in the third place, the League would amount to a super-state that might interfere with our domestic problems, such as our immigration policy.

Senator Henry Cabot Lodge of Massachusetts was one of the more temperate antagonists of Wilsonian moral leadership in world politics. He advocated American participation in some sort of world association, but attacked the proposed League Covenant as a revolution in American foreign policy and as an imminent danger to American peace and security. Under Article X, he insisted, we must guarantee the territorial integrity of practically every nation in the world. We should be bound to go to the relief of any country with our army and navy. American troops would thus fight the battles of the Balkans, prevent Arabian clashes in the Near East, and protect every part of the far-flung British Empire.[41] Lodge feared lest, through the League's machinery for international arbitration, jealous foreign countries should interfere with our domestic affairs. Japan would raise the question of our immigration laws and force us to submit the issue to arbitration; there must be, Lodge protested, no possible jurisdiction over the power that defends this country from a flood of Japanese, Chinese, and Hindu labor.[42] Nor can we permit international discussion of our protective tariffs, or of our control of the Panama Canal. Rather, argued Lodge, we must rely upon the historic Monroe Doctrine to maintain our peace and security.[43] Wars between na-

[41] Lodge, *The Senate and the League of Nations* (New York, C. Scribner's Sons), p. 391.
[42] *Ibid.*, pp. 236–237, 391–394.   [43] *Ibid.*, pp. 230–234.

tions come from contacts. A nation with which we have no contact is a nation with which we would never fight. The Covenant of the League creates for us a number of new contacts. We should, therefore, take the utmost care before we plunge into these strange relationships and abandon our tried policy of isolation.[44]

"Not even the wisest and most optimistic of reformers can change the geography of the globe. They say communication has quickened enormously. The Atlantic Ocean is not what it was as a barrier, or the Pacific either, I suppose. But do not forget that even under modern conditions the silver streak, the little channel only twenty miles wide, was England's bulwark and defense in the last war. Do not underrate the three thousand miles of Atlantic. It was on that that the Monroe Doctrine, the corollary of Washington's policy, rested."[45]

A second phase of the reaction against Wilsonian internationalism has been the growth of pessimism toward international affairs. The United States entered the war, so Wilson convinced the country, to save the world for democracy. The clash of arms became a holy crusade to preserve civilization against the threat of Teutonic barbarism. Once the war was over, however, the imperialistic nature of the struggle gradually leaked out. Philip Gibbs, the English journalist, exposed the Belgium atrocity stories as pure myths. Lasswell and Ponsonby [46] studied the technique of propaganda and demonstrated that the American public had "bit, hook, line and sinker" the stories spread by the Allies to whip up our hostility against the Germans. When the revolutions in Russia, Germany, and Austria opened the public archives of those countries, students learned of the secret negotiations that had preceded the war declarations of August, 1914, and exposed the treaties and agreements by which the Entente Allies had planned to crush Germany and to divide among themselves the spoils of war.[47] This new knowledge of the motive of the war and the technique of propaganda produced a reaction against Wilsonian idealism.

The political events in Europe since 1918 have not decreased, but deepened, this disillusionment. The continuation of Europe as an armed camp has led to a distrust of European diplomacy. The armies and navies of the Allied powers are to-day larger than those of 1913. The expenditures on armaments have increased. And the new states

[44] Lodge, *Lodge-Lowell Debate*, p. 12.
[45] *Ibid.*, p. 16.
[46] H. D. Lasswell, *Propaganda Technique in the World War;* A. Ponsonby, *Falsehood in War-Time.*
[47] See especially S. B. Fay, *Origins of the World War.*

of central Europe have joined the race for "preparedness." Governmental laboratories are experimenting with new explosives and deadly gases. Military aircraft has expanded in size and improved in efficiency. The attempts at disarmament have proved virtual failures. The Washington naval conference of 1921 resulted in the scrapping of a few capital ships and shifted construction to lighter war vessels. The Geneva conference of 1927 broke up over the question of the type of naval armament that the nations shall use. Each country fought for the particular type which would be most valuable to itself. The London conference of 1930 produced a tripartite agreement among the United States, Great Britain, and Japan that placed an upper limit in the naval construction race, but did not reduce the size of navies. Furthermore, Italy and France, apparently distrusting each other's international aims, refused assent to the London treaty. Attempts to control land armaments have proved even more colossal failures. The continuation of Europe as an armed camp has produced a sharp reaction in this country. It has led to increasing agitation for military, naval, and air preparedness. Admirals, generals, the National Security League, the American Legion, and a horde of other professional patriots have played upon this distrust of European armament.

The growth of nationalism in Europe has likewise contributed to the disillusionment. The development of Fascism in Italy and its spread to Poland and Germany have shaken the faith of Americans in the political reform of war-torn Europe. The blatant speeches of Mussolini against France, the sword-rattling of Pilsudski, the Hitlerite attack upon the Versailles Treaty, and Stalin's ranting about the world uprising of the proletariat—these manifestations do not encourage American optimism in the future of European peace. The continuation of the old dangerous techniques of diplomacy has enhanced distrust. Europe, not fully trusting the new machinery of world coöperation, still relies upon the balance of power. France and Italy have built up counter-alliances in central Europe. The Little Entente and the Italian group are as likely sources of a world explosion as were the Balkans in 1914. The German-Polish clash over the Danzig Corridor, the Italian demand for an African empire, the east European fear of the Russian bear, the German and Italian insistence upon the revision of the Versailles settlement—the resurgence of these old-style threats and controversies, sustained by pre-war methods of diplomacy, has made many an American skeptical as to the reality of the Wilsonian peace. The exposé of European

war aims, the piling up of armaments, the intensification of nationalism, and the continuation of diplomatic intrigue have practically
destroyed the desire for moral leadership on the part of the United
States.

All this has led to a fresh emphasis upon the Monroe Doctrine.
In theory, at least, the American nation should keep aloof from
European squabbles. The isolationists contend that our paramount
interest dictates "abstention from participation in European politics"
and requires also that "the machinations of foreign powers should
not have increased opportunity here." [48] The traditional policy of
isolation is no longer a defensive measure of a weak nation against
the threat of a powerful alliance. Rather, the continuation of the
Monroe Doctrine constitutes the employment of a political symbol
to register the disgust of a powerful state with the unreformed conduct of the world outside.

Possibly the best official interpretation of the new Monroe Doctrine comes from the lips of Charles Evans Hughes. As secretary of
state, he addressed the American Academy of Political and Social
Science on the centenary of the Monroe Doctrine. The United States,
he admitted, has increased its activities in world affairs. We have
become interested in the Orient; our war with Spain gave us wide
possessions in the Caribbean and the Pacific. But our emergence as
a world power has not led us to violate our tradition.

"We fought the Spanish War to put an end to an intolerable nuisance
at our very door, and to establish and make secure the independence of Cuba,
not to override it. And as a consequence of victory in that war we acquired
distant possessions, but not with the purpose of making there a basis for en-
croaching upon the territory or interfering with the political independence
of the peoples of the eastern nations. In safeguarding the integrity of China,
in securing equality of commercial opportunity, in endeavoring to forestall
efforts at exploitation and aggression, in seeking to remove suspicion and
allay apprehensions, and in enlarging through assured tranquillity the opportunities of peaceful commerce, we have been pursuing under different
conditions the same aim of independence, security, and peace which determined the declaration of Monroe." [49]

Hughes rationalized American participation in the World War on
the ground that the cause of liberty itself was at stake. We did not
violate our tradition. We have sought neither territory nor general
reparations. We did not seek to dictate to Europe or to deprive any

[48] C. E. Hughes, *The Centenary of the Monroe Doctrine*, p. 5. International Conciliation No. 194, January, 1924, Carnegie Endowment for International Peace.
[49] *Ibid.*, pp. 10-11.

one of rights.[50] The bitter controversy which followed the war showed with what tenacity we still hold to the principle of not meddling in the political strife of Europe. To be sure, we no longer fear the danger of organized efforts to extend to this continent the European political system of one hundred years ago. But Europe still has "a set of primary interests" which are not ours. Europe is engaged in political controversies the causes of which are essentially foreign to our concerns. .

"The preponderant thought among us undoubtedly is that our influence would not be increased by pooling it. The influence that is due to our detachment and impartiality could not long be maintained if we should substitute the rôle of a partisan in European quarrels, and the constant efforts of propagandists have brought vividly before us the fact that where the direct American interest is not clearly perceived foreign controversies afford abundant opportunity for the play among us of intense racial feeling. What was true in Monroe's day is even more true today in view of our vast population drawn from many countries and reproducing here the conflicts of European interests. It is not to our interest to adopt a policy by which we would create or intensify divisions at home without healing divisions abroad. And it must be always remembered that the moral force of our expressions depends upon the degree of the preponderance of the sentiments behind them. . . . The difficulties which beset Europe have their causes within Europe and not in any act or policy of ours." [51]

Hughes summarized our policies toward Europe as follows: (1) Opposition to alliances. "We refuse to commit ourselves in advance with respect to the employment of the power of the United States in unknown contingencies. We reserve our judgment to act upon occasion as our sense of duty permits." (2) Opposition to discrimination against our nationals. "We ask fair and equal opportunities in mandated territories as they were acquired by the Allies through our aid." (3) Judicial settlement of juristic questions. (4) Coöperation in humanitarian efforts which "aim to minimize or prevent those evils which can be met adequately only by community of action," as, for example, the attempt to stop the abuse of narcotic drugs. And (5) aid in the reëstablishment of sound economic conditions.[52]

The United States, on the other hand, has been called upon to exercise a guardianship over our sister republics in this hemisphere. Our policy, Hughes averred, makes available our friendly assistance to promote stability in neighboring states "which are especially afflicted with disturbed conditions involving their own peace and

[50] C. E. Hughes, *The Centenary of the Monroe Doctrine*, p. 11. International Conciliation No. 194, January, 1924, Carnegie Endowment for International Peace.
[51] *Ibid.*, pp. 12–13.   [52] *Ibid.*, p. 13.

that of their neighbors." "In promoting stability we do not threaten
independence but seek to conserve it. We are not aiming at control
but endeavoring to establish self-control." [53] The American policy
in the Caribbean is dictated by one other determinant—the protection
of the Panama Canal.

"Apart from obvious commercial consideration, the adequate protection
of this canal—its complete immunity from any adverse control—is essential
to our peace and security. . . . Disturbances in the Caribbean region are
therefore of special interest to us not for the purpose of seeking control over
others but of being assured that our own safety is free from menace." [54]

A third and highly important phase of the reaction against Wilsonian idealism in world affairs has been the growth of an imperialistic
sentiment in the United States. The economic interdependence of
this country for markets, raw materials, and investments has led
not only to a desire for a world community, but also to an insistence
upon our economic independence. The growth of American industries has resulted, on the one hand, in a demand for an "open door"
for our manufactures in such "backward" countries as China and,
on the other hand, in an insistence upon our share in the exploitation
of such raw materials as Mosul oil. The sudden accumulation of
capital during the World War and the consequent conversion of the
United States from a debtor to a creditor country has led to American
investments, not only in Europe, but in "backward" sections of the
world.

This reaction against the idealism of Wilsonian leadership comes
primarily from American business men. They feel the need for foreign trade and think that our new economic development will inevitably drive us into imperialism. Our need for markets, for raw
materials, for profitable fields for investment demand that we play
a larger part in world affairs—but not a rôle of unselfish disregard of
our own interests. Economic necessity must guide our policy. Imperialism, they argue, creates a nationally controlled source of raw
materials and provides new markets for our manufactures. National
industries will thus flourish, employment will become steadier, and
wages higher.

The foreign investments of the United States have inevitably had
repercussions upon our government. American investors—large and
small—desire that the countries to which they have loaned money

[53] C. E. Hughes, *The Centenary of the Monroe Doctrine*, p. 18. International Conciliation No, 194, January, 1924, Carnegie Endowment for International Peace.
[54] *Ibid.*, p. 22.

be protected against revolutions that threaten the safety of investments. They likewise desire stability to protect their investments in
private enterprises in foreign countries. Through the pressure brought
by American investors, our national government has become a silent
partner in the established order of the world. Our State Department
has concerned itself particularly with the maintenance of the *status
quo* in the Caribbean and in South America. This situation has become so important that the Department now has an agreement with
American bankers doing business abroad under which they inform
the government of their proposed loans, to the end that there may be
an opportunity to consider, in the light of public policy, the possible
national interests involved.[55] The Department of State considers it
obviously desirable that American capital going abroad be utilized
only for productive purposes. This is especially important at the
present time in view of the economic conditions in many foreign
countries as a result of the World War. Moreover, the national government cannot but object to the utilization of American capital for
militaristic ends. "In short, the Department of State could not be
expected to view with favor the utilization of American capital
abroad in such manner as to prevent or make difficult the carrying
out of essential American policies, not to promote the carrying out
abroad of policies inimical to the proper interests of the United
States." [56]

The influence of the new economic situation of America upon the
development of an imperialistic attitude was tersely stated by Curtis
Wilbur, then secretary of the navy, in a speech before the Connecticut
Chamber of Commerce on May 7, 1925.

"Americans have over twenty millions of tons of merchant shipping to
carry the commerce of the world, worth three billion dollars. We have loans
and property abroad, exclusive of government loans, of over ten billions of
dollars. If we add to this the volume of exports and imports for a single
year—about ten billion dollars—we have an amount almost equal to the entire property of the United States in 1868 and if we add to this the eight
billion dollars due us from foreign governments, we have a total of $31,000,-
000,000, being about equal to the total wealth of the nation in 1878. . . .
These vast interests must be considered when we talk of defending the flag.
. . . We fought not because Germany invaded or threatened to invade
America but because she struck at our commerce on the North Sea and
denied to our citizens on the high seas the protection of our flag. . . . To
defend America we must be prepared to defend its interests and our flag in

[55] Statement of Dr. A. N. Young, economic adviser of the State Department, at the
Institute of Politics, Williamstown, Mass., August 26, 1924.
[56] *Ibid.*

every corner of the globe. . . . An American child crying on the banks of the Yangtse a thousand miles from the coast can summon the ships of the American navy up that river to protect it from unjust assault." [57]

Many political speakers, representatives of chambers of commerce, and students of world politics have rationalized this imperialistic reaction against Wilsonian idealism. Possibly the most significant argument comes from C. K. Leith, professor of geology at the University of Wisconsin. Leith's major thesis is that world economic progress depends upon raw materials, especially mineral resources. Nature has allocated the important deposits of coal and iron in the North Atlantic countries. These countries, notably the United States, will continue to be the exploiters of mineral wealth. Economic self-determination in the field of natural resources is and will be possible only to them. "There is no use blinking the fact that we are now the world's chief mineral exploiters, and will continue so by virtue of the direction given to our activities by our environment." [58] Exploitation is essential to progress. By reason of their exploitation of power resources, the North Atlantic countries, Leith argues, are doing annually five times the combined mechanical work of Russia, China, and India, the three most populous countries, although the North Atlantic countries possess a population only a third as great. With a fifth of the world's population, the North Atlantic states are doing about two-thirds of the world's work. The United States alone is doing about 40 per cent of it. "This perspective reflects more or less the distribution of national wealth and the prevailing standards of living, as might be expected from the fact that wealth is essentially a product of work." [59] Leith accepts the principle that might makes right, "but only to the extent and in the sense that nature's environment creates might. Human volition plays little part, and it seems futile to argue this as a moral or ethical question. The concentration of power, with its consequences, is no more right or wrong than was nature's original distribution of resources." [60] Leith, however, maintains that there are good ways and bad ways of exploitation, and advocates an international conference to standardize methods of exploitation and to correct its abuses.[61]

[57] New York *Times*, May 8, 1925, p. 18.
[58] C. K. Leith, *Foreign Affairs*, October, 1927, pp. 136–137; also Leith, *World Minerals and World Politics*, pp. 9–21.
[59] Leith, *Foreign Affairs*, October, 1927, p. 133.
[60] *Ibid.*, p. 137.
[61] *Ibid.*, pp. 137–139; also *World Minerals and World Politics*, pp. 162–171.

II

Disillusioned Democracy

A second significant aspect of contemporary thought is the re-evaluation of democracy. Once the axiom of American institutions, democracy has fallen under the lash of a skeptical examination. And political methods in general are now subjected to a devastating distrust. The exposé of corruption in New York, Chicago, and elsewhere has shaken the faith of individuals; the debauch of the "Ohio Gang" during Harding's administration has undermined popular confidence and has developed an attitude of cynicism toward politics and politicians in general. The failure of direct democracy—direct primaries, election of senators, initiative and referendum—to cure the ills of government has produced a reaction against democracy. And prohibition—with its interference with the "personal liberty" of the individual, its methods of enforcement, and its rampant corruption of local and federal agents—has alienated the confidence of many in government. The causes and manifestations of this democratic disillusionment are various and interesting.

In the first place, American life has become increasingly complex. The transformation, described in the preceding chapter, from an agricultural-rural civilization to an industrial-urban culture has complicated not merely social institutions but politics and government as well. Historically, American democracy developed in small, local centers where industry was mainly agricultural and where production was carried on mainly with hand tools. Pioneer conditions put a high premium upon personal work, skill, ingenuity, initiative, adaptability, and neighborly sociability. The town, or some area not much larger, was the political unit; and the town meeting was the political arena. Genuine community life then existed.[62] The massing of population in urban centers, the herding of workers within factory walls, the expansion of the political unit have inevitably destroyed that original community of feeling out of which grew democracy. Political institutions have grown complex and hardly understandable. The conflicting economic and social interests affected by legislation and, in turn, attempting to mold legislation, have multiplied beyond the comprehension of the average man. So numerous have the representatives of these interest groups become that a United States senator has been heard to remark that he could not throw a stone out of his Washington office window without striking six of them.[63]

[62] J. Dewey, *The Public and its Problems* (New York, Henry Holt and Company), p. 111.
[63] E. P. Herring, *Group Representation before Congress*, p. 21.

The complexity of modern politics is well illustrated when we try to formulate a few general political principles. Formerly, a citizen could entertain a few such principles and apply them with some confidence. He believed in states' rights or in a centralized general government; in free trade or in protection. But for the average voter to-day the tariff question is a hodgepodge of infinite detail, schedules of rates specific and *ad valorem* on countless things, many of which he does not recognize by name, and with respect to which he can form no judgment. Probably not one voter in a thousand even reads the complex schedules of tariff duties, and he would be no wiser if he did. The average man gives it up as a bad job. Similarly, the problem of states' rights has grown incomprehensibly complicated. The voter may oppose centralization, but he also believes that the liquor traffic is a social crime. He finds that local attempts at prohibition are nullified by the importation of liquor from other states, made easy by modern means of transportation. He thus becomes an advocate of a constitutional amendment giving the national government power to prohibit the manufacture, transportation, and sale of intoxicating beverages. This, however, brings in its train a necessary extension of federal powers and an increase in federal officers. Thus to-day, the South, the traditional home of the states' rights doctrine, is the chief supporter of national prohibition. On the other hand, lifetime exponents of centralization are opposed to prohibition; hence they play a tune on the Jeffersonian flute. Another example of the complexity of modern political problems is the history of the doctrine of individualism. Originally, "liberals" cherished this principle in protest against the inherited régime; they wanted a minimum of governmental interference with their industry and trade; the vested interests, on the other hand, were mainly in favor of the old status of paternalism. To-day, the industrial-property régime being established, the doctrine of individualism is the intellectual bulwark of the standpatter.[64] The complexity of modern political interests and governmental machinery baffles many citizens, and has led to a declining interest in politics. The growth of non-voting has, with the exception of the religious and temperance fight of 1928, been shocking to the exponents of democracy. A few preach the impotence of all politics, while the many nonchalantly abstain from voting. Skepticism regarding the efficacy of voting characterizes the attitude both of the intellectual and of the man on the street. Some feel that their votes never change anything; others look upon politics merely

[64] Dewey, *op. cit.*, pp. 131–134.

as a fight between the ins and the outs for the plums of office; and still others visualize the party system as a protective coloration to conceal business control of government.[65] In brief, the intricacies of contemporary life have eclipsed the public.

A second important factor in the disillusionment as to politics and democracy is the corruption and inefficiency of government. During the last quarter of the nineteenth century, large-scale graft permeated politics. The franchise steals in cities and the looting of the national treasury during the Grant administration produced a bad odor. This earlier corruption did not, however, shake the general confidence in popular rule. The proposed solution was to make government even more democratic; bring the government closer to the people, the progressives argued, and the people will clean house; political graft and inefficiency are due to irresponsibility of government to the electorate. The progressive movements of Bryan, Roosevelt, and La Follette accordingly proposed the democratization of government. Popular election of United States senators, direct primaries, initiative and referendum, recall, women suffrage—these are the most important means adopted for the democratization of government. And yet government remains corrupt and inefficient. Crookedness in elections, continued domination of party machines, huge and dubious expenditures in campaigns, corruption in most large cities, the debauch of Harding's "Ohio Gang"—these are irrefutable evidence of the continuation of political corruption. Frank Kent, an outstanding political journalist, outlines the "heretofore unwritten laws, customs and principles of politics as practiced in the United States."[66] He emphasizes the continuation of inefficiency and crookedness. The successful politician, he says, is not necessarily a fellow of great shrewdness, subtlety, and resource; rather, in 999 cases out of 1000 what appears to be superhuman strategy is actually either an accident or a blunder.[67] Apropos of corruption, Kent employs several illuminating phrases: there is no nourishment in fighting the machine;[68] corruption is not a party liability;[69] you cannot win a campaign on a "shoe string";[70] "live up to the law and be licked."[71]

What is the consequence of this present-day corruption in politics? The democratization of government failed to solve the problem;

---

[65] Dewey, op. cit., p. 118.
[66] F. Kent, Political Behavior, title page; see also his Great Game of Politics.
[67] Kent, Political Behavior, p. 11. (New York, W. Morrow & Company.)
[68] Ibid., p. 31.   [70] Ibid., p. 196.
[69] Ibid., p. 120.   [71] Ibid., p. 217.

consequently, confidence in popular rule has decreased. The progressives can hardly urge the bringing of government any closer to the people; nor has the success of the initiative and referendum been such as to warrant an overwhelming confidence in the ability of the masses to rule. The direct election of senators has not produced a noticeably higher grade representative; the tirades of Heflin against the papal invasion of America have provided entertainment, but hardly encouragement, to visitors to the Senate gallery. Nor have the exposes of drinking on the part of congressmen sworn to uphold the Constitution increased confidence in government. The attack upon the democratic state by H. L. Mencken, the iconoclast editor of the *American Mercury*, is illustrative of a growing sentiment of disillusionment. He looks upon the House of Representatives and sees only a group of men who have compromised with honor, who have learned to leap through the hoops of professional job-mongers and Prohibitionist blackmailers. They keep silent in good causes, and speak in bad ones. Government is run chiefly by men whose first concern is for their offices, not for their obligations.[72]

A third factor of growing importance in the distrust of popular government is the enactment and enforcement of national prohibition. The temperance movement dates back to the last century. In 1874 the organization of the Women's Christian Temperance Union stimulated the attack upon the saloon. The movement at first was predominantly a moral one, but gradually it assumed an economic aspect. In the South, business men looked upon prohibition as a means of keeping the negro sober; and owners of large factories looked upon liquor as a menace to industrial safety and efficiency. The World War increased the economic significance of the movement; the feeding of troops demanded the conservation of grain supplies. As a result, a war-time act temporarily prohibited the liquor traffic, and at the same time Congress submitted the Eighteenth Amendment to the states. By 1920, when the states ratified the amendment, two-thirds of them had already adopted prohibition laws. The effort to prohibit all manufacture and sale of intoxicating beverages proved immediately unpopular with a large portion of the people. The populous industrial sections had never favored state prohibition acts, and the important group of organized labor emphatically opposed such legislation. Within the dry agricultural states the urban centers had remained predominantly wet. The cry soon arose that a belligerent minority of moral fanatics had seized upon the perturbed

[72] H. L. Mencken, *Notes on Democracy* (New York, Alfred A. Knopf), pp. 116-117.

war period to trick the country into prohibition. Nevertheless, even those who realized that a majority probably supported the Volstead Act questioned the right of the majority to deprive them of their personal liberties. The attempts at prohibition enforcement—with the consequences of corruption, "speak-easies," racketeering, gang murders, smuggling, and increased drinking by young men and women—have alienated many intelligent citizens not only from the prohibition movement but also from democratic government. They have felt that, if the majority could pass and retain on the statute-books such stupid attempts at moral reform, the majority might enact other legislation equally destructive of individual rights and clean government. The passage in some states of anti-evolution bills has similarly helped to raise this vital question of majority control. During the past decade, much has been written about majority democracy. The most searching inquiry into the right of the 51 per cent to regulate the lives of the other 49 per cent comes from the pen of Walter Lippmann.[73] Conservative men like A. Lawrence Lowell, president of Harvard University, have attacked the demoralizing consequences of the Eighteenth Amendment.

"That it has produced corruption among government agents, and in some states in the police, is universally believed. Like the policy of Reconstruction in the South, it has turned many respectable people who ought to be patterns of law and order into lawbreakers. It is responsible for no small amount of violence and crime. Men who are in a position to know assert that the murders in Chicago are mainly, if not wholly, due to quarrels among the bootleggers, and between them and the hi-jackers. Such conditions are certain to last so long as an illegal and lucrative traffic is conducted on a large scale, supported by sales to citizens in good standing, while the public authorities endeavor to suppress it by force. The country is at odds with itself. There is a lack of harmony in principles that causes friction, maladjustment, and confusion. It is not a healthy condition, or one that ought to continue." [74]

H. L. Mencken directs a characteristically vituperative attack against prohibition and its moralist exponents. The fanatics, he asserts, have converted the decent citizen into a criminal for performing acts that are natural to gentlemen everywhere, and have degraded the police and courts to the abhorrent office of punishing upright citizens. More than one judge, says Mencken, unable to square such loathsome duties with his private notions of honor, has stepped down from the bench, and left the business to a successor

---

[73] W. Lippmann, *Men of Destiny*, Ch. 5; *American Inquisitors*, Ch. 3.
[74] A. L. Lowell, "Reconstruction and Prohibition," *Atlantic Monthly*, February, 1929.

who was more a lawyer and less a man.[75] While the Prohibitionists advocated the Eighteenth Amendment in order to abate drunkenness, and so abolish crime, poverty, and disease, that millennium, Mencken complains, has not arrived. Not only are crime, poverty, and disease still prevalent, but drunkenness itself has greatly increased. Prohibition has made the use of alcohol fashionable, and so has vastly increased the number of drinkers, especially among the youth of both sexes. It has produced so many new evils that even the "mob" has turned against it; and yet the Prohibitionists, refusing to admit the obvious facts, demand more stringent enforcement measures.[76]

A fourth attack upon democracy comes from an entirely different quarter. During the past two decades, students of public affairs have turned to an analysis of public opinion. The theory of democracy posits the premise that government is or should be responsive to popular desires. But students of public opinion—Lippmann, Lowell, Dewey—demonstrate the irrational nature of that opinion. They show that stereotypes, symbols, and untrue pictures of the world outside are the determinants of opinion; and their demonstration of the ease with which propagandists can mold the so-called public to their way of thinking [77] has done much to shatter confidence in popular democracy as a method of government. Accepting the findings of this school and checking them with his own political observations, Frank Kent contends that anything like complete candor with the voters is fatal to any candidate.[78] "The cold fact is that in present-day politics when the American people decide an issue rightly it is an accident and not because of either an unerring instinct for the right or a clear comprehension of the facts, because they have neither." [79] Similarly, Dewey, in his search for the great community, believes that the prime condition of a democratically organized public is a kind of knowledge and insight which does not yet exist.[80]

Walter Lippmann, formerly an editor of the New York *World*, presents the clearest and most cogent analysis of public opinion and its relation to democratic government. His fundamental thesis is that—through incomplete knowledge, lack of access to information, censorship, lack of time and opportunity, the inadequacy of words, and the existence of stereotyped generalizations—the pictures of the world that we have in our heads differ fundamentally from the facts

---

[75] Mencken, *op. cit.*, pp. 165–166.
[76] *Ibid.*, pp. 162–163. This is probably the only time that Mencken has ever agreed with the "mob."
[77] Herring, *op. cit.*
[78] Kent, *op. cit.*, p. 74.
[79] *Ibid.*, p. 76.
[80] Dewey, *op. cit.*, p. 166.

of the world outside. We do not see first and then define, we define first and then see; in other words, in the great confusion of the outer world we tend to look at events through glasses colored for us by our culture.[81]

In the organization of government, says Lippmann, direct control is always impossible. The masses can merely choose between political machines, and answer yes or no on a concrete issue presented to them. The reason for the machine is not the perversity of human nature; rather it is that out of the private notions of any group no common idea emerges by itself. By mass action nothing can be constructed, devised, negotiated, or administered. A trade union, for example, can by mass action win a strike so that its officials can negotiate a settlement; but the negotiations can be carried on only through an organization, and the rank and file can merely approve or disapprove. When a number of people all say yes to a given project, they generally have all kinds of reasons, for the pictures in their minds are varied. There is no such thing as direct legislation; the voter can merely say yes or no to the proposals submitted by a smaller group, even though a brilliant amendment may occur to him. And in popular elections, the many elect only after the few have nominated.[82]

Public opinion does not arise spontaneously from the masses. Leaders often pretend that they have merely uncovered a program that existed in the public mind. When leaders actually believe this, they are usually deceiving themselves. Programs do not invent themselves simultaneously in a multitude of minds; rather, leaders put programs into the public mind. The mass is constantly exposed to suggestion; it reads, not the news itself, but the news with an aura of suggestion about it, indicating the line of action to be taken.[83] Leaders, knowing this, can manufacture consent. While the creation of consent is an old art which was supposed to have died out with the appearance of democracy, it has, rather, improved enormously in technique. As a result of psychological analyses and modern methods of communication, a revolution is taking place that is more significant than a shift of economic power. Persuasion has become a regular organ of government. The knowledge of how to create consent will, Lippmann predicts, alter every political calculation and modify every political premise. It is no longer possible, for example, to maintain the original dogma of democracy—that the knowledge needed for the management of government arises spontaneously from the human heart. The practice of democracy is now turning a corner.[84]

[81] Lippmann, *Public Opinion* (New York, The Macmillan Company), p. 81.
[82] *Ibid.*, pp. 229–233.   [83] *Ibid.*, p. 243.   [84] *Ibid.*, pp. 248–249.

A fifth and final attack upon democracy comes from the differential psychologists. While the exponents of democracy do not all insist upon human equality,—as did the framers of the Declaration of Independence, the Jacksonian democrats, or the radical abolitionists,—they do demand equality of opportunity for all men. All men should enjoy equal opportunity to exercise their unequal faculties. The democratic philosophers also insist that within the State there are divergent groups with divergent interests; the interests of each group can be secured only through its political participation. The new psychological school in politics questions both of these major contentions of democracy. They argue that men are unequal mentally; some are so inferior that they do not deserve equal opportunity with their superior brethren. The maximum human happiness and progress can be achieved by devoting the energies of society to the benefit of the superior mental groups. Thus in education, they argue, the compulsory school attendance laws fill the public schools with children who are incapable of imbibing more than a low minimum of knowledge and training. The presence of these subnormal children destroys the value of the public schools for those superior children from whom society can expect achievements. Democracy puts a stamp of uniformity upon its products and reduces its superior individuals to mediocrity. The psychological school attacks also the second contention of democracy. The masses, the argument runs, are so inferior mentally that they do not know what are their interests. The masses can not, by their political participation, take care of themselves. Moreover, through the doctrine of numerical majority these very masses control the interests of other and superior groups. This psychological analysis deserves attention.

H. L. Mencken and E. D. Martin are among the most vigorous American exponents of this psychological attack upon democracy. Mencken contends that there are all varieties of men. We now know a great deal more about the content and character of the human mind that we used to know; what we have learned, he says, has pretty well disposed of the old belief in its congenital intuitions and inherent benevolences. The human mind is mainly a function of purely physical and chemical phenomena, and its development and operation are subject to precisely the same natural laws that govern the development and operation of other human organs. There are thus minds which start out with a superior equipment, and proceed to high and arduous deeds; there are minds which never get any further than "a sort of insensate sweating, like that of a kidney."

Not only can we observe such differences, but through intelligence tests we can also begin to chart them with more or less accuracy.[85] Mencken portrays the world as a vast field of greased poles, flying gaudy and seductive flags. Up each an individual attempts to shin; some climb to high levels, but the great majority find the effort too much and never get very far from the ground. In an aristocratic society, government is a function of those who have reached the heights; in a democratic society, it is the function of all, and hence mainly of those who have hardly risen from the ground.[86]

In the psychological analysis of man, Mencken asserts, the emotion of fear stands out as the earliest and most profound.[87] Every other emotion is subordinate to that of fear; and none other shows itself so soon or enters so powerfully into the first functioning of the infant mind. The process of education is largely a process of getting rid of such fear.[88] But the vast majority of men are congenitally incapable of intellectual progress. They cannot take in new ideas; they cannot get rid of old fears. They are incompetent even to absorb the bald facts themselves.[89] This emotion of fear, says Mencken, dominates the political system in a democracy. The demagogues, who flourish in democratic states, are professors of mob psychology; they make the emotion of fear the corner-stone of their exact and puissant science. Politics with them consists almost wholly of the discovery and exploitation of bugaboos.[90] The whole history of the United States, Mencken believes, has been a story of melodramatic pursuits of imaginary monsters. His list includes the red-coats, the Hessians, the monocrats, again the red-coats, the Bank, the Catholics, Simon Legree, the Slave Power, Jeff Davis, Mormonism, Wall Street, the rum demon, John Bull, the hell hounds of plutocracy, the trusts, General Weyler, Pancho Villa, German spies, hyphenates, the Kaiser, Bolshevism. The plain people never vote for anything, but always against something.[91]

The mental inferiority of the masses, the political psychologists argue, is such that they can not take care of their own political interests. They lack the intelligence to know what is best for them. The whole progress of the world, even in the direction of ameliorating the lot of the masses, has always encountered the opposition of the masses. Mencken, following the example of Henry Adams,[92] points to the history of the Department of Agriculture. When, in 1830, the na-

[85] Mencken, *op. cit.*, pp. 9–11.
[86] *Ibid.*, pp. 16–17.
[87] *Ibid.*, pp. 18–19.
[88] *Ibid.*, p. 20.
[89] *Ibid.*, pp. 20–21.
[90] *Ibid.*, p. 22.
[91] *Ibid.*, pp. 22–23.
[92] H. Adams, *The Decay of Democratic Dogma*.

tional government started its agricultural work under a bureau of the Patent Office, the farmers opposed it almost unanimously; and for years their bitter derision kept the bureau feeble. When John Adams, during his presidency, proposed to set up a weather bureau, he was denounced as an idiot and a scoundrel. It is axiomatic, Mencken says, that all measures for safeguarding the public health are opposed by the majority, and that getting such legislation upon the statute books is mainly a matter of deceiving and checkmating the masses.[93]

Finally, argues this school, democracy, by permitting inferior men to participate in politics, lowers the average level of government. The quality of legislation, administration, and opinion sinks to a low level. Mencken, the supreme cynic and critic of the American people, depicts them as sheep. "Worse, they are donkeys. Yet worse, to borrow from their own dialect, they are goats." Small minorities, determined and ambitious individuals, and even exterior groups, constantly "bamboozle" and exploit them. The business of victimizing the people is a lucrative profession.[94] Thus, demagogues preach doctrines they know to be untrue to men they know to be idiots. And "demislaves" listen to what these idiots have to say and then pretend to believe it themselves. Every man who seeks elective office under democracy has to be either the one or the other, and most men have to be both. The whole process is one of false pretenses and ignoble concealments. No educated man who states plainly the elementary notions that he holds about government can win election to office in a democratic State, save perhaps by a miracle. His frankness would arouse fears, and those fears would be fatal to his chances.[95]

From his practical observation of politics, Frank Kent arrives at similar conclusions. Not more than one in sixty of those who go to the polls, he maintains, are accurately informed, keenly and continuously interested in either national or state politics.[96] One of the inherent and ineradicable traits of the American voters is that they infinitely prefer to vote against something or somebody than for them.[97] What the people want is "hokum."[98] If you want to get into a position to serve the people, it is necessary first to fool them.[99] For the candidate without the imagination or initiative necessary to supply an original brand of hokum for himself, there is always the Bible, the Constitution, and the Flag to fall back upon. These are the three "old reliables."[100]

[93] Mencken, op. cit., pp. 52–53.
[94] Ibid., p. 78.
[95] Ibid., pp. 102–103.
[96] Kent, Political Behavior, p. 79.

[97] Ibid., p. 81.
[98] Ibid., p. 146.
[99] Ibid., p. 304.
[100] Ibid., p. 149.

Democracy to-day is under fire. The complexity of political inter-ests and machinery discourages participation in government. The cor-ruption and inefficiency of government and the evils of prohibition have sapped much of the popular confidence in rule by the majority. The recent analysis of public opinion and the teachings of psychology have alienated the support of the intellectuals. In this country the problem has not yet become vitally important. But if the Fascist, Communist, and dictatorship attacks upon democracy in Europe [101] are at all pro-phetic of what may develop on this side of the Atlantic, the exponents of democracy must either rise in defense of their philosophy or reform their institutions of popular control to eliminate the recognized evils of democracy. Thus far they have silently remained in the background.

III

A Clash of Cultures

America has come of age in a third respect: a long and bitter clash of cultures is destined to characterize its life and thought for many generations. The old peoples against the new; the Anglo-Saxon Nordic against the Latin, Slav, and Jew; the Protestant against the Catholic—the conflict of these groups is cutting across economic and political lines. The old stocks are struggling to perpetuate their Anglo-American culture and to compel the later arrivals to accept their standards; the new stocks refuse to admit the inferiority of their contributions to civilization; they insist upon playing a rôle in fash-ioning American culture. Whereas the exponents of the doctrines of Karl Marx build up a philosophy of history and a program of eco-nomic and social reform based upon the reality of class conflict, we find in the United States a struggle between economic and ethnic factors for domination. The Italian trench-digger and the Italian merchant find more in common than do the Italian and Jewish pro-letarians. The election of 1928 amply illustrated that cultural align-ments play fully as significant a rôle in American politics as do eco-nomic factors. The Republican party had as its presidential candidate Herbert Hoover, a representative of the old, Nordic, Protestant stock; the Democratic party nominated Alfred E. Smith, Irish, Catholic, the idol of the new immigrants. This cleavage into ethnic and religious camps played probably a greater rôle in the balloting than did the issues of prohibition, water power, tariff, and farm relief.

[101] Disillusionment as to democracy and representative institutions is not the sole cause of Fascism, Communism, and dictatorships in Europe. Pressing economic prob-lems are of more immediate importance; but distrust of popular government has played a significant rôle.

During the past hundred years, America has witnessed one of the most spectacular movements of peoples in the world's history. The Irish famines and the German revolutions of 1848 caused an immigration wave to roll across the Atlantic. Between 1840 and 1880 almost ten million foreigners landed in the United States. The character of the American people visibly changed; it became less exclusively British and more German, Scandinavian, and Irish. The advent of the latter element introduced Catholicism on a large scale. After 1880 the wave of immigration changed. Between 1880 and 1914 almost twenty million immigrants arrived. But they were no longer predominantly northern Europeans; they came from southern and eastern Europe. Italy, Poland, Russia sent over the bulk of the new-comers. Latins, Slavs, and Jews became numerically important, especially in the industrial, urban centers.

The World War stimulated American nationalism. Immigration, formerly welcomed as an economic boon, was now scrutinized as a cultural, an eugenic, a national menace. Public opinion among the Anglo-Americans echoed almost to a man Roosevelt's blatant demand that immigrants be required at once to forget their past and cut themselves off from their heritages, to learn English and be naturalized, or to leave the country. The animus of the new nationalism was directed not only against the enemy alien, but against all foreigners who refused to "Americanize" themselves. Eugenists fostered theories of Nordic racial superiority. The fusion of the Slavs, Latins, and Jews with the native stock would prove an anthropological menace to the one hundred per cent integrity of the American. Madison Grant lamented the passing of the great Nordic race.[102] MacDougall questioned whether the infusion of the new inferior stocks rendered America unsafe for democracy.[103] With scientific precision and mathematical certainty, Brigham collected statistics from the army intelligence tests to demonstrate the dangers to American stock from the mentally inferior races.[104] And Laughlin studied the inmates of correctional and charitable institutions to convince himself and others of the alien menace that threatened the foundations of American life.[105] The eugenists theses were that racial, not individual, inferiority characterized the new immigrants

[102] *The Passing of the Great Race.*
[103] *Is America Safe for Democracy?*
[104] *A Study of American Intelligence.*
[105] *Europe as an Emigrant-exporting Continent, and the United States as an Immigrant-receiving Nation;* for a summary of the eugenic point of view, see W. W. Cook, *American Institutions and Their Preservation* (1929 edition), Ch. 33.

and that under the Mendelian law of the non-inheritance of acquired characteristics these new groups could never improve their inherent qualities. The Anglo-American fear of the immigrant resurrected the Ku Klux Klan. Its membership, recruited from every class that considered itself native, white, and Protestant, extended an animated hatred toward the Negro, Catholic, Jew, and alien. Everything variant from the traditional type of religion, race, culture, or morality fell under the lash of the Klan literature and raids. Stimulated by an aroused popular fear and encouraged by a group of eugenists, Congress revolutionized the American immigration policy. Through a plan of quota allotments and national origins, the United States dammed the flood of immigration and turned the current into a Nordic channel.

While the World War stimulated Anglo-American nationalism, it also produced a vigorous group-consciousness among the immigrants and their descendants. The old-world rivalries and passions aroused their sentiments, pro and con. The appalling conditions of starvation and disease in war-torn Europe stirred their interest in their relatives, friends, and compatriots in the lands of their origin. The nationalistic attack upon their hyphenism, the attempts to ram Americanization down their throats, the discrimination against them in immigration quotas, the restrictions against their employment and professional opportunities, produced a reaction not contemplated by the would-be assimilationists. Many of the new ethnic groups became more deeply conscious of their distinctive cultures. They demanded the right to play a rôle in fashioning American life.

The causes of their cultural awakening are complexly interwoven. The psychological reaction of Anglo-American prejudice stimulated the group consciousness of many Latins, Slavs, and Jews. Failure to find satisfaction in the humdrum of the economic struggle compelled many to seek cultural compensation. Frequently, the failure of their intellectual lights to find a recognized place in American letters or art forced them to stimulate their group cultures in order to develop an audience for their own abilities. The struggles of the Catholic churches and Jewish synagogues for survival and expansion forced their ministers to undertake a tremendous program of religious and cultural education. To a large degree, the new groups cherished a genuine love for their traditional cultures and, consequently, could not accept the monotony of American standardization.

The argument for cultural pluralism is based upon the democratic philosophy. The exponents of group survival in America go back to the intellectual school of democracy—to Emerson, Channing, Walt Whitman. To its new exponents, democracy is more than a system of government; it is a social philosophy. Democracy is primarily an individualistic philosophy. It values the individual above all else. The individual is not a mere social or political automaton with no mind, no desires, no aspirations of his own. He possesses personality; and personality is unique. Democracy recognizes and respects this personality of the individual; it permits its expression through the free use of the ballot, through political participation, through free speech, and through liberty in pursuit of happiness. "Self-determination is the quintessence of democracy. Values must be related to the self if they are to be in truth goods, and the individual must be regarded as his own end." "The extent to which it is possible in any given society to understand each individual's good and to include it in the social good becomes the limit of democracy." [106] Democracy considers personality as absolutely sacred and its exploitation as the worst form of sacrilege. But the individual does not exist save in a group. [107] The individual that lives an isolated existence, that never comes into contact with others, can not be found. Man is a social being; his full personality can be released only through group life. Consequently, democracy must recognize the place of group institutions in the life of the individual. Family, economic, and cultural groups all release some new side of the individual's personality and make for a fuller life. If democracy is to be true to its concept of individualism, it must give recognition to cultural groupings and permit their existence as distinct units in the pyschic organism of the nation.

The full development of our personality, reasons Berkson, depends upon "retaining those bonds of union between our differentiated self and the Universe." [108] A complete life, he holds, is possible only when the individual becomes conscious of the myriad relationships which join him with the world. Evolution teaches us that the line of development is not in "the attainment of homogeneous undifferentiation, but of integrated diversifications; not in a falling back to unconsciousness, but in the attainment of self-consciousness. [109]

"To regard each individual as an end in himself; to know that he is a growing organism and that the goal of his Being is already inherent in his distinctive endowment; to understand that as he grows he becomes more differentiated from his fellows and yet more dependent upon them; to realize that consciousness of himself and of his relationships to the world is what

[106] I. B. Berkson, *Theories of Americanization*, pp. 27, 28. (Teachers College, Columbia University.)
[107] M. P. Follett, *The New State.*   [108] Berkson, *op. cit.*, p. 37.   [109] *Ibid.*, p. 38.

keeps him whole—all these are of the democratic doctrine which looks for the goal of the world not in the fulfillment of any objective law or principle, but within man himself to the fulfillment of his Personality.

"In the endeavor to develop Personality three conditions must be held in mind:

1. That each unique individual be regarded as the point of reference for value;

2. That the environment present a diversity of possibilities accessible to all;

3. That there be a consciousness on the part of the individual of his dependence upon the intricate series of natural and social relationships upon which his individuality rests.

Since these three conditions may exist in an infinite variety of degrees, we must realize that democracy is no one definite state but a tendency of development. We can, therefore, speak of democracy only in comparative terms. It is the direction of the movement which will define any conditions as democratic or not. Where there is a progressive consideration of uniqueness, a multiplication of diverse possibilities, a growing consciousness of man's interdependence—there does democracy exist." [110]

Horace M. Kallen presents a similar democratic basis for cultural pluralism. The problem of democracy, he argues, is so to perfect the organization of society that every man and every group may have the freest possible opportunity to realize and perfect his nature, and to attain the excellence appropriate to his kind. In essence, therefore, democracy involves, not the elimination of differences, but the perfection and conservation of differences. It aims, through union, not at uniformity, but at variety. It involves a give and take between radically different types, and a mutual respect and coöperation based on a mutual understanding. [111]

Employing this democratic philosophy as a weapon, the cultural pluralists attack the doctrine of Anglo-Americanization. The "one hundred per centers" picture America as already populated with a fairly homogeneous type, which in race and culture has Anglo-Saxon affiliations. All new-comers from foreign lands must as quickly as possible divest themselves of their own characteristics, and, through intermarriage and the complete taking over of the language, customs, hopes, and aspirations of the Anglo-American type, obliterate all ethnic distinctions. They must utterly forget the land of their origin and completely lose from their memory all recollection of its traditions. The kind of life proper for America is regarded as a matter to be decided entirely by the Anglo-American and those who have al-

---

[110] Berkson, *op. cit.*, pp. 38–39.

[111] Kallen, *Culture and Democracy in the United States* (New York, Horace Liveright), p. 61.

ready become assimilated. The foreigners must mold themselves into the ready-made form. They must do all the changing; the situation is not to be changed by them.[112] The following statement by the superintendent of the New York public schools indicates the Anglo-Americanization view of assimilation:

"Americanization is a spiritual thing difficult of determination in mere language. Broadly speaking, we mean by it an appreciation of the institutions of this country, absolute forgetfulness of all obligations or connections with other countries because of descent or birth." [113]

Similarly, E. P. Cubberley, in his *Changing Conceptions of Education*, declares that:

"Our task is to break up their groups of settlements, to assimilate and amalgamate these peoples as a part of our American race, and to implant in their children, so far as can be done, the Anglo-Saxon conception of righteousness, law and order and popular government, and to awaken in them reverence for our democratic institutions and for those things in our national life which we as a people hold to be of abiding worth." [114]

The intellectual leaders of the new culture groups, supported by outstanding Anglo-American thinkers,[115] naturally resent such intimations of their cultural and racial inferiority. The eugenists argue that the success of the Anglo-American in intelligence tests and public life proves their inherent superiority. Kallen compares this Nordic argument to the Brahminical explanation of the Brahmins in India. The Brahmins are the highest caste because they sprang from the head of Brahma, and they know that they sprang from the head of Brahma because they are the highest caste.[116]

Berkson maintains that "the assumption of total and exclusive superiority on the part of one group amounts to the imposition of an external standard which does not reckon with those concerned and savors of a theocratic or of an aristocratic state rather than of a democratic one." No room is left for taking into consideration the nature and personality of the immigrant. "The most profound feeling in American tradition is violated, the fundamental intuition upon which American institutions and political organizations are based, namely, *a decent respect for the worth of personalities which are not altogether like ours and a sincere faith in their potentialities.*" [117] Berk-

[112] Berkson, *op. cit.*, p. 55.
[113] New York *Evening Post*, August 9, 1918.
[114] P. 16. (Boston, Houghton Mifflin Company.)
[115] John Dewey, Randolph Bourne, Van Wyck Brooks.
[116] Kallen, *op. cit.*, pp. 25–26.
[117] Berkson, *op. cit.*, p. 63.

son attacks the theory of Anglo-Americanization because of its emphasis upon negative values. It stresses the forgetting of other traditions and the destruction of other spiritual allegiances. To Berkson's mind, true Americanization is a positive task; it is "a constructive work of developing knowledge, ideas, social attitudes; conceptions of law, order, government; interpretations of duty, freedom and the meaning of life. It implies above all the creation of a psychological attitude of willingness to serve the nation rather than the self, the family, the class, or the group exclusively." [118] The underlying assumption of Anglo-Americanization is that the breaking up of a group loyalty leads of itself to a wider loyalty; but, it does not necessarily do so. Rather, it often breaks down deep-laid traditional social attitudes of respect for family and leads to serious problems of juvenile delinquency and crime. The most stupid thing in the Anglo-Americanization program is its failure to recognize that the morality, folkways, ideas, and aspirations of the new groups can be utilized for the development of true Americans.[119] Berkson weighs the Anglo-Americanization theory with his democratic scales and discovers its fundamental weaknesses.

"Weighed in the balance of our first and fundamental criterion of democracy—respect for personality—the 'Americanization' theory must be found wanting. The tendency to interpret Americanism as the culture of one definite race, something well established to which the newcomers must completely conform, falls into the category of an absolutistic conception which assumes beforehand what is good without relation to the persons affected. By tacitly, if not expressly, denying the right of the immigrant to modify and contribute to the development of Americanism, the 'Americanization' theory violates that notion which is the quintessence of democracy, namely that the person involved must be considered as the end. Neither is the second criterion of democracy—a diversity in the environment—fulfilled by the 'Americanization' theory. It idealizes a fixed type of culture as against a diversified culture enriched by the tradition of many peoples. By the elimination of foreign ideas it would indoctrinate the tenets of a nationalistic cult. True liberty is served by the enrichment of possibilities, not by the establishment of uniformity. Lastly the conception of socialization in the 'Americanization' theory is faulty. It breaks down loyalty to the immediate family and to the cultural institutions—language, customs, etc., with which it is affiliated. It fails to realize that much of what the man's character is depends upon the integrity of these relations. To cap the climax, it fails in relation to the problem of affiliating with the new social life. Its stress is so negative, constantly emphasizing the danger of the old associations, that too little attention is given to the positive task—and a task it is—of building up on a firm and profound basis the culture of the new land." [120]

[118] Berkson, *op. cit.*, p. 68.   [119] *Ibid.*, pp. 68–69.   [120] *Ibid.*, pp. 71–72.

The cultural pluralists refuse to accept the theory of Anglo-Americanization. Nor are they willing to adopt the "melting pot" method of assimilation, dramatized by Israel Zangwill.[121] This theory of adjustment does not fall into the psychological and democratic fallacies of the doctrine of Anglo-Americanization. It conceives of Americanism as in the making, something growing out of the people that live here, something much more of the future than of the past. Americanism is a new life to which all can contribute. "Out of the present heterogeneity of races a new superior race is to be formed; out of the present medley of cultures a new, richer, more humane civilization is to be created; out of the present ferment a new religion will develop representing the spiritual expression of the new people, a religion more relevant to modern conceptions of life than the historical creeds and more tolerant of the differences among humankind." [122] While this theory rests upon a better conception of the psychology of adjustment, and exhibits democratic tolerance for all groups, nevertheless the cultural pluralists can not accept it. The price of the "melting pot" theory is self-annihilation. While the foreign groups are permitted to contribute to the life of the nation, they do so by losing their own existence. The new strains of blood are mingled with the old stock through intermarriage, and the groups which have made the contributions to the composite American culture perish as they give forth the products of their own lives. This theory of assimilation is adequate only for those groups which are willing to surrender their identity completely in becoming incorporated into the life of America. It is no solution for those who wish to participate in American life, and yet desire to retain their ethnic identity.[123] Under the "melting pot" theory, the Jews, or any other ethnic group, would give forth one bright flash, and its light would go out forever. Social heredity, language, and thought, are, like all social characteristics, acquired. Culture needs institutions to perpetuate and transmit itself. A culture is a spiritual entity; it is the soul of a people. But as every spirit is the spirit of something, and every soul, the soul of something, so a culture cannot subsist without a people. The Hellenic culture of antiquity offered no new contributions after the overthrow of Athens and the fall of Greece. Roman jurisprudence is to-day scarcely further developed than it was in the Code of Justinian. Similarly, there can be no progressive Jewish

---

[121] *The Melting Pot;* also Mary Antin, *The Promised Land,* and Francis Kellor, *Straight America.*

[122] Berkson, *op. cit.,* p. 73.

[123] *Ibid.,* p. 76.

culture in America without a Jewish people here. The "melting pot" theory calls for the amalgamation and destruction of the distinctive peoples. Their cultural contributions would be dissipated and lost, as are our physical resources, such as forests and oil deposits. Cultural conservation for to-morrow demands the retention of ethnic groups, not their annihilation.

The cultural pluralists demand the preservation of their ethnic groups. Only through this method of adjustment can we achieve a truly democratic regard for the uniqueness of individual personalities. Cultural growth, reasons Kallen, is founded upon cultural pluralism.

"Cultural Pluralism is possible only in a democratic society whose institutions encourage individuality in groups, in persons, in temperaments, whose program liberates these individualities and guides them into a fellowship of freedom and coöperation. The alternative before Americans is Kultur Klux Klan or Cultural Pluralism." [124]

Kallen outlines the culture of a great and truly democratic commonwealth that he visualizes as the future America. Its form is that of the federal republic; its substance, a democracy of nationalities, coöperating voluntarily and autonomously through common institutions in the "enterprise of self-realization through the perfection of men according to their kind." The common language of the commonwealth is English, but each nationality has for its emotional life its own peculiar dialect or speech, its own individual and inevitable esthetic and intellectual forms. The political and economic life of the commonwealth is a single unit and serves as the foundation and background for the realization of the distinctive individuality of each group and for the pooling of these in a harmony above them all. [125]

"As in an orchestra every type of instrument has its specific *timbre* and *tonality*, founded in its substance and form; as every type has its appropriate theme and melody in the whole symphony, so in society, each ethnic group may be the natural instrument, its temper and culture may be its theme and melody and the harmony and dissonances and discords of them all make the symphony of civilization. With this difference: a musical symphony is written before it is played; in the symphony of civilization the playing is the writing, so that there is nothing fixed and inevitable about its progressions as in music, so that within the limits set by nature and luck they may vary at will, and the range and variety of the harmonies may become wider and richer and more beautiful—or the reverse." [126]

[124] Kallen, *op. cit.*, p. 43.
[125] *Ibid.*, p. 124. For a similar description of the proper cultural organization of America, see Berkson, *op. cit.*, p. 102, and Drachsler, *Democracy and Assimilation*, pp. 214–223.
[126] Kallen, *op. cit.*, pp. 124–125.

The philosophy of cultural pluralism has stimulated the imagination of some intellectual leaders of Anglo-American stock. Van Wyck Brooks typifies this group. He pictures the nationalities as the workshop of humanity, with each nationality having a special duty to perform, a special genius to exert, a special gift to contribute to the general stock of civilization.[127] The question of our immigration population affords, in his view, the most critical test for any merely pragmatic sociology.

"Our 'hyphenates,' bred in a richly poetic, a richly creative soil, desire to live poetically and creatively; but they come to us as the detached limbs of a tree that they have left behind. Has it never occurred to our awakeners that the only way in which we can absorb their life is by providing them with a new tree upon which they can engraft themselves?"[128]

The implications of cultural pluralism are important to American democracy and political institutions. This philosophy demands from the Americans of colonial origin a frank restatement of their traditional dogmas of democracy. If the latter are sincere in their cult of democratic liberties, then they must recognize the liberty of the non-Anglican Americans to express their lives through cultural devices most productive to their individual personalities and happiness. If the early Americans insist upon the enforcement of Anglo-American traits and upon the uprooting of all conflicting habits and ideas, then, insist the cultural pluralists, we must abandon our lip-service to the goddess of democracy. Cultural pluralism offers a challenge to the internationalists, too. If the exponents of American participation in world affairs are sincere in their desire for "diversity within a unity," then, to be consistent they must permit and encourage a cultural diversity within our own political unity. An internationalism of American cultures must parallel the proposed federation of nations; tolerance of differences at home can form the only firm foundation for tolerance of differences abroad.

WOODROW WILSON

The United States declared war against Germany in April, 1917. Wilson rationalized American entrance on the grounds of moral idealism. His famous "Fourteen Points" speech on January 8, 1918, outlined our purposes in the war and presented his view of the proper basis for a lasting peace. Upon the conclusion of the war, Wilson himself went to Paris and participated in the Versailles Conference. He did not secure the adoption of all his fourteen points, but compromised in order to win a victory for a

[127] *Letters and Leadership* (New York, The Viking Press), p. 60.
[128] *Ibid.*, pp. 111–112.

league of nations. Returning from Europe, he led the fight for the Versailles Treaty, the League Covenant, and the continued participation of the United States in world affairs.

THE FOURTEEN POINTS SPEECH, DELIVERED AT A JOINT SESSION OF THE TWO HOUSES OF CONGRESS, JANUARY 8, 1918.[129]

It will be our wish and purpose that the processes of peace, when they are begun, shall be absolutely open and that they shall involve and permit henceforth no secret understandings of any kind. The day of conquest and aggrandizement is gone by; so is also the day of secret covenants entered into in the interests of particular governments and likely at some unlooked-for moment to upset the peace of the world. It is this happy fact, now clear to the view of every public man whose thoughts do not still linger in an age that is dead and gone, which makes it possible for every nation whose purposes are consistent with justice and the peace of the world to avow now or at any other time the objects it has in view.

We entered this war because violations of right had occurred which touched us to the quick and made the life of our own people impossible unless they were corrected and the world secured once for all against their recurrence. What we demand in this war, therefore, is nothing peculiar to ourselves. It is that the world be made fit and safe to live in; and particularly that it be made safe for every peace-loving nation which, like our own, wishes to live its own life, determine its own institutions, be assured of justice and fair dealing by the other peoples of the world as against force and selfish aggression. All the peoples of the world are in effect partners in this interest, and for our own part we see very clearly that unless justice be done to others it will not be done to us. The program of the world's peace, therefore, is our program; and that program, the only possible program, as we see it, is this:

I. Open covenants of peace, openly arrived at, after which there shall be no private international understandings of any kind but diplomacy shall proceed always frankly and in the public view.

II. Absolute freedom of navigation upon the seas, outside territorial waters, alike in peace and in war, except as the seas may be closed in whole or in part by international action for the enforcement of international covenants.

III. The removal, so far as possible, of all economic barriers and the establishment of an equality of trade conditions among all the nations consenting to the peace and associating themselves for its maintenance.

IV. Adequate guarantees given and taken that national armaments will be reduced to the lowest point consistent with domestic safety.

V. A free, open-minded, and absolutely impartial adjustment of all colonial claims, based upon a strict observance of the principle that in determining all such questions of sovereignty the interests of the populations concerned must have equal weight with the equitable claims of the government whose title is to be determined.

[129] R. S. Baker and W. E. Dodd (editors), *The Public Papers of Woodrow Wilson: War and Peace* (New York, Harper & Brothers, 1925), I, 158–162. (Reprinted by permission of Mrs. Woodrow Wilson.)

VI. The evacuation of all Russian territory and such a settlement of all questions affecting Russia as will secure the best and freest coöperation of the other nations of the world in obtaining for her an unhampered and unembarrassed opportunity for the independent determination of her own political development and national policy and assure her of a sincere welcome into the society of free nations under institutions of her own choosing; and, more than a welcome, assistance also of every kind that she may need and may herself desire. The treatment accorded Russia by her sister nations in the months to come will be the acid test of their good will, of their comprehension of her needs as distinguished from their own interests, and of their intelligent and unselfish sympathy.

VII. Belgium, the whole world will agree, must be evacuated and restored, without any attempt to limit the sovereignty which she enjoys in common with all other free nations. No other single act will serve as this will serve to restore confidence among the nations in the laws which they have themselves set and determined for the government of their relations with one another. Without this healing act the whole structure and validity of international law is forever impaired.

VIII. All French territory should be freed and the invaded portions restored and the wrong done to France by Prussia in 1871 in the matter of Alsace-Lorraine, which has unsettled the peace of the world for nearly fifty years, should be righted, in order that peace may once more be made secure in the interest of all.

IX. A readjustment of the frontiers of Italy should be effected along clearly recognizable lines of nationality.

X. The peoples of Austria-Hungary, whose place among the nations we wish to see safeguarded and assured, should be accorded the freest opportunity of autonomous development.

XI. Rumania, Serbia, and Montenegro should be evacuated; occupied territories restored; Serbia accorded free and secure access to the sea; and the relations of the several Balkan states to one another determined by friendly counsel along historically established lines of allegiance and nationality; and international guarantees of the political and economic independence and territorial integrity of the several Balkan states should be entered into.

XII. The Turkish portions of the present Ottoman Empire should be assured a secure sovereignty, but the other nationalities which are now under Turkish rule should be assured an undoubted security of life and an absolutely unmolested opportunity of autonomous development, and the Dardanelles should be permanently opened as a free passage to the ships and commerce of all nations under international guarantees.

XIII. An independent Polish state should be erected which should include the territories inhabited by indisputably Polish populations, which should be assured a free and secure access to the sea, and whose political and economic independence and territorial integrity should be guaranteed by international covenant.

XIV. A general association of nations must be formed under specific covenants for the purpose of affording mutual guarantees of political independence and territorial integrity to great and small states alike.

In regard to these essential rectifications of wrong and assertions of right we feel ourselves to be intimate partners of all the governments and peoples associated together against the Imperialists. We cannot be separated in interest or divided in purpose. We stand together until the end.

For such arrangements and covenants we are willing to fight and to continue to fight until they are achieved; but only because we wish the right to prevail and desire a just and stable peace such as can be secured only by removing the chief provocations to war, which their program does remove. We have no jealousy of German greatness, and there is nothing in this program that impairs it. We grudge her no achievement or distinction of learning or of pacific enterprise such as have made her record very bright and very enviable. We do not wish to injure her or to block in any way her legitimate influence of power. We do not wish to fight her either with arms or with hostile arrangements of trade if she is willing to associate herself with us and the other peace-loving nations of the world in covenants of justice and law and fair dealing. We wish her only to accept a place of equality among the peoples of the world,—the new world in which we now live,—instead of a place of mastery.

Neither do we presume to suggest to her any alteration or modification of her institutions. But it is necessary, we must frankly say, and necessary as a preliminary to any intelligent dealings with her on our part, that we should know whom her spokesmen speak for when they speak to us, whether for the Reichstag majority or for the military party and the men whose creed is imperial domination.

We have spoken now, surely, in terms too concrete to admit of any further doubt or question. An evident principle runs through the whole program I have outlined. It is the principle of justice to all peoples and nationalities, and their right to live on equal terms of liberty and safety with one another, whether they be strong or weak. Unless this principle be made its foundation no part of the structure of international justice can stand. The people of the United States could act upon no other principle; and to the vindication of this principle they are ready to devote their lives, their honor, and everything that they possess. The moral climax of this the culminating and final war for human liberty has come, and they are ready to put their own strength, their own highest purpose, their own integrity and devotion to the test.

PRESENTING THE TREATY FOR RATIFICATION.
ADDRESS TO THE SENATE OF THE UNITED STATES,
JULY 10, 1919.[130]

Gentlemen of the Senate:

The treaty of peace with Germany was signed at Versailles on the twenty-eighth of June. I avail myself of the earliest opportunity to lay the treaty before you for ratification and to inform you with regard to the work of the Conference by which that treaty was formulated.

The treaty constitutes nothing less than a world settlement. It would not

[130] R. S. Baker and W. E. Dodd (editors), *The Public Papers of Woodrow Wilson: War and Peace* (New York, Harper & Brothers, 1925), I, 537-552. (Reprinted by permission of Mrs. Woodrow Wilson.)

be possible for me either to summarize or to construe its manifold provisions in an address which must of necessity be something less than a treatise. My services and all the information I possess will be at your disposal and at the disposal of your Committee on Foreign Relations at any time, either informally or in session, as you may prefer; and I hope that you will not hesitate to make use of them. I shall at this time, prior to your own study of the document, attempt only a general characterization of its scope and purpose.

In one sense, no doubt, there is no need that I should report to you what was attempted and done at Paris. You have been daily cognizant of what was going on there,—of the problems with which the Peace Conference had to deal and of the difficulty of laying down straight lines of settlement anywhere on a field on which the old lines of international relationship, and the new alike, followed so intricate a pattern and were for the most part cut so deep by historical circumstances which dominated action even where it would have been best to ignore or reverse them. The cross currents of politics and of interests must have been evident to you. It would be presuming in me to attempt to explain the questions which arose or the many diverse elements that entered into them. I shall attempt something less ambitious than that and more clearly suggested by my duty to report to the Congress the part it seemed necessary for my colleagues and me to play as the representatives of the Government of the United States.

That part was dictated by the rôle America had played in the war and by the expectations that had been created in the minds of the peoples with whom we had associated ourselves in that great struggle.

The United States entered the war upon a different footing from every other nation except our associates on this side the sea. We entered it, not because our material interests were directly threatened or because any special treaty obligations to which we were parties had been violated, but only because we saw the supremacy, and even the validity, of right everywhere put in jeopardy and free government likely to be everywhere imperiled by the intolerable aggression of a power which respected neither right nor obligation and whose very system of government flouted the rights of the citizens as against the autocratic authority of his governors. And in the settlements of the peace we have sought no special reparation for ourselves, but only the restoration of right and the assurance of liberty everywhere that the effects of the settlement were to be felt. We entered the war as the disinterested champions of right and we interested ourselves in the terms of the peace in no other capacity.

The hopes of the nations allied against the Central Powers were at a very low ebb when our soldiers began to pour across the sea. There was everywhere amongst them, except in their stoutest spirits, a somber foreboding of disaster. The war ended in November, eight months ago, but you have only to recall what was feared in midsummer last, four short months before the armistice, to realize what it was that our timely aid accomplished alike for their morale and their physical safety. The first, never-to-be-forgotten action at Chateau-Thierry had already taken place. Our redoubtable soldiers and marines had already closed the gap the enemy had succeeded in opening for their advance upon Paris,—had already turned the tide of battle back towards the frontiers of France and begun the rout that was to save Europe and the world. Thereafter the Germans were to be always forced back, back, were never to thrust successfully forward again. And yet there was no confident hope. Anxious men and women, leading spirits of France, attended the celebration of the Fourth of July last year in Paris out of generous courtesy,—with no heart for festivity, little zest for hope. But they came away with something new at their hearts; they have themselves told us so. The mere sight of our men,—of their vigor, of the confidence that showed itself in every movement of their stalwart figures and every turn of their swinging march, in their steady comprehending eyes and easy discipline, in the indomitable air that added spirit to everything they did,—made everyone who saw them that memorable day realize that something had happened that was much more than a mere incident in the fighting, something very different from the mere arrival of fresh troops. A great moral force had flung itself into the struggle. The fine physical force of those spirited men spoke of something more than bodily vigor. They carried the great ideals of a free people at their hearts and with that vision were unconquerable. Their very presence brought reassurance; their fighting made victory certain.

They were recognized as crusaders, and as their thousands swelled to millions their strength was seen to mean salvation. And they were fit men to carry such a hope and make good the assurance it forecast. Finer men never went into battle; and their officers were worthy of them. This is not the occasion upon which to utter a eulogy of the armies America sent to France, but perhaps, since I am speaking of their mission, I may speak also of the pride I shared with every American who saw or dealt with them there. They were the sort of men America would wish to be represented by, the sort of men every American would wish to claim as fellow countrymen and comrades in a great cause. They were terrible in battle, and gentle and helpful out of it, remembering the mothers and the sisters, the wives and the little children at home. They were free men under arms, not forgetting their ideals of duty in the midst of tasks of violence. I am proud to have had the privilege of being associated with them and of calling myself their leader.

But I speak now of what they meant to the men by whose sides they fought and to the people with whom they mingled with such utter simplicity, as friends who asked only to be of service. They were for all the visible embodiment of America. What they did made America and all that she stood for a living reality in the thoughts not only of the people of France but also of tens of millions of men and women throughout all the toiling nations of a world standing everywhere in peril of its freedom and of the loss of everything it held dear, in deadly fear that its bonds were never to be loosed, its hopes forever to be mocked and disappointed.

And the compulsion of what they stood for was upon us who represented America at the peace table. It was our duty to see to it that every decision we took part in contributed, so far as we were able to influence it, to quiet the fears and realize the hopes of the peoples who had been living in that shadow, the nations that had come by our assistance to their freedom. It was our duty to do everything that it was within our power to do to make the triumph of freedom and of right a lasting triumph in the assurance of which men might everywhere live without fear.

Old entanglements of every kind stood in the way,—promises which Governments had made to one another in the days when might and right were confused and the power of the victor was without restraint. Engagements which contemplated any dispositions of territory, any extensions of sovereignty that might seem to be to the interest of those who had the power to insist upon them, had been entered into without thought of what the peoples concerned might wish or profit by; and these could not always be honorably brushed aside. It was not easy to graft the new order of ideas on the old, and some of the fruits of the grafting may, I fear, for a time be bitter. But, with very few exceptions, the men who sat with us at the peace table desired as sincerely as we did to get away from the bad influences, the illegitimate purposes, the demoralizing ambitions, the international counsels and expedients out of which the sinister designs of Germany had sprung as a natural growth.

It has been our privilege to formulate the principles which were accepted as the basis of the peace, but they had been accepted, not because we had come in to hasten and assure the victory and insisted upon them, but because they were readily acceded to as the principles to which honorable and enlightened minds everywhere had been bred. They spoke the conscience of the world as well as the conscience of America, and I am happy to pay my tribute of respect and gratitude to the able, forward-looking men with whom it was my privilege to coöperate for their unfailing spirit of coöperation, their constant effort to accommodate the interest they represented to the principles we were all agreed upon. The difficulties, which were many, lay in the circumstances, not often in the men. Almost without exception the men who led had caught the true and full vision of the problem of peace as an indivisible whole, a problem, not of mere adjustments of interest, but of justice and right action.

The atmosphere in which the Conference worked seemed created, not by the ambitions of strong governments, but by the hopes and aspirations of small nations and of peoples hitherto under bondage to the power that victory had shattered and destroyed. Two great empires had been forced into political bankruptcy, and we were the receivers. Our task was not only to make peace with the Central Empires and remedy the wrongs their armies had done. The Central Empires had lived in open violation of many of the very rights for which the war had been fought, dominating alien peoples over whom they had no natural right to rule, enforcing, not obedience, but veritable bondage, exploiting those who were weak for the benefit of those who were masters and overlords only by force of arms. There could be no peace until the whole order of Central Europe was set right.

That meant that new nations were to be created,—Poland, Czecho-Slovakia, Hungary itself. No part of ancient Poland had ever in any true sense become a part of Germany, or of Austria, or of Russia. Bohemia was alien in every thought and hope to the monarchy of which she had so long been an artificial part; and the uneasy partnership between Austria and Hungary had been one rather of interest than of kinship or sympathy. The Slavs whom Austria had chosen to force into her empire on the south were kept to their obedience by nothing but fear. Their hearts were with their kinsmen in the Balkans. These were all arrangements of natural union or association. It was the imperative task of those who would make peace and make it intelligently to establish a new order which would rest upon the free choice of peoples rather than upon the arbitrary authority of Hapsburgs or Hohenzollerns.

More than that, great populations bound by sympathy and actual kin to Rumania were also linked against their will to the conglomerate Austro-Hungarian monarchy or to other alien sovereignties, and it was part of the task of peace to make a new Rumania as well as a new slavic state clustering about Serbia.

And no natural frontiers could be found to these new fields of adjustment and redemption. It was necessary to look constantly forward to other related tasks. The German colonies were to be disposed of. They had not been governed; they had been exploited merely, without thought of the interest or even the ordinary human rights of their inhabitants.

The Turkish Empire, moreover, had fallen apart, as the Austro-Hungarian had. It had never had any real unity. It has been held together only by pitiless, inhuman force. Its peoples cried aloud for release, for succor from unspeakable distress, for all that the new day of hope seemed at last to bring within its dawn. Peoples hitherto in utter darkness were to be led out into the same light and given at last a helping hand. Undeveloped peoples and peoples ready for recognition but not yet ready to assume the full responsibilities of statehood were to be given adequate guarantees of friendly protection, guidance and assistance.

And out of the execution of these great enterprises of liberty sprang opportunities to attempt what statesmen had never found the way before to do; an opportunity to throw safeguards about the rights of racial, national and religious minorities by solemn international covenant; an opportunity to limit and regulate military establishments where they were most likely to be mischievous; an opportunity to effect a complete and systematic internationalization of waterways and railways which were necessary to the free economic life of more than one nation and to clear many of the normal channels of commerce of unfair obstructions of law or of privilege; and the very welcome opportunity to secure for labor the concerted protection of definite international pledges of principle and practice.

These were not tasks which the Conference looked about it to find and went out of its way to perform. They were inseparable from the settlements of peace. They were thrust upon it by circumstances which could not be overlooked. The war had created them. In all quarters of the world old-established relationships had been disturbed or broken and affairs were at loose ends, needing to be mended or united again, but could not be made what they were before. They had to be set right by applying some uniform principle of justice or enlightened expediency. And they could not be adjusted by merely prescribing in a treaty what should be done. New states were to be set up which could not hope to live through their first period of weakness without assured support by the great nations that had consented to their creation and won for them their independence. Ill-governed colonies could not be put in the hands of governments which were to act as trustees for their people and not as their masters if there was to be no common authority among the nations to which they were to be responsible in the execution of their trust. Future international conventions with regard to the control of waterways, with regard to illicit traffic of many kinds, in arms or in deadly drugs, or with regard to the adjustment of many varying international administrative arrangements could not be assured if the treaty were to provide no permanent common international agency, if its execution in such matters was to be left to the slow and uncertain processes of coöperation by ordinary methods of negotiation. If the Peace Conference itself was to be the end of coöperative authority and common counsel among the governments to which the world was looking to enforce justice and give pledges of an enduring settlement, regions like the Saar basin could not be put under a temporary administrative régime which did not involve a transfer of political sovereignty and which contemplated a final determination of its political connections by popular vote to be taken at a distant date; no free city like Danzig could be created which was, under elaborate international guarantees, to accept exceptional obligations with regard to the use of its port and exceptional relations with a State of which it was not to form a part; properly safeguarded plebiscites could not be provided for where populations were at some future date to make choice what sovereignty they would live under; no certain and uniform method of arbitration could be secured for the settlement of anticipated difficulties of final decision with regard to many matters dealt with in the treaty itself; the long-continued supervision of the task of reparation which Germany was to undertake to complete within the next generation might entirely break down; the reconsideration and revision of administrative arrangements and restrictions which the treaty prescribed but which it was recognized might not prove of lasting advantage or entirely fair if too long enforced would be impracticable. The promises governments were making to one another about the way in which labor was to be dealt with, by law not only but in fact as well, would remain a mere humane thesis if there was to be no common tribunal of opinion and judgment to which liberal statesmen could resort for the influences which alone might secure their redemption. A league of free nations had become a practical necessity. Examine the treaty of peace and you will find that everywhere throughout its manifold provisions its framers have felt obliged to turn to the League of Nations as an indispensable instrumentality for the maintenance of the new order it has been their purpose to set up in the world,—the world of civilized men.

That there should be a League of Nations to steady the counsels and maintain the peaceful understandings of the world, to make, not treaties alone, but the accepted principles of international law as well, the actual rule of conduct among the governments of the world, had been one of the agreements accepted from the first as the basis of peace with the Central Powers. The statesmen of all the belligerent countries were agreed that such a league must be created to sustain the settlements that were to be effected. But at first I think there was a feeling among some of them that, while it must be attempted, the formation of such a league was perhaps a counsel of perfection which practical men, long experienced in the world of affairs, must agree to very cautiously and with many misgivings. It was only as the difficult work of arranging an all but universal adjustment of the world's affairs advanced from day to day from one stage of conference to another that it became evident to them that what they were seeking would be little more than something written upon paper, to be interpreted and applied by such methods as the chances of politics might make available if they did not provide a means of common counsel which all were obliged to accept, a common authority whose decisions would be recognized as decisions which all must respect.

And so the most practical, the most skeptical among them turned more and more to the League as the authority through which international action was to be secured, the authority without which, as they had come to see it, it would be difficult to give assured effect either to this treaty or to any other international understanding upon which they were to depend for the maintenance of peace. The fact that the Covenant of the League was the first substantive part of the treaty to be worked out and agreed upon, while all else was in solution, helped to make the formulation of the rest easier. The Conference was, after all, not to be ephemeral. The concert of nations was to continue, under a definite Covenant which had been agreed upon and which all were convinced was workable. They could go forward with confidence to make arrangements intended to be permanent. The most practical of the conferees were at last the most ready to refer to the League of Nations the superintendence of all interests which did not admit of immediate determination, of all administrative problems which were to require a continuing oversight. What had seemed a counsel of perfection had come to seem a plain counsel of necessity. The League of Nations was the practical statesman's hope of success in many of the most difficult things he was attempting.

And it had validated itself in the thought of every member of the Conference as something much bigger, much greater every way, than a mere instrument for carrying out the provisions of a particular treaty. It was universally recognized that all the peoples of the world demanded of the Conference that it should create such a continuing concert of free nations as would make wars of aggression and spoliation such as this that has just ended forever impossible. A cry had gone out from every home in every stricken land from which sons and brothers and fathers had gone forth to the great sacrifice that such a sacrifice should never again be exacted. It was manifest why it had been exacted. It had been exacted because one nation desired dominion and other nations had known no means of defense except armaments and alliances. War had lain at the heart of every arrangement of the Europe,—of every arrangement of the world,—that preceded the war. Restive peoples had been told that fleets and armies, which they toiled to sustain, meant peace; and they now knew that they had been lied to: that fleets and armies had been maintained to promote national ambitions and meant war. They knew that no old policy meant anything else but force, force, always force. And they knew that it was intolerable. Every true heart in the world, and every enlightened judgment demanded that, at whatever cost of independent action, every government that took thought for its people or for justice or for ordered freedom should lend itself to a new purpose and utterly destroy the old order of international politics. Statesmen might see difficulties, but the people could see none and could brook no denial. A war in which they had been bled white to beat the terror that lay concealed in every Balance of Power must not end in a mere victory of arms and a new balance. The monster that had resorted to arms must be put in chains that could not be broken. The united power of free nations must put a stop to aggression, and the world must be given peace. If there was not the will or the intelligence to accomplish that now, there must be another and a final war and the world must be swept clean of every power that could renew the terror. The League of Nations was not merely an instrument to adjust and remedy old wrongs under a new treaty of peace; it was the only hope for mankind. Again and again had the demon of war been cast out of the house of the peoples and the house swept clean by a treaty of peace; only to prepare a time when he would enter it again with spirits worse than himself. The house must now be given a tenant who could hold it against all such. Convenient, indeed, indispensable, as statesmen found the newly planned League of Nations to be for the execution of present plans of peace and reparation, they saw it in a new aspect before their work was finished. They saw it as the main object of the peace, as the only thing that could complete it or make it worth while. They saw it as the hope of the world, and that hope they did not dare to disappoint. Shall we or any other free people hesitate to accept this great duty? Dare we reject it and break the heart of the world?

And so the result of the Conference of Peace, so far as Germany is concerned, stands complete. The difficulties encountered were very many. Sometimes they seemed insuperable. It was impossible to accommodate the interests of so great a body of nations,—interests which directly or indirectly affected almost every nation in the world,—without many minor compromises. The treaty, as a result, is not exactly what we would have written. It is probably not what any one of the national delegations would have written. But results were worked out which on the whole bear test. I think that it will be found that the compromises which were accepted as inevitable nowhere cut to the heart of any principle. The work of the Conference squares, as a whole, with the principles agreed upon as the basis of the peace as well as with the practical possibilities of the international situations which had to be faced and dealt with as facts.

I shall presently have occasion to lay before you a special treaty with France, whose object is the temporary protection of France from unprovoked aggression by the Power with whom this treaty of peace has been negotiated. Its terms link it with this treaty. I take the liberty, however, of reserving it for special explication on another occasion.

The rôle which America was to play in the Conference seemed determined, as I have said, before my colleagues and I got to Paris,—determined by the universal expectations of the nations whose representatives, drawn from all quarters of the globe, we were to deal with. It was universally recognized that America had entered the war to promote no private or peculiar interest of her own but only as the champion of rights which she was glad to share with free men and lovers of justice everywhere. We had formulated the principles upon which the settlement was to be made,—the principles upon which the armistice had been agreed to and the parleys of peace undertaken,— and no one doubted that our desire was to see the treaty of peace formulated along the actual lines of these principles,—and desired nothing else. We were welcomed as disinterested friends. We were resorted to as arbiters in many a difficult matter. It was recognized that our material aid would be indispensable in the days to come, when industry and credit would have to be brought back to their normal operation again and communities beaten to the ground assisted to their feet once more, and it was taken for granted, I am proud to say, that we would play the helpful friend in these things as in all others without prejudice or favor. We were generously accepted as the unaffected champions of what was right. It was a very responsible rôle to play; but I am happy to report that the fine group of Americans who helped with their expert advice in each part of the varied settlements sought in every transaction to justify the high confidence reposed in them.

And that confidence, it seems to me, is the measure of our opportunity and of our duty in the days to come, in which the new hope of the peoples of the world is to be fulfilled or disappointed. The fact that America is the friend of the nations, whether they be rivals or associates, is no new fact; it is only the discovery of it by the rest of the world that is new.

America may be said to have just reached her majority as a world power. It was almost exactly twenty-one years ago that the results of the war with Spain put us unexpectedly in possession of rich islands on the other side of the world and brought us into association with other governments in the control of the West Indies. It was regarded as a sinister and ominous thing by the statesmen of more than one European chancellery that we should have extended our power beyond the confines of our continental dominions. They were accustomed to think of new neighbors as a new menace, of rivals as watchful enemies. There were persons amongst us at home who looked with deep disapproval and avowed anxiety on such extensions of our national authority over distant islands and over peoples whom they feared we might exploit, not serve and assist. But we have not exploited them. We have been their friends and have sought to serve them. And our dominion has been a menace to no other nation, We redeem our honor to the utmost in our dealings with Cuba. She is weak but absolutely free; and it is her trust in us that makes her free. Weak peoples everywhere stand ready to give us any authority among them that will assure them a like friendly oversight and direction. They know that there is no ground for fear in receiving us as their mentors and guides. Our isolation was ended twenty years ago; and now fear of us is ended also, our counsel and association sought after and desired. There can be no question of our ceasing to be a world power. The only question is whether we can refuse the moral leadership that is offered us, whether we shall accept or reject the confidence of the world.

The war and the Conference of Peace now sitting in Paris seem to me to have answered that question. Our participation in the war established our position among the nations and nothing but our own mistaken action can alter it. It was not an accident or a matter of sudden choice that we are no longer isolated and devoted to a policy which has only our own interest and advantage for its object. It was our duty to go in, if we were indeed the champions of liberty and of right. We answered to the call of duty in a way so spirited, so utterly without thought of what we spent of blood or treasure, so effective, so worthy of the admiration of true men everywhere, so wrought out of the stuff of all that was heroic, that the whole world saw at last, in the flesh, in noble action, a great ideal asserted and vindicated, by a Nation they had deemed material and now found to be compact of the spiritual forces that must free men of every nation from every unworthy bondage. It is thus that a new rôle and a new responsibility have come to this great Nation that we honor and which we would all wish to lift to yet higher levels of service and achievement.

The stage is set, the destiny disclosed. It has come about by no plan of our conceiving, but by the hand of God who led us into this way. We cannot turn back. We can only go forward, with lifted eyes and freshened spirit, to follow the vision. It was of this that we dreamed at our birth. America shall in truth show the way. The light streams upon the path ahead, and nowhere else.

JAMES T. SHOTWELL

James T. Shotwell has been a professor of history at Columbia University since 1907. He served under Wilson on the preparatory commission for the Versailles peace conference. Since 1924 he has been director of the division of economics and history of the Carnegie Endowment for International Peace. Shotwell has played an active part in the discussion of recent problems of American foreign affairs. He has occasionally acted as an unofficial liaison officer between the League of Nations and American officials. In addition to his historical studies, he has done much writing on international relations. His volume, *War as an Instrument of National Policy and its Renunciation in the Pact of Paris* (1929), presents the history, the underlying philosophy, and the possible future significance of the Kellogg-Briand treaty.

WAR AS AN INSTRUMENT OF NATIONAL POLICY [131]

CHAPTER IV

War in the New Era

Now it is time to see the bearing of this analysis upon the problem before us. War, too, has shared in the change which has come over social and political relationships. In the pre-scientific era—in which we are still rather deeply rooted, and in which some nations are still living—war partook of the nature of other industries; there were new inventions in it, as in the industries of peace, but it was conservative and localized, even more so than they. Thus, throughout most of European history, wars have been fought within fixed limits between the armed forces of two or more states, while the rest of mankind—even within the belligerent nations—looked on with more or less neutral indifference. Under such conditions war was controllable or relatively so. It was employed to conquer or defend this or that territory or to reduce or to aggrandize commerce. By land and sea the enemies were clearly discernible: there was no need to mistake either the aim of war or the limits of its operations. In the old isolated economy of nations, war was primarily a question of man-power. A nation which went to war simply called upon its citizens—or rather a monarch called upon his subjects—and each one came with his own arms and accouterments. The advancing armies lived off the supplies of the countryside through which they marched.

[131] J. T. Shotwell, *War as an Instrument of National Policy and its Renunciation in the Pact of Paris* (New York, Harcourt, Brace and Company, 1929), pp. 32–38, 220–226. (Reprinted by permission of the publishers.)

It was a straightforward operation, limited strictly to those engaged in it. A nation which did not wish to fight could remain aloof from the conflict by simply keeping its armies from the field.

Under these conditions the place of war in political theory was well defined. It was a legitimate exercise of sovereignty, the final argument, the *ultima ratio*, of governments. It established or enforced policies of state, and was therefore a usable instrument with calculable results. In such a world the only hope of peace was to use this final argument to impose a universal will; a hope like that which inspired the dreams of Dante. A superior power should coerce the anarchic and warring elements of civilization into a single empire. The restoration of the *pax Romana* proved impossible, however; and the modern states, hewn in every case out of this anarchy of war, continued to depend for their security upon the instrument which had been used for their creation.

Had war remained what it was in Dante's day, it is probable that the problem of international peace would still have to be stated in Dante's terms. But in the industrial and financial era of today, the nature of war has utterly changed from the simple strategy of man-power of earlier days. Not only does war involve the entire economic structure of the belligerent nations, but it spreads like a contagion throughout all those other countries whose economic life has become involved with that of the nations at war; which means more or less all the industrialized nations of the civilized world. As the armies advance in one direction, the ships go out in another for the raw materials of war, and the more the conflagration grows the more the belligerent becomes dependent on ever new supplies, and so, when the war is over, finds that the territory covered by the advance of its armies is perhaps of far less value to it than the wealth which it has sacrificed to win the victory. In other words, the direction of war in the modern world of industry and finance does not wholly follow that of military strategy; it follows rather that of economic needs satisfied only at the ruinous cost of war-time prices.

The World War offered an unparalleled opportunity for the study of these phenomena. This was seen early in the war by Professor John Bates Clark, who was then Director of the Division of Economics and History of the Carnegie Endowment for International Peace. From his suggestion has grown the *Economic and Social History of the World War*, to the preparation of which I have devoted nine years. Some two hundred contributors, among them thirty-five cabinet ministers of various governments, are contributing to its hundred and fifty volumes. The subject of this survey is what I have just indicated as the very heart of our problem. It avoids political controversy, leaves entirely aside such vexed questions as that of war-guilt, and deals with the World War from the angle of its displacement in the normal processes of civilization.

Viewing the World War from the historical standpoint just indicated it becomes growingly clear—and subsequent discussions on national security bear this out—that during the years 1914 to 1918, the industry of destruction, which is war, definitely passed into the industrial phase of economic history. This fact is disguised by the long deadlock of armies in the field, which gave many indications of a return to the war-economy of an earlier day. But when one deals with modern war, one is dealing with something larger than military facts. The survey covers—or may cover—every activity of those at war, in finance, industry, agriculture, housekeeping, engineering, even scientific research. For all these activities were more or less at war. Germany was the first to realize this. In all the literature of the war, there is nothing more striking than the little memoir in which Dr. Walter Rathenau describes the vision which he realized in the creation of the Division of Raw Materials of the War Office (*Rohstoffsabteilung*). When, in the early days of the war, the attention of the world was fastened upon the armies in the field, he saw in imagination the mobilization of factories and the belching furnaces instead of guns alone. It was because others did not have this vision that, when the war began, almost every one—including economists—said that it could not last more than a few months, because of the exhaustion of resources as well as of men.

Science falsified this prophecy. Medicine kept up the supply of lives for the front by reducing the death rate, by hygiene and surgery. Had the science of medicine been as primitive in 1914 as it was in 1870, or with us in the Spanish War of 1898, a war that cost a nation a million dead upon the field of battle would have cost it anywhere from ten to twenty times as many. The importance of this phase of the social and economic history of the war has not been fully appreciated. As for the parallel exhaustion of economic resources, similar surprises were sprung, too familiar to all of us now, however, to be described here. One need only recall the unrecognizable England of 1916 to 1918, in which almost every principle of its economic past was violated, as it has to be when a country becomes an arsenal; or the case of the United States, where still stranger transformations took place.

But the important point for us is that this economy of war followed the law of dynamics, change producing changes in geometric progression—with the whole process speeded up by the fact that the competition of war must follow a faster pace than that of peace, since in war the delay in adjustment may be fatal.

It is not so significant that the war involved so many people as that it involved them so completely. There was no keeping events within bounds, as in the simple economy of the past. The shifting map of economic interests was invaded to a far greater degree than the march of armies invaded any country on the geographic map, as the blockade and the financial dislocation of the war both clearly showed. Not only this, but sometimes the losses inflicted upon an enemy turned out to be one's own.

In its economy, therefore, the industry of war combines two techniques, both of them dynamic: the technique of peace which supplies war with its resources, and the technique of destruction. Now since both of these are progressively modified by every new development, war is as uncertain in its direction as in its intensity, or its spread. It is no longer a safe instrument for statesmanship under such circumstances; it is too dangerous to employ. It is no longer an *ultima ratio*, for it has lost its *raison d'être*. Victor and victim may suffer a common disaster. Its effects reach even into the unformed future, and rob the savings of generations yet unborn. Time, as well as space, levels its barriers to the march of destruction. This new dynamic world, the creation of human intelligence, containing as it does the most precious things in our heritage, has no other defense against it, once it is loosed, than that which endangers it as well. Such are the phenomena of war as revealed by a study of the tragic years 1914 to 1918. Moreover, it is equally clear from this analysis, that these phenomena are not merely incidental and temporary. They are typical and more and more true as civilization develops.

In short, war which was once a directable instrument of policy has now changed its nature with the nature of modern society and ceases to be controllable and directable in the hands of statesmen. By reason of its all-embracing needs, it becomes a contagion among the nations; and one cannot safely use a contagion as an instrument.

This was the supreme lesson of the World War. The fact was at last made clear that war had been industrialized,—war, that is, between the highly civilized nations. This means not only the complications of financial and industrial involvements, but it means something far more significant, that science has conquered nature not only for the welfare of civilization but also for its possible destruction. We talk about disarmament; but as long as war exists we must face the fact that the implements of war are also those of peace. We may limit our battleships in a Washington Conference, but there is no ratio of 5-5-3 or any other number in the capacities of chemistry or organized industry. These will vary with the vitality of the scientific or industrial development of nations and no arithmetic of limitations can set their bounds. There are, for instance, factories now in existence which can extract nitrate of ammonia from the air in thousands of tons each day to fertilize the farm land of their own country and of others; but these same factories can likewise produce high explosives in quantities no less enormous because the constituents of fertilizer and explosive are practically the same. The nitrate of the air is the base upon which both build. It needs no imagination but mere common sense to realize that this most essential industry for the maintenance of human life could produce and distribute *daily*, even with commercial airplanes, the material which could destroy entire cities. If there is to be another war between the highly civilized Powers, the laboratories of the universities and the workshops of towns and cities would be the arsenals of destruction and it would be a war of mutual extermination, since whatever nation is attacked would be compelled to make use of the same kind of chemical warfare in its own defense.

Can we prevent the use of such methods in war? Can we block the progress of science? No: Those same scientific processes which make life richer for us and supply bread in abundance for those who would otherwise be in need, processes particularly necessary in a world left with such misery as ours today, these processes are the very ones, with but minor changes in their apparatus, that are the modern equivalents for the armies of Caesar or Tamerlane. The same scientists, with the same formulae, can make both things—the life-saving and the life-destroying—in one and the same laboratory. I remember, for example, visiting an establishment where, during the war, poison gases were made, and found that other chemists working in that same laboratory had, at the same time, discovered the cure for sleeping sickness, by which it was hoped that at least as many lives might be saved as were lost through the instrument of death upon which their colleagues were working. Two laboratories side by side, men of science working in them in the same spirit of scientific inquiry,—so long as war is legitimate their services to society rest upon even terms. We have reached a place in history where we must choose between the dangers of the destruction of civilization in its entirety, and the possibility of making secure the happiness and well-being of nations by the abolition of war as the instrument of their policy.

CHAPTER XX

The Enforcement of Peace and the League of Nations

How can the United States support the cause of peace throughout the world without giving some guarantee that it will help to suppress violations of peace when they occur? This, next to its renunciation of war as an instrument of policy, is the most important thing for the United States to consider in connection with the Pact of Paris. It may be stated at once, and with the utmost emphasis, that the United States has no intention of accepting the duty of policeman even in the way laid down for Britain by the Treaty of Locarno. The formal obligation to intervene in the interests of peace when other nations go to war is a complication which the United States is not prepared to accept. It has registered this decision in ways which no statesman at home can overlook and which no foreign statesman should ignore. It was chiefly because this was believed to be the fundamental characteristic of the League of Nations that the opponents of the Covenant were able to carry the day. The mere apprehension of any possibility of this kind has been the chief argument for America's withdrawal from the whole peace movement of post-war Europe; for there, especially on the Continent, the emphasis has been upon enforcement.

It has, to say the least, been an unfair picture of the League of Nations which presented it to the American public as though the suppression of violence on the part of the League was merely war under another name and that the League actually perpetuated war in the name of peace. But the fear that this was so became almost a national obsession. Its basis, however, lay not in the reluctance of the United States to perform its duty as a civilized Power, but simply an abhorrence of entanglement in that kind of politics which played with war as an instrument of policy and that brought in peace-loving peoples to redress the balance of justice. While fully admitting the moral slump which this country suffered in withdrawing from the great experiment which other nations were working out, the reason for remaining aloof must not be interpreted as showing any sympathy with any Power which might attempt to overthrow the League by force or trickery. It was only because American opinion feared the continuance of these elements in international affairs and their possible use by League Powers themselves. The misunderstanding was chiefly due to the fact that the World War has so largely destroyed good faith among nations, and that the League seemed to many Americans still to emphasize this absence of good faith by its insistence upon measures of police, that the United States withheld its assent. Now the chief merit of the Pact of Paris is that it is a supreme assertion of international good faith and under it the moral purposes which persist in American outlook are finding a way of expressing themselves, clear of entanglement but in full harmony with the real purpose of the League.

There is no legal obligation in the Pact of Paris upon the United States or any other Power to join in police action against a state which runs amuck in the world, and no external body is called upon to point out the duty to the signatories in case violation occurs. The only reference to the problem is in that phrase added to the preamble in its final form which states that "any signatory Power which shall hereafter seek to promote its national interests by resort to war should be denied the benefits furnished by this treaty." The novelty in this method of approach is that instead of enumerating the duties of the law-abiding states it denies the aggressor the right to calculate upon the continuance of friendly relations. It does not say that those relations will be broken, but, in leaving the signatories free to take this step, points to it as a moral duty. No measures of coercion are provided beyond the fact that the aggressor states should receive no aid or comfort from the co-signatories. If the United States is unwilling to go to the extent of dissociating itself from a nation which goes to war in violation of its pledge of peace in a treaty to which the United States is a co-signatory, when that treaty leaves the United States its own judge as to whether the violation has actually occurred or not, then the United States has really put itself on the side of the aggressor. For to supply such a belligerent with the resources of war and to insist upon our right to do so would be making ourselves the accomplices in the aggression. The article in the preamble goes no farther than to warn a nation planning such aggression that it cannot calculate upon our joining it in this way. Our own good faith would count for little if we were to give it aid and comfort in such a violation of the peace. The treaty indicates that once convinced of the nature of its violation we could notify it that we recover full liberty of action with reference to it, and in view of the financial power and the control of resources at the command of the United States, a notification of this kind, that we regarded its act as canceling our obligation to remain at peace, would make any adventurous state pause on the threshold of its adventure. It is a way of using the influence of the United States for peace without assuming any obligations to join in positive measures of suppression.

It will be claimed by the legalist that this departs from the traditional policy of America in maintaining neutrality while other nations go to war. But the time has come to recognize that a concept of neutrality must now be changed to fit the conditions of modern warfare. When nations went to war dependent upon their own resources, and the conflict did not extend beyond the immediate scene of operations, neutrality was easy, for it meant simply remaining away from the actual fighting. Modern industrial warfare has changed this entirely, as the United States knows well. The arsenals of the European belligerents before we entered the war were to be found in Bridgeport, Pittsburgh and the Bethlehem Steel Works, as well as at Woolwich and Creusot. The existing international law permitted this because it had not been adjusted to the new era. We must recognize this fact if we are to deal honestly and squarely with the problem of war itself. If the nation whose forces are supplied with arms is in our opinion an aggressor nation, we become morally, if not legally, the accomplices in its aggression by the support rendered through finance and industry, upon which its chance of victory may depend. No one has seen this more clearly than Congressman Burton whose experience in the International Commission on the Export of Armament gives added authority to his proposal, which calls for a purely American pronouncement that it is an established policy of the United States not to supply with arms a nation which goes to war in violation of its specific pledges. Senator Burton's Resolution, however, is not up for discussion at this point other than to indicate what might be done by the United States to square itself with its moral duty in time of war. The Kellogg proposal does not go so far as this. But in releasing the signatories from the obligation to remain at peace with an aggressor, it procures that liberty of action which both saves us from involvement with the aggressor and enables us to perform the least of all moral duties, which is to refuse our aid in the perpetration of an international crime.

So far we have merely dealt with the negative consequences of the clause which reserves our liberty of action in case a nation goes to war in violation of the treaty, the point that we should not be helping the aggressor. But it is not likely that, in case of a perfectly clear violation, the United States would stop short with this. Senator Borah, in an interview in the New York *Times*, March 25, 1928, expressed the opinion that the country would not rest content with a merely negative sanction.

"Another important result of such a treaty would be to enlist the support of the United States in coöperative action against any nation which is guilty of a flagrant violation of this outlawry agreement. Of course, the Government of the United States must reserve the right to decide, in the first place, whether or not the treaty has been violated, and, second, what coercive measures it feels obliged to take. But it is quite inconceivable that this country would stand idly by in case of a grave breach of a multilateral treaty to which it is a part. . . . Of course, in such a crisis we would consult with the other signatories and take their judgment into account. But we should not bind ourselves in advance to accept their decision if it runs counter to our own conclusions."

Some sentences in later portions of the interview strengthen still further the statement, as, for instance, the following reply to the query as to what effect the Kellogg proposal would have upon the League of Nations:

"At present we have a network of treaties and understandings relative to peace—arbitration treaties, conciliation treaties, the Hague Tribunal, World Court, peace machinery of the League and peace machinery of Locarno. The effect of the Kellogg proposal is a solemn pledge to let all this peace machinery work."

We reach the conclusion, therefore, that the warning in the preamble to the Pact of Paris that any nation using war as an instrument of its national policy cannot in future depend upon our indifference, is the missing formula which solves for the present at least our relations with the League of Nations as well as with the individual governments of the world. There is a moral obligation not to frustrate measures of peace or to become an accomplice in any effort at frustration; but there are no involvements in police measures, no formal obligations of enforcement. The problem of the "sanctions," which had seemed at times insoluble, is at last nearing solution. If this alone were to the credit of the Pact of Paris, it would make it an outstanding milestone on the pathway of international peace. It is hardly to be wondered at that European countries concentrate their attention so largely upon it. At the same time, in their anxiety to secure American coöperation, there is some tendency to overstate what has been done. It is as important to emphasize the freedom of action which is reserved as the moral duty which is admitted.

It is impossible to close this discussion without appending a historical note. The suggestion of a negative instead of a positive sanction was first set forth in the plan of the American Committee which, in 1924, furnished some suggestions—especially the definition of aggression—embodied in the Geneva Protocol. The Protocol itself, however, definitely and emphatically rejected this particular idea and put all emphasis upon the obligations of joint action against the aggressor. The originator of the suggestion in the plan of the American Committee was Mr. David Hunter Miller. It was rejected in Geneva because the continental states felt the need of a more definite obligation to maintain the peace, an obligation which Locarno has since provided for the Continental Powers. But the British Empire as a whole has not been a member of the Locarno pact, the Dominions holding back from participation in the policing of Europe, much like the United States itself. The formula of 1924 left the aggressor state uncertain what action would be taken against it and decreased by that much the risk of aggression. The same conception is once more before us in different wording in the preamble of the Pact of Paris. The Continental Powers now recognize its validity in the support of the Covenant itself; thus it may serve to bridge the gulf not only between the League and the Powers outside it, but also that continuing difference of opinion within the League itself expressed by the reluctance of the British Empire to assume universal obligations of police on terms almost identical with the external reservations of the United States.

HENRY CABOT LODGE

For many years Lodge was a United States senator from Massachusetts and a leader of the Republican forces in the Senate. On the whole, he supported the propertied groups and the established order. During and immediately after the World War he was chairman of the Senate committee on foreign affairs. To him, consequently, fell the task of leading the Republican attack upon Wilson and the League Covenant. Lodge favored American participation in some form of international association of nations, and he proposed a series of reservations to the Covenant in order to eliminate those aspects of the proposed League that were incompatible with the traditional American policy of isolation.

THE LODGE–LOWELL DEBATE ON THE PROPOSED LEAGUE OF NATIONS, MARCH 19, 1919.

Opening Address of Henry Cabot Lodge.[132]

Senator from Massachusetts

. . . . . .

Now, ladies and gentlemen, we are all agreed in desiring the security of the peace of the world. I am not going to argue such a question as that.

[132] *The Lodge-Lowell Debate on the Proposed League of Nations, held in Boston, March 19, 1919* (Boston, Old Colony Trust Company, 1919), pp. 11–20. (Reprinted by permission of the publishers.)

We all hate war, and let me say to you that nobody can hate or abhor war more than those upon whose shoulders rested the dread responsibility of declaring war and sending forth the flower of our youth to battle. A man who has once borne that responsibility never can forget it. I should no more think of arguing to you that peace is better than war than I should think of insulting your intelligences by arguing that virtue is better than vice. We may dismiss it. We are equally desirous, I think—most of us certainly are desirous of doing all we can, through a union, or league, or alliance of the nations, to make the peace of the world secure—more secure, at all events, than it has ever been before. I will not stop to argue that.

The question before us, the only question of a practical nature, is whether the League that has been drafted by the Commission of the Peace Conference and laid before it will tend to secure the peace of the world as it stands, and whether it is just and fair to the United States of America. That is the question, and I want now, very briefly, to bring it to the test.

Wars between nations come from contacts. A nation with which we have no contact is a nation with which we should never fight. But contacts, foreign relations between nations are necessary and inevitable, and the object of all diplomacy and statesmanship is to make those contacts and relations as harmonious as possible, because in those contacts is found the origin of all war.

In this scheme for a League now before us we create a number of new contacts, a number of new relations, which nations have not undertaken before to create. There have been many leagues. There is nothing new in the idea of a league. They go back to the days of Greece. There is the peace of Westphalia, the League of Cambrai. I believe there are some thirty altogether in the pages of history, none of them very successful. And in the Holy Alliance of 1815 another attempt was made, and that time a league to preserve peace. But we are approaching this league on a different basis and on a different theory from any I believe ever attempted. We are reaching for a great object, playing for a great stake. But we are creating new contacts. Therefore, we should examine all the propositions with the utmost care before we give an assent to them.

I take first the form of the draft without regard to its substance. There were four drafts presented to the Commission, one by Italy, one by France, one by the United States and one by Great Britain. The British draft was the one selected. You can find in the treaty, if you will compare it with the plan put forth by General Smuts in January, that some paragraphs were taken from his plan with but slight changes. How nearly the draft presented conforms to the British draft I have no means of knowing.

The drafts offered by the other countries have never been discussed, although we are living in the era of open covenants openly arrived at. I hope in the course of a few years that those drafts may appear in the volumes published by Congress which contain an account of our foreign relations. The draft appears to me, and I think to any one who has examined it with care, to have been very loosely and obscurely drawn. It seems to me that Lord Robert Cecil, who, I believe, is principally responsible for it, should have put it in the hands of a parliamentary draftsman before it was submitted.

A constitution or a treaty ought to be in legal, statutory, or constitutional language, and not in the language selected for this purpose.

The language of that draft is of immense importance, because it is necessary that there should be just as few differences of opinion as to the meaning of the articles of that draft as human ingenuity can provide against. No man, be he president or senator, can fix what the interpretation of that draft is. The draft itself, the articles themselves, should answer as far as possible all questions. There is no court to pass upon them. They would have to be decided by the nine powers whose representatives compose the Executive Council. The people who are for this draft of a league and those who are against it differ about the construction of nearly every article. And, not only that, but those who are for it differ among themselves, and those who are against it differ among themselves, as to its construction. There will be differences arising out of that very porous instrument. There will be differences arising before a twelve-month has passed among the very nations that signed it.

Mr. Taft said on the 7th of March:

"Undoubtedly the covenant needs revision. It is not symmetrically arranged, its meaning has to be dug out, and the language is ponderous and in diplomatic patois."

I have said nothing about the draft as severe or as well put and as thoroughly descriptive as that.

Lately the phrase has been much used, especially when an answer was not very easy, that criticism must be constructive, not destructive. It was a convenient way of answering awkward questions, and evidently those who use it and use it freely have never stopped to think that there are some cases where criticism must be constructive as well as destructive and some where it must be destructive alone. For instance, in discussing slavery we criticise it in order to kill, and we do not expect that a substitute shall be offered for it. If a burglar breaks into my house and threatens the life of my wife and children, I should try if I could to shoot him. That is destructive criticism, and I should not think it necessary to precede with a proposition that he should engage in some other and less dangerous occupation.

Now this is a case where constructive criticism is clearly needed, and my first constructive criticism is that this League ought to be redrafted and put in language that everybody can understand. By doing that you will remove at once many causes of difference and dispute, and the instrument ought to diminish disputes, and increase harmony, because its purpose as to promote peace.

Another point which applies not only to the necessity of clear and definite language in the great instrument but to the whole treaty, or to any treaty or any alliance or league that we make, is to remember this—that the sanctity of treaties is above everything else important. Whatever a country agrees to, that the country must maintain.

The sanctity of treaties lies at the basis of all peace, and therefore we must be as careful as possible to remove all chances of disagreement arising out of conflicting interpretations of language.

As I have said, my first constructive criticism is that we should have a revision of the language and form of the draft.

Now, in discussing the draft of the League I can only deal with the most important points. To analyze all articles of that League as they should be analyzed would take many hours. But I will speak of one point which runs all through it—and that is, that there are so many places where it says that the Executive Council—which is the real seat of authority—the Executive Council shall recommend, or advise, or propose measures, and it fails to say by what vote they shall do it. There are one or two places where it is stated there shall be a two-thirds vote; another case where it shall be unanimous; but in most cases it is not stated.

Now, either there should be a clause in there saying that where not otherwise stated, the decision of the Executive Council shall be by a majority vote, or else it ought to be expressed in every article where they are called upon to make a recommendation, or a proposal, or a decision of any kind.

Again let me quote from Mr. Taft. He says, speaking of ambiguous phrases:

"One of these, for instance, is in respect to the Executive Council. Will it need a unanimous vote or will a majority vote be sufficient, where there is no specification?"

That puts the point extremely well, and I think there should be another change there. I offer that as a second constructive criticism.

I now come to what seems to me a very vital point indeed, and that is the Monroe Doctrine. I shall not undertake to trace the history of the Doctrine or its development since Mr. Monroe first declared it. But in its essence it rests upon the proposition of separating the Americas from Europe in all matters political. It rests on the differentiation of the American hemisphere from Europe, and therefore I have found it difficult to understand an argument first advanced with more confidence, perhaps, than it is now,—that we preserve the Monroe Doctrine by extending it. The Monroe Doctrine was the invisible line that we drew around the American hemisphere. It was the fence that we put around it to exclude other nations from meddling in American affairs, and I have never been able to get it through my head how you can preserve a fence by taking it down.

The Monroe Doctrine is the corollary of Washington's foreign policy declared in the Farewell Address. I am not going to base any argument upon it, but it is a mistake to consider the policy laid down by Washington and Monroe as ephemeral and necessarily transient. As Mr. Wilson well said, Washington's Doctrine was not transient. It may be wrong; the time may have come to discard it; but it is not ephemeral because it rests on two permanent facts,—human nature and geography.

Human nature, you may say, has changed. When you study the history of the past as far as we have a history there is a curious similarity in it at all stages. But one thing is certain,—not even the wisest and the most optimistic of reformers can change the geography of the globe. They say communication has quickened enormously. The Atlantic Ocean is not what it was as a barrier, or the Pacific either, I suppose. But do not forget that even under modern conditions the silver streak, the little channel only twenty miles wide, was England's bulwark and defense in this last war. Do not underrate the three thousand miles of Atlantic. It was on that that the Monroe Doctrine, the corollary of Wasington's policy, rested.

Great systems of morality and philosophy have been taught and preached, two thousand, twenty-five hundred, three thousand years ago. They may be wrong. But they are neither transient nor ephemeral because they rest upon the eternal verities. And when you come to discard a policy like that it is well to realize what you are abandoning and what its importance is.

The Monroe Doctrine has been expanded. A resolution was passed unanimously in the Senate a few years ago stating that the United States would regard it as an act of hostility for any corporation or association of any other nation to take possession of Magdalena Bay, being a post of great strategic, naval and military advantage. That did not rest on the Monroe Doctrine. It rested on something deeper than that. It rested on the basis of the Monroe Doctrine, the great law of self-preservation. They say that if we demand the exclusion of the Monroe Doctrine from the operation of the League, they will demand compensation. Very well. Let them exclude us from meddling in Europe. That is not a burden that we are seeking to bear. We are ready to go there at any time to save the world from barbarism and tyranny, but we are not thirsting to interfere in every obscure quarrel that may spring up in the Balkans. Mr. Taft says that the Covenant "should be made more definite by a larger reservation of the Monroe Doctrine."

I agree entirely. I offer that as my third constructive criticism, that there should be a larger reservation of the Monroe Doctrine, and when the leading advocate of this draft takes that position it seems to me it cannot be a very unreasonable one.

There is the question of immigration which this treaty reaches under the non-justiciable questions. I am told and I believe (I have followed it through all the windings) that a final decision could only be reached by unanimity, and it is said that the League would not be unanimous. I think that highly probable, but I deny the jurisdiction. I cannot personally accede to the proposition that other nations, that a body of men in executive council where we as a nation have but one vote, shall have any power, unanimous or otherwise, to say who shall come into the United States.

It must not be within the jurisdiction of the League at all. It lies at the foundation of national character and national well-being. There should be no possible jurisdiction over the power which defends this country from a flood of Japanese, Chinese, and Hindu labor.

The tariff is involved in the article for the boycott. The coastwise trade is involved in Article 21. I think we ought to settle our own import duties. They say it is a domestic question. So it is, so is immigration, but they are domestic questions with international relations.

Moreover—and I know some people think this as a far-fetched objection, but having other nations meddle with our tariff runs up against a provision of the Constitution. The Constitution provides that all revenue bills shall originate in the House of Representatives. Now I do not offer that as a final objection. No doubt we could amend our Constitution to fit the League, but it would take some time, and I think it is better to steer clear of the Constitution in cases like that. And I offer an amendment, already proposed by Senator Owen of Oklahoma, an ardent Democrat and a supporter of the League, to exclude international questions of the character of immigration and the tariff from the jurisdiction of the League. I present that as a fourth constructive criticism.

This treaty is indissoluble. There is no provision for withdrawal or termination. In the old days—very old days—they were in the habit of beginning treaties by swearing eternal friendship—which made them last no longer. That has been given up. In modern times almost all the treaties which we now have contain provisions for termination or withdrawal on notice. If there is no provision for withdrawal you are thrown back on denunciation or abrogation by one nation.

I have been surprised to hear in the Senate and elsewhere the statement that this was only a treaty and we could abrogate it by an act of Congress at any time, as we can under the decisions of the Supreme Court. Why, ladies and gentlemen, nothing could be worse than that. No greater misfortune could befall the peace of the world than to have a nation, especially a powerful nation, abrogate the treaty.

It is usually a preliminary to war. It is in many cases, at least. There ought to be some provision by which a withdrawal could be effected without any breach of the peace or any injury to the cause.

Mr. Taft says: "The covenant should also be made more definite as to when its obligations may be terminated." I offer this as a fifth constructive criticism.

I am obliged to move rapidly for my time is expiring, but there are two great points which I cannot leave wholly untouched.

One is Article 19, providing for mandatories. It does not say who shall select the mandatory. The provision is, that a nation may be selected to take charge of a weaker or a backward people and be appointed by the League to that work. It has been suggested that we should take charge of Constantinople; that we should take charge of Armenia and Mesopotamia and Syria. I am not going to argue it at length. I am not as deeply opposed to that provision as many others—as most other people are, as I believe the American people are. But it is a very grave responsibility to take charge of some distant people, furnish them with civilians to carry on their government, furnish them with an army to protect them, and send our young men away on that business. We have done it in Hayti, we have done it in San Domingo, we have done it in Nicaragua, and are doing it now. That is all within the Monroe Doctrine; that is all within our own "ring fence." We must do it; we owe it to the world; and we are quite capable of doing it successfully. But this is a demand to go out through Asia, Africa, and Europe and take up the tutelage of other people.

Then comes Article 10. That is the most important article in the whole treaty. That is the one that I especially wish the American people to consider, take it to their homes and their firesides, discuss it, think of it. If they commend it the treaty will be ratified and proclaimed with that in it. But think of it first, think well. This article pledges us to guarantee the political independence and the territorial integrity against external aggression of every nation a member of the League. That is, every nation of the earth. We ask no guarantees; we have no endangered frontiers; but we are asked to guarantee the territorial integrity of every nation practically in the world—it will be when the League is complete. As it is today, we guarantee the territorial integrity and political independence of every part of the far-flung British Empire.

Now mark! A guarantee is never invoked except when force is needed. If we guaranteed one country in South America alone, if we were the only guarantor, and we guaranteed but one country, we should be bound to go to the relief of that country with an army and navy. We, under that clause of this treaty—it is one of the few that is perfectly clear—under that clause of the treaty we have got to take our army and our navy and go to war with any country which attempts aggression upon the territorial integrity of another member of the League.

Now, guarantees must be fulfilled. They are sacred promises—it has been said only morally binding. Why, that is all there is to a treaty between great nations. If they are not morally binding they are nothing but "scraps of paper." If the United States agrees to Article 10 we must carry it out in letter and spirit; and if it is agreed to I should insist that we did so, because the honor and good faith of our country would be at stake.

Now, that is a tremendous promise to make. I ask the fathers and the mothers, the sisters and the wives and the sweethearts, whether they are ready yet to guarantee the political independence and territorial integrity of every nation on earth against external aggression, and to send the hope of their families, the hope of the nation, the best of our youth, forth into the world on that errand?

If they are, it will be done. If the American people are not ready to do it that article will have to go out of the treaty or be limited. If that League with that article had existed in the Eighteenth Century, France could not have assisted this country to win the Revolution. If that League had existed in 1898 we could not have interfered and rescued Cuba from the clutches of Spain; we should have brought a war on with all the other nations of the world.

Perhaps the time has come to do it. I only wish tonight to call your attention to the gravity of that promise. To what it means, that it is morally binding, that there is no escape when a guarantee of that sort is invoked. Think over it well; that is all I ask. Consider it. And remember that we must make no promise, enter into no agreement, which we are not going to carry out in letter and in spirit without restriction and without deduction.

CHARLES K. LEITH

Charles K. Leith has been a professor of geology at the University of Wisconsin since 1903, and has been interested in the relation of minerals to world politics. He was mineral adviser to the shipping and war industries boards in 1918 and to the American commission to negotiate peace in 1919. He has written many articles on mineral resources and their political consequences. His latest work is *World Minerals and World Politics* (1931).

EXPLOITATION AND WORLD PROGRESS [133]

The quest of iron and copper and flint for use as weapons, and of gold and silver and precious stones for adornment, runs far back into history and is associated with many stirring events of exploration and war. But they were

[133] *Foreign Affairs*, October, 1927, Vol. 6, pp. 128–139. (Reprinted by permission of the publishers.)

used on a relatively small scale and served only as a minor factor in the environmental conditions controlling human activities. With the advent of the industrial revolution of England, a century ago, began the real exploitation of earth materials in a way to influence essentially our material civilization. In this short time, at an ever accelerating rate, minerals have become the fundamental basis of industrialism, to be ranked with soil, climate, and other major influences on our activities. In these hundred years the output of pig iron has increased 100-fold, of mineral fuels 75-fold, and of copper 63-fold. In the last fifty years the per capita consumption of minerals in the United States has multiplied fifteen times. By harnessing up the power from coal, gas, and water we have multiplied our capacity for work. The acceleration of the rate of mineral exploitation may be realized from the fact that the world has exploited more of its resources in the last twenty years than in all preceding history.

In appraising the effect of this new element in human environment we have no historical precedent to guide us, for the change is too recent, too all-pervasive, for us to understand all its significance. Yet a few clear tendencies are beginning to be discernible.

The rising use of mineral resources has naturally led to an intensive search of the earth for adequate supplies, which is just beginning to give us some realization of their ultimate geographic distribution. Changes will still be made by discovery, usually in expected fields, but the main outlines are now pretty well fixed. The curve of geographic discovery is falling. The great discoveries of the future will in the main relate to better methods of recovery and use. As the insatiable appetite for minerals has risen, many sources of supply which formerly were adequate are beginning to look relatively small. As the demand multiplies, the sources known to be capable of meeting it become proportionally fewer. In short, it is being realized that nature has concentrated the really big sources of supply, adequate to meet present and future world demand, in a very few places on the globe, a fact which will play an increasingly important part in the future history of the world.

Thus, about thirty of the principal mineral districts account for three-fourths of the world's mineral production. Three-fourths of the world's iron comes from only half a dozen districts in the United States, England, France, Sweden, and Spain. Two-thirds of the world's coal comes from the eastern United States, England, and western Germany. Two-thirds of the world's copper comes from a half dozen districts in the western United States and Chile. The Union of South Africa produces over half the world's gold. And so on. A review of the entire list of commercial minerals would be merely a monotonous repetition of geographic facts of the same general import.

An obvious consequence of this inequality in the geographic distribution of minerals—of such practical bearing on world affairs, in peace and war,— is the interdependence of nations and their community of interest in regard to mineral supplies. There are not enough of the great primary sources to go around. Even the favored nations—among them the United States— lack a considerable number of them in sufficient quantity to meet modern demands, and many nations are conspicuously deficient. There is a high degree of specialization in production which, in the case of some nations and for some minerals, amounts practically to monopoly. A balanced ration of raw materials necessary for modern industry simply cannot be made up within the boundaries of any one nation. Immense international movements are therefore necessary. Reflecting this situation, the great commercial and industrial companies are becoming international in their scope, and to an increasing extent find it necessary to disregard national boundaries in securing supplies.

These are simple and more or less obvious facts of commercial geography. What is less generally understood is that this situation is essentially new in history. Only a few decades ago a state's dependence on mineral resources was much less marked. Nations could be more or less self-sufficing on the basis of smaller mineral supplies and of agricultural or other resources. A really new element in our environment now requires that nations work together if they are to advance along material and industrial lines. The pressure is inexorable and growing. It is a situation which cannot be changed by public will or for political motives. Neither will it be essentially changed by the substitution of chemical synthetics, nor by improvements in methods of mineral recovery, as now proclaimed by certain chemists. One must be hopeful indeed if he expects to synthesize substitutes on the stupendous scale of nature's laboratories, which have been on the job since the beginning of the earth's history. No, the nations actually stand today, and will continue to stand, in reciprocal and complementary relationships one to another in regard to mineral raw materials.

This is true not only as regards normal industrial development, but also as regards the requirements for a great war. War on the scale of the last one cannot be fought on the basis of the raw materials within any one national boundary. The United States is better supplied than any other nation, but for the prosecution of a great war it is necessary even for our nation to reach to the far quarters of the globe for many essential raw materials which cannot be either substituted for or stored in advance in sufficient quantities to last. Staff preparation for war now includes a study of how to control these far distant sources. The difficulties of this are so great that where they are realized they cannot fail to be real deterrents to hasty war. It is reassuring to know that there is now lively appreciation of these facts by our own and other war departments.

It is easy to infer that anything which tends to bind nations together materially is conducive to world peace. But it does not always follow that community of material interest eliminates friction, whether the family be that of nations or individuals. As a matter of fact, political reactions are on the whole away from any unification of international interest in minerals. One cause seems to be common inertia and opposition to anything new. Another is that it is no longer possible for nations to expand the areas of their political control to keep up with the expansion of commercial units, as was possible during much of the nineteenth century, when leading commercial nations, particularly of Europe, were rapidly opening up backward parts of the world, thereby giving outlet for commercial expansion. In Europe itself since the war political units have on the whole actually become more numerous and smaller, in the face of the marked tendency of commercial units to become larger and to expand their spheres of influence across international boundaries. Still another and powerful cause is the post-war flare of intensive nationalism, of "self-determination," coupled with a fresh realization of the vital part played by minerals in national economy, as a result of which there has been a world-wide wave of nationalization of resources, represented by measures ranging all the way from outright acquisition of minerals by nations to many measures of more indirect control, such as control of operations, prices, distributions, markets, tariffs, licenses, etc. The same tendency is manifest also in many kinds of prohibition against any foreign exploitation of minerals, covered by the general term "the closed door," and other attempts of nations to acquire or to protect resources by various political and military measures. These are powerful and usually justifiable reasons for these tendencies,—the desire to protect the future of the nations, to reap the benefits of any resources possessed, to prevent foreign exploitation hurtful to the nation, to avoid foreign political and military influence which often follows commercial investment, to aid "conservation" in a national sense, and for military protection.

We are therefore witnessing the conflict of two powerful opposing forces—on the one hand, world demand for raw materials, which knows no national boundaries and which is forcing coöperation in order that demand may be efficiently satisfied; on the other, the nationalistic forces directed toward partitioning resources for national gain or security. Many recent international episodes are an expression of this problem, and more are in store.

In our search for a solution of this problem a natural first thought is that one or other of the great opposing forces might be minimized or eliminated, but a little reflection will, I think, show the impracticability of accomplishing much along these lines. Nationalism is deeply rooted in history and ethnology; it is usually based on sound instincts of self-preservation; it involves many factors other than supplies of natural resources. There would have to be a radical change indeed in the national psychology to allow even the smallest alienation of political control of essential resources in favor of supernational or international control. Even if this difficulty were surmounted, it is doubtful if brains have yet developed capable of planning such administration in a way to provide for all contingencies.

It seems equally difficult to lessen the insistence of the demand for raw materials. "Industrial civilization" and "the machine age," are often disparaged, and disadvantageous comparisons are made with the intellectual or artistic accomplishments of earlier times, but no practicable method of changing its tendencies is suggested. The very people who take the view that commercial development should be curbed are not consistent when at the same time they buy household equipment made of materials from the other side of the globe. When one rides in an automobile, for instance, a demand is created for supplies coming from a dozen countries and by no possibility obtainable from one. Wholesale and world-wide self-denial in the use of common implements of human comfort is not likely to come about until the average material comfort of the world is on a much higher plane than at present. Rather is it more likely that the desire for them will harden into a belief in their urgent necessity. Even if it were possible, there remains the question whether there would be any ethical, moral, intellectual, or artistic gain in so curbing industrial demands. This is a topic of endless academic discussion, but academic it will doubtless remain.

It may be assumed, therefore, that, right or wrong, the demand for resources will continue to grow, which means also that the fundamental conflict with nationalism will remain. About the best that can be hoped for is
a working alliance of political and economic states, involving mutual compromise, and yet preserving the really essential rights of each. There is
being gradually worked out, through many commercial and political agreements, a certain adjustment in the international flow of mineral products
which is effecting a workable compromise between world demand on the
one hand and nationalistic policies on the other. There are also international
agreements of one kind or another, now under discussion, which promise
to minimize world friction. But one must be hopeful indeed to expect anything more than a slow amelioration of some of the grosser difficulties in
the problem. The essential conflict will remain and its course will continue
to be marked by flashes of international animosity. This need not lead to
pessimism and inaction. There is a wonderful opportunity for practical
accomplishments in this field. One, which seems to offer as much chance
for discouraging war as any yet suggested, is a better understanding of
foreign exploitation.

The primary meaning of the word "exploit" is to develop, or get the
value out of, but there has come to be attached to it the idea of unfairness,
selfishness, and force which is now reflected in supplementary definitions
in dictionaries. In the public mind the objectionable connotations so over-
shadow the primary meaning that the term has come to stand for one of the
most objectionable of human activities. I use the term here mainly in its
primary sense, but not exclusively so. If a less provocative term like "develop" were substituted, it would probably not be understood by most
people as covering essentially the same activity which has come historically
to be known as exploitation. A term is needed which will identify the facts,
whether they be regarded as good or bad. Even the best of *development* is
seldom completely free from selfishness and unfairness; the worst of *exploitation* is seldom without some underlying justification in world needs.

Much the larger part of the world's mineral production has come from
North Atlantic countries, and has served to build up the industrial and commercial supremacy of this part of the world. The concentration of heavy
industries about the North Atlantic is based primarily on the possession of
immense coal and iron deposits, together with adequate quantities of copper, lead, zinc, oil, gas and other essential minerals. The main industrial
power belt of the world crosses the United States, Great Britain, Germany,
Belgium, and Northern France, with minor extensions eastward to other
parts of Europe. From this belt originates the commercial, and in some
cases the political, control of a preponderant part of the mineral production
of the rest of the world. The United States originates and controls about 40
per cent of the world's mineral production, and the United States and Great
Britain together control at least 75 per cent.

By reason of their exploitation of power resources,—coal, oil, gas and
water—the North Atlantic countries, counting both man power and mineral
power, are doing annually five times the mechanical work of the combined
total of Russia, China and India, the three most populous countries of the
world, though the population of the North Atlantic countries is only a third

as great. With a fifth of the world's population, this group of countries is doing about two-thirds of the world's work. The United States alone is doing about 40 per cent of the world's work, and its next nearest competitor, Great Britain, about a quarter as much as the United States.

This perspective reflects more or less the distribution of national wealth and the prevailing standards of living, as might be expected from the fact that wealth is essentially a product of work. With certain qualifications, assuming equality of preparedness, skill, and courage, these figures probably also measure the relative ultimate power for sustaining war.

One frequently hears, particularly in connection with international debt discussions, that the present great wealth of the United States is due largely to the fortunes of war, that the United States came out of the Great War suddenly enriched. The student of natural resources sees that what really happened has been the partial emergence into world consciousness of the cumulative results of the rapidly growing volume of work by our country, based on use of resources, a tendency started long before the war, temporarily accelerated but later retarded by the war, easily and certainly predictable from pre-war curves, but only now reaching such towering proportions that it can no longer be ignored. The back of the monster can now be seen above the horizon, but its form and characteristics are not yet fully apparent. There are still many people who fail to understand that the mid-Victorian material standards of international comparison are gone and gone for good. The phrase "back to normal," implying as it does static conditions, becomes meaningless when applied to the present dynamic situation. There is no such thing as going back and reconstructing old conditions, much as we individually may have liked them.

In the past the leadership of the North Atlantic countries in mineral and power production has been regarded as a mere reflection of the initiative and energy of the North Atlantic races, and it has been more or less taken for granted that in time the development of other parts of the world would equalize the mineral situation; that, broadly speaking, one part of the earth would yield to human effort about as well as another. This belief was a natural one under commercial conditions existing in the past, when the requirement for minerals was on a much smaller scale. There were many parts of the world capable of yielding the supplies then needed. But the vastly increasing requirements of modern industrial civilization have brought a new perspective into the situation—new even to the special students in mineral resources. We see more and more clearly that the preponderant position of the North Atlantic countries is not a mere passing episode, but is based on a real concentration of mineral resources, of a quantity, distribution, grade, and availability which can hardly be duplicated elsewhere, and which assure primacy in heavy industry for hundreds of years to come.

It is to be emphasized that the building of the great industrial civilizations has not been based on any single mineral but on unusually fortunate associations of minerals, in very large amounts, particularly the combination of coal and iron necessary for the iron and steel industry. China has large undeveloped resources of coal, but it is very deficient in iron ore. The Philippines and the Dutch East Indies have considerable low grade iron ore, but no suitable coal. India has iron ore, but insufficient coking coal for a really great industry. Japan has neither coal nor iron in notable amounts; its control of the Manchurian coal is a great asset, but the necessary supply of iron ore has not yet been secured. Australia and South Africa have insufficient quantities of both coal and iron of proper grade and geographic association for the first rank of world industry, even though locally, as in eastern Australia, satisfactory local units of the iron and steel industry are developing. The countries bordering the Mediterranean Sea are conspicuously deficient in both coal and iron. There resources were adequate for an earlier civilization but not for the kind which has now developed around the North Atlantic. Southern Russia has moderate quantities of both coal and iron, which will in time be reflected by considerable industrial development, but not on a scale comparable with that of the Ruhr, England, or the United States.

While 80 per cent of the world's oil now comes from countries bordering the western North Atlantic, there are other centers of production in southeastern Europe, southwestern Asia, the Dutch East Indies, as well as potential fields in South America, Sakhalin Island, and in Africa, but these outlying sources are not likely to change the major geographic distribution of heavy industries, for several reasons. Oil cannot be substituted for coal for smelting except at increased cost; it is too valuable for other purposes. Even if it could, its volume is much too small to be used as a large scale substitute for coal. In recent periods of flush production in the United States, which has been by far the greatest oil producing country, oil has furnished only 28 per cent of the total energy units, as compared with 72 per cent for coal; and in the future, considering relative reserves, there is likely to be even a smaller ratio of the use of oil to the use of coal. There is little likelihood that any other region will produce oil in the huge amounts necessary to make up for the absence of coal. Moreover, because it is easy to transport, it is likely to flow toward industrial centers already established rather than to serve as a basis for local industries, except on a small scale.

As for other minerals—the copper of South America and central Africa, the gold of South Africa, the lead and silver of Burma, the iron ores of South America, the antimony of China, the tin of the Straits, and so on—in no case do they exist in a regional association with coal, iron and other essential minerals so as to furnish the basis of great industry. All of them are important to local industry, but there is no indication that any of them foretell the building of industries which will rival those of North Atlantic countries.

The recent rapid development of waterpower has led to a popular belief that this may cause a redistribution of heavy industry. As a matter of fact, when compared with coal, waterpower is even less important than oil. In the United States it furnishes only 5 per cent of the total energy, and a survey of potential waterpowers of this and other countries shows that when fully developed they can supply but a very small part of the energy necessary for the creation of heavy industry on a modern scale.

In summary, then, the mounting world demand for minerals has brought more and more centralization of industrial power in the North Atlantic countries. The outlying units of production have grown, but the large central units have grown faster. Nowhere on the horizon today is there any clear indication of decentralization in the mineral field, and consequently in industrial power. The mineral industries of the world will remain tributary to the North Atlantic countries for a long time to come. It does not follow that the rest of the world may not be prosperous, but its activities must take other lines, and as yet there is nothing in sight that promises to approximate the power that is based on the possession of mineral resources.

This is a lengthy preamble to a simple and bald conclusion, namely that the North Atlantic countries will continue to be the great exploiters of mineral wealth, as in the past. In these countries originate the necessary wealth, skill, and driving power. In these countries originates the main outward thrust, commercial and political, against the remainder of the world. From the standpoint of mineral resources, no such thing as equality of nations exists. Economic self-determination in the field of natural resources is and will be possible only to the North Atlantic nations.

In attempting to appraise the problem objectively the first step is to rid ourselves of the notion that our own nation is not exploiting, or that if it is exploiting it can stop. A large part of our American public seems to hold one or the other of these opinions, which is not surprising in view of some of the recent statements of our Government in relation to Mexico and Nicaragua. There is no use blinking the fact that we are now the world's chief mineral exploiters, and will continue so by virtue of the direction given to our activities by our environment.

The history of exploitation shows that our own and other governments have almost never frankly disclosed the exploitation being done by their nationals. They are keen to "protect legitimate interests" of their nationals, but deplore or ignore "exploitation." On the other hand, critics of suspected imperialistic tendencies (like Senator Borah), are likely to condemn all exploitation as pernicious, without recognition of its essential nature.

Our thesis, if you please, is acceptance of the principle that might makes right, but only to the extent and in the sense that nature's environment creates might. Human volition plays little part, and it seems futile to argue this as a moral or ethical question. This concentration of power, with its consequences, is no more right or wrong than was nature's original distribution of resources. One of the keenest philosophic writers on foreign affairs, Captain Mahan, has perhaps done as well as anybody in claiming this course as a natural right:

> "The claim of an indigenous population to retain indefinitely control of territory depends not upon a natural right, but upon political fitness . . . shown in the political work of governing, administering and developing, in such manner as to insure the natural right of the world at large that resources should not be left idle but be utilized for the general good. Failure to do this justifies in principle, compulsion from outside; the position to be demonstrated, in the particular instance, is that the necessary time and the fitting opportunity have arrived." [a]

Without exploitation our land would still be in the hands of the aborigines. Has the world benefited as a whole by the change? We hope it is for the good of the greatest number, and can make out a good case for this point of view, when all the elements of exploitation are taken into account; but we cannot prove it.

[a] Mahan, A. T., *Problem of Asia*, p. 98; Little, Brown & Co., 1900.

Having recognized that the international exploitation of minerals exists today, as in the past, and is inevitable for the future, the next step is to direct our attention to the *manner* of exploitation, to see that it is done intelligently, in the open, with due regard to the rights of people who must feel its brunt. In exploitation, as in most other fields of human activity, there are good ways and bad ways, fair and unfair ways, which are pretty well recognized by the people professionally in touch with it. In almost no other field of international relations is there such an opportunity today for nations to get together around the conference table, to standardize methods of exploitation and correct its abuses; in short, to bring the many exceptions and local causes of difficulty into conformity with well tried, fair, and effective measures developed by the long experience of many countries. If England and the United States alone could get together on this question, controlling as they do such a large and well assorted proportion of the world's mineral wealth, nearly three-quarters of the total, they could pretty well fix the procedure.

It evidently is the rôle of higher statecraft to make it clear that the demand for the open door is justified on a broader basis of world welfare. The closed door slows up mineral development and dams up commercial and political pressure from many sources, often to a dangerous point. Many backward countries have neither the capital nor the trained organizations for this work. Where the initiative lies with governments, there is often a conspicuous lack of imagination and venturesome spirit, so necessary for mineral exploration. Even where the factors of competence are apparently present back of the closed door, this policy in practice narrows participation and variety of attack to a notable degree. Unless the world turns backward from its present material habits of living, closed doors will increasingly become sources of international friction. Commercial and political pressure is likely to open the door, sometimes by force, sometimes by intrigue, by bribery, or by private bargaining, as shown in many striking recent episodes in Morocco, Mosul, Mexico, and elsewhere. In the interest of international good will, it ought to be possible for nations to agree on basic principles of procedure which in effect compromise legitimate national aspirations with insistent world pressure. Many recent specific bargains between nations and commercial companies seem to point the way to a better formulation of international agreements touching this important subject.

If this is too much to hope for in view of other elements in the political situation, the United States still has responsibility, as the world leader in mineral exploitation, to revise its own methods, to show that exploitation can be done with a decent regard to the rights of others, and to take advantage of its strength to help other nations placed by nature in a defensive position. In the long run it should accrue to our national self-interest even from a commercial standpoint. How far we are from taking that attitude is made evident by the mere mention of the belligerent way in which our so-called rights in the field of exploitation are sometimes "defended," the marvellous ways these rights are defined and construed, the way they are sometimes hidden under the skirts of the Monroe Doctrine, and the failure to acquaint the public with the real underlying needs and facts of exploitation. We need Mexico's minerals, and will get them. We believe that the exploitation of these minerals will in the long run accrue to the advantage of both countries. But cannot this be done without taking ruthless advantage of our weaker neighbors, often in a spirit of anger, and with an attitude of righteous self-complacency which ignores the abuses of our action or even denies its very existence? The international political methods now in vogue, which usually deal with this problem only in a spirit of narrow nationalism, afford little promise of early relief. Yet both as a scientist and an optimist I cannot but conclude that *ultimately* political arrangements must conform with the new environment.

EVERETT DEAN MARTIN

Everett Dean Martin is a lecturer and writer on social psychology. Formerly he was a Congregationalist minister, but since 1916 he has been connected with the Peoples Institute of New York City. In addition to his work with that organization, Martin has been a lecturer at the New School for Social Research and at the Cooper Union Forum. He has written a number of books on psychology, education, and religion; among them are: *The Behavior of Crowds, Psychology, The Meaning of a Liberal Education,* and *The Mystery of Religion.* Martin is one of the most vigorous critics of democracy.

PSYCHOLOGY [134]

LECTURE XIV

The Psychology of Propaganda and Public Opinion

What do we mean by public opinion? Whose opinion is it? What is the public? Much that I said in the lecture about the group mind applies here. You will remember that I said there is no such thing as a group mind or collective consciousness which exists independently of the persons who constitute a group. There are only individuals and individual opinions. Whatever the public is, therefore, it cannot be a group mind in the sense that the term is popularly used. Many people speak of the public as if it were a mysterious entity which held opinions different from the opinions of any person.

In fact, the word "public" is really an adjective used as a noun. "Public" is the opposite of "private." It simply characterises certain phases of the behavior and thinking of persons. As Walter Lippmann has shown, consultations with one's physician, the relations of lawyer and client, confessions to a priest or conversation between the members of a family are generally considered to be private matters; by which we mean that they are not the business of unknown persons. Public affairs are those to which we admit, as it were, a vast number of people. They are those things which are in a sense *on the street.* What I say in this lecture is public. It is given in a public meeting. It is published. But if I write a letter to my mother, that is private.

There would seem to be a difference between these two types of activities in which I as an individual am engaged. Of course, the public activities

[134] E. D. Martin, *Psychology: What It Has to Teach You About Yourself and Your World* (New York, W. W. Norton & Company, 1924), pp. 191–203, 228–233. (Reprinted by permission of the publishers.)

are my activities as truly as are the private ones. Yet I feel that in the things which I consider my own personal private affair, I am more truly myself than in the public activities. In a sense everyone performs these two types of behavior. Privately we may have an opinion about certain people. Publicly, we should be cautious, perhaps, in expressing such an opinion, if uncomplimentary, even though we were convinced it was true. That is, as a private person I have to *answer to my conscience* and must face the results of my behavior and experience. On my public side I must *keep up appearances*, have a record, keep that record straight. I am accountable to a great many persons who cannot know my experience and behavior as I know it privately.

On the public side of my nature I find myself trying to think of myself as I imagine other people think of me. As public we pay deference to beliefs and ideas which run current among people of our time without stopping to criticize them. We are more concerned with being like our neighbors than with being different from them. So we may say that the difference between the public and the private in us is really the difference between *two ways of thinking about ourselves*. When we think of ourselves and other people as part of an unknown multitude or mass, we are thinking of ourselves as public. When we think of ourselves in our concrete human relationships, we are thinking of ourselves as private persons. Think of humanity in the *concrete* and you think of individuals. Think of humanity in the *abstract*, and you think of the public.

It is on the side of the public self in us that we have membership in the various groups to which we belong. Each of these groups considers only part of our nature. It is interested only in certain aspects of our behavior and thought. It abstracts. Thus there is a reading public, an eating public, a riding public, and so forth. The sum-total of these so-called publics, we may speak of as "the public." But you can see that "the public" is not the same as the self of any of us. It is smaller rather than larger, since the life of every one of us contains more than is to be found in the sum-total of the various interests about which the groups to which we belong are organized. Therefore, the public in us is a pinching down of our real self, a standardizing of various aspects of our nature. In public we are always on parade, as it were. We emphasize those things in which men are similar and tend to ignore those in which they are unique. The public then is not a thing apart from us; it is simply one way of looking at people, a way in which we ignore their uniqueness. The public is, therefore, the abstract idea of everyone with all concrete individuals thought away. The public is everybody and nobody, since it does not represent the real self of any one. It is one of those fictions which we invent about ourselves, a fiction which may be either useful or harmful.

And now what is public opinion? Obviously it cannot be the opinion of some impersonal thing known as public. Public opinion consists of that opinion which goes along with the public-self of each of us. It is the opinion we try to hold when we are "on parade." It consists of those beliefs which we accept second-hand, which we strive to share with an undifferentiated number of unknown persons, beliefs we imagine such persons would approve. It consists of those ideas which we try to think because we imagine our neighbors are thinking them, when, as a matter of fact, our neighbors are trying to think the same ideas, because they imagine we are trying to think them.

Perhaps I can illustrate what I mean. When I was a college student I knew two men. One was a clergyman and the other the superintendent of the Sunday School in this clergyman's church. By and by the clergyman took me into his confidence, telling me that he did not believe certain articles of his creed but could not bring himself to challenge these dogmas openly because he was afraid he would deeply shock the good man who for fifteen years had been superintendent of his Sunday School and had always shown such implicit faith and devotion. A few years later I came somehow to be closely associated with this superintendent. By this time the clergyman had been called elsewhere. We were discussing him one day when the superintendent said to me: "He was such a good man; he had such simple faith. I never did believe his dogmas, but for years I refrained from discussing these matters with him for fear that I might give him pain." Here were two men who were in closest contact for fifteen years and neither knew that the other was a liberal. Liberalism in each case was the private judgment of these men. The creed was their public opinion.

I am inclined to think that in most cases our private judgments are sounder and more honest than our public opinion. When we in our thinking defer to the imagined judgment of the multitude we must remember that we are not deferring to people as they really are, for, as I have said, the public in us is a caricature of us. And so, public opinion is *a caricature* of the real opinion of everybody.

We live in a time when the public in us tends to eat up the man. The enormous increase in the means of publicity, the standardization and mechanization of our modern world, all tend to depersonalize our thought of ourselves. In the dissemination of information the attempt must be made to strike at the average level of opinion. So the imaginary average, the mediocre type, becomes the standard in most public opinion. The mass is worshipped because it is many and powerful. "The voice of the people is the voice of God." Great organizations, each with its propaganda and partial interest in us, control our life and our thought. The State is interested in us only as "citizens"; the newspapers, as "circulation"; the corporation, as "consumers."

Thus, in adapting ourselves to our present organized social world, there is a tendency to leave out something vital in the nature of each of us. Hence, the opinions which belong to and serve the interests of various standardized forms of human association are not our real opinions. I should say that our private judgment has to do with our own experience, with the opinions we have reached through criticism and analysis. Our public opinion has to do with those automatic forms of thought and behavior which are *imposed upon us from without*. When we exercise private judgment we are thinking with something inside our heads; when we give expression to public opinion we are thinking outside the head, as it were.

Our public opinions are largely the result of economic and geographic accidents. They are made up of things we have been taught. They vary with changes of time and place. What public opinion holds to be true in one place or age, it may with the same implicit faith hold to be untrue in another place or age. Public opinion in persons of the older generation, especially Protestant Americans, is very Puritanical. Candid discussion of sex is taboo. The fiction is maintained that ignorance is "purity." There is a general attempt to keep up an appearance of innocence. What is "decent" and what is "indecent" is held to be a matter beyond dispute. Certain "moral" judgments are held to be self-evident.

When I was chairman of the National Board of Review of Motion Pictures I had many occasions to see such public opinion at work. Certain people just could not be made to see that there might be any honest difference of opinion as to what is decent. Oftentimes very silly and childish notions were held to be the expression of eternal right. I recall one case in which the Board was severely criticised because it passed a picture which showed a lingerie shop in which a customer incidentally held up to view a woman's silk under-garment. The persons who objected to this picture were quite sure that all who did not agree with them were deliberately "wicked people." Now such a public opinion is not based on private judgment. The moral world is full of the self-appointed guardians of infantile taboos who strive to turn the dilemmas of mediocrity into universal truths or categorical imperatives. Public opinion of this nature is mere class opinion. It is not the result of private judgment.

Similarly there is a public opinion among certain business men with respect to organized labor which is not the result of private judgment. In the average Rotary Club, Chamber of Commerce, or advertising men's organization, there is an amazing unanimity about the alleged aims and ideals of labor. The arguments used are always the same, if arguments they can be called. "Unions mean inefficiency." "Walking delegates are always calling unwilling and loyal workingmen out on strikes." "Unions rob the honest working man of his divine right to work." "Organized labor is only another form of socialism and socialism means dividing up." "You cannot change human nature." It goes without saying that this piece of reasoning, though many persons may honestly think they are convinced by it, is not reasoning at all. It is not based upon evidence and its speciousness is perfectly obvious to any unprejudiced person.

Likewise there is a *class opinion* current among certain liberals and radicals. The question is often raised whether there is such a thing as "a working class psychology." I suspect there is for a large number of people. There is a current belief that "labor produces all wealth"; that all persons who live without performing actual labor are "wicked," deliberate exploiters who scheme day and night new and more diabolical measures for "reducing the workers to slavery." There is a notion that people may be divided into two great groups, the all-good and the all-bad; the capitalists belong to the latter group—notwithstanding the fact that few radicals perhaps would decline to belong to this group if they had the opportunity. This god-devil psychology is an "all-or-none" type of reaction and as such is not a matter of carefully scrutinized thinking.

This same characteristic of class opinion is seen in politics. A catch-phrase will always pass uncriticized. "Wall Street" is the modern devil. Whenever the policies of the present Mayor of New York are criticized, we are told that he is being persecuted by the "interests." These mysterious interests are very wonderful beings. The latest "public benefactors" who would save the people from the machinations of the "evil interests" are concerned with certain history text-books used in our public schools. The long suffering public is warned against a deep, dark conspiracy. Historians who honestly try to tell the facts about the American Revolution are "bought up" by the "interests" in a plot to lure this innocent Republic back into the jaws of the British Lion.

We had an excellent illustration of this type of opinion several years ago in New York. It will be remembered that the "Gary School," because the newspapers gave this name to the type of schools first established in Gary, Indiana, was called a "steel trust school." Men saw in it an attempt on the part of malefactors of great wealth to train up workingmen's sons to be wage slaves.

Likewise we should call attention to the nonsense that has for seven or eight years passed in this country as "Americanism." Most of this sort of thing was at bottom an attempt to bully and insult foreigners and to justify such behavior by an appearance of patriotic devotion. The wildest and silliest rumors circulated among a credulous section of the population. Perhaps the climax of this type of public opinion was reached when the Attorney-General of the United States assured us that there would be a Bolshevist revolution on a certain May morning.

As public opinion is largely class opinion, so it is a matter frequently a geographical accident. In the South, public opinion is anti-negro and anti-alcohol; which does not mean that private opinion, however, is always quite so "anti." In the Middle West public opinion is anti-Catholic, anti-Semitic, and anti-foreign. There is a psychological reason why public opinion is so often "against" someone. It is made up very largely of prejudices, and prejudice is hostility to that which is strange. Such hostility is seized upon and rationalized by crowds as I have tried to show, in the study of psychology of the crowd, in order to justify the escape of certain tendencies of cruelty in our nature. Public opinion as I will show later in this lecture has the function of creating a pseudo-social environment in which anti-social behavior may be made to appear as devotion to moral principles.

Crowd opinions, rumors and fictions become fixed. Crowd thinking tends to be at best rather banal and platitudinous, ungenerous and intemperate, because it is necessarily the appeal to the mediocre majority. Such an appeal is almost always a low appeal when the man in the street holds the power that he does today. Even those more clever persons who write for this man, speak for him and presume to think for him, gain his good-will by flattering him in his ignorance and by encouraging him in his prejudices. Many of the things which motivate the average man publicly may be absolutely irrelevant. Not many years ago in Illinois a candidate for the office of United States Senator chose as the leading issue in his campaign the menace of the Mormon Church. Often an issue is still debated and people are bitterly divided concerning it long after it is dead. Thus in the South they were still fighting the Civil War in the late nineties. Fundamentalists are quarreling over 17th century ideas after a century and more of science has modified the thinking of practically all educated people.

These persistent factors in public opinion are called by Walter Lippmann *stereotypes.* Most propaganda consists of such stereotypes. Stereotypes are not easily modified by new truths nor are they established by research and evidence in the first place. The popular ideas about prohibition are stereotypes. Recently an excellent man visited me to solicit my aid in some research work he was doing for a group of Protestant Churches. He was commissioned to make a study of the psychological effect of the 18th amendment. I was obliged to decline because I knew that the truth on this subject was not what these churches wanted and that they would not publish our findings, if they happened to run counter to their own pre-conceived opinions. When deTocqueville visited America in the early part of the 19th century, he was much impressed with this stereotype of American public opinion. He said:

"America is therefore a free country in which, lest anybody be hurt by your remarks, you are not allowed to speak freely of private individuals, of the State, or the citizens, or the authorities, or public or private undertakings, in short of anything at all, except perhaps the climate and the soil, and even then Americans will be found ready to defend both as if they had concurred in producing them."

"The American submits without a murmur to the authority of the pettiest magistrate. This truth prevails even in the trivial details of national life. An American cannot converse—he speaks to you as if he were addressing a meeting. If an American were condemned to confine himself to his own affairs, he would be robbed of one-half of his existence; his wretchedness would be unbearable. . . .

"I know of no country in which there is so little independence of mind and real freedom of discussion as in America. In America the majority raises formidable barriers around the liberty of opinion. Within these barriers an author may write what he pleases, but woe to him if he goes beyond them. Not that he is in danger of an *auto-da-fe*, but he is exposed to continued obloquy and persecution. His political career is closed for ever. Every sort of compensation, even that of celebrity, is refused him. Those who think like him have not the courage to speak out and abandon him to silence. He yields at length, overcome by the daily effort which he has to make, and subsides into silence as if he felt remorse for having spoken the truth."

This was many years ago, but the situation meanwhile has become much worse. There are many such stereotypes among us today,—the idea that America is the land of the free; that democracy means liberty; that the poorest among us has equal opportunity with the most favored; that progress is inevitable; that if you are not an optimist you are a traitor; that big cities are immoral; that what we get in the public schools is education; that the Republican party is a Grand Old Party. It is a regrettable fact that most of the councils of democracy consist in the repetition of such phrases. There is in this free land very little expression of genuine personal opinion concerning matters moral, religious, political. Such phrases as are repeated carry a certain stereotyped emotional significance but have helped us very little in solving the problems of our common life.

The Value of Public Opinion

Are we therefore to assume that public opinion has no value? I think such an assumption would be unwarranted, for although public opinion is nobody's opinion and although in most cases it is erroneous, yet the stereotypes of which I have spoken could under certain conditions be made to serve important social ends. The regularity and order of human affairs is to a great extent the result of the fact that men accept certain opinions second-hand. They learn to respect ideas which they do not wholly understand. Certain mental habits are formed which result in commonly accepted beliefs. But, we should strive to bring it about that these beliefs are true, for their effect in social behavior is something we cannot escape. But, it is essential that there should be some *common belief* among men and perhaps even false beliefs are better than none at all.

If all men were wise, if they were capable of forming private judgments of such a nature that they could coöperate advantageously with one another, public opinion would be unnecessary. But even the wisest of men have not the time nor the information to scrutinize all human ways or to settle for themselves all questions of faith. In fact, even the most critical and skeptical of men accepts a large portion of his opinions second-hand. Any social order at all rests upon such things as the commonly accepted respect for property, for human life, for law, and so forth. The beliefs upon which these respects rest may be very erroneous, yet in advance of correct opinion it is desirable that there be fairly wide-spread assent.

Many of the assumptions upon which our present social order rests will hardly stand the test of logical criticism. And our present social system is certainly anything but an adequate and just one. But some order is better than none. Many persons may not believe this—though we had a little hint of what may happen when the usual social regulation is absent, in the behavior of many persons in Boston during the police strike.

I recently met a man who had gone through the Great War as a Hungarian soldier. He had suffered very much from privation; had been under fire many times; in fact, had experienced all the horrors of war. He had also been in Hungary during the brief period of the dictatorship of Bela Kun. He told me that he would rather go through the entire war again than live three days in the midst of the chaos which followed that breakdown of social order in his country after the war.

Certainly there are many really valuable things in our society the survival of which depends upon the fact that there is a public opinion in their favor, even though there may not be a general and correct understanding of them. For instance, there is Science. There is a public opinion in favor of science. And science is possible only because people who are not scientists still believe that science is a good thing and allow it to proceed notwithstanding the fact that they have not mastered its technique and do not understand very well its general principles. I suppose most people believe that the earth is round and that it moves about the sun. There is a general acceptance of the doctrine of evolution, the law of gravitation, the bacteriological explanation of infectious diseases, the atomic theory, and so on. Yet I doubt if more than a very small portion of the population could give an intelligible account of the ground upon which these beliefs are founded. In fact, the public acceptance of science is an act of faith just as truly as belief in the Church or the Bible was in medieval times.

Even the most radical of radicals after all is a good deal of a conservative.

he accepts many things on faith. For instance, the popular belief in "Progress." Not only does he not criticize the concept of Progress; he accepts it as an unquestioned fact and does his best to accelerate it. As the late Prof. William Graham Sumner of Yale said, the great bulk of our popular beliefs is embedded in our "mores" of folkways. None of us is able wholly to emancipate himself from the folkways. Were it not for the folkways there could be no point of contact in our various social situations. There could be no communication or coöperation among men. Public opinion, therefore, even though it is full of errors, is indispensable.

Although public opinion is indispensable it is not necessary that it be left in *ignorance and folly*. Social progress consists in lifting public opinion to higher levels. The task of wisdom is not to abolish it, but to *correct* it wherever possible, subjecting it, as much as may be, to private judgment. This is why free speech, freedom of thought and assembly are so tremendously important. They are the very basis of social advance. This is why the liberal spirit of tolerance, that rare quality which came into the world with the 18th century free thinkers, and is today on the decline, is yet to be encouraged. Tolerance is not a mere sentiment of brotherly love or indifference to what people believe; but, once it is established among men it means that we have reached a turning point in history. After that, human advance may proceed at a pace never before possible.

A Criticism of Present Day Public Opinion

In discussing public opinion we should be much concerned about the low level on which it exists today. Why is it that on the whole the newspapers with the widest circulation are those which are the cheapest and least sincere? There are a few exceptions to this, but the exceptions only prove the rule. Note the captions that appear in the motion pictures, and for that matter the pictures themselves. Why is the motion picture what it is? The answer I think is obvious. *The trouble with the motion picture is the audience*. We have here a new fact in the history of art. All previous movements in art necessarily had to appeal to the cultured few, and hence the works of art reflected the mentality of the persons for whom they were created. With the coming of the motion picture and its "quantity production" it was necessary for the first time in history—at least modern history—that a form of art make its appeal to the man on the street. It was obliged, therefore, to present those things which reflected this man's mentality. If you want to know what public opinion in America is, go to a "movie"; read the fiction magazines; attend a religious revival; visit Coney Island; subscribe to the Saturday Evening Post; read the advertisements in the street-cars.

A number of my friends are trying to popularize psychology. They are sometimes able to secure an audience of a few hundred people for the scientific presentation of the subject. But irresponsible pseudo-psychologists can go about the country with a cheap, vulgar, caricature of this science and can attract many thousands to their psychological clown show. If a man can bat a base-ball over the Bull Durham sign at the back of the out field, the papers must devote many pages to him. If a man wins the Nobel prize for the most important work in Astronomical Physics, his name will remain unknown except to a few scientists who are his colleagues. If you wish to know what public opinion is, compare the popularity of John Dewey with that of Frank Crane. Ask yourself, what is the most popular song in America today?

Now the standards of public opinion revealed by the things I have mentioned characterize it in all its manifestations. Political opinion is not at all more reliable or intelligent than is the reaction of the public to the "movies," or to base-ball. One may wonder why public opinion is so persistently cheap and insincere. There are several reasons. First, the one I have suggested: *because of the type of thinker whose opinion becomes standardized.* We have learned from the intelligence tests one fact at least and that is that the mental level of the average person is fairly low. Yet the way the spiritual life of the community is now organized (especially since the circulation of books and the printing of newspapers, and so on, must be made to pay commercially), makes it necessary that all things appeal to and to some extent reflect the mentality of the duller minds in the community. Any organization of our cultural life which makes it possible that mediocrity have a voice in determining what shall survive, *degrades the values of civilization.*

I do not mean that the man on the street should not be permitted to choose his own amusements and to be free to think his own ideas. I think every effort should be made to educate him but he should not be put into a position where he decides what other people shall think and like.

Not only is the standardization of opinion according to the dilemmas of mediocrity being brought about by our present methods of quantity production, but it is also being achieved by the present trend of legislation. A number of southern legislatures have passed laws forbidding the teaching of Evolution in educational institutions supported by the public. We may yet see a constitutional amendment to this effect within a few years. The rapid growth of the censorship is another case in point. At one time there were over twenty State legislatures considering bills for the censorship of motion pictures. Now censorship is a form of propaganda. It means that any group which does not like itself to see certain things can, through political pressure, prevent any one else from seeing them. The same tendency is seen in the proposed legislation in New York, the aim of which is to establish a state censorship of books. On the pretext that they are suppressing "vice," representatives of "lowbrowism" are really doing their best to drag all intelligence down to the level of the lowest cranial altitude.

A second cause of the present low state of public opinion is the wide use of *propaganda.* The late Frank Cobb, editor of the New York World, said that public opinion in America is no longer free. He said that around all the sources of our information there is camped an army of press agents whose work it is to manipulate the public. He said that there were in 1919 about twelve hundred of these persons in New York City alone. During the war "the government suppressed the truth; the government distorted the truth; lied glibly and magnificently when occasion seemed to require." Now all sorts of agencies have learned the propagandist trick and have their special press agents. "The great corporations have them; the banks have them; the railroads have them. All the organizations of business and of social and political activity have them and they are the media through which news comes. Even statesmen have them."

He might have added that even churches have them. Vast sums of money are now spent, and the cleverest advertisers are employed, on the assumption that by cleverness it is possible to sell religion in the manner that soap is sold. A very illuminating fact was revealed in the recent trial of the superintendent of the Anti-Saloon League, where it was brought out that prohibition activities of the most far-reaching significance were supported in this State of New York by persons whose identity is kept a secret to this day. Mr. Cobb concludes that "What the United States needs more than anything else today is the restoration of the free play of public opinion."

One of the devises of propaganda is constant repetition. In order to get people to believe a lie it is only necessary to go on repeating it. As Prof. Santayana says. "This happy people can read. It supports a press conforming to the tastes of the common man, or rather to such tastes as common men can have in common; for the best in each is not diffused enough to be catered for in public. Moreover, this press is audaciously managed by some adventitious power, which guides it for its own purposes, commercial or sectarian. Superstitions old and new thrive in this infected atmosphere; they are now all treated with a curious respect, as if nobody could have anything to object to them. . . .

"A confused competition of all propaganda—those insults to human nature—is carried on by the most expert psychological methods, which the art of advertising has discovered; for instance, by always repeating a lie, when it has been exposed, instead of retracting it. The world at large is deafened; but each propaganda makes its little knot of proselytes, and inspires them with a new readiness to persecute and to suffer in the sacred cause. The only question is, which propaganda can first materially reach the greatest number of persons, and can most efficaciously quench all the others." . . .

"By giving a free rein to such propagandas, and by disgusting the people with too much optimism, toleration, and neutrality, liberalism has introduced a new reign of unqualified ill-will. Hatred and wilfulness are everywhere; nations and classes are called to life on purpose to embody them; they are summoned by their leaders to shake off the lethargy of contentment and to become conscious of their existence and of their terrible wrongs."

"These propagandas have taken shape in the blue sky of liberalism, like so many summer clouds; they seem airships sailing under a flag of truce; but they are engines of war, and on the first occasion they will hoist their true colours, and break the peace which allowed them to cruise over us so leisurely. Each will try to establish its universal ascendancy by force, in contempt of personal freedom, or the voice of majorities. . . ."

"Incipient formations in the body politic, cutting across and subverting its old constitution, eat one another up, like different species of animals; and the combat can never cease except some day, perhaps, for lack of combatants. Liberalism has merely cleared a field in which every soul and every corporate interest may fight with every other for domination. Whoever is victorious in this struggle will make an end of liberalism; and the new order, which will deem itself saved, will have to defend itself in the following age against a new crop of rebels."

Another device of propaganda is insinuation. People may be inveigled into accepting such beliefs as certain interested persons wish them to entertain by a sort of *flagrant duplicity*. While they are giving their assent to a proposition which in itself is quite innocent, it is made to appear that this proposition means something quite different. We had a great deal of this sort of thing during the war when it was common for certain sales organizations to exploit their own interests on a pretext that the customer in buying their particular brand of goods was helping to "win the war."

I have gathered a number of such advertisements. The following are typical: Here is a large picture of a beautiful child at the breakfast table. The advertisement reads: "Little Americans, you can do your bit"—Eat a certain brand of breakfast food. Another reads. "Have you a sweetheart, son, or brother in training camps in the American Army or Navy? If so, mail him a package of Allen's Foot Ease." Again, "Build fighting strength with Father John's remedy." The following is typical, I have it from a certain hotel in Western Pennsylvania. There was put on my table a card displaying a large picture of the American flag. The card read as follows:

"WAR
and
SERVICE

Labor is scarce—Our men are being called to serve their country—We will not replace those that leave but *will ask those who are left to work harder* and so do their share (the italics are mine). *Will you*, the guest, be considerate—It is one way in which YOU can help. . . ."

One of the most touching of all these war-time advertisements was a placard displayed in the subway after the armistice was signed. The sentiments here was 100% American: "When Johnny comes marching home again, give him a Tootsie Roll."

Public opinion is everywhere about on the level of commercial advertising. As a matter of fact, *propaganda is nothing but advertising*. We should always look for what the propagandist has to *sell* and should not be taken in by his big words. Professions of faith in ideals on the part of propagandists are only screens which hide their real intent. If you can get a number of people to agree to anything, true or false, you may turn that belief into a platitude, an abstraction, treat it as something final, something to be accepted uncritically. Then identify it with your own ulterior purpose, smear it all about your purpose like the sugar-coating about a dose of quinine, and in swallowing the sugar men will swallow your quinine also.

Most people will agree that murder is wicked. That being the case, those who wish to prevent any change of public opinion regarding the subject of "birth control" need only argue that birth control is murder, the murder of unborn children, even before they are conceived. Hence, those who advocate the change of the New York Statute do not only advocate something indecent; they are advocating "murder." So the Common Council of the City of Syracuse passes an ordinance prohibiting all discussion of the repeal of the present law. This is not an attack on free speech, of course. The city fathers are merely doing their duty in protecting human life.

Once men agree, as they properly do and should, that the laws must be obeyed, all that is necessary is to collect a large sum of money and bully or cajole our legislators to pass the 18th amendment, and straightway those who wish to take a drink are no longer merely "intemperate." Behold, they are "scofflaws." Had the advocates of sobriety put forth the same amount of effort in the attempt to persuade people to be temperate in their habits that they now put forth persuading them to obey an unpopular law, they might have been more successful, might have saved themselves a lot of trouble, and America today might have been a more law-abiding nation.

With the propagandists' use of such concepts as law, lawfulness, and nearly all the generalizations used in crowd propaganda,—"justice," "brotherly love," "truthfulness," "virtue" become *mere instruments for working the will of some sect* or group upon the community as a whole. There is probably no word to which men will so uniformly assent as "morality." Nietzche once said that the public may always be led by the nose in the name of morality.

Let the professional "reformer" then have his say and he will capitalize your morality in the interest of his own prejudices. He will tell you that a man is known by the company he keeps; that no man can be moral who habitually associates with immoral persons. A man, then, is an associate of evil people whether he knows such rascals personally or invites them into his house as fictitious characters to practice their evil deeds *between the covers of a book*. If you read Shakespeare you are the evil companion of Falstaff; if you read Flaubert, you are an associate of Madame Bovary. Hence morality demands that the police edit our literature.

All this means that public opinion becomes a device for coercion. It means that by the use of clever propaganda public opinion can be *manufactured like bricks* and delivered f. o. b. As I have said many times at Cooper Union, *all propaganda is lies;* it is insinuation. It should be looked in the face without "batting an eye." It should be met without compromise. It should be laughed off the stage by intelligent people. When I was chairman of the National Board of Review of Motion Pictures I once received a great bundle of letters. These letters all came from a large mid-western city. There were dozens of resolutions, practically identical, which had been passed by nearly every uplift organization in the community: churches, ministers' associations, women's clubs, school teachers, and so on. The resolutions stated that the motion pictures were very, very wicked and that I was personally to be held accountable henceforth for everything that appeared in them. Particularly the resolutions demanded that I personally see to it that no motion picture show anyone taking a drink of liquor, no woman smoking a cigarette, and in fine, nothing that in any way could be interpreted as making clergymen and social workers appear ridiculous.

Now the National Board was not a censorship organization. It was merely advisory, and its main task was to help producers to free their products of vulgarity and insincerity. In other words, to improve the artistic character of motion pictures. Yet the greatest pressure was brought to bear upon the secretary and the Chairman of the Board to use this agency to compel the whole American public to conform to all sorts of provincial pseudo-moral ideas. Had I yielded in the case just mentioned, those people would have demanded still more provincial restrictions. What I did and what I would advise should be done generally was to write these over-excited people a letter stating that their demands were essentially childish and provincial;

that I knew many splendid women who smoked cigarettes; that I thought, on the whole, that smoking was good for them. And furthermore, as to making clergymen and social workers appear ridiculous, that, as a matter of fact, they often were ridiculous, and never so much as in a case like this, when they were trying to preserve their imaginary dignity under the pretext that they were fighting in the cause of morality.

Finally, public opinion is today on a low level because of the *function of crowd ideas*. Crowd ideas are all rationalizations. They are not problem-solving ideas. To the crowd-mind there are no problems. The crowd always knows the answer. Crowd ideas have the function of justifying the anti-social behavior of the crowd itself. There are two aims that are always present when groups of men become crowd-minded. First, the crowd is a devise for preserving the egoism of its members. In lauding one's crowd, one praises oneself. Second, the crowd mind is always hostile to someone. The easiest way to get a crowd is to raise an issue, denounce someone, protest against some "evil." As I have elsewhere tried to show, public opinion is today of the same type as paranoia.

I wish to close this discussion with a little preachment on the right and duty of private judgment. If private judgment is to exist, there must be less standardization of opinion in this country. There must be more tolerance than the masses seem now disposed to exercise or permit. The mass must cease worshipping itself. And this spirit of tolerance must extend to all classes.

One of the most disillusioning facts which has come to my notice in recent years is the alacrity with which the communists in Russia, as soon as they gained power, became a propagandist organization and set up a rigid censorship, quite as intolerable as that under which they themselves had suffered under the old régime. This was bad enough, but the action was approved by a large number of the radical proletariat of America. I do not know how many times I have heard men say here in Cooper Union that ruthlessness, censorship, coercion on the part of the working class, should this class ever come into power, are quite justified by the fact that their opponents had resorted to the same practices.

Even the necessity of conserving the new order against counter-revolution could not justify this spirit. We had looked to labor once to help in freeing the world of tyranny and exploitation. When its proposed supremacy fails to hold out a promise of such liberation to mankind, labor necessarily must lose the sympathy of thinking men. When a society loses its spirit of tolerance that society is *going down*. I am not pointing to labor here as at all different from the other movements which exist in the world today. Catholics and Protestants and Prohibitionists and the Ku Klux Klan and the Fascisti are all evidence—evidence of the fact that a world controlled by the rank and file, a world in which uncultivated men scramble for power, in a word, a democratic world, cannot be a free world.

I am going to start a little revolution of my own. Not a violent revolution, but a spiritual revolution. I want to overthrow the present rulers of society: Mr. Babbitt and his less prosperous brother, Henry Dubb. While these men control opinions, and therefore control the world, our common life must remain a rather shoddy affair.

The Psychology of Politics

. . . . . .

The Place of Principle in Politics

The psychology of leadership in politics goes far to account for the fact that it is personalities, not principles, which, in the main, influence popular choice. Often, Merriam says, in fact, almost half of the time in the last 46 years, the people of this country have elected a president on one party and a congress of the opposing party, or have given the president's party so small a leadership in congress that he was practically powerless. Another proof that principles do not carry much weight is the fact of the geographical distribution of political opinion in America. In the campaign of 1920, out of 531 electoral votes 372 were decided before the campaign began and before any one knew what the issues in it would be. They would have been the same, no matter what the issues had been, for the vote of over half the people of this country was decided sixty years ago.

Merriam says that in the 32 campaigns in the history of this country, clean cut party issues dividing the voters have been presented in only 16 cases. He gives an outline of the typical party platform. It consists of:

1. The elaboration of the record of the party.
2. Denunciation of the opposition party.
3. General declarations regarding democracy and the nation.
4. General references to certain non-party issues.
5. Expressions of sympathy.
6. Non-committal reference to certain disputed issues.
7. Definite issues.

Our author says that in 1888 there were 19 planks in the republican platform and 12 in the democratic. Of these, nine were the same in both platforms, and in only one was there a significant difference. The parties agreed on the maintenance of the union (which must have been a live issue since the Civil War had been over 22 years!). They agreed on a homestead policy, on the early admission of territories, on civil service reform, on pensions, on the trusts, on sympathy with Ireland, on the exclusion of foreign contract labor. The Republican differed from the Democratic in declaring for personal rights and the free ballot. The Democratic brought out the important and relevant matter of adherence to a written constitution with specific powers. The Republican platform declared against Mormonism (obviously a national menace!) and in favor of bi-metallism, an issue upon which it took an opposite side eight years later. It declared for reduction of the cost of postage stamps, put itself on record in favor of the Monroe Doctrine and the protection of fisheries and added, to give the whole a still higher moral flavor, a non-committal prohibition plank which read as follows: "The first concern of all good government is the sobriety of the people and the purity of their homes. The Republican Party cordially sympathizes with all wise and well-directed efforts for the promotion of temperance and morality."

The two parties differed in only one important matter: the tariff. Of course, the tariff was the real issue. It meant business profits for somebody. Often the issue is not so clear as this. In the campaign of 1920 the issue seems to have been hatred of the person of Woodrow Wilson who was not, at that time, a candidate. You will remember seeing great signs posted on all the bill boards which read, "No more wibble and wobble." I am told that this was a campaign slogan to get which the party employed a great advertising company, and that it influenced thousands of votes. Its irrelevance is obvious. The slogan evidently referred to the record of Mr. Wilson, yet at the same time political speakers were saying that Mr. Wilson was a domineering, tyrannical, uncompromising idealist, who, once he made up his mind, could not be moved. And the pathos of such a slogan is that if "wibble and wobble" means anything it was the Harding Administration which later "wibbled and wobbled." What else could a wibbling and wobbling electorate expect?

The contemplation of party history makes it rather easy to predict some of the planks of the party platform in the campaign of 1924. Both parties will express sympathy for labor, while warning the public against the dangers of radicalism. Both will congratulate the Irish Free State on its successful establishment. Both will be non-committal about the Volstead act, pointing out the moral evils that follow disrespect for law. Both will deal with the oil scandal by warning the public of the dangers of corruption in high office. As to foreign policy, the Republicans will say that the peace of the world demands that America play her part in the fellowship of the nations; that some association of the peoples of the world for the preservation of peace would seem to be advisable, but that America must be saved from entangling alliances, the Monroe Doctrine protected and our domestic interests safeguarded. The Democrats will say that, whereas our domestic interests must be safeguarded, the Monroe Doctrine protected, and America kept from entangling alliances, nevertheless the Democratic party stands for the great principle that the peace of the world can only be maintained by some kind of a league or association among the nations of the world.

So far we have spoken only of general principles of political opinion and leadership. The history of political practice everywhere is unflattering to democracy. The great show of platitudinous principles professed by party organizations merely covers a thinly disguised effort to gain special advantages for some individuals. As Merriam says, "Each campaign consists of two parts: One is directed upon an appeal to the common interest on the theory that there are no classes, no races, no religions, no sections, no special interests, but that the common interest of all will be the criterion by which each voter will decide his party allegiance. The other section of the campaign is based upon the opposite theory: that the whole electorate is made up of a long series of special interests which must be shown their special advantage in the support of the particular party and its candidates to obtain their support."

In practice, therefore, politics both here and abroad is the story of a long series of acts of corruption and misgovernment, special favoritism, incompetence, shameful lobbying, hastily drawn and ill considered legislation, outrageous extravagance, the levying of tribute from the underworld for its protection, the insincere enforcement of laws, many of which should never have been passed and cannot honestly be enforced; in a word, the general misuse of the institution and functions of government by men who were incapable of statesmanship, and saw in political affairs nothing but the opportunity for advancement of someone's special interest. All this has been only too characteristic of political life everywhere, from the commonplace corruption in the government of most cities up to a recent cabinet of the "best minds."

It is a disheartening story. We may take some consolation in the fact that the life of the people goes on in spite of politics. A man recently returned from a business trip to Honduras tells me that on one occasion while talking to a merchant, he heard a great clatter in the street, together with much shooting. The American was frightened and asked the merchant what on earth was happening. Was it a revolution? The merchant said "Oh, yes, that is just the politicians passing by. We will close the blinds and do business as usual." We cannot, however, so blandly ignore the behavior of our politicians. For we have seen in recent years how politicians may well nigh wreck our civilization.

Politics and Democracy

What makes politics what it is? There are two ready-made answers, given from opposite standpoints and both inadequate. The first is the answer of the aristocrat. It says, that the trouble with politics is democracy; that democracy can never be anything but corrupt because it is government by the lower classes. But aristocracies too may be notoriously corrupt. Witness the behavior of the Russian aristocracy under the old régime. England, whose government is a combination of democracy and aristocracy, is doubtless the cleanest and most competent government in the world. It appears to fall below its high standard only during those periods when the business classes gain the upper hand.

The other answer is that of the socialists, who maintain that political corruption is a direct result of the capitalist system. There is much truth in this, but, like most socialist statements, it oversimplifies the case. There are many other factors, psychological in their nature, which, if I had time, I could show enter into the situation. Corruption is not the whole story in politics and may itself be correlated with the ignorance and cupidity of the average man. Capitalism may itself be an effect of the same psychological elements which have produced our present political forms of behavior. It is said that if we could remove the temptations set before our politicians by profit-seeking business men, all would be well. But those who say this forget that temptation would still exist. Wherever there is power over men, those who have such power will be tempted to make it a vested interest of their own. The situation in Russia today is proof of this fact.

There are three elements in politics which I wish to discuss very briefly. The first is the *politician*. There are, of course, many notable exceptions to what I am going to say. But, in a sense, politics has become a profession. This profession, however, differs from other professions in that it has few or no recognized professional standards. The physician, the professor (and to some extent even the lawyer) is answerable to his colleagues for his conduct. Each of these professions, therefore, has a certain professional ethic. I do not say that this ethic is universally lived up to. But if any one flagrantly betrays a professional trust he is answerable to his colleagues, answerable, that is, to men who are specially trained, have a sense of responsibility for the profession, and know enough to pass rather intelligent judgment upon one another. The rogue may be expelled from the practice of his profession and the incompetent excluded. It is not so with the politician or the labor leader. The politician makes his appeal to the undifferentiated mass. Moreover, there are, for entrance into the profession of politics, no intellectual standards or requirements as in other professions. Consequently, the men who enter this profession are, on the whole, men of a lower type of mentality. Psychologically speaking, they belong to a lower type of men. Now, when these two factors enter into the selection of the personnel of a profession, they cannot but degrade it. The fact is that a high-minded, well-educated sincere man is at a decided disadvantage in politics as in all things where he must make his appeal to the mass as a whole. Victory is on the side of sensation, superficiality, and humbug.

Second, let us consider briefly politics as an expression of the *psychology of the people*. It is often said that people have the government they deserve. I am not sure that this is the case. It is not true that the masses are necessarily corrupt, though there is a certain amount of "cussedness" in the nature of us all. The difficulty lies in the type of appeal to which the masses uniformly respond. This is due not only to popular ignorance, but also to the desire of crowds to be flattered. The very sense of power which men have when they get together in a party gives strength to their feeling of self-importance. They wish to hear those things which encourage them in their protest against the feeling of inferiority. Again, popular thinking is highly irrelevant, substituting for the results of behavior various made-in-advance principles which really have nothing to do with the case in hand. Consequently, political thought and propaganda seldom rise above the level of commercial advertising. There is a touch of insincerity in almost everything with which men strive to reach the masses. Catch phrases, over-statement of fact, broad generalizations, the trite, the obsolete, the platitudinous, commonly determine our political choices, and I do not see how this situation may be remedied except by a new and more self-analytical type of education.

In an earlier lecture we learned that there are two kinds of thinking—*problem-solving* thinking and *rationalization*. The latter does not have the function of adapting the organism to environmental situations; it is the mere fabrication of ideas which will at once disguise and make plausible some unconscious wish. Public opinion concerning political matters is seldom problem-solving thinking. It is rationalization—men do not think out political problems, they merely repeat their dogmas, resort to special pleading, cleverly impute to their opponents the unconscious motives they themselves entertain. The function of party opinion is to hold the members in the crowd, make converts of the credulous, represent the party's will to rule as the triumph of a great cause. Its function is to protest the "purity" of the party's aims, justify and intensify an artificial fervor of partisan strife and enable the average man to keep up his fiction of superiority. "The People" thinking in these ways imagines its voice to be the voice of God, believes it is giving expression to sacred truths, when it is merely priding itself on the sheer power of its numbers and pooling the manifestation of its egotism. As

I have said, when numbers alone count, it is the mediocre man who must be cajoled, his mental qualities set the standard and must be glorified with big words. True distinction of worth is rated low, even resented. The real interest of the public is not good government, but that which causes the average man to feel himself important. Perhaps it was an error to extend the franchise to all men regardless of their mental capacity; though, I do not see just how, at present, we could find a criterion of mental capacity which could be justly applied in determining who should vote.

Finally, there is *politics as a method of government*. Certainly the party system, as we have worked it out in America, makes the party itself an end, and is to be held accountable for much of the misgovernment in this country. Government as government has very little to do with the ends of practical politics as we have known those ends. Strangely enough, though the average American is indifferent to politics, yet he is politically minded to an unfortunate degree. We look to the government for all sorts of things which government can never, by its very nature, satisfactorily perform. In fact, government *is perhaps the least lovely thing that democracy has achieved*, though democratic government has doubtless been conducive to the achievement of whatever human advancement in other directions society has in recent years attained. Even this, however, is a debatable point. I am anything but an anarchist, but I hold with Jefferson that "that government is best which governs least." Government must be rigidly restricted or majorities will utterly crush the life out of the minorities which oppose them. And certainly the will of the majority is a poor method of determining the right policy of government. A project should gain no sanctity because a thousand stupid and uneducated men may favor it in opposition to the judgment of 100 wise men. And under our present political methods, not only majorities, but also organized minorities may practice coercion in support of ill-advised measures.

The world today is so highly organized, political policy may have such far-reaching and unforeseen effects, a bit of stupidity may be so universally disastrous, that it stands to reason that the control of affairs can no longer, with safety, be left to the mercy of political practices, as we have known them. If politics cannot in some way be made to encourage the leadership and control of the higher types of men and women in communities, democracy probably will not survive the century. Thinking people must make an effort to see that the profession of politics acquires a professional ethic, in the light of which certain practices become reprehensible. The public must be taught to stop worshipping itself. If it must have its self-flattery, it should get it otherwise than at the expense of the future of the state. It must not forget the psychological fact that *social behavior is conditioned by the kind of man in whose interest it is performed*. In politics as elsewhere, the important question is "Who goes there?"

ISAAC B. BERKSON

Isaac B. Berkson has been engaged in Jewish educational work since 1911. He was formerly director of the Central Jewish Institute of New York City and supervisor of the Bureau of Jewish Education of New York City. His book, *Theories of Americanization: A Critical Study*, is an analysis and criticism of the various theories of assimilation that have been proposed in this country. Berkson examines each with his democratic measuring rod and favors that of cultural pluralism. It is interesting to note that in recent years the most enthusiastic defense of democracy has come from Americans who are descendants of recent immigrants.

THEORIES OF AMERICANIZATION [135]

CHAPTER I

The Doctrines of Democracy

· · · · · · ·

IV

The Criteria of Democracy

Uniqueness of Evaluation

It is fundamental to remember that each individual is a unique specimen; human individuals are not copies of each other like so many buttons turned out by the same machine. Our doctrine of evolution would impress upon us the heterogeneity within each species and the tendency for greater individual diversification as the species reaches higher levels. This primary fact of individual differences must be taken into the first reckoning in our evaluation of the good. The unique nature of the particular individual involved must become the reference point if we are seeking a real benefit for him. The extent to which it is possible in any given society to understand each individual's good and to include it in the social good becomes the limit of democracy.

The traditional tendency has been to pass judgment on persons in accordance with some group in which they were classed. Race, sex, social class or church were for the most part considered to be the determining factors in assigning to the individual a place in society. The presumption was that difference in some characteristics carried with it similar differences in respect to the total character. Classification seems to have the result of investing a person with a sort of quality which makes him what he is. Against this attitude of mind the democratic conception would insist that the character of each individual should be directly examined in order to ascertain what he is. A person is what he is, because he is so, not because he belongs to a certain class.

This tendency in democracy, to approach the matter in hand directly, is matched by a similar development in the conception of cause. In primitive stages of thought when men sought the cause of a phenomenon, they did not seek it in the phenomenon under examination, but in some other object or process. To control, little interest or study was given to the matter to be controlled; the endeavor was to exert influence through something external which was considered as having a dominating potency. The disease which had come over a man was considered as quite separate from the man. It had entered into him. The ensuing activity, therefore, was to do something not to the man but to the evil spirits which needed to be expelled. In the cosmic scheme, God and creation were considered as quite distinct and the world was to be controlled not by mastering creation, but by appealing in some way to God.

[135] I. B. Berkson, *Theories of Americanization: A Critical Study* (New York, Teachers College, Columbia University, 1920), pp. 28–39, 61–72, 97–98, 117–118. (Reprinted by permission of the publishers.)

In science to-day the tendency is to seek the cause in the very subject under consideration, not in the distant far-off external relationships. We find the 'cause' in the immediately preceding and surrounding conditions; i.e., we find it more useful from the point of view of control to know what immediately precedes and surrounds. We refuse to be satisfied with the intuition of a connection between this before us and that remote ultimate. Even if the ultimate can influence the immediate object at hand, it must be through intermediate connections which must in the last analysis be contiguous with the immediate object. So we begin with the matter at hand and seek to gain control over the nearby conditions.

Cause, therefore, is to be sought *in the peculiar organization of the specific instance in question,* not in any external fact or object, which on account of some overt similarity or some other process of association or some mystical connection is assumed to exercise potency over it. So closely have cause and effect approached each other in modern thinking that the use of these words tends to give a false connotation of disparateness, when in reality they have come to mean two aspects of or stages in the same process.

The mechanistic interpretation of the universe as against an idea of creator and creation; the attempt to get at heredity not on the basis of external resemblances of relatives, but through a study of the germ plasm; the explanation of human nature not by means of 'faculties,' but in terms of the organization of the nervous system; the analysis of historical phenomena by examining the local and contemporaneous conditions rather than harking back to supposed 'origins'; and in philosophy the finding of purposes not in some external Authority or Law or Society, but in the functioning organism—all these seem to be products of working with intrinsic, immediately related conditions.

This attitude of seeking the 'cause' in the sphere of efficient condition, in the particular, immediate, internal, specific organization of the business in question rather than primarily in the realm of 'final causes' in the general, ultimate, external, mystical relationships, is the attitude to be borne in mind when we approach the task of understanding the nature of any individual. To come as near home as possible, to endeavor to begin from within, is part of the democratic doctrine of self-determination.

Race, color, class, sex, social position are themselves at best only hints concerning the individuals to whom we wish to refer. They are not powers or spirits which enter into the individual and make him what he is. To understand, for instance, what place a person who happens to be a woman ought to play in our social organization, it would be in the democratic spirit to ascertain just what she could do from an impartial test of her capabilities, rather than to assign a preconceived status, determined altogether by one factor, that of sex. The movement of democracy is to get away from such prejudgments on the basis of one factor (a procedure which is bound to bring about a judgment by an external standard) and to get as close as possible to the actual individual, as near as possible to his own unique nature. The same line of reasoning which forbids absolute values, related to a conceptual God, precludes values related to conceptual Classes.

It is the unique person to whom values must be related. We fulfill the demands of our relativistic conception of value only in the degree that we give due consideration to the individual's nature involved. *In thinking about the good, the point of departure from which our reckoning begins must be the individual persons who are most closely concerned in the situation*—that is the first prerequisite of a democratic procedure. Because we are incapable of realizing in its fullness and intensity the experience of others (we seem, too, naturally disinclined to do so) the practical application of democracy involves the setting up of machinery which will enable men to control the policies that govern them. For this reason "consent of the governed" is regarded as the basic principle in political democracy. Participation in the control of any activity which vitally affects the course of one's life becomes the safeguard of human liberty. The word 'self-determination' expresses so happily the essential meaning of democracy because it implies that the ultimate judgment of the good and the final power over one's fate must rest with the living subject of experience.

Since the individual undergoing an experience is alone capable of realizing to the full value of any experience, we might conclude (granting that he accords to every other individual the respect of personality which he demands for himself) that the individual himself must in the last analysis be the ultimate and only judge of the salvation which is in accordance with his own nature. Such is perhaps the case, but it will be well to see in what important directions the validity of his judgment must be practically limited.

Diversity in the Environment

We can speak of judgment on the part of the individual only when he has a variety of possibilities of experience from which to choose. When there is only one possible mode of responding either in act or in imagination there can be no judgment in the true sense. In accordance with the biological conception underlying this discussion the individual is conceived as an organism responding to an environment and learning through the satisfactions and dissatisfactions accompanying his reactions to choose what for him is the good and to reject the evil. There must be present a multiplicity of material and ideal objects to which to respond before a free choice becomes possible.

The removal of governmental and social restraints which prevent some from enjoying the benefits already conferred upon others is only the first step in the attainment of freedom. For its full development it is necessary to create continuously new possibilities in the surroundings. A richly diversified natural mental and social environment must be present before the individual can be thought of as reacting in accordance with his own nature. America must be justly considered democratic even more because it is the golden land of opportunity than because it opposes privilege. The popular conception colored by the long, difficult struggle for equal rights naturally emphasizes most the personal aspect implied in the phrase *equality* of opportunity. But equality alone is negative and empty when not joined to a *multiplicity* of opportunity. "The troubles of the many—that is half consolation," so runs a Hebrew proverb. The individual human undoubtedly finds some measure of satisfaction in realizing that he is no worse off than his fellow. An intelligent and positive conception, however, will stress the impersonal condition of freedom—a manifold diverse opportunity.

The presence of a variety of possibilities is the *sine qua non* of freedom, and defining from the point of view of the environment the only real meaning that the term can have.

The mere existence of objects and ideas obviously does not imply that all will react; to be present in the environment signifies also potentiality on the part of the organism. Fundamentally important differences of instinctive endowment affect the possibility of response. Original nature, therefore, gives both the possibility of freedom and its limitations. So, too, the modifications upon the nervous system known as habit formation have their effect upon the possibilities of reaction. Habit, too, makes possible, but at the same time may limit freedom. The establishment of fixed modes of reaction permits the organism to engage the attention in new fields. Fixed habits are necessary to relieve the mind from the many harassing details of the daily routine of physical and social living. The number of situations into which we are thrown is so great that it would be impossible to consider in each case what would be the best type of reaction. In many cases nearly any mode of reaction would do nearly as well; in other cases age-long experimentation has evolved customs which have justified themselves in practice. In all such instances the development of habits serves freedom. The danger lurks when habits are established in reference to matters where freedom of choice is all important. For this reason individualists have often warned that the only habit to form is the habit to form no habit.

In any matter in which freedom is considered of great moment fixation of habit setting up an unalterable reaction amounts really to a limitation of environment. Habit formation can even be used as a means for the suppression of freedom. By bringing about an immediate and fixed response the organism becomes less able to choose, for as a matter of fact it no longer has the possibility of several reactions. When the series of habits acquired was originally contrived with little consideration of the person in whom the habit is later fixed and the process is calculated to further the interests of those who implant them, habit formation becomes indoctrination. Indoctrination limits freedom by closing the imagination to any but the ideas which have been indoctrinated. When one comes under the influence of only one language, one literature, one church or one school system, the tendency in a sense is toward indoctrination. A good illustration is the parochial school which takes all the child's time, sets up definite ideas as exclusively the true ones, and prevents the child from coming under other influences than its own. Similar, too, may be the effect of state control of the public schools, although in a different direction. If the public school demands practically all of the child's time, education can avoid becoming indoctrination only when the diversity and richness of the curriculum matches with the uniqueness of each child's nature.

An understanding of the organic nature of the individual would make us insist that greater diversification of possibilities to react to can alone lead to freedom. Since the organism cannot react to nothingness, it is only by offering additional ways of doing things that liberation from the necessity of reacting in one way can come. The mediæval serf, whose slavery depended upon the fact that he was bound to the land, would not have received freedom if land were, so to speak, abolished; only by being permitted to move from place to place, i.e., to be in many lands, could freedom be attained. To be relieved from the hardship that expression imposes upon thought, it would be necessary not to be ignorant of all language, but to know more of the languages. To be a free thinker it is necessary to understand and at least in a sense believe in many religions, not to be ignorant and skeptical of all. Especially if we have in mind any high degree of individual uniqueness, as we have in our conception of the self-conscious individual, we must assume an environment with diversified possibilities. Organic uniqueness and dependence upon a diversified environment proceed together. The conception of the individual as an organic entity must immediately lead us to the positive conception of freedom, and to the insistence upon a diversification of environment as well as upon a uniqueness of evaluation. In addition, then, to the necessity of regarding each individual as unique, a second prerequisite of self-determination will be *an environment rich in possibilities of thought and act.*

The term 'organism' includes the ideas of an environment and of a relationship between the organism and the environment. The distinctions, 'organism,' 'environment,' 'reaction,' are mental discriminations; in nature these three are aspects of one unitary process. Any one of the terms must imply the other two, for they are all correlative. It is the interest of the particular discussion that will determine the standpoint from which to view the whole process. In the discussion above, conceiving the process from the point of view of the individual organism, we were led to emphasize the need of each individual organism as unique. Taking the environmental attitude, it was shown that diversity of possibilities is necessary if the organism is to have freedom to react. Our third criterion will be developed by examining the question from the point of view of the relating principle, the interdependence of organism and environment.

Socialization

The first standard of democracy stressed the importance of the realization of the uniqueness of each individual as basic to any meaningful conception of value. This argument will have been completely misunderstood, however, if the idea of uniqueness has been confused with that of disparateness. Each moment in a lifetime is a unique experience, but time would be inconceivable if the moment were regarded as separate and unrelated to the preceding and succeeding moments. Each act and each thought, though unique, has its background and its references, its 'causes' and 'results.' So, too, uniqueness of the individual does not imply a separation from, and lack of relation to, other things and men. Quite the contrary. Uniqueness depends upon the peculiar organization of relationships, and no great degree of uniqueness can exist without a corresponding complexity of organization which of course involves a multiplicity and complexity of relationships. Organic uniqueness and dependence upon a diversified environment must proceed *pari passu* because they are in fact the same things. The individuality of a man consists in the relationship that he bears to the world; it is the world from his point of view.

Man's dependence is upon the whole of Nature—things, ideas and persons. The individual can exist neither physically nor as the figment of a conception without dependence in some measure on one or all of these three aspects of the environment. As his individuality develops, the dependence upon ideas and persons becomes of more significant importance. In so far as any individual at any moment recalls the relevant happenings, and in degree that he realizes in true measure the dependencies upon which his own individuality rests, he will be true to his own nature. Man does not live by bread alone; a complexity of social and spiritual relationships is necessary for his welfare. To understand that all relationships have significances wider than the present application and to assume the responsibility that they imply, is a part of democracy. Nothing in the world that we can discover is irrelevant to our existence, and nothing that we do or neglect to do can fail to influence ourselves and the world. *The extent to which the individual realizes his many interdependences* becomes the third criterion of democracy.

Democratic thought has in view especially our relations to other persons. A natural view of things unbiased by anthropomorphism, as we have noted earlier in this chapter, would regard all nature as sacred and all beings as ends in themselves. The democratic view, accepting this outlook, nevertheless assumes the prior importance of human life and insists on the sanctity of each person as the highest good. So also here, logically insisting on the importance of all dependencies, the crucial interest of the democratic aspiration turns about mankind and on the relation of men to each other.

Our first doctrine of the sacredness of each unique personality already implies that each man must respect the personality of the other. If a conflict of interest ensues, an adjustment is necessary which will consider in equal measure all concerned, and which will avoid the exploitation of the one at the expense of the other. In addition to this, our concept of interdependence demands from the individual the responsibility to maintain those social relations and organizations upon which his welfare rests. To know that every action of his has reference to other persons and to consider the effect of his activities upon the social institutions is a duty which he must fulfill not only by virtue of the doctrine of the inviolability of all persons, but also because natural conditions make him dependent upon social life for his very existence.

It will be realized from this emphasis placed upon socialization that the need of unique evaluation does not imply selfishness or unbridled individualism. Undoubtedly danger lurks in the over-emphasis of either of the two factors to the exclusion of the other—democracy is a balance of forces. We are entering upon a period in which socialization will for the time being be considered the more important factor in many plans of economic and political life. The change is from an emphasis upon rights to emphasis upon duties. Nor are we yet ripe for that exalted conception of 'mutual aid' implied in the theory of Anarchy. Evidently since all individuals have not accepted the responsibility of *noblesse oblige* involved in the democratic doctrine it will be necessary to have means of restraint to use against those who would attempt to violate the personalities of others. Furthermore, the relations upon which we are dependent are far from being obvious. It has taken hundreds of generations of human living to fully realize many of them and it may take a lifetime to rediscover them. Respect for social institutions and obedience to them until more adequate ones can be established will follow as a corollary from a realization of the individual's dependence upon social life. Here education has an important function in making explicit the significance and deep roots of social institutions. Moreover, since the dependencies of man upon other men and upon nature are not of a definite and limited number but are really infinite, always multiplying in number and increasing in complexity, the social relation cannot be confined only to adjustment to existing institutions and traditions. Education has the additional function of extending the social idea in new directions to apply to wider and more complex societies and to find embodiment in new and more highly developed institutions. The process of socialization is never complete. In no sense is the individual to be conceived of as disparate, a law unto himself, self-sustaining and self-sufficient; at every point it will be seen that he must reckon with other forces and with other men, and with his future as well.

The unification of the individual with the World is an abiding thought in philosophy and religion. The longing to become merged with the All, to save oneself from the loneliness of a dissociated life, is at the heart of the notion of Salvation. The quest of life is a quest for the unification of the individual soul with the soul of the world. Born from the World, we are yet, so to speak, bound by an umbilical cord from the very center of our being to the womb of Mother Earth and we dare not break the bond without cutting off the sustenance of the nourishing mother.

Differentiation, a separating from the total matrix, never means an absolute separation from the body. It is as if with every diversification the bond that unifies us with earth undergoes a subdivision; a new finely spun thread appears with each differentiation. Never is the individual in reality cut off from the world from which he was born. The higher the differentiation, the more numerous are the bonds, the more finely spun, the more closely interwoven; they cannot be neglected or broken without hurt to the being. The full development of our personality depends upon retaining these bonds of union between our differentiated self and the Universe.

Our new outlook has not suppressed the deep human longing for unification with the world; but the conception of what constitutes union has been transformed. In the philosophies of the East the unification is to be attained by merging again into the Infinite from which we have sprung. Through a loss of consciousness we are to be unified again with the world of the unconscious. The whole work of evolution is to be undone and the self is to lapse again into an undifferentiated state of unconsciousness. In accordance with our own conception a complete life is possible neither when the bonds are broken nor when they are merged into indiscrimination, but only when the Individual becomes conscious of the myriad relationships which join him with the World. The union of the self with the World cannot be attained by falling back into the undifferentiated state, by going back into the womb, as it were. Once born we must continue to grow, that is, to become differentiated. Only one process can save us. We must become *conscious* of the bonds that hold us to the world; see clearly every relationship; discover more and more how we are bound to the world. Our own notion of evolution teaches us that the line of development is not in the attainment of homogeneous undifferentiation, but of integrated diversifications; not in a falling back to unconsciousness, but in the attainment of self-consciousness. The progress of our salvation is in the continued differentiation of each self and in the progressive, conscious realization of the bonds of union that the differentiating self bears to the rest of the world.

To regard each individual as an end in himself; to know that he is a growing organism and that the goal of his Being is already inherent in his instinctive endowment; to understand that as he grows he becomes more differentiated from his fellows and yet more dependent upon them; to realize that consciousness of himself and of his relationships to the world is what keeps him whole—all these are of the democratic doctrine which looks for the goal of the world not in the fulfillment of any objective law or principle, but within man himself to the fulfillment of his Personality.

In the endeavor to develop Personality three conditions must be held in mind:

1. That each unique individual be regarded as the point of reference for value;

2. That the environment presents a diversity of possibilities accessible to all;

3. That there be a consciousness on the part of the individual of his dependence upon the intricate series of natural and social relationships upon which his individuality rests.

Since these three conditions may exist in an infinite variety of degrees, we must realize that democracy is no one definite state but a tendency of development. We can, therefore, speak of democracy only in comparative terms. It is the direction of the movement which will define any condition as democratic or not. Where there is a *progressive consideration of uniqueness, a multiplicity of diverse possibilities, a growing consciousness of man's interdependence*—there does democracy exist.

CHAPTER II

Theories of Ethnic Adjustment

. . . .

II

The 'Americanization' Theory

. . . . . .

Apart from the dubious assumption of the superiority of one race over another, whatever evidence we have should utterly refute the idea that knowing a man's race you could know very much about his mental and moral characteristics. The variability amongst individuals of the same race and the overlapping of one race with another are so great in the measurement of any trait in original nature, that 'race' becomes a useless criterion for determining an individual's place on any scale that one might choose to measure. The one fact of racial origin (at any rate, with reference to all white races) means nothing. This is the scientific testimony which together with a democratic faith in the value of all human personalities might have led to a more tolerant attitude. Such wholesale condemnation runs counter current to the first requisite condition of democracy, that the unique make-up of individuals be taken into consideration.

It is erroneous to fly to the conclusion that the inferiorities and evils when they do exist are caused by the 'race' of the immigrant. What is more probable is that social and governmental conditions in other lands are to be blamed. In that case our theory of amelioration would certainly be affected. Indeed, it is also possible that some measure of the evils of crowded tenements and poor sanitation are to be traced to our own failure to deal adequately with the problem and perhaps even to our desire to exploit the immigrant. To throw the entire blame on the vague 'race' of the immigrant often serves merely to obscure the real causes and to hinder an adequate solution. It tends to shift attention from the true evils involved and from the reforms really required. Sociological theorists are only too often innocent supporters of what are in actuality the prejudices and interests of the classes.

America, it should be remembered, does not exist for the benefit of any one class of persons, whether we consider the grouping economic, political, or racial. The idea that the predominating stock of the inhabitants of the United States is Anglo-Saxon is a myth. The composite American is a multiform hyphenate: Scotch-Irish-English-German-Polish-Jewish-Italian-Russian, etc., etc. All of these are represented in fair numbers in the new "Galilee of the Nations." To conceive of America as belonging exclusively to one race, because priority of habitation has given it a divine right to possession of the land, is a notion contrary to democracy. Indeed, this minority, due to its priority and to the undoubted excellence of native gifts, has stamped its culture ineffaceably upon American life, its language, its political organization and spiritual aspirations. The influence of this group outweighs, justly, that to which its numerical strength would entitle it. To say, however, that American institutions and forms of life have once for all been fixed by the fathers of our country and that the newcomers, the majority, must mould themselves into these forms, is itself contradictory to the principle of freedom upon which these forms are built and of which they are but a particular and perhaps inadequate expression. Our newcomers had no voice in the formation of these institutions, and to force them upon the immigrant without regard to his consent and without permitting his own personality to modify them in the least is an arbitrariness suggestive of tyranny rather than democracy. Many of these foreigners fleeing from religious, cultural, and political oppression come to America to seek the spiritual freedom which the constitution grants but which an interpretation in accordance with this line of thought completely abrogates. Of what significance is the opportunity of economic advancement, if it must be bought at the price of suppression of individuality? Even under the conditions of Russian persecution the Jew was permitted to speak his own language and to live in many senses an independent cultural life. But if a conception of Americanism as here outlined is to be followed, such rights would be taken from him, in this country whose distinct and peculiar excellence lies in its gift of freedom. The result of such a program of Americanization is a tyranny over the beliefs and minds of men worse than the economic and political slavery from which they fled. Those who would put the immigrant into an American straight-jacket may be superficially American in that they attempt to adjust to the established forms of American life; they are not true to the fundamental spirit of American life and American institutions, which is to liberate and not to suppress the individuality of men.

Thus again this conception of Americanization fundamentally transgresses the first doctrine of democracy, that the unique individual must be taken into account in considering the end of his own development and the standard of his own good. The theory under discussion implies the unquestionable superiority of one group, of the Anglo-Saxon race and culture, and proceeds to judge the value of the other groups by their approximation to this standard. There is no question here regarding the desirability of institutions and conceptions objectively demonstrable to be beneficial to the generality of men. Cleanliness and righteousness must be enforced because they are universally admitted to be good, not because they are peculiarly Anglo-Saxon virtues. Obedience to these cannot be regarded as an external criterion, for they serve for the food of all men. Perhaps it is even necessary in practice to go a little further and to maintain—although this may not be altogether rationally defensible—that priority of occupation does give a certain preference to the established group apart from or in addition to any inherent excellence. But the tendency to believe that America exists solely and exclusively for the type of life represented by one particular group, must be challenged. The assumption of total and exclusive superiority on the part of one group amounts to the imposition of an external standard which does not reckon with those concerned and savors of a theocratic or of an aristocratic state rather than of a democratic one. No room is left for taking the nature and personality of the immigrant into consideration; his physical characteristics, his individuality, his ideals and culture are contemptuously ignored as unworthy of consideration. The most profound feeling in American tradition is violated, the fundamental intuition upon which American institutions and political organizations are based, namely, *a decent respect for the worth of personalities which are not altogether like ours and a sincere faith in their potentialities.*

But not even in a democracy, one might say, are all individuals to be tolerated and every inclination permitted to have its way. Perhaps the tenor of the argument even thus far will carry the conviction that no individualistic position is proposed here and more will be said later explicitly on this question. The point urged, however, is that no neglect of interests or suppression of personalities is permissible in a democracy without some definite demonstration of the evil effects. Even criminals cannot be convicted without due process of law and in accordance with democratic notions they are to be considered innocent until proved guilty. In the face of the fact that the United States is richer, more powerful, more highly cultured, and its moral outlook as lofty as it was in the days of the fathers of our country in spite of a continuous stream of immigration, positive evidence would, be needed to prove that our fundamental institutions are being threatened. Problems have been created; but who can say that even these problems have not within them the seed of a contribution? The evil result is often due to the lack of understanding in meeting the new problem presented rather than to something inherent in the situation. The difference between the democratic attitude and the autocratic one would be just this: *the democratic attitude would have faith in the worth of a personality until positive proof of its inferiority were presented: the autocratic would condemn without proof. What is America if not liberal and generous? Not that which is the least, but that which is the most compatible with its integrity must be done.*

III

Americanization as Likemindedness

The emphasis on homogeneity which characterizes the Americanization theories undoubtedly finds justification in the need for national unity. If the citizens of the state are to act upon their affairs with reference to each other's interests and for the common good of the whole community, a certain degree of likemindedness must undoubtedly exist among them. Without common interests crystallized into common purposes, without the means of communicating these purposes and the relevant facts and ideas through a common language, without opportunity for general discussion of common problems and for participation in common tasks the democratic ideal of government by the people remains impossible of attainment. More than this the nation may fall prey to dissension from within and present a weakened front to inimical forces from without. Apart from the cultivating and humanizing influence that the inculcation of any great tradition may have, Americanization finds its irrefutable defense in the need of likemindedness to safeguard the very existence of the state.

However proper in its motives the current 'Americanization' theory with its connotation of "breaking up communities," of "ironing out differences," of casting the immigrant into the mould of a standardized American is false in effect, not only because it does not give consideration to the personality of the immigrant, not only because its method is psychologically indefensible, but especially because it fails to grasp adequately the basic principle of its own purpose, that of creating likemindedness. Its conception of likemindedness is superficial and primitive. It is the application of a primitive idea of what 'like' means to a complex modern social situation that makes the 'Americanization' theory, as ordinarily understood and advocated, so tragically erroneous.

The hiatus between the means applied and the results expected, which is so striking to the civilized person when he observes the manipulations of magic among primitive men, in all likelihood does not at all disturb the savage. No feeling of a gap is present in his mental reaction toward these ceremonies. According to his mental categories likeness of sense and emotional appeal gives the impression of complete similarity, and similarity somehow has a causative potency. To make an effigy of the enemy and stick daggers into it, is felt to be 'like' doing the real thing, and is accompanied by a feeling of satisfaction and accomplishment. A discriminating intellect, intent upon the practical outcome, would not feel such an action as relevant to or 'like' the real task. When it seems apparent even to the primitive mind that the two actions are not identical, there is attributed to the similar action a potency which causes the desired action to occur. It is vaguely felt that the dagger piercing the effigy in some way causes the destruction of the human object of hatred. Similarity to senses and emotions assumes a causative power.

Whenever a new problem occurs in a highly emotional situation, undiscriminating minds will tend to respond in the fashion characteristic of primitive men. Burning and burying the Kaiser in effigy undoubtedly gave those who participated in such ceremonies a feeling of satisfaction, as if they had really accomplished something. What is satisfying to the senses and the emotions tends to be totally satisfying even when the rational end of the action is not fulfilled. Naturally such emotional and sensory responses often prevent the attention from centering itself upon the real work to be done.

The conception of likemindedness underlying the current 'Americanization' theory partakes of the primitive notion that 'like' means similar to senses and emotions and that it implies causative potency. The attention centres upon outward conformity, which is conceived as likemindedness and as being productive of unity. Men are thought of as being alike when they look alike, when they dress alike, when they speak the same language, and these external similarities seem to be considered sufficient for bringing about an inner national unity. Differences in manner, speech and dress have a disturbing effect upon the attention, and if only these distinctions could be eliminated, it is felt, what harmony there would be! Hence the tremendous anxiety to have the races fuse, to do away with dissimilar customs, to abolish foreign languages. If all Americans could be made to seem alike, unity would be assured. Similarity will bring about unity somehow, even if in itself it is not unity.

This desire for conformity, an emotional response in a situation which is felt as dangerous, is increased further by the apprehension of public opinion. It is good to be able to *demonstrate* Americanization. Directors of social settlements and principals of schools are anxious to be able to *show* that those in their charge are American. To permit or promote differences is not quite safe; they may imply divergencies not in harmony with a one hundred per cent patriotism. To level down to an accepted standard which everyone can recognize and no one question is the easiest and the most practical plan.

There is a third force, perhaps, in addition to a primitive psychology and the apprehension of public opinion, that tends to stress the importance of conformity, namely the American aptitude for standardization. Machinery has been standardized; clothes, food, school buildings, handwriting have all been standardized. Why not standardize personalities? And educational thought forthwith busies itself with the standard American, to be produced with the minimum of effort and most quickly by the appropriate educational machinery.

A conception of likemindedness which identifies it with conformity is both inadequate and erroneous. It permits outward resemblances to hide inward disunities; it crushes inner unities for the sake of outward conformities. In accordance with such a notion the unscrupulous politician and the exploiter of the social good may be considered the best Americans, and the foreign-tongued social reformer, even were both his theory and practiced plan valid, would tend to be considered un-American.

A more adequate conception of a true Americanization policy will appear if we scrutinize somewhat more carefully the word 'likemindedness.' 'Like,' if it is to mean anything, must signify not a vague general resemblance, but similarity in reference to the specific interest. Sticking daggers into an effigy is not 'like' killing the man, because in reference to the essential purpose there is no resemblance. Were we interested in race likeness, language likeness, or dress likeness the current Americanization notion might satisfy. But what we are interested in is *likemindedness*.

The word 'mindedness' implies a likeness not alone in reference to means. Mind signifies purposeful action, and the term 'likemindedness' when used as a justification of Americanism must direct itself to a unity of social aims, beyond all else. In so far as likemindedness requires conformities in manner and language as prerequisites, it will be necessary to insist on these. But sheer destruction of divergencies without reference to the ultimate purpose cannot be defended on grounds of 'likemindedness.' What the promotion of unity implies is an emphasis upon the deep-lying purposes of American tradition rather than an exclusive attention upon its instruments or upon the negative task of the elimination of possible disturbances.

Americanization is a positive task, not a negative one. *Forgetting* other languages and other traditions, *destruction* of other spiritual allegiances is not an essential part of it, or if it is truly seen any part of it at all. Americanization is a constructive work of developing knowledge, ideas, social attitudes; conceptions of law, order, government; interpretations of duty, freedom and the meaning of life. It implies above all the creation of a psychological attitude of willingness to serve the nation rather than the self, the family, the class, or the group exclusively. How inadequate is that notion which identifies training for citizenship with 'coaching' on the answers to questions which will be asked of the applicant for citizen papers! How meagre is the plan which looks only to conformities in dress and speech. But even more objectionable is the current 'Americanization' theory, which regards the uprooting of foreign tradition as a necessary antecedent to true assimilation. If Americanism has to do with social ideals, is it not quite possible that it will have kinship with other traditions? May not understanding of another tradition be an aid rather than a hindrance?

A little thought would reveal that not only is there a possibility of common elements in two traditions: there is rather a necessity. Any social tradition which has lived for some time embodies institutions, customs, ideas which promote the living together of men. These may have reference to local conditions, to particular periods, to certain types of men. But it would argue a disparateness which is untenable in human affairs, to maintain that all of these are sectional and particularistic and that there are not some which embody elements of the universal. With the length of a tradition and with the breadth of its experience, the chances for possibility of wide application become greatly increased. Undoubtedly there will be found elements in the European tradition which can be of service in the upbuilding of American life. For Americanism itself is not exclusive and sectarian; its ends are broadly human. A sympathetic and constructively minded statesman or educator with insight into the nature of social tradition would immediately recognize that every foreign system has within it possibilities of interpretation in terms of American life. The most stupid thing in the 'Americanization' program is the failure to recognize that the morality, folkways, ideas and aspirations of the immigrant groups could be utilized for the development of true Americans out of immigrants.

With contemptuous neglect, often with direct opposition, the current 'Americanization' theory has tended to break down deep-laid traditional social attitudes of respect for family, for kin and for the ethnic community; for the ideas of duty, service and self-restraint that such loyalties involve. The public school system has not succeeded in implanting equally deep-rooted conceptions of service; it has not realized how interwoven with the integrity of the family, and of the "consciousness-of-kind" groups, is the loyalty to the state and to society as a whole. The assumption was that breaking down a loyalty of seemingly smaller range leads of itself to a wider loyalty. It does not, necessarily. More often it leads to license and to individualism in the bad sense of that word. The notorious increase of criminality in the American-born second generation is due to the breach made in the social tradition of the family. Very often the foreign system of traditional morality breaks down not because it is inferior in aspiration but because it cannot adapt itself to apply to the new conditions. In such cases it should be the policy to reinterpret and apply in reference to the new conditions, not to destroy it or to permit it to disintegrate in the transition from one environment to another. Once morality and idealism have been implanted these attitudes may be transferred from one social situation to another much more easily than they can be developed altogether anew. Much of the lofty idealism and exalted loyalty among Americans of foreign near-ancestry are attitudes transferred from their ethnic tradition to the new life. It is possible to speak of justice, duty, service and loyalty, of law, order and government in other languages than English. Yet too often does the 'Americanization' theory imply that righteousness is Anglo-Saxon exclusively and that foreign languages ought therefore not to be tolerated. If the concept of likemindedness be carefully borne in mind it must lead to the realization that Americanization will be served very often by a conservation of social ideals even when they are foreign rather than by a destruction of them.

If we turn our attention from the objective aspect—ideas, aspirations, purposes—implied in likemindedness to the inner personal organic common feeling connoted in the phrase, "to be minded alike," the need for a sympathetic attitude toward the foreigner again becomes clear. The immigrant must be made to feel American; it is not sufficient that he strive in an objective way or mechanically for ends which can be identified as American. For it is such whole-hearted emotional identification with the body of citizens which is at the basis of a lasting allegiance. Now the current 'Americanization' theory, which contemptuously places the immigrant outside of the group and gives him a share in the people's heritage only when he diverts himself of his most significant characteristics, is not calculated to promote that feeling of common ownership and responsibility which is the *sine qua non* of the community spirit. How can the immigrant feel himself part of the people when those who are recognizedly of the people place him outside? Such a course must drive the self-respecting among the immigrants to a heightened self-consciousness which divides his group, in heart, from the American people. This attitude taken towards the immigrant acts like anti-Semitism toward the Jew, impressing upon him a feeling of separateness from the general body of citizens.

The more the immigrant is permitted to retain and to develop his own type of life, when these are not detrimental to the general good, the more likely will he be drawn to feel that this really is his country. The splendid loyalty that immigrants have shown toward America and their heartfelt reverence for the new Promised Land are the results of no 'Americanization' program, but of living under institutions which by their very nature permitted economic advance, educational opportunities, and individual freedom in a degree unknown to them in the lands of their birth. It is the excellence of American tradition working indirectly and spontaneously which Americanizes, not the direct application of strict methods. The general work of the public schools, giving the individual a better start in life, permitting him to make more out of himself, has in all likelihood done more for the inculcation of a desire to maintain these institutions than any direct teaching could have done. High-handed artificial methods negate the natural effect of democratic American life which is to identify the good of the individual with the good of the state. If the immigrant is to attain to a whole-hearted allegiance and undivided loyalty to America, he must be regarded as kin with the other citizens, i.e., as a man whose personality must be respected, not as an inferior being whose individuality must be obliterated.

In yet a third way can the term 'likemindedness' help to a better conception of what proper assimilation means, namely through a consideration of the educational method that a developing mind implies. In the development of mind, it is necessary to start with the present mental situation, with the apperceptive mass of ideas, interests and associations. In general education it is the pupil that furnishes the method; in the Americanization of the foreigner, the latter is the starting point. The teacher must understand the tradition and past experiences of the immigrant if he is really to develop his mind. He cannot neglect these and get his own thought across. The process, too, requires patience, and will be slow and developmental rather than hasty and forced. The terms 'break up' and 'iron out' should be expunged from the vocabulary of assimilation. These are not words which are congruous with the ideas of growth, implied in the living mind. They savor of the methods of Russification that used to be practiced by Russia and of Prussianism that used to be practiced by Germany, rather than of the technique of democracy in education. Were Americanism conceivable as a completed doctrine, handed down through generations by authoritative interpreters, it would be easier to think of Americanization as conformity to a certain fixed type or standard. But, since the democratic faith looks upon the living forces in human nature as primary and respects personality above all else, standardization of men must be recognized as the cardinal sin.

Weighed in the balance of our first and fundamental criterion of democracy—respect for personality—the 'Americanization' theory must be found wanting. The tendency to interpret Americanism as the culture of one definite race, something well established to which the newcomers must completely conform, falls into the category of an absolutistic conception which assumes beforehand what is good without relation to the persons affected. By tacitly, if not expressly, denying the right of the immigrant to modify and contribute to the development of Americanism, the 'Americanization' theory violates that notion which is the quintessence of democracy, namely that the person involved must be considered as the end. Neither is the second criterion of democracy—a diversity in the environment—fulfilled by the 'Americanization' theory. It idealizes a fixed type of culture as against a diversified culture enriched by the tradition of many peoples. By the elimination of foreign ideas it would indoctrinate the tenets of a nationalistic cult. True liberty is served by the enrichment of possibilities, not by the establishment of uniformity. Lastly the conception of socialization in the 'Americanization' theory is faulty. It breaks down loyalty to the immediate family and to the cultural institutions—language, customs, etc., with which it is affiliated. It fails to realize that much of what the man's character is depends upon the integrity of these relations. To cap the climax, it fails in relation to the problem of affiliating with the new social life. Its stress is so negative, constantly emphasizing the danger of the old associations, that too little attention is given to the positive task—and a task it is—of building up on a firm and profound basis the culture of the new land.

Thus the public school graduate grows up to know that he must despise his parents with their poor knowledge of English, that he must be thoroughly conversant with the batting averages, and that he must possess a large quantity of Americanism—100 per cent at least! But how shall he know the profound quality of America? Whether from the point of view of democracy (which may be considered idealistic) or from the point of view of efficiency, the current 'Americanization' theory fails to qualify. Neither reason nor praticality can justify it. It can be explained only by an emotional hysteria which bids us do *something*, by the superficial intelligence which confuses the uniform with the unified, by the will to mastery which sometimes makes us brutally intolerant. . . .

CHAPTER III

The Community Theory

The 'Community' theory which is proposed as the constructive suggestion is in reality the formulation of a process already shaping itself among some of our immigrant groups as a result of the confluence of the ethnic will to live with the conditions of American life. To the writer the suggestion has come from the experience of the Jewish group; and, although there are many indications of this scheme of organization among other immigrant nationalities, the Jews have undoubtedly gone furthest in its development. In fact, it may be regarded as the response of the Jewish group to the problem of adjustment. While many among the Jews would differ with our proposal or with some of its features, the tendency of Jewish institutional development would indicate that the 'Community' theory is the acceptable mode of adjustment for the Jewish group as an ethnic entity. Confidence in the validity of this plan should be the greater because it represents the resultant of many intricate social forces working slowly upon each other under democratic conditions. It will be apt to escape the basic unsoundness of an *a priori* plan built upon the interest of certain classes, the undiscerning emotionalism misunderstood as patriotism or the romantic imagination of sociological litterateurs. The formulation presented below comes after the process and is an attempt to build a consistent theory out of dissociated methods to the end that the further course of adjustment may be guided more directly in line with the ideal. Drawn from Jewish life, it will undoubtedly apply most closely to Jewish life. Nevertheless, it is hoped that the Jewish experience may form the basis of a theory of adjustment which will be applicable to all groups which desire to maintain their ethnic identity in the conditions of democratic life in America.

Like the 'Federation of Nationalities' theory, our position insists on the value of the ethnic group as a permanent asset in American life. The 'Community' theory differs from the 'Americanization' and 'Melting Pot' theories in that it refuses to set up as an ideal such a fusion as will lead to the obliteration of all ethnic distinctions. Furthermore, it regards a rich social life as necessary for the development and expression of the type of culture represented by the foreign ethnic group. There is, however, a fundamental difference in what is conceived to be the ultimate sanction for maintaining the identity of the foreign ethnic group. In the 'Federation of Nationalities' theory the assumed identity of race is pivotal; the argument is made to rest primarily upon the proposition that "we cannot change our grandfathers." The 'Community' theory, on the other hand, would make the history of the ethnic group its æsthetic, cultural and religious inheritance, its national self-consciousness the basic factor. This change of emphasis from race to culture brings with it a whole series of implications rising from the fact that culture is psychical, must be acquired through some educational process, and is not inherited in the natural event of being born. The 'Community' theory is to be understood as an analysis of what is implied for the theory of adjustment by considering culture as central in the life of the ethnos. Community of culture possible of demonstration becomes the ground for perpetuation of the group, rather than an identity of race, questionable in fact and dubious in significance. . . .

Summary

The 'Community' theory endeavors to meet all the justifiable considerations presented in each of the other proposals. It seeks especially to avoid such a scheme of adjustment as would tend to force the individual to accept one solution as against another. It leaves all the forces working; they are to decide what the future is to be. Both the 'Americanization' and 'Federation of Nationalities' theories presume too much to 'fix' conditions; the one would make the citizen conform to the nature of a mythical Anglo-Saxon, and the other to harmonize with the soul assumed to reside in the ethnos. The contention of the 'Community' theory is that neither of these facts can so easily be taken for granted, and urges that all forces be given a just opportunity to exert their influence. If these conditions are granted and the ethnic group perpetuates itself, only then does it become justified to the reason. On the other hand, if the ethnic group finally disintegrates, the 'Community' theory really resolves itself into the 'Melting Pot' theory, accomplishing the fusion without the evils of hasty assimilation. Its essential merit is that it rejects the doctrine of predestination; it conceives the life of the individual to be formed not in accordance with some preconceived theory but as a result of the interaction of his own nature with the richest environment. In this it satisfies the basic notion of democracy that the individual must be left free to develop through forces selected by the laws of his own nature, not moulded by factors determined upon by others either in the interest of themselves or in accordance with an assumed good.

So, too, a comparison with our three criteria, the unique individual, enrichment of environment, and dependence upon social institutions, finds the 'Community' theory the most adequate solution. It provides in greatest measure for conceiving the individual as creator of and participant in the culture to be evolved, and allows at the same time for a great degree of individual diversification. It strives for a culture enriched by the contributions from many cultures and thus multiplies the possibilities of varied experience. It intensifies the idea of duty and responsibility to social life and institutions by adding the ethnic group and all the significant institutions connected with its history to the burden of civilization that each developed citizen must bear. It offers the greatest opportunity for the creation of a free, rich and lofty Personality.

SELECTED BIBLIOGRAPHY

J. Addams, *Democracy and Social Ethics* (1902).

R. S. Baker and W. E. Dodd (ed.), *Public Papers of Woodrow Wilson: War and Peace* (2 vols., 1927).

I. B. Berkson, *Theories of Americanization* (1920).

J. H. Clarke, *America and World Peace* (1925).

J. Dewey, *The Public and its Problems* (1927).

R. Fosdick, *The Old Savage in the New Civilization* (1929).

H. F. Fraser, *Foreign Trade and World Politics* (1926).

J. M. Jacobson, "The Right to Survive," *The Reflex* 5: 40–46, January, 1930.

H. Kallen, *Culture and Democracy in the United States* (1924).

C. K. Leith, *World Minerals and World Politics* (1931).

W. Lippmann, *Public Opinion* (1927).
    Phantom Public (1925).

H. C. Lodge, *The Senate and the League of Nations* (1925).

H. L. Mencken, *Notes on Democracy* (1926).

R. T. Moon, *Imperialism and World Politics* (1926).

C. C. Morrison, *The Outlawry of War* (1927).

J. H. Randall, *A World Community* (1930).

J. T. Shotwell, *War as an Instrument of National Policy and its Renunciation in the Pact of Paris* (1929).

INDEX

Abolitionists, 319–324, 327, 329–333, 350–354, 635

Adair v. U. S., 514, 550

Adams, H. C., 517, 525, 531–533, 636

Adams, J., 246, 411
  on the American Revolution, 94, 96, 97–99, 113–125
  attitude on democracy, 186–188, 191–199
  attitude on aristocracy, 187–188, 192–194
  on theory of checks and balances, 188–189
  attack upon by J. Taylor, 252–253, 283

Adams, S., 95, 102–103, 164

Adamson Act, 517

Adkins v. Children's Hospital, 515–516, 549–554

Agrarian-commercial conflict,
  during American Revolution, 92–93
  during post-Revolutionary period, 165–168
  during Jeffersonian period, 244–245
  during Jacksonian period, 254–257
  and the slavery controversy, 327–329
  and particularism, 408, 425, 426
  in contemporary politics, 497–498, 505, 517

Alien and Sedition Acts, 246, 327, 411

Amendment of Constitution, difficulty of, 175

American Economic Association, 531

American Revolution,
  causes of, 88–93
  political theory of, 94–106

Americanization, theories of,
  Anglo-Americanization, 639–640, 642–643
  attack upon Anglo-Americanization, 643–644, 706–714
  "melting-pot" theory, 645–646
  cultural pluralism, 646–647, 714–716

Anti-Federalists, 178–179, 234–243

Anti-Masonic Party, 259

Anti-slavery arguments,
  of radical abolitionists, 319–324, 329–333, 350–354
  of free-soil group, 333–335, 376–384
  of W. E. Channing, 335–341, 354–366
  of F. Wayland, 335–340, 366–376

Anti-slavery movement, 325–329, 333–334

Antin, M., 645

Aristocracy, theories of,
  of the Puritans, 5, 9–10, 35–39
  of A. Hamilton, 170
  of J. Adams, 186–188, 192–194
  attack upon by J. Taylor, 252–253, 283–297
  pro-slavery theories on, 341–342, 346–347, 347–349, 385–386, 387–390, 394–395, 395–397, 399–407
  recent theories of, *see* H. Spencer, W. G. Sumner, H. L. Mencken

Articles of Confederation, 164, 167, 175, 177, 178, 218, 219, 223, 415, 416, 418, 432, 459, 468, 473

Bellamy, E., 525, 528–530, 539, 562–572

Berkson, I. B., 641–642, 643–644, 646, 699–716

Bill of Rights,
  in early state constitutions, 16, 110–111
  in federal Constitution, 178, 235–237

Blackstone, W., 100, 125, 126, 132

Bluntschli, J. K., 434, 489

Borah, W. E., 611, 665

Boucher, J., 107–109, 153–162

Bourne, R., 643

Brandeis, L. D., 539, 540–541

Brigham, C. C., 639

Briscoe v. The Commonwealth's Bank of the State of Kentucky, 261

Brook Farm, 262

Brooks, V. W., 643, 647

Brownson, O. A., 434

Bryan, W. J., 518, 630

Burgess, J. W., 434–435, 489–496, 512–513

Burke, E., 95

Butler, N. M., 523

Calhoun, J. C.,
  on slavery, 341, 342, 343, 346, 348, 350, 384–386
  on state sovereignty, 414–417, 419, 420–425, 427, 431–432, 433, 435, 437–449, 479, 487
  on concurrent majority, 420–425, 443–449

Calvin, J., 6, 23
  political theories of, 6–8, 11–12, 23–31
  on predestination, 6–7, 23–26
  on spiritual aristocracy, 7
  on civil government, 11–12, 26–31

Campbell, J., 346

717

Cardozo, B. N., 539
Channing, W. E., 262, 264–266, 329, 334, 335–341, 354–366, 641
Charles River Bridge Case, 261, 308–310
Checks and balances,
  in early state constitutions, 111–112
  in federal Constitution, 174–175
  J. Adams on, 188–189
  The Federalist on, 183–186, 220–228
Cherokee Nation v. Georgia, 412
Chisholm v. Georgia, 410
Church and state,
  in the Puritan colonies, 8–13, 32–39, 59–61
  Roger Williams on, 18–19, 72–87
  during the Revolutionary period, 90–91, 112
City of N. Y. v. Miln, 260–261
Clarke, J. B., 505
Clarke, J. H., 608–610
Clayton Act, 517, 519
Compromises in the Constitution, 169
Concurrent majority theory of Calhoun, 421–425, 443–449
Confession of Faith, 8
Congregationalism, 20, 22
Constitution of the United States,
  creation of, 173–177, 415–416, 461
  ratification of, 177–179, 209–211, 416–417, 420, 462, 466
  political theory of, 173–177, 417–419
  difficulty of amendment of, 175
  powers granted to central government, 175–177
  interpretation of by J. Story, 466–478
  interpretation of by A. P. Upshur, 417–419, 444–455
  early opposition to, 178–179, 234–243
Constitutional Convention of 1787,
  reasons for, 164–168, 415–417
  attitude of members of, 168–173
  results of, 173–179
  compromises at, 169
  attitude on democracy, 170–173, 203–212
  Randolph plan at, 201–203
  debates of, 200–212
Cooper, T., 344
Coppage v. Kansas, 514, 550
Corruption in politics, 628, 630–631
Cotton, J., 10, 12, 13, 17, 32–39, 70, 76, 80–87
Cotton gin, influence on slavery problem, 325
Cubberley, E. P., 643
Culbertson, W. S., 616
Cultural pluralism, 640–647, 699–716

Dartmouth College v. Woodward, 191
Davis, J., 328, 414–417, 419–420, 427, 459–466
De Bow, J. D. B., 346

Declaration of Independence, 99, 100, 102, 249, 635
  use of in slavery controversy, 330, 334–335, 341, 342, 344, 351, 376, 379–382, 390, 395
  use of in particularistic arguments, 415
Democracy, theories of,
  Puritan theories of, 9, 13–17, 22, 35–39, 61–65
  Roger Williams on, 19–20, 77–78, 86
  during the American Revolution, 99–106, 109–112
  J. Adams on, 186–188, 191–199
  attitude of Constitutional Convention on, 170–174, 203–212
  T. Jefferson on, 246, 248–250, 270–273, 274–282
  during Jacksonian period, 254, 257–260, 301–308
  intellectual defense of, 262–269, 310–324
  and slavery arguments, 340–345, 349–350, 363–366, 384–386, 391–401
  contemporary distrust of, 628–638, 681–698
  H. L. Mencken on, 631, 632–633, 635–637
  cultural pluralism and, 640–647, 699–716
  I. B. Berkson, 641–642, 643–644, 699–716
Dew, F. R., 348, 394
Dewey, J., 628–630, 633, 643
Dickinson, J.,
  on the American Revolution, 94
  speeches at Constitutional Convention, 172–173, 205–206
Disarmament, 610–611, 621–622, 662
Divided sovereignty, theory of, 409–410
Divine right, theory of, 14, 108–109, 157–162
Douglas, S. A., 334, 377–383
Drachsler, L., 646
Dred Scott Case, 334, 377–383
Due process of law, *see* Supreme Court, on social legislation

Eighteenth Amendment, *see* Prohibition
Electoral College, 174, 185, 189, 259, 418
Eleventh Amendment, 410
Ely, R. T., 525, 531
Emerson, R. W., 262–264, 311–319, 641
Eugenists and Nordicism, 639–640

Farm Loan Act, 517, 519
Farmer-Labor Party, 518
Federal Farm Board, 519
Federal Reserve Banks, 517, 519
Federal Trade Commission, 517, 519
Federalism, theory of,
  The Federalist on, 180–182, 213–218, 409
  Particularists on, 418, 449–455

Federalist, The, 167, 179–186, 213–228
  on factions, 180–182, 213–218
  on large republics, 180–182, 213–218
  on private property rights, 182–183, 218–220
  on checks and balances, 183–186, 220–228
  on the legislature, 183–184, 220–221
  on the executive, 185, 221–223
  on the judiciary, 185–186, 223–228
  on divided sovereignty, 409
  interpretation of by J. Story, 469, 474
Fichte, J., 432
Fifth Amendment, 505, 513, 549
Filmer, R., 108, 153
Fisher, S., 433
Fitzhugh, G., 343–344, 348, 350, 387–394
Fletcher v. Peck, 191
Follett, M. P., 641
Fosdick, R. B., 614, 616–617, 618–619
Fourier, C., 262
"Fourteen Points" of W. Wilson, 605, 647, 648–650
Fourteenth Amendment, 497, 505, 513, 540
Franklin, B., 94, 173
Fraser, H. F., 613, 614–615, 617–618
Free silver movement, 497
Free Soil Party, 328, 329, 333, 376
Freedom of contract, 506–511, 513–516, 521–522, 546–554
French Revolution, influence of, 245–246, 326
Freund, E., 541
Frontier, influence of,
  on the American Revolution, 91, 93, 109–110
  on Jeffersonian democracy, 244
  on Jacksonian democracy, 254–257
  passing of, 500, 504
Fugitive Slave Act, 327
Fundamental Orders of Connecticut, 15, 20, 61–65

Garrison, W. L., 327, 329–333, 341, 350–354
Gary, E. H., 511–512
Geography, influence of on political institutions,
  on Puritanism, 8
  on the American Revolution, 88–89
  on Jeffersonian democracy, 244–245
  on Jacksonian democracy, 255–256
George, H., 525, 527–528
Gerry, E., 172, 203, 210
Gibbons v. Ogden, 190
Godwin, W., 262, 264, 354
Gorham, M., 210–211
Government in business, 519–520, 532–533, 537–538
Governors, early powers of, 111–112
  later increase in powers of, 259

Granger movement, 497, 517, 518
Grant, M., 639
Greenback movement, 497, 518

Hamilton, A., 246
  on the American Revolution, 94, 96–97, 100–101, 125–134
  speeches at Constitutional Convention, 170–171, 208–209
  fiscal program of, 179, 244, 245
  The Federalist by, 179, 185–186, 220–228
  attack upon by J. Taylor, 252, 253–254, 283
Hammond, J. H., 346–349
Harding, W. G., 610, 628, 630
Harlan, J. M., 514, 550
Harper, W., 342, 345–346, 349, 394–407
Hartford Convention, 411
Hay, J., 603
Hayne, R. Y., 479, 480, 481
Hegel, G. W. F., 432, 434
Henry, Patrick, 164, 178, 235–239
Hepburn Act, 519, 585
Herring, E. P., 628, 633
Hill, D. J., 511
Hobbes, T., 106, 143
Holmes, O. W., Jr., 539–540
Hooker, T., 17, 20, 65–70
Hoover, H., 513, 610, 638
Hosmer, W., 329
Hudson, M. O., 608, 610
Hughes, C. E., 623–625
Hurd, J. C., 434
Hutchinson, T., 102

Immigration, 639
Imperialism, 346–347 fn., 625–627, 672–681
Implied powers, 190, 421, 458
Income tax, 518
Independence, growth of idea of, 103–104
Individualism, theories of,
  during the American Revolution, 109–110
  during the Jeffersonian period, 249–250, 252, 276
  during the Jacksonian period, 256
  R. W. Emerson on, 263–264, 317–319
  H. D. Thoreau on, 266, 319–324
  W. E. Channing on, 264–266, 361–363
  Walt Whitman on, 267–269
  in contemporary economic thought, 505–516, 519, 521, 546–554
  new social concepts of, 641–642, 699–706
  see also Democracy, Natural rights, *Laissez-faire*
Industrial revolution, 257, 325–326, 500–504, 613
Inheritance tax, 518
Initiative and referendum, 628, 630

Internal improvements, 255–256, 261, 304–305, 308–310
International interdependence, growth of, 602–603, 614–617, 674
Internationalism,
League of Nations, 606–610, 647–659
World Court, 610
disarmament, 610–611
outlawry of war, 610–613, 659–666
international coöperation, 613–619
reaction against, 619–627, 666–681
Interstate Commerce Commission, 517, 520, 585, 589
Isolation, 606, 617, 621, 624, 667, 669

Jackson, A., 254, 256, 259, 260, 301–305, 412, 413
Jacksonian democracy, 254–262, 267, 269, 301–310, 635
James, E. J., 531
Jameson, J. A., 434
Jay, J., 179, 212
Jefferson, T., 165, 189, 244, 246, 341, 411, 414
on post-Revolutionary conditions, 165
on agrarianism, 246–247, 273–274
on natural rights, 249–250, 270–273
on decentralization, 250–251, 280
on *laissez-faire*, 251, 276
on democracy, 248, 249–250, 270–273, 274–282
influence on contemporary thought, 505
Jhering, R. von, 539, 544–545
Judicial review, 174, 175, 185–186, 223–228, 248, 512
J. Marshall on, 189–190, 228–231

Kallen, H. M., 642, 643, 646
Kellogg-Briand treaty, 611, 612, 659, 663–666
Kellor, F., 645
Kent, F., 630, 633, 637
Ku Klux Klan, 640, 693

Labor legislation, 497, 518, 519
Labor movements, 257, 497–498, 517
La Follette, R. M., 517, 518, 535–536, 539, 581–589, 630
Laissez-faire, theories of,
T. Jefferson on, 251, 269, 276
during the Jacksonian period, 256, 269
R. W. Emerson on, 263–264, 317–319
W. E. Channing on, 265
H. D. Thoreau on, 266, 319–320
Walt Whitman on, 268
G. Fitzhugh on, 392–394
L. F. Ward on, 523–525
H. D. Lloyd on, 525–527, 554–562
E. Bellamy on, 528–530, 562–572
H. C. Adams on, 531–533
W. Wilson on, 521, 533–535, 577–581
R. M. La Follette on, 535–536, 581–589

Laissez-faire, theories of—*Continued*
N. Thomas on, 536–538
O. W. Holmes on, 539–540
L. D. Brandeis on, 540–541
R. Pound on, 541–545, 589–600
E. A. Ross on, 533, 572–576
influence on recent politics and thought, 497, 505–516, 517–518, 546–554
attack upon in contemporary thought, 519–545, 554–600
Laughlin, H. H., 639
League of Nations, 606, 619–620, 647
W. Wilson on, 606–608, 649–659
H. C. Lodge on, 620–621, 666–672
other writers on, 610, 618–619, 663–666
Leith, C. K., 627, 672–681
Leonard, D., 99, 106–107, 143–153
Liberal Republican Party, 518
Liberator, The, see W. L. Garrison
Lieber, F., 432–433, 435
Lincoln, A., 329, 333–335, 376–384, 433
Lippmann, W., 253, 632, 633–634
Lloyd, H. D., 525–527, 539, 554–562
Lochner v. N. Y., 514–515
Locke, J., 100, 155, 158, 159
"Locofocos," 257
Lodge, H. C., 620–621, 666–672
Lowell, A. L., 632, 633
Loyalists in the American Revolution, 92, 106–109, 143–162
Lundy, B., 350

MacDougall, W., 639
Madison, J., 246
on post-Revolutionary conditions, 165
speeches at Constitutional Convention, 171–172, 204–205, 207–208, 211, 212, 220
The Federalist by, 179, 180–184, 212–221
on divided sovereignty, 409–410
Mahan, A. T., 679
Marbury v. Madison, 174, 189–190, 228–231
Marshall, J., 174, 175, 189–191, 228–234, 248, 252, 254, 260–261, 283, 412–413, 466
Martin, E. D., 635, 681–698
Martin v. Hunter's Lessee, 469
Marxian socialism in the United States, 537
Mason, G., 178, 204, 209, 212, 239–243
Massachusettensis, *see* D. Leonard
Massachusetts Body of Liberties, 15, 16, 110
Mather, C., 20
Mayflower Compact, 15, 61
McCulloch v. Maryland, 190
"Melting-pot" theory, 645–646, 715
Mencken, H. L., 631, 632–633, 635–637
Merriam, C. E., 694, 695
Minerals, importance of in world politics, 627, 672–681

Minimum wage, Supreme Court opinion on, 549–554
Missouri Compromise, 325
Monroe Doctrine, 617, 620–621, 623–625, 669–670, 671, 680
Montesquieu, C., 111
Morris, G., 172, 211–212
Mulford, E., 434

National Anti-Slavery Society, 327, 329, 330, 350–354
Nationalism,
  F. Lieber on, 432–433
  D. Webster on, 426–432, 479–487
  J. Story on, 426–432, 466–478
  J. W. Burgess on, 434–435
  after the Civil War, 432–435, 487–496
  recent growth of, 619–627, 666–672, 639–640
Natural law and rights,
  J. Wise on, 20–22
  during American Revolution, 99–100, 104–105, 125–127, 132–134
  T. Paine on, 104–105
  A. Hamilton on, 125–127, 132–134
  T. Jefferson on, 249–250, 270–273
  N. S. Townshend on, 305–308
  F. Lieber on, 433
  J. W. Burgess on, 435
  and the slavery controversy, 341–345, 390–401
Navigation Acts, 89–90
Nedham, M., 191
Neutrality, 613, 664
New England Confederation, 88
Nineteenth Amendment, 630
Non-Partisan League, 518
Nordicism, 639–640, 642–643
Nott, J. C., 346
Nullification, 413, 424–425, 429–431, 486

"Open-door" policy, 603
Osborn v. The Bank, 190
Otis, J., 94
Outlawry of war, 610–613, 659–666
Owen, R., 262

Paine, T., 94, 101, 103–106, 108, 135–143, 164
Particularism, see States' rights
Peckham, R. W., 515
Permanent Court of International Justice, 610, 665
Pinkney, C., 203, 206
Pitney, M., 514, 550
Platform of Church Discipline, 10, 12–13, 15–16, 39–61
Plato, influence on pro-slavery exponents, 346, 347
Police power, 513–516, 539–541, 549–554

Popular sovereignty, theories of,
  during the Puritan period, 19, 21–22, 77–78, 86
  during the Revolutionary period, 100–101
  D. Webster on, 426–432, 481–484
Populist Party, 518
Potter, P. B., 608
Pound, R., 541–545, 589–600
Preamble to Constitution, origin of, 427–428
Progressive Party, 518
Prohibition and democracy, 631–633
Prohibition movement, 631–632
Pro-slavery arguments,
  attack upon equality, 341–342, 385–386, 395–397
  attack upon liberty, 343–344, 384–386
  attack upon natural rights, 344–346, 390–394, 395–401
  racial superiority, 346–347
  slavery and human progress, 347–349, 387–390, 394–395, 399–407
  slavery and democracy, 349–350, 391–394
Psychology and democracy, 635–637, 681–698
Public opinion and democracy, 633–634, 681–698
Public utilities, government regulation of, 517–518
Pufendorf, S., 20, 100
Puritans, Old World influences on, 3–8
  political theory of, 8–17

Quebec Act, 91, 123

Railways, regulation of, see Public utilities
Randall, J. A., 614, 615–616
Randolph, E., 167, 169–170, 200–203, 209–210
Raw materials, importance of in world politics, 627, 672–681
Read, G., 206, 207, 208
Referendum, 19, 628, 630
Regionalism, 436
Religion, influence of on American Revolution, 91–92
Religious tolerance,
  Roger Williams on, 17–18, 71–75, 81–87
  during Jacksonian period, 258
Right of revolution, 101–102, 249, 320
Roosevelt, T., 517, 518, 630, 639
Root, E., 521–522, 610
Ross, E. A., 533, 572–576
Rotation in office, 259–260, 301–302
Rousseau, J. J., 262, 264, 354

Seabury, S., 125
Secession, theory of, 419–420, 425, 458–459, 465–466
Self-determination, 605, 649

Separation of powers, 111–112, 174–175, 183–186, 188–189, 220–228
Seventeenth Amendment, 628, 630
Shays's Rebellion, 166, 168, 176, 249
Sherman, J., 172, 204, 208
Sherman Anti-Trust Act, 517, 519, 587
Shotwell, J. T., 608, 611–613, 659–666
Single tax, 527–528
Singletary, A., 178, 234–235
Slavery,
    beginnings of controversy over, 325–329
    territorial expansion and, 327–329
    pro-slavery theories, 341–350, 384–407
    anti-slavery theories, 319–324, 329–341, 350–384
Smith, Adam, 505
Social contract theory,
    during the Puritan period, 13–16, 17, 20–22
    during the Revolutionary period, 99–102, 104–110, 125–127, 136, 157–159, 164
    post-Revolutionary development of, 248–250, 270–273
    and the slavery controversy, 341–345, 390–401
    F. Lieber on, 433
    J. W. Burgess on, 435
Social legislation, 518, 519
Socialist theory, 528–530, 536–538
Sociological jurisprudence, 539–545, 589–600
South Carolina, tariff controversy in, 328, 408, 413
"South Carolina Exposition," 384, 413, 414, 437, 479–481
Sovereignty, theories of,
    Roger Williams on, 19, 77–78
    divided sovereignty, 409–410
    state sovereignty, 414–425, 437–466
    national sovereignty, 432–435, 487–496
    D. Webster on, 426–432, 479–487
    J. Story on, 426–432, 466–478
Spencer, H., 505–506, 511, 513, 523, 524, 540, 546
Spoils system, 259
Stamp Act, 94
Stephens, A. 419, 421, 455–459
State constitutions, creation of, 108–112
States' rights,
    the practice of, 410–414
    antecedent to theory of, 414
    theory of, 414–425, 437–466
    historical arguments for, 414–417, 459–464
    legal arguments for, 417–420, 449–455, 465–466
    philosophical arguments for, 420–425, 437–449, 456–459
Stevens, T., 434
Stone, H. F., 511 fn.
Story, J., 426–432, 466–478, 487
Sturges v. Crowninshield, 191, 228, 231–234

Suffrage, widening of, 112, 173, 258, 305–309, 630
Sumner, C., 434, 487–489
Sumner, W. G., 506–511, 513, 523, 546–549
Supreme Court,
    creation of, 174–175, 202
    The Federalist on, 185–186, 223–228
    under J. Marshall, 189–191, 228–234
    under R. Taney, 260–261, 308–310
    on divided sovereignty, 410
    on social legislation, 513–516, 539–541, 549–554
Sutherland, G., 515–516, 549–554

Taft, W. H., 668, 669, 671
Taney, R., 260–261, 308–310, 377–383
Tariff, 179, 245, 295–300, 302–303, 328, 408, 412, 413, 425, 497
Taxation, colonial theory of, 94–95
Taylor, J., 252–254, 283–300, 411, 414
Tenth Amendment, 410, 464
Texas, annexation of, 412
Thomas, N., 536–538, 539
Thoreau, H. D., 266, 319–324, 333
Tories, see Loyalists
Town meeting, 16, 251
Townshend, N. S., 305–308
Transportation Act of 1920, 520
Trusts, regulation of, 517, 519–520, 533–536
Turgot, J., 191

Upshur, A. P., 417–419, 449–455
Utopian socialism, 262, 528–530

Veblen, T., 525, 530–531
Versailles conference and treaty, 604, 605, 619, 622, 647–648, 650–651, 653–659
Virginia and Kentucky Resolutions, 246, 411, 414
Volstead Act, see Prohibition

Ward, L. F., 523–525, 539
Wayland, F., 329, 334, 335–340, 366–376
Webster, D., 426–432, 479–487
Westward expansion, 254–256, 327
Whiskey Insurrection, 177, 245
Whitman, Walt, 262, 267–269, 641
Wilbur, C., 626–627
Williams, Roger, 17, 70,
    on religious tolerance, 17–18, 71–75
    on separation of church and state, 18–19, 72–87
    on democracy, 19–20, 77–78, 86
Willoughby, W. W., 520
Wilson, J., 203, 206
Wilson, W.,
    on laissez-faire and individualism, 517, 518, 521, 533–535, 539, 577–581
    on internationalism, 604–608, 619, 621, 647–659
Winthrop, J., 11
Wise, J., 17, 20–22

Wollstonecraft, M., 354
Women's suffrage, 258, 305, 630
Woolsey, T. D., 520
Worcester v. Georgia, 412
World Court, *see* Permanent Court of International Justice
World War,
  causes of American entrance into, 603–604

World War—*Continued*
  reasons for American entrance into, 604–605, 621, 623, 648
  consequences of, 608–610, 612, 660–662

Young, A. N., 626

Zangwill, I., 645